PHILIP'S

C000258354

STREET

Hampshire

Bournemouth and Poole

First published in 2006 by

Philip's, a division of
Octopus Publishing Group Ltd
2-4 Heron Quays, London E14 4JP

First edition 2006
First impression 2006
HAMAA

ISBN-10   0-540-08776-9 (spiral)
ISBN-13   978-0-540-08776-1 (spiral)

© Philip's 2006

Ordnance Survey®

This product includes mapping data licensed
from Ordnance Survey® with the permission of
the Controller of Her Majesty's Stationery Office.
© Crown copyright 2006. All rights reserved.
Licence number 100011710.

Printed and bound in Spain
by Cayfosa-Quebecor

Contents

III   **Key to map symbols**

IV   **Key to map pages**

VI   **Route planning**

X   **Administrative and Postcode boundaries**

1   **Street maps** at 3½ inches to 1 mile

404   **Street map of Portsmouth city centre** at 7 inches to 1 mile

405   **Index** of towns and villages

408   **Index** of streets, hospitals, industrial estates, railway stations, schools, shopping centres, universities and places of interest

Digital Data

The exceptionally high-quality mapping found in this atlas is available as digital data in TIFF format, which is easily convertible to other bitmapped (raster) image formats.

The index is also available in digital form as a standard database table. It contains all the details found in the printed index together with the National Grid reference for the map square in which each entry is named.

For further information and to discuss your requirements, please contact Philip's on 020 7644 6932 or james.mann@philips-maps.co.uk

22a	**Motorway** with junction number
	Primary route – dual/single carriageway
	A road – dual/single carriageway
	B road – dual/single carriageway
	Minor road – dual/single carriageway
	Other minor road – dual/single carriageway
	Road under construction
	Tunnel, covered road
	Rural track, private road or narrow road in urban area
	Gate or obstruction to traffic (restrictions may not apply at all times or to all vehicles)
	Path, bridleway, byway open to all traffic, road used as a public path
	Pedestrianised area
DY7	**Postcode boundaries**
	County and unitary authority boundaries
	Railway, tunnel, railway under construction
	Tramway, tramway under construction
	Miniature railway
Walsall	**Railway station**
	Private railway station
South Shields	**Metro station**
	Tram stop, tram stop under construction
	Bus, coach station

◆	Ambulance station
◆	Coastguard station
◆	Fire station
◆	Police station
✛	Accident and Emergency entrance to hospital
H	Hospital
+	Place of worship
i	Information Centre (open all year)
🛒	Shopping Centre
P P&R	Parking, Park and Ride
PO	Post Office
⚕ 🚐	Camping site, caravan site
▶ ✕	Golf course, picnic site
Prim Sch	Important buildings, schools, colleges, universities and hospitals
	Built up area
	Woods
River Medway	Water name
	River, weir, stream
	Canal, lock, tunnel
	Water
	Tidal water
Church	Non-Roman antiquity
ROMAN FORT	Roman antiquity
87	Adjoining page indicators and overlap bands
237	The colour of the arrow and the band indicates the scale of the adjoining or overlapping page (see scales below)

Enlarged mapping only

	Railway or bus station building
	Place of interest
	Parkland

Abbr.	Full	Abbr.	Full	Abbr.	Full
Acad	Academy	Inst	Institute	Recn Gd	Recreation Ground
Allot Gdns	Allotments	Ct	Law Court		
Cemy	Cemetery	L Ctr	Leisure Centre	Resr	Reservoir
C Ctr	Civic Centre	LC	Level Crossing	Ret Pk	Retail Park
CH	Club House	Liby	Library	Sch	School
Coll	College	Mkt	Market	Sh Ctr	Shopping Centre
Crem	Crematorium	Meml	Memorial	TH	Town Hall/House
Ent	Enterprise	Mon	Monument	Trad Est	Trading Estate
Ex H	Exhibition Hall	Mus	Museum	Univ	University
Ind Est	Industrial Estate	Obsy	Observatory	W Twr	Water Tower
IRB Sta	Inshore Rescue Boat Station	Pal	Royal Palace	Wks	Works
		PH	Public House	YH	Youth Hostel

■ The small numbers around the edges of the maps identify the 1 kilometre National Grid lines
■ The dark grey border on the inside edge of some pages indicates that the mapping does not continue onto the adjacent page

The scale of the maps on the pages numbered in blue is 5.52 cm to 1 km • 3½ inches to 1 mile • 1: 18103	0 ¼ ½ ¾ 1 mile 0 250 m 500 m 750 m 1 kilometre
The scale of the maps on pages numbered in red is 11.04 cm to 1 km • 7 inches to 1 mile • 1: 9051	0 220 yards 440 yards 660 yards ½ mile 0 125 m 250 m 375 m ½ kilometre

IV

Key to map pages

220	Map pages at 3½ inches to 1 mile
404	Map pages at 7 inches to 1 mile

Scale

0 — 5 — 10 — 15 km
0 — 5 — 10 miles

Calne

Marlborough

Hungerford

A4

A342 A3102 A4 A4 A34

Pewsey

Hamstead Marshall
3
North End

4 Broad Laying

Rivar **17**
Oxenwood

Buttermere **18**
Linkenholt

Combe **19**

Highclere **20**
Faccombe

21

Vernham Street **37**

38
Upton

39

Ashmansworth **40**
Woodcott

41

Upper Chute **57**
Ludgershall

Tangley **58** **59**
Hatherden

Hurstbourne Tarrant **60** **61**
Stoke

62
St Mary Bourne

Westbury

Tidworth 78 **79**

Appleshaw **80** **81**
Fyfield   Weyhill

Enham Alamein **82** **83**
Charlton

84 **85**
Picket Piece

Warminster

Wiltshire & Swindon STREET ATLAS

Durrington

Shipton Bellinger **101**
Cholderton

Thruxton **102** **103**
Quarley

Monxton **104** **105**
Upper Clatford

Andover 106 **107**
Forton

Longparish **108**

Amesbury

Newton Tony **123**

124 **125**
Over Wallop

Palestine **126** **127**
Kentsboro

Wherwell **128** **129**
Chilbolton

Barton Stacey

130

Middle Wallop **145** **146** **147**

Nether Wallop **148** **149**
Stockbridge

Leckford **150** **151**

152
Crawley

A36 A303 A303 A343 A3067

A350 A36 A345 A338 A30 A30

Wilton

Salisbury

Middle Winterslow **168** **169**
West Tytherley

Broughton **170** **171**
Horsebridge

Up Somborne **172** **173**
King's Somborne

174
Sparsholt

190 **191**
West Dean   Lockerley

Brook **192** **193**
Mottisfont

194 **195**

Standon **196**

Croucheston **210** **211**

212 **213**
Whiteparish
Sherfield English

Timsbury **214** **215**
Awbridge

Braishfield **216** **217** **218**
Ampfield   Hiltingbury
A3090

Martin Drove End
230 **231**
Martin   Rockbourne

232 **233**
Whitsbury

Wick **234** **235**
Hale   Landford

Lover **236** **237**

East Wellow **238** **239**
West Wellow

Romsey 240 **241**
North Baddesley

Chandler's Ford **242** **243**
Eastleigh

255

Damerham **256** **257**
Fordingbridge   Godshill

Woodgreen **258** **259**

Nomansland **260** **261**
Bramshaw   Newbridge

Ower **262** **263**
Calmore

Rownhams **264** **265**

Bassett **266** **267**
Swaythling

279
Edmondsham

Alderholt **280** **281**

Stuckton **282** **283**

284 **285**
Stoney Cross

Bartley **286** **287**
Minstead

Totton 288 **289**
Marchwood

Shirley **290** **291**
Southampton

Verwood 302 **303**

Ellingham **304** **305**
Rockford

Linwood **306** **307**
Linford

Emery Down **308** **309**
Bank

Lyndhurst 310 **311**
Clayhill

312 **313**
Dibden Purlieu

314
Hythe

Three Legged Cross
326 **327**
St Leonards

Ringwood 328 **329**
Kingston

Burley Street **330** **331**
Burley

332 **333**
Brockenhurst

334 **335**
Balmerlawn

336 **337**
Hill Top
Beaulieu

338
Blackfield

Pamphill **350** **351**
Wimborne Minster

Colehill **352** **353**
Ferndown

Trickett's Cross **354** **355**
Avon

356 **357**
Thorney Hill
Ripley

358 **359**
Wootton

Setley **360** **361**
Sway   Pilley

East Boldre **362** **363**
Bull Hill

364 **365**
Exbury
Lepe

Corfe Mullen **374** **375**
Broadstone

Bearwood **376** **377**
East Howe

Hurn **378** **379**
Charminster

Bransgore 380 **381**
Burton

Bashley **382** **383**
New Milton   Hordle

384 **385**
Bucklers Hard

East End **386** **387**
Waterford

Thorns Beach **388**

Upton **389**
Hamworthy

Newtown **390** **391**
Poole

392 **393**
Boscombe

394 **395**
Southbourne

Christchurch 396 **397**

Barton on Sea **398** **399**
Milford on Sea

Downton **400**
Lower Pennington
Keyhaven

Dorset STREET ATLAS

Blandford Forum

Wareham

401
Brownsea Island

402
Sandbanks

Bournemouth

Totland

Calne A4 Marlborough Hungerford Pewsey Westbury Warminster Durrington Amesbury Wilton Salisbury Blandford Forum Wareham Poole Bournemouth Totland

Berkshire STREET ATLAS

Surrey STREET ATLAS

West Sussex STREET ATLAS

Isle of Wight STREET ATLAS

Ascot
Sunninghill
Bracknell
Crowthorne
Chobham
Woking
Guildford
Shalford
Godalming
Milford
Elstead
Frensham
Chiddingfold
Haslemere
Kingsley Green
Petworth
Midhurst
Chichester
Bosham
Middleton-on-Sea
Bognor Regis
East Wittering
Selsey
Cowes
Ryde
Newport
Bembridge

Shaw **2**
1
Newbury **Thatcham**
Wokingham
Greenham
5 **6** **7**
Aldermaston
Headley
Brimpton
Newtown
8 **9**
Mortimer
10 **11** **12** **13**
Stratfield Mortimer
Beech Hill
Pamber Heath
Arborfield Garrison
14 **15** **16**
Riseley
Finchampstead

Burghclere
22 **23**
Ecchinswell
Axmansford
24 **25**
Kingsclere
Tadley
26 **27**
Little London
Fair Oak Green
28 **29**
Bramley
Heckfield
30 **31**
Turgis Green
Eversley Cross
32 **33**
Yateley
34 **35**
Blackwater
Camberley
36
Frimley

Sydmonton
42 **43**
44 **45**
Hannington
Ibworth
Ramsdell
46 **47**
Sherborne St John
Church End
48 **49**
Chineham
Rotherwick
50 **51**
Hook
Hartley Wintney
52 **53**
Fleet
Fox Lane
54 **55**
Pondtail
Frimley Green
56
Mytchett

Litchfield
63 **64** **65**
Quidhampton
Wootton St Lawrence
66 **67**
Oakley
Basingstoke
68 **69**
Cranbourne
Old Basing
70 **71**
Greywell
72 **73**
Odiham
Church Crookham
74 **75**
Mill Lane
Aldershot
Ash Vale
76 **77**
Tongham

Laverstoke
86 **87**
Whitchurch
Overton
88 **89**
North Waltham
90 **91**
Farleigh Wallop
Dummer
Cliddesden
92 **93**
Tunworth
Upton Grey
94 **95**
Long Sutton
Crondall
96 **97**
Well
Hog Hatch
98 **99**
Farnham
100
Seale

109
110 **111**
Micheldever Station
112 **113**
Popham
Ellisfield
114 **115**
Axford
116 **117**
Golden Pot
Lasham
118 **119**
Lower Froyle
Upper Froyle
Wrecclesham
120 **121** **122**
Bentley
Millbridge

Sutton Scotney
131
132 **133**
Stoke Charity
Micheldever
134 **135**
East Stratton
Brown Candover
Bradley
136 **137**
Upper Wield
Bentworth
138 **139**
Alton
Binsted
140 **141**
East Worldham
Dockenfield
142 **143**
Sleaford
Frensham
144
Churt

153
South Wonston
154 **155**
Northington
Old Alresford
156 **157**
Medstead
158 **159**
Bighton
Chawton
160 **161**
Four Marks
West Worldham
162 **163**
Oakhanger
Arford
164 **165**
Bordon
Beacon Hill
166 **167**
Grayshott

175
Kings Worthy
176 **177**
Avington
New Alresford
178 **179**
Ovington
180 **181**
Bishop's Sutton
Ropley
Monkwood
East Tisted
182 **183**
Selborne
184 **185**
Greatham
Conford
186 **187**
Longmoor Camp
Liphook
188 **189**

403
Winchester
197 **198** **199**
Cheriton
200 **201**
Kilmeston
West Tisted
202 **203**
Bramdean
204 **205**
Privett
High Cross
206 **207**
Hawkley
Liss
Langley
208 **209**
Rake
Milland

219
Twyford
220 **221**
Owslebury
Beauworth
222 **223**
West Meon
224 **225**
Warnford
226 **227**
Langrish
East Meon
Steep
228 **229**
Petersfield

Crowdhill
244 **245**
Bishopstoke
Upham
246 **247**
Lower Upham
Droxford
Corhampton
248 **249**
Coombe
250 **251**
Buriton
252 **253**
Nursted
254

Horton Heath
268 **269**
West End
Durley
Bishop's Waltham
270 **271**
Shirrell Heath
Soberton
272 **273**
Hambledon
274 **275**
Clanfield
276 **277**
Chalton
278
Compton

Hedge End
292 **293**
Newtown
Shedfield
Botley
294 **295**
Wickham
Newtown
296 **297**
Anthill Common
298 **299**
Denmead
Horndean
300 **301**
Rowlands Castle

Netley
315
Bursledon
316 **317**
Locks Heath
Crockerhill
318 **319**
Fareham
Southwick
320 **321**
Wymering
Waterlooville
322 **323**
Purbrook
Havant
324 **325**
Westbourne

Newtown
339 **340**
Fawley
Titchfield
341 **342**
Stubbington
Portchester
343 **344** **345**
Bridgemary
North End
Cosham
346 **347**
Southbourne
348 **349**
North Hayling

Calshot
366
Lee-on-the-Solent
367
Hardway
368 **369**
Gosport
370 **371**
404
Portsmouth
Fleet
372 **373**
West Town

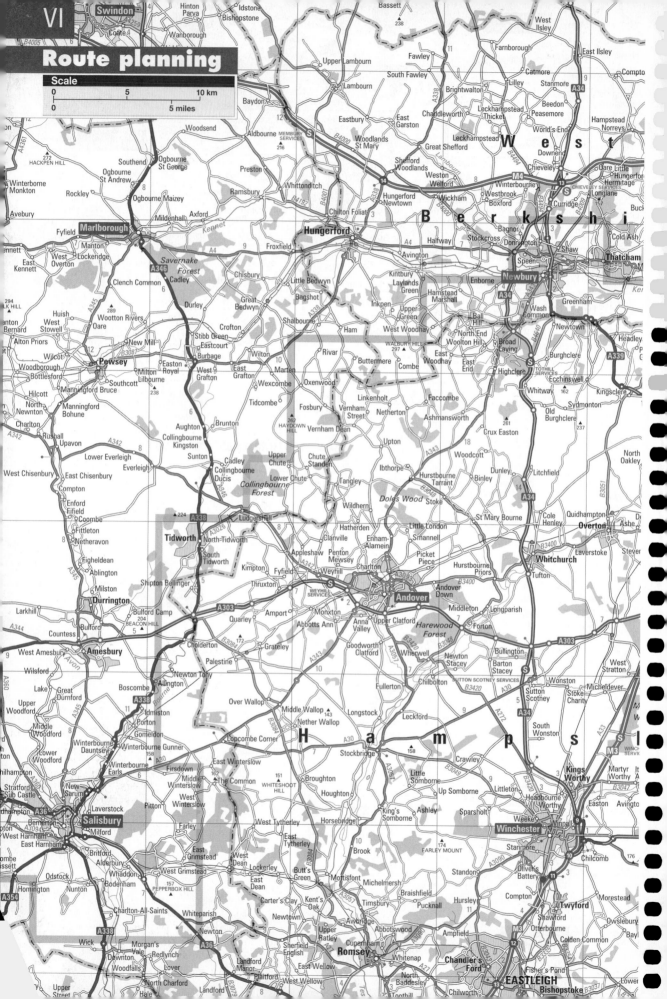

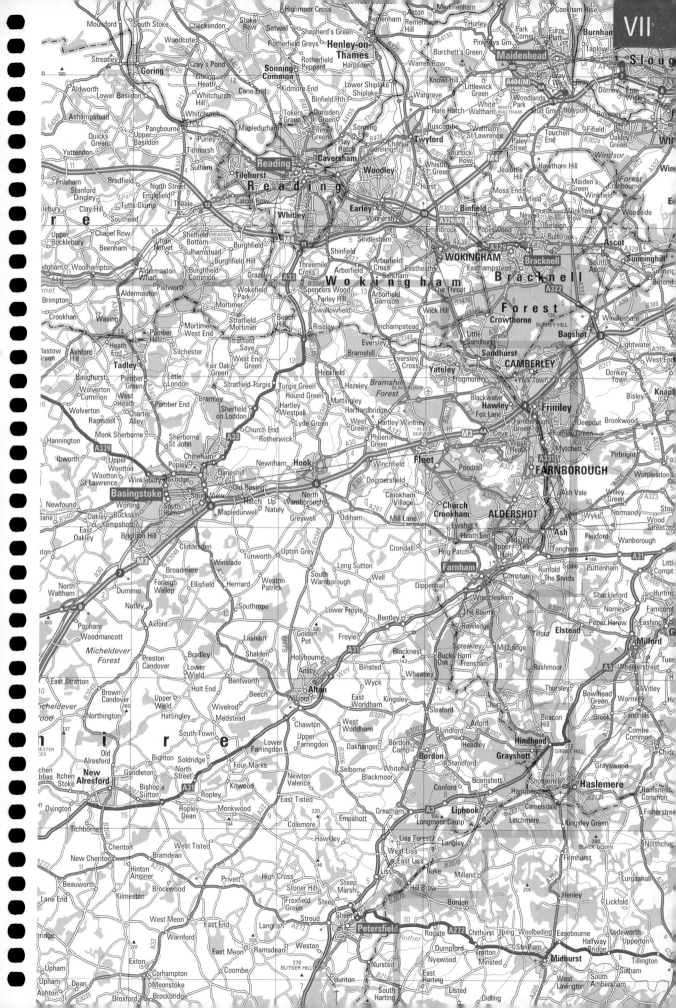

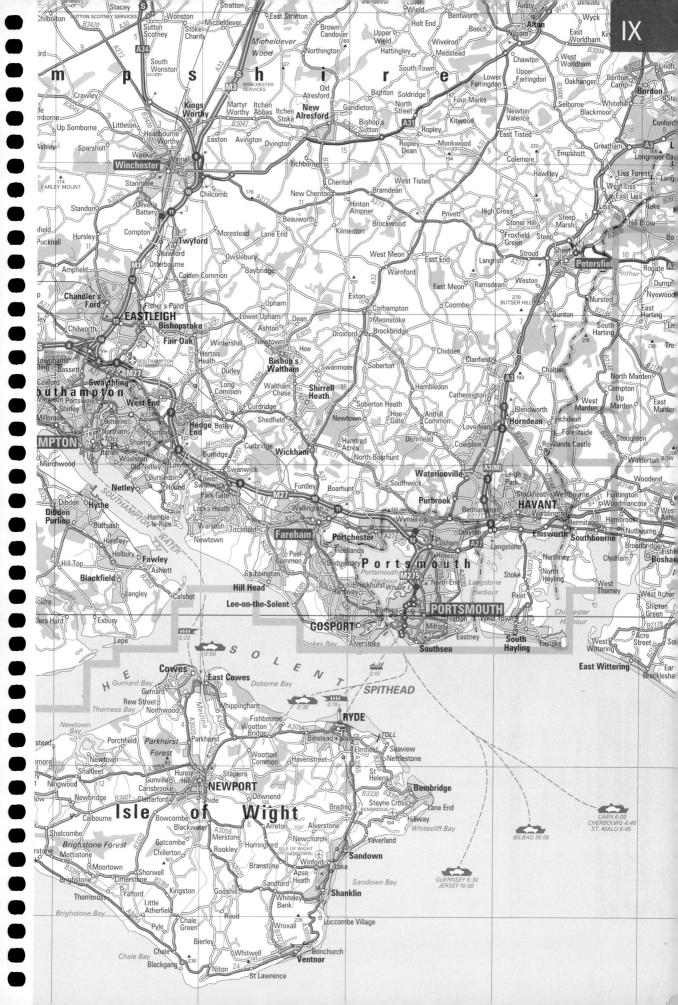

Major administrative and Postcode boundaries

Scale

| County and unitary authority boundaries |
| District boundaries |
| Postcode boundaries |

0   5   10   15 km
0   5   10 miles

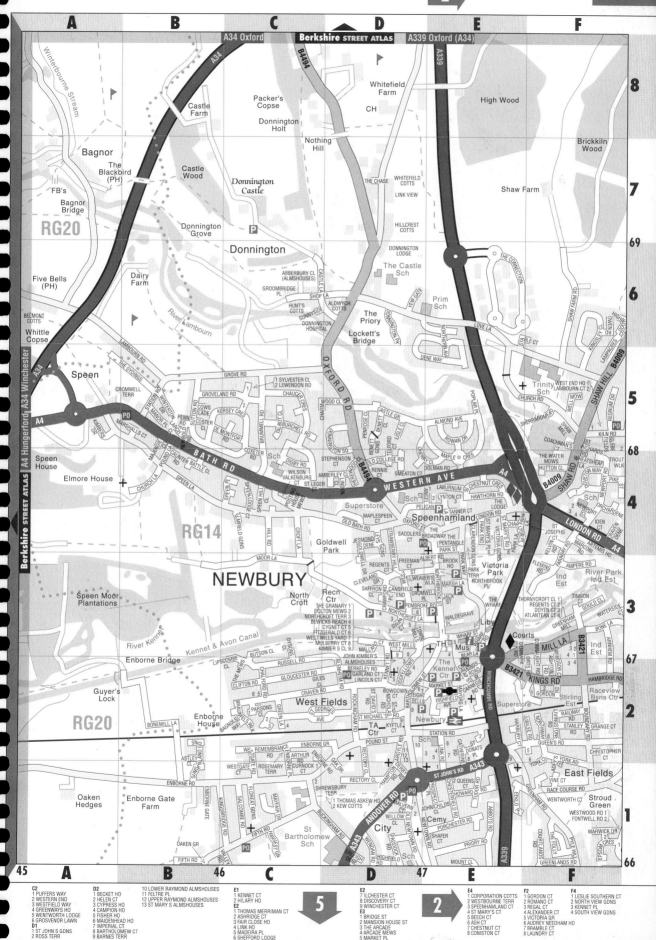

1

2 →

C2
1 PUFFERS WAY
2 WESTERN END
3 WESTFIELD WAY
4 GREENWAYS HO
5 WENTWORTH LODGE
6 GROSVENOR LAWN
D1
1 ST JOHN S GDNS
2 ROSS TERR

D2
1 BECKET HO
2 HELEN CT
3 CYPRESS HO
4 CAMPION HO
5 FISHER HO
6 MAIDENHEAD HO
7 IMPERIAL CT
8 BARTHOLOMEW CT
9 BARNES TERR

10 LOWER RAYMOND ALMSHOUSES
11 FELTRE PL
12 UPPER RAYMOND ALMSHOUSES
13 ST MARY S ALMSHOUSES

E1
1 KENNET CT
2 HILARY HO
E2
1 THOMAS MERRIMAN CT
2 ASHRIDGE CT
3 FAIR CLOSE HO
4 LINK HO
5 MADEIRA PL
6 SHEFFORD LODGE

E2
1 ILCHESTER CT
7 DISCOVERY CT
9 WINCHESTER CT
E3
1 BRIDGE ST
2 MANSION HOUSE ST
3 THE ARCADE
4 ARCADE MEWS
5 MARKET PL

E4
1 CORPORATION COTTS
2 WESTBOURNE TERR
3 SPEENHAMLAND CT
4 ST MARY'S CT
5 BEECH CT
6 ASH CT
7 CHESTNUT CT
8 CONISTON CT

F2
1 GORDON CT
2 ROMANO CT
3 REGAL CT
4 ALEXANDER CT
5 VICTORIA GR
6 AUDREY NEEDHAM HO
7 BRAMBLE CT
8 LAUNDRY CT

F4
1 LESLIE SOUTHERN CT
2 NORTH VIEW GDNS
3 KENNET PL
4 SOUTH VIEW GDNS

5

2 →

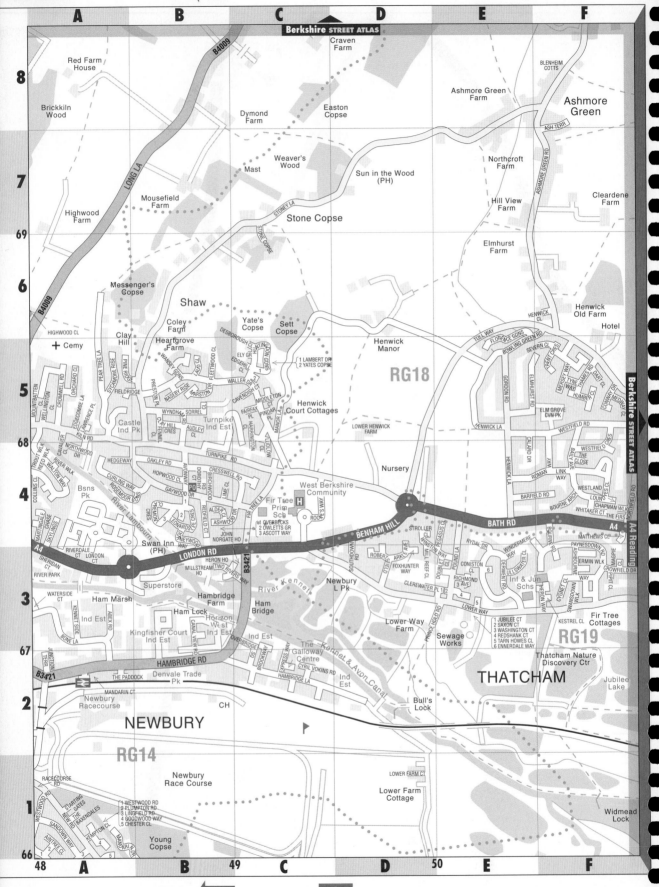

Berkshire STREET ATLAS

Berkshire STREET ATLAS

A B C D E F

Horn Copse
Queenhills Copse
Kintbury Holt Farm
Hankin's La
Mason's Farm
Barr's Farm
OLD LA
White Hill Farm
PARK LA
8

Hightree Copse
TINKER'S CNR
Hamstead Marshall
White Hart Inn (PH)

Old Hat
FORBURY LA
The Oaks
Elm Farm Research Ctr
Plumb Farm
7

RG17
Curr Copse
Little Holt Copse
Great Holt Copse
Briff's Copse
ASH TREE GR
65

Skew-whiff
Milkhouse Copse
Waterman's Copse
HOLTWOOD RD
6

Holt Lodge
The Alders
BURGESS LA
Burgess Farm
Holt Manor Farm
Waterman's Farm
Mayhouse Gullies

Holtwood Farm
Little Farm
5

Holly La
Malt House
WATERY LA
RG20
Smith's Bridge
Holtwood
64

Holly Copse
River Enborne
Gore End Bridge
4

Weir
Hazelby House
Gore End
Studland Ind Est

Green Farm Copse
Malthouse Farm
Smart's Copse
Hillier's Farmhouse
NEW VILLAS
GORE END RD
KNIGHTS LEA
3

West Woodhay
Fishpond Farm
Green Plantation
Hatch House Farm
Ansell's Copse
GRAVELLY CL
63

Wilmot's Farm
Old Rectory
Hatch House Plantations
North End
Burlyns Farm
Burlyns
WELLINGTON COTTS
2

Woodcut Copse
Berries Copse
Northenby House
Oakhurst

Hayes
Berries Farm
North End Farm
Heath End
Farm Copse
1

39 A B 40 C D 41 E F 62

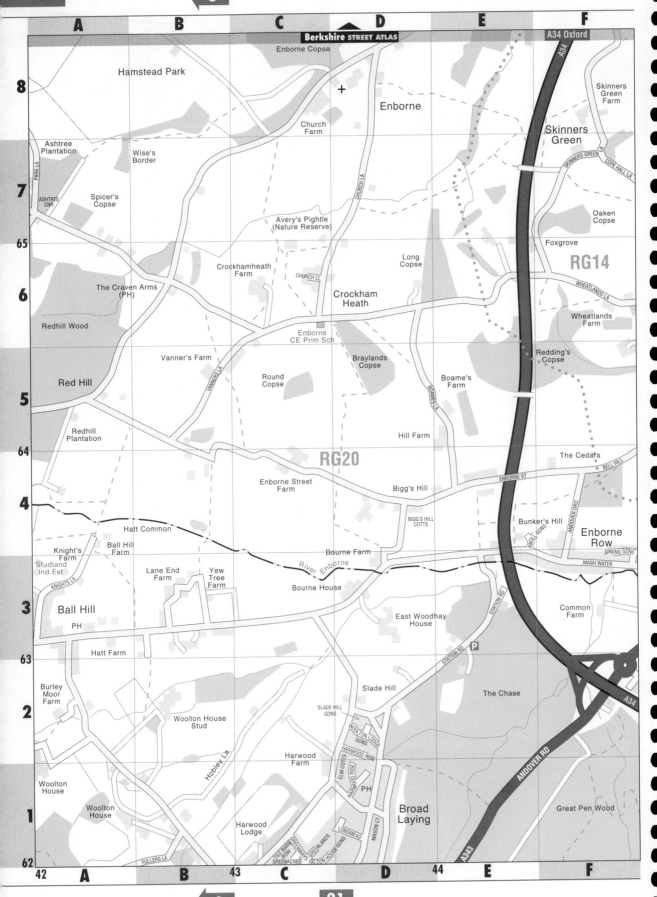

Berkshire STREET ATLAS

A B C D E F

A34 Oxford

Enborne Copse

Hamstead Park

Enborne

Church Farm

Skinners Green Farm

Skinners Green

SKINNERS GREEN LA

COPE HALL LA

Ashtree Plantation

Wise's Border

PARK LA

ASHTREE CNR

Spicer's Copse

Avery's Pightle (Nature Reserve)

CHURCH LA

Oaken Copse

Foxgrove

RG14

Crockhamheath Farm

CHURCH CL

Long Copse

WHEATLANDS LA

The Craven Arms (PH)

Crockham Heath

Wheatlands Farm

Redhill Wood

Enborne CE Prim Sch

Redding's Copse

VANNER'S LA

Vanner's Farm

Braylands Copse

Boame's Farm

Round Copse

BOAME'S LA

Red Hill

Redhill Plantation

Hill Farm

The Cedars

BELL HILL

RG20

Enborne Street Farm

Bigg's Hill

ENBORNE ST

Bigg's Hill

Bunker's Hill

ANDOVER DRO

Enborne Row

KNOLL GDNS

SPRING GDNS

Hatt Common

Ball Hill Farm

Bourne Farm

WASH WATER

Knight's Farm

Studland Ind Est

KNIGHTS LA

Lane End Farm

Yew Tree Farm

River Enborne

Bourne House

East Woodhay House

Common Farm

Ball Hill

PH

STATION RD

Hatt Farm

P

Burley Moor Farm

Slade Hill

The Chase

Woolton House Stud

SLADE HILL GDNS

A34

HOBLEY LA

Harwood Farm

WOOLTON LODGE GDNS

HARWOOD RISE

ELM COTTS

HARWOOD RISE

ANDOVER RD

Woolton House

Woolton House

PH

Broad Laying

Great Pen Wood

Harwood Lodge

LONGMEAD

MASON CT

FULLERS LA

TILL BARN ROW

GREENWAYS

GREENLANDS

GREENACRES

FALCON HOUSE GDNS

A343

42 A B 43 C D 44 E F

8

7

65

6

5

64

4

63

3

2

1

62

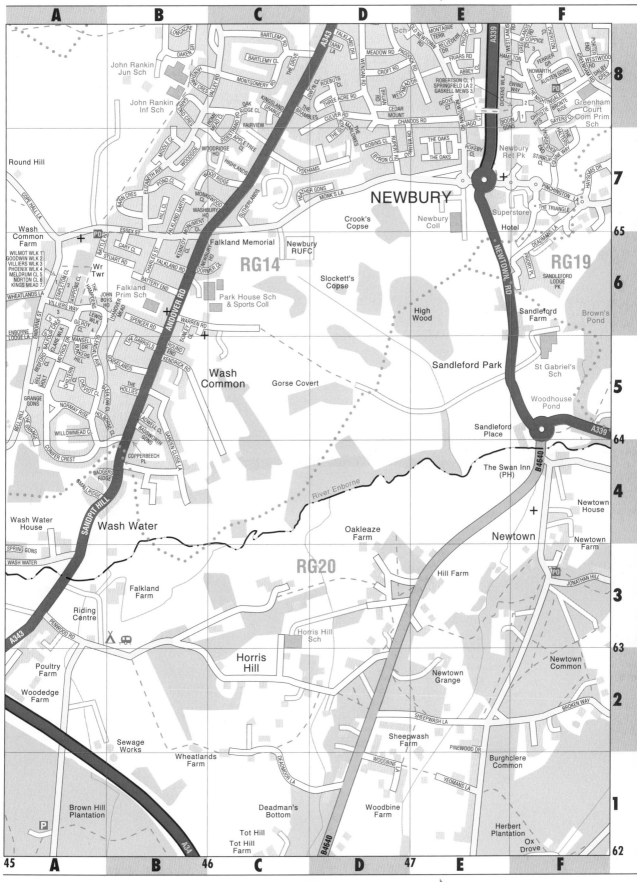

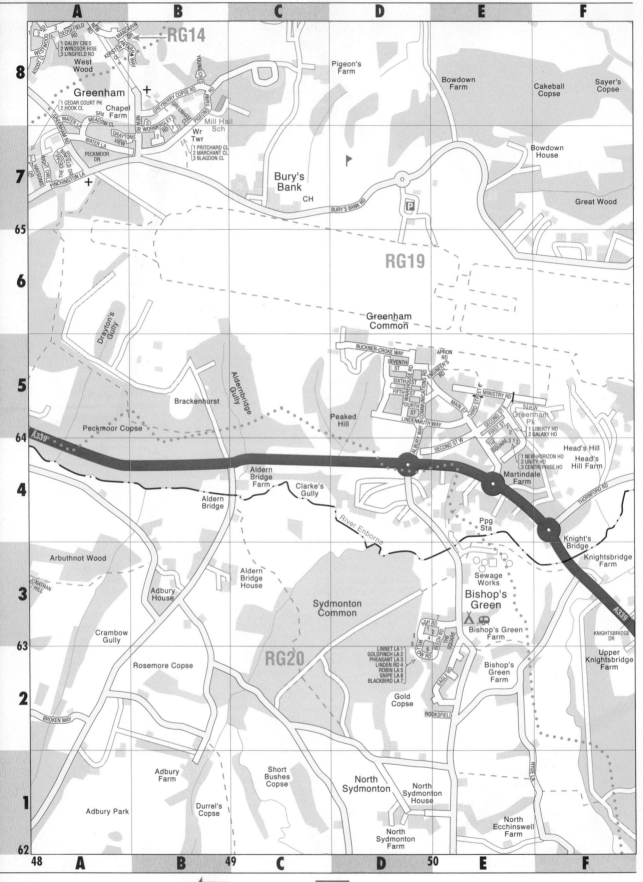

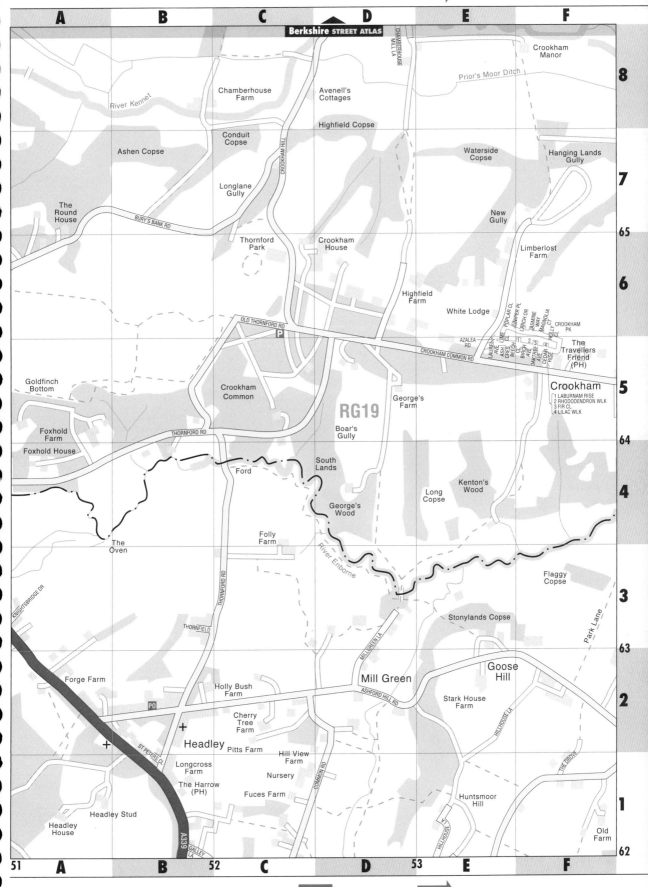

Berkshire STREET ATLAS

A B C D E F

Crookham Manor

Prior's Moor Ditch

Chamberhouse Farm

Avenell's Cottages

River Kennet

Highfield Copse

Conduit Copse

Waterside Copse

Hanging Lands Gully

Ashen Copse

CROOKHAM HILL

Longlane Gully

New Gully

The Round House

BURY'S BANK RD

Thornford Park

Crookham House

Limberlost Farm

Highfield Farm

White Lodge

OLD THORNFORD RD

P

CROOKHAM COMMON RD

AZALEA RD

LABURNEY AVE
ASH CL
LIME
CHES
BEECH CL
POPLAR PL
JUNIPER PL
LARCH DR
BIRCH CL
JASMINE WAY
MAGNOLIA
HOLLY CT
CROOKHAM PK

OAKTREE AVE
CEDAR RISE

The Travellers Friend (PH)

Goldfinch Bottom

Crookham Common

George's Farm

Crookham
1 LABURNAM RISE
2 RHODODENDRON WLK
3 FIR CL
4 LILAC WLK

RG19

Foxhold Farm

THORNFORD RD

Boar's Gully

Foxhold House

Ford

South Lands

Kenton's Wood

Long Copse

George's Wood

River Enborne

Folly Farm

The Oven

Flaggy Copse

THORNFORD RD

Park Lane

Stonylands Copse

THORNFIELD

MILLGREEN LA

KNIGHTSBRIDGE DR

Forge Farm

Mill Green

Goose Hill

ASHFORD HILL RD

Stark House Farm

PO

Holly Bush Farm

ST PETERS CL

Cherry Tree Farm

HILLHOUSE LA

Headley

Pitts Farm

Hill View Farm

Longcross Farm

COMMON RD

Nursery

THE DROVE

The Harrow (PH)

Fuces Farm

Huntsmoor Hill

A339

Headley Stud

HILLHOUSE

Old Farm

Headley House

GALLEY LS

51 A B 52 C D 53 E F

8 7 65 6 5 64 4 3 63 2 1 62

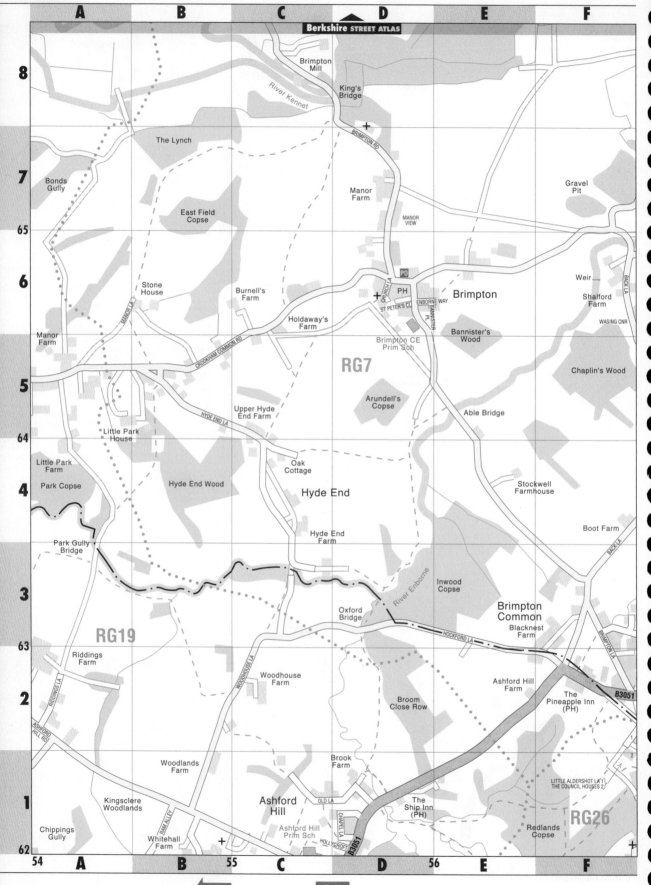

Berkshire STREET ATLAS

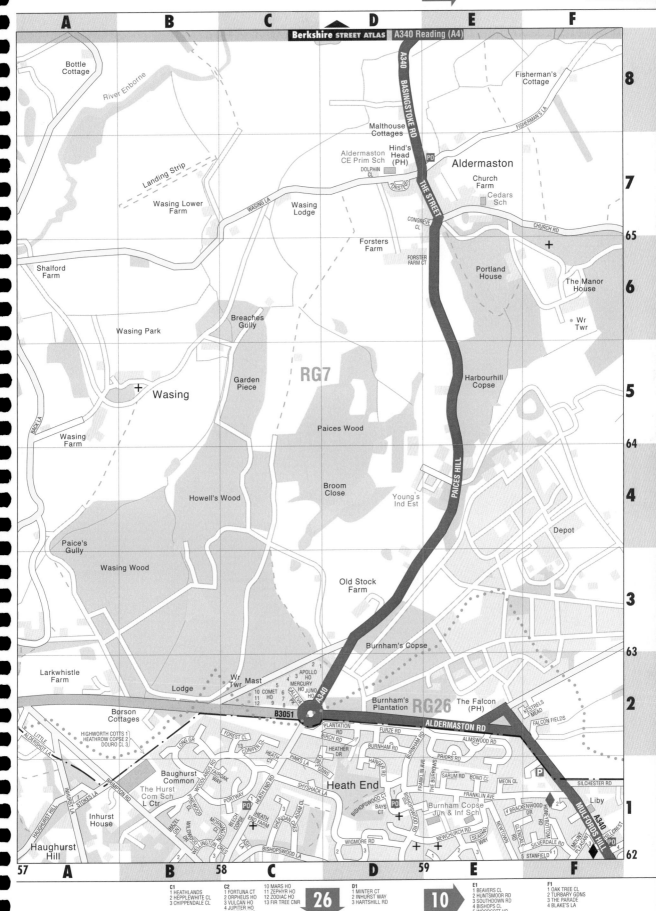

Berkshire STREET ATLAS A340 Reading (A4)

RG7

RG26

C1
1 HEATHLANDS
2 HEPPLEWHITE CL
3 CHIPPENDALE CL

C2
1 FORTUNA CT
2 ORPHEUS HO
3 VULCAN HO
4 JUPITER HO
5 MINERVA HO
6 TITAN HO
7 BACCHUS HO
8 MIDAS HO
9 SATURN HO
10 MARS HO
11 ZEPHYR HO
12 ZODIAC HO
13 FIR TREE CNR

D1
1 MINTER CT
2 INHURST WAY
3 HARTSHILL RD

E1
1 BEAVERS CL
2 HUNTSMOOR RD
3 SOUTHDOWN RD
4 BISHOPS CL
5 WOODCOTT HO

F1
1 OAK TREE CL
2 TURBARY GDNS
3 THE PARADE
4 BLAKE'S LA

Berkshire STREET ATLAS

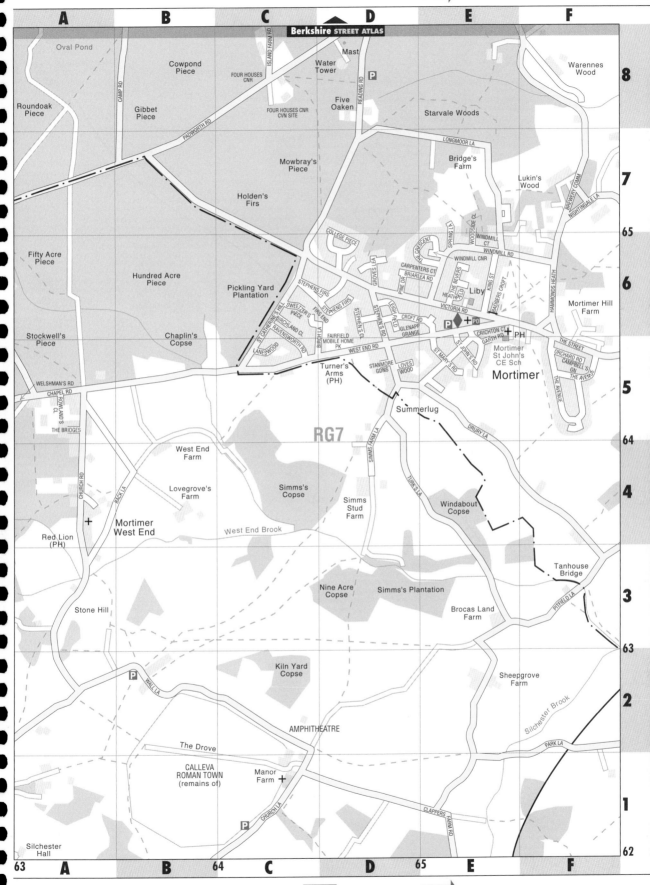

Berkshire STREET ATLAS

A **B** **C** **D** **E** **F**

Oval Pond

Roundoak
Piece

Cowpond
Piece

FOUR HOUSES
CNR

Water
Tower

Mast

8

Warennes
Wood

CAMP RD

ISLAND FARM RD

READING RD

P

Gibbet
Piece

FOUR HOUSES CNR
CVN SITE

Five
Oaken

Starvale Woods

PADWORTH RD

Mowbray's
Piece

LONGMOOR LA

Bridge's
Farm

Lukin's
Wood

BREWERY COMM

NIGHTINGALE LA

7

Holden's
Firs

COLLEGE PIECE

WOODSIDE CL

SPRING LA

WINDMILL
CT

65

Fifty Acre
Piece

STEPHENS FIRS

GROVES LEA

CRESCENT

CARPENTERS CT

PINE DR

BRIARLEA RD

WINDMILL CNR

WINDMILL RD

HAMMONDS HEATH

6

Hundred Acre
Piece

Pickling Yard
Plantation

SWEEFER'S
PIECE

FIRS END

STEPHENS FIRS

THE BEVERS

KING ST

BADGERS CROFT

Liby

Mortimer Hill
Farm

Chaplin's
Copse

ST CATHERINE'S HILL

BIRCHLAND CL

RAVENSWORTH RD

BIRCH LA

STEPHEN'S CL

STEPHEN'S RD

LEIGH FIELD

CROFT RD

VICTORIA RD

HEATHLANDS

CRICHTON CL

GARTH RD

PH

ORCHARD RD

CAMPBELL'S
GN

THE STREET

Stockwell's
Piece

LANESWOOD

WEST END RD

GLENAPP
GRANGE

ST MARY'S RD

ST JOHN'S RD

P PO

Mortimer
St John's
CE Sch

THE AVENUE

5

WELSHMAN'S RD

Turner's
Arms
(PH)

STANMORE
GDNS

LOVES
WOOD

Mortimer

CHAPEL RD

ROWLAND'S
CL

THE BRIDGES

Summerlug

DRURY LA

64

West End
Farm

RG7

SIMMS FARM LA

Windabout
Copse

4

CHURCH RD

BACK LA

Lovegrove's
Farm

Simms's
Copse

Simms
Stud
Farm

TURK'S LA

Red Lion
(PH)

Mortimer
West End

West End Brook

Tanhouse
Bridge

Nine Acre
Copse

Simms's Plantation

Brocas Land
Farm

PITFIELD LA

3

Stone Hill

63

P

WALL LA

Kiln Yard
Copse

Sheepgrove
Farm

SILCHESTER BROOK

2

AMPHITHEATRE

The Drove

PARK LA

CALLEVA
ROMAN TOWN
(remains of)

Manor
Farm

1

P

CHURCH LA

CLAPPERS
FARM RD

Silchester
Hall

62

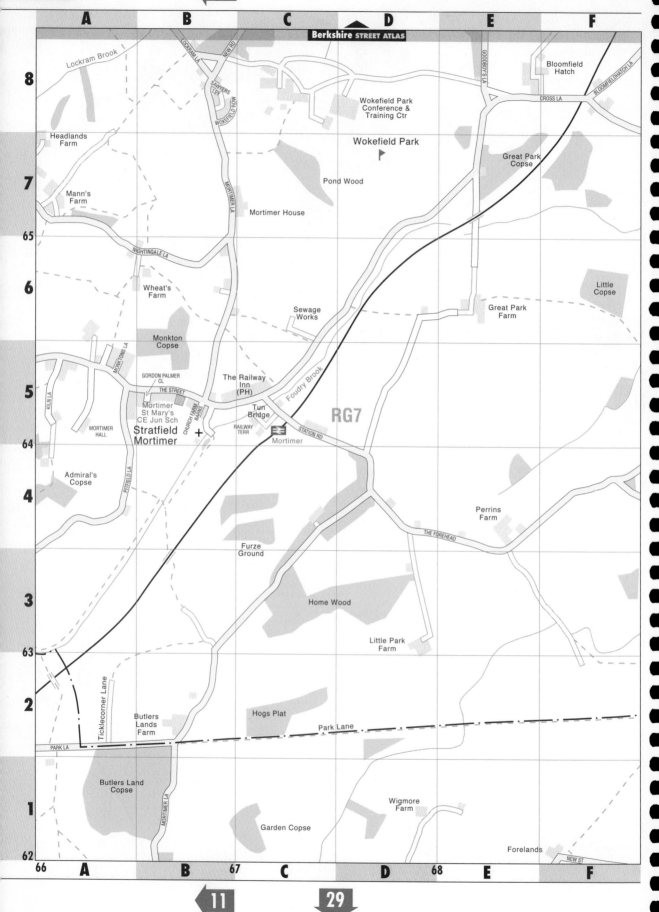

Berkshire STREET ATLAS

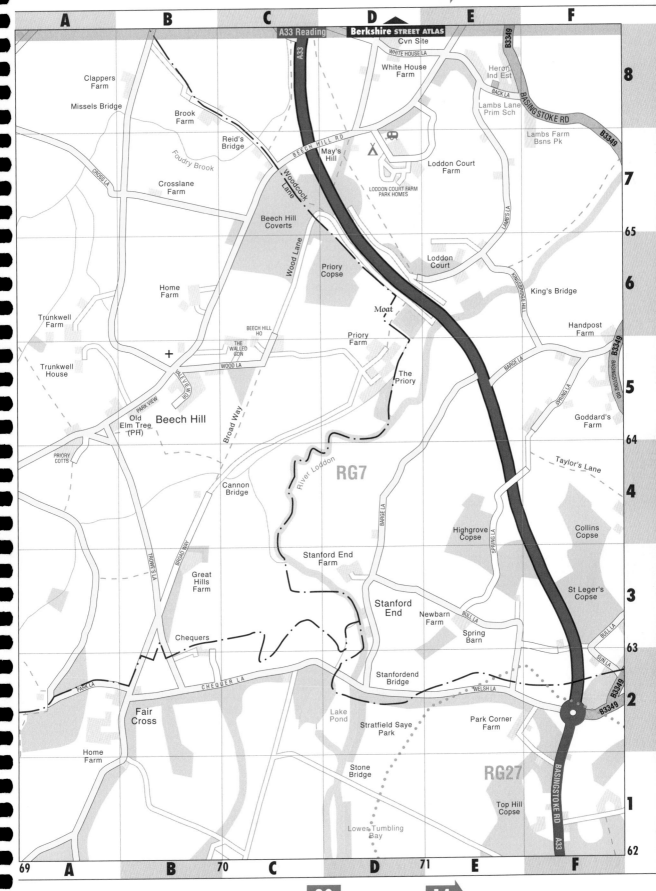

Berkshire STREET ATLAS

A33 Reading

Clappers Farm
Missels Bridge
Brook Farm
Reid's Bridge
Crosslane Farm
Foudry Brook
CROSS LA
Beech Hill Coverts
Woodcock Lane
Wood Lane
Home Farm
Trunkwell Farm
Trunkwell House
THE WALLED GDN
BEECH HILL HO
WOOD LA
VALE VIEW DR
PARK VIEW
Old Elm Tree (PH)
Beech Hill
PRIORY COTTS
Broad Way
BROAD WAY
TROWE'S LA
Great Hills Farm
Chequers
PARK LA
Fair Cross
Home Farm
CHEQUER LA
Cannon Bridge
River Loddon
RG7
Stanford End Farm
BARGE LA
Stanford End
Newbarn Farm
Spring Barn
BULL LA
Stanfordend Bridge
WELSH LA
Lake Pond
Stratfield Saye Park
Stone Bridge
Lower Tumbling Bay
RG27
Priory Copse
Priory Farm
Moat
The Priory
A33
Cvn Site
WHITE HOUSE LA
White House Farm
BACK LA
Lambs Lane Prim Sch
Loddon Court Farm
LODDON COURT FARM PARK HOMES
May's Hill
BEECH HILL RD
Loddon Court
LAMB'S LA
KINGSBRIDGE HILL
King's Bridge
Handpost Farm
BARGE LA
SPRING LA
Goddard's Farm
Taylor's Lane
Highgrove Copse
SPRING LA
Collins Copse
St Leger's Copse
BULL LA
SUN LA
Park Corner Farm
Top Hill Copse
Heron Ind Est
BASINGSTOKE RD
Lambs Farm Bsns Pk
B3349
B3349
B3349
B3349
BASINGSTOKE RD
B3349

69 70 71

62 63 64 65 66 67 68

8
7
65
6
5
64
4
3
63
2
1
62

13

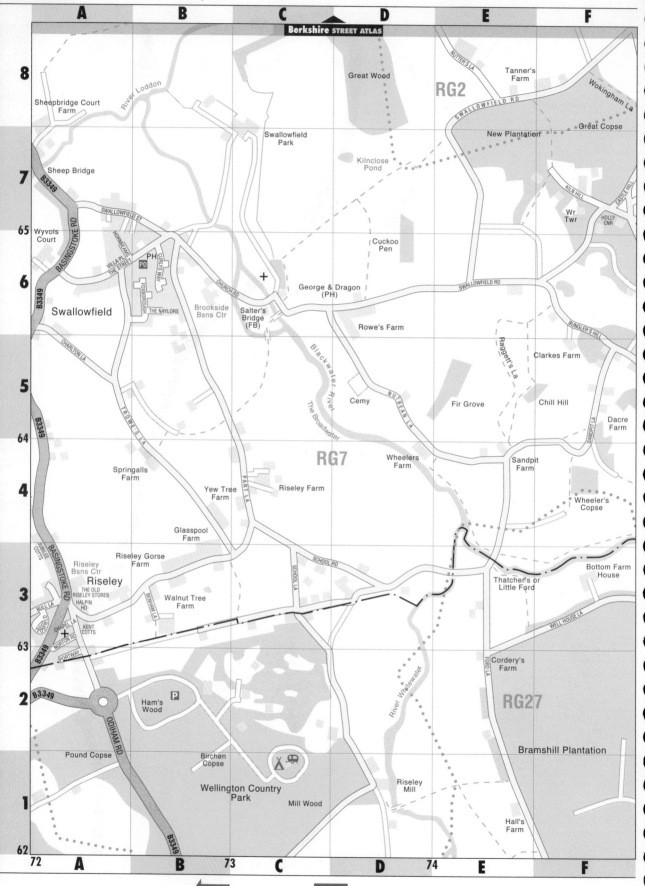

Berkshire STREET ATLAS

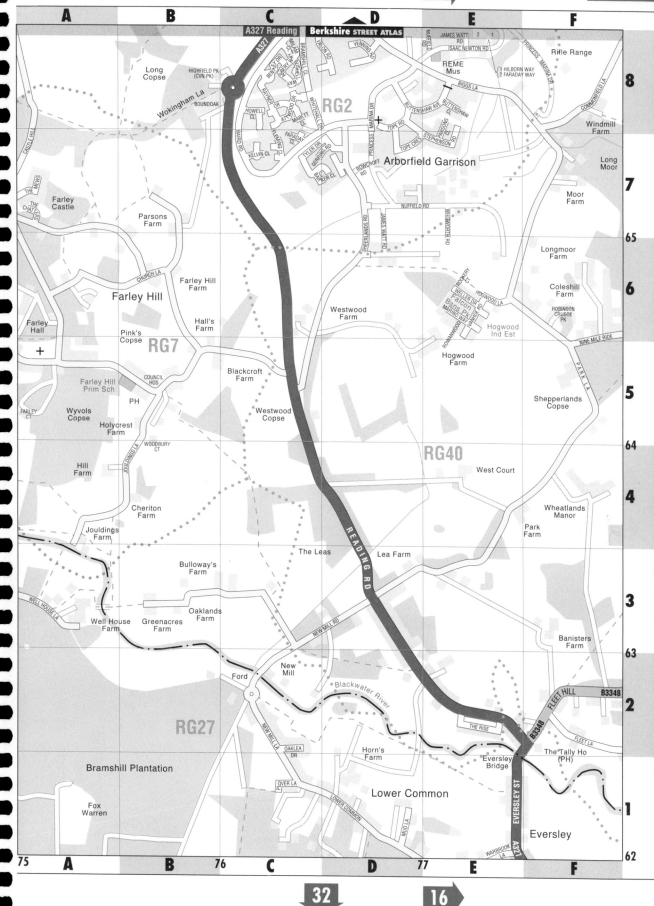

A327 Reading **Berkshire** STREET ATLAS

RG2

Rifle Range

JAMES WATT RD
ISAAC NEWTON RD

REME
Mus

1 HILBORN WAY
2 FARADAY WAY

Windmill
Farm

BIGGS LA

Arborfield Garrison

Long
Moor

Long
Copse

HIGHFIELD PK
(CVN PK)

Wokingham La

BOUNDOAK

NUFFIELD RD

Moor
Farm

THE MEWS

Farley
Castle

THE CHATTS EAS

Parsons
Farm

Longmoor
Farm

Coleshill
Farm

ROBINSON
CRUSOE
PK

NINE MILE RIDE

CHURCH LA

Farley Hill
Farm

Westwood
Farm

Hogwood
Ind Est

Farley Hill

Hall's
Farm

Hogwood
Farm

Farley
Hall

Pink's
Copse

RG7

PARK LA

Shepperlands
Copse

COUNCIL
HOS

Blackcroft
Farm

Farley Hill
Prim Sch

PH

Westwood
Copse

RG40

West Court

FARLEY
CT

Wyvols
Copse

Holycrest
Farm

WOODBURY
CT

Wheatlands
Manor

Hill
Farm

Park
Farm

Cheriton
Farm

Jouldings
Farm

The Leas

Lea Farm

WELL HOUSE LA

Bulloway's
Farm

Banisters
Farm

Well House
Farm

Greenacres
Farm

Oaklands
Farm

NEW MILL RD

Blackwater River

FLEET HILL

B3348

RG27

Ford

New
Mill

THE RISE

B3348

FLEET LA

The Tally Ho
(PH)

OAKLEA
DR

Horn's
Farm

Eversley
Bridge

Bramshill Plantation

OVER LA

Lower Common

EVERSLEY ST

Fox
Warren

LOWER COMMON

Eversley

WARBROOK LA

Berkshire STREET ATLAS

18

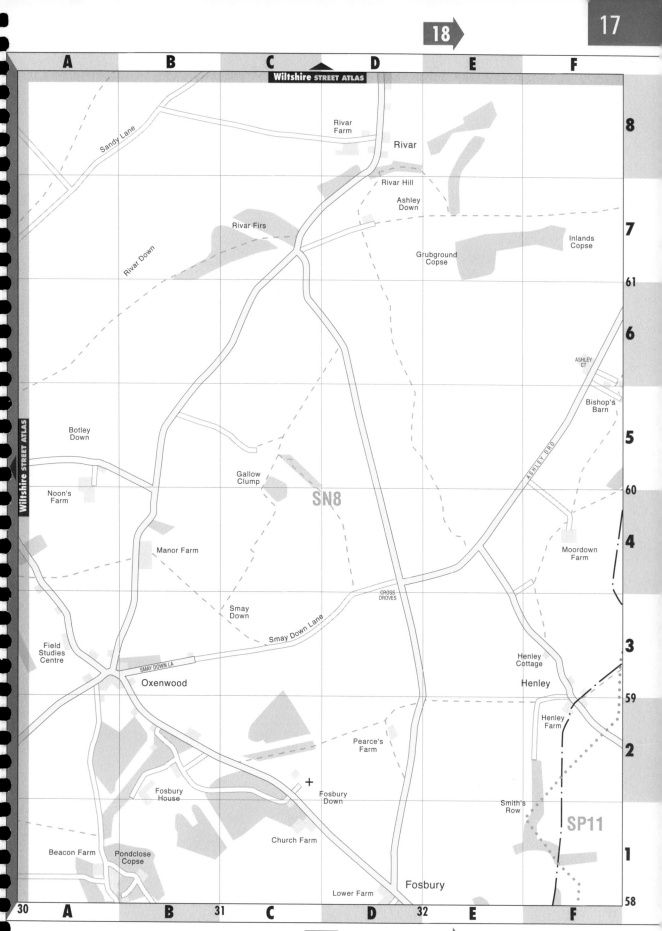

Wiltshire STREET ATLAS

37
18

17

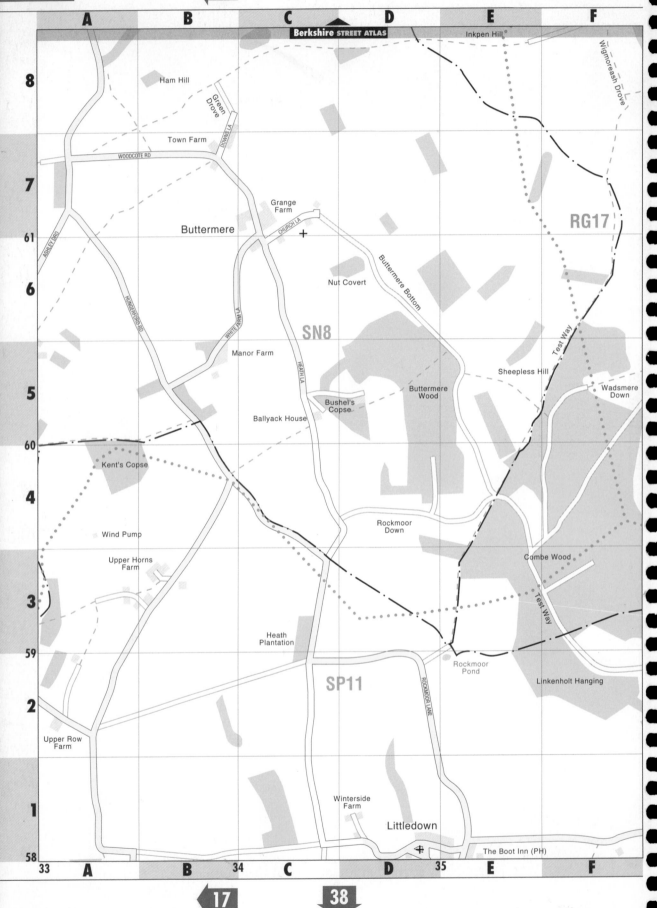

Berkshire STREET ATLAS

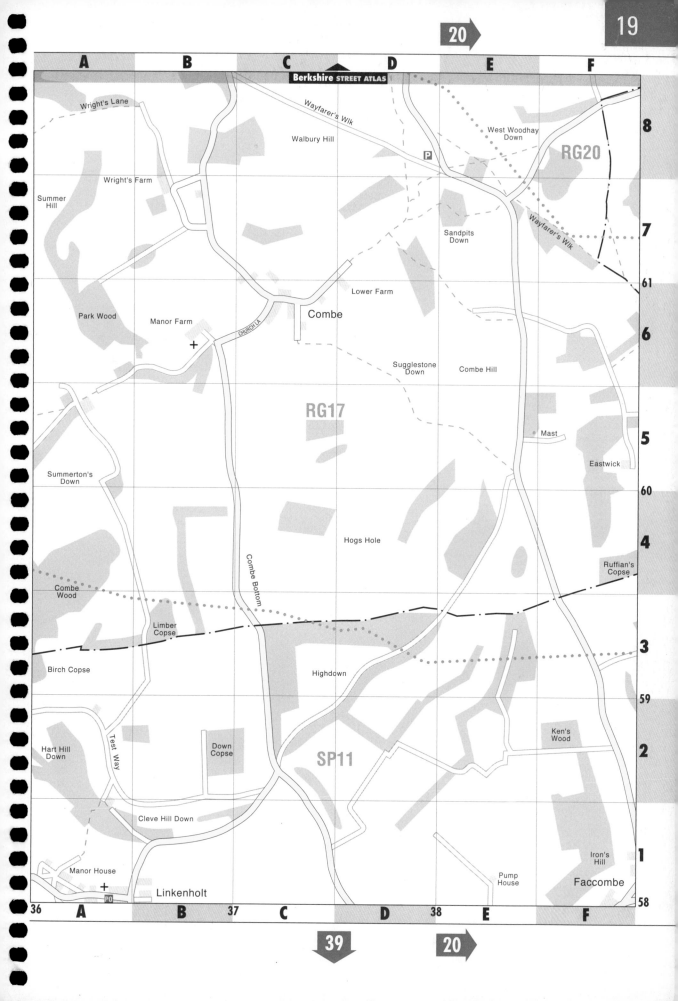

Berkshire STREET ATLAS

A B C D E F

8
7
61
6
5
60
4
3
59
2
1
58

Wright's Lane

Waytarer's Wlk

Walbury Hill

West Woodhay Down

RG20

Wright's Farm

Summer Hill

Waytarer's Wlk

Sandpits Down

Park Wood

Manor Farm

Lower Farm

Combe

CHURCH LA

Sugglestone Down

Combe Hill

RG17

Mast

Eastwick

Summerton's Down

Hogs Hole

Combe Bottom

Ruffian's Copse

Combe Wood

Limber Copse

Birch Copse

Highdown

SP11

Ken's Wood

Hart Hill Down

Test Way

Down Copse

Cleve Hill Down

Manor House

Pump House

Iron's Hill

Faccombe

Linkenholt

PO

36 A B 37 C D 38 E F 58

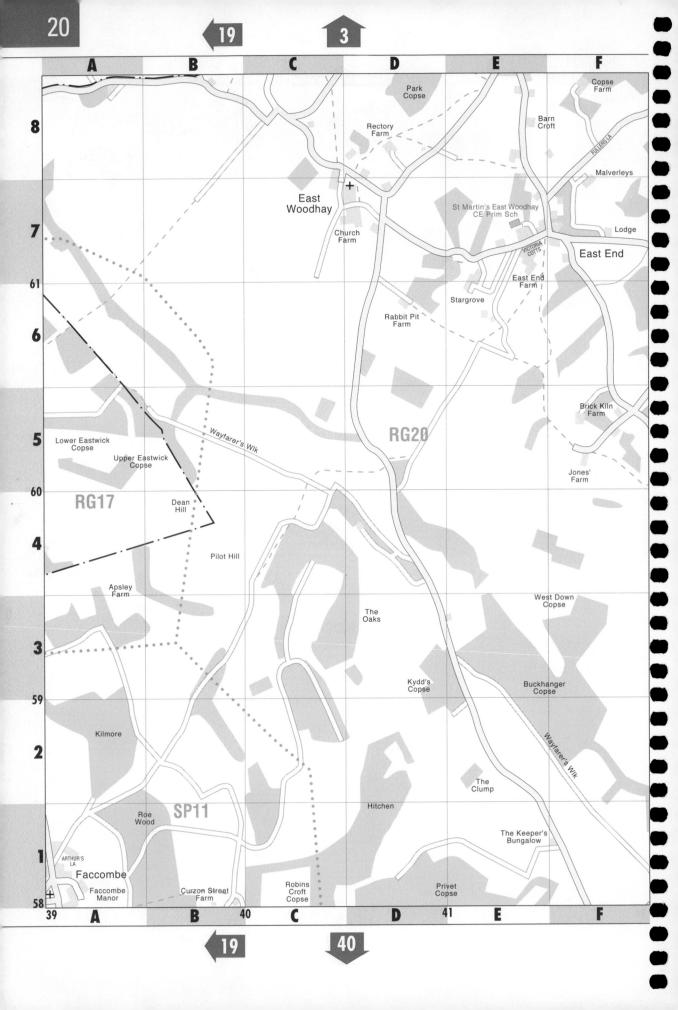

A B C D E F

8

Park Copse

Copse Farm

Rectory Farm

Barn Croft

FULLERS LA

Malverleys

East Woodhay

7

Church Farm

St Martin's East Woodhay CE Prim Sch

Lodge

VICTORIA COTTS

East End

61

East End Farm

Stargrove

6

Rabbit Pit Farm

RG20

Brick Kiln Farm

Lower Eastwick Copse

Wayfarer's Wlk

5

Upper Eastwick Copse

Jones' Farm

RG17

Dean Hill

60

4

Pilot Hill

Apsley Farm

West Down Copse

The Oaks

3

Kydd's Copse

Buckhanger Copse

59

Kilmore

Wayfarer's Wlk

2

The Clump

Roe Wood

SP11

Hitchen

The Keeper's Bungalow

1

ARTHUR'S LA

Faccombe

Faccombe Manor

Curzon Street Farm

Robins Croft Copse

Privet Copse

58

39 A B 40 C D 41 E F

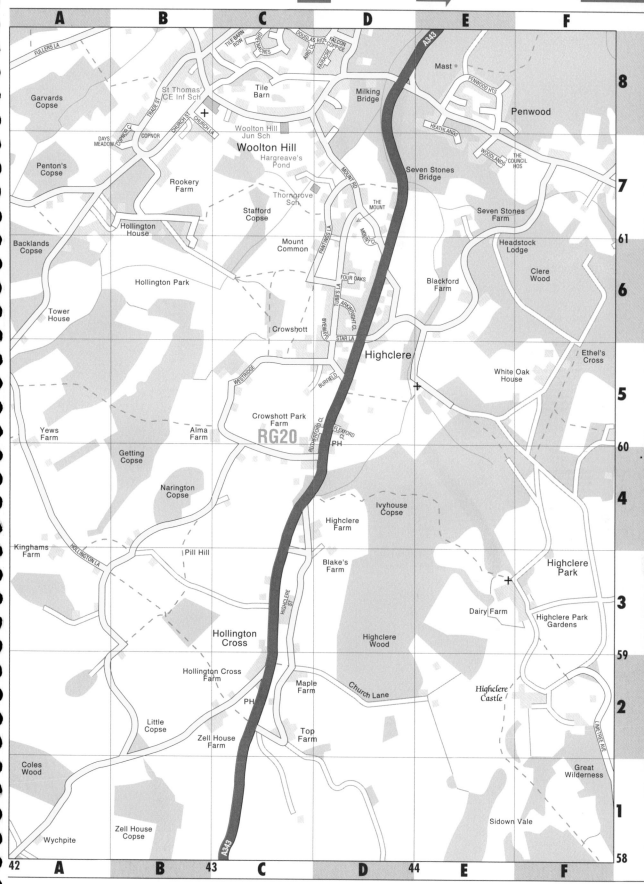

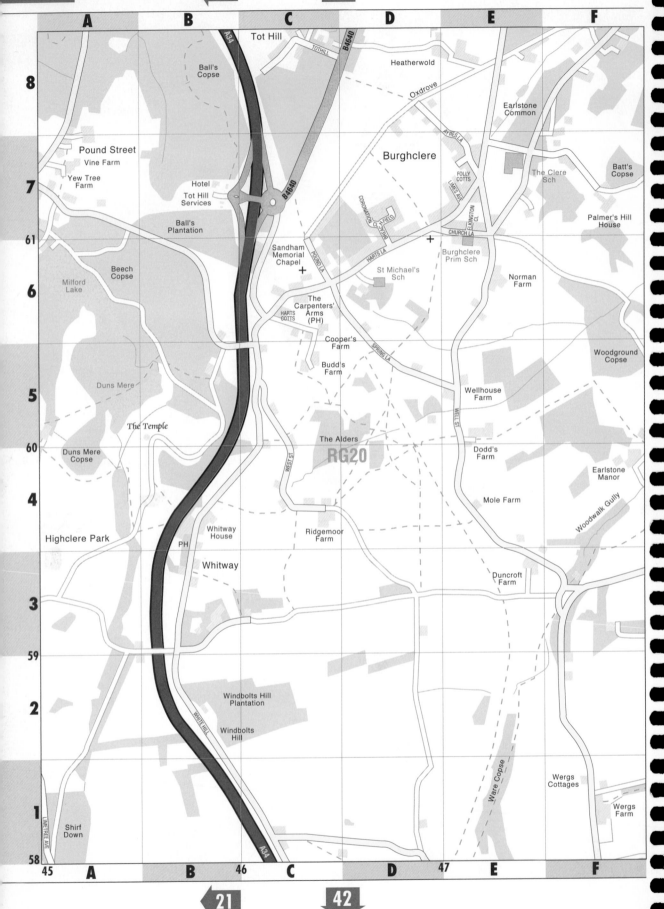

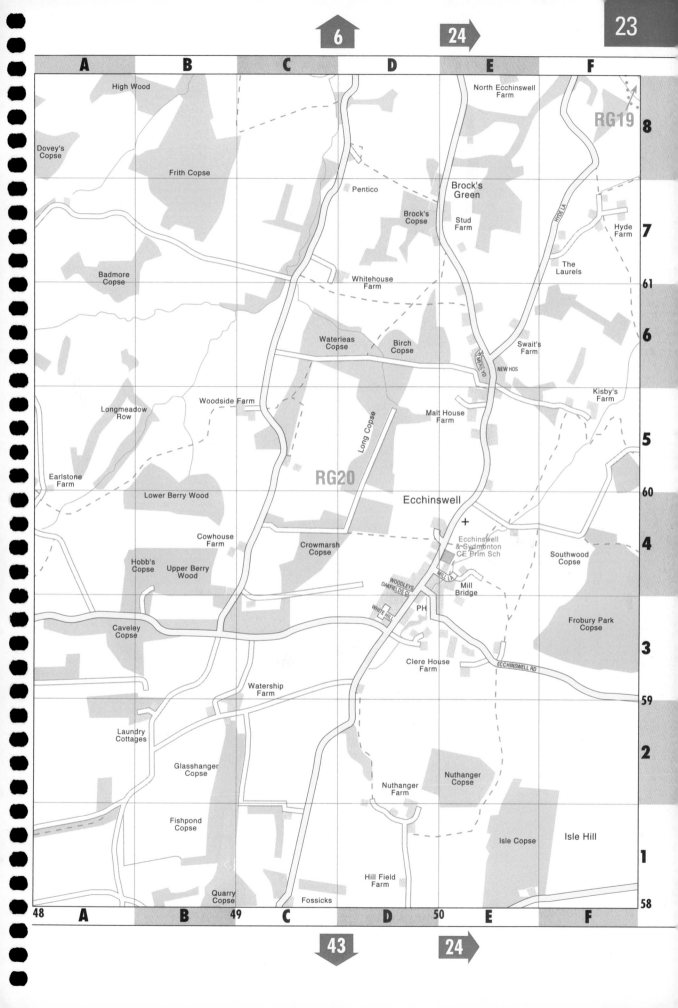

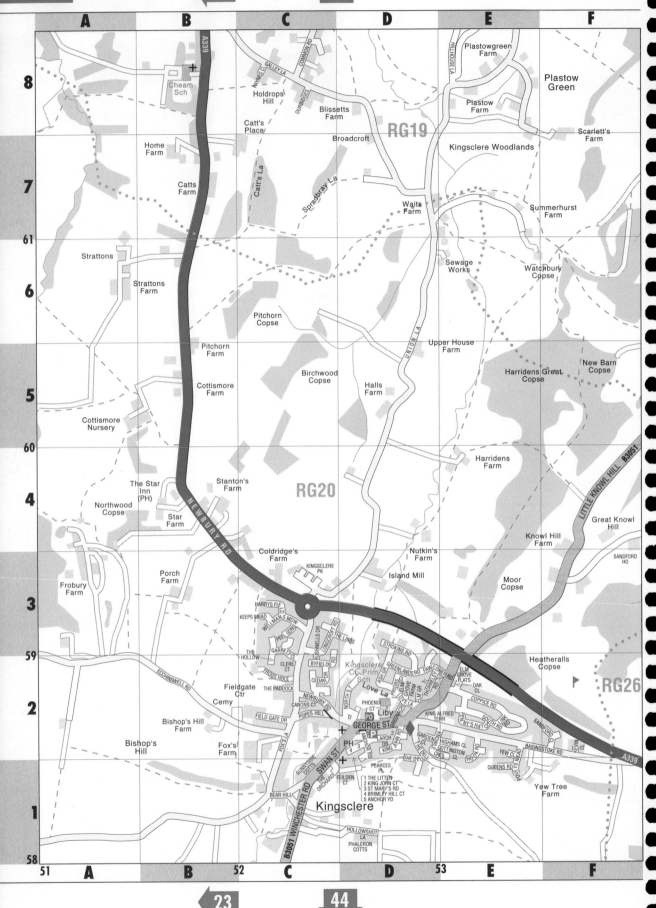

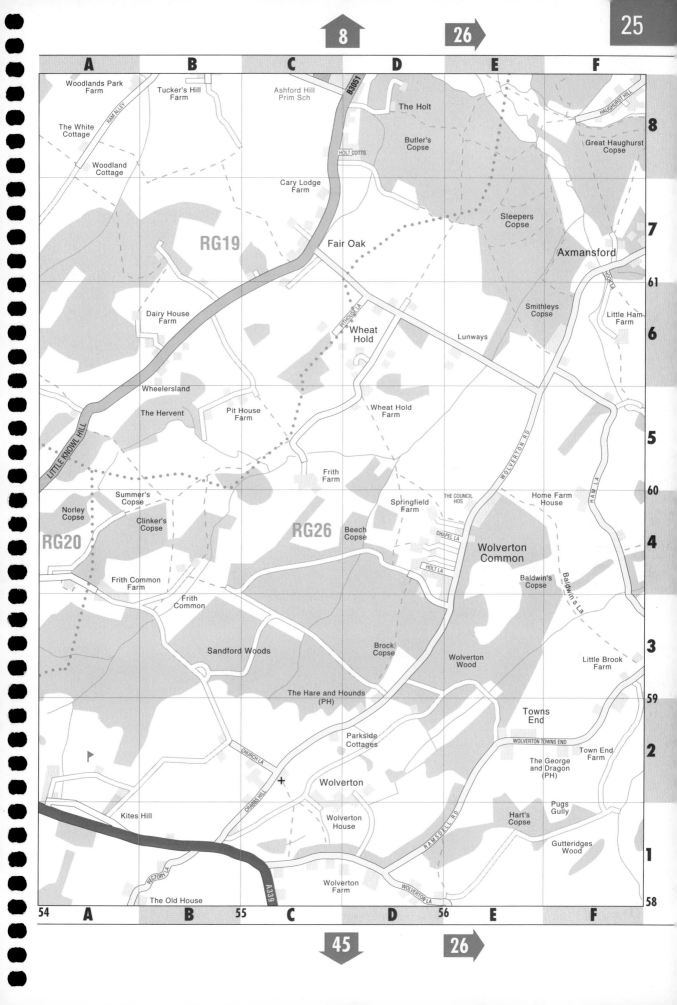

A B C D E F

8

Woodlands Park Farm

Tucker's Hill Farm

Ashford Hill Prim Sch

The Holt

Butler's Copse

Haughurst Hill

Great Haughurst Copse

The White Cottage

RAM ALLEY

HOLT COTTS

Woodland Cottage

Cary Lodge Farm

B3051

7

RG19

Fair Oak

Sleepers Copse

Axmansford

61

Dairy House Farm

Wheat Hold

Lunways

Smithleys Copse

Little Ham Farm

6

P.HOUSE LA

HOLT CR

Wheelersland

The Hervent

Pit House Farm

Wheat Hold Farm

WOLVERTON RD

5

LITTLE KNOWL HILL

HAM LA

Frith Farm

Summer's Copse

THE COUNCIL HOS

Home Farm House

60

Norley Copse

Clinker's Copse

RG26

Springfield Farm

CHAPEL LA

Wolverton Common

4

RG20

Beech Copse

HOLT LA

Baldwin's Copse

Baldwin's La

Frith Common Farm

Frith Common

Brock Copse

Wolverton Wood

Little Brook Farm

3

Sandford Woods

59

The Hare and Hounds (PH)

Towns End

CHURCH LA

Parkside Cottages

WOLVERTON TOWNS END

Town End Farm

2

CRABBS HILL

+

Wolverton

RAMSDELL RD

The George and Dragon (PH)

Kites Hill

Wolverton House

Hart's Copse

Pugs Gully

RECTORY LA

A339

Gutteridges Wood

1

The Old House

Wolverton Farm

WOLVERTON LA

58

54 A B 55 C D 56 E F

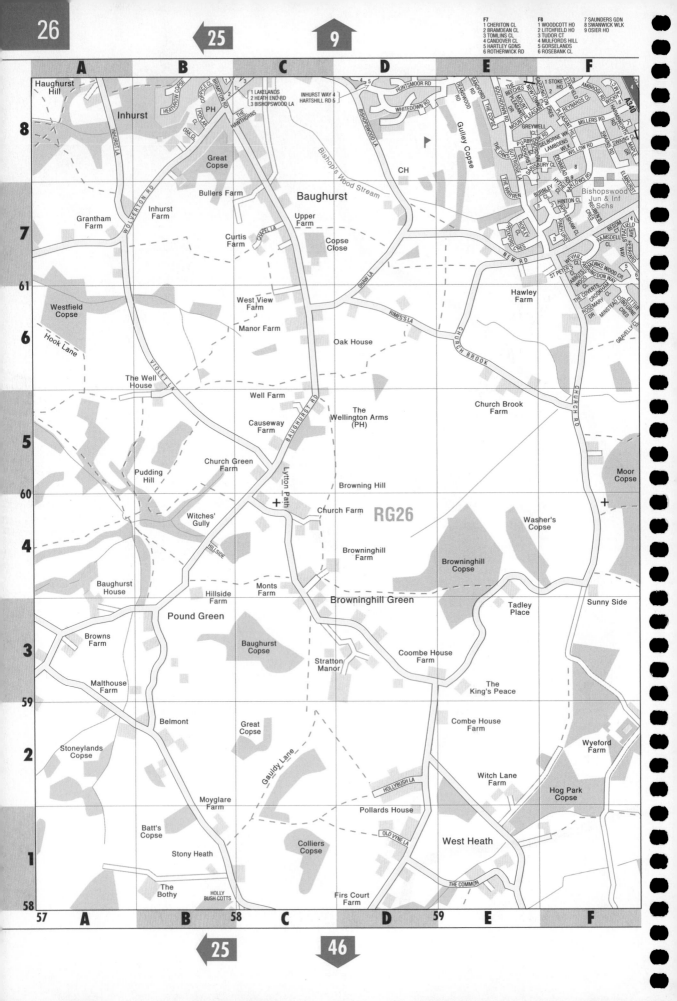

F7
1 CHERITON CL
2 BRAMDEAN CL
3 TOMLINS CL
4 CANDOVER CL
5 HARTLEY GDNS
6 ROTHERWICK RD

F8
1 WOODCOTT HO
2 LITCHFIELD HO
3 TUDOR CT
4 MULFORDS HILL
5 GORSELANDS
6 ROSEBANK CL

7 SAUNDERS GDN
8 SWANWICK WLK
9 OSIER HO

Haughurst Hill

Inhurst

Grantham Farm

Westfield Copse

Hook Lane

The Well House

Pudding Hill

Baughurst House

Browns Farm

Malthouse Farm

Stoneylands Copse

Belmont

Pound Green

Moyglare Farm

Batt's Copse

Stony Heath

The Bothy

HOLLY BUSH COTTS

Great Copse

Bullers Farm

Inhurst Farm

Curtis Farm

West View Farm

Manor Farm

Well Farm

Causeway Farm

Church Green Farm

Witches' Gully

Hillside Farm

Monts Farm

Baughurst Copse

Great Copse

Gauldy Lane

Colliers Copse

Firs Court Farm

1 LAKELANDS
2 HEATH END RD
3 BISHOPSWOOD LA

INHURST WAY 4
HARTSHILL RD 5

Baughurst

Upper Farm

Copse Close

Oak House

The Wellington Arms (PH)

Browning Hill

RG26

Church Farm

Browninghill Farm

Browninghill Green

Stratton Manor

Coombe House Farm

The King's Peace

Combe House Farm

Pollards House

OLD VYNE LA

West Heath

THE COMMON

Huntsmoor Rd

Whitedown Rd

CH

Gulley Copse

Hawley Farm

Church Brook Farm

Browninghill Copse

Tadley Place

Witch Lane Farm

Hog Park Copse

Wyeford Farm

Washer's Copse

Moor Copse

Sunny Side

THE BEECHES

Bishopswood Jun & Inf Schs

A340

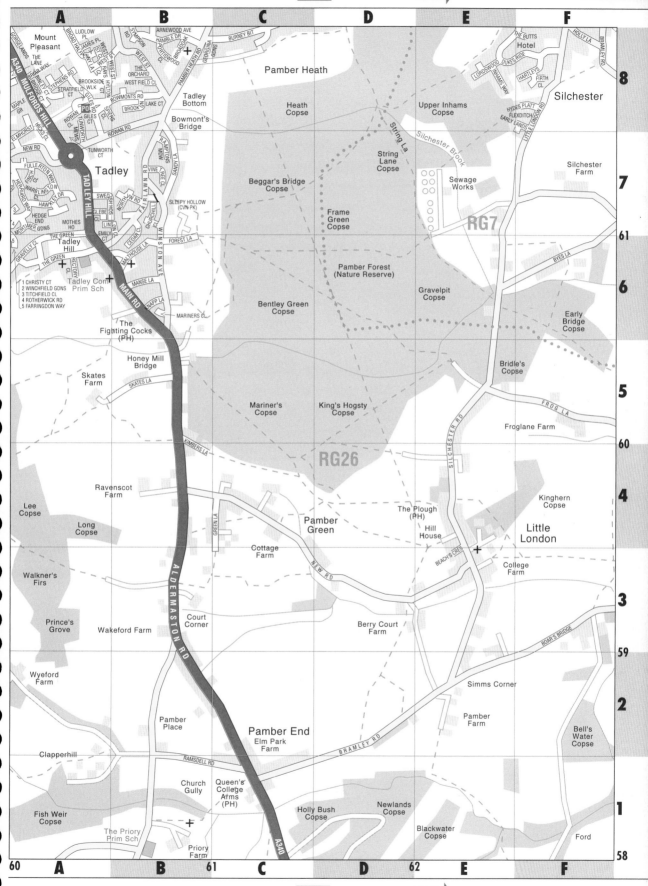

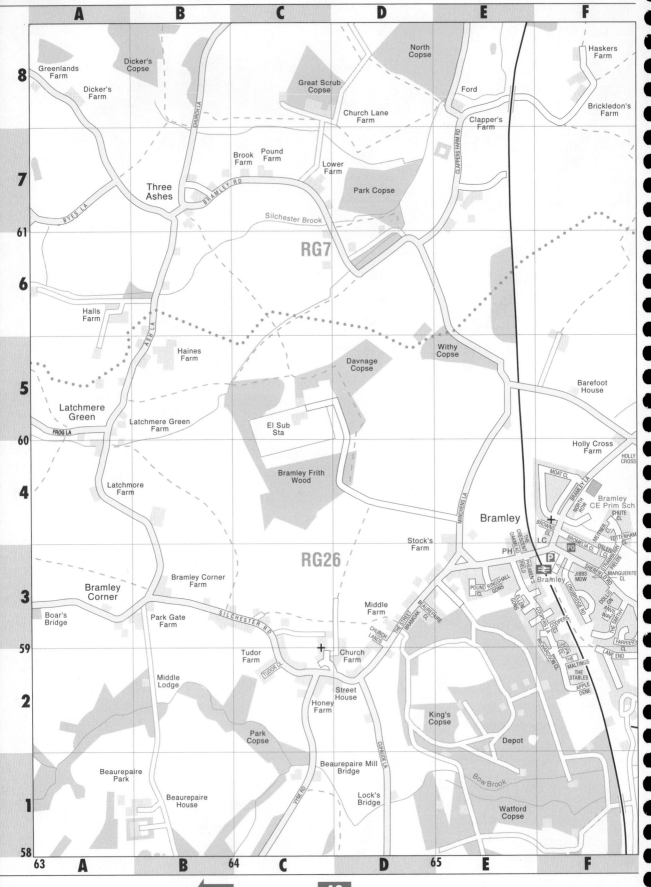

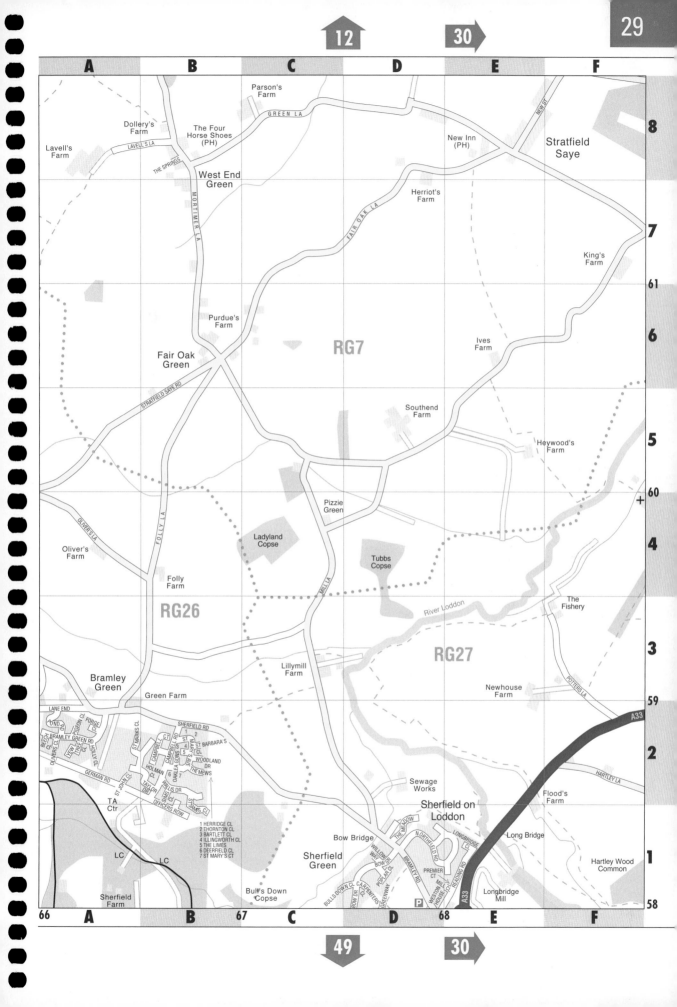

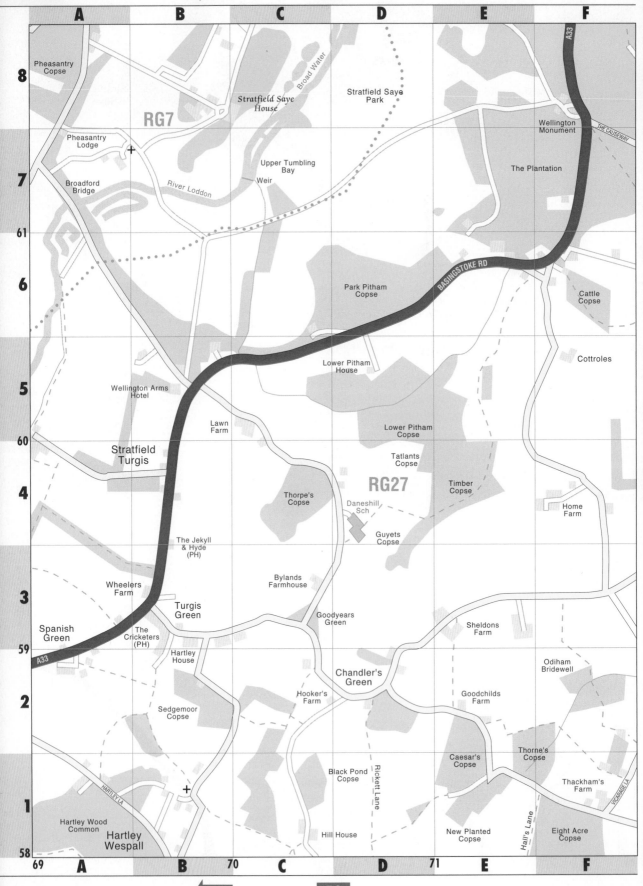

RG7

Pheasantry
Copse

Pheasantry
Lodge

Broadford
Bridge

River Loddon

Stratfield Saye
House

Broad Water

Upper Tumbling
Bay

Weir

Stratfield Saye
Park

Wellington
Monument

The Causeway

The Plantation

Basingstoke Rd

Park Pitham
Copse

Cattle
Copse

Cottroles

Lower Pitham
House

Wellington Arms
Hotel

Lawn
Farm

Lower Pitham
Copse

Stratfield
Turgis

Tatlants
Copse

RG27

Thorpe's
Copse

Timber
Copse

Home
Farm

Daneshill
Sch

The Jekyll
& Hyde
(PH)

Guyets
Copse

Bylands
Farmhouse

Wheelers
Farm

Turgis
Green

Goodyears
Green

Sheldons
Farm

Spanish
Green

A33

The
Cricketers
(PH)

Hartley
House

Chandler's
Green

Odiham
Bridewell

Goodchilds
Farm

Sedgemoor
Copse

Hooker's
Farm

Caesar's
Copse

Thorne's
Copse

Black Pond
Copse

Rickett Lane

Thackham's
Farm

Vicarage La

Hartley La

Hartley Wood
Common

Hartley
Wespall

Hill House

New Planted
Copse

Hall's Lane

Eight Acre
Copse

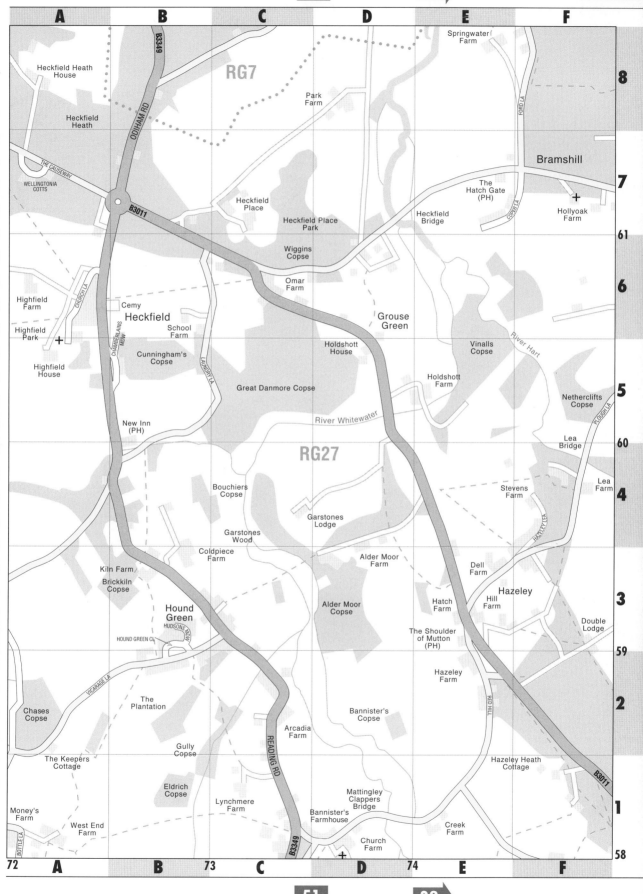

A B C D E F

8
St Neot's Sch
WARBROOK LA
Warbrook (Con Ctr)
A327
B3272
READING RD
Bramshill Plantation
Warren Farm
GLASTON HILL RD

7
ST NEOT'S RD
Yalden's Farm
Church Farm
A327

61
Refuse Tip

6
PLOUGH LA
Moor Place Farm
Heath Warren

Cudbury Clump

RG27

5

60
Peatmoor Copse
THE QUADRANGLE
LAKESIDE DR
READING DEN
READING DR S
The Welsh Drive

4
GREENRIDE DR
LOWER FOOL RD
Bramshill House (Police Coll)
MANSION DR
PHEASANTRY DR
Warren Heath
Three Castles Path
Sir Richard's Drive

Bramshill Park

Deer Park
Long Water
Birch Bottom
Sand & Gravel Pit

3
High Bridge

59
River Hart
Chalwin's Copse

2
Hazeley Heath
Crabtree Copse
Hulford's Copse
Warren Hill Plantation

Crabtree Lodge
A30
STAR HILL

1
B3011
Purdies Farm
Warren Hill Farm
Star Hill

58
B3011
Hatts Cottage
Hazeley Heath
SPRINGWELL LA
HULFORDS LA
A30

75 A B 76 C D 77 E F

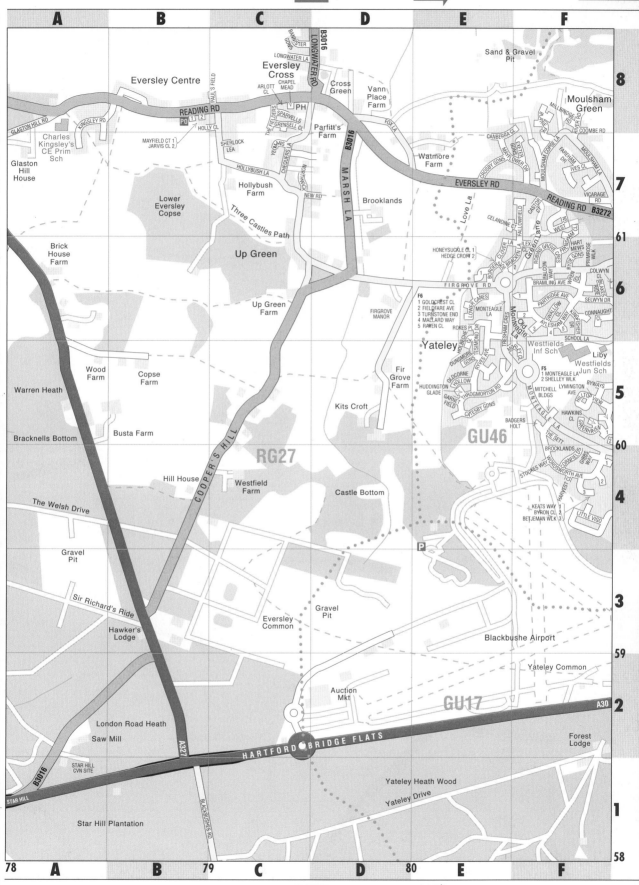

A B C D E F

8
7
61
6
5
60
4
3
59
2
1
58

Sand & Gravel Pit

Moulsham Green

Eversley Centre

PAUL'S FIELD

BANISTER GDNS

LONGWATER LA

Eversley Cross

B3016

LONGWATER RD

Cross Green

Vann Place Farm

MILLBRIDGE RD

PACK LA

COOMBE RD

CHAPEL MEAD

ARLOTT CL

READING RD

SPARVELLS

GRENSELL CL

PH

PO

CHEQUERS LA

HOLLY CL

THE FIELDERS

YEOMANS

Parfitt's Farm

Watmore Farm

FOX LA

CANBERRA CT

CROSBY GDNS

CHESTER GDNS

MAY FLOWER DR

FARNHAM

IVES CL

MOULSHAM LA

MAYFIELD CT 1
JARVIS CL 2

SHERLOCK LEA

HOLLYBUSH LA

NORTHWICK

NEW RD

Hollybush Farm

Brooklands

EVERSLEY RD

READING RD

B3272

VICARAGE RD

Charles Kingsley's CE Prim Sch

GLASTON HILL RD

KINGSLEY RD

Glaston Hill House

Lower Eversley Copse

Three Castles Path

MARSH LA

Love La

CELANDINE CT

FALLOWFIELD

VINE

WEST

CASTOR

PRIMROSE WLK

HART MEWS

GREEN LANE

RYDE GDNS

PERSIMMON

Up Green

Brick House Farm

HONEYSUCKLE CL 1
HEDGE CROFT 2

BODEN'S

BRACKEN CL

CLOVER LA

ALEX

FALCON

ROBIN'S GROVE

COLWYN CL

FIRGROVE RD

F6
1 GOLDCREST CL
2 FIELDFARE AVE
3 TURNSTONE END
4 MALLARD WAY
5 RAVEN CL

LOWER CANES

BRAMLING AVE

SWALLOW CL

PARTRIDGE AVE

SELWYN DR

BLAKES

KINGFISHER

CONNAUGHT CL

Up Green Farm

FIRGROVE MANOR

MONTEAGLE LA

OLDE MONTEAGLE

SWALLOW

AYLESHAM

WREN

FISHER DR

SCHOOL LA

Westfields Inf Sch

Liby

Westfields Jun Sch

ROKES PL

TRESHAM CRES

DUNSMORE GDNS

Yateley

DESMOND DR

OLDCORNE

HOLLOW

RYE'S AVE

MOSS

F5
1 MONTEAGLE LA
2 SHELLEY WLK

BYWAYS

Wood Farm

Copse Farm

Warren Heath

Fir Grove Farm

HUDDINGTON GLADE

GARNET FIELD

THROGMORTON RD

CATESBY GDNS

LYMINGTON AVE

MITCHELL BLDGS

TOP VIEW

HAWKINS CL

GRENHAM

Bracknells Bottom

Busta Farm

Kits Croft

GU46

BADGERS HOLT

THE SETT

BROCKLANDS

GIBBS WAY

MONTEAGLE LA

COOPER'S HILL

RG27

Castle Bottom

STOOKES WAY

WORDSWORTH AVE

CORNFIELDS

HARVEST

Hill House

Westfield Farm

LITTLE VIGO

KEATS WAY 1
BYRON CL 2
BETJEMAN WLK 3

The Welsh Drive

Gravel Pit

P

Sir Richard's Ride

Blackbushe Airport

Yateley Common

Hawker's Lodge

Eversley Common

Gravel Pit

GU17

A30

London Road Heath

A327

BLACKBUSHES RD

Auction Mkt

Saw Mill

HARTFORD BRIDGE FLATS

Forest Lodge

STAR HILL CVN SITE

B3016

STAR HILL

Yateley Heath Wood

Yateley Drive

Star Hill Plantation

78 A B 79 C D 80 E F

33

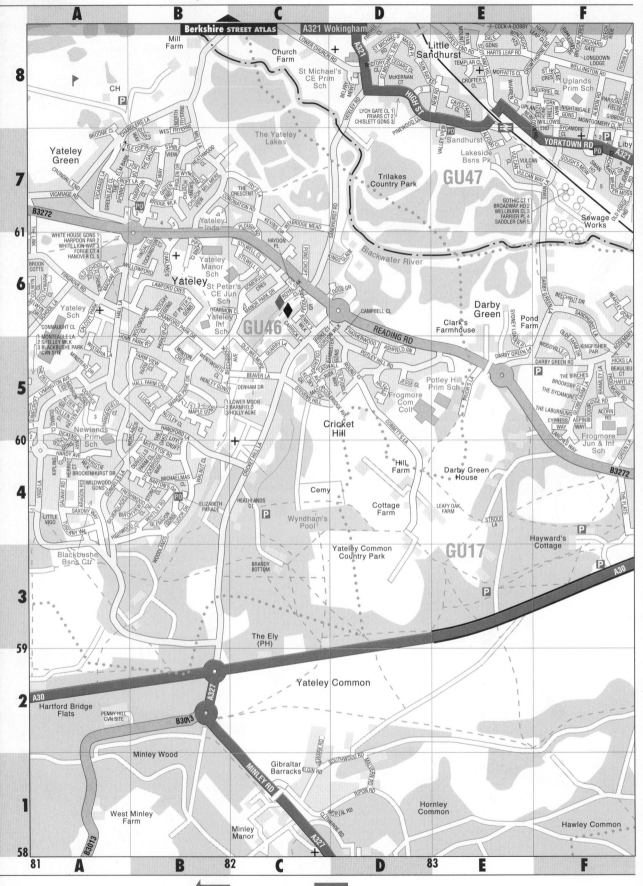

33
54

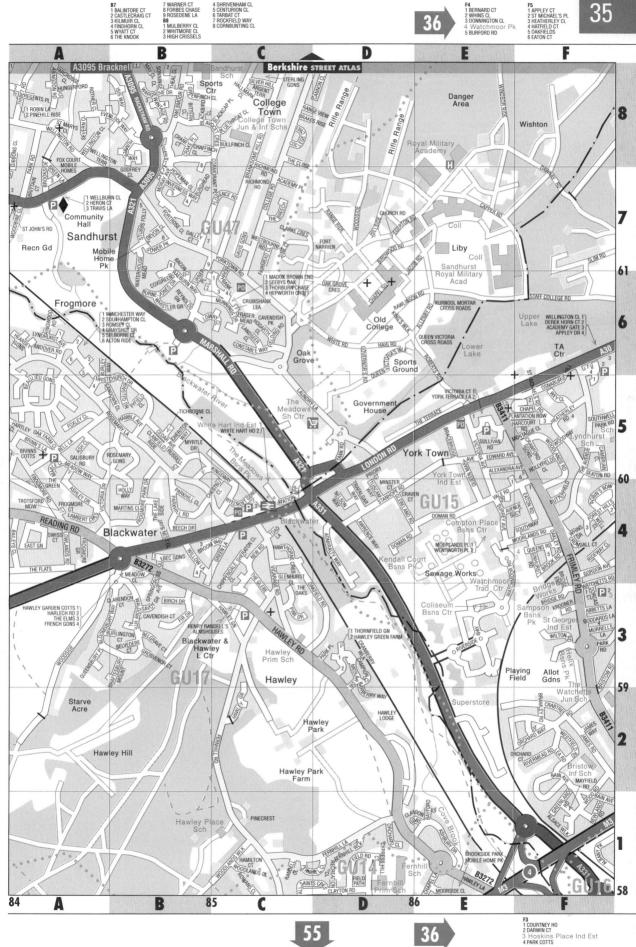

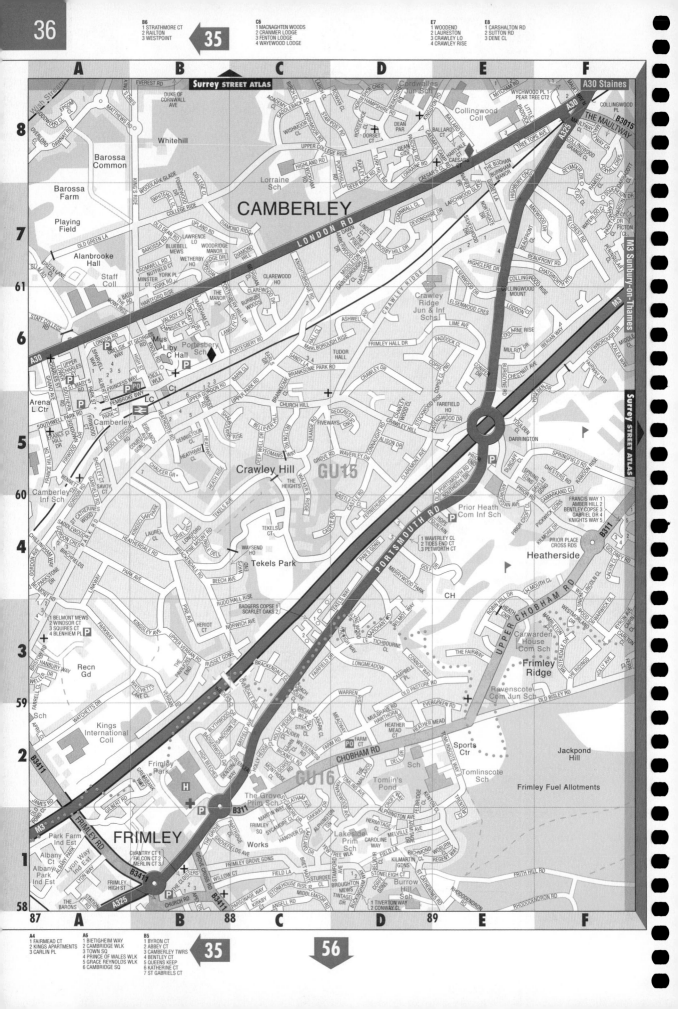

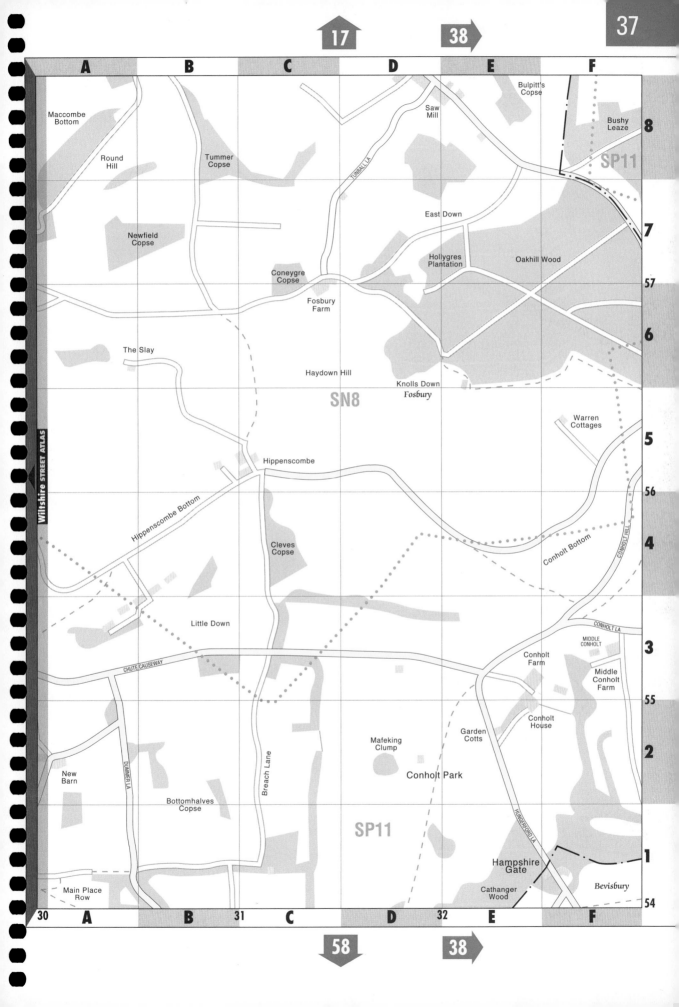

17
38

A B C D E F

8
7
57
6
5
56
4
3
55
2
1
54

Wiltshire STREET ATLAS

Maccombe Bottom
Round Hill
Tummer Copse
Newfield Copse
Coneygre Copse
Fosbury Farm
The Slay
Haydown Hill
SN8
Knolls Down
Fosbury
Saw Mill
Bulpitt's Copse
Bushy Leaze
SP11
East Down
Hollygres Plantation
Oakhill Wood
TUNBALL LA
Warren Cottages
Hippenscombe
Hippenscombe Bottom
Cleves Copse
Little Down
Conholt Bottom
CONHOLT HILL
CHUTE CAUSEWAY
New Barn
DUMMER LA
Bottomhalves Copse
Breach Lane
Mafeking Clump
Conholt Park
Garden Cotts
Conholt House
Conholt Farm
MIDDLE CONHOLT
CONHOLT LA
Middle Conholt Farm
SP11
HUNGERFORD LA
Hampshire Gate
Cathanger Wood
Bevisbury

Main Place Row

30 A B 31 C D 32 E F

58
38

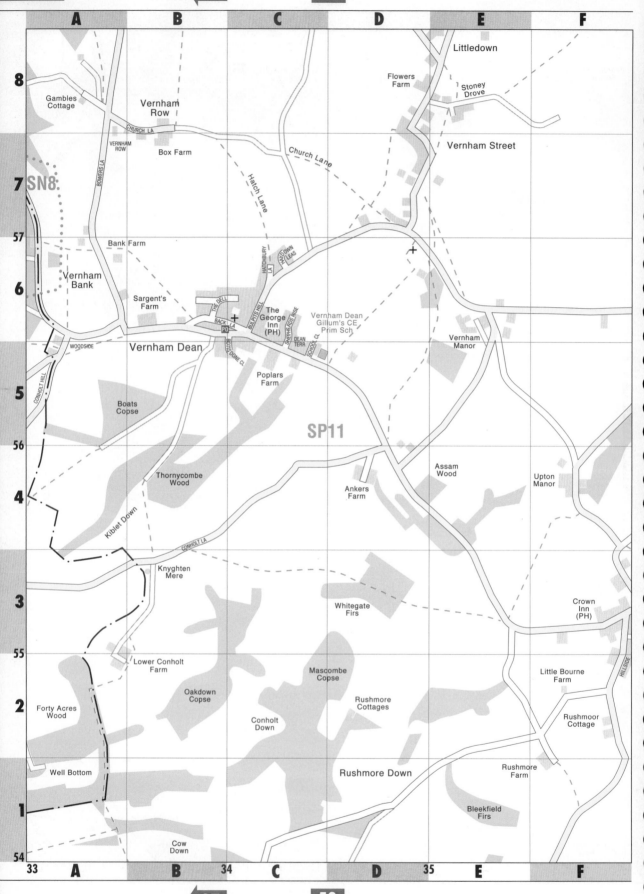

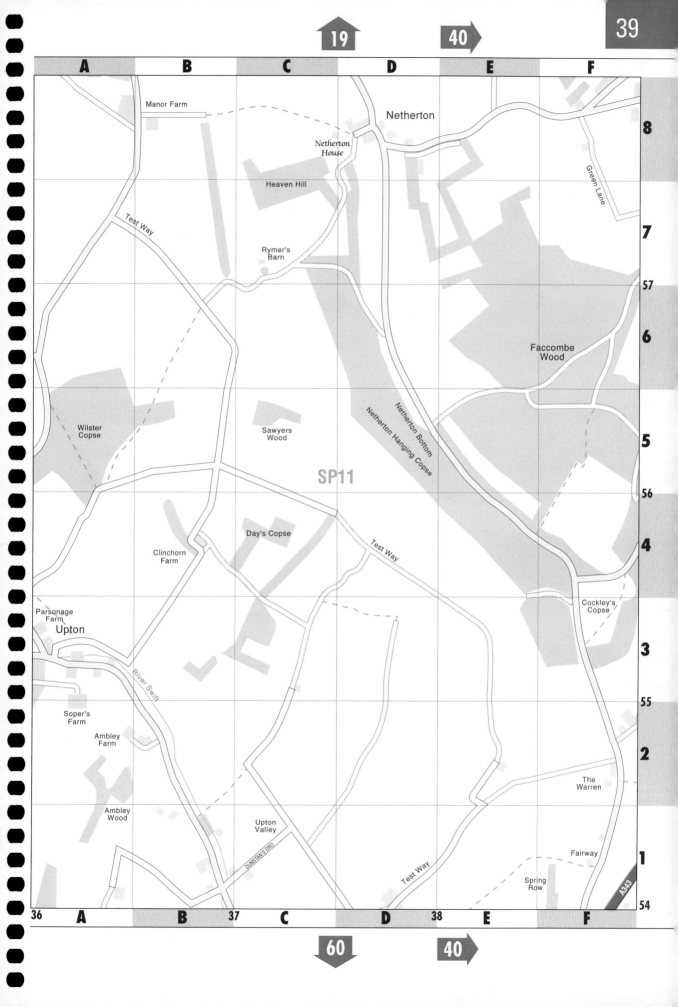

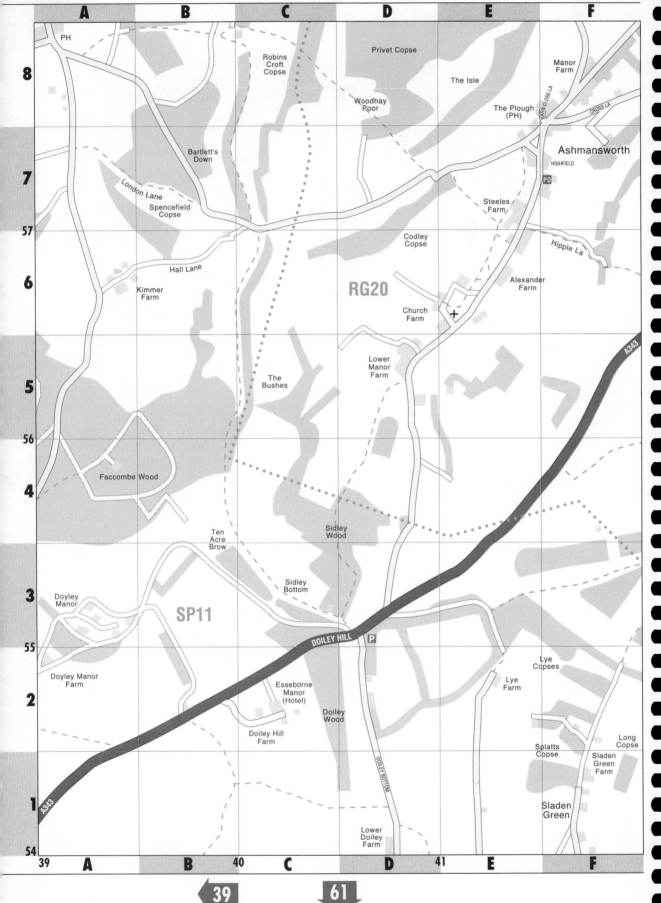

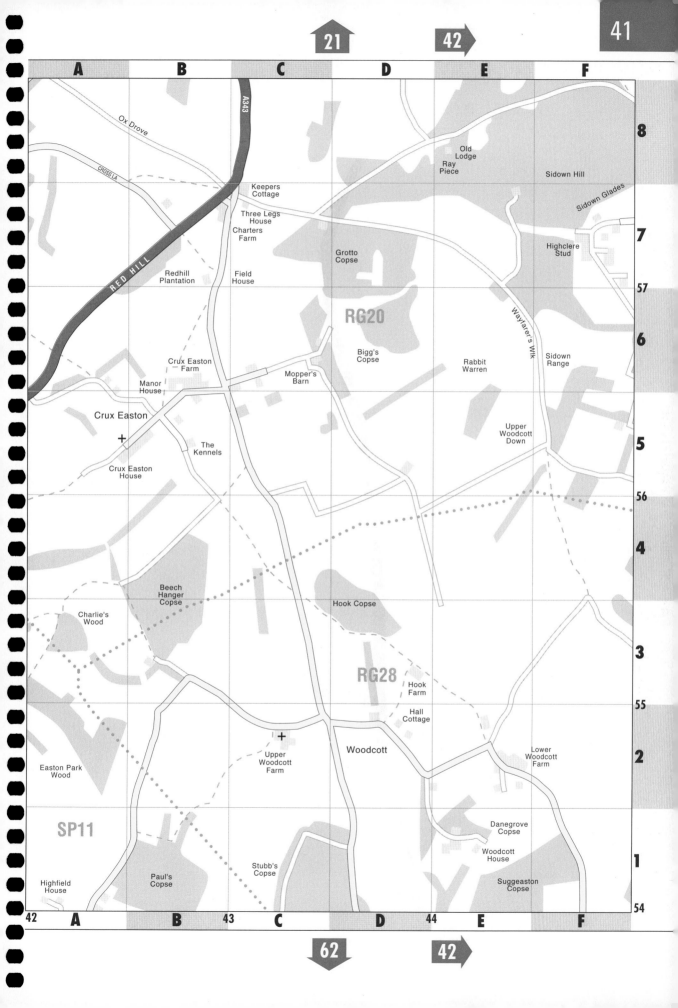

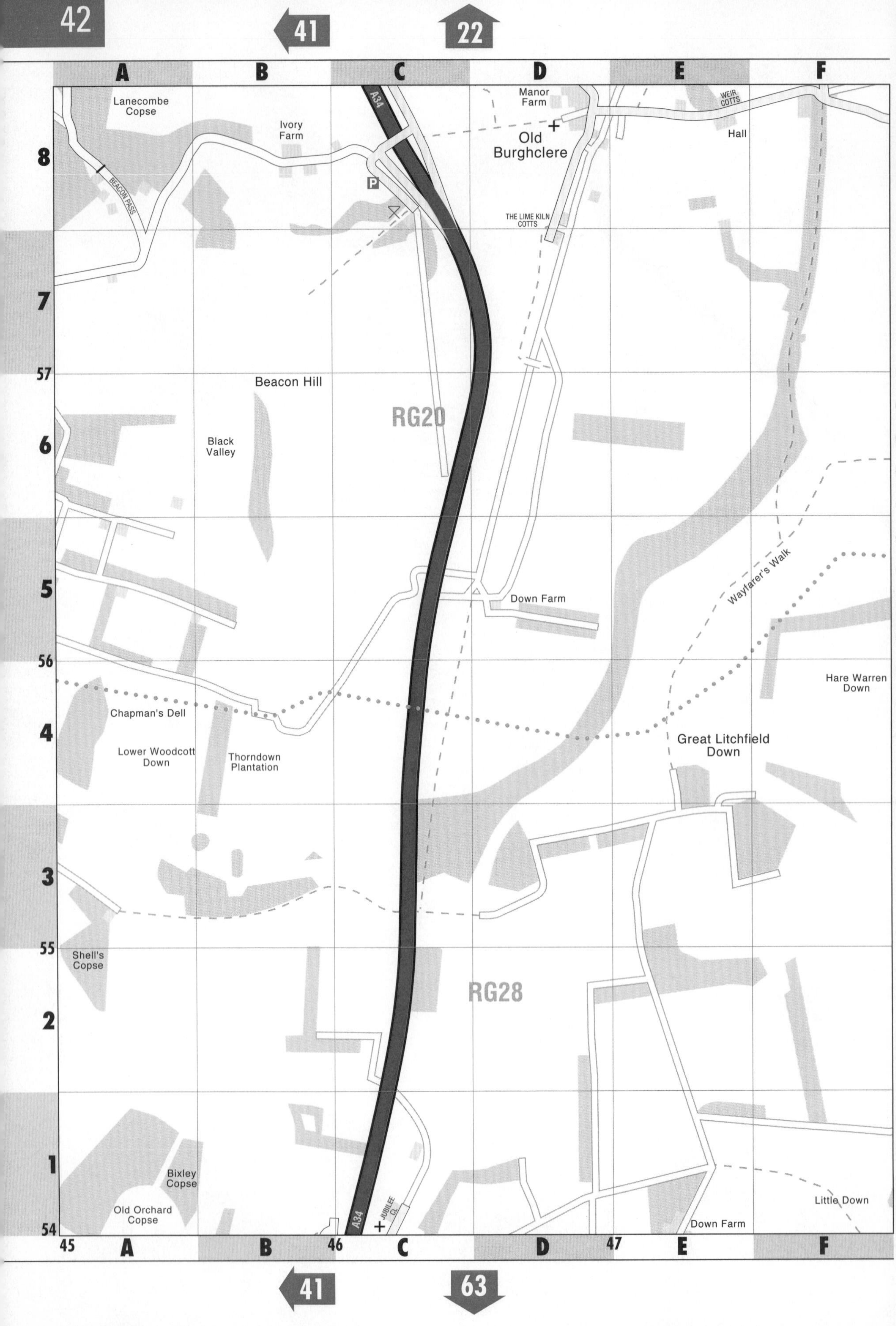

A B C D E F

8

Lanecombe Copse

Ivory Farm

A34

Manor Farm

WEIR COTTS

Old Burghclere

Hall

BEACON PASS

P

THE LIME KILN COTTS

7

57

Beacon Hill

RG20

6

Black Valley

5

Down Farm

Wayfarer's Walk

56

Hare Warren Down

Chapman's Dell

4

Lower Woodcott Down

Thorndown Plantation

Great Litchfield Down

3

55

Shell's Copse

RG28

2

1

Bixley Copse

Little Down

Old Orchard Copse

A34

JUBILEE CL

Down Farm

54

45 A B 46 C D 47 E F

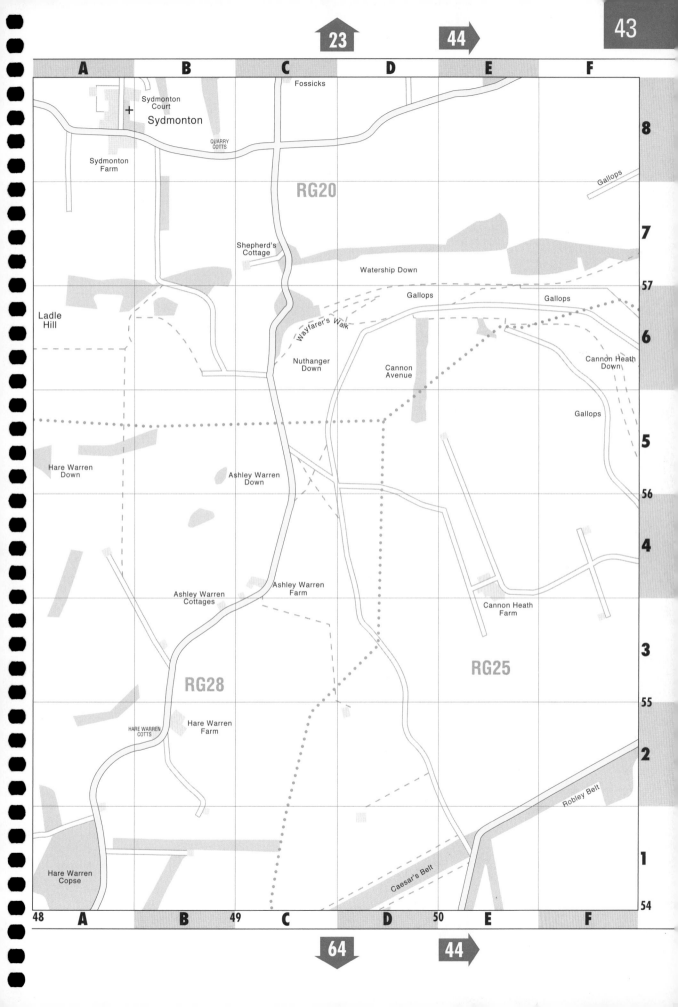

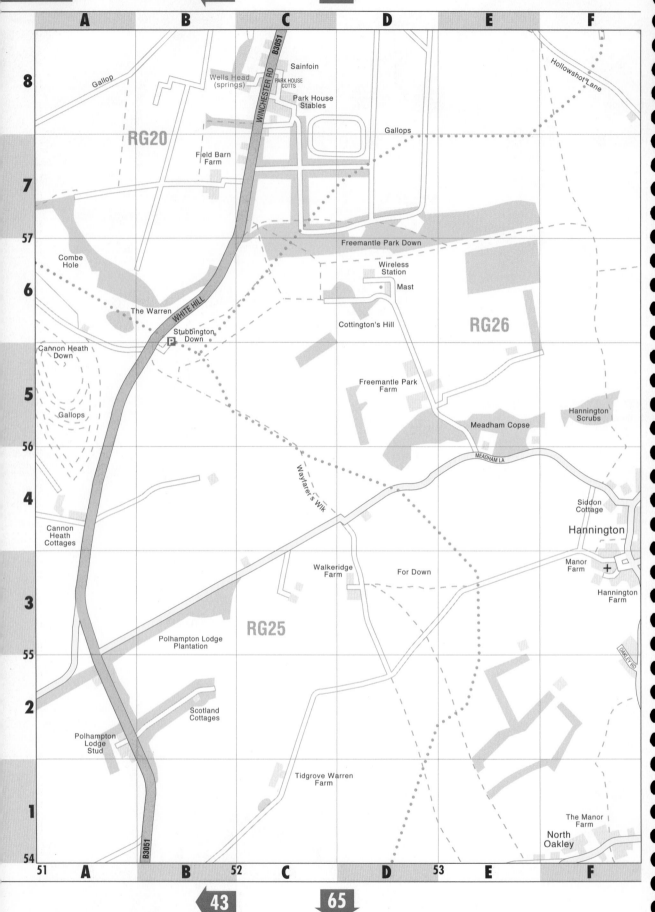

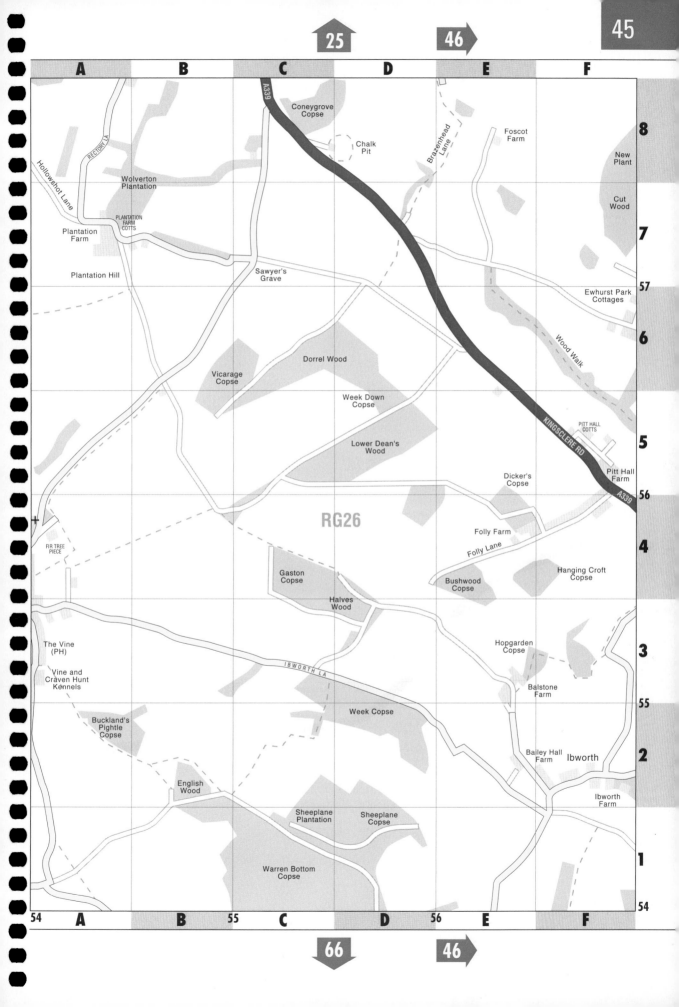

A   B   C   D   E   F

Coneygrove
Copse

8

Chalk
Pit

New
Plant

RECTORY LA

Foscot
Farm

Brazenhead Lane

A339

Wolverton
Plantation

Cut
Wood

7

Hollowshot Lane

PLANTATION
FARM
COTTS

Plantation
Farm

Sawyer's
Grave

Ewhurst Park
Cottages

57

Plantation Hill

Wood Walk

6

Dorrel Wood

Vicarage
Copse

Week Down
Copse

KINGSCLERE RD

PITT HALL
COTTS

5

Lower Dean's
Wood

Dicker's
Copse

Pitt Hall
Farm

A339

56

RG26

Folly Farm

FIR TREE
PIECE

Folly Lane

4

Gaston
Copse

Bushwood
Copse

Hanging Croft
Copse

Halves
Wood

The Vine
(PH)

Hopgarden
Copse

3

IBWORTH LA

Balstone
Farm

Vine and
Craven Hunt
Kennels

55

Buckland's
Pightle
Copse

Week Copse

Bailey Hall
Farm   Ibworth

2

English
Wood

Ibworth
Farm

Sheeplane
Plantation

Sheeplane
Copse

1

Warren Bottom
Copse

54

54   A   55   B   C   56   D   E   F

A B C D E F

8
Sandpits Copse
Round Copse
Bushy Copse
Lily Lake
Hollybush Farm
Little Wyford Farm
The White Hart (PH)
Fir Tree Farm
PAMBER RD
BAUGHURST RD
WHITE HART LA
MONK SHERBORNE RD
Charter Alley

7
Dogkennel Wood
Park Copse
Lloyd's Copse
Ramsdell
The Old Brick Kiln Trad Est
Wither's Copse
Brocas Bridge
PEAL'S PIGHTLE

Skyer's Farm

57
Home Farm
Ewhurst Park
Ewhurst Pond
SHERWASH LA
Six Acre Copse

6
Ewhurst House
LLOYD'S LA
Skyer's Wood
May's Cottage
Privett Copse

May's Copse

5
Wood Walk
Lodge
Spilman's Copse
RG26
Lower Farm
BASINGSTOKE RD

56
A339

4

3
Pierce's Copse
Pithall
Woodgarston Farm
Piccadilly Hill
Field Barn Farm

55

2
Upper Wootton
Manor Farm
KINGSCLERE RD
A339

HOOK LA

Woodgarston La

1
Ebenezer Cottage
RG23

54
Whitedown
57 58 59

A B C D E F

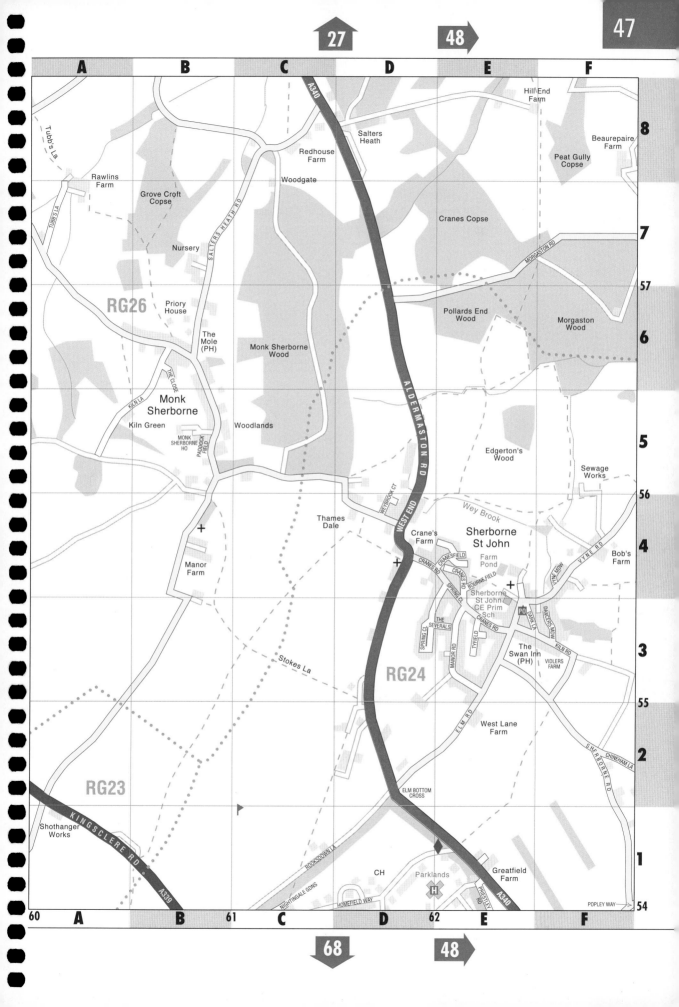

47 28

A B C D E F

8

Baker's Farm House

Cufaude Bsns Pk

Bushyplatt Copse

Pepper Wood

Vyne Lodge Farm

Cufaude Farm

Beech Lodges

MORGASTON RD

Cufaude

7

RG26

P

Upper Cufaude Farm

CUFAUDE LA

57

Vyne Park

The Lake

VYNE RD

6

The Vyne

Gallary Pightle Copse

Gallaries Copse

Vyne Farm

MARL'S LA

5

Collet's Copse

Razor's Farm

SAFFRON CL 1
PETTY'S BROOK RD 2
GREENWOOD DR 3
PARKWOOD CL 4.

Long Swains Row

THORNHILL W

56

RG24

Hampshire Int Bsns Pk

CUFAUDE LA

THYME

Martin's Bushes

AJAX CL

ACHILLES WAY

PENGWIN WAY

BOWMAN RD

4

Marl's Copse

Chineham Bsns Pk

SPINDLEWOOD

MAYBROOK

FOREST DR

TANGWAY

Spier's Copse

LINDENWOOD

LIME TREE WAY

STAG OAK LA

HAZELWOOD

CHERRYWOOD

HAMMORE RD

OAKWOOD

OAKWOOD

BIRCHWOOD

MALLERY WAY

Four Lanes Inf & Com Jun Schs

CIBBONS RD

SORRELL'S

CATKIN RD

ELMWOOD

LARCHWOOD 1
AGHEMUND CL 2

Crockford's Farm

CEDARWOOD

BEECHWOOD

ROSEWOOD

Chineham

THUMWOOD

3

Kiln Farm

Parrott's Copse

PINEWOOD

MERRYFIELD

SOUTHAMS

WOODVILLE CL 1

WHITEWOOD

KINGS PIGHTLE

ASHFIELD

55

Carpenter's Down Wood

MAPLEWOOD

KINGS WOOD

HIGHMOORS

WOODVILLE

LARFIELD

HAZELDENE RD

MATTOCK WAY

Long Copse

LONG COPSE CHASE

THUMBER 2

Marlborough Trad Mews

JERSEY CL

GUERNSEY CL

CROCKFORD LA

LITTLE COPSE CHASE

FRANKLINS COPSE

READING GLADE

JOSEPH'S CL

CLERE GDNS

2

Marnel Dell

Popley Fields House

TASMANIA CL

CARPENTER'S DOWN

MONTSERRAT PL

MONT-SERRAT RD

DOMINICA CL

BASINGSTOKE

Com Ctr

P

GREAT OAKS CHASE

MORRIS RISE

UPPER READING RD

HARDS-WOOD

REMEMBRANCE GDNS

A33

Great Binfields Copse

CHINEHAM LA

BERMUDA CL

ANGLESEY CL

FALKLAND RD

PITCAIRN CL

STROUD

SIMONS RD

SIMONS CT

Wellfield Farm

SPECKLED WOOD RD

MALTA

TIMOR CL

GILBERT CL

Marnel Inf & Jun Schs

ASCENSION CL

MADEIRA CL

MINDEN CL

BINFIELDS RDBT

MAGNOLIA HOUSE

St Bede's RC Prim Sch

ABBEY CT

COSTAR O

TRINIDAD

POPLEY WAY

CATMAN RD

SHETLAND RD

MALONEY RD

ORKNEY RD

CROCKFORD LA

READING RD

Kingsland Ind Pk

Lutyens Ind Ctr

BILTON RD

Chineham District Ctr

P

Liby

GREAT BINFIELDS RD

CENTRE DR

HERON PK

1

BUCKFAST CL

ROMSEY CL

FOUNTAINS CL

ABBEY RD

PERSHORE RD

EVESHAM WLK

SELBY WALK

FAWKESBURY CL

Popley

John Hunt of Everest Com Sch

SHAKESPEARE RD

LAWRENCE RD

CHINEHAM PARK

FARDE CL

LUNDY

BYRON CL

Gaston's Wood Ind Est

STEWART RD

LUTYENS CL

WADE RD

54

63 A B 64 C D 65 E F

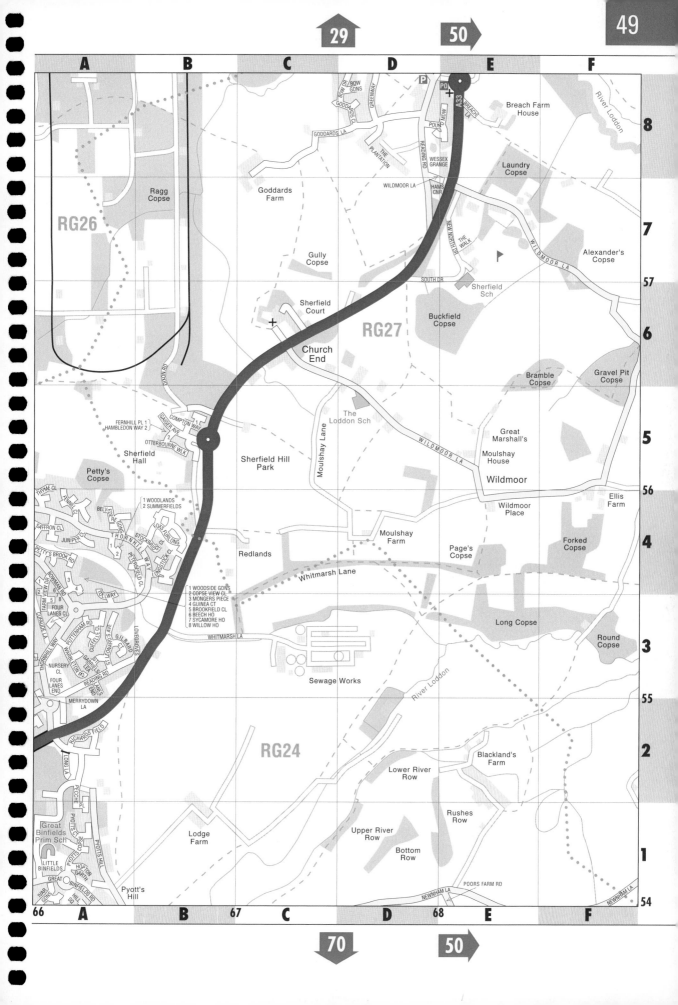

49
30

A B C D E F

8

Topford Cottage

Webb's Hill

Kilnclose Copse

Hall's Lane

Peter's Copse

Webb's Copse

Lower Home Copse

Cooper's Farm

ROTHERWICK LA

Allen Moor

Poplars Farm

Upper Home Copse

7

Hays Farm

Mill Farm

Cooper's Copse

The Fox (PH)

Lyde Green Farm

Lyde Green

Allenmoor Lane

Lance Levy Farm

MILL LA

Black Wood

57

FROG LA

Wedman's Farm

6

Soperslip Copse

River Loddon

Lyde River

Winnells Copse

Rooks Farm

Rotherwick

WEDMAN'S PL

LAMPARDS CL

WEDMAN'S LA

COWFOLD LA

Whitewater CE Prim Sch

THE STREET

HOOK RD

Summerstead Farm

Tim's Copse

The Old Rectory

The Coach and Horses (PH)

5

Wildmoor Farm

RG27

POST HORN LA

56

The Old House

GREEN LA

Optrex Bsns Pk

Runten's Farm

4

CH

Cedar Clump

North Runten's Copse

Tylney House

3

Tylney Park

Home Farm

Shirlen's Copse

55

Tylney Hall Hotel

College Copse

Beehive Farm

Outdoor Education Centre

College Copse

Hill Copse

2

Compfield Copse

TYLNEY LA

RIDGE LA

Owen's Farm

GOOSE GN

SHELDON ST

PAINTERS PIGHTLE

SWAN ST YD

BROWN CROFT

Hale Farm

Deanlands Farm

Newnham

1

Newnham Green Farm

PH

BOWLING GREEN DR

HOP GARDEN RD

CARLETON CL

NEWNHAM LA

Lyde Mill

Webb's Copse

54

49
71

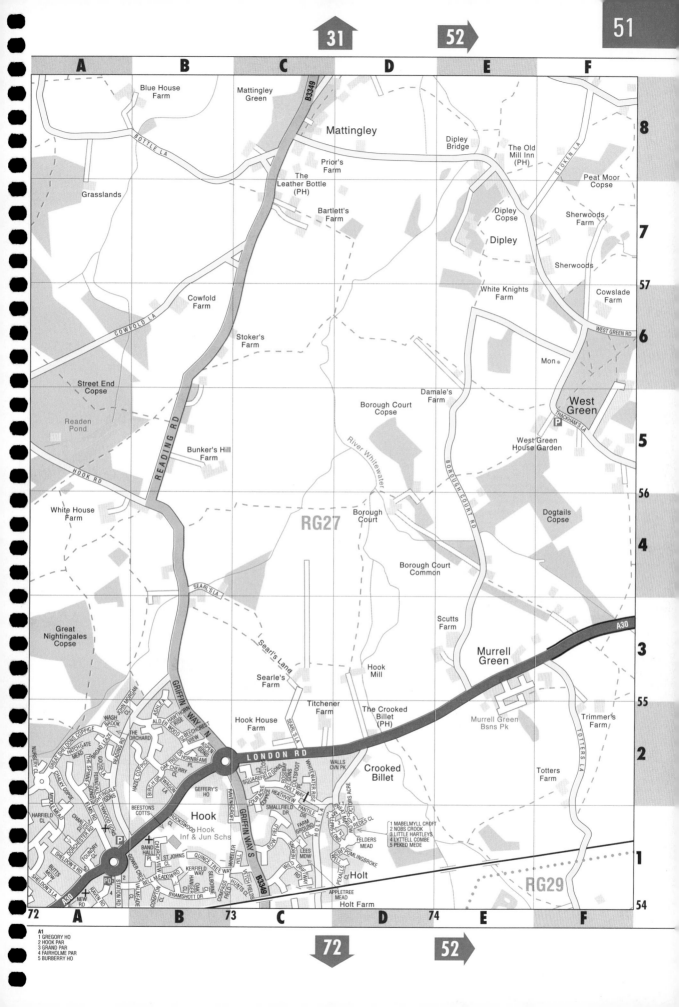

A   B   C   D   E   F

8

7

57

6

56

4

3

55

2

1

54

Blue House Farm

Mattingley Green

Mattingley

Dipley Bridge

The Old Mill Inn (PH)

Peat Moor Copse

BOTTLE LA

Prior's Farm

The Leather Bottle (PH)

Grasslands

Bartlett's Farm

Dipley Copse

Sherwoods Farm

Dipley

Cowfold Farm

White Knights Farm

Sherwoods

Cowslade Farm

COWFOLD LA

Stoker's Farm

WEST GREEN RD

Street End Copse

Mon

Readen Pond

READING RD

Borough Court Copse

Damale's Farm

West Green

B3349

Bunker's Hill Farm

River Whitewater

West Green House Garden

THACKHAM'S LA

HOOK RD

White House Farm

Borough Court

RG27

Dogtails Copse

BOROUGH COURT RD

Borough Court Common

SEARL'S LA

Great Nightingales Copse

Searl's Lane

Scutts Farm

A30

Murrell Green

Hook Mill

Searle's Farm

Titchener Farm

The Crooked Billet (PH)

Murrell Green Bsns Pk

Trimmer's Farm

55

GRIFFIN WAY N

LONDON RD

WALLS CVN PK

Crooked Billet

TOTTERS LA

Hook House Farm

SEARL'S LA

Totters Farm

JOHN MORGAN

WASH BROOK

ASHLEA

HAWTHORN RISE

ALDER WOOD DR

BEECHCREST

ASPEN GDNS

HATCHGATE

THE ORCHARD

BROAD LEAZE

GOOSELA

NIGHTINGALE GDNS

TREE DR

HORNBEAM PL

OAK CHERRY LA

WAGON LA

Geffery's Ho

SQUAREFIELD GDNS

ROSEBAY GDNS

HOLT WAY

HOLTSFOOT

WHITEWATER RISE

MOTORS CL

1 MABELMYLL CROFT
2 NOBS CROOK
3 LITTLE HARTLEYS
4 LYTTELL COMBE
5 PEKED MEDE

Great Sheldons Coppice

NURSERY CL

THE SPINNEY

FERNDALE

GOSSETT GDNS

NIGHTINGALE GDNS

MIDDLEMEAD

CHALKY COPSE

BIRCH GR

BRANKSOME HILL RD

HAZEL COPPICE

PINES RD

Hook

Beestons Cotts

BROOKSWOOD

HEATHVIEW

SMALLFIELD DR

PANTILE DR

FARM GROUND

FELDERS MEAD

HARFIELD CL

DORCHESTER

CHARLES RD

FOUNDRY CL

BOWER GREEN

CHURCH VIEW

ST JOHNS PL

KERFIELD WAY

MEADOWD

BELL MEADOW

Hook Inf & Jun Schs

GRIFFIN WAY S

QUINCE TREE WAY

SELBORNE CL

RAVEL RD

BOW FIELD

SHERFIELD CL

WILD DRUFTWAY

LEES MDW

REDFIELDS

WILLS MEAD

PENALLERS

FELDERS MEAD

POMLINGBROKE

Holt

BUTTS MDW

SHELDON'S LA

NEW RD

RAVEN RD

STATION RD

VALMEADE CL

COMPTON

BRAMSHOTT DR

OAK HANGER CL

COMPASS FIELD

TILN

WITHER

VETCH FIELDS

B3349

APPLETREE MEAD

Holt Farm

A30

P

P

72   73   74

A   B   C   D   E   F

72   52

72

51 32

A   B   C   D   E   F

8   7   57   6   5   56   4   3   55   2   1   54

B3013

Minley Warre

Minley Farm

Minley Home Farm

Minley Wood

GU17

Hawley Common

Hawley Lake

A327

Lower Minley Cottages

MINLEY RD

Crown and Cushion (PH)

LINKLATER'S COTTS

BLACKBUSHES RD

Mallards Copse

Brook House

Tobridge Copse

M3

4a   M3

Bramshot Copse

GU14

A327

ELVETHAM HEATH WAY

B3013

Ancels Copse

The Bungalow

Great Bramshot Farm

Ash Copse

BARLEY WAY   HARVEST CRES

1 RYELAND CL.
2 COLBRED CNR.
3 FALLOWFIELD

4 ELLEN DR.
5 LIME DR.
6 CHERBERRY CL.
7 ARGENTE CL.
8 TUDOR CT.

ANCELLS CT

THE GATES

MILL HOUSE DR

ANCELLS RD

KERRY   SHETLAND WAY

THRESHERS CNR

CH

MINLEY RD

ANGORA WAY

SWALEDALE GDNS

CHEVIOT FARM DR

DEXTERS WAY

TAMWORTH

GUERNSEY DR

JERSEY

SUSSEX GDNS

AYRSHIRE

FRIESIAN

DEVON CL

ROAD MEAD

GALLOWAY CL

HANOVER DR

FOREST DEAN

HIGHLAND

SHIRE AVE

FOXWOOD

WOODGATE

FALKNER HO

CHESTNUT CL

DROVERS

GU51

Little Bramshot Farm

SANKEY LA

Hotel

A3013

B3014

A327

FLEET RD   SUMMIT   B3014

FENNEL CL

MARJORAM CL

LYNDSEY RD   NANWICH DR

AVE   A327

OLDWOOD CHASE

A3013

CYGNET CT 1
WATERSIDE MEWS 2

COVE RD

SOUTHWOOD LA

KENNELS LA

MINLEY GR

1 OLD COVE RD
2 WATERSIDE CT

LAKESIDE CT

PETERBOROUGH

KNOLL CT

Fleet Waterfront Bsns Pk

Station Ind Est

Fleet Pond (Nature Reserve)

Gelvert Stream

P

ELVETHAM RD

COACH HOUSE GDNS

HILLCREST

CRANBROOK CT

THE MOUNT

WENSLEYDALE DR

KNOLL RD

HIGHDOWN

DARSET AVE

Fugelmere Wlk

WEIR RD

CONSTANT RD

Bramshot Gate

Sewage Works

LINGFIELD

ELVETHAM CL

WAVERLEY

KNOLL CL

Seymour CT

Bramshot Dr

CHESTNUT GR

WELLINGTON AVE

KENILWORTH RD

FUGELMERE RD

POND DR

PINEWOOD HILL

DUNMOW HILL

AVONDALE RD

KENT RD

KENILWORTH RD

KENILWORTH RD

BROOK GDNS

PRIMROSE CT

COMPASS

WOODSIDE GDNS

COX RD

BOXBEE

ROYDEN

THE ROMANY

THE HOWE

Cody Tech Pk

THE FAIRWAY

IVELY RD

FLEET RD

STOCKTON

KNOLL CL

BRICKFIELD LA

A3013

B3010

Wks

OLD SCHOOL CL

CLARENCE RD

KINGS RD

SOUTHBY DR

NEVINS RD

ADAMS DR

COMBE

WOOD LA

WOODSIDE RD

WESTOVER RD

FENWICK

LESTOCK WAY

GUILDFORD RD

HOWARD CL

HERBES

CYPRESS RD

CEDAR DR

FARNHAM RD

PONDTAIL RD

ROMAN CL

LYNDALE DR

PONDPENNY LA

ARMSTRONG WAY

Pyestock

Playing Field

FLEET

Oakley Park

ALBERT ST

OLD SCHOOL CL

CHURCH PL

CONNAUGHT RD

BRINSWAY

ABBOTS BURN

THE LAURELS

GEORGE GDNS

KEATS GDNS

ALBANY CT

ALBANY RD

ALTON RD

ELMS RD

CAMP

FRESHAM

DENMARK

COWARD RD

GEORGE RD

PO

Pondtail

WEIR RD

81   A   B   82   C   D   83   E   F

A1
1 OLD DAIRY CL
2 ARGYLL CT
3 CLARENCE CT
4 GEORGINA CT
5 WINDSOR CT
6 KINGSWOOD CT
7 BEARWOOD GDNS
8 OLD SCHOOL TERR
9 CONSORT PL
10 SWIFT CT
11 WESTFIELD CT
12 ST JOHN'S CT
13 VINCENT CT
14 CLARE CT

A2
1 WESTMINSTER CL
2 PINEWOOD CT
3 ST PHILIPS CT
4 KINGS PAR
5 GAINSBOROUGH CT

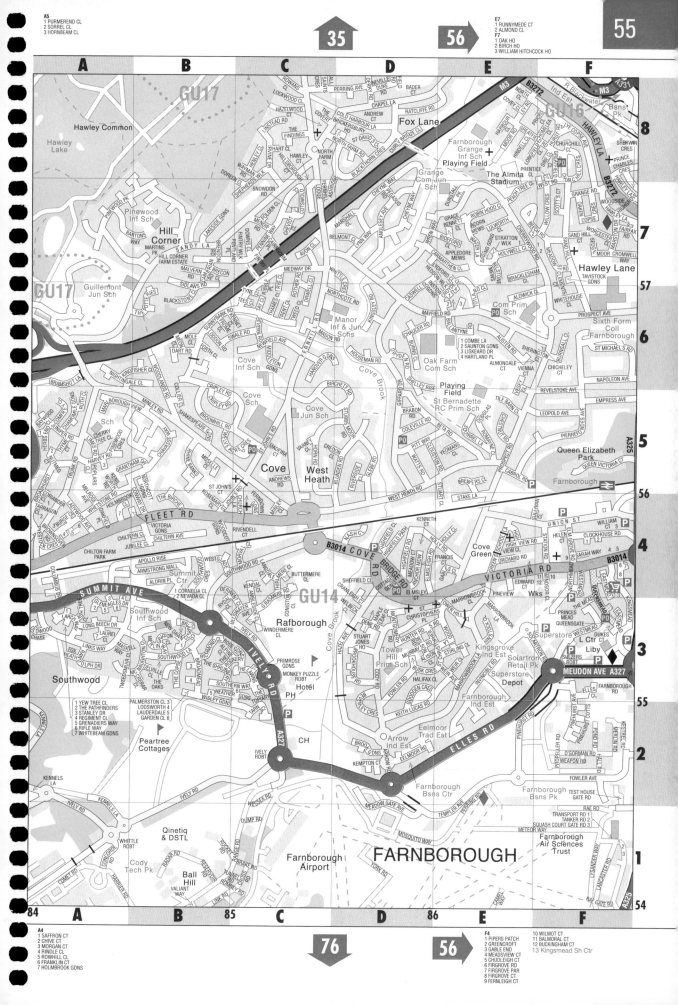

55 36

FRIMLEY

Factory

Frimley Bsns Pk

Frimley CE Jun Sch

Frimley Green

Richmond Hill

St Cross

The Grange

Loen

Frimhurst Farm

Clewborough House Sch

Aqueduct

The Kings Head (PH)

Frimley Lodge

The Old Mill

Four Winds

Water Works

GU16

GU14

FARNBOROUGH

Farnborough Green

Henry Tyndale Sch

North Farnborough Inf Sch

Farnborough Street

Farnborough Hill (Girls Sch)

Farnborough Park

Jubilee Hall Rd

Coleford Bridge

Coleford Farm

Mytchett

Mytchett Prim Sch

Basingstoke Canal

Basingstoke Canal Ctr

Playing Field

South Farnborough

King George's Field

South Farnborough Jun Sch

Farnborough Coll of Tech

Linsford Farm

Linsford Bsns Pk

Mytchett Farm CVN Pk

Potters (PH)

Mytchett Place

Keogh CL

The Glade

Rushmoor Ind Sch

Salesian Coll

Mast

Grove Farm

Grove Farm Pk

Mytchett Lake

GU12

Keogh Barracks

Playing Field

B3165

A331

A325

A331

B3403

Guildford Rd

Mytchett Rd

Frimley Green Rd

Blackwater River

Surrey STREET ATLAS

55 77

A1
1 CAMBRIDGE CT
2 BARTON CT
3 WILLIAM CT
4 DENBY CT
5 REDE CT
6 NEELEM CT
7 KASHMIR CT
8 BULLER CT
9 WYKEHAM HO
10 ALEXANDRA CT
11 WETHERBY GDNS
12 SOMERSET CT

58

Wiltshire STREET ATLAS

Wiltshire STREET ATLAS

A B C D E F

Grubground Copse
Shaw Farm
Bauks Hill
Green Farm
Chute Ride
The Cross Keys (PH)
TRIGG MDW
MALTHOUSE LA
8

Merrylawn Copse
Rudge Copse
Shaw Bottom
Chute Down
PO
Upper Chute

New Ride
Hopgood's Copse
Crystal Palace

SN8
Collingbourne Wood

FOREST LA
7

Oakety Copse
Waterlane Bottom
Water Lane

Collingbourne Wood
53

Blackmore Lane
Cowcommon Bottom
6

Great Wickheath Copse
Coldridge Wood
Honey Bottom
Ladies Lawn

Cockshord Ride
Wickheath Copse
Sawpit Ride
Sawpit Copse

Cockshord Copse
Oxdown Copse
Stert Copse
Coldridge Bottom
SP11
Coldridge End
5

Pigstye Copse
Coldridgedown Copse
52

Coldridge Down
4

Crawlboys Farm

Busheydown Copse
Biddesden Park
3

Crawlboys Row
Crawlboys LA
Marlins Farm
Biddesden House
LONG BOTTOM
51

Old Common Way
Ludgershall Castle Prim Sch
HYSON CRES 1
MAPLE CRES 2
ELM CL 3
Biddesden Farm

PERHAM CRES
BEARD CT
LINDEN CL
ST NICHOLAS CL
WOOD PK
Bulls Drove
BIDDESDEN LA
2

SHORT ST
MEADE CORONATION RD
BEST ST
CHALLIS CT
SPRAY LEAZE
ABBATT CT

A342 Devizes
A342
1 2 3 4

LARKIN CL 1
DAIRY HO 2
BLANE HO 3
PEARL HO 4
GRASSMT RD
PRETORIA RD
Faberstown
Hillfield Copse
Lambourne's Hill

Ludgershall
ANDOVER RD
P
Biddesden Bottom

NEWTON VILLAS 1
ELMAY HO 2
SHOPPEDEN LA
LC
A342
1

Andover Lane Farm
50

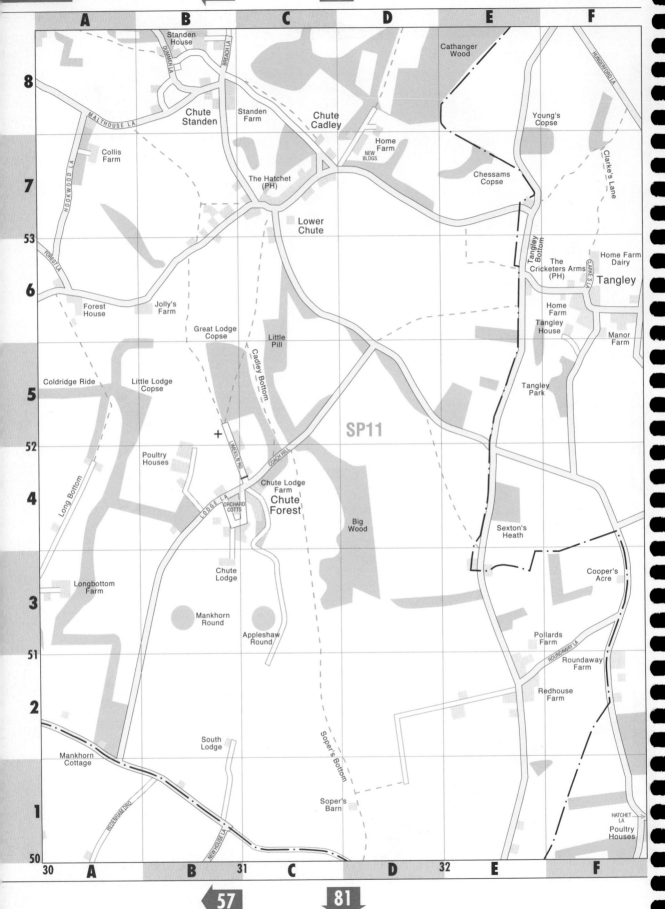

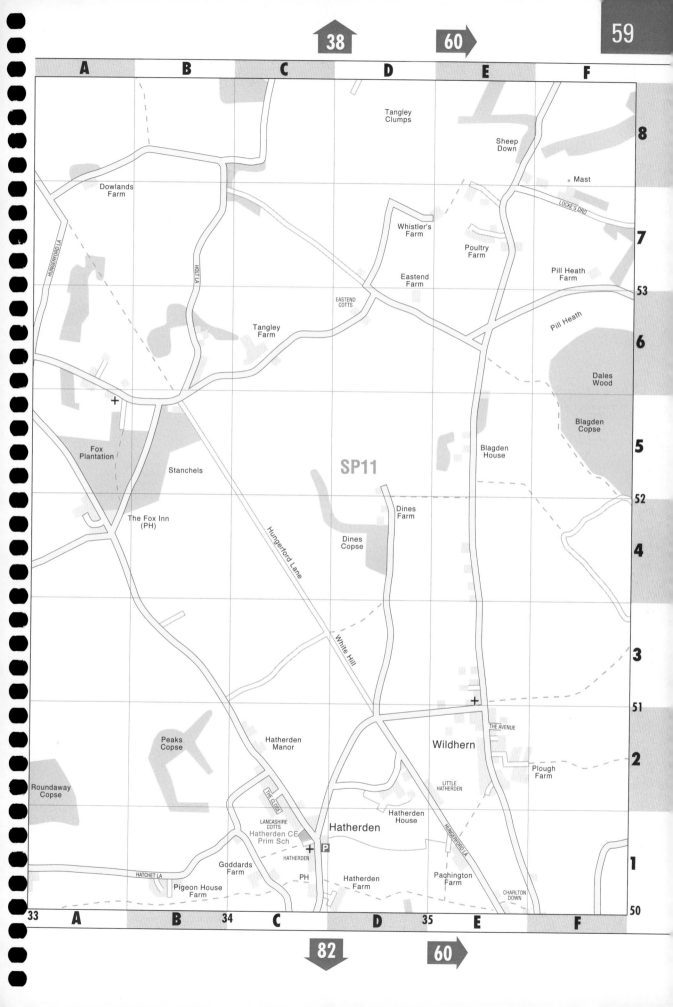

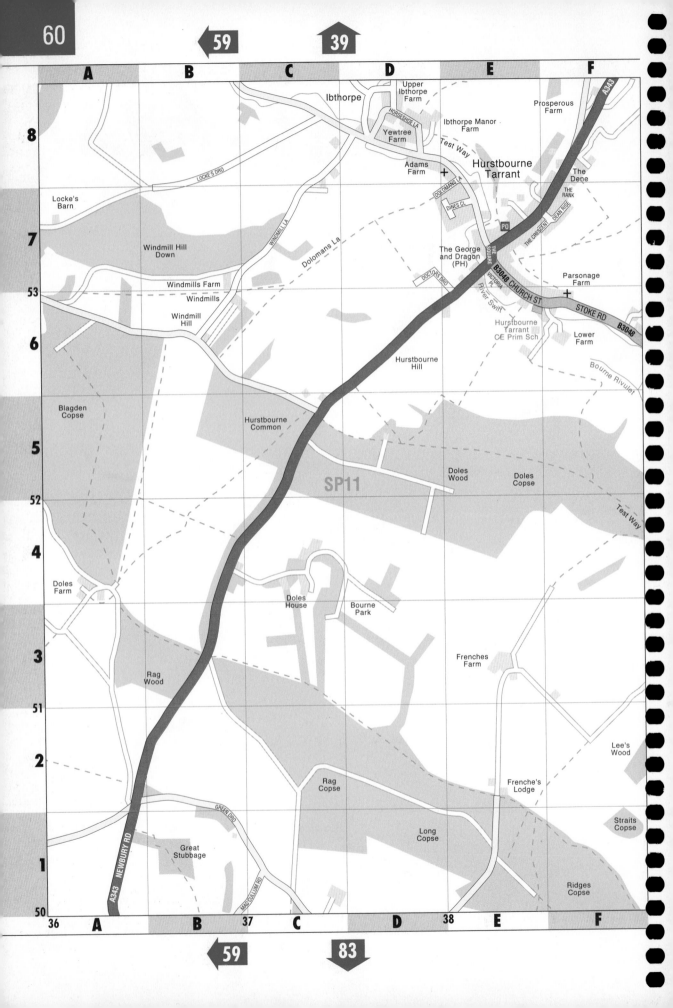

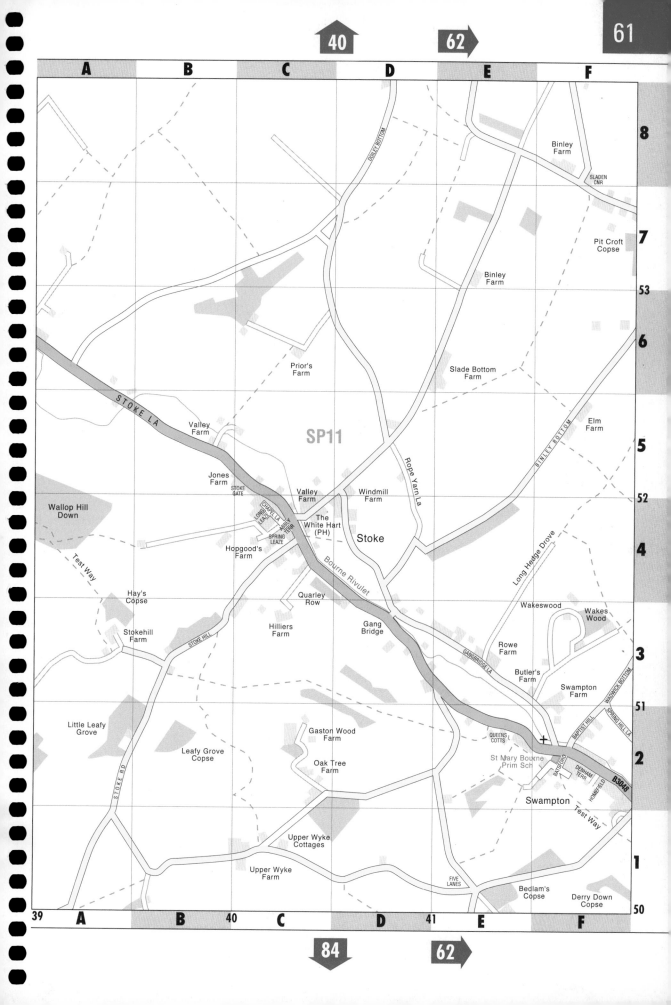

40 62

A B C D E F

8

Binley Farm

SLADEN CNR

7

Pit Croft Copse

53

Binley Farm

6

DIDLEY BOTTOM

STOKE LA

Slade Bottom Farm

Prior's Farm

BINLEY BOTTOM

Elm Farm

Valley Farm

SP11

5

Jones Farm

STOKE GATE

Rope Yarn La

52

Wallop Hill Down

CHAPEL LA
LONG LEAZE
ABBEY TERR
SPRING LEAZE

Valley Farm

Windmill Farm

Long Hedge Drove

The White Hart (PH)

Stoke

4

Hopgood's Farm

Test Way

Bourne Rivulet

Wakeswood

Wakes Wood

Hay's Copse

Quarley Row

Rowe Farm

Stokehill Farm

STOKE HILL

Hilliers Farm

Gang Bridge

GANGBRIDGE LA

Butler's Farm

3

Swampton Farm

WADWICK BOTTOM

51

Little Leafy Grove

STOKE RD

Gaston Wood Farm

QUEENS COTTS

BAPTIST HILL

SPRING HILL LA

Leafy Grove Copse

Oak Tree Farm

St Mary Bourne Prim Sch

BATSFORD

DENHAM TERR

HOMEFIELD

B3048

2

Swampton

Test Way

1

Upper Wyke Cottages

Upper Wyke Farm

FIVE LANES

Bedlam's Copse

Derry Down Copse

50

39 A B 40 C D 41 E F

84 62

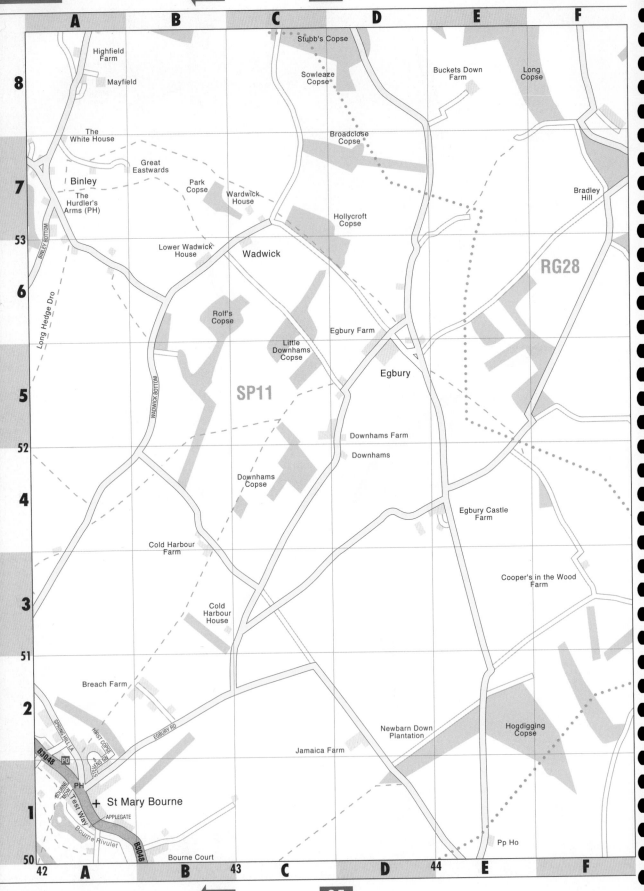

8 Highfield Farm
Mayfield

Stubb's Copse
Sowleaze Copse
Buckets Down Farm
Long Copse

The White House
Great Eastwards
Broadclose Copse

7 Binley
Park Copse
Wardwick House
Bradley Hill

The Hurdler's Arms (PH)
Hollycroft Copse

53 Lower Wadwick House
Wadwick

6 Long Hedge Dro
Rolf's Copse
Egbury Farm
RG28

Little Downhams Copse
Egbury

5 Wadwick Bottom
SP11

Downhams Farm
Downhams

52
Downhams Copse
Egbury Castle Farm

4
Cold Harbour Farm
Cooper's in the Wood Farm

3 Cold Harbour House

51
Breach Farm

2 Spring Hill La
Egbury Rd
Newbarn Down Plantation
Hogdigging Copse

Hurst Copse
Stevens La
Jamaica Farm

B3048
PO
Steven
PH
St Mary Bourne
Applegate

1 Bourne Mdw
Test Way
Pp Ho

Bourne Rivulet
B3048

50
Bourne Court

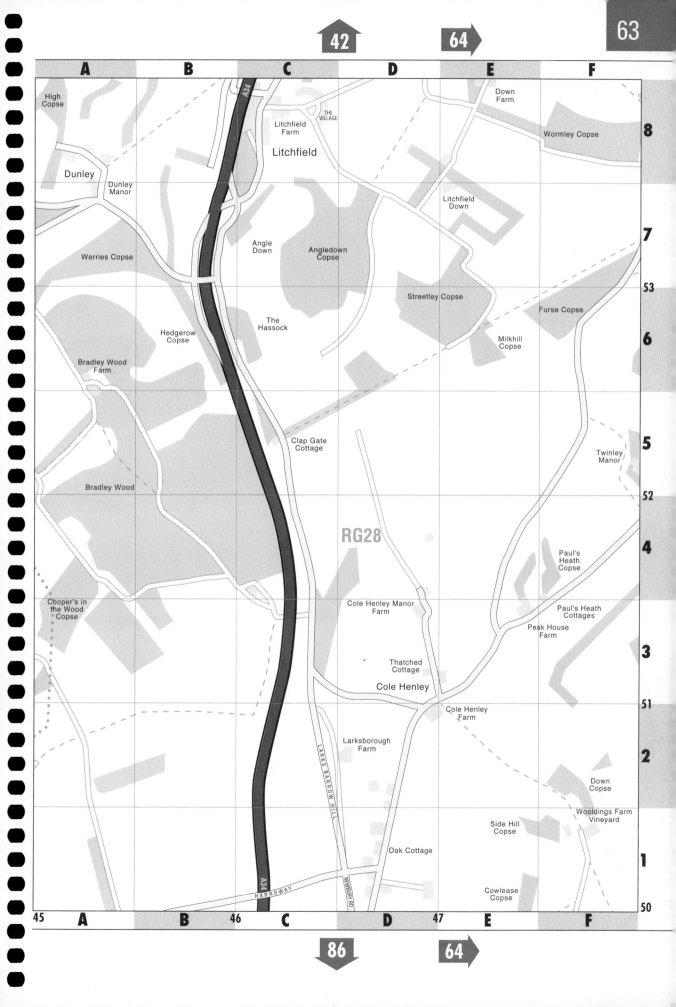

63
43

A B C D E F

8

Owls
Lodge

Caesar's Belt

Palmer's
Bushes

Robley Belt

7

Ridgeway
Copse

53

Keeper's Cottage

Old Farmhouse

6

Dunn's
Wood

Ridgeway
Farm

Willesley Warren
Farm

Willesley Warren
Cottages

Paul's
Wood

RG25

5

Twinley
Manor

52

Little Twinley's
Copse

RG28

The
Peak

4

Whitnal

New
Barn

La
Bresse

3

51

TWINLEY LA

COURT DRO

2

Harroway Belt

The
Orchards

The
Cottage

Lordsfield
Plantation

1

Ash Bed
Plantation

Northfield
Plantation

Northington Belt

Sewage
Works

50

48 A B 49 C D 50 E F

63
87

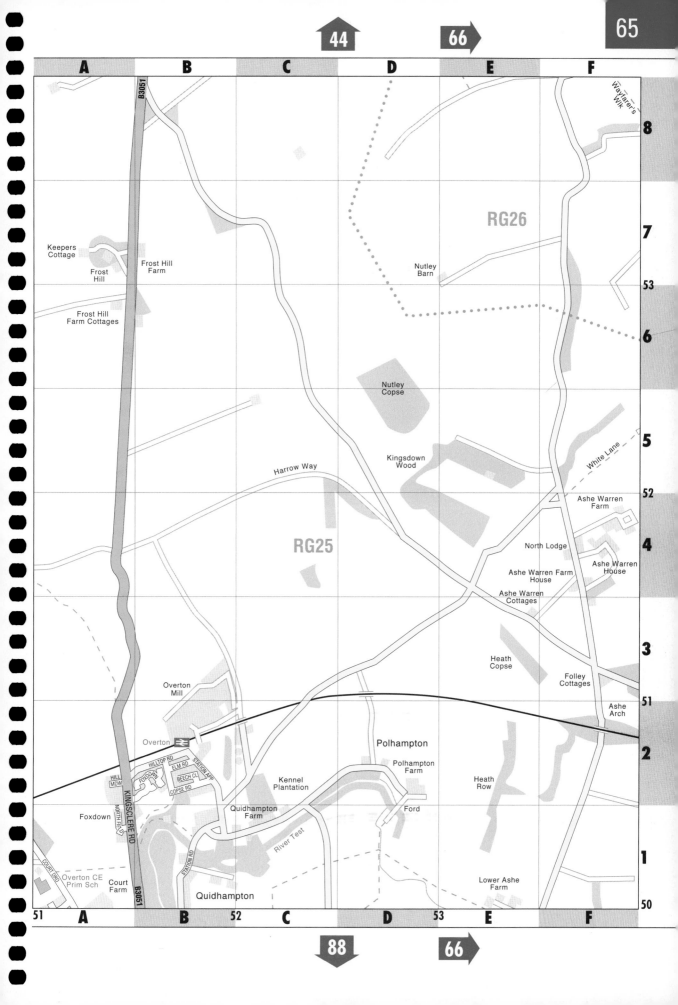

65
45

A B C D E F

8

Warren Bottom Copse

Freemantle Farm

Freemantle Farm Cottages

Sunny View

The Gables

7

Hay Wood

Wayfarer's Walk

RG26

Lynwood

Pamelia

Lockley Copse

53

Shear Down Farm

Frith Wood

Rosemont

WHITE LA

MALSHANGER COTTS

6

White Lane

Patchbourne Wood

Malshanger House

SUMMER DOWN LA

Summer Down Copse

Malshanger Park

Great Deane Wood

5

Wayfarer's Walk

Home Farm Cottages

Home Farm

52

Blandy's Farm

MALSHANGER LA

Sourley Row

4

SUMMERDOWN COTTS

Summerdown House

RG23

Little Deane Wood

IVY DOWN LA

3

Stubb's Copse

Deane Down Farm

Deane Down

Sewage Works

RG25

HARROW WAY

B3400

51

Motel

Clarken Green

2

Wayfarer's Walk

The Spinney

STATION RD

Park Farm

Church Oakley

Deane House Cottages

RECTORY RD

Deane House

DEANE COTTS

ANDOVER RD

Oakley Park

1

Deane

Manor Farm

Deane Park

B3400

50

54 A B 55 C 56 D E F

65
89

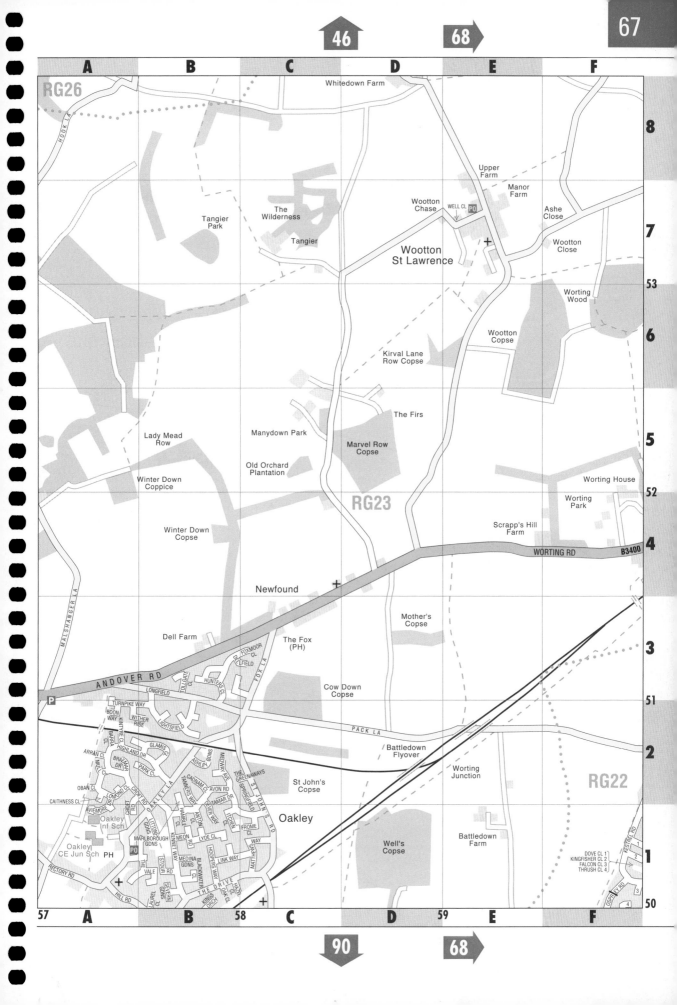

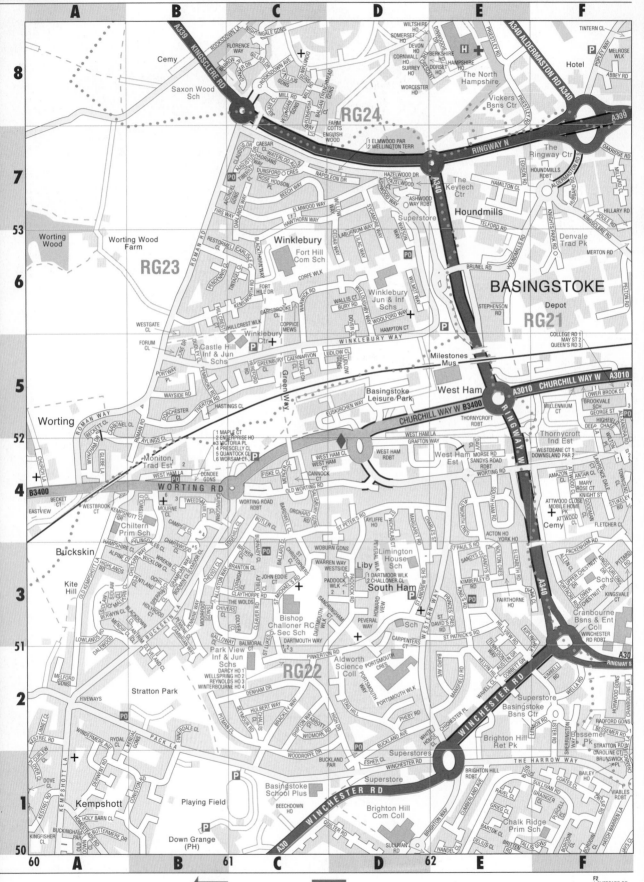

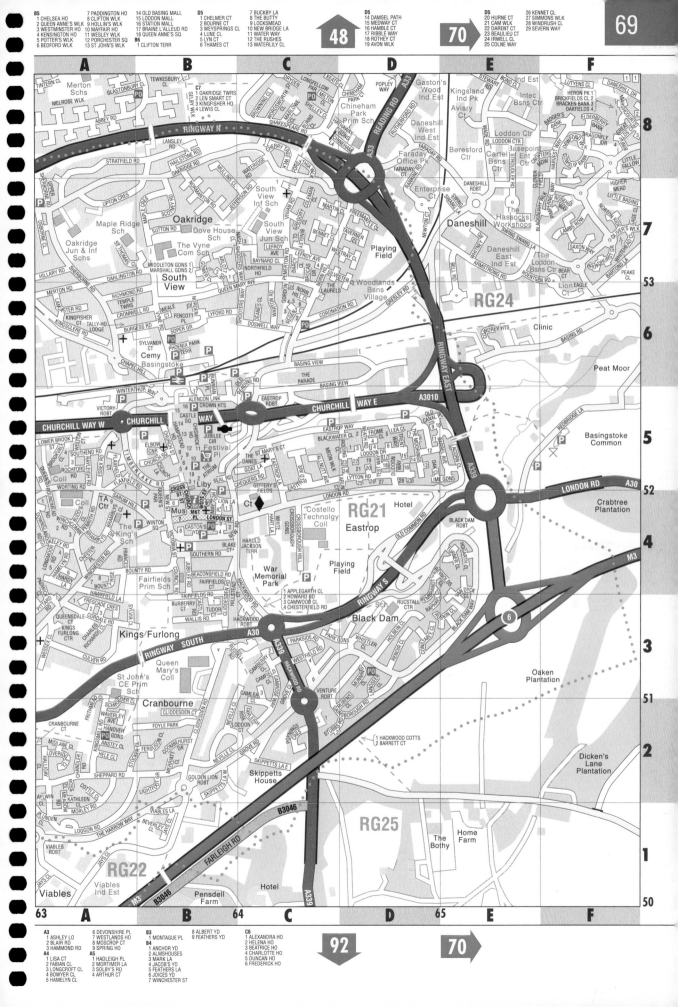

A   B   C   D   E   F

8

ar GDNS
PRIVETT CL   THE TOP
HEDGEROWS   PAYNE'S MDW
INKPEN GDNS   BARTONS LA
DAMESHILL DR   PYOTTS HILL
GREAT BINFIELDS RD   RIVERSIDE CL

Lower Mill
Lower Mill Farm

Newnham La

Bain's Wood

Elliot's Copse

Poors Farm

Newnham La

Gold's Farm

Little Fallow
Little Basing
OLIVERS WLK
BARTONS LA

Oliver's Battery
Motte & Baileys

Wildwood Farm

Round Copse

WATER END LA

7

Barton's Mill

River Loddon

PADDOCKFIELDS
PRIORY GDNS

1 POPPY FIELDS
2 GREAT BINFIELDS CRES
3 AMPORT CL
4 BRICKFIELDS CL
5 CHARLDON GN
6 TRELLIS DR
7 CAVEL CT
8 COPSE FIELD
9 BEDDINGTON CT

RILEY LA

Cemy

1 CHESTNUT BANK
2 CHAPEL CL
3 POWER HO

Bushy Lease Copse

Hodd's Copse

Virnell's Copse

ASHMOOR LA

POORS FARM RD
POT LA

A30

53

MOOR VIEW
THE STREET
BURTON'S GDNS
CHURCH LA

MANOR LA
ST MARY'S CL
MILKINGPEN LA

Hodd's Farm

Hodd's Hill

6

Grange Farm

BEAUMONT WAY
CROWN CRES

St Mary's CE Jun Sch

Brown's Farm

RG24

Old Basing

RG27
Priory Farm

Lyde River

REDBRIDGE LA
BASING RD

The Crown (PH)

Basing House
(remains of)

ALMOND CL
CROWN LA
MUSKET COPSE

THE MEAD

Old Basing Inf Sch

PAWLETT PL
CROMWELL CL
LOYALTY LA

FRASER CL
ASH GR
HOLLY DR
BELLE VUE RD

CAVALIER RD

BRAMBLE WAY
ST MARY
FAIRTHORNE RISE

Swannill Nursery

East Moor

Andwell Moor

M3

5

Basingstoke Common

PARK LA
APPLE WAY
BYFLEET AVE
LINDEN CT
LINDEN AVE

THE DELL
BLENHEIM RD
CHALK VALE

HATCH LA
LINGFIELD CL
RAINBOW CL

Hatch
BATCHELOR

Hatch

LONDON RD

PH
GREYWELL RD

OAK TREE COTTS

GREYWELL RD

COB TREE COTTS

52   A30

Crabtree Plantation

P

PELHAM CL
PARK AVE

CRAB TREE WAY
OLIVER WAY
BASINGFIELD CL

Basingfield

KEMBERS LA

TUNWORTH RD
FROG LA

4   M3

DICKENS LA

Huish Farm

3

New Park

Dicken's Lane Plantation

HUISH LA

Huish House

Moorhams Cottage

Moorhams Copse

Sheetlands Copse

Webb's Farm

Mapledurwell

The Gamekeepers (PH)

RG25

Nunnery Hill

Manor Farm

DOWN LA

51

2

TUNWORTH RD

Gray's Farm

1

Blackdown Farm

POLECAT CNR

Ragmore

50
66   A   B   67   C   68   D   E   F

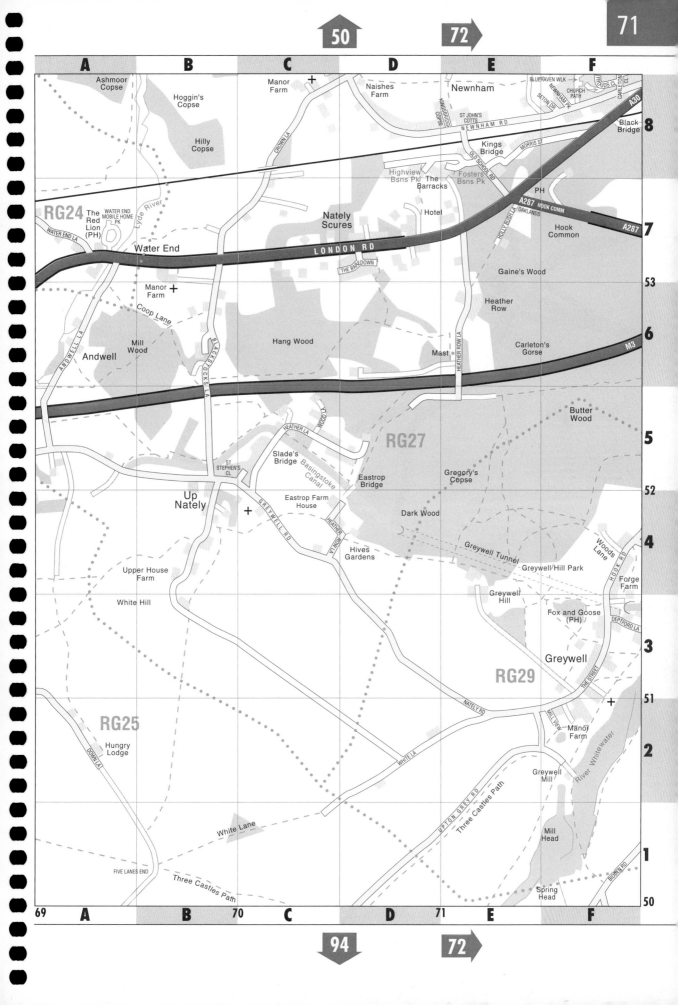

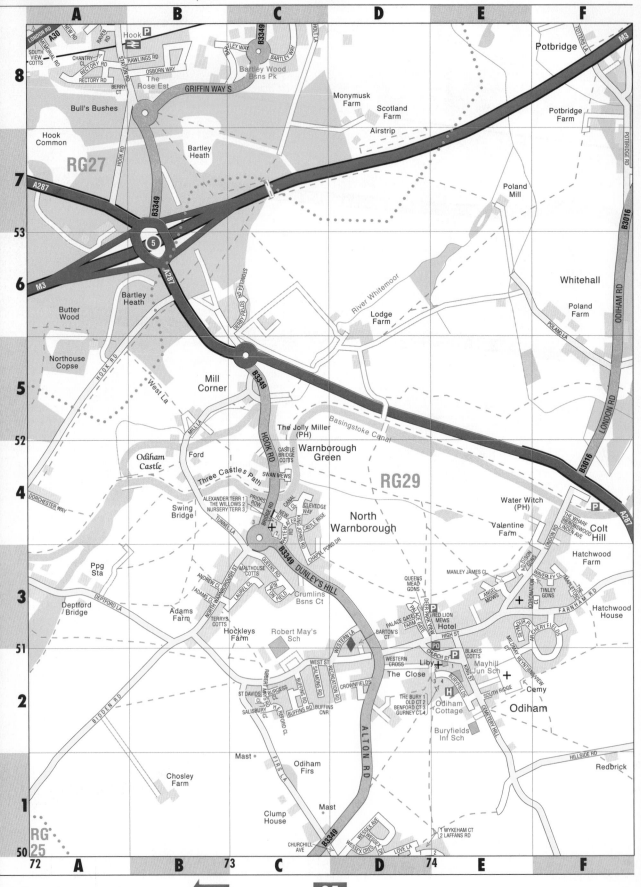

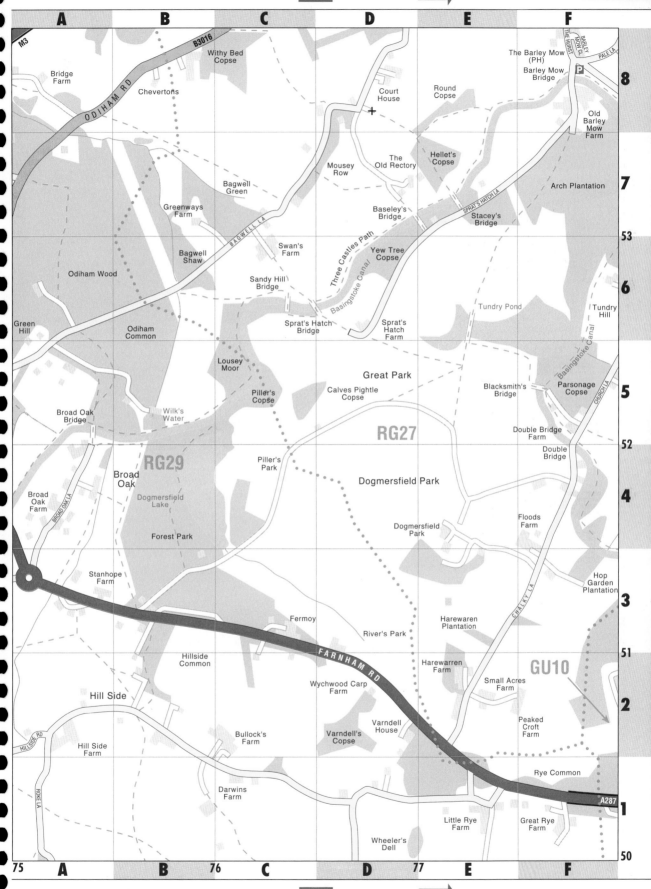

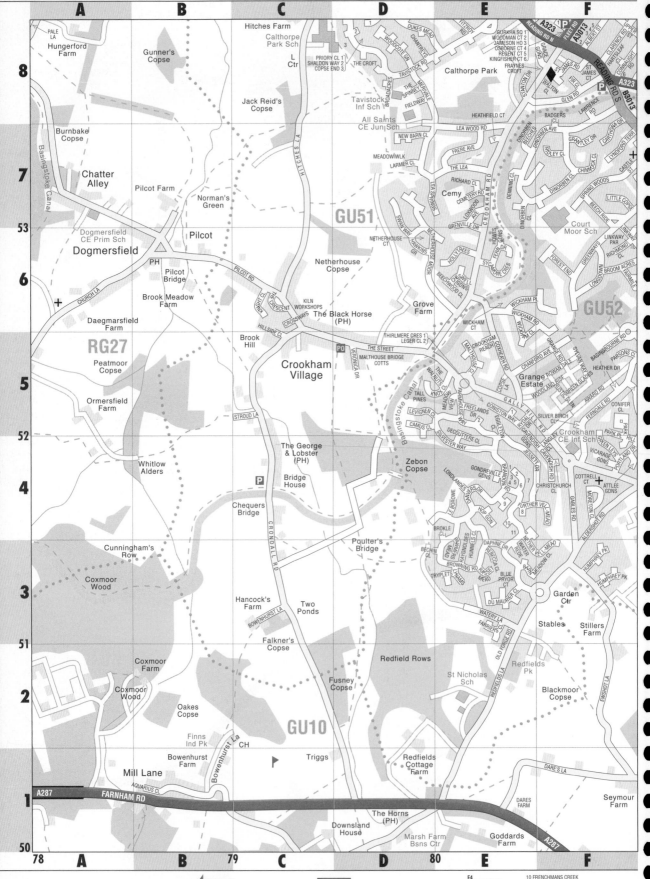

E4
1 WOOLAND CT
2 ANNETTES CROFT
3 HOUSE PLAT CT
4 HORNES FIELD CT
5 NICOTIANA CT
6 RYE CROFT
7 MELLERSH CL
8 SEPEN MEADE
9 TWISELL THORNE
10 FRENCHMANS CREEK
11 CONSTANTIUS CT

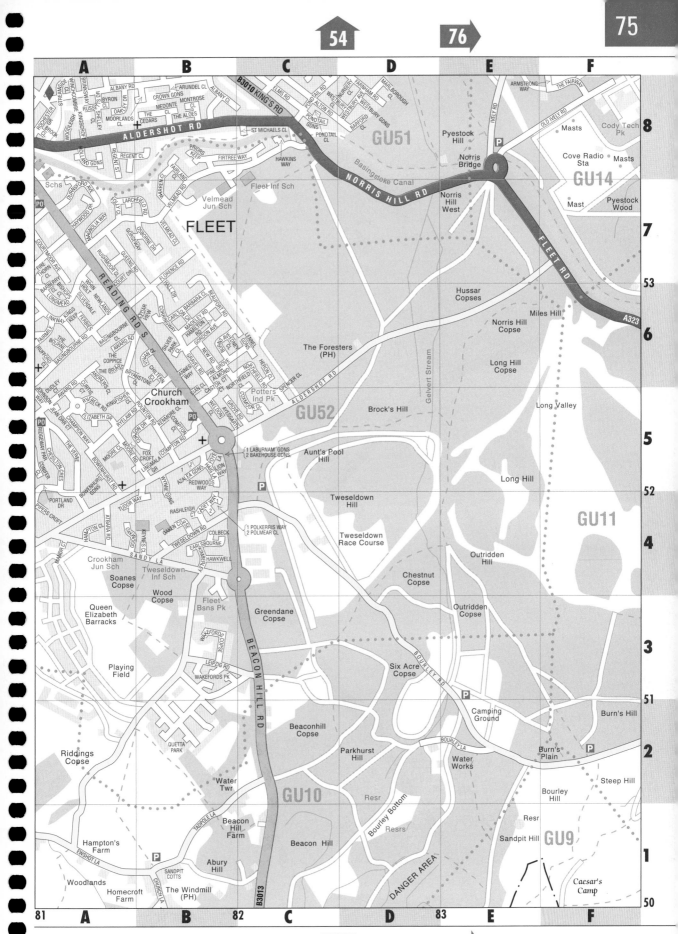

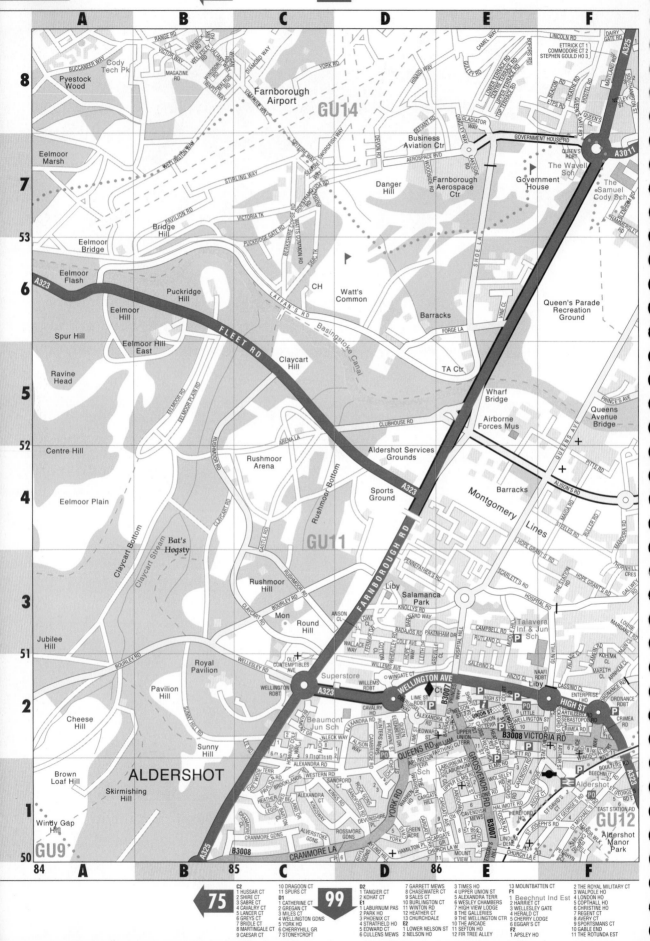

C2
1 HUSSAR CT
2 SHIRE CT
3 SABRE CT
4 CAVALRY CT
5 LANCER CT
6 GREYS CT
7 BRIDLE CT
8 MARTINGALE CT
9 CAESAR CT
10 DRAGOON CT
11 SPURS CT
D1
1 CATHERINE CT
2 GREGAN CT
3 MILES CT
4 WELLINGTON GDNS
5 YORK HO
6 CHERRYHILL GR
7 STONEYCROFT

D2
1 TANGIER CT
2 KOHAT CT
E1
1 LABURNUM PAS
2 PARK HO
3 PHOENIX CT
4 STRATFIELD HO
5 EDWARD CT
6 CULLENS MEWS
7 GARRETT MEWS
8 CHASEWATER CT
9 SALES CT
10 BURLINGTON CT
11 WINTON RD
12 HEATHER CT
13 CHURCHDALE
E2
1 LOWER NELSON ST
2 NELSON HO

3 TIMES HO
4 UPPER UNION ST
5 ALEXANDRA TERR
6 WESLEY CHAMBERS
7 HIGH VIEW LODGE
8 THE GALLERIES
9 THE WELLINGTON CTR
10 THE ARCADE
11 SEFTON HO
12 FIR TREE ALLEY

13 MOUNTBATTEN CT
F1
1 Beechnut Ind Est
2 HARRIET CT
3 WELLESLEY GATE
4 HERALD CT
5 CHERRY LODGE
6 EGGAR'S CT
F2
1 APSLEY HO

2 THE ROYAL MILITARY CT
3 WALPOLE HO
4 LONDON HO
5 COPTHALL HO
6 CHRISTINE HO
7 REGENT CT
8 AVERY CT
9 SPORTSMANS CT
10 GABLE END
11 THE ROTUNDA EST

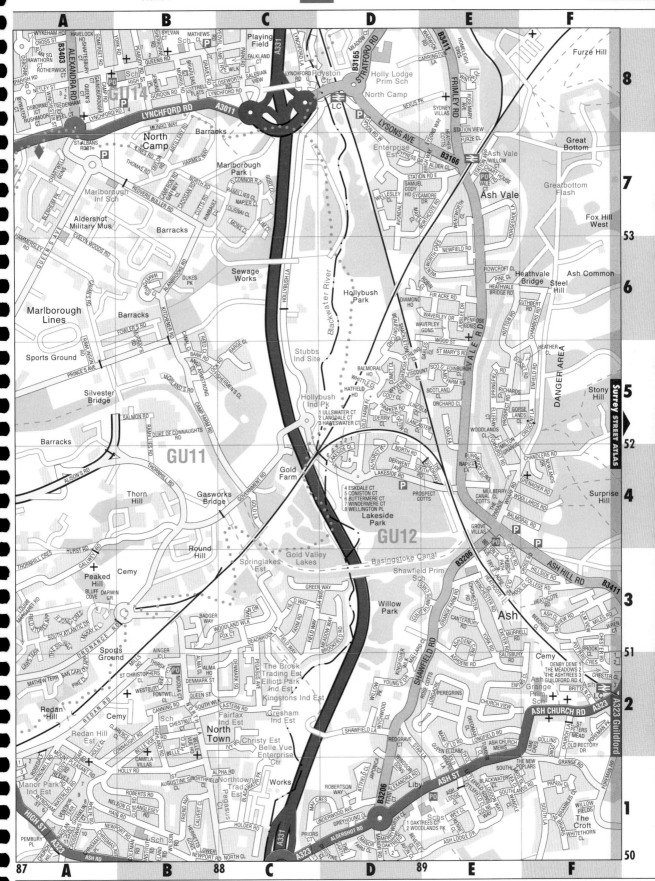

A8
1 KINGS CT
2 PRINCESS CT
3 GRESHAM CT

B8
1 GROSVENOR HO
2 ARNELL CT
3 THE FERNS
4 KINGDOM HO
5 MORRIS HO

A1
1 REDAN GDNS
2 AMBER CT
3 POUND RD
4 YORK LODGE
5 WINDMILL CT
6 WHEELWRIGHT HO
7 SUNNY VIEW CL
8 PARK CL
9 BEMBRIDGE CT
10 RYDE CT
11 WAVELL CT
12 TEMPLAR LODGE

Wiltshire STREET ATLAS

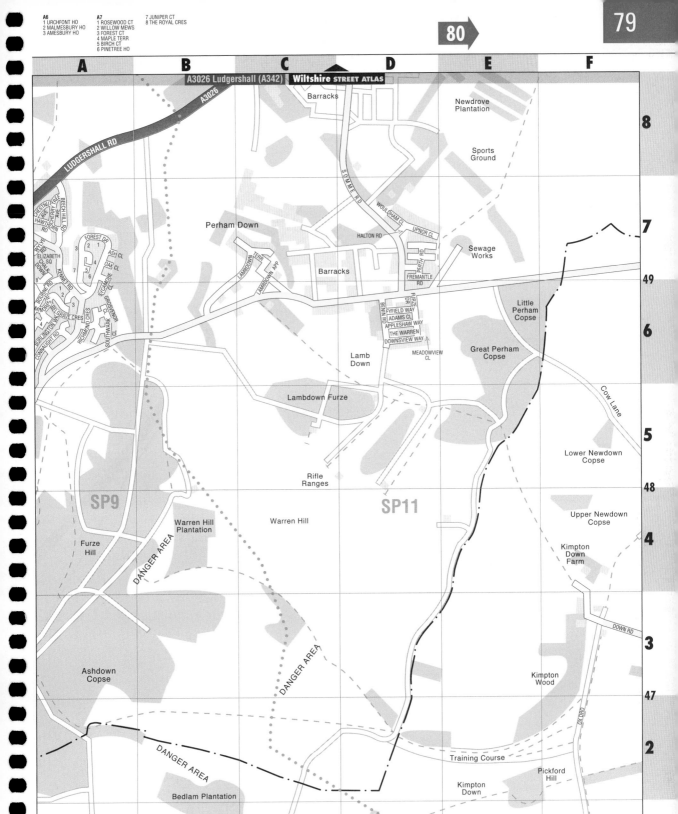

80 ▶

A6
1 URCHFONT HO
2 MALMESBURY HO
3 AMESBURY HO

A7
1 ROSEWOOD CT
2 WILLOW MEWS
3 FOREST CT
4 MAPLE TERR
5 BIRCH CT
6 PINETREE HO

7 JUNIPER CT
8 THE ROYAL CRES

A   B   C   D   E   F

A3026 Ludgershall (A342)   **Wiltshire STREET ATLAS**

Barracks

Newdrove
Plantation

8

LUDGERSHALL RD

A3026

Sports
Ground

SOMME RD

WOULDHAM CL

UPNOR CL

7

Perham Down

HALTON RD

PEBB RD

Sewage
Works

49

FREMANTLE
RD

Barracks

Little
Perham
Copse

6

LAMBDOWN TERR

LAMBDOWN APP

FURZE DRO

BENIN RD

FYFIELD WAY
ADAMS CL
APPLESHAW WAY
THE WARREN
DOWNSVIEW WAY

MEADOWVIEW
CL

Great Perham
Copse

Lamb
Down

Cow Lane

Lambdown Furze

5

Lower Newdown
Copse

48

Rifle
Ranges

SP9

SP11

Upper Newdown
Copse

Warren Hill
Plantation

Warren Hill

Kimpton
Down
Farm

4

Furze
Hill

DANGER AREA

Kimpton
Wood

DOWN RD

OXDRO

3

DANGER AREA

Ashdown
Copse

Kimpton
Down

47

Training Course

2

DANGER AREA

Pickford
Hill

Bedlam Plantation

Kimpton
Down

Markway Firs

Kimpton Farm

1

OLD COACH RD

46

24   25   26

A   B   C   D   E   F

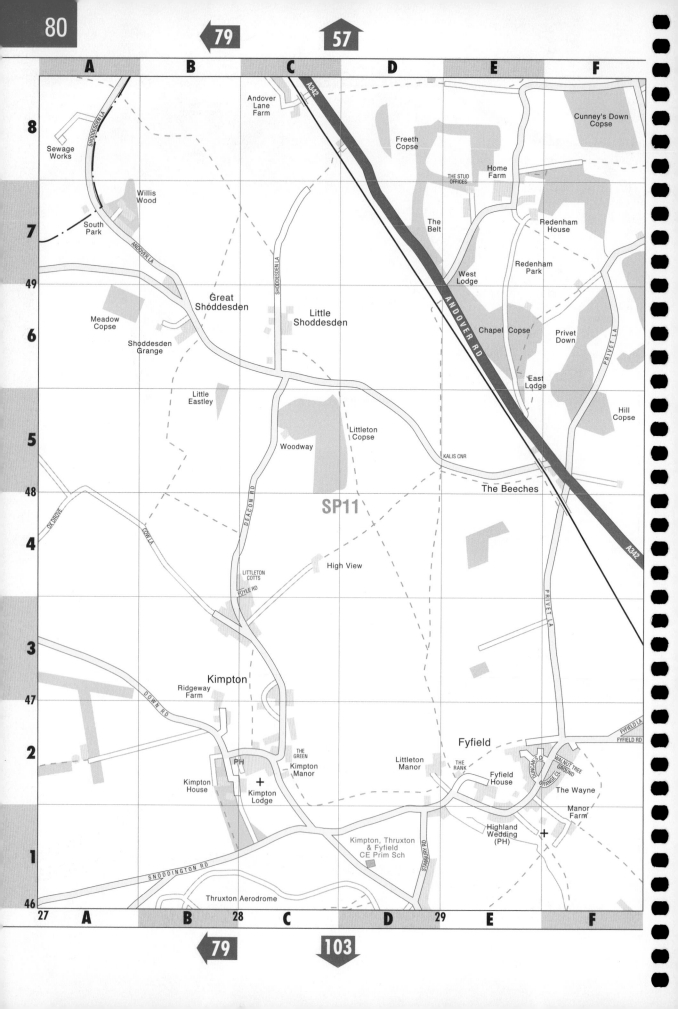

58
82

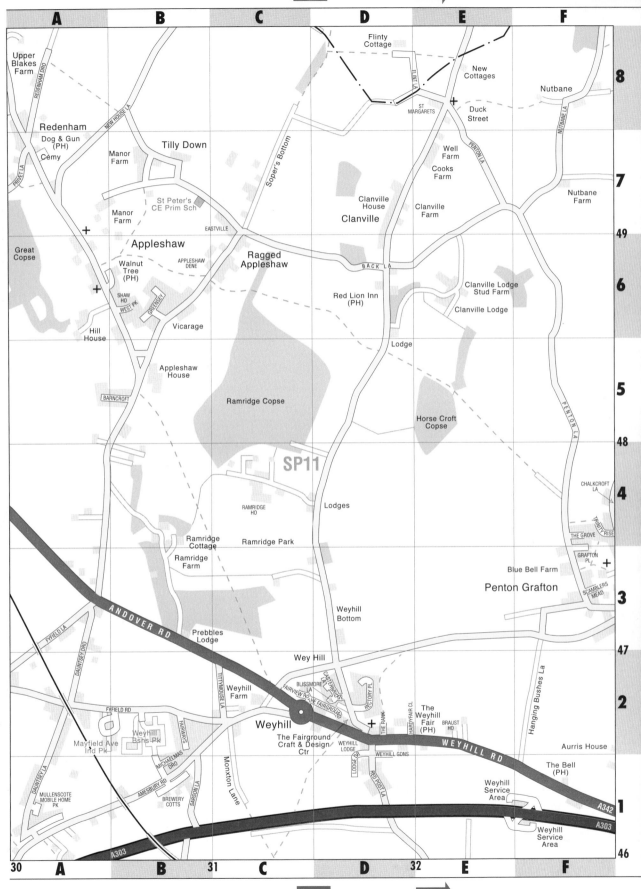

81 59

A B C D E F

8

Nutbane
Copse

Hatherden
Farm Cottages

Charlton
Down
Farm

May's
Wood

Breach Row

Hare and Hounds
(PH)

Hungerford La

7

49

Little
Bilgrove
Copse

Penton
Copse

SP11

6

Chalk Croft
Farm

Penton
Saw Mill

Cemy

5

Chalkcroft La

48

STADDLESTONES
COTTS

Old Nursery
Cottage

MARSUM CL 1
OLD ENGLISH DR 2
ANDEFERAS RD 3
OLDENBURG CL 4
LINGEN CL 5

4

Penton
Mewsey

Saxon Way

Rune Dr

River Anton

Foxcotte
Farm

Foxcotte

Charlton

St Benedict's
Convent Sch

PH

Foxcotte La

Foxcotte
Manor

Richborough

Recluver Way

Mercia Ave

Brancaster

Home
Farm
Gdns

Augustine Way

Bede Dr

Dorchester

Rochester Cl

Hengest Cl

Broxhill Cl

St Birinus
Gdns

Enham La

Aldrin
Cl

Armstrong

Altona
Gdns

Bremen Gdns

Holland

Kiel Ct

Emden Rd

Flensburg

Verden

Hamburg

Lubeck Dr

Borkum

Elbe Way

St Alphege
Gdns

3

1 MALTHOUSE COTTS
2 PENTON LA

Penton Park

Gorse
Plantation

Ethelbert

Tower Cl

Dacre

Litchfield Cl

Bartin

St Thomas
Cl

Collins La

The Green

Wetherby Gdns

Goch Way

Alfred Gdns

1 HOGARTH CT
2 MUNNINGS CT
3 STUBBS CT
4 GAINSBOROUGH CT
5 REYNOLDS CT
6 LANDSEER CT
7 TURNER CT
8 LOWRY CT
9 LINFON DR
10 LANCASTER CL
11 THE ROWANS

47

Chalkcroft La

Foxcotte Rd

Lakeside Cl

Cotte Cl

Sunnyside Cl

Kimberley La

PO

Carter's Mdw

Hillside
Villas

2

Harrow La

Andover
Fball Club

Mark La

SP10

Charlton
Sp and L Ctr

West Portway

Basepoint
Bsns Ctr

Harrow
Way
Com Sch

Silche

Churchill Way W

Park View Cl

Lawrence Cl

Artists Way

Andover
War Meml

Brooks
Rise

H

Redon Way

A343

Hopkinson Way

Arkwright
Gate

Telford
Gate

Brunel
Gate

Smeaton Rd

Macadam Way

Harrow Way

Sterling
Pk

Caxton
Cl

Harrow Way

Chaucer Ave

Milton Ave

Apple Tree Cl

Orange Tree Rd

May Tree Rd

Thistledown
Cl

Charlton Rd

The Laurels

Nestor Cl

1

Short La

Harrow Way

Harrow Way

Penton
Corner

Homestead
Farm

Derby
Gate

Newton
Pk

Faraday
Pk

Mitchell Way

Galileo
Pk

Watt Cl

Sterling Pk

Shakespeare Ave

Bleadon Dr

The Drive

Brackenbury

Silver Birch

Ferndale Rd

Mylen Rd

Hanson

Manor Rd

Wellington Rd

Halifax Cl

Old Down Rd

Cricklade

Charlton
Rd

Portway
Ind Est

Telford
Gate

Sopwith
Pk

Royce Cl

Parnell
Ct

Eardley Ave

Orchard Rd

Junction
Rd

BEECH CL

ELIZABETH
CT

A342
A303

Weyhill Rd

Keith Way

Whittle Rd

Joule Rd

Stephenson Cl

East Portway

Upper Dro

Cherry Tree Dr

Beckett Cl

46

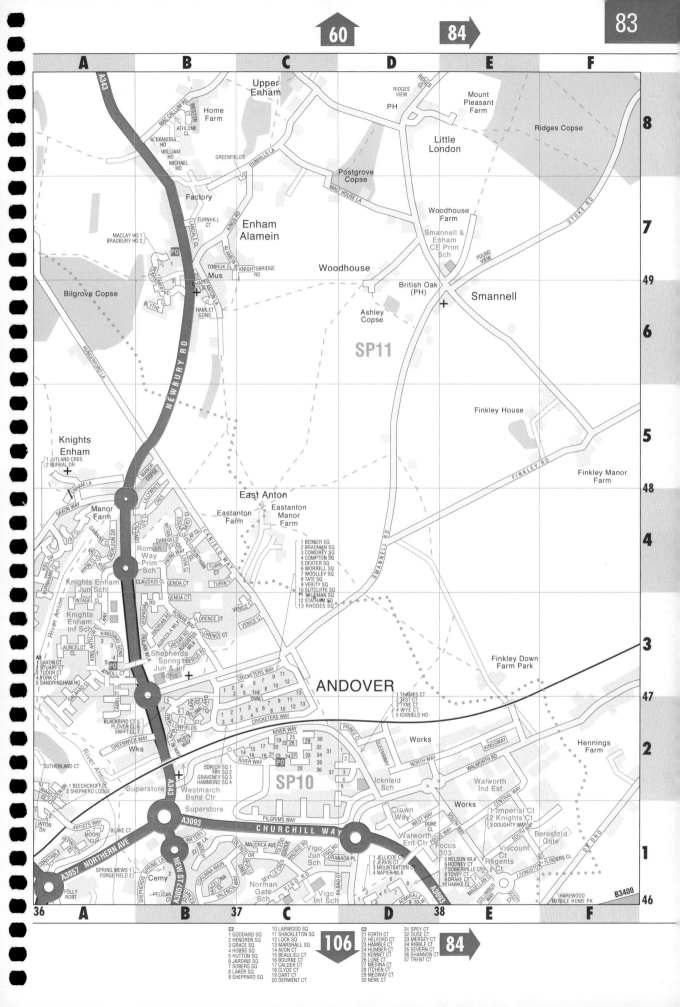

83
61

| | A | B | C | D | E | F |

8

Mongomble Copse

STOKE RD

Test Way

Hackwood Copse

Middle Wyke Farm

Moors Wood

Lower Wyke Barn

7

FINKLEY RD

49

Trinley Wood

Middle Wyke Cottages

Trinley Buildings

6

Lower Wyke Farm

Lesleys Cottage

5

SP11

Apsley Clump

48

Pepper Hill Firs

4

Test Way

WALWORTH RD

Lower Wyke Down Farm

3

The Commercial Ctr

PO

OX DROVE RISE

Tinker's Hill

Faulkner's Down Farm

Lapstone Farm

Village Hall

47

Picket Piece

OX DRO

2

Melrose Farm

Fox Cottages

Andover Down Farm

Harewood Peak

B3400

Harewood Farm

Fox Farm

1

Down House Farm

Folly Copse

Down House

LONDON RD

THE MIDDLEWAY

Test Way

46

B3400

| 39 | A | | B | 40 | C | | D | 41 | E | | F |

83
107

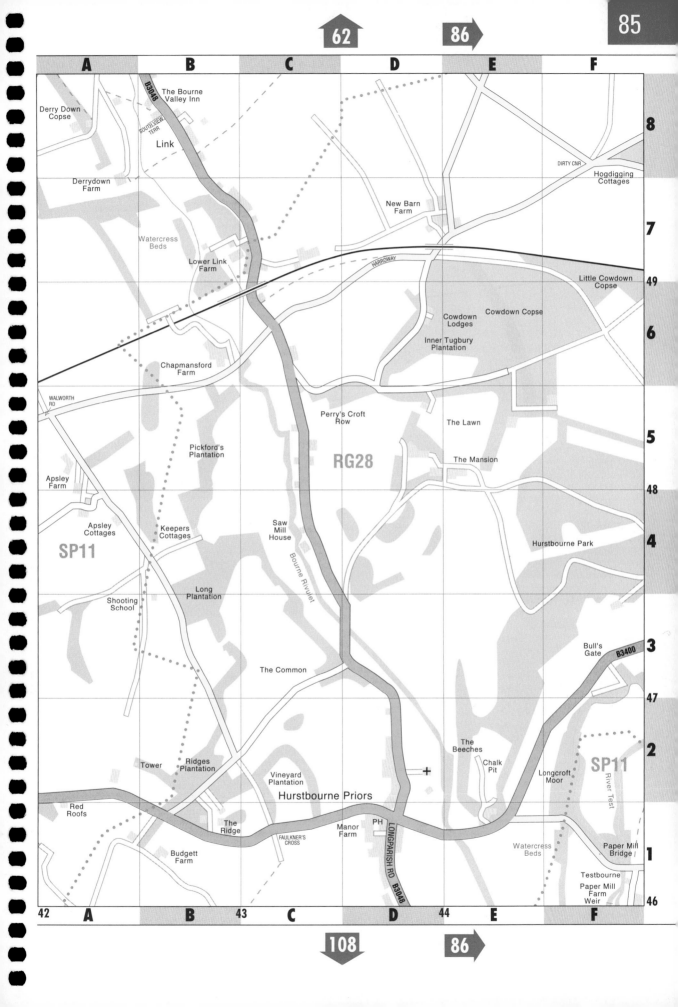

85
63

A B C D E F

8

Down Farm

HARROWAY

Sheepcrook
Cottages

7

Bere Hill
Farm

HARROWAY

Winterhill
Plantation

49

Whitchurch

BLOSWOOD LA

NEWBURY RD

6

Whitchurch
GREENWOODS CROSSWAYS

Water
Twr

STATION RD

BERE HILL

Whitchurch

BERE HILL
CVN SITE

Wells-in-the-Field
Farm

B3400

SKYLARK RISE
PEGASUS CT
BEECH CT
ARGLISEN RD
EVINGAR RD
KINGSLEY PK
WITIAN CT
BRADBURY CL
CAESARS WAY
Evingar
Ind Est
MEADOW VIEW
BICESTER
EVINGAR GDNS
FIRS WAY
DANCES LA
BURGAGE FLD

RG28

5

MEADOW DR
OAKLAND RD
KINGS WLK
THE CROOKERY
LYNCH HILL
KINGS WLK
LYNCH HILL PK

LONDON RD

Manor
Farm
GROVES ORCH
HARTLEY MDW
BLOSWOOD LA
Liby
TOWN HALL
BELL ST
JOBSON RD
LONDON ST
THE LYNCH
POUND MDW
THE GREEN
HILL SVS
THE GABLES

48

WARWICK CL
SEEVIOUR'S
FAIRCLOSE TERR
WELLS LA
CHURCH ST
BELL ST
SHELLEY CT
LONG'S MEWS
PAGES YD
CLARK MEWS
TEST RD
WINCHESTER ST
PO
1 WATERLOO CT
2 MULBERRY MEAD
3 KINGFISHER CL
4 CHATTER LA
5 LORD DENNING CT

River Test

Whitchurch
CE Prim Sch

Lynch Hill

Cemy

Whitchurch Silk Mill

Great
Town
Bridge

HIDES CL
SHEPPARD RD
THE GUILD
DANIEL RD
RAMPTON RD
NEUVIC WAY
WHEELER CL
BROOKS CL

4

Hurstbourne Park

THE KNOWLINGS

Coombedown
Hanger

THE WEIR
WINCHESTER RD
WEBBS FARM CL
CHARLCOT CL
BROADWAY LA
QUEENS RD
CHERRY ORCH
MICHELDEVER GDNS
MICHELDEVER CL

Southfield
Farm

3

B3400

Fulling
Mill

Testbourne
Com Sch

MICHELDEVER RD

47

2

RIVERSIDE COTTS
Manor
House
Manor Farm

Sewage
Works

Knowle
Clump

Tufton

1

SP11

Buftons

46

45 A B 46 C D 47 E F

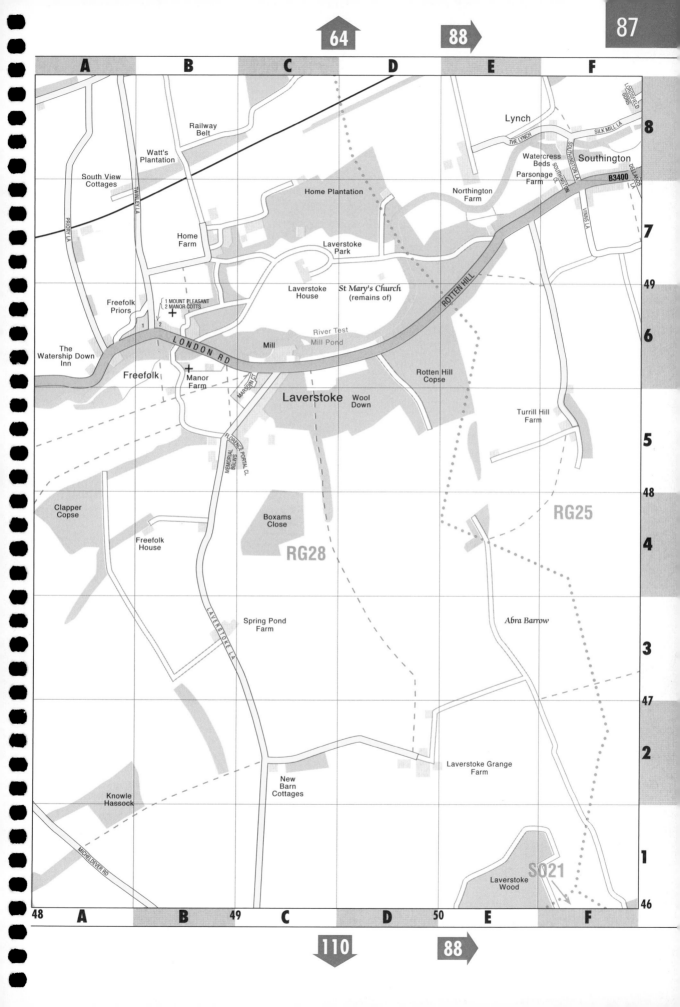

87
65

A B C D E F

8

Lordsfield Gdns
Silk Mill La
Glebe Mdw
Court Drove
Church Rd
Court Farm
Kingsclere Rd
Bridge St
Riverside Cl
Station Rd
Lambs Cl
Turnpike Cotts

1 TOWN MILL
2 NORRIS HO
3 OVERTON HO
4 LAMPOOL HO
5 BUTLER LODGE
6 WALTHAM CT

Source of the River Test

Ashe House
Ash Hill Row
Ashe

Hyde Hill Plantation

B3400

River Test
B3051
London Rd
Liby
P
PO
High St
B3400

7

King's Field
Horley's Field
Woodl
Oak Cl
Dellands La
Kerchers Field
Red Lion La
Lion Cl
The Orchard
Greyhound La
Alexander
Battens
Elm Piece Ho
Sprents
Papermakers La
Winchester St
Highfields
Waltham Rd
The Green
Two Gate Mdw
Two Gate La
Nightingale Rise
Hazeloomb

Berrydown La
Berrydown Court

Water Tower

Berrydown Farm

Tidnock Farm

Burley La

49

Charledown Cl
Charle Down Rd
Crawts Rd
Poultons Rd
Crks Cl
Pond Cl

Smith's Field

Overton

1 DALLENCE HO
2 MILLDOWN HO

Berrydown Copse

Burley Wood

Lampacre Plantation

6

Jackson's Copse

Sapley Farm House

Upper Ashe

5

Woodside

Waltham La

RG25

48

4

White Hill

Bramdown Copse

3

Lower Whitehill Cottages

Northdown Plantation

Hazeldown Copse

47

2

Southley Farm

Bramdown

Quidhampton Southley Copse

Shelter Plantation

1

Upper Whitehill Farm

Southley Copse

Pilgrim's Copse

Copse Farm

Litchfield Tunnel

Litchfield Copse

Keepers Cottage

Pilgrim's Farm

Cowage Copse

46

51 A B 52 C 53 D E F

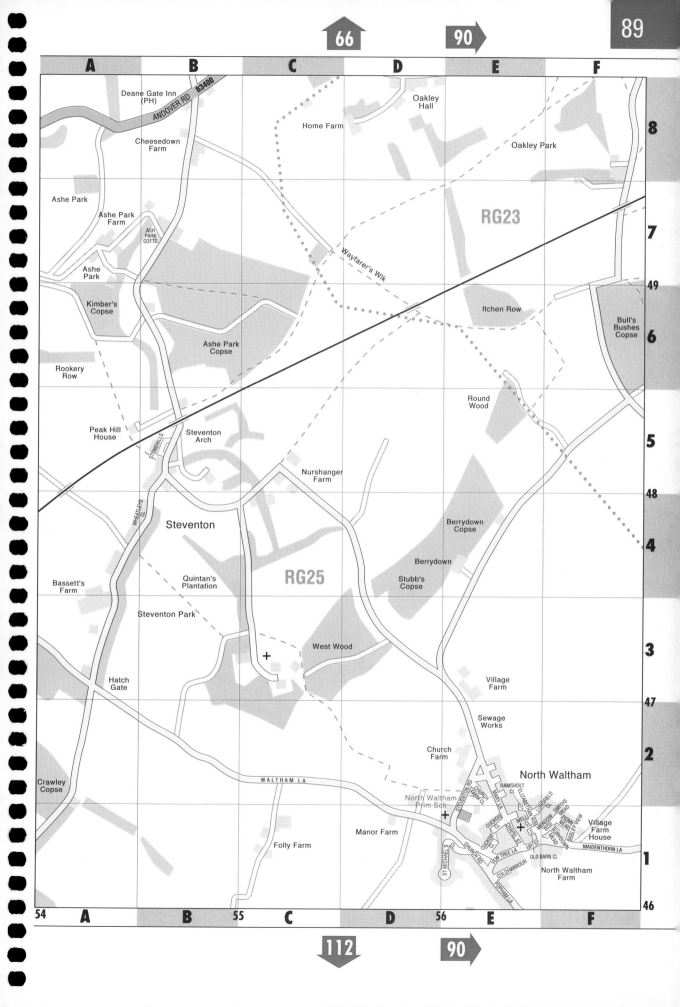

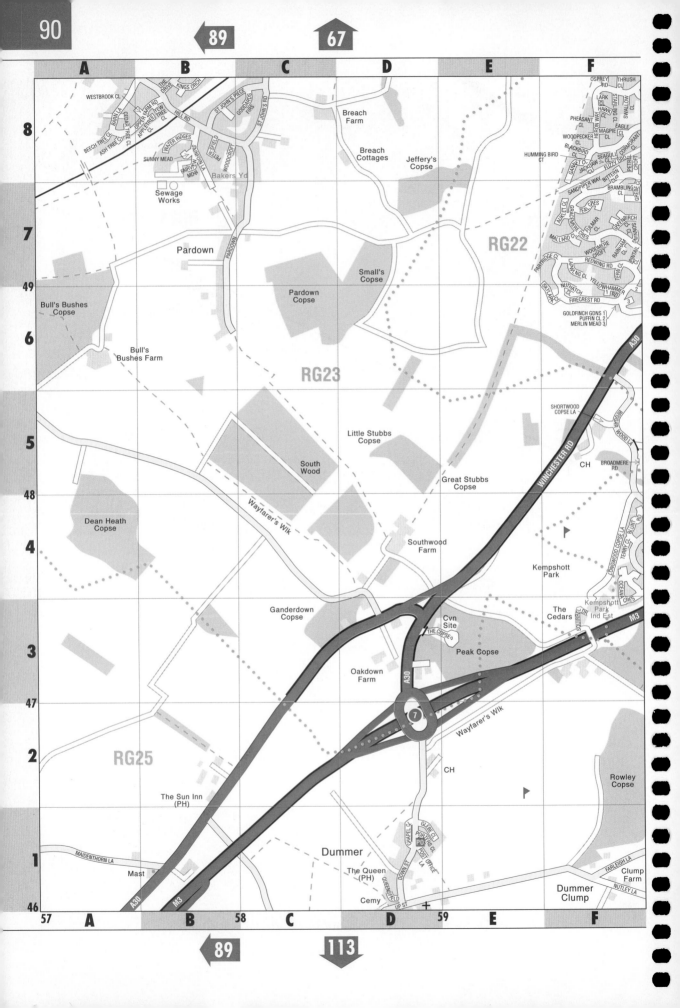

A B C D E F

8

WESTBROOK CL
THE DRIVE
KINGS ORCH
ST JOHN'S PIECE
GODDARDS FIRS
ST JOHN'S RD
Breach Farm

UPPER FARM RD
APPLEBEE CL
YEW TREE CL
BEECH TREE CL
CEDAR TREE CL
ASH TREE CL
BARN LA
HILL RD
Breach Cottages
Jeffery's Copse

WATER RIDGES
SAXFORD LA
Bakers Yd
WOODCROFT
SUNNY MEAD
DAIRY CL
MDW

Sewage Works

OSPREY RD
THRUSH CL
LARK CL
STARLING CL
HAWK CL
PHEASANT CL
HERON WAY
EAGLE CL
WOODPECKER CL
BLACKBIRD CL
SEAGULL CL
CORMORANT
HUMMING BIRD CT
GANNET CL
JACDAW CL
FUZZY DRO
PETRI CL
SANDPIPER WAY
BITTERN CL
BRAMBLING CL
GREBE CL

7

Pardown
Pardown

Small's Copse

RG22

TERN CL
CRES
GRACEMERE CRES
FULMAR CL
GREEN
BIRCH
SISKIN CL
MALLARD CL
WOODMERE CROFT
RAMBAM CL
CENTRAL
PARTRIDGE CL
LAPWING CL
YELLOWHAMMER
REDWING RD
TERI CL

49

Pardown Copse

NUTHATCH CL
FIRECREST RD
SKYLARK

6

Bull's Bushes Copse

Bull's Bushes Farm

RG23

GOLDFINCH GDNS 1
PUFFIN CL 2
MERLIN MEAD 3

SHORTWOOD COPSE LA

5

Little Stubbs Copse

South Wood

CH
BROADMERE RD

48

Wayfarer's Wlk

Great Stubbs Copse

WINCHESTER RD
BEGGARWOOD LA

4

Dean Heath Copse

Southwood Farm

Kempshott Park

LONGWOOD COPSE LA
TERRY CL
OCEAN DR
FLINT RD

Kempshott Park Ind Est

3

Ganderdown Copse

Cvn Site
THE COPSE

Peak Copse

The Cedars

GIBBONS
CRES

47

Oakdown Farm

A30

7

Wayfarer's Wlk

M3

2

RG25

CH

Rowley Copse

The Sun Inn (PH)

1

MAIDENTHORN LA

Mast

Dummer

The Queen (PH)

CHAPEL CL
GLEBE CL
PORTERS CL
POST OFFICE LA
PO
DOWN ST

FARLEIGH LA
Clump Farm

Dummer Clump
NUTLEY LA

46

Cemy
QUEENSFIELD
UP ST

57 A B 58 C D 59 E F

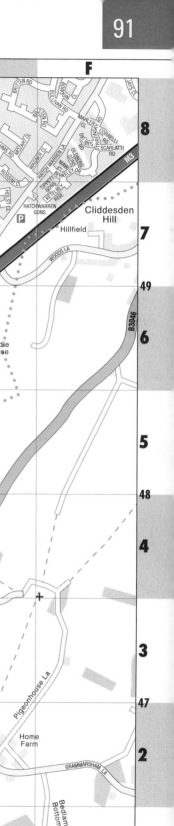

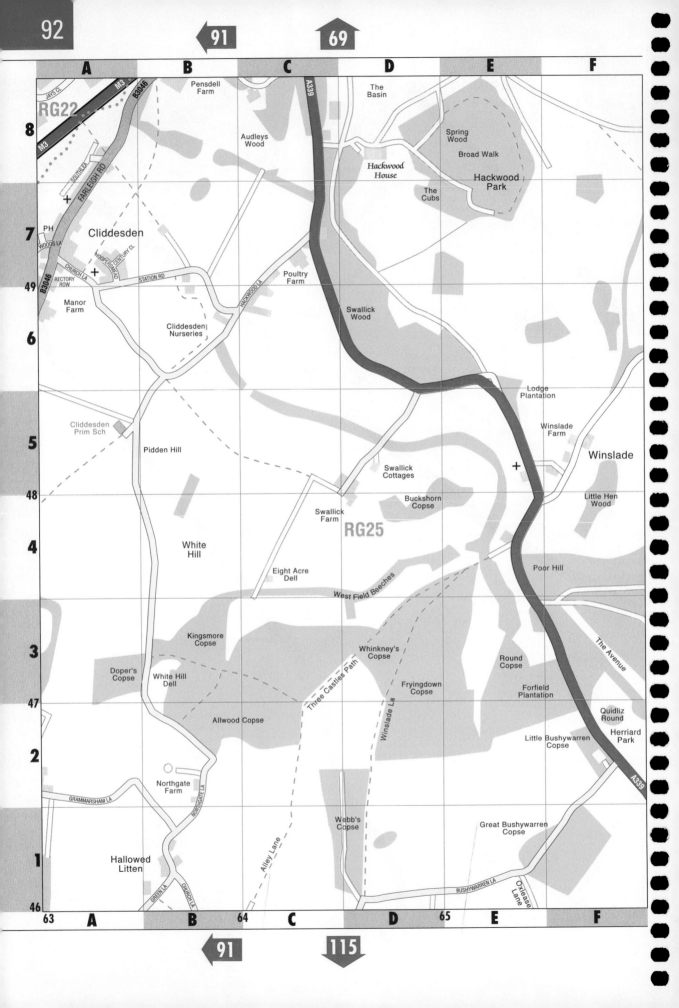

A   B   C   D   E   F

RG22

JAYS CL

M3

B3046

Pensdell Farm

The Basin

Spring Wood

Broad Walk

Audleys Wood

Hackwood House

The Cubs

Hackwood Park

8

SOUTHSEA

FARLEIGH RD

PH

Cliddesden

7

WOODS LA

B3046

CHURCH LA

HOOPERSMEAD

CENTURY CL.

STATION RD

RECTORY ROW

49

Manor Farm

Cliddesden Nurseries

HACKWOOD LA

Poultry Farm

Swallick Wood

A339

6

Cliddesden Prim Sch

Pidden Hill

Lodge Plantation

Winslade Farm

Winslade

5

Swallick Cottages

Buckshorn Copse

Little Hen Wood

48

Swallick Farm

RG25

White Hill

4

Eight Acre Dell

West Field Beeches

Poor Hill

Kingsmore Copse

Whinkney's Copse

Round Copse

The Avenue

3

Doper's Copse

White Hill Dell

Three Castles Path

Fryingdown Copse

Forfield Plantation

Quidliz Round

47

Allwood Copse

Winslade La

Little Bushywarren Copse

Herriard Park

2

GRAMMARSHAM LA

Northgate Farm

NORTHGATE LA

Alley Lane

Webb's Copse

Great Bushywarren Copse

A339

1

Hallowed Litten

GREEN LA

CHURCH LA

BUSHYWARREN LA

Oxlease Lane

46

63   A   B   64   C   D   65   E   F

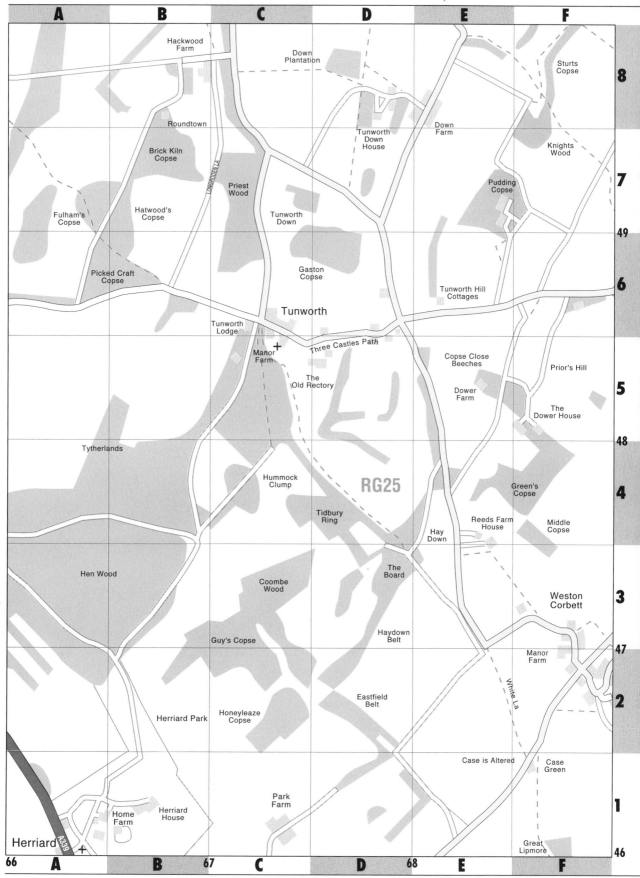

A	B	C	D	E	F

8
7
49
6
5
48
4
47
2
1
46

Hackwood Farm

Down Plantation

Sturts Copse

Roundtown

Tunworth Down House

Down Farm

Knights Wood

Brick Kiln Copse

Priest Wood

Pudding Copse

Fulham's Copse

Hatwood's Copse

Tunworth Down

Picked Craft Copse

Gaston Copse

Tunworth Hill Cottages

Tunworth

Tunworth Lodge

Three Castles Path

Copse Close Beeches

Prior's Hill

Manor Farm

The Old Rectory

Dower Farm

The Dower House

Tytherlands

Hummock Clump

RG25

Green's Copse

Tidbury Ring

Reeds Farm House

Middle Copse

Hay Down

Hen Wood

Coombe Wood

The Board

Weston Corbett

Guy's Copse

Haydown Belt

Manor Farm

White La

Honeyleaze Copse

Eastfield Belt

Herriard Park

Case is Altered

Case Green

Park Farm

Herriard House

Home Farm

Herriard

A339

Great Lipmore

LONGBRIDGE LA

66   67   68

A B C D E F

Three Castles Path

Three Castles Path

Four Lanes End

UPTON GREY RD

Bidden Water

Ford Farm

FORD LA

Bidden Grange Farm

BIDDEN RD

Lower Bidden Farm

Bidden

Dean Plantation

GASTON LA

RG25

Cleves Farm

CLEVES LA

THE ARBORETUM

Upton Grey House

Manor Farm

WOODMANFIELD

Little Dean Farm

LITTLE DEAN LA

Gaston Copse

CEMETERY LA

Upton Grey

PO

LITTLE HODDINGTON

SOUTH HILL

Little Hoddington

The Hoddington Arms (PH)

USTON CL

WESTON RD

The Village Farm

LIMBREY HILL

Hoddington Park

HODDINGTON COTTS

Tile Barn Farm

Weston Mark

Hoddington House

THE OLD ORCH 1
NASH MDWS 2

1
2

Hoddington Farm

Lee's Farm

Dean Farm House

LEES HILL

RG29

Weston Patrick House

CHURCH VIEW

ALTON ROAD
COTTS

B3349

Manor Farm

Weston Patrick

Dean Copse

Hoddington

Wood Lane End

Privett Copse

Westers Lane

Long La

Little Park Copse

PICKAVEL LA

B3349

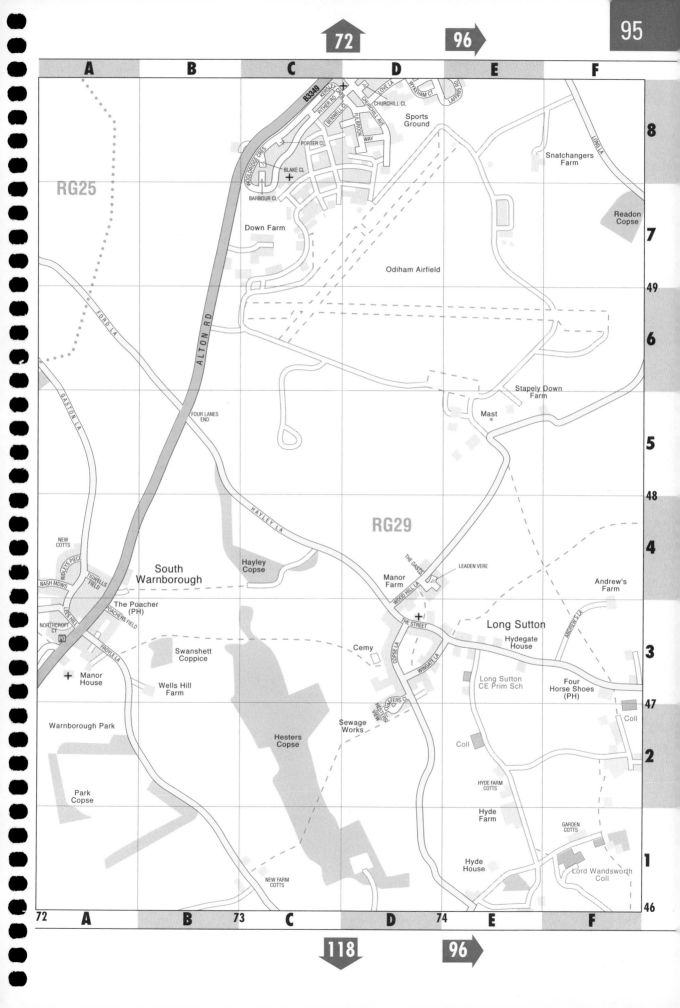

A B C D E F

8
7
49
6
5
48
4
3
47
2
1
46

RG25

RG29

B3349
KERSLEY CRES
PITHER RD
BENWELL CL
FULBROOK WAY
PORTER CL
BLAKE CL
BARBOUR CL
WOOLDRIDGE CRES

LOVE LA
CHURCHILL CL
CHURCHILL AVE
WYKEHAM CT
LAPTONS CL
LONG LA

Sports Ground

Snatchangers Farm

Readon Copse

Down Farm

Odiham Airfield

ALTON RD
FORD LA
GASTON LA

FOUR LANES END

Stapely Down Farm

Mast

HAYLEY LA

Hayley Copse

NEW COTTS
RIDLEY'S PIECE
TIGWELLS FIELD
NASH MDWS
LEES HILL
NORTHCROFT CT
PO
FROYLE LA

South Warnborough

The Poacher (PH)
POACHERS FIELD

Manor House

Swanshett Coppice

Wells Hill Farm

Hesters Copse

Warnborough Park

Park Copse

Manor Farm
THE OASTS
LEADEN VERE
WOOD HILL LA

Andrew's Farm
ANDREW'S LA

Long Sutton

Hydegate House
HYDEGATE LA

THE STREET
COPSE LA
WINGATE LA
CRAFERS CL
HESTERS VIEW

Cemy

Sewage Works

Long Sutton CE Prim Sch

Four Horse Shoes (PH)

Coll

Coll

HYDE FARM COTTS

Hyde Farm

GARDEN COTTS

Hyde House

Lord Wandsworth Coll

NEW FARM COTTS

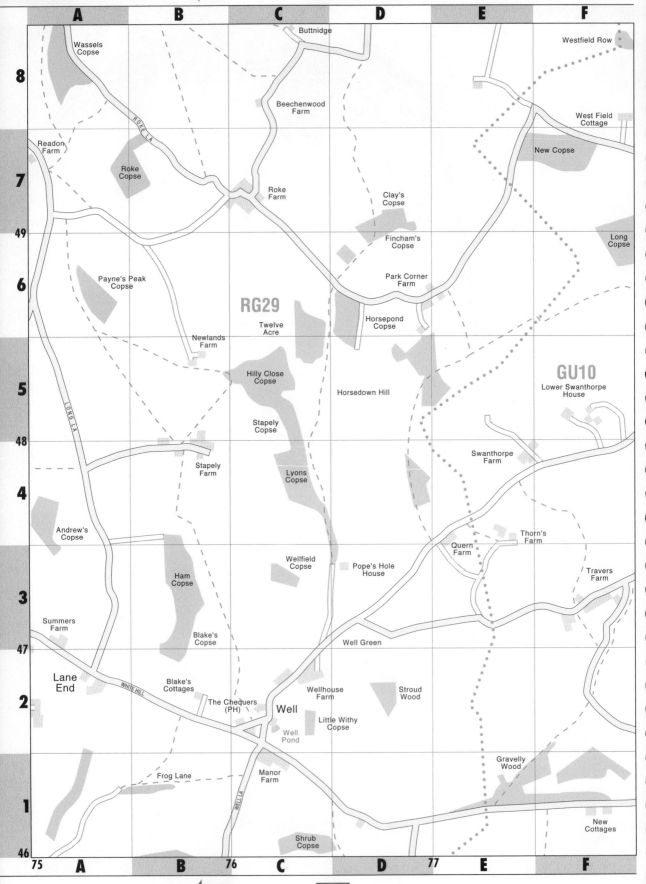

Wassels Copse

Readon Farm

Roke Copse

ROKE LA

Buttnidge

Beechenwood Farm

Roke Farm

Clay's Copse

Fincham's Copse

Westfield Row

West Field Cottage

New Copse

Long Copse

Payne's Peak Copse

Newlands Farm

Twelve Acre

RG29

Park Corner Farm

Horsepond Copse

GU10

Hilly Close Copse

Horsedown Hill

Lower Swanthorpe House

Stapely Copse

Swanthorpe Farm

LONG LA

Stapely Farm

Lyons Copse

Andrew's Copse

Ham Copse

Wellfield Copse

Pope's Hole House

Quern Farm

Thorn's Farm

Travers Farm

Summers Farm

Blake's Copse

Well Green

Lane End

WHITE HILL

Blake's Cottages

The Chequers (PH)

Well

Wellhouse Farm

Stroud Wood

Little Withy Copse

Well Pond

WELL LA

Gravelly Wood

Frog Lane

Manor Farm

Shrub Copse

New Cottages

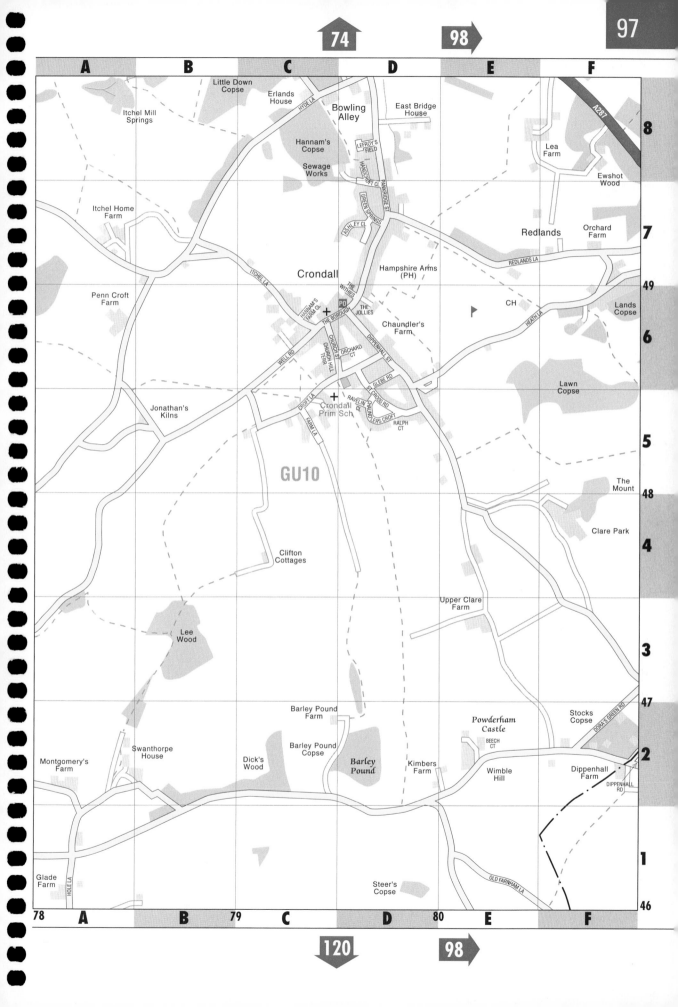

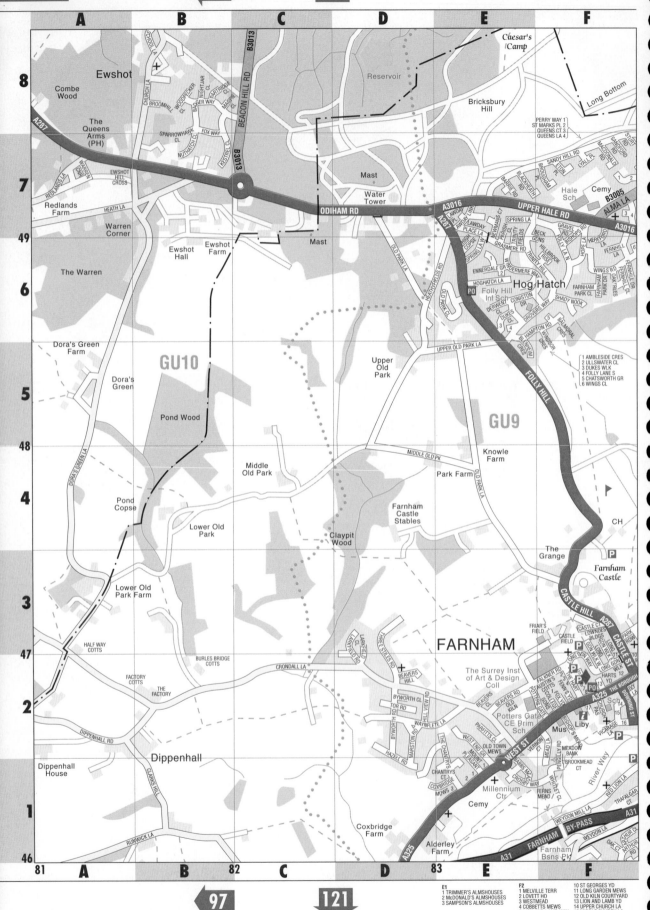

E1
1 TRIMMER'S ALMSHOUSES
2 McDONALD'S ALMSHOUSES
3 SAMPSON'S ALMSHOUSES

F2
1 MELVILLE TERR
2 LOVETT HO
3 WESTMEAD
4 COBBETTS MEWS
5 LION AND LAMB WAY
6 TIMBER CL
7 CRAVEN HO
8 ARUNDELL PL
9 THE MEWS

10 ST GEORGES YD
11 LONG GARDEN MEWS
12 OLD KILN COURTYARD
13 LION AND LAMB YD
14 UPPER CHURCH LA
15 MIDDLE CHURCH LA
16 LOWER CHURCH LA
17 KINGHAM PL

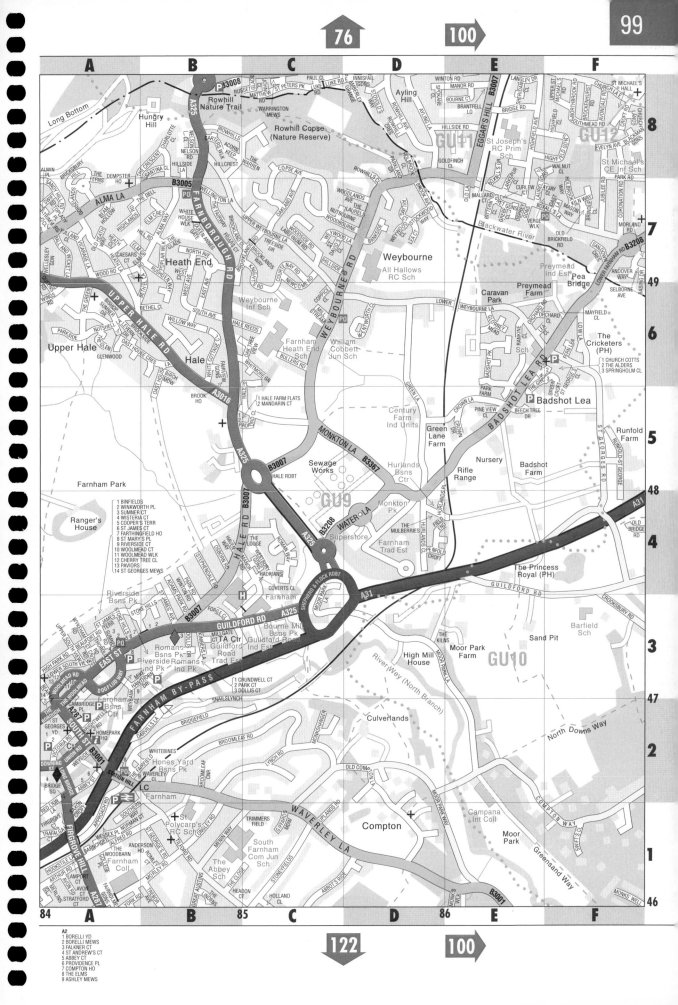

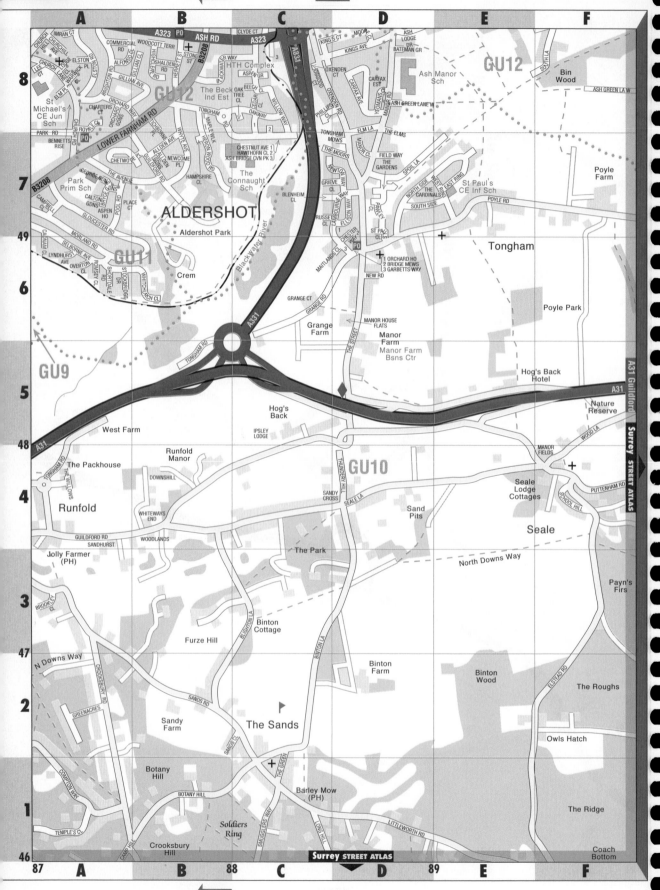

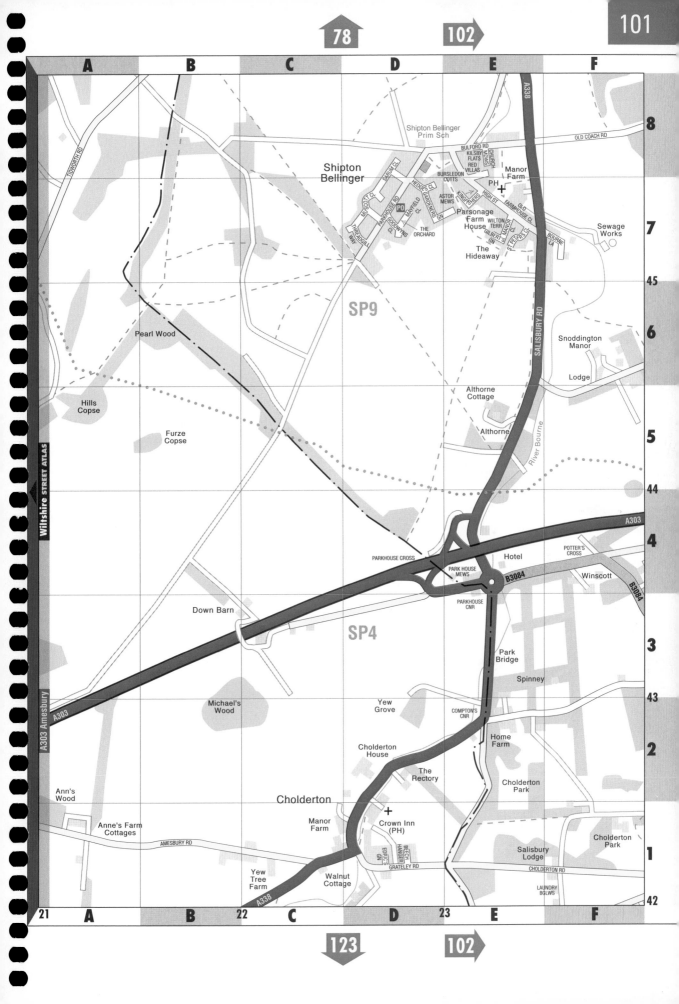

A B C D E F

8
45
6
5
44
4
43
3
2
1
42

Wiltshire STREET ATLAS

Shipton Bellinger Prim Sch
OLD COACH RD
BULFORD RD
KILSBY FLATS
RED VILLAS
BURSLEDON COTTS
CHURCH MDWS
Manor Farm
PH
Shipton Bellinger
SARUM CL
HEDGES GDNS
ASTOR MEWS
KINGFISHERS
HIGH ST
FARMHOUSE CL
OLD
MAYFIELD CL
THE ORCHARD
PO
GODDWYNS CL
THREADGILL WAY
PARKHOUSE RD
MUSCOTT CL
Parsonage Farm House
WILTON TERR
MANOR CL
GILBERT'S GN
ST PETER'S CL
BOURNE LA
SALISBURY RD
A338
Sewage Works
The Hideaway

SP9

Pearl Wood

Snoddington Manor
Lodge

Hills Copse

Furze Copse

Althorne Cottage
Althorne

River Bourne

A303
A303 Amesbury

Parkhouse Cross
PARKHOUSE MEWS
PARK HOUSE MEWS
Hotel
POTTER'S CROSS
Winscott
B3084
B3084
PARKHOUSE CNR

Down Barn

SP4

Park Bridge
Spinney

Michael's Wood

Yew Grove
COMPTON'S CNR

Home Farm

Cholderton House
The Rectory
Cholderton Park

Ann's Wood

Cholderton

Manor Farm
Crown Inn (PH)
Anne's Farm Cottages
AMESBURY RD

Cholderton Park

BEECH HANGER
EDRIC'S GN
GRATELEY RD
CHOLDERTON RD

Salisbury Lodge

Yew Tree Farm
Walnut Cottage
A338

LAUNDRY BGLWS

21 A B 22 C D 23 E F

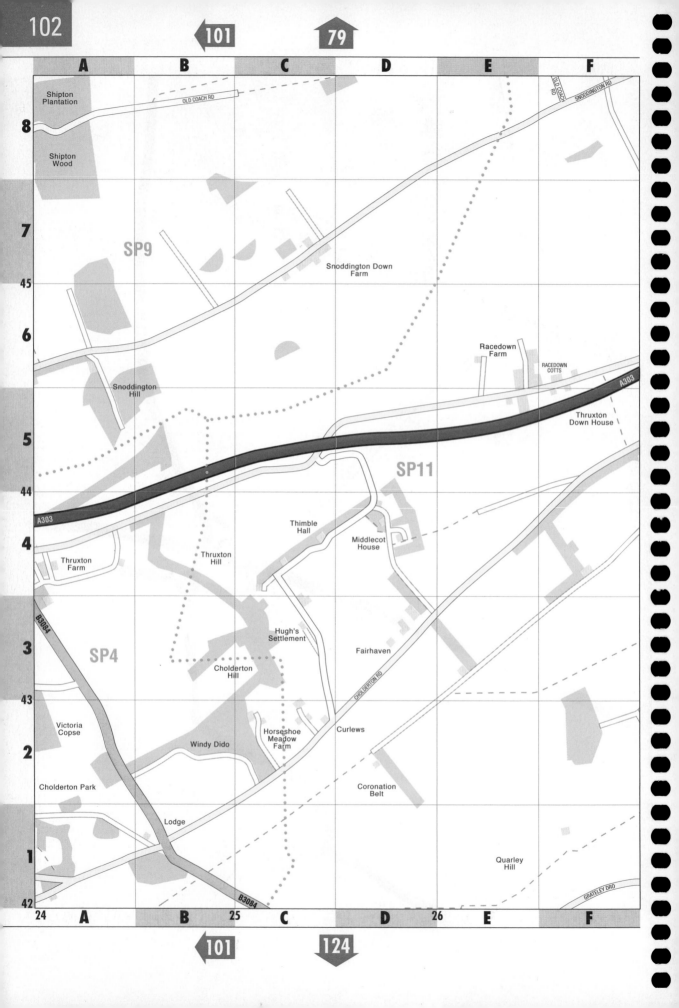

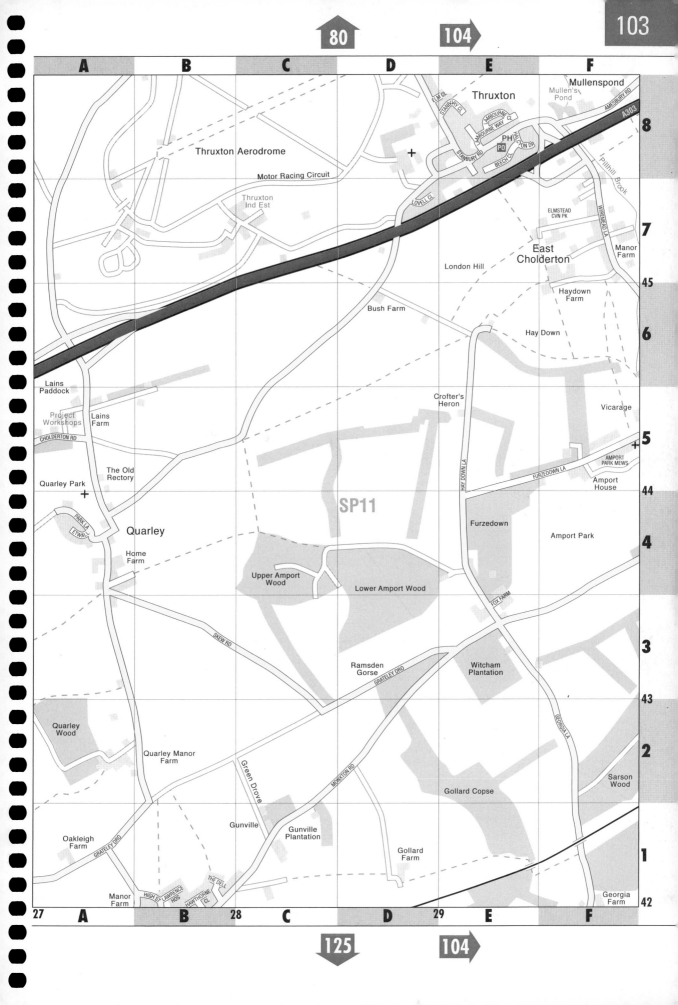

103
81

A B C D E F

8

AMESBURY RD
A303

THE LIMES

The Hawk
Conservancy

SARSON LA

Works

Monxton Lane

7

MONXTON RD

RED POST LA

RED POST
BRIDGE

45

Hunt's
Lane

Piper's Hill

SUNNYBANK

ANDOVER RD

6

SARSON CL

Manor
Farm

Amport
Inn
(PH)

MOUNT
PLEASANT

Upper Mill
Farm

CHAPEL CL

THE EIGHTS

Amport

The Black Swan
(PH)

Pillhill Brook

WIREMEAD LA

Watercress
Beds

COBB
MEWS

Sarson

SARSONS
BARNS

GREEN LA

ABBOTTS ANN RD

CHALKPIT LA

Watercress
Beds

CATTLE LA

THE GREEN

FURZEDOWN LA

5

Amport CE
Prim Sch

SHEPPARD
ALMSHOUSES

Monxton

AMPORT
FIRS

KEEPER'S HILL

The
Triangle

44

SP11

Two Rivers
Farm

4

Manor
Farm

HILLSIDE

BROAD RD

Church
Lane

PO

Hook Lane

CATHERINES WAY

Abbott's Ann
CE Prim Sch

1

3

Sarsons Wood

DUNKIRT LA

MANOR CL 1
TIMOTHY'S FIELD 2

WARREN DR

2

BILBERY

43

Great Wood

The Drove

CRISWICK
CL

2

Keeper's
Cottage

Dunkirt Lane

Eastover
Farm

1

Woodlands Prospect
Farm

Dunkirt
Barn

Eastover Farm
Cottages

SALISBURY RD

A343

Sarson Furze
Down

The Groves

The Morrells

Eastover Copse

42

30 A B 31 C D 32 E F

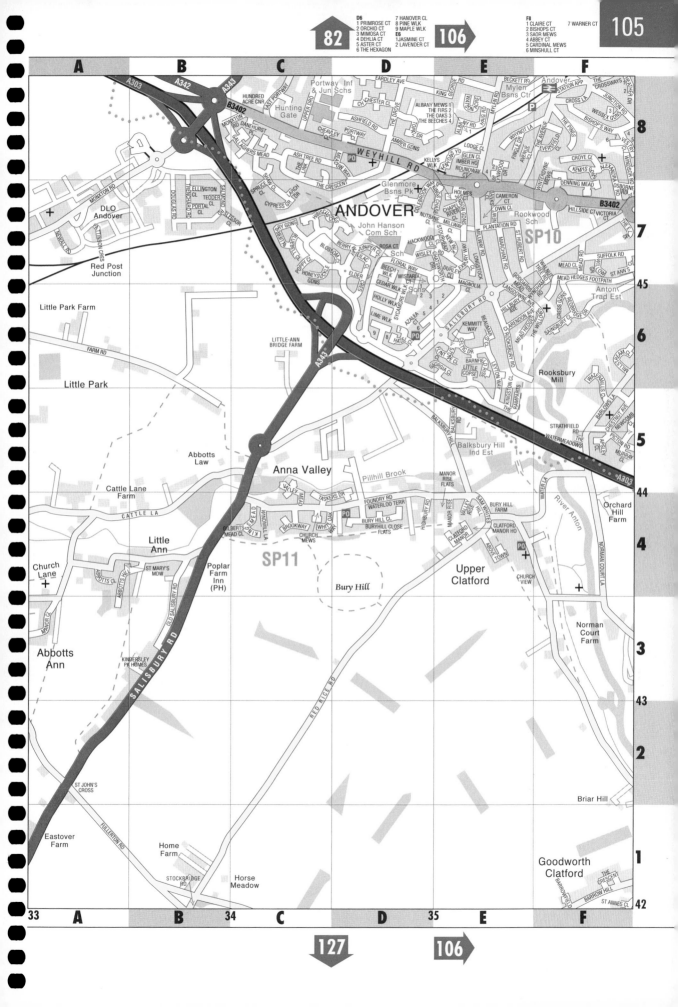

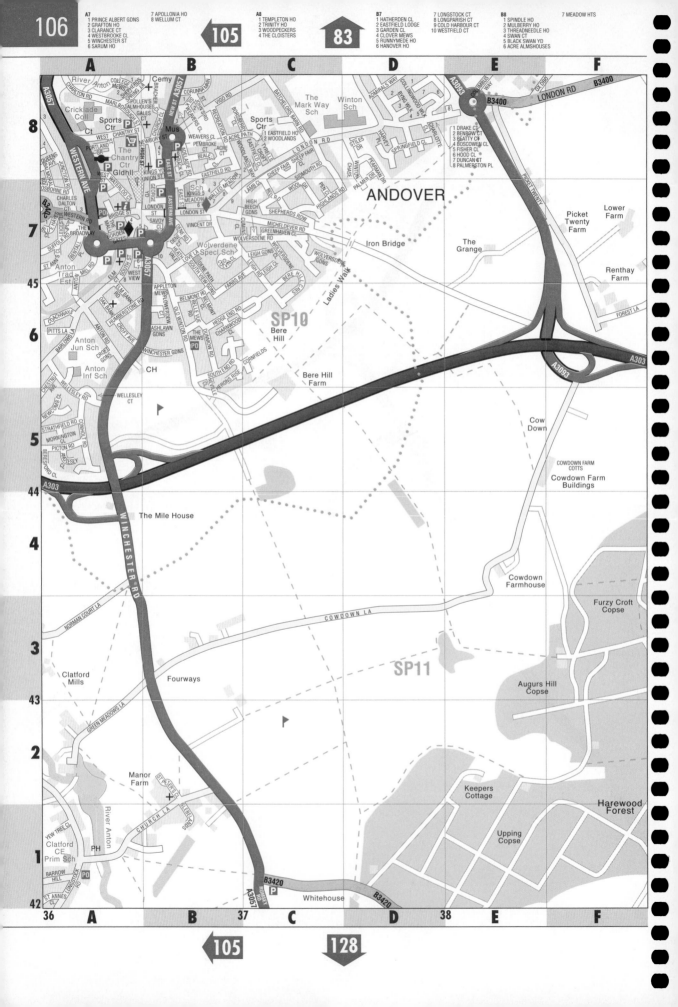

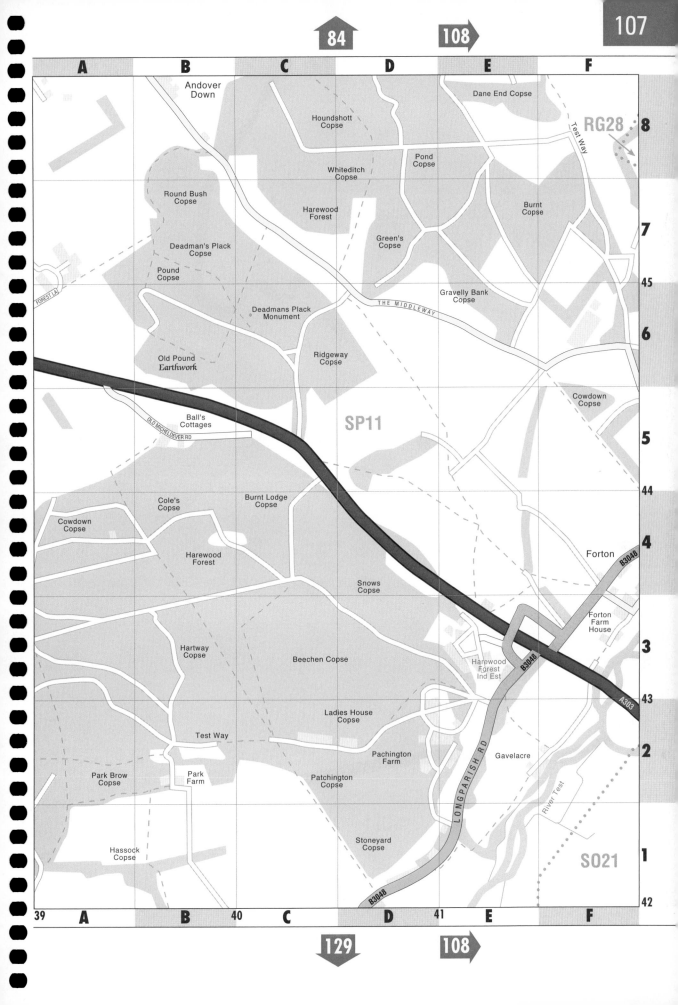

A B C D E F

Andover Down

Dane End Copse

Houndshott Copse

RG28 8

Whiteditch Copse

Pond Copse

Test Way

Round Bush Copse

Harewood Forest

Burnt Copse

7

Deadman's Plack Copse

Green's Copse

45

Pound Copse

Gravelly Bank Copse

THE MIDDLEWAY

Deadmans Plack Monument

6

Old Pound Earthwork

Ridgeway Copse

Cowdown Copse

FOREST LA

Ball's Cottages

SP11

5

OLD MICHELDEVER RD

44

Cole's Copse

Burnt Lodge Copse

Forton 4

B3048

Cowdown Copse

Snows Copse

Forton Farm House

Harewood Forest

B3048

Hartway Copse

Beechen Copse

Harewood Forest Ind Est

3

B3048

A303

43

Ladies House Copse

Test Way

Gavelacre

2

Pachington Farm

LONGPARISH RD

River Test

Park Brow Copse

Park Farm

Patchington Copse

Stoneyard Copse

SO21

1

Hassock Copse

B3048

42

39 A B 40 C D 41 E F

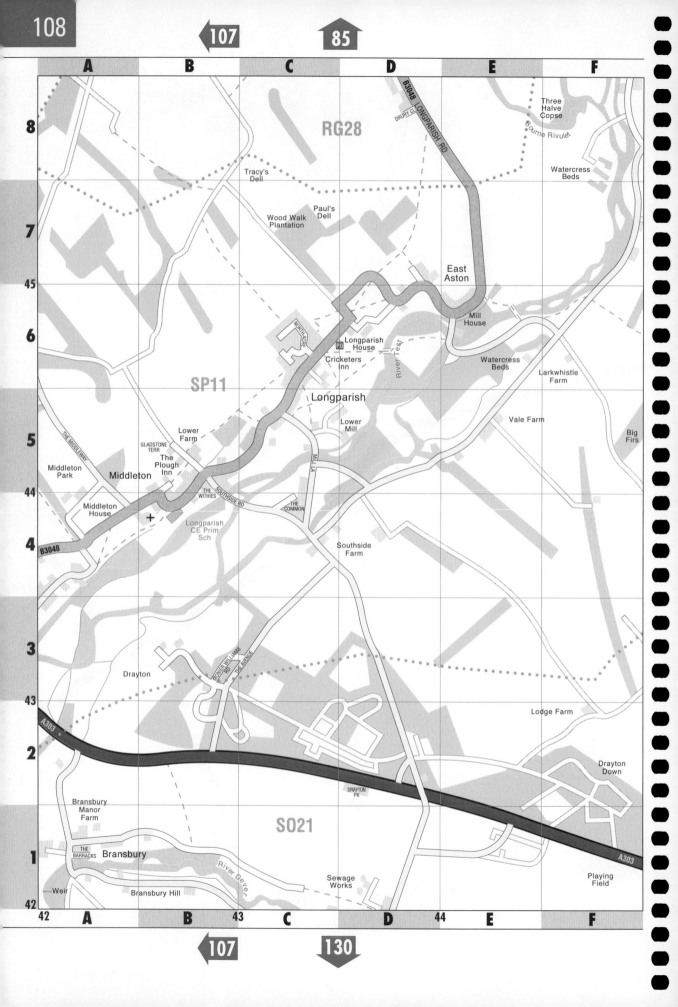

A   B   C   D   E   F

8

RG28

B3048 LONGPARISH RD

DRURY CL

Three Halve Copse

Bourne Rivulet

7

Tracy's Dell

Paul's Dell

Wood Walk Plantation

Watercress Beds

45

East Aston

6

NORTHACRE

Longparish House

PO

Cricketers Inn

Mill House

River Test

Watercress Beds

Larkwhistle Farm

SP11

Longparish

Vale Farm

5

Lower Farm

Lower Mill

Big Firs

GLADSTONE TERR

The Plough Inn

MILL LA

44

Middleton Park

Middleton

THE WITHIES

SOUTHSIDE RD

THE COMMON

Middleton House

Longparish CE Prim Sch

Southside Farm

4

B3048

3

Drayton

MONIER WILLIAMS RD

THE AVENUE

43

Lodge Farm

A303

2

Drayton Down

DRAYTON PK

Bransbury Manor Farm

SO21

A303

1

THE BARRACKS

Bransbury

River Dever

Sewage Works

Playing Field

42

Weir

Bransbury Hill

42   A   B   43   C   D   44   E   F

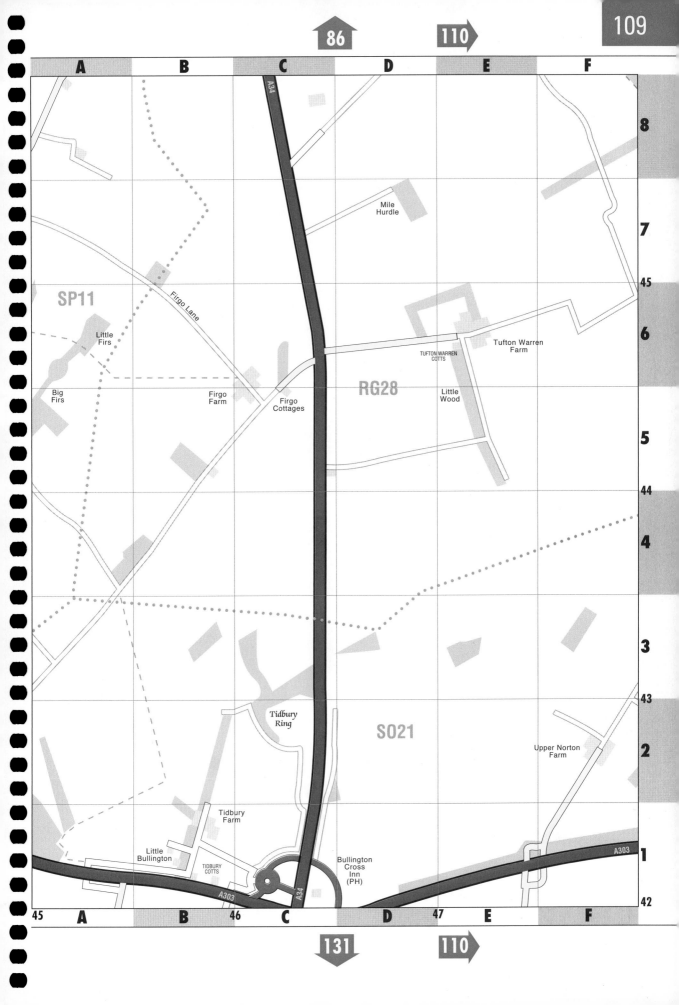

A B C D E F

8
7
45
6
5
44
4
3
43
2
43
1
42

Mile
Hurdle

SP11

Firgo Lane

Little
Firs

Tufton Warren
Farm

TUFTON WARREN
COTTS

RG28

Big
Firs

Firgo
Farm

Firgo
Cottages

Little
Wood

A34

Tidbury
Ring

SO21

Upper Norton
Farm

Tidbury
Farm

Little
Bullington

TIDBURY
COTTS

Bullington
Cross
Inn
(PH)

A303

A303

A34

109
87

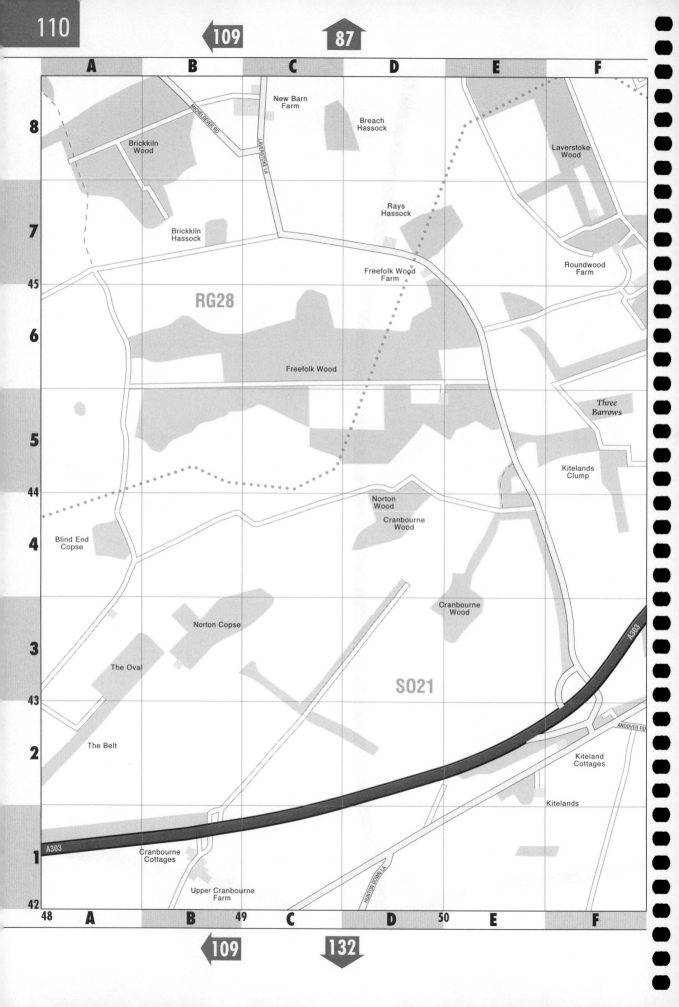

109
132

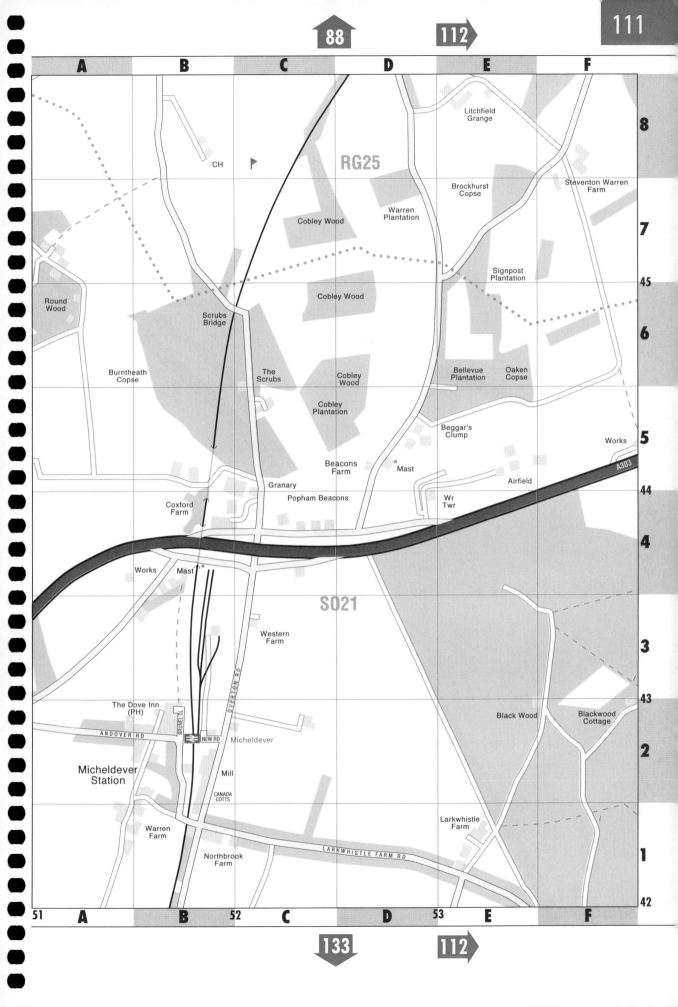

111
89

A B C D E F

8

RG25

Ashen Grove Copse

The Fox (PH)

POPHAM LA

Wheatsheaf Hotel

A38

7

A303

WOODSIDE COTTS

M3

45

Crem

Misholt Copse

Waltham Trinleys

Hellier's Copse

6

Bramley Wood

Cocksford Firs East

Cocksford Down

5

A303

West Farm

44

Popham Court Farm

4

Popham Court Farm

Popham

Bittley Copse

3

SO21

The Old Vicarage

Black Wood

College Wood

43

Vicarage Farm

2

BRADLEY COTTS

Bradley Farm

Manor Farm

Woodmancott

Rownest Wood

1

London Lodge

The Calvert Ctr

42

Innersdown Farm

A303 M3

54 A 55 B C 56 D E F

111
134

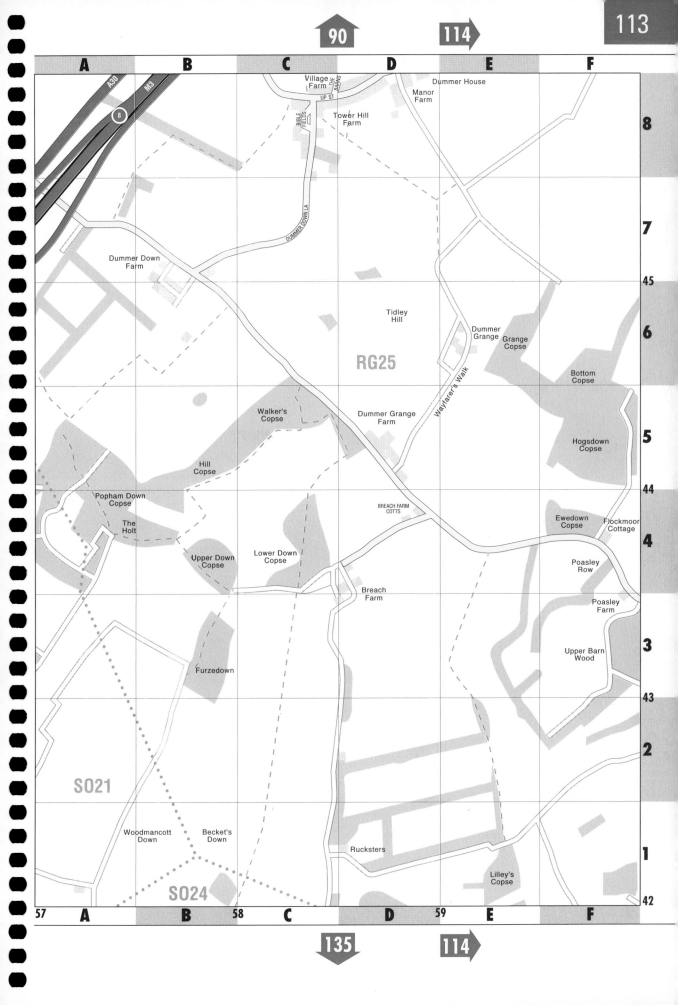

A B C D E F

8
7
45
6
5
44
4
43
2
1
42

A30
M3
8

Village Farm
THE BARNS
Dummer House
Manor Farm
UP ST
Tower Hill Farm
BIBLE FIELDS
DUMMER DOWN LA

Dummer Down Farm

Tidley Hill

RG25

Dummer Grange
Grange Copse
Bottom Copse

Walker's Copse
Dummer Grange Farm
Wayfarer's Walk
Hogsdown Copse

Hill Copse

Popham Down Copse

The Holt
BREACH FARM COTTS
Ewedown Copse
Flockmoor Cottage

Upper Down Copse
Lower Down Copse
Poasley Row

Breach Farm
Poasley Farm

Furzedown
Upper Barn Wood

SO21

Woodmancott Down
Becket's Down
Rucksters

SO24
Lilley's Copse

57 A B 58 C D 59 E F

113
91

A B C D E F

8

Nutley La

Inwood Copse

B3046

Lowe's Wood

Great Wood

Cow Down Gate

Nutley House

Round Copse

Nutley Wood

Gobley Hole

Norton's Wood

7

Wr Twr

45

6

Great Reid's Copse

Nutleydown Wood

Rabbits Row

Nutley Down

Berrydown Copse

Nutley

Windmill Hill

5

Manor Farm

Berrydown Copse

Chapell's Wood

Warwicks Row Copse

Berry Down

44

RG25

Bermondspit House

Wellclose Gate

Berrydown Farm

4

BERRYDOWN RD

The Crown Inn (PH)

Moundsmere Farm

3

Axford Large Farm

KENWARD BGLWS

Inham's Copse

Moundsmere Manor

Pescot Hole Copse

Axford House

Axford

43

Fawkners

DAMSEL LANE

2

Allen's Copse

Oak Hill La

Bradley Park

Preston House

East Park

Coombe Plantation

1

West Park

SO24

Home Farm

B3046

P

GARDEN CL

42

60 A B 61 C D 62 E F

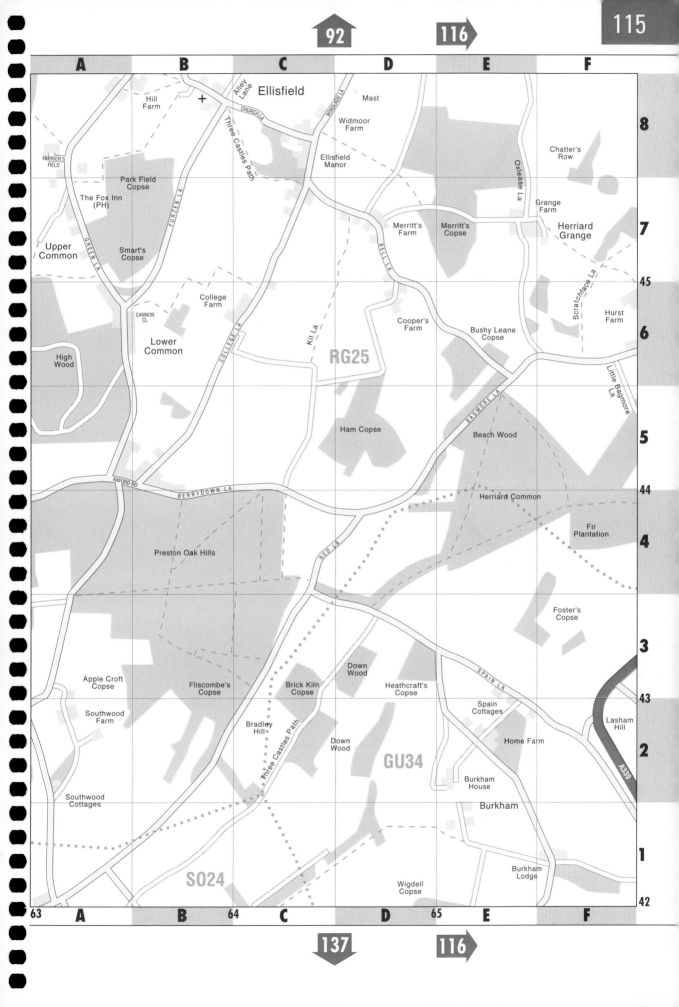

92
116
137
116

Ellisfield

Alley Lane
Hill Farm
CHURCH LA
WINSLADE LA
Mast
Widmoor Farm
Three Castles Path
Ellisfield Manor
FARRIER'S FIELD
Park Field Copse
The Fox Inn (PH)
FURZEN LA
GREEN LA
Oxlease La
Chatter's Row
Grange Farm
Herriard Grange
Upper Common
Smart's Copse
College Farm
Merritt's Farm
Merritt's Copse
Scratchface La
Hurst Farm
CANNON CL
Lower Common
COLLEGE LA
Kit La
BELL LA
Cooper's Farm
Bushy Leane Copse
High Wood
RG25
Ham Copse
Beach Wood
BAGMORE LA
Little Bagmore La
AXFORD RD
BERRYDOWN LA
Herriard Common
Fir Plantation
Preston Oak Hills
RED LA
Foster's Copse
Apple Croft Copse
Fliscombe's Copse
Brick Kiln Copse
Down Wood
Heathcraft's Copse
SPAIN LA
Spain Cottages
Lasham Hill
A339
Southwood Farm
Bradley Hill
Three Castles Path
Down Wood
GU34
Home Farm
Southwood Cottages
Burkham House
Burkham
Wigdell Copse
Burkham Lodge
SO24

A   B   C   D   E   F

8

Manor Farm
Scratchface La
A339
Herriard Park
Square Lipmore

Kennel Row
Park Corner
Breeches Row
Little Wood

7

Elderfield House
HOCKLEYS LA
Nashes Green
Lee Farm

45

SOUTHROPE GN
Southrope

Bagmore
BAGMORE LA

6

Fur & Feathers (PH)
Hyde Farm
Summerlea Ct
RG25
Hale Farm
High Wood

Bull's Copse
LIPSCOMBE CL
Bull's Farm
Cotterpin's Copse
BACK LA

Great Matt's Copse
Little Matt's Copse
Brick Kiln Common
Whitewood Cottage

5

Clark's Copse
White Wood

Nursery Copse
Cold Harbour

44

Middle Common Wood
New Inn Copse
THE AVENUE
Mus

4

New Inn Brow
Avenue Farm
East Common Wood

Hovena Copse
Lasham Airfield
Masts

3

A339
GU34

Lasham Hill Farm
New Copse
Highfield House

43

Lasham Hill
Royal Oak (PH)
White Hill
Lasham Wood

2

CAMONS MEAD
New Farm
Church Farm

A339
New Farm House
Lasham

1

42

66   A   B   67   C   D   68   E   F

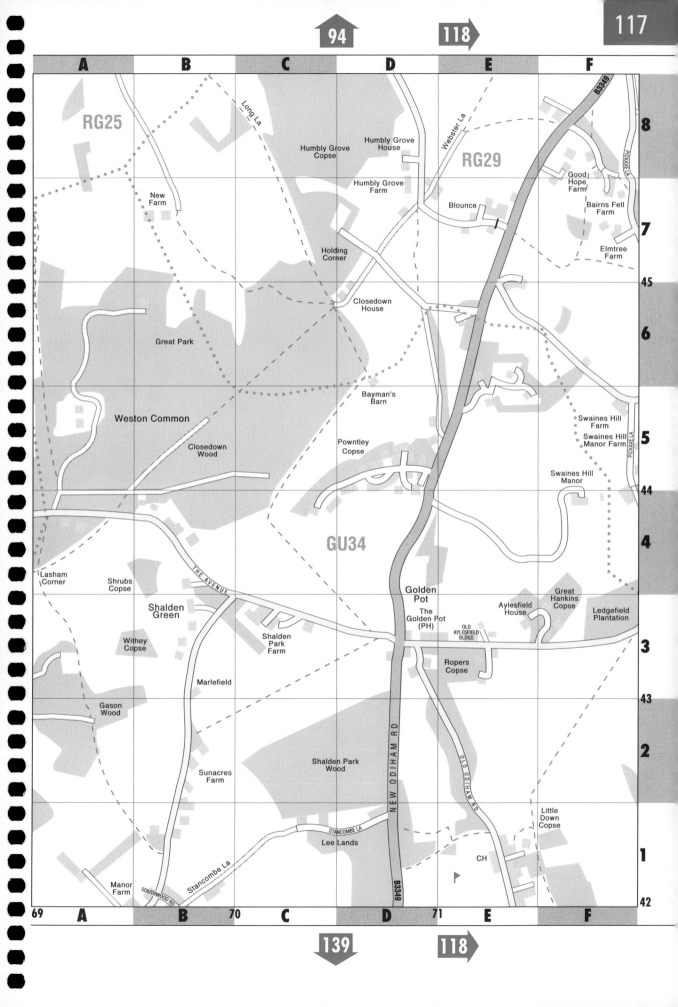

117 95

A B C D E F

8

Vinney
Copse

New Farm

Sheephouse
Copse

Pickaxe
Copse

White House
Farm

Highnam
Copse

7

Sutton
Common

45

RG29

6

West
View

Great
Wood

Gaston
Copse

PICKAXE LA

Broadlands
Copse

Little
Wood

5

SOXCROFT LA

Yarnhams
Farm

Hawkins
Wood

44

4

Mast

Beech Hangers La

Liddenfield
Copse

Stowell
Copse

Dicket's
Plantation

Yarnhams
Cottages

Stowell
Cottage

Fielders
Copse

Shrub Croft
Copse

3

Masts

Ham Wood

GU34

43

Spollycombe
Copse

2

Peakham
Copse

Holybourne
Down

Brockham Hill
Farm Cottages

BROCKHAM HILL LA

Brockham Hill
Barn

New La

1

Round
Wood

Howard's
La

42

72 A B 73 C D 74 E F

117 140

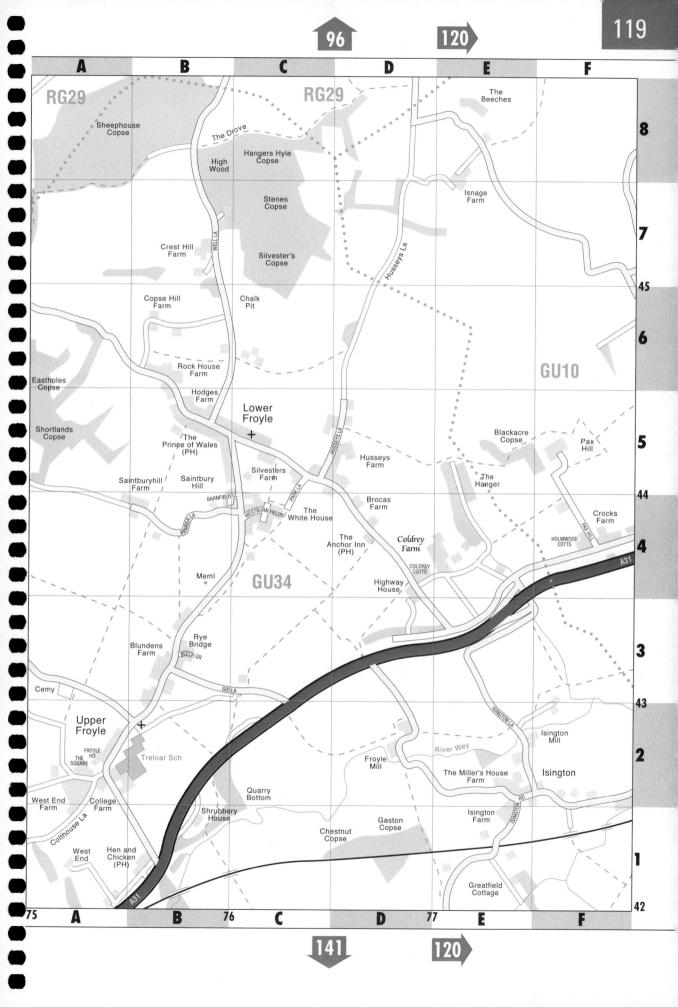

A B C D E F

8

RG29

RG29

The Beeches

Sheephouse Copse

The Drove

High Wood

Hangers Hyle Copse

Isnage Farm

7

Stenes Copse

Crest Hill Farm

WELL LA

Silvester's Copse

Husseys La

45

Copse Hill Farm

Chalk Pit

6

Eastholes Copse

Rock House Farm

GU10

Shortlands Copse

Hodges Farm

Lower Froyle

Blackacre Copse

Pax Hill

5

The Prince of Wales (PH)

Husseys La

Husseys Farm

The Hanger

Saintburyhill Farm

Saintbury Hill

Silvesters Farm

BARNFIELD CL.

PARK LA

Brocas Farm

44

WESTBURN FIELDS

The White House

Crocks Farm

PAMBER LA

The Anchor Inn (PH)

Coldrey Farm

HOLMWOOD COTTS

4

Meml

GU34

Highway House

COLDREY COTTS

A31

Rye Bridge

BEECH GR

Blundens Farm

3

Cemy

GID LA

43

Upper Froyle

ISINGTON LA

Isington Mill

FROYLE HO

THE SQUARE

Treloar Sch

River Wey

Isington

2

West End Farm

College Farm

Froyle Mill

The Miller's House Farm

Colthouse La

Quarry Bottom

Shrubbery House

Chestnut Copse

Gaston Copse

Isington Farm

ISINGTON RD

1

West End

Hen and Chicken (PH)

Greatfield Cottage

A31

42

119
97

A B C D E F

8

Locks Grove
Gasson's Coppice
Highcombes Farm
Cheek's Farm
Grover's Farm
Willey Copse

7
BURY COURT COTTS
Bury Court
Hill Farm

45
Perryland
Wallfield Copse
IDLEFIELD COTTS

6
+
Irelands
East Green
Northbrook Farm
Northbrook
A31

Jenkyn Place
CHURCH LA
HOLE LA
Broadhatch House
Welche's House
Marsh House
The Bull Inn (PH)
GU10
CRONDAL RD

5
LONGCROFT
EGGARS FIELD
SCHOOL LA
BAGS HELLIS
Bentley
Bentley CE Prim Sch
Bentley Bsns Pk
Turk's Mill

44
OAKWAY
SOUTH VIEW COTTS
BONNERS FIELD
BROADLANDS CL
PH PO
RECTORY LA
THE POLLARDS
Bentley Ind Ctr
Marelands
White Bridge
Cotton's Copse

4
A31
THE DRIFT
South Green Farm
Sewage Works
River Wey
Holt Pound Inclosure

Bentley Green Farm
STATION RD
Alice Holt Forest

3
Anstey Bridge
NEY BANK
Forest Wlks
P

43
P Bentley
Mast
Alice Holt Farm
ALICE HOLT COTTS
A325

2
ISINGTON RD
Isington Close
Aldix Copse Farm
Westminster House
PARK CL
Alice Holt Lodge
GRAVEL HILL RD
GU34
THROAKMEAD
BLACKNEST RD
Lodge Inclosure
Plain Piece

1
Catham Copse
Redcap Copse
Broadview Farm
THE GLADE
BACK LA
A325

42
Blacknest Ind Pk

78 A B 79 C D 80 E F

119
142

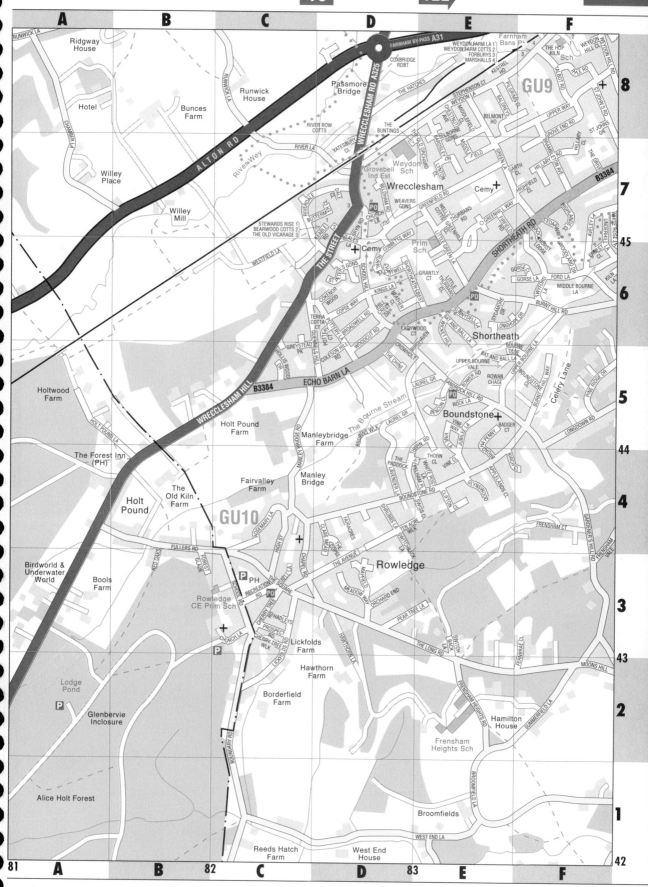

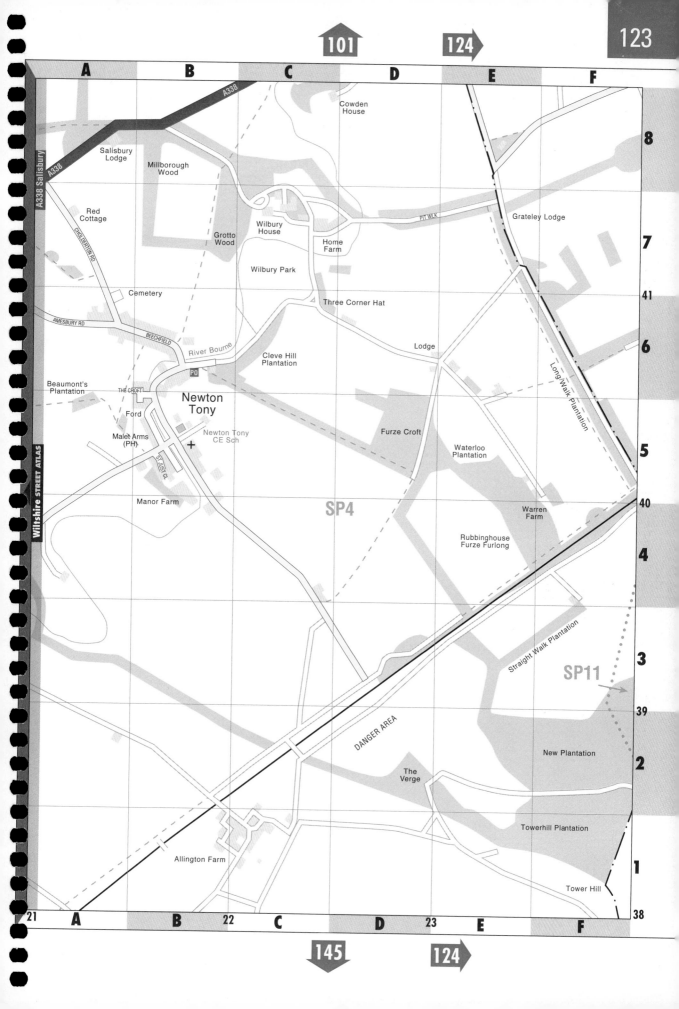

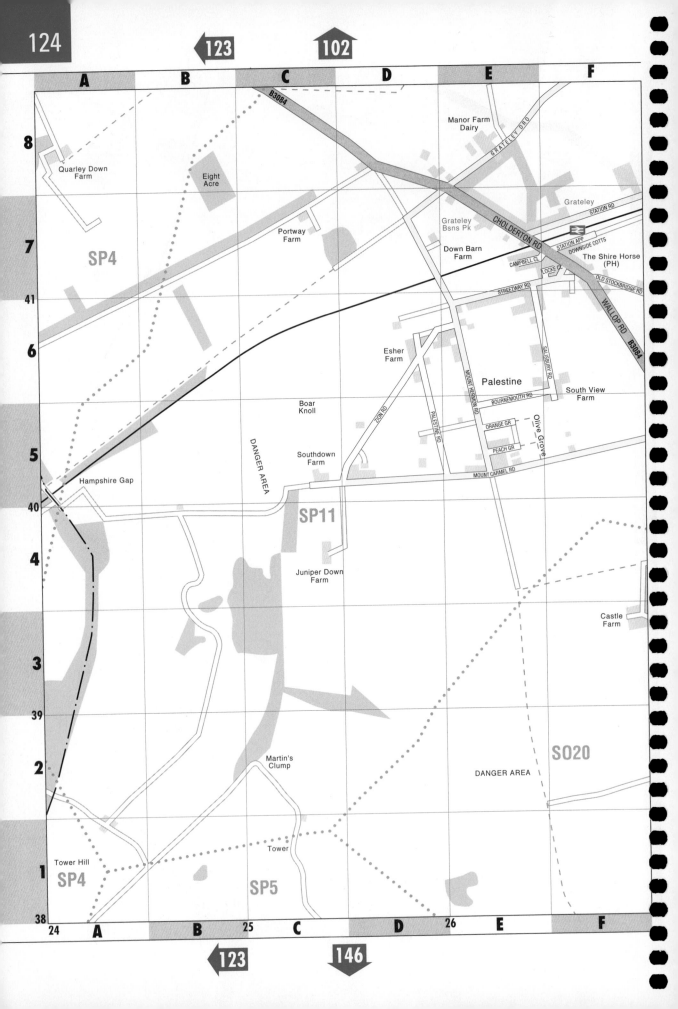

A   B   C   D   E   F

8

Quarley Down
Farm

Eight
Acre

Manor Farm
Dairy

GRATELEY DRO

B3084

Grateley

STATION RD

7

SP4

Portway
Farm

Grateley
Bsns Pk

Down Barn
Farm

CHOLDERTON RD

CAMPBELL CL

LOCKE CL

STATION APP

DOWNSIDE COTTS

The Shire Horse
(PH)

41

STREETWAY RD

OLD STOCKBRIDGE RD

6

Esher
Farm

MOUNT HERMON RD

Palestine

SALISBURY RD

WALLOP RD

B3084

Boar
Knoll

ZION RD

PALESTINE RD

BOURNEMOUTH RD

South View
Farm

DANGER AREA

Southdown
Farm

ORANGE GR

PEACH GR

Olive Grove

5

Hampshire Gap

40

SP11

MOUNT CARMEL RD

4

Juniper Down
Farm

3

Castle
Farm

39

SO20

2

Martin's
Clump

DANGER AREA

1

Tower Hill

SP4

Tower

SP5

38

24   A   B   25   C   D   26   E   F

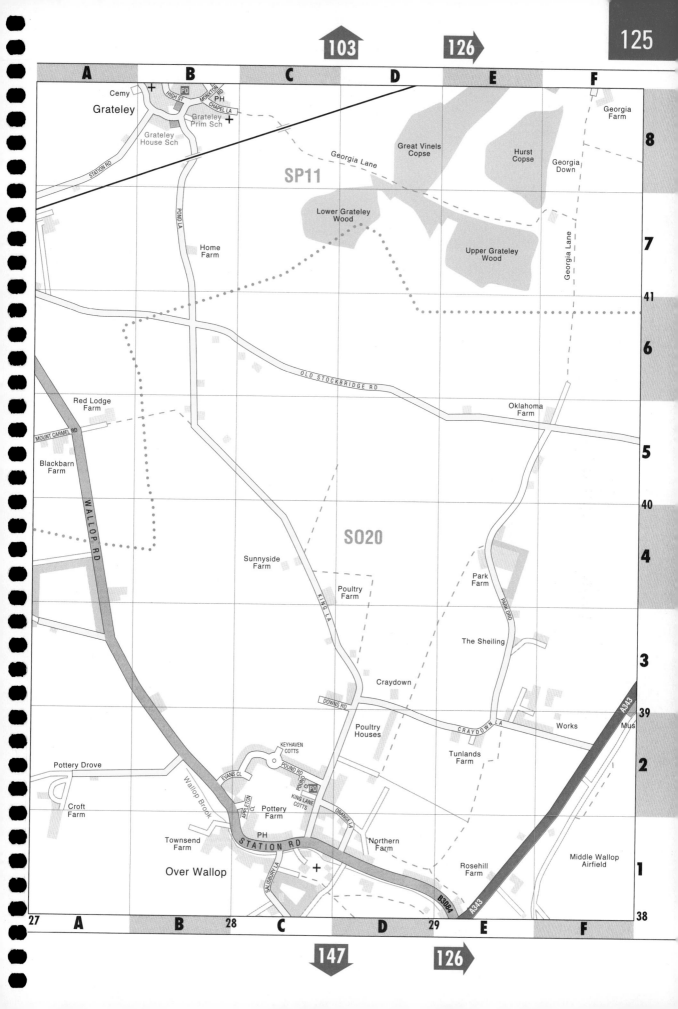

103
126

A B C D E F

8

Grateley
Cemy
Grateley House Sch
Grateley Prim Sch
HIGH ST
MONKTON RD
CHAPEL LA
PO
PH
STATION RD

Georgia Farm

Georgia Lane

Great Vinels Copse

Hurst Copse

Georgia Down

SP11

Home Farm

POND LA

Lower Grateley Wood

Upper Grateley Wood

Georgia Lane

7

41

6

OLD STOCKBRIDGE RD

Red Lodge Farm

MOUNT CARMEL RD

Oklahoma Farm

Blackbarn Farm

WALLOP RD

5

40

SO20

Sunnyside Farm

Poultry Farm

Park Farm

PARK DRO

KING LA

4

The Sheiling

Craydown

3

DOWNS RD

Poultry Houses

CRAYDOWN LA

Works

Mus

A343

39

Pottery Drove

Croft Farm

Wallop Brook

EVANS CL

KEYHAVEN COTTS

POUND RD

PO

KING LANE COTTS

Tunlands Farm

2

APPLETON CL

Pottery Farm

POUND LA

ORANGE LA

Northern Farm

Rosehill Farm

Middle Wallop Airfield

Townsend Farm

PH

STATION RD

SALISBURY LA

Over Wallop

B3084

A343

1

38

147
126

125 | 104

A B C D E F

8

Old Prospect Farm

Eastover Copse

Cossical Copse

Prospect Farm

Stonehanger Copse

7

Abbotts Ann Down

SALISBURY RD

A343

41

Down Farm

SP11

Chestnut Cottage

Dunkirt House

6

Monxton Oakcuts

5

OLD STOCKBRIDGE RD

Saxley Farm

IPOH CL
TAIPING PL
BENTA PL
SEREMBAN CL
BELANGA CL

Married Quarters

Kentsboro

40

WILSON CL
SEK KONG CL
FALAISE RD

Towers

Kentsboro Farm

THE GREEN
MEAD PK SQ
LOWER UPPER
MEAD CL
CHESTNUT SQ
BEECHES
THE AVENUE
OLD PARK LA
HARVEST WAY
THE FURROWS

1 CHESTNUT PL
2 MEAD PARK SQ
3 FARRIERS LA
4 THE FOX COVER
5 BIRCHEN COPPICE

Upper Oakcuts Copse

4

• Mast

SO20

3

A343

39

Mus of Army Flying
Explorers World

Knock Wood

Down Farm

2

Middle Wallop Airfield

1

Sewage Works

38

30 A B 31 C D 32 E F

125 | 148

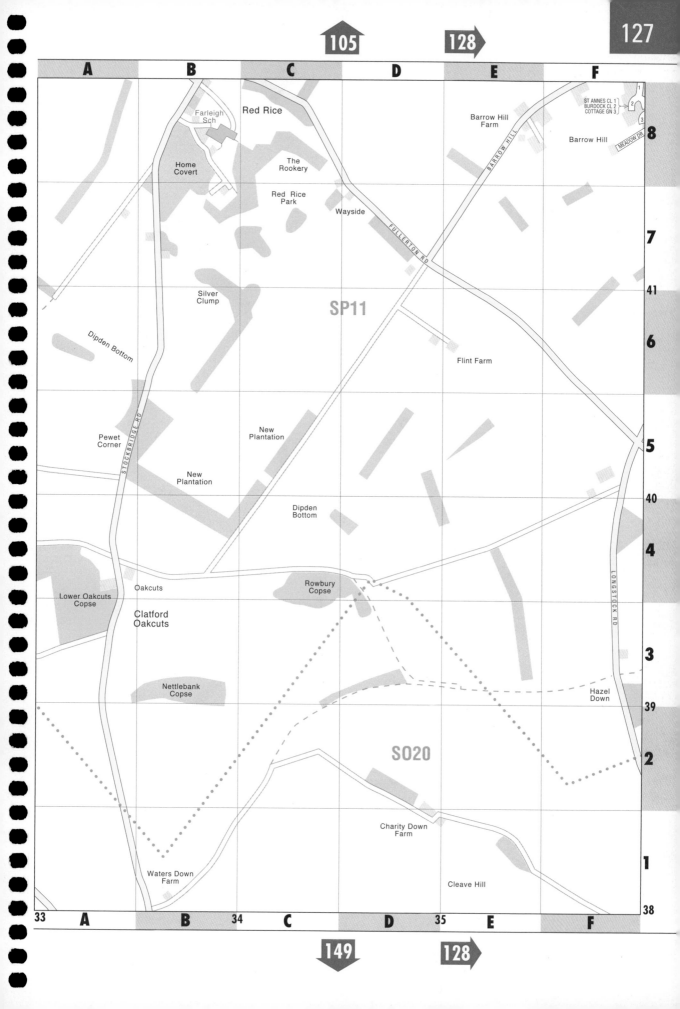

A B C D E F

Red Rice

Farleigh Sch

Home Covert

The Rookery

Red Rice Park

Wayside

Barrow Hill Farm

ST ANNES CL 1
BURDOCK CL 2
COTTAGE GN 3

Barrow Hill

MEADOW DR.

BARROW HILL

FULLERTON RD

SP11

Silver Clump

Dipden Bottom

Flint Farm

Pewet Corner

New Plantation

STOCKBRIDGE RD

New Plantation

Dipden Bottom

LONGSTOCK RD

Lower Oakcuts Copse

Oakcuts

Rowbury Copse

Clatford Oakcuts

Nettlebank Copse

Hazel Down

SO20

Charity Down Farm

Waters Down Farm

Cleave Hill

8 7 41 6 5 40 4 3 39 2 1 38

33 34 35

A **B** **C** **D** **E** **F**

1 COTTAGE GN
2 MEADOW DR

8

Sewage Works

New Barn

Wind Whistle
Cottage

WINCHESTER RD

B3420

A3057

7

LONGSTOCK RD

Mackrel's Down

41

NEW BARN LA

THE OLD THE

BEECH GR

FAIR PIECE

B3420

Red Hill

Wherwell

6

SP11

Westover
Farm

Wallis
Bottom

ROMSEY RD

CHAN CL

CHAPEL
CT

White Lion
(PH)

River Anton

FULLERTON RD

5

Chilbolton
Bottom

40

Test Way

4

Cottonworth

Cottonworth
Cotts

Cottonworth
Farm

COLE LA

FULLERTON RD

River Test

STATION RD

RIVER VIEW

Fullerton

Fullerton
Manor

3

Fullerton
Grange

The Mill
House

P

BRANKSOME GL

Sewage
Works

Test
Valley
Farm

Hazel Down

The Mayfly
(PH)

Testcombe

39

West
Down

Poultry
Houses

2

Longstock
House

Longstock Park

Water
Wheel

Ivy
Farm

Weir

SO20

Hazeldown
Farm

Water
Copse

1

A3057

38

36 **A** **B** 37 **C** **D** 38 **E** **F**

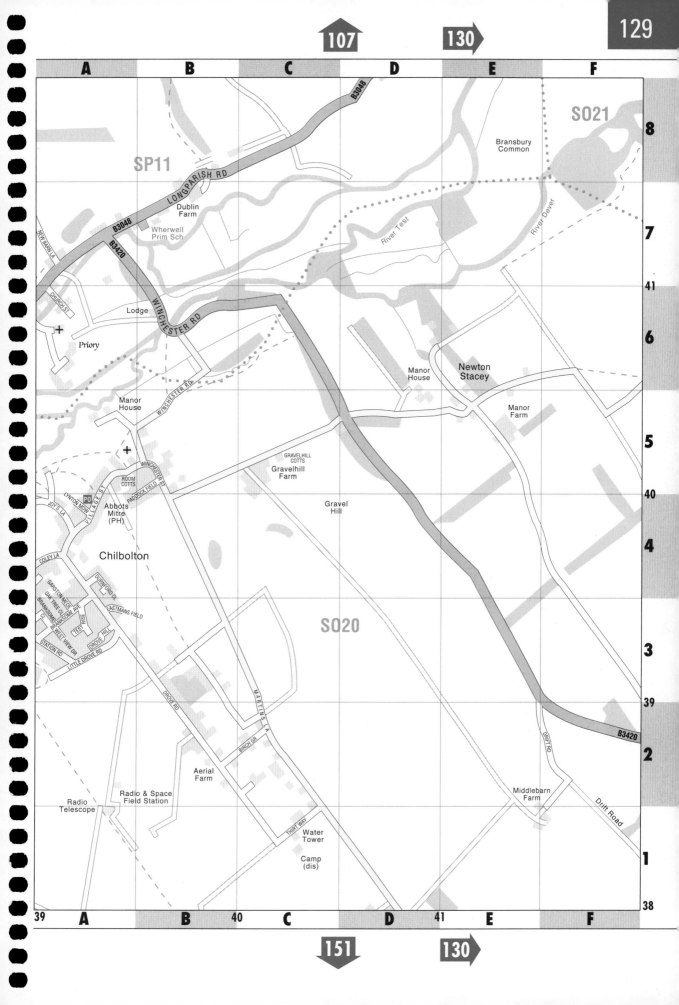

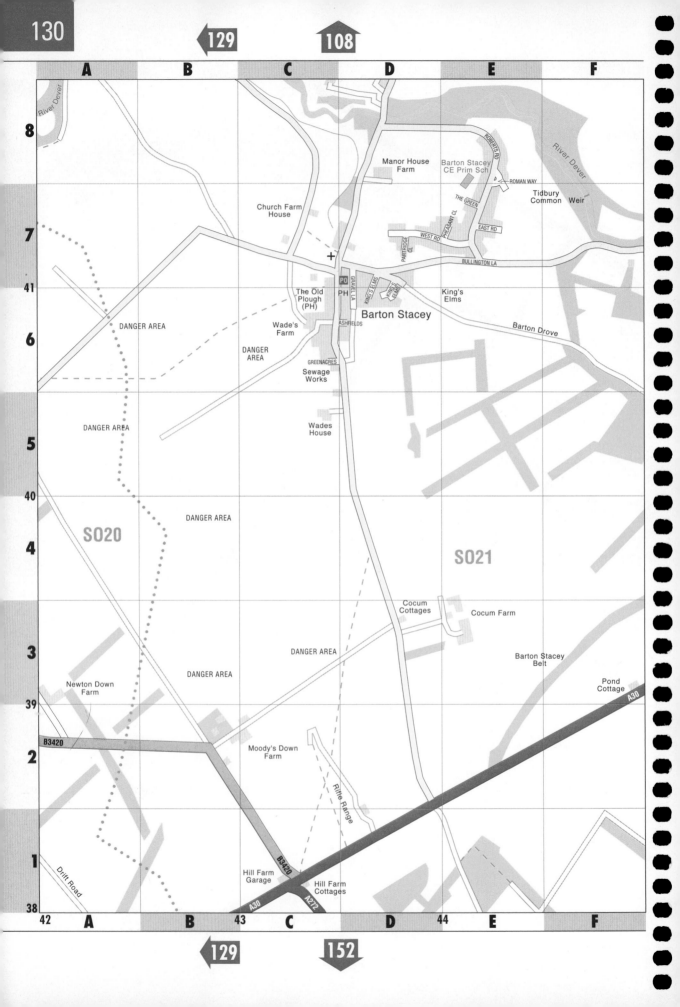

A   B   C   D   E   F

8

River Dever

Manor House
Farm

Barton Stacey
CE Prim Sch

ROBERTS RD

Roman Way

River Dever

Tidbury
Common   Weir

Church Farm
House

THE GREEN

7

PHEASANT CL

WEST RD

EAST RD

BULLINGTON LA

41

PO

The Old
Plough
(PH)

GRAVEL LA

PH

KING'S ELMS

KING'S
ELMS

King's
Elms

Barton Stacey

6

DANGER AREA

Wade's
Farm

ASHFIELDS

Barton Drove

DANGER
AREA

PARTRIDGE CL

GREENACRES

Sewage
Works

DANGER AREA

5

Wades
House

40

SO20

DANGER AREA

4

SO21

Cocum
Cottages

Cocum Farm

3

DANGER AREA

Barton Stacey
Belt

DANGER AREA

Pond
Cottage

Newton Down
Farm

A30

39

B3420

2

Moody's Down
Farm

Rifle Range

A30

1

Drift Road

B3420

Hill Farm
Garage

Hill Farm
Cottages

A272

38

42   A   B   43   C   D   44   E   F

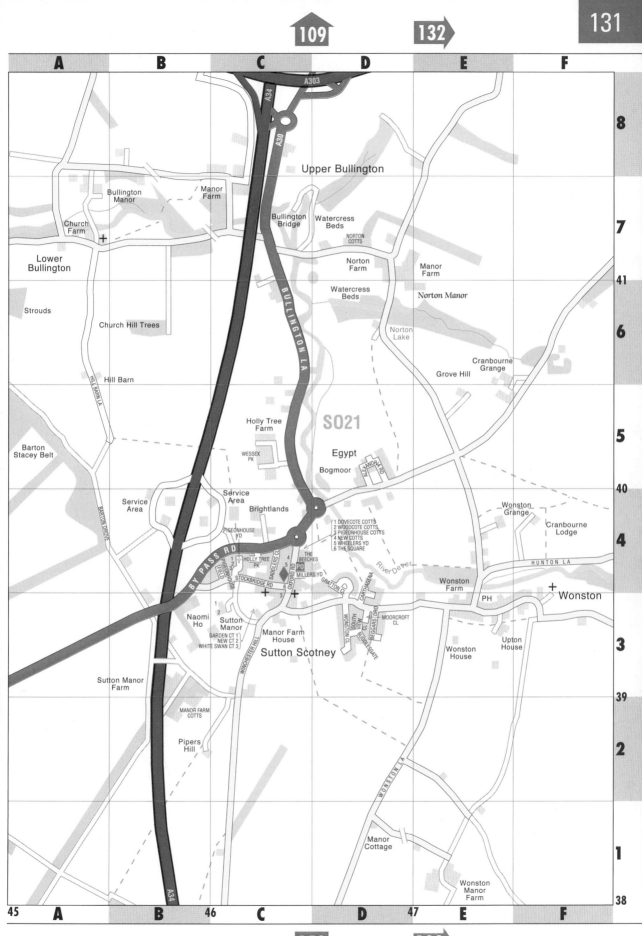

131
110

A B C D E F

8

Hunton Down Farm

Victoria Cottages

7

Counsellor's Walk

41

HUNTON DOWN LA

Hunton Grange Farm

Weston Down Cottages

6

New Cottages

Chestnut Villas

Northbrook House

5

Norsebury Ring

WESTON DOWN RD

40

SO21

Hunton Manor Farm

Hunton

Norsebury Farm

Northbrook

NORTHBROOK

4

Hunton Manor

Lower Norsebury

Norsebury House

Weston Colley

HUNTON LA

Norsebury Cottages

WESTON COLLEY COTTS

Weston Farm

River Dever

3

GLEBE COTTS

Stoke Charity

Michaels

PO

MEASURES GATE

39

OLD STOKE RD

2

Borough Farm

1

38

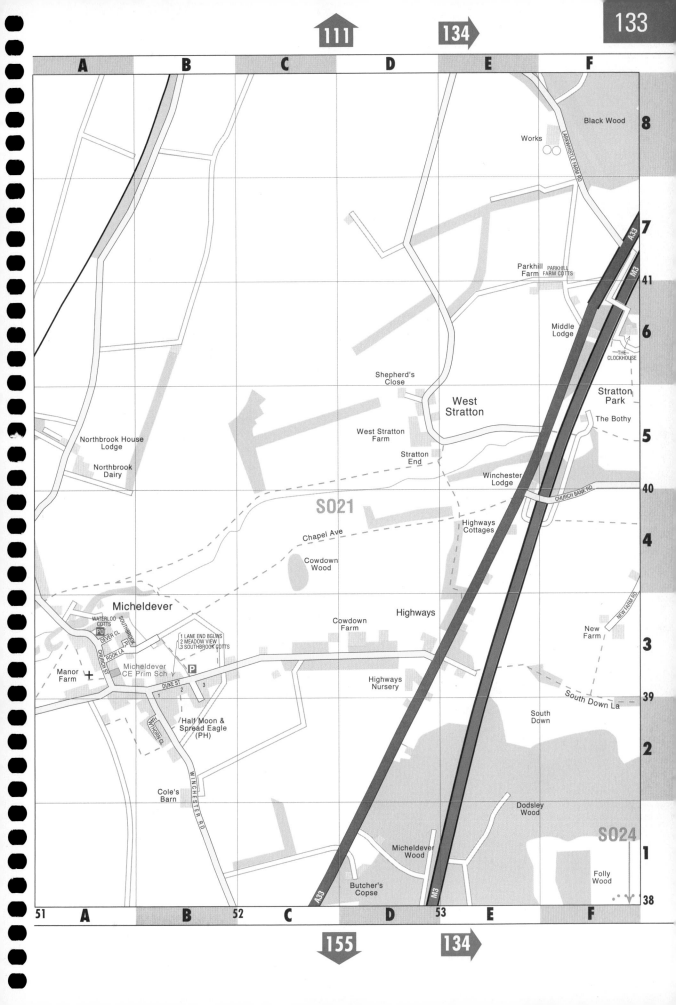

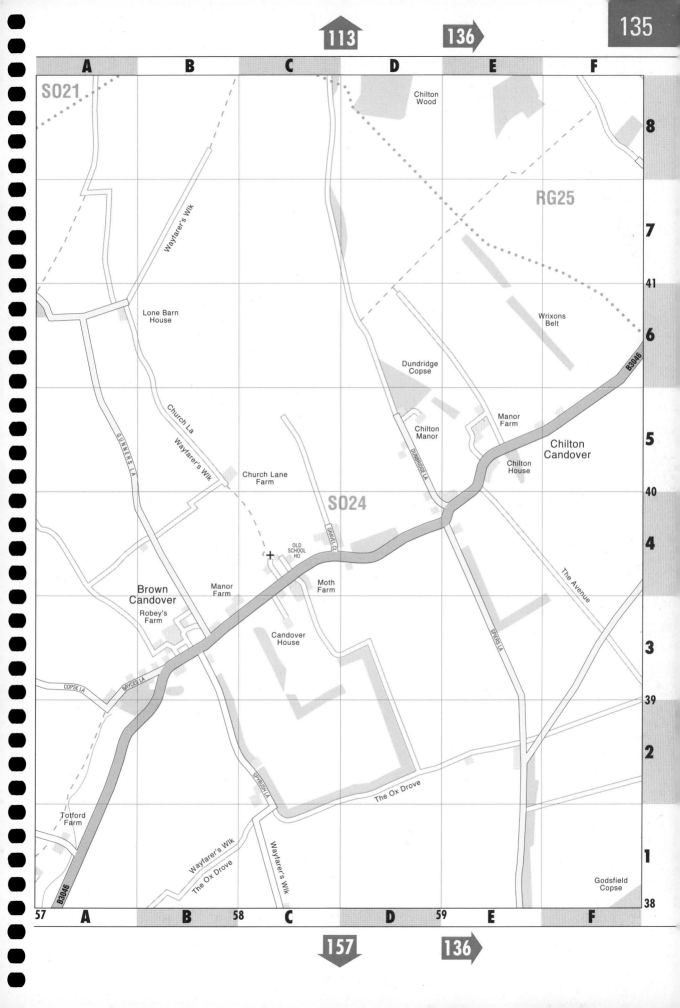

135
114

A　　　B　　　C　　　D　　　E　　　F

8

B3046

North Hall

The Purefoy Arms (PH)

Preston Candover CE Prim Sch

STENBUR DR

Preston Candover

Manor Farm

South Hall

Fairview Farm

Bradley Corner

Down La

7

Lower Farm

Preston Down

Three Castles Path

RG25

41

Preston Grange

Down Farm

Park Copse

6

B3046

Buds Hill

Windmill Hill

5

The Ox Drove

Down Farm Dairy

40

4

3

Bangor Copse

SO24

Wield Wood Lodge

Caigers Farm

39

Chilton Down

Wield Wood

Wield Wood Farm

Wield Manor Farm

2

Dandelys Copse

Wield Wood

Upper Wield

Wield House Farm

PO

HOME CL

Juniper Hill

1

Godsfield Copse

Armsworth Hill Farm

Three Castles Path

Barton Copse

38

60　　A　　　B　　61　　C　　　D　　62　　E　　　F

135
158

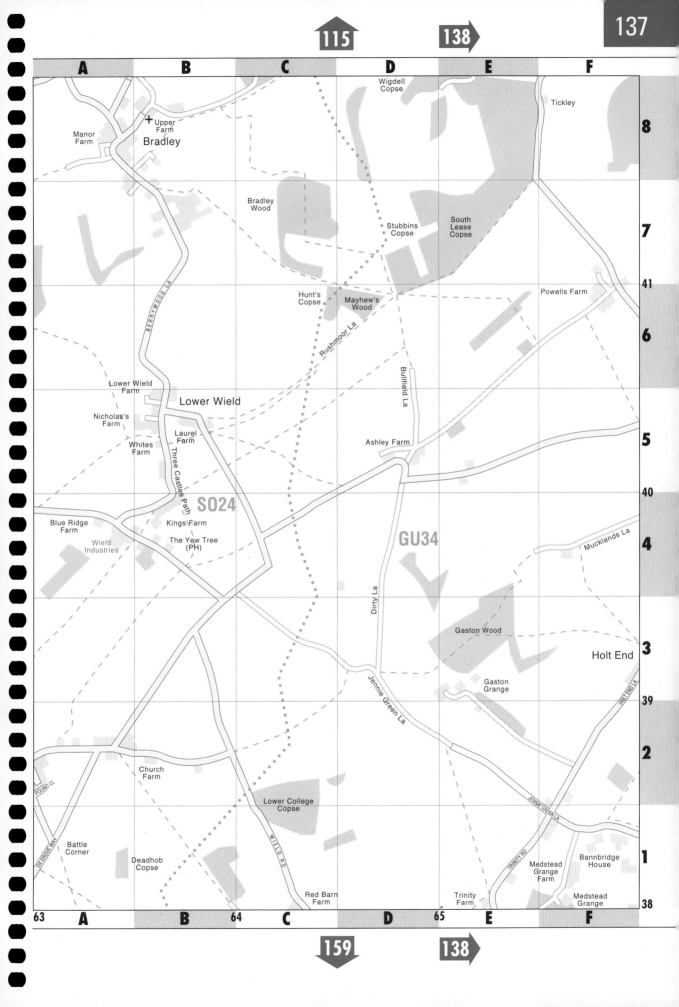

115
138
159
138

A B C D E F

8
7
41
6
5
40
4
3
39
2
1
38

Wigdell Copse
Tickley
Manor Farm
Upper Farm
Bradley
Bradley Wood
Stubbins Copse
South Lease Copse
Powells Farm
Hunt's Copse
Mayhew's Wood
BERRYWOOD LA
Rushmoor La
Bullfield La
Lower Wield Farm
Lower Wield
Nicholas's Farm
Laurel Farm
Ashley Farm
Whites Farm
Three Castles Path
SO24
Blue Ridge Farm
Kings Farm
The Yew Tree (PH)
Wield Industries
GU34
Mucklands La
Dirty La
Gaston Wood
Holt End
Gaston Grange
HOLT END LA
Jennie Green La
Church Farm
Lower College Copse
Deadhob Copse
POUND CL
OX GROVE WAY
Battle Corner
WIELD RD
Red Barn Farm
Jennie Green La
Trinity Farm
TRINITY RD
Medstead Grange Farm
Bannbridge House
Medstead Grange

63 A B 64 C D 65 E F

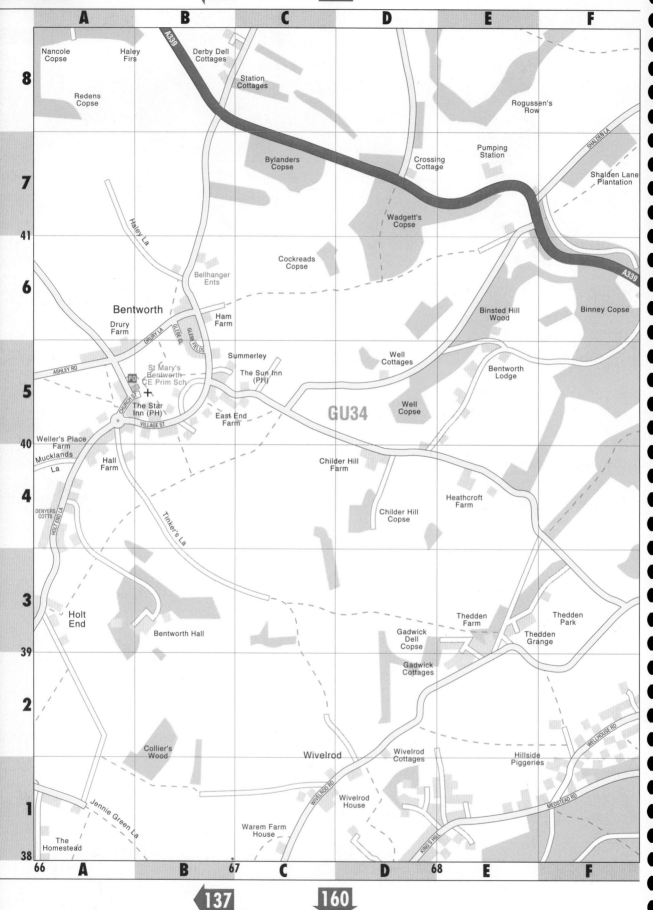

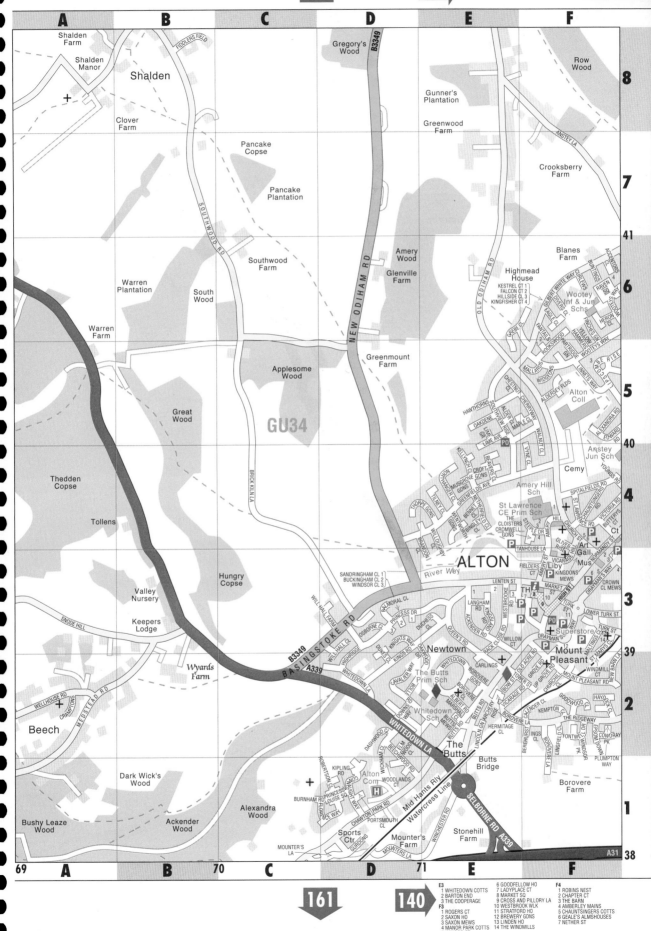

117
140

161
140

E3
1 WHITEDOWN COTTS
2 BARTON END
3 THE COOPERAGE

F3
1 ROGERS CT
2 SAXON HO
3 SAXON MEWS
4 MANOR PARK COTTS
5 INWOOD CT
6 GOODFELLOW HO
7 LADYPLACE CT
8 MARKET SQ
9 CROSS AND PILLORY LA
10 WESTBROOK WLK
11 STRATFORD HO
12 BREWERY GDNS
13 LINDEN HO
14 THE WINDMILLS

F4
1 ROBINS NEST
2 CHAPTER CT
3 THE BARN
4 AMBERLEY MAINS
5 CHAUNTSINGERS COTTS
6 GEALE'S ALMSHOUSES
7 NETHER ST

139
118

A · B · C · D · E · F

8

Row Wood

Bonham's Farm

Howard's La

BROCKHAM HILL LA

New La

Cuckoo's Corner

A31

7

Cadnam Farm

Howards Farm

Manor Farm

Haw Bridge

41

1 GILMOUR GDNS
2 GOODWYNS GN

Holybourne

HOWARD'S LA

CHURCH LA

Wisteria Mews

PO

Hawbridge Farm

BONHAMS

VINDOMIS GL

DOWNS VIEW

PEACEMAKERS

LOWER NEATHAM MILL LA

6

BAKERS
GERALD SQ

HAZEL RD

TOCKS

MANOR RD

LINK RD

WOOTEYS WAY

JENNER WAY

ANSTEY LA

Alton Convent Sch

Treloar Coll

Eggar's Sch

NEW PADDOCK CL

Andrews Endowed CE Prim Sch

CAMPBELL CT

COMPLINS

MALTHOUSE MEWS

BINFORD DRI

GASKELL CL

THORNTON END

UPPER NEATHAM MILL LA

LONDON RD

PH

Upper Neatham Mill Farm

River Wey

Neatham

Manor Farm

SWALLOW CL

ROBIN CL

DOVE CL

PO

PLOVERS RD

WREN CL

ALLEN CL

PLOVERS WAY

DOWDEN GR

POLRO

WILLIAM WAY

HAROLD CL

GL SPEARS

MARY ROSE MEWS

JOHN EGGARS SQ

Anstey

B3004

Copt Hill

Stirvill's Copse

5

EDWARD RD

MARTINS

GEALE'S CT

CHALCRAFTS

ANSTEY CRES

SHIPLEY

ADAMS WAY

NEWMAN LA

ANSTEY MILL CL

Lynch Hill

GU34

40

Sch

NURSERY RD

PARK CLOSE RD

LANSDOWNE RD

ADAMS HO

Riverwey Ind Est

MILL LA

Grove Pk Ind Est

WATERBROOK

OB LA

Golden Chair Hill

EASTBROOKE RD

VICTORIA RD

GARTH

LITTLEFIELD

THE AMPORTS

Kerridge Ind Est

P

Alton

SYCAMORE CL

Alton Station Rd

WATERCRESS

PK

CAKER STREAM RD

Sewage Works

Golden Chair Farm

Monk Wood

4

VICTORIA RD

YORK MEWS

KNOX RD

GARTH

NORMANDY ST

THE AMPORTS

WATERSIDE

SPITALHATCH

DICKER'S LA

Mill La Ind Est

THE KILNS

Spitalhatch

Omhi Bsns Ctr

Neatham Down

MANOR PK COTTS

BRAMLEY

RUSSELT RD

KINGSHEAD

Mid Hants Rly Watercress Line

ASHDEL RD

WILSOM CL

Alton Bsns Ctr

OMEGA PK

Delta Bsns Pk

Clay's Farm

3

MORELAND CL

GALVAIN CL

STOCERS RD

GOODYERS

WILSOM RD

Wilsom

1 FERNDOWN CT
2 PROSPECT PL
3 ASHLEY CT
4 ROSETREE COTTS
5 ORCHARD TERR
6 RIVER VIEW COTTS
7 ORCHARD HO
8 BLENHEIM CL
9 KINGSMEAD COTTS
10 SHERWOOD TERR

39

THE RIDGEWAY

SALISBURY RD

HUNTSMEAD

CURTIS RD

CROWLEY DR

WINDMILL HILL

WINDMILL LA

Hurdles

CAT'S LA

2

1 SANDOWN CL
2 ASCOT CL

WINCANTON CL

Water La

CH

Wixes

CAKER'S LA

Shelley's Barn

Old House Farm

Mast

Little Caker Bridge

Cox's Copse

SHELLEY'S LA

WICK LA

1

Kiln House

Park Farm

PH

BLANKET ST

B3004

38

A31

72 · A · B · 73 · C · D · 74 · E · F

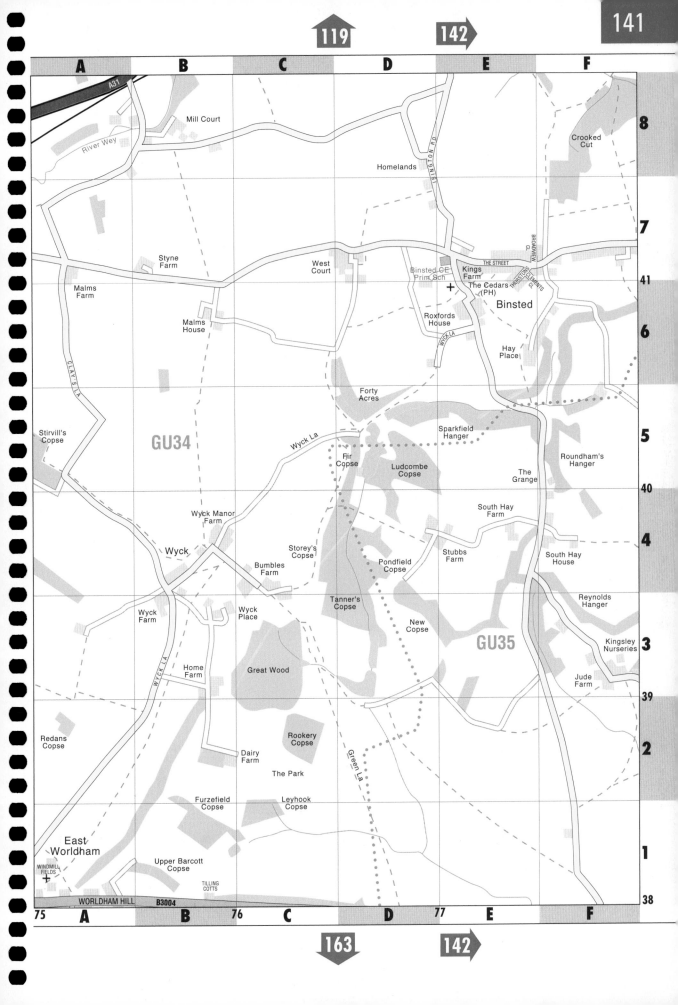

	A	B	C	D	E	F

8

Betty King's Copse

Home Hanger

Blacknest Ind Pk

Recn Gd

Lodge Inclosure

Bucks Horn Oak

THE GLADE

Halfway Farm

The Halfway House (PH)

BLACKNEST RD

Blacknest

PH

Longfield

BINSTEAD RD

FOUR WAYS

BACK LA

A325

GU10

DOCKENFIELD ST

7

River Hill Farm

Cobden's Copse

Boxall's Copse

Buckshot Hole

41

Camices Farm

Binsted Place

GU34

CH

Goose Green Inclosure

Binsted Place Farm

WHEATLEY LA

6

Gasen Copse

Woodlands Farm

FRITH END RD

THE KILNS

Round Copse

Forest Lodge

5

Clement's Hanger

Clements Farm

HOLT BARNS

Goose Green Farm

Wheatley

40

Wheatley Farm

Straits Inclosure

Frith End Farm

Frithend House

4

Hoggatts

Mowlands Farm

3

Stephenfield Copse

GU35

Grooms Farm

Jude Copse

THE STRAITS

SICKLES LA

39

Straits Farm

Osbornes Farm

Trottsford Farm

Pear Tree Cottage

2

Malthouse Farm

River Slea

SUNNYSIDE

Old Park Farm

Bordan Farm

PICKETTS HILL

1

Kingsley

WOOLMER

GOLD HILL

PARK

B3004

FORGE RD

Sleaford Bridge

The New Inn (PH)

SCHOOL FIELDS

PO

CHURCHFIELDS

Kingsley Bsns Pk

Sleaford Farm

A325

Sleaford

38

Dean Farm

B3004

PH

OCKHAM HALL

Kingsley Pond

Kingsley Common

Gold Hill

78	A	B	79	C	D	80	E	F

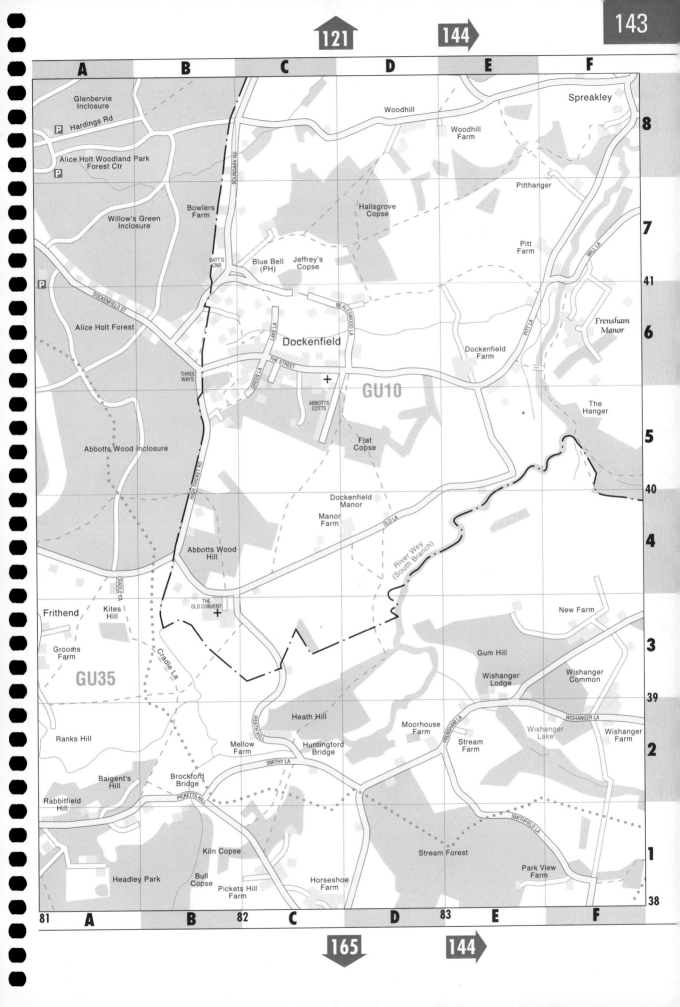

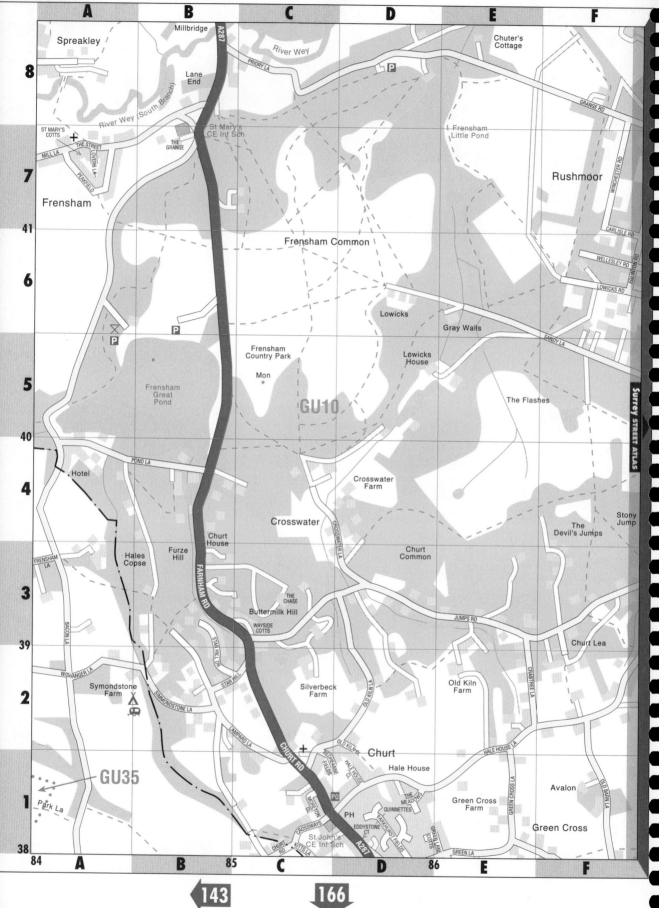

Spreakley
Millbridge
River Wey
PRIORY LA
Chuter's Cottage
A287
Lane End
River Wey (South Branch)
St Mary's CE Inf Sch
St Mary's Cotts
THE GRANGE
THE STREET
LOVERS LA
MILL LA
PEASFIELD
Frensham
Frensham Little Pond
GRANGE RD
Rushmoor
Frensham Common
CARLISLE RD
WINCHESTER RD
WELLESLEY RD
EGGARS RD
NUTLEY LA
LOWICKS RD
Lowicks
Gray Walls
SANDY LA
Frensham Country Park
Mon
Lowicks House
The Flashes
Frensham Great Pond
GU10
Surrey Street Atlas
POND LA
Hotel
Crosswater Farm
FRENSHAM LA
Hales Copse
Furze Hill
Churt House
Crosswater
CROSSWATER LA
Churt Common
The Devil's Jumps
Stony Jump
BACON LA
FARNHAM RD
THE CHASE
Buttermilk Hill
WAYSIDE COTTS
JUMPS RD
Churt Lea
CRABTREE LA
WISHANGER LA
Symondstone Farm
SIMMONDSTONE LA
STAR HILL DR
STAR MILL
Silverbeck Farm
OLD KILN LA
Old Kiln Farm
HALE HOUSE LA
LAMPARD LA
CHURT RD
Churt
Hale House
GREEN CROSS LA
OLD BARN LA
Avalon
GU35
Park La
MICKETON
PO
HEDGERNE FIELDS
REDGERNE FIELDS
HALE HOUSE
Green Cross Farm
Green Cross
PH
THE MEADOWS
Quinnettes
PARKSHOTT FIELDS
EDDYSTONE CT
CROSSWAYS
CHURT RD
KITTS LA
St John's CE Inf Sch
A287
GREEN LANE COTTS
GREEN LA

84   85   86

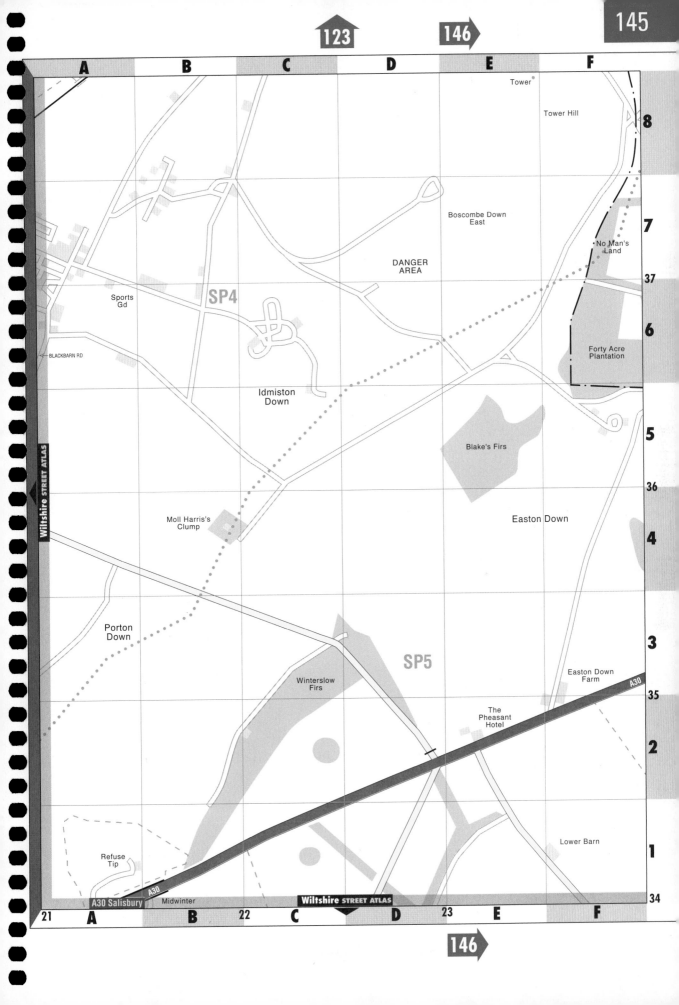

Tower

Tower Hill

Boscombe Down
East

No Man's
Land

DANGER
AREA

Forty Acre
Plantation

SP4

Sports
Gd

BLACKBARN RD

Idmiston
Down

Blake's Firs

Moll Harris's
Clump

Easton Down

Porton
Down

SP5

Winterslow
Firs

Easton Down
Farm

A30

The
Pheasant
Hotel

Lower Barn

Refuse
Tip

A30

A30 Salisbury   Midwinter

Wiltshire STREET ATLAS

Wiltshire STREET ATLAS

SP4

SO20

A B C D E F

8

Isle of Wight Hill

Suddern Hill

7

37

DANGER AREA

6

Jack's Bush Farm

A343

Bush Farm

5

36

Roche Court Down

Little Firs Farm

Easton Down

Little Firs

4

SP5

Hollom Down Farm

Firs Farm

The Anchorage

LOPCOMBE CNR

A343

MOUNT HTS

Lopcombe Corner Farm

Cherry View Farm

3

A30

Popple Light Copse

35

A30

2

Gutteridge Farm

Ashley's Copse

Bussle Wood

1

Ramshill Drove

Burretts Grove

Warren Court Farm

Roche Court Farm

Roche Court

34

24 A B 25 C D 26 E F

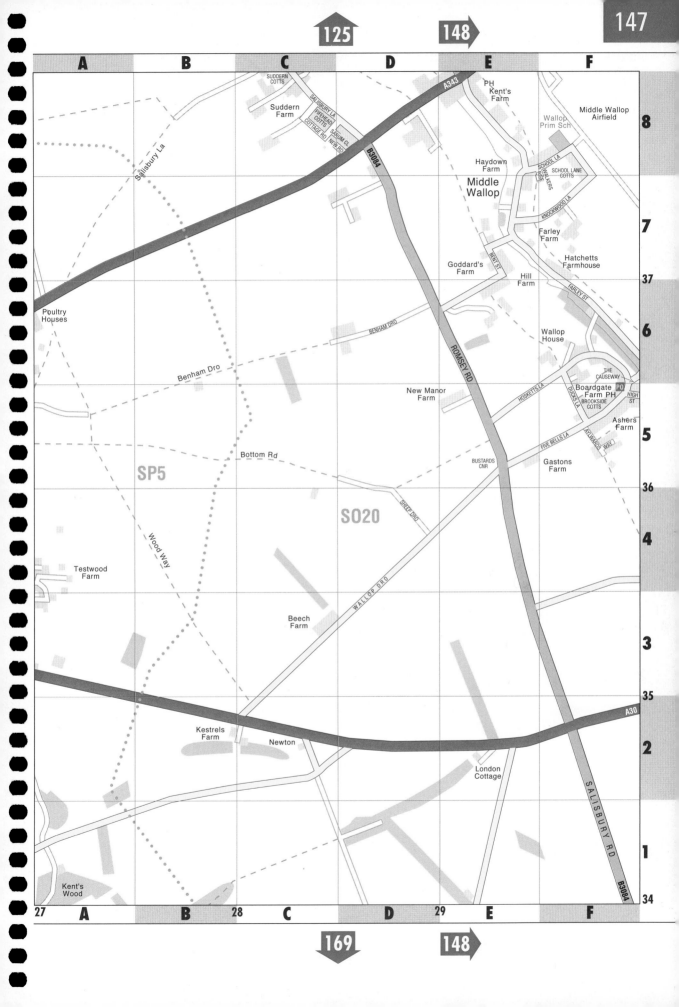

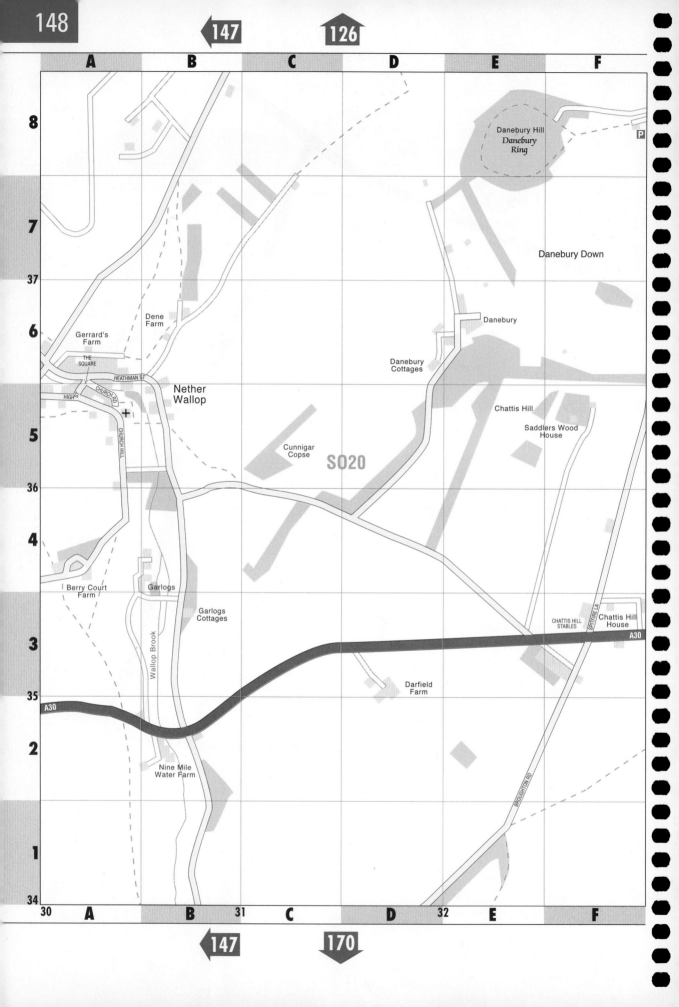

	A	B	C	D	E	F

8

Danebury Hill
Danebury Ring

P

7

Danebury Down

37

6

Dene Farm

Gerrard's Farm

Danebury

THE SQUARE

Danebury Cottages

HEATHMAN ST

CHURCH RD

Nether Wallop

HIGH ST

Chattis Hill

Saddlers Wood House

CHURCH HILL

+

5

Cunnigar Copse

SO20

36

4

Berry Court Farm

Garlogs

Garlogs Cottages

CHATTIS HILL STABLES

SPITFIRE LA

Chattis Hill House

Wallop Brook

3

A30

Darfield Farm

35

A30

2

Nine Mile Water Farm

BROUGHTON RD

1

34

30	A	B	31	C	D	32	E	F

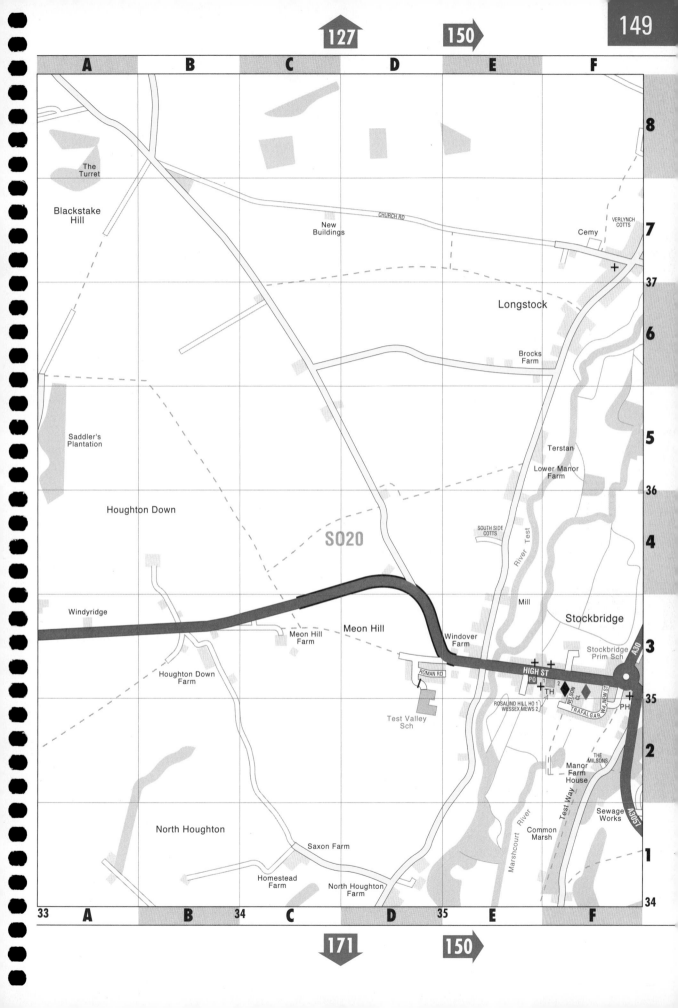

A B C D E F

The Turret

Blackstake Hill

CHURCH RD

New Buildings

VERLYNCH COTTS

Cemy

Longstock

8

7

37

Brocks Farm

6

Saddler's Plantation

Terstan

Lower Manor Farm

5

36

Houghton Down

SO20

SOUTH SIDE COTTS

River   Test

4

Mill

Stockbridge

Windyridge

Meon Hill Farm

Meon Hill

Windover Farm

Stockbridge Prim Sch

A30

3

35

Houghton Down Farm

ROMAN RD

HIGH ST

PO

TH

2

NELSON CL

NEW ST

TRAFALGAR WA

PH

ROSALIND HILL HO 1
WESSEX MEWS 2

Test Valley Sch

THE MILSONS

Manor Farm House

2

North Houghton

Marshcourt   River

Test Way

Common Marsh

Sewage Works

A3057

Saxon Farm

Homestead Farm

North Houghton Farm

1

34

33 A B 34 C D 35 E F

149
128

A **B** **C** **D** **E** **F**

A3057

8

Little Common

Abbotts Manor Farm

Leckford

Leckford Dairy

River Test

Great Common

PO Leckford

Leckford Plantation

Leckford Abbas

THE OLD RECTORY

7

Charity Farm House

Baker's Farm

37

Aqueduct

PH

Lone Barn

6

CH

LECKFORD LA

Riches Plantation

Chilcombe Copse

Atners Hill

Test Way

Atners Towers

5

Leckford Camp

SO20

36

London Hill Farm

A30

4

Wynrush

LONDON RD

Fair View Farm

A3057

Sandydown Farm

Little Dean Farm

Woolbury Ring

SANDYDOWN COTTS

3

OLD LONDON RD

LITTLE DEAN HO

LITTLE DEAN CT

A30

Sch

35

B3049

WIWTON HILL

Cemy

Stockbridge Down

2

Home Farm

SOMBORNE PARK RD

P

Lamberts

The Plantation

Ridge's Grove

P

B3049

1

A3057

FERNY LA

Teg Down

Windovers

34

36 **A** **B** 37 **C** **D** 38 **E** **F**

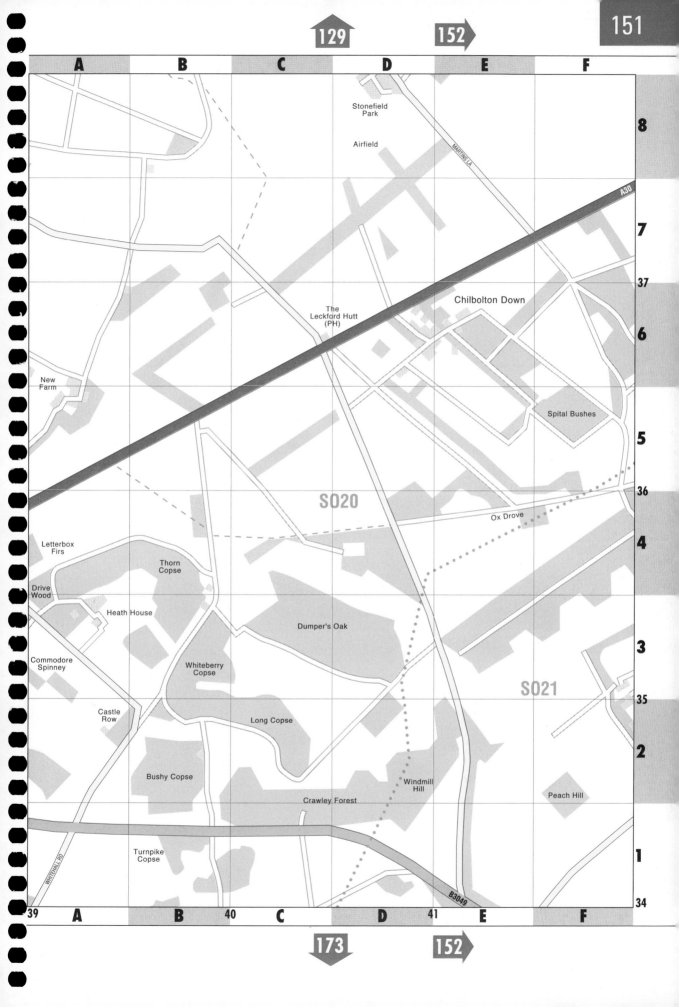

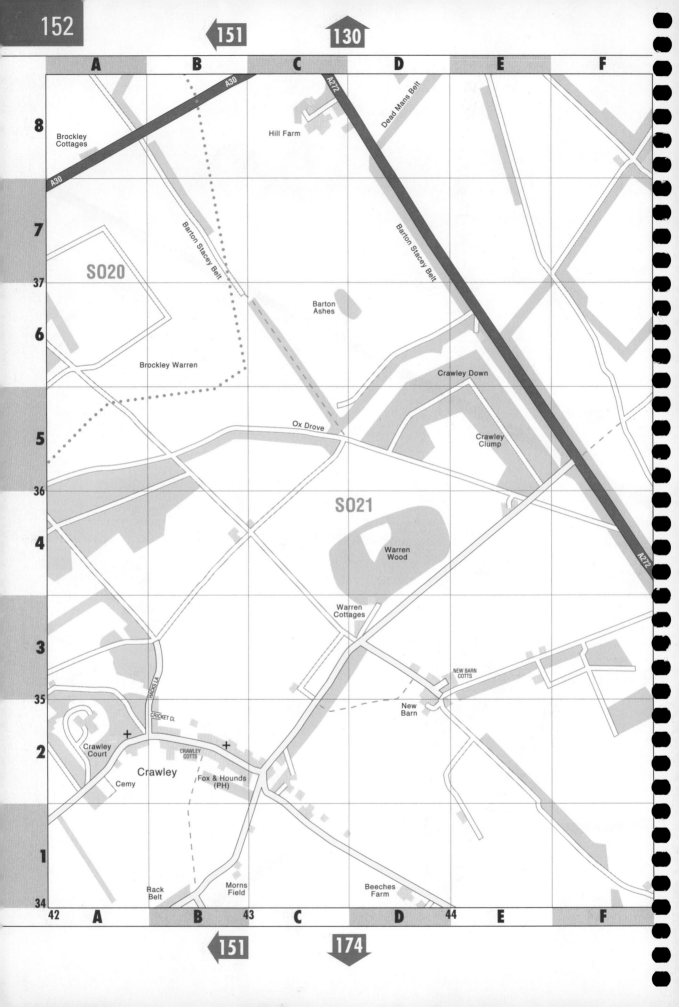

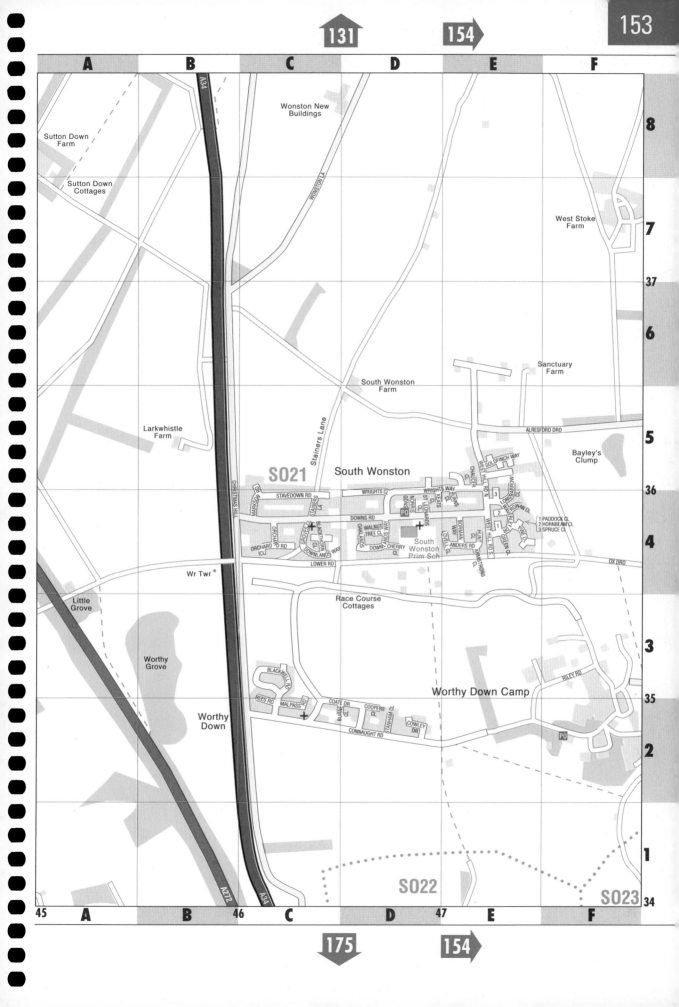

131
154
175
154

Wonston New
Buildings

Sutton Down
Farm

Sutton Down
Cottages

WONSTON LA

West Stoke
Farm

Sanctuary
Farm

South Wonston
Farm

Larkwhistle
Farm

ALRESFORD DRO

Bayley's
Clump

Stainers Lane

SO21

South Wonston

GOLDFINCH WAY

WEST HILL RD N

CHAUCER CL

CHRISTMAS HILL

MARKSM CL

STAVEDOWN RD

STAINERS LA

WRIGHTS CL

WRIGHTS WAY

ST LEONARDS CL

KEATS CL

BURNS CL

LONGBARROW CL

WAVERLEY CL

ROWAN CL

1 PADDOCK GL
2 HORNBEAM CL
3 SPRUCE CL

GROVE CL

BLACKTHORN

NORRIS GDNS

PO

DOWNS RD

ORCHARD CL

ORCHARD RD

DOWNLANDS WAY

WALNUT TREE CL

OAKLANDS

ANDS WAY

CHERRY CL

DOWN CL

South
Wonston
Prim Sch

LOVELL CL

ANDERS RD

BORMAN WAY

HUNT CL

ARMSTRONG CL

WEST HILL RD S

GREEN CL

TYNE CL

LOWER RD

OX DRO

Wr Twr

Little
Grove

Race Course
Cottages

Worthy
Grove

A34

Worthy Down Camp

RILEY RD

Worthy
Down

BLACKWELL RD

REES RD

MALPASS RD

COATE DR

BURNE CL

COOPERS CL

STANHAM CL

COWLEY DR

CONNAUGHT RD

PO

A272

A34

SO22

SO23

45   46   47
34   35   36   37

153
132

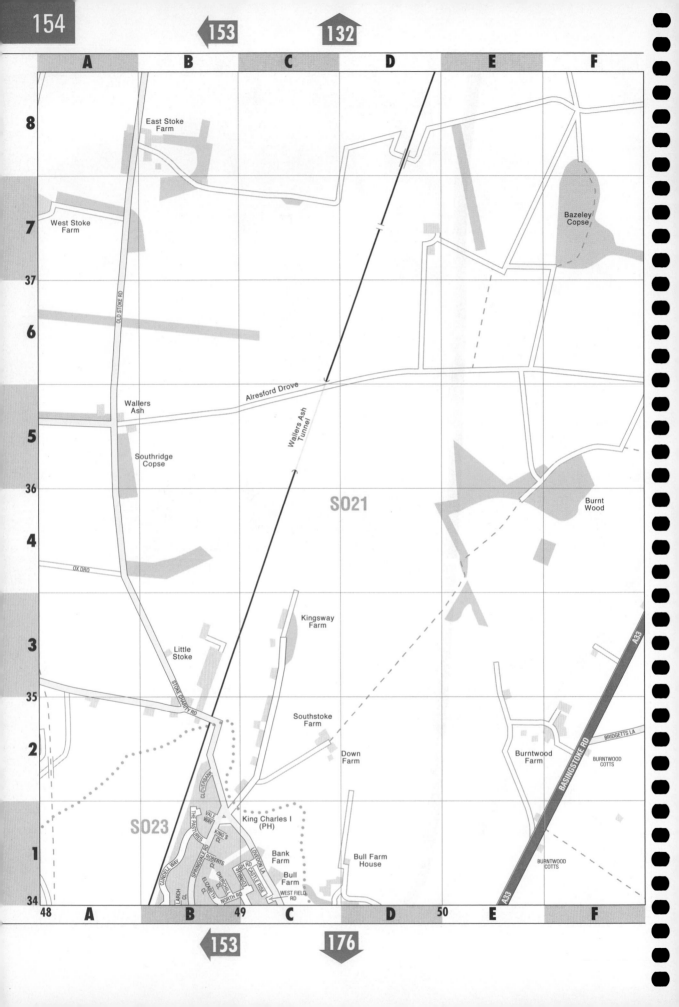

East Stoke Farm

West Stoke Farm

Bazeley Copse

OLD STOKE RD

Wallers Ash

Alresford Drove

Wallers Ash Tunnel

Southridge Copse

SO21

Burnt Wood

OX DRO

Kingsway Farm

Little Stoke

STOKE CHARITY RD

Southstoke Farm

Burntwood Farm

BASINGSTOKE RD

BRIDGETTS LA

BURNTWOOD COTTS

A33

Down Farm

SO23

King Charles I (PH)

CLOVERBANK

QUIDELL WAY

THE PASTURES

VALE WAY

KING'S CL

SPRINGVALE RD

ROBERTS CL

ASH RD

CHURCHILL RD

LOVEDON LA

CASTLE FIELD

Bank Farm

Bull Farm

Bull Farm House

LARCH CL

ELIZABETH CL

NORTH RD

WEST FIELD RD

BURNTWOOD COTTS

A B C D E F

8

7

37

6

Micheldever
Wood

Long Wlk

Mill Lane
Copse

Newdown
Farm

Alresford Drove

SO24

Micheldever Wood
Archaeological
Trail

P

Hassock
Copse

5

SO21

Chillandham La

36

Winchester
Services (North)

Itchen
Wood

4

BASINGSTOKE RD

WINCHESTER RD

A33

M3

Shroner
Wood

Shroner Wood
House

Winchester
Services (South)

Courtney's
Copse

Shroner Hill
Farm

The
Scrubbs

3

35

Rutherley
Copse

Chillandham
Farm

Chillandham La

2

BRIDGETS LA

1

Bridget's
Farm

Lone
Farm

34

M3

51 A B 52 C D 53 E F

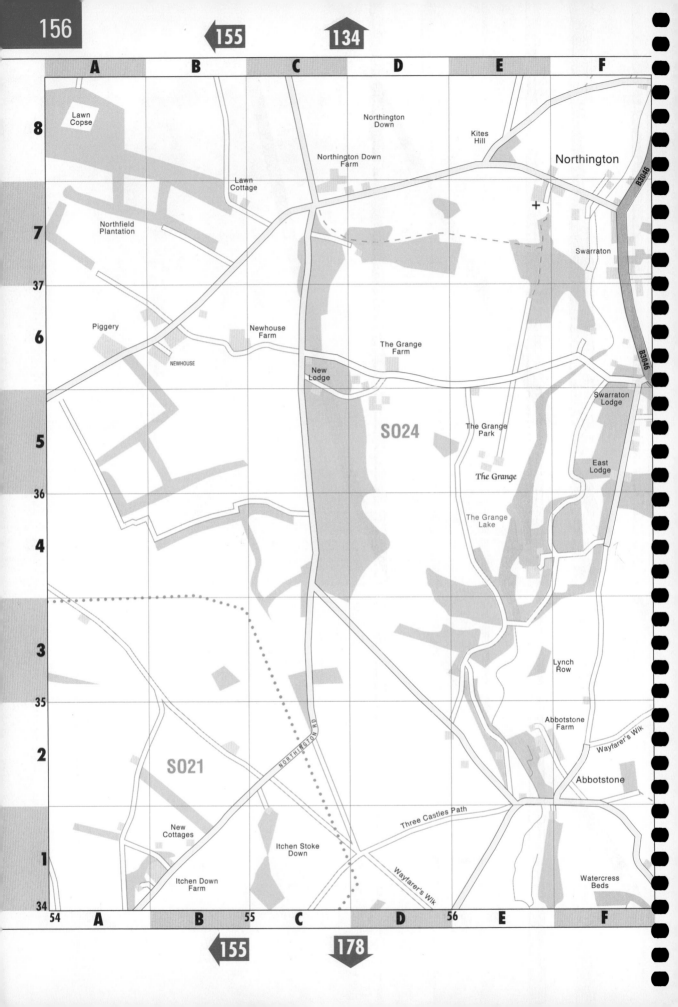

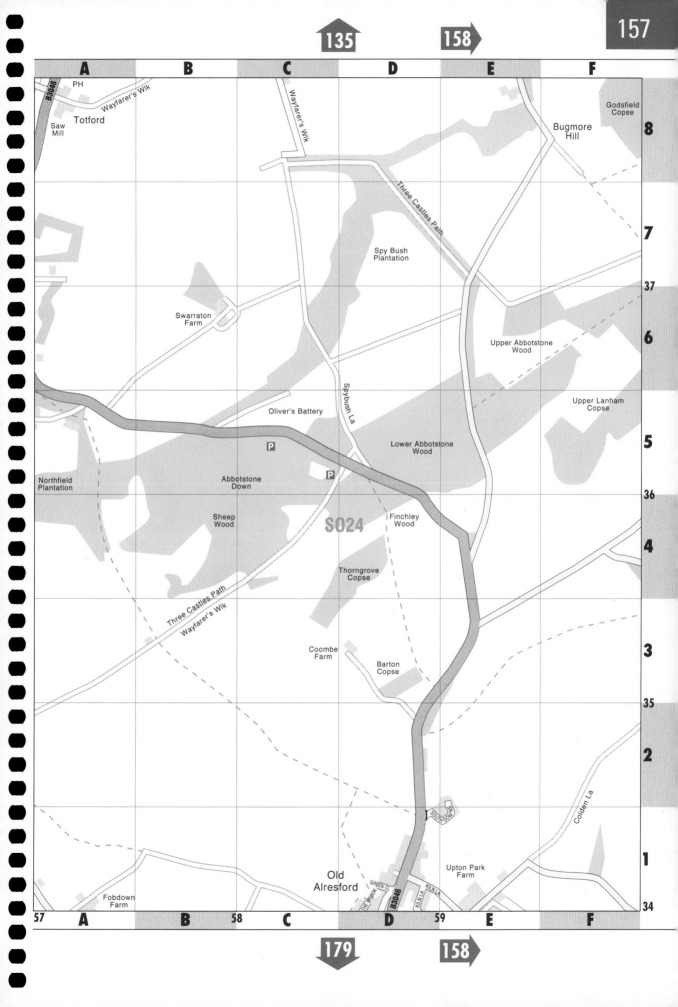

8
Godsfield Copse
Bugmore Hill

7

37

6
Upper Abbotstone Wood

Upper Lanham Copse

5

36

4

3

35

2

1

34

B3046
PH
Wayfarer's Wlk
Totford
Saw Mill

Wayfarer's Wlk

Three Castles Path

Spy Bush Plantation

Swarraton Farm

Spybush La

Oliver's Battery

P

Lower Abbotstone Wood

P

Northfield Plantation

Abbotstone Down

SO24

Sheep Wood

Finchley Wood

Thorngrove Copse

Three Castles Path
Wayfarer's Wlk

Coombe Farm

Barton Copse

SOUTH DOWN

Colden La

Old Alresford

Upton Park Farm

THE BROOK
GREEN CL
B3046
KILN LA
KILN LA

Fobdown Farm

157
136

A **B** **C** **D** **E** **F**

Godsfield
Copse

Three Castles Path

8

Long
Plantation

Armsworth
House

Armsworth Park

Armsworth
Park
Farm

Park
House

Hoggs
Lodge

UPPER LANHAM LA

Barton Copse

Barton
Ind Est

Barton
House

Newmer
Farm

FERNEY LA

OX DROVE WAY

7

Godsfield
Farm

+

Upper
Abbotstone
Wood

37

Upper
Lanham
Copse

Lower Lanham
Copse

Upper
Lanham
Farm

Woodridden
Wood

GU
34

6

The
Border

Bighton
Wood

5

Marks
Wood

Lower Lanham
Farm

Lucys
Wood

SO24

36

Scrivens
Copse

Bighton
Wood

Breach
Farm

4

Nettlebeds
Farm

The
Plantation

Nettlebeds
Farm
Stables

COLDEN LA

Bighton
House

Gardeners
Cottage

Inner
Lodge

3

35

NETTLEBEDS LA

High
Dell
Farm

2

Cricket
Ground

The
Three
Horse Shoes
(PH)

Bighton
Manor

+

MALTHOUSE LA

BIGHTON LA

Manor Farm

BIGHTON DEAN LA

BARNETTS WOOD
LA

1

Bighton

34

60 **A** **B** 61 **C** **D** 62 **E** **F**

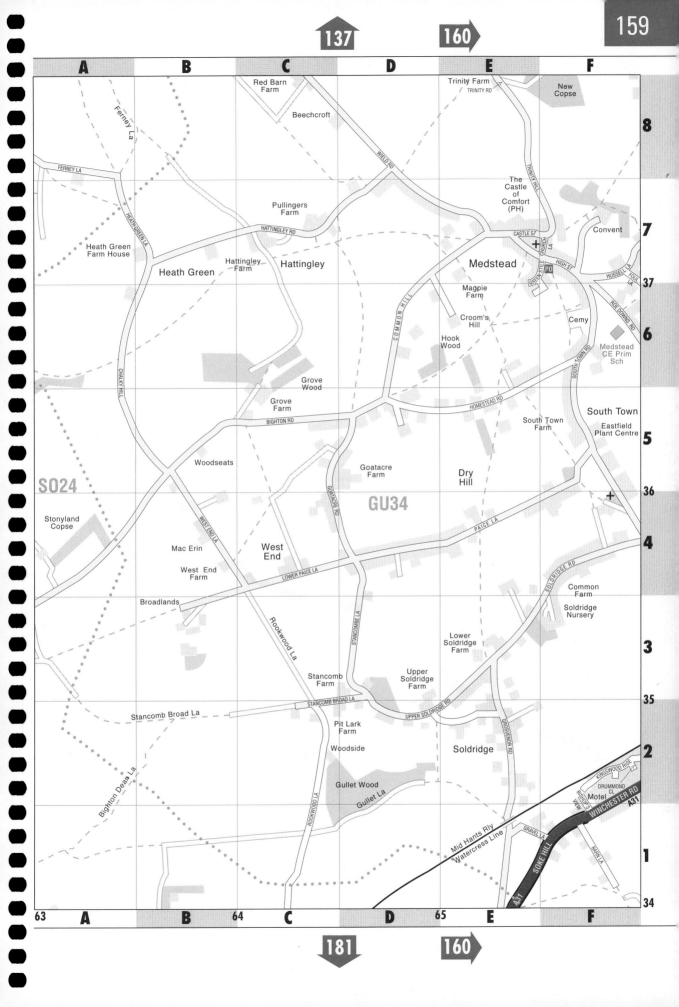

A B C D E F

8
7
37
6
5
36
4
3
35
2
1
34

Red Barn Farm

Beechcroft

Ferney La

FERNEY LA

Heath Green Farm House

Pullingers Farm

HATTINGLEY RD

Heath Green

Hattingley Farm

Hattingley

HEATH GREEN LA

WELD RD

Trinity Farm
TRINITY RD

New Copse

TRINITY HILL

The Castle of Comfort (PH)

CASTLE ST

Medstead

Convent

HIGH ST

CHURCH LA

GREEN STILE

PO

HUSSELL LA

FOUL LA

Magpie Farm

Croom's Hill

Hook Wood

Cemy

ROE DOWNS RD

Medstead CE Prim Sch

COMMON HILL

CHALKY HILL

Grove Wood

Grove Farm

BIGHTON RD

HOMESTEAD RD

South Town Farm

South Town

Eastfield Plant Centre

SO24

Woodseats

Stonyland Copse

WEST END LA

Mac Erin

West End

Goatacre Farm

GOATACRE RD

GU34

Dry Hill

PAICE LA

+

West End Farm

LOWER PAICE LA

SOLDRIDGE RD

Common Farm

Soldridge Nursery

Broadlands

Rookwood La

STANCOMBE LA

Lower Soldridge Farm

Stancomb Farm

Upper Soldridge Farm

Soldridge

GROSVENOR RD

Bighton Dean La

Stancomb Broad La

STANCOMB BROAD LA

UPPER SOLDRIDGE RD

Pit Lark Farm

Woodside

ROOKWOOD LA

Gullet Wood

Gullet La

KINGSWOOD RISE

DRUMMOND CL

Motel

BISHOPS VIEW

WINCHESTER RD

A31

Mid Hants Rly
Watercress Line

GRAVEL LA

SOKE HILL

BARN LA

A31

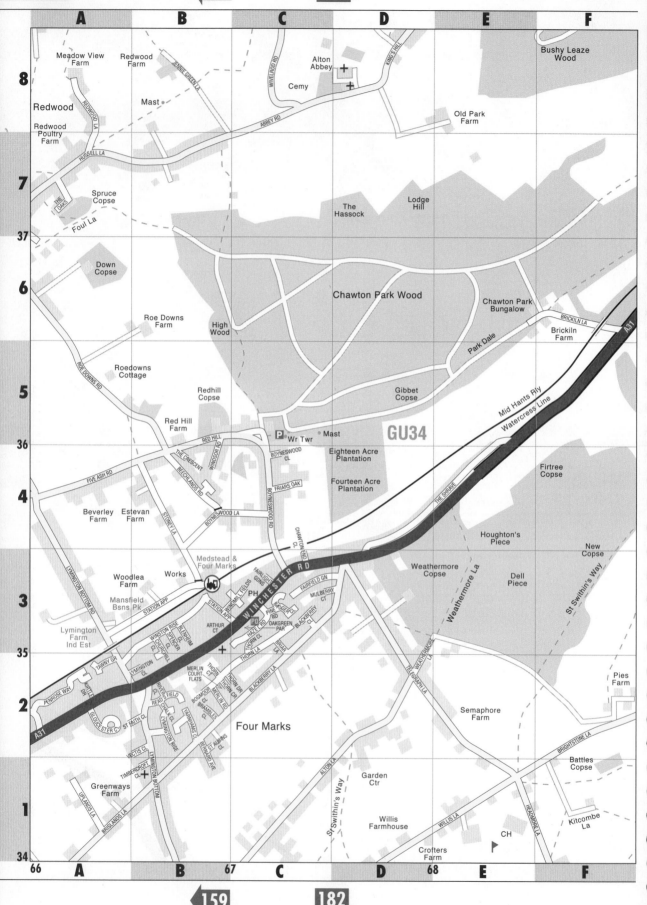

159 138

A B C D E F

8

Meadow View Farm
Redwood Farm
Alton Abbey
Bushy Leaze Wood
Cemy
JENNIE GREEN LA
WIVELROD RD
KING'S HILL

Redwood
Mast
ABBEY RD
Old Park Farm

Redwood Poultry Farm
REDWOOD LA

7
HUSSELL LA
THE OAKS
Spruce Copse
The Hassock
Lodge Hill

Foul La

37

Down Copse

6
ROE DOWNS RD
Chawton Park Wood
Chawton Park Bungalow
BRICKILN LA
A31

Roe Downs Farm
High Wood
Park Dale
Brickiln Farm

Roedowns Cottage
Redhill Copse
Gibbet Copse

5
Red Hill Farm
RED HILL
Mid Hants Rly
Watercress Line
Firtree Copse

THE CRESCENT
WINDSOR RD
BOYNESWOOD CL
Wr Twr
Mast
GU34

36
FIVE ASH RD
BEECHLANDS RD
FRIARS OAK
Eighteen Acre Plantation

4
Beverley Farm
Estevan Farm
STONEY LA
BOYNESWOOD RD
Fourteen Acre Plantation
THE SHRAVE
Houghton's Piece
New Copse

BOYNES-WOOD LA
CHAWTON END CL
Weathermore Copse
Dell Piece

Medstead & Four Marks
Woodlea Farm
Works
ST SWITHIN'S WAY

3
LYMINGTON BOTTOM RD
STATION APP
WINDMILL FIELDS
PH
FAIRLIGHT
FAIRFIELD GN
PINE RD
BADGER CL
MULBERRY CT
Weathermore
Weathermore La

Mansfield Bsns Pk
STATION APP
WINCHESTER RD
HAZEL RD
OAKGREEN PAR
BLACKBERRY
Semaphore Farm
Pies Farm

Lymington Farm Ind Est
WINSTON RISE
BLENHEIM
SPENCER
ARTHUR CT
THORN CL
BRIAR
BLACKBERRY LA

35
TAWNY GR
CHURCHILL
THORN LA
TELEGRAPH LA

2
PENROSE WAY
GLOUCESTER C
MYRTLE DR
LYMINGTON CL
READ'S FIELD
BOGMOOR CL
BRAMBLES
THORN DR
MERLIN COURT FLATS

A31
ST FAITH CL
CHALK LA
LYMINGTON RISE
Four Marks

VECTIS CL
LYMINGTON BOTTOM
BERNARD AVE
ST ALBANS
ALTON LA
ST SWITHIN'S WAY
Garden Ctr
Battles Copse
BRIGHTSTONE LA

TIMBERCROFT CL
Greenways Farm

1
UPLANDS LA
BROSLANDS LA
Willis Farmhouse
WILLIS LA
HEADMORE LA
Kitcombe La

CH
Crofters Farm

34
66 A 67 B C 68 D E F

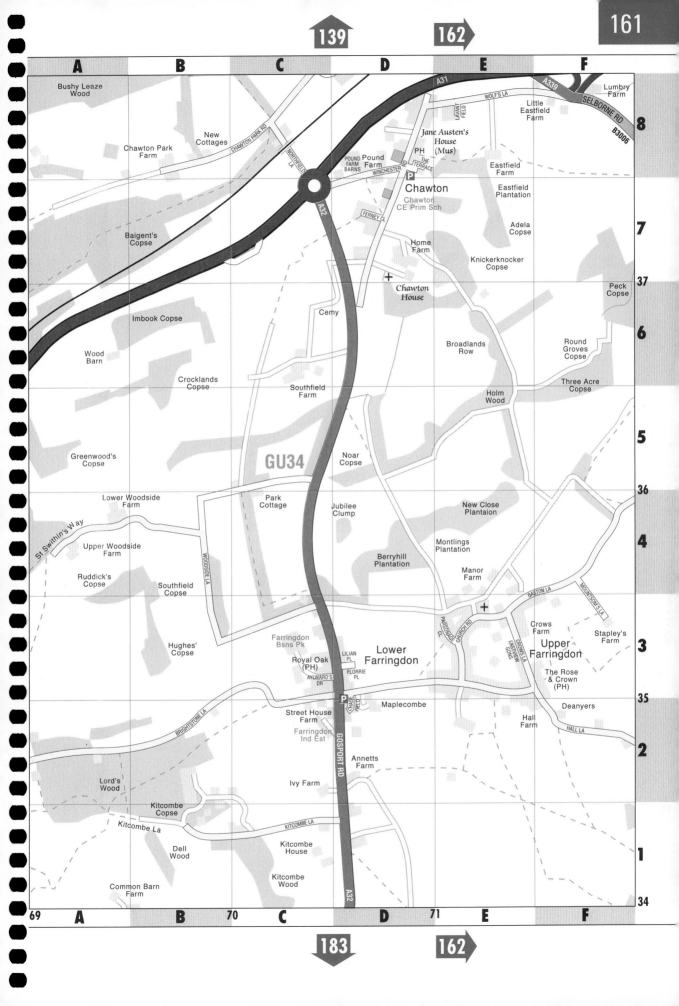

139
162
183
162

A B C D E F

8 7 37 6 5 36 4 3 35 2 1 34

Bushy Leaze Wood

Chawton Park Farm

New Cottages

CHAWTON PARK RD

NORTHFIELD LA

A31

A339

SELBORNE RD

B3006

Lumbry Farm

WOLF'S LA

LAVANT FIELD

Little Eastfield Farm

POUND FARM BARNS

Pound Farm

WINCHESTER RD

THE TERRACE

PH

Jane Austen's House (Mus)

Eastfield Farm

Chawton

Chawton CE Prim Sch

Eastfield Plantation

FERNEY CL

Home Farm

Adela Copse

Knickerknocker Copse

Peck Copse

Baigent's Copse

A32

Chawton House

Cemy

Broadlands Row

Round Groves Copse

Imbook Copse

Three Acre Copse

Wood Barn

Crocklands Copse

Southfield Farm

Holm Wood

GU34

Noar Copse

Greenwood's Copse

Lower Woodside Farm

Park Cottage

Jubilee Clump

New Close Plantaion

St Swithin's Way

Upper Woodside Farm

WOODSIDE LA

Montlings Plantation

Ruddick's Copse

Southfield Copse

Berryhill Plantation

Manor Farm

BASTON LA

MOUNTSINS LA

Crows Farm

Stapley's Farm

Hughes' Copse

Farringdon Bsns Pk

LILIAN PL

Royal Oak (PH)

AYLWARD'S DR

FLORRIE PL

Lower Farringdon

PARSONAGE CL

CHURCH RD

EASTVIEW GDNS

CROWS LA

Upper Farringdon

The Rose & Crown (PH)

Street House Farm

BRIGHTSTONE LA

Farringdon Ind Est

CHASE FIELD

Maplecombe

Deanyers

HALL LA

Hall Farm

GOSPORT RD

Annetts Farm

Lord's Wood

Ivy Farm

Kitcombe Copse

Kitcombe La

KITCOMBE LA

Dell Wood

Kitcombe House

Kitcombe Wood

Common Barn Farm

A32

161 140

A **B** **C** **D** **E** **F**

8
Westbrook Grange
Trencheaunts
East Worldham
BLANKET ST
DROVE COTTS
Manor Farm
B3006
Whitehouse Farm
Hamble Pits Copse
Water La

7
Caker Stream
Wild Duck Copse
Warner's Hanger

37
Derby's Dell
West Worldham
Manor Farm
West Worldham Farm

6
Copse Close
Little Wood Copse
Hartley Mauditt

5
Barleywood Farm
Round House
SELBORNE RD
Old Elm
Hartley Mauditt Village
Hartley Pond
Hartley Park

36
GU34

4
Hartley Park Bsns Ctr
Hartley Park Farm

3
Windmill Cottages
Wick Hill Cottages
Milking Hanger

35
Frenchmare Copse
Norton Farm
Long Copse

2
HALL LA
Fielder's Farm

1
Noar Copse
Bush Down
Long Lythe
Hangers Way
Oakhanger Stream
Dorton
Noar Plantation
Nine Acres
B3006
GOSLINGS CROFT

34
72 **A** 73 **B** **C** 73 **D** 74 **E** **F**

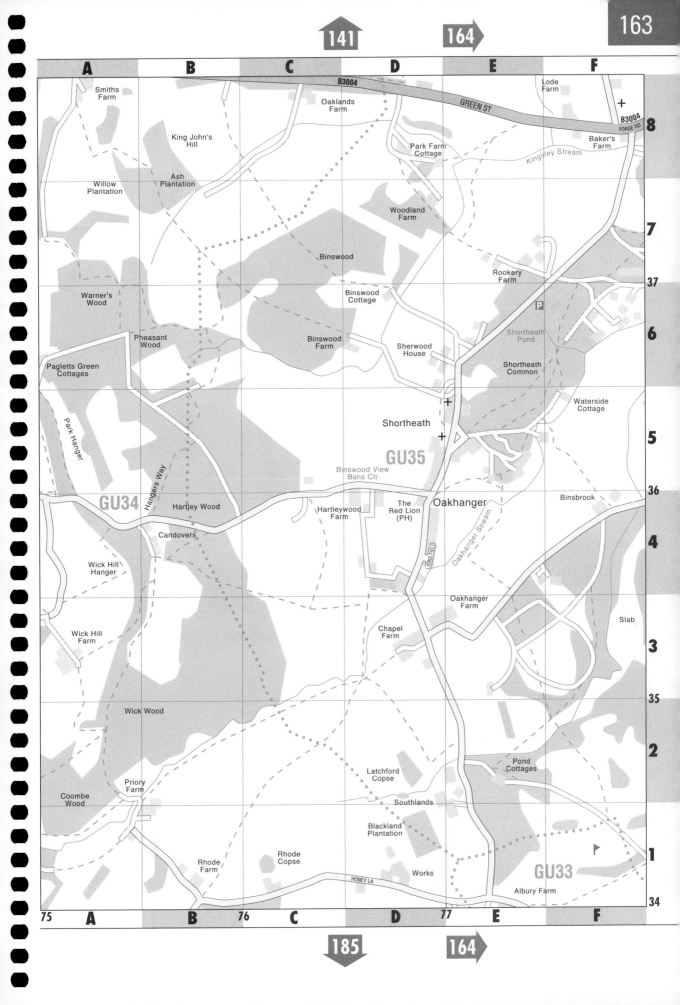

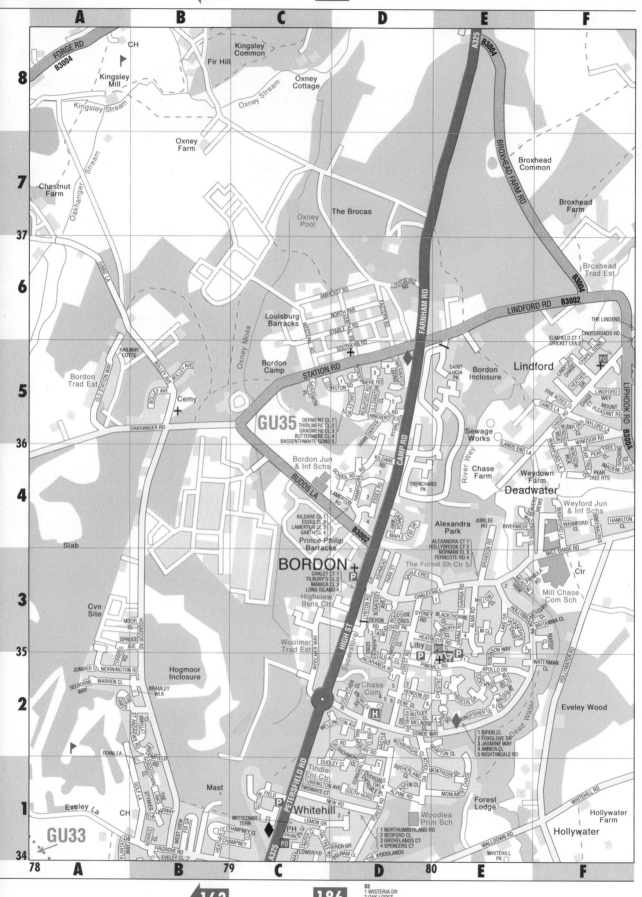

D2
1 WISTERIA DR
2 OAK LODGE
3 SHAFTESBURY CT
4 ASHLEY HO
5 COOPER HO
6 JOHN POUNDS HO
7 CONNAUGHT CL
8 BLUE TIMBERS CL

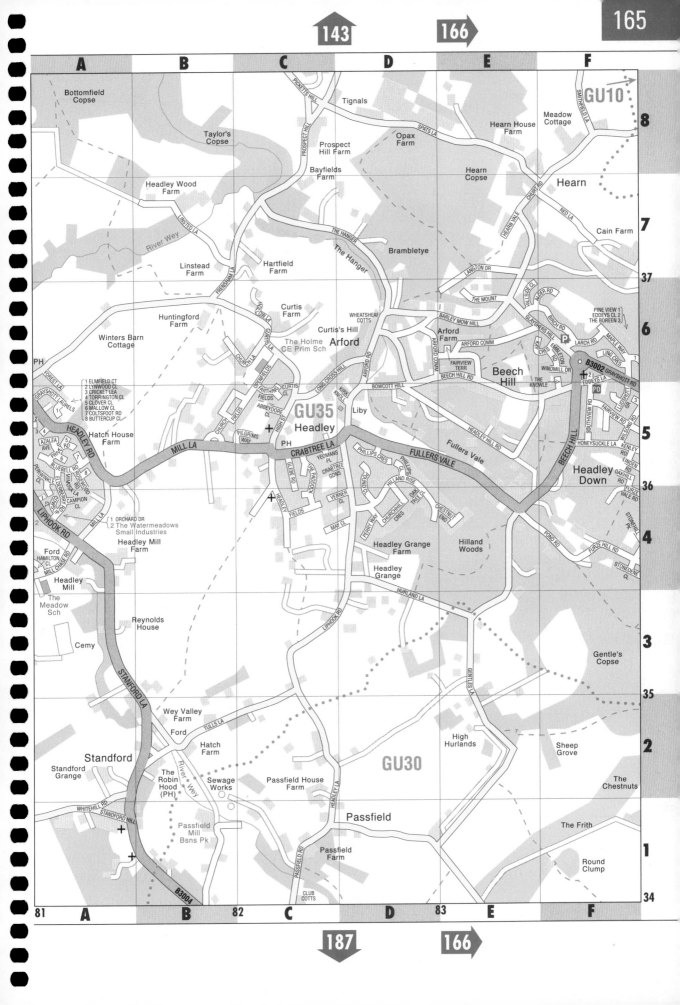

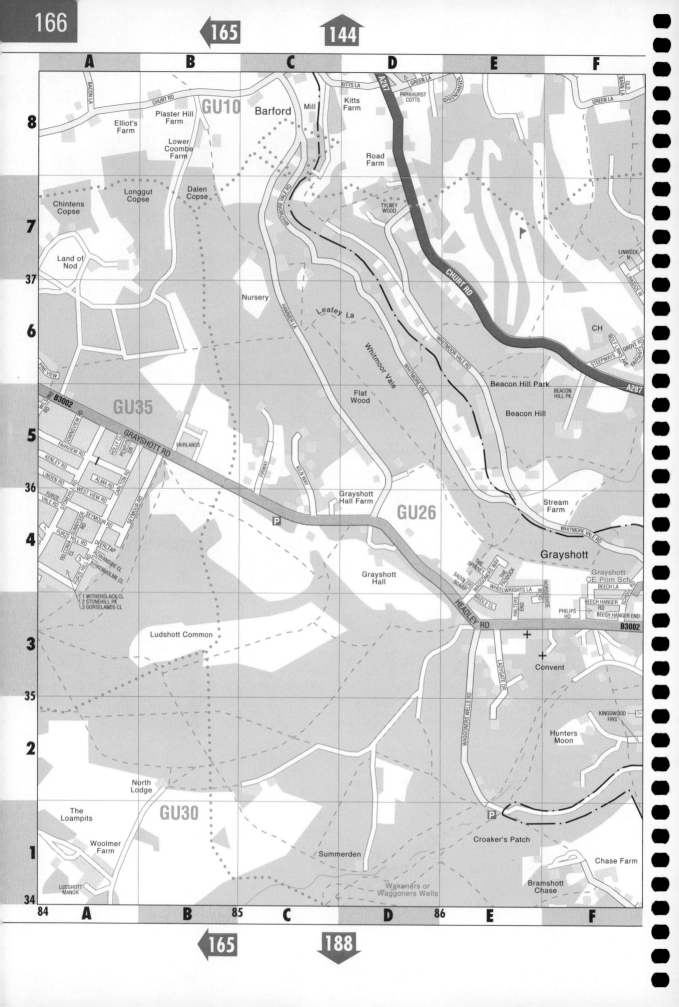

165
144

GU10

Barford

Mill

Kitts La

Kitts Farm

Parkhurst Cotts

Green La

A287

Green La

Old Barn La

Churt Rd

Elliot's Farm

Plaster Hill Farm

Lower Coombe Farm

Road Farm

Tylney Wood

Chintens Copse

Longgut Copse

Dalen Copse

Land of Nod

Nursery

Leafey La

Churt Rd

CH

Linkside N

Linkside W

Golf Links Ave

Grove Rd

Fairway

Steepways

A287

Beacon Hill Park

Beacon Hill Pk

Beacon Hill

Whitmoor Vale Rd

Whitmoor Vale

Flat Wood

Whitmore Vale

Hammer La

Pine View

GU35

B3002

Wilsons Rd

Downinsview Rd

Grayshott Rd

Fairlands

Firway

Kiln Way

Grayshott Hall Farm

GU26

Stream Farm

Whitmore Vale Rd

Fairview Rd

Kenley Rd

Linden Rd

Holly Cl

Perry Hill Dr

Alma Rd

Carlton Rd

Seymour Rd

Stonehill Rd

West View Rd

Furze Vale Rd

Telconia Cl

Furze Hill Rd

Seymour Rd

Deerleap

Rowanside Cl

Birkenholme Cl

1 Witherslack Cl
2 Stonehill Pk
3 Gorselands Cl

Furze Hill Rd

Grayshott Hall

Grayshott

Grayshott CE Prim Sch

Beech La

The Spinney

Waggoners Way

Saddlers Scarp

The Paddock

Wheelwrights La

Bridle Cl

Halters End

Horseshoe

Beech Hanger Rd

Beech Hanger End

Philips Ho

B3002

Headley Rd

Convent

Ludshott Common

Waggoners Wells Rd

Ladygate Dr

Kingswood Firs

Hunters Moon

North Lodge

GU30

Croaker's Patch

The Loampits

Woolmer Farm

Summerden

Wakeners or Waggoners Wells

Bramshott Chase

Chase Farm

Ludshott Manor

84

85

86

165
188

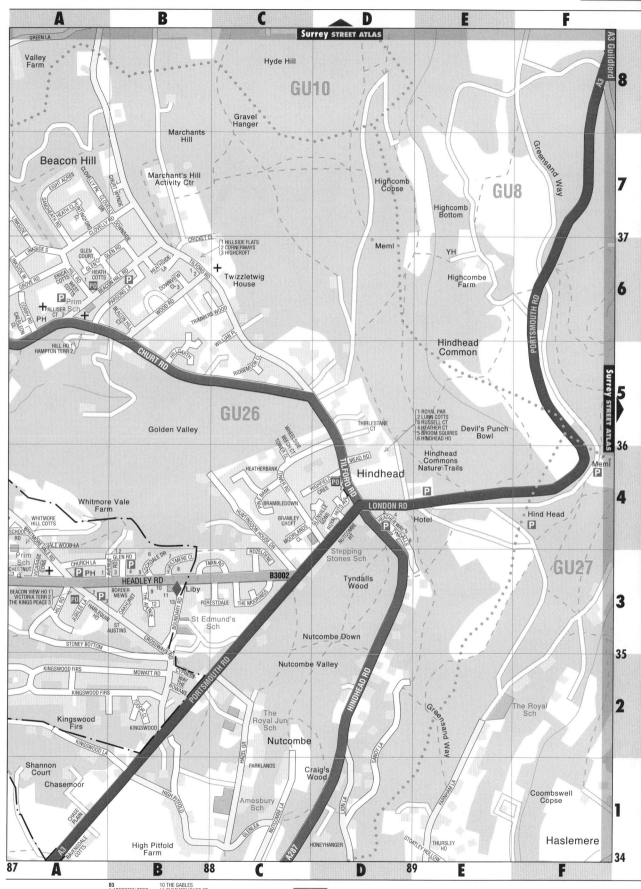

B3
1 ABERDEEN TERR
2 CORNER COTTS
3 THE SQUARE
4 OAKLEA HO
5 ROCKDALE
6 ROCKDALE HO
7 OAK HO
8 HURSTMERE HO
9 OAK COTT
10 THE GABLES
11 SUMMERHOUSE CT
12 WOOLMER VIEW
13 HOLMES CT

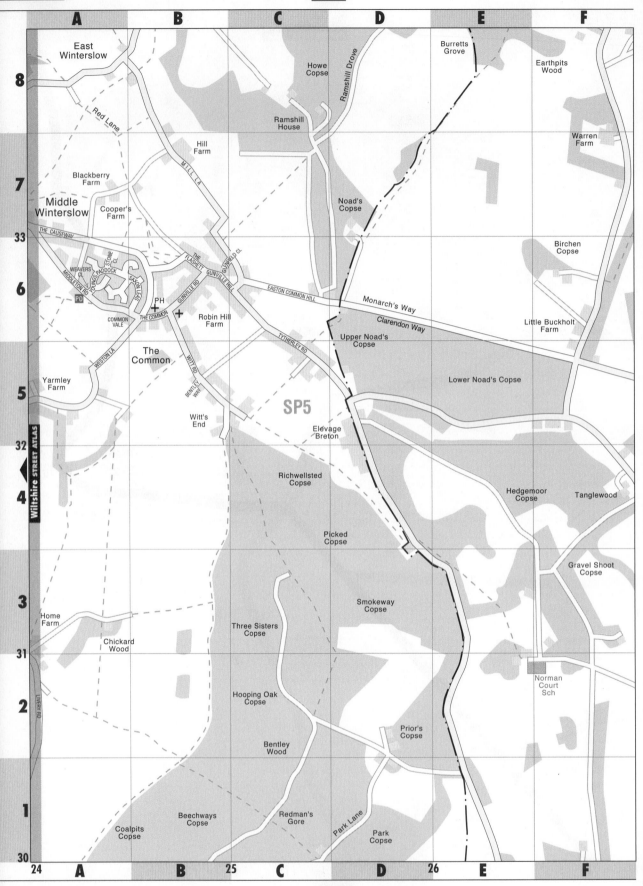

Wiltshire STREET ATLAS

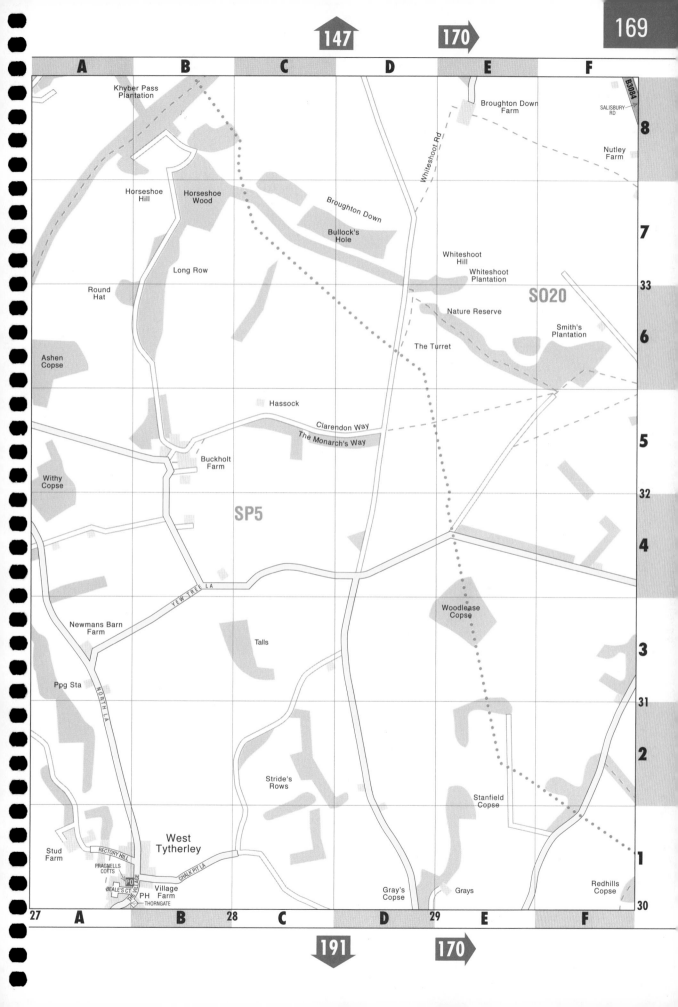

A   B   C   D   E   F

Khyber Pass
Plantation

B3084

SALISBURY
RD

Broughton Down
Farm

Whiteshoot Rd

Nutley
Farm

8

Horseshoe
Hill

Horseshoe
Wood

Broughton Down

Long Row

Bullock's
Hole

Whiteshoot
Hill

Whiteshoot
Plantation

7

Round
Hat

Nature Reserve

SO20

33

Smith's
Plantation

The Turret

6

Ashen
Copse

Hassock

Clarendon Way

The Monarch's Way

5

Withy
Copse

Buckholt
Farm

32

SP5

4

YEW TREE LA

Woodlease
Copse

Newmans Barn
Farm

Talls

3

Ppg Sta

NORTH LA

31

Stride's
Rows

Stanfield
Copse

2

West
Tytherley

Stud
Farm

RECTORY HILL

PRAGNELLS
COTTS

PO

BEALE'S CT

PH

Village
Farm

THORNGATE

Gray's
Copse

Grays

Redhills
Copse

1

CHALK PIT LA

27   A   B   28   C   D   29   E   F   30

169
148

A   B   C   D   E   F

8

Waterloo Farm
Works
Nutley Farm
Manor Farm
The Buildings
Eveley Wood

7

B3084
SALISBURY RD
Broughton Prim Sch
NORTH END
VENISON TERR
DIXONS LA
SCHOOL LA
THE GARDENS
THINWOOD CL
PAYNES LA
PAYNES CL
Everley Farm
Broughton Drove

33

Cemy
WHITESHOOT
CHAPEL CT
HIGH ST
CHAPEL LA
OLD FORGE GDN
RECTORY LA
Broughton
Steven's Drove
PLOUGH GDNS
GREENACRE
QUEENWOOD RD
QUEENWOOD RISE
PO
Broughton House

6

Church Farm
THE POUND
BUCKHOLT RD
BEECHCROFT COTTS
PH
Monarch's Way
ROOKERY LA
Clarendon Way
ROMSEY RD
The Manse
COOLERS FARM
Wallop Brook

5

Coolers Farm
SOUTH RD
Hyde Farm
Ford
Hayter's Farm
Hayter's Copse
Clarendon Way

32

Broughton Hill
SO20
THE HOLLOW
Roake Farm
HORSEBRIDGE RD
Balls Plantation

4

Avenue Cottages
Honeycomb

3

BEECH TREE WLK
Little Wood
Fir Hill

31

Queenwood Farm
Hildon House

2

Queenwood Avenue
Acorn Ground
Heywood Farm

1

Redhills Copse
Dumore Copse
Straits Copse
Crown Farm
Copse Corner

30

SP5
SO51
B3084

30   A   31   B   C   31   D   32   E   F

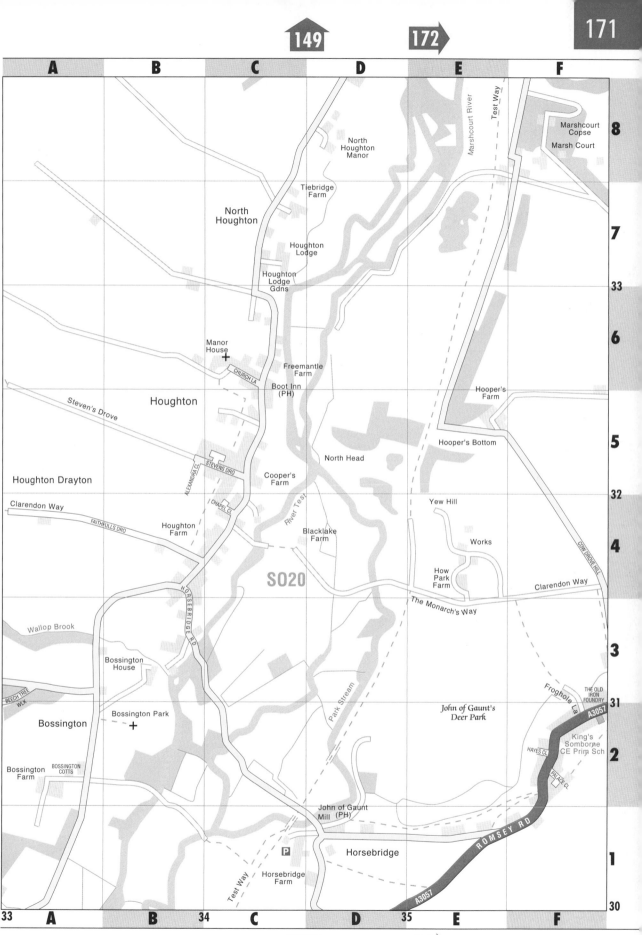

A   B   C   D   E   F

8

7

33

6

5

32

4

3

31

2

1

30

Marshcourt River
Test Way
Marshcourt Copse
Marsh Court

North Houghton Manor

Tiebridge Farm

North Houghton

Houghton Lodge

Houghton Lodge Gdns

Manor House

Freemantle Farm

Boot Inn (PH)

CHURCH LA

Houghton

Hooper's Farm

Hooper's Bottom

Steven's Drove

Houghton Drayton

ALEXANDRA CL
STEVENS DRO

North Head

Cooper's Farm

Yew Hill

Works

Clarendon Way

FAITHFULLS DRO

CHAPEL CL

Houghton Farm

River Test

Blacklake Farm

SO20

How Park Farm

Clarendon Way

COW DROVE HILL

The Monarch's Way

HORSEBRIDGE RD

Wallop Brook

Bossington House

Park Stream

John of Gaunt's Deer Park

Froghole La

THE OLD IRON FOUNDRY

A3057

BEECH TREE WLK

Bossington

Bossington Park

King's Somborne CE Prim Sch

HAYES CL

Bossington Farm

BOSSINGTON COTTS

PALACE CL

John of Gaunt Mill (PH)

ROMSEY RD

P

Horsebridge

Test Way

Horsebridge Farm

A3057

33   A   B   34   C   D   35   E   F

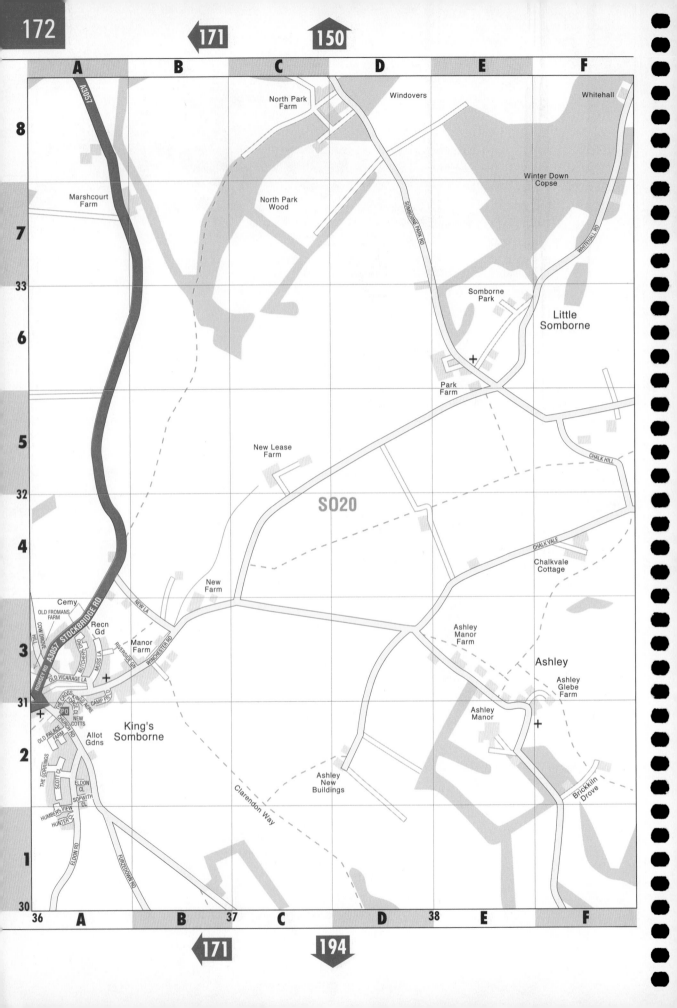

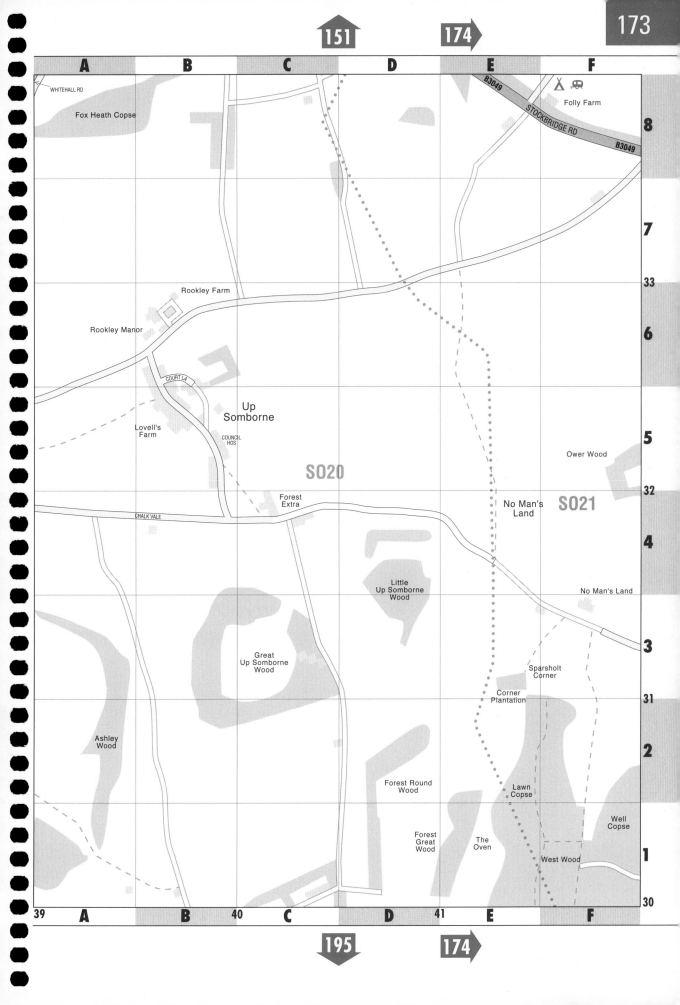

A | B | C | D | E | F

WHITEHALL RD

Fox Heath Copse

B3049
STOCKBRIDGE RD
B3049

Folly Farm

8

7

33

Rookley Farm

Rookley Manor

6

COURT LA

Up
Somborne

Lovell's
Farm

COUNCIL
HOS

5

Ower Wood

SO20

32

Forest
Extra

No Man's
Land

SO21

CHALK VALE

4

Little
Up Somborne
Wood

No Man's Land

Great
Up Somborne
Wood

3

Sparsholt
Corner

Corner
Plantation

31

Ashley
Wood

2

Forest Round
Wood

Lawn
Copse

Well
Copse

Forest
Great
Wood

The
Oven

West Wood

1

30

39 | A | B | 40 | C | D | 41 | E | F

A   B   C   D   E   F

8

Rack Belt

B3049

PH
RACK & MANGER
COTTS

Kirton
Farm

7

STOCKBRIDGE RD

Long
Park

Littleton
House

33

6

BALLDOWN CVN &
CAMPING PK

Cradle
Copse

Long
Wood

Ball Down
House

Northwood Park
Farm

5

HATCHERY HILL

FISH LA

GARSTONS TK

Bushmoor
Copse

Northwood
Park

B3049

32

MEADOWVIEW

MEADOWBANK

FARM RD

LONG BARN RD

HILLSIDE
COTTS

HILLSIDE RD

Sparsholt Coll
Hampshire

WESTLEY COURT RD

LIBRARY LA

WESTLEY LA

SO21

4

CHUTE HILL 1
SAXONY CRES 2

Privet
Copse

WATLEY LA

Lainston
House
Hotel

Lainston
Farm

3

Moorcourt
Farm

MOOR COURT LA

LOCK'S LA

HOME LA

CHURCH LA

LAMBOURNE CL

The Plough Inn
(PH)

Church
Farm

Dean

Dean
Farm

DEAN LA

Sparsholt CE
Prim Sch

Sparsholt

PO

31

WOODMAN LA

WOODMAN CL

BOSTOCK CL

STOCKWELL
PL

SHEDDON
PL

2

Ham Green

Well Copse

1

Burrow Road

Stockers Down

Lanham
Plantation

SO22

30

West Wood

Heath's
Copse

Rabbit
Warren

42   A   B   43   C   D   44   E   F

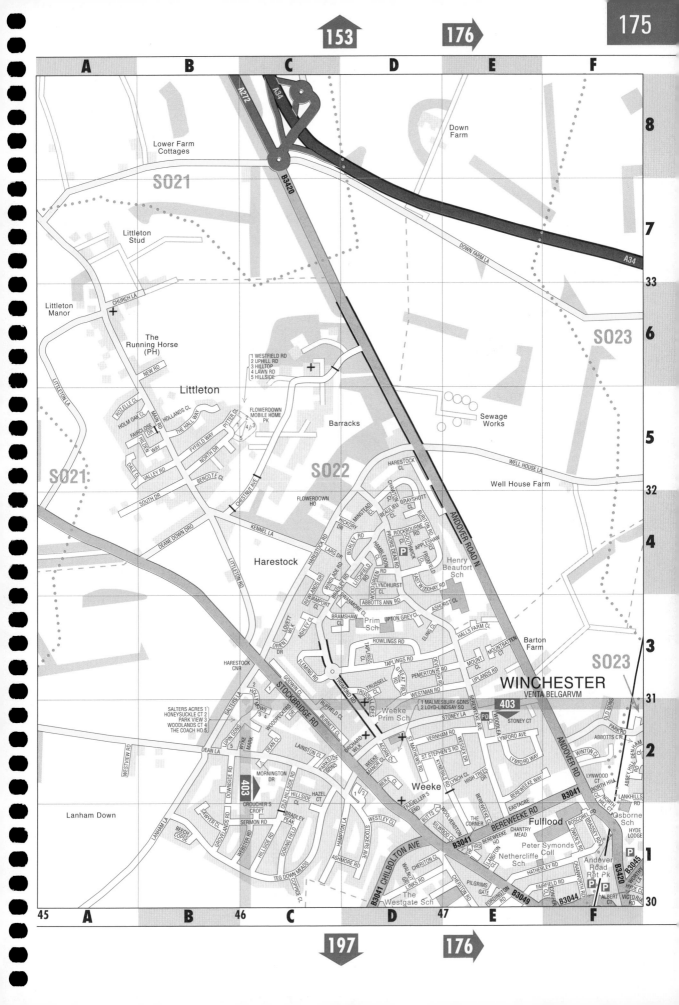

A B C D E F

8

Springvale

Meadow
Farm House

Cemy

1 GILLINGHAM CL
2 CEDARWOOD

Woodhams
Farm

7

A34

Recn
Gd

33

Hinton
House

B3047

Springvale Ave

Kings
Worthy
Prim Sch

Prince's Mead
Sch

Worthy
Park

6

Kings
Worthy

B3047

Abbots
Worthy

Worthy Park
Home Farm

Headbourne
Worthy

Upper
Farm

HEADBOURNE
WORTHY
HO

PH

PO

St Mary's Cl

5

Foresters
Pk

Lower
Farm

Pudding
House
Farm

Easton
Down

SO21

Three Castles Path
Itchen Way

Dairy
Farm

Lone
Barn

32

SO23

4

SO22

3

St Swithuns Way

Kings Way

River Itchen

WINCHESTER BY PASS

Winnall
Cottage Farm

Abbotts
Barton

31

Abbotts Lea
Cotts

WOODPECKERS

PARK RD

403

Abbots
Barton
Farm
House

Shoulder of Mutton
Farm

2

Abbotts
Barton

WINCHESTER
VENTA BELGARVM

403

The
Wykeham
Ind Est

9

North Walls
Recn
Gd

1

P

B3045

HYDE ST

Hyde

River Park
L Ctr

Chaucer Bsns Pk 1
Winchester Trad Pk 2
Sun Valley Bsns Pk 3
Winnall Trad Est 4

ERASMUS PARK
STUDENT VILLAGE

2

Superstore

Balfour Red
Cross Mus

Winnall Down
Copse

Dykes
Farm

M3

A33

30

48 A 49 B C 50 D E F

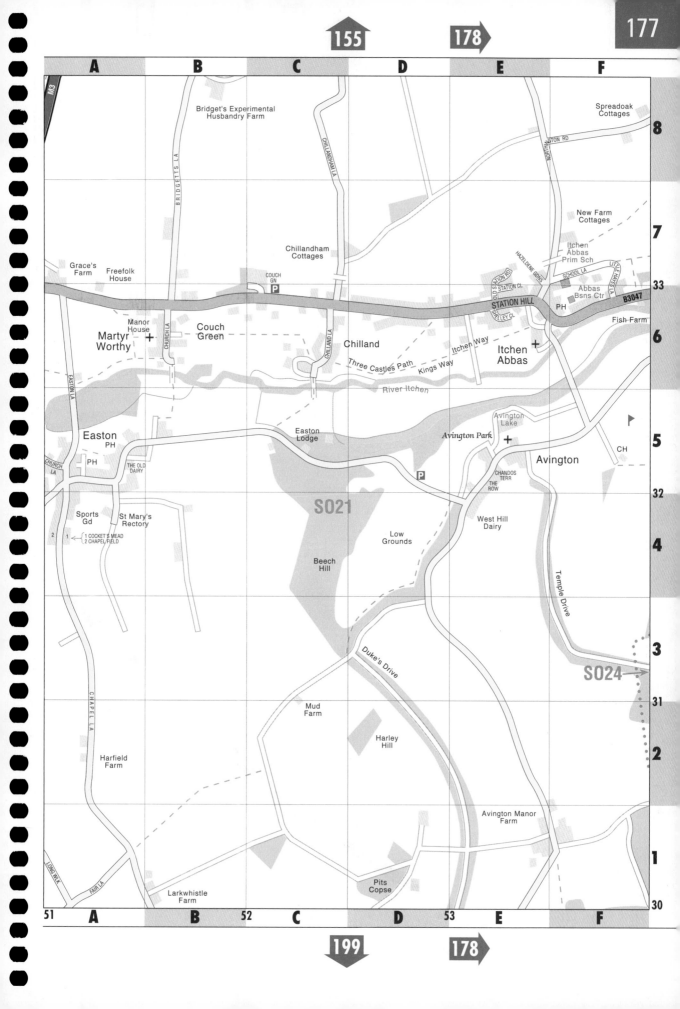

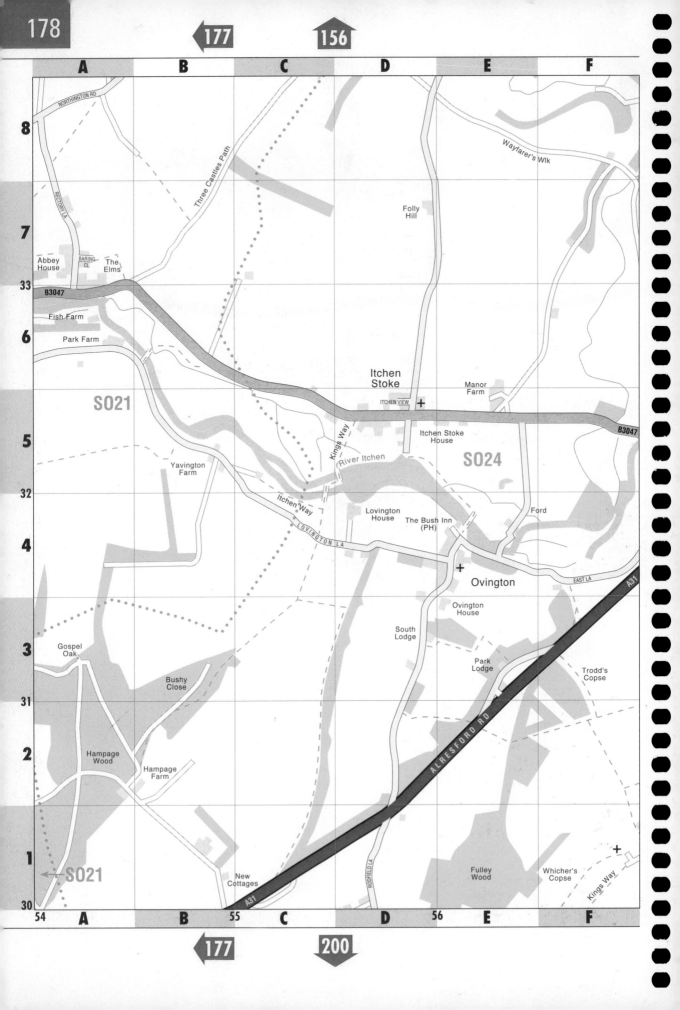

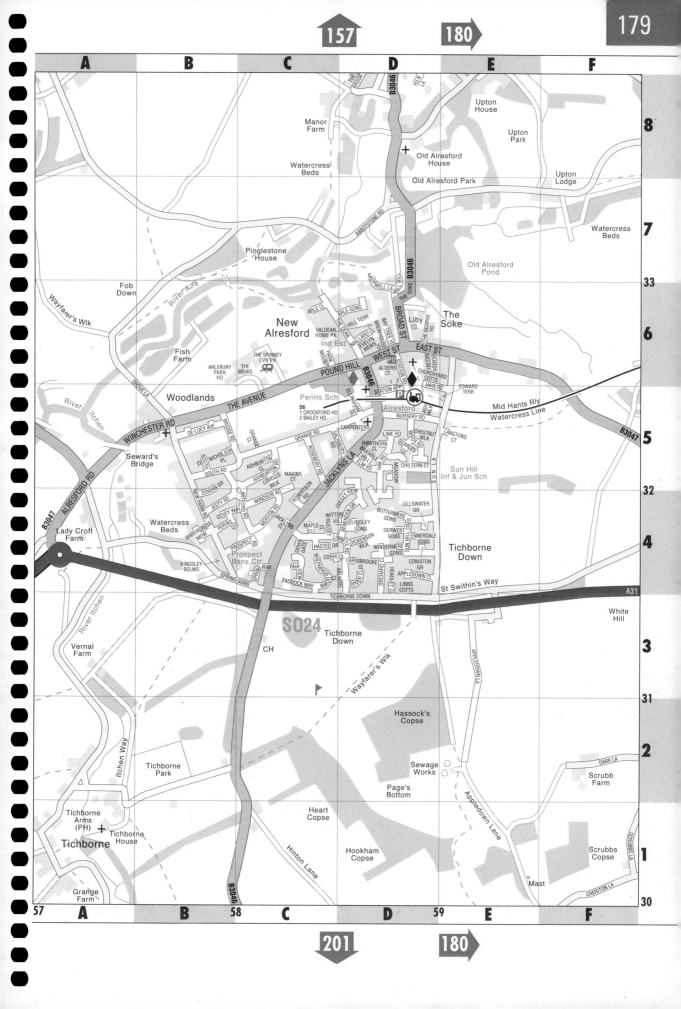

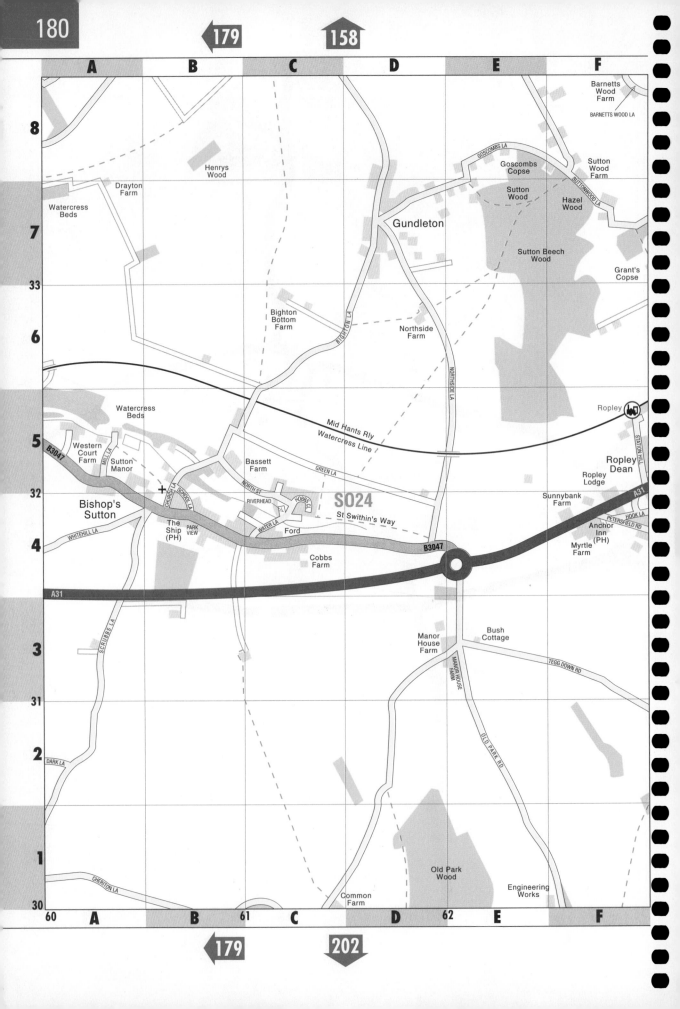

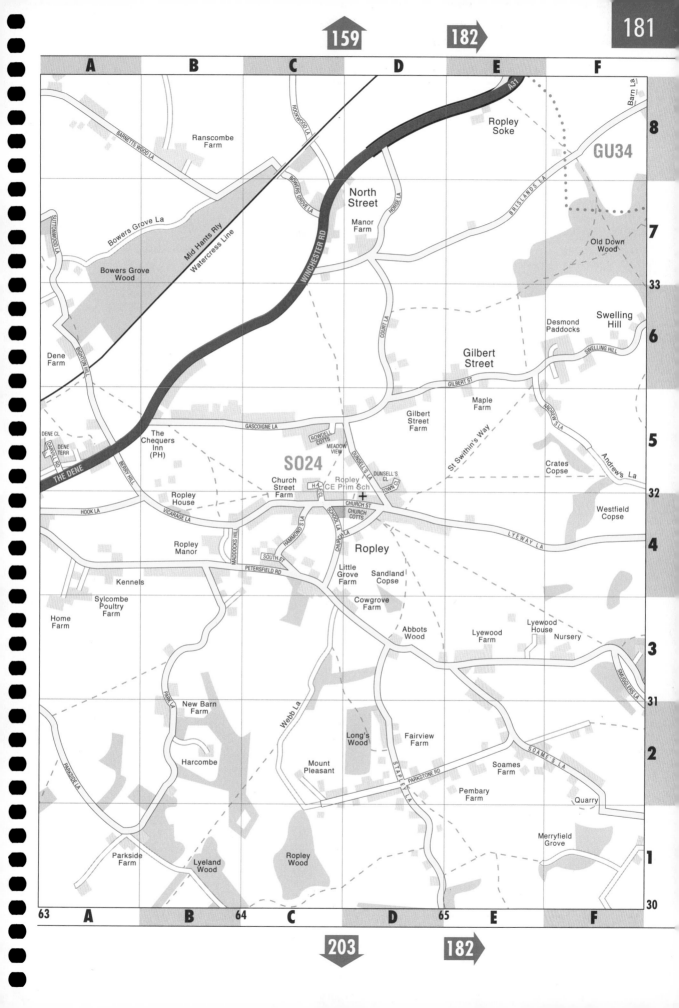

181 160

A B C D E F

8

Green La
Brislands La
GRADWELL LA
LYMINGTON BOTTOM
ALTON LA
KITWOOD RD
Kitfield Farm
Homestead Farm
Four Marks CE Prim Sch
HAWTHORN RD
Hawthorn Farm
WILLIS LA
Old Hawthorn Farm
Hawthorn
HAWTHORN LA
Ashurst Farm
HEADMORE LA
Headmore Farm
MARY LA
Newton Common
Hawthorn Plantation

7

Old Down Wood
Kitwood
KITWOOD LA
Kitwood Farm
Kitwood Plantation
Newtonwood Farm

33

SWELLING HILL
Shalfleet
Carter's Copse

6

Swelling Hill Pond
Dogford Wood
The Mountains Plantation

LYEWAY RD

Gillswood Farm Cottage

5

Lyeway Farm
GU34
Winchester Wood

Andrew's La

32

REDBRIDGE LA
LYEWAY LA
Green La
Charlwood Farm
Plain Farm

4

SO24
CHARLWOOD LA
Charlwood
Avenue Bungalow
Pine Cottages

Plaindell

Oak Wood

3

Treetops Farm

31

PETERSFIELD RD
Dunn's Plantation
Stonybrow Plantation

2

Vale Farm
SMUGGLERS LA
Maybank Farm
Monkwood
Farley Farm
Broomfield Plantation
Stony Brow
Stonybrow Wood
A32

HILL FARM RD

SOAME'S LA
THE PRIORS WAY
Short Wood

1

Merryfield Farm
Inham's Wood
Knight's Wood
West Tisted Common
Brewer's Farm
BREWERS LA
A32

30

66 A B 67 C D 68 E F

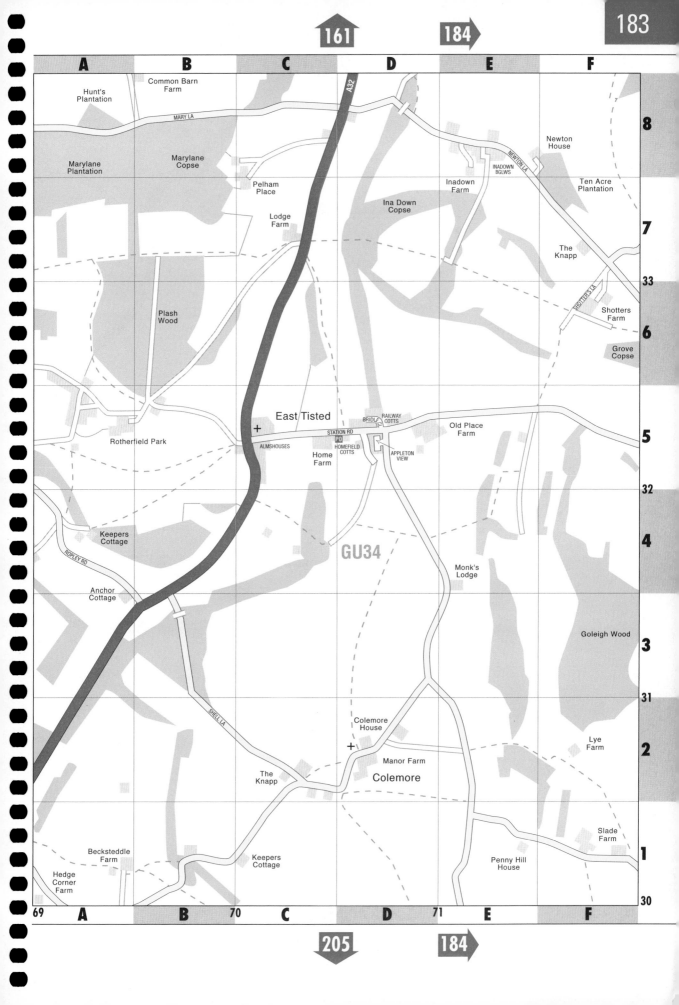

183
162

A   B   C   D   E   F

8

Wood Lane

Selborne

GRANGE FARM

GOSLINGS CROFT

1 NEW RD COTTS
2 GANDERS CL

SELBORNE RD

GRACIOUS ST

B3006

Mus

HIGH ST

HUCKERS LA

HASTARDS LA

MALTBYS

Sewage
Works

Pleasure Row
Plantation

Coneycroft
Hill

Selborne Hanger

Selborne
CE Prim
Sch

WAKES
COTTS

PO

Selborne
Arms
(PH)

P

HONEY LA

7

Newton Valence
Place Farm

Nature Reserve

Selborne Common

Selborne Hill

FOUNTAIN RD

PLUM FELL LA

Ketcher's
Farm

33

Newton
Valence Place

Hangers Way

Galley Hill
Farm

KETCHERS
FIELD

SOTHERINGTON LA

6

NEWTON LA

Newton
Valence

BARNFIELD
COTTS

Longhope

Homestead
Farm

Galley Hill

B3006

HULLAM LA

Green Lane

Lower Noar
Hill Farm

Brunstable
Farm

5

Hale
Copse

High Wood
Hanger

32

Bridleway
Copse

Noar
Hill

Heards Farm

GU34

Charity
Farm

High
Common

4

Cuckoo
Copse

King's
Farm

Nature Reserve

Holtham Lane

3

Goleigh
Manor

Noar Hill
Common

Hangers Way

Noar Hill
Hanger

GU33

Empshott
Green

House Lands
Plantation

Abbot's
Copse

31

Goleigh
Farm

Quarry
Farm

2

Herrings
Land
Copse

Barefield
Copse

Watercress
Beds

Lye Wood

BUTTON'S LA

Vann
Farm

Shadwell
Copse

MILL LA

Keyham
Farm

1

GU32

Mill Lane
Copse

Lowergreen
Farm

30

Church
Farm

72   A   73   B   C   73   D   74   E   F

183
206

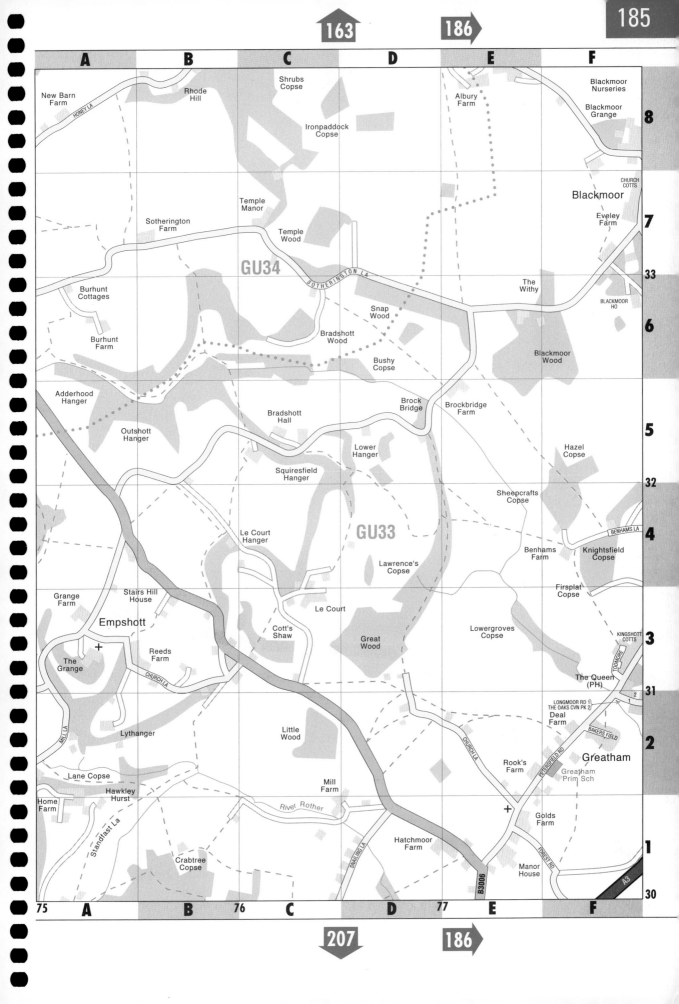

A B C D E F

8

7

33

6

5

32

4

3

31

2

1

30

St Matthew's CE Prim Sch

The Vicarage

Keepers Cottage

BENHAMS LA
WOLMER TERR
PO
Forest Side Farm
DIGBY WAY
Inn

King's Holt

HOPESWOOD
WOLFMERE LA
Forest Side

Greatham Moor

A3

Palmer's Ball

Longmoor Inclosure

Broad Hill

MOOR RD

Longmoor Camp

WHITE AVE
KIMBERLEY RD
ROBERTS RD
BADEN POWELL RD
PATERSON RD
PRETORIA RD
LINCOLN RD
ST SMITS CT
KITCHENER RD
WARREN RD
FRENCH RD
OLD HUNTERS RD
HAM

METHUEN RD
QUORN TERR
PLUMER RD
RAILWAY RD

LONGMOOR RD
WOOLMER RD A325

PETERSFIELD RD

BLACKMOOR RD

PLANTATION WAY
BRACKEN LA
EVERLEY CL
DRIFT RD

A325

MAYFLOWER RD

OAK TREE RD
FOREST RD
THE WOODLANDS
LIPHOOK RD
WALLDOWN RD

WHITEHILL PK
HOLLYWATER RD
PH

Hollywater Green

Hollywater Clump

Round Hill

DANGER AREA

Rifle Range

GU35

Fern Hill

Park Hill

Horsebush Hill
Linchborough Park

Cranmer Bottom

DANGER AREA

Woolmer Forest

DANGER AREA

Queen's Bank

Long Down

Brimstone Inclosure

GU30

Woolmer Pond Cottage

GU33

Woolmer Pond

Woolmer Down

Heifers Down

Rifle Range

DANGER AREA

A3

Weavers Down

WOLMER COTTAGES

DANGER AREA

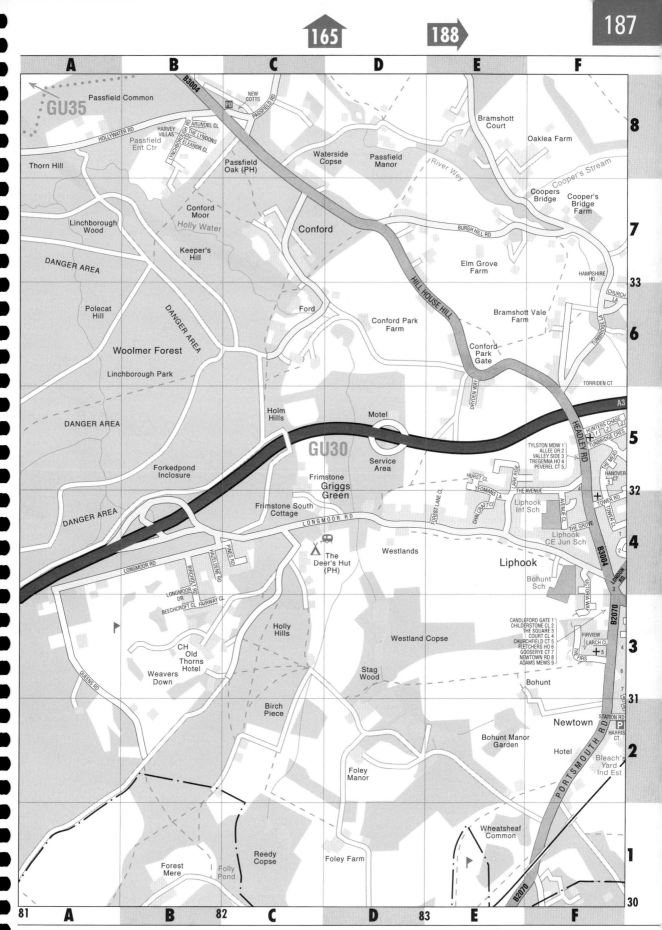

A2
1 ADAMS MEWS
A3
1 SHIPLEY CT
2 COURT CL
A4
1 CHILDERSTONE CL
2 LINCOLN CT

The Hanger
Spring Pond Hanger
Cooper's Stream
Glebe House Farm
WOOLMER LA
RECTORY LA
LIMES CL
33
CHURCH LA
Bramshott
CHURCH RD
B2171
6
A3
TUNBRIDGE CRES
WEYLAND CL
LONDON RD
5
1 PADDOCK WAY
2 GREENFIELD CL
3 TOWER RD
MEADOW END
Penally Farm
Hewshott Lodge
32
MEADOW WAY
MEADOW CL
MALTHOUSE MDWS
CALVECROFT
WEY LODGE
LOCKE RD
CLOSE RD
ST JOHNS
HAWKSHAW CL
THE MALTINGS
WEY WOOD
MANOR FIELDS
B2171
Liby
ERLES MALTHOUSE CT
CHILTEE CL
GRENVILLE
CHAPPELL
HAZELBANK CL
COLLIERS CRES
HASLEMERE RD
Super store
B2131
WHITLEE MANOR
OTTAWA DR
HAZELBANK MEWS
Liphook
Montreal WLK
WINNIPEG CL
CANADA
QUEBEC
HUDSON DR
HILTON DR
WILLOW CL
SHEPHERDS WAY
WILLOW GDNS
GOLDENFIELDS CL
CHESTNUT CL
DEVILS LA
Brookham Plantation
Beaver Ind Est
FLETCHERS FIELD
NEWTOWN RD
CHILTLEY WAY
SHEPHERDS WAY
CHILTLEY LA
31
STATION RD
REDHOUSE MEWS
Liphook
Bleach's Yard Ind Est
HEATHERLEY MEWS
THE CLOSE
GUNNS FARM
ADMERS CRES
HOLLYCOMBE CL
MIDHURST RD
HIGHFIELD LA
Brookham Sch
Highfield Sch
2
SOUTH RD
Churcher's Coll Jun Sch
North Lodge Ind Pk
30

Coach House Copse
Spring Pond
Downlands Farm
Downlands House
P
P
Woodlands
Cold Ash Hill
Old Barn Farm
Hewshott Farm
HEWSHOTT LA
HEWSHOTT GR
Hewshott House
GU30
Bridge
Bridge Lodge
Lower Brookham
Brookham Plantation
Sussex Border Path
Stanley Common

Kent's Hill
Bramshott Chase
A3
Bramshott Common
GU26
The Spaniard Inn (Hotel)
Prince of Wales (PH)
HAMMER LA
River Wey
Hammer Bottom
Gillham's Moor
GILLHAM'S LA
Gillham's Farm
GU27
B2131
LIPHOOK RD
Linchmere Common
DANLEY LA
Danley Farm
Linchmere
Church Farm
THE COURTYARD
Poison Copse
Ash Copse
Golden Valley
Hazel Piece
Hilly Field Copse

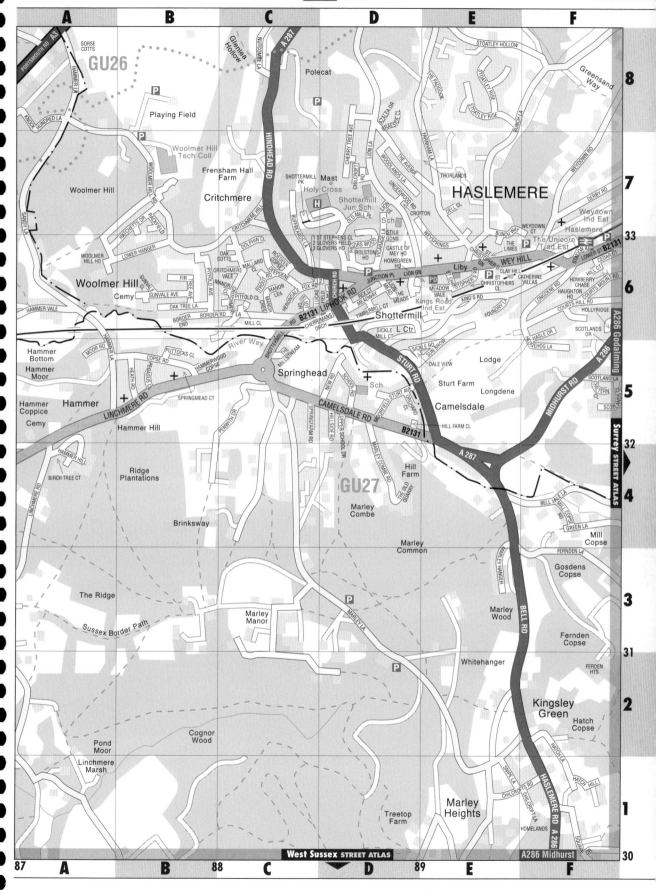

A   B   C   D   E   F

8

West Tytherley
CE Prim Sch
THE VILLAGE
THORNGATE
Church
Farm
Stony
Batter
Stride's
Farm
Manor
Farm
East
Tytherley

DEAN RD
Poplar
Farm
Lodge
Farm
Sopp's
Farm
MANOR
RD
7
The Green
THE COACH RD
Summer Lodge
CEDARS VIEW
BONNER
COTTS
Oaklands
Farm
29
RED LA
PUG'S HOLE

RED LA
BULL'S DROVE
Drove
6

FRENCHMOOR LA
SP5
Lockerley Hall
Park

Frenchmoor
Upper Frenchmoor Copse
Lower
Frenchmoor
Copse
Bulls Drove
Lain
Copse
5
Pug's Hole
Lockerley
Hall
28
Home Farm
Bsns Ctr
Holbury Wood
The Star Inn
(PH)
4

Holbury
Farm
MARK WAY
SO51
Holbury LA
PARK
VIEW
3
Holbury Mill
Lockerley Water
Farm
27
Mill Farm
Manor
Farm
GLEBE MDW
LC
River Dun
EAST DEAN RD
PO
2
East Dean
Lockerley

Dean Hill Barn
Farm
Top Green
PENDLE GREEN
Deangate
Farm
Butt's
Green
1
Dean Hill
Curlew's
Farm
Critchell's
Green
COOKS LA
BUTTS CL
26

27   A   B   28   C   D   29   E   F

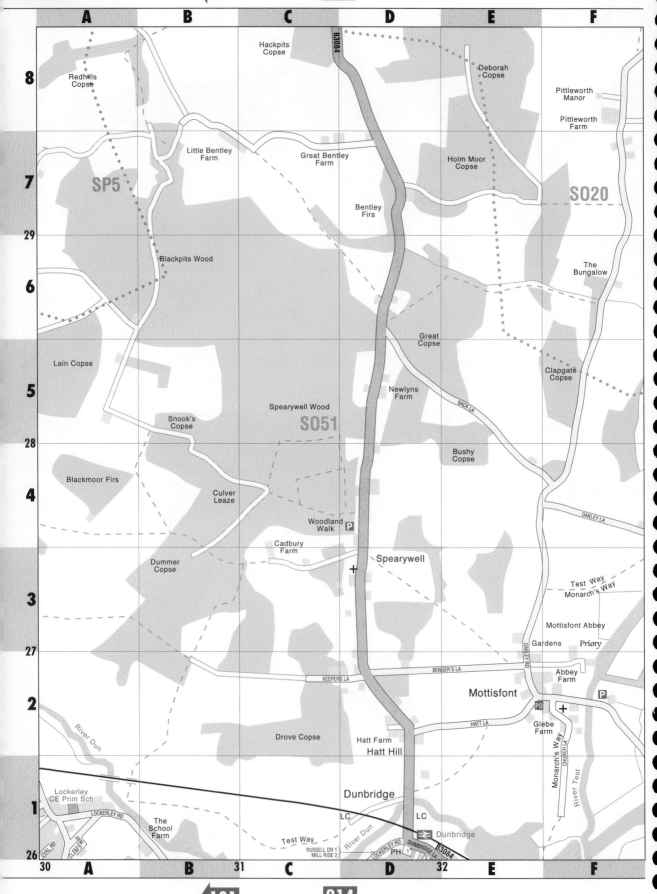

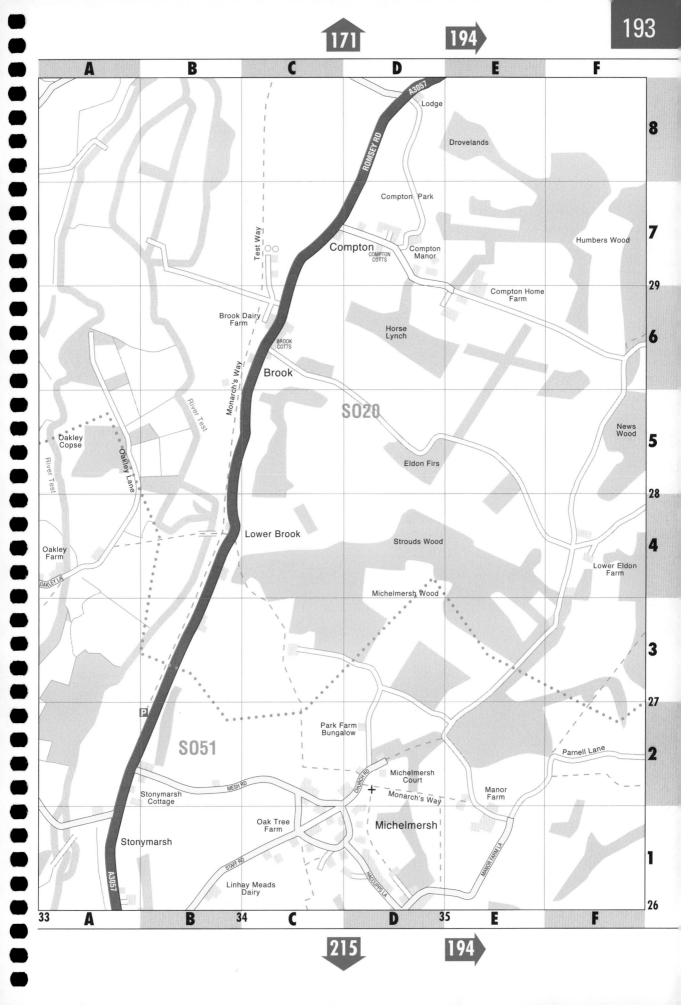

193
172

A **B** **C** **D** **E** **F**

8

Hoplands

Charlwood
Copse

Clarendon Way

Bourne
Farm

FURZEDOWN RD

Hoplands
Cottages

7

FURZEDOWN
COTTS

Combe
Bottom

29

Furzedown
Farm

Luke Copse

Humbers
Wood

FURZEDOWN
HO

6

Dirty Mount

Parnholt Wood

SO20

5

News
Wood

ELDON RD

28

The
Bungalow

Bailey's
Down

Taunton
Vale

Eldon
House

+

4

Fishponds
Farm

Bailey's Down
Farm

SO51

3

Stubb's Copse

Farley
House

27

Bull Grove
Copse

Blue Haze
Farm

2

Parnell La

KINGSOMBORNE RD

Windmill
Cottages

FARLEY LA

Monarch's Way

Hall
Place

Pitt
Farm

Fernhill
Farm

Fern Hill La

1

Braishfield
Manor

PAYNES HAY RD

BRAISHFIELD RD

26

36
A 37 **B** **C** 38 **D** **E** **F**

193
216

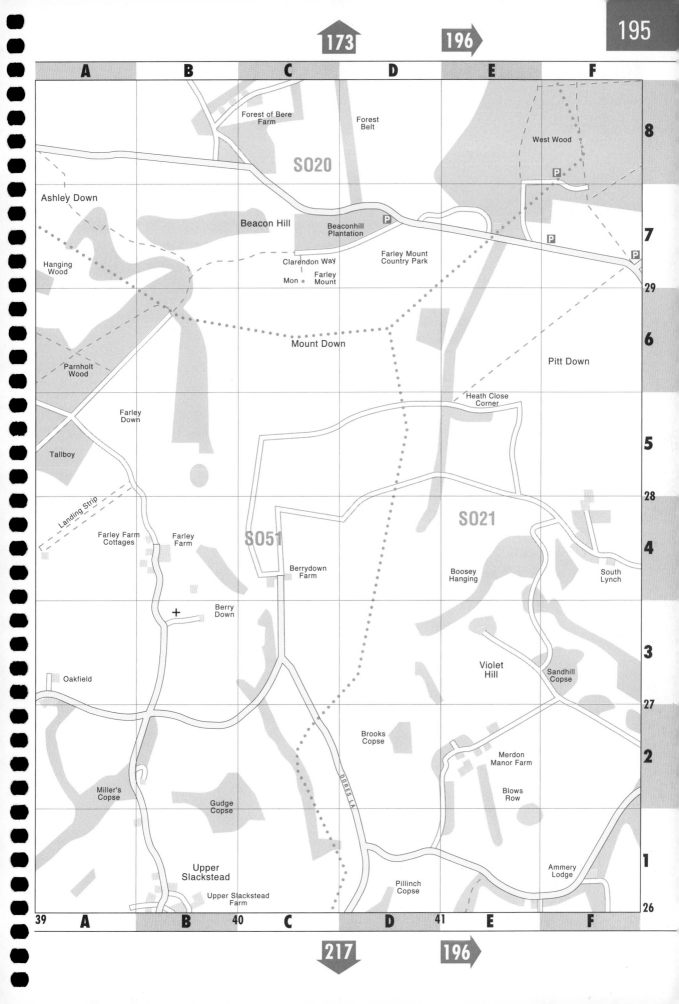

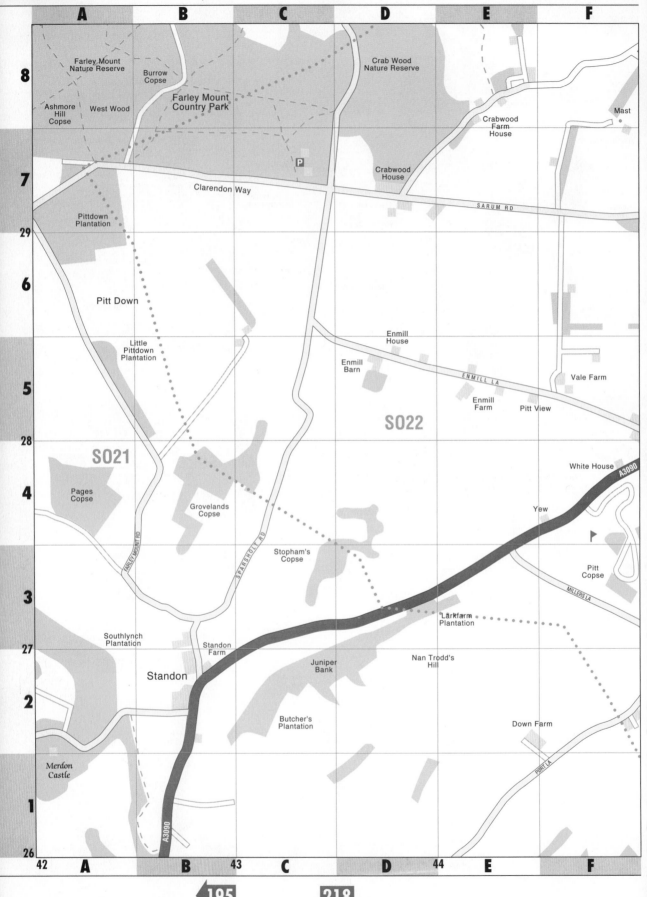

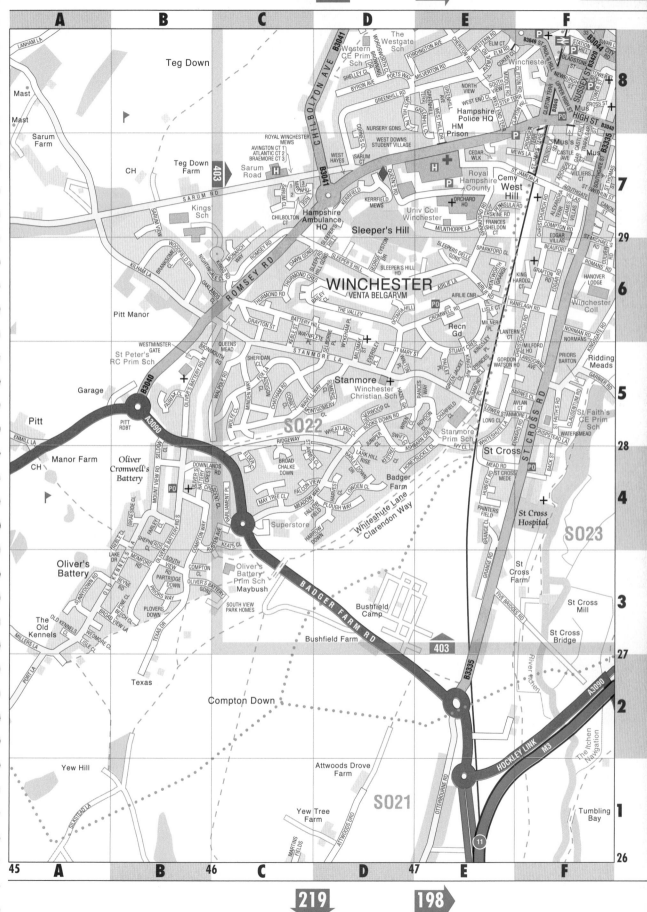

198

197 176

C8
1 BRAXTON HO
2 CRADDOCK HO
3 ROUNDHUTS RISE
4 PEACOCK PL
5 RINGLET WAY
6 LONGHOUSE GN

7 GATEKEEPER CL

D8
1 EARLE HO
2 SPITFIRE END
3 LIMETREE WLK

A B C D E F

8

St Martins Trad Pk
Winnall Trad Est
Winchester Sch of Art
Bsns Ctr
L Ctr St Bede CE Prim Sch
SWAN · HYDE ST
B3047
GORDON RD
CITY RD
NORTH WALLS
Liby's
ST PETER ST
PARCHMENT ST
Winnall
Winnall Prim Sch
Fairdown
Winnall Valley Ind Est
Easton Lane Bsns Ctr
Easton La
NICKEL CL · FIONA CL
COLSON RD · WALES ST
EDEN RD
GARBETT RD
SHEPHERDS RD
LONGFIELD RD
WARREN RD
WINNALL MANOR RD
IMBER RD
M3
A33
A33

No Man's Land
Winnall Down Farm
FAIR LA

St Swithun's Sch
Leigh House
H
ALRESFORD RD
B3404
Magdalen Hill Farm

Magdalen Hill Down

7

FRIARSGATE
EASTGATE ST
B3330
B3331
Mus
Cath
The Close
The Pilgrims' Sch
Palace
B3404
YH
Mill
St Giles Hill
The Soke
STRATTON RD
HIGHMOUNT
NORTHBROOKE CT
CHALK RD
QUARRY RD
CHESIL WOOD
PETERSFIELD RD
A31
A31
KINGS LA
Magdalen Hill Down

29

Winchester Coll
EAST HILL
HIGHCLIFFE RD
ST CATHERINE'S RD
PORTAL RD
DELL RD
FIVEFIELDS RD
GORDON AVE
FIVEFIELDS CL
Highcliffe
All Saints CE Prim Sch
NELSON RD
ST LEONARD'S LA
South Downs Way
Chilcomb

6

Wharf Hill
Wharf Bridge
MILLAND RD
TEST HO · MEON HO
SO23
Playing Field
Chilcomb House
CHILCOMB LA
The Manor House

5

WINCHESTER
VENTA BELGARVM
Bar End
Bar End Ind Est
Works
P&R
B3330
404
10
A31
CHILCOMB LA
Chilcomb Ranges
Chilcomb Manor
CLARENDON WAY
River Itchen
Tun Bridge
GARNIER RD
BULL DRO
Sewage Works

28

4

The Itchen Navigation
Itchen Way
Sewage Works
MORESTEAD RD
SO21
Deacon Hill

3

St Catherine's Hill
Nature Reserve
Pilgrim's Trail
Twyford Down
MORESTEAD RD

27

2

M3
403

Morestead Down

1

B3335
CH
White La
Morestead Farm

26

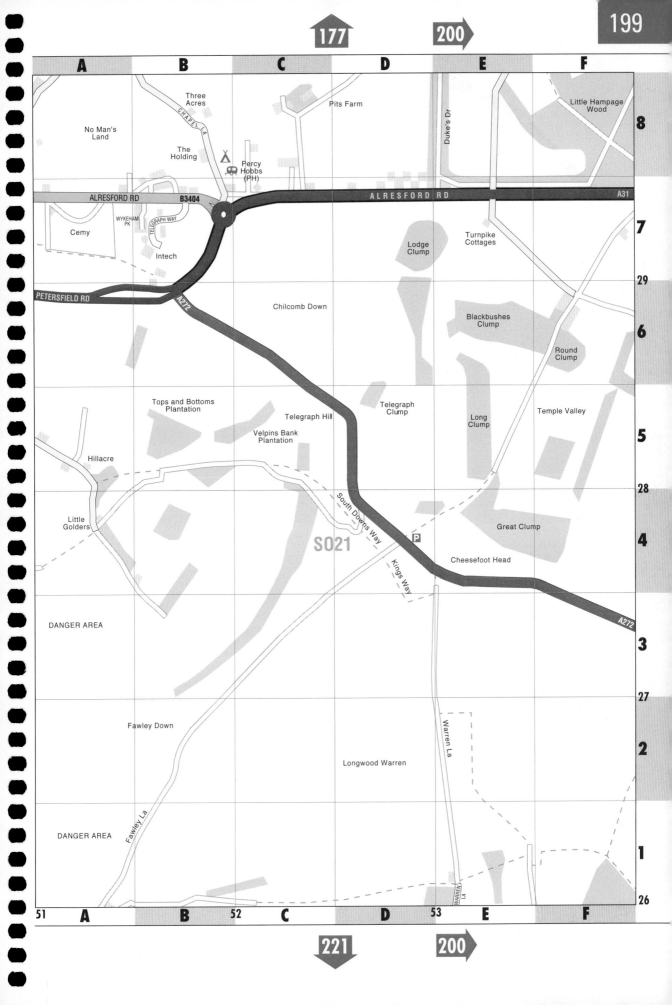

177
200

A B C D E F

8

Little Hampage Wood

No Man's Land

Three Acres

Pits Farm

Duke's Dr

The Holding

CHAPEL LA

Percy Hobbs (PH)

ALRESFORD RD   B3404   ALRESFORD RD   A31

7

Cemy

WYKEHAM PK

TELEGRAPH WAY

Intech

Turnpike Cottages

Lodge Clump

29

PETERSFIELD RD

A272

Chilcomb Down

Blackbushes Clump

6

Round Clump

Tops and Bottoms Plantation

Telegraph Hill

Telegraph Clump

Long Clump

Temple Valley

Velpins Bank Plantation

5

Hillacre

28

Little Golders

South Downs Way

SO21

P

Great Clump

4

Kings Way

Cheesefoot Head

A272

3

DANGER AREA

27

Fawley Down

Warren La

2

Longwood Warren

DANGER AREA

Fawley La

1

WARREN LA

26

51   A   B   52   C   D   53   E   F

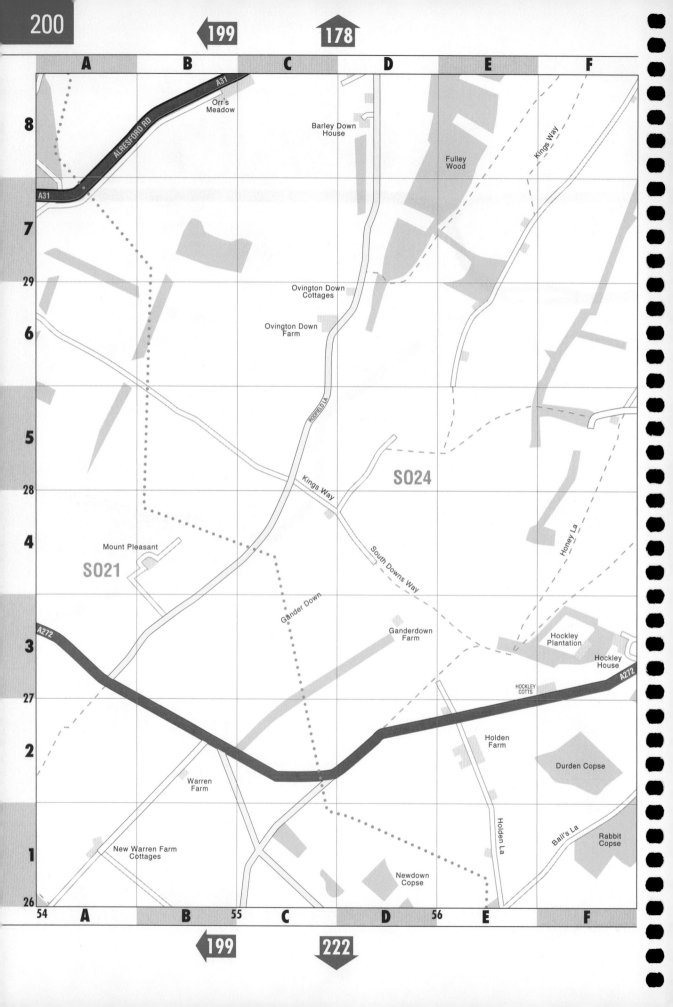

A B C D E F

A31
ALRESFORD RD
Orr's Meadow
Barley Down House
Fulley Wood
Kings Way
8

A31
7

Ovington Down Cottages
29

Ovington Down Farm
6

ROCHELD LA
SO24
5

Kings Way
28

Honey La
Mount Pleasant
South Downs Way
4

SO21
Gander Down
Ganderdown Farm
Hockley Plantation
Hockley House
A272
A272
3

HOCKLEY COTTS
27

Holden Farm
Durden Copse
Warren Farm
2

Holden La
Ball's La
Rabbit Copse
New Warren Farm Cottages
Newdown Copse
1

26

54 A B 55 C D 56 E F

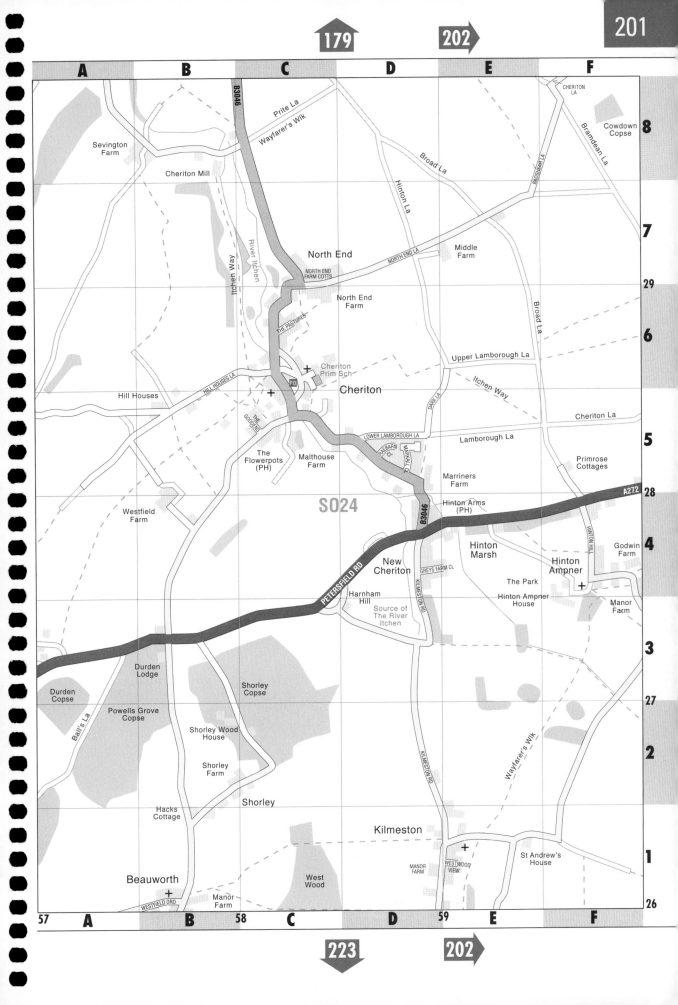

A   B   C   D   E   F

8

Bullbeck
Copse

Tenant
Woods

Common
Farm

Old Park
Wood

Cheriton Wood

Breach Plain
Cottages

7

Wood Farm
Cottages

29

Marriners
Farm

Wood
Farm

Alresford La

6

Bramble
Farm

WOOD LA

Cheriton La

Kalamunnda
Farm

Woodlane
Farm

5

Lacey's
Farm

New
Cottages

PETERSFIELD RD

West End
Farm

THE SPINNEY

WOODLANE CL

SO24

A272

28

Bramdean

CHURCH LA

WOODCOTE
COTTS

Woodcote Manor
House

4

Bramdean
Manor

Manor
Farm

Bramdean
Farm

Hinton
Ampner

The Malthouse

TITHELANDS LA

Manor Farm

3

A272

27

Godwin's
Plantation

Humpty's Down

2

New Pond
Cottages

Joan's
Acre

Brockwood
Park Sch

1

Broom
Wood

Joan's
Acre Wood

Brockwood
Park Farm

DELL
COTTS

GU32

BROCKWOOD
BOTTOM

26

60   A   B   61   C   D   62   E   F

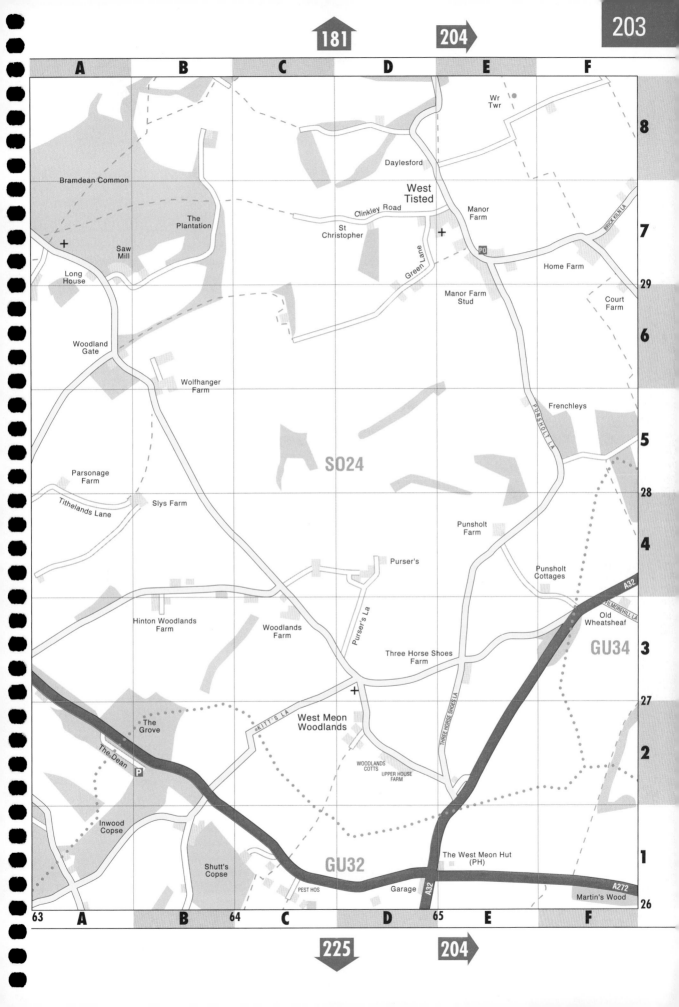

203
182

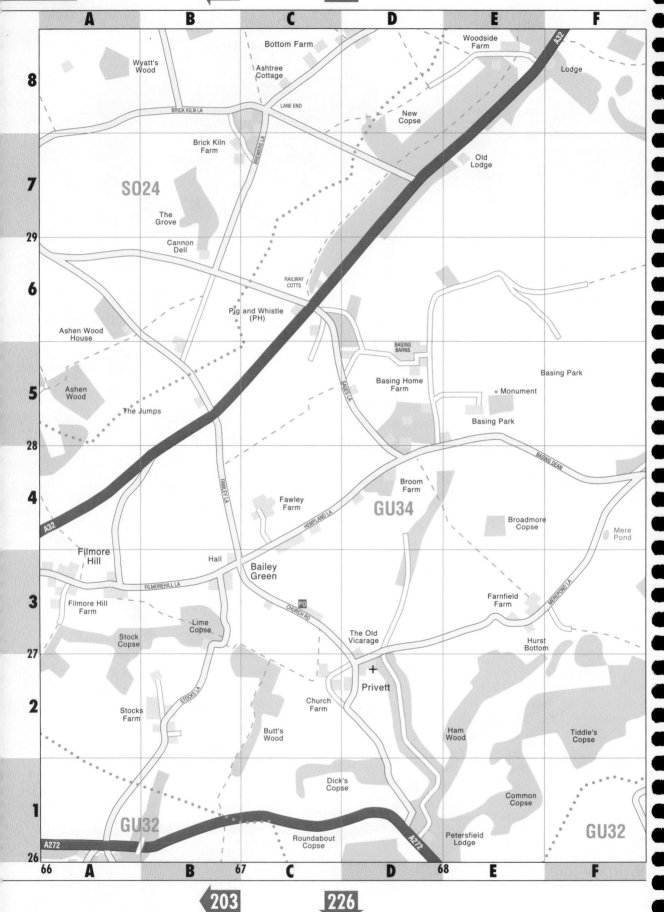

203
226

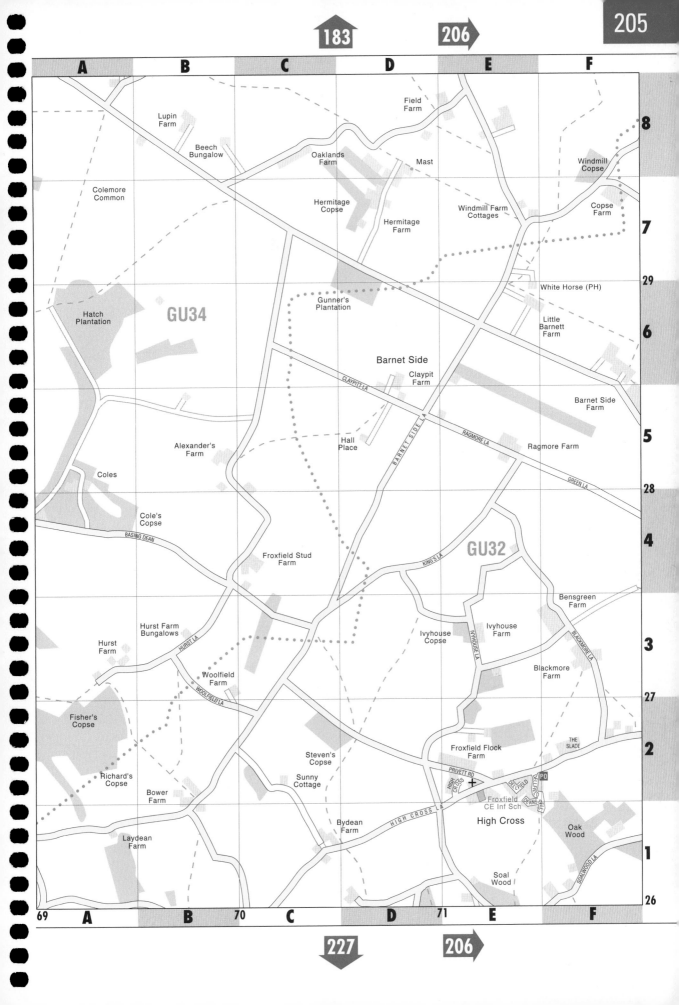

205
184

A **B** **C** **D** **E** **F**

8

Church Farm

Manor House

GU34

Lowergreen Farm

Lower Green

Champlers Farm

7

Five Ash Farm

Hawkley Hanger

Hawkley

29

UPPER GN

PH

POCOCKS LA

ROMEFIELD COTTS

MILL LA

LEARS LA

HAWKLEY RD

6

Warren Farm

Tubb's Farm

Cheesecombe Farm

CHEESECOMBE FARM LA

Oakshott Stream

5

The Warren

Reston Hanger

Oakshott Farm

Moore's Copse

GU33

Warren Corner

Shaw Wood

Roundhills Hanger

28

Windmill Cottage

WARREN LA

Parsons

Happersnapper Hanger

Oakshott

4

GREEN LA

GU32

Hill Farm

Lower Oakshott Farmhouse

HONEYCRITCH LA

Oakshott Hanger

Harder's Way

COTTAGE LA

3

Ringsgreen Copse

PH

TROOPER BOTTOM

WOODFIELD COTTS

Wheatham Hill

Rings Green

Ringsgreen Lane

Woodfield Copse

OLD LITTEN LA

Old Litten Lane

27

Ashford Hill

Shoulder of Mutton Hill

2

HIGH CROSS LA

COCKSHOTT LA

Southdean Farm

Ashford Farm

Week Green Farm

Lutcombe Bottom

ASHFORD CHACE

MILL LA

SOALWOOD LA

Wyke Green Farm

Bushy Hill

1

Pipers Farm

Wyke Green Cottage

STONER HILL RD

Little Langleys

26

72 **A** **B** 73 **C** **D** 74 **E** **F**

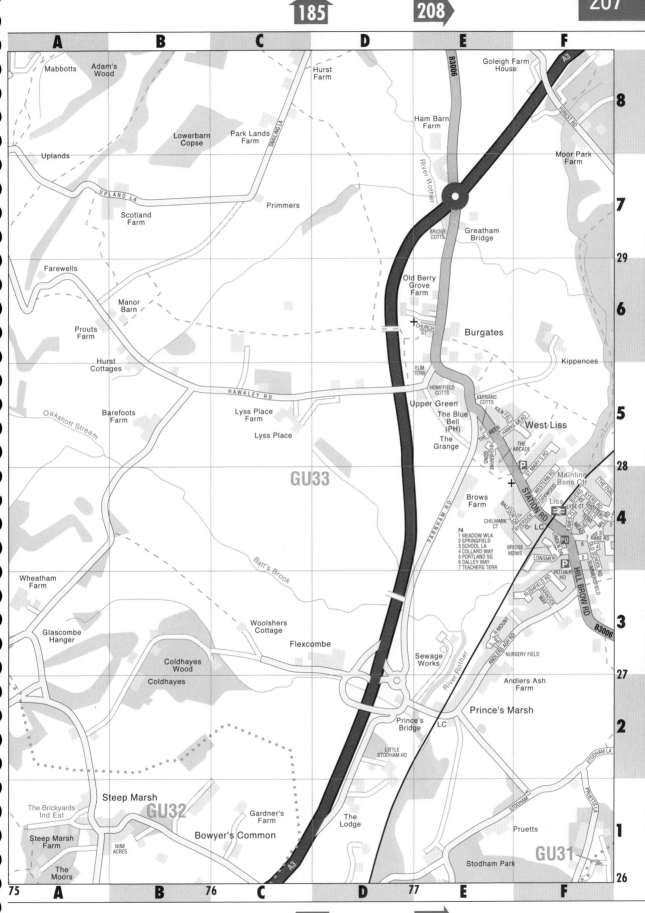

185
208

Mabbotts
Adam's Wood
Hurst Farm
Goleigh Farm House
B3006
A3
Uplands
Lowerbarn Copse
Park Lands Farm
SWAILING LA
Moor Park Farm
UPLAND LA
Scotland Farm
Primmers
River Rother
8
Farewells
BRIDGE COTTS
Greatham Bridge
29
Manor Barn
Old Berry Grove Farm
FOREST RD
Prouts Farm
CHURCH ST
Burgates
7
Hurst Cottages
ELM TERR
Kippences
6
Oakshott Stream
HAWKLEY RD
HOMEFIELD COTTS
Upper Green
KEENANS COTTS
KILN FIELD
West Liss
Barefoots Farm
Lyss Place Farm
The Blue Bell (PH)
HAWKS MEAD
Lyss Place
The Grange
THE GREEN
THE ARCADE
Mainline Bsns Ctr
5
BISHEARNE GDNS
ST MARY'S RD
THE OVAL
GU33
Brows Farm
P
WESTERN RD
YORKWOOD
28
FARNHAM RD
BALFOUR CR
STATION RD
Liss
RIVERSIDE
LC
4
CHILMARK CT
LIMES CT
RAKE RD
F4
1 MEADOW WLK
2 SPRINGFIELD
3 SCHOOL LA
4 COLLARD WAY
5 PORTLAND SQ
6 DALLEY WAY
7 TEACHERS TERR
BRIDGE MDWS
LONGMEAD
P
RUSHFIELD RD
ROTHER HO
SUMMERSFIELD
HILL BROW RD
Wheatham Farm
Batt's Brook
ELM MOUNT
ANDLERS ASH RD
BARNSIDE WAY
B3006
3
Woolshers Cottage
Flexcombe
Nursery Field
27
Glascombe Hanger
Sewage Works
River Rother
Andlers Ash Farm
Coldhayes Wood
Coldhayes
Prince's Marsh
2
Prince's Bridge
LC
LITTLE STODHAM HO
STODHAM LA
The Brickyards Ind Est
Steep Marsh
GU32
Gardner's Farm
Bowyer's Common
The Lodge
Pruetts
PRUETTS LA
1
Steep Marsh Farm
NINE ACRES
STODHAM
GU31
The Moors
A3
Stodham Park
26

75   A   B   76   C   D   77   E   F

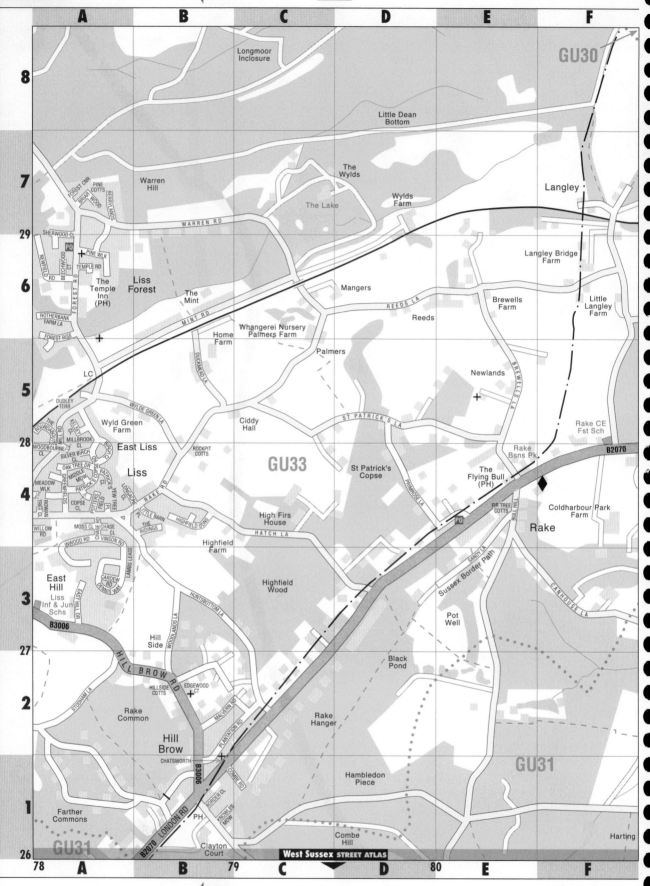

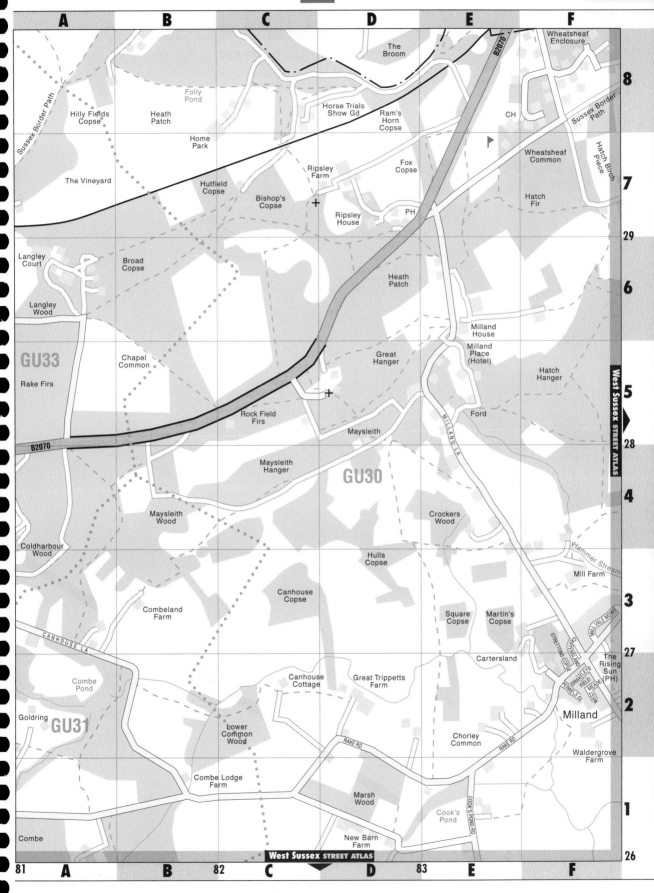

The Broom

Wheatsheaf Enclosure

Folly Pond

Horse Trials Show Gd

Ram's Horn Copse

CH

Sussex Border Path

Hilly Fields Copse

Heath Patch

Home Park

Wheatsheaf Common

Hatch Birch Piece

Ripsley Farm

Fox Copse

The Vineyard

Hutfield Copse

Bishop's Copse

Ripsley House

PH

Hatch Fir

Langley Court

Broad Copse

Heath Patch

Milland House

Langley Wood

Milland Place (Hotel)

GU33

Chapel Common

Great Hanger

Hatch Hanger

Rake Firs

Rock Field Firs

Maysleith

Ford

Maysleith Hanger

GU30

Maysleith Wood

Coldharbour Wood

Crockers Wood

Hammer Stream

Mill Farm

Hulls Copse

Canhouse Copse

Square Copse

Martin's Copse

Combeland Farm

CANHOUSE LA

Cartersland

STREETONS COPSE

MILL VALE MDWS

The Rising Sun (PH)

Combe Pond

Canhouse Cottage

Great Trippetts Farm

Milland

Goldring

GU31

Lower Common Wood

RAKE RD

Chorley Common

RAKE RD

Waldergrove Farm

Combe Lodge Farm

Marsh Wood

COOK'S POND RD

Cook's Pond

Combe

New Barn Farm

B2070

Milland La

B2070

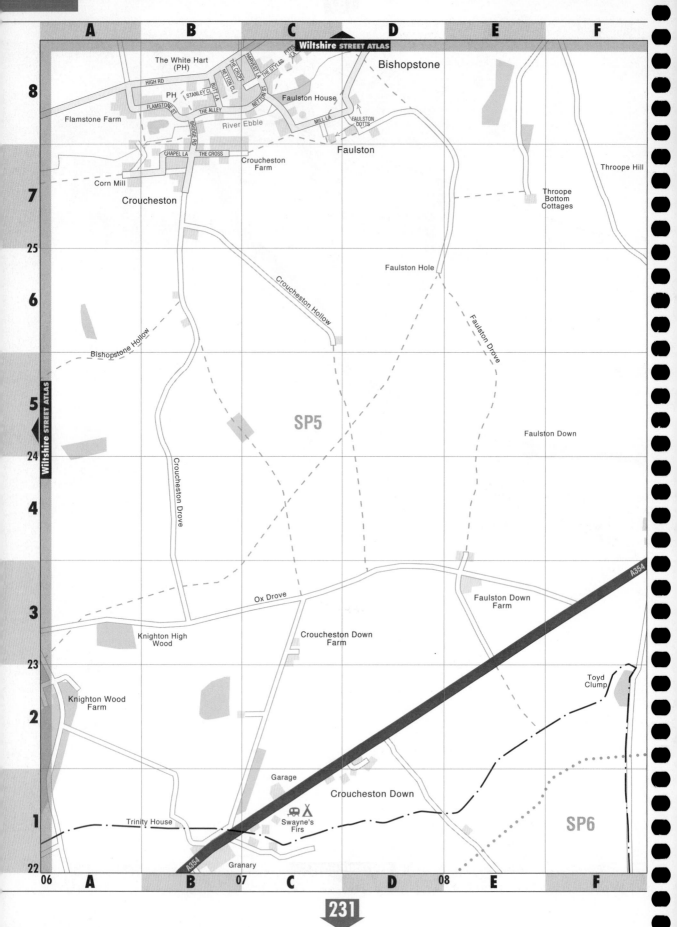

Bishopstone

The White Hart (PH)

HIGH RD

PH

STANLEY CL

THE CROFT

NETTON CL

BUTT LA

HARVEST LA

THE STYLES

PITTS LA

NETTON ST

Faulston House

MILL LA

FAULSTON COTTS

The Alley

FLAMSTONE ST

BRIDGE RD

River Ebble

Flamstone Farm

CHAPEL LA

THE CROSS

Croucheston Farm

Faulston

Corn Mill

Croucheston

Throope Hill

Throope Bottom Cottages

Faulston Hole

Croucheston Hollow

Faulston Drove

Bishopstone Hollow

SP5

Faulston Down

Croucheston Drove

Ox Drove

Faulston Down Farm

Knighton High Wood

Croucheston Down Farm

A354

Toyd Clump

Knighton Wood Farm

Garage

Croucheston Down

SP6

Trinity House

Swayne's Firs

A354

Granary

Wiltshire STREET ATLAS

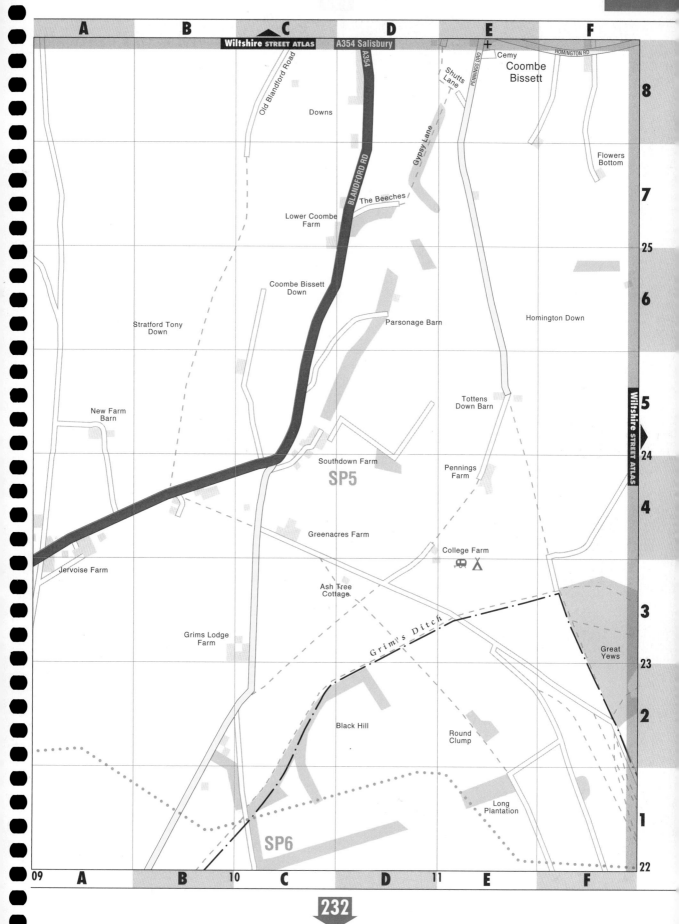

A354 Salisbury

Old Blandford Road

Downs

BLANDFORD RD

A354

The Beeches

Lower Coombe Farm

Gypsy Lane

Shutts Lane

PENNINGS DRO

Cemy

Coombe Bissett

HOMINGTON RD

Flowers Bottom

Coombe Bissett Down

Stratford Tony Down

Parsonage Barn

Homington Down

New Farm Barn

Tottens Down Barn

Southdown Farm

SP5

Pennings Farm

Greenacres Farm

College Farm

Jervoise Farm

Ash Tree Cottage

Grims Ditch

Grims Lodge Farm

Great Yews

Black Hill

Round Clump

Long Plantation

SP6

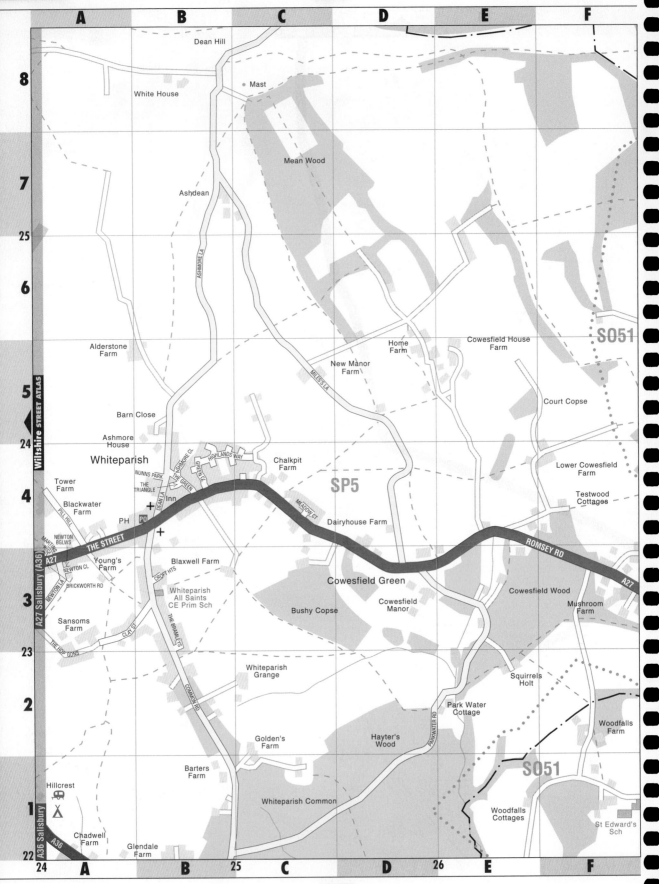

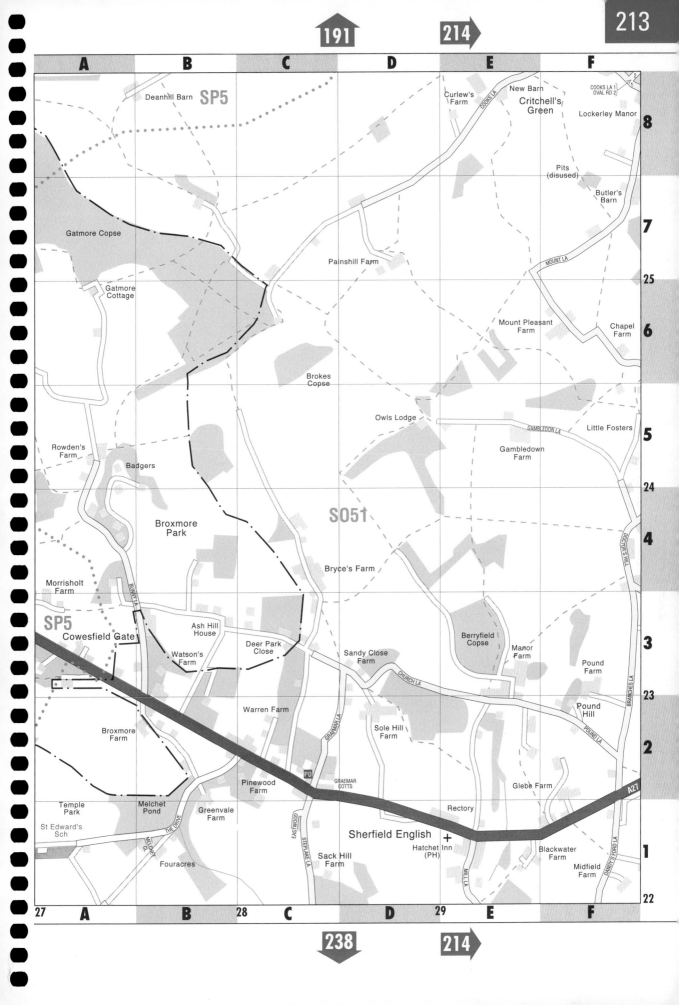

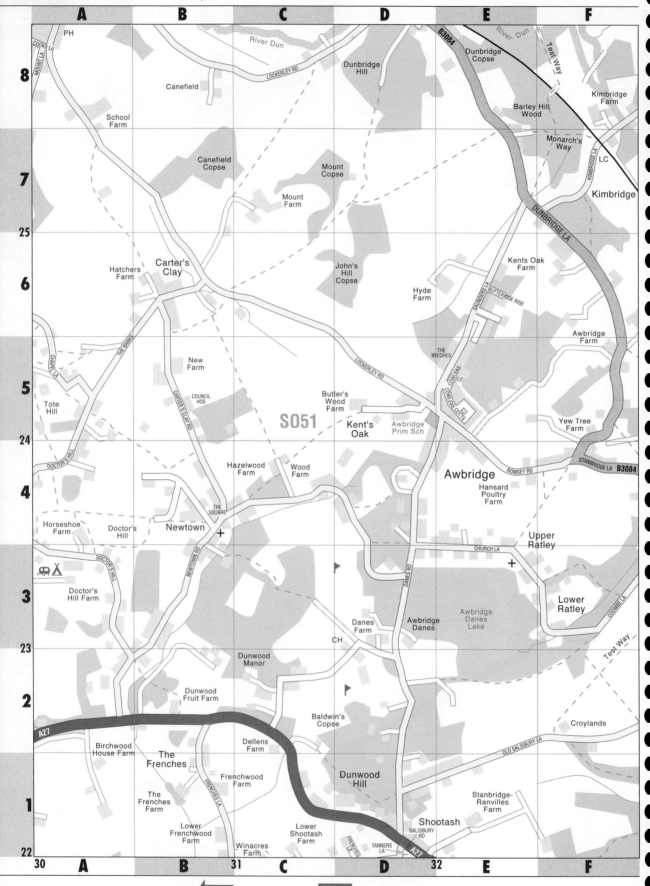

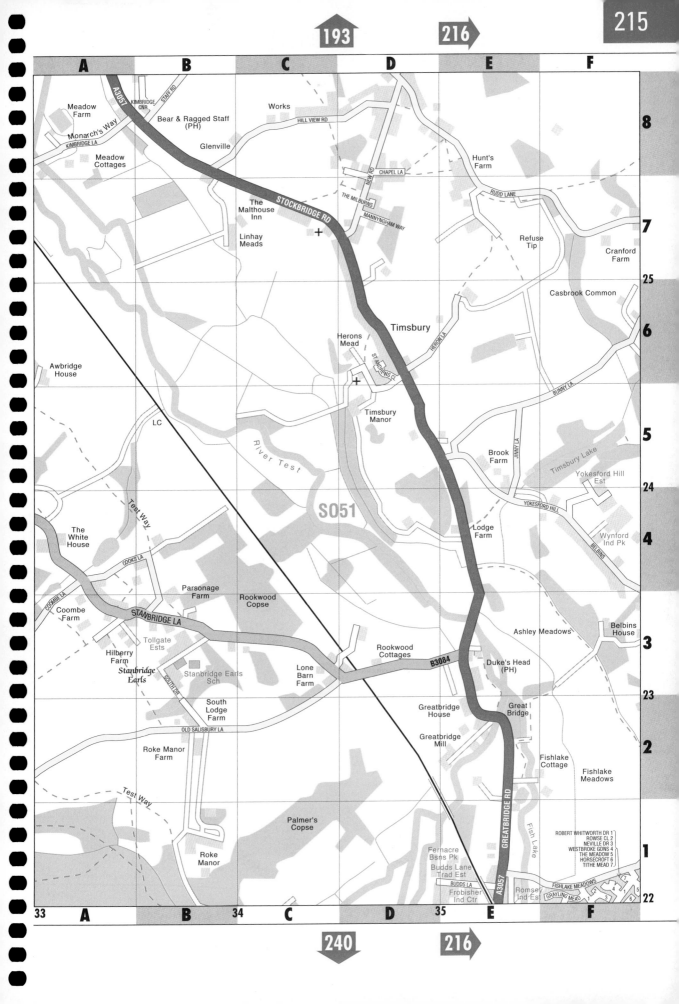

215
194

A | B | C | D | E | F

8

Malthouse Farm

Monarch's Way

Merrie Meade Farm

FERN HILL LANE

ELDON RD

PAYNES HAY RD

Paynes Hay Farm

7

RUDD LA

WHITE LADIES

Sharpes Farm

LOWER ST

Braishfield

CHURCH LA

DUMMERS RD

Monarch's Way

Hawkes Farm

Churchers Barn

25

BUNNY LA

NEWPORT LA

The Newport Inn (PH)

CHAPEL CL

BLACKTHORN CL

HILL VIEW RD

GARDINERS CNR

P

DORES LA

Pucknall

COMMON HILL RD

Pucknall Farm

6

Fairbourne Lake

KILN LA

Braishfield Prim Sch

The Wheatsheaf Inn (PH)

Round Copse

Fairbournes Farm

The Homestead

SO51

5

Dog & Crook (PH)

MEGANA WAY

24

Abbotswood Farm

BRAISHFIELD RD

Crookhill Farm

Sir Harold Hillier Gardens & Arboretum

4

The Bog

Jermyns House

JERMYNS LA

Outwood Lodge

A3090

BELBINS

SANDY LA

Belbins Bsns Pk WESTLINK

P

Cemy

Bracken Wood

3

CUPERNHAM LA

Abbotswood

Abbotswood House

Nursery

THE STRAIGHT MILE

South Holmes Copse

23

WOODLEY CLOSE FLATS

WOODLEY CL

Ganger Farm

2

Oxlease

ROMSEY

Cupernham

WOODLEY LA

GANGER FARM LA

WOODLEY WAY

GANGER RD

FOOTNER CL

ANDERSON CL

NORRIS CL

Woodley

Woodlands

Ganger Wood

Crampmoor Farm

GROVELY WAY

CRAMPMOOR LA

1

THE MEADOW

FISHLAKE MDWS

OXLEASE

CANALSIDE RD

RICHMOND LA

BROOK WAY

CAVENDISH CL

KINVER CL

STAPLEFORD CL

WARREN GDNS

AINSLIE RD

OAKWOOD

ABBOTS CL

BRAISLEY

WAVERLEY

LINCOLN CL

ADDISON

BEVERLEY GDNS

WESTERING

PINEWOOD CL

CEDAR LAWN

SHORT HILL

SCHOOL RD

NORTH CL

THE GREEN

HUNTER CL

SOUTH CL

DIBBEN WLK

THE COPSE

PEEL CL

1 GRANGE MEWS
2 COWSLIP WAY
3 HALTERWORTH LA
4 ST SWITHUN'S CL

Crampmoor

GREEN LA

22

FISHLAKE MDWS

SMITH'S FIELD

DURBAN CL

CUPERNHAM LA

Cupernham Inf & Jun Schs

RALPH LA

CARISBROOKE CL

FAIRVIEW DR

FAIRVIEW CL

WINTERBOURNE RD

WINCHESTER HILL

PO

PRIMROSE WAY

A3090 WINCHESTER RD

BRIAR WAY

SORREL CL

CONFREY CL

COLNSWOOD WLK

CAMPION DR

CLOVER WAY

BRAMBLE DR

36 | A | 37 | B | C | 37 | D | 38 | E | F

215
241

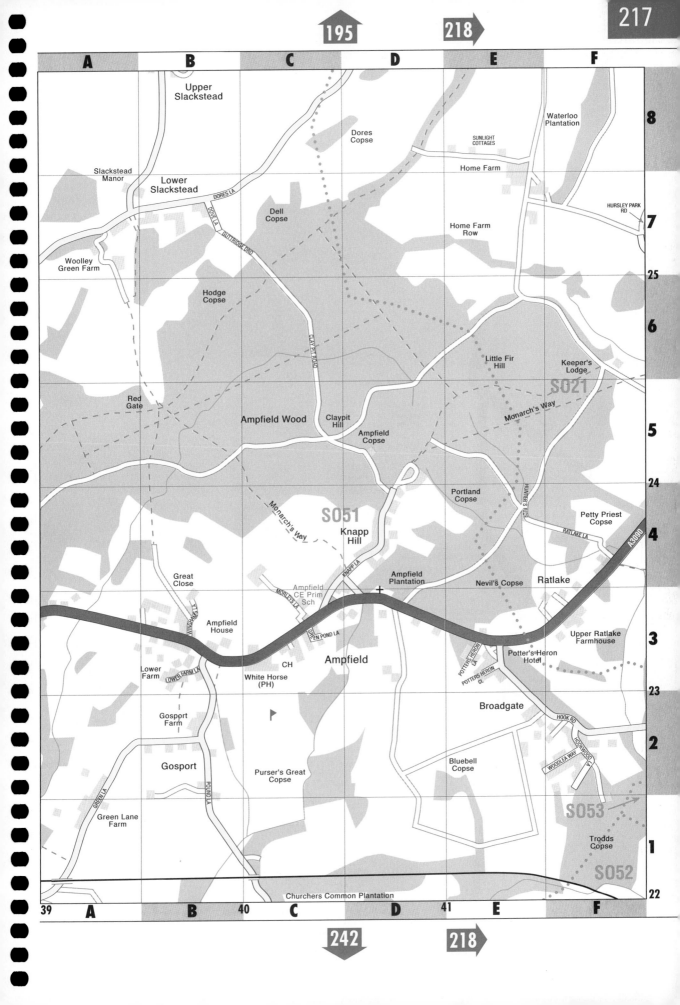

217 196

A B C D E F

8

7

25

6

5

24

4

3

23

2

1

22

42 43 44

A B C D E F

217 243

A3090

Hursley Park Rd
King's Head Inn
KEBLE CL
CATWAYS
HEATHCOTE PL
COLLINS LA
PORT LA
Shawlands Farm
Cemy
PO
Hursley Park
Hursley
MERCROW CL
SOUTH END CL
PELICAN CT
Parsonage Farm
BUNSTEAD LA
Monarch's Way
Silkstead La
Shepherds La
Hursley Park Rd
John Keble CE Prim Sch
Bunstead
POLES LA
Upper Silkstead Farm
Silkstead
B3043
Brooks Copse
Brooks Way
SO21
Hursley Forest
Weedacre Copse
Lower Silkstead Farmhouse
P
Windmill Copse
Ladwell
Strowdens Copse
Freemantles Copse
Red House
A3090
Kent's Copse
Field House
Wells Row
Cranbury Park
Hawstead Farm
Home Farm
Cranbury House
Great Pond
SO53
Hocombe Plantation
Hocombe
ROTHVILLE PL
Hocombe Bridge
Upper Pond
Hocombe Upper Plantation
HOOK RD
HOOK WATER CL
HOOK WATER RD
HOOK CRES
HOCOMBE WOOD RD
HURSLEY RD
HOCOMBE DR
HOCOMBE PARK CL
TITHEWOOD CL
CHARNWOOD GDNS
CHARNWOOD CRES
CHARNWOOD CL
ASHDOWN CL
ASHDOWN RD
ASHDOWN DR
HOCOMBE RD
Castle Copse
Lower Pond
The Castle
SO51
STANTON CLE
BEECHWOOD CRES
RICHMOND CL
ELM CT
HAZEL CL
WALNUT
HEATHFIELD
MAYTREE RD
HEATHFIELD RD
NICHOLAS RD
WOODLANDS CL
RANDALL RD
COULTAS RD
LAKEWOOD RD
MALCOLM RD
SHERWOOD RD
MARLBOROUGH RD
THORNBURY WOOD
THE GLADE
KINGSWAY
ST MARKS CL
SO52
BEECHWOOD CL
BADDESLEY RD
AVEBURY GDNS
RAMSDOWN GDNS
THE TANYARDS
N MILLERS DALE
SYCAMORE AVE
Hiltingbury
Stewart Ho
PO
Queen's Rd
HILTINGBURY CL
Hiltingbury Inf Sch
Hiltingbury Jun Sch
WESTERN RD
HEATHERDENE RD
MALCOLM RD
FRESHWATER CT
THOROLD RD
GROSVENOR RD
BROXBURN CL
THORNBURY
WINCHESTER RD
MALIBRES RD
Wheelhouse CVN PK
St James CVN PK
THE KING EDWARD CVN PK
FLIPFORD CT
THE WOODLANDS
BRIDGE RISE
ROSEMOOR GR
MILLERS DALE
PINE RD
Cemy
LAIDLAW GDNS
B3043
Cuckoo Bushes
PINE RD
PINE CRES
Recn Gd
Hiltingbury Rd
OAKWOOD
BEECH CL
OAKWOOD CL
OAKWOOD RD
Gordon Rd

B1
1 AMPFIELD CT
2 HURSLEY CT
3 ASHTON PL
4 HILTINGBURY CT
5 CHILLINGTON GDNS
6 VANBURGH WAY
7 LAURISTON DR
8 CRANBORNE GDNS
9 STRATFIELD DR
10 ALBURY PL
11 APSLEY PL
12 ORMESBY DR
13 SIMPKINS CT
14 OAKLANDS

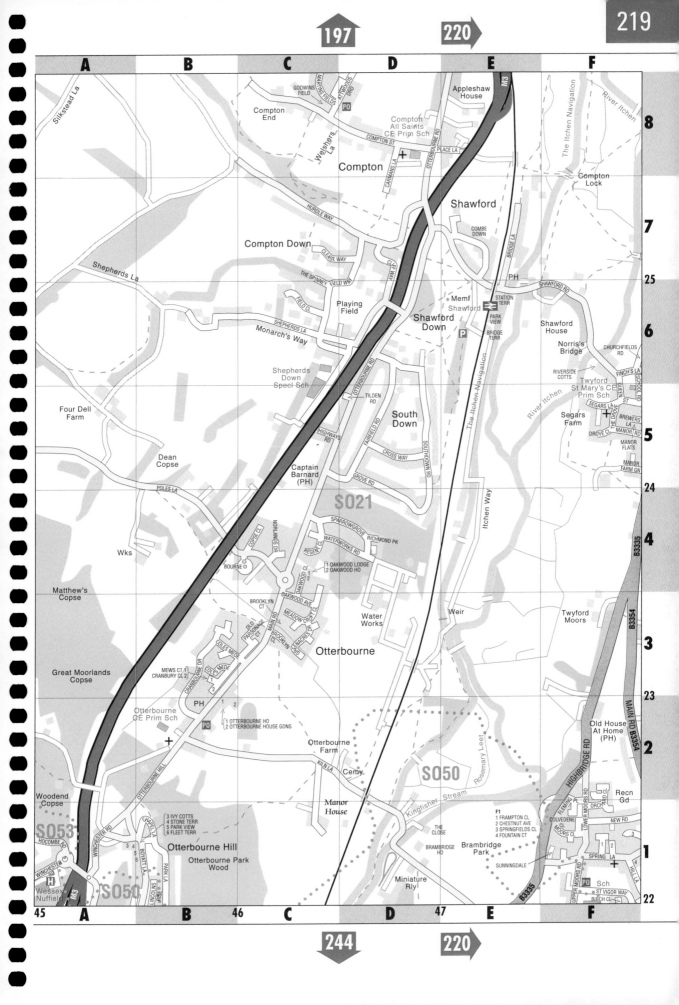

219
198

A B C D E F

8

B3335

Hockley Farm

New Barn Farm

Works

HOCKLEY COTTS

River Itchen

COXS HILL

Hazeley Down

MORESTEAD RD

Morestead

FAWLEY LA

Twyford Lodge

CHURCH LA

HIGH ST

COLES CL

NEWTON RD

KINGS

SHIPLEY RD

North Fields Farm

1 PENTON RD
2 FRANKLIN RD
3 NORTH FIELDS COTTS

Morestead Grange

7

Meml

Pilgrim's Trail

25

BERRY LA

BOURNE FIELDS

Northfields

OLD RECTORY LA

BOURNE LA

HAZELEY RD

HAZELEY FARM COTTS

6

CHURCHFIELDS

SEARLES HILL

Twyford Sch

Twyford

Works

Hazeley Copse

Hazeley Farm

MARE LA

CHURCHFIELDS RD

THE AVENUE

1 ST MARY'S TERR
2 THE CRESCENT

WHATLEY LA

PO

NURSE'S PATH

DOLPHIN HILL

HIGHFIELD

Monarch's Way

HILL RISE

HIGH ST

HIGHFIELD LA

ROMAN RD

LOVE LA

PARK LA

5

HIGH ST

1 THE OLD LAUNDRY
2 QUEEN ST
3 BREWERS LA
4 MANOR RD

P

Roundbushes Copse

HATCHERS LA

Colleton House

Knighton

24

Cockscomb Hill Farm

Hazelwood Farm

SO21

HARE LANE

4

Hensting Valley Farm

Gabriel's Copse

Cockscomb Hill Copse

WHITES HILL

Watley Lane

3

WOODLAND DROVE

Hill View Farm

Whites Hill Farm

23

Meadow View Farm

2

B3354

Taylor's Copse

Colden Common Park

HENSTING LA

Boyes' Copse

SO50

NEW RD

MAIN RD

BOYES LA

P

Park Copse

Hensting Farm

Water Lane

1

SPRING LA

Colden Common

SPRING HOUSE CL

King's Copse

Elm Farm

ASH CL

AVONDALE MOBILE HOME PK

B3354

Hensting

Horsham Copse

22

48 A B 49 C D 50 E F

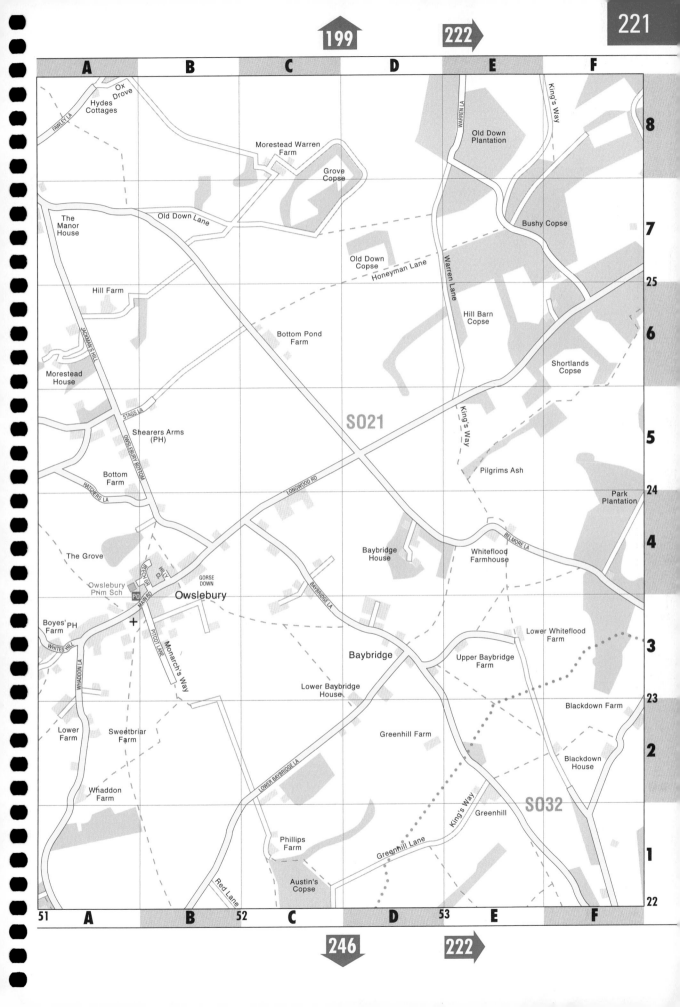

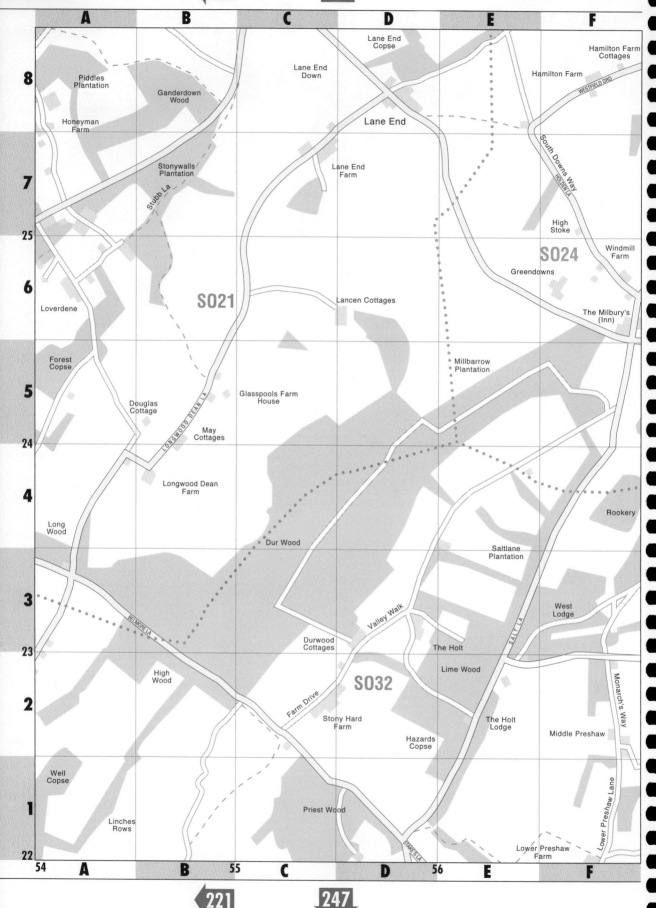

A B C D E F

8 Piddles Plantation
Ganderdown Wood
Lane End Copse
Lane End Down
Hamilton Farm Cottages
Honeyman Farm
Hamilton Farm
WESTFIELD DRO
Lane End

7 Stonywalls Plantation
Lane End Farm
Stubb La
South Downs Way
HOLDEN LA

25 High Stoke

6 Loverdene
SO21
Lancen Cottages
SO24
Greendowns
Windmill Farm

The Milbury's (Inn)
Forest Copse
Millbarrow Plantation

5 Douglas Cottage
Glasspools Farm House
LONGWOOD DEAN LA
May Cottages

24 Longwood Dean Farm

4 Long Wood
Rookery
Dur Wood
Saltlane Plantation

3 BELMORE LA
Valley Walk
West Lodge
SALT LA

23 Durwood Cottages
The Holt
Lime Wood

2 High Wood
SO32
Farm Drive
Stony Hard Farm
The Holt Lodge
Middle Preshaw
Monarch's Way
Hazards Copse
Lower Preshaw Lane

1 Well Copse
Priest Wood

22 Linches Rows
STARE'S LA
Lower Preshaw Farm

54 A B 55 C D 56 E F

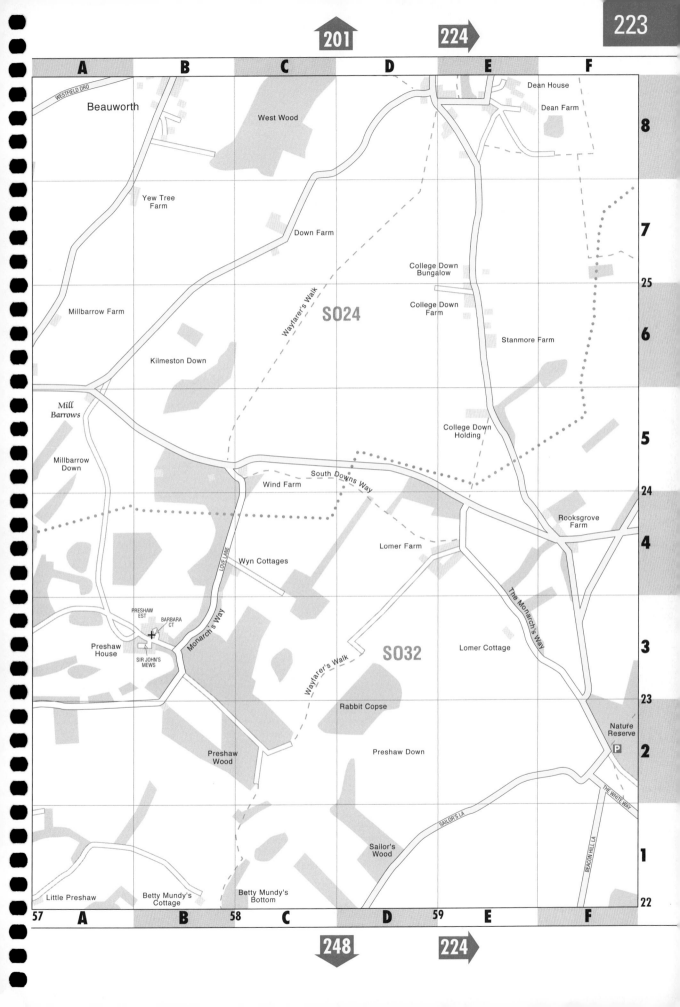

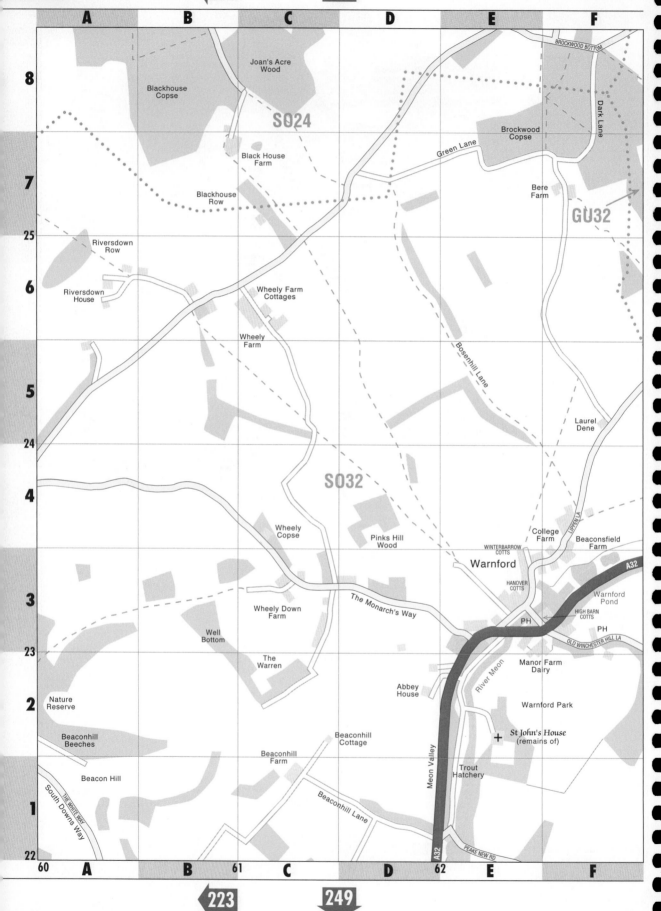

SO24

GU32

Joan's Acre Wood

Blackhouse Copse

BROCKWOOD BOTTOM

Brockwood Copse

Dark Lane

Green Lane

Black House Farm

Bere Farm

Blackhouse Row

Riversdown Row

Riversdown House

Wheely Farm Cottages

Wheely Farm

Bosenhill Lane

Laurel Dene

SO32

Wheely Copse

Pinks Hill Wood

College Farm

LIPPEN LA

Beaconsfield Farm

WINTERBARROW COTTS

Warnford

A32

HANOVER COTTS

Warnford Pond

PH

HIGH BARN COTTS

PH

Wheely Down Farm

The Monarch's Way

OLD WINCHESTER HILL LA

Well Bottom

Manor Farm Dairy

The Warren

Abbey House

River Meon

Warnford Park

Nature Reserve

St John's House (remains of)

Beaconhill Beeches

Beaconhill Cottage

Beaconhill Farm

Meon Valley

Trout Hatchery

Beacon Hill

THE WHITE WAY

South Downs Way

Beaconhill Lane

A32

PEAKE NEW RD

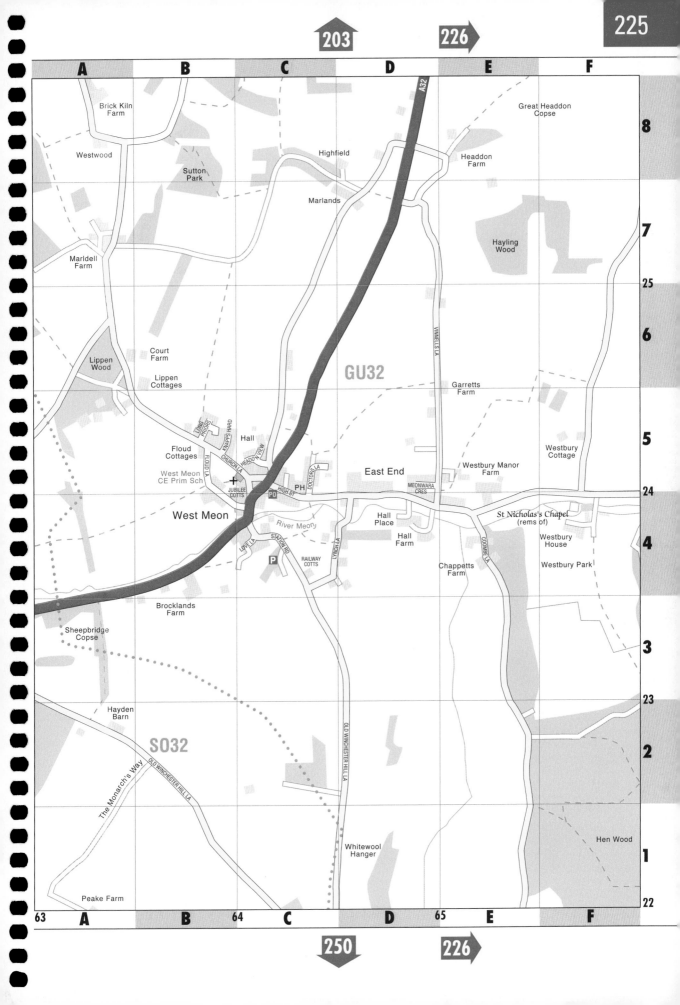

203
226

A B C D E F

8

Brick Kiln Farm

Great Headdon Copse

Westwood

Highfield

Sutton Park

Headdon Farm

Marlands

7

Marldell Farm

Hayling Wood

25

6

Court Farm

Lippen Wood

GU32

Lippen Cottages

Garretts Farm

LONG PRIVETT
KNAPPS HARD

Hall

Westbury Cottage

5

Fleud Cottages

HEADON VIEW

Westbury Manor Farm

FLOUD LA

CHURCH LA

DOCTORS LA

East End

West Meon CE Prim Sch

HIGH ST

PH

MEONWARA CRES

JUBILEE COTTS

PO

St Nicholas's Chapel
(rems of)

24

West Meon

River Meon

Hall Place

Westbury House

4

LOVE LA

STATION RD

Hall Farm

LYNCH LA

COOMBE LA

Westbury Park

P

RAILWAY COTTS

Chappetts Farm

Brocklands Farm

3

Sheepbridge Copse

23

Hayden Barn

OLD WINCHESTER HILL LA

2

SO32

The Monarch's Way

OLD WINCHESTER HILL LA

Hen Wood

1

Whitewool Hanger

Peake Farm

22

A32
VINNELLS LA

225
204

A B C D E F

8

7

25

6

5

24

4

3

23

2

1

22

Arbor Trees Farm

Redwood Cottage

Red Wood

Peak Farm

Kingsland Copse

Great Copyhold Copse

Old Down

Old Down Farm

GU34

A272

War Hill

Warhill Cottage

Park House

Upper Bordean House

Upper Bordean Farm

Bordean Barn

Tigwell Copse

Mare Pond

Trenleygrove Plantation

Trenley Grove

Burrow Plantation

GU32

Tigwell Cottages

Tigwell Farm

East Lodge

Bereleigh Cottage

Orchard Plantation

Riplington

River Meon

Drayton House

Drayton Farm

Bereleigh House

Park Cottages

Park Farm

Park Cottages

Riplington Hanger

Drayton Cottages

Drayton

Horsedown Farm

Drayton Mill

Mascoombe Bottom

Emmet's Down

Drayton Down

Halnaker Lane

Chalk Dell Cottages

Park Hill

Park Hill

Vineyard Hole

Hen Wood

Middle Down

Sewage Works

Yew Down

1 FORBES ALMSHOUSES
2 TEMPLE LA
3 WESTBROOKE COTTS

Frogmore

Gravel Lane

East Meon

East Meon CE Prim Sch

WORKHOUSE LA

PARK VISTA

THE CROSS

THE GREEN

CHIDDEN

HILL VIEW

CHAPEL ST

GLENTHORNE MEADOW

CHURCH ST

HIGH ST

Court House

PH

PO

EAME'S COTTS

GREENWAY

66 A B 67 C D 68 E F

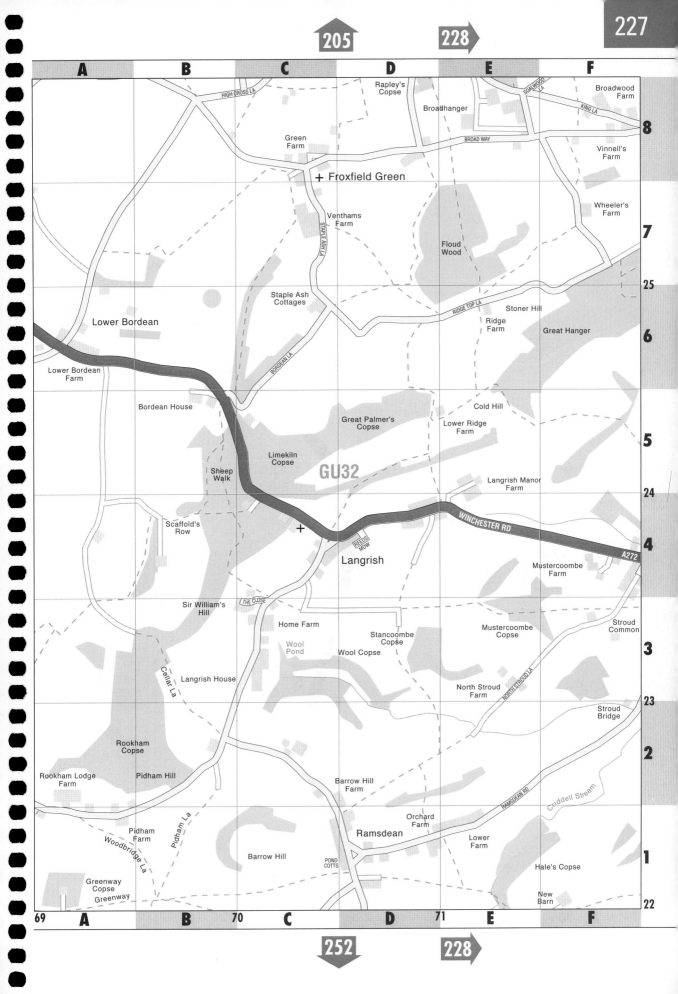

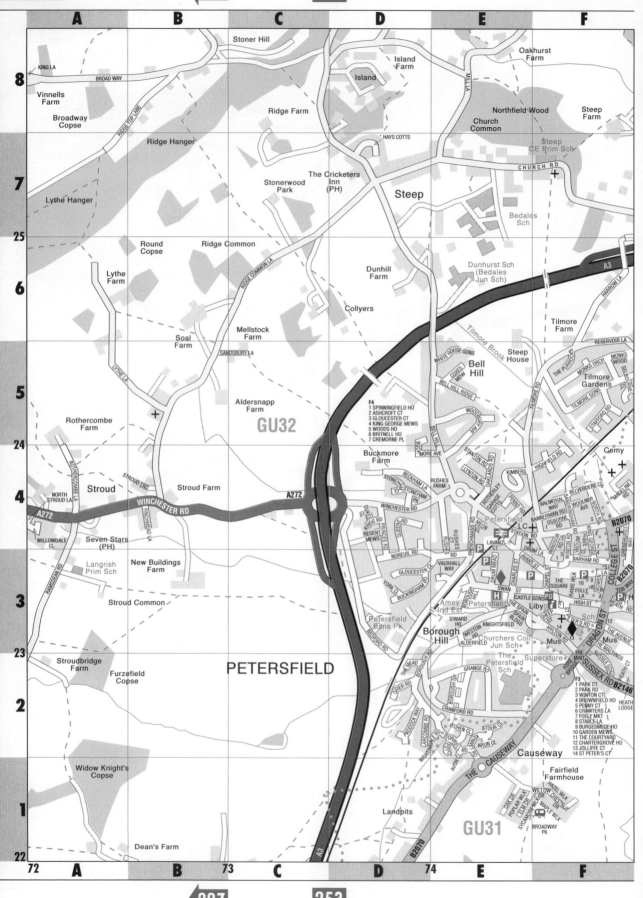

A	B	C	D	E	F

8 King La — BROAD WAY — Stoner Hill — Island Farm — Island — Oakhurst Farm

Vinnells Farm — Broadway Copse — RIDGE TOP LANE — Ridge Farm — Northfield Wood — Church Common — Steep Farm

Ridge Hanger — HAYS COTTS — Steep CE Prim Sch

CHURCH RD

7 Lythe Hanger — Stonerwood Park — The Cricketers Inn (PH) — Steep — Bedales Sch

25

Round Copse — Ridge Common — Dunhill Farm — Dunhurst Sch (Bedales Jun Sch) — A3

6 Lythe Farm — RIDGE COMMON LA — Collyers — Tilmore Farm — HARROW LA — RESERVOIR LA

Soal Farm — Mellstock Farm — SANDSBURY LA — WHITE HOUSE GDNS — Steep House — MONKS ORCH — MONKS WOOD — Tilmore Gardens — TILMORE GDNS

LYTHE LA — Bell Hill — BELL HILL RIDGE — Bell Hill

5 Rothercombe Farm — Aldersnapp Farm — **GU32** — F4
1 SPINNINGFIELD HO
2 ASHCROFT CT
3 GLOUCESTER CT
4 KING GEORGE MEWS
5 WOODS HO
6 BRITNELL HO
7 CREMORNE PL — Cemy

24 ROTHERCOMBE LA — STROUD END — Buckmore Farm — MORE AVE — STANTON RD — KIMBERS — HIGHFIELD RD — B2070

NORTH STROUD LA — Stroud — Stroud Farm — A272 — BECKHAM LA — STONEHAM — RUSHES FARM — LYNTON RD — OAKLANDS RD — BELVEDERE CL — WOOLNER AVE — NORTH RD — MADELINE

4 A272 — WINCHESTER RD — WINCHESTER RD — BALMORAL WAY — BANNERMAN RD — OSBORNE RD — KING GEORGE — B2070

WILLOWDALE CL — Seven Stars (PH) — FINCHDEAN LA — DUKES KINGS CL — REGENT MEWS — S RD — MEON — Petersfield — STATION RD — DRUM LA — BARHAM RD

3 RAMSDEAN RD — Langrish Prim Sch — New Buildings Farm — NOREUIL RD — RUSHES — PRENCHAM — LAVANT — CHARLES ST — CHAPEL ST — HIGH ST — FOLLY LA — HEATH RD — PTH

GLOUCESTER CL — SWAN ST — THE SQUARE — RAMS WLK — TOR WAY

Stroud Common — YORA CL — BUCKINGHAM RD — VAUXHALL WAY — Amey Ind Est — Petersfield — Liby — THE AVENUE — DRAGON ST

23 Stroudbridge Farm — Petersfield Bsns Pk — BEDFORD RD — Borough Hill — WESTON KNIGHTSFIELD — SIWARD RD — ALDERFIELD — Churchers Coll Jun Sch — Mus — The Mint — Mus — THE MALTINGS

PETERSFIELD — Furzefield Copse — The Petersfield Sch — GRANGE RD — Superstore — SUSSEX RD — B2146

2 OSIER RD — BOROUGH RD — CRANFORD RD — F3
1 PARK CT
2 PARK RD
3 WINTON CT
4 BROWNFIELD HO
5 PENNY CT
6 CRAWTERS LA
7 FOLLY MKT
8 STABLE LA
9 BURGESMEDE HO
10 GARDEN MEWS
11 THE COURTYARD
12 CHARTERGROVE HO
13 JOLLIFFE CT
14 ST PETER'S CT — HEATH LODGE

THE MEAD — PADDOCK WAY — LARCOMBE RD — NIGHTINGALE RD — ITCHEN CL — ORELL RD — ARUN CL — STOUR CL — Causeway — Fairfield Farmhouse

1 Widow Knight's Copse — Landpits — THE CAUSEWAY — OAK CRES — POPLAR WLK — WILLOW DR — HAZEL WLK — CHESTNUT DR — BROADWAY PK — **GU31**

MAPLE WLK — SYCAMORE WLK

22 Dean's Farm — B2070 — A3

72	A	B	73	C	D	E	74	F

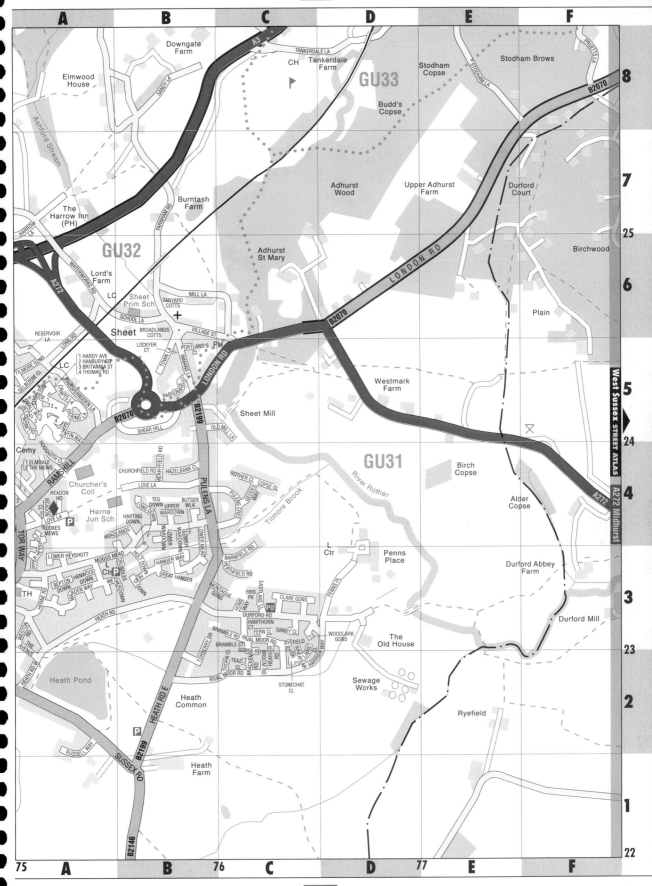

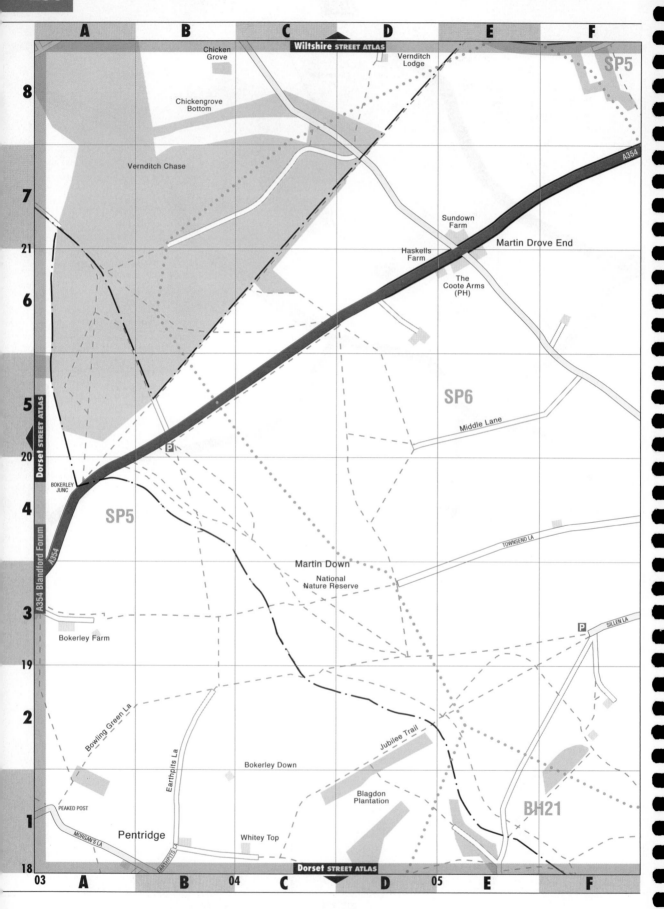

SP5

A354

8

7

21

Vernditch Chase

Chicken Grove

Chickengrove Bottom

Vernditch Lodge

Sundown Farm

Haskells Farm

Martin Drove End

The Coote Arms (PH)

6

SP6

5

Middle Lane

20

BOKERLEY JUNC

SP5

4

Bokerley Farm

Martin Down

National Nature Reserve

TOWNSEND LA

SILLEN LA

3

19

Bowling Green La

Earthpits La

Bokerley Down

Jubilee Trail

Blagdon Plantation

BH21

2

1

PEAKED POST

Pentridge

MORGAN'S LA

EARTHPITS LA

Whitey Top

18

Dorset STREET ATLAS

A354 Blandford Forum

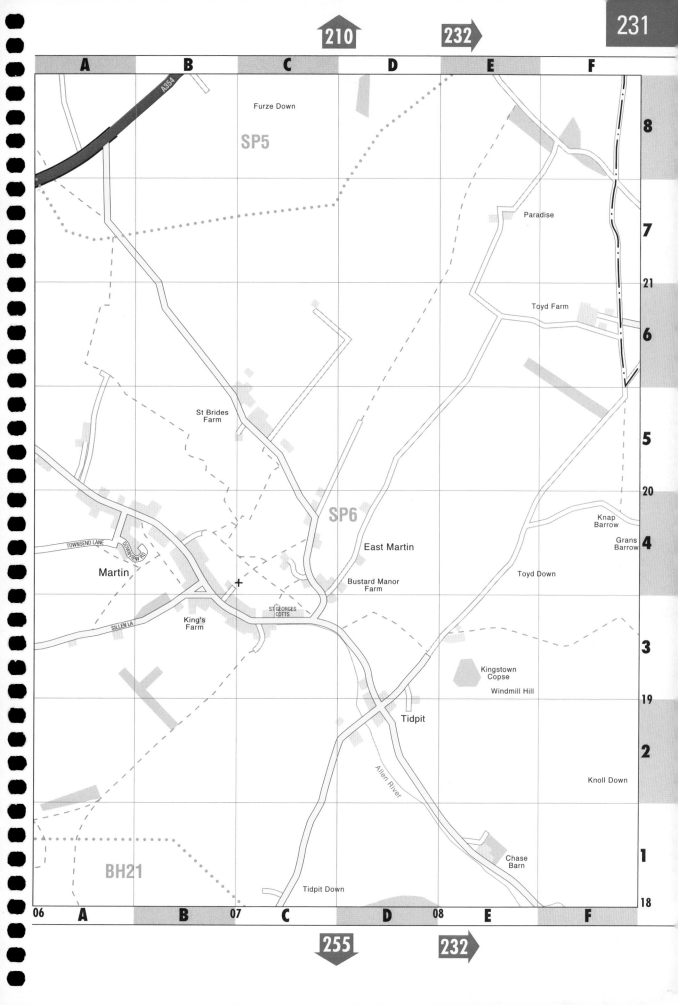

232

A B C D E F

8

Furze Down

SP5

Paradise

7

21

Toyd Farm

6

St Brides
Farm

5

20

SP6

Knap
Barrow

East Martin

Grans
Barrow

4

TOWNSEND LANE

DOWNTOWN RD

Toyd Down

Martin

Bustard Manor
Farm

ST GEORGES
CDTTS

King's
Farm

SILLEN LA

Kingstown
Copse

3

Windmill Hill

19

Tidpit

2

Allen River

Knoll Down

Chase
Barn

1

BH21

Tidpit Down

18

231
211

A B C D E F

8

Little Toyd
Farm

Whitsbury Down

Rockbourne Down

Tenantry
Farm

7

21

Northayes
Farm

Dairy
Buildings

Cranway
Farm

6

Scotland Farm
Cottage

5

Duck's Nest
Long Barrow

SP6

20

DOWN FARM
COTTS

4

Down
Farm

3

Glebe Farm
Cottages

Glebe
Farm

Provost
Farm

Dunberry
Hill

Knoll Down

19

Bokerley Dyke
Plantation

2

Honeysuckle
Farm

Lime Kiln
Farm

MANOR FARM
COTTS

Newbourne
Farm

The Mushroom
Farm

Damerham
Knoll

NEW RD

Manor Farm
Manor House

The Rose & Thistle
(PH)

1

Rockbourne

Western Downland
CE Prim Sch

BOURNE
COTTS

18

09 A B 10 C D 11 E F

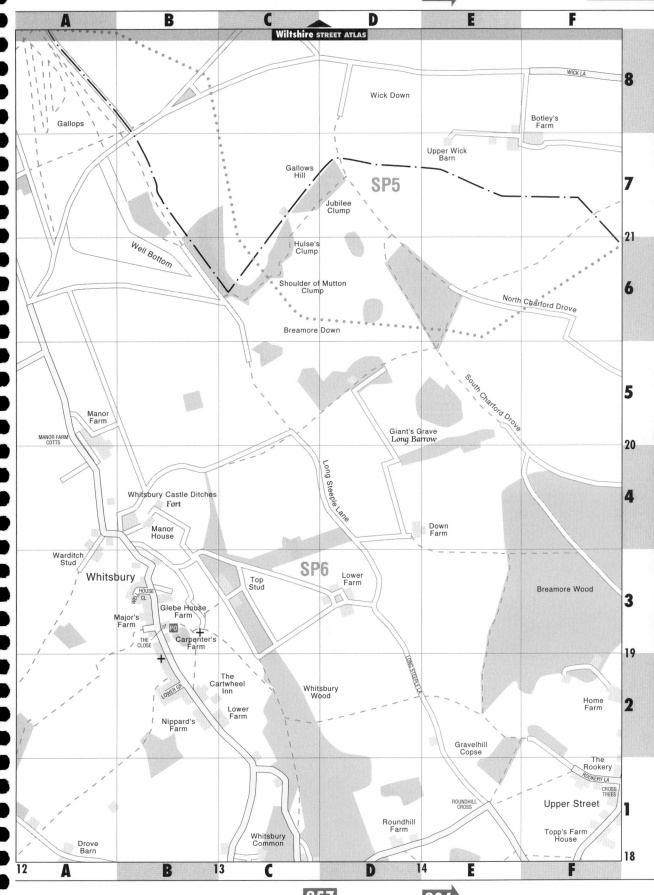

A B C D E F

8

Wick Down

Botley's
Farm

Upper Wick
Barn

SP5

7

21

Gallops

Gallows
Hill

Jubilee
Clump

Well Bottom

Hulse's
Clump

6

North Charford Drove

Shoulder of Mutton
Clump

Breamore Down

South Charford Drove

5

Manor
Farm

20

MANOR FARM
COTTS

Giant's Grave
Long Barrow

4

Whitsbury Castle Ditches
Fort

Long Steeple Lane

Manor
House

Down
Farm

Breamore Wood

Warditch
Stud

Whitsbury

SP6

3

WELL
HOUSE
CL

Top
Stud

Lower
Farm

Major's
Farm

Glebe House
Farm

PO

THE
CLOSE

Carpenter's
Farm

19

LOWER GR

The
Cartwheel
Inn

LONG STEEPLE LA

Home
Farm

2

Nippard's
Farm

Lower
Farm

Whitsbury
Wood

Gravelhill
Copse

The
Rookery

ROOKERY LA

CROSS
TREES

Roundhill
Farm

ROUNDHILL
CROSS

Upper Street

1

Drove
Barn

Whitsbury
Common

Topp's Farm
House

18

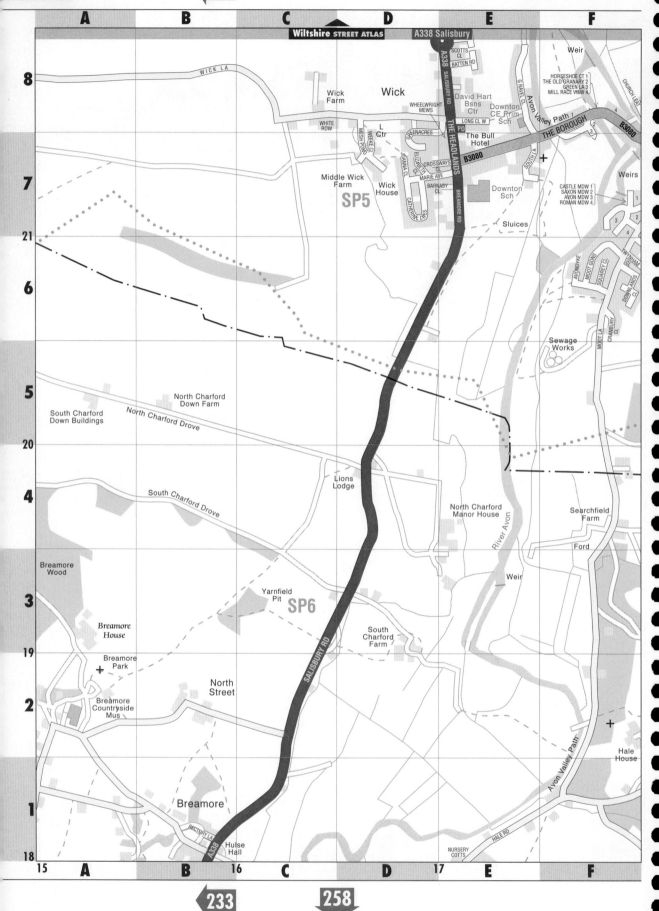

Wiltshire STREET ATLAS | A338 Salisbury

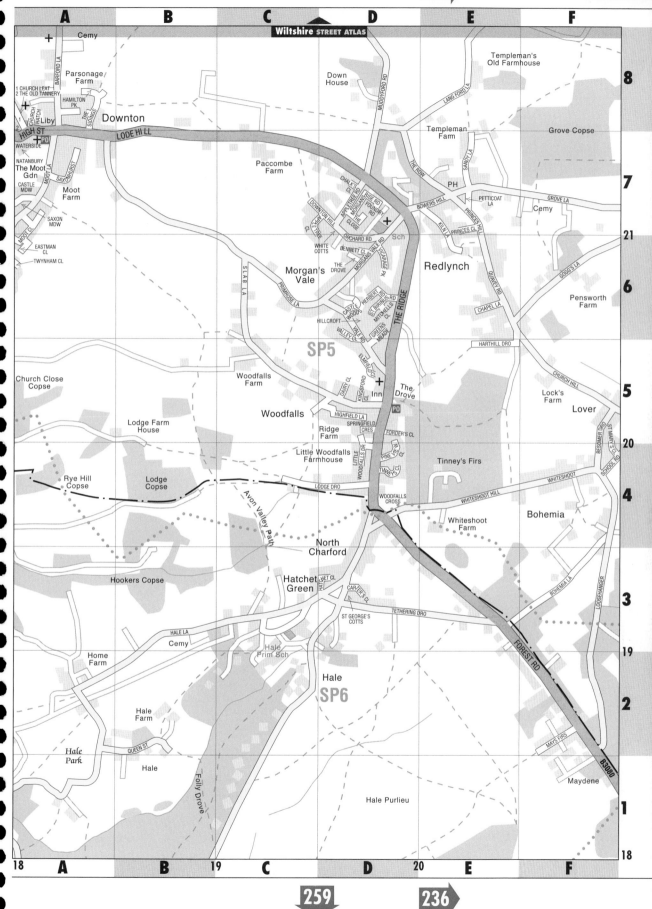

Wiltshire STREET ATLAS

A **B** **C** **D** **E** **F**

Cemy

8
Templeman's
Old Farmhouse

Parsonage
Farm
Down
House

1 CHURCH LEAT
2 THE OLD TANNERY
Hamilton
PK
Grove Copse

HAMILTON
Liby
Templeman
Farm
Downton
LODE HI LL
PH

HIGH ST
PO
7
WATERSIDE
PETTICOAT
LA
NATANBURY
The Moot
Gdn
Paccombe
Farm
Cemy
CASTLE
MDW
CHALK'S
BOWERS HILL
GROVE LA

Moot
Farm
DOWNTON HILL
21
SAXON
MDW
ORCHARD RD
Sch

EASTMAN
CL
WHITE
COTTS
BENNETT CL
Redlynch

TWYNHAM CL
Morgan's
Vale
THE DROVE
6
SLAB LA
Pensworth
Farm
PRIMROSE LA
CASTLE
WOODS
CHAPEL LA

HILLCROFT
HARTHILL DRO

SP5
VALLEY CL

Woodfalls
Farm
DAIRY CL
The
Drove
Lock's
Farm
5
Lover
Woodfalls
Inn
PO
20
Church Close
Copse
HIGHFIELD LA
SPRINGFIELD
CRES
FORDER'S CL

Ridge
Farm
Lodge Farm
House
Little Woodfalls
Farmhouse
PINE CL
Tinney's Firs

TIMMS
LODGE DRO
WHITESHOOT
4
Rye Hill
Copse
Lodge
Copse
Avon Valley Path
Woodfalls
Cross
WHITESHOOT HILL
Bohemia
Whiteshoot
Farm
North
Charford

Hookers Copse
Hatchet
Green
HATCHET CL
3
CARTER'S RD
TETHERING DRO
19
HALE LA
ST GEORGE'S
COTTS

Cemy
Hale
Prim Sch
FOREST RD

Home
Farm
Hale
2
Hale
SP6

Hale
Farm
Hale
MAYS FIRS
QUEEN ST

Hale
Park
Hale
B3080

Folly Drove
Maydene
1

Hale Purlieu

18

235

Wiltshire STREET ATLAS

212
238

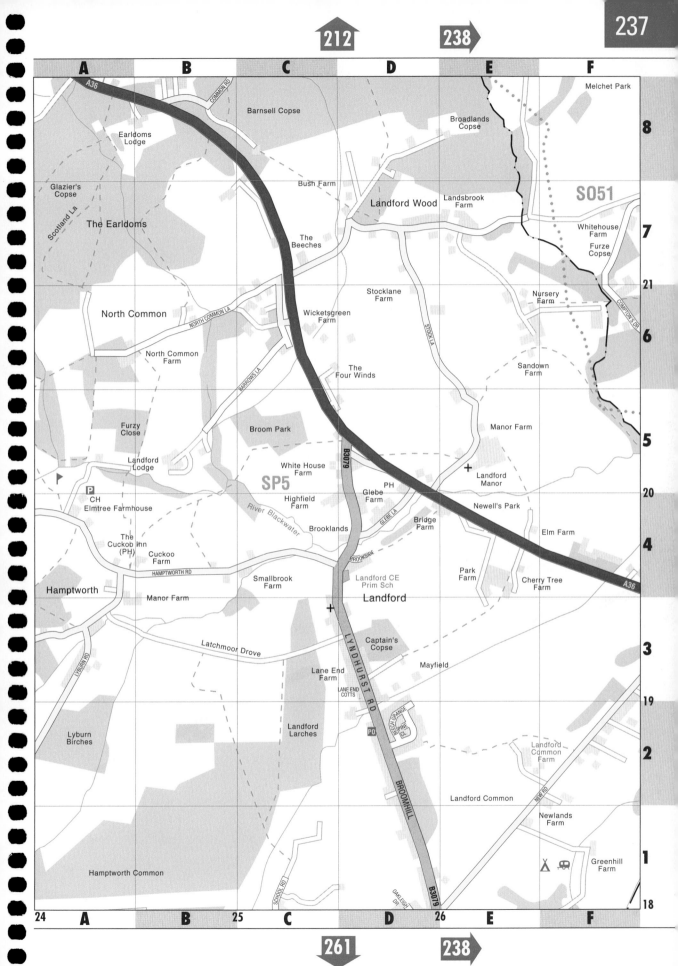

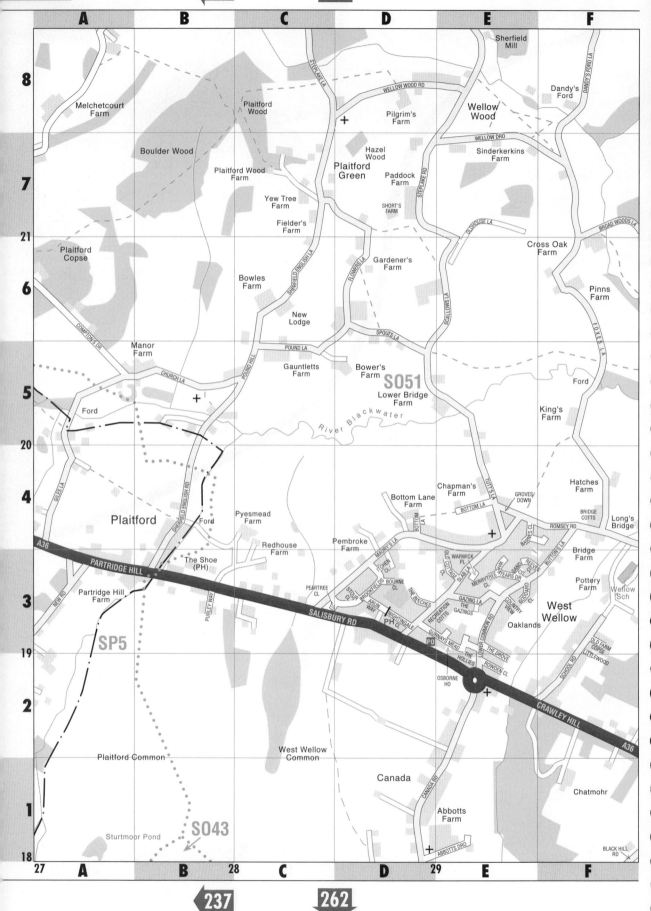

Melchetcourt Farm

Boulder Wood

Plaitford Wood

Plaitford Wood Farm

Yew Tree Farm

Plaitford Copse

Fielder's Farm

Bowles Farm

New Lodge

Manor Farm

COMPTON'S DR

CHURCH LA

Ford

POUND LA

POUND HILL

Gauntletts Farm

SHERFIELD ENGLISH LA

GILES LA

Plaitford

SHERFIELD ENGLISH RD

Ford

Pyesmead Farm

Redhouse Farm

Pembroke Farm

PURLEY WAY

NEW RD

The Shoe (PH)

Partridge Hill Farm

A36

PARTRIDGE HILL

SP5

SALISBURY RD

PEARTREE CL

STOUR CL

Plaitford Common

West Wellow Common

Sturtmoor Pond

S043

Canada

CANADA RD

Abbotts Farm

ABBOTTS DRO

STEEPLAKE LA

WELLOW WOOD RD

Plaitford Green

Pilgrim's Farm

Hazel Wood

Paddock Farm

SHORT'S FARM

SHERFIELD ENGLISH LA

FLOWERS LA

Gardener's Farm

SPOUT'S LA

Bower's Farm

River Blackwater

S051

Lower Bridge Farm

Bottom Lane Farm

Chapman's Farm

BOTTOM LA

BOTTOM LA

MABEY'S LA

ITCHEN CL

BROOKFIELDS

BOURNE CL

THE BEECHES

NIGHTINGALE CL

PH CL

ARLIN WAY

GURNAYS MEAD

THE HOLLIES

OSBORNE HO

PO

Sherfield Mill

Wellow Wood

Dandy's Ford

DANDY'S FORD LA

WELLOW DRO

Sinderkerkins Farm

STEEPLAKE RD

OLDHOUSE LA

Cross Oak Farm

BROAD WOODS LA

SCALLOWS LA

Pinns Farm

FOXES LA

King's Farm

Ford

Hatches Farm

GROVES DOWN

TUTT'S LA

ROMSEY RD

BRIDGE COTTS

Long's Bridge

BARNES CL

WARWICK PL

OLD COTTAGE

SUB LA

MERRYTREE CL

REEVES CL

BUTTON'S LA

SANDY CL

GODDARD CL

YEARS DR

COUNTRY VIEW

GAZING LA

THE GAZINGS

RECREATION COTTS

LOWER COMMON RD

THE DROVE

ROWDEN CL

SCHOOL RD

Bridge Farm

Pottery Farm

Wellow Sch

West Wellow

Oaklands

OLD FARM CORSE

LITTLEWOOD

CRAWLEY HILL

A36

Chatmohr

BLACK HILL RD

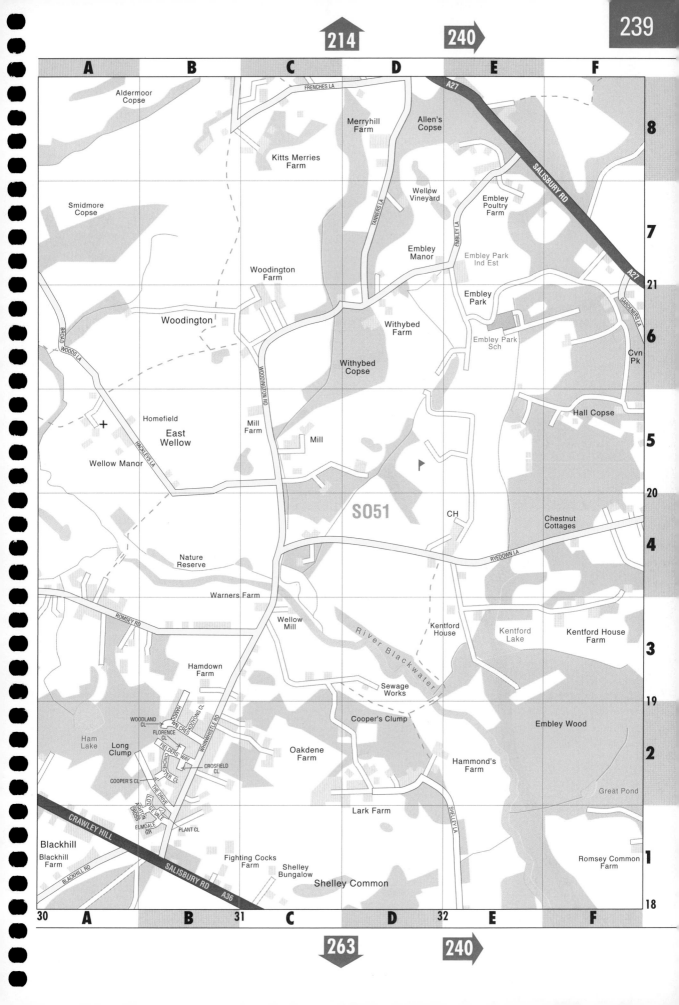

239
215

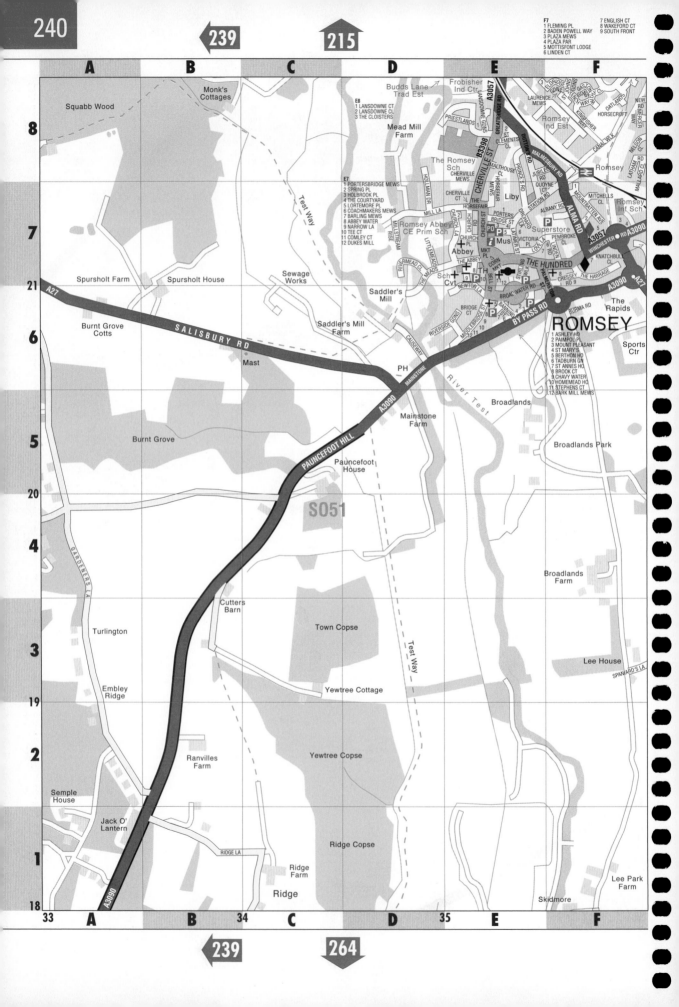

239
264

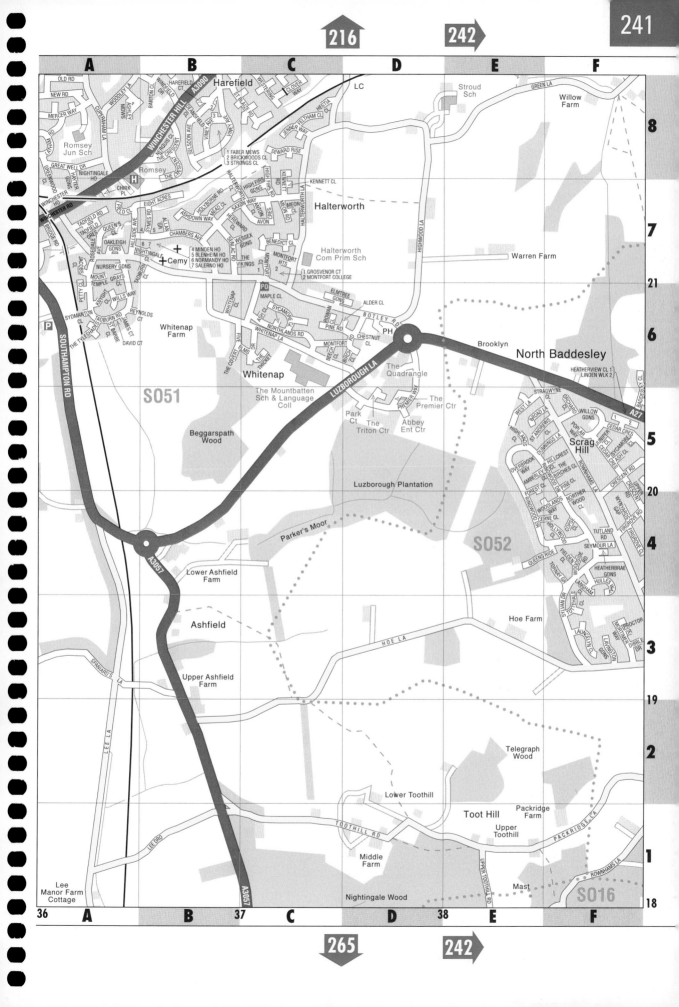

241
217

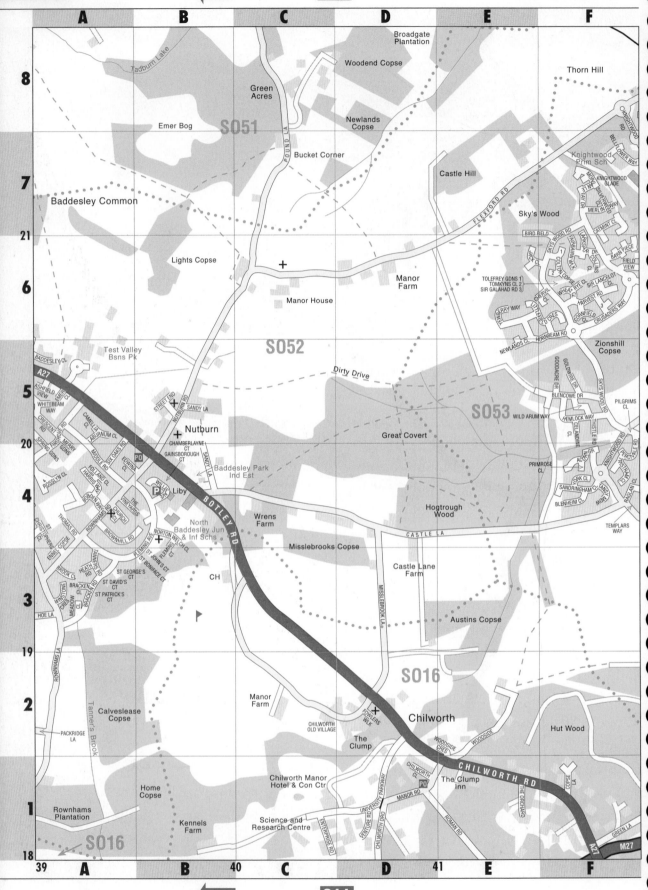

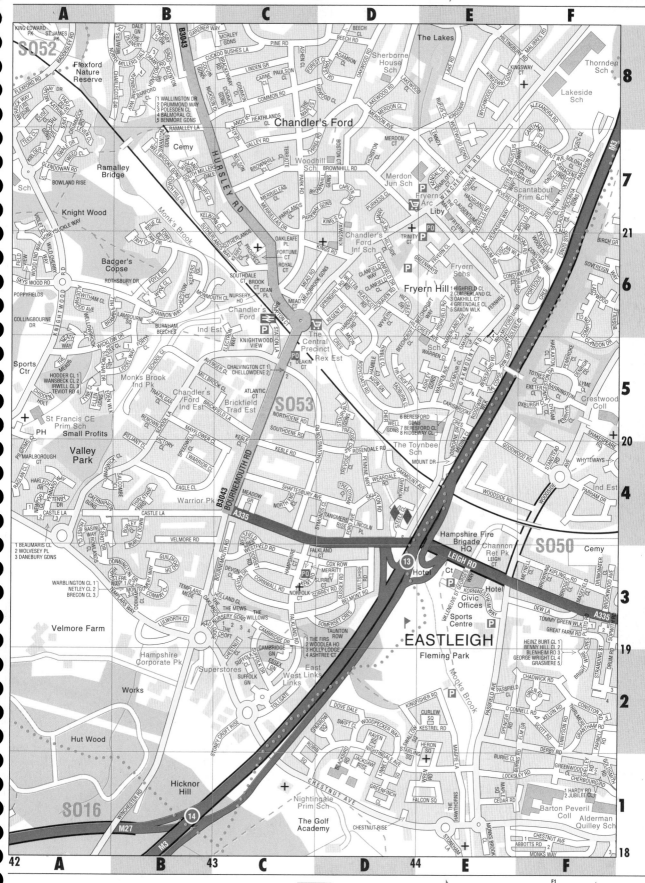

F1
1 PRIORY RD
2 FRIARS RD
3 CHERITON RD

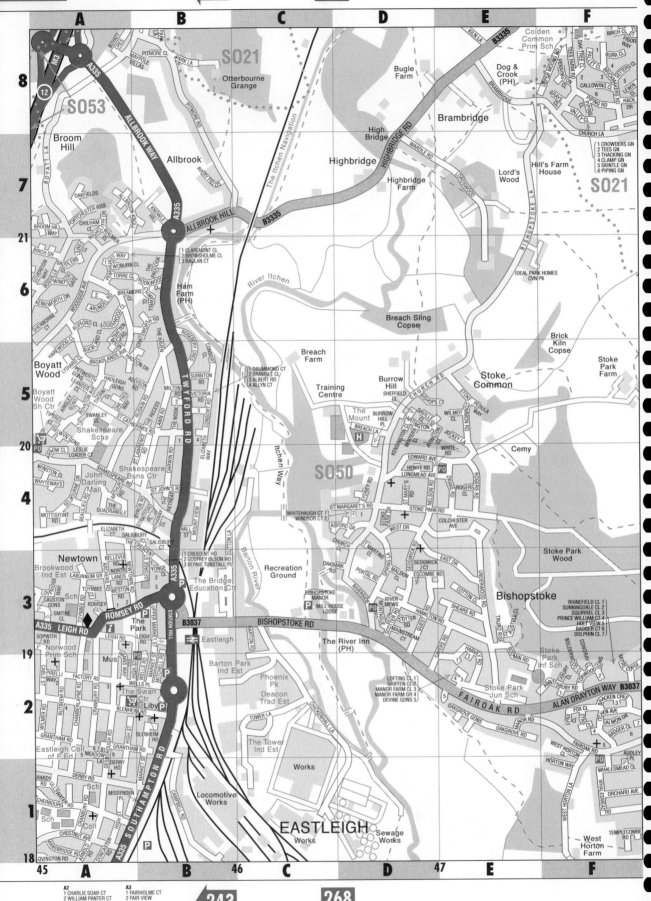

A2
1 CHARLIE SOAR CT
2 WILLIAM PANTER CT
3 ERRINGTON HO
4 SOVEREIGN CT
5 MAPLELEAF GDNS
6 THE PASTURES
7 THE CROFT
8 THE SPINNEY
9 GRANTHAM CT

A3
1 FAIRHOLME CT
2 FAIR VIEW

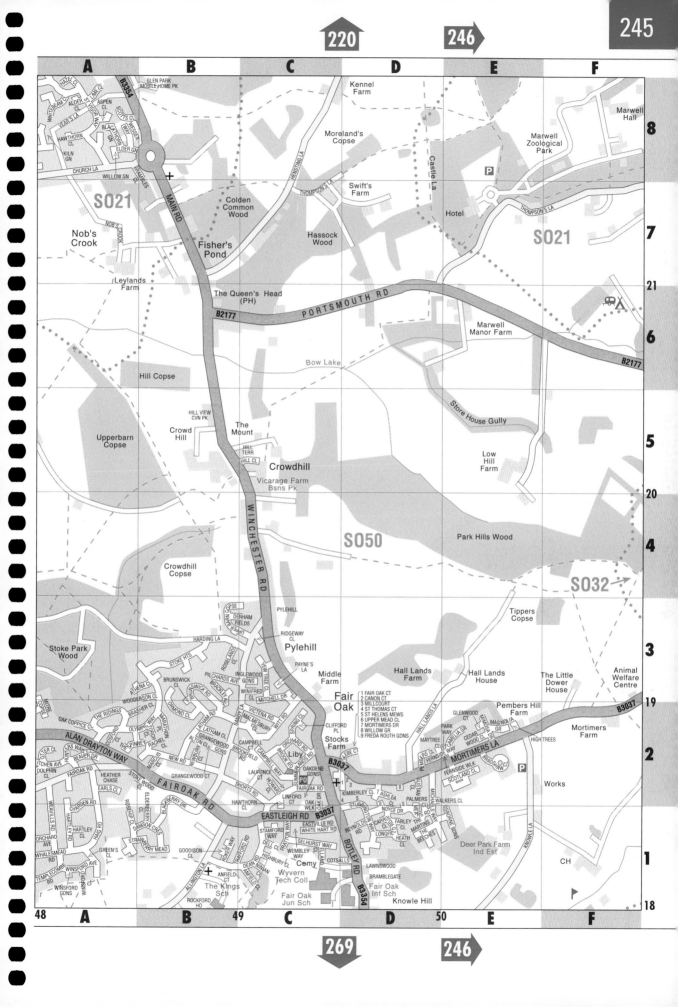

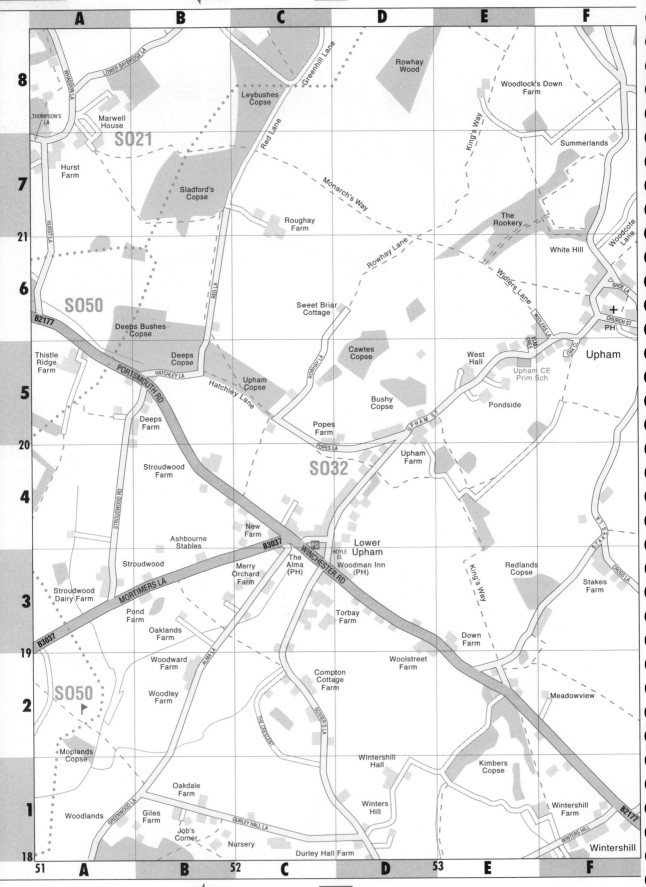

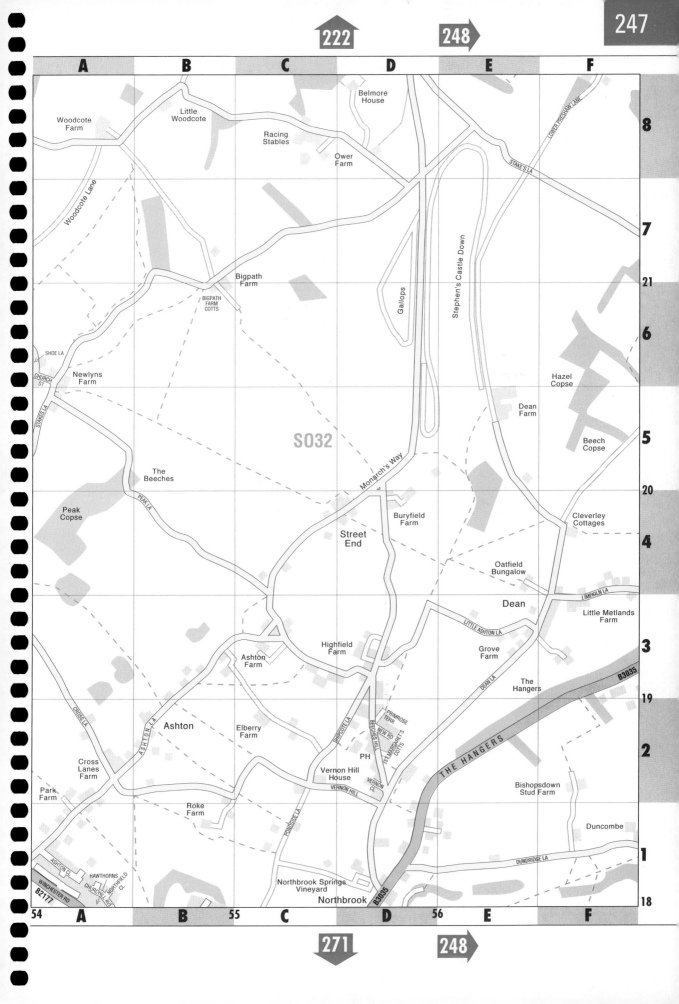

222
248

A   B   C   D   E   F

8

7

21

6

5

20

4

3

19

2

1

18

Woodcote Farm
Little Woodcote
Belmore House
Racing Stables
Ower Farm
LOWER PRESHAW LANE
STAKE'S LA

Woodcote Lane

Bigpath Farm
BIGPATH FARM COTTS

Stephen's Castle Down
Gallops

Hazel Copse

SHOE LA
CHURCH ST
STAKE'S LA
Newlyns Farm

Dean Farm

Beech Copse

SO32

Monarch's Way

The Beeches

PEAK LA

Peak Copse

Buryfield Farm

Cleverley Cottages

Street End

Oatfield Bungalow

Dean
LIMEKILN LA

Little Metlands Farm

Highfield Farm

LITTLE ASHTON LA

Grove Farm

Ashton Farm

The Hangers

B3035

CROSS LA

DEAN LA

ASHTON LA

Ashton

Elberry Farm

SHIPCOTE LA
PRIMROSE TERR
NEW RD
ST MARGARET'S COTTS
BEECHES HILL

PH

THE HANGERS

Cross Lanes Farm

Vernon Hill House

VERNON CL

Bishopsdown Stud Farm

Park Farm

Roke Farm

VERNON HILL

PONDSIDE LA

Duncombe

DUNDRIDGE LA

ASHTON CL
WINCHESTER RD
CHURCHILL AVE
HAWTHORNS
NORTHFIELD CL
B2177

Northbrook Springs Vineyard

B3035

Northbrook

54   A   B   55   C   D   56   E   F

271
248

247
223

A **B** **C** **D** **E** **F**

8

Sargeant's Copse

King's Copse

SAILORS LA

Downleaze Copse

Punch Bowl

Shellets Farm

Winters Down

LONE BARN LA

7

Littleton Copse

St Clair's

STAKE'S LA

21

Franklin Lane

Corhampton Forest

BEACON HILL LA

Warners Cottage

6

Wyndham Lodge

CORHAMPTON LA

Bottom Copse

Corhampton Lane Farm

5

Wayfarer's Walk

SO32

Steynes Farm

Greenacres

B3035

Franklin Farm

Corhampton Down

20

Droxford Down

CH

4

LIMEKILN LA

Hazel Holt

Shepherds Down Farm

SHEEP POND LA

3

B3035 THE HANGERS

Hazel Holt Farm

19

Galley Down

DUNDRIDGE LA

Shepherds Down

Peak Down

HACKETTS LA

2

Lycroft Farm

Wayfarer's Walk

Dundridge

Hampshire Bowman (PH)

PARK LA

Swanmore Barn Farm

1

Dundridge Farm

DAMSON HILL

Beechen Copse

Fir Down

Field Farm

Swanmore Park Farm

18

57 **A** **B** 58 **C** **D** 59 **E** **F**

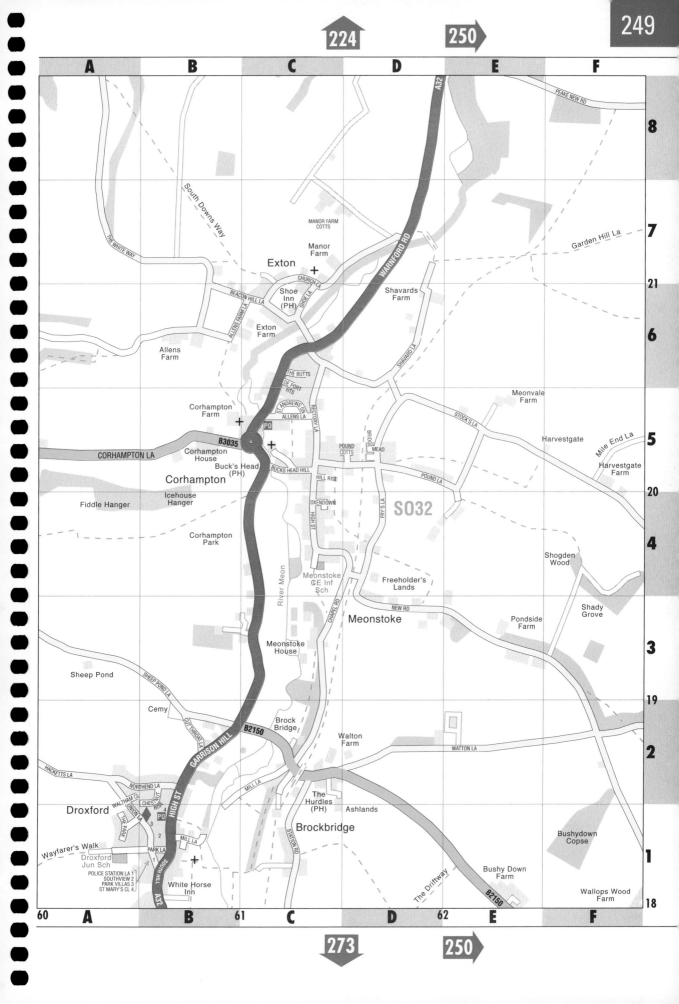

249
225

A B C D E F

8

Peake New Rd

Peake Farm

Bullshead Copse

OLD WINCHESTER HILL LA

OLD WINCHESTER HILL LA

Whitewool Hanger

Hen Wood

Peake Wood

Whitewool Farm

Monarch's Way

7

Garden Hill La

Roll's Copse

P

South Downs Way

21

Nature Trail

GU32

6

Old Winchester Hill

Nature Reserve

5

Mile End La

Castle Cottages

Monarch's Way

20

SO32

Stocks Farm

4

STOCK'S LA

Teglease Down

Little West End Farm

3

Teglease Copse

PO7

19

2

Westend Down

Sheepbarn Copse

Teglease Farm

SHEARDLEY LA

WHITELEAF LA

1

Stoke Wood

Little Sheardley Wood

18

Wallops Wood Farm

63 A 64 B C 64 D E 65 F

249
274

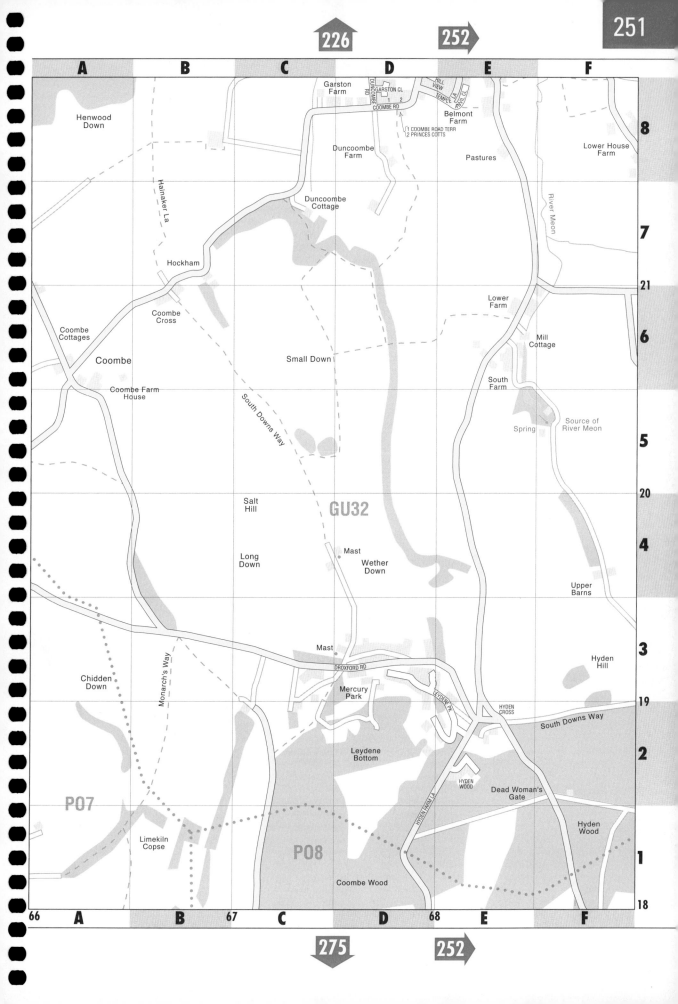

A   B   C   D   E   F

Henwood
Down

Garston
Farm

DUNCOMBE RD

GARSTON CL
1   2

COOMBE RD

HILL
VIEW

TEMPLE LA

YEOVIL CL

Belmont
Farm

Lower House
Farm

8

Duncoombe
Farm

Pastures

Halnaker La

Duncoombe
Cottage

River Meon

7

Hockham

21

Coombe
Cross

Lower
Farm

6

Coombe
Cottages

Small Down

Mill
Cottage

Coombe

South
Farm

Coombe Farm
House

South Downs Way

Source of
River Meon

Spring

5

20

Salt
Hill

GU32

Long
Down

Mast

Wether
Down

4

Upper
Barns

Mast

Hyden
Hill

3

Chidden
Down

DROXFORD RD

Mercury
Park

LEYDENE PK

HYDEN
CROSS

19

Monarch's Way

South Downs Way

Leydene
Bottom

2

HYDEN FARM LA

HYDEN
WOOD

Dead Woman's
Gate

P07

Limekiln
Copse

Hyden
Wood

P08

1

Coombe Wood

18

66   A   B   67   C   D   68   E   F

1 COOMBE ROAD TERR
2 PRINCES COTTS

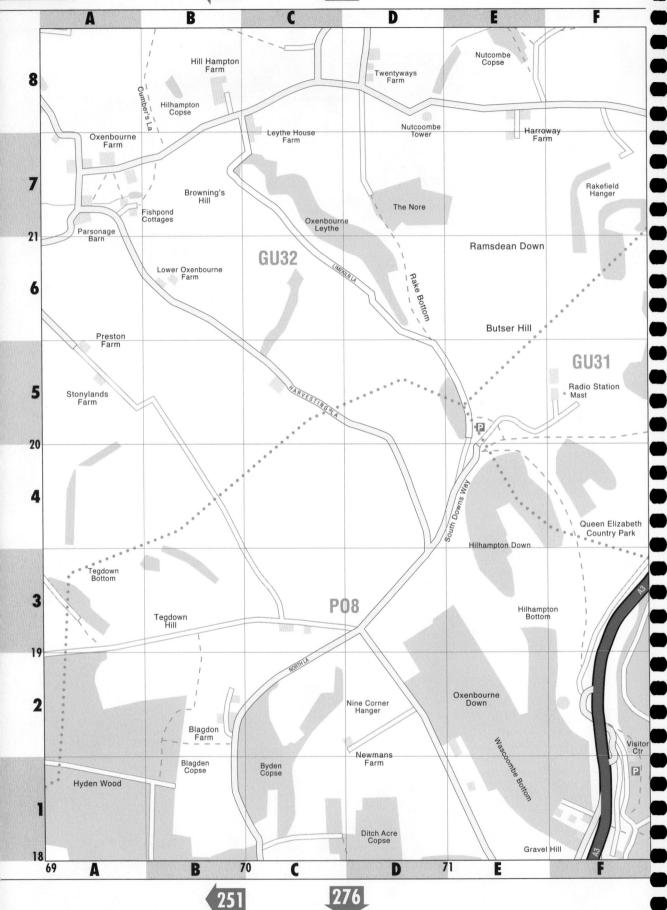

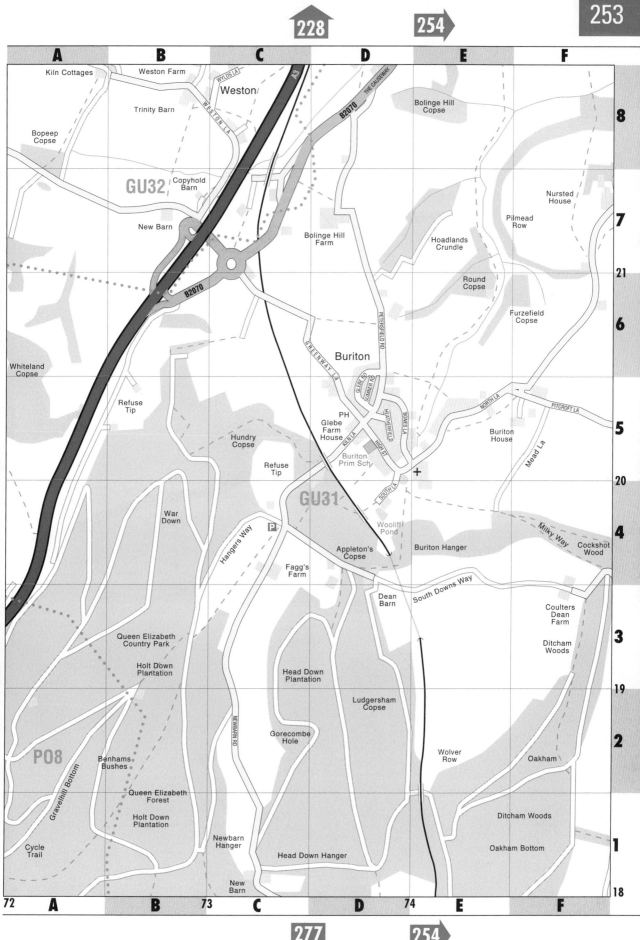

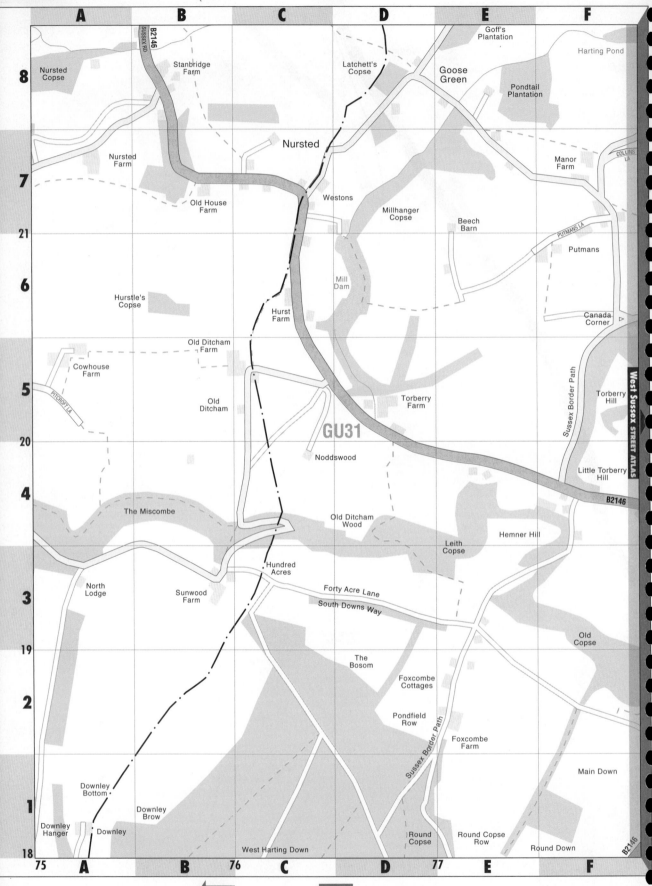

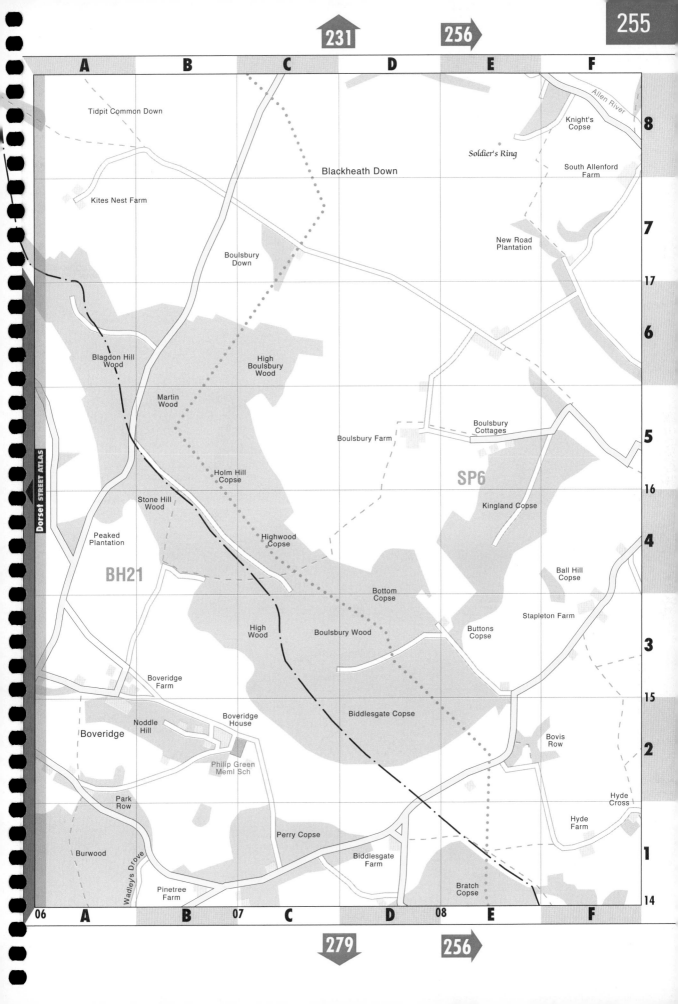

231
256

A B C D E F

8

7

17

6

5

16

4

15

3

2

1

14

Tidpit Common Down

Blackheath Down

Allen River

Knight's Copse

Soldier's Ring

South Allenford Farm

Kites Nest Farm

New Road Plantation

Boulsbury Down

Blagdon Hill Wood

High Boulsbury Wood

Martin Wood

Boulsbury Farm

Boulsbury Cottages

SP6

Holm Hill Copse

Kingland Copse

Stone Hill Wood

Peaked Plantation

Highwood Copse

Ball Hill Copse

BH21

Stapleton Farm

Bottom Copse

High Wood

Boulsbury Wood

Buttons Copse

Boveridge Farm

Biddlesgate Copse

Bovis Row

Noddle Hill

Boveridge House

Boveridge

Philip Green Meml Sch

Hyde Cross

Park Row

Hyde Farm

Burwood

Perry Copse

Biddlesgate Farm

Bratch Copse

Pinetree Farm

Wadley's Drove

Dorset STREET ATLAS

06 A B 07 C D 08 E F

279
256

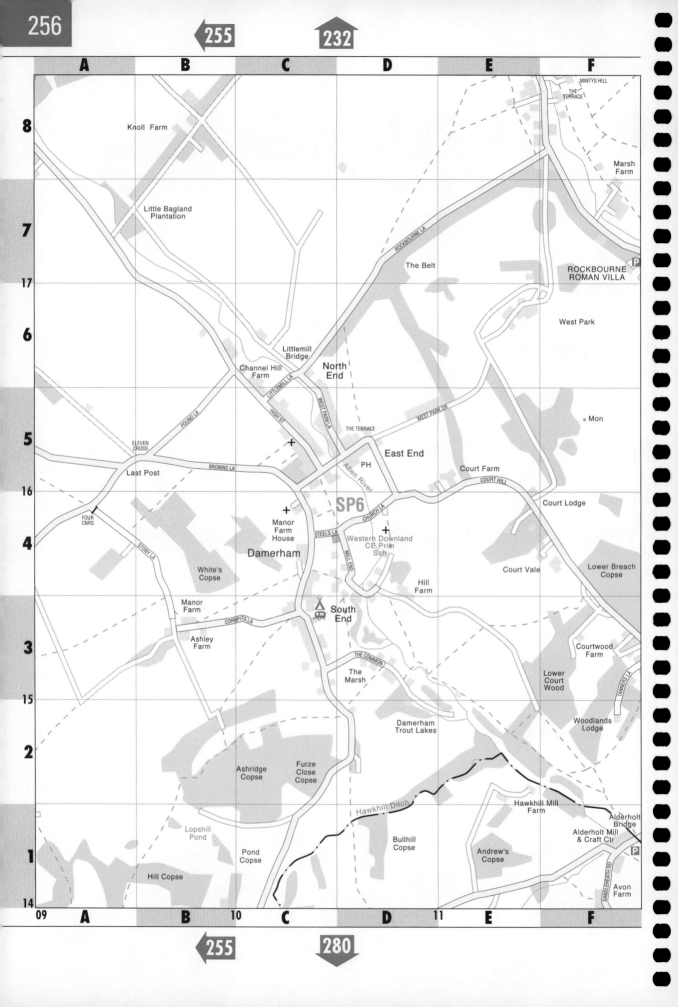

A B C D E F

8

Knoll Farm

7

Little Bagland
Plantation

17

ROCKBOURNE LA

The Belt

ROCKBOURNE
ROMAN VILLA

West Park

6

Littlemill
Bridge

Channel Hill
Farm

North
End

LITTLEMILL LA

HIGH ST

WEST PARK LA

WEST PARK DR

Mon

5

POUND LA

ELEVEN
CROSS

THE TERRACE

Allen River

East End

Last Post

BROWNS LA

PH

Court Farm

COURT HILL

16

FOUR
CNRS

STONY LA

Manor
Farm
House

SP6

STEELS LA

CHURCH LA

Western Downland
CE Prim
Sch

Court Lodge

4

Damerham

MILL END

Hill
Farm

Court Vale

Lower Breach
Copse

White's
Copse

3

Manor
Farm

CORNPITS LA

Ashley
Farm

South
End

THE COMMON

Courtwood
Farm

Lower
Court
Wood

TANNERS LA

15

The
Marsh

Damerham
Trout Lakes

Woodlands
Lodge

2

Ashridge
Copse

Furze
Close
Copse

Hawkhill Ditch

Hawkhill Mill
Farm

Alderholt
Bridge

Alderholt Mill
& Craft Ctr

Lopshill
Pond

Bullhill
Copse

Andrew's
Copse

SANDLEHEATH RD

1

Pond
Copse

Hill Copse

Avon
Farm

14

09 A B 10 C D 11 E F

MINTYS HILL
THE
TERRACE

Marsh
Farm

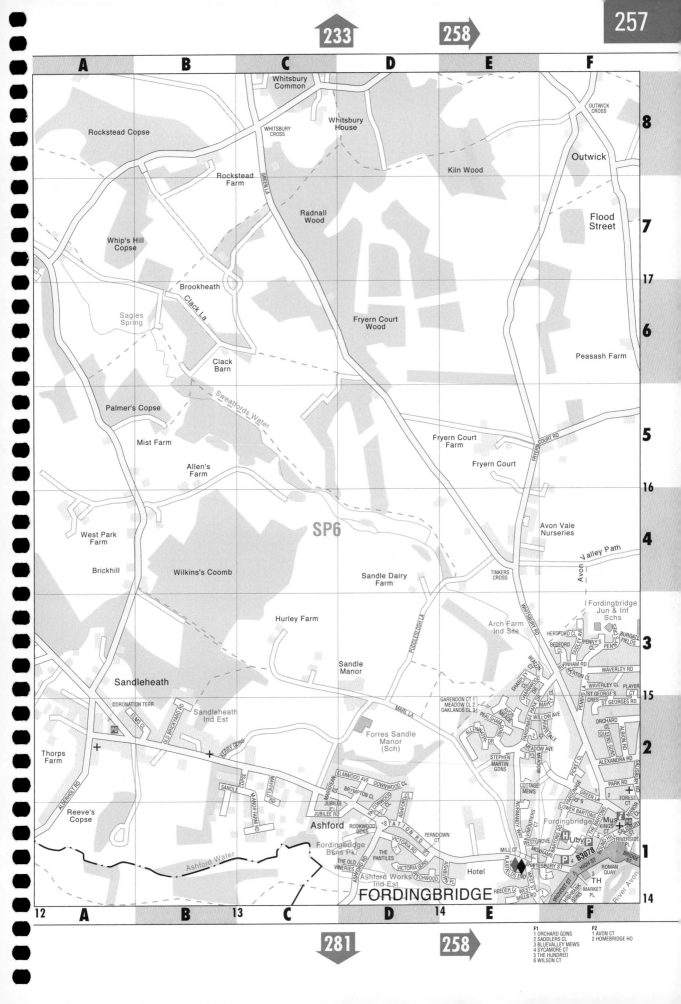

F1
1 ORCHARD GDNS
2 SADDLERS CL
3 BLUEVALLEY MEWS
4 SYCAMORE CT
5 THE HUNDRED
6 WILSON CT

F2
1 AVON CT
2 HOMEBRIDGE HO

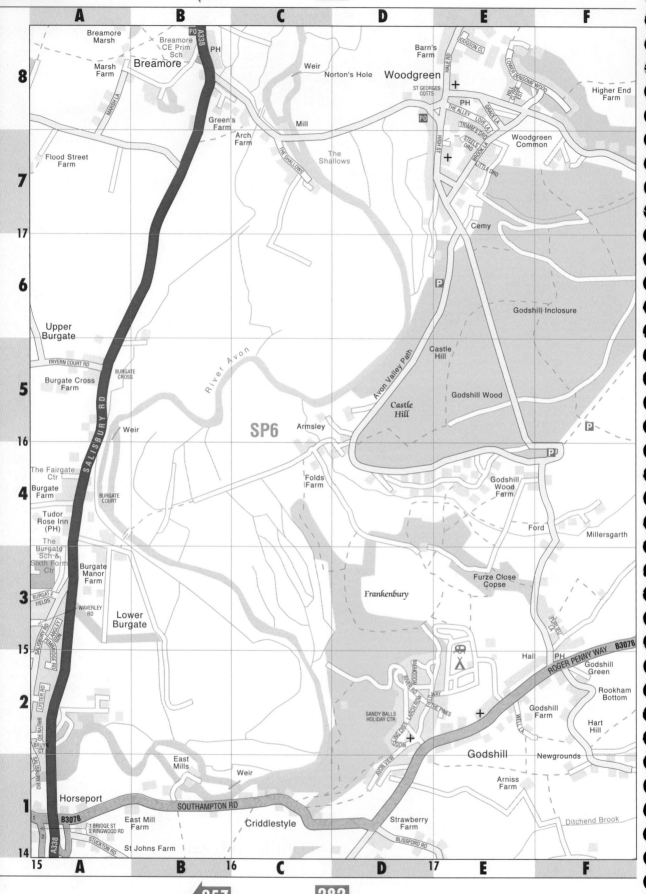

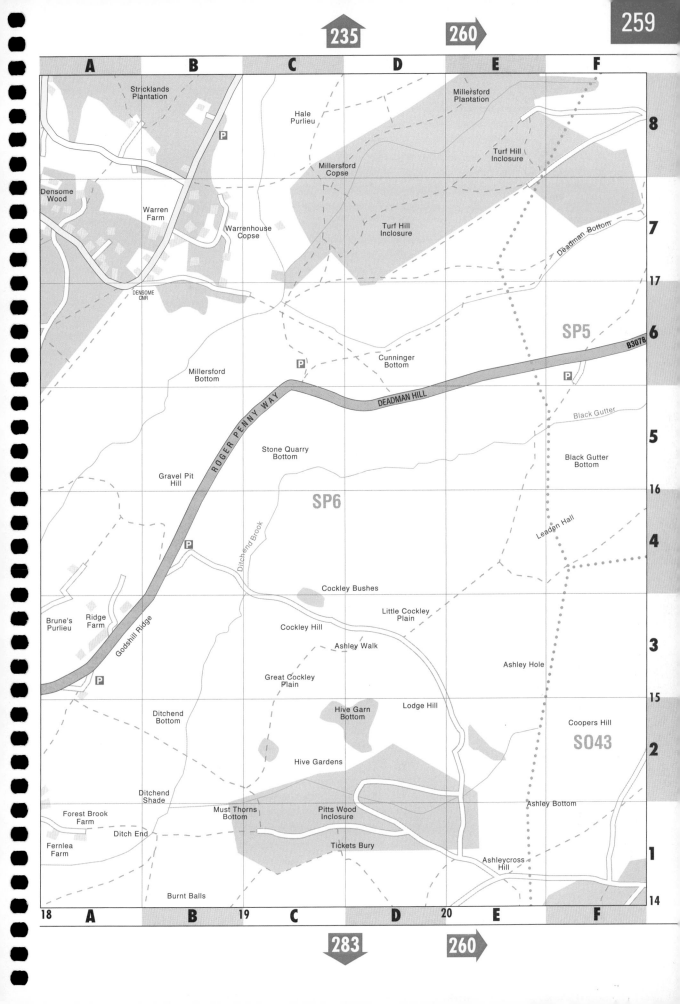

259
236

A B C D E F

8

Golden Cross
Jacob's Barrow

B3080

LYBURN RD

Pound
Bottom

Cloven Hill Plantation

Franchises
Common

Tinney's
Plantation

Rushy
Flat

FOREST RD

7

Burnt Ground Wood

Franchises
Lodge

Franchises
Wood

17

B3080

6

B3078

ROGER PENNY WAY

Hope
Cottage

Firs Hill
Copse

SP5

Bramshaw
Telegraph

Tucker's
Hat

Picket
Corner

Studley
Head

Black Gutter

5

Bur
Bushes

Studley
Wood

Claypits Bottom

Homy Ridge

16

Studley
Castle

4

The Butts

Howen Bottom

3

Eyeworth Wood

Islands Thorns Inclosure

15

SO43

2

Crock Hill

Latchmore Brook

Eyeworth
Pond

Irons
Well

Eyeworth
Lodge

P

Howen
Bushes

1

Fritham
Bridge

Fritham
Farm

The Royal Oak
(PH)

Fritham

14

Gorley Bushes

259
284

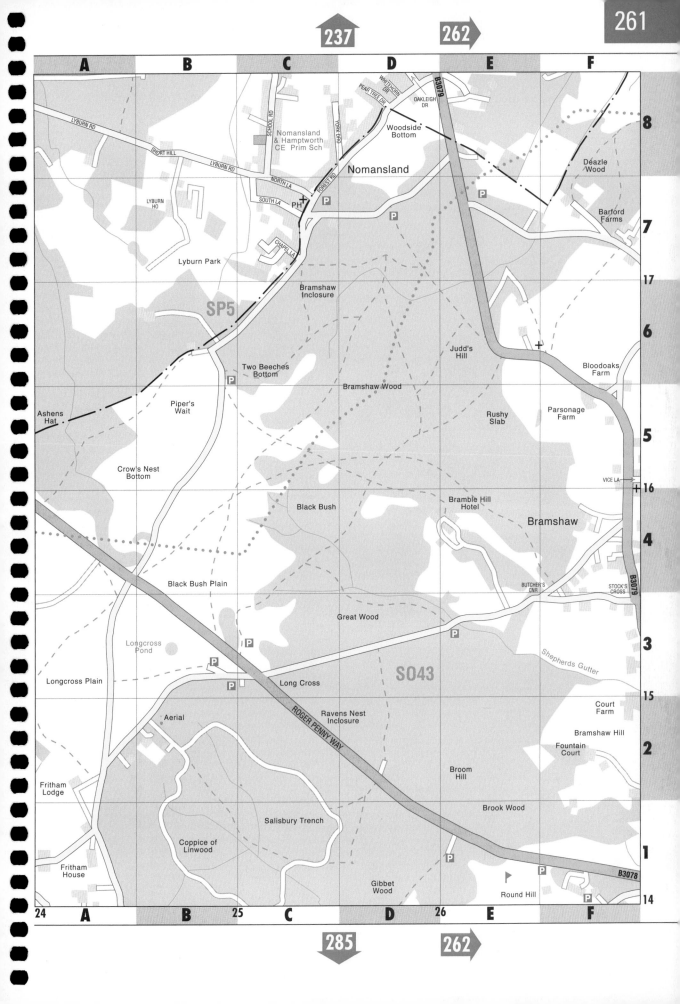

A   B   C   D   E   F

8
7
17
6
5
16
4
3
15
2
1
14

LYBURN RD
SHORT HILL
LYBURN RD
LYBURN HO
NORTH LA
SOUTH LA
CHAPEL LA
PH
SCHOOL RD
YORK DRO
FOREST RD
Nomansland & Hamptworth CE Prim Sch
Lyburn Park
Bramshaw Inclosure
SP5
Two Beeches Bottom
Piper's Wait
Ashens Hat
Crow's Nest Bottom
Black Bush
Black Bush Plain
Longcross Pond
Longcross Plain
Aerial
Fritham Lodge
Fritham House
Coppice of Linwood
Salisbury Trench
ROGER PENNY WAY
Long Cross
Ravens Nest Inclosure
Great Wood
Broom Hill
Brook Wood
Gibbet Wood
Round Hill
SO43
WHITCHORN DR
PEAR TREE DR
OAKLEIGH DR
B3079
Woodside Bottom
Nomansland
Deazle Wood
Barford Farms
Judd's Hill
Bramshaw Wood
Rushy Slab
Bloodoaks Farm
Parsonage Farm
Bramble Hill Hotel
VICE LA
Bramshaw
BUTCHER'S CNR
STOCK'S CROSS
B3079
Shepherds Gutter
Court Farm
Bramshaw Hill
Fountain Court
B3078

24   A   B   25   C   D   26   E   F

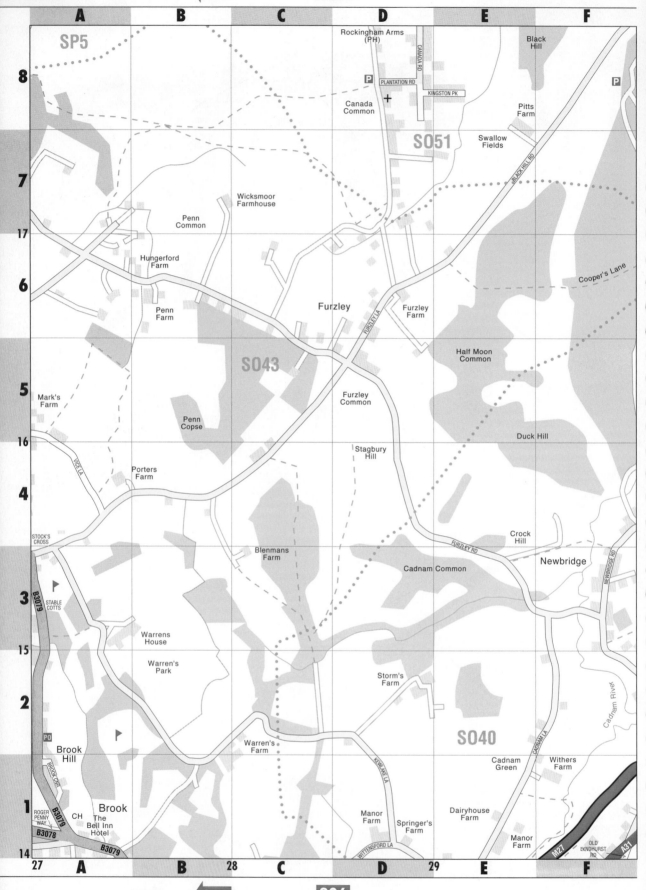

SP5

Rockingham Arms (PH)

Black Hill

CANADA RD

PLANTATION RD

KINGSTON PK

SO51

Canada Common

Swallow Fields

Pitts Farm

BLACK HILL RD

Wicksmoor Farmhouse

Penn Common

Cooper's Lane

Hungerford Farm

Furzley

FURZLEY LA

Furzley Farm

Penn Farm

Half Moon Common

SO43

Furzley Common

Duck Hill

Mark's Farm

Penn Copse

Stagbury Hill

Porters Farm

VICE LA

Crock Hill

FURZLEY RD

Newbridge

NEWBRIDGE RD

STOCK'S CROSS

Blenmans Farm

Cadnam Common

B3079

STABLE COTTS

Warrens House

Warren's Park

Storm's Farm

Cadnam River

SO40

PO

CADNAM LA

Brook Hill

Warren's Farm

Cadnam Green

Withers Farm

BROCK CNR

KENWAKE LA

Manor Farm

Dairyhouse Farm

ROGER PENNY WAY

B3079

CH

Brook

The Bell Inn Hotel

Springer's Farm

Manor Farm

M27

OLD LYNDHURST RD

A31

B3078

B3079

WITTENSFORD LA

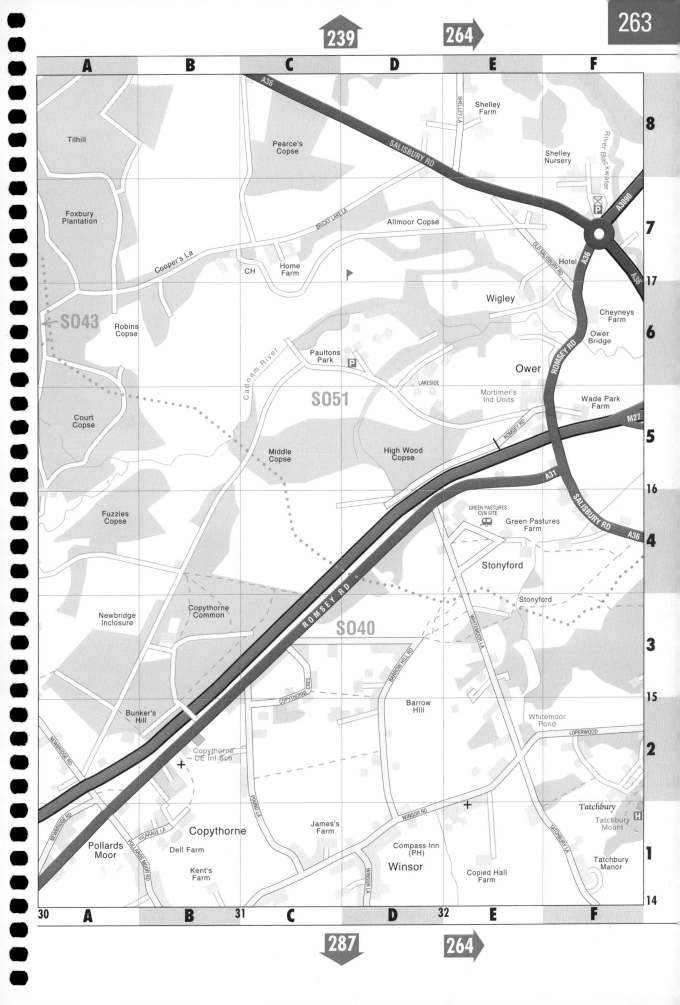

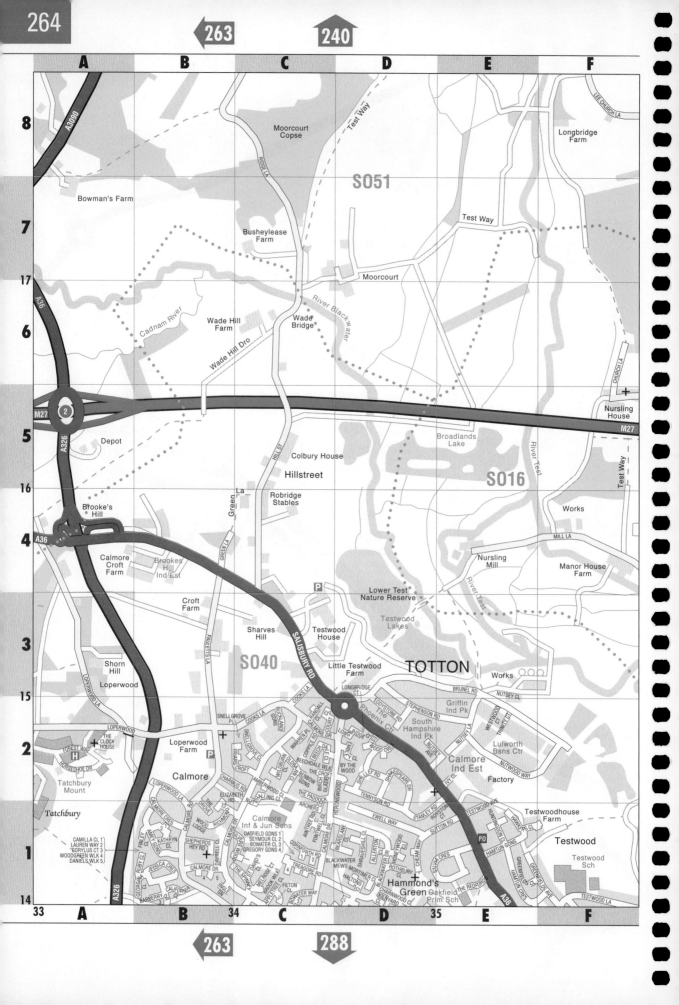

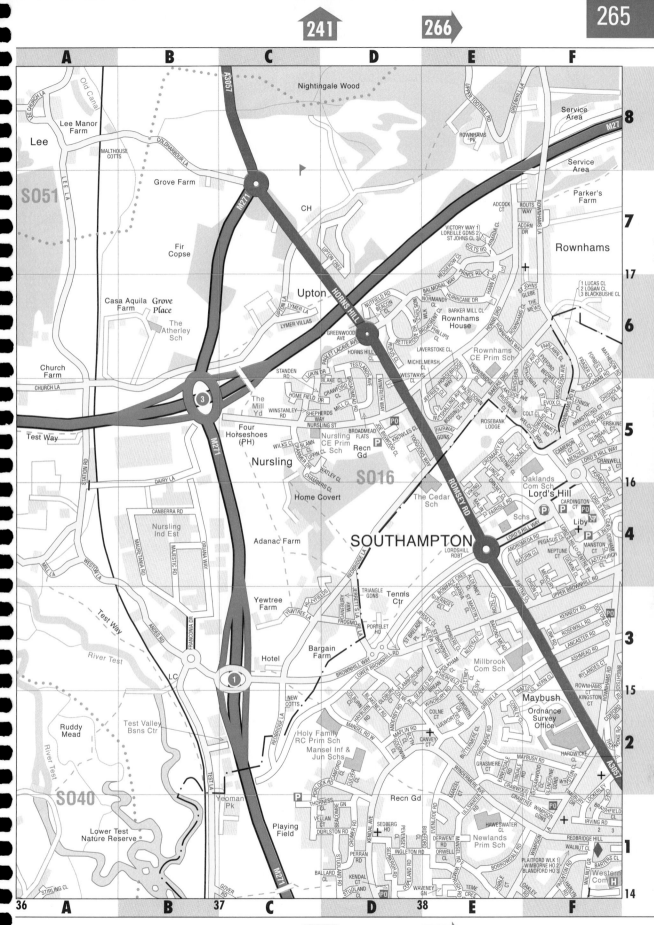

A B C D E F

SO52

M27

Chilworth Tower

Dymer's Wood

Chilworth Common

Chilworth Road A27

Chilworth Common

Heatherlands Rd
Pinelands Rd
Roman Rd
Hadrian Way
Pine Wlk
Pine Ho
Dale Ho
Ling Ho
Maple Beech
M27
A33
Fitzroy

Lord's Wood

Roman Dr
The Ring
Chilworth Ring

Bassett Heath Ave
Birch Rd
Links View Way
Saxholm Way
Saxholm Dale
Bassett Row

Castle Hill

Golf Course Rd
CH

SO16

Greenbank Cres
Ridgemount Ave
Ridgemount La
Chelwood Gate
Brampton Twr
Brampton Manor

Bassett Ave

Lordswood

Oakwood Schs

Oakwood Dr

Grafton Gdns

Holly Hill Dell

Sports Ctr

Vermont Sch

Red Lodge Sch

Chetwynd Dr
A35
A33
Bassett Cres E
Oaklands Way
Univ A35

Sinclair Prim Sch

Lord's Hill Way

Aldermoor Rd

Lordswood Rd

Burgess Rd

Cutthorn

A3035 Highfield Ave

Tanner's Brook

Aldermoor

Princess Anne H

Cemy

Holly Brook

Schs
PO
Winstone Bldgs
A35

SOUTHAMPTON

Coronation Ave

Southampton Common

The Lake

SO15

SO17

Northbrook Ind Est

Southampton Gen H

Shirley Warren

Chalybeate H

Super store

Shirley Park

Bellemoor Sch (Boys)

Winchester Rd

Coxford

Romsey Rd
A3057

Old Shirley

Wordsworth Inf Schs

Upper Shirley

Taunton's Coll

Redbridge Hill

Cemetery Lake

The Cowherds (PH)

A33

39 A 40 B C 41 D E F

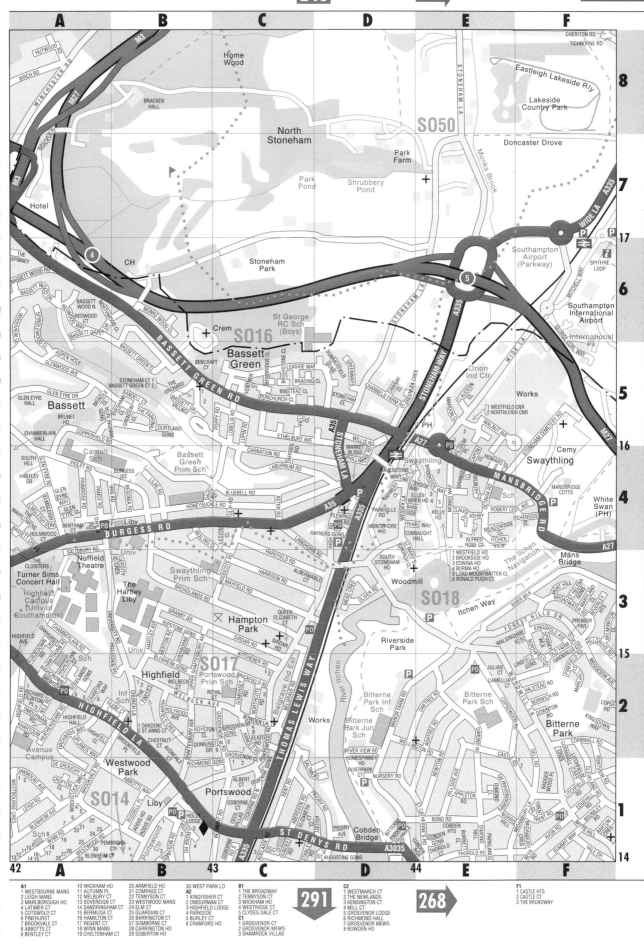

243

268

291

268

A1
1 WESTBOURNE MANS
2 LEIGH MANS
3 MARLBOROUGH HO
4 LATIMER CT
5 COTSWOLD CT
6 PINEHURST
7 BROOKVALE CT
8 ABBOTTS CT
9 BENTLEY CT

10 WICKHAM HO
11 AUTUMN PL
12 MELBURY CT
13 SOVEREIGN CT
14 SANDRINGHAM CT
15 BERMUDA CT
16 HAMILTON CT
17 REGENT CT
18 WINN MANS
19 CHELTENHAM CT

20 ARMFIELD HO
21 COMPASS CT
22 TENNYSON CT
23 WESTWOOD MANS
24 ELM CT
25 GUARDIAN CT
26 BARRINGTON CT
27 SOMBORNE CT
28 CARRINGTON HO
29 SOBERTON HO

30 WEST PARK LO
A2
1 KINGFISHER CT
2 OMDURMAN CT
3 HIGHFIELD LODGE
4 PARKSIDE
5 BURLEY CT
6 CRANFORD HO

B1
1 THE BROADWAY
2 TENNYSON CT
3 WICKHAM HO
4 WESTRIDGE CT
5 CLYDES DALE CT
C1
1 GROSVENOR CT
2 GROSVENOR MEWS
3 SHAMROCK VILLAS

C2
1 WESTMARCH CT
2 THE NEWLANDS
3 KENSINGTON CT
4 MILL CT
5 GROSVENOR LODGE
6 RICHMOND HALL
7 GROSVENOR MEWS
8 BOWDEN HO

F1
1 CASTLE HTS
2 CASTLE CT
3 THE BROADWAY

267 244

A B C D E F

8
7
17
6
5
16
4
3
15
2
1
14

SO50

West Horton Farm

Allington Manor Farm Bsns Ctr

ALINGTON MANOR FARM COTTS

Southampton International Airport

Allington Manor Sch

Hog Wood

Railway Cottage

Decoy Covert

River Itchen

Milkmead Copse

SEDDUL-BAHR

Itchen Valley Country Park

High Hill

White Harmony Acres Ind Est

High Wood

Oaklands House

Visitor Ctr

SO18

Water Works

Winslowe House

Moorgreen Farm

Gaters Mill

MILL HO

SO30

MANSBRIDGE RD

The Manor House

Garden Ctr

STOUR CL 1
CREEDY GDNS 2
WEBBURN GDNS 3

Sch

Townhill Park

Schs

The King's Prim Sch

Brookside Way

Southampton Arms (PH)

St James' CE Prim Sch

Moorgreen

1 THE GATEHOUSE
2 LANCASTER CT
3 HALIFAX CT
4 WELLINGTON CT
5 LINCOLN CT

Liby

Hatch Bottom

Hatch Grange

West End

Moorgreen

B3035

CHURCH HILL

HIGH ST

The Hampshire Health & Tennis Club

SWAYTHLING RD

Mus

BOTLEY RD
B3035

Dog Kennel Farm

The Rose Bowl

Midanbury

45 A B 46 C D 47 E F

267 292

A1
1 GRASDEAN CL
2 WAKEFIELD CT
3 CLEVELAND CT
4 BENHAMS FARM CL

A2
1 LONGMEAD RD
2 ROWLANDS WLK
3 DEWSBURY CT
4 CORNWALL CL

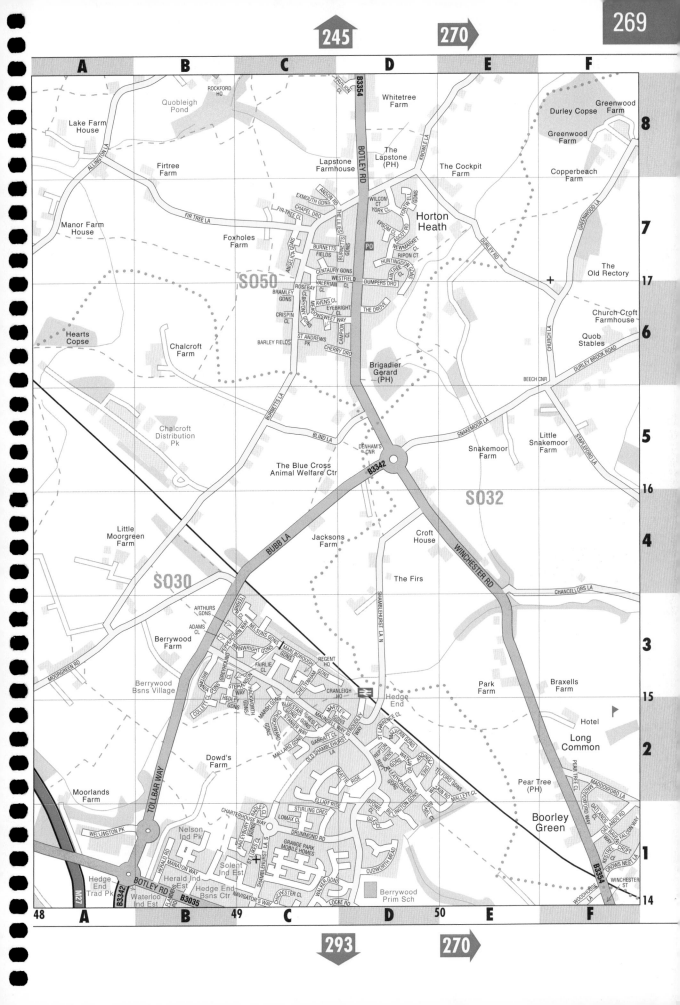

269
246

A B C D E F

8

Greenwood

Winters Hill

Wintershill

Laurel Farm

Woodlea Nursery

Kings Way

Trullingham Farm

Robin Hood (PH)

The Drove

Durley Street

MANOR TERR.

7

DURLEY ST

Durley Manor Farm

Tangier Farm

VICTORIA CT

MANOR RD

17

6

DURLEY BROOK RD

Durley Lodge

Perlins Farm

Durley CE Prim Sch

PO

Durley

KYLES LA

Broom Farm

Lower Farm

PARSONAGE LA

Millstone Farm

Mincingfield Farm

MINCINGFIELD LA

MILLWAY

Brownheath Park

Brown Heath

5

THE SAWMS

WHITE GATES

Farmer's Home (PH)

MINCINGFIELD TERR

16

Stapleford Farmhouse

Gregory Farm

GREGORY LA

S032

Brokes Copse

STAPLEFORD LA

HEATHER ST

4

Blundell's Copse

Brokes Farm

River Hamble

Harfields Bungalow

B3035

CHANCELLORS LA

Hill Farm

NETHERHILL

MILL LA

Calcot House

Harfields Farm

3

Ford Lake

Netherhill Farm

Durley Mill

Calcot Farm

CALCOT LA

15

NETHERHILL LA

BLIND LA

BOTLEY RD

2

Frogmill Farm

Breach Hill

Cricketer's Inn (PH)

Maddoxford Farm

THE PLANTATION

CURDRIDGE LA

HYLE LA

CREEPERS END LA

MADDOXFORD LA

Long Acres Farm

Hill Farm

Curdridge Firs

CROWS NEST LA

WANGFIELD LA

The Paddocks

LOCKHAMS RD

GORDON RD

1

Boorley Green

Holly Tree Farm

Lower Wangfield Farm

Parklands

Firs Farm

PO

Boorley Green Farm

S030

B3035

CHAPEL LA

14

51 A B 52 C D 53 E F

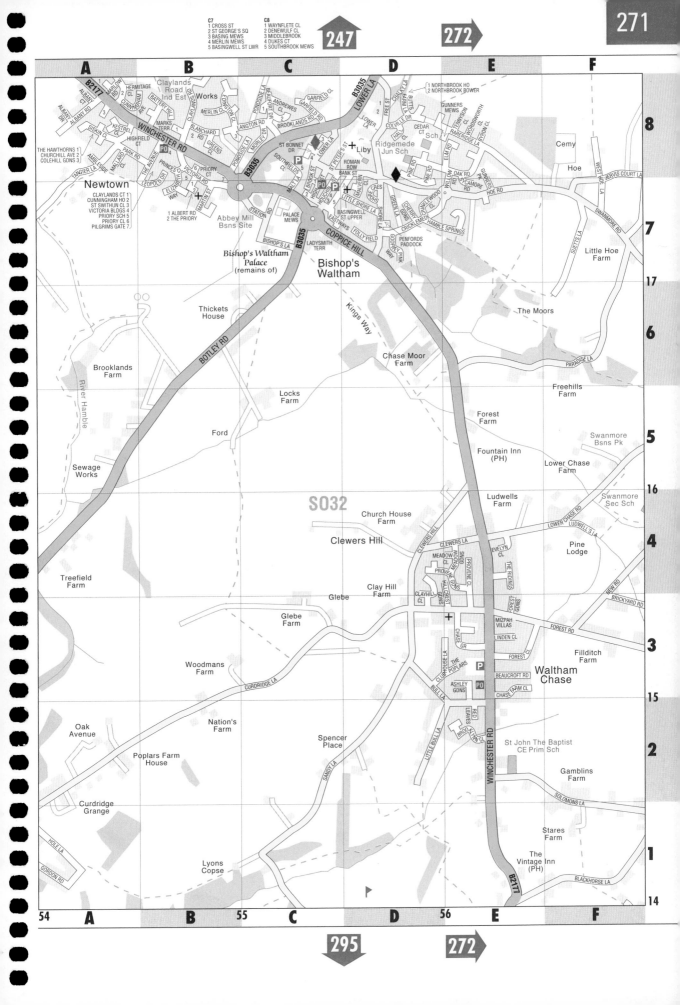

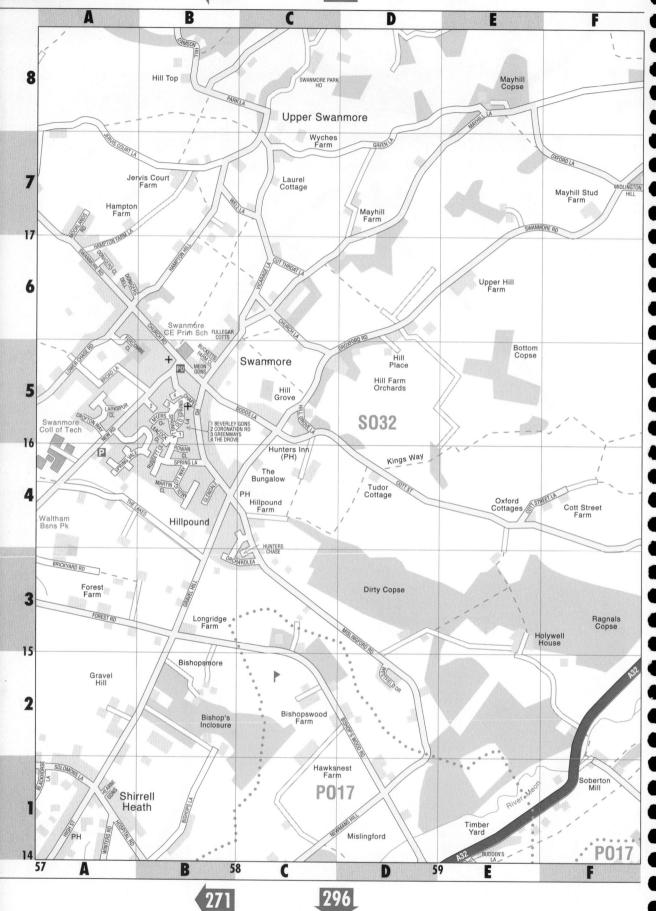

A B C D E F

8 Hill Top

DAMSON HILL

PARK LA

Upper Swanmore

Swanmore Park Ho

Mayhill Copse

Wyches Farm

GREEN LA

OXFORD LA

MAYHILL LA

7 Jervis Court Farm

JERVIS COURT LA

Laurel Cottage

Mayhill Farm

Mayhill Stud Farm

MIDLINGTON HILL

Hampton Farm

MOORLANDS RD

HAMPTON FARM LA

WELL LA

17 SWANMORE RD

SWANMORE RD

DOWNGERS CL

BELL

HAMPTON HILL

VICARAGE LA

CUT THROAT LA

6 Upper Hill Farm

CHURCH LA

DROXFORD RD

Swanmore CE Prim Sch

FULLEGAR COTTS

Bottom Copse

CHURCH RD

FOXCOMBE CL

BUCKETTS FARM CL

Swanmore

Hill Place

PO

MEON GDNS

Hill Farm Orchards

LOWER CHASE RD

BROAD LA

Hill Grove

SO32

5 CHAPEL RD

DODDS LA

HILL GROVE LA

LARKSPUR CL

4 MYERS CL

SPRING LA

SNIPES RD

CROFTON WAY

NEW RD

1 BEVERLEY GDNS
2 CORONATION RD
3 GREENWAYS
4 THE DROVE

16 Swanmore Coll of Tech

P

SPRING VALE

BACOCK CL

RUSSETS CL

ROWAN CL

SPRING LA

Hunters Inn (PH)

Kings Way

COTT ST

4 MARTIN CL

MEDSTEAD

GLENDALE

The Bungalow

Tudor Cottage

COTT STREET LA

Oxford Cottages

Cott Street Farm

THE OAKES

PH Hillpound Farm

Hillpound

GRAVEL HILL

ORCHARDLEA

HUNTERS CHASE

BRICKYARD RD

3 Forest Farm

FOREST RD

Dirty Copse

Ragnals Copse

Longridge Farm

MISLINGFORD RD

Holywell House

15 Bishopsmore

Gravel Hill

WESTFIELD DR

A32

2 Bishop's Inclosure

Bishopswood Farm

BISHOP'S WOOD RD

BISHOPS LA

1 Shirrell Heath

SOLOMONS LA

BLACKHORSE LA

HEARNE GDNS

Hawksnest Farm

PO17

River Meon

Soberton Mill

Timber Yard

HIGH ST

PH

WINTERS RD

HOSPITAL RD

NEWMANS HILL

Mislingford

A32

BUDDEN'S LA

14 PO17

57 A 58 B C 58 D 59 E F

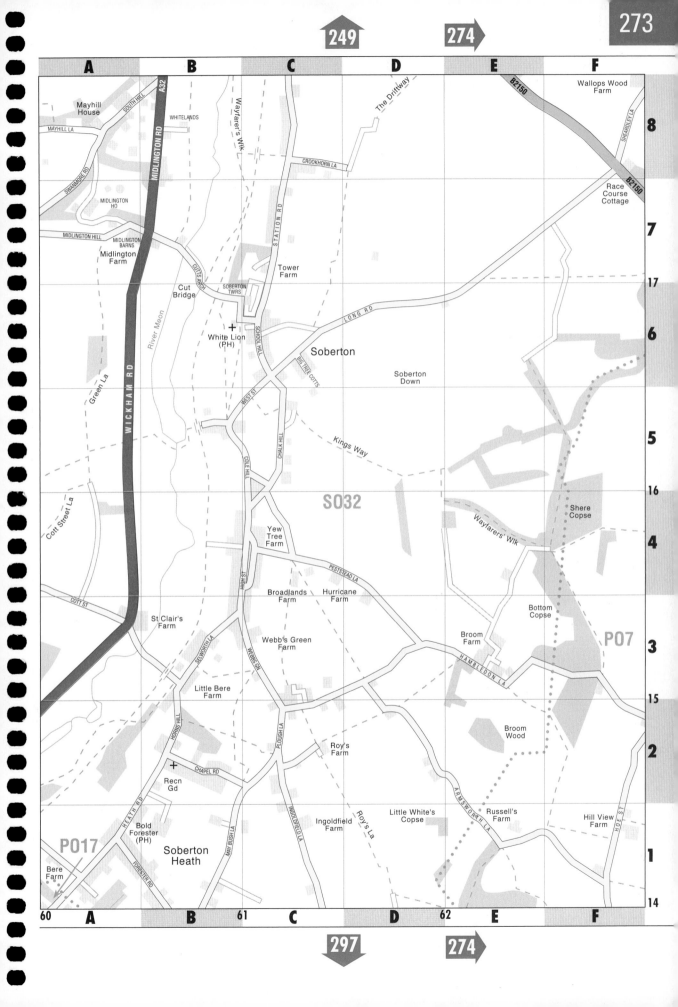

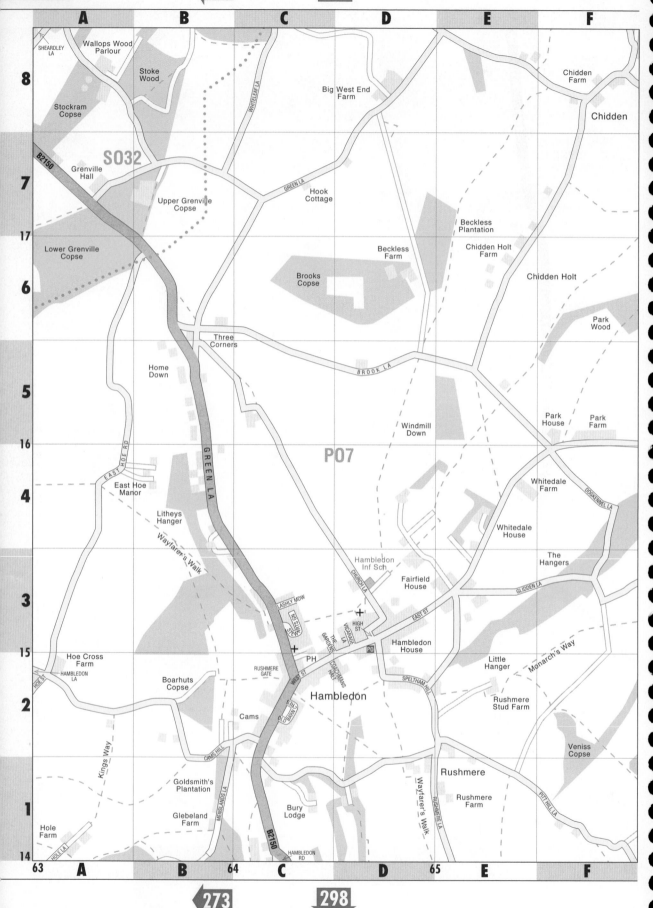

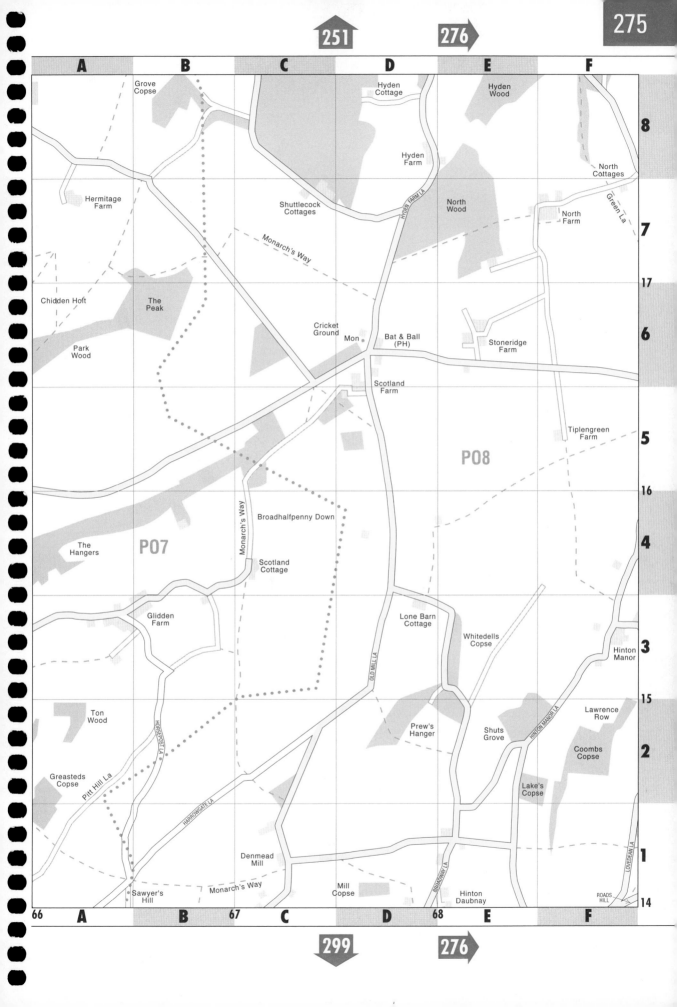

275
252

A B C D E F

8
7
17
6
5
16
4
3
15
2
1
14

Smith's Copse
Lowton's Copse
Ditch Acre Copse
Chapel Farm
A3
Hog's Lodge Inn (PH)
Green La
HORS LODGE LA
Thieves Lane
PETERSFIELD RD
Bramble La
Clanfield Jun Sch
Swallow Ct
Ivy Orch La
East Mean Rd
PH
Church End
Kingsbury Ct
Wilkins Cl
Homefield Way
Manor Farm
Petersfield La
Green Lane
CHALTON LA
Chalton La
Hambledon Rd
Pook La
South La
Sword Cl
Nickleby Rd
Pond La
Windmill Cl
Maple Cres
Beech Rd
Down Farm
Clanfield Down
Butser Ancient Farm
Green La
Picks Mead
Clanfield
Sunderton La
Rosewood Gdns
Sandlewood Cl
White Cl
Oak Rd
Sycamore Cl
Maple Cres
Beam Rise
P08
London Rd
Hinton Manor La
Downhouse Rd
Farm View Ave
Aldridge Cl
New Rd
Hazel Cl
Hazelgrove
Meadow Croft Farm
Chalton Windmill
Windmill Hill
St David's Rd
Jacobs Cl
Jasmine Way
Pine Dr
Storrington Rd
Tillington Rd
1 Slindon Cl
2 Amberley Rd
3 Middleton Rise
4 Heyshott Gdns
Windmill Hill Farm
Ridge Cl
Fieldfare Cl
Redwing Cl
Kestrel Cl
Goring Ave
Walburton Way
Chilworth Gdns
Blackberry Cl
Goring Ave
Windmill Down
Charity Farm
St James Cl
Harting Cl
Singleton Gdns
Loseworth Cl
Elderberry Cl
Kennels
Petersgate Inf Sch
Meon Cl
Valle Cl
Park Dr
PO
Main Cres
Arle Cl
Drift Rd
Horndean Down
Court La
White Dirt La
Noxes Rd
First Ave
Dell Ridge
Snell's Cnr
Hill Top Gdns
Hillside
Viking Way
Butser Ct
Blendworth Down
Draycote
Wode Cl
Wessex Rd
Glamorgan Rd
Wrexham Gr
Francis Rd
Belmont Rd
St Christophers Mobile Home Pk
White Dirt La
White Dirt Farm
Southdown Rd
Catherington La
Romsey Rd
The Hollies
Munday's Row
Derwent Cl
Thornfield Cl
St Hilda Ave
New Barn Farm
Northfield Cl
St Giles Way
St Michaels Way
Loveden La
Old Lane
Tarn Rise
Escdale Cl
Hawthorn Rd
Ennerdale Cl
St Andrew Cl
North Hd Rd
Claire Gdns
London Rd
Southdown Rd
St Hubert Rd
Catherington Down
Catherington La
P
Catherington CE Inf Sch
South Rd
Well Cl
South Rd
Holdenhurst Cl
Crabden La
Nature Reserve
St Catherines
PH
Down La
The Vale
Lith La
Lynwood Way
Chervil La
Juniper Cl
Comfrey Cl
Down Farm La
Cvn Pk
Stubbins Down
Kings Court Sch
Catherington
A3(M)
A3
Blendworth Lith
Crabden Row
Crabden La

69 70 71

A B C D E F

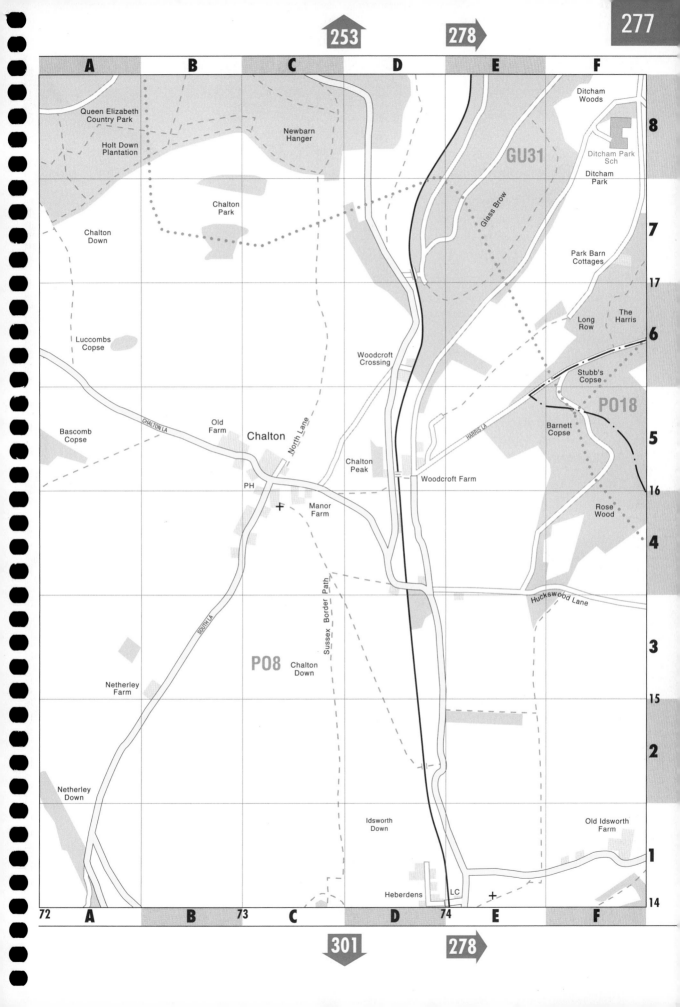

253
278

A   **B**   **C**   **D**   **E**   **F**

Queen Elizabeth
Country Park

Holt Down
Plantation

Ditcham Woods

Newbarn
Hanger

GU31

Ditcham Park
Sch

Chalton
Park

Ditcham
Park

8

Chalton
Down

Glass Brow

7

Park Barn
Cottages

17

Luccombs
Copse

Woodcroft
Crossing

Long
Row

The
Harris

6

Stubb's
Copse

Bascomb
Copse

CHALTON LA

Old
Farm

Chalton

North Lane

Barnett
Copse

PO18

5

Chalton
Peak

HARRIS LA

PH

Woodcroft Farm

16

Manor
Farm

Rose
Wood

4

Sussex Border Path

Huckswood Lane

SOUTH LA

3

PO8

Chalton
Down

Netherley
Farm

15

2

Netherley
Down

Idsworth
Down

Old Idsworth
Farm

1

Heberdens

LC

14

72   **A**   **B**   73   **C**   **D**   74   **E**   **F**

301
278

GU31

Booker Down

Booker Down Rough

Hudsons Copse

Upper West Wood

Uppark (National Trust)

Harehurst Wood

Sussex Border Path

Nightingale Bottom

Grass Piece

Lower West Wood

The Harrows

Star Copse

Park Copse

The Harris

Hale Wood

Killing Wood

Ladyholt

Eckensfield

Hucksholt Farm

Ladyholt Park

Wills Wood

Little Down Copse

Littlegreen Wood

Compton Park

PO18

Littlegreen Sch

Cowdown La

Cowdown La

Hundred Acre Farm

Cowdown Farm

Huckswood

Compton Farm

Huckswood Copse

Jubilee Clump

Compton

PO8

THE SQUARE

PO CHURCH LA

Robin Wood

Compton Down

SCHOOL LA

PH

Compton & Up Marden CE Prim Sch

Hill Barn

Drift Road Plantation

West Hanger

Bottom Copse

B2146

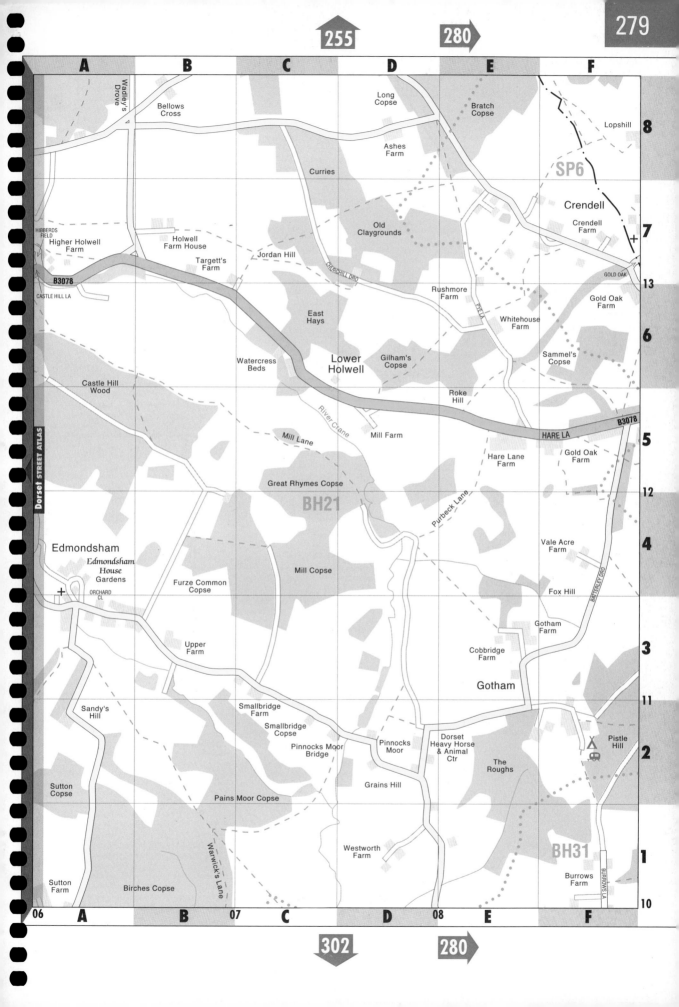

Dorset STREET ATLAS

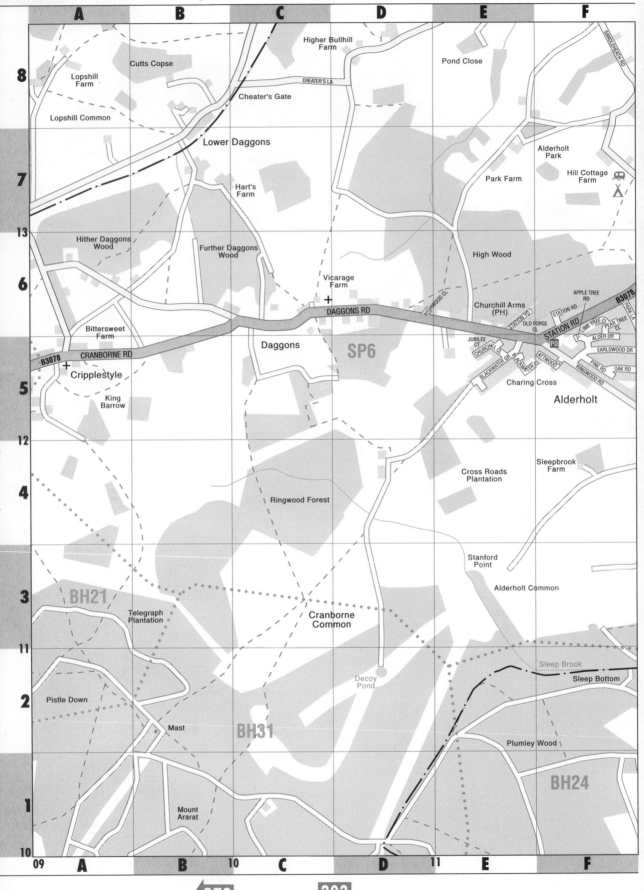

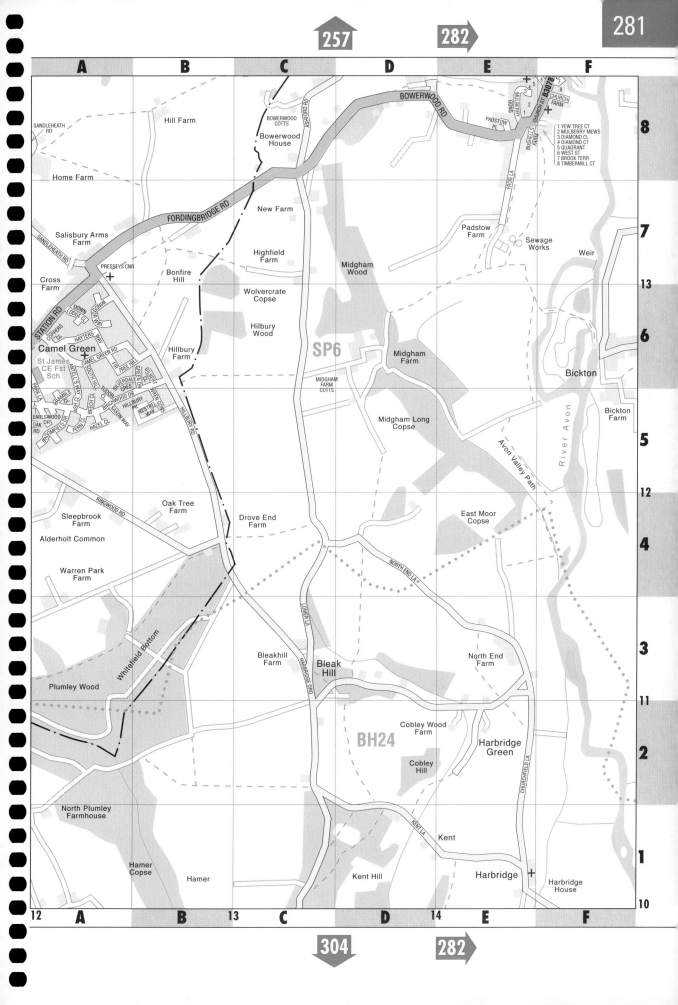

281 258

	A	B	C	D	E	F

8

Cemy

B3078
A338

Winnall's Wood

BROADHILL LA

BLISSFORD RD

Blissford Hill

The Merrie Thought

Newfoundland

Blissford

BLISSFORD CROSS

Redbrook

Rose Farm

The Three Lions (PH)

CHILLY HILL

STUCKTON RD

7

Redbrook Farm

REDBROOK COTTS

Stuckton

Ditchend Brook

Frogham

BLISSFORD HILL

ABBOTS WELL RD

13

Flaxfield Farm

THE CLOSE

BARTLETTS COMM

The Foresters Arms (PH)

Bickton Ash

FROGHAM CROSS

THE PADDOCK

6

HERN LA

FENTONS HILL

HYDE LA

Frogham Hill

P

Abbots Well

Hyde

Hyde Common

Ogdens Farm

5

RINGWOOD RD

SP6

Hungerford

HUNGERFORD HILL

Hyde CE Prim Sch

Ogdens

12

Hern Gate Farm

Dairy Farm

4

RINGWOOD RD

The Royal Oak (PH)

Gunville

GORLEY LYNCH

Holland Bottom

LAWRENCE LA

GORLEY CROSS

BUDDLE HILL

Buddle

Gorley Common

North Gorley

Huckles Brook

Dorridge Hill

3

Knutley Copse

Gorley Hill

Furze Hill

Brogenslade Bottom

11

King's Copse

Ford

2

Hucklesbrook Farm

South Gorley

BROOKSIDE

Cuckoo Hill

Huckles Bridge

Cuckoo Hill Rly

1

SALISBURY RD A338

BH24

IBSLEY DRO

BLIND LA

Newtown Farm

NEWTOWN LA

Little Chibden Bottom

Ibsley Common

10

Merrilea Farm

15	A	16	B	C	17	D	E	F

281 305

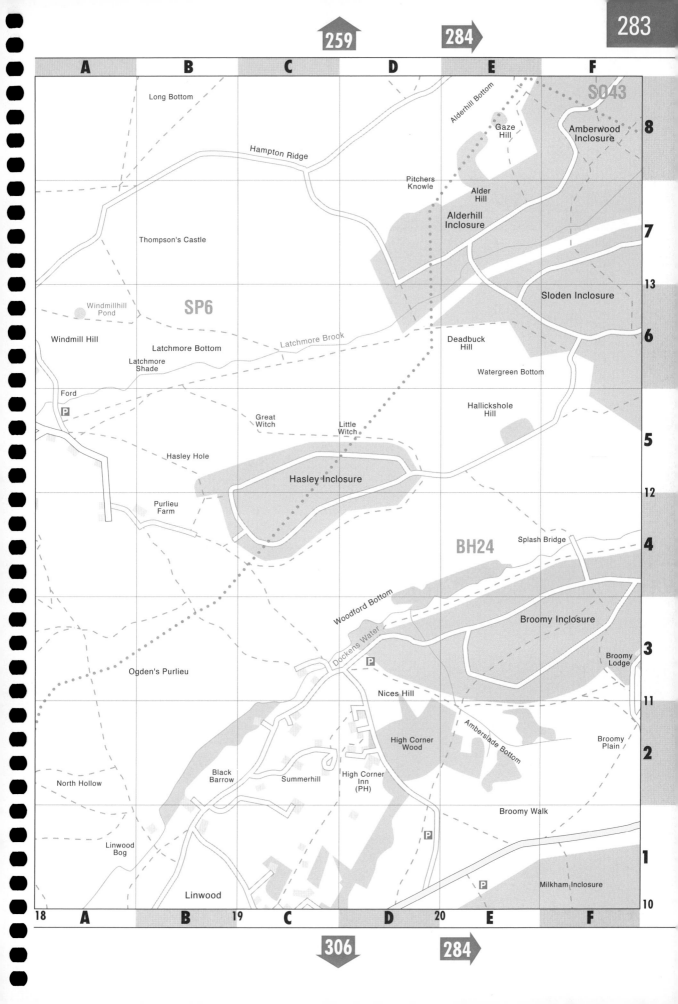

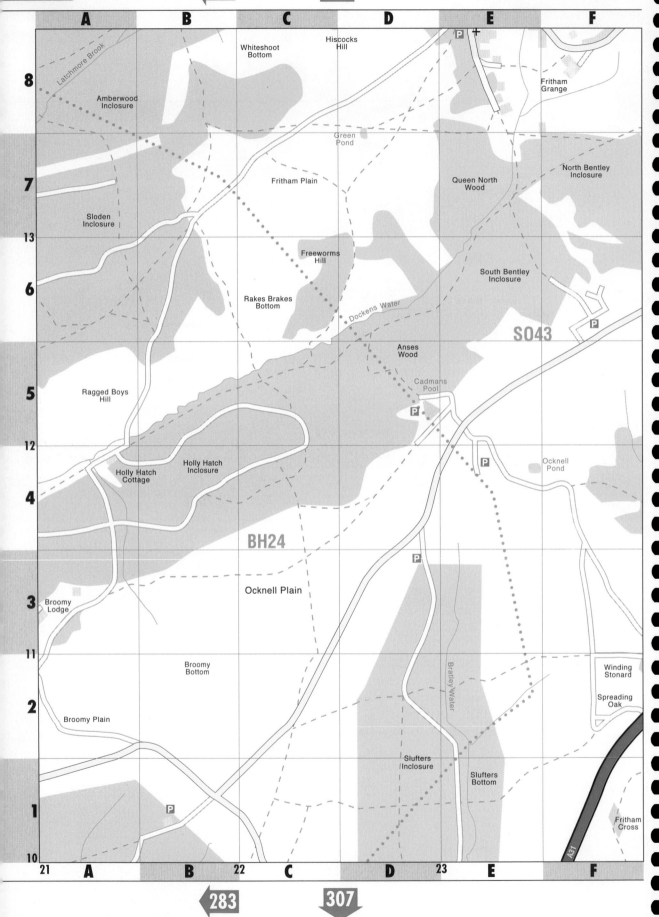

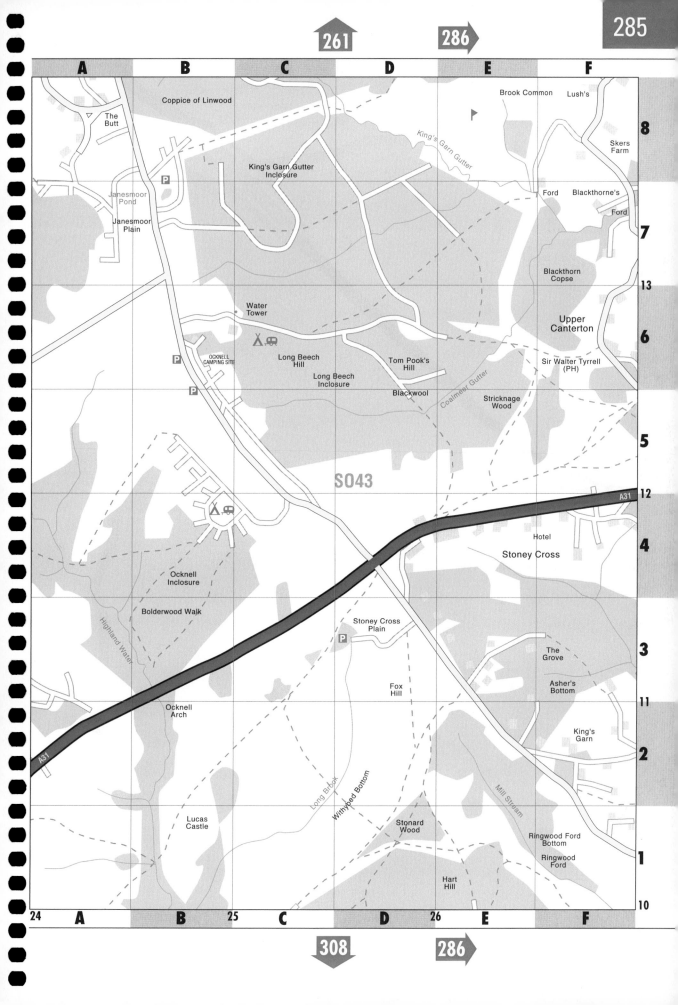

261
286

A   B   C   D   E   F

The Butt

Coppice of Linwood

Brook Common Lush's

8

King's Garn Gutter

Skers Farm

King's Garn Gutter Inclosure

Janesmoor Pond

Ford Blackthorne's

Ford

Janesmoor Plain

7

Blackthorn Copse

13

Water Tower

Upper Canterton

6

Long Beech Hill

OCKNELL CAMPING SITE

Tom Pook's Hill

Sir Walter Tyrrell (PH)

Long Beech Inclosure

Blackwool

Strcknage Wood

Coalmeer Gutter

5

SO43

A31

12

Hotel

4

Stoney Cross

Ocknell Inclosure

Bolderwood Walk

Highland Water

Stoney Cross Plain

The Grove

3

Asher's Bottom

Fox Hill

11

Ocknell Arch

King's Garn

2

Long Brook

Withybed Bottom

Mill Stream

Lucas Castle

Stonard Wood

Ringwood Ford Bottom

Ringwood Ford

1

Hart Hill

10

308
286

285
262

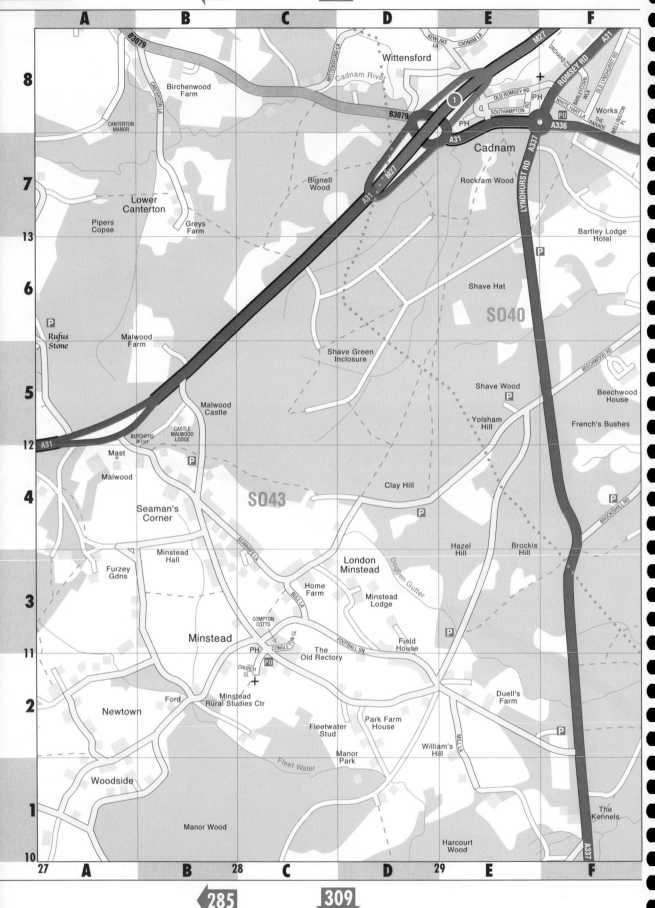

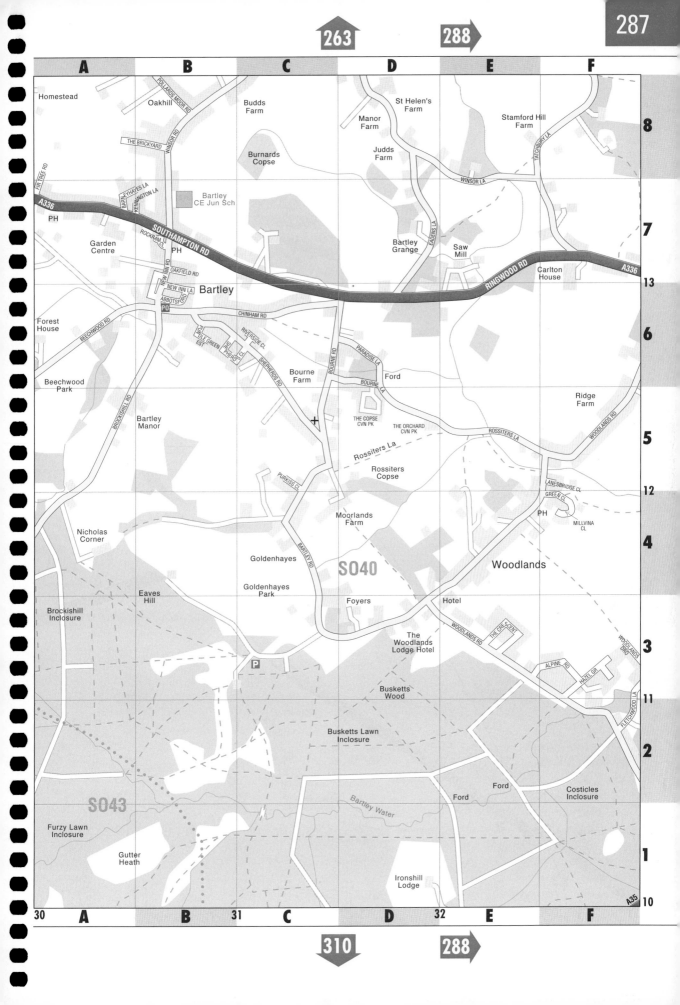

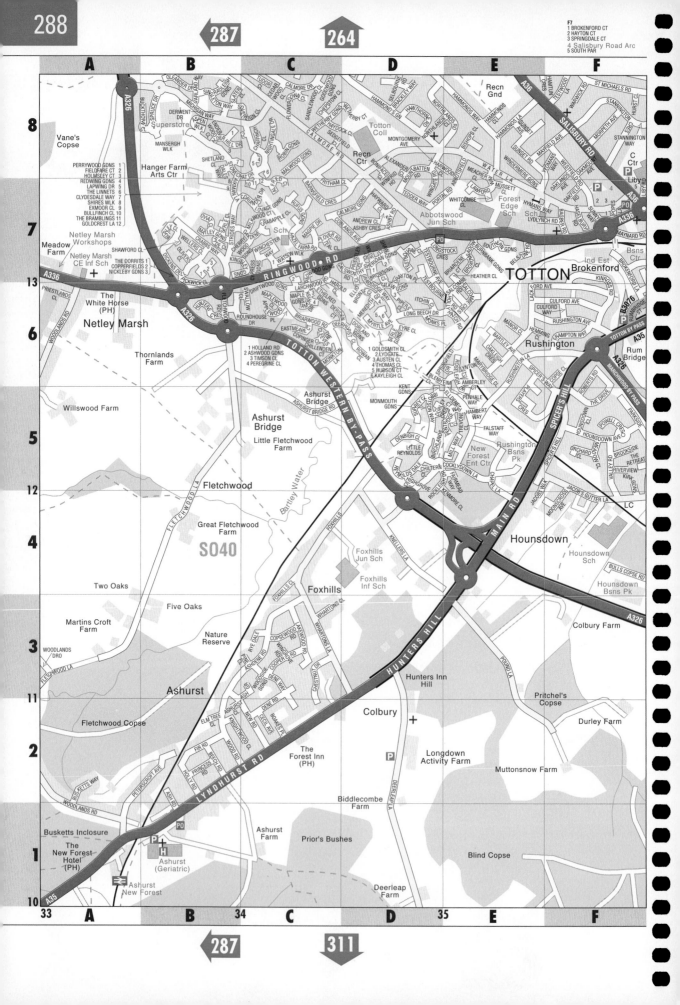

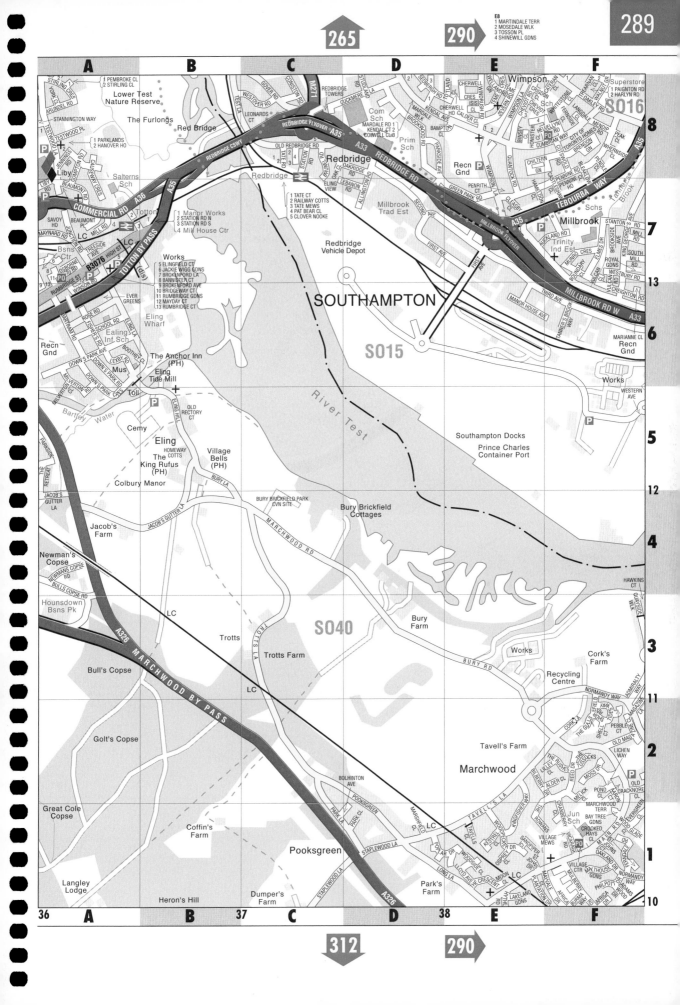

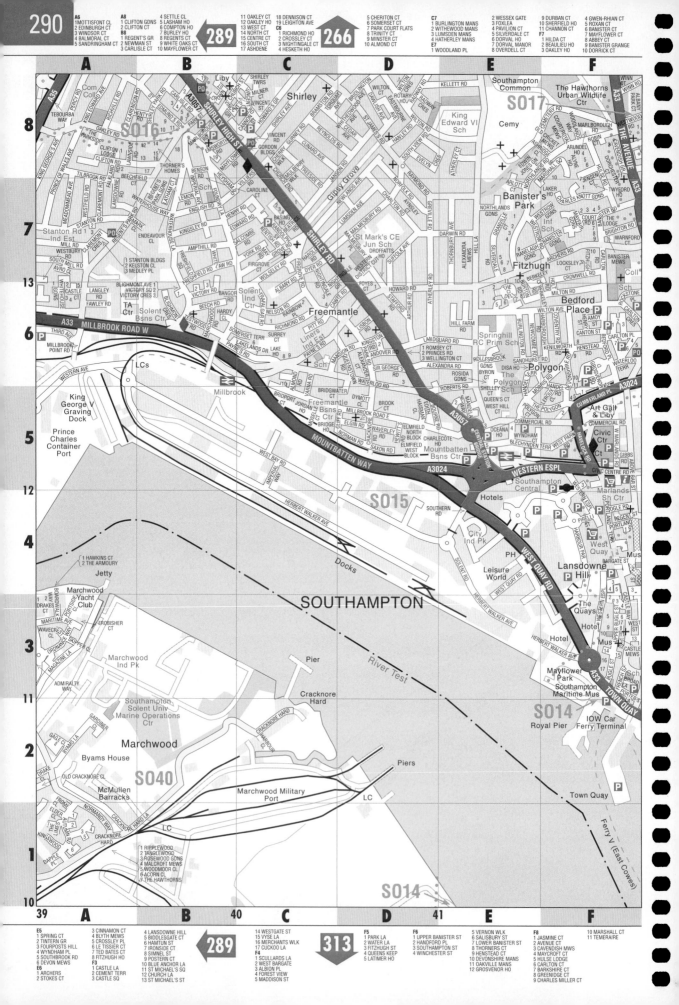

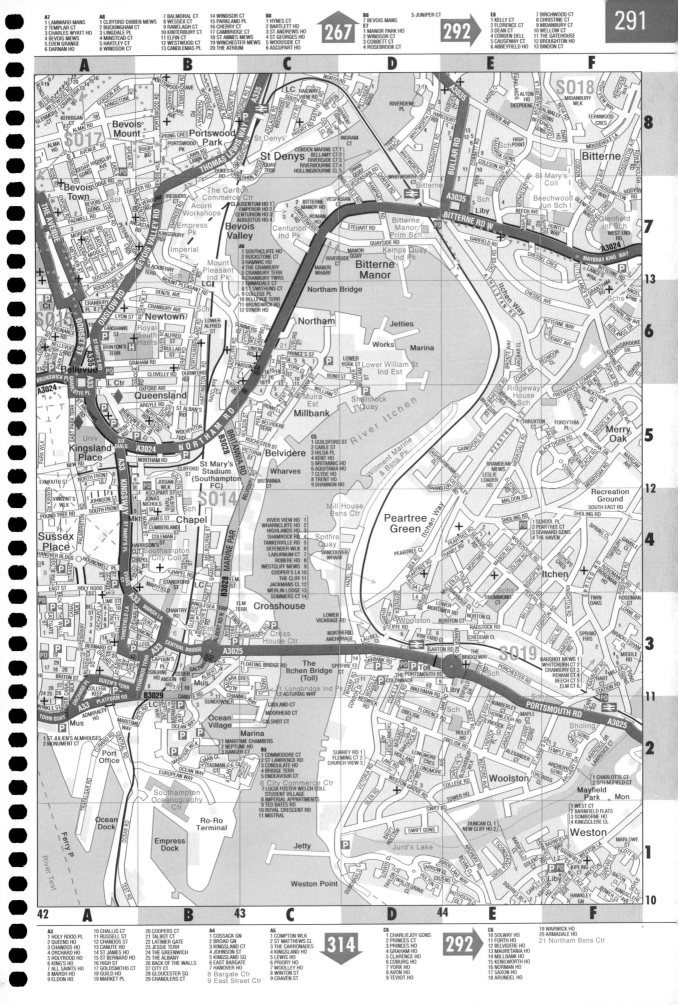

267 292

A7
1 LAMWARD MANS
2 TEMPLAR CT
3 CHARLES WYATT HO
4 BEVOIS MEWS
5 EDEN GRANGE
6 DARNAN HO

A8
1 CLIFFORD DIBBEN MEWS
2 BUCKINGHAM CT
3 LINGDALE PL
4 MINSTEAD CT
5 HARTLEY CT
6 WINDSOR CT

7 BALMORAL CT
8 WESSEX CT
9 RANELAGH CT
10 KINTERBURY CT
11 ELFIN CT
12 WESTWOOD CT
13 CANDLEMAS PL

14 WINDSOR CT
15 PARKLAND PL
16 CHERRY CT
17 CAMBRIDGE CT
18 ST ANNES MEWS
19 WINCHESTER MEWS
20 THE ATRIUM

B8
1 HYNES CT
2 BARTLETT HO
3 ST ANDREWS HO
4 ST GEORGES HO
5 WOODSIDE CT
6 ASCUPART HO

B8
7 BEVOIS MANS
E7
1 MANOR PARK HO
2 WINDSOR CT
3 GOBBETT CT
4 ROSEBROOK CT

5 JUNIPER CT

E8
1 KELLY CT
2 FLORENCE CT
3 DEAN CT
4 CORDEN DELL
5 MILLBANK HO
6 ABBEYFIELD HO

7 BIRCHWOOD CT
8 CHRISTINE CT
9 MIDANBURY CT
10 WELLOW CT
11 THE GATEHOUSE
12 BROUGHTON CT
13 BINDON CT

314 292

A3
1 HOLY ROOD PL
2 QUEENS HO
3 CHANDOS HO
4 ORCHARD HO
5 HOLYROOD HO
6 KING'S HO
7 ALL SAINTS CT
8 MARSH HO
9 ELDON HO

10 CHALLIS CT
11 RUSSELL ST
12 CHANDOS ST
13 CANUTE HO
14 ST JAMES HO
15 ST BERNARD HO
16 HIGH ST
17 GOLDSMITHS CT
18 GUILD HO
19 MARKET PL

20 COOPERS CT
21 TALBOT CT
22 LATIMER GATE
23 JESSIE TERR
24 THE GREENWICH
25 THE ALBANY
26 BACK OF THE WALLS
27 CITY CT
28 GLOUCESTER SQ
29 CHANDLERS CT

A4
1 COSSACK GN
2 BROAD GN
3 KINGSLAND CT
4 JOHNSON ST
5 KINGSLAND SQ
6 EAST BARGATE
7 HANOVER HO
8 Bargate Ctr
9 East Street Ctr

A5
1 COMPTON WLK
2 ST MATTHEWS CL
3 THE CARRONADES
4 KINGSLAND HO
5 LEWIS HO
6 PRIORY HO
7 WOODSIDE CT
8 WINTON ST
9 CRAVEN ST

C6
1 CHARLIEJOY GDNS
2 PRINCES CT
3 PRINCES HO
4 GRAHAM HO
5 CLARENCE HO
6 COBURG HO
7 YORK HO
8 AVON HO
9 TEVIOT HO

C6
10 SOLWAY HO
11 FORTH HO
12 BELVIDERE HO
13 MAURETANIA HO
14 MILLBANK HO
15 KENILWORTH HO
16 NORMAN HO
17 SAXON HO
18 ARUNDEL HO

19 WARWICK HO
20 ARMADALE HO
21 Northam Bsns Ctr

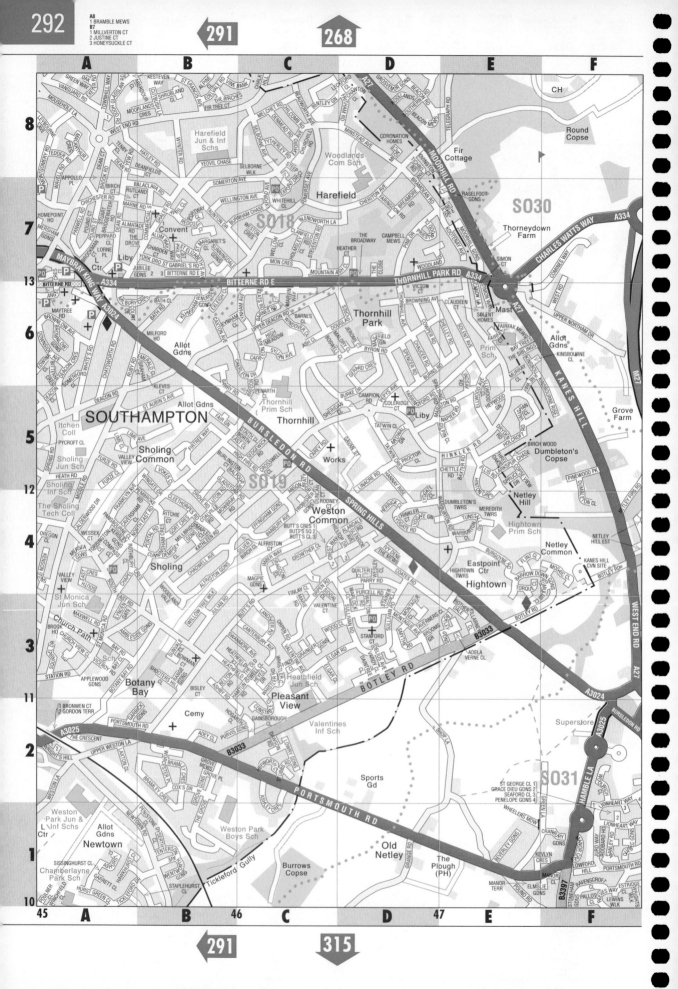

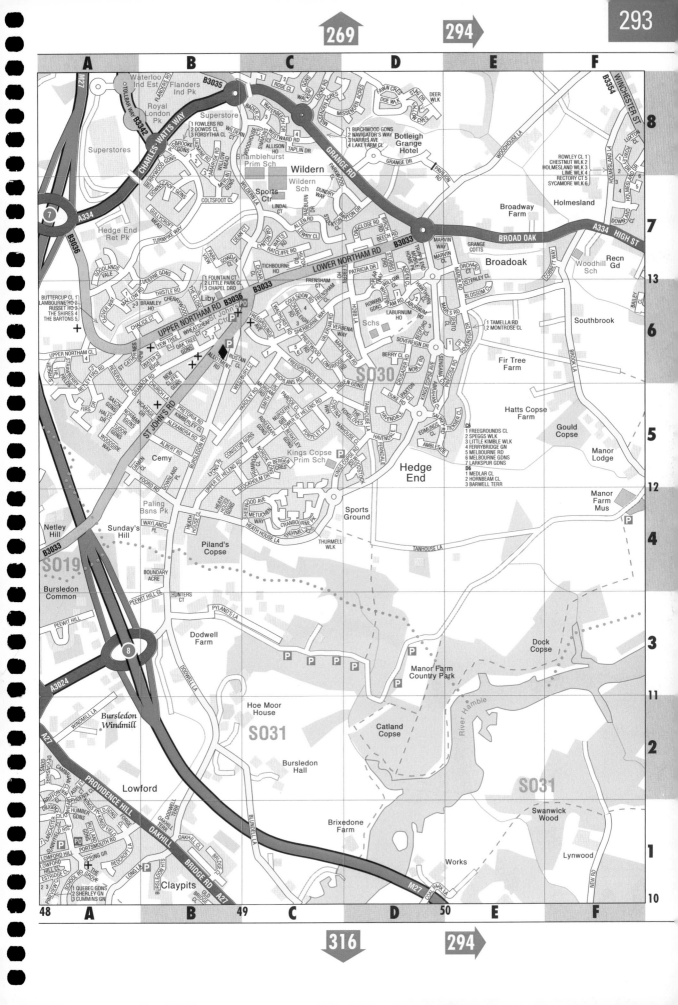

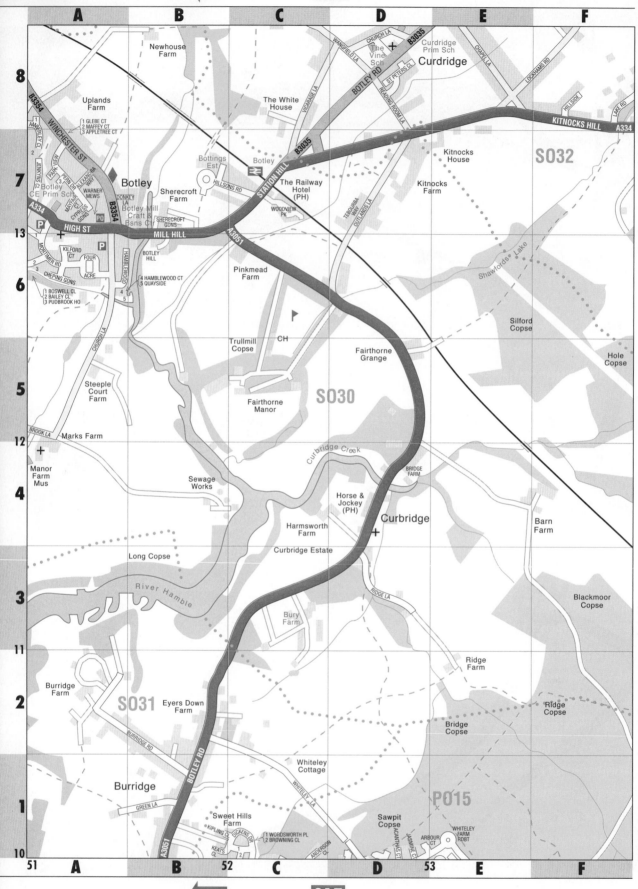

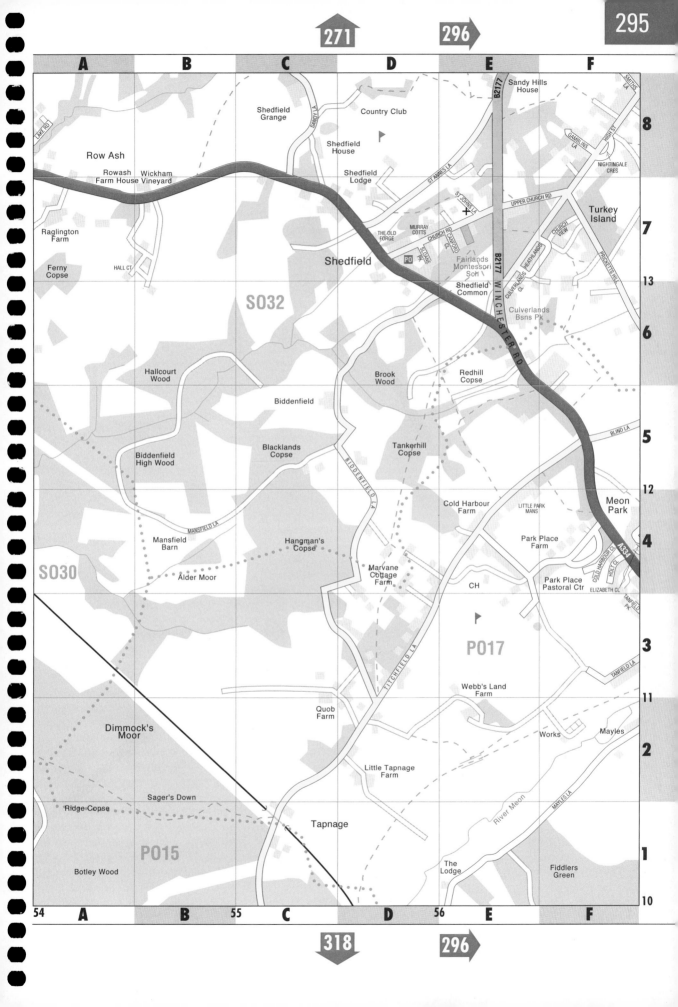

271
296

A B C D E F

8
7
13
6
5
12
4
3
11
2
1
10

Sandy Hills House
B2177
SMITHS LA
Shedfield Grange
SANDY LA
Country Club
Shedfield House
GAMBLINS LA
HIGH ST
NIGHTINGALE CRES
Row Ash
Rowash Farm House
Wickham Vineyard
Shedfield Lodge
ST ANNES LA
UPPER CHURCH RD
Turkey Island
Raglington Farm
HALL CT
THE OLD FORGE
MURRAY COTTS
ST JOHNS LA
CHURCH RD
CANFORD
CL
CHURCH
VIEW
PRICKETTS HILL
Ferny Copse
Shedfield
PO
SLOANE PK
Fairlands Montessori Sch
B2177
CULVERLANDS CL
HEATHLANDS
SO32
Shedfield Common
Culverlands Bsns Pk
WINCHESTER RD
Hallcourt Wood
Brook Wood
Redhill Copse
Biddenfield
BLIND LA
Blacklands Copse
Tankerhill Copse
BIDDENFIELD LA
Biddenfield High Wood
12
Cold Harbour Farm
LITTLE PARK MANS
Meon Park
MANSFIELD LA
Park Place Farm
A334
Mansfield Barn
Hangman's Copse
Marvane Cottage Farm
COLD HARBOUR CL
HOLT CL
TANFIELD PK
Alder Moor
CH
Park Place Pastoral Ctr
ELIZABETH CL
SO30
PO17
TITCHFIELD LA
Dimmock's Moor
Webb's Land Farm
TANFIELD LA
Quob Farm
Works
Mayles
Little Tapnage Farm
River Meon
MAYLES LA
Sager's Down
Ridge Copse
Tapnage
PO15
The Lodge
Fiddlers Green
Botley Wood

54 A B 55 C D 56 E F

318
296

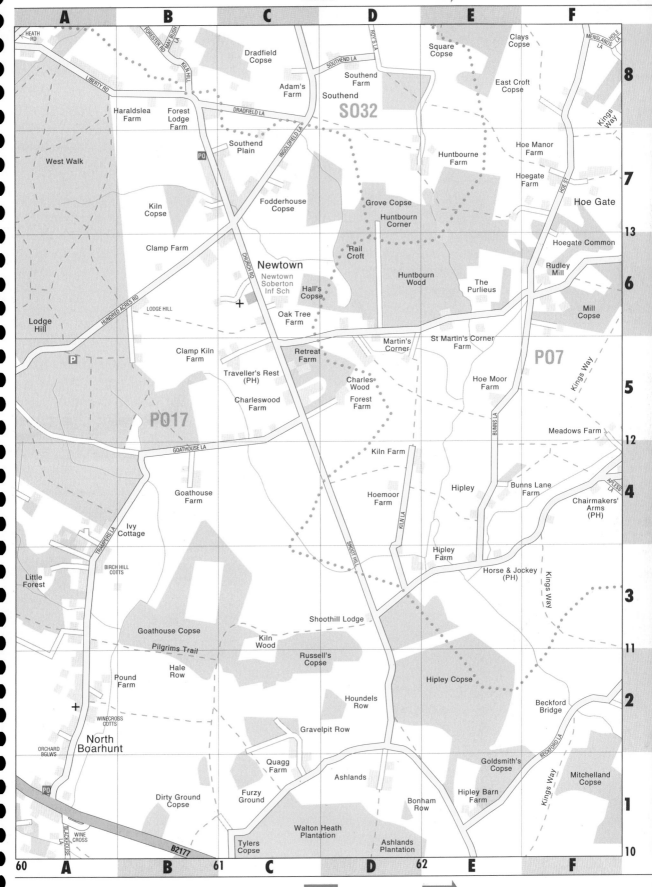

297
274

	A	B	C	D	E	F

8

Hole La

Kings Way

Menslands Lane

Madam's Copse

Bury Lodge Farm

Menslands Lane

Harwood House

B2150

Pithill Farm

The Paddocks

Menslands Lane

Habens Lane

Kidburn

Bittles Farm

HAMBLEDON RD

Vinnell's Wood

Port Copse Plantation

RUSHMERE LA

Steane Copse

7

Bent Farm

BENT LA

WELL HILL

Rookwood Farm

Pithill Farm

13

Kings Way

Great Ervills Farm

BROAD LA

Forest Gate

Waytarer's Walk

KILMORE LA

6

Mill Plain

Cherryhill Copse

Cherryhill Farm

The Plantation

UPPER CRABBICK LA

UPLANDS RD

THOMPSONS LA

ANTHILL CL

Alexandra House

Anthill Common

Anthill Farm

High Wood

Pyles Farm

PH

SCHOOL LA

Harts Copse

Inn

TANNER'S LA

5

LOWER CRABBICK LA

Inhams

INHAMS LA

GLASSPOOL

Rookwood View

Cemy

CEMETERY LA

Park Rd

Worlds End

Crabbick Farm

P07

HAMBLEDON RD

CLARENDON CL

PO

B2150

12

Collyers Farm

Woodlake Farm

Lower Crabbick Farm

FOREST RD

HARVEST RD

HAWTHORN RD

YEW TREE

GREEN LA

SOUTHWICK RD

FRENCHIES

ASHLING CL

FAIRFIELD

PH

4

APLESS LA

PH

ROMAN GN

THE SMITHY

LOYLAND RD

PURDIES

PEAKFIELD

BUNKERS HILL

THE ORCHARD

BERE RD

Denmead Jun Sch

Apless Farm

BECKFORD LA

Creech Wood

Forest Farm

THE WILLOWS

THE MEADOW

CORNER MEAD

WHITE WINGS HO

FIELD WAY

Old River

3

THE LIBERTY

Bunkers Hill

P

Creech Wood Forest Walk

Creech House

Parklands Bsns Pk

FALCON CT

THE SPINNEY

11

Lower Beckford

Creech Lodge

MOUNT PLEASANT

FURZELEY RD

CH

2

Wiggs Wood

Furzeley Corner

NEW LANDS LA

1

Lovelocks

P017

Creech Farm

Furzehill Farm

SHEEPWASH LA

Three Oaks Farm

BLENHEM BARN

Jays Copse

Jays Hummock

BELNEY LA

Hallsfield Farm

10

63	A	B	64	C	D	65	E	F

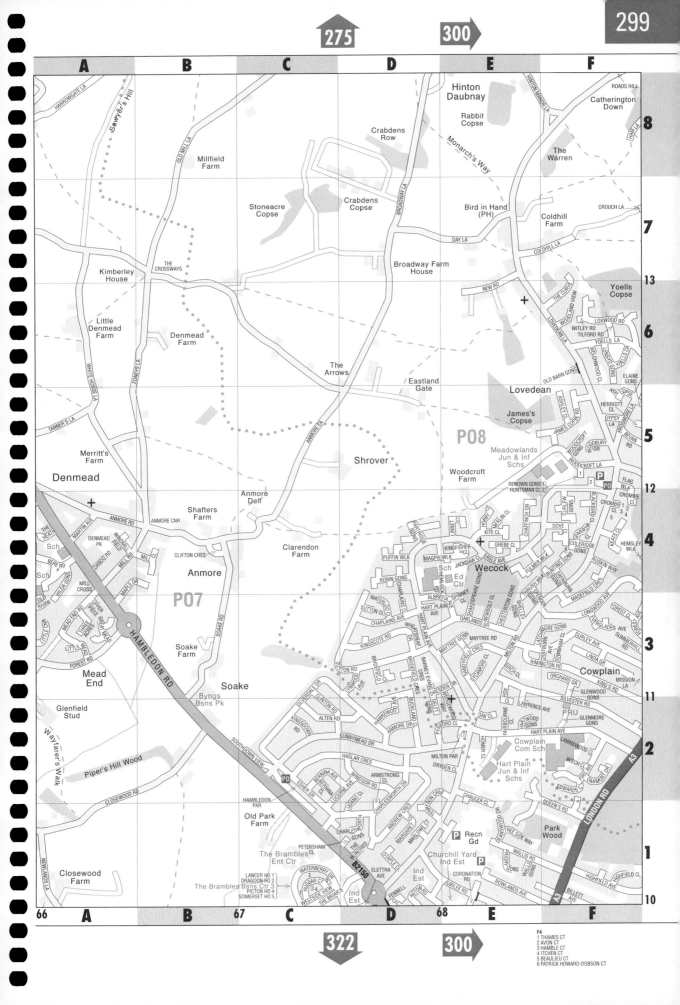

299
276

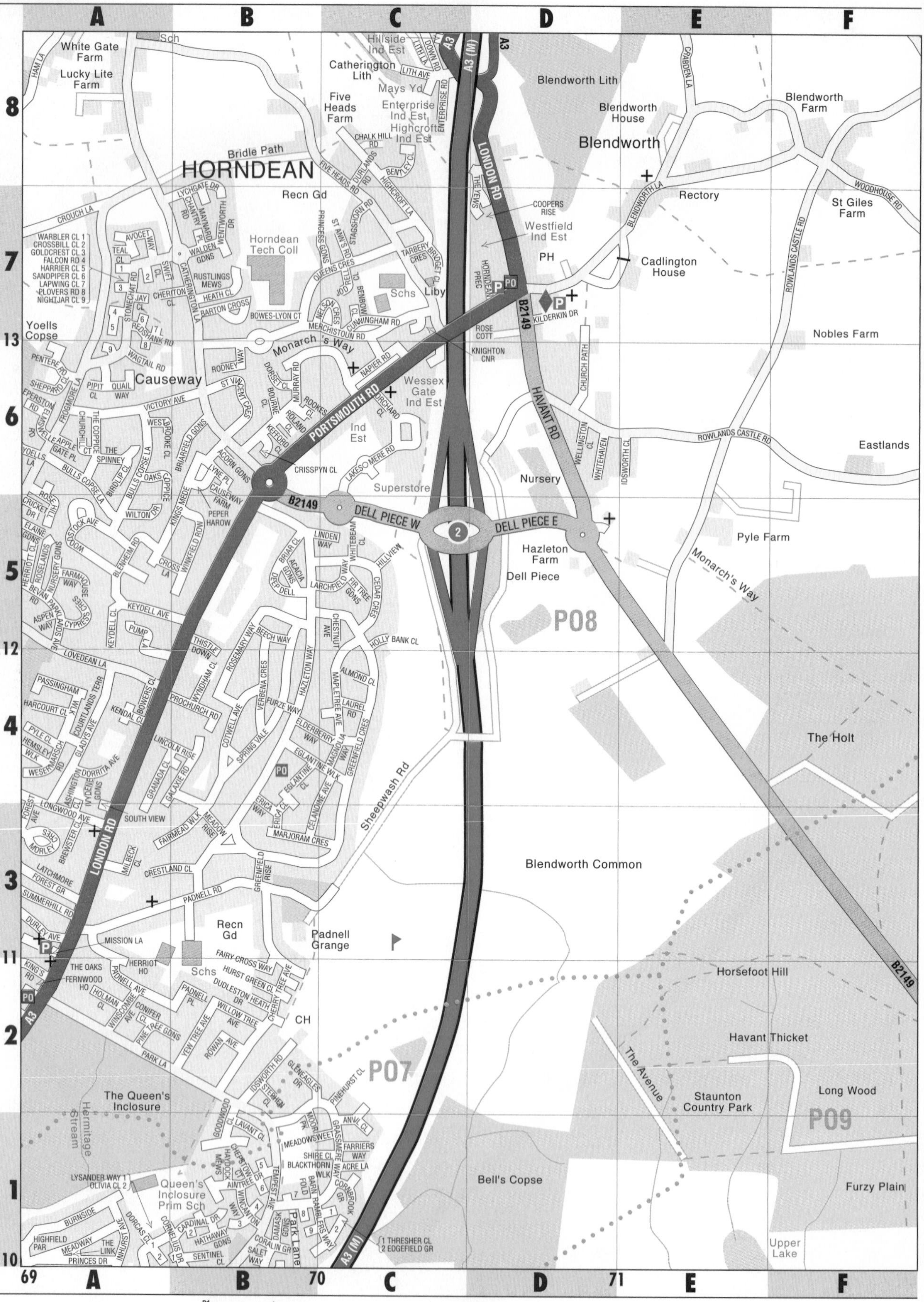

299
323

B1
1 JESSICA CL
2 OCTAVIUS CT
3 KEMPTON PK
4 PLUMPTON GR
5 FONTWELL MEWS
6 RIPON GDNS
7 THE WESTBROOK CTR
8 BRACKEN HEATH
9 HITHERWOOD CL

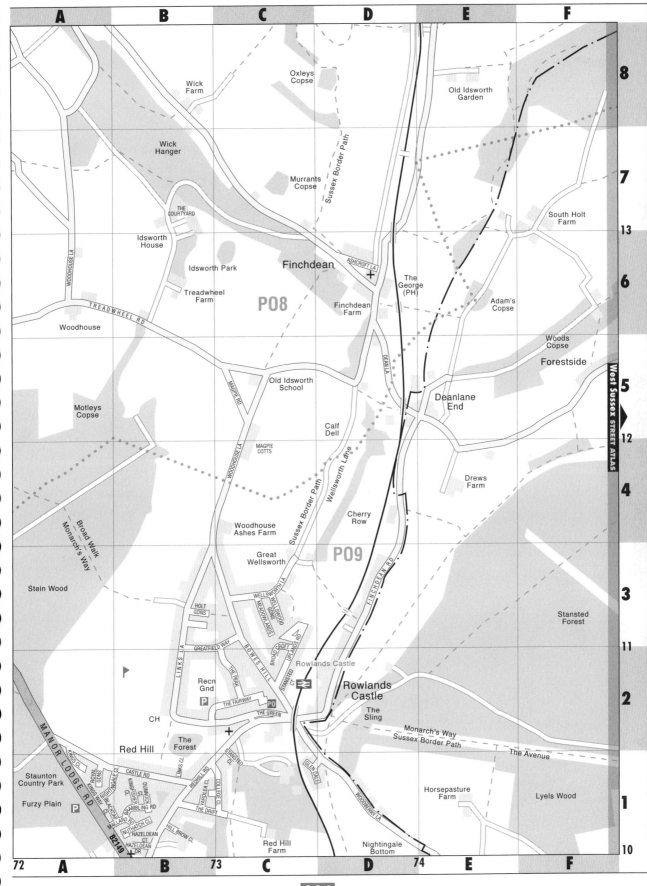

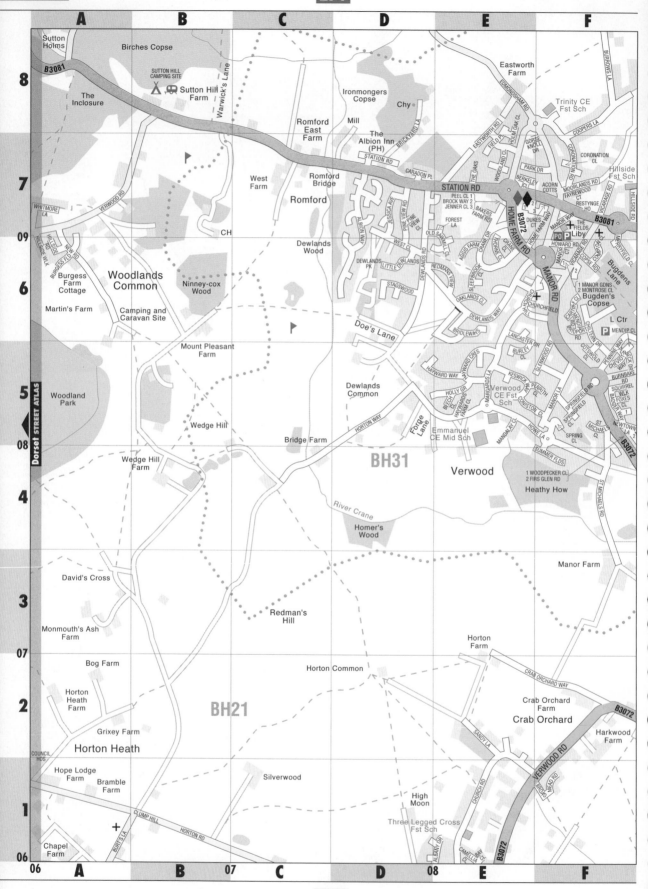

Dorset STREET ATLAS

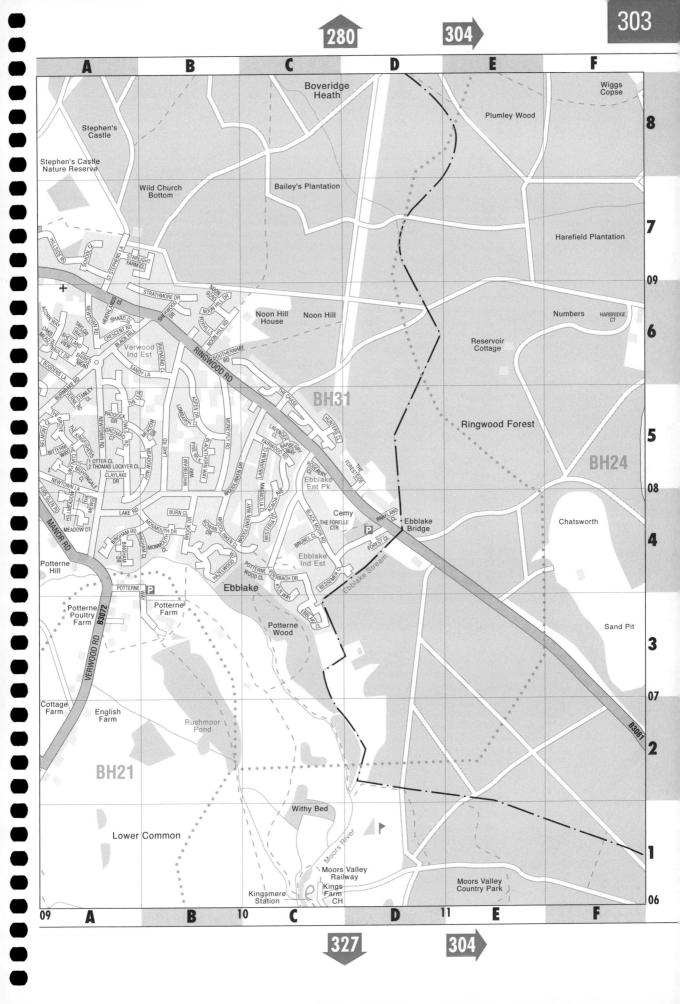

303
281

A B C D E F

8

Gravel Pit

Turmer
Hill

Harbridge
Farm

Ibsley
Bridge

Avon Valley Path

Weir

Turmer

Harbridge
Lodge

Hamer Brook

Plumley
Farm

7

Lower
Turmer

Mill Stream

A338

PH

09

Turmer Brook

6

SHEPHERDS LA

Shepherds
Cottage

Shepherds Hill

Home
Wood

Dog Kennel
Wood

Gravel
Pit

Ibsley
Water

Riverbank
Covert

CHESTNUT AVE

Whitehoe
Cottages

New Barn
Cottages

Old
Somerley

Ellingham

5

NEA DR

Somerley
Park

The
Bothy

ELLINGHAM DR

New
Bridge

Ellingham
Farm

ELLINGHAM CROSS

ELLINGHAM DRO

SALISBURY RD

Nursery
Cottages

BH24

08

Broad Close
Covert

4

Old Laundry
Cottage

Somerley

Gravel
Works

Park
Cottage

The Belt

3

Ringwood
Forest

Meadow
Lake

River Avon

Blashford
Farm

A338

07

Sand
Pit

DUNCOMBE DR

ASHLEY DR

Dockens Water

SALISBURY RD

2

B3081

Sunderton
Wood

Weir

Lifeland
Copse

Upper Hurst
Farm

Duncombe
Lodge

Ashley
Farm

King Stream

Gouldings
Farm

1

VERWOOD RD

B3081

Up
Mead

Hurst Old
Farm

06

Baker's
Hanging

Lin Brook

12 A B 13 C D 14 E F

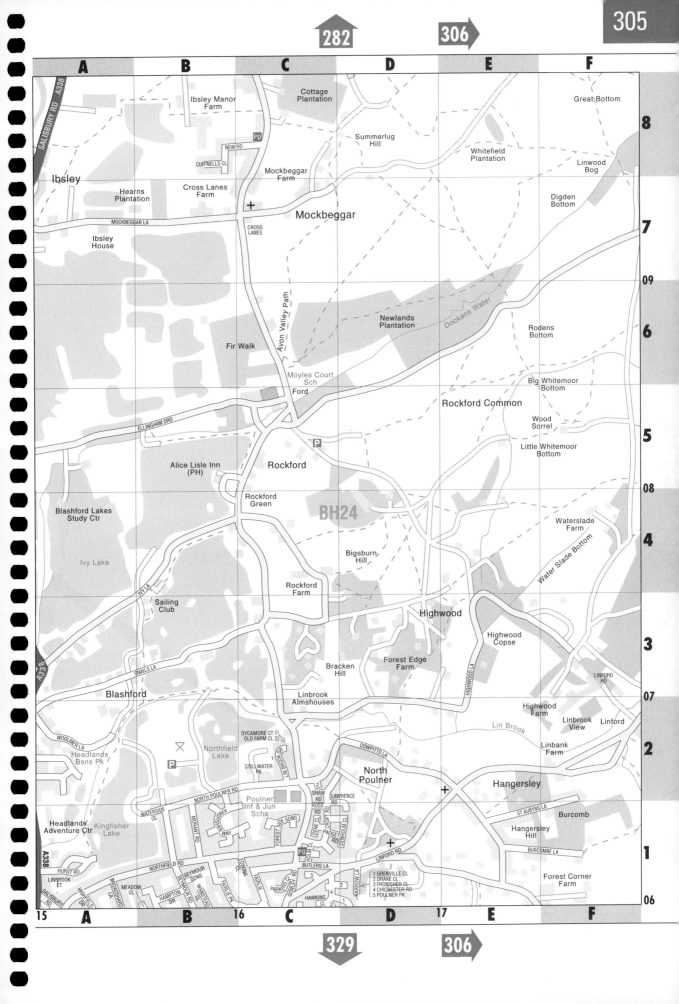

282 306

A B C D E F

SALISBURY RD A338

Ibsley Manor Farm

Cottage Plantation

Great Bottom

8

NEW RD

Summerlug Hill

Whitefield Plantation

Linwood Bog

CUFFNELLS CL

Mockbeggar Farm

Ibsley

Hearns Plantation

Cross Lanes Farm

Digden Bottom

Mockbeggar

MOCKBEGGAR LA

Mockbeggar

7

CROSS LANES

09

Ibsley House

Dockens Water

Avon Valley Path

Newlands Plantation

Rodens Bottom

6

Fir Walk

Big Whitemoor Bottom

Moyles Court Sch

Ford

Rockford Common

Wood Sorrel

5

Alice Lisle Inn (PH)

ELLINGHAM DRO

P

Rockford

Little Whitemoor Bottom

08

Rockford Green

BH24

Waterslade Farm

4

Blashford Lakes Study Ctr

Bigsburn Hill

Water Slade Bottom

Ivy Lake

Rockford Farm

IVY LA

Sailing Club

Highwood

Highwood Copse

3

SNAILS LA

Bracken Hill

Forest Edge Farm

HIGHWOOD LA

LINFORD HO

A338

Blashford

Linbrook Almshouses

Highwood Farm

07

WOOLMER LA

Lin Brook

Linbrook View

Linford

Headlands Bsns Pk

Northfield Lake

SYCAMORE CT 1
OLD FARM CL 2

LIN BROOK DR

COWPITTS LA

Linbank Farm

2

P

STILLWATER PK

North Poulner

Hangersley

Headlands Adventure Ctr

Kingfisher Lake

NORTH POULNER RD

WATERSIDE CL

MORANT RD

FORESTSIDE WAY

Poulner Inf & Jun Schs

SHAW RD

ROSS RD

LAWRENCE RD

ST AUBYNS LA

Burcomb

FOREST SIDE GDNS

DENE CL

PROFT RD

PADGET RD

DENHOLM CL

Hangersley Hill

HURST RD

LINBROOK CT

SALISBURY RD

HIGHFIELD DR

BROADSHARD LA

MEADOW CL

HAMPTON DR

SCHMOUR RD

WANSTEAD

SEYMOUR GDNS

EDWINA CL

FAIRLIE

NORTHFIELD RD

FAIRLIE PK

PARK RD

GORLEY RD

PO

BUTLERS LA

HOLM CL

HAWKINS

LINFORD RD

NARROW LA

BURCOMBE LA

Forest Corner Farm

1 GRENVILLE CL
2 DRAKE CL
3 FROBISHER CL
4 CHICHESTER RD
5 POULNER PK

06

15 A B 16 C D 17 E F

A338

329 306

305
283

A **B** **C** **D** **E** **F**

8

Milkham
Inclosure

Linwood

Amie's
Wood

Webb's
Copse

Toms
Farm

Appleslade
Farm

The
Red Shoot Inn
(PH)

Linwood
Farm

7

Amie's
Corner

King's
Garden

Appleslade
Bottom

Lin Wood

Mount
Hill

09

Castle
Piece

Roe
Inclosure

Appleslade
Inclosure

6

Linford Brook

Red Shoot
Plain

Red Shoot
Wood

Buckherd
Bottom

5

Green
Ford

Greenford
Bottom

08

Great Linford
Inclosure

White
Hill

BH24

Collier's
Thorns

4

Pinnick
Wood

Akercombe
Bottom

Handy
Cross

A31

Linford Bottom

3

Little Linford
Inclosure

Handy Cross Plain

Ridley Plain

Marrowbones
Hill

07

Linford

2

Picket
Bottom

Old
Gate

Little
Wood

Harvest
Slade

Brook
Farm

Picket
Hill

Ridley
Bottom

1

Shobley

Ridley
Wood

Shobley
Bottom

A31

Picket
Post

06

18 **A** **B** 19 **C** **D** 20 **E** **F**

305
330

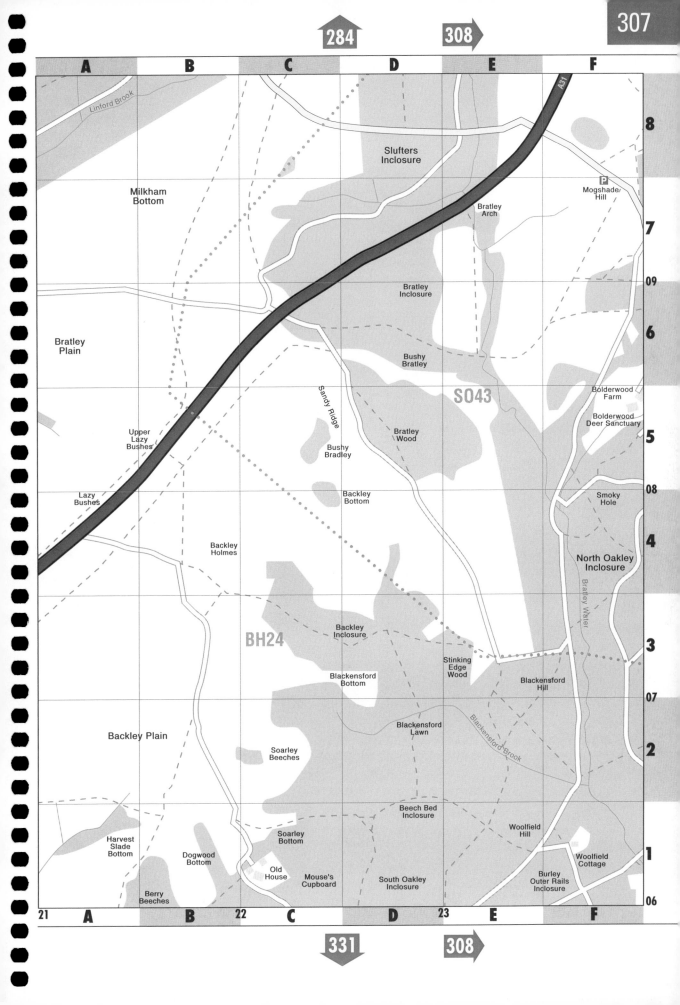

284
308
308

A31

Linford Brook

Slufters
Inclosure

Milkham
Bottom

Bratley
Arch

Mogshade
Hill

Bratley
Inclosure

Bushy
Bratley

Bratley
Plain

SO43

Bolderwood
Farm

Bolderwood
Deer Sanctuary

Sandy Ridge

Bratley
Wood

Upper
Lazy
Bushes

Bushy
Bradley

Backley
Bottom

Smoky
Hole

Lazy
Bushes

North Oakley
Inclosure

Backley
Holmes

Bratley Water

BH24

Backley
Inclosure

Stinking
Edge
Wood

Blackensford
Hill

Blackensford
Bottom

Blackensford Brook

Backley Plain

Blackensford
Lawn

Soarley
Beeches

Beech Bed
Inclosure

Woolfield
Hill

Harvest
Slade
Bottom

Soarley
Bottom

Dogwood
Bottom

Woolfield
Cottage

Old
House

Mouse's
Cupboard

South Oakley
Inclosure

Burley
Outer Rails
Inclosure

Berry
Beeches

21   22   23

06 07 08 09

307
285

A B C D E F

8

7

09

6

5

08

4

07

3

2

1

06

24 25 26

Acres Down House

Puckpits Inclosure

Bolderwood Walk

Coneygear Bottom

Cross

Woolsmoor Meads

Highland Water Inclosure

Wick Wood

Bagshot Gutter

Holm Hill

The Knowles

Forest Walks

Holmhill Inclosure

Deer Sanctuary

Bolderwood Cottage

Highland Water

SO43

Bolderwood Grounds

Wooson's Hill

Portuguese Fireplace

Millyford Bridge

Pound Hill

Mark Ash Wood

Holidays Hill

North Oakley Inclosure

Wooson's Hill Inclosure

Holidays Hill Inclosure

Barrow Moor

Dark Hat

Church Moor

Bolderwood Arboretum Ornamental Dr

Warwickslade Cutting

BH24

Winding Shoot

Knightwood Oak

A35

Hart Hill

Knightwood Inclosure

Anderwood Inclosure

Eagle Oak

A35

Rhinefield Ornamental Dr

307
332

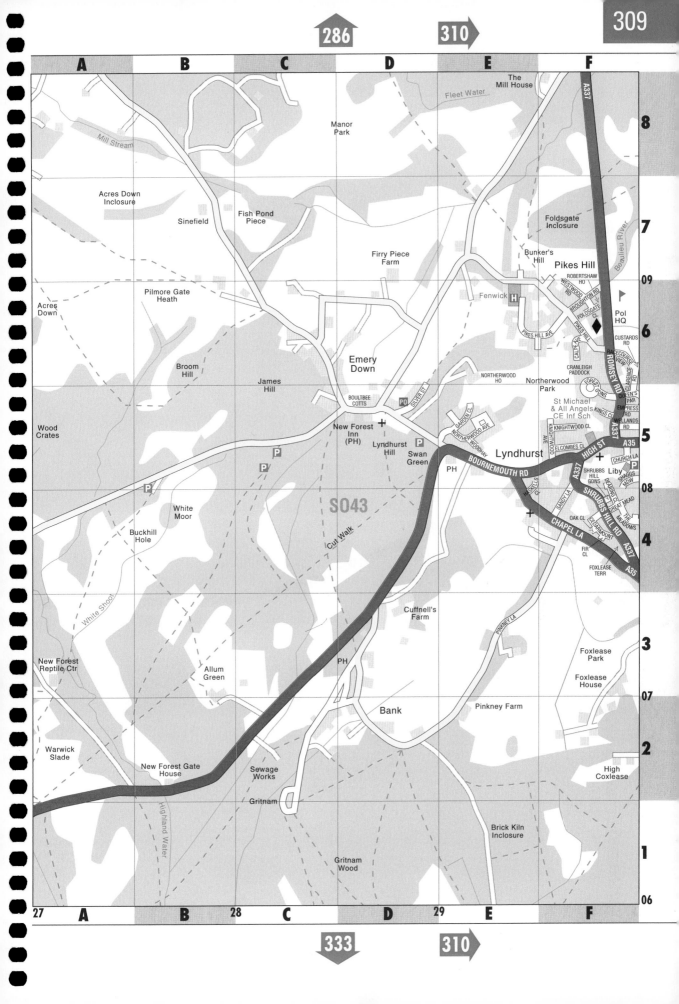

309
287

A B C D E F

8
7
09
6
5
08
4
07
3
2
1
06

Fox Hill

Rushpole Wood

Redbridge Hill

Ironshill Inclosure

Lodgehill Inclosure

A35

Fair Cross

Whitebridge Hill

Lodgehill Cottage

Beaulieu River

Mallard Wood

Beaulieu River

SO40

Dunces Arch Inclosure

CH

Dunces Arch

Longwater Lawn

THE CUSTARDS

Custards

THATCHED COTTAGE CVN PK

SOUTHAMPTON RD

Fox Hill

Row Hill

1 QUEEN'S PAR
2 EMPRESS RD

QUEENS RD

PRINCES CRES

PEMBERTON RD

WELLANDS RD

PO

HIGH ST

A35

B3056

Meml

PRINCES CT

Cemy

White Moor

SO43

RUFUS CT

Hotel
New Forest Mus

Bolton's Bench

The Ridge

SHAGGS MDW

THE MEADOWS

The Bench

BEAULIEU RD

GOSPORT LA

Goose Green

A35

BROOKLANDS

A337

Irons Hill Walk

B3056

Matley Ridge

Clayhill

Pondhead Inclosure

Parkhill (Hotel)

Pondhead

Holmhill Passage

BEECHEN LA
HILLARY CL
PARK CL

CLAY HILL

The Crown & Stirrup (PH)

Beechen La

Parkhill Lawn

Little Holmhill Inclosure

Park Ground Inclosure

Denny Inclosure

Little Holmhill

Park Hill

A337

30 A B 31 C D 32 E F

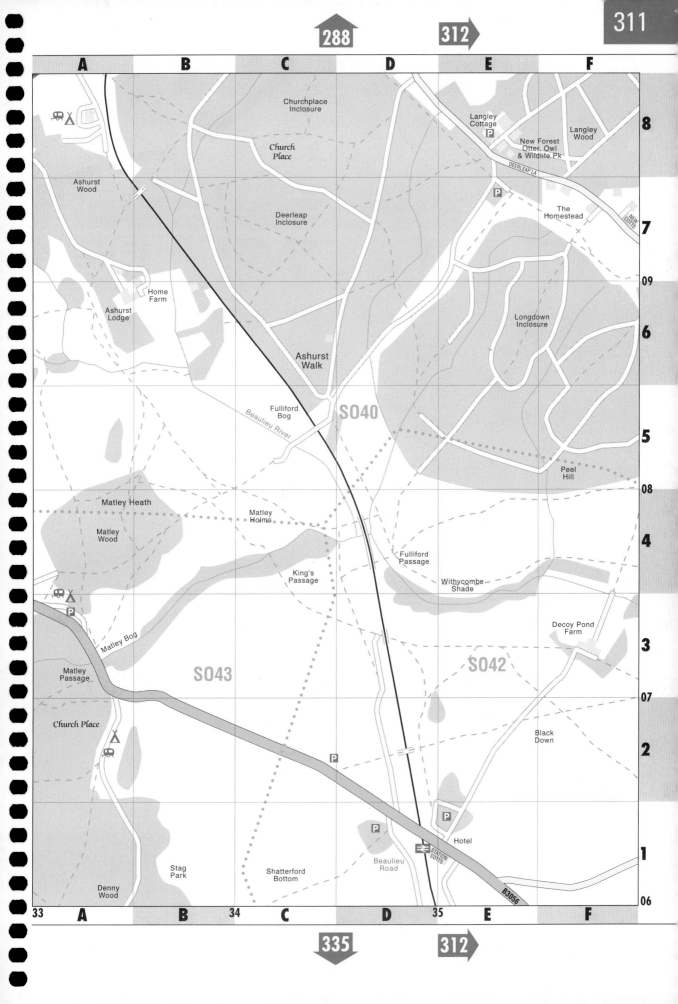

A B C D E F

8

7

09

6

5

08

4

3

07

2

1

06

Ashurst Wood

Churchplace Inclosure

Church Place

Deerleap Inclosure

Langley Cottage

New Forest Otter, Owl & Wildlife Pk

Langley Wood

DEERLEAP LA

The Homestead

NEW COTTS

Home Farm

Ashurst Lodge

Ashurst Walk

Longdown Inclosure

Fulliford Bog

Beaulieu River

SO40

Peel Hill

Matley Heath

Matley Holms

Matley Wood

King's Passage

Fulliford Passage

Withycombe Shade

Decoy Pond Farm

Matley Bog

SO43

Matley Passage

SO42

Church Place

Black Down

Stag Park

Shatterford Bottom

Beaulieu Road

Hotel

STATION COTTS

Denny Wood

B3056

311
289

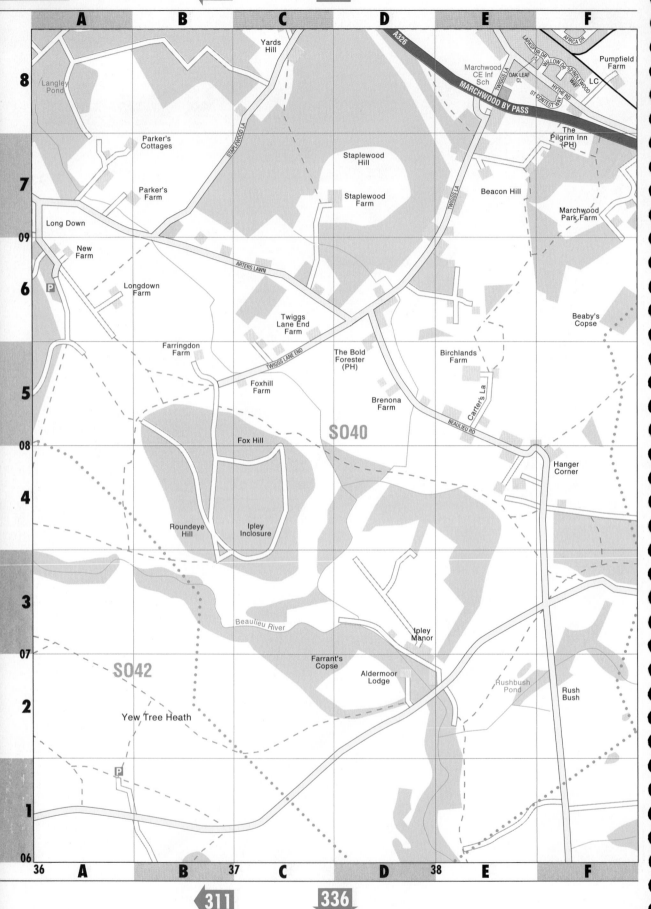

311
336

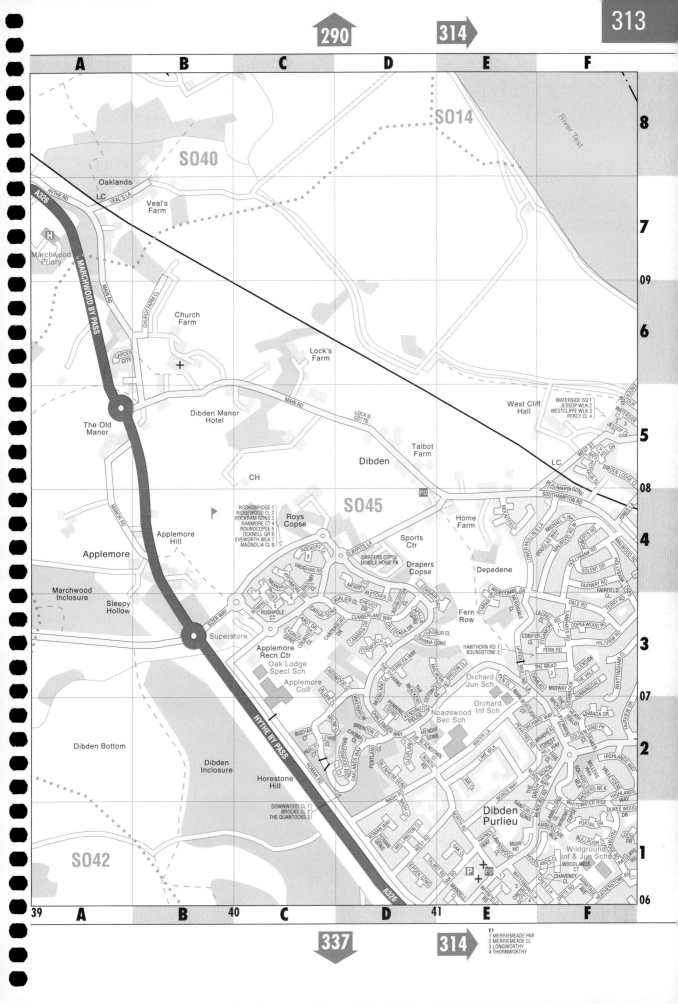

290
314

A **B** **C** **D** **E** **F**

8

SO14

River Test

SO40

Oaklands
LC
VEAL'S LA
HYTHE RD
Veal's
Farm

7

A326
H
Marchwood
Priory

MAIN RD
MARCHWOOD BY PASS
CHURCH FARM CL

09

Church
Farm

6

GARDEN
CITY

Lock's
Farm

Dibden Manor
Hotel
MAIN RD
LOCK'S
COTTS

West Cliff
Hall
WATERSIDE SQ 1
JESSOP WLK 2
WESTCLIFFE WLK 3
PERCY CL 4

WATERSIDE
JESSOP CL

The Old
Manor

Talbot
Farm

WEST ST
WESTHILL DR
DIBDEN LODGE CL

5

MANOR RD

CH

Dibden
LC

BEAUMARIS GDNS
SOUTHAMPTON RD

08

Applemore
Hill

SO45

PO

Home
Farm

MOUNTFIELD
LOWER MULLINS LA
DOUGLAS WAY
MICHAEL'S WAY
MALWOOD RD
ROBERTS RD
HOLLYBANK RD

4

Applemore

ROOKSBRIDGE 1
RIDGEWOOD CL 2
ROCKRAM GDNS 3
RANMORE CT 4
ROUNDCOPSE 5
OCKNELL GR 6
EVEWORTH WLK 7
MAGNOLIA CL 8

Roys
Copse

Sports
Ctr

Drapers
Copse

Depedene

WIDECOMBE DR
MEERVALE
CL

SOLENT DR
FAIRWAY RD
FAIRFIELD
CL

HOLLYBANK CRES

Marchwood
Inclosure

Sleepy
Hollow

ROCKERY
CL
CLAYPITS LA
DRAPERS COPSE
MOBILE HOME PK

Fern
Row

TAMAR
CL

LAUREL
CL
SYCAMORE
CL
CONIFER CL

DALE RD
LAURELS RD
COPSEWOOD RD

FERRY RD
HILLVIEW RD

3

SIZER WAY
Superstore

VAUGHAN RD
HASKALL
CL
RYCHMORE
DR
BROOMY
ROWHILL DR
RUSHPOLE
CT

MORRS
FLETCHER CL
CAVALIER CL
CHEVIOT
DR
ASHBURTON
CAPELLA
CORSAIR DR

Hawthorn Rd 1
Boundstone 2

UPPER MULLINS LA

FERN RD
THE MEAD

GLENSIDE
THE VALE
WHITTINGHAM CL

Applemore
Recn Ctr
Oak Lodge
Specl Sch
Applemore
Coll

CYGNUS
GDNS
CABOT DR
COURTIER
CL
CANTERBURY
DR
CAMBRIN
CL
COSWORTH
CL
CUMBERLAND WAY
CALEDONIA DR
CARDELIA CL
CORINNA GDNS

MIDWAY
SUNNINGDALE

07

REDWOOD
ALDER CL

OAKENBROW
BUCHAN
CT
LEWIS
CL
HUXLEY CT

THE ST IVANS
CLEVER LA
THE KENSINGTON
FIELDS
THE
BRACKENS
THE COTSWOLDS
MALCROFT
BRECON CL
Orchard
Jun Sch
Orchard
Inf Sch
Noadswood
Sec Sch

N CL
MARLBOROUGH
TREAD
GOLDEN HIND PK
FOREST
ARMADA DR

07

BLENHEIM GDNS
CHALLENGER WAY
PENNINE
GDNS
CROMARTY
RD
CLEVER LA
BRENDON CL
MENDIP
GDNS
BUCKDOWN

ORCHARD WAY
FIR TREE RD
WICKEL
RD

BRAEHEAD
HIGHLANDS WAY

2

Dibden Bottom

Dibden
Inclosure

Horestone
Hill

HYTHE BY PASS
ROMAN RD

OAKLANDS WAY
PENTLAND
CL
BRABAZON CL
BLENHEIM GDNS
LEVER RD
WATER LA
LIME WLK
LIME CL

NOADS WAY
THE GABLES
BEAULIEU RD
LANDGUARD
WINDOMET
FOXTAIL DR
MILLERS
WAY
SQUIRRELS WLK
BADGERS WLK
WHITEWATER RISE
DUKES WOOD
DR

VALLETORE
HIGHLANDS
WAY

DOWNWOOD CL 1
BROCKS CL 2
THE QUANTOCKS 3

Dibden
Purlieu

RANFURLY
GDNS
AMBERSLADE

BULLRUSH CL
PARTRIDGE RD
LODGE
DR

1

SO42

ROMAN WAY
ROMAN
GDNS
WELLINGTON CL
WEST RD
WEST RD
NASH RD
NASH CL
NORTH RD
HAYNES
WAY
LANNINGTON
OAK CL
MUIR
HO
WOODLANDS CL

Wildground
Inf & Jun Schs

WOODLANDS
CT
CHAVENEY
CL
ARMITAGE
HEATHERSTONE AVE

06

DEPDEN GDNS
TALBOT RD
OAK RD
MANSELL
WHITNEY
RD
CRETE LA
CHETE RD
CRETE COTTS
CRETE CL
CRETE LA

A326

39 **A** **B** 40 **C** **D** 41 **E** **F**

337
314

E1
1 MERRIEMEADE PAR
2 MERRIEMEADE CL
3 LONGWORTHY
4 THORNWORTHY

A B C D E F

8

SO14

Docks

QE2
Passenger
Terminal

Mast

Weston Shelf

Weston
Hard

SO19

ROTHSCHILD
CL

SEAFORD CL
WESTON
HOLT
CT

INTERNATIONAL WAY

HAWKLEY GN
SPARSHOLT RD
KINGSCLERE AVE
BRAMSHOTT
CROOKHORN

HURSTBOURNE
PL

CANBERRA
TWRS

Weston
Shore
Inf Sch

Weston
Park

RIVERSDALE CL 1
SQUIRES WLK 2
HAMPTON TWRS 3
HAVRE TWRS 4
OSLO TWRS 5
COPENHAGEN TWRS 6
ROTTERDAM TWRS 7
WESTON CT 8
GRATELEY CL 9
DRAYTON CL 10

Ferry
P

7

Solent Way

SO31

MARINA
VIEW

ABBEY HILL

09

Hythe
Marina

Southampton Water

6

WHITE
HEATHER
CT

ENDEAVOUR WAY

VELSHEDA
CT

ASTRA
CT

SHAMROCK WAY

ENDEAVOUR WAY

WEST ST

Hythe Pier Rly

Hythe Pier

5

P

P

Hythe
Hard

DIBDEN
LODGE CL

BRINTON

PROSPECT PL

P

HIGH

Hythe

1 WATERSIDE
2 MOUNT HOUSE CL
3 HAZELDALE VILLAS
4 HOMEBOROUGH HO
5 DRUMMOND CT
6 ADMIRALS WAY
7 MARSH PAR
8 NEW MARSH HO
9 DRUMMOND RD

10 COURT HOUSE CL
11 LAWRENCE HO
12 MARINER MEWS
13 HANOVER CT
14 THE SYCAMORES
15 FAIRFIELD CL
16 GREEN CL
17 HOLLYBANK CL
18 TRAFALGAR HO

08

Hythe
Prim Sch

THE PROMENADE

THE MARSH

ST JOHN'S ST

SIR
CHRISTOPHER CT

DAVIDSON CL

GENERAL CT

SCOTT CL

Pier

LC

Liby

JONES CL

STEWART

JEWELL RD

NEW RD

SCHOOL RD

ALEXANDRA RD

ST CHRISTOPHER

SCOTT CL

PALMERSTONE DR

BELTAN CL

DINE DR

Waterside
Heritage
Ctr

4

HOLLIDAY CL

EDWARD

ALEXANDRA

RD

LOWMEADOW

WADMORE CL

GINS

SELTAN CL

SOUTHAMPTON CL

ATHELING RD

CAPSTONE

FREEDOM CL

SPRING
RD

PARK CL

SO45

MALWOOD RD

MOUSEHOLE LA

GINS

HOBART DR

SHORE RD

3

HOLLYBANK CRES

KELVIN

GINS

ABBEY
CL

ASHFORD CRES

LANGDOWN RD

TATES

HARVEY
GINS

Howard
Oliver
Ho

P

CAT

LANGDOWN

Solent Way

FAIRVIEW DR

FAIRVIEW CL

Langdown
Firs

WINDRUSH WAY

ELGIN CL

QUEENS RD

DEERLEAP

DEER LEAF WAY

LANGDOWN LAWN

WILDWOOD

HOME FARM

Langdown

LC

07

LANGDOWN
LAWN CL

WHITECROFT

ILLEY WAY

ADAMS RD

LADYCROSS RD

BURLETON

BURNETT

KIMBER

TATES
RD

KENNET CL

FULMAR RD

CORMORANT DR

2

BEAULIEU RD

H

Hythe

ROSE GREATWOOD CL

LINWOOD

FOXBURY CL

FURZEY
AVE

FURZEY
Piece

Waterside
Prim Sch

BIRCH DALE

PINEWOOD
CRES

CURLEW
WLK

CURLEW CL

CURLEW
CL

HIGHLANDS CL

BELVEDERE RD

ST MONT

BUTTS BRIDGE HILL

ROSEBERY AVE

LAMMAS
RD

LYNTON RD

FURZEDALE
GINS

SPINNEY
GINS

SPINNEY
DALE

HART HILL

1

FROG LA

CALLERS LA

OLD CRACKNORE

DUE

BUTTSBRIDGE RD

FERNHILLS CL

PINEWOOD

FURZEDALE RD

HARDY DR

Hotel

Furzedown
Farm

Frostlane

LODGE DR

WILDGROUND LA

HEATHERSTONE AVE

Elizabeth

CHALONERS CL

GRENVILLE GINS

BUTTS ASH LA

FAWLEY RD

FROST LA

Kitcher's
Copse

Crampool Copse

WEST RD

EAST RD

Works

06

Forest Lodge

Forest Lodge

A1
1 HARTLEY WLK
2 SILVERS END
3 ANDREW CL
4 WILDGROUND LA
5 NORTHBOURNE CL
6 SHOBLANDS WAY
7 SANDILANDS WAY

A2
1 FAIRVIEW PAR
2 KNIGHTSTONE GRANGE
3 HIGHLANDS WAY
4 FRAYSLEA

B1
1 NELSON CT
2 FURZEDOWN MEWS
3 TRAFALGAR WAY
4 HAMILTON MEWS

◁ 313

338

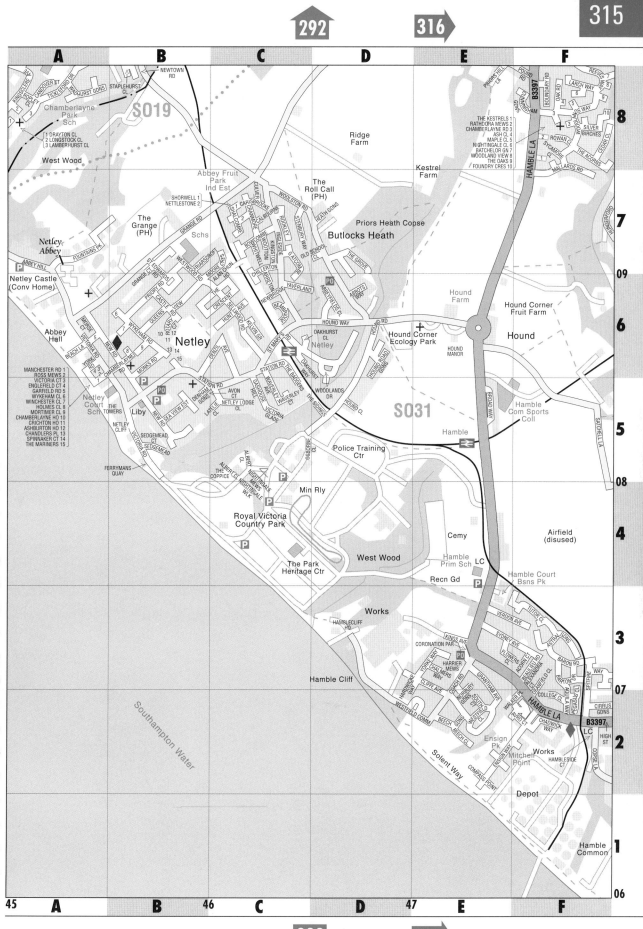

A B C D E F

1 DRAYTON CL
2 LONGSTOCK CL
3 LAMBERHURST CL

West Wood

Chamberlayne
Park Sch

SO19

NEWTOWN
RD

Ridge
Farm

THE KESTRELS 1
RATHDORA MEWS 2
CHAMBERLAYNE RD 3
ASH CL 4
MAPLE CL 5
NIGHTINGALE CL 6
BATCHELOR GN 7
WOODLAND VIEW 8
THE OAKS 9
FOUNDRY CRES 10

Kestrel
Farm

SILVER
BIRCHES

8

Abbey Fruit
Park
Ind Est

SHORWELL 1
NETTLESTONE 2

The Grange
(PH)

Schs

GRANGE RD

The
Roll Call
(PH)

Priors Heath Copse

Butlocks Heath

7

09

Netley
Abbey

FOUNTAINS PK

Netley Castle
(Conv Home)

The Grange

Netley

Hound
Farm

Hound Corner
Fruit Farm

Hound

6

Abbey
Hall

Hound Corner
Ecology Park

Hound
MANOR

MANCHESTER RD 1
ROSS MEWS 2
VICTORIA CT 3
ENGLEFIELD CT 4
GARFIELD RD 5
WYKEHAM CL 6
WINCHESTER CL 7
HOLMES CL 8
MORTIMER CL 9
CHAMBERLAYNE HO 10
CRICHTON HO 11
ASHBURTON HO 12
CHANDLERS PL 13
SPINNAKER CT 14
THE MARINERS 15

Netley
Court
Sch

Liby

Netley
Cliff

OAKHURST
CL
Netley

Station RD

Netley Lodge
CL

SO31

Hamble

Hamble
Com Sports
Coll

5

08

FERRYMANS
QUAY

Police Training
Ctr

The
Coppice

Min Rly

Royal Victoria
Country Park

Cemy

Airfield
(disused)

4

The Park
Heritage Ctr

West Wood

Hamble
Prim Sch

LC

Recn Gd

Hamble Court
Bsns Pk

Works

TUTOR CL

VERDON AVE

HAMBLECLIFF
HO

SYDNEY AVE

Hamble Cliff

KINGS AVE

Coronation Par

HARRIER
MEWS

CHALMERS
WAY

FLOWERS
CL

BARON RD

SPITFIRE
WAY

3

07

COACH RD

HAMBLE LA

Ensign
Pk

Works

Mitchell
Point

HAMBLESIDE
CT

B3397

LC

2

Southampton Water

Solent Way

COMPASS POINT

Depot

Hamble
Common

1

06

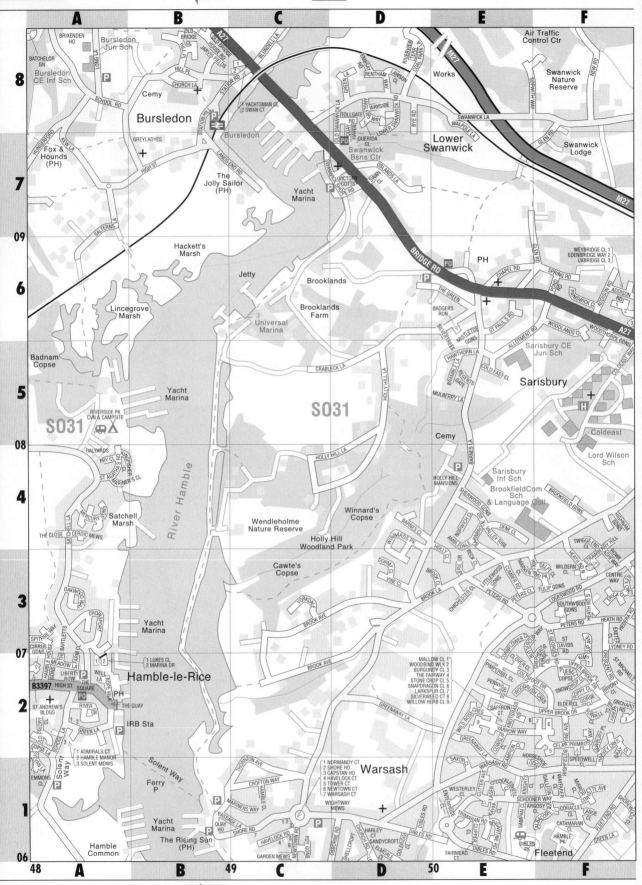

315
293
315
340

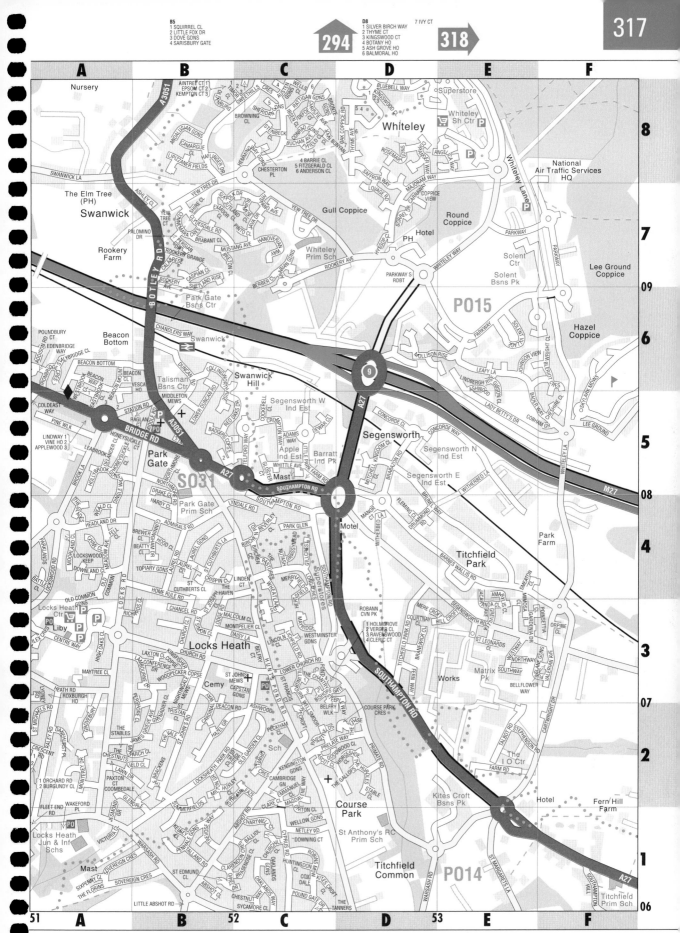

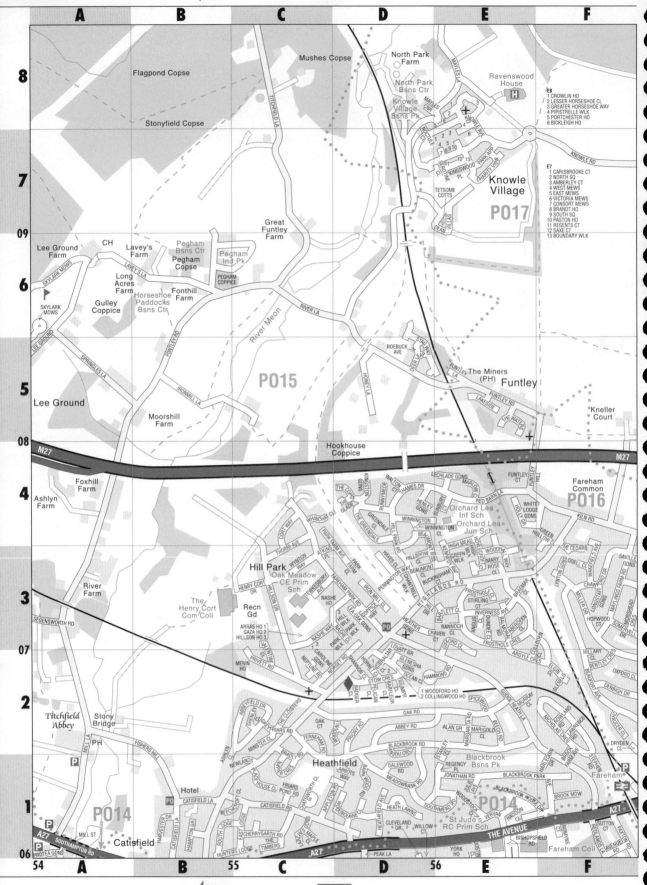

317
295

A B C D E F

8 Flagpond Copse
Mushes Copse
North Park Farm
North Park Bsns Ctr
Knowle Village Bsns Pk
Ravenswood House
Stonyfield Copse

E8
1 CROWLIN HO
2 LESSER HORSESHOE CL
3 GREATER HORSESHOE WAY
4 PIPISTRELLE WLK
5 PORTCHESTER HO
6 BICKLEIGH HO

7 Knowle Village
PO17

E7
1 CARISBROOKE CT
2 NORTH SQ
3 AMBERLEY CT
4 WEST MEWS
5 EAST MEWS
6 VICTORIA MEWS
7 CONSORT MEWS
8 BRANDT HO
9 SOUTH SQ
10 PASTON HO
11 REGENTS CT
12 SAXE CT
13 BOUNDARY WLK

09 Great Funtley Farm
Lee Ground Farm
CH Lavey's Farm
Pegham Bsns Ctr
Pegham Ind Pk
Pegham Copse
Pegham Coppice

6 Long Acres Farm
Fonthill Farm
Horseshoe Paddocks Bsns Ctr
Gulley Coppice
River Meon
River La
SKYLARK MDWS
Roebuck Ave
Funtley La
The Miners (PH)
Funtley

5 Lee Ground
PO15
Moorshill Farm
Lakeside
Funtley Rd
The Water
Kneller Court

08 M27
Hookhouse Coppice
M27

4 Foxhill Farm
Ashlyn Farm
Orchard Lea Inf Sch
Orchard Lea Jun Sch
Fareham Common
PO16

3 River Farm
Segensworth Rd
Hill Park
Oak Meadow CE Prim Sch
The Henry Cort Com Coll
Recn Gd

ARRAS HO 1
GAZA HO 2
HILLSON HO 3

07 MENIN HO
1 WOODFORD HO
2 COLLINGWOOD HO

2 Titchfield Abbey
Stony Bridge
PH
Heathfield
Blackbrook Bsns Pk
Blackbrook Park
Fareham

1 PO14
Hotel
St Jude's RC Prim Sch
PO14
THE AVENUE
Fareham Coll

06 A27
Catisfield
PROTEA GDNS
SOUTHAMPTON RD
A27
PEAK LA
Bishopsfield Rd

54 A 55 B C 56 D E F

317
342

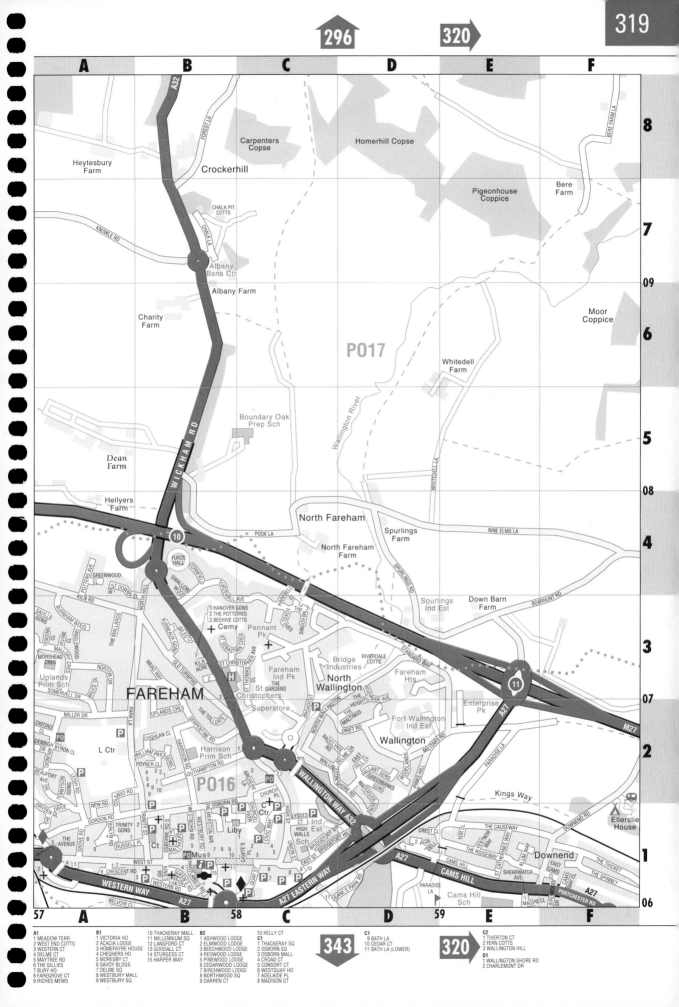

A1
1 MEADOW TERR
2 WEST END COTTS
3 WESTERN CT
4 DELME CT
5 MAYTREE RD
6 THE GILLIES
7 BURY HO
8 FAREGROVE CT
9 RICHES MEWS

B1
1 VICTORIA HO
2 ACACIA LODGE
3 HOMEFAYRE HOUSE
4 CHEQHERS HO
5 MORESBY CT
6 SAVOY BLDGS
7 DELME SQ
8 WESTBURY MALL
9 WESTBURY SQ

10 THACKERAY MALL
11 MILLENNIUM SQ
12 LANGFORD CT
13 GOODALL CT
14 STURGESS CT
15 HARPER WAY

B2
1 ASHWOOD LODGE
2 ELMWOOD LODGE
3 BEECHWOOD LODGE
4 REDWOOD LODGE
5 PINEWOOD LODGE
6 CEDARWOOD LODGE
7 BIRCHWOOD LODGE
8 NORTHWOOD SQ
9 DARREN CT

10 KELLY CT
C1
1 THACKERAY SQ
2 OSBORN SQ
3 OSBORN MALL
4 CROAD CT
5 CONSORT CT
6 WESTQUAY HO
7 ADELAIDE PL
8 MADISON CT

C1
9 BATH LA
10 CEDAR CT
11 BATH LA (LOWER)

C2
1 TIVERTON CT
2 FERN COTTS
3 WALLINGTON HILL

D1
1 WALLINGTON SHORE RD
2 CHARLEMONT DR

296   320

343   320

8
B2177
Carmans Copse
STAPLE CROSS
Staplecross Copse
Walton Heath
Mitchelland
Kings Way
BLACKHOUSE LA
Prior's Hold Farm
Carmans Farm
Lodge Farm
Vernons Farm
Lodge Coppice
Friar's Coppice
COMMON LA

7
Wallington River
Boarhunt Mill
Grub Coppice
Mill Coppice
Ham Coppice
BRIDGE ST
Newman's Bridge
Castle Farm
NORTON RD
NORTON CL
CASTLE RD

09
Kings Way
BOARHUNT RD
Dirtystile Copse
Ham Farm
BACK LA
WEST ST
Royal Naval Cotts
NORTH DR

6
Ashleydown Coppice
FAREHAM RD
HIGH ST
Southwick
PO PH P
The Wilderness

5
Manor Farm
Boarhunt
Ashley Down Farm
Stroud Coppice
Perrige's Coppice
B2177

08
P017
Marls Rows

4
MONUMENT LA
Damson Row
Offwell Farm
PORTCHESTER LA
CROOKED WALK LA

3
SWIVELTON LA
Monument Farm
Royal Armouries Mus of Artillery
Mountemoor's Coppice
Fort Southwick

07
DOWNEND RD
Fort Nelson
Nelson's Monument
PORTSDOWN HILL RD
Mast
JAMES CALLAGHAN DR

M27
The Mount
NELSON LA
Ports Down
SKEW RD
High Tor
PO6
WINTERBOURNE RD
1 2 3 4 5 6 7 8 9 10 11
KINGSCOTE RD
ALMONDSBURY RD
HILLSLEY RD
RIDGEWAY CL

2
LECKFORD CL
EXTON GDNS
WALTHAM CL
CAER PERIS VIEW
NYEWOOD AVE
PORTCHESTER HTS
ANSON GR
BENEDICT WAY
BROWNING AVE
KEATS AVE
CHAUCER AVE
COLERIDGE RD
MACAULAY AVE
KALAMOUTH AVE

PO16
Winnham Farm
KILMISTON DR
DORE AVE
STEEP CL
ROGATE GDNS
HILL RD
BURITON CL
CARLTON RD
EDWARD GR
SHELLEY AVE
MASEFIELD AVE
DRYDEN AVE
BRIDGES AVE
BUDE CL
HELSTON RD

1
TUDOR CL
DANES RD
PIPER CORNWAY LA
SAXON CL
LANCASTER CL
NORTHFIELD PK
CAMP LOT
MERLIN GDNS
JUTE CL
HIGH WLK
HARTING GDNS
ISLAND VIEW WLK
FROXFIELD GDNS
LAVEROCK LEA
MORNINGSIDE AVE
SEAVIEW AVE
LEITH AVE
NEWBOLT RD
HILLSIDE CRES
TRURO RD
MOUSEHOLE RD
PENDENNIS RD
Portchester
Cams Bridge
THE PINES
THE THICKET
TAMAR DR
WINDSOR
SOLENT VIEW
GRINDLE CL
RED BARN AVE
Northern Schs
ROBINSON CT
CANON'S BARN CL
HILL VIEW RD
RICHMOND RISE
PORTSVIEW GDNS
COLLINGTON RD
RAYMOND RD
SAUNDERS HO
PAMELA CL
CORNAWAY LA
HAWTHORN CL
LINDEN LEA
Crem
BOXWOOD CL
Sch

06
60 A 61 B C 62 D E F

F2
1 TRINIDAD HO
2 ST LUCIA HO
3 BERMUDA HO
4 ST KITTS HO
5 ANTIGUA HO
6 FOXCOTE HO
7 KINGSCOTE HO
8 ALMONDSBURY HO
9 OAKLANDS HO
10 THORNBURY HO
11 PARKFIELD HO

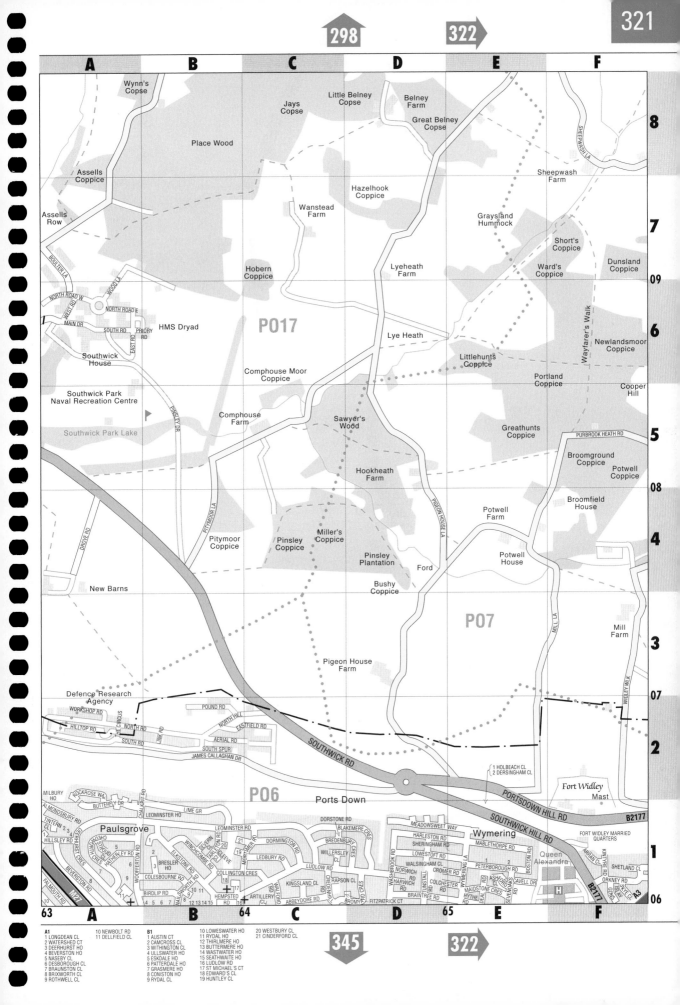

Wynn's Copse

Jays Copse

Little Belney Copse

Belney Farm

Great Belney Copse

Place Wood

Assells Coppice

Assells Row

Hazelhook Coppice

Sheepwash Farm

Graysland Hummock

Wanstead Farm

Short's Coppice

Ward's Coppice

Dunsland Coppice

Hobern Coppice

BOULTER LA

NORTH ROAD W

WEST RD

WOOD LA

NORTH ROAD E

MAIN DR

SOUTH RD

EAST RD

PRIORY RD

HMS Dryad

Lyeheath Farm

Lye Heath

P017

Wayfarer's Walk

Newlandsmoor Coppice

Southwick House

Comphouse Moor Coppice

Littlehunts Coppice

Portland Coppice

Cooper Hill

Southwick Park Naval Recreation Centre

Comphouse Farm

Sawyer's Wood

Greathunts Coppice

PURBROOK HEATH RD

Southwick Park Lake

PINSLEY DR

Hookheath Farm

Broomground Coppice

Potwell Coppice

PITYMOOR LA

PIGEON HOUSE LA

Broomfield House

Potwell Farm

Pitymoor Coppice

Pinsley Coppice

Miller's Coppice

Pinsley Plantation

Ford

Potwell House

DROVE RD

New Barns

Bushy Coppice

P07

MILL LA

Mill Farm

WIDLEY WLK

Pigeon House Farm

Defence Research Agency

WORKSHOP RD

HILLTOP RD

THE CIRCUS

NORTH RD

SOUTH RD

POUND RD

NORTH HILL

LINK RD

EASTFIELD RD

AERIAL RD

SOUTH SPUR

JAMES CALLAGHAN DR

SOUTHWICK RD

1 Holbeach Cl
2 Dersingham Cl

Fort Widley Mast

PORTSDOWN HILL RD

MILBURY HO

ROCKROSE WA

BUTTERFLY DR

CHALKPIT RD

LIME GR

P06

Ports Down

SOUTHWICK HILL RD

B2177

Fort Widley Married Quarters

ALMONDSBURY RD

LEOMINSTER HO

Paulsgrove

LEOMINSTER RD

DORSTONE RD

BLAKEMERE CRES

BREDENBURY CRES

MEADOWSWEET WAY

HARLESTON RD

Wymering

MABLETHORPE RD

ARGALL CL

KINTYRE RD

SHETLAND CL

TINTERN CL

HILLSLEY RD

CHAWTON CL

STROUD GREEN

HATHERLEY RD

WINCHCOMBE RD

ELKSTONE RD

MORTIMER RD

LEDGLEVE

DORMINGTON RD

WILLERSLEY RD

LEDBURY RD

LUDLOW RD

SHERINGHAM RD

LOWESTOFT RD

WASHBROOK RD

NORWICH RD

HARWICH RD

WALSINGHAM CL

CROMER RD

WYMERING LA

PETERBOROUGH RD

MAIDSTONE CRES

ASHCROFT RD

BOSTON RD

Queen Alexandra

A3

ORKNEY RD

SKYE CL

FALMOUTH RD

M27

BEVERSTON RD

WOOFFERTON RD

BRESLER HO

COLESBOURNE RD

BIRDLIP RD

WALLSEND RD

COLLINGTON CRES

WALFORD RD

KINGSLAND CL

RAPSON CL

BRAINTREE RD

CHESHAM CL

BROMYARD CRES

FITZPATRICK CT

TUNSTALL RD

COLCHESTER RD

CAVELL DR

SEVENOAKS RD

HYTHE CL

H

B2177

HEMPSTED RD

ABBEYDORE RD

ARTILLERY CL

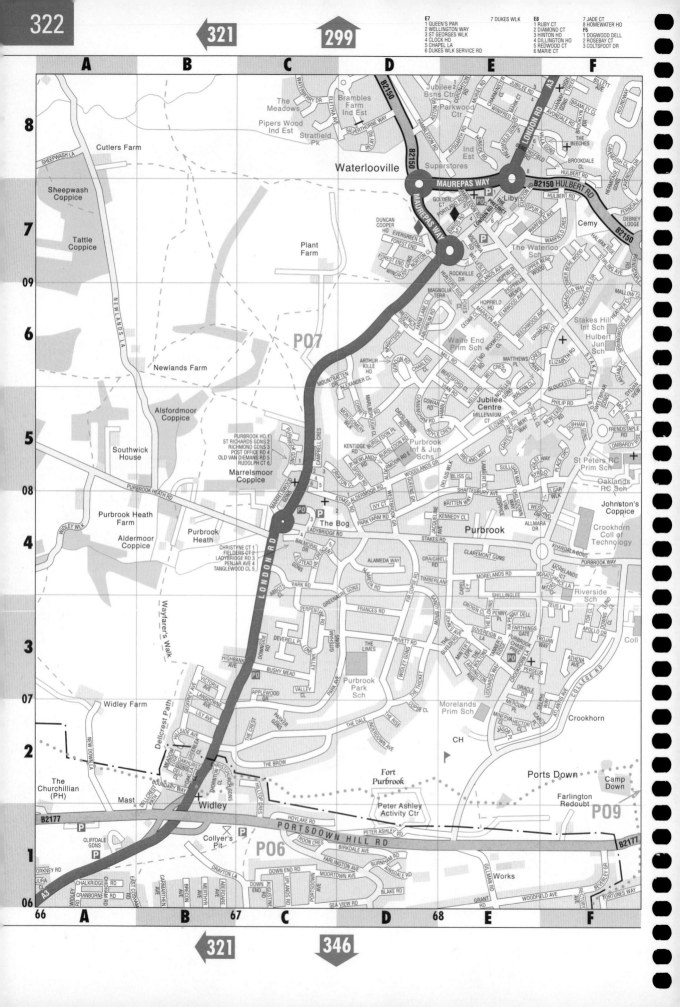

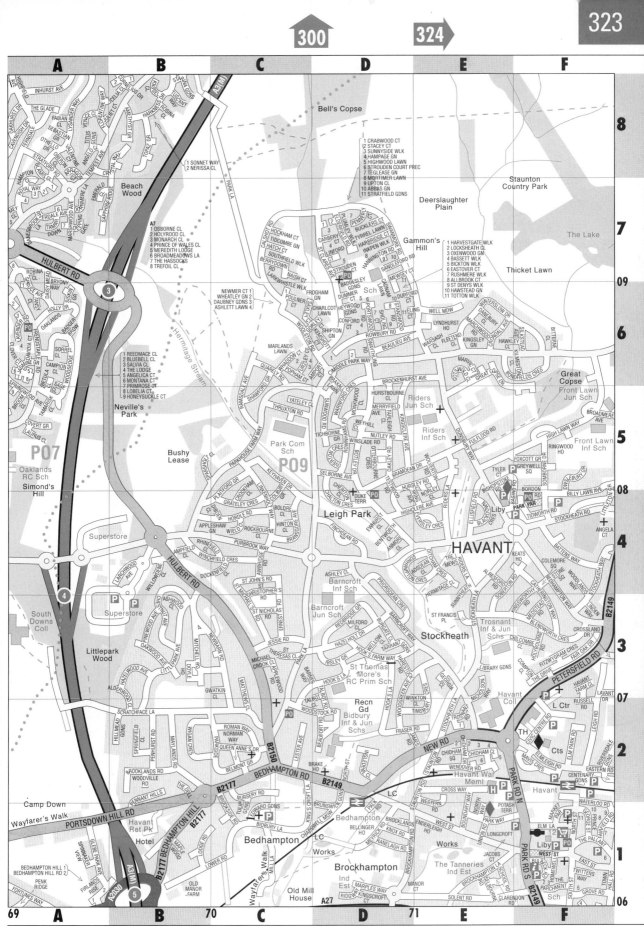

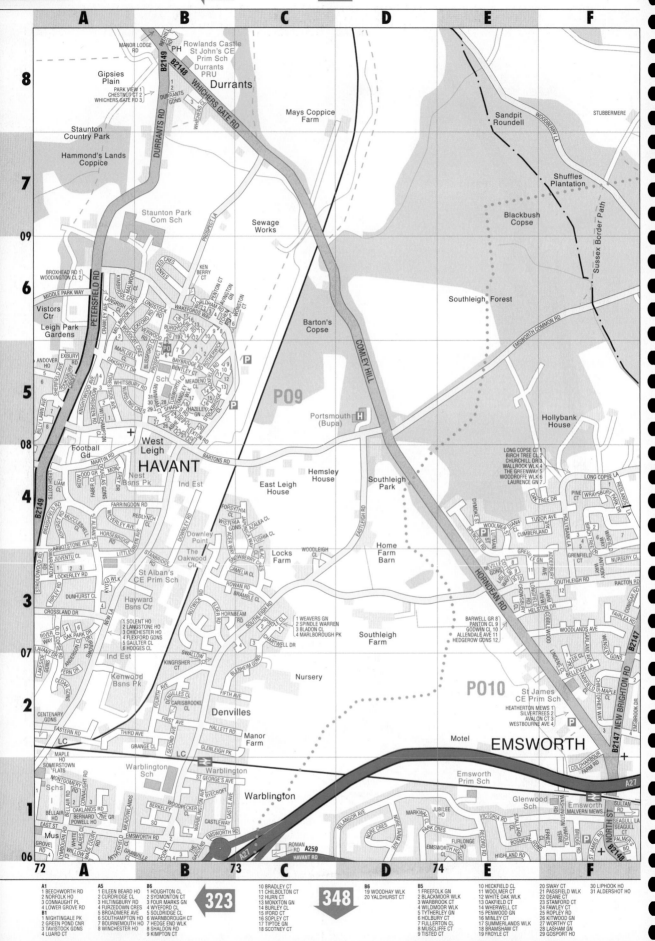

A   B   C   D   E   F

8

Rowlands Castle
St John's CE
Prim Sch
Durrants
PRU
Durrants

Gipsies
Plain

MANOR LODGE
RD

PARK VIEW 1
CHESTNUT CT 2
WHICHERS GATE RD 3

B2149
B2148
WHICHERS GATE RD
DURRANTS RD
DURRANTS GDNS
REDHILL
PH

Mays Coppice
Farm

Sandpit
Roundell

WOODBERRY LA

STUBBERMERE

Staunton
Country Park

Hammond's Lands
Coppice

Shuffles
Plantation

7

Staunton Park
Com Sch

PROSPECT LA

STAINER CRES

Sewage
Works

Blackbush
Copse

Sussex Border Path

09

BROXHEAD RD 1
WOODINGTON CL 2

MIDDLE PARK WAY

Vistors
Ctr

Leigh Park
Gardens

PETERSFIELD RD

KIMBROOK CRES
MALWOOD
LANGRISH
CRAWLEY CL
MILLBROOK DR
LONGSTOCK
ECKFORD
KENWOOD
BLISSFORD CL

WAKEFORDS WAY

KEN
BERRY
CT

OLDHAM RD 3
LAVINGTON CT 4
MONXTON GN

Barton's
Copse

COMLEY HILL

Southleigh Forest

LONG COPSE CT 1
BIRCH TREE CL 2
CHURCHILL DR 3
WALLROCK WLK 4
THE GREENWAY 5
WOODROFFE WLK 6
LAURENCE GN 7

6

ANDOVER
HO
EXBURY
SHEFFIELD
AVE

NIGHTINGALE AVE
WITCHAMPTON

MARLDELL
OAKSHOTT DR
WHITSBURY RD
NURSLING CRES
WENWOOD
WOODCOTE CRES
PROSPECT CL
BENTLEY CT
BAYBRIDGE RD
Sch
MEADEND
NETHERWICK
HAZELEY
STOCKBRIDGE

PO9
6
5
4

Portsmouth
(Bupa)
H

Hollybank
House

5

BILLY LAWN AVE
LOWER GROVE RD
KINGSWOOD AVE
FORESTSIDE AVE

MARTIN RD
DOUGLAS
MONT FREY DR

SHARP'S RD
EXTON RD

BARTONS RD

West
Leigh

HAVANT

Football
Gd

Nest
Bsns Pk

Ind Est

East Leigh
House

Hemsley
House

Southleigh
Park

DYMONE ST
WOOLMER ST
SPENCER RD
DIANA CL
CUMBERLAND
TUDOR AVE
HOLLYBANK LA
PINE CT
BIRCH TREE CT

WRAYSBURY RD
REDLANDS
BIRCH TREE
WINFIELD
WAY
ANTHONY
WAY
NURSERY CL

08

LEIGH COTTS
B2149

ABBOTSTONE AVE
BRASHFIELD
SHIRLEY
MUCCLESHELL
HORSEBRIDGE
WAVERLEY AVE
REDLYNCH
FARRINGDON RD

DOWNLEY RD
WISTERIA ACER WAY
JAPONICA WAY
FORSYTHIA CL
AZALEA CL
FUSCHIA CL

EASTLEIGH RD
WOODLEIGH
CL

Home
Farm
Barn

GREVILLE GN
NEVILLE
GDNS
ALDERBURY
AVE
SOUTHLEIGH RD
GRENFIELD
CT

LONG COPSE LA
OAK TREE DR
RACTON RD
FAIRLEA RD
DONIGER RD

4

STROUDWOOD RD
SNAPHATCH
HIPLEY RD
JUVENTU CL
LOCKERLEY RD
DUNHURST CL
CROSSLAND DR
KEEL CL

LITTLEWOOD
STANBRIDGE
KYDE
ROWAN RD
BRAMBLE CL

NUTWICK RD
ELDER RD
SOUTHLEIGH RD
CAMELIA CL
SNOWBERRY CRES

Locks
Farm

CROWSBURY CL
LONG RD
FARM
VIEW
HELSTON RD
COBBLEWOOD

WOODLANDS AVE
WENSLEY
RD
B2147

3

RIVER
WAY
OLD COPSE RD
OAK PARK DR
LAVANT DR
LAKESIDE GDNS
FERN DR
CENTENARY
GDNS

The
Oakwood
Ctr

St Alban's
CE Prim Sch

Hayward
Bsns Ctr

1 SOLENT HO
2 LANGSTONE HO
3 CHICHESTER HO
4 FLEXFORD GDNS
5 GAULTER CL
6 HODGES CL

HORNBEAM
RD
SPINDLE CL
CHARTWELL DR

1 WEAVERS GN
2 SPINDLE WARREN
3 BLADON CL
4 MARLBOROUGH PK

Southleigh
Farm

BARWELL GR 8
PANTON CL 9
GODWIN CL 10
ALLENDALE AVE 11
HEDGEROW GDNS 12

HORNDEAN RD

UNDINE CL
BELLEVUE LA
FARFIELD
GARLAND RD
BRIGHTON
CHRISTOPHER WAY
MAPLE
CL

PO10

NEW BRIGHTON RD
EMSBROOK DR
B2147

07

Ind Est

Kenwood
Bsns Pk

SWALLOW

KINGFISHER
CT

FOURTH AVE
FIFTH AVE

BLENHEIM GDNS

Nursery

St James
CE Prim Sch

HEATHERTON MEWS 1
SILVERTREES 2
AVALON CT 3
WESTBOURNE AVE 4

P

2

EASTERN RD

THIRD AVE
SECOND AVE
FIRST AVE
DENVILLES CL
CARISBROOKE CL
FOURTH AVE

Denvilles

HALLETT RD

Manor
Farm

Motel

EMSWORTH

COLDHARBOUR
FARM RD

B2147

MAPLE
RD
SOMERSTOWN
FLATS

Warblington
Sch

GRANGE CL
GLENLEIGH PK

ST GEORGE'S AVE

Warblington

Emsworth
Prim Sch

Glenwood
Sch

WASHINGTON
RD
HAROLD RD
Emsworth
Malvern Mews

NORTH ST

1

MONTGOMERY RD
BELAIR RD
CONNAUGHT RD
BELLAIR HO
BERNARD
POWELL HO
Schs

OAKLANDS RD
ANNE GR

MEADOWLANDS
WARBLINGTON AVE
RYECROFT
WOODPECKER WLK
CASTLE WAY

EMSWORTH RD

SELANGOR AVE
NORE CRES
NORE FARM AVE
MARKWAY
JUBILEE
HO
PARK CRES
FURLONGE

VICTORIA RD
STALLARD
RECORD RD
HIGHLAND RD

BOSMERE
GDNS
ERNEST RD
BRIDGE RD
ST JAMES RD

SULTAN
RD
SEAGULL LA
SEAGULL
RD
PALMER'S

P
B2148

06

EAST ST
Mus
GROVE
RD
LYMBOURN
WHITE
LADIES
CL
WILLOW

NETHERFIELD CL
EMSWORTH RD
WADE CT
GRANVILLE RD
PARK LA

ROMAN
RD
A259
HAVANT RD

A27

EMSWORTH HOUSE
CL

HIGHLAND RD

72   A   73   B   73   C   74   D   74   E   F

← 323   348

West Sussex STREET ATLAS

A **B** **C** **D** **E** **F**

8

Holme Farm

Sussex Border Path

PO9

The Groves

Stubbermere

New Barn Cottage

Sindle's Farm

PO18

Newbarn La

Park La

Monument La

Racton Mon

7

B2147

Racton Common

Pond Cottage

09

Brickkiln Ponds

Pond Copse

Emsworth Common Rd

Aldsworth

Ell Bridge

6

Woodberry La

Valley Farm

Ellbridge Buildings

Westbourne Common

Aldsworth Manor

Ractonpark Wood

Longcopse Hill

Cricket Gd

Aldsworth Common

Common Rd

5

Monk's Hill

1 SILVERLOCK PL
2 LANSDOWN TERR

Didmans Copse

Monk's Farm

Sydenham Terr

Covington Rd

Commonside

River Ems

Foxbury La

08

Hollybank Farm

School La

Willow Gdns

River St

Byerley Cl

Ellesmere Orch

Whitley Cl

Commonside

Westbourne Prim Sch

4

Long Copse La

Beckenham Terr

Nightingale Ct

PO10

Woodmancote

Westbourne

Manchester Terr

North St

Mill Rd

Shert Rd

Homefield

Grebe Cl

Lark

Mallard Way

Deepsprings

Woodmancote Farm

Bishop Barn Farm

Manor House

Church

Crockford Rd

Harold Rd

Edgell Rd

Kings Rd

Woodmancote La

The Woodmancote Arms (PH)

3

Racton Rd

B2147

The Wren Ctr

King St

East St

New Rd

Chantry Farm

Cemy

Cemetery La

Duffield La

South Lane Farm

A27 Chichester

WESTBOURNE RD

Old Church Rd

Rectory Rd

The Grove

Whitechimney Row

Lumley Farm

Walnut Tree Dr

07

New Brighton

Lewis Rd

Wyko Cres

Oakmeadow Cl

Elderfield

Rivermead Ct

CHURCH VIEW 1
VICTORIA TERR 2
JUBILEE TERR 3
DUKES CL 4

Brook Cotts

South La

South La

Old Farm La

A27

West View Cotts

2

Wickor Way

Wickor Cl

Westbourne Ave

Westwood

Sussex Border Path

Mill La

Lumley Croft

Hither Grn

South La

Lauder Rd

Cheshire Tway

Fraser Gdns

PO18

Danbury Ct

Haslemere Rd

Bourne View

Stein Rd

Breach Ave

Kelsey Ave

Hurstwood Ave

1

Westbourne Cl

Lumley

Lumley Mill Farm

Bourne Com Coll

Park Rd

Clovelly Rd

Works

Mountwood

Merrivale Rd

Smallcutts Ave

Barnfield Dr C

Field Cl

Glenwood Rd

Overton Rd

Flinstone Gr

Breach

Loveders Farm

06

1 VICTORIA TERR
2 RAGLAN TERR
3 LUMLEY TERR

Lumley Rd

The Rookery

Woodfield Park Rd

St John's Rd

Roman Ct

Hartland Ct

Manor Rd

Priors Cl

PO

Manor Gdns

Manor Way

Cooks La

Guildford Cl

Priors Leaze La

Inlands Rd

Inlands Farm

Inlands

A **B** **C** **D** **E** **F**

75 76 77

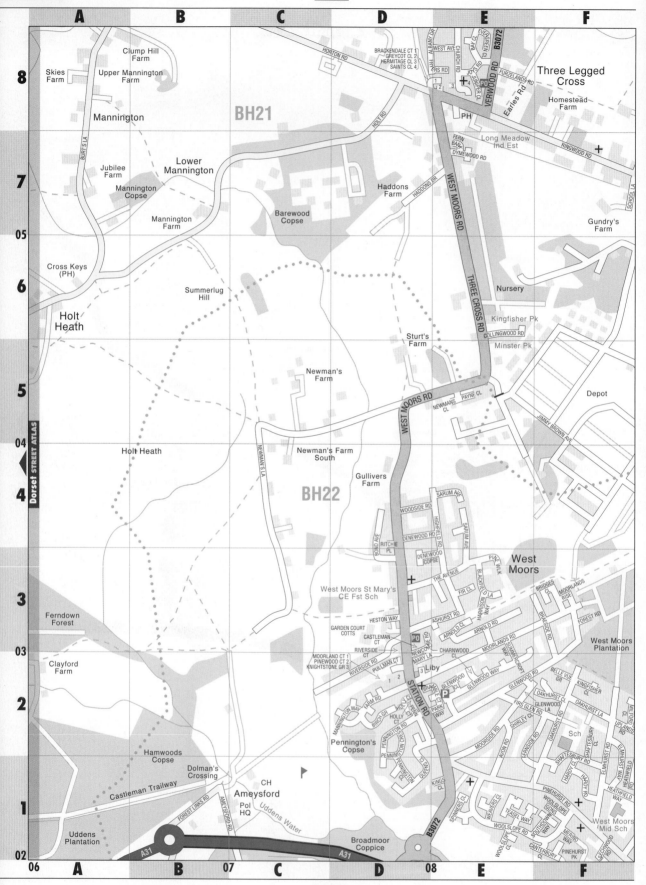

Dorset STREET ATLAS

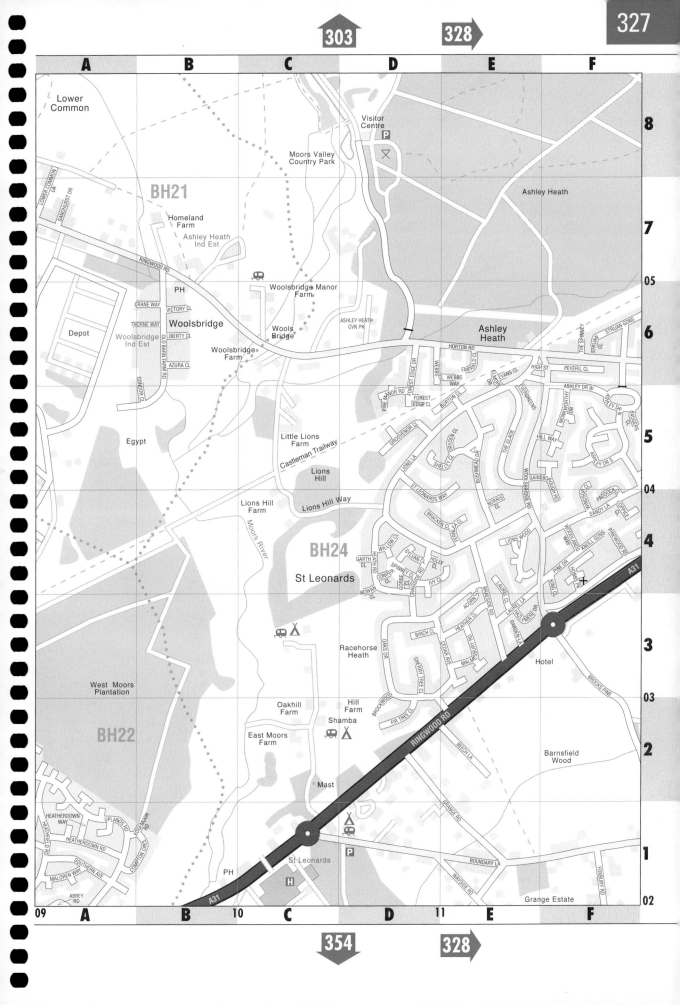

A B C D E F

8
05
7
6
5
04
4
03
3
02
2
1

Lower Common

BH21

Homeland Farm

Ashley Heath Ind Est

Moors Valley Country Park

Visitor Centre

Ashley Heath

RINGWOOD RD

LOWER COMMON LA
SANDHURST DR

PH

CRANE WAY

VICTORY CL

THORNE WAY

LIBERTY CL

Woolsbridge

Woolsbridge Ind Est

Depot

AZURA CL

OLD BARN FARM RD
CONDOR CL

Egypt

Woolsbridge Manor Farm

Wools Bridge

Woolsbridge Farm

ASHLEY HEATH CVN PK

Ashley Heath

HORTON RD

WEBBS WAY
WEBBS CL

FOREST EDGE DR
FOREST EDGE CL
PINE MANOR RD

EMERALD CL
ELMORE DR
EVANS CL

HIGH ST

EVERGREENS
MONKWORTHY DR

THE SPINNEY
STRUAN GDNS
STRUAN CL

PEVERIL CL

ASHLEY DR W
ASHLEY DR N
ASHLEY DR S
BADGERS

BURTON CL
GROSVENOR CL

SHELLEY CL
DRYDEN CL
BUSHMEAD DR

THE GLADE
HILL WAY

WOODSBRIDGE RD
GAINSBOROUGH RD

WINDSOR CL
SANDY LA
PADDOCK
COPPICE

Little Lions Farm

Castleman Trailway

LIONS LA

ST LEONARDS WAY

NORRIS CL

PINEWOOD RD

Lions Hill

BH24

St Leonards

Lions Hill Farm

Lions Hill Way

Moors River

West Moors Plantation

BH22

MOORS RIVER

BRACKEN CL
FERN LA CL

WILLOW CL
GARTH CL
HEATH RD
CONIFER CL

SYLVAN CL
SPINNEY CL
GORSE CL
CRAIGMOOR CL

HOLLY CL
IVY CL

ROWAN CL

LIONS WOOD

WOODLANDS WAY
KNOLL GDNS

PINE DR
PINE CL
HOBBS CL

BRAESIDE RD
LAUREL LA
HAZELMERE DR

Racehorse Heath

BIRCH CL

OAKS DR

CEDAR AVE
CHERRY TREE CL

HEATHER RD
MALMESBURY RD

ACORN CL
LAUREL CL
GARDEN LA

BROCKS PINE

Hotel

A31

Oakhill Farm

East Moors Farm

Hill Farm

Shamba

Mast

BROCKWOOD
FIR TREE CL

RINGWOOD RD

BEECH LA

GRANGE RD

Barnsfield Wood

HEATHERDOWN WAY
UPLANDS RD

HEATHFIELD RD
HEATHERDOWN RD

SOUTHERN AVE
MALOREN WAY

ABBEY RD

COMPTON CRES
FROGMORE RD

PH

St Leonards

H

St Leonards

A31

P

BOUNDARY LA

WAYSIDE RD

FOXBURY RD

Grange Estate

09 A B 10 C D 11 E F 02

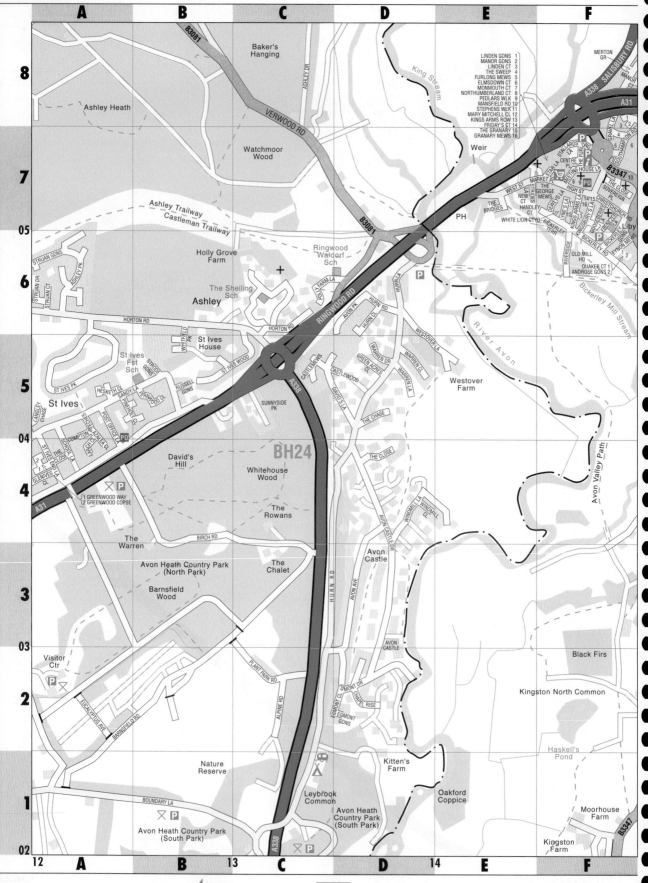

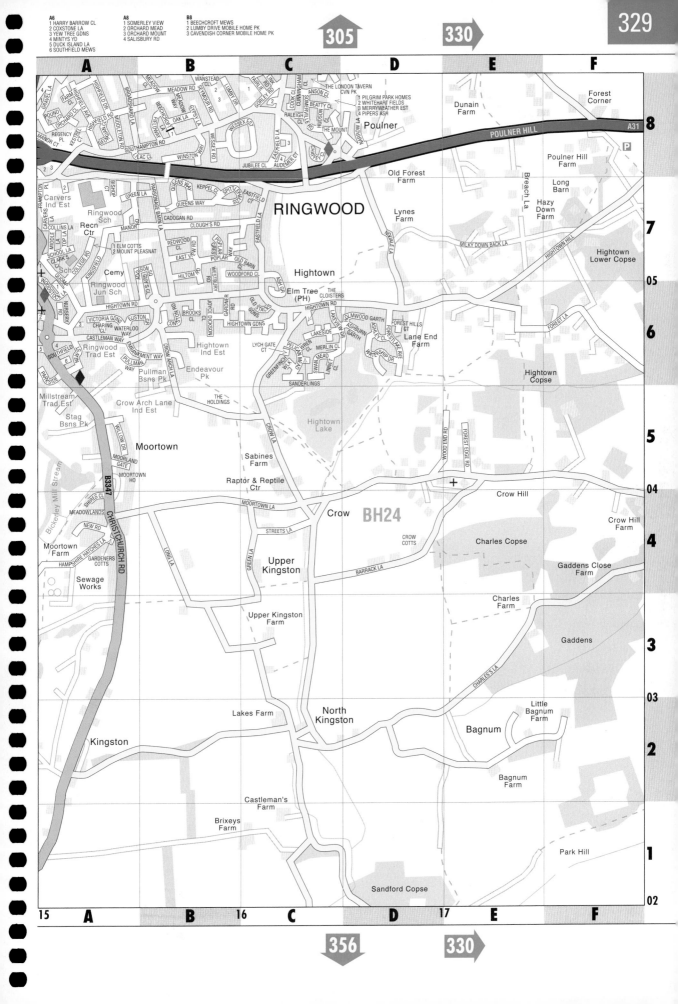

329
306

A | **B** | **C** | **D** | **E** | **F**

A31

8

Picket Plain

Ridley Wood

Picket Hill

Ridley Green

Foulford

Foulford Bottom

Mill Lawn Brook

7

Vereley Wood

Turf Croft Farm

Foulford Farm

Vereley Farm

Vereley

05

Mast

Vereley Hill

Box Berry Hill

6

Burley Croft

Whitemoor House

Hurn Farm

Smugglers Road

Common Moor

FOREST LA

COACH HILL LA

FOREST RD

5

Forest Farm

Vales Moor

Broad Bottom

RINGWOOD RD

PO

THE BARRACKS

04

Knaves Ash

Little Castle Common

RANDALL'S LA

Burley Street

TYRELL'S LA

CROW HILL TOP

Castle Hill

Stock's Farm

Sandys

4

CHARLES'S LA

BH24

Black Bush

LONGMEAD RD

Critenbury Farm

Strodgemoor Bottom

Sandy Shoot

3

Burley Hill House

ESDAILE LA

CLOUGH

GARDEN RD

Coffins Holms

CASTLE HILL LA

HONEY LA

Campden House

COPSE RD

03

Church Moor

2

Bagnum Rough

Cranes Moor

Burley Beacon

WARNES LA

POUND LA

Burnt Axon

MEADON CL

Shappen

Kingston Great Common

SHAPPEN HILL LA

Pound Farm

Bagnum Bog

Muddy Lane

1

Brown Loaf

Chubb's Farm

Slap

02

18 | **A** | **B** | 19 | **C** | **D** | 20 | **E** | **F**

329
357

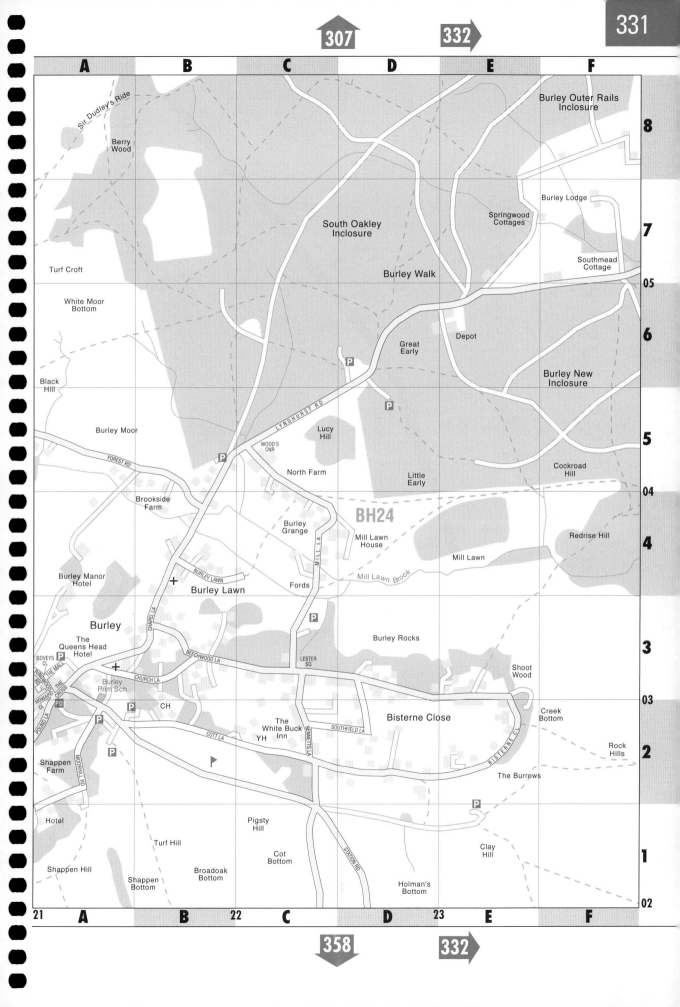

A　B　C　D　E　F

8

Longmead Cottage

P

Anderwood
Cottage

Brock Hill
Forest Walks

SO43

Vinney
Ridge

A35

P

P

7

Dames Slough
Inclosure

Dames Slough
Hill

Vinney Ridge
Inclosure

Rhinefield Ornamental Dr

05

Dogkennel
Bridge

Forest Walks

6

Blackwater
Bridge

Black Water

P

5

Burley Old
Inclosure

Rhinefield Sandy's
Inclosure

Fletchers Thorns
Inclosure

Rhinefield
Cottage

BH24

04

Fletchers
Hill

4

Red Rise

Redrise
Shade

Mill Lawn Brook

Markway
Bridge

Ober Water

SO42

Rhinefield House
(Hotel)

RHINEFIELD RD

Redrise Furze
Brake

3

Ferny Knapp
Inclosure

Clumber
Inclosure

P

03

P

Markway Hill

2

Crab Tree
Bog

Spy Holms

Markway
Inclosure

Crab Tree
Earth

Silver Stream

1

Duckhole
Bog

Holm Hill

Duck Hole

BH25

Holmhill Bog

02

A35

A　B　25　C　D　26　E　F
24

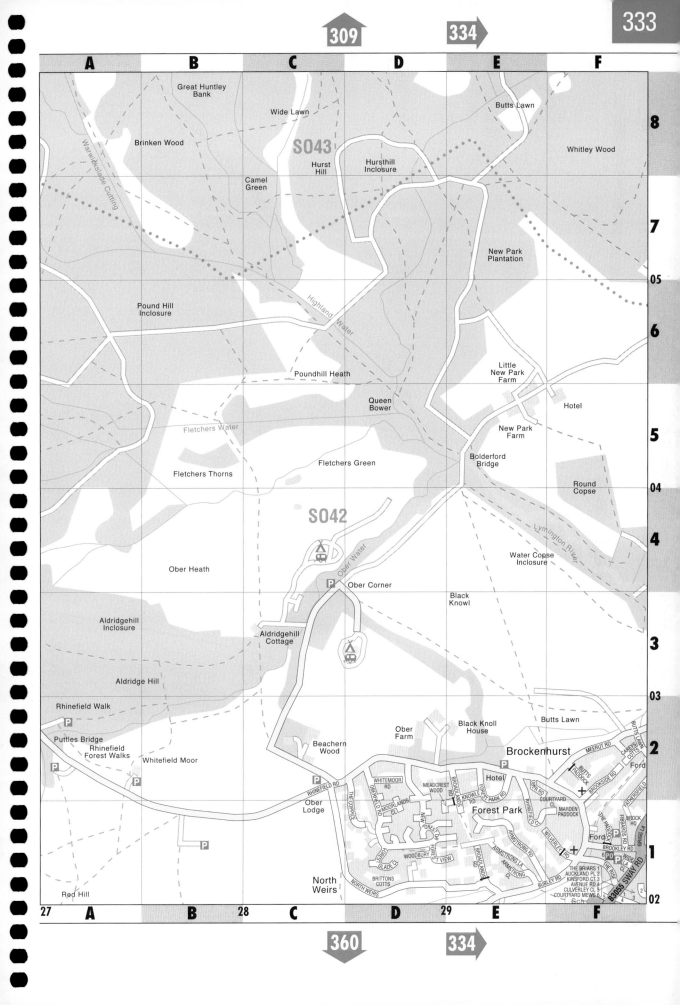

333
310

A   B   C   D   E   F

A337

8
Spaniards
Hole

P

King's
Hat

SO43

7
Parkhill
Inclosure

05

6
Hollands
Wood

Ramnor
Inclosure

5
Stubby Copse
Inclosure

04
Pignal
Inclosure

4
SO42

HOLLANDS WOOD
CVN & CAMPING
SITE

P

Balmer Lawn

Standing
Hat

Pound

Perrywood
Haseley
Inclosure

Victoria
Tilery
Cottage

Pignalhill
Inclosure

3
Ford   Hotel

P

BALMER LAWN RD

Jacks
Wood

B3055

03
Balmerlawn

Bridge
Farm

Warren
Farm

Whitley Ridge

Hotel

New Copse
Inclosure

MEERUT RD

WATERS GN

PARK CL

RINGWOOD
TERR

2
BURFORD LA

Hotel

Brockenhurst

1 FATHERSFIELD
2 WATERS GN
3 WATERS GREEN CT

Old Mill
House

Perrywood
Ivy
Inclosure

B3055

HOBLOCK
RD

SPRIGG LA

CHESTNUT
RD

FOREST

LYNDHURST RD

Brockenhurst
Coll

Lymington River

Longbow

B3055

1
HOMEFORDE
HO

BROOKLEY RD

A337

GREEN JAYS RD

NORTH RD

LC

MILL LA

P

Ivy
Wood

Irons
Hill

Perrywood
Ironshill
Inclosure

AUCKLAND AVE

AUCKLAND
CL

02
1 STATION APP
2 LYMINGTON RD

B3055

30   A   B   31   C   D   32   E   F

333
361

311
336
362
336

SO43

Denny
Wood

Denny
Lodge

Woodfidley
Passage

B3056

B3056

Stephill
Bottom

Furzy
Brow

Bishop of
Winchester's
Purlieu

Denny Lodge
Inclosure

Penny
Moor

Woodfidley

Rowbarrow

SO42

LC

Frame Heath
Inclosure

Frame
Wood

Ladycross
Inclosure

Moon
Hill

Ladycross
Lodge

Worts Gutter

Hawkhill
Inclosure

Lodge
Heath

B3055

Stockley
Inclosure

Little
Wood

A B C D E F

8

SO40

King's Hat
Cottage

Buck Hill

Ferny Crofts
(Scout Ctr)

King's Hat
Inclosure

7

B3056

Gurnetfields
Furzebrake

P

Starpole
Pond

05

P

Culverley
Old Farm

NORTH LA

Pig
Bush

Culverley
Farm

P

Foxhunting
Inclosure

6

P

Gurnet
Fields

North
Gate

Honey
Hill

Shepton
Bridge

Shepton Water

The House
in the Wood

Halfpenny
Green

Penerley Water

Penerley
Wood

Beaulieu River

5

Little Goswell
Copse

SO42

04

Little Honeyhill
Wood

Penerley
Gate

Penerley
Farm

Hides Hill La

4

Tantany
Wood

Penerley
Lodge

Leygreen
Farm

Hartford
Bridge

Hides
Close

Stubbs Wood

Black
Bridge

3

Hartford
Copse

03

Abbotstanding
Wood

P

Wood La

P

The National
Motor Mus

2

Beaulieu Abbey
(remains of)

Works Gutter

Palace
House

FURZEY LA

Palace La   B3054

PALACE LA

Furzey
Lodge

1

Pit
Copse

Hotel

Mill

SOLENT WAY

PONDSIDE FLATS 1
DITTON COTTS 2
CLITHEROE COTTS 3

B3054

HIGH ST

PO

02

B3056

B3054

Beaulieu
Village
Prim Sch

Beaulieu

36 A 37 B C 37 D 38 E F

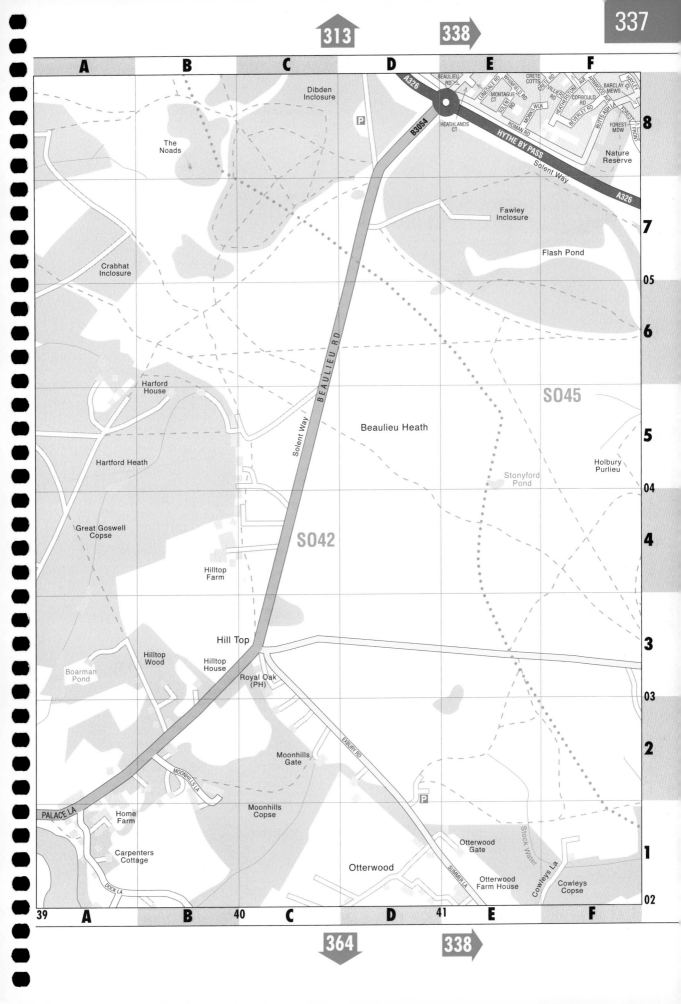

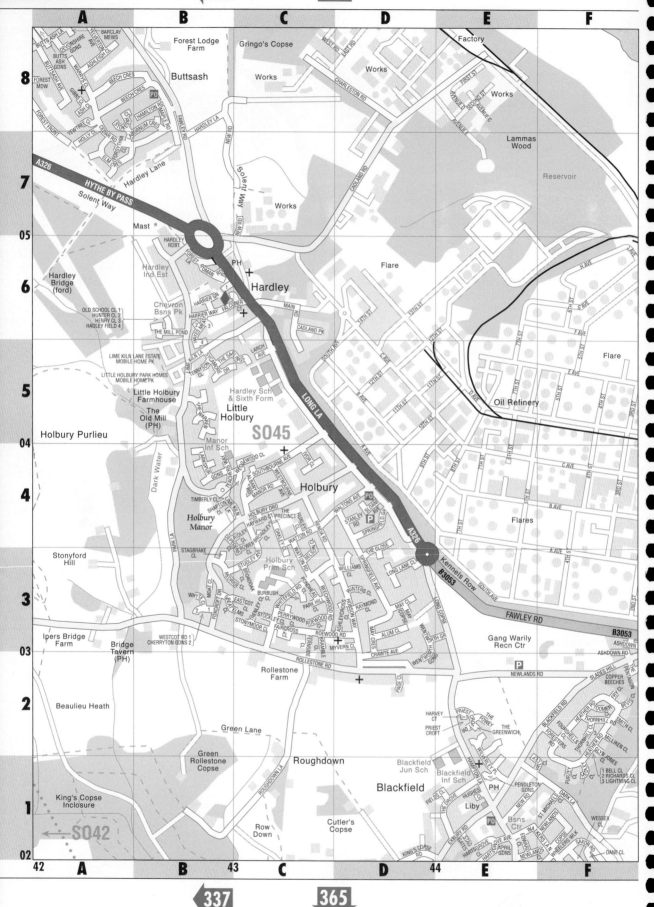

315
340

A B C D E F

8
05
7
6
05
5
04
4
03
3
03
2
02
1
02

Southampton Water

Jetty

Marine Terminal

Pier

Pier

Pier

Cadland Creek

FORESHORE N

FORESHORE S
PI.PH.RD
NORTH TRESTLE RD
BURMAH RD N
BURMAH ROAD S
SOUTH TRESTLE RD
CADLAND RD
JETTY RD
OLD AGWI RD
AGITATOR RD
BITUMEN RD
FLUME RD
SEPS 4 RD

SO45

Ashlett Creek

LANE JAVE
C AVE
D AVE
2ND ST
1ST ST
C AVE
B AVE
A AVE
SOUTH AVE
CHURCH LA
Fawley Inf Sch
Fawley Bsns Ctr
SCHOOL RD

Fawley

MARSH LA
CHURCHFIELDS
RYE PADDOCK LA
COPTHORNE COTTS
COPTHORNE LA
ORCHARD CL
EDGE
7
WOODVILLE RD
LINDA RD
COLE VILLE AVE
WYNTON CL
SHERRIN CL
ADMIRALS CL
ASHLETT CL
Liby
THE SQ
10 9
FALCON
DENNY CL
5
CASTNOT RD
8
SCHOOL RD
FIELDS
ASHLETT RD
STONEHILLS

The Jolly Sailor (PH)

Ashlett

STONEHILLS

P.O

FAWLEY RD
BLACKFIELD RD
THE PENTAGON
CHAPEL LA
FAWLEY BY PASS

HAMLET CT   1
MEADOW WAY   2
THE PADDOCKS   3
CHARLES LEY CT   4
WHITES LA   5
FORGE LA   6
ASHLETT MEWS   7
RHYME HALL MEWS 8
THE LANE   9
MERLIN COTTS   10

Stonehills

Stone Hill Farm

NORTHERN ACCESS RD

Fields Farm

Badminston Farm

Fields Heath

BADMINSTON LA

EASTERN RD
NORTHERN RD
SWITCH HOUSE RD
CENTRAL WAY N
HALEVIA
WESTERN RD
BOILER RD
WRIGHT WAY
CHANNEL MOUTH RD

Fawley Power Station

Chy

Swing Bridge

Tom's Down

Badminston Common

BADMINSTON DRO
B3053
TOWER LA
SOUTHERN RD
QUAYSIDE RD

45 A B 46 C D 47 E F

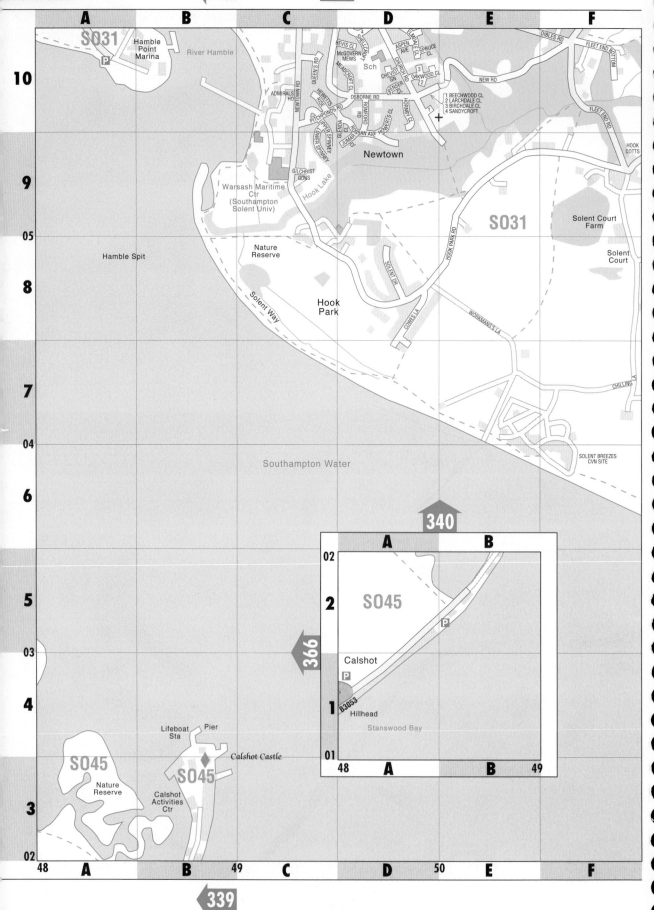

A **B** **C** **D** **E** **F**

SO31

Hamble Point Marina

River Hamble

10

BEVIS CL
SKELLCROFT
McGOVERN MEWS
ASPEN
ELMDALE CL
SPRUCE CL
DIBLES RD
FLEET END BOTTOM
Sch
NEW RD
MEADCROFT CL
CHRISTOT RD
CHURCH RD
GN
OAKWOOD CL
FLEET END RD
HOOK COTTS

QUEEN'S RD
HEWETTS RISE
ADMIRALS HO
NEWTOWN RD
PITCHPONDS RD
OSBORNE RD
ROMFORD RD
HORNBY CL
HOWERTS CL
SPENCER RD
1 BEECHWOOD CL
2 LARCHDALE CL
3 BIRCHDALE CL
4 SANDYCROFT

UPPER SPINNEY
LOWER SPINNEY
GLORIA DR
JUMAR SSAN AVE

Newtown

9

Warsash Maritime Ctr (Southampton Solent Univ)

GILCHRIST GDNS

Hook Lake

SO31

Solent Court Farm

05

Hamble Spit

Nature Reserve

Solent Court

HOOK PARK RD

8

Solent Way

Hook Park

SOLENT DR

CONES LA

WORKMANS'S LA

CHILLING LA

7

04

Southampton Water

SOLENT BREEZES CVN SITE

6

340

A **B**

02

SO45

2

P

366

Calshot

03

P

4

B3053

1

Hillhead

Stanswood Bay

01

48 **A** 49 **B**

5

03

SO45

Nature Reserve

Pier

Lifeboat Sta

Calshot Castle

SO45

Calshot Activities Ctr

3

02

48 **A** 49 **B** **C** 50 **D** **E** **F**

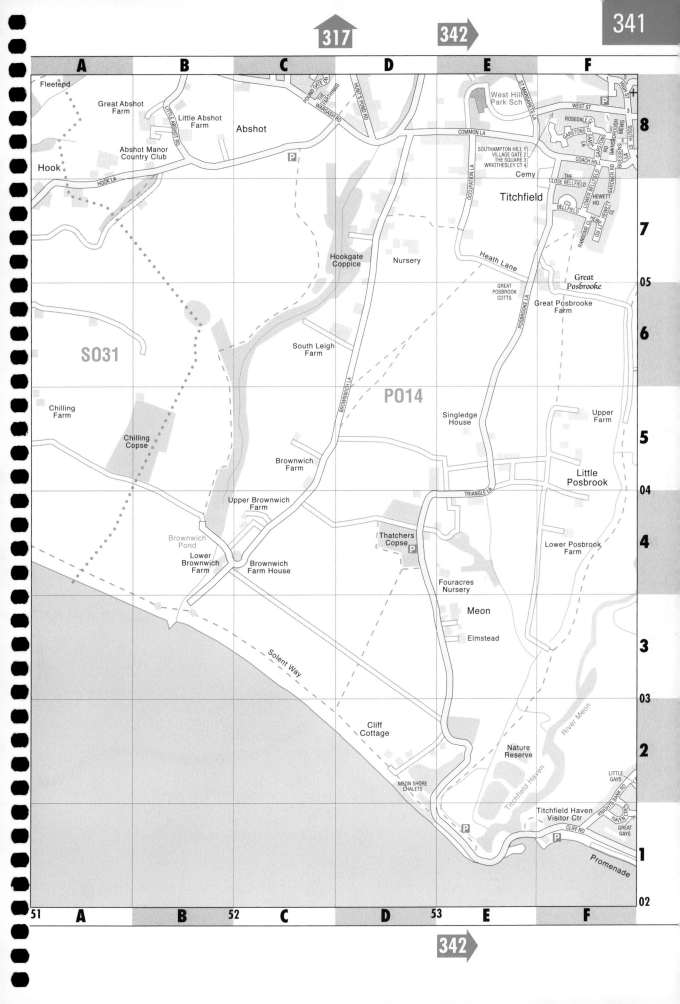

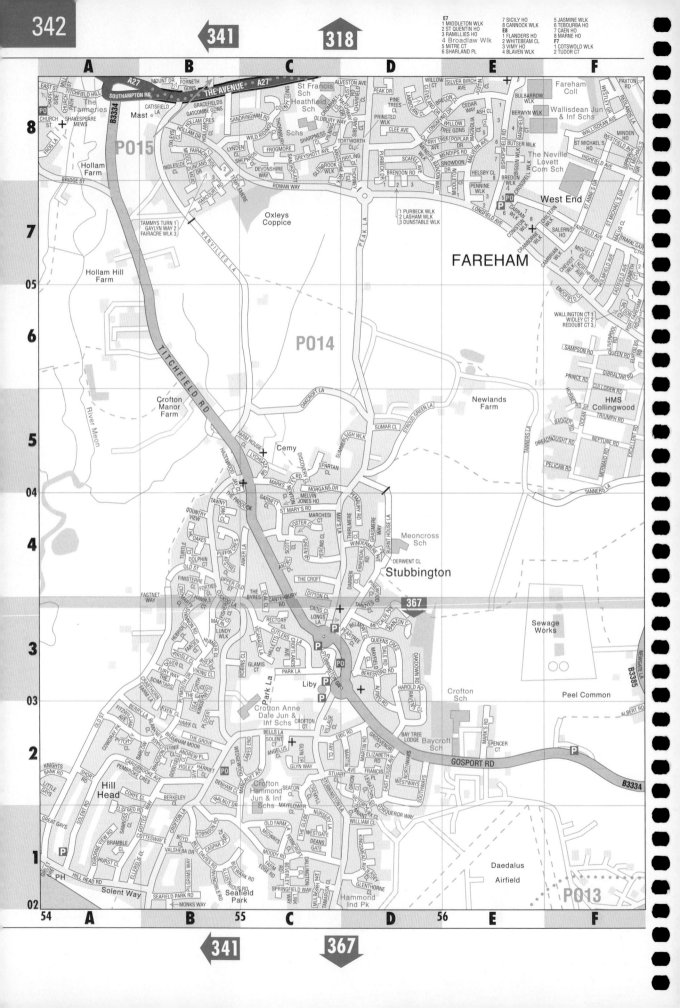

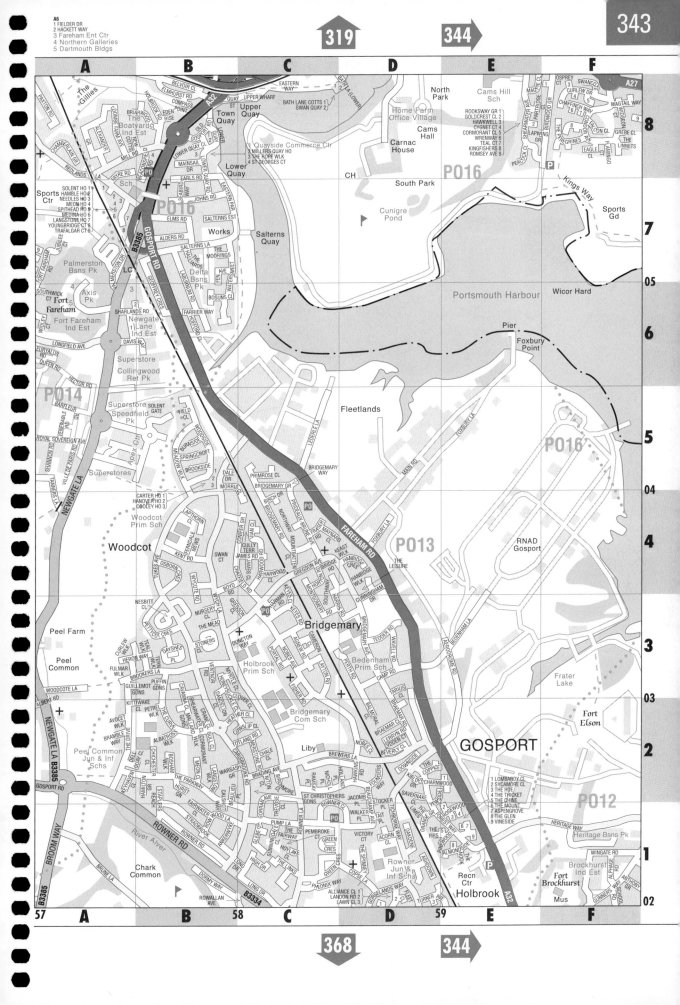

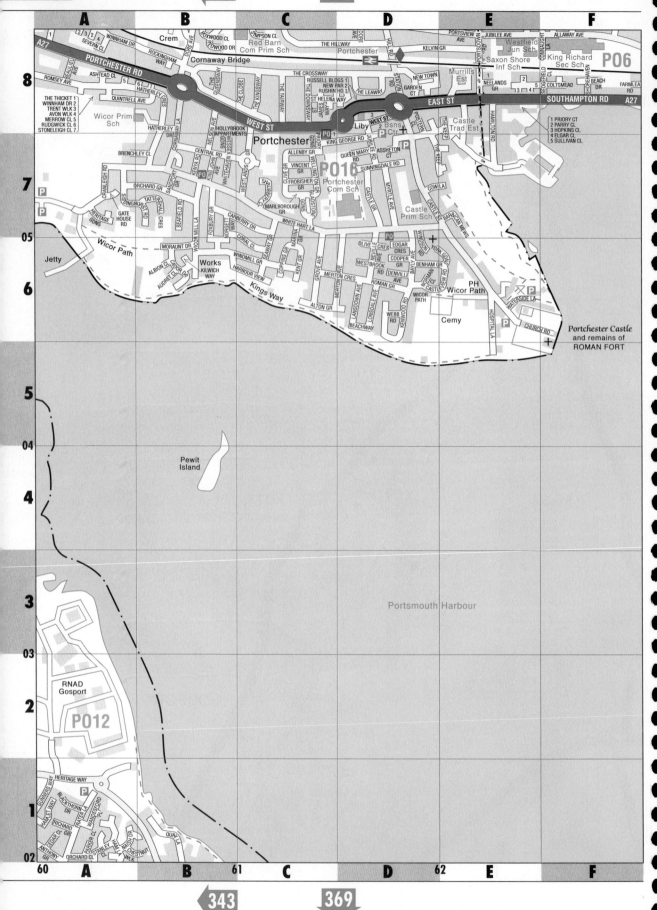

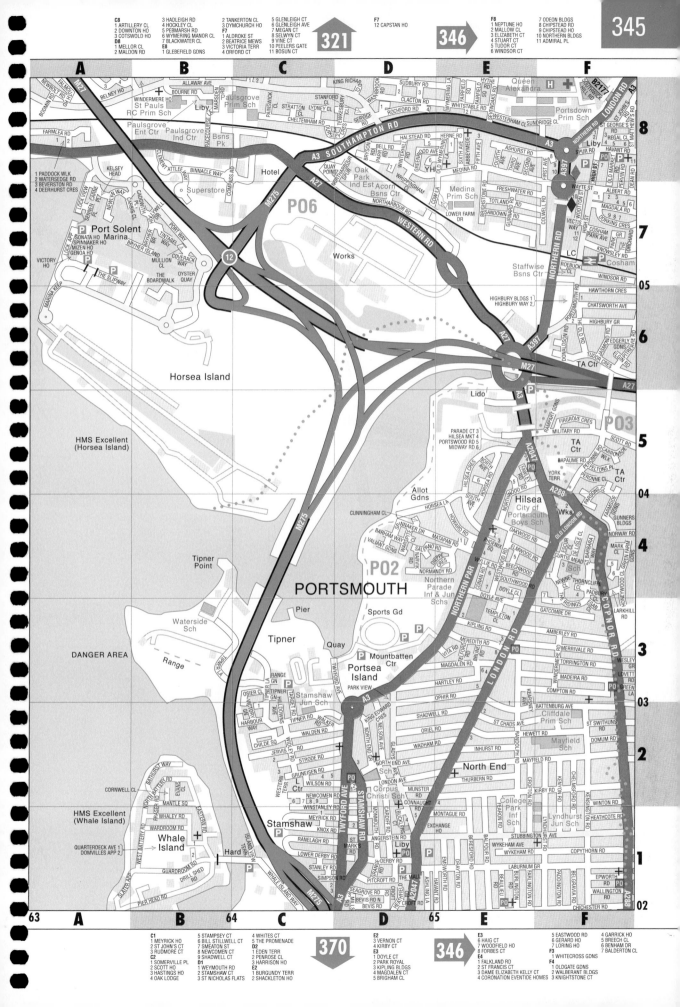

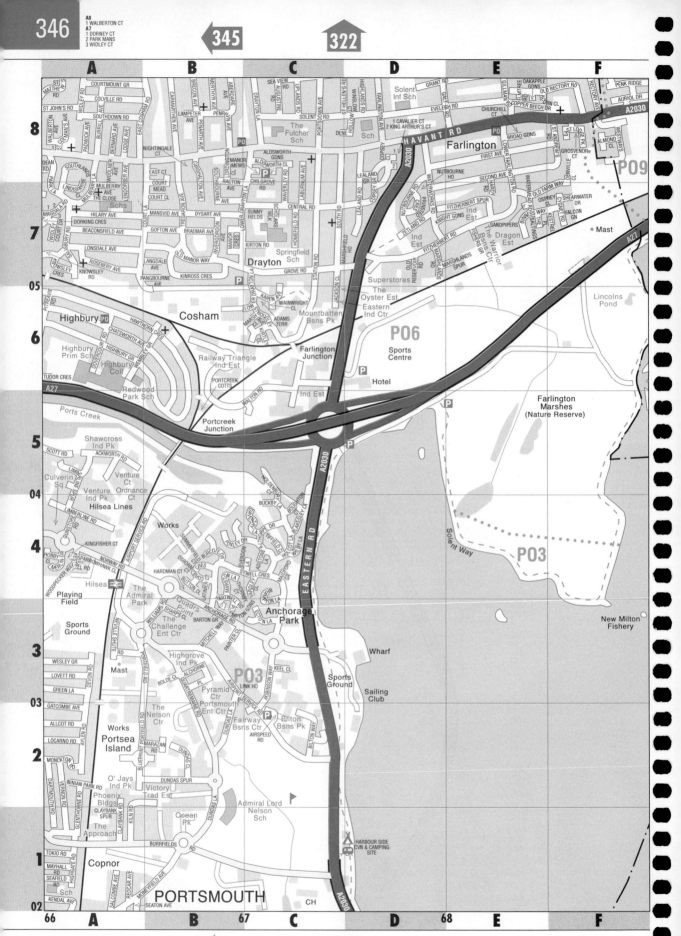

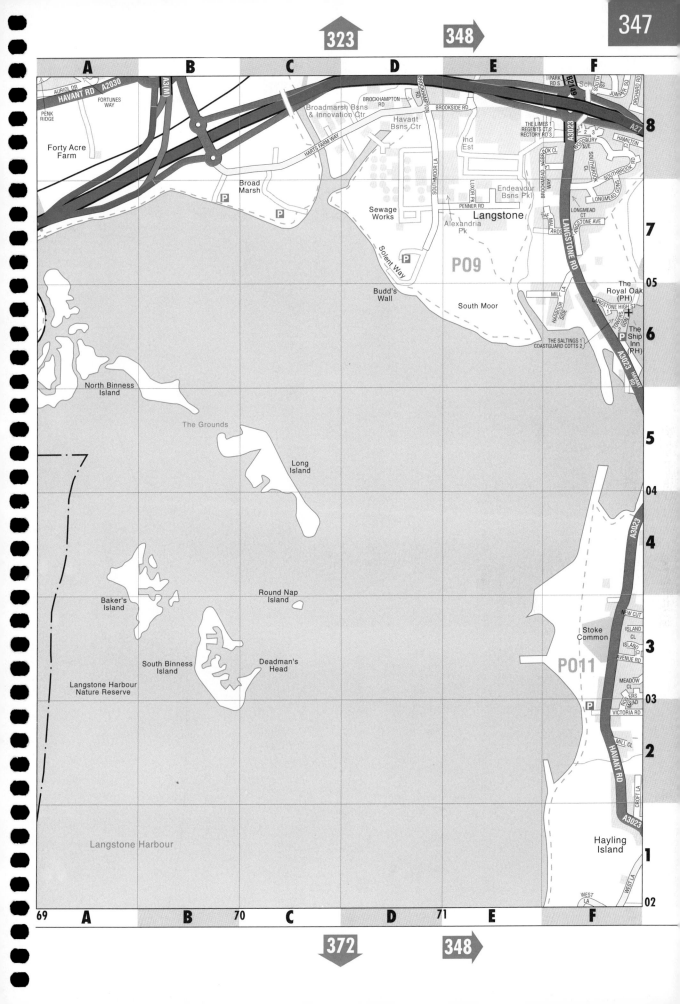

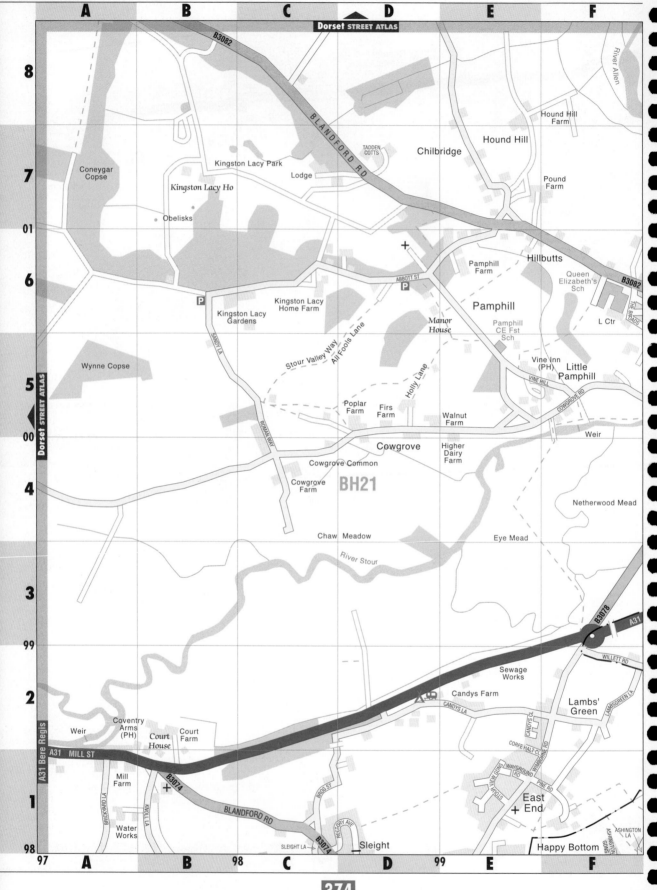

B3082

Coneygar Copse

Kingston Lacy Park

Kingston Lacy Ho

Lodge

Obelisks

TADDEN COTTS

BLANDFORD RD

Chilbridge

Hound Hill

Hound Hill Farm

Pound Farm

Pamphill Farm

Hillbutts

Queen Elizabeth's Sch

B3082

THE BROADS

Pamphill

L Ctr

Kingston Lacy Home Farm

Kingston Lacy Gardens

ABBOTT ST

Manor House

Pamphill CE Fst Sch

Wynne Copse

SANDY LA

Stour Valley Way

All Fools Lane

Holly Lane

Vine Inn (PH)

Little Pamphill

VINE MILL

COWGROVE RD

Poplar Farm

Firs Farm

Walnut Farm

Weir

ROMAN WAY

Cowgrove

Higher Dairy Farm

Cowgrove Common

BH21

Cowgrove Farm

Netherwood Mead

Chaw Meadow

Eye Mead

River Stour

B3078

A31

Sewage Works

WILLETT RD

Candys Farm

Lambs' Green

LAMBSGREEN LA

Candys Farm

CANDYS LA

CANDYS CL

CORFE HALT CL

WIMBORNE RD

PINE RD

Coventry Arms (PH)

Court House

Court Farm

A31 Bere Regis

Weir

A31 MILL ST

Mill Farm

B3074

BRICKYARD LA

KNOLL LA

BLANDFORD RD

Water Works

BROB ST

REGORY AVE

B3074

SLEIGHT LA

Sleight

WAYGROUND RD

STOUR VIEW GDNS

East End

Happy Bottom

ASHINGTON LA

ASHINGTON GDNS

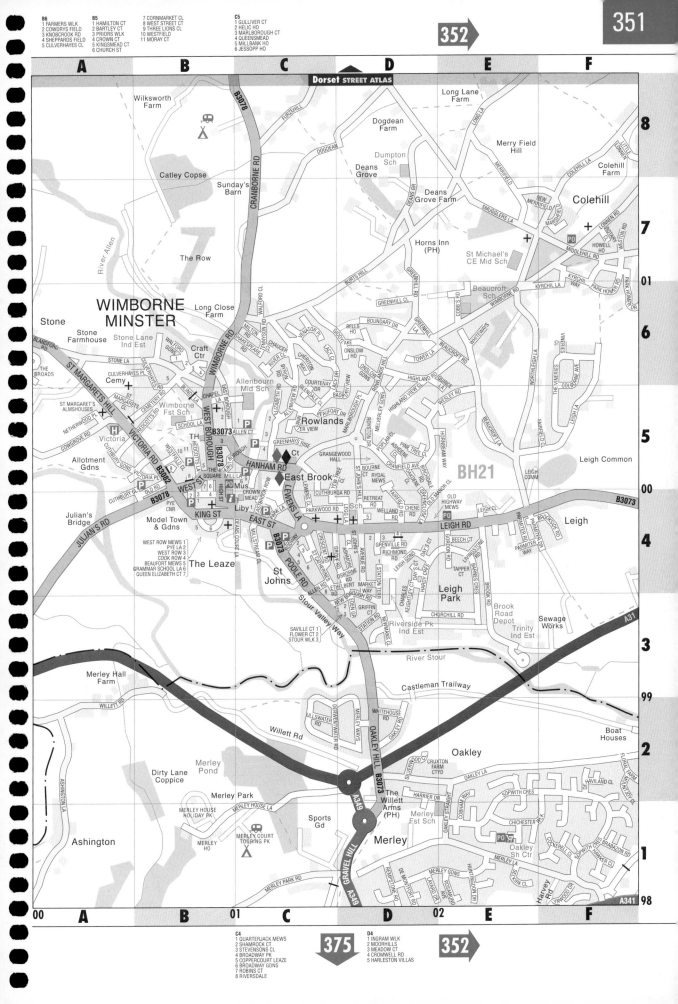

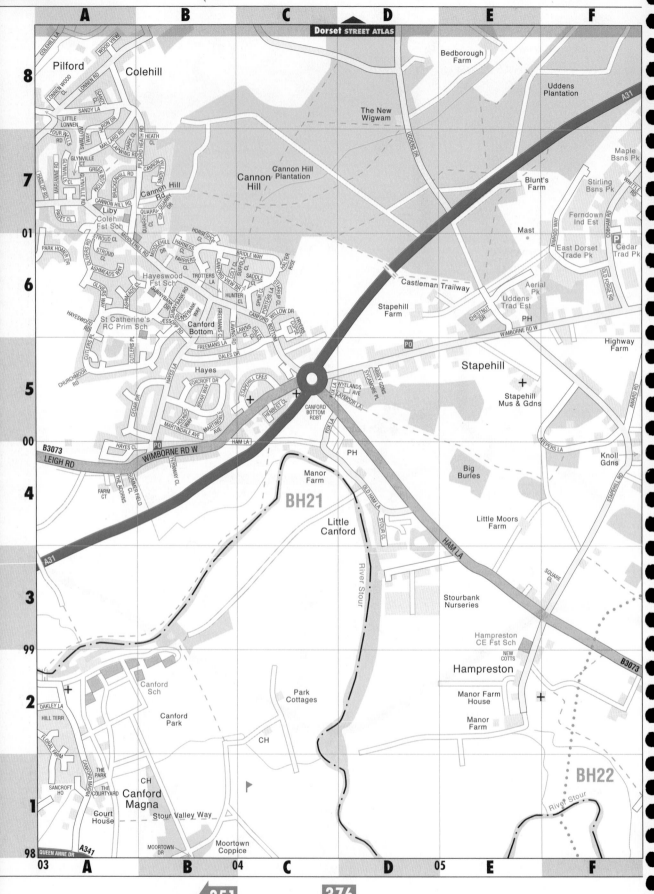

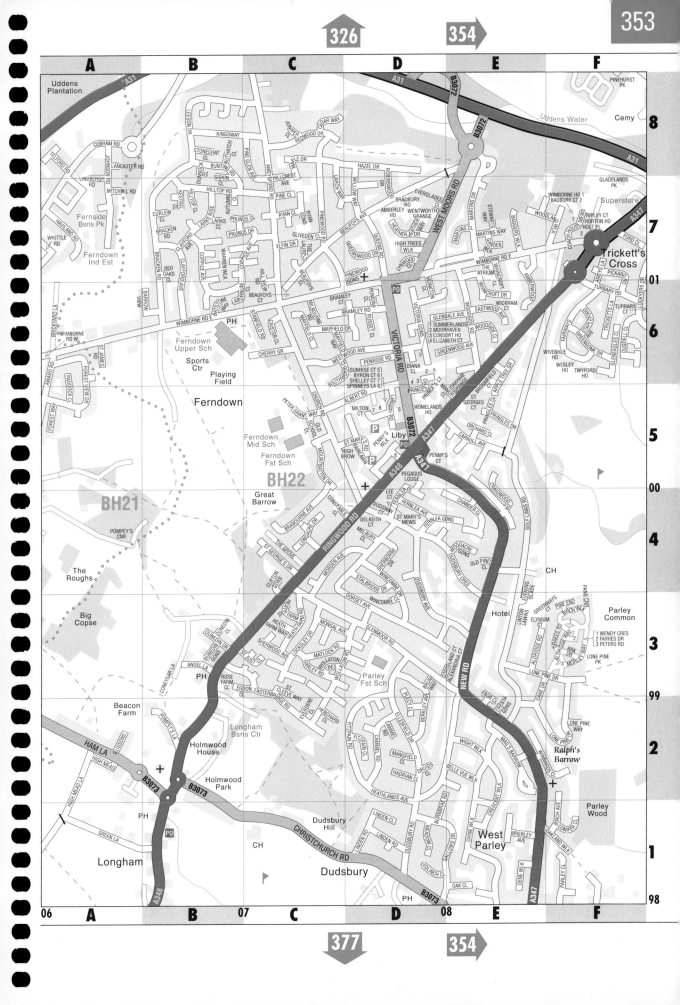

353
327

A   B   C   D   E   F

UPLANDS RD
PINEHURST RD
ABBEY RD
MONKS CL
A31
St Leonard's Bridge
H
St Leonards
Grange Estate

PRIORY RD
UPLANDS CL
ABBOTTS WAY
NORTH DR
THE SQUARE
MOOR SIDE
THE AVENUE
Dorset Ambulance Service HQ
White Ranch
WAYSIDE RD
FOXBURY RD

ASHLEY CT
P.O.
RINGWOOD RD
THE ACORNS
WEST DR
CENTRAL DR
8

PRIORY GDNS
A31
St Leonards Farm Pk
SOUTH DR
EAST DR
THE COPSE
THE PADDOCK
Palmers Ford Farm

A347
Superstore

Trickett's Cross
7

P
EMBERLEY CL
FORD LA
Palmer's Ford
BH24

CORBIN AVE
01

BOLTON CRES
THAMES CL
01

LOCKYERS DR
MEDWAY RD
HUMBER RD
TRENT CL
WAY
Foxbury Road

PETWYN CL
BANKS RD
DERWENT CL
6

SEVERN RD
Works
Heath Road West
Barnsfield Heath

TAMAR CL

Parley Common
5
Fir Grove Farm

BH22
Barnsfield Heath

00
00

Gibbet Firs
4
Moors River
Hurn Forest

East Parley Common
3

99
99

BH23

2
Bournemouth International Airport

BARRACK RD

Heathfield Farm
1
Basepoint Bsns Ctr
Aviation Park W

CAPEL LA
ENTERPRISE WAY

The Oaks
98

09   A   10   B   C   10   D   11   E   F

353
378

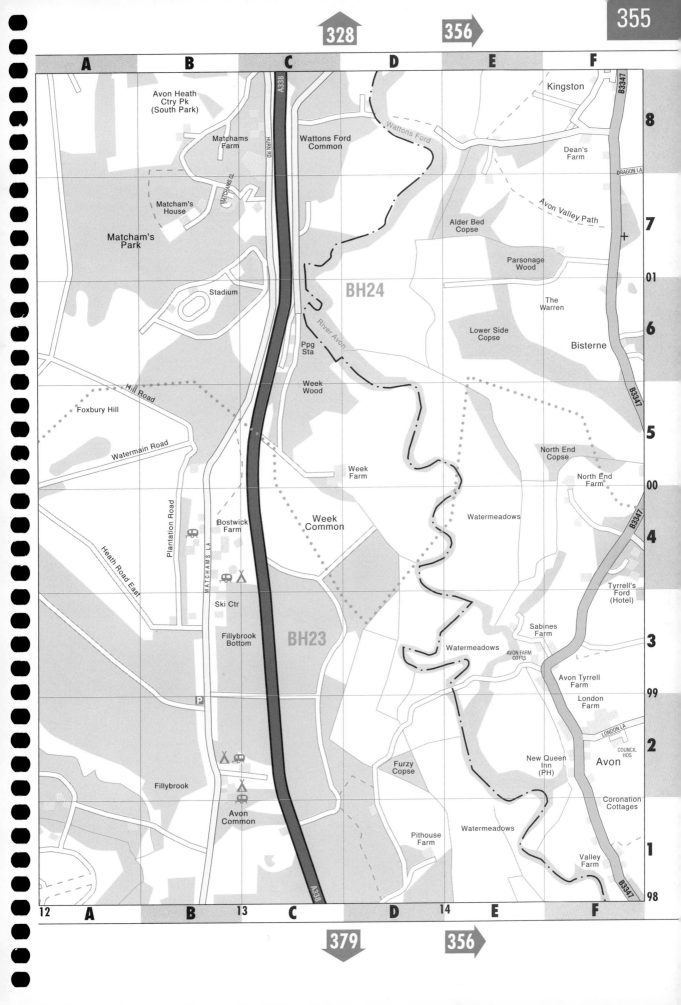

328
356
379
356

Avon Heath
Ctry Pk
(South Park)

Kingston

B3347

Matchams
Farm

Wattons Ford
Common

Wattons Ford

Dean's
Farm

DRAGON LA

HURN RD

MATCHAMS CL

Matcham's
House

Avon Valley Path

Alder Bed
Copse

Matcham's Park

Parsonage
Wood

BH24

Stadium

The
Warren

River Avon

Lower Side
Copse

Bisterne

Ppg
Sta

Week
Wood

Hill Road

Foxbury Hill

North End
Copse

Watermain Road

Week
Farm

North End
Farm

B3347

Plantation Road

Bostwick
Farm

Week
Common

Watermeadows

MATCHAMS LA

Heath Road East

Ski Ctr

Tyrrell's
Ford
(Hotel)

Fillybrook
Bottom

BH23

Sabines
Farm

Watermeadows

AVON FARM
COTTS

Avon Tyrrell
Farm

P

London
Farm

LONDON LA

COUNCIL
HOS

Fillybrook

Furzy
Copse

New Queen
Inn
(PH)

Avon

Avon
Common

Coronation
Cottages

Pithouse
Farm

Watermeadows

Valley
Farm

B3347

A338

8
01
7
6
5
00
4
3
99
2
1
98

12 A   B   13   C   D   14   E   F

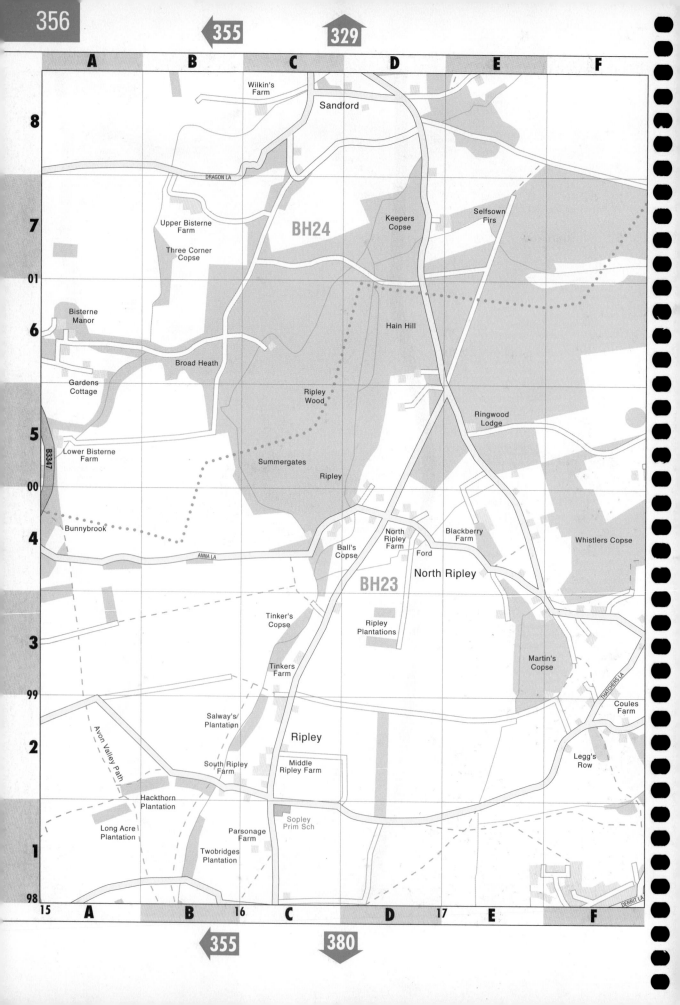

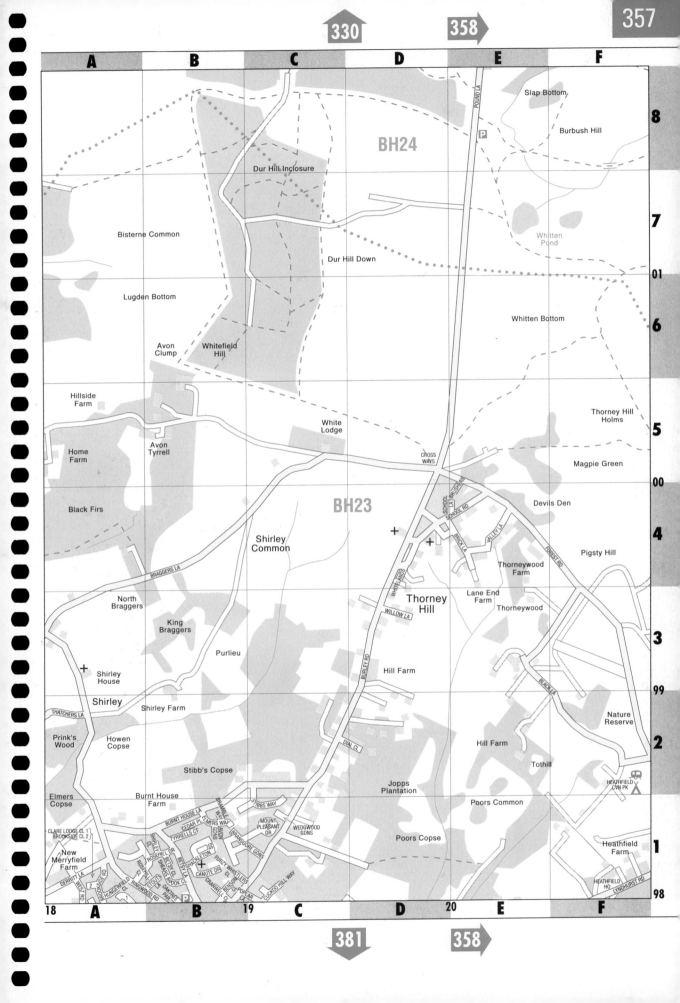

A B C D E F

8

BH24

Slap Bottom

Burbush Hill

Dur Hill Inclosure

7

Bisterne Common

Whitten
Pond

Dur Hill Down

01

Lugden Bottom

Whitten Bottom

6

Avon
Clump

Whitefield
Hill

Hillside
Farm

5

Thorney Hill
Holms

White
Lodge

Avon
Tyrrell

CROSS
WAYS

Magpie Green

Home
Farm

00

BH23

Devils Den

4

Black Firs

SCHOOL LA
SCHOOL RD

BRICK LA
VALLEY LA
BRUSHERS

Pigsty Hill

Shirley
Common

Thorneywood
Farm

FOREST RD

Braggers La

Lane End
Farm

Thorneywood

North
Braggers

WHITE LADS

Thorney
Hill

King
Braggers

WILLOW LA.

3

Purlieu

BURLEY RD

Hill Farm

BLACK LA

99

Shirley
House

Nature
Reserve

Shirley

Shirley Farm

2

THATCHERS LA

Prink's
Wood

Howen
Copse

DIAL CL

Hill Farm

Tothill

Stibb's Copse

Jopps
Plantation

HEATHFIELD
CVN PK

Elmers
Copse

Burnt House
Farm

TIBBS WAY

Poors Common

BURNT HOUSE LA
BRAMBLE
ELMERS WAY
AVON
BRANSGORE GDNS

MOUNT
PLEASANT
DR.

WEDGWOOD
GDNS

Poors Copse

1

CLARE LODGE CL 1
BROOKSIDE CL 2

New
Merryfield
Farm

CEDAR PL
TYRRELLS CT
SHACKLETON

FURZY WHISTLERS

Heathfield
Farm

DERRITT LA
WEST RD
BRUNGENFIELD
RINGWOOD RD
SHIRLEY DR
ROSEHILL DR
ROSEHILL CL
STOTTS LA
BETSY CL
SPEARS BROOK CL
OAKTREE
CRANWELL CL
BENSON
POPLAR
CANUTE DR

CHANNEL HILL WAY

HEATHFIELD
HO
LYNDHURST RD

98

18 A B 19 C D 20 E F

357
331

A B C D E F

8

7

01

6

5

00

4

99

2

98

Holmsley
Bog

Goatspen
Plain

Clayhill
Bottom

Scrape
Bottom

Greenberry
Bridge

Anthony's Bee
Bottom

BH24

Scrape Rd

Holmsley
Walk

Gravel
Pit

Wilverley
Cottage

Holmsley Ridge

Holmsley
Lodge

Little
Holmsley

Lodge
Hill

The
Old Station

Cardinal
Hat

Avon Water

Mill

Holmsley
Inclosure

Hanging
Shoot

Holmsley
Toll House

Brownhill Inclosure

Magpie Bottom

Great
Hat

Stony Moors

Wootton Copse
Inclosure

Pigsty
Hat

B3058

Wootton
Old Farm

Bell's
Hat

BROWNHILL RD

Mast

BH23

RHINEFIELD RD

WILVERLEY RD

99

Little Wootton Inclosure

BH25

HOLMSLEY RD

Wattons
Farm

Wootton Heath
Farm

Plain Heath

WOTTON FARM RD

B3058

Manor
Farm

NORTH DR

Valesmoor
Farm

FOREST RD

Willie's
Holms

LYNDHURST RD

Forest
Lodge

A35

Hole Copse

Portnall's
Farm

21 A 22 B C 23 D E F

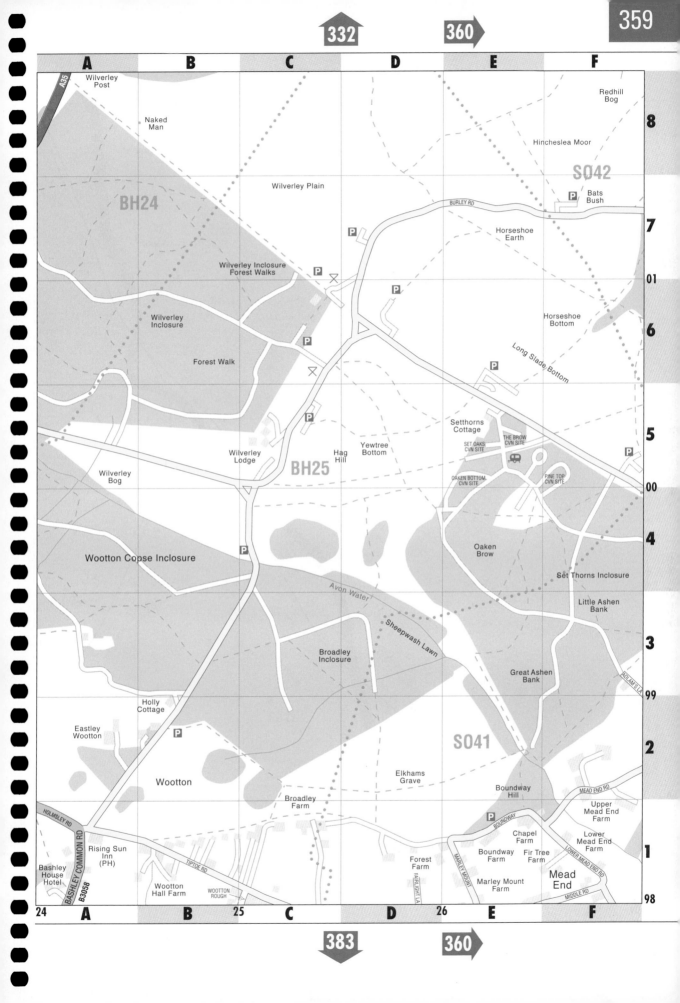

A B C D E F

8

White Moor

Furzey Cottage

Pound Farm

Brockenhurst CE Prim Sch

Brookley Farm

RAILWAY TERR 1
AVENUE RD 2

PARTRIDGE RD

HIGHWOOD RD

B3055

Five Thorns Hill

BURLEY RD

Furzy Hill

South Weirs

SOUTH WEIRS

Brockenhurst

TATTENHAM RD

THE LAURELS

ADDISON RD

7

01

P

Farm Cottage

Trenley Lawn

Worthys Farmhouse

West Beams Farm

SWAY RD

COLLYERS RD

WOODLANDS RD

Brokenhurst Copse

TILEBARN LA

6

Hincheslea Wood

SO42

Blackhamsley House

CH

Brokenhurst Manor Golf Club

Lymington Junction

Latchmoor House

5

Hincheslea Bog

BH25

P

Blackhamsley Hill

Cater's Cottage

B3055

Three Beech Bottom

Setley Plain

00

P

4

P

3

Cemy

QUARR HO

BULDOWNE WLK

GILPINS FOLLY

FOREST EDGE CL

BRIGHTON RD

OAKENBROW

ISLAND VIEW

GILPIN HILL

KITCHERS CL

HAWTHORNE DR

MANCHESTER RD

HIGHFIELD CL

BOND LA

LITTLE BRM

JORDANS LA

OXFORD TERR

Widden Bottom

SO41

Milking Pound Bottom

99

THE CLOSE

NORMANDY CL

ADLAMS LA

MEAD END RD

STAG CL

FORD RISE

MIDDLE RD

CRUSE CL

ANDERWOOD DR

GURRANT WAY

HIGHFIELD GDNS

WIDDEN CL

HYDE CL

SET THORNS RD

BADGERS CL

CHRITAL CL

CENTENARY CL

ST JAMES RD

DURNSTOWN

PH

Durns Town

BACK LA

2

St Luke's CE Prim Sch

HERON CL

Sway

Hotel

PO

ROWAN CL

STATION RD

CHURCH LA

WESTBEAMS RD

BIRCHY HILL

COOMBE LA

CHAPEL LA

Little Purley Farm

PITMORE LA

SHIRLEY HOLMS

Hilltop

P

1

Rushcroft Farm

Sway Park Ind Est

Sway

HOLLIES CL

TEBOURBA COTTS

JUBILEE CT

B3055

OLD VICARAGE LA

Manor Farm

Eastwoods

98

27 A B 28 C D 29 E F

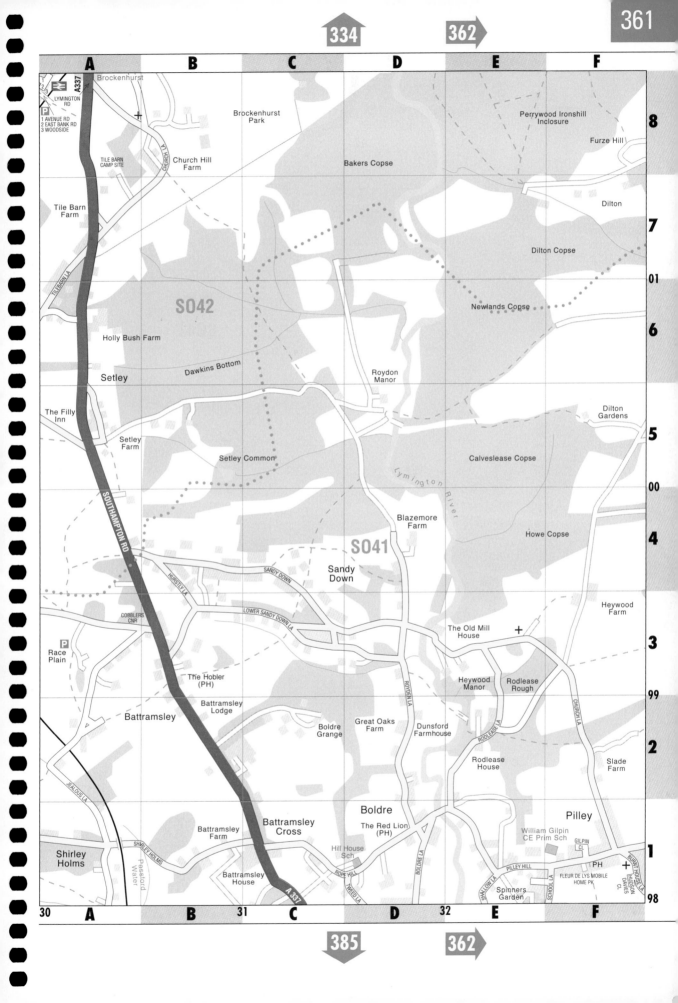

334
362

Brockenhurst

LYMINGTON RD

1 AVENUE RD
2 EAST BANK RD
3 WOODSIDE

Brockenhurst
Park

Perrywood Ironshill
Inclosure

Furze Hill

8

Bakers Copse

Church Hill
Farm

TILE BARN CAMP SITE

Dilton

Tile Barn
Farm

7

Dilton Copse

01

SO42

Newlands Copse

6

Holly Bush Farm

Dawkins Bottom

Roydon
Manor

Setley

Dilton
Gardens

The Filly
Inn

Calveslease Copse

5

Setley
Farm

Lymington River

00

Setley Common

Blazemore
Farm

Howe Copse

4

SO41

Sandy Down

Sandy
Down

SOUTHAMPTON RD

Heywood
Farm

COBBLERS CNR

Lower Sandy Down La

The Old Mill
House

3

HURSTLY LA

Race
Plain

The Hobler
(PH)

Heywood
Manor

Rodlease
Rough

99

Battramsley
Lodge

RODLEASE LA

CHURCH LA

Battramsley

Boldre
Grange

Great Oaks
Farm

Dunsford
Farmhouse

Rodlease
House

Slade
Farm

2

ROYDEN LA

Boldre

Pilley

JEALOUS LA

William Gilpin
CE Prim Sch

Battramsley
Farm

Battramsley
Cross

The Red Lion
(PH)

GILPIN CL

1

SHIRLEY HOLMS

Hill House
Sch

PILLEY HILL

PH

BURNT HOUSE LA
HUDSON DAVIES CL

Shirley
Holms

Passford Water

Battramsley
House

BOLDRE LA

SCHOOL LA

FLEUR DE LYS MOBILE HOME PK

A 337

ROPE HILL

NEEDS LA

SHALLOW LA

Spinners
Garden

98

30

A

B

31

C

D

32

E

F

385
362

361
335

A B C D E F

8

B3055

Stockley
Inclosure

Stockley
Cottage

Hawkhill
Inclosure

Lodge Heath

P

P

B3055

7

Dilton
Common

Hatchet Moor

01

Dilton
Farm

SO42

6

Beaulieu Heath

P

5

Little Dilton
Farm

B3054

Two Bridges
Bottom

00

Greenmoor

Deep Moor

Sheffield
Copse

4

SO41

Crockford Stream

3

Whitemoor
Rough

Crockford Bridge

P

99

Allot
Gdns

Lower Crockford Bottom

P

Pilley
Bailey

Fords

2

Wooden House La

Bull
Hill

Norley Inclosure

Wormstall
Wood

May La

Pilley Gn

Jordans La

Pilley Bailey

Pilley St
PO

Bull Hill

1

Lucky La

Burnt House La

Pilley

P

B3054

Norleywood Rd

Norley
Farm

98

Warborne La

33 A B 34 C D 35 E F

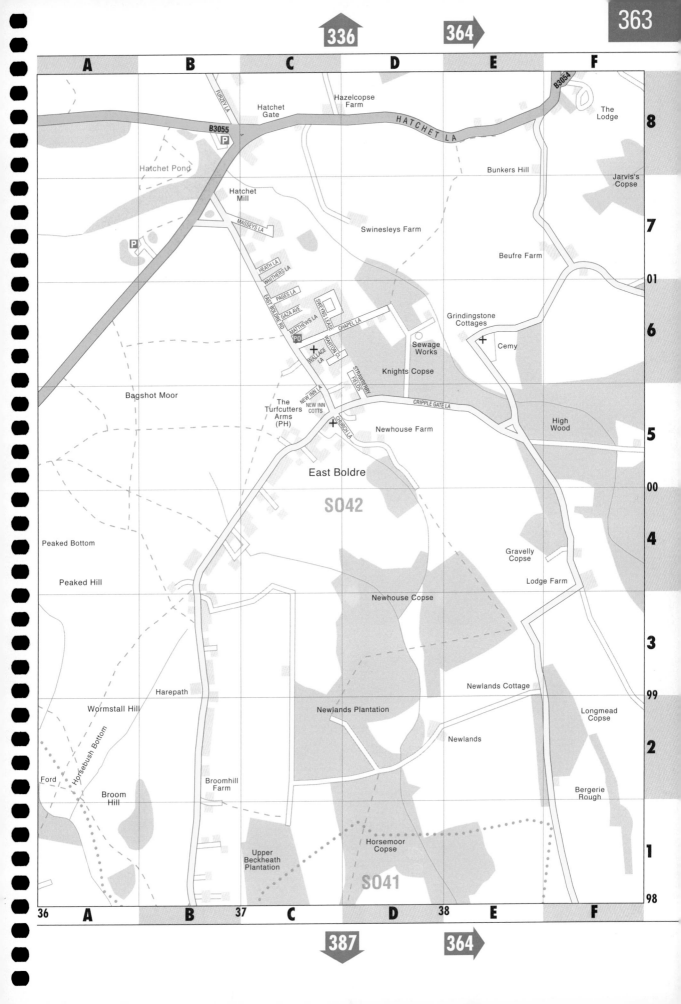

336
364

A B C D E F

8
7
6
5
4
3
2
1

01
00
99
98

The Lodge

B3054

Jarvis's Copse

Hatchet Gate

Hazelcopse Farm

HATCHET LA

Bunkers Hill

FURZEY LA

B3055

Hatchet Pond

Hatchet Mill

MASSEYS LA

Swinesleys Farm

Beufre Farm

HEATH LA
WHITHERS LA
PAGES LA
GAZA AVE
EAST BOLDRE RD
MATTHEWS CL
SWEINS LEASE
CHAPEL LA
WARTON CL

Grindingstone Cottages

Cemy

Sewage Works

Knights Copse

WALLACE LA
STRAWBERRY FIELDS

Bagshot Moor

NEW INN LA
NEW INN COTTS
CHURCH LA

The Turfcutters Arms (PH)

CRIPPLE GATE LA

High Wood

Newhouse Farm

East Boldre

SO42

Peaked Bottom

Gravelly Copse

Lodge Farm

Peaked Hill

Newhouse Copse

Newlands Cottage

Harepath

Wormstall Hill

Newlands Plantation

Longmead Copse

Newlands

Horsebush Bottom

Ford

Broomhill Farm

Broom Hill

Bergerie Rough

Upper Beckheath Plantation

Horsemoor Copse

SO41

36 A B 37 C D 38 E F

363
337

A **B** **C** **D** **E** **F**

8

Carpenters Dock

Oxleys

THE HUMMICKS

SO42

DOCK LA

Oxleys Copse

Landing Stage

Bailey's Hard

7

Spearbed Copse

Sims Wood

Steerleys Copse

Cowleys Lane

Stock Copse

SUMMER LA

Keeping Copse

01

Solent Way

6

Keeping Marsh

SO45

Keeping Farm

Keeping

Beaulieu River

Gilbury Hard

5

Dungehill Copse

Marina

Quay

Jetty

Ashen Wood

00

Hotel

Bucklers Hard Maritime Mus

P

Little Purnel

Bucklers Hard

Clobb Copse

4

SO42

Clobb Gorse

Solent Way

Salternshill Copse

Foul Bush

Clobb Farm

3

Tylers Copse

Old Park Wood

Salternshill

99

Coopers Wood

Lodge Plantation

Kitchers Rough

Drokes

2

Shadebush Copse

Landing Stages

1

St Leonards Grange

Gins

GINS LA

Chapel

Tithe Barn

St Leonard's Farm

WARREN LA

98

363
388

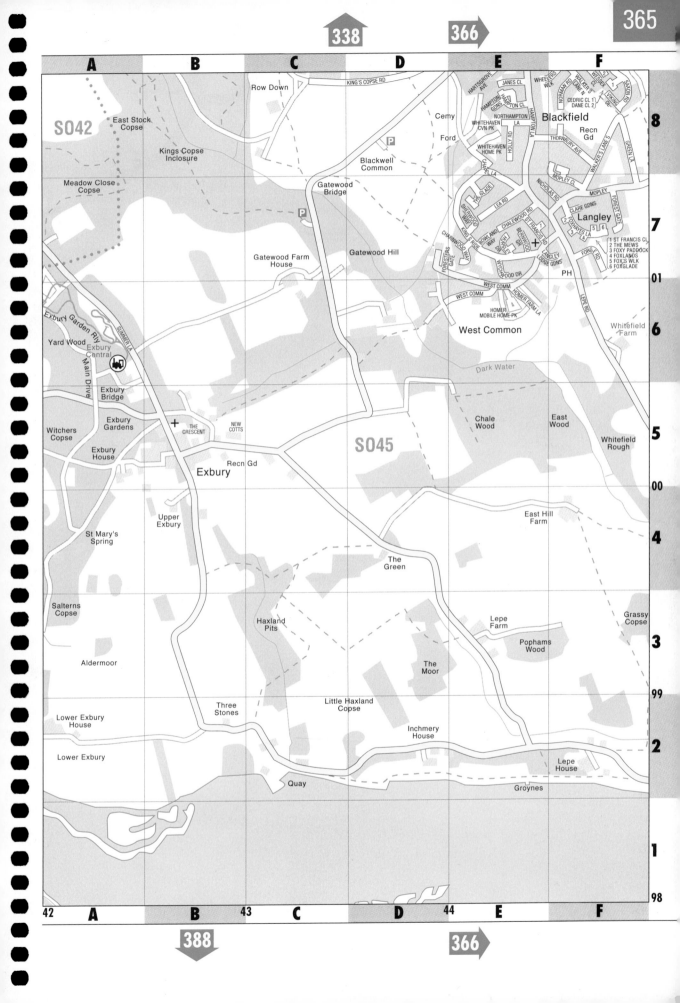

338
366
388
366

SO42

East Stock Copse

Kings Copse Inclosure

Meadow Close Copse

Row Down

KING'S COPSE RD

Blackwell Common

Gatewood Bridge

Gatewood Hill

Gatewood Farm House

HARTSGROVE AVE
HAMPTON GDNS
JANES CL
HAMPTON CL
WHEELERS WLK
WALKER'S
LANE N
NORMAN RD
WESSEY
LUKING
GR
SAXON RD
CEDRIC CL 1
DANE CL 2
Cemy
Ford
Blackfield
NORTHAMPTON LA
WHITEHAVEN CVN PK
HOLLY RD
THORNBURY AVE
Recn Gd
WALKER'S LANE S
GREEN LA
WHITEHAVEN HOME PK
CHAPEL LA
HAMPTON LA
MOPLEY CL
NICHOLAS RD
MOPLEY
FOREST GATE
THE GLADE
LEA RD
CLARE GDNS
Langley
SHERWOOD WAY
CHALEWOOD RD
ST FRANCIS RD
LANGLEY
FOXHAYES LA
BOWLAND
BENWOOD
3
FORESTERS GATE
CHARNWOOD WAY
KING'S RIDE
WYCH RD
WYCHWOOD DR
LANGLEY LODGE GDNS
FORG'F RD
PH
WEST COMM
LEPE RD
WEST COMM
HOMER FARM LA
HOMER MOBILE HOME PK

1 ST FRANCIS CL
2 THE MEWS
3 FOXY PADDOCK
4 FOXLANDS
5 FOX'S WLK
6 FOXGLADE

West Common

Whitefield Farm

Exbury Garden Rly
Yard Wood
Exbury Central
SUMMER LA
Main Drive
Exbury Bridge
Exbury Gardens
Witchers Copse
THE CRESCENT
NEW COTTS
Exbury House
Exbury
Recn Gd

Dark Water

Chale Wood
East Wood
Whitefield Rough

SO45

East Hill Farm

Upper Exbury

St Mary's Spring

The Green

Salterns Copse

Haxland Pits

Aldermoor

Lepe Farm
Pophams Wood
Grassy Copse

The Moor

Three Stones

Little Haxland Copse

Lower Exbury House

Inchmery House

Lower Exbury

Quay

Lepe House

Groynes

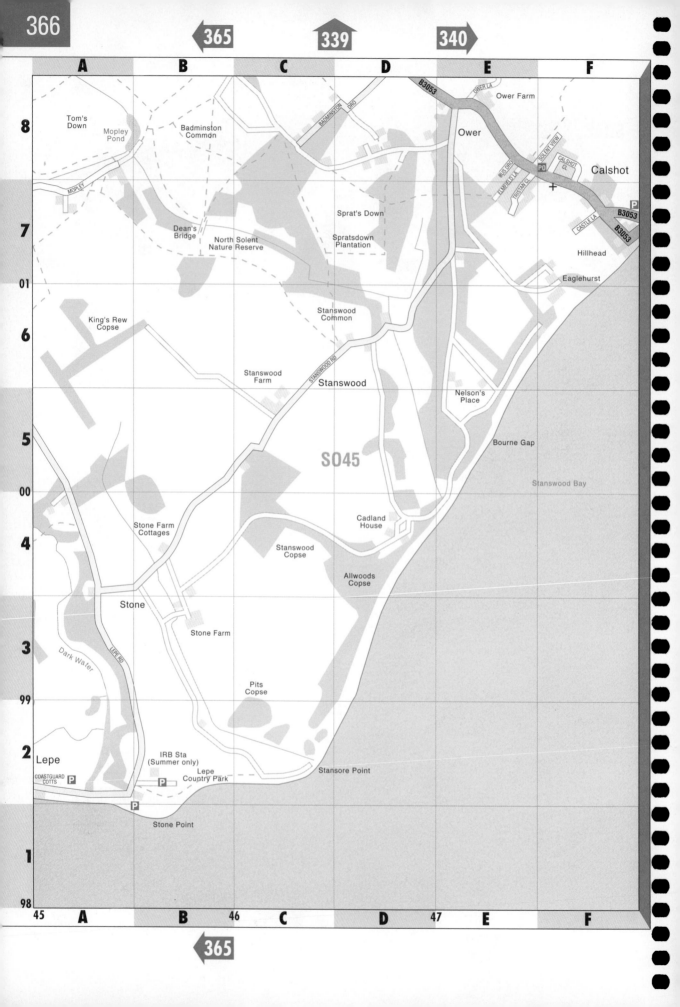

365 339 340
365

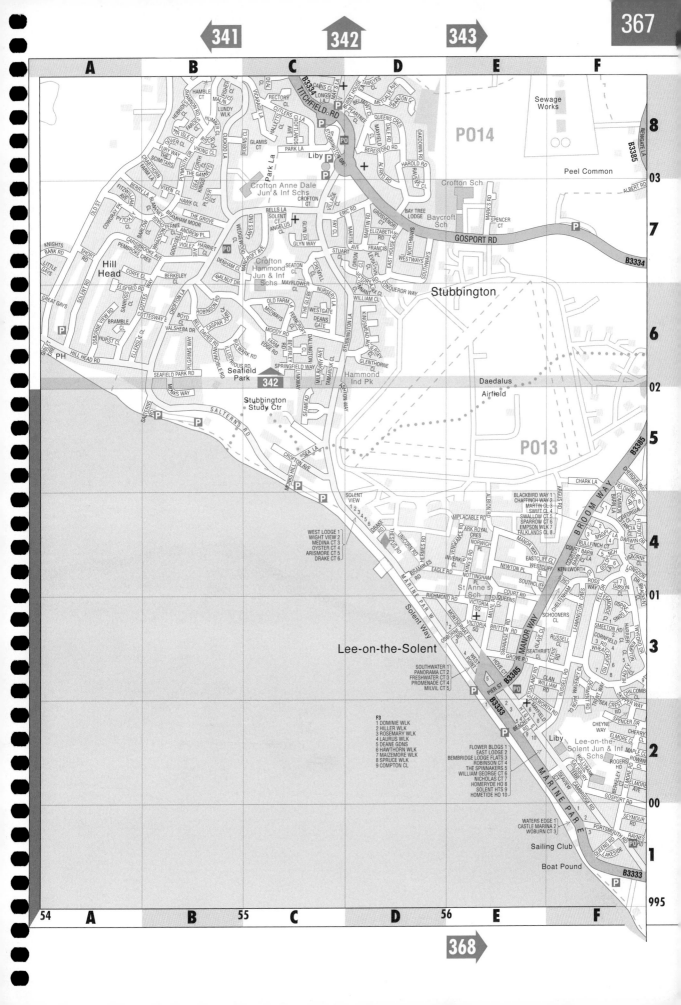

367
343

C6
1 JADE CT
2 JASMINE CT
3 COBALT CT
4 MAGENTA CT
5 CARMINE CT
6 CORAL CT

7 BATH AND WELLS CT
8 BRADFORD CT
9 WORCESTER CT
10 HEREFORD CT
11 SHEFFIELD CT
12 DERBY CT
13 LOVELOCK TERR

14 SHEPPERD TERR

D5
1 ROCHESTER CT
2 LIVERPOOL CT
3 OTTER CT
4 LICHFIELD CT
5 BLACKBURN CT
6 ST EDMONDSBURY CT

7 BIRMINGHAM CT
8 ELY CT
9 LINCOLN CT
10 MANCHESTER CT
11 LEICESTER CT
12 PETERBOROUGH CT
13 WINCHESTER CT

14 ST ALBANS CT
15 GUILDFORD CT

Map labels

Shoot Farm
Rowner
Grange Inf & Jun Schs
Fort Brockhurst
Brockhurst
Fort Rowner
HMS Sultan
Brune Park Cem Coll
Wild Grounds Nature Reserve
Siskin Inf & Jun Schs
Works
Grange Farm
17th Century Experience
Fort Grange
PO13
PO12
Cemy
Ann's Hill
Westfield Ind Est
Lee-on-the-Solent
The Seagulls
Carter's Copse Nature Trail
Fairview CT
Privett
DANGER AREA
Browndown
Kingfisher CVN PK
Browndown Training Camp
Browndown Point
Solent Way
Browndown Battery
Stokes Bay Mobile Home PK
Bay House Sch
Hotel
The Pebble Beach (PH)
Sailing Club
Stokes Bay
Promenade

1 BRACKEN CL
2 TWYFORD DR
3 COMPTON CL
4 SHERBROOKE CL

1 LARCH CL
2 SPENCER DR
3 CHERRY CL
4 MAPLE CL

1 FAIRLEAD DR
2 COMPASS CL
3 RALEIGH WLK
4 COVENTRY CT

1 NASMITH CL
2 WHITECLIFFE CT
3 MOAT CT

1 WAVERLEY PATH
2 GOMER CT
3 BROADSANDS WLK

CHAPEL SQ 1
THAMESMEAD CT 2
CLARE HO 3
RUSSELL CHURCHER CT 4
GOYDA HO 5
BAGOT HO 6

BURNETT RD 1
CLIFTON ST 2
CLAUDIA CT 3

D3
1 MILFORD CT
2 CHURCHER WLK
3 WICKHAM CT
4 WOOLSTON CT
5 FAIR OAK CT
6 CADNAM CT
7 SHIRREL CT
8 MARCHWOOD CT
9 SEAVIEW CT

10 ASHURST CT

F4
1 NORMANDY GDNS
2 DROXFORD CL
3 SELBORNE GDNS
4 WARNFORD CL
5 WILTON CL
6 ARDEN CL
7 CANBERRA CT
8 PILBROW CT

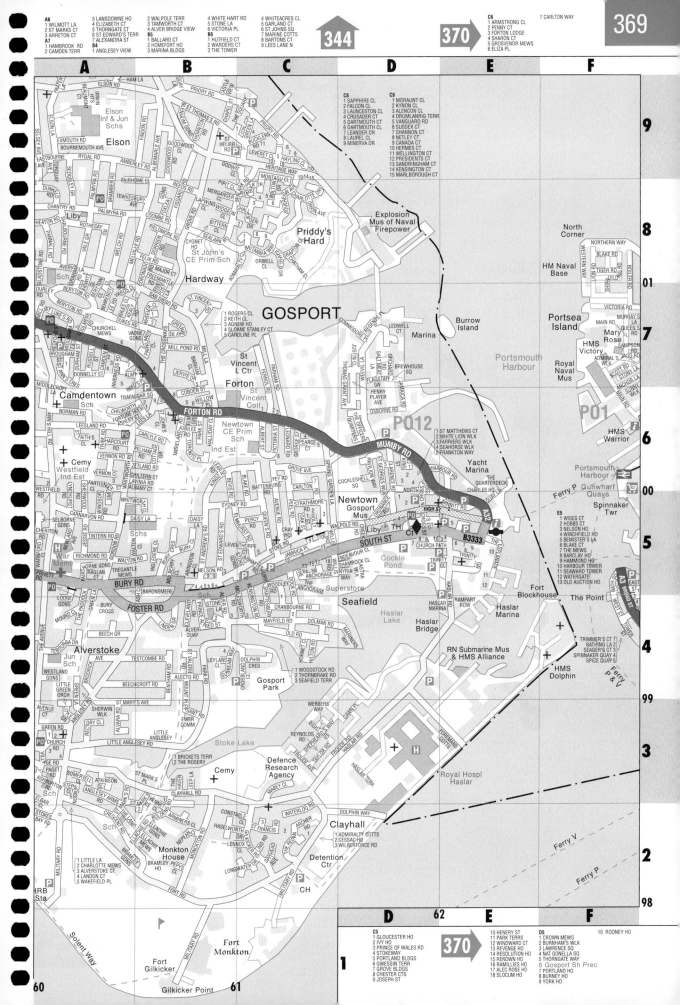

A6
1 WILMOTT LA
2 ST MARKS CT
3 ARRETON CT
A7
1 HAMBROOK RD
2 CAMDEN TERR

3 LANSDOWNE HO
4 ELIZABETH CT
5 THORNGATE CT
6 ST EDWARD'S TERR
7 ALEXANDRA ST
B4
1 ANGLESEY VIEW

2 WALPOLE TERR
3 TAMWORTH CT
4 ALVER BRIDGE VIEW
B5
1 BALLARD CT
2 HOMEFORT HO
3 MARINA BLDGS

4 WHITE HART RD
5 STONE LA
6 VICTORIA PL
B6
1 HUTFIELD CT
2 WARDERS CT
3 THE TOWER

5 WHITEACRES CL
5 GARLAND CT
6 ST JOHNS SQ
7 MARINE COTTS
8 BARTONS CT
9 LEES LANE N

C6
1 ARMSTRONG CL
2 PENNY CT
3 FORTON LODGE
4 SHARON CT
5 GROSVENOR MEWS
6 ELIZA PL

7 CARLTON WAY

C8
1 SAPPHIRE CL
2 FALCON CL
3 LAUNCESTON CL
4 CRUSADER CT
5 DARTMOUTH CT
6 DARTMOUTH CL
7 LEANDER DR
8 LAUREL CL
9 MINERVA DR

C9
1 MORAUNT CL
2 KYNON CL
3 ALENCON CL
4 DRUMLANRIG TERR
5 VANGUARD RD
6 SUSSEX CT
7 SHANNON CT
8 NETLEY CT
9 CANADA CT
10 HERMES CT
11 WELLINGTON CT
12 PRESIDENTS CT
13 SANDRINGHAM CT
14 KENSINGTON CT
15 MARLBOROUGH CT

1 ROGERS CL
2 KEITH CL
3 AGNEW HO
4 SLOANE STANLEY CT
5 CAROLINE PL

1 ST MATTHEWS CT
2 WHITE LION WLK
3 FARRIERS WLK
4 SEAHORSE WLK
5 FRANKTON WAY

E5
1 WISES CT
2 HOBBS CT
3 NELSON HO
4 WINCHFIELD HO
5 BEMISTER'S LA
6 BLAKE CT
7 THE MEWS
8 BARCLAY HO
9 HAMMOND HO
10 HARBOUR TOWER
11 SEAWARD TOWER
12 WATERGATE
13 OLD AUCTION HO

TRIMMER'S CT 1
BATHING LA 2
SEAGER'S CT 3
SPINNAKER QUAY 4
SPICE QUAY 5

1 WOODSTOCK RD
2 THORNBRAKE RD
3 SEAFIELD TERR

1 ADMIRALTY COTTS
2 CESSAC HO
3 WILBERFORCE RD

1 BRICKETS TERR
2 THE ROSERY

1 LITTLE LA
2 CHARLOTTE MEWS
3 ALVERSTOKE CT
4 LANDON CT
5 WAKEFIELD PL

C5
1 GLOUCESTER HO
2 IVY HO
3 PRINCE OF WALES RD
4 STOKEWAY
5 PORTLAND BLDGS
6 GWESSIN TERR
7 GROVE BLDGS
8 CHESTER CTS
9 JOSEPH ST
10 HENERY ST
11 PARK TERRS
12 WINDWARD CT
13 REVENGE HO
14 RESOLUTION HO
15 RENOWN HO
16 RAMILLIES HO
17 ALEC ROSE HO
18 SLOCUM HO

D5
1 CROWN MEWS
2 BURNHAM'S WLK
3 LAWRENCE SQ
4 NAT GONELLA SQ
5 THORNGATE WAY
6 Gosport Sh Prec
7 PORTLAND HO
8 BURNEY HO
9 YORK HO

10 RODNEY HO

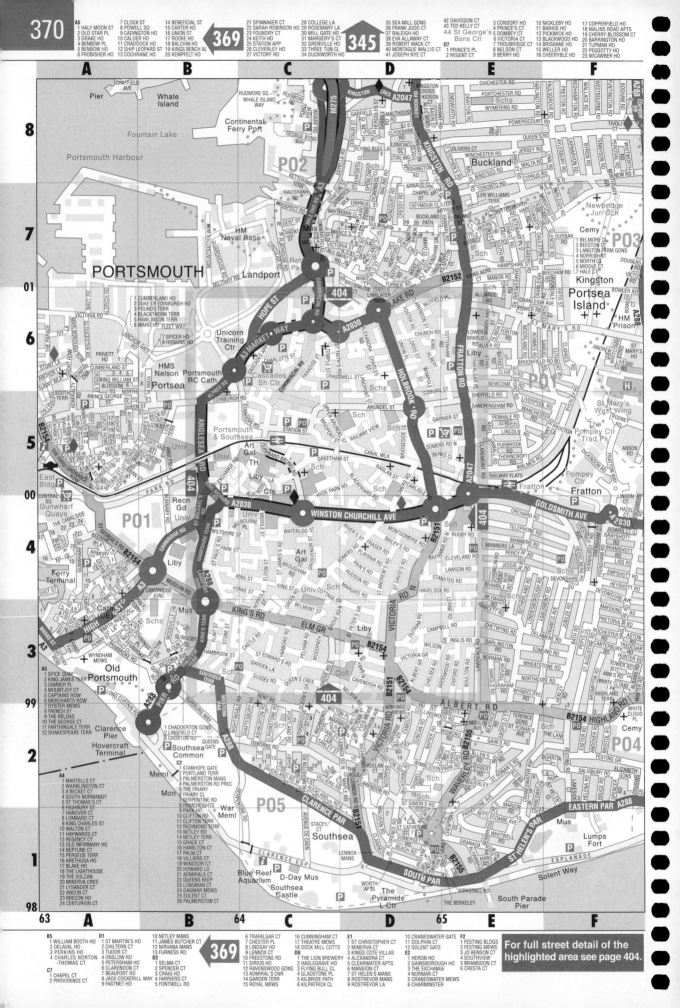

For full street detail of the highlighted area see page 404.

346
372

A5
1 ANSON RD
2 VERNON MEWS
3 MILTON CT
4 WASHINGTON CT

A8
1 SIDMOUTH AVE
2 MONEYFIELD AVE
3 MONEYFIELD LA
4 CONISTON AVE
5 MANOR PARK AVE
6 STAPLETON RD

B5
1 BLENDWORTH RD
2 AVOCET HO
3 CURLEW PATH
4 CHEVENING CT
5 OXTED CT
6 TERN WLK

A | B | C | D | E | F

PORTSMOUTH

Langstone Harbour

Great Salterns Lake

Portsea Island

Great Salterns Quay

Westover Prim Sch

Baffins

Portsmouth Coll

Liby

1 DUDLEY RD
2 WALFORD BLDGS

Baffins Pond

PO3

HAYLING AVE

JENKINS GR

CEDAR GR

Central Point
East Shore Sch

1 SCHOONER WAY
2 SOVEREIGN CL
3 ATALANTA CL
4 WAYFARER CL
5 MAYFLOWER DR
6 LONGFIELD CL

St Mary's
East Wing

Langstone Rd

Moorings Way
Inf Sch

Miltoncross Sch

Cemy

Cluster Ind Est

St Georges Ind Est

Ind Est

THE HAVEN

SOVEREIGN DR

Univ of Portsmouth (Langstone Campus)

SANDERLING RD

Fratton Ind Est
MILTON LA
Football Gd

St James

H

PO4

Waterside Sch (Unit)

Milton

BROOM SQ

Landing Stage

Ferry (F)

Landing Stage

Liby

1 RHYS CT
2 ANVIL CT

LOCKSWAY RD

1 COACH-HOUSE MEWS
2 TOWPATH MEAD
3 MAURICE RD
4 FAIR OAK RD
5 OAKDEAN CT
6 CHERITON RD

IRB Sta

The Ferry Boat Inn (PH)

CH

PO11

GOLDSMITH AVE

Schs

Bransbury Park

EASTLAKE HTS 1
HORSE SANDS CL 2
LANGSTONE MARINA HTS 3
SPITHEAD 4
SOLENT HTS 5
VANGUARD CT 6

Marina

Allot Gdns

Friendly Societies' Homes

Fort Cumberland

HIGHLAND RD B2154

Eastney

Royal Marines Mus

SEA BREEZE GDNS

FORT CUMBERLAND RD

CENTURION GATE

MELVILLE RD

SOUTHSEA CVN PK

Solent Way

ESPLANADE

EASTERN PAR

66 | A | B | 67 | C | D | 68 | E | F | 98

372

A2
1 NETTLESTONE RD
2 CULVER RD
3 EASTERN TERR
4 HIGHLAND ST
5 PRIORY RD
6 EASTNEY ST

A3
1 HATFIELD RD
2 COVINDALE HO
3 WYN SUTCLIFFE CT
4 CARPENTER CL

B2
1 CLOCKTOWER DR
2 TEAPOT ROW
3 CHURCHILL SQ
4 FLINDERS CT
5 SAUNDERS MEWS
6 MOUNTBATTEN SQ
7 DRYSDALE MEWS
8 PITCAIRN MEWS
9 BAMFORD HO

10 DOWELL HO
11 FINCH HO
12 HALLIDAY HO
13 HARVEY HO
14 PRETTYJOHN HO
15 WILKINSON HO

B3
1 GRAND DIVISION ROW

B4
1 MILTON PARK AVE
2 ARTILLERY TERR
3 OLD CANAL
4 MILFORD CT
5 WILLIAM CT

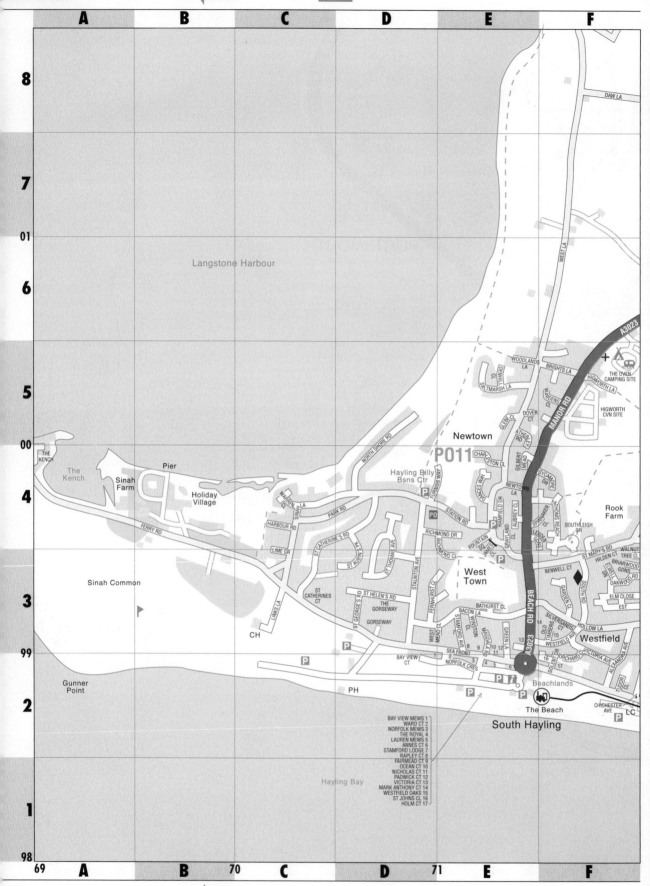

A B C D E F

8

7

01

Langstone Harbour

6

5

00

The Kench

The Kench

Pier

Sinah Farm

Holiday Village

4

Ferry Rd

Sinah Common

Sinah La

Warren Cl

Harbour Rd

Park Rd

Lime Gr

St Catherine's Rd

St Aubin's Pk

St Thomas Ave

Staunton Ave

North Shore Rd

Furniss Way

Dukes Way

Station Rd

Richmond Dr

Richmond Cl

Fountain Sq

Grayland Cl

Hamfield Dr

Aubrey Cl

Newtown La

Mead Cl

St Mary's Rd

Hilden Ct

Walnut Tree Cl

Briarwood Gdns

Oakwood Rd

Elm Close Est

Saltmarsh La

Woodlands La

Brights La

Higworth La

The Oven Camping Site

A3023

Manor Rd

Gardens Cl

Dover Ct

Glebe Cl

Gilbert Mead

Sycamore Dr

Solent Rd

Thomas Reach

Southleigh Gr

Higworth Cvn Site

Rook Farm

Newtown

P011

Hayling Billy Bsns Ctr

West Town

Westfield

3

Links La

CH

St George's Rd

St Helen's Rd

St Catherines Ct

The Gorseway

Gorseway

Fernhurst Rd

West Mead Cl

Stamford Rd

Winston Ave

Bacon La

Magdala Rd

Green La

Bathurst Cl

14

Old Timbers

Silversands Gdns

Hollow La

South Cl

Garden Cl

Benwell Ct

Victoria Ave

Alexandra Ave

Orchard Cl

Westfield Ave

13

99

P

P

P

Bay View Ct

Sea Front

Norfolk Cres

1

2

3

4 5

6

10 12

11

7

9

16

17

Beachlands

Gunner Point

PH

P

The Beach

Tudor Cl

Chichester Ave

LC

2

South Hayling

Hayling Bay

BAY VIEW MEWS 1
WARD CT 2
NORFOLK MEWS 3
THE ROYAL 4
LAUREN MEWS 5
ANNES CT 6
STAMFORD LODGE 7
RAPLEY CT 8
FAIRMEAD CT 9
OCEAN CT 10
NICHOLAS CT 11
PADWICK CT 12
VICTORIA CT 13
MARK ANTHONY CT 14
WESTFIELD OAKS 15
ST JOHNS CL 16
HOLM CT 17

1

98

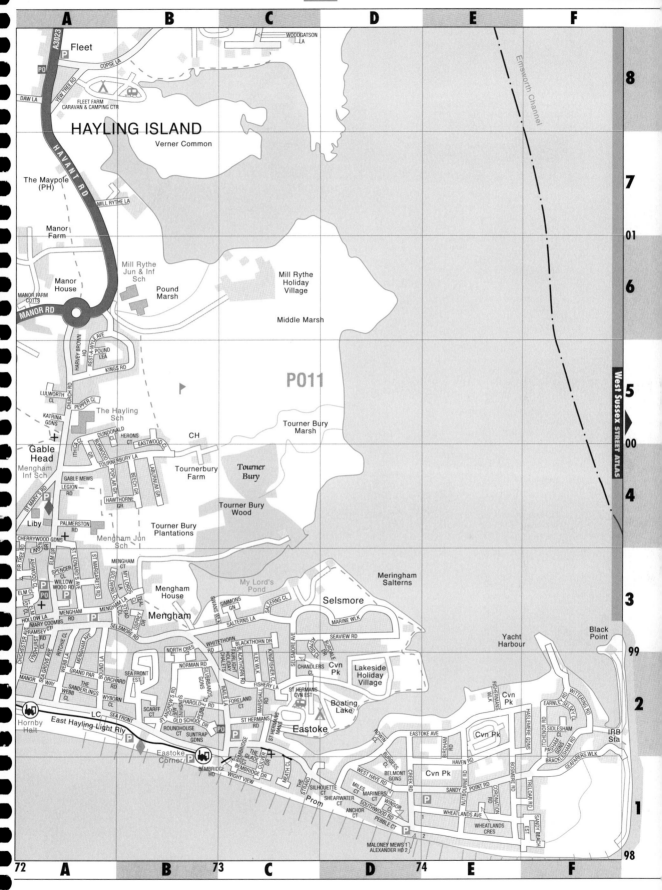

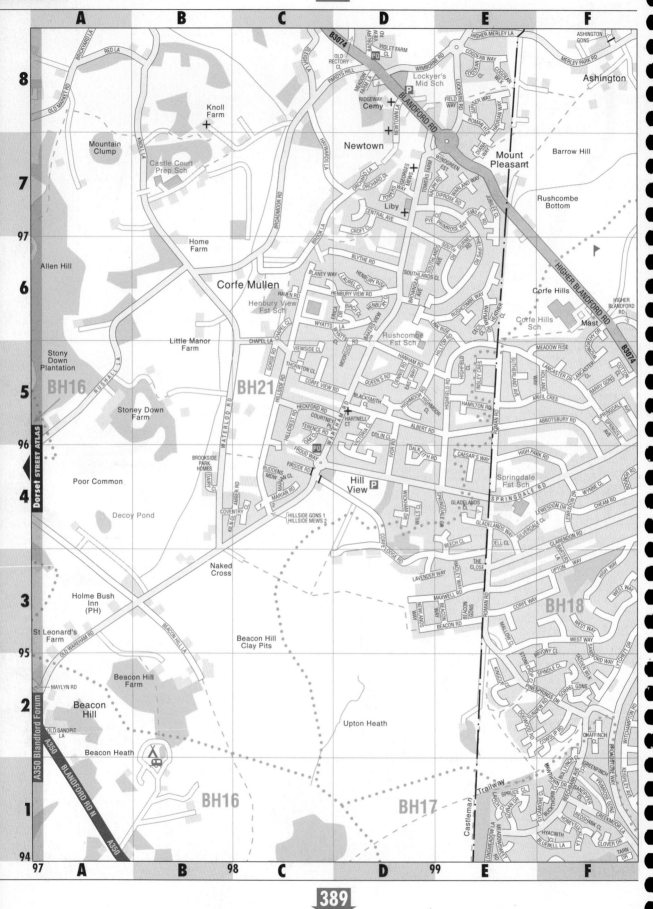

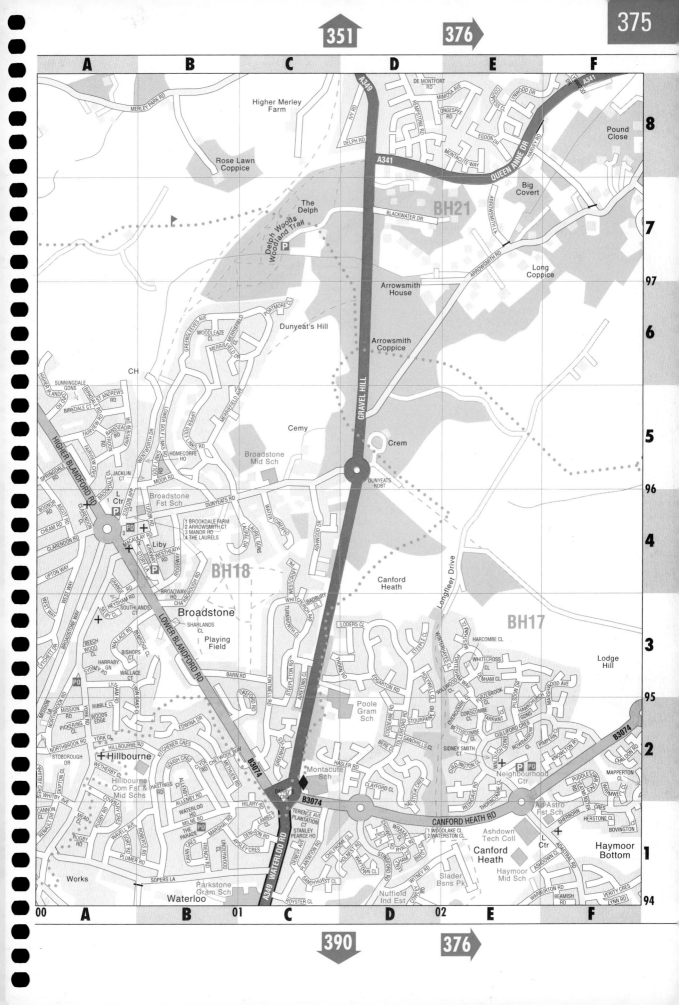

375 352 375 391

A341

MOORTOWN FARM

River Stour

Knighton House

Knighton Farm

Knighton

Bartlett's Cliff

BH22

Brake Hills

Longfleet Drive

MOORTOWN DR

BH21

MAGNA RD

Stour Valley Way

River Stour

A348

Stoat's Hill

Canford Park Events Arena & Sports Gd

KNIGHTON LA

Withy Bed

New Covert

THE ORCHARD

Bearwood

Bear Wood

BEAR CROSS RDBT
1 QUAYLE DR 2
BEAR CROSS GDNS 3

ROUNDHAYE

WHEELERS LA

Knighton Lodge

Bearwood Prim Sch

WOOD LEA WAY

CUDNELL AVE

WIMBORNE RD

A341

Merton Grange

BEAR CROSS AVE

MAGNA GDNS

RUNNYMEDE AVE

BARONS RD

Eastlands Farm

WHEELERS LA

VISCOUNT

Wheelers Lane

KNIGHTS RD

DUKES DR

Bear Cross

BH11

ROSS GDNS

VISCOUNT CT

KING JOHN AVE

WELDON AVE

VENNING AVE

FULWOOD AVE

RIVERFORT

1 HOLLY GREEN RISE
2 GAYDON RISE
3 KNIGHTON HEATH CL
4 CRANWELL CL
5 HIGH OAKS GDNS

MONKS WAY

ANTAGENET CRES

KING RICHARD DR

SHAPLAND AVE

DALEWOOD AVE

MARQUIS WAY

DE COURTENAI

SPICER LA

Oakmead Coll of Tech

CRUSADER RD

HULL RD

HIGH HOWE LA

RINGWOOD RD

6 HICKES CL
7 CHERRETT CL
8 BURGESS CL

Canford Heath Nature Reserve

WOODGREEN DR

MILL CRES

HIGH HOWE

MEADOW VIEW

West Howe

POOLE LA

CH

PADDINGTON GR

GOLDENLEAS CT 1
SAFFRON CT 2
BEXINGTON CL 3

Pool Lane RDBT

Works

Mast

AUTUMN

GOLDENLEAS DR

STILLMORE RD

DOMINION RD

Ringwood Road Ret Pk

West Howe Ind Est

FRANCIS AVE

Francis Avenue Ind Est

Turbary Ret Pk

Dominion Ctr

Roundways

POOLE

Mast

Drewitt Ind Est

Knighton Heath Ind Est

Turbary Common

BH17

CANFORD HEATH RD

Mannings Heath RDBT

BELBEN RD

A3049

TA Ctr

B3074

B3074

FARWELL RD

BREMBLE CL

BOWDEN RD

RINGWOOD RD

WALLISDOWN RD

Turbary Hts

CANFORD WAY

1 CRANBOURNE CT
2 STOCKBRIDGE CL

The Fulcrum Ctr

HUDSON CL

A3049

LOCKYER RD

A348

Discovery Court Bsns Ctr

RALEIGH RD

Haymoor Bottom

DORSET WAY

Superstore

Alderney

Bloom Road Bsns Pk

BEDFORD RD S

DOLBERY RD

B3068

ALDERNEY RDBT

LOEWY CRES

BH12

BYNBOW CRES

MOSSLEY AVE

Tower Park

L Complex

LING RD

The Courtyard

BROOM RD

PO

B3068

Alderney

ST HELIER RD

GUERNSEY RD

CORBIERE AVE

Bourne Bottom

Specl Sch Manorside Comb Sch

PLEMONT CL

EVERING AVE

HILLSIDE RD

A3049

VERITY CRES

MANOR AVE

HERM RD

ALDERNEY AVE

EVERING GDNS

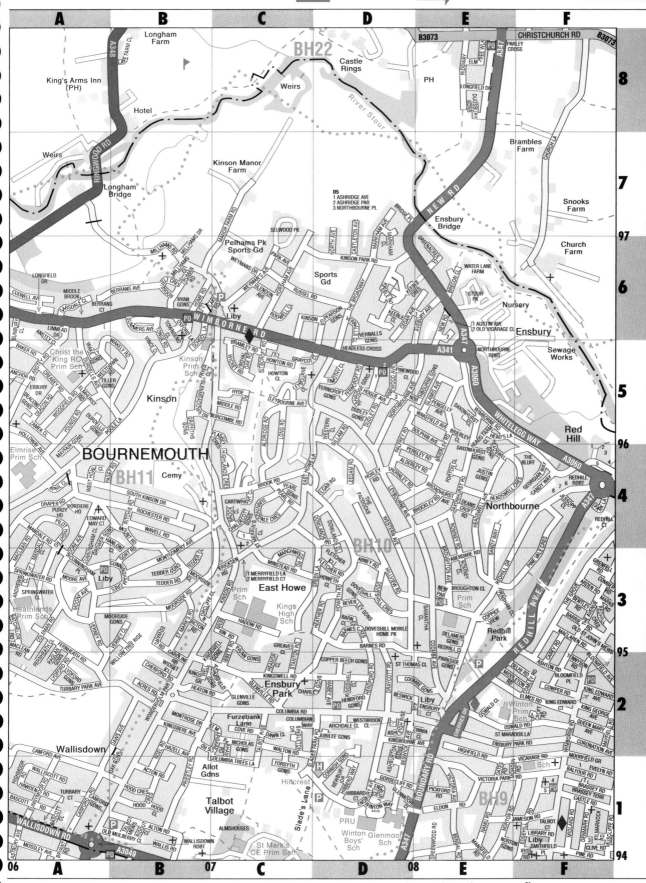

353
378
392
378

F1
1 EVELYN MEWS
2 ST JOHN'S GDNS
3 NORWAY CL
4 VICTORIA PARK PL
5 LAMPTON GDNS

F4
1 REDHILL PARK HOMES
2 WHEATPLOT PARK HOMES
3 KINGFISHER PARK HOMES
4 RIVERSIDE
5 WIMBORNE RD
6 MAGNOLIA HO
7 WISTERIA HO
8 LABURNUM HO

D5
1 ASHRIDGE AVE
2 ASHRIDGE PAR
3 NORTHBOURNE PL

BOURNEMOUTH

BH22 · BH23 · BH10 · BH9 · BH8

East Parley · Portfield Sch · Aviation Park W · Enterprise Way · Chapel Gate · Chapel La

Bournemouth International Airport

College of Air Traffic Control · Parley La · B3073

New Cottages · Parley Court · Parley Green La · Parley Green

Alice in Wonderland Family Fun Park · Merritown · Dales La · West Hurn

River Stour · Stour Valley Way · Hurn Court La · Hurn Court Farm · West Lodge

Works · Berry Hill · Muccleshell Farm · Hicks Farm · Wood Row · Weir · Leaden Stour · Pig Shoot La

Muscliffe La · Nursery · Musgliff · Muscliff Prim Sch · Cemy · River Farm · Throop · Throop Mill · Blue Roof Farm

Westover Retail Pk · A3060 · The Grove

Castle La W · B3061 · B3062 · Ashstead Gdns · Luckham Gdns · Charminster Rd

Moordown · Charminster · Bournemouth Sch for Girls · Bournemouth Sch · Sports Ctr

Castlepoint · Liby · Yeomans Ind Pk · Eventide Homes

Queen's Park Jun & Inf Schs · The Bishop of Winchester Comp Sch · Strouden · Haddon Hill

B3063 · Cemy · Wessex Way · A3060

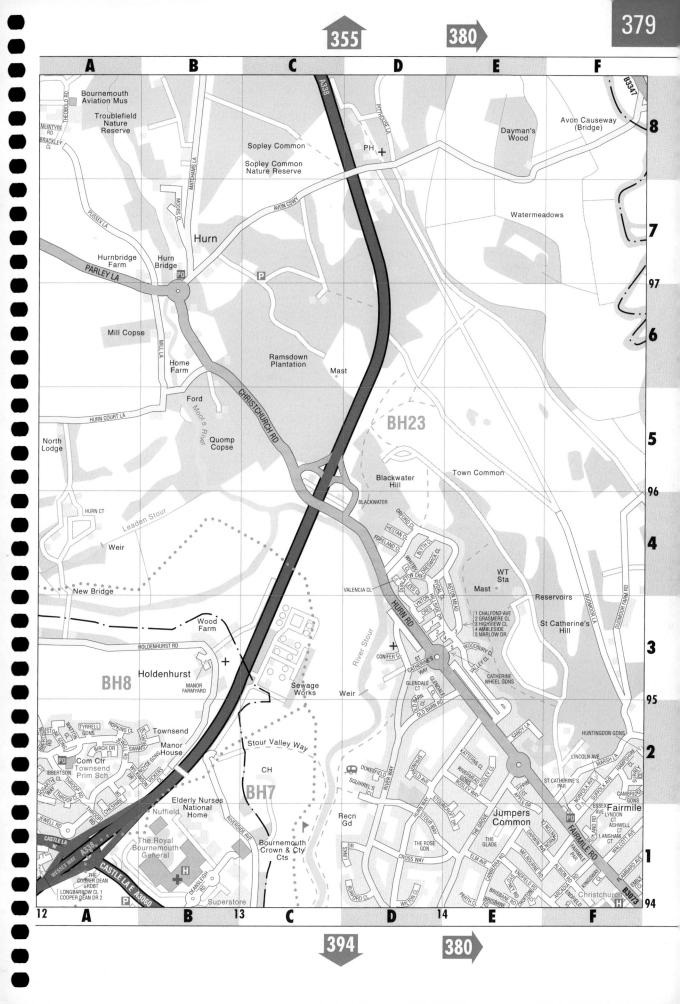

379
356

A B C D E F

8

7

97

6

5

96

4

3

95

2

1

94

15 A B 16 C D 17 E F

379
395

B3347
Court Farm
Cemy
Mill Race
RINGWOOD RD
MEADOW
PRIEST LA
Priest House
PO
Sopley
The Wool Pack (PH)
SOPLEY FARM BLDGS
Sopley Park
Moorlands Coll
SALISBURY RD
Winkton Acre
Winkton
PH
AVON COTTS
WINKTON GN
HARE WAY LA
New Barn
Barrett's Copse
WILTSHIRE GDNS
WILTSHIRE RD
Higher Clockhouse Farm
North Bockhampton
Clockhouse Copse
DERRITT LA
Lower Clockhouse Farm
BURLEY RD
TWIN OAK PK
Holfleet
Bockhampton Farm
BOCKHAMPTON RD
Middle Bockhampton
The Lamb Inn (PH)
Avon Valley Path
South Bockhampton
Hawthorn Farm
HAWTHORN RD
LYNDHURST RD
Hawthorn Farm
Waterditch Farm
WATERDITCH RD
Dudmoor Farm
Ogber
River Avon
Cowards Marsh
Winkton Common
WINKTON HO
JOPPS CNR
Old Mill Stream
BH23
BURTONCROFT
MORLEY CL
CHESTNUT WAY
KIRKHAM AVE
HARRISON CL
BIRCH AVE
AVON VIEW PAR
CAMPBELL RD
PAR CL
TARWELL CL
KATHERINE CHANCE CL
Burton CE Prim Sch
Burton Hall
FRIDAY RD
WINKTON CL
BURTON HALL PL
HENRY AVE
KINGSWELL
THE LINDENS
VICARAGE WAY
SALISBURY RD
PRESTON LA
HILL LA
REDCLIFFE RD
COWLEYS RD
PITTMORE RD
WOODSTOCK RD
VINNEYS CL
MEADER CL
Burton Green Farm
SUMMERFIELD CL 1
BARLANDS CL 2
BURNHAM RD
FERN CL
CRABTREE CL
FOOTNERS LA
WHITEHAYES RD
WHITEHAYES CL
THE GREEN
PO
Burton
BODOWEN CL
BODOWEN RD
STONY LA
WHITEHAYES RD
MARTINS HILL LA
SHORTS CL
MARTINS HILL CL
REEBYS CL
HOLLY GDNS
SUMMERS LA
Burton HO
Works
HUNTINGDON GDNS
SUFFOLK AVE
MARSH LA
WALCOTT AVE
FLAMBARD AVE
WILDELL CL
HAWORTH CL
EMILY CL
BRONTE AVE
BRAMWELL CL
VILLETTE CL
MINE CL
CALKIN CL
RIMBURY WAY
QUEENSMEAD
MED CL
BORDAN AVE
AV CL
BURTON CL
SANDY PLOT
Burton Farm
PH
AMBURY LA
B3347

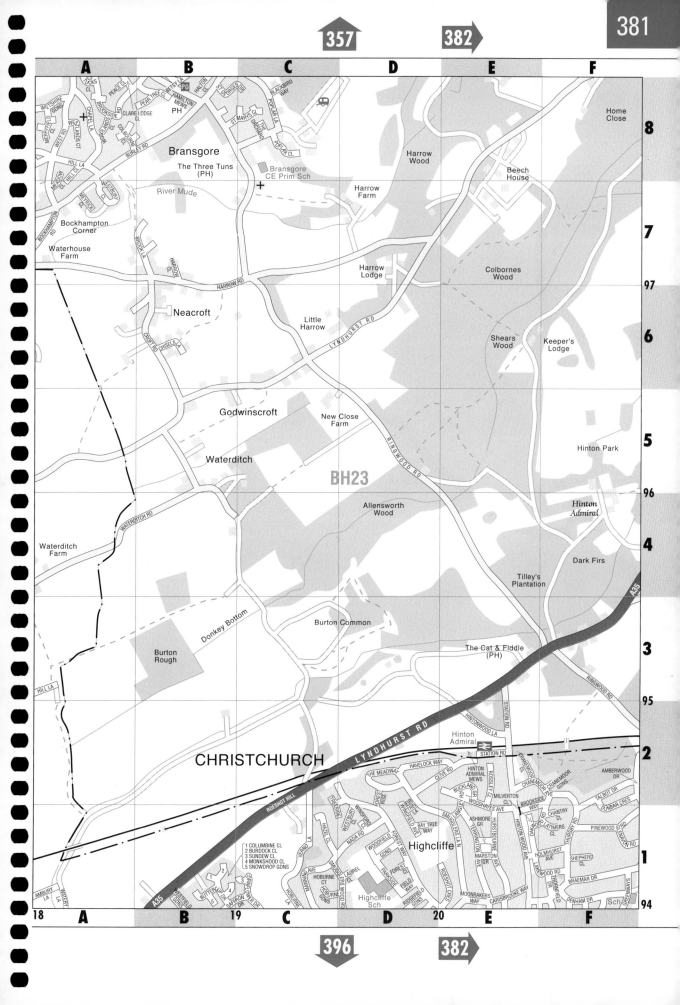

A B C D E F

Home
Close

8

Bransgore

Harrow
Wood

Beech
House

The Three Tuns
(PH)

Bransgore
CE Prim Sch

Harrow
Farm

River Mude

Bockhampton
Corner

7

Waterhouse
Farm

Harrow
Lodge

Colbornes
Wood

97

HARROW RD

Neacroft

Little
Harrow

LYNDHURST RD

Shears
Wood

Keeper's
Lodge

6

Godwinscroft

New Close
Farm

5

Waterditch

RINGWOOD RD

Hinton Park

BH23

96

Allensworth
Wood

Hinton
Admiral

Waterditch
Farm

WATERDITCH RD

4

Dark Firs

Tilley's
Plantation

A35

Donkey Bottom

Burton Common

The Cat & Fiddle
(PH)

3

Burton
Rough

RINGWOOD RD

HILL LA

95

STATION RD

HINTONWOOD LA

Hinton
Admiral

LYNDHURST RD

CRANEMOOR AVE

2

CHRISTCHURCH

STATION RD

Amberwood
Dr

ROESHOT HILL

Havelock Way

Hinton
Admiral
Mews

The Meadway

Clive Rd

Highcliffe

1 COLUMBINE CL
2 BURDOCK CL
3 SUNDEW CL
4 MONKSHOOD CL
5 SNOWDROP GDNS

A35

Highcliffe
Sch

Sch

1

94

18 A B 19 C D 20 E F

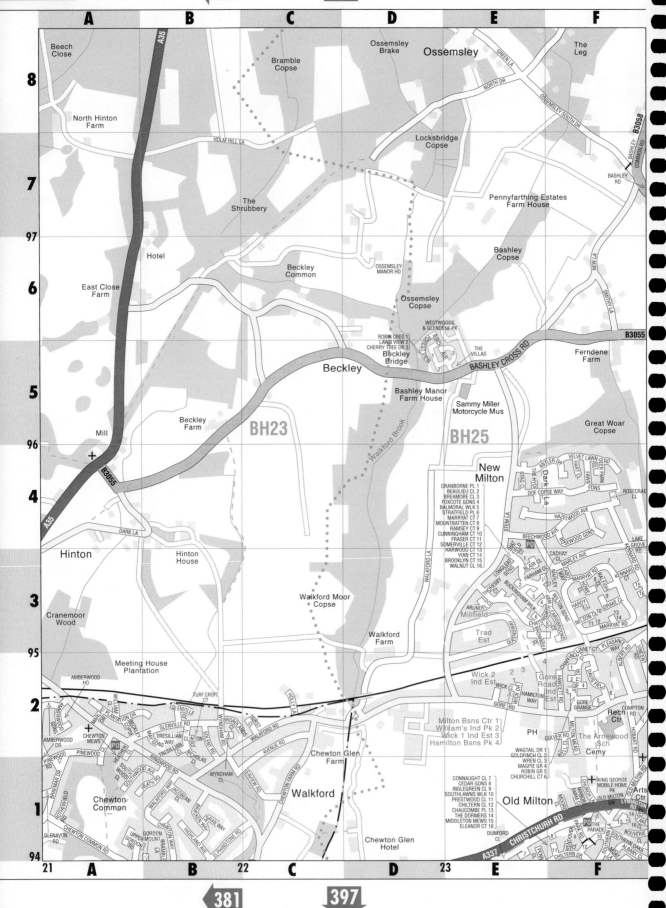

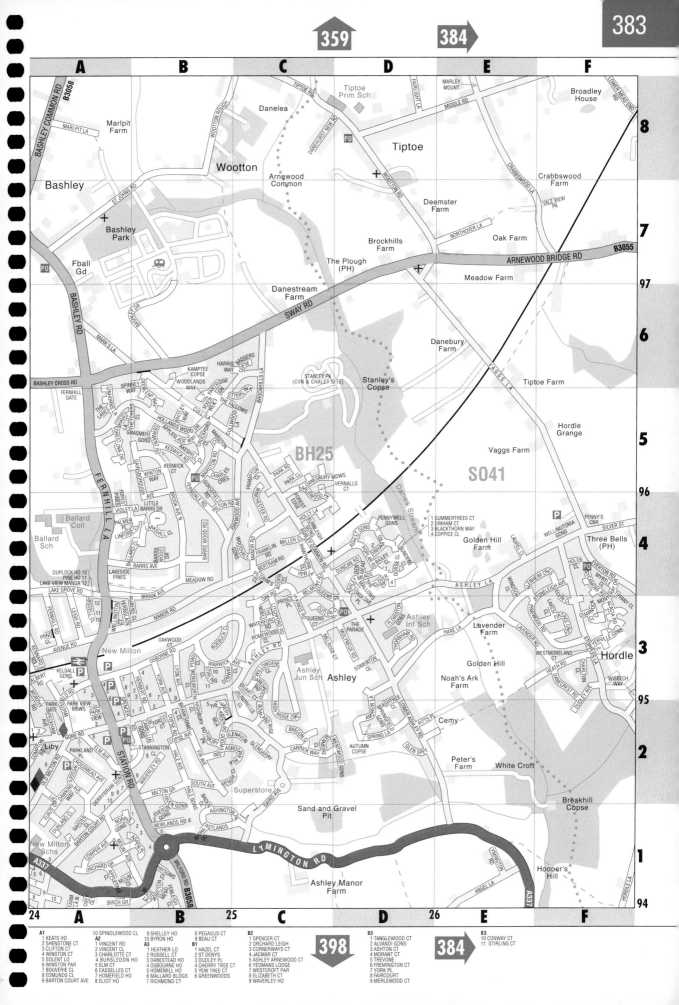

359
384

A1
1 KEATS HO
2 SHENSTONE CT
3 CLIFTON CT
4 WINSTON CT
5 SOLENT LO
6 WINSTON PAR
7 BOUVERIE CL
8 EDMUNDS CL
9 BARTON COURT AVE
10 SPINDLEWOOD CL

A2
1 VINCENT RD
2 VINCENT CL
3 CHARLOTTE CT
4 BURSLEDON HO
5 ELM CT
6 CASSELLES CT
7 HOMEFIELD HO
8 ELIOT HO
9 SHELLEY HO
10 BYRON HO

A3
1 HEATHER LO
2 RUSSELL CT
3 DANESTEAD HO
4 OSBOURNE HO
5 HOMEMILL HO
6 MALLARD BLDGS
7 RICHMOND CT

B1
1 HAZEL CT
2 ST DENYS
3 DUDLEY PL
4 CHERRY TREE CT
5 YEW TREE CT
6 GREENWOODS
7 RICHMOND CT
8 PEGASUS CT
9 BEAU CT

B2
1 SPENCER CT
2 ORCHARD LEIGH
3 CORNERWAYS CT
4 JACMAR CT
5 ASHLEY ARNEWOOD CT
6 YEOMANS LODGE
7 WESTCROFT PAR
8 ELIZABETH CT
9 WAVERLEY HO

B3
1 TANGLEWOOD CT
2 ALVANDI GDNS
3 ASHTON CT
4 MORANT CT
5 TREVONE
6 FREMINGTON CT
7 YORK PL
8 FAIRCOURT
9 MERLEWOOD CT
10 CONWAY CT
11 STIRLING CT

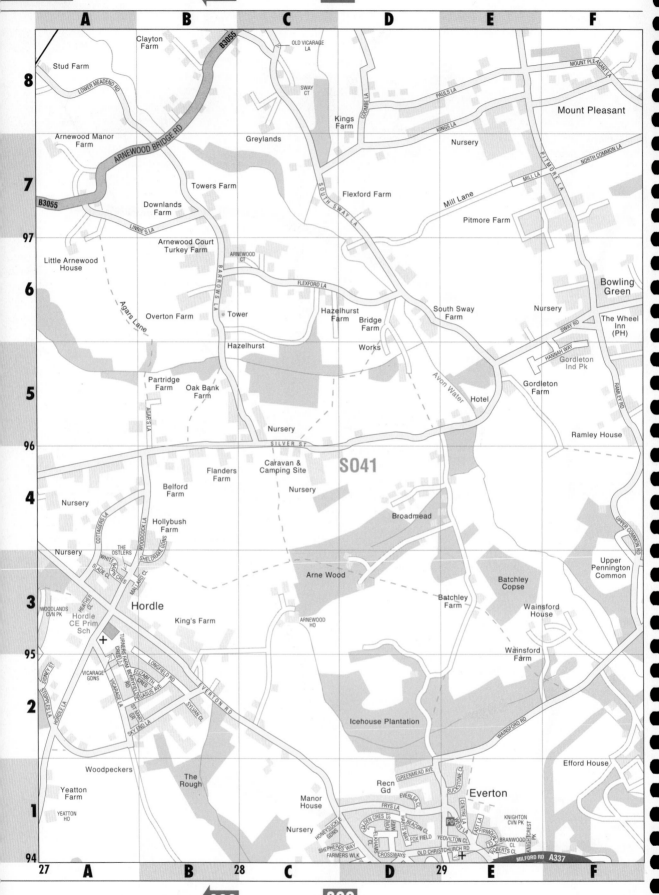

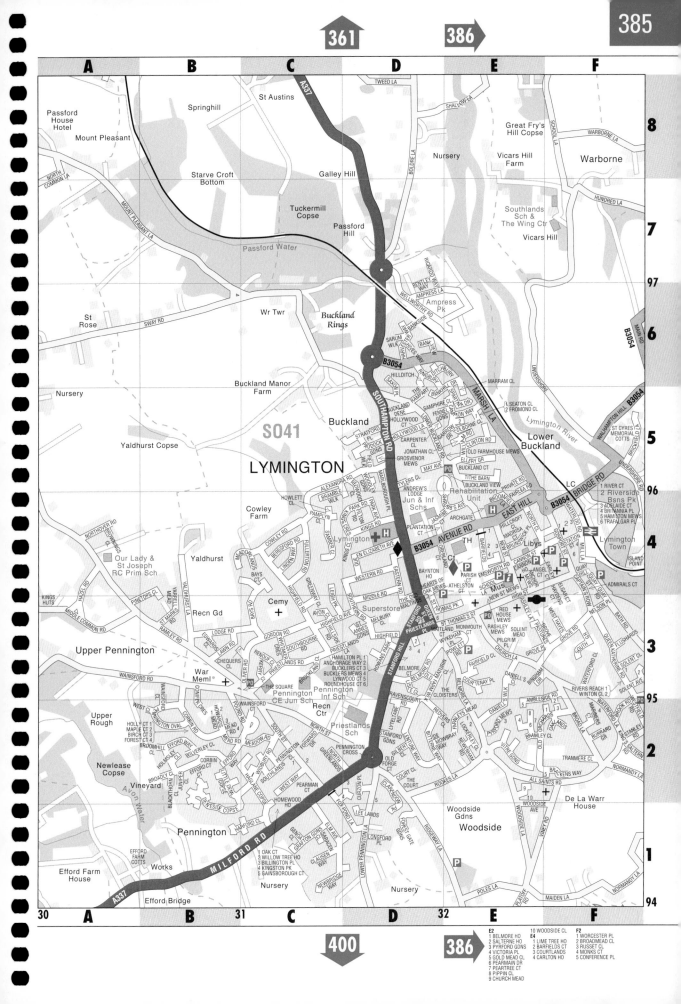

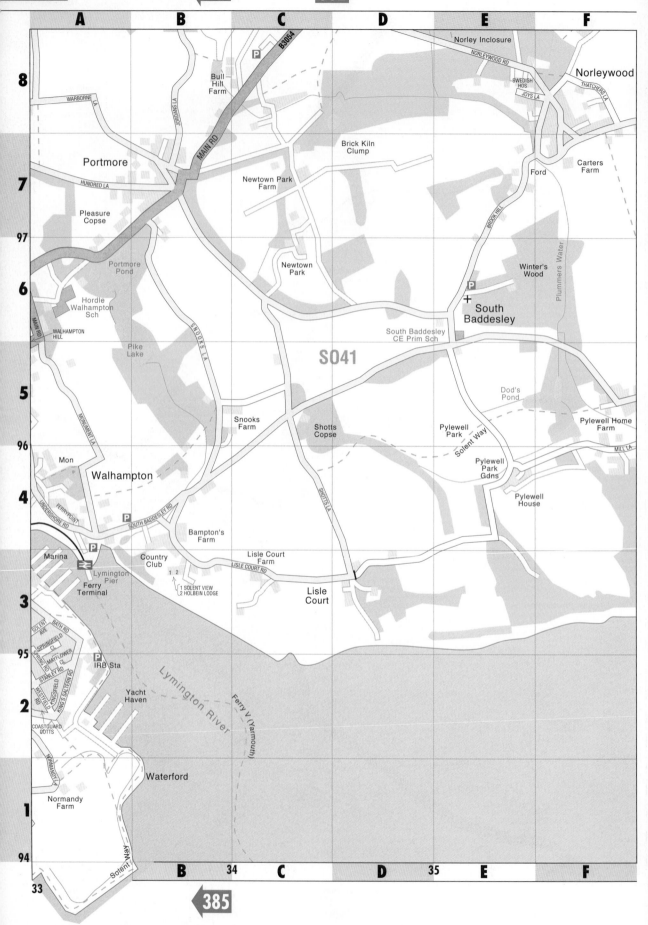

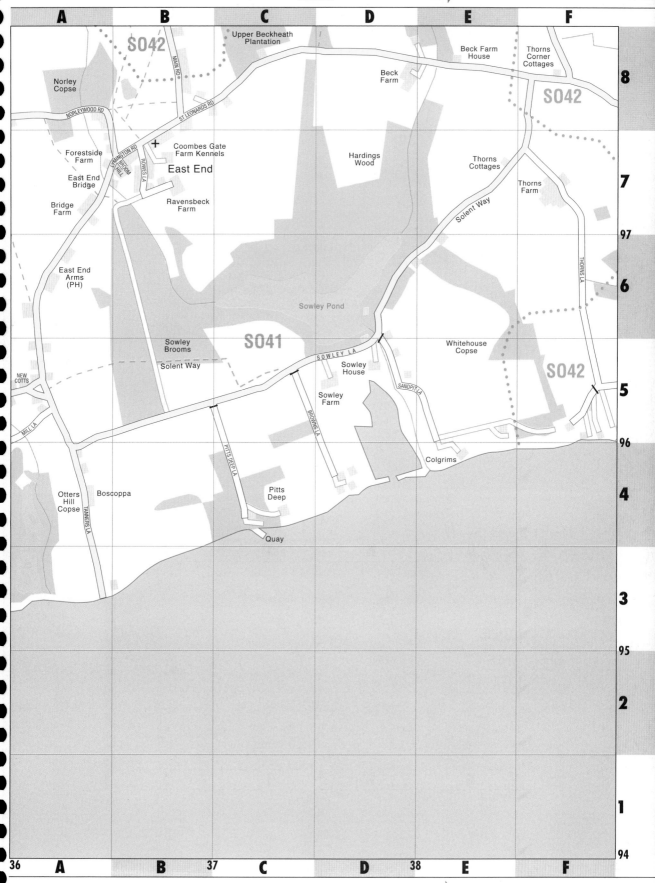

387
364
365
388
387

A B C D E F

8

7

97

6

5

96

4

3

95

2

1

94

39 A B 40 C D 41 E F

Bergerie
Farm

Solent Way

The Log
House

Gins
House

Black Water

Rye
Errish

Park

Black Water
House

WARREN LA

Thorns
Copse

PARK LA

Rye Errish
Copse

Warren
Farm

SO41

SO42

Park
Farm

Great
Marsh

Gravelly
Marsh

Thorns
Marsh

Thorns
Beach

Warren
House

Park Shore

THORNS LA

Little
Marsh

365

G H I J

SO42

Beaulieu River

Bird
Sanctuary

Gull
Island

Needs Ore
Cottages

Needs Ore
Point

Bird
Sanctuary

WARREN LA

8

7

97

42 G H 43 I J

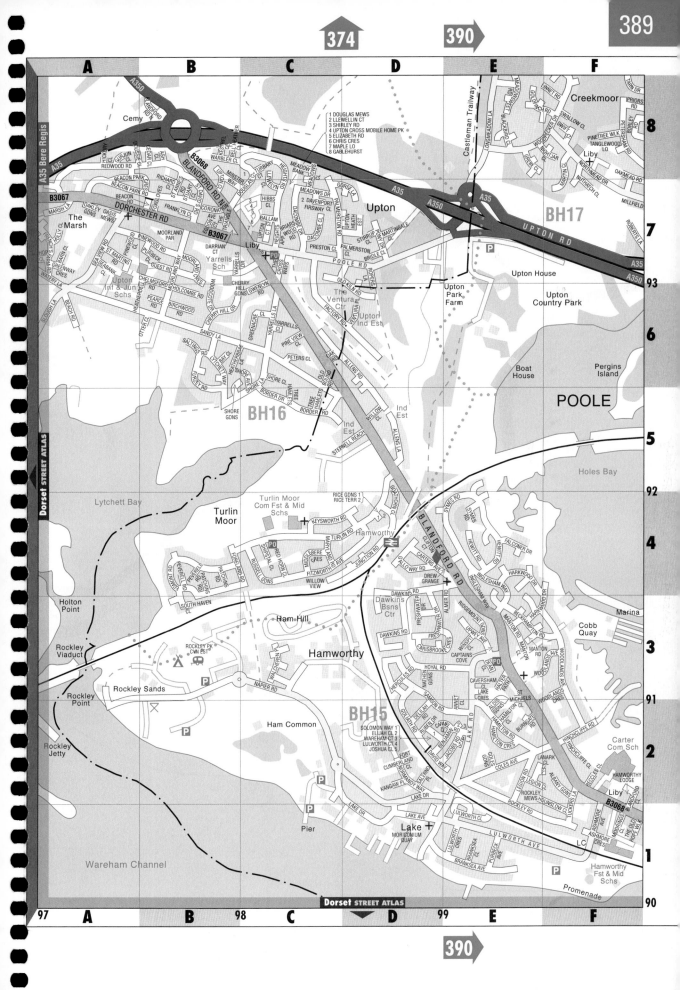

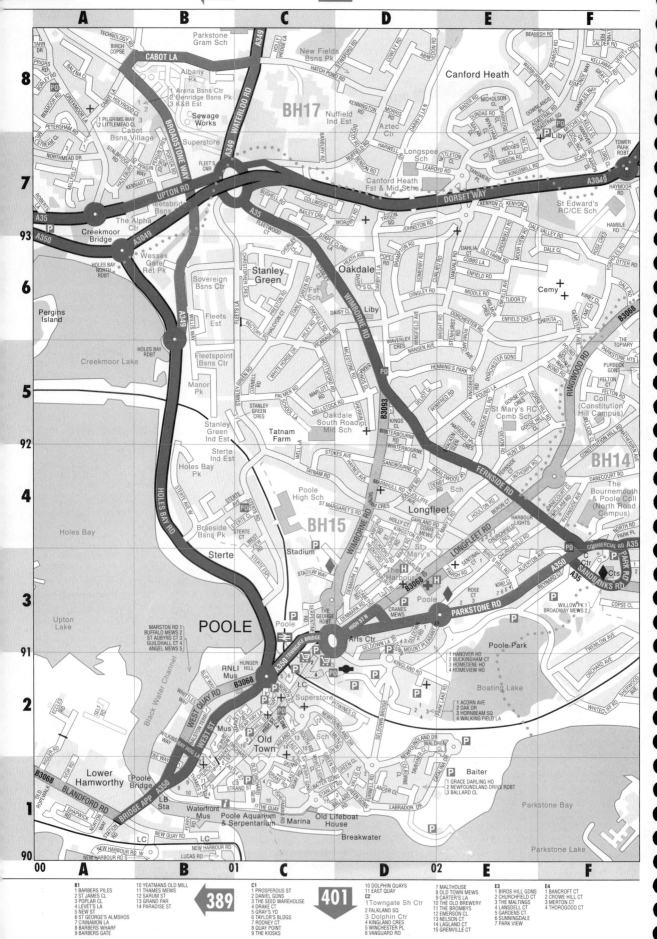

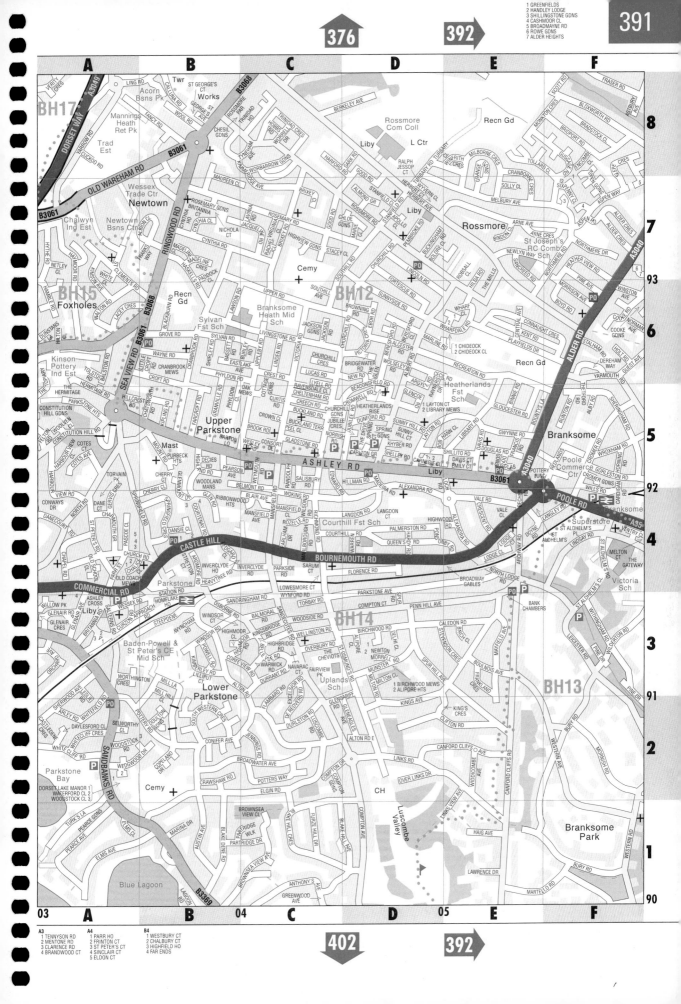

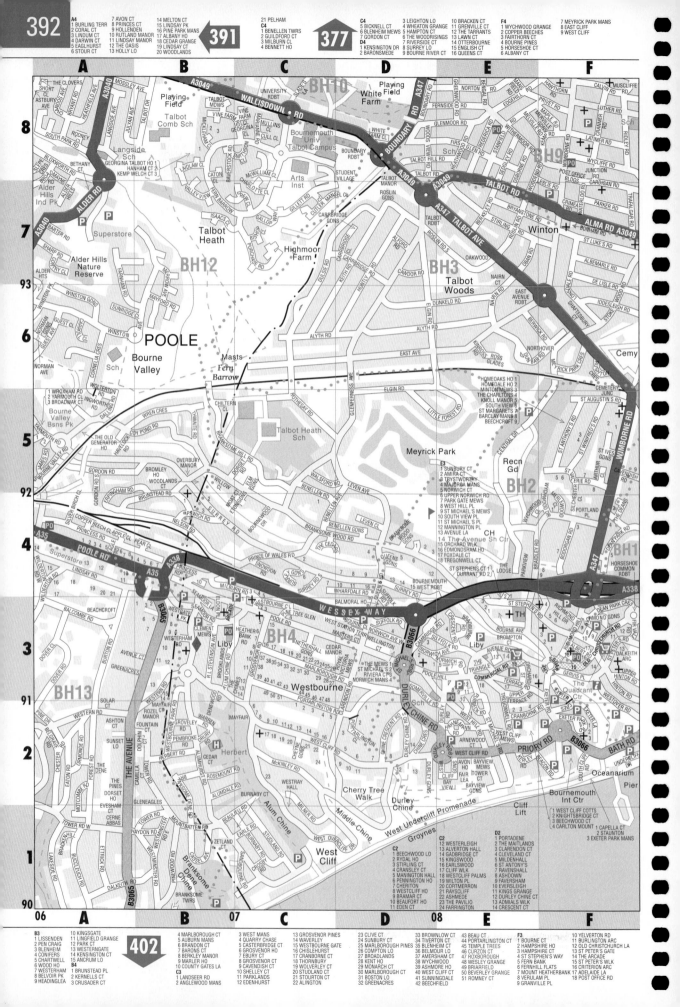

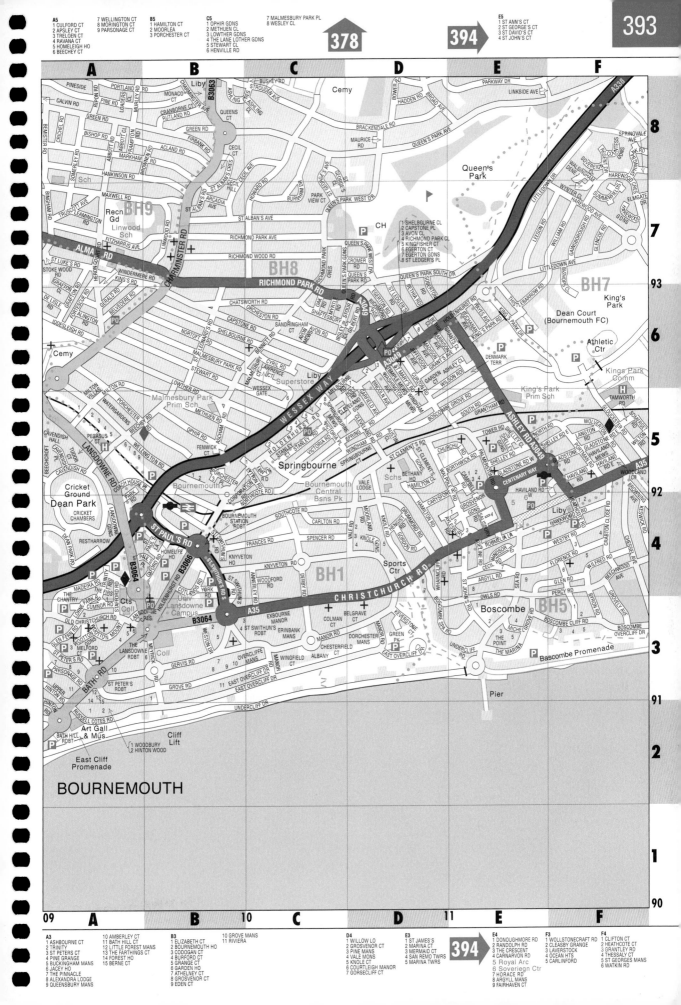

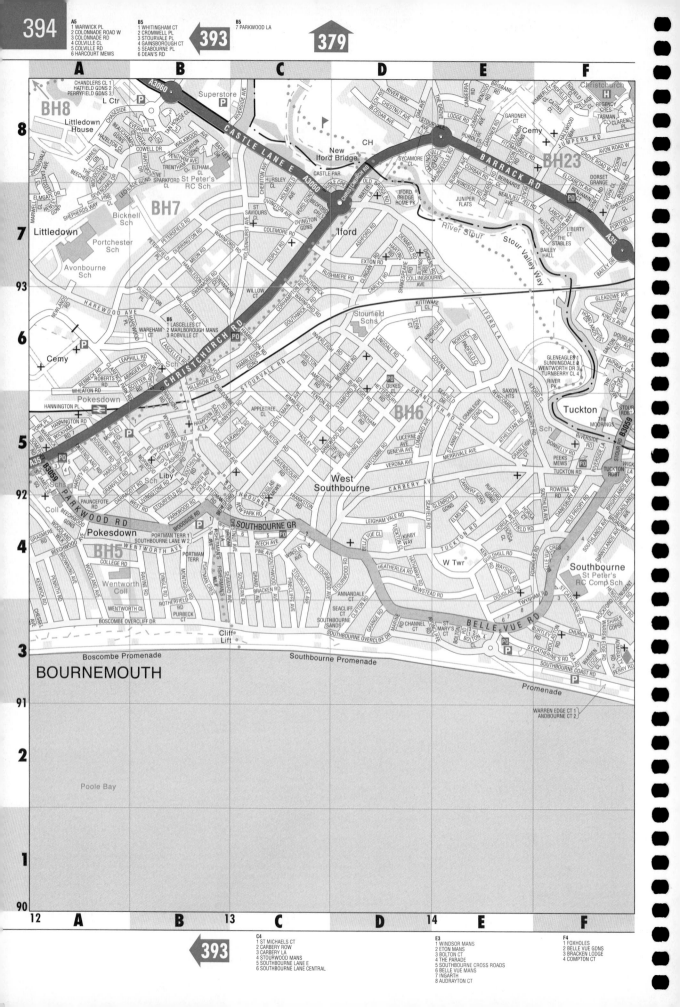

A5
1 WARWICK PL
2 COLONNADE ROAD W
3 COLONNADE RD
4 COLVILLE CL
5 COLVILLE RD
6 HARCOURT MEWS

B5
1 WHITINGHAM CT
2 CROMWELL PL
3 STOURVALE PL
4 GAINSBOROUGH CT
5 SEABOURNE PL
6 DEAN'S RD

B5
7 PARKWOOD LA

393

379

BH8

Littledown House

CHANDLERS CL 1
HATFIELD GDNS 2
PERRYFIELD GDNS 3

L Ctr

Superstore

A3060

CASTLE LANE E

New Iford Bridge

CH

A3060

CASTLE LANE E

BARRACK RD

BH23

Christchurch

H
Regency Cres

Cemy

Littledown

BH7

St Peter's RC Sch

Bicknell Sch

Portchester Sch

Avonbourne Sch

Iford

CHRISTCHURCH RD

Iford Bridge Home Pk

Juniper Flats

River Stour

Stour Valley Way

Bailey Hall

The Stables

A35

HAREWOOD AVE

Cemy

WAREHAM CT

B6
1 LASCELLES CT
2 MARLBOROUGH MANS
3 ROBVILLE CT

Stourfield Schs

Gleneagles 1
Sunningdale 2
Wentworth Dr 3
Turnberry Cl 4

River Pk

Pokesdown

Hannington Pl

BH6

Tuckton

The Moorings

B3059

Riverside Rd

Tuckton Rdbt

West Southbourne

Liby

Pokesdown

BH5

Wentworth Coll

Wentworth Cl

Boscombe Overcliff Dr

SOUTHBOURNE GR

PORTMAN TERR 1
SOUTHBOURNE LANE W 2

Portman Terr

W Twr

Southbourne

St Peter's RC Comp Sch

Cliff Lift

Boscombe Promenade

Southbourne Promenade

BELLE VUE RD

BOURNEMOUTH

Promenade

WARREN EDGE CT 1
ANDBOURNE CT 2

Poole Bay

C4
1 ST MICHAELS CT
2 CARBERY ROW
3 CARBERY LA
4 STOURWOOD MANS
5 SOUTHBOURNE LANE E
6 SOUTHBOURNE LANE CENTRAL

E3
1 WINDSOR MANS
2 ETON MANS
3 BOLTON CT
4 THE PARADE
5 SOUTHBOURNE CROSS ROADS
6 BELLE VUE MANS
7 INGARTH
8 AUDRAYTON CT

F4
1 FOXHOLES
2 BELLE VUE GDNS
3 BRACKEN LODGE
4 COMPTON CT

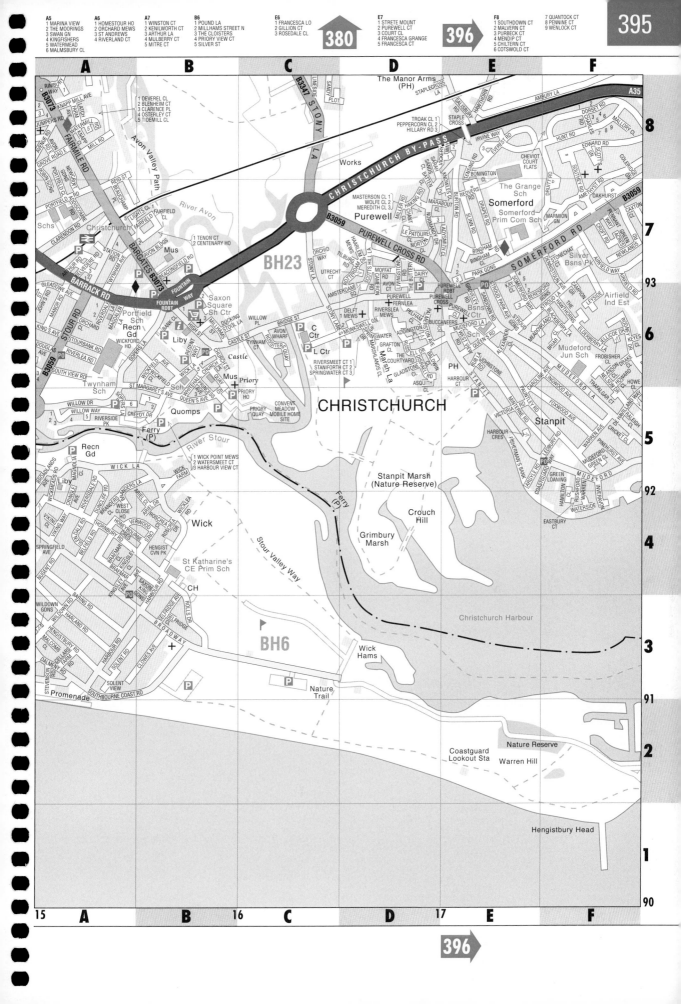

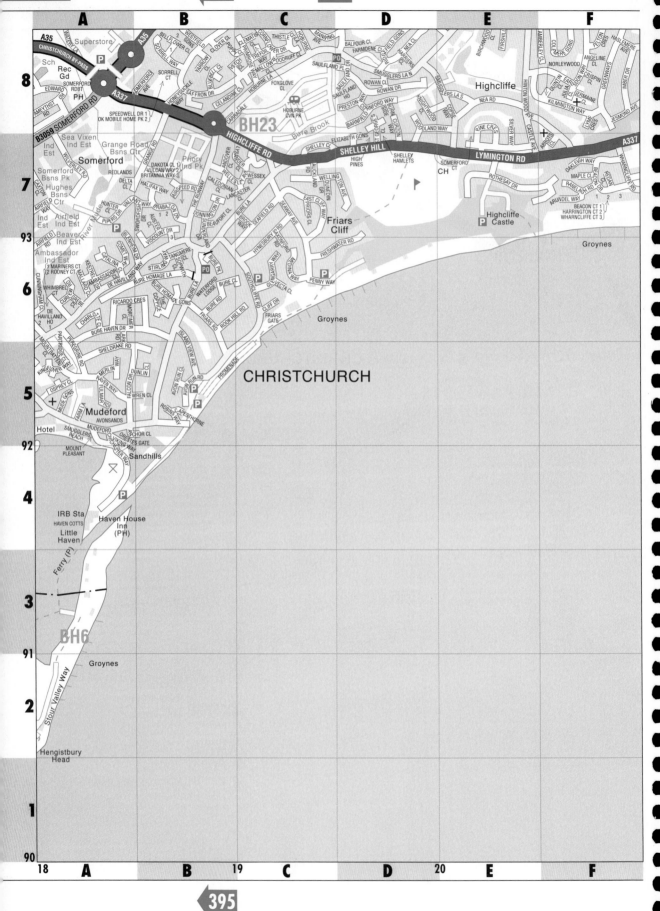

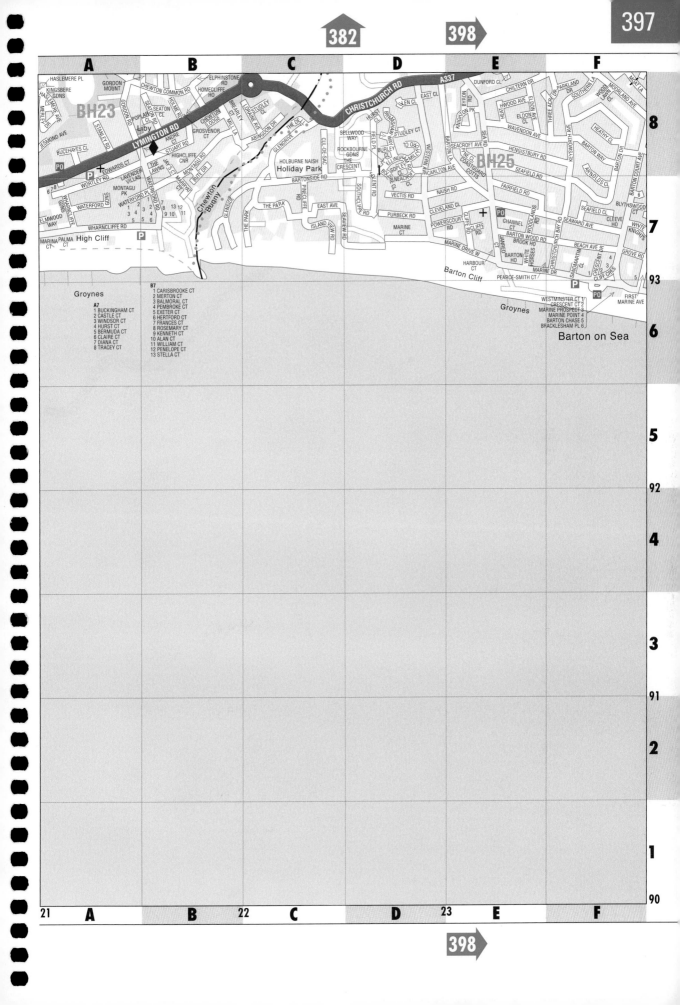

397
383

A B C D E F

8
7
93
6
5
92
4
3
91
2
1
90

24 A B 25 C D 26 E F

ALBANY MOAT CL
BARTON CT
COURT DR
FRIARS WLK
FARM LA N
CHESTNUT AVE
UPLANDS AVE
WESTBURY CL
LANGTON CL
BASHMORE AVE
HEDGERLEYS
GREEN LA
GREENFIELD
NEWTON RD
FENLEIGH CL
B3058
HIGHLANDS RD
SWANFIELD RD
GREENACRE
THE CLOSE
SPINACRE
ATKINSON CL
REDDON CL
ROYSTON PL
ARLINGTON CT
SEAWAY
BARTON CROFT
DANES CL
FARM LA S
DILLY LA
MITCHELL CL
GROVE RD
MEADOW WAY
THE FA WAY
MAPLE
THE WILLOWS
SILVERDALE
THE MARTELLS
BARTON COMMON LA
BARTON COMMON RD
RECTON LA
WILLOW WLK
BARTON GN
Durlston Court Sch

1 LYNRIC CL
2 WHITE KNIGHTS
3 HIGH MARRYATS
4 DOLPHIN PL
5 ALDBURY CT
6 GROVE GDNS
7 MARINERS REACH
8 SECOND MARINE AVE
9 GAINSBOROUGH HO

DOLPHIN MANS
MARINE DR E
GREENSIDE CT

SOLENT DR

Barton Common

Barton Cliff

Barton on Sea

BH25

MILFORD RD

CH

Becton Bunny

Christchurch Bay

Angel Cottage

ANGEL LA

HOME FARM

Ashley Clinton House

Danes Stream

Taddiford Farm

Hordle Manor Farm

A337 LYMINGTON RD

Ashley Bridge

CHRISTCHURCH RD A337

PH

Downton

SO41

Hordle Bridge

DANEHURST

SHOREFIELD RD

DOWNTON LA

HORDLE LA

CLIFF RD

B 3058

A B C D E F

8

Leagreen

Leagreen
Farm

CHRISTCHURCH RD

FARMERS WLK
EVERTON RD
BEECH
CEDAR DR
LIME GR

MILFORD RD A337

THE GRANGE

Everton
Grange

MILFORD RD A337

GRANGE CL
GRANGE LA

B3058

RODBOURNE CL 1
ASH GR 2
OAK GDNS 3
CHERRY TREE CL 4
CYPRESS GR 5
LABURNUM DR 6
MULBERRY GR 7
PLANTATION 8

Buona Vista
Farm

BRAXTON
CTYD

Downton Manor
Farm

Newlands
Manor

Newlands
Manor

7

DOWNTON
CVN PK

Barnes
Farm

Cox's
Bridge

Lymore

LYMINGTON RD

LYMORE VALLEY

LYMORE LA

93

SHOREFIELD
RD
SEABREEZE WAY
WARREN
PK
DANE RD
DANEHURST

Blackbush
Copse

SO41

Nursery

Hotel

Milford on Sea
CE
Prim Sch

SCHOOL LA

LYMEFIELDS

Lymore
Farm

AGARTON LA

6

BARNES LA

D5
1 ADDINGTON CT
2 BLANDFORD CT
3 DACRES WLK
4 DRYDEN PL
5 WINDMILL CL
6 GLEBEFIELDS

Knold

SHOREFIELD
COUNTRY PK

Danes Stream

BLACKBUSH RD

MANOR RD

MANOR
LA

KNOWLAND DR

The
Vicarage

1 MOLEFIELDS
2 MILFORD HO

5

AMBERWOOD

Studland
Common

SHOREFIELD
WAY
GEORGE RD
GREENWAYS

Shorefield

SHOREFIELD
CRES

SYCAMORE CT
WAYSIDE CT

KITWALLS
LA

Recn
Gd

BROADFIELDS
CL
DEANS CT

CANONS
WLK

KNOWLAND DR

SHELLEY WAY

LYNDALE

MILFORD CRES

CARRINGTON
CL

NORTHFIELD RD

92

THE BUCKLERS

WEST RD
NORTH HEAD

SHARVELLS RD

STUDLAND DR

VINEGAR
HILL
NEW VALLEY RD
MILL MDW

HOLLY
GDNS
WOOD LA

WOODLAND
WAY

CHAUCER LA
KEATS AVE
WOOLF RD
LOVE LA

THE
ORCHARD
GREENBANKS

SOUTH
CT

MILFORD
PO

PARK RD
MILFORD
PL

LAWN
RD
LAWN RD

CARRINGTON LA

CHAMPION
CL

EASTERN
WAY
AUBREY CL

SOLENT WAY

KEYHAVEN RD

4

1 LYDGATE
2 SEAWINDS

PLESS RD

WESTMINSTER
RD

MARYLAND
GDNS

WHITBY RD
CORNWALLIS
RD

VICTORIA RD

HAMILTON
CT
KENSINGTON PK
ROCKCLIFF

KIVERNELL RD

PARK LA

DANESTREAM
CL

LUCERNE RD

River GDNS

WESTOVER RD

HIGH ST

DANESTREAM
CT

War
Meml

Liby

Milford
Trad Est

LAUNDRY LA
SWALLOW DR
GREBE CL
PLOVER DR

KEYHAVEN RD

CARRINGTON
CVN PK

NEW LA

Hordle Cliff

CLIFF RD

P

B4
1 CAMDEN HURST
2 SOLENT PINES
3 MARYLAND CT
4 WHITBY CT
5 BEATRICE CT
6 ALLISON CT

WHITBY RD

DE LA WARR RD

1 2 3 4 5 6

OAKTREE
CT

3 CT
4 5 6
7 8 9 10

11

12 13 14

Rook Cliff

P

HOMEGRANGE
HO

SHINGLE BANK DR

NEEDLES
WAY
POINT

RAVENS WAY

THE BOLTONS

THE
SHORE

GILLINGHAM RD

OVERSTAND

ISLAND
VIEW
GDNS

ISLAND VIEW CL

MANDERLEY

HENLEY CL

CASTLE
CL

Sturt
Pond

P

P

P

91

Solent Way

C4
1 KIVERNELL PL
2 HOLLY GDNS
3 ROOKWOOD
4 HAVEN CT
5 HURST CT
6 SOLENT CT
7 OSBORNE CT
8 TOTLAND CT
9 SEA PINES
10 PINEHURST
11 NEEDLES CT
12 RICHMOND CT
13 ROOKCLIFF
14 PARK CT

Milford on Sea

HURDLES
MEAD

HURST RD

3

2

1

90

27 A 28 B C 28 D 29 E F

399
385

A   B   C   D   E   F

MILFORD RD
A337

8

Efford Experimental
Horticulture Station

Lower Pennington

Sadlers Farm

Great Newbridge
Copse

The Salterns

The Chequers Inn
(PH)

Lower Farm

7

Pennington
House

Iley La

Oxey Marsh

93

Avon Water

6

SO41

Saltworks

Nature
Reserve

Pennington
Marshes

Jetty

5

Solent Way

Vidle Van
Farm

92

Saltworks

LYMORE LA

Keyhaven Marshes

4

Keyhaven

AUBREY FARM
COTTS

KEYHAVEN RD

HAREWOOD GN

Lyndon

NEW RD

Aubrey
House

SHIPWRIGHTS
WLK

P

Jetty

PH

Keyhaven
House

SALTGRASS LA

3

Salt
Grass

91

Ferry (F)
(Summer Only)

2

The Mount

1

Solent Way

Hurst Beach

Hurst
Castle

90

30   A   31   B   C   32   D   E   F

399

A　B　C　D　E　F

Marina

BH15

NEW HARBOUR RD S

NEW HARBOUR RD

New Quay

8

Ferry (V) routes to
St. Malo
Guernsey
Jersey
Cherbourg

Main Channel

Ferry (P)
(April to September)

7

Poole Harbour

89

6

Cambridge Wood

Nature Reserve

Oxford Wood

5

Maryland

The Villa

West Lake

East Lake

Middle Street

Elizabeth Hill

Pottery Pier

Rough Brake

88

Brownsea Island
National Trust

BH13

St Michael's Mount

Fire Twr

Harley Wood

Church Hill

4

Lincoln Cliff

Mon

Farm Buildings

William Pit

Harry Point

3

Slipway

Landing Stage

Oil Well

BH15

Oil Well

Furzey Island

87

Slipway

Landing Stage

2

BH15

Green Island

Goathorn Pier

1

South Deep

Goathorn Point

BH19

Jerry's Point

BH20

Goathorn Plantation

Brand's Bay

BH19

86

00　A　B　01　C　D　02　E　F

Dorset STREET ATLAS

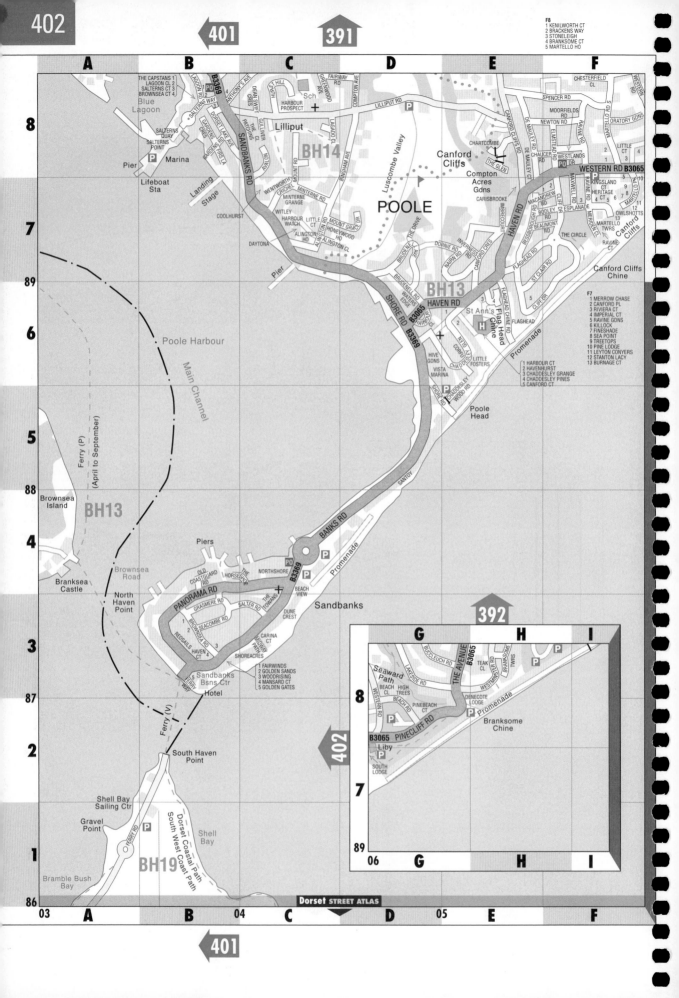

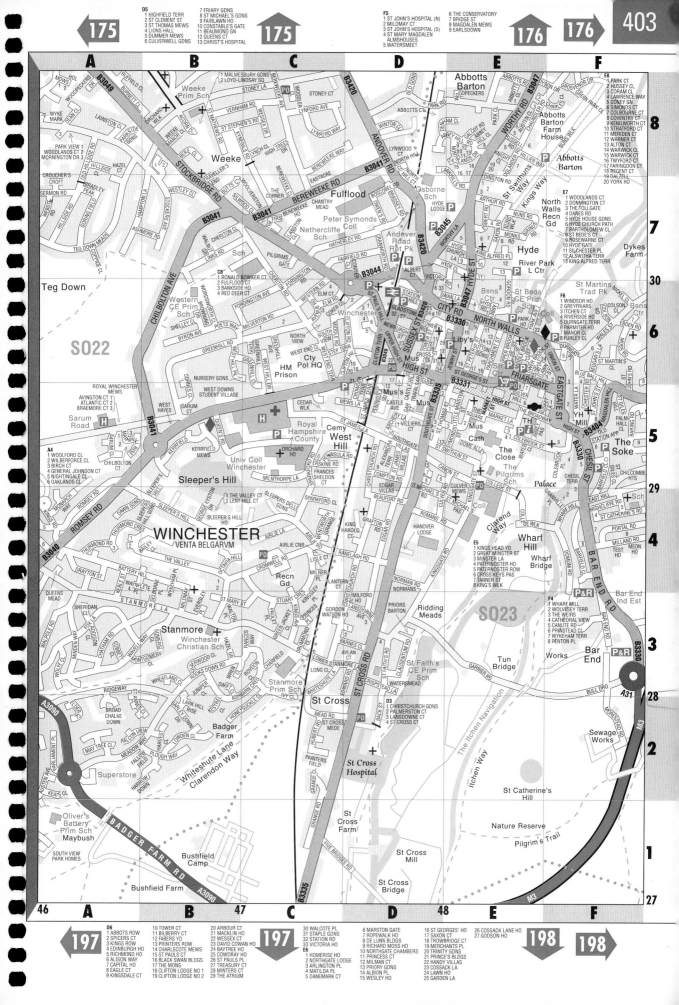

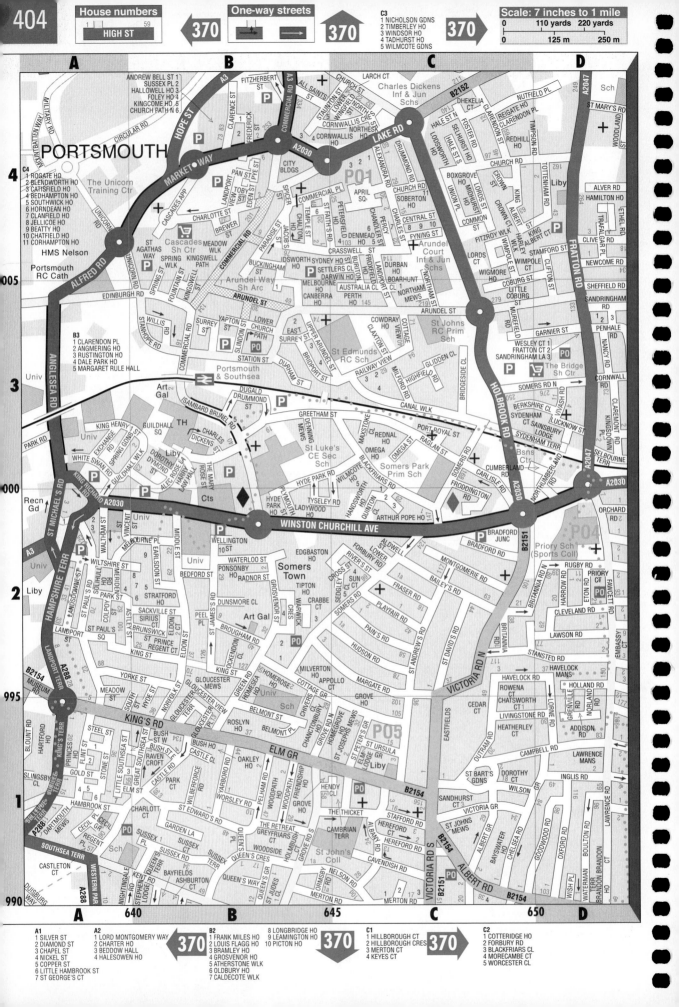

House numbers
1   59
HIGH ST

One-way streets
370

C3
1 Nicholson Gdns
2 Timberley Ho
3 Windsor Ho
4 Tadhurst Ho
5 Wilmcote Gdns
370

Scale: 7 inches to 1 mile
0   110 yards   220 yards
0   125 m   250 m

C4
1 Rogate Ho
2 Blendworth Ho
3 Catisfield Ho
4 Bedhampton Ho
5 Southwick Ho
6 Horndean Ho
7 Clanfield Ho
8 Jellicoe Ho
9 Beatty Ho
10 Chatfield Ho
11 Corhampton Ho

B3
1 Clarendon Pl
2 Angmering Ho
3 Rustington Ho
4 Dale Park Ho
5 Margaret Rule Hall

Index

Place name May be abbreviated on the map	→	**Church Rd** **6** Beckenham BR2..........**53** C6

Location number Present when a number indicates the place's position in a crowded area of mapping

Locality, town or village Shown when more than one place has the same name

Postcode district District for the indexed place

Page and grid square Page number and grid reference for the standard mapping

Public and commercial buildings are highlighted in magenta   **Places of interest** are highlighted in blue with a star★

Abbreviations used in the index

Acad	Academy	Comm	Common	Gd	Ground	L	Leisure	Prom	Promenade
App	Approach	Cott	Cottage	Gdn	Garden	La	Lane	Rd	Road
Arc	Arcade	Cres	Crescent	Gn	Green	Liby	Library	Recn	Recreation
Ave	Avenue	Cswy	Causeway	Gr	Grove	Mdw	Meadow	Ret	Retail
Bglw	Bungalow	Ct	Court	H	Hall	Meml	Memorial	Sh	Shopping
Bldg	Building	Ctr	Centre	Ho	House	Mkt	Market	Sq	Square
Bsns, Bus	Business	Ctry	Country	Hospl	Hospital	Mus	Museum	St	Street
Bvd	Boulevard	Cty	County	HQ	Headquarters	Orch	Orchard	Sta	Station
Cath	Cathedral	Dr	Drive	Hts	Heights	Pal	Palace	Terr	Terrace
Cir	Circus	Dro	Drove	Ind	Industrial	Par	Parade	TH	Town Hall
Cl	Close	Ed	Education	Inst	Institute	Pas	Passage	Univ	University
Cnr	Corner	Emb	Embankment	Int	International	Pk	Park	Wk, Wlk	Walk
Coll	College	Est	Estate	Intc	Interchange	Pl	Place	Wr	Water
Com	Community	Ex	Exhibition	Junc	Junction	Prec	Precinct	Yd	Yard

Index of localities, towns and villages

A

Abbotstone........156 F2
Abbotswood........216 A3
Abbots Worthy......176 D6
Abbotts Ann.......105 A3
Abbotts Barton...403 E8
Abshot............341 C8
Alderholt.........280 F5
Aldermaston........9 E7
Aldermaston Soke..10 D3
Aldermoor.........266 A3
Alderney..........376 C1
Aldershot..........76 B1
Aldsworth.........325 D6
Allbrook..........244 B7
Alton.............139 E3
Alverstoke........369 A4
Ameysford.........326 C1
Ampfield..........217 C3
Amport............104 B6
Anchorage Park....346 C3
Andover...........106 D7
Andwell............71 A6
Anmore............299 B4
Anna Valley.......105 C5
Ann's Hill........368 F5
Anstey............140 B5
Anthill Common....298 D6
Applemore.........313 A4
Appleshaw..........81 B6
Appleslade Bottom 306 A2
Arborfield Garrison 15 D7
Arford............165 D6
Ash................77 E3
Ashe...............88 F8
Ashfield..........241 B3
Ashford...........257 C1
Ashford Hill
 Hawkley........206 C2
 Thatcham..........8 C1
Ashington.........351 A1
Ashlett...........339 D3
Ashley
 New Milton.....383 D3
 St Leonards....328 B6
Ashley Heath......327 E6
Ashmansworth......40 F7
Ashmore Green......2 F8
Ashton............247 B2
Ashurst...........288 B3
Ashurst Bridge....288 C5
Ash Vale..........77 E7
Avington..........177 E5
Avon..............355 F2
Avon Castle.......328 D3

Awbridge..........214 E4
Axford............114 C3
Axmansford.........25 F7

B

Badshot Lea........99 F5
Baffins...........371 B7
Bagmore...........116 A6
Bagnor.............1 A7
Bagnum............329 E2
Bailey Green......204 C3
Ball Hill...........4 A3
Balmerlawn........334 B3
Banister's Park...290 E7
Bank..............309 D2
Bar End...........403 F3
Barford...........166 C8
Barnet Side.......205 D6
Bartley...........287 B6
Barton on Sea.....397 F6
Barton Stacey.....130 D6
Bashley...........383 A7
Basingstoke........68 E6
Bassett...........267 A5
Battramsley.......361 B2
Battramsley Cross.361 C1
Baughurst.........26 C7
Baybridge.........221 D3
Beacon Hill
 Haslemere......167 A7
 Poole..........374 A2
Bear Cross........376 F5
Bearwood..........376 E6
Beaulieu..........336 E1
Beauworth.........201 B1
Beckley...........382 C5
Bedford Place.....290 F6
Bedhampton........323 C1
Beech.............139 A2
Beech Hill
 Bordon.........165 E6
 Mortimer........13 B5
Bellevue..........291 A6
Bell Hill.........228 E5
Belvidere.........291 C5
Bentley...........120 B5
Bentworth.........138 A4
Bevois Mount......291 A8
Bevois Town.......291 A7
Bevois Valley.....291 B7
Bickton...........281 F6
Bidden............94 D7
Bighton...........158 B1
Binsted...........141 E6
Bishop's Green.....6 E3

Bishop's Sutton...180 A4
Bishopstoke.......244 E3
Bishopstone.......210 D8
Bishop's Waltham..271 C7
Bisterne..........355 F6
Bisterne Close....331 D2
Bitterne..........291 F8
Bitterne Manor....291 D7
Bitterne Pk.......267 E2
Black Dam..........69 D3
Blackfield........338 D1
Blackmoor.........185 F7
Blacknest.........142 D8
Blackwater
 Bournemouth....379 D4
 Camberley.......35 B4
Blashford.........305 A3
Bleak Hill........281 C3
Blendworth........300 D8
Blissford.........282 F8
Boarhunt..........320 B5
Bohemia...........235 F4
Boldre............361 D1
Boorley Green.....269 F2
Bordon............164 C3
Borough Hill......228 E3
Boscombe..........393 E3
Bossington........171 A2
Botany Bay........292 A3
Botley............294 B7
Boundstone........121 E5
Bournemouth.......393 A4
Bourne Valley.....392 B6
Boveridge.........255 A2
Bowling Alley......97 D8
Bowling Green.....384 F6
Boyatt Wood.......244 A5
Bradley...........137 B8
Braishfield.......216 C7
Brambridge........244 E8
Bramdean..........202 D4
Bramley............28 E4
Bramley Corner.....28 A3
Bramley Green......29 A3
Bramshaw..........261 F4
Bramshill..........31 F7
Bramshott.........188 A6
Branksome.........391 F5
Branksome Park....391 F1
Bransbury.........108 A1
Bransgore.........381 B8
Breach............325 E1
Breamore..........258 B8
Bridgemary........343 C3
Brighton Hill......91 E8
Brimpton...........8 E6
Brimpton Common....8 E3

Broadgate.........217 E2
Broad Laying.......4 D1
Broadoak..........293 E7
Broad Oak..........73 B4
Broadstone........375 B3
Brockbridge.......249 C1
Brockhampton......323 D1
Brockhurst........368 E7
Brock's Green......23 E7
Brokenford........288 F7
Brook.............262 A1
Brook Hill........262 A2
Broom Hill........244 A7
Broughton.........170 C7
Brown Candover....135 B3
Brown Heath.......270 D5
Browninghill Green 26 D3
Buckland
 Lymington......385 D5
 Portsmouth.....370 E8
Bucklers Hard.....388 D4
Bucks Horn Oak....142 E8
Buckskin..........68 A3
Bull Hill.........362 C2
Bunstead..........218 D6
Burgates..........207 E6
Burghclere........22 D7
Buriton...........253 D6
Burkham...........115 E1
Burley............331 E1
Burley Lawn.......331 B4
Burley Street.....330 E5
Burridge..........294 B1
Bursledon.........316 B8
Burton............380 D2
Butlocks Heath....315 D7
Buttermere.........18 B7
Buttsash..........338 B8
Butt's Green......191 F1

C

Cadnam............286 E7
Calmore...........264 B2
Calshot...........366 F8
Camberley..........36 C7
Camdentown........369 A6
Camel Green.......281 A6
Camelsdale........189 E5
Canada............238 D1
Canford Cliffs....402 E8
Canford Heath....375 E1
Canford Magna.....352 A1
Carter's Clay.....214 B6
Catherington......276 B1

Catisfield........318 A1
Causeway
 Horndean.......300 A6
 Petersfield....228 F2
Chalton...........277 C5
Chandler's Ford...243 C8
Chandler's Green..30 D2
Chapel............291 B4
Charlton..........82 E3
Charminster.......378 C2
Charter Alley......46 E8
Chatter Alley......74 A7
Chawton...........161 D7
Cheriton..........201 D5
Chidden...........274 F8
Chilbolton........129 A4
Chilbridge........350 E7
Chilcomb..........198 F6
Chilland..........177 D6
Chilton Candover..135 F5
Chilworth.........242 D2
Chineham...........48 F3
Cholderton........101 C2
Christchurch......395 D5
Church Crookham...75 B5
Church End........49 C6
Church Oakley......66 F1
Churt.............144 D1
Chute Cadley.......58 C8
Chute Forest.......58 C4
Chute Standen......58 B8
City...............1 D1
Clanfield.........276 B5
Clanville..........81 D7
Clarken Green......66 E2
Clatford Oakcuts..127 B3
Clayhall..........369 D2
Clayhill..........310 A3
Claypits..........293 B1
Clewers Hill......271 D4
Cliddesden........92 A7
Cliddesden Hill...91 F7
Colbury...........288 D2
Colden Common.....220 A1
Cold Harbour......116 A5
Cole Henley.......63 D3
Colehill..........352 B8
Colemore..........183 D2
College Town......35 C8
Colt Hill.........72 F4
Combe..............19 C6
Compton
 Farnham.........99 D1
 Horndean.......278 E1
 King's Somborne 193 D7
 Shawford.......219 D8
Compton Down.....219 C7

Conford...........187 C7
Coombe Bissett....211 E8
Copnor............346 A1
Copythorne........263 B1
Corfe Mullen......374 C6
Corhampton........249 B5
Cosham............346 B6
Cottonworth.......128 C4
Couch Green.......177 B6
Course Park.......317 D2
Cove..............55 C5
Cove Green........55 E4
Cowesfield Gate...213 D1
Cowgrove..........350 D4
Cowplain..........299 F3
Coxford...........266 A2
Crab Orchard......302 F2
Crampmoor.........216 F1
Cranbourne........69 B2
Crawley...........152 B2
Crawley Hill.......36 C5
Creekmoor.........389 F8
Crendell..........279 F7
Cricket Hill.......34 D5
Criddlestyle......258 C1
Cripplestyle......280 A5
Critchell's Green.213 F8
Critchmere........189 C7
Crockerhill.......319 B8
Crockham Heath.....4 D6
Crondall...........97 C7
Crooked Billet.....51 D2
Crookham...........7 F5
Crookham Village...74 C5
Crosshouse........291 C3
Crosswater........144 C4
Croucheston.......210 B7
Crow..............329 C4
Crowdhill.........245 C5
Crowesfield Green.212 D3
Crux Easton........41 A5
Cuckoo's Corner...140 E7
Cufaude...........48 D7
Cupernham.........216 B2
Curbridge.........294 D4
Curdridge.........294 D8
Curdridge Firs....270 F1
Custards..........310 A6

D

Daggons...........280 C5
Damerham..........256 C4
Daneshill..........69 E7
Darby Green........34 E6
Deadwater.........164 E4

Dean
Bishop's Waltham . . . 247 E3
Winchester 174 E3
Deane. 66 B1
Deanlane End 301 E5
Dean Park 393 A4
Denmead 299 A5
Denvilles 324 B2
Dibden 313 D5
Dibden Purlieu. 313 E1
Dipley. 51 E7
Dippenhall. 98 B1
Dockenfield 143 C6
Dogmersfield. 74 A6
Donnington. 1 C6
Downend 319 F1
Downton
Milford on Sea. . . . 398 F7
Redlynch 235 A8
Drayton
Cosham 346 C7
East Meon 226 C3
Droxford 249 A1
Dudsbury 353 C1
Dummer 90 D1
Dunbridge 192 D1
Dundridge 248 B1
Dunley. 63 A8
Dunwood Hill 214 D1
Durley 270 B5
Durley Street 270 D7
Durns Town 360 D2
Durrants 324 B2

E
East Anton. 83 C4
East Aston. 108 E7
East Boldre 363 C5
East Brook 351 C5
East Cholderton . . . 103 F7
East Dean 191 B2
East End
Corfe Mullen 350 E1
Damerham. 256 D5
East Boldre 387 B7
Wootton Hill 20 F7
East Fields. 1 F1
East Green 120 D6
East Hill 208 A3
East Howe 377 C3
Eastleigh 244 C1
East Liss 208 B4
East Meon 226 D1
Eastney. 371 C4
Eastoke 373 C2
Easton 177 A5
East Parley 378 B8
Eastrop 69 D4
East Stratton 134 A4
East Tisted 183 C5
East Tytherley 191 E8
East Winterslow . . . 168 A8
East Woodhay 20 C7
East Worldham 141 A1
Ebblake 303 C3
Ecchinswell. 23 D4
Edgeborough 122 A3
Edmondsham 279 A4
Egbury 62 D5
Egypt. 131 D5
Eling 289 B5
Ellingham 304 E5
Ellisfield. 115 C8
Elson 369 A9
Elvetham. 53 B5
Elvetham Heath . . . 53 D3
Emery Down 309 D6
Empshott. 185 A3
Empshott Green . . . 184 F3
Emsworth 324 E2
Enborne. 4 D8
Enborne Row 4 F4
Enham Alamein 83 C7
Ensbury 377 F6
Ensbury Park 377 C2
Eversley 15 F1
Eversley Centre . . .33 B8
Eversley Cross . . . 33 C8
Everton 384 E1
Ewshot 98 A8
Exbury 365 B5
Exton. 249 C7

F
Faberstown. 57 C1
Faccombe 20 A1
Fair Cross. 13 B2
Fairmile 379 F1
Fair Oak
Eastleigh 245 D2
Kingsclere 25 C7
Fair Oak Green. 29 B6
Fareham 319 B3
Farleigh Wallop. 91 E2
Farley Hill. 15 B6
Farlington 346 E8
Farnborough 55 D1
Farnborough Green. 56 A6
Farnborough Park . 56 A5
Farnborough Street .56 B5
Farnham. 98 E3
Faulston 210 D7
Fawley 339 A3
Ferndown 353 B5

Filmore Hill. 204 A3
Finchampstead 16 C2
Finchdean 301 D6
Fisher's Pond 245 B7
Fitzhugh. 290 E7
Fleet
Farnborough 54 B1
Hayling Island . . . 373 A8
Fleetend. 316 F1
Fletchwood 288 B5
Flood Street 257 F7
Fordingbridge 257 D1
Forest Gate 298 E6
Forest Park 333 E1
Forestside 301 F5
Forton
Andover. 107 F4
Gosport 369 C7
Fosbury 17 D1
Foulford 330 A7
Four Marks 160 C2
Foxcotte 82 D3
Foxhills 288 C4
Foxholes 391 A6
Fox Lane 55 D8
Fratton 370 F5
Freefolk 87 B6
Freemantle 290 C6
Frenchmoor 191 A6
Frensham 144 A7
Friars Cliff 396 D7
Frimley 36 B1
Frimley Green 56 D7
Frimley Ridge. 36 F3
Fritham 260 F1
Frithend 143 A3
Frogham 282 E7
Frogmore 35 A6
Frostlane 314 C1
Froxfield Green . . . 227 D8
Fryern Hill 243 E6
Fulford 403 D7
Fullerton 128 D3
Funtley 318 E5
Furzeley Corner. . . 298 E2
Furzey Lodge 336 B1
Furzley 262 C6
Fyfield. 80 E2

G
Gable Head 373 A4
Gilbert Street . . . 181 E6
Gobley Hole 114 C7
Godshill 258 E2
Godwinscroft 381 C5
Golden Pot 117 D3
Gong Hill 122 B4
Goodworth Clatford 105 F1
Goose Green 310 A4
Goose Hill 7 E2
Gore End 3 F4
Gosden Green 349 C8
Gosport
Ampfield 217 B2
Portsmouth 369 C7
Gotham 279 E3
Grange Estate 354 F8
Grateley 125 B8
Grayshott 166 F4
Greatham 185 F2
Great Shoddesden . 80 B6
Green Cross 144 F1
Greenham 6 A8
Greywell 71 F3
Grouse Green 31 D6

H
Haddon Hill 378 E1
Hale
Downton. 235 D2
Farnham 99 B6
Halterworth 241 C7
Hambledon 274 C2
Hamble-le-Rice . . . 316 B2
Hammer 189 A5
Hammond's Green . . 264 D1
Hampreston 352 E2
Hampshire Gate. . . .37 E1
Hamptworth 237 A4
Hamstead Marshall . 3 F8
Hamworthy 389 C3
Hangersley 305 E2
Hannington. 44 F4
Happy Bottom 350 F1
Harbridge 281 E1
Harbridge Green . . 281 E2
Hardley 338 C6
Hardway 369 B8
Harefield
Romsey. 241 B8
Southampton 292 C7
Harestock 175 C4
Hartfordbridge. . . .52 F8
Hartley Mauditt . . 162 E6
Hartley Wespall . . 30 A1
Hartley Wintney. . .52 E6
Haslemere 189 E7
Hatch Bottom 268 C5
Hatchet Green 235 C3
Hatch Warren 91 C6
Hatherden 59 D1
Hatt Hill 192 D2
Hattingley 159 C7
Havant 323 E4

Hawkley 206 E7
Hawley 35 C3
Hawley Lane. 55 F7
Hawthorn 182 D8
Hayling Island . . . 371 A8
Haymoor Bottom. . . 375 F1
Hazeley. 31 E3
Hazeley Bottom . . .52 A8
Headbourne
Worthy. 176 B5
Headley
Bordon. 165 C5
Kingsclere 7 B2
Headley Down 165 F5
Head's Hill 6 F4
Hearn 165 F7
Heath End
Farnham 99 B7
Tadley 9 D1
Woolton Hill 3 E1
Heatherside. 36 F4
Heathfield 318 C1
Heath Green 159 B7
Heckfield 31 B6
Hedge End 293 D5
Henley 17 F3
Hensting 220 C1
Hermitage 349 A8
Herriard 93 A1
Highbridge 244 D7
Highbury 346 A6
Highclere 21 D5
Highcliffe 396 E8
High Cross 205 E1
Highfield 267 B2
Highrown 329 C7
Hightown 292 E4
Highways 133 D3
High Wood 305 D3
Hillbourne 375 A2
Hill Brow 208 B2
Hillbutts 350 F6
Hill Head 367 A4
Hill Park 318 C3
Hillpound 272 B4
Hillstreet 264 C5
Hill Top 337 B3
Hill View 374 D4
Hilsea 345 E4
Hiltingbury 218 C1
Hindhead 167 D4
Hinton
Christchurch 382 A3
New Alresford . . . 201 E4
Hinton Ampner . . . 201 F4
Hinton Daubnay . . . 299 E8
Hocombe 218 C2
Hoe Gate 297 F7
Hog Hatch 98 E6
Holbrook 343 E1
Holbury 338 C4
Holdenhurst 379 B3
Hollington Cross . 21 C3
Hollywater 164 F1
Holt 51 D1
Holt End 138 A3
Holt Heath 326 A6
Holt Pound 121 B4
Holtwood 3 F5
Holybourne 140 B7
Hook
Basingstoke 51 B1
Fareham 341 A8
Hoplands 194 C8
Hordle 383 F3
Horndean 300 B8
Horris Hill 5 C2
Horsea Island 345 B6
Horsebridge 171 D1
Horseport 258 A1
Horton Heath
Fair Oak. 269 D7
Three Legged Cross 302 A2
Houghton 171 B5
Hound 315 F6
Hound Green. 31 B3
Hound Hill 350 E7
Houndmills 68 E7
Houndsdown 288 E4
Hungerford 282 C5
Hunton 132 B4
Hurn 379 B7
Hursley 218 B7
Hurstbourne Priors . 85 C2
Hurstbourne Tarrant .60 E8
Hyde
Frogham 282 D6
Winchester 403 E7
Hyde End 8 C4
Hythe 314 B5

I
Ibsley 305 A8
Ibthorpe 60 D8
Ibworth 45 F2
Idmiston Down 146 C5
Iford 394 D7
Inhurst 26 A8
Inlands 325 F1
Isington 119 F2
Itchen 291 F4
Itchen Abbas 177 E6
Itchen Stoke 178 D6

J
Jumpers Common . 379 E1

K
Keeping 364 C5
Kempshott. 68 A1
Kentsboro 126 C5
Kent's Oak 214 D5
Keyhaven 400 B4
Kilmeston 201 D1
Kimbridge 214 F7
Kimpton 80 B3
Kingsclere 24 C1
Kings Furlong 69 A3
Kingsland Place . . 291 A5
Kingsley 142 B1
Kingsley Green . . . 189 D5
Kingsmead 296 C7
King's Somborne . . 172 B2
Kingston
Portsmouth 370 F7
Ringwood 329 A2
Kings Worthy 176 C6
Kinson 377 B5
Kitwood 182 A7
Knapp Hill 217 D4
Knighton 376 D8
Knights Enham 83 A5
Knowle Village. . . 318 E7

L
Lake 389 D1
Lambs' Green 350 F2
Landford 237 D3
Landford Wood . . . 237 D7
Landport 370 C7
Lane End 222 D8
Langdown 314 C2
Langley
Blackfield 365 F7
Liss 208 F7
Langrish 227 D4
Langstone 347 E2
Lansdowne Hill . . . 290 F4
Lasham 116 D1
Latchmere Green . . 28 A5
Laverstoke 87 C5
Leagreen 399 B8
Leckford 150 D8
Leckford Abbas . . . 150 D7
Lee 265 A8
Lee-on-the-Solent. 367 C4
Leigh 351 F4
Leigh Park
Havant 323 D4
Wimborne Minster . 351 E4
Lepe 366 A2
Liliput 402 C8
Linchmere 188 F2
Lindford 164 F5
Linford 306 A2
Link 85 B8
Linkenholt 19 B1
Linwood 306 B8
Liphook 188 B3
Lisle Court 386 C5
Liss 208 B4
Liss Forest 208 B6
Litchfield 63 C8
Little Ann 105 B4
Little Canford . . . 352 D4
Littledown
Andover 18 D1
Bournemouth . . . 394 A7
Little Hoddington . 94 C5
Little Holbury . . . 338 C5
Little London
Andover 83 E8
Tadley 27 F4
Little Pamphill . . 350 F5
Little Posbrook . . 341 F5
Little Sandhurst. . .34 E8
Little Shoddesden . 80 C6
Little Somborne . . 172 F6
Littleton 175 B5
Lockerley 191 E1
Locks Heath 317 B3
London Minstead . . 286 D3
Long Common 269 F2
Longfleet 390 C6
Longham 353 A1
Longparish 108 C5
Longstock 149 E6
Long Sutton 95 E3
Lord's Hill 265 F4
Lordswood 266 D5
Lovedean 299 C5
Lover 236 A5
Lower Bordean 227 A4
Lower Bourne 122 C6
Lower Brook 193 C4
Lower Buckland . . . 385 E5
Lower Bullington . 131 A7
Lower Burgate 258 A3
Lower Canterton . . 286 B7
Lower Chute 58 C7
Lower Common
Basingstoke 115 B6
Sandhurst 15 D1
Lower Daggons 280 B7
Lower Farringdon . 161 D3
Lower Froyle 119 C5

Lower Green 206 E8
Lower Hamworthy . 390 A1
Lower Holwell 279 D6
Lower Mannington . 326 B7
Lower Parkstone . . 391 B3
Lower Pennington . 400 D8
Lower Ratley 214 F3
Lower Slackstead . 217 B7
Lower Swanwick . . . 316 E7
Lower Upham 246 D3
Lower Wield 137 B5
Lowford 293 A2
Ludgershall 57 A1
Lumley 325 A1
Lyde Green 50 E7
Lymington 385 C5
Lymore 399 F2
Lynch 87 E8
Lyndhurst 309 E5

M
Mannington 326 A8
Mapledurwell. 70 E3
Marchwood 289 E2
Marley Heights . . . 189 E1
Martin 231 A4
Martyr Worthy 177 A6
Maybush 265 F2
Mead End
Horndean 299 A3
Sway 359 F1
Medstead 159 E7
Mengham 373 B3
Meon 341 E3
Meon Park 296 A4
Meonstoke 249 D3
Merley 351 D1
Merritown 378 E7
Merry Oak 291 F5
Micheldever 133 A3
Michelmersh 193 D1
Midanbury 268 A1
Middle
Bockhampton . . . 380 F6
Middle Bourne . . 122 A7
Middleton 108 A5
Middle Wallop 147 E7
Middle Winterslow. 168 A7
Milford on Sea . . . 399 D3
Milland 47 B2
Millbank 291 C6
Millbridge 122 C1
Millbrook 289 F7
Mill Corner 72 B5
Mill Green 7 D2
Mill Lane 74 B1
Milton 371 C4
Minstead 286 B3
Mockbeggar 305 C7
Monk Sherborne . . .47 B6
Monkwood 182 B2
Monxton 104 C5
Moordown 378 A2
Moorgreen 268 F2
Moortown 329 B5
Morestead 220 F8
Morgan's Vale 235 C5
Mortimer 11 E5
Mortimer West End .11 B4
Mottisfont 192 E2
Moulsham Green. . . .33 F8
Mount Pleasant
Alton 139 F2
Corfe Mullen . . . 374 C4
Lymington 384 F8
Mudeford 396 A5
Mullenspond 103 F8
Murrell Green 51 E3
Muscliffe 378 C4
Mytchett 56 C3

N
Nashes Green 116 C7
Nately Scures 71 C7
Neacroft 381 B6
Neatham 140 E6
Netherton 39 D8
Nether Wallop . . . 148 B5
Netley 315 B6
Netley Marsh 288 A5
New Alresford 179 C6
Newbridge 262 F3
New Brighton 325 A3
Newbury 1 C3
New Cheriton 201 D4
Newfound 67 C4
New Milton 382 E5
Newnham 50 C1
Newton Stacey . . . 129 E6
Newton Tony 123 B5
Newton Valence . . 184 A6
Newtown
Alton 139 E3
Awbridge 214 B4
Bishop's Waltham . 271 A7
Corfe Mullen . . . 374 D7
Eastleigh 244 A3
Gosport 369 D5
Liphook 187 F2
Minstead 286 A2
Newbury 5 F4
North Boarhunt . 297 C6
Poole 391 B7

Southampton 291 B6
South Hayling . . . 372 E5
Warsash 340 D9
Weston 292 A1
Nob's Crook 245 A7
Nomansland 261 D8
No Man's Land 198 F8
Norleywood 386 F8
Northam 291 C6
North Baddesley . 241 F6
North Boarhunt . . 297 A2
North
Bockhampton . . . 380 F7
Northbourne 377 E4
Northbrook
Bishop's Waltham . 247 D1
Micheldever 132 F4
North Camp 77 B7
North Charford . . . 235 D3
North Common 237 B6
North End
Damerham 256 C6
New Alresford . . 201 C7
Portsmouth 345 E2
Woolton Hill 3 E2
North Fareham . . . 319 C4
Northfields 220 B7
North Gorley 282 B3
North Hayling . . . 348 C3
North Houghton . . 171 C7
Northington 156 F8
North Kingston . . 329 C2
Northney 348 C4
North Oakley 44 F1
North Poulner . . . 305 D2
North Ripley 356 F4
North Street
Fordingbridge . . 234 B2
Ropley 181 D7
North Sydmonton . . .6 D1
North Tidworth . . .78 F7
North Town 77 B2
North Wallington . 319 C3
North Waltham 89 F2
North Warnborough. 72 D4
North Weirs 333 C1
Nursling 265 C5
Nursted 254 C7
Nutbourne 349 F7
Nutburn 242 B5
Nutcombe 167 C2
Nutley 114 C3

O
Oakdale 390 D6
Oakhanger 163 E4
Oakley
Basingstoke 67 C1
Wimborne Minster . 351 E2
Oakridge 69 B7
Oakshott 206 D4
Odiham 72 E2
Ogdens 282 F5
Old Alresford . . . 157 C1
Old Basing 70 C6
Old Burghclere . . . 42 D8
Old Milton 382 E1
Old Netley 292 D1
Old Portsmouth . . 370 A3
Old Shirley 266 B1
Old Town 390 C3
Oliver's Battery . 197 A3
Ossemsley 382 E8
Otterbourne 219 C3
Otterbourne Hill . 219 B1
Otterwood 337 C1
Outwick 257 F8
Overton 88 B7
Over Wallop 125 B1
Ovington 178 E4
Ower
Calshot 366 E8
Romsey 263 E6
Owslebury 221 B3
Oxenwood 17 B3

P
Padworth 10 E8
Padworth Common . .10 E6
Palestine 124 E6
Pamber End 27 C2
Pamber Green 27 D4
Pamber Heath 10 D1
Pamphill 350 E6
Pardown 90 B7
Park Gate 317 B5
Parley Green 378 C7
Passfield 165 D1
Paulsgrove 321 A1
Peartree Green . . . 291 D4
Pennington 385 B1
Penton Corner 82 A1
Penton Grafton . . .81 F3
Penton Mewsey . . .82 A4
Pentridge 230 B1
Penwood 21 F8
Petersfield 228 C2
Phoenix Green 52 B4
Picket Piece 84 A2
Pikes Hill 309 F7
Pilcot 74 B6
Pilford 352 A8
Pilley 362 A1
Pilley Bailey 362 A2

Plaitford... 238 B4
Plaitford Green... 238 D7
Pleasant View... 292 C3
Pokesdown... 394 A4
Polhampton... 65 D2
Pollards Moor... 263 A1
Polygon... 290 E6
Pondtail... 54 D1
Pooksgreen... 289 C1
Poole... 390 B3
Popham... 112 E4
Popley... 48 C1
Portchester... 344 C7
Portmore... 386 A7
Porton Down... 145 A3
Ports Down... 322 F2
Portsea... 370 B6
Portsea Island... 370 F6
Portsmouth... 404 A4
Port Solent... 345 A7
Portswood... 267 C1
Portswood Park... 291 B8
Potbridge... 72 F8
Poulner... 329 D8
Pound Green... 26 B3
Pound Street... 22 A7
Preston Candover... 136 B8
Priddy's Hard... 369 C8
Prince's Marsh... 207 E2
Prinsted... 349 C7
Privett
  Gosport... 368 F3
  Petersfield... 204 D2
Pucknall... 216 F6
Purbrook... 322 E4
Purewell... 395 D7
Pyestock... 54 F1
Pylehill... 245 C3

Q
Quarley... 103 B4
Queensland... 291 B5
Quidhampton... 65 B1

R
Rafborough... 55 C3
Ragged Appleshaw... 81 C6
Rake... 208 F4
Ramsdean... 227 D1
Ramsdell... 46 D7
Ratlake... 217 F4
Redbridge... 289 C8
Redbrook... 282 A7
Redenham... 81 A8
Red Hill
  Bournemouth... 377 F5
  Rowlands Castle... 301 B2
Redlands... 97 F7
Redlynch... 235 E6
Red Rice... 127 C8
Redwood... 160 A8
Ridge... 240 C1
Ringwood... 329 C7
Ripley... 356 C2
Riseley... 14 A3
Rivar... 17 D8
Rockbourne... 232 F1
Rockford... 305 C5
Romford... 302 C7
Romsey... 240 F6
Ropley... 181 D4
Ropley Dean... 180 F5
Ropley Soke... 181 E8
Rossmore... 391 E7
Rotherwick... 50 E6
Rotten Green... 53 C4
Roughdown... 338 C1
Row Ash... 295 A8
Rowlands... 351 C5

Rowlands Castle... 301 D2
Rowledge... 121 D3
Rowner... 368 C8
Rownhams... 265 F7
Runfold... 100 A4
Rushington... 288 F6
Rushmere... 274 E1
Rushmoor... 144 F7

S
St Cross... 403 C2
St Denys... 291 C8
St Giles' Hill... 198 C7
St Ives... 328 A5
St Johns... 351 C4
St Leonards... 327 C4
St Mary Bourne... 62 A1
Sandbanks... 402 C3
Sandford... 356 C8
Sandhurst... 35 A7
Sandleheath... 257 A3
Sandy Down... 361 C4
Sarisbury... 316 F5
Scrag Hill... 241 F5
Seafield... 369 D4
Seale... 100 F4
Seaman's Corner... 286 B4
Segensworth... 317 D5
Selborne... 184 E8
Selsmore... 373 D3
Setley... 361 A6
Shalden... 139 B8
Shalden Green... 117 B3
Shaw... 2 B6
Shawford... 219 E7
Shawford Down... 219 D6
Shedfield... 295 D7
Sherborne St John... 47 E4
Sherfield English... 213 D1
Sherfield Green... 29 C1
Sherfield on Loddon... 29 D1
Shipton Bellinger... 101 D8
Shirley
  Bransgore... 357 A2
  Southampton... 290 C8
Shirley Holms... 361 A1
Shirley Warren... 266 B2
Shobley... 306 A1
Sholing... 292 B4
Sholing Common... 292 B5
Shootash... 214 D1
Shorley... 201 C2
Shortfield Common... 122 A1
Shortheath
  Bordon... 163 D5
  Wrecclesham... 121 E6
Shottermill... 189 D6
Shrover... 299 D5
Silchester... 10 F1
Silkstead... 218 F5
Skinners Green... 4 F7
Sladen Green... 40 F1
Sleaford... 142 E1
Sleeper's Hill... 403 B5
Sleight... 350 D1
Smannell... 83 E6
Soake... 299 B3
Soberton... 273 C6
Soberton Heath... 273 B1
Soldridge... 159 E2
Somerford... 395 E7
Sopley... 380 B7
Southampton... 290 D3
South Baddesley... 386 E6
South
  Bockhampton... 380 E4
Southbourne
  Bournemouth... 394 F4
  Havant... 349 E8
South Down... 219 D5

South End... 256 D3
South Farnborough... 56 B2
South Gorley... 282 C2
South Ham... 68 D3
South Hayling... 372 E2
Southington... 87 F8
Southrope... 116 C6
Southsea... 370 C1
South Tidworth... 78 B1
South Town... 159 F5
South View... 69 B7
South Warnborough... 95 B4
South Weirs... 360 D7
South Wonston... 153 D5
Southwood... 55 A3
Spanish Green... 30 A3
Sparsholt... 174 C3
Spearywell... 192 D3
Speen... 1 A5
Speenhamland... 1 E4
Spitalhatch... 140 B3
Spreakley... 144 A8
Springbourne... 393 C5
Springhead... 189 C5
Springvale... 176 B8
Stamshaw... 345 C1
Standford... 165 A2
Standon... 196 B2
Stanford End... 13 D3
Stanley Green... 390 C6
Stanmore... 403 B3
Stanpit... 395 F5
Stanswood... 366 D6
Stapehill... 352 E5
Steep... 228 D7
Steep Marsh... 207 B1
Sterte... 390 B3
Steventon... 89 B4
Stockbridge... 149 F3
Stockheath... 323 E3
Stoke
  Andover... 61 D4
  Hayling Island... 348 A1
Stoke Charity... 132 B3
Stoke Common... 244 E5
Stone
  Langley... 366 A3
  Wimborne Minster... 351 A6
Stone Copse... 2 C7
Stoney Cross... 285 E4
Stony Batter... 191 D8
Stonyford... 263 E4
Stonymarsh... 193 B1
Stratfield Mortimer... 12 B5
Stratfield Saye... 29 B4
Stratfield Turgis... 30 B4
Stratfield Turgis... 30 B4
Street End... 247 D4
Stroud... 228 A4
Strouden... 378 E1
Stubbington... 342 D4
Stuckton... 282 B7
Sussex Place... 291 A4
Sutton Scotney... 131 C3
Swallowfield... 14 A6
Swampton... 61 F2
Swanmore... 272 C5
Swanwick... 317 A7
Sway... 360 B1
Swaythling... 267 F4
Swelling Hill... 181 F6
Sydmonton... 43 B8

T
Tadley... 27 A7
Talbot Heath... 392 B7
Talbot Village... 377 C1
Talbot Woods... 392 E7
Tangley... 58 F6
Tapnage... 295 C1

Teg Down... 403 A6
Testcombe... 128 E3
Testwood... 264 F1
Thatcham... 2 E2
The Beeches... 80 E5
The Bourne... 122 B6
The Butts... 139 E2
The Common... 168 B5
The Earldoms... 237 A7
The Frenches... 214 B1
The Green... 191 B7
The Marsh... 389 A7
The Sands... 100 C2
The Soke
  New Alresford... 179 E6
  Winchester... 403 A5
The Straits... 142 B3
Thorney Hill... 357 D3
Thorney Island... 349 B3
Thornhill... 292 C5
Thornhill Park... 292 D6
Thorns Beach... 388 B6
Three Ashes... 28 B7
Three Legged
  Cross... 326 F8
Throop... 378 E4
Thruxton... 103 E8
Tichborne Down... 179 E4
Tidworth... 78 E6
Tilford... 122 F4
Tilford Reeds... 122 E3
Tilly Down... 81 B7
Timsbury... 215 D6
Tipner... 345 C3
Tiptoe... 383 D8
Titchfield... 341 E7
Titchfield Common... 317 D1
Titchfield Park... 317 E4
Tongham... 100 E6
Toot Hill... 241 E1
Totford... 157 A8
Tot Hill... 22 C8
Totton... 288 E7
Townhill Park... 268 A2
Towns End... 25 E7
Trickett's Cross... 353 F7
Tuckton... 394 F5
Tufton... 86 B2
Tunworth... 93 C6
Turgis Green... 30 B3
Turkey Island... 295 F7
Turlin Moor... 389 B4
Turmer... 304 B8
Twyford... 220 A6
Tye... 348 C1

U
Up Green... 33 C6
Upham... 246 F5
Up Nately... 71 B4
Upper Bullington... 131 D8
Upper Burgate... 258 A6
Upper Canterton... 285 F6
Upper Chute... 57 F8
Upper Clatford... 105 E4
Upper Common... 115 A7
Upper Enham... 83 C8
Upper Farringdon... 161 F3
Upper Froyle... 119 A2
Upper Hale... 99 A6
Upper Kingston... 329 C4
Upper Parkstone... 391 B5
Upper Pennington... 385 C2
Upper Ratley... 214 E4
Upper Shirley... 266 D1
Upper Slackstead... 195 B1
Upper Street... 233 F1
Upper Swanmore... 272 C8
Upper Wield... 136 F2
Upper Wootton... 46 B2
Up Somborne... 173 C5

Upton
  Andover... 39 A3
  Poole... 389 D7
  Southampton... 265 C6
Upton Grey... 94 A5

V
Valley Park... 243 A4
Vernham Bank... 38 A6
Vernham Dean... 38 B5
Vernham Row... 38 B8
Vernham Street... 38 E7
Verwood... 302 E4
Viables... 69 A1

W
Wadwick... 62 C6
Walhampton... 386 A4
Walkford... 382 C1
Wallington... 319 D2
Wallisdown... 377 A2
Waltham Chase... 271 F3
Warblington... 324 C1
Warborne... 385 F8
Wardley... 47 C4
Warnborough Green... 72 C4
Warnford... 224 A3
Warren Corner... 206 B5
Warsash... 316 D1
Wash Common... 5 C5
Wash Water... 5 B4
Wasing... 9 B5
Waterditch... 381 B5
Water End... 71 B7
Waterloo... 375 B1
Waterlooville... 322 D8
Waterford... 386 B1
Wecock... 299 E4
Weeke... 404 B8
Westbourne
  Bournemouth... 392 C3
  Emsworth... 325 B4
West Cliff... 392 C1
West Common... 365 E6
West Dean... 190 D3
West End
  Fareham... 342 F7
  Four Marks... 159 C4
  Southampton... 268 E2
West End Green... 29 B8
Westfield... 372 F3
West Fields... 1 D2
West Green... 51 F5
West Ham... 68 E5
West Heath
  Farnborough... 55 C5
  Tadley... 26 E1
West Hill... 403 C5
West Howe... 376 E4
West Hurn... 378 F6
West Leigh... 324 B4
West Liss... 207 F5
West Meon... 225 B4
West Meon
  Woodlands... 203 C2
West Moors... 326 B3
Weston
  Petersfield... 253 C8
  Southampton... 291 F1
Weston Colley... 132 E4
Weston Common... 292 C4
Weston Corbett... 93 F3
Weston Patrick... 94 A2
West Parley... 353 E1
West Southbourne... 394 D5
West Stratton... 133 E5
West Thorney... 349 D2
West Tisted... 203 D7
West Town... 372 E3

West Tytherley... 169 B1
West Wellow... 238 F3
West Woodhay... 3 A3
Westwood Park... 267 B1
West Worldham... 162 E6
Weybourne... 99 D7
Weyhill... 81 C2
Whale Island... 345 B1
Wharf Hill... 403 E4
Wheat Hold... 25 D6
Wheatley... 142 A5
Wherwell... 128 F6
Whitchurch... 86 D6
Whitehall... 72 F6
Whitehill... 164 C1
Whiteley... 317 D8
Whitenap... 241 C6
Whiteparish... 212 A4
Whitsbury... 233 B3
Whitway... 22 B3
Wick
  Bournemouth... 395 B4
  Downton... 234 C8
Wickham... 296 B3
Widley... 322 B1
Wigley... 263 E6
Wildern... 293 C8
Wildhern... 59 E2
Wildmoor... 49 E5
Wilsom... 140 B3
Wimborne Minster... 351 A6
Wimpson... 289 E8
Winchester... 403 B4
Winchfield... 52 C2
Winchfield Hurst... 52 F1
Winklebury... 68 C6
Winkton... 380 C5
Winnall... 198 C8
Winslade... 92 F5
Winsor... 263 D1
Wintershill... 270 E8
Winton... 392 F7
Wittensford... 286 D8
Wivelrod... 138 C2
Wolverton... 25 C2
Wolverton Common... 25 E4
Woodcot... 343 A4
Woodcott... 41 D2
Woodend... 296 F8
Woodfalls... 235 C5
Woodgreen... 258 D8
Woodhouse... 83 D7
Woodlands
  New Alresford... 179 B5
  Totton... 287 E4
Woodlands
  Common... 302 B6
Woodley... 216 C2
Woodmancote... 325 E4
Woodmancott... 112 E1
Woodside
  Lymington... 385 E1
  Minstead... 286 A1
Woolmer Hill... 189 A6
Woolsbridge... 327 B6
Woolston... 291 E2
Woolton Hill... 21 C7
Wooton St Lawrence... 67 D7
Wootton... 383 B8
Worlds End... 298 A5
Worthy Down
  Camp... 153 E3
Worting... 68 A5
Wrecclesham... 121 D7
Wyck... 141 B4
Wymering... 321 E1

Y
Yateley... 34 B6
Yateley Green... 34 A7
York Town... 35 E5

408 1st–Ali

1st St SO45 . . . . **339** A4
2nd St SO45 . . . . **339** A4
3rd St SO45 . . . . **338** F4
4th St SO45 . . . . **338** F4
5th St
　Blackfield SO45 . . . . **338** E4
　Fawley SO45 . . . . **338** F5
6th St
　Fawley SO45 . . . . **338** E4
　Fawley SO45 . . . . **338** E6
7th St
　Fawley SO45 . . . . **338** E4
　Fawley SO45 . . . . **338** E5
8th St SO45 . . . . **338** E4
9th St SO45 . . . . **338** D4
10th St SO45 . . . . **338** D5
11th St SO45 . . . . **338** D5
12th St SO45 . . . . **338** D5
13th St SO45 . . . . **338** D6
14th St SO45 . . . . **338** D6
17th Century
Experience ✷
　PO13 . . . . **368** C5

A

Aaron Cl BH17 . . . . . **390** F7
Aaron Ct SO40 . . . . . **289** F2
A Ave SO45 . . . . **338** D4
Abbas Bsns Ctr SO21 **177** F6
Abbas Gn PO9 . . . . . . **323** D7
Abbatt Cl SP11 . . . . **57** B2
Abberbury Cl
　(Almshouses) RG14 . .1 C6
Abbetts La GU15 . . . . .**35** F3
Abbey Bsns Pk GU9 . **122** E8
Abbey Cl
　Hythe SO45 . . . . **314** A3
　Newbury RG14 . . . . .5 E8
Abbey Ct
　2 Camberley GU15 . . **36** B5
　4 Andover SP10 . . . **105** F8
　5 Farnham GU9 . . . . . **99** A2
　8 Southampton
　SO15 . . . . **290** F7
　Basingstoke RG24 . . . . **48** A1
Abbeydore Cl GU35 . **165** C5
Abbeydore Rd PO6 . . **321** C1
Abbey Ent Ctr SO51 . **241** D5
Abbeyfield Dr PO15 . **318** C2
Abbeyfield Ho **6**
　SO18 . . . . **291** E8
Abbeyfields Cl SO31 . **315** D6
Abbey Fruit Park Ind Est
　SO31 . . . . **315** C7
Abbey Gdns BH21 . . . **352** D5
Abbey Hill SO31 . . . . **315** A7
Abbey Hill Cl SO23 . . **403** E8
Abbey Hill Rd SO23 . . **403** E8
Abbeymede PO6 . . . . **345** E8
Abbey Mill Bsns Site
　SO32 . . . . **271** C7
Abbey Pas SO23 . . . . **403** E5
Abbey Rd
　Basingstoke RG24 . . . . **69** A8
　Fareham PO15 . . . . . **318** D2
　Medstead GU34 . . . . **160** C8
　West Moors BH22 . . . **354** A8
Abbey Sch The GU9 . . **99** B1
Abbey St GU9 . . . . **99** A2
Abbey Terr SP11 . . . . . **61** C4
Abbey The SO51 . . . . **240** E7
Abbey Water **8**
　SO51 . . . . **240** E7
Abbey Way GU14 . . . . **56** A4
Abbotsbury Rd
　Bishopstoke SO50 . . . **244** A2
　Corfe Mullen BH18 . . **374** F5
Abbots Cl
　Christchurch BH23 . . **396** F7
　Fleet GU51 . . . . **54** A1
　Waterlooville PO7 . . . **322** C4
Abbotsfield SO40 . . . **288** E8
Abbotsfield Cl SO16 . . **266** C5
Abbotsford SO40 . . . **287** B6
Abbots Lea Cotts
　SO23 . . . . **176** B3
Abbots Rd RG14 . . . . . . .1 E1
Abbot's Ride GU9 . . . . **99** C1
Abbots Row **1** SO22 **403** D6
Abbotstone Ave PO9 **324** A4
Abbotstone Rd SO24 **179** D7
Abbots Way
　Fareham PO15 . . . . . **318** D1
　Netley SO31 . . . . **315** D6
Abbots Well Rd SP6 . **282** F7
Abbotswood Cl
　Romsey SO51 . . . . . . **216** C1
　Tadley RG26 . . . . **26** F7
Abbotswood Jun Sch
　SO40 . . . . **288** E2
Abbott Cl
　Basingstoke RG22 . . . . **68** C2
　Bournemouth BH9 . . . **393** A8
Abbott Rd BH9 . . . . . **393** A8
Abbott's Ann CE Prim
Sch SP11 . . . . **104** F3

Abbotts Ann Rd
　Monxton SP11 . . . . . **104** C5
　Winchester SO22 . . . **175** D3
Abbotts Cl
　Abbotts Ann SP11 . . . **105** A4
　North Tidworth SP9 . . . **78** E7
　Winchester SO23 . . . **403** E8
Abbotts Cotts GU10 . **143** C5
Abbotts Ct
　8 Southampton
　SO17 . . . . **267** A1
　Winchester SO22 . . . **403** D8
Abbotts Dro SO51 . . . **238** E1
Abbotts Hill SP11 . . . **105** A4
Abbotts Rd
　Eastleigh SO50 . . . . . **243** F1
　North Tidworth SP9 . . . **78** E7
　Winchester SO23 . . . **403** E8
Abbott St BH21 . . . . . **350** D6
Abbotts Way
　Southampton SO17 . . **267** B1
　West Moors BH22 . . . **354** A8
A'Becket Ct **3** PO1 . **370** A4
Abercrombie Gdns
　SO16 . . . . **266** A4
Aberdare Ave PO6 . . **346** B8
Aberdare Rd BH10 . . **377** E3
Aberdeen Cl PO15 . . . **318** E3
Aberdeen Rd SO17 . . **267** C1
Aberdeen Terr **1**
　SO26 . . . . **167** B3
Aberdour Cl SO18 . . . **292** B8
Abex Rd RG14 . . . . .2 A3
Abingdon Cl PO12 . . . **369** B5
Abingdon Dr BH23 . . **397** C8
Abingdon Gdns
　SO16 . . . . **266** E3
Abingdon Rd
　Poole BH17 . . . . **390** D8
　Sandhurst GU47 . . . . . **35** A8
Abinger Rd BH7 . . . . **394** B6
Abney Rd BH10 . . . . . **377** D3
Above Bar St SO14 . . **290** F5
Above Town SP11 . . . **105** E4
Abraham Cl SO30 . . . **293** D5
Abshot Cl PO14 . . . . . **317** B1
Abshot Rd PO14 . . . . **317** C1
Acacia Ave BH31 . . . **303** C4
Acacia Gdns PO8 . . . **300** B5
Acacia Lodge **2**
　PO16 . . . . **319** B1
Acacia Rd
　Hordle SO41 . . . . **383** F3
　Southampton SO19 . . **291** F5
Academy Cl GU15 . . . .**35** F6
Academy Gate GU15 . **35** F6
Acanthas Ct PO15 . . . **294** D1
Accentors Cl GU34 . **139** F6
Acer Way PO9 . . . . . . **324** B4
Acheulian Cl GU9 . . . **122** A7
Achilles Cl RG24 . . . . . **48** F4
Ackender Rd GU34 . . **139** E3
Ackworth Rd PO3 . . . **346** A5
Acland Rd BH9 . . . . . **393** B8
Acorn Ave BH15 . . . . **390** D2
Acorn Bsns Ctr PO6 . **345** D7
Acorn Bsns Pk BH12 **391** B8
Acorn Cl
　Basingstoke RG21 . . . . **69** E5
　Christchurch BH23 . . **394** F8
　Farlington PO6 . . . . . **346** E8
　Gosport PO13 . . . . . . **343** D1
　Marchwood SO40 . . . **290** A1
　New Milton BH25 . . . **383** C4
　St Leonards BH24 . . . **327** E3
　Winchester SO22 . . . **403** B8
Acorn Cotts BH31 . . . **302** F7
Acorn Ct SO31 . . . . . **315** F3
Acorn Dr SO16 . . . . . **265** F7
Acorn Gdns PO8 . . . . **300** B6
Acorn Gr SO53 . . . . . **242** F4
Acorn Keep GU9 . . . . . **99** B8
Acorn Mews GU14 . . . **55** F7
Acorn Rd GU17 . . . . . . **34** F5
Acorns The
　Bursledon SO31 . . . . **315** F8
　West Moors BH24 . . . **354** B8
　Wimborne Minster
　BH21 . . . . **352** B4
Acorn Way BH31 . . . . **303** A6
Acorn Workshops
　SO14 . . . . **291** B7
Acre Almshouses **6**
　SP10 . . . . **106** B8
Acre Ct SP10 . . . . **106** A7
Acre La PO7 . . . . **300** C1
Acre Path SP10 . . . . . **106** C8
Acres Rd BH11 . . . . . **377** B2
Acton Ho RG22 . . . . . . **68** E4
Acton Rd BH10 . . . . . **377** B1
Adair Rd PO4 . . . . **371** A2
Adam Cl RG26 . . . . .9 C1
Adames Rd PO1 . . . . **370** E6
Adampur Rd SP9 . . . . . **78** C4
Adams Cl
　Hedge End SO30 . . . . **269** B3
　North Tidworth SP11 . . **79** D6
　North Warnborough
　RG29 . . . . **72** B3
Adams Dr GU51 . . . . . **54** C1

Adamsfield Gdns
　BH10 . . . . **377** C2
Adams Ho GU34 . . . . **140** A4
Adams Mews **1**
　GU30 . . . . **188** A2
Adamson Cl SO53 . . . **243** D8
Adams Park Rd GU9 . . **99** B3
Adams Rd SO45 . . . . **314** A2
Adams Terr PO6 . . . . **346** C6
Adams Way
　Alton GU34 . . . . **140** A4
　Locks Heath PO15 . . . **317** C5
Adams Wood Dr
　SO40 . . . . **289** F1
Adastral Rd BH17 . . . **390** F8
Adastral Sq BH17 . . . **390** F8
Ad Astra Fst Sch
　BH17 . . . . **375** F1
Adcock Ct SO16 . . . . **265** E7
Adderbury Ave PO10 **324** F3
Addington Ct **1**
　SO41 . . . . **399** D5
Addington Pl BH23 . . **395** D6
Addiscombe Rd
　BH23 . . . . **395** A7
Addis Ho SO17 . . . . . **267** B1
Addison Cl
　Romsey SO51 . . . . . . **216** B1
　Winchester SO22 . . . **403** A3
Addison Gdns RG29 . . .**72** E3
Addison Rd
　Brockenhurst SO42 . . **360** F4
　Camberley GU15 . . . . . **56** C8
　Eastleigh SO50 . . . . . **244** B5
　Locks Heath SO31 . . . **317** A6
　Portsmouth PO4 . . . . **404** D1
　Sarisbury SO31 . . . . . **316** F6
Adela Sq BH24 . . . . . **329** B7
Adelaide Cl BH23 . . . **394** F8
Adelaide Ct SO41 . . . **385** F4
Adelaide La **17** BH1 . **392** F3
Adelaide Pl **7** PO16. **319** C1
Adelaide Rd
　Andover SP10 . . . . . . **106** B8
　Southampton SO17 . . **291** C8
Adela Verne Cl SO19 **292** E3
Adeline Rd BH1,BH5 . **393** E4
Adey Cl SO19 . . . . **292** B2
Adey's Cl RG14 . . . . . . .1 F2
Adhurst Rd PO9 . . . . **324** A4
Adlam's La SO41 . . . . **360** A2
Adlington Pl GU14 . . . **56** C2
Admers Cres GU30 . . **188** A2
Admiral Lord Nelson Sch
　PO3 . . . . **346** B1
Admiral Park The
　PO3 . . . . **346** A4
Admiral Pl **11** PO6 . . **345** F8
Admirals Cl SO45 . . . **339** B3
Admiral's Cnr **13**
　PO5 . . . . **370** D2
Admirals Ct
　21 Portsmouth
　PO5 . . . . **370** C2
　Hamble-le-R SO31 . . . **316** A2
　Lymington SO41 . . . . **385** F4
Admirals Ho SO31 . . **340** C10
Admirals Rd SO31 . . . **317** B4
Admirals Way
　Andover SP10 . . . . . . **106** D8
　Hythe SO45 . . . . **314** A5
Admirals Wlk
　13 Bournemouth
　BH2 . . . . **392** D2
　Gosport PO12 . . . . . . **368** F3
Admiral's Wlk PO1 . . **369** F7
Admiralty Cl PO12 . . **369** C8
Admiralty Cotts
　PO12 . . . . **369** C2
　Portsmouth PO5 . . . . **404** C1
Admiralty Rd
　Bournemouth BH6. . . **394** F3
　Portsmouth PO1 . . . . **370** A5
Admiralty Way
　Camberley GU15 . . . . . **35** D4
　Marchwood SO40 . . . **289** F2
Adrian Cl RG27 . . . . . . **52** D5
Adsdean Cl PO9 . . . . **323** E4
Adstone Cl PO3 . . . . **346** C4
Adur Cl
　Gosport PO12 . . . . . . **368** F7
　West End SO18 . . . . . **268** B1
Aerial Pk BH1 . . . . . . **352** E6
Aerial Rd PO6 . . . . . . **321** B7
Aerodrome Rd PO13 **343** C5
Aerospace Bvd GU14. **76** D7
Africa Dr SO40 . . . . . **312** F8
Agar's La SO41 . . . . . **384** B5
Agarton La SO41 . . . . **399** F6
Aggis Farm BH31 . . . **302** E6
Aghemund Cl RG24 . . **48** E3
Agincourt Rd PO2 . . . **370** D7
Agitator Rd SO45 . . . **339** C4
Agnew Ho PO12 . . . . **369** B7
Agnew Rd PO13 . . . . **343** C3
Agra Rd SP9 . . . . **78** C4
Agricola Wlk SP10 . . . **83** A2
Aikman La SO40 . . . . **288** B7
Ailsa La SO19 . . . . . . **291** D4
Ainger Cl GU12 . . . . . . **77** B3
Ainsdale Rd PO6 . . . . **322** D1

Ainsley Gdns SO50 . . **244** A5
Aintree Cl
　Horton Heath SO50 . . **269** D7
　Newbury RG14 . . . . .2 A1
Aintree Ct SO31 . . . . **317** B8
Aintree Dr PO7 . . . . . **300** B1
Aintree Rd SO40 . . . . **264** C1
Airborne Forces Mus ✷
　GU11 . . . . **76** E5
Aircraft Espl GU14 . . . **56** A1
Aird Cl RG20 . . . . **21** C8
Airetons Cl BH18 . . . . **375** C3
Airfield Ind Est
　Christchurch BH23 . . **395** F6
　Christchurch BH23 . . **396** A7
Airfield Rd BH23 . . . . **395** F6
Airfield Way BH23 . . **395** F7
Airlie Cnr SO22 . . . . . **403** C4
Airlie La SO22 . . . . . . **403** C4
Airlie Rd SO22 . . . . . . **403** C4
Airport Service Rd
　Portsmouth PO3 . . . . **346** A4
　Portsmouth PO3 . . . . **346** B3
Airspeed Rd
　Christchurch BH23 . . **396** B7
　Portsmouth PO3 . . . . **346** C2
Ajax Cl
　Chineham RG24 . . . . . . **48** F4
　Stubbington PO14 . . . **367** D6
Akeshill Cl BH25 . . . . **383** B5
Alameda Rd PO7 . . . . **322** D4
Alameda Way PO7 . . **322** D4
Alamein Rd
　Aldershot GU11 . . . . . . **76** F2
　Enham Alamein SP11 . **83** B7
　Hythe SO45 . . . . **313** C2
　Marchwood SO40 . . . **289** F2
　Newbury RG14 . . . . .2 B4
　Romsey SO51 . . . . . . **216** A4
Alan Chun Ho SO31 . **315** C7
Alan Ct **10** BH23 . . . . **397** B7
Alandale Rd SO19 . . . **292** D4
Alan Drayton Way
　SO50 . . . . **244** F2
Alan Gr PO15 . . . . . . **318** E2
Albacore Ave SO31 . . **316** F1
Albany BH1 . . . . **393** C3
Albany Bsns Ctr
　PO17 . . . . **319** B7
Albany Cl
　Fleet GU51 . . . . **55** B8
　Old Milton BH25 . . . . **382** F1
Albany Ct
　6 Bournemouth
　BH2 . . . . **392** F4
　Bishop's Waltham
　SO32 . . . . **271** A8
Albany Dr
　Bishop's Waltham
　SO32 . . . . **271** A8
　Three Legged Cross
　BH21 . . . . **302** E1
Albany Gdns BH15 . . **389** F2
Albany Ho **17** BH13. . **392** A4
Albany Mews SP10 . . **105** E8
Albany Park Ct SO17 **290** E8
Albany Park Ind Est
　GU16 . . . . **36** A1
Albany Pk
　Camberley GU16 . . . . . **35** F1
　Frimley GU16 . . . . **36** A1
　Poole BH17 . . . . **390** B8
Albany Rd
　Andover SP10 . . . . . . **105** E8
　Bishop's Waltham
　SO32 . . . . **271** A8
　Fleet GU51 . . . . **75** A8
　Holbury SO45 . . . . . . **338** C4
　Romsey SO51 . . . . . . **240** F7
　Southampton SO15 . . **290** C6
Albany The **25** SO16 **291** A4
Albatross Wlk BH23 . **343** B2
Albemarle Ave PO12 **369** B9
Albemarle Rd BH3 . . **392** F7
Albemarle Ct SO17 . **267** C3
Albert Cl SO31 . . . . . **315** C5
Albert Ct
　Southampton SO17 . . **267** C1
　Winchester SO23 . . . **403** D7
Albert Gr PO5 . . . . . . **404** C1
Albert Rd
　Aldershot GU11 . . . . . . **76** F2
　Alton GU34 . . . . **139** E2
　Bishop's Waltham
　SO32 . . . . **271** B7
　Bournemouth BH1 . . **392** F3
　Camberley GU15 . . . . . **36** A5
　Corfe Mullen BH21 . . **374** D5
　Cosham PO6 . . . . **345** F7
　Eastleigh SO50 . . . . . **244** B5
　Farnborough GU14 . . . **56** A2
　Ferndown BH22. . . . . **353** D5
　Hedge End SO30 . . . . **293** B5
　Newbury RG14 . . . . .1 E3
　New Milton BH25 . . . **382** F2
　Poole BH12 . . . . **391** D6
　Portsmouth PO4,PO5 **370** C2
　Stubbington PO14 . . . **367** F7
Albert Rd N SO14 . . . **291** B3
Albert Rd S SO14 . . . **291** B3

Albert St
　Fleet GU51 . . . . **53** F1
　Gosport PO12 . . . . . . **369** C6
Albert Yd **8** RG21 . . . **69** B4
Albion Cl
　Poole BH15 . . . . **391** B7
　Portchester PO16 . . . **344** B6
Albion Pl
　14 Winchester
　SO23 . . . . **403** E6
　3 Southampton
　SO14 . . . . **290** F4
　Hartley Wintney RG27 . **52** C6
Albion Rd
　Christchurch BH23 . . **379** E1
　Fordingbridge SP6 . . . **257** F2
　Lee-on-t-S PO13 . . . . **367** E4
　Sandhurst GU47 . . . . . **34** F8
Albion Twrs SO14 . . . **291** B4
Albion Way BH31 . . . **302** D7
Albretia Ave PO8 . . . **299** E3
Albury Pl **10** SO53 . . **218** B1
Albury Way RG19 . . . . .**6** D4
Alby Rd BH12 . . . . . . **391** F5
Alcantara Cres SO14 **291** B3
Alcester Rd BH12 . . . **391** D6
Alchorne Pl PO3 . . . . **346** B3
Aldbury Ct BH25 . . . . **398** A7
Alder Cl
　Alton GU34 . . . . **139** E5
　Ash Vale GU12 . . . . . . **77** E7
　Burton BH23 . . . . **380** C1
　Colden Common
　SO21 . . . . **245** A8
　Hythe SO45 . . . . **313** C2
　Marchwood SO40 . . . **289** F2
　Newbury RG14 . . . . .2 B4
　Romsey SO51 . . . . . . **216** A4
Alder Cres BH12 . . . . **391** F7
Alder Dr SP6 . . . . **280** F5
Alderfield GU32 . . . . . **228** E3
Alder Gr GU46 . . . . **34** A5
Alder Hill Dr SO40 . . **288** B8
Alder Hills BH12 . . . . **392** A7
Alder Hills Ind Pk
　BH12 . . . . **392** A7
Alder Hills Nature
Reserve ✷ BH12 . . . **392** A7
Alderholt Mill & Craft
Ctr ✷ SP6 . . . . **256** F1
Alderholt Rd SP6 . . . **257** A2
Alder Hts BH12 . . . . . **392** A7
Alder La PO12,PO13. . **368** D5
Alderley Rd BH10 . . . **377** D4
Alderman Quilley Sch
　SO50 . . . . **243** F1
Alderman Quilley Sch
The SO50 . . . . **244** A1
Aldermaston CE Prim
Sch RG7 . . . .**9** D7
Aldermaston Rd
　Basingstoke RG24 . . . . **68** F8
　Pamber End RG26 . . . . **27** B3
　Pamber Heath RG26 . . .9 E2
　Sherborne St John RG24,
　RG26 . . . . **47** D5
Aldermaston Rd S
　RG21 . . . . **68** F7
Aldermoor Ave
　SO16 . . . . **266** A4
Aldermoor Cl SO16. . **266** C4
Aldermoor Rd
　Gosport PO13 . . . . . . **368** D7
　Southampton SO16 . . **266** B4
　Waterlooville PO7 . . . **322** D4
Aldermoor Rd E
　PO7 . . . . **322** D5
Alderney Ave
　Basingstoke RG22 . . . . **91** B7
　Poole BH12 . . . . **376** D1
Alderney Cl SO16 . . . **265** E4
Alderney Hospl
　BH12 . . . . **376** C2
Alderney Rdbt BH12. **376** D2
Alder Rd
　Headley GU35 . . . . . . **165** F6
　Poole BH12 . . . . **391** F6
　Southampton SO16 . . **266** A4
Alders Ct SO24 . . . . . **179** D6
Aldersey Flds GU34 . **139** F5
Aldershot Ho **31**
　PO9 . . . . **324** B5
Aldershot Military Mus ✷
　GU11 . . . . **77** A7
Aldershot Rd
　Ash GU12 . . . . **77** D1
　Fleet,Church Crookham
　GU52 . . . . **75** C5
　Fleet GU51 . . . . **75** B8
Aldershot Sta GU11 . . **76** F1
Alders Rd PO16 . . . . . **343** B2
Alders The GU9 . . . . . . **99** F6
Alderwood RG24 . . . . **48** F3
Alderwood Ave
　SO53 . . . . **243** A6
Alderwood Cl PO9 . . **323** D3
Alder Wood Dr RG27 . **51** B2
Aldis Gdns BH15 . . . . **389** E2
Aldrich Rd PO1 . . . . . **370** A6
Aldridge Cl PO8 . . . . **276** C5
Aldridge Rd
　Bournemouth BH10 . . **377** C5

Aldridge Rd *continued*
　Ferndown BH22. . . . . **353** E3
Aldridge Way BH22 . **353** F3
Aldrin Cl SP10 . . . . **82** E3
Aldrin Pl GU14 . . . . **55** B4
Aldroke St **1** PO6 . . . **345** F7
Aldsworth Cl PO6 . . . **346** E8
Aldsworth Common Rd
　PO10 . . . . **325** C6
Aldsworth Gdns PO6 **346** C8
Aldwell St PO5 . . . . . **404** C2
Aldwick Cl GU14 . . . . . **55** E6
Aldworth Cres RG22 . . .**68** E4
Aldworth Science Coll
　RG22 . . . . **68** D2
Aldwych Cotts RG14 . . .1 D6
Alec Rose Ho **17**
　PO12 . . . . **369** C5
Alec Rose La PO1 . . . **404** B3
Alecto Rd PO12 . . . . **369** B4
Alec Wintle Ho PO2 . **370** D8
Alencon Cl **3** PO12 . **369** C9
Alencon Link RG21 . . . **69** B5
Alexander Cl
　Christchurch BH23 . . **395** E6
　Houghton SO20 . . . . . **171** B5
　Totton SO40 . . . . **288** D8
　Waterlooville PO7 . . . **322** D6
Alexander Ct
　4 Newbury RG14 . . . . .1 F2
　Southampton SO15 . . **290** D6
　Southampton,Woolston
　SO19 . . . . **291** E2
Alexander Gr PO16 . . **343** A8
Alexander Ho
　6 North Tidworth
　SP9 . . . . **78** E8
　South Hayling PO11 . . **373** E1
Alexander Rd RG25 . . . **88** B7
Alexander Terr RG29 . **72** C4
Alexandra Ave
　Camberley GU15 . . . . . **35** E5
　South Hayling PO11. . **372** F2
Alexandra Cl SO45 . . **314** A4
Alexandra Ct
　10 Farnborough
　GU14 . . . . **56** A1
　4 Portsmouth PO4. . **370** E1
　Aldershot GU11 . . . . . . **76** C1
　Bordon GU35 . . . . . . **164** E3
　Hamble-le-R SO31 . . . **315** F3
Alexandra Ho
　1 Basingstoke
　RG21 . . . . **69** C6
　Enham Alamein SP11 . **83** B8
Alexandra Lodge **8**
　BH1 . . . . **393** A3
Alexandra Mews
　SO15 . . . . **290** E7
Alexandra Rd
　Aldershot GU11 . . . . . . **76** C1
　Alton GU34 . . . . **139** F5
　Andover SP10 . . . . . . **105** F8
　Ash GU12 . . . . **77** D1
　Basingstoke RG21 . . . . **68** F5
　Bournemouth BH6. . . **394** C5
　Chandler's Ford SO53 **243** F8
　Farnborough GU14 . . . **56** A1
　Fordingbridge SP6. . . **257** F2
　Hedge End SO30 . . . . **293** B5
　Hythe SO45 . . . . **314** A4
　Lymington SO41 . . . . **385** C5
　Poole BH14 . . . . **391** D5
　Portsmouth PO1 . . . . **404** C4
　Southampton SO15 . . **290** E6
Alexandra St **7**
　PO12 . . . . **369** A7
Alexandra Terr
　6 Aldershot GU11 . . . **76** C2
　Winchester SO23 . . . **403** D5
Alexandra Way SO30 **294** A7
Alexandria Ct BH22 . **353** E3
Alexandria Pk PO9. . **347** E7
Alexandria Rd SO21 . **131** D5
Alfonso Cl GU12 . . . . **100** A8
Alford Cl GU47 . . . .**34** E7
Alford Rd BH3 . . . . . . **392** D7
Alfred Cl
　Fleet GU51 . . . . **53** D3
　Totton SO40 . . . . **288** C7
Alfred Gdns SP10 . . . .**82** D7
Alfred Rd
　Farnham GU9 . . . . **99** A4
　Portsmouth PO1 . . . . **404** A4
　Stubbington PO14 . . . **367** D8
Alfred Rose Ct SO18. **267** E4
Alfred St SO14 . . . . . **291** B6
Alfrey Cl PO10 . . . . . **349** D8
Alfriston Ct SO19 . . . **292** C4
Alfriston Gdns SO19. **292** B4
Algiers Rd PO3 . . . . . **371** B8
Alhambra Rd PO4 . . . **370** C1
Alice Holt Cotts
　GU10 . . . . **120** F2
Alice Holt Woodland
Park Forest Ctr ✷
　GU10. . . . . **143** A8
Alice in Wonderland
Family Fun Park ✷
　BH23. . . . . **378** E7
Alice Rd GU11 . . . .**76** F2
Alington **22** BH4 . . . **392** C3

Alington Cl BH14..... 402 C7
Alington Ho BH14..... 402 C7
Alington Manor Farm
  Cotts SO50....... 268 F7
Alington Rd
  Bournemouth BH3... 393 A6
  Poole BH14....... 402 C7
Alipore Cl BH14.. 391 D3
Alipore Hts BH14 .. 391 D3
Alison Cl GU14..... 55 D3
Alison Dr GU15..... 36 D5
Alison's Rd GU11....76 F4
Alison Way
  6 Winchester
  SO22........... 403 D6
  Aldershot GU11.....76 D2
Allan Gr SO51...... 241 B7
Allaway Ave PO6..... 345 B8
Allbrook Hill SO50.. 244 A7
Allbrook Knoll SO50. 244 A7
Allbrook Way SO50.. 244 B7
Allcot Rd PO3....... 346 A2
Allden Ave GU12... 100 B7
Allden Gdns GU12... 100 B7
Allee Dr GU30...... 187 F5
Allenbourn Mid Sch
  BH21........... 351 C5
Allenby Cl BH17.... 375 B2
Allenby Gr PO16.... 344 C7
Allenby Rd
  Gosport PO12...... 368 E6
  Poole BH17....... 375 B2
  Sandhurst GU15.....35 E6
Allen Cl
  Alton GU34....... 140 A5
  Basingstoke RG21....68 F3
Allen Ct BH21...... 351 C5
Allendale Ave GU14. 324 E3
Allen Gallery★ GU34 139 F3
Allen Rd
  Hedge End SO30.... 293 C7
  Wimborne Minster
  BH21........... 351 C4
Allens Farm La SO32 249 B6
Allens La
  Meonstoke SO32.... 249 C5
  Upton RG21....... 389 D5
Allens Rd BH16..... 389 D6
Allen's Rd PO4..... 370 E2
Allenview Rd BH21.. 351 C5
Allenwater Dr SP6.. 257 E2
Allerton Cl SO40.... 264 D1
Alley The
  Bishopstone SP5.... 210 B8
  Woodgreen SP6..... 258 E8
All Hallows RC Sch
  GU9............. 99 D7
Alliance Cl PO13.... 368 D8
Alliance Ho PO1.... 370 E6
Allington La SO30... 268 C5
Allington Manor Farm
  Bsns Ctr SO50..... 268 E7
Allington Manor Sch
  SO50........... 268 F7
Allington Rd SO15.. 289 D7
Allison Ct **6** SO41.. 399 B4
Allison Ho SO30.... 293 C8
Alliston Way
  Basingstoke RG22... 68 B3
  Whitchurch RG28....86 D4
Allmara Dr PO7..... 322 F4
Allnutt Ave RG21.... 69 C5
Allotment Rd
  Hedge End SO30.... 293 B6
  Sarisbury SO31.... 316 C6
All Saints CE Jun Sch
  GU51............ 74 D8
All Saints CE Prim Sch
  SO23........... 403 F4
All Saints Cres **4** SO14. 35 C1
All Saints Ho **7**
  SO14........... 291 A3
All Saints Rd SO41.. 385 F2
All Saint's Rd PO1.. 370 D7
All Saint's St PO1... 404 B4
Allyn Ct SO50...... 244 B5
Alma Cl GU12.......77 B2
Alma Ho
  Aldershot GU12.....77 B2
  Southampton SO14.. 291 A8
Alma La
  Farnham GU9...... 99 A7
  Upham SO32...... 246 B2
Alma Rd
  Bordon GU35...... 164 E3
  Bournemouth BH9... 393 A7
  Headley GU35..... 166 A6
  Romsey SO51...... 240 F7
  Southampton SO14.. 291 A8
Alma Sq GU14.......77 A8
Alma St PO12...... 369 B7
Almatade Rd SO18... 292 A4
Alma Terr PO4...... 371 A3
Alma Way GU9.......99 B7
Almer Rd BH15..... 389 E3
Almondale Ct GU14...55 E6
Almond Ave RG14.....1 E5
Almond Cl
  2 Farnborough
  GU14........... 55 E7
  Havant PO9....... 346 F8
  Old Basing RG24....70 A6
  Waterlooville PO8.. 300 C4
Almond Ct
  10 Southampton
  SO15........... 290 C6
  Fleet GU52........ 75 B6

Almond Gr BH12.... 391 D7
Almond Rd SO15.... 290 C6
Almondsbury Ho **8**
  PO6............. 320 F2
Almondsbury Rd
  PO6............. 320 F2
Almondside PO13.... 343 D6
Almshouses
  2 Basingstoke
  RG21........... 69 B4
  Bournemouth BH10.. 377 C1
  East Tisted GU34... 183 C5
Almswood Rd RG26...75 E2
Aloes The GU51......75 B8
Alpha Ctr The BH17. 390 B7
Alphage Rd PO12.... 343 F1
Alpha Rd GU12.......77 B1
Alphington Ave GU16. 36 D1
Alphington Gn GU16. 36 D1
Alpine Cl
  Farnborough GU14... 55 B3
  Southampton SO18.. 292 B8
Alpine Ct RG22......68 B3
Alpine Rd
  Bordon GU35...... 164 D1
  St Leonards BH24... 328 C2
  Woodlands SO40... 287 F3
Alresford Dro SO21. 153 F5
Alresford Rd
  Chilcomb SO21.... 199 D7
  Havant PO9....... 323 E4
  Ovington SO24..... 178 E2
  Winchester SO23... 198 D7
Alresford Sta★
  SO24........... 179 D5
Alsace Wlk GU15.....35 F1
Alsford Rd PO7..... 322 D5
Alswitha Terr **12**
  SO23........... 403 E7
Alten Rd PO7....... 299 C2
Althorpe Dr PO3.... 346 C4
Altona Gdns SP10....82 F3
Alton Bsns Ctr GU34 140 B3
Alton Cl SO50...... 245 B2
Alton Coll GU34.... 139 F5
Alton Com Hospl
  GU34........... 139 D1
Alton Convent Sch
  GU34........... 140 A6
Alton Ct **13** SO23.... 403 E8
Alton Gr PO16..... 344 C6
Alton Ho SO18..... 291 E8
Alton Inf Sch GU34.. 140 A4
Alton La GU34..... 160 C1
Alton Rd
  Bournemouth BH10.. 377 B1
  Farnham GU10.... 121 C7
  Fleet GU51....... 75 C8
  Odiham RG29..... 95 B6
  Poole BH14...... 391 C3
Alton Rd E BH14... 391 D2
Alton Ride GU17.....35 A6
Alton Road Cotts
  RG29............ 94 F3
Alton Sta GU34.... 140 A4
Alum Chine Rd BH4. 392 B3
Alum Cl SO45...... 338 D3
Alumdale Rd BH4... 392 B2
Alumhurst Rd BH4.. 392 B2
Alum Way
  Portchester PO16... 319 E1
  Southampton SO18.. 292 B7
Alvandi Gdns **2**
  BH25........... 383 B3
Alvara Rd PO12.... 369 A3
Alver Bridge View **4**
  PO12........... 369 B4
Alvercliffe Dr PO12.. 368 F2
Alver Quay PO12... 369 B4
Alver Rd
  Gosport PO12..... 369 B4
  Portsmouth PO1... 370 E6
Alverstoke CE Jun Sch
  PO12........... 369 A4
Alverstoke Com Inf Sch
  PO12........... 369 A4
Alverstoke Ct PO12. 369 A3
Alverstoke Gdns
  GU11........... 76 C1
Alverstone Rd PO4.. 371 A5
Alverton Ave BH15.. 390 F3
Alverton Hall **13**
  BH4............ 392 C2
Alveston Ave PO14.. 342 D8
Alwin Pl GU9.......99 A7
Alyne Ho SO15..... 290 F4
Alyth Rd BH3...... 392 D6
Amarylis Cl PO15... 317 E4
Amazon Cl RG21.....68 F4
Ambassador Cl
  BH23........... 396 A6
Ambassador Ind Est
  BH23........... 396 A6
Amber Cl GU35..... 164 E2
Amber Ct **2** GU12.... 77 B1
Amber Gdns SP10... 105 D8
Amber Hill GU15.....36 F1
Amberley Cl
  Botley SO30...... 294 A8
  Christchurch BH23.. 396 F6
  Newbury RG14......1 D4
  North Baddesley
  SO52........... 241 E5
Amberley Ct
  10 Bournemouth
  BH1............ 393 A3
  3 Knowle Village
  PO17........... 318 E7

Amberley Ct continued
  Totton SO40...... 288 E6
Amberley Grange
  GU11............ 99 D8
Amberley Ho BH22.. 353 D7
Amberley Mains **4**
  GU34........... 139 E4
Amberley Rd
  Bournemouth BH6... 276 D5
  Gosport PO12..... 369 A9
  Portsmouth PO2... 345 F3
Amber Rd BH21..... 374 C4
Amberslade Wlk
  SO45........... 313 F1
Amberwood
  Ferndown BH22.... 353 E7
  Milford on S SO41.. 399 B5
Amberwood Cl SO40 264 C2
Amberwood Dr
  Camberley GU15.... 36 D7
  Christchurch BH23.. 381 F2
Amberwood Gdns
  BH23........... 382 A2
Amberwood Ho
  BH23........... 382 A2
Ambleside
  Bishop's Waltham
  SO32........... 271 A8
  Christchurch BH23.. 379 E3
  Hedge End SO30... 293 D5
Ambleside Cl
  Farnborough GU14.. 55 C3
  Mytchett GU16.....56 E2
Ambleside Cres GU9 .98 E6
Ambleside Gdns
  SO19........... 292 A3
Ambleside Rd SO41. 385 F3
Ambrose Rd RG26... 26 F8
Ambury La BH23.... 395 F8
Amersham Ct PO12. 368 E4
Amersham Ct **37**
  BH4............ 392 C3
Amery Hill GU34.... 139 E4
Amery Hill Sch GU34 139 F4
Amery St GU34..... 139 F4
Amesbury Ho **3** SP9 . 79 A6
Amesbury Rd
  Bournemouth BH6... 394 C6
  Cholderton SP4.... 101 B1
  Newton Tony SP4... 123 A6
  Weyhill SP11...... 81 B1
Amethyst Gr PO7... 323 B8
Amethyst Rd BH23.. 395 F7
Amey Gdns SO40... 264 D1
Amey Ind Est GU32. 228 E3
Ameysford Rd
  Ameysford BH22... 326 B1
  Ferndown BH22.... 353 C7
Ameys La BH22..... 353 F7
Amherst Rd GU35... 164 D6
Amira Ct **2** BH2.... 392 E3
Amoy St SO15...... 290 F6
Ampere Rd RG14......1 F1
Ampfield CE Prim Sch
  SO51........... 217 C3
Ampfield Cl PO9.... 323 B4
Ampfield Ct **1** SO53 218 B1
Ampfield Rd BH8... 378 D3
Amport CE Prim Sch
  SP11........... 104 A5
Amport Cl
  Old Basing RG24....70 A8
  Winchester SO22... 175 C3
Amport Ct PO9..... 323 D6
Amport Firs SP11... 104 A5
Amport Park Mews
  SP11........... 103 F5
Ampress La SO41... 385 D6
Ampress Pk SO41... 385 D6
Ampthill Rd SO15... 290 D7
Amsterdam Sq BH23 395 D6
Amyas Ct PO4..... 371 C4
Ancasta Rd SO14... 291 B7
Ancells Ct GU51.....54 C5
Ancells Rd GU51.....54 C5
Anchorage Rd PO3.. 346 B3
Anchorage The
  PO12........... 369 C5
Anchorage Way
  SO41........... 385 D3
Anchor Cl
  Bournemouth BH11.. 376 F6
  Christchurch BH23.. 396 A5
Anchor Ct PO11.... 373 C7
Anchor Gate Rd PO1 370 A6
Anchor La PO1..... 370 A6
Anchor Mdw GU12.. 77 B1
Anchor Mews SO41. 385 E4
Anchor Rd
  Bournemouth BH11.. 376 F5
  Kingsclere RG20....24 D2
Anchor Yd
  1 Basingstoke
  RG21........... 69 B4
  Kingsclere RG20....24 D2
Ancrum Lo **15** BH4.. 392 B3
Andalusian Gdns
  PO15........... 317 B8
Andbourne Ct BH6.. 394 F3
Andeferas Rd SP10...82 E7
Anderby Rd SO16... 265 D2
Anderson Cl
  Havant PO9....... 324 A3
  Romsey SO51..... 216 C2
  Swanwick PO15.... 317 C8
Anderson Ho GU9...99 B1

Anderson's Rd SO14 291 B3
Anders Rd SO21.... 153 A3
Anderwood Dr SO41 360 B2
Andes Cl SO14..... 291 C3
Andes Rd SO16..... 265 B3
Andlers Ash Rd
  GU33........... 207 E3
Andover CE Prim Sch
  SP10........... 106 B7
Andover Cl BH23... 396 B7
Andover Dr **3** GU51.. 53 D3
Andover Dro RG20...4 F4
Andover La SP11.....80 A7
Andover Rd
  Blackwater GU17... 35 A6
  Fyfield SP11...... 80 E6
  Ludgershall SP11... 57 B1
  Micheldever SO21.. 111 A2
  Monxton SP11.... 104 D6
  Newbury RG20......5 B6
  Oakley RG23,RG25.. 66 D1
  Portsmouth PO4... 370 F2
  Southampton SO15.. 290 D6
  Wash Water RG20.....4 E1
  Winchester SO23... 403 D8
Andover Road N
  SO22........... 175 E4
Andover Road Ret Pk
  SO23........... 403 D7
Andover Sta SP10.. 105 F8
Andover War Meml
  Hospl SP10....... 82 E1
Andover Way GU11...99 F7
Andre Ct BH23..... 397 B8
Andrewartha Rd
  GU14........... 56 C2
Andrew Bell St PO1. 404 B4
Andrew Cl
  3 Hythe SO45.... 314 A1
  North Warnborough
  RG29........... 72 B3
  Portsmouth PO1... 370 F6
  Totton SO40...... 288 D7
Andrew Cres PO7... 299 D1
Andrew Ct GU14.... 55 B8
Andrewes Cl SO32.. 271 C8
Andrew La BH25.... 383 D2
Andrew Pl PO14.... 367 B7
Andrews Cl
  Bournemouth BH11.. 377 A3
  Fleet GU52....... 75 A6
Andrews Endowed CE
  Prim Sch GU34... 140 C6
Andrew's La
  Gilbert Street SO24. 181 F5
  Long Sutton RG29... 95 F3
Andrew's Lodge
  SO41........... 385 D5
Andrews Rd SO41... 385 D5
Andrews Way SO31.. 316 B8
Androse Gdns BH24. 328 F6
Andwell La RG24,RG27 71 A6
Anfield Cl SO50.... 245 C1
Anfield Ct SO50.... 245 B1
Angela Cl PO9..... 323 F4
Angel Cres SO18... 292 A6
Angel Ct
  Lymington SO41... 385 E4
  Newbury RG14......1 E4
Angelica Ct PO7.... 323 A6
Angelica Gdns SO50. 269 C7
Angelica Way PO15. 317 E8
Angeline BH23..... 396 F8
Angel La
  Barton on S BH25.. 398 D8
  Ferndown BH22.... 353 B3
Angel Mdws RG29...72 E3
Angel Mews BH15... 390 B2
Angelo Cl PO7..... 323 A8
Angelus Cl PO14... 367 C7
Angerstein Rd PO2.. 345 D1
Anglers Way SO31.. 316 B8
Anglesea Pl PO1.... 370 B5
Anglesea Ct SO15.. 266 B1
Anglesea Rd
  Lee-on-t-S PO13... 368 A4
  Portsmouth PO1... 404 A3
  Southampton SO15.. 266 B1
Anglesea Terr SO14. 291 B3
Anglesey Arms Rd
  PO12........... 369 A3
Anglesey Ave GU11.. 55 D7
Anglesey Cl
  Andover SP10.... 106 A5
  Basingstoke RG24.. 48 C2
Anglesey Rd
  Aldershot GU12.....77 B1
  Gosport PO12.... 369 A3
Anglesey View **1**
  PO12........... 369 B4
Anglewood Mans **2**
  BH4............ 392 C3
Anglo-European Coll of
  Chiropractic BH5.. 394 A4
Angmering Ho **2**
  PO1............ 404 B3
Angora Way GU51... 54 B4
Angus Cl PO15..... 318 E3
Anjou Cl BH11..... 376 D5
Anjou Cres PO15... 318 D2
Anker La PO14..... 342 C4
Ankerwyke PO13.... 343 B1
Anmore Cl PO9..... 323 C5
Anmore Cnr PO7... 299 B4
Anmore Dr PO7.... 299 D2
Anmore La PO7,PO8. 299 C5
Anmore Rd PO7.... 299 A4

Anna La BH23...... 356 B4
Annandale Cl BH23. 394 D4
Annandale Dr GU10. 122 B6
Anne Armstrong Cl
  GU11............ 77 B5
Anne Cl BH23..... 380 A1
Anne Cres PO7.... 322 E6
Annerley Rd BH1... 393 C4
Annes Ct PO12.... 372 E2
Annes Way GU52....75 B6
Annet Cl BH15.... 389 E2
Annettes Croft **2**
  GU52........... 74 E4
Ann's Hill Rd PO12. 369 A6
Ansell Rd GU16.....36 C1
Anson Cl
  Aldershot GU11.....76 D3
  Christchurch BH23.. 395 F6
  Gosport PO13.... 368 D5
  Ringwood BH24... 329 C8
Anson Ct **22** PO1... 370 A4
Anson Dr SO19.... 292 C5
Anson Gr PO16.... 320 E1
Anson Ho SO14.... 291 B3
Anson Rd
  1 Portsmouth
  PO4............ 371 A5
  Horton Heath SO50. 269 C7
Anstey Cl
  Basingstoke RG21... 69 A2
  Bournemouth BH11.. 377 A6
Anstey Jun Sch
  GU34........... 139 F4
Anstey La GU34.... 140 A4
Anstey Mill Cl GU34. 140 B5
Anstey Mill La GU34. 140 B5
Anstey Rd
  Alton GU34...... 140 A5
  Bournemouth BH11.. 377 A5
  Romsey SO51.... 216 B1
Antar Cl RG21..... 68 F8
Antell's Way SP6... 281 A6
Anthill Cl PO7..... 298 C6
Anthony Gr PO12... 344 A1
Anthony's Ave BH14. 391 C1
Anthony Way PO10.. 324 F3
Antigua Ho **5** PO6.. 320 F2
Antler Dr BH25.... 382 E4
Anton Cl
  Oakley RG23..... 67 B1
  Romsey SO51.... 241 C7
Anton Inf Sch SP10. 106 A6
Anton Jun Sch SP10 106 A6
Anton La SP11.....83 B6
Anton Mill Rd SP10. 106 A7
Anton Rd SP10.... 106 A7
Anton Trad Est SP10 106 A7
Antrim Cl RG22.....68 B3
Anvil Cl
  East Meon GU32... 251 E8
  Waterlooville PO7.. 300 C1
  West End SO30.... 268 C2
Anvil Cres BH18.... 374 F5
Anvil Ct PO4...... 371 A4
Anvil Way RG26.....28 F3
Anzac Cl PO14.... 342 C4
Apex Ctr PO14.... 343 A5
Apex Dr GU16......36 B1
Apless La PO7..... 298 A4
Apollo Cl BH12.... 391 D7
Apollo Dr
  Bordon GU35..... 164 E2
  Waterlooville PO7.. 322 F1
Apollo Ho RG7......9 C2
Apollonia Ho **7**
  SP10........... 106 A7
Apollo Rd SO53.... 243 F7
Apollo Rise GU14... 55 B4
Apple Cl BH13..... 392 A4
Apple Dene RG26...28 F2
Apple Gr
  Christchurch BH23.. 379 E2
  Emsworth PO10.... 349 B8
Apple Ind Est PO15. 317 D4
Applelands Cl GU10. 121 E4
Applemore Coll
  SO45........... 313 C3
Appleshaw Cl
  Fareham PO15.... 318 D1
  Southampton SO18.. 267 E1
Appleshaw Dene
  SP11........... 81 B6
Appleshaw Way SP11 79 D6
Appleslade Way
  BH25........... 383 B5
Appleton Cl SO20.. 125 C2
Appleton Mews
  SP10........... 106 B6
Appleton Rd
  Fareham PO15.... 318 D1
  Southampton SO18.. 267 E1
Appleton View GU34 183 D5
Appletree Cl
  Bournemouth BH5.. 395 C5
  New Milton BH25... 383 A1
  Oakley RG23......90 B8
  Totton SO40...... 264 C1
Apple Tree Cl
  Newbury RG14.....5 C7

Apple Tree Cl continued
  Redlynch SP5..... 235 D7
Appletree Ct SO30.. 294 A7
Apple Tree Gr
  Andover SP10.....82 E1
  Ferndown BH22.... 353 E6
Appletree Mead RG27 51 C1
Appletree Rd SP5... 235 D7
Apple Tree Rd SP6.. 280 F5
Apple Way RG24.....70 B5
Applewood SO31... 317 A5
Applewood Gdns
  SO19........... 292 A3
Applewood Gr PO7.. 322 C3
Applewood Pl SO40 288 C6
Applewood Rd PO9. 323 C3
Appley Ct **1** GU15...35 F5
Appley Dr GU15.....35 F6
Appollo Ct PO5.... 404 B2
Appollo Pl SO18.... 292 A7
Approach Rd
  Farnham GU9...... 99 A1
  Poole BH14...... 391 B3
Approach The PO3.. 346 A1
April Cl
  Bournemouth BH11.. 377 A4
  Camberley GU15....36 A2
  Southampton SO18.. 292 B7
April Gdns SO45.... 338 C1
April Gr SO31..... 316 E3
April Sq PO1...... 404 C4
Apron Rd RG19......6 E5
Apsley Cl SP10.... 105 F5
Apsley Cres BH17.. 375 C4
Apsley Ct **2** BH8... 393 A5
Apsley Ho **1** GU11...76 F2
Apsley Pl **11** SO53. 218 B1
Apsley Rd PO4..... 371 A4
Aquarius Cl GU10...74 B2
Aquila Way SO31... 315 F2
Aquitania Ho **6**
  SO14........... 291 C5
Arabian Gdns PO15. 317 C7
Aragon Rd GU46....34 A4
Aragon Way BH9... 378 B4
Arbery Way RG2.... 15 C8
Arboretum The RG25 .94 B6
Arbour Ct
  20 Winchester
  SO22........... 403 E6
  Whiteley PO15.... 294 E1
Arcade BH4....... 392 B3
Arcade Mews **4** RG14..1 E3
Arcade The
  10 Aldershot GU11.. 76 E2
  14 Bournemouth BH1 392 F3
  3 Newbury RG14.....1 E3
  Liss GU33....... 207 E5
Arcadia Ave BH8... 393 B7
Arcadia Cl
  Basingstoke RG22... 91 A4
  Southampton SO16.. 266 B3
Arcadia Rd BH23... 379 F1
Archdale Cl BH10... 377 D2
Archer Ho PO12.... 369 C2
Archers **1** SO15.... 290 E6
Archers Cl SO40... 264 C1
Archers Rd
  Eastleigh SO50.... 244 A3
  Southampton SO15.. 290 F7
Archery Fields SO23 .72 F3
Archery Gdns SO19. 291 F2
Archery Gr SO19... 291 F2
Archery La
  Fareham PO16.... 319 C2
  Winchester SO23... 403 D5
Archery Rd SO19... 291 E1
Archery Rise GU34. 139 E2
Arch Farm Ind Site
  SP6............ 257 C2
Archgate SO41..... 385 E4
Archway Rd BH14.. 391 E4
Arcot Rd SP9......78 E3
Arden Cl
  6 Gosport PO12.. 368 F4
  Southampton SO18.. 268 B1
Arden Rd BH9..... 377 F3
Arden Wlk BH25... 383 B2
Ardglen Rd RG28....86 C6
Ardingly Cres SO30. 269 D2
Ardington Rise PO7. 322 E3
Ardmore Rd BH14.. 391 D4
Ardnave Cres SO16.. 266 F5
Ardrossan Ave GU15 .36 E5
Arena Bsns Ctr BH17 390 B8
Arena La GU11..... 76 C5
Arena L Ctr GU15...36 A5
Arethusa Ho **18** PO1. 370 A4
Arford Comm
  Headley GU35.... 165 D6
  Headley GU35.... 165 E6
Arford Rd GU35.... 165 D5
Argente Cl GU51.....54 B4
Argent Terr GU47....35 C8
Argosy Cl SO31.... 316 F1
Argus Rd PO13.... 367 F4
Argyle Cl GU35.... 164 D2
Argyle Cres PO15.. 318 F2
Argyle Rd
  Christchurch BH23.. 395 E5
  Newbury RG14......1 D2
  Southampton SO14.. 291 B5
Argyll Ct **2** GU51... 54 A1
Argyll Mans **8** BH5. 393 E4

Argyll Rd
Bournemouth BH5......393 E4
Poole BH12.........391 D6
Ariel Cl BH6.........395 B4
Ariel Dr BH6.........395 B4
Ariel Rd PO1........370 E5
Arismore Ct PO13....367 D4
Ark Dr BH22.........353 F3
Ark Royal Cres PO13 367 E4
Arkle Ave RG19.......2 D3
Arkwright Cl RG20....21 D6
Arkwright Gate SP10..82 B2
Arlebury Park Ho
SO24.............179 B6
Arle Cl
Clanfield PO8.......276 C4
New Alresford SO24 .179 C8
Arle Gdns SO24......179 D6
Arley Rd BH4........391 E7
Arlington Ct BH25...398 B8
Arlington Pl [3] SO23 403 E6
Arlington Terr GU11 .76 D1
Arliss Rd SO16......266 A1
Arlott Cl RG27.......33 C8
Arlott Ct SO15......290 E7
Arlott Dr RG21........69 B7
Armada Cl SO16......265 E7
Armada Dr SO45......313 F2
Armadale Ho [20]
SO14.............291 C6
Armfield Ho [20]
SO17.............267 A1
Arminers Cl PO12....369 B2
Armitage Ave SO45 .313 F1
Armitage Dr GU16....36 D1
Armory La PO1.......290 A3
Armoury The SO40...290 A3
Armstrong Cl
[1] Gosport PO12.....369 C6
Brockenhurst SO42...333 E1
South Wonston SO21.153 E4
Waterlooville PO7....299 D1
Armstrong Ct SO16...265 F5
Armstrong La SO42...333 E1
Armstrong Mall GU14 .55 B4
Armstrong Rd
Basingstoke RG24....69 E7
Brockenhurst SO42...333 E1
Armstrong Rise SP10..82 E3
Armstrong Way GU14 .75 F8
Armsworth La PO7,
SO32.............273 E1
Arnaud Cl PO2.......370 D7
Arne Ave BH12.......391 E7
Arne Cl RG22.........91 D7
Arne Cres BH12.......391 F7
Arnell Ct [2] GU14...77 B8
Arnett Ave RG40......16 D7
Arnewood Ave RG26 ..27 B8
Arnewood Bridge Rd
SO41.............384 B7
Arnewood Ct SO41...384 C6
Arnewood Ct BH2....392 E2
Arnewood Ho SO41 .384 C3
Arnewood Rd BH6....394 D5
Arnewood Sch The
BH25.............382 F2
Arnheim Cl SO16......266 D4
Arnheim Rd SO16......266 D4
Arnhem Cl GU11.......76 F2
Arnhem Rd RG14.......1 F3
Arnold Cl BH22.......326 E3
Arnold Rd
Eastleigh SO50....268 A8
Southampton SO17...267 C2
West Moors BH22....326 E3
Arnolds Cl BH25.....397 F8
Arnside Rd PO7.......322 E8
Arnwood Ave SO45...337 F8
Arragon Ct PO7......323 A8
Arran Cl
Oakley RG23.........67 A2
Portsmouth PO6.....321 F1
Arran Way BH23.......382 B1
Arras Ho PO15.......318 C3
Arreton SO31.........315 C6
Arreton Ct [3] PO12 .369 A6
Arrow Cl
Eastleigh SO50....244 A4
Southampton SO19...291 D1
Arrow Ind Est GU14..55 D2
Arrow La RG27........52 B7
Arrow Rd GU14.......55 D2
Arrowsmith Ct BH18 375 A4
Arrowsmith La BH21 375 E7
Arrowsmith Rd
BH21.............375 E7
Artemis Rd RG14.......1 F4
Arters Lawn SO40....312 C6
Arthur Cl
Bournemouth BH2....392 F6
Farnham GU9.........98 F1
Arthur Ct
[4] Basingstoke
RG21.............69 A5
Four Marks GU34....160 B3
Arthur Kille Ho PO7 .322 D6
Arthur La [3] BH23...395 A7
Arthur Pope Ho PO7 404 C2
Arthur Rd
Christchurch BH23...395 A7
Eastleigh SO50.....244 A4
Farnham GU9........99 A1
Newbury RG14.........1 C2
Southampton SO15...290 D6

Arthur Rd continued
Winchester SO23....403 E7
Arthurs Gdns SO30...269 B3
Arthur's La SP11......20 A1
Arthur St
Aldershot GU11.......76 F2
Portsmouth PO2.....370 D7
Artillery Cl [1] PO6 .345 C8
Artillery Rd
Aldershot GU11.......76 F2
Farnborough GU14....77 B3
Artillery Terr [2] PO4 371 B4
Artists Way SO41.....83 A1
Arts Inst of Bournemouth
The BH12...........392 C8
Arun Cl GU31.........228 E2
Arun Ct RG21.........69 D5
Arundel
Fleet GU51..........75 B8
Liphook GU30.......187 B8
New Alresford SO24 .179 D4
New Milton BH25....382 E3
Arundel Ct Inf Sch
PO1..............404 C4
Arundel Ct Jun Sch
PO1..............404 C4
Arundel Dr PO16.....319 A2
Arundel Gdns RG23 ..68 B7
Arundel Ho
[18] Southampton,Northam
SO14.............291 C6
Southampton,Banister's Pk
SO15.............290 F8
Arundel Pl [8] GU9...98 F2
Arundel Rd
Eastleigh SO50.....244 A6
Gosport PO12.......368 F5
Totton SO40.......289 A8
Arundel St PO1......404 C3
Arundel Way BH23...396 F7
Arundel Way Sh Arc
PO1..............404 B3
Arun Rd SO18........268 B2
Arun Way SO51.......238 D3
Ascension Cl RG24....48 D1
Ascham Rd BH8......393 B6
Ascot Cl
Alton GU34.........140 A2
Newbury RG14........6 A8
Titchfield PO14.....317 C2
Ascot Ct GU11.......76 E1
Ascot Rd
Broadstone BH18...375 A4
Horton Heath SO50..269 D7
Portsmouth PO3.....371 A7
Ascott Way RG14.......2 B4
Ascupart Ho [6]
SO17.............291 B8
Ascupart St SO14....291 B4
Asford Gr SO50.......244 D4
Ashbarn Cres SO22 ..403 C3
Ashbourne Ct [1]
BH1..............393 A3
Ashbourne Rd BH5...396 B5
Ashbourne Way RG19 .2 E3
Ash Bridge Cvn Pk
GU12.............100 C8
Ashbridge Rise
SO53.............218 B1
Ashburn Garth BH24 329 D6
Ashburnham Cl
SO19.............291 D5
Ashburn Pl SP6......257 E1
Ashburton Cl
Hythe SO45........313 D3
New Alresford SO24 .179 C5
Ashburton Ct PO5....404 B1
Ashburton Gdns
BH10.............377 D1
Ashburton Ho SO31 .315 B6
Ashburton Rd
Gosport PO12.......368 F2
New Alresford SO24 .179 C5
Portsmouth PO5.....370 C2
Ashbury Dr GU47......35 E1
Ashbury Rd GU35....164 D2
Ashby Cres SO40.....288 D2
Ashby Pl PO5........370 C2
Ashby Rd
Southampton SO19...292 B3
Totton SO40.......288 D2
Ash Church Mews
GU12.............77 E2
Ash Church Rd GU12 .77 E2
Ash Cl
Alderholt SP6......281 A5
Ash GU12..........77 F3
Blackwater GU17....35 A5
Bursledon SO31....315 F8
Colden Common
SO21.............220 A1
Fareham PO14......342 E8
Gosport PO12.......369 B5
Hythe SO45........338 A8
North Baddesley
SO52.............241 F5
North Tidworth SP9..79 A7
Romsey SO51.......241 C6
Southampton SO19...292 C6
Upton BH16.......389 B8
Waterlooville PO8...299 C2
Ash Copse PO8.......299 F5
Ash Cres RG19........7 E5
Ashcroft Ct [2] SO22 228 F4
Ashcroft La PO8......301 D6
Ash Ct [8] RG14......1 E4
Ashdell Rd GU34....140 A3
Ashdene [17] SO15...290 B8

Ashdene Cl BH21.....351 D5
Ashdene Cres GU12...77 E3
Ashdene Rd
Ash SO41...........77 E2
Ashurst SO40......288 C3
Ashdown
[8] Bournemouth
BH2..............392 D2
Fawley SO45.......338 F3
Gosport PO13......343 D1
Ashdown Ave GU14 ..56 C2
Ashdown Cl
Chandler's Ford
SO53.............218 C2
Ashdown Dr SO53.....218 C2
Ashdown Rd
Blackfield SO45....338 F2
Chandler's Ford SO53 218 C2
Ashdown Tech Coll
BH17.............375 D4
Ashdown Terr SP9...78 F5
Ashdown Way SO51...241 B7
Ashdown Wlk BH25...383 C2
Ashen Cl SO53.......243 C8
Ashe Rd PO9.........324 B5
Ashfield RG24........48 F3
Ashfield Gn GU46....34 D5
Ashfield Rd SP10....105 D8
Ashfields SO21......130 D6
Ashfield View SO52..242 A5
Ashford Chace GU32 206 E1
Ashford Cl
Fordingbridge SP6...257 D1
Portsmouth PO6.....321 E1
Ashford Cres SO45...314 B3
Ashford Hill Prim Sch
RG19...............8 C1
Ashford Hill Rd RG19...7 D2
Ashford Rd
Bournemouth BH6...394 D7
Fordingbridge SP6...281 C8
Ashford Works Ind Est
SP6..............257 D1
Ash Gr
Ashurst SO40......288 C3
Hordle SO41.......399 D8
Kingsclere RG20.....24 D2
Liphook GU30......188 B3
Old Basing RG24.....70 C6
Ringwood BH24.....329 C6
Ash Grange Prim Sch
GU12.............77 F2
Ash Green La W GU10,
GU12.............100 C8
Ash Grove Ho [5]
PO15.............317 D8
Ash Hill Rd GU12.....77 D1
Ashington Cl PO8...300 A3
Ashington Gdns
BH21.............374 F8
Ashington La BH21...351 A1
Ashington Pk BH25..383 B1
Ash La
Bramley RG7,RG26...28 B6
Pamber Heath RG26...9 C1
Ashlawn Gdns SP10..106 B6
Ashlea RG27.........51 B2
Ashlea Cl SO50......245 D2
Ashleigh Cl SO45....338 A8
Ashleigh Rise BH10 .377 D2
Ashlet Gdns BH25...383 D4
Ashlett Cl SO45......339 C3
Ashlett Lawn PO9....323 C6
Ashlett Mews SO45 .339 B3
Ashlett Rd SO45....339 C3
Ashley Arnewood Ct [5]
BH25.............383 B2
Ashley Cl
Bournemouth BH1....393 E6
Camberley GU15.....56 E6
Crondall GU10......97 D7
Havant PO9........323 D4
Horndean PO8......299 F5
Ringwood BH24.....329 D6
Swanwick SO31.....317 B7
Winchester SO22....175 C3
Ashley Common Rd
BH25.............383 C4
Ashley Cres SO19....292 C1
Ashley Cross BH14...391 A4
Ashleycross Cl SO45 338 D3
Ashley Ct
Alton GU34........140 A4
Bursledon SO31....293 A2
Buttermere SN8.....17 F6
Gosport PO12......369 A6
West Moors BH22...354 A8
Ashley Dr
Blackwater GU17....35 A4
Ellingham BH24....304 C3
Ashley Drive N BH24 327 F5
Ashley Drive S BH24 327 F5
Ashley Drive W
BH24.............327 F5
Ashley Dro SN8......17 F5
Ashley Gdns
Chandler's Ford
SO53.............243 E5
Oakley RG23........67 A2
Waltham Chase SO32 271 E3
Ashley Heath Cvn Pk
BH24.............327 D6
Ashley Heath Ind Est
BH21.............327 B7
Ashley Ho
[4] Bordon GU35....164 D2
Romsey SO51......240 E6

Ashley Inf Sch BH25..383 D3
Ashley Jun Sch
BH25.............383 C3
Ashley La
Hordle BH25,SO41...383 E4
Lymington SO41.....385 E3
Ashley Lodge [1]
RG21.............69 A3
Ashley Mdws SO51...241 A8
Ashley Meads BH25 .383 D4
Ashley Mews [9] GU9 .99 A2
Ashley Pk RG24......328 A6
Ashley Rd
Bentworth GU34....138 A5
Bournemouth BH1....393 E5
Farnborough GU14...56 B3
New Milton BH25...383 C4
Poole BH14........391 C5
Ashling Cl
Bournemouth BH8...393 C8
Denmead PO7......298 A4
Ashling Cres BH8....393 B8
Ashling Gdns PO7...298 A4
Ashling La PO2......345 D1
Ashling Park Rd PO7 298 A4
Ash Lodge Cl GU12...77 E1
Ash Lodge Dr GU12 ..77 E1
Ashlyn Cl PO15......318 C2
Ash Manor Sch
GU12.............100 D8
Ashmead
[22] Bournemouth
BH4..............392 C2
Bordon GU35.......164 D3
Ashmead Rd SO16....265 F3
Ashmeads Cl BH21...352 A6
Ashmeads Way
BH21.............352 A6
Ashmoor La RG24....70 E7
Ashmore BH21.......351 D4
Ashmore Ave
Barton on S BH25...398 B8
Hamworthy BH15....389 F1
Ashmore Cl SP5......212 B4
Ashmore Cres BH15..389 F1
Ashmore Gr BH23...381 E1
Ashmore Green Rd
RG18...............2 F7
Ashmore Ho [39] BH4. 392 C3
Ashmore La
West Dean SP5.....190 C1
West Dean SP5.....212 B6
Ashmore Rd BH10....377 D5
Ash Park Cotts RG25 .89 B7
Ash Rd
Aldershot GU12....100 B8
Ashurst SO40......288 B2
Bishop's Green RG20 ..6 D3
Ashridge GU14......55 C7
Ashridge Ave [1]
BH10.............377 D5
Ashridge Cl SO15...290 F8
Ashridge Ct [2] RG14 ..1 F2
Ashridge Gdns BH10 377 D5
Ashridge Par [2]
BH10.............377 D5
Ash St GU12.........77 E1
Ash Sta GU12........77 F2
Ashstead Gdns BH8 .378 C3
Ashtead PO16.......344 A8
Ash Terr RG18........2 F8
Ashton Cl SO32......247 A1
Ashton Cross SO51 .239 B1
Ashton Ct
[3] New Milton
BH25.............383 B3
Poole BH13........392 A2
Ashton Ho SO19.....291 F1
Ashton La SO32......247 B2
Ashton Pl [3] SO53...218 B1
Ashton Rd
Bournemouth BH9...377 C2
Newbury RG14........1 F2
Ashton Way PO14....367 C5
Ashtree Cl BH25....383 D2
Ash Tree Cl
Farnborough GU14...55 A3
Oakley RG23........90 A8
Ash Tree Gr RG20.....3 F7
Ashtree Rd SO18....267 E2
Ashtrees The GU12...77 F2
Ashurst Bridge Rd
SO40.............288 C5
Ashurst Cl
Ashurst SO40......288 C3
Southampton SO19 ..292 A1
Tadley RG26........26 E8
Winchester SO22...175 D3
Ashurst Ct [10] PO12..368 D3
Ashurst Dro SN8.....17 F5
Ashurst Hospl (Geriatric)
SO40.............288 B1
Ashurst New Forest Sta
SO40.............288 A1
Ashurst Rd
Ash Vale GU12......77 D4
Bournemouth BH8...378 D3
Cosham PO6.......345 E8
West Moors BH22...326 E3
Ash Vale Sta GU12...77 E7
Ashwell Ave GU15....36 D6
Ashwell Rd BH23....379 F1
Ash Wlk SO24.......179 D5
Ashwood
Titchfield SO31....317 C5
Whiteley PO15.....317 E5

Ashwood Cl
Havant PO9........323 B3
South Hayling PO11. .373 A3
Ashwood Dr
Broadstone BH18...375 C4
Newbury RG14.......2 B4
Ashwood Gdns
[6] Southampton
SO16.............266 E3
Totton SO40.......288 C7
Ashwood Lodge [1]
PO16.............319 B2
Ashwood Way RG23 ..68 D7
Ashwood Way Rdbt
RG23.............68 D7
Aspen Ave SO31.....340 D10
Aspen Cl
Bordon GU35.......164 D1
Colden Common
SO21.............245 A8
Hedge End SO30....293 D7
Aspen Dr BH31......303 B5
Aspen Gdns
Hook RG27.........51 B2
Poole BH12........391 F7
Aspen Gr GU12......100 C8
Aspengrove PO13....343 E1
Aspen Ho GU11......100 A8
Aspen Holt SO16....267 A5
Aspen Pl SO25......383 B1
Aspen Rd BH12......391 F7
Aspen Way
Poole BH12........391 F7
Waterlooville PO8...300 A5
Aspen Wlk SO40.....288 B8
Aspin Way GU17......34 F5
Asquith Cl BH23.....395 D6
Assheton Ct
[3] North Tidworth
SP9..............78 F7
Portchester PO16...344 D7
Astbury Ave BH12...392 A8
Aster Cl [3] SP10...105 C6
Aster Rd
Basingstoke RG22...91 A7
Southampton SO16 ..267 C4
Astley Cl RG14........1 B2
Astley St PO5........404 A2
Aston Mead BH23...379 E4
Aston Rd
Portsmouth PO4....370 F3
Waterlooville PO7...299 D1
Astor Mews SP9.....101 E7
Astra Ct SO45.......314 A5
Astral Gdns SO31....315 F3
Astra Wlk PO12.....369 D5
Astrid Cl PO11......373 C3
Asturias Way SO14..291 C3
Asylum Rd SO15.....291 A6
Atalanta Cl PO4.....371 C5
Atbara Rd GU52.....75 A4
Atheling Rd SO45....314 A4
Athelney Ct [7] BH1 393 B3
Athelstan Rd
Bournemouth BH6...394 E5
Southampton SO19 ..291 E6
Athelston Ct SO41...385 D3
Athena Ave PO7.....322 F3
Athena Cl SO45......314 A5
Atherfield Rd SO16..265 E3
Atherley Ct SO15....290 E8
Atherley Rd
Southampton SO15...290 D6
South Hayling PO11. .372 E5
Atherley Sch The
SO18.............268 A2
Atherstone Wlk [5]
PO5..............404 B2
Athlone Cl SP11......83 B8
Atholl Ct SP10.......83 A3
Atholl Rd GU35......164 D1
Atkinson Cl
Barton on S BH25...398 B8
Gosport PO12......369 A3
Atkins Pl PO15......318 C3
Atlantean Ct RG14....1 F3
Atlantic Cl SO14....291 B2
Atlantic Ct
Chandler's Ford
SO53.............243 C5
Winchester SO22 ...403 A5
Atlantic Park View
SO18.............268 A2
Atlantis Ave PO7....322 F2
Atrium The
[20] Southampton
SO17.............291 A8
[29] Winchester SO23 403 D6
Basingstoke RG21...69 B5
Ferndown BH22.....353 E7
Attenborough Cl
GU51..............54 B3
Attfield Cl GU12......77 D1
Attlee Gdns GU52....74 F4
Attwood Cl
Aldershot SP6.....280 F5
Basingstoke RG21...68 F4
Attwood Close Mobile
Home Pk RG21......68 F4
Attwood Dr RG2......15 C8
Attwoods Dro SO21 .197 D1
Aubrey Cl
Milford on S SO41...399 F4
South Hayling PO11. .372 E4
Aubrey Farm Cotts
SO41.............400 A4
Auburn Mans [5]
BH13.............392 B4

Auchinleck Ho [3] SP9 78 F8
Auchinleck Way GU11 76 C2
Auckland Ave SO42 ..334 A1
Auckland Pl SO42....334 A1
Auckland Rd
Christchurch BH23...396 C7
Southampton SO15 ..289 F7
Auckland Rd E PO5 .370 C2
Auckland Rd W PO5. 370 C2
Audemer Ct BH24....329 C8
Audley Cl RG14......2 B5
Audley Ho GU9......122 B7
Audley Pl SO50.....244 F1
Audrayton Ct [8]
BH6..............394 E3
Audret Cl PO16.....344 B6
Audrey Needham Ho [6]
RG14..............1 F2
Augustine Rd
Cosham PO6.......346 C8
Southampton SO14 ..291 B6
Augustine Way SP10 ..82 D3
Augustus Cl SO53....243 E7
Augustus Dr RG23....68 C7
Augustus Ho SO18...291 C7
Augustus Way SO53..243 D7
Augustus Wlk SP10 ..83 B3
Auklet Cl RG22.......90 F7
Auriol Dr PO9........347 A8
Aurora Dr RG22......91 A4
Austen Ave
Bournemouth BH10..377 E6
Winchester SO22 ...403 A2
Austen Cl
Totton SO40.......288 D6
Winchester SO23...403 E8
Austen Gdns
Newbury RG14.......5 F8
Swanwick PO15....317 C8
Austen Gr RG22.......68 E2
Austen Rd GU14......55 E6
Austerberry Way
PO13.............368 E8
Auster Cl BH23......396 B7
Austin Cl BH23......396 B7
Austin Ct BH1.......393 D5
Austin [1] PO6......321 B1
Austin's Cotts GU9...98 E1
Australia Cl PO1....404 C3
Aust Rd PO14.......342 D8
Autumn Cl BH22....353 B7
Autumn Copse BH25 383 D2
Autumn Pl [11] SO17..267 A1
Autumn Rd
Bournemouth BH11..376 D3
Marchwood SO40...290 A1
Avalon BH14........402 C8
Avalon Ct PO10.....324 C7
Avebury Ave BH10...377 E6
Avebury Gdns SO53 218 A1
Aveley La GU9.......122 A7
Avenger Cl SO53.....243 B5
Avens Cl SO50......269 C6
Avenue C SO45......338 E8
**Avenue Campus (Univ of
Southampton)**
SO17.............267 A2
Avenue Cl
Andover SP10......105 E8
Liphook GU30......187 F4
Avenue Ct
[2] Southampton
SO17.............290 F8
Gosport PO12......369 A3
Poole BH13........392 B3
Avenue D SO45......338 E8
Avenue De Caen
PO5..............370 C1
Avenue E SO45......338 E8
Avenue La [13] BH2. .392 E3
Avenue Rd
Bournemouth BH2...392 E3
Brockenhurst SO42..360 F8
Christchurch BH23...394 F7
Farnborough GU14...56 B3
Fleet GU51........53 F2
Gosport PO12......369 C5
Grayshott GU26....167 A3
Lymington SO41....385 E4
New Milton BH25...383 A3
North Hayling PO11. .348 A3
Southampton SO14 ..291 A8
Walkford BH23.....382 C2
Wimborne Minster
BH21.............351 D4
Winchester SO22 ...403 C6
Avenue Sh Ctr The [14]
BH2..............392 E3
Avenue Sucy GU15....35 E4
Avenue The
Aldershot GU12....100 A7
Andover SP10......105 F8
Barton Stacey SP11..108 C3
Bishop's Waltham
SO32.............271 B8
Bournemouth BH9...377 F3
Camberley GU15....35 F4
Fareham PO14......318 E1
Farleigh Wallop RG22 .91 D2
Fleet GU51........53 E1
Golden Pot GU34...117 B4
Gosport PO12......369 A4
Grayshott GU26....167 B3
Haslemere GU27...189 C1
Hatherden SP11.....59 E2
Liphook GU30......187 F4
Middle Wallop SO20 126 B4
Mortimer RG7......11 F5

Avenue The *continued*
New Alresford SO24 179 C5
Petersfield GU31 228 F3
Poole BH13 392 A2
Rowledge GU10 121 D3
Southampton SO17 266 F2
Southrope RG25, GU34 116 D4
South Tidworth SP9 78 E4
Twyford SO21 220 A6
West Moors BH22 326 E3
West Moors BH24 354 B8
Avery Cl RG40 16 D6
Avery Ct 8 GU11 76 F2
Avery Fields SO50 244 B7
Avery La PO12 369 A8
Aviary Ct RG24 69 E8
Aviation Park W
East Parley BH23 378 C8
Hurn BH23 354 D1
Aviemore Dr RG23 67 A1
Avington Cl SO50 244 D5
Avington Ct
Southampton SO16 266 F4
Winchester SO22 403 A5
Avington Gn PO9 324 B6
Avington Park★ SO21 177 E5
Avlan Ct SO23 403 D3
Avocet Cl PO4 371 B5
Avocet Cres GU47 35 C8
Avocet Ho 2 PO4 371 B5
Avocet Quay PO10 349 A7
Avocet Way PO8 300 A7
Avocet Wlk PO13 343 A2
Avon Ave BH24 328 D3
Avon Bldgs BH23 395 B7
Avonborne Way SO53 243 B8
Avonbourne Sch BH7 394 A7
Avon Castle BH24 328 D3
Avon Castle Dr BH24 328 D3
Avon Cl
Ash GU12 77 D1
Bournemouth BH8 393 D6
Farnborough GU14 55 C7
Lee-on-t-S PO13 367 F2
Lymington SO41 385 C3
Petersfield GU31 228 E2
Avoncliffe Rd BH6 394 E3
Avon Cotts BH23 380 C5
Avon Cres SO51 241 C7
Avon Cswy BH23 379 C7
Avon Ct
14 Andover SP10 83 C2
1 Fordingbridge SP6 257 F2
2 Waterlooville PO8 299 F4
7 Poole BH13 392 A4
Christchurch BH23 395 C6
Farnham GU9 99 A1
Netley SO31 315 C5
Avondale GU12 77 D7
Avondale Ct SO17 267 B2
Avondale Mobile Home Pk SO21 220 A1
Avondale Rd
Aldershot GU11 99 F8
Fleet GU51 54 B2
Portsmouth PO1 370 F7
Waterlooville PO7 322 F8
Avondyke SP5 234 F6
Avon Farm Cotts BH23 355 E3
Avon Gdns BH23 357 B1
Avon Gn SO53 243 D5
Avon Heath Ctry Park Visitor Ctr★ BH24 328 A2
Avon Heath Ctry Pk (North Pk)★ BH24 328 B3
Avon Heath Ctry Pk (South Pk)★ BH24 355 B8
Avon Ho
8 Southampton SO14 291 C6
Bournemouth BH2 392 E2
Avon Mdw SP5 234 F7
Avon Meade SP6 257 E2
Avon Mews BH8 393 C6
Avon Pk BH24 328 D6
Avon Rd
Bournemouth BH8 393 C6
Farnham GU9 99 A1
Oakley RG23 67 B2
Southampton SO18 267 F1
South Tidworth SP9 78 E5
West Moors BH22 326 E2
Avon Road E BH23 395 A8
Avon Road W BH23 394 F8
Avon Run Cl BH23 396 B5
Avon Run Rd BH23 396 B5
Avonsands BH23 396 A5
Avon View SP6 258 D1
Avon View Par BH23 380 C3
Avon View Rd BH23 380 C3
Avonway RG14 2 B4
Avon Way SO30 268 E2
Avon Wharf BH23 395 C5
Avon Wlk
19 Basingstoke RG21 69 D5
Portchester PO16 344 A8
Avro Cl SO15 290 A7
Avro Ct SO31 315 F2
Award Rd
Ferndown BH21 352 F5
Fleet GU52 75 A5
Award Rd *continued*
Wimborne Minster BH21 353 A6
Awbridge Prim Sch SO51 214 D5
Awbridge Rd PO9 323 C4
Axford Cl BH8 378 D3
Axford Rd RG25 115 A5
Axis Pk PO14 343 A6
Ayesgarth GU52 75 B5
Ayjay Cl GU11 99 F7
Aylen Rd PO3 346 A2
Aylesbury Rd
Bournemouth BH1 393 E4
Portsmouth PO2 370 F8
Aylesham Way GU46 33 F6
Ayliffe Ho RG22 68 D4
Ayling Cl PO13 368 C7
Ayling Ct GU9 99 D7
Ayling Hill GU11 76 D1
Ayling La GU11 99 D8
Aylings Cl RG22 68 B3
Aylward's Dr GU34 161 C3
Aylward St PO1 370 A5
Aylwards Way SO20 147 F5
Aylwin Cl RG21 69 A2
Aynsley Ct SO15 290 D7
Ayres La RG20 22 E8
Ayrshire Gdns GU51 54 B4
Aysgarth Rd PO7 322 E8
Aysha Cl BH25 383 B1
Azalea Ave GU35 165 A5
Azalea Cl
Havant PO9 324 C4
St Leonards BH24 328 A5
Azalea Ct SP10 105 D6
Azalea Dr GU27 189 D8
Azalea Gdns GU52 75 B5
Azalea Rd RG19 7 E5
Azalea Way GU15 36 F6
Aztec Ctr BH17 390 D8
Azura Cl BH21 327 B6

B

Babbs Mead GU9 98 E1
Babs Fields GU10 120 A5
Bacchus Ho 7 RG7 9 C2
Bach Cl RG22 91 D7
Back La
Appleshaw SP11 81 D6
Brimpton RG7 9 A5
Bucks Horn Oak GU10 142 F8
Mottisfont SO51 192 E5
Silchester RG7 11 B4
Southrope RG25, GU34 116 D5
Southwick PO17 320 E6
Swallowfield RG7 13 E8
Sway SO41 360 C2
Vernham Dean SP11 38 C6
Back of the Walls 26 SO14 291 A3
Back St SO23 403 D2
Bacon Cl
Sandhurst GU47 35 B6
Southampton SO19 291 F1
Bacon La
Churt GU10 144 A3
South Hayling PO11 372 E3
Badajos Rd GU11 76 D3
Badbury Cl BH18 375 C3
Badbury Ct BH22 353 F7
Badbury View BH21 351 D5
Badbury View Rd BH21 374 D8
Baddesley Cl SO52 241 F6
Baddesley Gdns PO9 323 D6
Baddesley Park Ind Est SO52 242 B4
Baddesley Rd SO53 218 A1
Baden Cl BH25 383 B1
Baden Powell Rd GU33 186 D2
Baden-Powell & St Peter's CE Mid Sch BH14 391 B3
Baden Powell Way 2 SO51 240 F7
Bader Cl SO30 293 C8
Bader Ct GU14 55 D8
Bader Rd BH17 390 E8
Bader Way PO15 317 F5
Badger Brow PO7 323 A6
Badger Cl
Bishopstoke SO50 244 F2
Fareham PO15 318 D2
Four Marks GU34 160 C3
Badger Ct
Bishopstoke SO50 244 F2
Farnham GU10 121 E5
Badger Farm Rd SO22 403 B1
Badger Rd PO14 342 F5
Badger's Bank RG24 69 F8
Badgers Cl
Fleet GU52 74 F8
St Leonards BH24 327 F5
Sway SO41 360 C2
Badgers Copse
Camberley GU15 36 C4
Locks Heath SO31 317 B5
New Milton BH25 383 C6
Badgers Croft RG7 11 E6
Badgers Holt GU46 33 F5
Badgers Ridge RG20 5 B4
Badgers Run SO31 316 E6
Badgers The SO31 315 C6
Badgers Wlk
Ferndown BH22 353 E7
Hythe SO45 313 F2
Badger Way
Aldershot GU12 77 B3
Ewshot GU10 98 B8
Verwood BH31 302 F5
Badgerwood Dr GU16 36 B2
Badger Wood Pl SO18 267 F1
Badminston Dro SO45 366 C8
Badminston La SO45 339 C1
Badshear La SO24 201 F8
Badshot Lea Rd GU9 99 E5
Badshot Lea Village Inf Sch GU9 99 E6
Badshot Pk GU9 99 E6
Badsworth Gdns RG14 5 B5
Baffins Rd PO3 371 A6
Bagber Rd SO40 288 F7
Bagmore La
Ellisfield RG25 115 E5
Herriard RG25 116 A6
Bagnols Way RG14 1 C2
Bagot Ho PO12 368 F6
Bagshot Mews SO19 291 F3
Bagwell La RG27,RG29 73 C7
Baigent Cl SO23 198 C8
Bailey Cl
Botley SO30 294 A6
Camberley GU16 56 B8
New Milton BH25 383 D4
Winchester SO22 403 B4
Bailey Cres BH15 390 C7
Bailey Dr BH23 394 F7
Bailey Gn SO18 268 A2
Bailey Hall BH23 394 F7
Bailey Ho
2 New Alresford SO24 179 D6
Basingstoke RG21 68 F1
Baileys Cl GU17 35 A4
Bailey's Rd PO5 404 C2
Baily Ave RG18 2 F4
Bain Ave GU15 35 F2
Baird Ave RG22 68 E2
Baird Rd
Arborfield Garrison RG2 15 C7
Farnborough GU14 56 A6
Baiter Gdns BH15 390 C1
Bakehouse Gdns GU52 75 B5
Baker Rd BH11 377 A5
Bakers Dro SO16 265 E5
Bakers Farm Rd BH31 302 E7
Bakers Field GU33 185 F2
Baker St PO1 370 D7
Bakers View BH21 374 D6
Bakers Yd RG23 90 B8
Balaclava Rd SO18 292 B7
Balchin Ho 18 PO1 370 A5
Balcombe Rd BH13 392 A3
Balderton Cl 7 PO2 345 F4
Baldreys GU9 121 E8
Baldwin Cl BH23 395 D6
Balena Cl BH17 390 A8
Balfour Cl
Christchurch BH23 396 D8
Gosport PO13 368 D6
Balfour Cres RG14 5 A6
Balfour Dr GU33 207 F4
Balfour Rd
Bournemouth BH9 377 F1
Portsmouth PO2 345 E1
Southampton SO19 292 C5
Balfour Red Cross Mus★ SO23 176 C1
Balintore Ct 1 GU47 35 B7
Balksbury Hill SP11 105 E5
Balksbury Hill Ind Est SP11 105 E5
Balksbury Inf Sch SP10 105 D7
Balksbury Jun Sch SP10 105 D6
Balksbury Rd SP11 105 E5
Ballam Cl BH16 389 C7
Ball And Wicket La GU9 99 A7
Ballantyne Rd GU14 55 E6
Ballard Cl
Basingstoke RG22 68 C3
New Milton BH25 383 B4
Poole BH15 390 D1
Southampton SO16 265 D1
Ballard Coll BH25 383 A4
Ballard Ct
1 Gosport PO12 369 B5
Camberley GU15 36 E8
Ballard Rd
Camberley GU15 36 E8
Poole BH15 390 D1
Ballard Sch BH25 383 A4
Balldown Cvn & Camping Pk SO21 174 C6
Balliol Cl PO14 317 C1
Balliol Rd PO2 370 E8
Balmer Lawn Rd SO42 334 B3
Balmoral Ave BH8 378 E1
Balmoral Cl
Alton GU34 139 D3
Chandler's Ford SO53 243 B8
Balmoral Cl *continued*
Gosport PO13 343 D2
Southampton SO16 266 C5
Balmoral Cres GU9 98 F6
Balmoral Ct
11 Farnborough GU14 55 F4
3 Christchurch BH23 397 B7
4 Southampton,Millbrook SO15 290 A6
7 Southampton SO17 291 A8
Basingstoke RG22 68 C3
Balmoral Dr
Camberley GU16 56 D8
Waterlooville PO7 322 C4
Balmoral Ho
6 Whiteley PO15 317 D8
Ash Vale GU12 77 D5
Bournemouth BH2 392 D3
Balmoral Rd
Andover SP10 106 A8
Ash Vale GU12 77 E4
Fareham PO15 318 E3
Poole BH14 391 C3
Balmoral Way
Basingstoke RG25 91 A6
Petersfield GU32 228 F4
Rownhams SO16 265 E6
Balmoral Wlk BH25 382 F3
Balsan Cl RG24 68 C8
Balston Rd BH14 391 A6
Balston Terr BH15 390 B2
Baltic Rd SO30 268 E1
Bamber La GU34 119 B4
Bambridge Pk Gdn Ctr Miniature Rly★ SO50 219 D1
Bamford Ho 9 PO4 371 B2
Bampton Cl SO16 289 E8
Bampton Ct SO53 243 C6
Banbury Ave SO19 292 C4
Banbury Cl GU16 56 E7
Banbury Rd BH17 390 C7
Bancroft Ct 1 BH15 390 E4
Band Hall Pl RG27 51 A1
Bangor Rd SO15 290 B6
Banister Ct 6 SO15 290 F7
Banister Gdns SO15 290 F7
Banister Grange 9 SO15 290 F7
Banister Inf Sch SO15 290 F7
Banister Mews SO15 290 F7
Banister Rd SO15 290 F7
Bank Chambers BH14 391 E3
Bank Cl BH23 395 B6
Bankhill Dr SO41 385 D5
Bank Rd GU11 77 B5
Banks Cl SP10 105 E7
Bankside
Farnham GU9 99 D7
Lymington SO41 385 D6
Bank Side
Finchampstead RG40 16 D6
Southampton SO18 267 D4
Bankside Ho 3 SO22 403 C6
Bankside Rd BH9 378 A3
Banks Rd BH13 402 C4
Bank St SO32 271 D8
Banks The SO51 214 A5
Bankview SO41 385 D6
Bannerman Rd GU32 228 F4
Banning St SO51 240 E6
Bannister Ct SO40 289 A7
Bannister Gdns
Eversley Cross RG27 33 C8
Yateley GU46 34 D5
Bannister Pl RG7 8 D6
Banstead Rd BH18 375 A5
Bapaume Rd PO3 345 F5
Baptist Hill SP11 61 F2
Barbara Cl GU52 75 B6
Barbara Ct SO32 223 B3
Barbe Baker Ave SO30 268 D2
Barbel Ave RG21 69 E5
Barberry Cl GU52 75 A6
Barberry Dr SO40 264 B1
Barberry Way
Farnborough GU17 35 D2
Verwood BH31 303 C5
Barbers Gate 9 BH15 390 B1
Barbers Piles 1 BH15 390 B1
Barbers Wharf 8 BH15 390 B1
Barbican Mews PO16 344 E7
Barbour Cl RG29 95 C8
Barcelona Cl SP10 83 B1
Barclay Ho 8 PO12 369 E5
Barclay Mans BH2 392 F5
Barclay Mews
Hythe SO45 337 F8
Hythe SO45 338 A8
Bardon Way PO14 342 D8
Bardsley Dr GU9 121 E7
Bardwell Cl RG22 68 C4
Baredown The RG27 71 D7
Bar End Ind Est SO23 403 F3
Bar End Rd SO23 403 F4
Barentin Way GU31 229 A5
Barfield Cl SO23 403 F4
Barfield Rd RG18 2 E4
Barfields SO41 385 E4
Barfield Sch GU10 99 F3
Barfields Ct 2 SO41 385 E4
Barfleur Cl PO15 318 D2
Barfleur Rd PO14 343 A5
Barford Cl
Chandler's Ford SO53 243 B8
Fleet GU51 75 D8
Barford La SP5 235 A8
Bargate Ctr 8 SO14 291 A4
Bar Gate Mus★ SO14 290 F4
Bargates BH23 395 B7
Bargate St SO14 290 F4
Barge Cl GU11 77 C5
Barge La
Swallowfield RG7 13 E5
Swallowfield,Stanford End RG7 13 D4
Barham Cl PO12 369 B7
Barham Rd GU32 228 F3
Barham Way PO2 345 D4
Baring Cl
East Stratton SO21 134 A4
Itchen Abbas SO21 178 A7
Baring Rd
Bournemouth BH6 395 A3
Winchester SO23 403 F5
Barker Cl RG2 15 C7
Barker Mill Cl SO16 265 E6
Barkham Ride RG40 16 C8
Barkis Ho 11 PO1 370 D7
Bark Mill Mews SO51 240 E6
Barkshire Ct 7 SO15 290 F8
Barlands Cl BH23 380 C2
Barle Cl SO18 268 B1
Barleycorn Wlk SO40 286 F8
Barley Down Dr SO22 403 B2
Barley Fields SO50 269 C6
Barley Mow Cl RG27 73 F8
Barley Mow Hill GU35 165 E6
Barley View RG25 89 F1
Barley Way GU51 54 B5
Barling Mews 7 SO51 240 E7
Barlow Cl PO14 367 B7
Barlows La SP10 105 F5
Barlows Rd RG26 26 F7
Barnaby Cl SP5 234 D7
Barnard Cl GU16 56 D8
Barnard Way GU11 76 D3
Barnbrook Rd SO31 316 E4
Barn Cl
Camberley GU15 36 C6
Emsworth PO10 348 D8
Upton BH16 389 A7
Barn Close La RG20 40 F8
Barn Cres RG14 5 B7
Barncroft
Appleshaw SP11 81 B5
Farnham GU9 99 A1
Barncroft Inf Sch PO9 323 D3
Barncroft Jun Sch PO9 323 D3
Barncroft Way PO9 323 D3
Barnes Cl
Bournemouth BH10 377 D3
Farnborough GU14 56 B4
Sarisbury SO31 316 D4
Southampton SO18 292 C6
West Wellow SO51 238 E4
Winchester SO23 403 D3
Barnes Cres
Bournemouth BH10 377 D3
Wimborne Minster BH21 351 E4
Barnes La
Milford on S SO41 399 C6
Sarisbury SO31 316 E4
Barnes Rd
Bournemouth BH10 377 D3
Camberley GU16 56 C8
Portsmouth PO1 370 E6
Southampton SO19 292 C6
Barnes Terr 9 RG14 1 D2
Barnes Wallis Rd PO15 317 E4
Barnes Way PO9 323 C3
Barnet Side La GU32, GU34 205 D5
Barnetts Wood La SO24 181 A8
Barney Evans Cres PO8 299 D3
Barneyhayes La SO40 287 A7
Barnfield
Christchurch BH23 396 D8
Yateley GU46 34 B5
Barnfield Cl
Breach PO10 325 E1
Lower Froyle GU34 119 C4
Southampton SO19 291 E1
Barnfield Cotts GU34 184 A6
Barnfield Ct
Fareham PO14 342 E8
Southampton SO19 291 F1
Barnfield Flats SO19 291 F1
Barnfield Rd
Petersfield GU31 229 C3
Southampton SO19 291 F1
Barnfield Rise SP10 105 E6
Barnfield Way SO19 291 F1
Barn Fold PO7 300 B1
Barn Green Cl PO7 298 F4
Barn La
Four Marks GU34 159 F1
Oakley RG23 90 A8
Barn Meadow Cl GU52 74 E3
Barn Piece SO53 242 F6
Barn Rd BH18 375 B3
Barnsfield Cres SO40 288 C7
Barnsfield Rd BH24 328 B2
Barnside Way GU33 207 F3
Barnsland SO30 268 C2
Barnsley Cl GU12 56 F2
Barns Rd BH22 354 A6
Barns The RG25 113 C8
Barn The 3 GU34 139 F4
Barnwells Ct RG27 52 D7
Barn Wood Rd PO15 318 D1
Baroda Rd SP9 78 C4
Baron Rd SO31 315 F3
Barons Ct 7 BH12 392 B4
Barons Mead SO16 265 F4
Baronsmede 2 BH2 392 D4
Baronsmere PO12 369 A5
Barons Rd BH11 376 D6
Barons The GU16 36 A1
Barossa Rd GU15 36 B7
Barrack La BH24 329 D4
Barrack Rd
Aldershot GU11 76 E2
Christchurch BH23 394 E8
Ferndown BH22 354 A2
Barracks The
Bransbury SO21 108 A1
Burley Street BH24 330 E5
Barra Cl RG23 67 A2
Barracuda Rd GU11 76 C7
Barratt Ind Pk PO15 317 C5
Barrett Ct RG21 69 C2
Barrie Cl PO15 317 C8
Barrie Rd
Bournemouth BH9 377 F3
Farnham GU9 98 E7
Barrington Cl SO50 243 F5
Barrington Ct 26 SO17 267 A1
Barrington Ho 20 PO1 370 D7
Barron Pl RG24 68 C8
Barrow Down Gdns SO19 292 E4
Barrow Dr BH8 378 F2
Barrowfield SP11 105 F1
Barrowgate Rd BH8 378 D3
Barrowgate Way BH8 378 D3
Barrow Hill SP11 127 E8
Barrow Hill Rd SO40 263 D3
Barrow Rd BH8 378 F2
Barrows La
Landford SP5 237 C6
Sway SO41 384 B6
Barrow View BH22 353 B6
Barrow Way BH8 378 F2
Barrs Ave BH25 383 B4
Barrs Wood Dr BH25 383 B4
Barrs Wood Rd BH25 383 B4
Barry Gdns BH18 374 F5
Barry Rd SO19 292 B5
Barry Way RG22 91 D7
Barter Rd BH12 392 A7
Barters Cl SO16 265 F1
Barters La BH18 374 F3
Bartholomew Cl 7 SO23 403 E7
Bartholomew Ct 8 RG14 1 D2
Bartholomew St RG14 1 D2
Bartlemy Cl RG14 5 C8
Bartlemy Rd RG14 5 C8
Bartlett Cl
Bramley RG26 29 B2
Fareham PO15 318 E3
Bartlett Dr BH7 394 B8
Bartlett Ho 2 SO17 291 B8
Bartlett Pl GU16 56 D5
Bartletts Comm SP6 282 E7
Bartletts The SO31 316 A2
Bartley Ave SO40 288 E6
Bartley CE Jun Sch SO40 287 B7
Bartley Ct 2 BH21 351 B5
Bartley Rd SO40 287 C4
Bartley Way RG27 72 C8
Bartley Wood Bsns Pk RG27 72 C8
Bartok Cl RG22 68 E1
Barton Chase BH25 397 F7
Barton Cl
Aldershot GU11 76 C1
Andover SP10 82 D3
Romsey SO51 241 B8
Barton Common La BH25 398 B8
Barton Common Rd BH25 398 B7

Barton Court Ave BH25 398 A8
Barton Court Rd BH25 383 A1
Barton Cres SO18 267 F1
Barton Croft BH25 398 A7
Barton Cross PO8 300 B7
Barton Ct 2 GU14 56 A1
Barton Dr
Barton on S BH25 397 F8
Hamble-le-R SO31 315 F3
Hedge End SO30 293 D7
Barton Dro SO21 131 A4
Barton End 2 GU34 139 E3
Barton Gn BH25 398 B6
Barton Gr PO3 346 B3
Barton Ho BH25 397 E7
Barton Ind Est SO24 158 F8
Barton La BH25 397 E8
Barton Lo BH12 391 B5
Barton Park Ind Est SO50 244 B2
Barton Peveril Coll SO50 243 F1
Barton Rd SO50 244 C3
Bartons Ct 8 PO12 369 B6
Barton's Ct RG29 72 D3
Barton's Dr GU46 34 B4
Bartonside Rd BH25 397 C7
Bartons La RG24 70 A7
Bartons Rd
Fordingbridge SP6 257 F1
Havant PO9 324 B4
Barton Stacey CE Prim Sch SO21 130 E8
Bartons The
Fordingbridge SP6 257 F1
Hedge End SO30 293 A6
Bartons Way GU14 55 B7
Barton Way BH25 397 F8
Barton Wood Rd BH25 397 E7
Bartram Rd SO40 289 A6
Barwell Gr PO10 324 E3
Barwell Terr 3 SO30 293 D6
Bascott Cl BH11 377 A1
Bascott Rd BH11 377 A1
Basepoint Bsns Ctr
Andover SP10 82 D2
Hurn BH23 354 C1
Basepoint Ent Ctr
Basingstoke RG24 69 E8
Southampton SO14 291 B3
Bashley Common Rd BH25 383 A8
Bashley Cross Rd BH25 382 E5
Bashley Dr BH25 383 B6
Bashley Rd BH25 383 A6
Basing Barns GU34 204 D5
Basingbourne Cl GU52 75 A6
Basingbourne Rd GU52 75 A6
Basing Dean GU34 204 E4
Basing Dr GU11 99 A7
Basingfield Cl RG24 70 C4
Basing Ho SO15 290 C7
Basing House★ RG24 70 A6
Basing Mews 3 SO32 271 C7
Basing Rd
Havant PO9 323 E4
Old Basing RG24 69 F6
Basingstoke Bsns Ctr RG22 68 E2
Basingstoke Canal Ctr★ GU16 56 E3
Basingstoke Coll of Tech RG21 69 A4
Basingstoke Rd
Aldermaston RG7 9 D8
Alton GU34 139 C2
Itchen Abbas SO21 155 A4
Kingsclere RG20 24 E2
Kings Worthy SO21, SO23 176 D7
Ramsdell RG26 46 E5
Riseley RG7 14 A3
Stratfield Turgis RG27 30 E6
Swallowfield RG7 14 A6
Basingstoke School Plus RG22 68 C1
Basingstoke Sta RG21 69 B6
Basing View RG21 69 C6
Basing Way SO53 243 A4
Basingwell St Lwr 5 SO32 271 C7
Basingwell St Upper SO32 271 D7
Basin St PO2 370 D8
Bassenthwaite Gdns GU35 164 D5
Bassett Ave SO16 266 F5
Bassett Cl
Camberley GU16 56 C8
Southampton SO16 266 F4
Bassett Cres E SO16 266 F4
Bassett Cres W SO16 266 F3
Bassett Ct SO16 266 F4
Bassett Dale SO16 266 F6
Bassett Gdns SO16 266 F4
Bassett Gn Village SO16 267 B5
Bassett Green Cl SO16 267 B5
Bassett Green Ct SO16 267 B5
Bassett Green Dr SO16 267 A6
Bassett Green Prim Sch SO16 267 B4
Bassett Green Rd SO16 267 B5
Bassett Heath Ave SO16 266 F6
Bassett Mdw SO16 266 F4
Bassett Mews SO16 266 F5
Bassett Rd BH12 391 B6
Bassett Row SO16 266 F6
Bassett Wlk PO9 323 D6
Bassett Wood Dr SO16 267 A6
Bassett Wood Mews 7 SO16 266 F4
Bassett Wood N SO16 267 A6
Bassett Wood Rd SO16 267 A6
Bat and Ball La GU10 121 E6
Batchelor Cres BH11 376 F3
Batchelor Dr RG24 70 C5
Batchelor Gn SO31 315 F8
Batchelor Rd BH11 377 A3
Batchelors Barn Rd SP10 106 C8
Batcombe Cl BH11 376 E3
Bateman Gr GU12 100 D8
Bath and Wells Ct 7 PO13 368 C6
Bath Cl SO19 292 B6
Bath Hill Ct 11 BH1 393 A3
Bath Hill Rdbt BH1 393 A2
Bathing La PO1 369 F5
Bath La 9 PO16 319 C1
Bath La (lower) 11 PO16 319 C1
Bath Lane Cotts PO16 343 C8
Bath Rd
Bournemouth BH1 393 A3
Camberley GU15 36 B6
Emsworth PO10 348 F8
Lymington SO41 386 A3
Newbury RG14 1 B4
Portsmouth PO4 370 F3
Southampton SO19 292 B6
Thatcham RG18 2 E4
Bath Sq PO1 369 F5
Bath St SO14 291 A7
Bathurst Cl PO11 372 E3
Bathurst Way PO2 345 B2
Batsford SP11 61 F2
Batstone Way BH22 353 B6
Battenburg Ave PO2 345 F2
Battenburg Rd PO12 369 C6
Batten Cl BH23 395 D7
Batten Rd SP5 234 E8
Battens Ave RG25 88 B8
Battens Way PO9 323 F4
Batterley Dro BH21 279 F4
Battery Cl PO12 368 F8
Battery End RG14 5 B6
Battery Hill
Bishop's Waltham SO32 271 B8
Winchester SO22 403 A4
Battery Row PO1 370 A3
Battle Cl
Locks Heath SO31 317 A4
Newbury RG14 1 B4
Battle Rd RG14 5 A6
Battramsley Cross SO41 361 C1
Batt's Cnr GU10 143 B7
Baughurst Rd
Baughurst RG26 26 C5
Padworth RG7 10 E6
Ramsdell RG26 46 D8
B Ave
Fawley SO45 338 F4
Holbury SO45 338 D5
Baveno Ho GU14 56 A1
Baverstock Rd BH12 392 B8
Baverstocks GU34 140 A6
Baxendales The RG14 2 A1
Baxter Rd SO19 292 E5
Baybridge La SO21 221 C4
Baybridge Rd PO9 324 B5
Bay Cl
Southampton SO19 292 A3
Three Legged Cross BH21 326 E8
Upton BH16 389 B6
Baycroft Sch PO14 367 E7
Bayfield Ave GU16 36 C2
Bayfields PO5 404 B1
Bayford Cl GU17 35 E1
Bay Hog La BH15 390 B2
Bay House Sch PO12 368 E2
Bayly Ave PO16 344 D6
Baynard Cl RG21 69 C7
Baynton Ho SO41 385 D4
Bay Rd
Gosport PO12 368 F3
Southampton SO19 292 A3
Bays Ct
Lymington SO41 385 C4
Pamber Heath RG26 9 D1
Bays Rd SO41 385 C3
Bayswater Ho PO5 404 C1
Baythorn Cl PO2 370 D7
Bay Tree Gdns SO40 289 F1
Baytree Ho 24 SO23 403 D6
Bay Tree Lodge PO14 367 D7
Bay Trees SO19 292 E6
Bay Tree Way BH23 381 D1
Bay Tree Yd SO24 179 D6
Bay View BH2 392 E2
Bay View Ct PO11 372 D2
Bayview Gdns BH2 392 E2
Bayview Mews BH2 392 E2
Bay View Mews PO11 372 D2
Baywood Cl GU14 55 A5
Bazaar Rd SP9 78 D5
Beach Ave BH25 397 F7
Beach Cl BH13 402 G8
Beachcroft BH13 392 A3
Beach Dr PO6 344 F8
Beach La SO31 315 A6
Beachlands Sta★ PO11 372 F2
Beach Piece Way RG22 91 B7
Beach Rd
Emsworth PO10 348 E8
Lee-on-t-S PO13 367 E2
Poole BH13 402 G8
Portsmouth PO5 370 D1
South Hayling PO11 372 E3
Upton BH16 389 A6
Beach's Cres RG26 27 E3
Beach View BH13 402 C4
Beachway PO16 344 D6
Beacon Bottom SO31 317 A6
Beacon Cl
Everton SO41 384 D1
Farnham GU10 121 E5
Locks Heath SO31 317 A6
Rownhams SO16 265 D6
Beacon Ct
Christchurch BH23 396 F7
Fordingbridge SP6 257 E3
Beacon Dr BH23 396 F7
Beacon Gdns BH18 374 E3
Beacon Hill Com Prim Sch GU26 167 A6
Beacon Hill Ct GU26 167 B6
Beacon Hill La
Corfe Mullen BH21 374 B3
Droxford SO32 248 F6
Meonstoke SO32 249 C6
Beacon Hill Rd
Beacon Hill GU26 167 B6
Ewshot GU10 98 C8
Fleet GU10,GU52 75 C3
Beacon Mews SO30 292 D8
Beacon Mount SO31 317 A6
Beacon Park Cres BH16 389 A8
Beacon Park Rd BH16 389 B7
Beacon Pass RG20 42 A8
Beacon Rd
Bournemouth BH2 392 F2
Broadstone BH18 374 E3
Farnborough GU14 76 F8
Upton BH16 389 B7
West End SO30 292 D8
Beaconsfield Ave PO6 346 A7
Beaconsfield Rd
Basingstoke RG21 69 B4
Christchurch BH23 395 B7
Fareham PO16 343 B8
Poole BH12 391 D6
Waterlooville PO7 322 E8
Beacon Sq PO10 348 F7
Beacon View Ho GU26 167 A3
Beacon Way
Broadstone BH18 374 E3
Locks Heath SO31 317 A6
Beale's Cl SP10 106 B8
Beale's Ct SP5 169 A1
Beales La GU10 121 D7
Bealeswood La GU10 143 D6
Bealing Cl SO16 267 B4
Beal's Pightle RG26 46 F8
Beam Hollow GU9 99 A7
Beamish Rd BH17 390 F8
Bear Cross Ave BH11 376 F6
Bear Cross Rdbt BH11 376 F6
Bear Ct RG24 69 F7
Beard Ct SP11 57 A2
Bear Hill RG20 24 C1
Bear La
Farnham GU9 99 A3
Newbury RG14 1 E3
Bear Mus The★ GU31 228 F3
Bearslane Cl SO40 264 D1
Bearwood Cotts GU10 121 D7
Bearwood Gdns 7 GU51 54 A1
Bearwood Prim Sch BH11 376 C6
Beasant Cl PO3 371 B6
Beatrice Ct 5 SO41 399 B4
Beatrice Ho 3 RG21 69 C6
Beatrice Mews 2 PO6 345 F7
Beatrice Rd
Portsmouth PO4 370 E2
Southampton SO15 290 C7
Beattie Rise SO30 269 D2
Beatty Cl
Locks Heath SO31 317 B4
Ringwood BH24 329 C8
Beatty Ct SP10 106 C7
Beatty Dr PO12 368 F2
Beatty Ho 9 PO1 404 C4
Beatty Rd BH9 378 B1
Beaty Ct SO19 292 C5
Beauchamp Ave PO13 343 D1
Beauchamp Pl BH23 395 A7
Beauchamps Gdns BH7 394 A8
Beauclerk Gn RG27 52 C1
Beaucroft La BH21 351 E5
Beaucroft Rd
Waltham Chase SO32 271 E3
Wimborne Minster BH21 351 E6
Beaucroft Sch BH21 351 E6
Beau Ct
43 Bournemouth BH4 392 C3
9 New Milton BH25 383 A3
Beaufort Ave PO16 318 F2
Beaufort Cl
Christchurch BH23 396 B7
Lee-on-t-S PO13 368 A6
Beaufort Dr
Bishop's Waltham SO32 271 C8
Wimborne Minster BH21 351 C5
Beaufort Ho 10 BH4 392 C2
Beaufort Mews BH21 351 B4
Beaufort Rd
7 Portsmouth PO5 370 D1
Ash Vale GU12 77 D6
Bordon GU35 164 D5
Bournemouth BH6 394 D6
Farnham GU9 99 A3
Fleet GU52 75 B6
Havant PO9 323 D2
Winchester SO23 403 D4
Beaufoys Ave BH22 353 D7
Beaufoys Cl BH22 353 C7
Beaufoys Ct BH22 353 C6
Beaufront Cl GU15 36 E7
Beaufront Rd GU15 36 F7
Beaulieu Abbey★ SO42 336 F2
Beaulieu Ave
Christchurch BH23 394 E7
Havant PO9 323 D6
Portchester PO16 344 A8
Beaulieu Cl
New Milton BH25 382 E3
Southampton SO16 266 B5
Winchester SO22 175 D4
Beaulieu Ct
15 Andover SP10 83 C2
23 Basingstoke RG21 69 D5
5 Waterlooville PO8 299 F4
Blackwater GU17 34 F5
Beaulieu Gdns GU17 35 A5
Beaulieu Ho 2 SO15 290 F7
Beaulieu Pl PO13 343 B2
Beaulieu Rd
Beaulieu SO42, SO45 337 C6
Bournemouth BH4 392 B1
Christchurch BH23 394 E7
Dibden Purlieu SO45 313 F1
Eastleigh SO50 244 A4
Hamble-le-R SO31 315 F3
Hythe SO45 313 F1
Lyndhurst SO43 310 C4
Marchwood SO40 312 E5
Portsmouth PO2 345 E1
Beaulieu Road Sta SO42 311 D1
Beaulieu Village Prim Sch SO42 336 F1
Beaumaris Cl
Andover SP10 105 E6
Chandler's Ford SO53 243 A4
Beaumaris Gdns SO45 313 F5
Beaumaris Par GU16 56 D8
Beaumond Gn 11 SO23 403 D5
Beaumont Cl
Fareham PO15 318 D3
Southampton SO16 266 E3
Beaumont Ct PO12 369 A9
Beaumont Gr GU11 76 C2
Beaumont Jun Sch GU11 76 D2
Beaumont Pl SO40 289 A7
Beaumont Rd
Poole BH13 402 F7
Totton SO40 289 A7
Beaumont Rise PO15 318 D4
Beaurepaire Cl RG26 28 D3
Beauworth Ave SO18 292 C8
Beaver Dr SO50 245 A2
Beaver Ind Est
Christchurch BH23 396 A7
Liphook GU30 188 A3
Beaver La GU46 34 C5
Beavers Cl
1 Pamber Heath RG26 9 E1
Alton GU34 139 E4
Farnham GU9 98 E2
Beavers Hill GU9 98 D2
Beavers Mews GU35 164 E4
Beavers Rd GU9 98 E2
Beccles Cl BH15 389 F2
Becher Rd BH14 391 E4
Bechin Cl GU52 74 D3
Beck Cl SO31 316 E3
Beckenham Terr PO10 325 B4
Becket Ct RG23 68 A4
Becket Ho 1 RG14 1 D2
Beckett Cl RG23 68 A5
Beckett Rd SP10 105 E8
Becketts RG27 52 C6
Beckford La PO17 297 F2
Beck Gdns GU9 98 E6
Beckham La GU32 228 D4
Beckhampton Rd BH15 389 E3
Beck Ind Est The GU12 100 B8
Beckley Copse BH23 382 A2
Beck St PO1 370 B5
Becton La BH25 398 B7
Becton Mead BH25 383 B1
Bedales Sch GU32 228 E7
Bedale Way BH15 390 F5
Beddington Ct RG24 70 A8
Beddow Hall 3 PO5 404 A2
Bede Dr SP10 82 D3
Bedenham La PO13 343 E3
Bedenham Prim Sch PO13 343 D3
Bedfield Ho SO23 176 B5
Bedfield La SO23 176 B5
Bedford Ave
Camberley GU16 56 D5
Southampton SO19 291 E2
Bedford Cl
Bordon GU35 164 D1
Fordingbridge SP6 257 F3
Havant PO9 348 B8
Hedge End SO30 293 D6
Newbury RG14 5 A5
Bedford Cres
Bournemouth BH7 394 C7
Camberley GU16 56 D6
Bedford La GU16 56 D6
Bedford Pl SO15 290 F6
Bedford Rd GU32 228 D3
Bedford Rd N BH12 376 C2
Bedford Rd S BH12 376 C2
Bedford St
Gosport PO12 369 A7
Portsmouth PO5 404 B2
Bedford Wlk 6 RG21 69 B5
Bedhampton Hill PO9 323 B1
Bedhampton Hill Rd PO9 323 A1
Bedhampton Ho 4 PO1 404 C4
Bedhampton Rd
Havant PO9 323 C2
Portsmouth PO2 370 F8
Bedhampton Sta PO9 323 D1
Bedhampton Way PO9 323 F4
Bedser Sq SP10 83 B3
Bedwell Cl SO16 265 F6
Beecham Berry RG22 91 D7
Beecham Rd PO1 370 F7
Beech Ave
Bournemouth BH6 394 C4
Camberley GU15 36 B4
Christchurch BH23 394 D8
Farnham GU10 122 A5
Middle Wallop SO20 126 B4
Southampton SO18 291 E7
Beechbank Ave BH17 374 F1
Beechbrook Ave GU46 34 C5
Beech Cl
Alderholt SP6 281 A5
Aldershot GU12 100 C8
Bramley RG26 29 A2
Broadstone BH18 374 E4
Chandler's Ford SO53 243 D8
Hamble-le-R SO31 315 E2
Hordle SO41 399 D8
Overton RG25 65 B2
Penton Corner SP11 82 A1
Romsey SO51 241 C6
Thatcham RG19 7 F5
Thruxton SP11 103 E8
Verwood BH31 302 E5
Waterlooville PO8 299 F3
Winchester SO22 197 B3
Beech Cnr SO32 269 F6
Beech Copse
Pamber Heath RG26 9 C1
Winchester SO22 175 B1
Beech Cres SO45 338 A8
Beechcrest View RG27 51 B2
Beechcroft BH1 393 A5
Beechcroft Cl
Andover SP10 83 A1
Chandler's Ford SO53 243 D6
Beechcroft Cl *continued*
Fareham PO15 318 C1
Liphook GU30 187 B3
Beechcroft Cotts SO20 170 B6
Beechcroft La BH24 329 B8
Beechcroft Mews 1 BH24 329 B8
Beechcroft Rd PO12 369 B4
Beechcroft Way SO53 243 E6
Beech Ct
5 Newbury RG14 1 E4
Crondall GU10 97 E2
Hindhead GU26 167 C4
Southampton SO19 291 F3
Whitchurch RG28 86 C6
Wimborne Minster BH21 351 E4
Beechdale Cl SO40 264 D2
Beechdale Wlk SO40 264 C2
Beechdown Ho RG22 68 C1
Beech Dr GU17 35 B4
Beechen La SO43 310 A3
Beeches Hill SO32 247 D2
Beeches The
Andover SP10 105 E8
Ash Vale GU12 56 D1
Awbridge SO51 214 E5
Basingstoke RG22 91 D6
Bournemouth BH7 394 A8
Fair Oak SO50 245 D1
Sutton Scotney SO21 131 C4
Tadley RG26 26 E8
Waterlooville PO7 322 F8
West Wellow SO51 238 D3
Beechey Ct 6 BH8 393 A5
Beechey Rd BH8 393 A5
Beechfield
42 Bournemouth BH4 392 C3
Newton Tony SP4 123 B6
Beechfield Ct SO15 290 B8
Beech Gdns SO31 315 E2
Beech Gr
Gosport PO12 369 A4
Owslebury SO21 221 B4
South Hayling PO11 373 B4
Upper Froyle GU34 119 B3
Wherwell SP11 128 F7
Beech Grange SP5 237 D2
Beech Hanger SP4 101 D1
Beech Hanger End GU26 166 F3
Beech Hanger Rd GU26 166 F3
Beech Hill GU35 165 F5
Beech Hill Ho RG7 13 C6
Beech Hill Rd
Headley GU35 165 E6
North Tidworth SP9 79 A7
Swallowfield RG7 13 C7
Beech Ho
Chineham RG24 49 A4
Southampton SO16 266 F7
Beeching Cl GU12 77 F3
Beech La
Grayshott GU26 166 F4
St Leonards BH24 327 E2
Beechlands Rd GU34 160 B4
Beechmount Rd SO16 266 F5
Beechnut Dr GU17 34 F6
Beechnut Ind Est 1 GU11 76 F1
Beechnut Rd GU12 76 F1
Beech Rd
Ashurst SO40 288 B2
Bishop's Green RG20 6 E3
Camberley GU16 56 D6
Chandler's Ford SO53 243 D8
Clanfield PO8 276 D5
Fareham PO15 318 E2
Farnborough GU14 55 E7
Hedge End SO30 293 D7
New Alresford SO24 179 D5
Southampton SO15 290 B6
Beech Ride
Fleet GU52 74 F7
Sandhurst GU47 34 F8
Beech Tree Cl RG23 90 A8
Beech Tree Dr GU9 99 E5
Beech Tree Wlk SO20 170 D3
Beech Way
Basingstoke RG23 68 C7
Waterlooville PO8 300 B5
Beech Wlk SP10 105 D7
Beechwood
Chineham RG24 48 E3
Fordingbridge SP6 257 D1
Beechwood Ave
Bournemouth BH5 394 A4
New Milton BH25 382 F4
Waterlooville PO7 322 E6
Beechwood Cl
Basingstoke RG22 91 C6
Chandler's Ford SO53 218 A1
Fleet GU51 74 E6
Warsash SO31 340 D10
Beech Wood Cl BH18 375 A3
Beechwood Cres SO53 218 B2
Beechwood Ct
Bournemouth BH2 392 E2

Beechwood Ct *continued*
Liss GU33 208 A6
Beechwood Gdns
Bournemouth BH5 394 A4
Southampton SO18 291 F8
Beechwood Ho SO17 291 C8
Beechwood Jun Sch SO18 291 F7
Beechwood La BH24 331 B3
Beechwood Lo 1 BH4 392 C2
Beechwood Lodge 3 PO16 319 B2
Beechwood Rd
Alton GU34 139 D2
Bartley SO40 287 A6
Holbury SO45 338 C3
Portsmouth PO2 345 E4
West Moors BH22 326 F1
Beechwood Rise SO18 268 C1
Beechwood Way SO45 313 C2
Beechworth Rd 1 PO9 324 A1
Beehive Cotts PO16 319 B3
Beehive Wlk PO1 370 A4
Beeston Ct PO1 370 E7
Beestons Cotts RG27 51 A1
Beethoven Rd RG22 91 E7
Beeton's Ave GU12 77 E4
Beggars Dro SO21 131 D3
Beggar's La SO23 403 F6
Beggarwood La RG22 91 B5
Begonia Cl RG22 91 A7
Begonia Rd SO16 267 B4
Behrendt Cl PO12 369 A7
Belaga Cl SO20 126 A5
Belben Cl BH12 376 D2
Belben Rd BH12 376 C2
Belbins SO51 215 F4
Belbins Bsns Pk SO51 216 A3
Beldham Rd GU9 121 D7
Belfield Rd BH6 395 A4
Belfry Ct SO31 317 C3
Belfry Mews GU47 34 D8
Belfry Sq RG22 91 A5
Belfry Wlk PO14 317 C2
Belgrave Cres SP9 79 A6
Belgrave Ct
Blackwater GU17 35 B3
Bournemouth BH1 393 D3
Belgrave Ind Est SO17 267 C2
Belgrave Mews RG27 52 D6
Belgrave Rd
Poole BH13 392 A2
Southampton SO17 267 C2
Belgravia Rd PO2 345 F1
Bellair Ho PO9 324 A1
Bellair Rd PO9 324 A1
Bellamy Ct SO17 291 D8
Belland Dr GU11 76 C1
Bell Cl
Blackfield SO45 338 F2
Farnborough GU14 56 A6
Bell Cres PO7 322 E6
Bell Ct PO18 349 F7
Bell Davies Rd PO14 367 B6
Bellemoor Rd SO15 266 D1
Bellemoor Sch (Boys) SO15 266 D2
Bellever Hill GU15 36 C5
Bellevue RG28 86 C5
Belle Vue Cl
Aldershot GU12 77 B2
Bournemouth BH6 394 D4
Belle Vue Cres BH6 394 F4
Belle Vue Ent Ctr GU12 77 C2
Belle Vue Gdns 2 BH6 394 F4
Belle Vue Gr BH22 326 F2
Belle Vue Ho GU12 77 B2
Belle Vue Inf Sch GU12 77 B2
Bellevue La PO10 324 F2
Belle Vue Mans 6 BH6 394 E3
Bellevue Rd
Eastleigh SO50 244 A3
Southampton SO15 291 A6
Belle Vue Rd
Aldershot GU12 77 B2
Andover SP10 106 B6
Bournemouth BH6 394 E3
Old Basing RG24 70 C6
Poole BH14 391 C3
Bellevue Terr
10 Southampton SO14 291 A6
Portsmouth PO5 404 A1
Belle Vue Wlk BH22 353 E2
Bellew Rd GU16 56 F7
Bellfield PO14 341 F7
Bellflower Cl BH23 396 B8
Bellflower Way
Chandler's Ford SO53 242 F7
Titchfield PO15 317 F3
Bellhanger Ents GU34 138 B6
Bell Heather Cl BH16 389 B8
Bell Hill
Newbury RG14,RG20 4 F4
Bell Hill *continued*
Petersfield GU32 228 E5
Bell Hill Ridge GU32 228 E5
Bell Holt RG14 5 A5
Bellinger Ho PO9 323 D1
Bell La
Blackwater GU17 35 A5
Ellisfield RG25 115 D7
Rowledge GU10 121 C3
Bell Meadow Rd RG27 51 B1
Bell Rd
Andover SP10 106 C7
Basingstoke RG24 69 E7
Cosham PO6 345 D8
Haslemere GU27 189 F3
Bells Ho BH21 351 D6
Bells La PO14 367 C7
Bell St
Ludgershall SP11 57 A2
Romsey SO51 240 E7
Southampton SO14 291 A3
Whitchurch RG28 86 C5
Bell Vale La GU27 189 F4
Bell Yd RG28 86 C5
Belmont Ave BH8 378 C2
Belmont Cl
Andover SP10 106 B6
Farnborough GU14 55 D7
Horndean PO8 276 C3
Hythe SO45 314 A2
Stubbington PO14 367 D8
Verwood BH31 303 A5
Belmont Cotts RG20 1 A6
Belmont Gdns PO11 373 D1
Belmont Gr PO9 323 C2
Belmont Ho GU9 121 E8
Belmont Hts RG22 91 C5
Belmont Mews GU15 36 A3
Belmont Pl PO5 404 B1
Belmont Rd
Andover SP10 106 B6
Camberley GU15 36 A4
Chandler's Ford SO53 243 D3
New Milton BH25 383 C4
Poole BH14 391 C5
Southampton SO17 267 C1
Belmont St PO5 404 B1
Belmore Cl PO1 370 E7
Belmore Ct SO41 385 D3
Belmore Ho 1 SO41 385 E2
Belmore La
Lymington SO41 385 E3
Owslebury SO21 221 E4
Upham SO21,SO32 222 B3
Belmore Rd SO41 385 D3
Belmour Lo 36 BH4 392 C3
Belney Ho PO6 345 A8
Belney La PO7 298 E1
Belsize Rd GU14 56 A1
Belstone Mews GU14 55 E7
Belstone Rd SO40 288 E7
Belton Rd
Camberley GU15 36 C5
Southampton SO19 292 B3
Belvedere Cl GU51 53 C1
Belvedere Ct GU17 35 B3
Belvedere Dr RG14 5 E8
Belvedere Gdns RG24 49 A4
Belvedere Rd
Bournemouth BH3 393 A6
Christchurch BH23 395 A7
Farnborough GU14 56 A2
Hythe SO45 314 A2
Belverdere Cl GU32 228 F4
Belvidere Ho 12 SO14 291 C6
Belvidere Rd SO14 291 C5
Belvidere Terr SO14 291 C5
Belvoir Cl
Fareham PO16 343 B8
Frimley GU16 36 D1
Belvoir Pk 8 BH13 392 B3
Bembridge SO31 315 C6
Bembridge Cl SO16 267 C5
Bembridge Cres PO4 370 E1
Bembridge Ct
9 Aldershot GU12 77 A1
South Hayling PO11 373 C1
Bembridge Dr PO11 373 C1
Bembridge Ho PO11 373 C1
Bembridge Lodge Flats PO13 367 E2
Bemister Rd BH9 393 A8
Bemister's La 5 PO12 369 E5
Benbow Cl PO8 300 C7
Benbow Cres BH12 376 E1
Benbow Ct SP10 106 C7
Benbow Gdns SO40 264 C2
Benbow Ho 5 PO1 370 A5
Benbow Pl 4 PO1 370 A5
Benbridge Ave BH11 376 F5
Bencraft Ct SO16 267 B5
Bendeng Cl 2 GU51 53 E3
Bendigo Rd BH23 394 E8
Benedict Cl SO51 241 C7
Benedict Way PO16 320 E1
Beneficial St 14 PO1 370 A5
Benellen Ave BH4 392 C4
Benellen Gdns BH4 392 D4
Benellen Rd BH4 392 C5
Benellen Twrs 1 BH4 392 C4
Benenden Gn SO24 179 D4
Benett Cl RG14 1 D5
Benett Gdns RG14 1 D5
Benford Ct RG29 72 E2
Bengal Rd BH9 392 E8
Benger's La SO51 192 E2
Benham Dr 6 PO3 345 F4
Benham Dro SO20 147 D6
Benham Gr PO16 344 D6
Benham Hill RG18 2 D4
Benham La RG7 14 B3
Benhams Farm Cl 4 SO18 268 A1
Benhams La GU33 186 A4
Benhams Rd SO18 268 A2
Benin Rd SP11 79 D6
Benjamin Ct BH23 394 F7
Benjamin Rd BH15 389 D2
Benmoor Rd BH17 390 A8
Benmore Cl BH25 383 C2
Benmore Gdns SO53 243 B8
Benmore Rd BH9 378 A1
Bennet Cl
Alton GU34 139 E4
Basingstoke RG21 69 C7
Bennett Cl SP5 235 D6
Bennett Ct GU15 36 A5
Bennett Ho 4 BH4 392 C4
Bennett Rd BH8 393 C6
Bennetts La BH24 331 C2
Bennetts Rise GU11 100 A8
Bennion Rd BH10 377 C3
Benny Hill Cl SO50 243 F3
Benridge Bsns Pk BH17 390 B8
Benridge Cl BH18 375 A3
Benson Cl BH23 357 B1
Benson Rd
Poole BH17 390 D7
Southampton SO15 290 B8
Benta Cl SO20 126 A5
Bentall Pl SP10 106 A7
Bentham Ct SO16 267 A4
Bentham Rd PO12 369 B4
Bentham Way SO31 316 D8
Bent La PO7 298 A7
Bentley Bsns Pk GU10 120 B5
Bentley CE Prim Sch GU10 120 B5
Bentley Cl
Horndean PO8 300 C8
Kings Worthy SO23 176 B6
Bentley Copse GU15 36 F4
Bentley Cres PO16 318 F2
Bentley Ct
4 Camberley GU15 36 B5
9 Southampton SO17 267 A1
Havant PO9 324 B5
Bentley Dr RG2 15 C8
Bentley Gn SO18 292 C8
Bentley Ind Ctr GU10 120 B4
Bentley Lodge GU51 53 D3
Bentley Rd BH9 377 F3
Bentley Sta GU10 120 C3
Bentley Way
Lymington SO41 385 D6
Middle Winterslow SP5 168 B5
Bent St SO20 147 E7
Bentworth Cl PO9 323 D4
Benwell Cl RG29 95 C8
Benwell Ct PO11 372 F3
Bepton Down GU31 229 A3
Berber Cl PO15 317 C7
Bercote Cl SO22 175 B5
Bere Cl
Chandler's Ford SO53 243 A8
Poole BH17 375 D2
Winchester SO22 403 B8
Bere Farm La PO17 319 F8
Bere Hill RG28 86 D6
Bere Hill Cl RG28 86 D6
Bere Hill Cres SP10 106 C7
Bere Hill Cvn Site RG28 86 D6
Berehurst GU34 139 F2
Bere Rd PO7 298 F4
Beresford Cl
Andover SP10 106 A5
Camberley GU16 56 D6
Chandler's Ford SO53 243 E5
Poole BH12 391 D6
Waterlooville PO7 322 E6
Beresford Ctr RG24 69 E8
Beresford Gate SP10 83 F1
Beresford Gdns
Chandler's Ford SO53 243 E5
Christchurch BH23 395 E6
Beresford Rd
Bournemouth BH5 394 B4
Chandler's Ford SO53 243 E5
Lymington SO41 385 C4
Poole BH12 391 D6
Portsmouth PO2 345 E1
Stubbington PO14 367 D8
Bereweeke Ave SO22 403 C8
Bereweeke Cl SO22 403 C7
Bereweeke Ho SO22 403 C7
Bereweeke Rd SO22 403 C7
Bereweeke Way SO22 403 C8
Berewyk Cl RG22 91 A7
Bergen Cres SO30 293 C5
Berkeley Ave BH12 391 D8
Berkeley Cl
Fleet GU51 54 B1
Southampton SO15 290 E7
Stubbington PO14 367 B7
Verwood BH31 302 E7
Berkeley Cres GU16 56 E8
Berkeley Ct PO13 367 F2
Berkeley Dr RG22 91 F8
Berkeley Gdns SO30 293 C5
Berkeley Rd
Bournemouth BH3 392 E7
Newbury RG14 1 D2
Southampton SO15 290 F6
Berkeley Sq PO9 324 B1
Berkeley The PO5 370 E1
Berkley Ave BH22 353 D2
Berkley Manor 8 BH13 392 B4
Berkshire Bsns Pk RG7 10 C4
Berkshire Cl PO1 404 D3
Berkshire Copse Rd GU11 76 C7
Berkshire Ho RG24 68 E8
Berkshire Rd GU15 36 D8
Bermuda Cl RG24 48 C2
Bermuda Ct
15 Southampton SO17 267 A1
5 Christchurch BH23 397 A7
Bermuda Ho 3 PO6 320 F2
Bernard Ave
Cosham PO6 346 A8
Four Marks GU34 160 B2
Bernard Ct 1 GU15 35 F4
Bernard Ho 7 GU51 53 E3
Bernard Powell Ho PO9 324 A1
Bernards Cl BH23 394 E8
Bernard St SO14 291 A3
Berne Ct 15 BH1 393 A3
Berney Rd PO4 371 C4
Bernie Tunstall Pl SO50 244 B3
Bernina Ave PO7 299 C2
Bernina Cl PO7 299 C2
Bernstein Rd RG22 91 C8
Bernwood Gr SO45 365 E7
Beron Ct BH15 390 E4
Berrans Ave BH11 377 B6
Berrans Ct BH11 377 A6
Berrybank GU47 35 C6
Berry Cl SO30 293 D6
Berry Ct RG27 72 A8
Berrydown La
Axford RG25 114 E4
Ellisfield RG25 115 B4
Overton RG25 88 C7
Berrydown Rd PO9 323 C7
Berryfield Rd SO41 384 A2
Berry Hill SO24 181 A5
Berry Ho 9 PO1 370 D7
Berry La
Stubbington PO14 367 A7
Twyford SO21 220 A7
Berrylands GU33 208 A7
Berry Way SP10 105 D7
Berrywood Bsns Village SO30 269 B3
Berrywood Gdns SO30 293 B8
Berrywood La SO24 137 B6
Berrywood Prim Sch SO30 269 D1
Berthon Ho SO51 240 E6
Bertie Rd PO4 371 B4
Bertram Rd BH25 383 C4
Berwick Rd BH3 392 E6
Berwyn Cl RG22 68 A3
Berwyn Wlk PO14 342 E8
Beryl Ave PO12 368 F8
Beryton Cl PO12 369 A7
Beryton Rd PO12 369 A7
Besom Ct RG26 26 F7
Besomer Dro SP5 235 F5
Bessborough Rd BH13 402 E7
Bessemer Cl BH31 303 C4
Bessemer Pk RG21 68 F2
Bessemer Rd RG21 68 F2
Beswick Ave BH10 377 D2
Beta Rd GU14 55 E5
Bethany Ct BH12 392 A7
Bethany Ho BH1 393 D5
Bethany Jun CE Sch BH1 393 D5
Bethel Cl GU9 99 B6
Bethel La GU9 99 B6
Bethia Cl BH8 393 D6
Bethia Rd BH8 393 D6
Betjeman Wlk GU46 33 F4
Betsy Cl BH23 357 B1
Betsy La BH23 357 B1
Betteridge Dr SO16 265 D6
Bettesworth Rd PO1 370 E7
Bettiscombe Cl BH17 375 E2
Betula Cl PO7 323 A6
Beulah Rd SO16 266 A1
Bevan Cl SO19 291 E1
Bevan Rd PO8 299 F5
Beveren Cl GU51 54 B4
Beverley Cl
Ash GU12 77 D1
Basingstoke RG22 69 B1
Locks Heath SO31 317 C4
Beverley Cres GU14 55 D2
Beverley Gdns
Bournemouth BH10 377 D3
Bursledon SO31 292 E1
Romsey SO51 216 B1
Swanmore SO32 272 B5
Beverley Gr PO6 322 F1
Beverley Grange 50 BH4 392 C3
Beverley Hts SO18 267 F3
Beverley Rd
Hythe SO45 337 F8
Stubbington PO14 367 C6
Beverly Cl PO13 343 D2
Bevers The RG7 11 E6
Beverston Ho 4 PO6 321 A1
Beverston Rd PO6 321 A1
Bevis Cl
Blackfield SO45 338 F2
Warsash SO31 340 D10
Bevis Rd
Gosport PO12 369 B6
Portsmouth PO2 345 D1
Bevis Rd N PO2 345 D1
Bevois Gdns SO14 291 A7
Bevois Hill SO14 291 B8
Bevois Mans 7 SO14 291 B8
Bevois Mews 4 SO14 291 A7
Bevois Town Prim Sch SO14 291 A7
Bevois Valley Rd SO14 291 B7
Bewicks Reach RG14 1 D3
Bexington Cl BH11 376 E3
Bexmoor RG24 70 A6
Bexmoor Way RG24 70 A6
Beyne Rd SO22 197 B3
Bible Fields RG25 113 C8
Bicester Cl RG28 86 C5
Bickerley Gdns BH24 328 F6
Bickerley Rd BH24 328 F6
Bickerley Terr BH24 328 F7
Bickleigh Ho 6 PO17 318 E8
Bicknell Ct 5 BH4 392 C4
Bicknell Rd GU16 36 C2
Bicknell Sch BH7 394 A7
Bickton Ash SP6 282 A6
Bickton Wlk PO9 323 D6
Bicton Rd BH11 377 B3
Bidbury Inf Sch PO9 323 D2
Bidbury Jun Sch PO9 323 D2
Bidbury La PO9 323 C1
Biddenfield La SO32, PO17 295 D5
Bidden Rd
Odiham RG29 72 A2
Upton Grey RG25 94 D7
Biddesden La SP11 57 D2
Biddlecombe Cl PO13 368 C8
Biddlesgate Ct 5 SO14 290 F3
Bideford Cl
Farnborough GU14 55 E7
Southampton SO16 265 E1
Bietigheim Way 1 GU15 36 A6
Biggin Wlk PO14 342 E8
Bigg's Hill Cotts RG20 4 D4
Biggs La RG2 15 E8
Bighton Dean La SO24 158 E1
Bighton Hill SO24 181 A6
Bighton La SO24 180 D6
Bighton Rd GU34 159 C5
Bigpath Farm Cotts SO32 247 B6
Big Tree Cotts SO32 273 C6
Bilbao Ct SP10 83 D1
Bilberry Cl SO31 316 F2
Bilberry Ct 11 SO22 403 D6
Bilberry Dr SO40 289 E2
Billett Ave PO7 299 F1
Billing Ave RG40 16 D6
Billing Cl PO4 371 B3
Billington Gdns SO30 269 D1
Billington Pl SO41 385 D2
Bill Stillwell Ct 6 PO2 345 C2
Billy Lawn Ave PO9 323 F4
Bilton Bsns Pk PO3 346 C2
Bilton Rd RG24 48 E1
Bilton Way PO3 346 C2
Bindon Cl
Poole BH12 391 E7
Southampton SO16 266 A2
Bindon Ct 13 SO18 291 E8
Bindon Rd SO16 266 A2
Binfields GU9 99 A3
Binfields Cl RG24 48 F1
Binfields Rdbt RG24 48 E1
Bingham Ave BH14 402 D8
Bingham Cl
Christchurch BH23 395 E7
Verwood BH31 303 B4
Bingham Dr
Lymington SO41 385 E3
Verwood BH31 303 A4
Bingham Rd
Bournemouth BH9 393 A7
Christchurch BH23 395 E7
Verwood BH31 303 A4
Bingley Cl
Alton GU34 139 E4
Basingstoke RG21 69 C7
Binley Bottom SP11 61 F5
Binley Ct RG26 27 A8
Binnacle Way PO6 345 B8
Binness Way PO6 346 E7
Binnie Rd BH12 391 E5
Binsey Cl SO16 289 E8
Binstead Cl SO16 267 C5
Binstead Rd GU34, GU10 142 E8
Binsted CE Prim Sch GU34 141 E7
Binsted Dr GU17 35 B5
Binsteed Rd PO2 370 E8
Binswood View Bsns Ctr GU35 163 D5
Binton La GU10 100 C3
Birch Ave
Beckley BH25 382 D5
Burton BH23 380 C3
Ferndown BH22 353 F1
Fleet GU51 53 F1
Thatcham RG19 7 F5
Birch Cl
Bordon GU35 164 E2
Camberley GU15 36 C8
Colden Common SO21 244 F8
Corfe Mullen BH21 374 D6
Liss GU33 208 A4
Poole BH14 391 E3
Romsey SO51 241 D6
Rowledge GU10 121 E4
Southampton SO16 266 A2
St Leonards BH24 327 D3
Waterlooville PO8 299 E3
Birch Copse BH17 390 A8
Birch Ct
3 Winchester SO22 403 A4
5 North Tidworth SP9 79 A7
Lymington SO41 385 B2
Southampton SO18 292 A7
Tidworth SP9 78 E7
Birch Dale SO45 314 B2
Birchdale Cl SO31 340 D10
Birchdale Rd BH21 351 D5
Birch Dr
Blackwater GU17 35 B3
Bournemouth BH8 379 A2
Gosport PO13 343 C4
Birchen Cl SO31 317 C4
Birchen Coppice SO20 126 B4
Birchen Rd SO31 317 C4
Birches Cl The SO52 241 F5
Birches Crest RG22 91 D6
Birches The
Blackwater GU17 34 F5
Farnborough GU14 55 B4
Southampton SO18 292 B8
Birchett Rd
Aldershot GU11 76 E2
Farnborough GU14 55 D6
Birchfields GU15 36 A4
Birchglade SO40 264 C2
Birch Gr
Bordon GU35 164 D1
Chilbolton SO20 129 C2
Eastleigh SO50 244 A6
Hook RG27 51 B2
Old Milton BH25 383 A1
West Moors BH22 326 D2
Birch Hill Cotts PO17 297 A3
Birch Ho
2 Farnborough GU14 55 F7
Southampton SO16 266 F7
Birch La RG7 11 D6
Birchland Cl RG7 11 C6
Birchlands SO40 288 D5
Birch Mdw GU9 99 B6
Birchmore Cl PO13 343 C2
Bircholt Rd GU30 187 B4
Birch Rd
Chilworth SO16 267 A8
Finchampstead RG40 16 E7
Headley GU35 165 F6
Hedge End SO30 293 D7
Pamber Heath RG26 9 D2
Southampton SO16 266 A3
St Leonards BH24 328 B4
Birch Tree Cl PO10 324 F4
Birch Tree Ct GU27 189 A4
Birch Tree Dr PO10 324 F4
Birchview Cl GU46 34 B4
Birch Way GU12 77 E7
Birch Wlk BH22 353 F3
Birchwood RG24 48 F3
Birch Wood SO19 292 E5
Birchwood Cl BH23 396 E8
Birchwood Ct 7 SO18 291 E8
Birchwood Dr SP6 281 A5
Birchwood Gdns SO30 293 C8
Birchwood Lodge 7 PO16 319 B2
Birchwood Mews BH14 391 D3
Birchwood Rd
Newbury RG14 2 B4
Poole BH14 391 D3

Birchwood Rd continued
Upton BH16.........**389** B6
Birchy Hill SO41....**360** C1
Bird Field SO53.......**242** F7
Birdham Rd PO11...**373** E2
Birdhaven GU10......**121** E6
Birdlip Cl PO8........**300** A6
Birdlip Rd PO6.......**321** B1
Birds Hill Gdns **1**
  BH15..............**390** E3
Bird's Hill Rd BH15...**390** E3
Birdwood Gr PO16....**343** F8
Birdwood Rd GU15....**35** D7
Birdworld & Underwater
  World★ GU10......**121** A3
Birinus Rd SO23......**403** E7
Birkdale Ave PO6.....**322** C1
Birkdale Cl BH18......**375** A5
Birkdale Rd BH18.....**375** A5
Birkenholme Cl
  GU35..............**166** A4
Birmingham Ct **7**
  PO13..............**368** D5
Biscay Cl PO14........**367** B8
Bishearne Gdns
  GU33..............**207** E5
Bishop Challoner RC Sec
  Sch RG22...........**68** C3
Bishop Cl BH12.......**392** C7
Bishop Ct BH24.......**329** A8
Bishop of Winchester
  Comp Sch The
  BH8...............**378** D1
Bishop Rd BH9........**393** A8
Bishops Cl
  4 Pamber Heath
  RG26................**9** E1
  Bournemouth BH7...**393** F7
  Fleet GU52..........**75** A6
  South Tidworth SP9...**78** F4
  Totton SO40........**288** E8
Bishops Cres SO19....**291** F4
Bishops Ct
  2 Andover SP10...**105** F8
  Bishopstoke SO50....**244** D5
  Broadstone BH18....**375** A3
Bishopsfield Rd
  PO14..............**342** E8
Bishops Gate PO14...**317** D3
Bishops La SO32......**272** B1
Bishop's La SO32.....**271** C7
Bishop's Mead GU9....**98** F2
Bishops Rd
  Farnham GU9........**98** F1
  Southampton SO19...**291** E4
Bishop St PO1........**370** A5
Bishopstoke La
  SO50..............**244** E7
Bishopstoke Manor
  SO50..............**244** C3
Bishopstoke Rd
  Eastleigh SO50.....**244** C3
  Havant PO9.........**323** C5
Bishop Sumner Dr
  GU9................**99** A6
Bishop's View GU34..**159** F1
Bishop's Waltham Inf
  Sch SO32..........**271** D8
Bishop's Waltham
  Palace★ SO32.....**271** C7
Bishop's Way SO32....**105** F8
Bishopswood Ct RG26..**9** D1
Bishopswood Jun Sch
  RG26...............**26** F7
Bishopswood La
  Baughurst RG26......**26** C8
  Pamber Heath RG26...**9** C1
Bishopswood Rd RG26..**9** D1
Bishop's Wood Rd PO17,
  SO32..............**272** D2
Bishopwood Inf Sch
  RG26...............**26** F7
Bisley Ct SO19.......**292** B3
Bisterne Cl BH24.....**331** E2
Bittern Cl
  Aldershot GU11......**99** C4
  Basingstoke RG22....**90** F8
  Gosport PO12......**369** B8
  Sandhurst GU47......**35** B8
Bitterne CE Inf Sch
  SO19..............**291** F6
Bitterne CE Jun Sch
  SO19..............**291** F6
Bitterne Cl PO9......**323** F6
Bitterne Cres SO19...**292** A6
Bitterne Manor Ho
  SO18..............**291** C7
Bitterne Manor Prim Sch
  SO18..............**291** C7
Bitterne Park Inf Sch
  SO17..............**267** D2
Bitterne Park Jun Sch
  SO17..............**267** D2
Bitterne Park Sch
  SO18..............**267** E2
Bitterne Park Triangle
  SO18..............**267** D1
Bitterne Rd SO18.....**292** A6
Bitterne Rd E SO18...**292** C7
Bitterne Rd W SO18...**291** E7
Bitterne Sta SO18....**291** D7
Bitterne Way
  Lymington SO41.....**385** D2
  Southampton SO19...**291** F6
  Verwood BH31......**303** A5

Bitumen Rd SO45.....**339** B4
Blackbarn Rd SP4....**145** A6
Blackberry Cl
  Clanfield PO8.......**276** D4
  Four Marks GU34....**160** C3
Blackberry Dr SO50...**245** B1
Blackberry La
  Christchurch BH23...**395** F6
  Four Marks GU34....**160** C2
Blackberry Terr
  SO14..............**291** B7
Blackberry Wlk RG24..**69** E7
Blackbird Cl
  Basingstoke RG22.....**90** F8
  Broadstone BH17....**389** E8
  Sandhurst GU47......**35** B8
  Waterlooville PO8...**299** F4
Blackbird Ct SP10....**83** B2
Blackbird La RG20......**6** E3
Blackbird Rd SO50...**243** D2
Blackbird Way
  Bransgore BH23.....**381** C8
  Lee-on-t-S SO31....**367** F4
Blackbrook Bsns Pk
  PO15..............**318** E1
Blackbrook House Dr
  PO14..............**318** E1
Blackbrook Park Ave
  PO15..............**318** E1
Blackbrook Rd PO15..**318** D2
Blackburn Ct **5**
  PO13..............**368** D5
Blackburn Rd BH12...**391** B6
Blackbushe Bsns Ctr
  GU46...............**34** A4
Blackbushe Cl SO16..**265** F5
Blackbushe Park Cvn
  Site GU46..........**34** A4
Blackbushes Rd RG27..**53** D7
Blackbush Rd SO41..**399** B5
Blackcap Cl PO9.....**301** A1
Blackcap Pl GU47......**35** C8
Black Dam Rdbt RG21..**69** E4
Black Dam Way RG21..**69** E3
Blackdown Cl
  Basingstoke RG22....**68** B3
  Hythe SO45.........**313** D2
Blackdown Cres
  PO9................**323** E4
Blackfield Inf Sch
  SO45..............**338** D1
Blackfield Jun Sch
  SO45..............**338** E1
Blackfield La BH22...**326** E3
Blackfield Rd
  Blackfield SO45.....**338** F2
  Bournemouth BH8...**378** D1
Blackfriars Cl **3**
  PO5................**404** C2
Blackfriars Rd PO5...**404** C3
Blackheath Rd GU9....**98** E7
Black Hill BH31.......**303** A6
Black Hill Rd SO43,
  SO51..............**262** E7
Blackhorse La SO32..**271** F1
Blackhouse La
  North Boarhunt
  PO17..............**320** A8
  Soberton PO17......**297** A1
Black La
  Bransgore BH23....**357** E3
  Redlynch SP5.......**236** B4
Blackman Gdns GU11..**99** F8
Blackmoor Ho GU33..**185** F6
Blackmoor Rd GU33..**186** A6
Blackmoor Wlk **2**
  PO9................**324** B5
Blackmore La GU34...**205** F3
Blacknest Ind Pk
  GU34..............**142** C8
Blacknest Rd GU34...**120** C1
Black Pond La GU10..**122** A6
Blacksmith BH21.....**374** D5
Blackstocks La RG27..**71** B6
Blackstone Cl GU14...**55** B6
Black Swan Bldgs **16**
  SO22..............**403** D6
Black Swan Yd **5**
  SP10..............**106** B8
Blackthorn Cl
  Braishfield SO51....**216** D6
  Lymington SO41.....**385** B2
  Southampton SO19...**291** F5
  South Wonston SO21..**153** C4
Blackthorn Cres
  GU14...............**55** D8
Blackthorn Dr
  Gosport PO12......**344** A1
  South Hayling PO11..**373** C3
Blackthorne Cl GU35..**164** E3
Blackthorn Gn SO21..**245** A8
Blackthorn Rd
  Southampton SO19...**291** F5
  South Hayling PO11..**373** C2
Blackthorn Terr PO1..**370** A6
Blackthorn Way
  Basingstoke RG23....**68** C6
  New Milton BH25...**383** D4
  Verwood BH31......**303** B5
Blackthorn Wlk PO7..**300** C1
Blackwater BH23....**379** D4
Blackwater Cl
  7 Cosham PO6...**345** D8
  Alderholt SP6......**280** C5
  Ash GU12..........**77** E1
  Basingstoke RG21....**69** C5
  Oakley RG23.........**67** B1

Blackwater Dr
  Oakley BH21........**375** D7
  Totton SO40........**264** D1
Blackwater Gr SP6...**280** E5
Blackwater Mews
  SO40..............**264** D1
Blackwater Pk GU12..**77** C1
Blackwater Sta GU17..**35** C4
Blackwater View
  RG40...............**16** F2
Blackwater Way
  GU12..............**100** B8
Blackwell Rd SO21...**153** C3
Blackwood Ho **13**
  PO1................**370** D7
Bladon Cl PO9........**324** C3
Bladon Rd SO16......**266** C2
Blagdon Cl RG19.......**6** B7
Blair Ave BH14.......**391** C4
Blair Cl BH25........**382** E3
Blaire Pk GU46.......**33** F8
Blair Rd **2** RG21...**69** A3
Blaise Cl GU14.......**56** B3
Blake Cl
  Nursling SO16......**265** D5
  Odiham RG29.........**95** C8
Blake Ct
  6 Gosport PO12...**369** E5
  Andover SP10.......**83** A1
  Basingstoke RG21....**69** E8
Blake Dene Rd BH14..**391** B4
Blake Hill Ave BH14..**391** D1
Blake Hill Cres BH14..**391** C1
Blake Ho **17** PO1...**370** A4
Blakemere Cres
  PO6................**321** D1
Blakeney Rd SO16....**265** D2
Blake Rd
  Cosham PO6........**322** D1
  Hedge End SO30....**293** E6
  Gosport PO12......**369** C6
  Portsmouth PO1....**369** F8
Blakes Cotts RG29....**72** E2
Blake's La
  4 Pamber Heath
  RG26................**9** F1
  Tadley RG26........**10** A1
Blakesley La PO3....**346** C4
Blakes Ride GU46.....**33** F6
Blanchard Rd SO32..**271** B8
Blandford Cl BH15...**389** F2
Blandford Ct **2**
  SO41..............**399** D5
Blandford Ho SO16..**265** F1
Blandford Rd
  Coombe Bissett
  SP5................**211** D7
  Corfe Mullen BH21..**374** D8
  Hamworthy BH16...**389** D4
  Pamphill BH21......**350** D7
Blandford Rd N
  Upton BH16........**389** B7
  Upton BH16........**389** B8
Blaney Way BH21....**374** C6
Blanket St GU34......**162** F8
Blankney Cl PO14....**367** B7
Blann Cl SO16.......**265** C5
Blashford Lakes Study
  Ctr BH24..........**305** A4
Blaven Wlk **4** PO14..**342** E8
Bleach's Yard Ind Est
  GU30..............**188** A2
Bleaklow Cl SO16....**289** F8
Blechynden Terr
  SO15..............**290** E5
Bledlow Cl RG14......**5** A5
Blencowe Dr SO53...**242** F5
Blendon Dr SP10.....**82** D1
Blendworth Cres
  PO9................**323** F3
Blendworth Ho **2**
  PO1................**404** C4
Blendworth La
  Blendworth PO8....**300** E7
  Horndean PO8......**292** C7
Blendworth Rd **1**
  PO4................**371** B5
Blenheim **3** BH13..**392** B3
Blenheim Ave SO17..**267** A1
Blenheim Cl
  Alton GU34........**140** A3
  Chandler's Ford SO53..**242** F4
  Four Marks GU34...**160** B3
  Tongham GU10.....**100** C7
  Totton SO40........**288** E4
Blenheim Cotts RG18...**2** F1
Blenheim Cres
  Farnham GU9........**98** E5
  Hordle SO41.......**383** F4
Blenheim Ct
  35 Bournemouth
  BH4................**392** C4
  Christchurch BH23..**395** A8
  Farnborough GU14...**56** A7
  Portsmouth PO4....**371** A3
  South Hayling PO11..**373** C2
Blenheim Dr BH23...**396** B6
Blenheim Gdns
  Gosport PO12......**369** B8
  Havant PO9........**324** C2
  Hythe SO45.........**313** D2
  Southampton SO17..**267** D2
Blenheim Ho
  Eastleigh SO50.....**244** B4
  Romsey SO51.......**241** B7
Blenheim Mews **6**
  BH4................**392** C4
Blenheim Pk GU11...**77** A7

Blenheim Rd
  Eastleigh SO50.....**244** A2
  Farnborough GU11....**76** F7
  Newbury RG14........**1** D2
  Old Basing RG24......**70** C5
  Waterlooville PO8...**300** A5
Blenhem Barn PO7...**298** F1
Bleniem Pl GU15......**36** A3
Bleriot Cres PO15....**318** F2
Blighmont Ave SO15..**290** B6
Blighmont Cres
  SO15..............**290** B6
Blighton La GU10....**100** C3
Blind La
  Curdridge SO32.....**270** C2
  Horton Heath SO30..**269** C5
  Ibsley SP6..........**282** C1
  Wickham PO17......**295** F5
  Wimborne Minster
  BH21..............**351** B5
Bliss Cl
  Basingstoke RG22....**68** E1
  Waterlooville PO7...**322** E5
Blissford Cl PO9.....**324** B5
Blissford Cross SP6..**282** E8
Blissford Hill SP6....**282** E7
Blissford Rd SP6.....**282** E8
Blissmore La SP11....**81** D2
Block Cotts RG7......**10** F6
Bloomfield Ave BH9..**377** F2
Bloomfieldhatch La
  RG7................**12** F8
Bloomfield Pl BH9...**377** F2
Bloomsbury Way
  GU17...............**35** B3
Bloomsbury Wlk
  SO19..............**291** E2
Blossom Cl
  Andover SP10......**105** D7
  Hedge End SO30....**293** E6
Blossom Sq PO1.....**370** A6
Bloswood Dr RG28....**86** B5
Bloswood La RG28....**86** A6
Blount Rd PO1.......**370** B3
Bloxworth Rd BH12..**391** F8
Blue Anchor La **10**
  SO14..............**290** F3
Blue Ball Hill SO23..**403** F6
Bluebell Cl
  Andover SP10......**105** C7
  Christchurch BH23..**396** B8
  Waterlooville PO7...**323** A6
Bluebell Copse SO31..**316** F2
Bluebell La SO31.....**316** F2
Bluebell Mews GU15..**36** B7
Bluebell Rd
  Lindford GU35......**165** A5
  Southampton SO16..**267** C4
Bluebell Way PO15...**317** D8
Bluebell Wlk GU51...**53** F2
Blueberry Gdns
  SP10..............**105** C7
Bluehaven Wlk PO27..**50** F1
Blue Hayes Cl SP10..**106** A7
Blueprint Portfield Rd
  PO3................**346** A2
Blue Pryor Ct **12**
  GU52...............**74** E3
Blue Reef Aquarium★
  PO5................**370** C1
Bluestar Gdns SO30..**269** C2
Bluethroat Cl GU47...**35** C8
Blue Timbers Cl **8**
  GU35..............**164** C2
Bluevalley Mews **3**
  SP6................**257** F1
Bluff Cove GU11......**77** A3
Bluff The BH10......**377** F4
Blundell La SO31....**293** C1
Blunden Cl RG21......**69** A1
Blunden Rd GU14.....**55** D5
Blunt Rd RG22........**90** F4
Blyth Cl
  Christchurch BH23..**379** D4
  Southampton SO16..**265** D2
Blythe Cl SP11.......**83** B6
Blythe Rd BH21......**374** D6
Blyth Mews **4** SO25..**290** E6
Blythswood BH25.....**397** F7
Blythwood Dr GU16...**36** B2
Boakes Pl SO40......**288** C2
Boames La RG20.......**4** E5
Boardmark The PO6..**345** B7
Boardwalk Way
  SO40..............**290** A3
Boarhunt Cl PO1.....**404** C3
Boarhunt Rd
  Boarhunt PO17.....**320** A6
  Fareham PO17......**319** E3
Boar's Bridge PO14...**27** F3
Boatyard Ind Est The
  PO16..............**343** A8
Bob Hann Cl BH12...**391** D5
Bockhampton Rd
  BH23..............**380** E6
Bodin Gdns RG14......**5** F8
Bodley Rd BH13......**402** F7
Bodmin Cl RG22......**68** B3
Bodmin Rd
  Bishopstoke SO50...**244** E2
  Portchester PO6....**345** A8
Bodorgan Rd BH2....**392** F4
Bodowen Cl BH23...**380** E2
Bodowen Rd BH23...**380** D1
Bodycoats Rd SO53..**243** D5
Bofors Rd GU14......**56** C8
Bogmoor Cl GU34...**160** B2
Bognor Rd BH18.....**374** F4

Bohemia La SP5,SP6..**235** F3
Bohunt Sch GU30....**187** F4
Boiler Rd
  Fawley SO45.......**339** E1
  Portsmouth PO1....**369** F8
Bokerley Junc SP5...**230** A4
Bolde Cl PO3.........**346** B3
Boldens Rd PO12....**369** B2
Bolderwood Arboretum
  Ornamental Dr★ BH24,
  SO43..............**308** C2
Bolderwood Cl SO40..**244** F2
Bolderwood Deer
  Sanctuary★ SO43..**308** A6
Boldre Cl
  Barton on S BH25...**397** D8
  Havant PO9........**323** C4
  Poole BH12........**391** D7
Boldre La SO41......**385** D8
Boldrewood Rd
  SO16..............**266** E4
Boleyn Cres BH9....**378** E4
Bolhinton Ave SO40..**289** F1
Bolle Rd GU34.......**139** D2
Bolley Ave GU35....**164** B5
Bolton Cl BH6........**394** E3
Bolton Cres
  Basingstoke RG22....**68** E1
  Ferndown BH22.....**354** A6
Bolton Ct **3** BH6....**394** E3
Bolton Dr PO12......**369** C8
Bolton Rd BH6.......**394** E3
Boltons The
  Milford on S SO41...**399** D4
  Waterlooville PO7...**322** E3
Bonchurch Cl SO16..**267** C5
Bonchurch Rd PO4...**371** A5
Bond Ave BH22......**326** D4
Bond Cl
  Basingstoke RG24....**69** E8
  Pamber Heath RG26...**9** E1
  Sway SO41.........**360** B3
Bondfields Cres PO9..**323** F6
Bond Rd
  Poole BH15........**390** F5
  Southampton SO18..**267** E1
Bond St SO14........**291** C6
Bone La RG14...........**2** A3
Bonemill La RG20......**1** B2
Bonham Rd BH9......**392** F7
Bonhams Cl GU34...**140** E7
Boniface Cl SO40....**288** D8
Boniface Cres SO16..**265** E4
Bonington Cl BH23..**395** E8
Bonner Cotts SP5....**191** F7
Bonners Field GU10..**120** A5
Boon Way RG23.......**67** A2
Boothby Cl SO40....**289** A6
Bordean La GU32....**227** C6
Border Cl GU33......**208** B1
Border Dr BH16......**389** C5
Border End GU27....**189** B6
Border Mews GU26..**167** B3
Border Rd
  Haslemere GU27....**189** B6
  Upton BH16........**389** C5
Borderside GU46......**33** E6
Bordon Cl RG26.......**26** E8
Bordon Jun & Inf Schs
  GU35..............**164** C4
Bordon Rd PO9......**323** F5
Bordon Trad Est
  GU35..............**164** A5
Boreen The GU35....**165** F5
Boreham Rd BH6.....**394** D5
Borelli Mews **2** GU9..**99** A2
Borelli Yd **1** GU9.....**99** A2
Borkum Cl SP10.......**82** E3
Borland Ho PO17....**296** F1
Borman Way SO21...**153** E4
Borodin Cl RG22......**91** F8
Borough Court Rd
  RG27...............**51** E5
Borough Gr GU32....**228** E2
Borough Hill GU32...**228** D3
Borough Rd GU32....**228** D2
Borough The
  Crondall GU10.......**97** C6
  Downton SP5.......**234** F8
  Farnham GU9........**98** F2
Borovere Cl GU34...**139** E2
Borovere Gdns GU34..**139** E2
Borovere La GU34...**139** E2
Borrowdale Rd SO16..**265** E1
Borsberry Cl SP10...**106** B8
Borthwick Rd BH1...**393** C5
Boscobel Rd SO22...**403** D7
Boscombe Cliff Rd
  BH5................**393** F3
Boscombe Grove Rd
  BH1................**393** D5
Boscombe Overcliff Dr
  BH5................**394** A4
Boscombe Spa Rd
  BH5................**393** D4
Boscowen Cl SP10...**106** C7
Bosham Rd PO2......**370** F8
Bosham Wlk PO13...**343** B2
Bosley Cl BH23......**379** E2
Bosley Way BH23....**379** E2
Bosmere Gdns PO10..**324** C1
Bosmere Jun Sch
  PO9................**347** F8
Bosmere Rd PO11...**373** E1

Bossington Cl SO16..**265** E5
Bostock Cl SO21.....**174** D3
Boston Cl SO53.......**243** D7
Boston Lo **31** BH4...**392** C3
Boston Rd PO6.......**321** E1
Bosun Ct **11** PO6....**345** E7
Bosuns Cl PO16......**343** B6
Bosville SO50.........**244** A6
Boswell Cl
  Botley SO30........**294** A6
  Southampton SO19..**292** C6
Bosworth Mews BH9..**378** E4
Botany Bay Rd SO19..**292** A3
Botany Hill GU10.....**100** D1
Botany Ho **4** PO15..**317** D8
Botisdone Cl SP11.....**38** C5
Botley CE Prim Sch
  SO30..............**294** A6
Botley Dr PO9........**323** D5
Botley Gdns SO19....**292** E3
Botley Hill SO30......**294** B7
Botley Mill Craft & Bsns
  Ctr SO30...........**294** B7
Botley Rd
  Bishop's Waltham
  SO32..............**271** B6
  Curdridge SO32.....**270** F2
  Fair Oak SO50.....**245** D1
  Hedge End SO30....**269** B1
  Horton Heath SO50..**269** D7
  North Baddesley
  SO52..............**242** B4
  Romsey SO51,SO52..**241** D6
  Southampton SO19..**292** D3
  Swanwick SO31.....**317** B7
Botley Sta SO30......**294** B7
Bottings Est SO30....**294** B7
Bottle La RG27.......**51** B8
Bottom La
  West Wellow SO51...**238** D4
  West Wellow SO51...**238** E4
Boughton Ct PO3....**346** C4
Boulnois Ave BH14...**391** E3
Boultbee Cotts
  SO43..............**309** D5
Boulter La PO17.....**321** A7
Boulters Rd GU11.....**76** F1
Boulton Rd PO5......**404** D3
Boundary Acre SO31..**293** B4
Boundary Cl SO15....**289** F7
Boundary Dr BH23...**351** D6
Boundary La BH24...**327** C1
Boundary Oak Prep Sch
  PO17..............**319** C3
Boundary Rd
  Bournemouth BH10..**377** E1
  Bursledon SO31....**315** F8
  Dockenfield GU10...**143** B8
  Farnborough GU14...**56** A2
  Grayshott GU26....**167** B3
  Newbury RG14........**1** F2
  Rowledge GU10....**121** C2
Boundary Rdbt BH3,
  BH10..............**392** D8
Boundary Way
  Cosham PO6........**322** B2
  Havant PO9.........**323** E1
Boundary Wlk **13**
  PO17..............**318** E7
Bound La PO11......**373** A2
Boundoak RG2........**15** B8
Boundstone SO45....**313** F3
Boundstone Cl GU10..**121** F5
Boundstone Rd
  GU10..............**121** E4
Boundway SO41......**359** E1
Bounty Rd RG21......**69** A4
Bounty Rise RG21.....**69** A4
Bountys La BH12.....**391** E5
Bourley La GU10......**75** E2
Bourley Rd
  Aldershot GU11.....**76** C3
  Fleet GU9,GU10,GU11,
  GU52...............**75** D3
Bourne Arch RG18.....**2** F4
Bourne Ave
  Bournemouth BH2...**392** E3
  Southampton SO15..**266** C1
Bourne Cl
  Bournemouth BH2...**392** D3
  Otterbourne SO21..**219** C4
  Waterlooville PO8...**300** B6
  West Wellow SO51...**238** D3
Bourne Com Coll
  PO10..............**325** D1
Bourne Cotts SP6....**232** E3
Bourne Ct
  16 Andover SP10...**83** C2
  1 Bournemouth BH2 **392** F4
  2 Basingstoke RG21..**69** D5
  Aldershot GU11......**99** E8
  Wimborne Minster
  BH21..............**351** D5
Bourne Dene GU10..**121** E5
Bourne Field RG24....**47** E4
Bourne Fields SO21..**220** B3
Bourne Firs GU10....**122** B5
Bourne Gr GU10.....**122** C7
Bourne Grove Cl
  GU10..............**122** C7
Bourne Grove Dr
  GU10..............**122** C7
Bourne Hts GU9.....**122** A8
Bourne Inf Sch The
  GU10..............**122** B6
Bourne La
  Bartley SO40......**287** D6
  Shipton Bellinger SP9 **101** F7

Bourne La *continued*
Twyford SO21 . . . . . . **220** B6
Bourne Mdw SP11 . . . **62** A1
Bourne Mill Bsns Pk
GU9 . . . . **99** C3
Bournemouth Ave
PO12 . . . . **369** A9
Bournemouth Aviation
Mus★ BH23 . . . . **379** A8
Bournemouth Central
Bsns Pk BH1 . . . . . . **393** C5
Bournemouth Ho
2 Bournemouth
BH1 . . . . **393** B3
7 Havant PO9 . . . . . **324** A5
Bournemouth Int Ctr★
BH2 . . . . **392** F2
Bournemouth
International Airport
BH23 . . . . **378** E8
Bournemouth Learning
Support Centre PRU
BH10 . . . . **377** D1
Bournemouth Memorial
Homes BH8 . . . . **378** F1
Bournemouth Nuffield
Derwent Suite
BH7 . . . . **379** B1
Bournemouth Nuffield
Hospl The BH8 . . . . . **393** A5
Bournemouth & Poole
Coll Annexe The
BH1 . . . . **393** A3
Bournemouth & Poole
Coll (Constitution Hill
Campus) The BH14 . **390** F5
Bournemouth & Poole
Coll (North Road
Campus) The BH14 . **390** F4
Bournemouth & Poole
Coll The BH1 . . . . . . **393** B3
Bournemouth Rd
Chandler's Ford
SO53 . . . . **243** C4
Lyndhurst SO43 . . . . . **309** E5
Over Wallop SP11 . . . **124** E5
Poole BH14 . . . . **391** D4
Bournemouth Sch
BH8 . . . . **378** C1
Bournemouth Sch for
Girls BH8 . . . . **378** C2
Bournemouth Sta
BH8 . . . . **393** B4
Bournemouth Station
Rdbt BH8 . . . . **393** B4
Bournemouth Univ
(Lansdowne Campus)
BH1 . . . . **393** B3
Bournemouth Univ
(Talbot Campus)
BH12 . . . . **392** C8
Bournemouth West Rdbt
BH2 . . . . **392** D3
Bourne Pines 4
BH2 . . . . **392** F4
Bourne Rd
Bartley SO40 . . . . **287** C6
Cosham PO6 . . . . **345** B8
North Tidworth SP9 . . . **78** F6
Southampton SO15 . . **290** D5
Thatcham RG19 . . . . **2** F4
Bourne River Ct 9
BH4 . . . . **392** D4
Bourne The GU52 . . . . **75** A6
Bourne Valley Bsns Pk
BH12 . . . . **392** A5
Bourne Valley Rd
BH12 . . . . **392** A5
Bourne View SP9 . . . . . **78** F7
Bourne View Cl
PO10 . . . . **325** D2
Bournewood Dr BH4 **392** C4
Bournewood Pk
GU10 . . . . **122** C7
Bourton Gdns BH7 . . **394** B8
Bouverie Cl 7 BH25 **383** A1
Boveridge Gdns BH9 **378** B4
Bovington Cl BH17 . . **375** F1
Bowater Cl SO40 . . . **264** C1
Bowater Way SO40 . . **264** C1
Bowcombe SO31 . . . . **315** C7
Bowcott Hill GU35 . . **165** D5
Bowden Ho 8 SO17 . **267** C2
Bowden La SO17 . . . . **267** C2
Bowden Rd BH12 . . . **376** C2
Bowdown Ct RG14 . . . . . **1** D2
Bow Dr RG27 . . . . **49** D8
Bowenhurst Gdns
GU52 . . . . **75** A5
Bowenhurst La GU51 . **74** C3
Bowenhurst Rd GU52 . **75** A5
Bowen La GU31 . . . . . **228** F3
Bower Cl
Holbury SO45 . . . . . . **338** C3
Southampton SO19 . . **291** F1
Bower Rd
Bournemouth BH8 . . . **393** D8
Farnham GU10 . . . . . . **121** E5
Bowers Cl PO8 . . . . . . **300** A4
Bowers Grove La
SO24 . . . . **181** C8
Bowers Hill SP5 . . . . **235** E7
Bowers La SP11 . . . . . . **38** A7
Bowerwood Cotts
SP6 . . . . **281** C8
Bowerwood Rd SP6 . **281** D8
Bowes Hill PO9 . . . . . **301** C3
Bowes-Lyon Ct PO8 . **300** B7
Bow Field RG27 . . . . . . **51** C1
Bow Gdns RG27 . . . . . . **49** D8
Bow Gr RG27 . . . . **29** D1
Bowland Rise
Chandler's Ford
SO53 . . . . **243** A7
New Milton BH25 . . . **383** C2
Bowland Way SO45 . . **365** E7
Bowler Ave PO1 . . . . **370** F6
Bowler Ct PO1 . . . . . . **370** F6
Bowling Green Ct
GU16 . . . . **56** C7
Bowling Green Dr
RG27 . . . . **50** F1
Bowling Green Rd
RG18 . . . . **2** E5
Bowlings The GU15 . . **36** A6
Bowman Ct SO19 . . . **292** B3
Bowman Rd RG24 . . . . **49** A4
Bowmonts Rd RG26 . . . **27** B8
Bow St GU34 . . . . **139** E2
Bowyer Cl 4 RG21 . . . **69** A4
Boxall's Gr GU11 . . . . . **99** E8
Boxall's La GU11 . . . . . **99** F7
Box Cl BH17 . . . . **390** B7
Boxgrove Ho PO1 . . . **404** C4
Boxwood Cl
Portchester PO16 . . . **320** B1
Waterlooville PO7 . . . **322** E6
Boyatt Cres SO50 . . . **244** A8
Boyatt La SO50 . . . . . **244** A7
Boyatt Wood Sh Ctr
SO50 . . . . **244** A5
Boyce Cl RG22 . . . . **91** C8
Boyd Cl PO14 . . . . **367** B6
Boyd Rd
Gosport PO13 . . . . . . **343** B4
Poole BH12 . . . . **391** F6
Boyes La SO21 . . . . . . **220** A1
Boyle Cres PO7 . . . . . **322** D5
Boyne Mead Rd
SO23 . . . . **176** C7
Boyne Rise SO23 . . . . **176** B8
Boyneswood Cl
GU34 . . . . **160** C4
Boyneswood La
GU34 . . . . **160** B4
Boyneswood Rd
GU34 . . . . **160** C4
Boynton Cl SO53 . . . . **243** B8
Brabant Cl PO15 . . . . **317** B7
Brabazon Dr BH23 . . **396** B7
Brabazon Rd
Locks Heath PO15 . . . **317** D5
Merley BH21 . . . . **351** F1
Brabon Rd GU14 . . . . . **55** D5
Brabourne Ave
BH22 . . . . **353** C4
Bracebridge GU15 . . . . **35** E5
Bracher Cl SP10 . . . . **106** B8
Bracken Bank RG24 . . . **69** F8
Brackenbury SP10 . . . **82** D1
Bracken Cl
Lee-on-t-S PO13 . . . . **368** A6
North Baddesley
SO52 . . . . **242** A3
St Leonards BH24 . . . **327** D4
Bracken Cres SO50 . . **244** F2
Bracken Ct 10 BH4 . . **392** D4
Brackendale Cl GU15 . **36** C3
Brackendale Ct
BH21 . . . . **326** E8
Brackendale Rd
Bournemouth BH8 . . . **393** D8
Camberley GU15 . . . . . **36** B4
Bracken Glen BH15 . **390** E5
Bracken Hall SO16 . . **267** B8
Bracken Heath 8
PO7 . . . . **300** B1
Brackenhill BH13 . . . **392** A1
Brackenhill Rd BH21 **352** A7
Bracken La
Bordon GU35 . . . . **186** A8
Southampton SO16 . . **266** A1
Yateley GU46 . . . . **33** F6
Bracken Lodge 3
BH6 . . . . **394** F4
Bracken Pl SO16 . . . . **267** A7
Bracken Rd
Bournemouth BH6 . . . **394** C4
Ferndown BH22 . . . . . **353** B7
North Baddesley
SO52 . . . . **242** A3
Petersfield GU31 . . . . **229** C2
Brackens The
Basingstoke RG22 . . . . **91** C6
Hythe SO45 . . . . **313** D3
Locks Heath SO31 . . . **317** B2
Brackens Way
2 Poole BH13 . . . . . **402** F8
Lymington SO41 . . . . **385** F2
Bracken Way BH23 . . **382** B1
Brackenway Rd
SO53 . . . . **243** C8
Brackenwood Dr RG26 . **9** E1
Bracklesham Cl
Farnborough GU14 . . . **55** E7
Southampton SO19 . . **291** F3
Bracklesham Pl
BH25 . . . . **397** F7
Bracklesham Rd
Gosport PO13 . . . . . . **368** D8
South Hayling PO11 . . **373** F2
Brackley Ave
Fair Oak SO50 . . . . . . **245** B3
Hartley Wintney RG27 . **52** C6
Brackley Cl BH23 . . . **379** A8
Brackley Way
Basingstoke RG22 . . . . **68** C2
Totton SO40 . . . . **288** D8
Bracknell La RG27 . . . **52** C7
Bradburne Rd BH2 . . **392** E3
Bradbury Cl RG28 . . . . **86** B5
Bradbury Ho
Enham Alamein SP11 . . **83** B6
Ferndown BH22 . . . . . **353** D7
Bradford Ct 8 PO13 **368** C6
Bradford Junc PO5 . . **404** C2
Bradford Rd
Bournemouth BH9 . . . **378** C4
Portsmouth PO5 . . . . **404** C2
Brading Ave
Gosport PO13 . . . . . . **343** C2
Portsmouth PO4 . . . . **371** A2
Brading Cl SO16 . . . . **267** C5
Bradley Cotts SO21 . . **112** B2
Bradley Ct 10 PO9 . . . **324** B6
Bradley Gn SO16 . . . . **266** B4
Bradley Peak SO22 . . **403** A7
Bradley Rd SO22 . . . . **175** C4
Bradly Rd PO15 . . . . . **318** C1
Bradman Sq SP10 . . . . **83** B3
Bradpole Rd BH8 . . . **378** E1
Bradshaw Cl SO50 . . . **245** E2
Bradstock Cl BH12 . . **391** F8
Bradwell Cl SP10 . . . . **82** D3
Braehead SO45 . . . . . **313** F2
Braemar Ave
Bournemouth BH6 . . . **395** A4
Cosham PO6 . . . . **346** B7
Braemar Cl
Bournemouth BH6 . . . **395** A4
Camberley GU16 . . . . . **56** D8
Fareham PO15 . . . . . . **318** E3
Gosport PO13 . . . . . . **343** D2
Braemar Dr
Christchurch BH23 . . **381** F1
Oakley RG23 . . . . **67** A2
Braemar Rd PO13 . . . **343** D2
Braemore Ct SO22 . . **403** A5
Braeside Bsns Pk
BH15 . . . . **390** B4
Braeside Cl
Haslemere GU27 . . . . **189** D8
Southampton SO19 . . **291** E5
Winchester SO22 . . . . **197** B4
Braeside Cres SO19 . **291** E5
Braeside Rd
Southampton SO19 . . **291** E5
St Leonards BH24 . . . **327** E3
West Moors BH22 . . . **326** F3
Braggers La BH23 . . . **357** B4
Brahms Rd RG22 . . . . . **91** E8
Braidley Rd BH2 . . . . **392** E4
Brailswood Rd BH15 **390** E4
Braine L'Alleud Rd 17
RG21 . . . . **69** B5
Braintree Rd PO6 . . . **321** D1
Braishfield Cl SO16 . **265** F1
Braishfield Gdns
BH8 . . . . **378** D2
Braishfield Prim Sch
SO51 . . . . **216** D6
Braishfield Rd
Braishfield SO51 . . . . **194** D1
Havant PO9 . . . . **324** A4
Romsey SO51 . . . . **216** C4
Brake Ho PO9 . . . . . . **323** D2
Brake Rd GU14 . . . . . . **55** C1
Brakes Rise GU47 . . . . **35** C8
Bramar Ct 9 BH4 . . . **392** C2
Bramber Rd PO12 . . . **369** A8
Bramble Bank GU16 . . . **56** E6
Bramble Cl
Alderholt SP6 . . . . . . **281** A5
Eastleigh SO50 . . . . . . **244** B5
Havant PO9 . . . . **324** C3
Holbury SO45 . . . . . . **338** C3
Stubbington PO14 . . . **367** A6
Bramble Ct
7 Newbury RG14 . . . . . . **1** F2
Petersfield GU31 . . . . **229** C3
West Moors BH22 . . . **326** E2
Brambledown GU26 . **167** C4
Bramble Dr SO51 . . . **216** C1
Bramblegate SO50 . . **245** D1
Bramble Hill
Chandler's Ford
SO53 . . . . **243** A6
New Alresford SO24 . **179** D5
Bramble La
Clanfield PO8 . . . . **276** B7
Sarisbury SO31 . . . . . **316** E5
Walkford BH23 . . . . . **382** B1
Bramble Mews 1
SO18 . . . . **292** A8
Bramble Rd
Petersfield GU31 . . . . **229** C3
Portsmouth PO4 . . . . **370** E4
Brambles Bsns Ctr The
PO7 . . . . **299** C1
Brambles Cl
Ash GU12 . . . . **77** F1
Colden Common
SO21 . . . . **245** A8
Four Marks GU34 . . . **160** B2
Brambles Ent Ctr The
PO7 . . . . **299** C1
Brambles Farm Ind Est
PO7 . . . . **322** D8
Brambles Rd PO13 . . **367** D4
Brambles The RG14 . . . . **5** C8
Brambleton Ave
GU9 . . . . **121** F7
Bramble Way
Bransgore BH23 . . . . **357** B1
Gosport PO13 . . . . . . **343** A2
Old Basing RG24 . . . . . **70** C6
Bramble Wlk SO41 . . **385** C4
Bramblewood Pl
GU51 . . . . **53** E1
Brambling Cl
Basingstoke RG22 . . . . **90** F7
Southampton SO16 . . **266** B6
Brambling Rd PO9 . . . **301** B1
Bramblings The
SO40 . . . . **288** C7
Bramblys Cl RG21 . . . . **69** A4
Bramblys Dr RG21 . . . . **69** A4
Brambridge SO50 . . . **244** E8
Brambridge Ho
SO50 . . . . **219** D1
Bramdean Cl 2 RG26 . **26** F7
Bramdean Dr PO9 . . . **323** D5
Bramdean Mews
SO19 . . . . **291** E5
Bramdean Rd SO18 . . **292** D7
Bramdown Hts RG22 . . **91** B7
Bramham Moor
PO14 . . . . **367** B7
Bramley CE Prim Sch
RG26 . . . . **28** F4
Bramley Cl
Alton GU34 . . . . **140** A3
Lymington SO41 . . . . **385** E2
Waterlooville PO7 . . . **322** F8
Bramley Cres SO19 . . **292** B2
Bramley Croft GU26 . **167** C4
Bramley Ct BH22 . . . . **353** C6
Bramley Gdns
Emsworth PO10 . . . . . **349** B8
Gosport PO12 . . . . . . **369** B2
Horton Heath SO50 . . **269** C6
Bramley Green Rd
RG26 . . . . **29** A2
Bramley Ho
3 Portsmouth PO5 . . **404** B2
Gosport PO12 . . . . . . **369** B2
Hedge End SO30 . . . . **293** B6
Bramley La
Blackwater GU17 . . . . . **34** F5
Bramley RG26 . . . . **28** F4
Bramley Rd
Bournemouth BH10 . . **377** C5
Camberley GU15 . . . . . . **35** F2
Ferndown BH22 . . . . . **353** D6
Pamber End RG26 . . . . . **27** D2
Sherfield on L RG27 . . **29** D1
Silchester RG7 . . . . **10** F1
Three Ashes RG7 . . . . . **28** B7
Bramley Sta RG26 . . . . . **28** F3
Bramleys The SP5 . . **212** B3
Bramley Wlk GU35 . . **164** B2
Bramling Ave GU46 . . . **33** F6
Bramoak RG26 . . . . **28** D3
Brampton Gdns RG22 **91** C5
Brampton La PO3 . . . **346** C4
Brampton Manor
SO16 . . . . **266** F5
Brampton Rd BH15 . . **390** D6
Brampton Twr SO16 . **266** F5
Bramsdon Ct 5 PO4 **370** F2
Bramshaw Cl SO22 . . **175** C3
Bramshaw Ct 18
PO9 . . . . **324** B5
Bramshaw Gdns
BH8 . . . . **378** D3
Bramshaw Way
BH25 . . . . **397** D8
Bramshill Cl RG2 . . . . . **15** C8
Bramshill Ho (Police
Coll) RG27 . . . . **32** B4
Bramshot Dr GU51 . . . **54** A2
Bramshot La
Farnborough GU14 . . . **55** A6
Farnborough GU51 . . . **54** E5
Bramshott Dr RG27 . . . **51** B1
Bramshott Rd
Farnborough GU51 . . . **54** E2
Portsmouth PO4 . . . . **370** F4
Southampton SO19 . . **314** F8
Bramston Rd SO15 . . **290** C8
Brancaster Ave SP10 . **82** D3
Branches La SO51 . . . **213** F3
Branders Cl BH6 . . . . **395** A4
Branders La BH6 . . . . **395** B5
Brandon Cl GU34 . . . **139** E4
Brandon Ct
6 Poole BH12 . . . . . **392** B4
Portsmouth PO5 . . . . **404** D1
Brandon Ho PO5 . . . . **404** D1
Brandon Rd
Crookham Village
GU52 . . . . **74** E4
Portsmouth PO5 . . . . **370** D2
Brandt Ho 8 PO17 . . **318** E7
Brandwood Ct 4
BH14 . . . . **391** A3
Brandy Bottom GU46 **34** C3
Brandy Mount SO24 . **179** D6
Branewick Cl PO15 . . **317** D3
Branksea Ave BH15 . **389** E1
Branksea Cl BH15 . . . **389** E1
Branksome Ave
Chilbolton SO20 . . . . . **129** A3
Southampton SO15 . . **266** C1
Branksome Cl
Camberley GU15 . . . . . **36** C6
Chilbolton SO20 . . . . . **129** A3
New Milton BH25 . . . **383** B2
Winchester SO22 . . . . **197** B6
Branksome Ct 4
BH13 . . . . **402** F8
Branksome Dene Rd
BH4 . . . . **392** B2
Branksome Heath Mid
Sch BH12 . . . . **391** C6
Branksome Hill Rd
Bournemouth BH4 . . . **392** B5
Sandhurst GU47 . . . . . **35** C8
Branksome Park Rd
GU15 . . . . **36** C6
Branksome Sta
BH12 . . . . **391** F4
Branksome Twrs
BH13 . . . . **402** H8
Branksome Walk Manor
4 GU51 . . . . **53** F1
Branksome Wood Gdns
BH2 . . . . **392** D4
Branksomewood Rd
GU51 . . . . **53** F1
Branksome Wood Rd BH2,
BH4 . . . . **392** C4
Bransbury Cl SO16 . . **266** C4
Bransbury Rd PO4 . . **371** B3
Bransgore Ave PO9 . . **323** C4
Bransgore CE Prim Sch
BH23 . . . . **381** C8
Bransgore Gdns
BH23 . . . . **357** C1
Bransley Cl SO51 . . . . **216** B1
Branson Rd GU35 . . . **164** E3
Brantfell Lo GU11 . . . . **99** E8
Branton Cl RG22 . . . . . **68** C3
Branwell Cl BH23 . . . **380** A1
Branwood Cl SO41 . . **384** E1
Brasenose Cl PO14 . . **317** C1
Brasher Cl SO50 . . . . **245** A2
Brassey Cl BH9 . . . . . **378** A1
Brassey Rd
Bournemouth BH9 . . . **378** A1
Winchester SO22 . . . . **403** D7
Brassey Terr BH9 . . . **377** F1
Brasted Ct PO4 . . . . **371** C5
Braunfels Wlk RG14 . . . **1** C2
Braunston Cl 7 PO6 **321** A1
Braust Ho SP11 . . . . . . **81** E2
Braxall Lawn PO9 . . . **323** D6
Braxton Ctyd SO41 . . **399** E7
Braxton Ho 1 SO23 . **198** C8
Breach Ave PO10 . . . . **325** E2
Breach Farm Cotts
RG25 . . . . **113** D4
Breachfield RG20 . . . . . **22** D7
Breach La
Bishopstoke SO50 . . . **244** D5
Sherfield on L RG27 . . . **49** E8
Upper Chute SP11 . . . . **58** B8
Breadels Ct RG22 . . . . . **91** B4
Breadels Field RG22 . **91** A4
Breamore CE Prim Sch
SP6 . . . . **258** B8
Breamore Cl
Eastleigh SO50 . . . . . . **244** A6
New Milton BH25 . . . **382** E3
Breamore Countryside
Mus★ SP6 . . . . **234** A2
Breamore Ho★ SP6 . **234** A3
Breamore Rd
Downton SP5 . . . . **234** E7
Southampton SO18 . . **292** D7
Brean Cl SO16 . . . . . . **265** E2
Brearley Ct BH23 . . . **397** B8
Brecon Ave PO6 . . . . **346** B8
Brecon Cl
Bournemouth BH10 . . **377** E6
Chandler's Ford SO53 **243** B3
Fareham PO14 . . . . . . **342** E8
Farnborough GU14 . . . **55** B7
Hythe SO45 . . . . **313** E3
New Milton BH25 . . . **383** C2
Brecon Ho 23 PO1 . . **370** A4
Brecon Rd SO19 . . . . **292** C5
Bredenbury Cres
PO6 . . . . **321** C1
Bredon Wlk PO14 . . . **342** E8
Bredy Cl BH17 . . . . . . **375** D1
Breech Cl 5 PO3 . . . . **345** F4
Breech The GU47 . . . . **35** C7
Bremble Cl BH12 . . . . **376** C2
Bremen Gdns SP10 . . . **82** F3
Brenchley Cl PO16 . . **344** B7
Brendon Cl SO45 . . . **313** D2
Brendon Gn SO16 . . . **289** F8
Brendon Rd
Fareham PO14 . . . . . . **342** D8
Farnborough GU14 . . . **55** B7
Brent Ct PO10 . . . . . . **348** E7
Brentwood Cres
SO18 . . . . **268** A1
Bret Harte Rd GU16 . . . **36** C1
Breton Cl PO15 . . . . . **317** B7
Brewells La GU33 . . . **208** E5
Brewer Cl
Basingstoke RG22 . . . . **68** C3
Locks Heath SO31 . . . **317** B4
Brewers Cl GU14 . . . . . **55** E5
Brewers La
Gosport PO13 . . . . . . **343** D2
Twyford SO21 . . . . . . **219** F5
West Tisted SO24 . . . **204** C7
Brewer St PO1 . . . . . . **404** B4
Brewery Comm RG7 . . . **11** F7
Brewery Cotts SP11 . . . **81** B1
Brewery Gdns 12
GU34 . . . . **139** F3
Brew House La RG27 . **52** D6
Brewhouse Sq PO12 . **369** D7
Brewhouse Yd SO24 . **179** D6
Brewster Cl PO8 . . . . **300** A3
Briar Cl
Christchurch BH23 . . **395** F6
Gosport PO12 . . . . . . **368** E3
Poole BH15 . . . . **390** E5
Waterlooville PO8 . . . **300** B5
Briardene Ct SO40 . . **288** E7
Briarfield 49 BH4 . . . . **392** C3
Briarfield Gdns PO8 . **300** B6
Briar La GU34 . . . . **160** C3
Briarlea Rd RG7 . . . . . . **11** E6
Briarleas Ct GU14 . . . . **77** B8
Briars Cl GU14 . . . . **55** B3
Briars The
Ash GU12 . . . . **77** F1
Brockenhurst SO42 . . **333** F1
Fleet GU52 . . . . **75** A6
Briar's The PO7 . . . . . **299** C1
Briarswood SO16 . . . . **266** B1
Briarswood Rd BH16 **389** C7
Briarswood Rise
SO45 . . . . **313** D2
Briar Way
Romsey SO51 . . . . **216** C1
Tadley RG26 . . . . **27** A8
Wimborne Minster
BH21 . . . . **352** B5
Briarwood RG40 . . . . . . **16** C6
Briar Wood GU33 . . . . **208** A7
Briarwood Cl PO16 . . **343** B8
Briarwood Gdns
PO11 . . . . **372** F3
Briarwood Rd SO40 . . **288** C6
Brickersbury Ho
GU14 . . . . **55** D8
Brickets Terr PO12 . . **369** B3
Brickfield La
Chandler's Ford
SO53 . . . . **243** C5
Lymington SO41 . . . . **385** F5
Brickfield Rd SO17 . . **267** C2
Brickfields Cl RG24 . . . **70** A8
Brickfield Trad Est
SO53 . . . . **243** C5
Brickiln La GU34 . . . . **160** F6
Brick Kiln Ind Est
RG26 . . . . **10** A1
Brick Kiln La
Alton GU34 . . . . **139** C4
West Tisted SO24 . . . **204** B8
Brick La
Bransgore BH23 . . . . **357** E4
Fleet GU51 . . . . **54** A2
Brickmakers Rd
SO21 . . . . **244** F8
Bricksbury Hill GU9 . . **99** A8
Brickwoods Cl SO51 . **241** B8
Brickworth Rd SP5 . . **212** A3
Brickyard La
Corfe Mullen BH21 . . **350** A1
Ferndown BH22 . . . . . **353** A6
Verwood BH31 . . . . . . **302** D7
Brickyard Rd SO32 . . **272** A3
Brickyards Ind Est The
GU32 . . . . **207** A1
Brickyard The SO40 . **287** B8
Bricky Lake La SO51 **263** C7
Bridefield Cl PO8 . . . **299** D3
Bridefield Cres PO8 . **299** D3
Bridge App BH15 . . . . **390** B1
Bridge Cl SO31 . . . . . **293** B1
Bridge Cotts
Liss GU33 . . . . **207** E7
West Wellow SO51 . . **238** F4
Bridge Ct
Romsey SO51 . . . . **240** E6
Tadley RG26 . . . . **27** A8
Bridge Education Ctr The
SO50 . . . . **244** B3
Bridge End GU15 . . . . . **35** F4
Bridge Farm SO30 . . . **294** D4
Bridgefield GU9 . . . . . . **99** B2
Bridgefoot Dr PO16 . **319** C1
Bridgefoot Hill PO16 **319** C1
Bridgefoot Path
PO10 . . . . **348** F8
Bridge Ho
Gosport PO13 . . . . . . **343** C4
Southampton SO15 . . **290** C5
Bridge Industries
PO16 . . . . **319** C3
Bridge La SO21 . . . . . . **219** E7
Bridgemary Ave
PO13 . . . . **343** D3
Bridgemary Com Sch
PO13 . . . . **343** C2
Bridgemary Gr PO13 **343** C5
Bridgemary Rd
PO13 . . . . **343** C4
Bridgemary Way
PO13 . . . . **343** C5
Bridge Mdws GU33 . . **207** F4
Bridgemead GU16 . . . . **56** B8
Bridge Mead SO32 . . **249** D5
Bridge Mews GU10 . . **100** D7
Bridge Pl BH10 . . . . . **377** D7
Bridge Rd
Aldershot GU11 . . . . . . **99** E8
Bishopstone SP5 . . . . **210** B8
Bursledon SO31 . . . . . **293** B1
Camberley GU15 . . . . . **35** F3
Emsworth PO10 . . . . . **324** F1
Farnborough GU14 . . . **55** D4
Locks Heath SO31 . . . **317** B5

Bridge Rd *continued*
Lymington SO41 .... **385** F5
New Alresford SO24 .. **179** B5
North Warnborough
RG29 .... **72** C4
Romsey SO51 ...... **241** A7
Sarisbury SO31 ..... **316** D6
Southampton SO19 .. **291** D3
Bridgers Cl SO16.... **265** E5
Bridges Ave PO6.... **320** F1
Bridges Cl
Eastleigh SO50 ..... **243** F3
West Moors BH22.... **326** F3
Bridge Sh Ctr The
PO1................ **404** D3
Bridgeside Cl PO1 .. **404** D3
Bridge Sq GU9...... **99** A2
Bridge St
◗ Newbury RG14...... **1** E3
◗ Winchester SO23.. **403** F5
Andover SP10 ...... **106** A4
Christchurch BH23 .. **395** C6
Fordingbridge SP6... **257** F1
Overton RG25 ...... **88** A8
Southwick PO17 .... **320** E6
Titchfield PO14 .... **342** A7
Wickham PO17 ..... **296** A3
Bridges The
Ringwood BH24..... **328** E7
Silchester RG7 ..... **11** A5
Bridget Cl PO8...... **300** C7
Bridge Terr
◗ Southampton
SO14............. **291** B3
Compton SO21...... **219** E6
Bridgetts La SO21... **155** B2
Bridgewater Rd
BH12 .... **391** D6
Bridgeway Ct SO40.. **289** F4
Bridgeway The SO19 **291** E3
Bridge Wlk GU46.... **34** B7
Bridgwater Ct SO15. **290** D5
Bridle Cl
East Tisted GU34.... **183** D5
Grayshott GU26..... **166** E3
Upton BH16........ **389** D7
Bridle Cres BH7.... **394** D7
Bridle Ct ◗ GU11.... **76** C2
Bridle Way BH21.... **352** C6
Bridleways BH31.... **302** E6
Bridlington Ave
SO15 .... **290** D8
Bridport Ct SO15.... **290** C5
Bridport Rd
Poole BH12 .... **391** F8
Verwood BH31...... **302** F6
Bridport St PO1..... **404** B3
Brierley Ave BH23... **353** E1
Brierley Cl BH10.... **377** E4
Brierley Rd BH10... **377** E4
Brigantine Rd SO31.. **316** C4
Brigham Cl ◗ PO2... **345** E3
Brighstone Cl SO16 **267** C5
Brightlands Ave BH6 **394** F5
Brighton Ave PO12.. **368** F6
Brighton Hill Com Coll
RG22............. **68** D1
Brighton Hill Ctr
RG22............. **91** D8
Brighton Hill Rdbt
RG22............. **68** E1
Brighton Hill Ret Pk
RG22............. **68** E2
Brighton Rd
Aldershot GU12.... **100** A8
Southampton SO15 . **290** F7
Sway SO41 .... **360** A3
Brighton Way RG22.. **91** D8
Bright Rd BH15 ... **390** E6
Brightside Rd SO16 **265** F3
Brights La PO11..... **372** F5
Brightstone La GU34 **161** B2
Brightstone Rd PO6. **345** E7
Brightwells Rd GU9 . **99** A2
Bright Wire Cres
SO50 .... **243** F4
Brimley Hill Ct RG24 **24** D2
Brimpton CE Prim Sch
RG7.............. **8** D6
Brimpton La RG7 ... **8** F3
Brimpton Rd
Baughurst RG26 ... **26** B8
Brimpton RG7 ..... **8** D7
Pamber Heath RG26 .. **9** A1
Brindle Cl
Aldershot GU11..... **99** F7
Southampton SO16 .. **267** A5
Brinksway GU51 .... **75** A8
Brinns Cotts GU17 .. **35** A5
Brinn's La GU17..... **35** A5
Brinsons Ct BH23 ... **380** C3
Brinton La SO45 .... **314** A5
Brinton's Rd SO14 .. **291** B5
Brinton's Terr SO14 **291** A6
Brisbane Ho ◗ PO1. **370** D7
Brisbane Rd BH23... **379** E1
Brislands La GU34 .. **181** E7
Bristol Ct PO13 .... **368** C6
Bristol Rd PO4...... **370** F2
Bristow Inf Sch GU15 **.35** F1
Bristow Rd GU15.... **36** A3
Britain St PO1...... **370** A4
Britannia Cl GU35... **164** F3

Britannia Ct
Poole BH12 .... **391** B7
Southampton,Bitterne
Manor SO14....... **291** C5
Britannia Dr RG22... **91** A4
Britannia Gdns SO30 **269** B3
Britannia Pl SO41... **385** F4
Britannia Rd
Poole BH14 .... **391** A3
Portsmouth PO5 .... **404** C2
Southampton SO14 .. **291** D3
Britannia Rd N PO5 . **404** D2
Britannia St GU31... **229** A5
Britannia Way
Christchurch BH23 .. **396** B7
Gosport PO12 ..... **369** C8
Britannic Ho ◗
SO14 .... **291** C5
Britnell Ho ◗ GU31 . **228** F4
Briton St SO14...... **291** A3
Brittain Ct GU47.... **35** A7
Britten Cl GU12.....**77** F2
Britten Rd
Basingstoke RG22... **91** E8
Lee-on-t-S PO13 .... **367** E3
Britten Way PO7.... **322** E4
Brittons Cotts SO42 **333** D1
Brixey Cl BH12...... **391** C7
Brixey Rd BH12..... **391** C7
Brixworth Cl ◗ PO6. **321** A1
Broadacres
GU51 .... **74** D8
Broad Ave BH8 .... **393** D8
Broadbent Cl SO16.. **265** E6
Broad Chalke Down
SO22 .... **403** A2
Broad Croft PO9.... **301** C3
Broadfield Cl PO16 .. **319** C2
Broadfields Cl SO41 **399** D5
Broad Gdns PO6 ... **346** E8
Broad Gn ◗ SO14... **291** A4
Broadhalfpenny La
RG26 .... **10** A1
Broad Ha'penny
GU10 .... **121** E5
Sandhurst GU47 ... **34** B7
Southampton,Thornhill Pk
SO18.............. **292** D7
Winchester SO23 ... **403** E5
Broadwell Rd GU10 . **121** D6
Broad Wlk GU16 .... **36** C2
Broad Woods La
SO51 .... **239** A6
Brocas Dr RG21..... **69** C7
Brockenhurst Ave
PO9 .... **323** D6
Brockenhurst CE Prim
Sch SO42......... **360** F8
Brockenhurst Coll
SO42 .... **334** A2
Brockenhurst Dr
GU46 .... **.34** B5
Brockenhurst Rd
Aldershot GU11..... **99** F8
Bournemouth BH9... **378** B2
Brockenhurst Sta
SO42 .... **361** A8
Brockham Hill La
GU34 .... **118** A2
Brockhampton La
PO9 .... **323** E1
Brockhampton Rd
Havant PO9........ **323** D1
Langstone PO9 ..... **347** D8
Brock Hill Forest Wlks★
SO43.............. **332** F8
Brockhills La BH25.. **383** C6
Brock Ho SO42 ..... **333** F1
Brockhurst Ind Est
PO12.............. **343** F1
Brockhurst Inf Sch
PO12.............. **368** F7
Brockhurst Jun Sch
PO12.............. **369** A8
Brockhurst Lodge
GU9 .... **121** F7
Brockishill Rd SO40 **287** A5
Brocklands
Havant PO9........ **323** D1
Yateley GU46....... **33** F4
Brockley Rd BH10... **377** E4
Brocks Cl SO45 .... **313** D2
Brocks Pine BH24... **327** F3
Brock Way BH31.... **302** E7
Brockwood BH24 ... **327** D2
Brockwood Bottom
Bramdean SO24 .... **202** E1
Bramdean SO24 .... **224** F8
Brockwood Park Sch
SO24.............. **202** F1
Brodrick Ave PO12.. **369** A4
Brog St BH21....... **350** C1
Brokenford Ave
SO40 .... **289** A7
Brokenford Bsns Ctr
SO40.............. **288** F7
Brokenford Ct ◗
SO40.............. **288** F7
Brokenford La SO40. **288** F7
Broken Way RG20.... **5** F2
Brokle Cl GU52.....**74** E4
Brombys The ◗
BH15 .... **390** C2
Bromelia Cl RG26 ... **28** F4
Bromley Ho BH12 ... **392** B5
Bromley Rd SO18... **267** F1
Brompton Cl BH2.... **392** E8
Brompton Rd PO4... **370** F3
Bromyard Cres PO6. **321** D1

Broadstone Mid Sch
BH18.............. **375** C5
Broadstone Way
Broadstone BH17 ... **374** F1
Poole BH17 .... **390** B7
Broadview Cl GU34. **141** E7
Broad View La SO22. **197** A3
Broadwater Ave
BH14 .... **391** C2
Broadwater Rd
Romsey SO51 ...... **240** E6
Southampton SO18 .. **267** F3
Broadway
Southbourne BH6 ... **395** B3
Whitchurch RG28 ... **86** D4
Broad Way
Beech Hill RG7 ...... **13** B3
Froxfield Green GU32 **227** E8
Hamble-le-R SO31... **315** E5
Southampton SO17 .. **267** B1
Broadway Ct BH12 .. **392** A5
Broadway Gables
BH14 .... **391** E4
Broadway Gdns ◗
BH21 .... **351** C4
Broadway Ho
Broadstone BH18 ... **375** B4
Sandhurst GU47 ... **34** F7
Broadway La
Bournemouth BH8... **378** C4
Horndean PO8...... **299** D2
Broadway Mews
BH14 .... **390** F3
Broadway Pk
◗ Wimborne Minster
BH21 .... **351** C4
Petersfield SO31.... **228** F1
Broadway The
◗ Portswood
SO15.............. **267** B1
◗ Bitterne Pk SO18.. **267** F1
Andover SP10 ..... **106** A7
Bournemouth BH10.. **377** D6
Newbury RG14 ......**1** E4
Broadwell Rd GU10 . **121** D6
Broad Wlk GU16 .... **36** C2
Broad Woods La
SO51 .... **239** A6
Brocas Dr RG21..... **69** C7
Brockenhurst Ave
PO9 .... **323** D6
Brockenhurst CE Prim
Sch SO42......... **360** F8
Brockenhurst Coll
SO42 .... **334** A2
Brockenhurst Dr
GU46 .... **.34** B5
Brockenhurst Rd
Aldershot GU11..... **99** F8
Bournemouth BH9... **378** B2
Brockenhurst Sta
SO42 .... **361** A8
Brockham Hill La
GU34 .... **118** A2
Brockhampton La
PO9 .... **323** E1
Brockhampton Rd
Havant PO9........ **323** D1
Langstone PO9 ..... **347** D8
Brock Hill Forest Wlks★
SO43.............. **332** F8
Brockhills La BH25.. **383** C6
Brock Ho SO42 ..... **333** F1
Brockley Rd BH10... **377** E4
Brocks Cl SO45 .... **313** D2
Brocks Pine BH24... **327** F3
Brock Way BH31.... **302** E7
Brockwood BH24 ... **327** D2
Brockwood Bottom
Bramdean SO24 .... **202** E1
Bramdean SO24 .... **224** F8
Brockwood Park Sch
SO24.............. **202** F1
Brodrick Ave PO12.. **369** A4
Brog St BH21....... **350** C1
Brokenford Ave
SO40 .... **289** A7
Brokenford Bsns Ctr
SO40.............. **288** F7
Brokenford Ct ◗
SO40.............. **288** F7
Brokenford La SO40. **288** F7
Broken Way RG20.... **5** F2
Brokle Cl GU52.....**74** E4
Brombys The ◗
BH15 .... **390** C2
Bromelia Cl RG26 ... **28** F4
Bromley Ho BH12 ... **392** B5
Bromley Rd SO18... **267** F1
Brompton Cl BH2.... **392** E8
Brompton Rd PO4... **370** F3
Bromyard Cres PO6. **321** D1

Bronte Ave BH23... **380** A1
Bronte Cl SO40 .... **288** D6
Bronte Gdns PO15 .. **317** C8
Bronte Rise RG14 ....**5** F8
Bronte Way SO19 ... **291** E6
Bronwen Ct SO19 ... **292** A2
Bronze Cl RG22 ..... **91** A4
Brook Ave
Farnham GU9 ...... **99** D7
New Milton BH25 ... **383** B4
Warsash SO31 ..... **316** D5
Brook Ave N BH25 .. **383** B4
Brook Cl
Ash GU12.......... **77** F3
Bournemouth BH10.. **377** C4
Fleet GU51 .... **75** A8
North Baddesley
SO52............. **242** A3
Sarisbury SO31..... **316** E3
Brook Cnr SO43..... **262** A1
Brook Cotts
King's Somborne
SO20............. **193** C6
Westbourne PO10... **325** B3
Yateley GU46....... **34** A6
Brook Ct
Chandler's Ford
SO53............. **243** C6
Romsey SO51 ...... **240** E6
Southampton SO15 .. **290** D5
Brookdale Cl
Broadstone BH18 ... **375** A4
Waterlooville PO7 ... **322** F8
Brookdale Farm
BH18 .... **375** A4
Brook Dr BH31..... **303** B4
Brooke Cl SO23 .... **176** B8
Brooke Ct GU16.... **56** D6
Brookers La SO31... **343** B3
Brookes Hill Ind Est
SO40.............. **264** B4
Brook Farm Ave
PO15 .... **318** F1
Brookfield Cl
◗ Havant PO9 ..... **323** E2
Chineham RG24...... **49** A3
Brookfield Com Sch &
Language Coll
SO31............. **316** E4
Brookfield Gdns
SO31............. **316** F4
Brookfield Pl SO17.. **267** B2
Brookfields Cl
Aldershot GU12..... **77** D3
Fair Oak SO50 ..... **245** B2
Portsmouth PO1 .... **370** E6
Brookfields SO51.... **238** D3
Brook Gdns
Emsworth PO10..... **348** D8
Farnborough GU14 .. **55** D2
Brook Gn RG26......**27** B8
Brookham Sch GU30 **188** C2
Brook Hill SO41..... **386** E7
Brook Ho
Barton on S BH25 ... **397** E7
Farnham GU9 ...... **99** B6
Newbury RG14 ...... **1** E4
Southampton SO19 .. **292** A3
Brookhouse Rd GU14. **55** D3
Brook La
Botley SO30........ **293** F6
Bransgore BH23 .... **381** F6
Corfe Mullen BH21.. **374** C6
Hambledon PO7..... **274** D5
Locks Heath SO31... **317** A5
Warsash SO31..... **316** D3
Woodgreen SP6..... **258** E7
Brookland Cl SO41.. **385** C3
Brooklands
Aldershot GU11..... **76** C1
Bournemouth BH4... **392** B3
Lyndhurst SO43..... **310** A4
Brooklands Cl GU9...**99** B7
Brooklands Rd
Bishop's Waltham
SO32............. **271** C8
Farnham GU9 ...... **99** C7
Havant PO9........ **323** D2
Brooklands Way GU9. **99** C7
Brookley Cl GU10 ... **100** A8
Brookly Gdns GU51 .. **54** B2
Brooklyn Cl SO21 ... **219** C3
Brooklyn Ct
New Milton BH25 ... **382** F3
Otterbourne SO21... **219** F2
Brooklyn Dr PO7.... **322** F8
Brooklyn Cl SO32... **271** E2
Brookman Ct SO18... **292** A4
Brook Mdw PO15 ... **318** F1
Brookmead Way
PO9 .... **347** F8

Brookside
Farnham GU9 ...... **99** B6
Gosport PO13 ..... **343** B5
Ibsley SP6......... **282** C2
Landford SP5....... **237** D4
Sandhurst GU47 .... **35** A7
Totton SO40........ **288** F5
Brookside Ave SO15. **289** F7
Brookside Bsns Ctr
RG7.............. **14** B6
Brookside Cl
Bransgore BH23 .... **357** A1
Denmead PO7 ..... **298** F4
Brookside Cotts
SO20 .... **147** F5
Brookside Ho SO18 . **267** E4
Brookside Park Homes
BH21 .... **374** B4
Brookside Park Mobile
Home Pk GU14....**35** E1
Brookside Rd
Bransgore BH23 .... **381** A8
Brockenhurst SO42.. **333** F2
Havant,Bedhampton
PO9 .... **323** C1
Langstone PO9 ..... **347** E8
Wimborne Minster
BH21 .... **351** F4
Brookside Way
Christchurch BH23 .. **381** E1
Southampton SO18 .. **267** E4
West End SO30 .... **268** E3
Brookside Wlk RG26 **27** A8
Brooks Rise RG10 ...**82** E1
Brooks Sh Ctr The
SO23.............. **403** E6
Brook St SO32 ..... **271** C8
Brook Terr SP6 ..... **281** F8
Brook The SO24 .... **179** D8
Brook Trad Est The
GU12.............. **77** D3
Brookvale Cl RG21 .. **69** A5
Brookvale Ct ◗
SO17 .... **267** A1
Brookvale Rd SO17.. **267** A1
Brookvale Sch GU17 **.68** F5
Brook Valley SO16 .. **266** A2
Brookway
Anna Valley SP11 ... **105** C4
Newbury RG14 ...... **2** C2
Brook Way
Christchurch BH23 .. **396** C7
Romsey SO51 ...... **216** A1
Brook Wlk SO40 .... **264** C1
Brookwood Ave
SO50 .... **243** F3
Brookwood Ind Est
SO50.............. **244** A3
Brookwood Rd
Farnborough GU14 .. **56** B4
Southampton SO16 . **289** D8
Broom Acres
Fleet GU51 .... **74** F6
Sandhurst GU47 ... **34** F8
Broom Cl
Portsmouth PO4 .... **371** D4
Waterlooville PO7 ... **323** A5
Broome Cl GU46 ... **34** A7
Broomfield Cres
PO13 .... **368** B7
Broomfield Cl SO41. **385** B2
Broomfield Dr SP6.. **281** A5
Broomfield La
Lymington SO41 .... **385** E4
Rowledge GU10..... **121** E1
Broomfield Rd GU35 **164** B2
Broomhill
Ewshot GU10....... **98** B8
Landford SP5....... **237** D2
Broom Hill SO41.... **387** B7
Broomhill Cl SO41... **385** B2
Broomhill Rd GU14... **55** B5
Broom Hill Way
SO50 .... **244** A7
Broomhurst La ◗
GU51 ....**53** E5
Broom La BH6...... **394** B4
Broomleaf Cnr GU9..**99** B2
Broomleaf Rd GU9 ..**99** B2
Broom Rd
Petersfield GU31.... **229** C2
Poole BH12 .... **376** C1
Broom Road Bsns Pk
BH12.............. **376** C1
Brooms Gr SO19 ... **292** D3
Broom Sq PO4...... **371** D5
Broom Squires
GU26 .... **167** D4
Broom Way
Blackwater GU17 ... **35** C4
Gosport PO13,PO14 . **343** A1
Lee-on-t-S PO13 .... **367** F4
Broomwood Way
GU10 .... **122** A6
Broomy Cl SO45 .... **313** C4
Broomy Lodges SO51 **53** C4
Brougham La PO12.. **369** A7
Brougham Pl GU9...**99** F7
Brougham Rd PO5... **404** B2
Brougham St PO12.. **369** A7
Broughton Ave BH10 **377** D4
Broughton Cl
◗ Southampton
SO16.............. **266** A1
Bournemouth BH10.. **377** D4
Broughton Ho ◗
SO18 .... **291** E8

Broughton Mews
GU16 .... **36** D1
Broughton Prim Sch
SO20.............. **170** B7
Broughton Rd
Broughton SO20 .... **148** E2
Lyndhurst SO43 .... **309** F6
Brow Cvn Site The
BH25 .... **359** E6
Brown Croft RG27....**50** F1
Browndown Rd
PO13 .... **368** C3
Brownen Rd BH9.... **393** B8
Brownfield Ho ◗
GU31 .... **228** F3
Brownhill Cl SO53... **243** C7
Brownhill Ct SO16 .. **265** E3
Brownhill Gdns
SO53 .... **243** D7
Brownhill Rd
Chandler's Ford
SO53............. **243** D7
New Milton BH25 ... **358** E3
North Baddesley
SO52............. **242** A4
Brownhill Way SO16 **265** D3
Browning Ave
Bournemouth BH5... **394** A4
Portchester PO6 .... **320** E1
Southampton SO19 . **292** D6
Browning Cl
Basingstoke RG24... **69** C8
Eastleigh SO50 .... **243** F3
Swanwick PO15..... **317** C8
Totton SO40........ **288** D7
Browning Dr SO22 .. **403** B6
Browning Rd
Crookham Village
GU52 .... **74** E3
Poole BH12 .... **391** D6
Brownings Cl SO41.. **385** A4
Brownlow Ave SO19. **292** A6
Brownlow Cl PO1 ... **370** D7
Brownlow Ct ◗ BH4 **392** C3
Brownlow Gdns
SO19 .... **292** A6
Browns Cl RG26.....**28** F4
Brownsea Ave BH21. **374** D6
Brownsea Cl BH25 .. **382** E3
Brownsea Ct BH14 .. **402** B8
Brownsea Island (NT)★
BH15.............. **401** D4
Brownsea Rd BH13.. **402** B3
Brownsea View Ave
BH14 .... **391** C1
Brownsea View Cl
BH14 .... **391** C1
Browns La
Damerham SP6..... **256** B5
East End SO41...... **387** C5
Brownsover Rd GU14. **55** A4
Browns Wlk GU10... **121** D5
Brownwich La PO14. **341** D5
Browsholme Cl
SO50 .... **244** A6
Brow The PO7...... **322** C2
Broxburn Cl SO53... **218** E1
Broxhead Farm Rd
GU35.............. **164** F2
Broxhead Rd PO9 ... **324** A6
Broxhead Trad Est
GU35.............. **164** F6
Bruan Rd RG14......**5** D8
Bruce Cl PO16 ..... **319** A3
Bruce Rd PO4 ..... **370** F2
Brudenell Ave BH13. **402** D7
Brudenell Rd BH13.. **402** D6
Brue Cl SO53 ...... **243** B7
Brummell Rd RG14....**1** D7
Brune Ho SO16..... **267** A5
Brune La PO13 .... **368** C8
Brunel Cl
Hedge End SO30 ... **269** D1
Micheldever SO21... **111** B2
Verwood BH31...... **303** C4
Brunel Gate SP10 ... **82** B2
Brunel Rd
Basingstoke RG21... **68** E6
Portsmouth PO2 .... **345** E3
Southampton SO15 . **289** C8
Totton SO40........ **264** C3
Brunel Way PO15 ... **317** C8
Brune Park Com Coll
PO12.............. **368** E8
Brune Way BH22.... **353** D3
Brunstead Pl ◗
BH12 .... **392** B4
Brunstead Rd BH12 . **392** B4
Brunswick Cl SO50.. **245** B3
Brunswick Gdns
PO9 .... **323** D2
Brunswick Ho ◗
SO15 .... **291** A6
Brunswick Pl
Basingstoke RG21... **68** F1
Lymington SO41 .... **385** E4
Southampton SO15 . **291** A6
Brunswick Rd SO50. **245** B3
Brunswick Sq SO14 . **291** A3
Brunswick St PO5... **404** B2
Bruntile Cl GU14....**56** E1
Brushers BH23...... **357** E4
Bruyn Ct SP6 ...... **258** A2
Bruyn Rd SP6...... **258** A3
Bryanstone Cl GU52. **75** A6
Bryanstone Rd BH3 . **392** E7
Bryanston Rd SO19.. **291** E5
Bryant Rd BH12..... **392** A8

Bryce Gdns GU11 ... 100 A7
Bryces La SO24 ... 135 A3
Bryher Br PO6 ... 345 B7
Bryher Island PO6 ... 345 B7
Brympton Cl SP6 ... 257 D2
Bryn Rd GU10 ... 121 D7
Bryony Cl
Broadstone BH18 ... 374 F3
Locks Heath SO31 ... 316 F2
Bryony Gdns SO50 ... 269 C6
Bryony Way PO7 ... 323 A7
Bryson Cl PO13 ... 368 A6
Bryson Rd PO6 ... 345 D8
Bubb La SO30 ... 269 C4
Bub La BH23 ... 395 E6
Buccaneers Cl BH23 395 E6
Buccaneer Way GU14 76 A8
Buccleuch Rd BH13 . 392 A1
Bucehayes Cl BH23 . 397 A8
Buchanan Ave BH7 .. 393 E6
Buchanan Dr RG40 ... 16 C7
Buchanan Rd SO16 .. 265 F5
Buchan Ave PO15 ... 317 C8
Buchan Ct SO45 ... 313 C2
Buchan The GU15 ... 36 E8
Buckby La
7 Basingstoke RG21 ... 69 D5
Portsmouth PO3 ... 346 C4
Bucketts Farm Cl SO32 ... 272 B5
Buckfast Cl RG24 ... 48 A1
Buckholt Rd SO20 ... 170 A6
Buckhurst Rd GU16 .. 56 D6
Buckingham Cl GU34 ... 139 D3
Buckingham Ct
12 Farnborough GU14 ... 55 F4
1 Christchurch BH23 ... 397 A7
2 Southampton SO17 ... 291 A8
Basingstoke RG22 ... 91 A8
Fareham PO15 ... 318 E3
Poole BH15 ... 390 D3
Buckingham Gn PO1 ... 370 D7
Buckingham Mans 5 BH1 ... 393 A3
Buckingham Par RG22 ... 68 A1
Buckingham Rd
Newbury RG14 ... 1 D1
Petersfield GU32 ... 228 D3
Poole BH12 ... 391 D7
Buckingham St PO1. 404 B4
Buckingham Way GU16 ... 56 D8
Buckingham Wlk BH25 ... 382 E3
Buckland Ave RG22 .. 68 D2
Buckland Cl
Eastleigh SO50 ... 244 A5
Farnborough GU14 ... 56 A7
Waterlooville PO7 ... 299 D2
Buckland Ct SO41 ... 385 E5
Buckland Dene SO41 ... 385 D5
Buckland Gdns SO40 ... 264 C2
Buckland Gr BH23 .. 381 E2
Buckland Par RG22 ... 68 D1
Buckland Path PO2 . 370 D7
Buckland Rd BH12 .. 391 C5
Buckland St PO2 ... 370 E7
Buckland Terr BH12. 391 C5
Buckland View SO41 385 E5
Bucklers Ct
Havant PO9 ... 323 D7
Lymington SO41 ... 385 D3
Portsmouth PO2 ... 345 D1
Bucklers Hard Maritime Mus* SO42 ... 364 D5
Bucklers Mews SO41 ... 385 D3
Bucklers Rd PO12 ... 369 C9
Bucklers The SO41 .. 399 A5
Bucklers Way BH8 .. 378 D3
Buckley Ct SO16 ... 266 B1
Buckmore Ave GU32 228 D4
Buckner-Croke Way RG19 ... 6 D5
Bucksey Rd PO13 ... 368 C8
Bucks Head Hill SO32 ... 249 C5
Buckskin La RG22 ... 68 B3
Buckstone Cl SO41 .. 384 E1
Buckthorn Cl
Broadstone BH17 ... 374 F1
Totton SO40 ... 288 B8
Budden's La PO17 ... 296 E8
Buddens Mdw BH21. 374 C4
Buddens Rd PO17 ... 296 A4
Buddle Hill SP6 ... 282 C4
Buddlesgate SO21 .. 131 D3
Budd's Cl RG21 ... 69 A4
Budds La
Bordon GU35 ... 164 C4
Romsey SO51 ... 215 E1
Budds Lane Trad Est SO51 ... 215 E1
Bude Cl PO6 ... 320 F1
Buffalo Mews BH15 . 390 B2
Buffbeards La GU27. 189 C7
Buffins Cnr RG29 ... 72 C2
Buffins Rd RG29 ... 72 C2
Bufton Field RG29 ... 72 C3
Bugdens La BH31 ... 303 A6
Bugle St SO14 ... 290 F3
Bulbarrow Wlk PO14 342 E8
Bulbeck Rd PO9 ... 323 F1
Bulbery SP11 ... 104 F3
Buldowne Wlk SO41. 360 B3
Bulford Rd
Shipton Bellinger SP9 ... 101 E8
South Tidworth SP9 ... 78 D4
Bullar Rd SO18 ... 291 E8
Bullar St SO14 ... 291 B6
Bull Dro SO23 ... 403 F3
Buller Ct 8 GU14 ... 56 A1
Buller Rd GU11 ... 76 F4
Bullers Rd GU9 ... 99 C6
Bullfinch Cl
Broadstone BH17 ... 374 F1
Sandhurst GU47 ... 35 C8
Totton SO40 ... 288 C7
Bullfinch Ct PO13 ... 367 F4
Bull Hill
Boldre SO41 ... 362 B1
Rake GU33 ... 208 E4
Bullington La
Barton Stacey SO21 . 130 E7
Upper Bullington SO21 ... 131 C6
Bull La
Minstead SO43 ... 286 C3
Swallowfield RG7 ... 13 E3
Waltham Chase SO32 271 D3
Bullrush Cl SO45 ... 313 F1
Bulls Copse La PO8 . 300 A6
Bulls Copse Rd SO40 ... 289 A4
Bulls Down Cl RG27 .. 29 D1
Bulls Dro SP5 ... 191 A6
Bulpits Hill SP11 ... 38 C6
Bulwark Rd PO14 ... 367 B6
Bunch La GU27 ... 189 E8
Bunch Way GU27 ... 189 E7
Bungler's Hill RG7 ... 14 F6
Bunkers Hill
Denmead PO7 ... 298 D4
Newbury RG14 ... 5 A5
Bunnian Pl RG21 ... 69 B6
Bunns La PO7 ... 297 E5
Bunny La
Michelmersh SO51 .. 215 F5
Sherfield English SO51 ... 213 A4
Bunstead La SO21 ... 218 D7
Bunting Gdns PO8 ... 299 F4
Bunting Mews RG22 ... 91 A7
Bunting Rd BH22 ... 353 B8
Buntings GU34 ... 139 F6
Buntings The GU9 ... 121 D7
Burberry Ct RG21 ... 69 B3
Burberry Ho 5 RG27 . 51 A1
Burbidge Gr PO4 ... 371 A2
Burbridge Cl BH17 ... 390 E8
Burbury Woods GU15 36 C6
Burbush Cl SO45 ... 338 C3
Burchell Rd RG14 ... 1 C5
Burchett Coppice RG40 ... 16 D8
Burcombe La BH24 .. 305 F1
Burcombe Rd BH10 . 377 C5
Burcote Dr PO3 ... 346 B4
Burdale Dr PO11 ... 373 D3
Burdock Cl
Christchurch BH23 .. 381 B1
Goodworth Clatford SP11 ... 127 F8
Bure Cl BH23 ... 396 B6
Bure Haven Dr BH23 396 A6
Bure Homage Gdns BH23 ... 396 B6
Bure Homage La BH23 ... 396 B6
Bure La BH23 ... 396 B6
Bure Pk BH23 ... 396 B6
Bure Rd BH23 ... 396 B6
Burfield RG20 ... 21 D5
Burford Cl BH23 ... 379 D1
Burford Ct 4 BH1 .. 393 B3
Burford La SO42 ... 334 A2
Burford Rd 5 GU15 ... 35 F4
Burgage Field RG28 .. 86 D6
Burgate Cl PO9 ... 323 D3
Burgate Cross SP6 .. 258 A5
Burgate Ct SP6 ... 258 A4
Burgate Fields SP6 . 258 A3
Burgate Sch & Sixth Form Ctr The SP6 .. 258 A3
Burge Cl GU14 ... 55 A4
Burgesmede Ho 9 GU32 ... 228 F3
Burgess Cl
Bournemouth BH11 ... 376 F4
Odiham RG29 ... 72 C2
South Hayling PO11 . 373 D1
Burgess Ct SO16 ... 267 B4
Burgess Fld BH21 ... 302 A6
Burgess Gdns 5 SO16 ... 266 E3
Burgess La RG20 ... 3 B6
Burgess Rd
Basingstoke RG21 ... 69 B6
Southampton SO16 .. 267 B4
Upper Shirley SO16 . 266 D3
Burghclere Prim Sch RG20 ... 22 E6
Burghclere Rd
Havant PO9 ... 324 B6
Southampton SO19 .. 314 F8
Burghead Cl GU47 ... 35 B7
Burgh Hill Rd GU30 . 187 E7
Burgoyne Rd
Camberley GU15 ... 36 E6
Portsmouth PO5 ... 370 D1
Southampton SO19 .. 292 E4
Burgundy Cl SO31 ... 316 F2
Burgundy Terr 1 PO2 ... 345 E2
Buriton Cl PO16 ... 320 D1
Buriton Ct SO19 ... 291 E3
Buriton Prim Sch GU31 ... 253 D5
Buriton Rd SO22 ... 175 D4
Buriton St PO1 ... 404 C4
Burkal Dr SP10 ... 83 A4
Burke Dr SO19 ... 292 D5
Burleigh Rd
Bournemouth BH6 ... 394 D5
Camberley GU16 ... 56 B8
Portsmouth PO1 ... 370 F7
Burles Bridge Cotts GU10 ... 98 A1
Burley Cl
14 Havant PO9 ... 324 B6
Barton on S BH25 ... 397 D8
Chandler's Ford SO53 243 B4
Totton SO40 ... 288 B7
Verwood BH31 ... 302 E5
Burley Ct 5 SO17 ... 267 A2
Burley Down SO53 ... 243 B4
Burley Ho 7 SO16 ... 290 B8
Burley La RG25 ... 88 E6
Burley Lawn BH24 ... 331 B4
Burley Prim Sch BH24 ... 331 A3
Burley Rd
Bransgore BH23 ... 381 A8
Bransgore,Thorney Hill BH23 ... 357 D3
Brockenhurst SO42 .. 360 C8
Poole BH12 ... 391 C6
Winchester SO22 ... 175 D4
Winkton BH23 ... 380 D6
Burley Way GU17 ... 35 A6
Burling Terr 1 BH13 ... 392 A4
Burlington Arc 11 BH1 ... 392 F3
Burlington Ct
10 Aldershot GU11 ... 76 E1
Blackwater GU17 ... 35 B3
Southampton SO19 .. 292 B5
Burlington Mans 1 SO15 ... 290 C7
Burlington Rd
Portsmouth PO2 ... 345 E1
Southampton SO15 .. 290 E6
Burlington Wlk SP9 .. 79 A6
Burma Ho SO18 ... 267 E4
Burmah Road N SO45 ... 339 C5
Burmah Road S SO45 ... 339 B5
Burma Rd SO51 ... 240 F6
Burma Way SO40 ... 289 F1
Burmese Cl PO15 ... 317 C7
Burnaby Cl RG22 ... 68 C3
Burnaby Ct BH4 ... 392 C1
Burnaby Rd
Bournemouth BH4 ... 392 C1
Portsmouth PO1 ... 370 B4
Burnage Ct 13 BH13. 402 F7
Burnbake Rd BH31 ... 303 A5
Burnbank Gdns SO40 ... 288 E7
Burnbrae Rd BH22 ... 353 D1
Burn Cl BH31 ... 303 B4
Burne Cl SO21 ... 153 C2
Burne-Jones Dr GU47 35 B6
Burnett Ave BH23 ... 394 E8
Burnett Cl
Hythe SO45 ... 314 B2
Southampton SO18 .. 267 E1
Winchester SO22 ... 403 A8
Burnett Rd
Christchurch BH23 .. 394 F7
Gosport PO12 ... 368 F6
Burnetts Fields SO50 ... 269 C7
Burnetts Gdns SO50. 269 D7
Burnetts La SO30 ... 269 C5
Burney Bit RG26 ... 27 C8
Burney Ho 8 PO12 .. 369 D5
Burney Rd PO12 ... 368 E3
Burngate Rd BH15 ... 389 E2
Burnham Beeches SO53 ... 243 B6
Burnham Chase SO18 ... 292 C7
Burnham Copse Jun & Inf Sch RG26 ... 9 E1
Burnham Dr BH8 ... 393 C7
Burnham Manor GU15 ... 36 E8
Burnham Rd
Alton GU34 ... 139 C1
Burton BH23 ... 380 C2
Cosham PO6 ... 322 D1
Fordingbridge SP6 ... 257 F3
Pamber Heath RG26 ... 9 D2
Burnhams Cl SP10 ... 83 A4
Burnham's Wlk 2 PO12 ... 369 D5
Burnham Wood PO16 ... 319 A3
Burnleigh Gdns BH25 ... 383 C4
Burnley Cl RG26 ... 26 F7
Burnmoor Mdw RG40 16 C2
Burnsall Cl GU14 ... 55 F6
Burns Ave GU52 ... 75 B6
Burns Cl
Basingstoke RG24 ... 69 C8
Eastleigh SO50 ... 243 E1
Farnborough GU14 ... 55 D6
South Wonston SO21. 153 E4
Burnside
Christchurch BH23 .. 396 D8
Fleet GU51 ... 54 A1
Gosport PO13 ... 343 B5
Waterlooville PO7 ... 300 A1
Burns Pl SO16 ... 266 A2
Burns Rd
Bournemouth BH6 ... 394 D7
Eastleigh SO50 ... 243 F1
Southampton SO19 .. 292 D6
Burnt Hill Rd GU10 .. 121 F6
Burnt Hill Way GU10 121 F5
Burnt House La
Boldre SO41 ... 362 A1
Bransgore BH23 ... 357 B1
Stubbington PO14 ... 342 D4
Burnt Oak RG40 ... 16 D8
Burntwood Cotts SO21 ... 154 F2
Burrard Gr SO41 ... 385 F2
Burr Cl SO21 ... 244 F8
Burrell Rd GU16 ... 56 A8
Burrfields Rd PO3 ... 346 B1
Burridge Rd SO31 ... 294 A2
Burrill Ave PO6 ... 346 A8
Burrowfields RG22 ... 91 B5
Burrow Hill Pl SO50. 244 D5
Burrow Hill Sch GU16 36 D1
Burrows Cl PO9 ... 324 A3
Burrows La BH31 ... 302 F8
Burrows The RG26 ... 9 E1
Burrwood Gdns GU12 77 E4
Bursledon CE Inf Sch SO31 ... 316 A8
Bursledon Cotts SP9 101 E8
Bursledon Ho 4 BH25 ... 383 A2
Bursledon Hts SO31. 293 B1
Bursledon Jun Sch SO31 ... 316 A8
Bursledon Pl PO7 ... 322 D5
Bursledon Rd
Hedge End SO30 ... 293 B5
Southampton SO19, SO31 ... 292 C5
Waterlooville PO7 ... 322 D5
Bursledon Sta SO31. 316 B8
Bursledon Windmill* SO31 ... 293 A2
Burtley Rd BH6 ... 394 F3
Burton CE Prim Sch BH23 ... 380 C3
Burton Cl
Burton BH23 ... 380 C1
St Leonards BH24 ... 327 E5
Burtoncroft BH23 ... 380 C3
Burton Hall BH23 ... 380 C3
Burton Hall Pl BH23. 380 D3
Burton Ho BH23 ... 380 D1
Burton Rd
Christchurch BH23 .. 395 E7
Poole BH13 ... 392 A3
Southampton SO15 .. 290 E6
Burton's Gdns RG24 ... 70 B7
Burt's Hill BH21 ... 351 D7
Burt's La BH21 ... 326 A7
Burwood Gr PO11 ... 373 A4
Bury Brickfield Park Cvn Site SO40 ... 289 C4
Bury Cl PO12 ... 369 B5
Bury Court Cotts GU10 ... 120 A7
Bury Cres PO12 ... 369 B5
Bury Cross PO12 ... 369 A5
Burydown Mead RG25 89 F1
Bury Farm SO30 ... 294 C3
Buryfields RG29 ... 72 E2
Buryfields Inf Sch RG29 ... 72 E2
Bury Hall La PO12 ... 368 F3
Bury Hill Cl SP11 ... 105 D4
Buryhill Close Flats SP11 ... 105 D4
Bury Hill Farm SP11. 105 E4
Bury Ho 7 PO16 ... 319 A1
Bury La SO40 ... 289 B5
Bury Rd
Basingstoke RG23 ... 68 D6
Gosport PO12 ... 369 A5
Marchwood SO40 ... 289 E3
Poole BH13 ... 391 F1
Poole BH13 ... 391 F2
Bury's Bank Rd RG19 .. 6 D7
Bury The RG29 ... 72 E2
Bus Dro SO45 ... 366 E8
Bushell Rd BH15 ... 390 C7
Bushells Farm SP6 .. 281 E8
Bushell Way RG2 ... 15 C8
Bushey Rd BH8 ... 378 C1
Bush Ho PO5 ... 404 B1
Bushmead Dr BH24 .. 327 E5
Bushnells Dr RG20 ... 24 C3
Bush St E PO5 ... 404 B1
Bush St W PO5 ... 404 B1
Bushy Mead PO7 ... 322 C3
Bushywarren La RG25 92 E1
Busk Cres GU14 ... 55 D3
Busket La SO23 ... 403 E5
Busketts Way SO40 .. 288 A2
Bustards Cnr SO20 .. 147 E5
Butchers Bush SO43 286 B5
Butcher's Cnr SO43 . 261 E4
Butcher St PO1 ... 370 A5
Bute Dr BH23 ... 397 B8
Butler Cl RG22 ... 68 C4
Butler Lodge RG25 ... 88 B8
Butlers Cl SO51 ... 191 F1
Butlers La BH24 ... 305 C1
Butser Ancient Farm* PO8 ... 276 F6
Butser Ct PO8 ... 276 D3
Butser Wlk
Fareham PO14 ... 342 E8
Petersfield GU31 ... 229 B4
Butson Cl RG14 ... 1 C3
Buttenshaw Ave RG2. 15 D8
Buttenshaw Cl RG2 ... 15 E8
Buttercup Cl
Hedge End SO30 ... 293 A6
Hythe SO45 ... 314 A1
Lindford GU35 ... 165 A5
Buttercup Dr BH23 .. 381 B1
Buttercup Way SO31 316 E3
Butterfield GU15 ... 35 F4
Butterfield Rd SO16 . 266 E3
Butterfly Dr PO6 ... 321 A1
Butteridge Rise SO51 ... 214 E6
Buttermer Cl GU10 .. 121 D7
Buttermere Cl
Bordon GU35 ... 164 D5
Farnborough GU14 ... 55 C4
Southampton SO16 .. 265 E2
Buttermere Ct GU12 .. 77 D4
Buttermere Dr RG22 . 68 A1
Buttermere Gdns SO24 ... 179 D4
Buttermere Ho 13 PO6 ... 321 B1
Butterys Ct GU34 ... 139 F4
Buttery The BH23 ... 395 D7
Butt La SP5 ... 210 B8
Button's La
Hawkley GU34 ... 184 C2
West Wellow SO51 .. 238 F3
Buttsash Ave SO45 .. 338 A8
Butts Ash Gdns SO45 ... 314 A1
Butts Ash La SO45 ... 338 A8
Butts Bridge Hill SO45 ... 314 A2
Buttsbridge Rd SO45 ... 314 A1
Butts Cl SO22 ... 403 B7
Butt's Cl SO19 ... 292 D4
Butt's Cres SO19 ... 292 C4
Butts Farm La SO32 . 271 D8
Butts Lawn SO42 ... 333 F2
Butts Mdw RG27 ... 51 A1
Butts Mews GU34 ... 139 E2
Butts Paddock SO42 333 F2
Butts Prim Sch The GU34 ... 139 E2
Butts Rd GU34 ... 139 E2
Butt's Rd SO19 ... 292 C3
Butt's Sq SO19 ... 292 C4
Butts The
Meonstoke SO32 ... 249 C6
Silchester RG7 ... 27 F8
Butty The 8 RG21 ... 69 D5
Byams La SO40 ... 290 A2
Bye Rd SO31 ... 316 D8
Byerley Cl PO10 ... 325 B5
Byerley Rd PO1 ... 370 F5
Byes La RG7 ... 27 F6
Byeways
Highclere RG20 ... 21 D6
Hythe SO45 ... 313 F2
Byfields Rd RG20 ... 24 C2
Byfleet Ave RG24 ... 70 B5
Byfrons The GU14 ... 56 A2
Byngs Bsns Pk PO7 .. 299 B2
Byng Wlk SP10 ... 106 D8
By Pass Rd
Romsey SO51 ... 240 E6
Sutton Scotney SO21. 131 B4
Byrd Cl PO7 ... 322 E5
Byrd Gdns RG22 ... 91 C7
Byres The PO14 ... 342 C4
Byron Ave
Frimley GU15 ... 36 F3
Winchester SO22 ... 403 B6
Byron Cl
Basingstoke RG24 ... 48 D1
Bishop's Waltham SO32 ... 271 E8
Fareham PO16 ... 319 A2
Fleet GU51 ... 75 A8
Newbury RG14 ... 5 D7
Yateley GU46 ... 33 F4
Byron Ct
1 Camberley GU15 .. 36 B5
Ferndown BH22 ... 353 D5
Southampton SO15 .. 290 E6
Byron Ho 10 BH25 ... 383 A2
Byron Rd
Barton on S BH25 ... 397 E8
Bournemouth BH5 ... 393 F3
Eastleigh SO50 ... 244 B4
Portsmouth PO2 ... 370 F8
Southampton SO19 .. 292 D6
Wimborne Minster BH21 ... 351 C6
By The Wood SO40 ... 264 D2
Bywater Ct GU14 ... 77 A8
Byways GU46 ... 33 F5
Byworth Cl GU9 ... 98 D2
Byworth Rd GU9 ... 98 D2

C

Cable St
2 Southampton SO14 ... 291 C5
Eastleigh SO50 ... 244 A2
Cabot Bsns Village BH17 ... 390 A7
Cabot Dr SO45 ... 313 C3
Cabot La BH17 ... 390 B8
Cabot Way BH25 ... 382 F3
Cabrol Rd GU14 ... 55 E5
Cabul Rd SP9 ... 78 D4
Cadet Way GU52 ... 75 B4
Cadgwith Pl PO6 ... 345 B7
Cadham Ct GU51 ... 53 C4
Cadhay Cl BH25 ... 382 E3
Cadington Ho 9 PO1 ... 370 A5
Cadland Ct SO14 ... 291 C2
Cadland Pk SO45 ... 338 C6
Cadland Rd
Fawley,Buttsash SO45 ... 338 D7
Fawley SO45 ... 339 B5
Cadnam Cl
Aldershot GU11 ... 100 A6
Oakley RG23 ... 67 B2
Cadnam Ct 6 PO12 . 368 D3
Cadnam La SO40 ... 262 F2
Cadnam Lawn PO9 .. 323 D6
Cadnam Rd PO4 ... 371 B3
Cadnam Way BH8 ... 378 D3
Cadogan Rd
Farnborough GU11 ... 77 B7
Ringwood BH24 ... 329 B7
Cador Dr PO16 ... 344 B6
Caen Ho 7 PO14 ... 342 E8
Caerleon Ave SO19 .. 292 C6
Caerleon Cl GU26 ... 167 A6
Caerleon Dr
Andover SP10 ... 83 A4
Southampton SO19 .. 292 C6
Caernarvon GU16 ... 56 D8
Caernarvon Cl RG23 .. 68 C5
Caernarvon Gdns SO53 ... 243 A4
Caer Peris View PO16 ... 320 C2
Caesar Cl RG23 ... 68 C7
Caesar Ct 9 GU11 ... 76 C2
Caesar Rd SP10 ... 83 B3
Caesar's Camp Rd GU15 ... 36 E8
Caesar's Cl GU15 ... 36 E8
Caesars Ct
Camberley GU15 ... 36 E8
Farnham GU9 ... 99 A7
Caesar's Way
Broadstone BH18 ... 374 E4
Whitchurch RG28 ... 86 B6
Cains Cl PO14 ... 367 C8
Caird Ave BH25 ... 383 C2
Cairn Cl GU15 ... 36 F3
Cairngorm Cl RG22 ... 68 B4
Cairngorm Pl GU14 ... 55 C7
Cairns Cl BH23 ... 394 F8
Cairo Terr PO2 ... 370 D7
Caister Cl BH22 ... 353 C6
Caistor Cl SO16 ... 266 A4
Caithness Cl RG23 ... 67 A2
Caker's La GU34 ... 140 D1
Caker Stream Rd GU34 ... 140 B4
Calabrese SO31 ... 317 B7
Calard Dr RG18 ... 2 E5
Calbourne SO31 ... 315 C7
Calcot La SO32 ... 270 E3
Calcott Pk GU46 ... 34 A6
Caldecote Wlk 7 PO5 ... 404 B2
Calder Cl SO16 ... 289 E8
Calder Ct 17 SP10 ... 83 C2
Calder Ho 10 PO1 ... 370 A5
Calder Rd BH17 ... 390 F8
Calderwood Dr SO19 ... 292 A4
Caledonia Dr SO45 .. 313 D3
Caledonian Cl BH23 . 396 B7
Caledon Rd BH14 ... 391 E3
Calender Cl GU34 ... 139 F2
California Cl SO40 ... 264 B1
California Ctry Pk* RG40 ... 16 A7
Calkin Cl BH23 ... 380 A1
Calleva Cl RG22 ... 91 B7
Calleva Mus* RG7 ... 10 F1
Calleva Pk RG7 ... 9 C2
Calleva Roman Town* RG7 ... 11 B1
Callowing Cl SO21 ... 244 F8
Calluna Rd BH12 ... 391 B8
Calmore Cl BH8 ... 378 D3
Calmore Cres SO40 .. 264 B1
Calmore Dr SO40 ... 288 C8
Calmore Gdns SO40. 288 D7
Calmore Ind Est SO40 ... 264 E2
Calmore Inf Sch SO40 ... 264 C1
Calmore Jun Sch SO40 ... 264 C1
Calmore Rd SO40 ... 288 C8

Calne Ho **3** SP9 . . . . . .78 F6
Calpe Ave SO43 . . . . . 309 F6
Calshot Activities Ctr
SO45 . . . . 340 B3
Calshot Castle★
SO45 . . . . 340 B3
Calshot Cl SO45 . . . . . 366 F7
Calshot Ct SO14 . . . . . 291 C2
Calshot Dr SO53 . . . . . 243 A4
Calshot Rd
Fawley SO45 . . . . 339 B3
Havant PO9 . . . . 323 C7
Calshot Way
Camberley GU16 . . . . . 56 E7
Gosport PO13 . . . . . . 343 B1
Calthorpe Hos RG27 . . .52 F8
Calthorpe Park Sch
GU51 . . . . .74 C8
Calthorpe Rd GU51 . . .53 E2
Calton Gdns GU11 . . . 100 A7
Calvecroft GU30 . . . . 188 A4
Calvert Cl GU12 . . . . . .77 B1
Calvert Ctr The
SO21 . . . . 112 D1
Calvin Cl GU15 . . . . . .36 F4
Calvin Rd BH9 . . . . . . 392 F8
Camargue Cl PO15 . . . 317 B8
Camberlet Twrs **3**
GU15 . . . . .36 B5
Camberley Inf Sch
GU15 . . . . .36 A5
Camberley Sta GU15 . . 36 B5
Camberley Towers
GU15 . . . . .36 A5
Camber Pl **3** PO1 . . . 370 A3
Camberry Cl RG21 . . . .69 C3
Cambria Dr SO45 . . . . 313 D3
Cambrian Cl
Bursledon SO31 . . . . . 293 A2
Camberley GU15 . . . . . 35 F5
Cambrian Rd GU14 . . . .55 B7
Cambrian Terr PO5 . . . 404 C1
Cambrian Way
Basingstoke RG22 . . . . 68 B3
Finchampstead RG40 . . 16 E8
Cambrian Wlk PO14 . . 342 F7
Cambridge Ct
17 Southampton
SO14 . . . . 291 A8
1 Farnborough GU14 . 56 A1
Cambridge Dr SO53 . . 243 C2
Cambridge Gdns
BH23 . . . . 379 F2
Cambridge Gn
Chandler's Ford
SO53 . . . . 243 C2
Titchfield PO14 . . . . . 317 C2
Cambridge Junc
PO1 . . . . 370 B4
Cambridge Pl GU9 . . . 99 A2
Cambridge Rd
Aldershot GU11 . . . . . . 76 C4
Bournemouth BH2 . . . 392 D3
Gosport PO12 . . . . . . 368 F6
Lee-on-S PO13 . . . . . . 367 F2
Portsmouth PO1 . . . . . 370 B4
Southampton SO14 . . 291 A8
Cambridge Rd E
GU14 . . . . .56 B1
Cambridge Rd W
GU14 . . . . 56 A1
Cambridge Sq **6**
GU15 . . . . 36 A6
Cambridge Wlk **2**
GU15 . . . . 36 A6
Camcross Cl **2** PO6 . 321 E1
Camden Cl BH9 . . . . . 378 B1
Camden Hurst **1**
SO41 . . . . 399 B4
Camden St PO12 . . . . 369 A7
Camden Terr **2**
PO12 . . . . 369 A7
Camden Wlk GU51 . . . 54 C1
Camela Villas GU12 . . .77 B1
Camel Green Rd
SP6 . . . . 281 A6
Camelia Cl PO9 . . . . . 324 C3
Camelia Gdns SO18 . . 268 A2
Camelia Gr SO50 . . . . 245 E2
Camellia Cl
North Baddesley
SO52 . . . . .242 A5
Three Legged Cross
BH21 . . . . 302 E1
Camellia Ct SO18 . . . . 267 E2
Camellia Gdns BH25 . 383 B2
Camelot Sp SP10 . . . . .83 E7
Camelot Cres PO16 . . 320 B1
Camelsdale Fst Sch
GU27 . . . . .189 D5
Camelsdale Rd
GU27 . . . . .189 D5
Camel Way GU14 . . . .55 E1
Cameron Cl PO13 . . . 343 C3
Cameron Ct
Andover SP10 . . . . . . 105 E7
Southampton SO16 . . 265 F5
Cameron Rd
Christchurch BH23 . . 395 D7
Farnborough GU11 . . . 77 B7
Camfield Cl RG21 . . . . 69 C3
Camford Cl RG22 . . . . 91 A4
Camilla Cl SO40 . . . . . 264 B1
Camilla Ct BH13 . . . . 392 B2
Camlea Cl RG21 . . . . . 69 C2

Camley Cl SO19 . . . . . 291 E1
Cammel Rd BH22 . . . . 353 D2
Camoys Mead GU34 . . 116 C2
Campana Int Coll
GU10 . . . . .99 E2
Campbell Cl
Aldershot GU11 . . . . . 100 A7
Fleet GU51 . . . . 53 E1
Grateley SP11 . . . . . . 124 E7
Yateley GU46 . . . . 34 D6
Campbell Cres PO7 . . 322 C5
Campbell Ct
Bramley RG26 . . . . 29 B2
Fair Oak SO50 . . . . . . 245 C2
Holybourne GU34 . . . 140 C6
Campbell Fields GU11 76 F1
Campbell Mews
SO18 . . . . .292 D7
Campbell Pl GU16 . . . . 36 D3
Campbell Rd
Aldershot GU11 . . . . . . 76 E3
Bournemouth BH1 . . . 393 E6
Bramley RG26 . . . . 29 B2
Burton BH23 . . . . 380 C3
Eastleigh SO50 . . . . . 244 B1
Portsmouth PO5 . . . . 404 D1
Campbell's Gn RG7 . .11 F5
Campbell St SO14 . . . 291 C6
Campbell Way SO45 . 345 C2
Camp Farm Rd GU11 . .77 B5
Camp Field SO20 . . . 172 A3
Camp Hill GU11 . . . . 100 A1
Campion Cl
Blackwater GU17 . . . . 35 D3
Horton Heath SO50 . . 269 D6
Lindford GU35 . . . . . 165 A4
Locks Heath SO31 . . . 316 E2
Waterlooville PO7 . . . 323 A6
Campion Ct SO21 . . . 216 C1
Campion Gr BH23 . . . 395 F6
Campion Ho **4** RG14 . .1 D2
Campion Rd SO19 . . . 292 D5
Campion Way
Hartley Wintney
RG27 . . . . 52 D7
Kings Worthy SO23 . . 176 C7
Lymington SO41 . . . . 385 E5
Camp Rd
Bordon GU35 . . . . . . .164 D4
Farnborough GU14 . . . 77 A8
Gosport PO13 . . . . . . 343 D3
Padworth RG7 . . . . 11 B8
Campsie Cl RG22 . . . . .68 B4
Camrose Way RG21 . . 69 C3
Cams Bay Cl PO16 . . . 319 F1
Cams Hill
Hambledon PO7 . . . . 274 B2
Portchester PO16 . . . 319 E1
Cams Hill Sch PO16 . 343 E8
Camus Cl GU52 . . . . . 74 D5
Cam Wlk **21** RG21 . . . 69 D5
Camwood Cl RG21 . . . 69 D5
Canada Cotts SO21 . . 111 B2
Canada Ct **9** PO12 . . 369 C9
Canada Pl **6** SO16 . . 266 F4
Canada Rd
Southampton SO19 . . 291 E2
West Wellow SO51 . . 238 D1
Canada Way
Bordon GU35 . . . . . . .164 D4
Liphook GU30 . . . . . . 188 A3
Canal Cl
Farnborough GU11 . . . 77 B5
North Warnborough
RG29 . . . . 72 C4
Romsey SO51 . . . . . . 216 A1
Canal Cotts GU12 . . . .77 E4
Canalside The PO16 . . 370 A4
Canal View Rd RG14 . .2 B3
Canal Wlk
Portsmouth PO1 . . . . 404 D1
Romsey SO51 . . . . . . 240 F8
Southampton SO14 . . 291 A3
Canberra Cl
Gosport PO13 . . . . . . 368 F4
Yateley GU46 . . . . 33 E7
Canberra Ct **7** PO12 368 F4
Canberra Ho PO1 . . . . 404 B3
Canberra Rd
Christchurch BH23 . . 379 E1
Nursling SO16 . . . . . . 265 B4
Thorney Island PO10 . 349 A3
Canberra Towers
SO19 . . . . 314 F8
Canberra Way RG21 . . 91 A4
Candleford Gate
GU30 . . . . .187 F4
Candlemas Pl **18**
SO17 . . . . 291 A8
Candover Cl **4** RG26 . .26 F7
Candover Ct SO19 . . . 315 A8
Candy Cl SO18 . . . . . . 292 E6
Candys Cl BH21 . . . . . 350 E2
Candys La BH21 . . . . . 350 E2
Canes La GU35 . . . . . 164 F5
Canford Ave BH11 . . . 377 A2
Canford Bottom
BH21 . . . . 352 C6
Canford Bottom Rdbt
BH21 . . . . 352 C5
Canford Cl
Shedfield SO32 . . . . . 295 E7
Southampton SO16 . . 265 D2
Canford Cliffs Ave
BH14 . . . . 391 C2
Canford Cliffs Rd
BH13 . . . . 391 C2
Canford Cres BH13 . . 402 E7

Canford Ct BH13 . . . . 402 E6
Canford Gdns BH11 . . 377 A1
Canford Heath Fst & Mid
Schs BH17 . . . . 390 D7
Canford Heath Nature
Reserve★ BH11 . . . . 376 B4
Canford Heath Rd
BH17 . . . . 375 E1
Canford Magna
BH21 . . . . 352 A1
Canford Park Events
Arena & Sports Gd★
BH21 . . . . 376 B7
Canford Pl **2** BH13 . . 402 E7
Canford Rd
Bournemouth BH11 . . 377 A1
Poole BH15 . . . . 390 D4
Canford Sch BH21 . . . 352 B2
Canford View Dr
BH21 . . . . 352 B6
Canford Way BH11 . . . 376 C2
Canhouse La
Rake GU31,GU33 . . . . 208 F3
Rake GU31,GU33 . . . . 209 A3
Canning Rd GU12 . . . .77 B2
Cannock Ct RG22 . . . . 68 C4
Cannock Wlk **8**
PO14 . . . . 342 E7
Cannon Cl
Broadstone BH18 . . . . 375 A1
Ellisfield RG25 . . . . . . 115 B6
Sandhurst GU47 . . . . . 35 D8
Cannon Hill Gdns
BH21 . . . . 352 B7
Cannon Hill Rd
BH21 . . . . 352 A7
Cannon Ho SO41 . . . . 385 E4
Cannon St
Lymington SO41 . . . . 385 E4
Southampton SO15 . . 290 C8
Canoe Cl SO31 . . . . . . 316 F1
Canon Ct SO50 . . . . . 245 C2
Canon's Barn Cl
PO16 . . . . 320 C1
Canons Cl SP9 . . . . . . .78 F4
Canons Ct RG20 . . . . . 24 C2
Canon's Ct RG20 . . . . 24 C2
Canons St SO23 . . . . . 403 E5
Canons Wlk SO41 . . . 399 D5
Cansfield End RG14 . . 1 D3
Cantell Sch SO16 . . . . 267 A4
Canterbury Ave
SO19 . . . . 292 C3
Canterbury Cl
Basingstoke RG22 . . . 91 B8
Lee-on-S PO13 . . . . . . 368 B4
West Moors BH22 . . . 326 F1
Canterbury Dr SO45 . 313 C3
Canterbury Gdns
GU14 . . . . .56 B2
Canterbury Rd
Ash GU12 . . . . 77 E3
Farnborough GU14 . . . 56 B2
Portsmouth PO4 . . . . 370 F3
Stubbington PO14 . . . 342 C4
Canterton La SO43 . . 286 B8
Canterton Manor
SO43 . . . . 286 A8
Canton St SO15 . . . . . 290 F6
Canute Dr BH23 . . . . . 357 B1
Canute Ho **13** SO14 . . 291 A3
Canute Rd
5 Winchester
SO23 . . . . .403 F4
Southampton SO14 . . 291 B3
Canvey Ct SO16 . . . . . 265 E2
Capella Ho BH2 . . . . . 392 F2
Capel Gdns SO45 . . . 313 D3
Capel Ley PO7 . . . . . . 322 E4
Capers End La SO32 . 278 E1
Capesthorne BH23 . . . 396 B5
Capital Ho **7** SO22 . . 403 D6
Capon Cl SO18 . . . . . . 267 E4
Capper Rd GU15 . . . . 35 E7
Capstan Gdns SO31 . . 317 C3
Capstan Ho
12 Cosham PO6 . . . 345 F7
Warsash SO31 . . . . . . 316 C1
Capstans The BH14 . . 402 B8
Capstone Pl BH8 . . . . 393 D6
Capstone Rd BH8 . . . 393 B6
Captains Cl PO12 . . . . 368 F7
Captains Cove BH15 . 389 E3
Captains Pl SO14 . . . . 291 B3
Captains Row **5**
PO1 . . . . 370 A3
Captain's Row SO41 . 385 F4
Caradon Pl BH31 . . . . 302 D7
Carberry Dr PO16 . . . 344 C7
Carbery Ave BH6 . . . . 394 D5
Carbery Ct PO9 . . . . . 323 D7
Carbery Gdns BH6 . . . 394 E5
Carbery La **3** BH6 . . . 394 C4
Carbery Row **2** BH6 394 C4
Carbis Cl PO6 . . . . . . 345 A7
Carbonel Cl RG23 . . . . 68 A5
Cardew Rd GU33 . . . . 208 A3
Cardigan Rd
Bournemouth BH9 . . . 392 F8
Poole BH12 . . . . 391 F4
Cardinal Cl
Shedfield SO32 . . . . . 295 E7
Southampton SO16 . . 265 D2
Cardinal Mews **5**
SP10 . . . . 297 E8
Cardinals The GU10 . . 100 D7
Cardinal Way SO31 . . 317 B2
Cardington Ct SO16 . . 265 F4
Carey Rd
Bournemouth BH9 . . . 377 F1

Carey Rd continued
Southampton SO19 . . 292 C5
Careys Cotts SO42 . . . 333 F2
Careys Rd BH8 . . . . . . 378 D4
Carfax Ave GU10 . . . . 100 D8
Carfax Est GU10 . . . . 100 D8
Cargate Ave GU11 . . .76 E1
Cargate Gr GU11 . . . . 76 E1
Cargate Hill GU11 . . . 76 D1
Cargate Terr GU11 . . . 76 D1
Carina Ct BH13 . . . . . 402 C3
Carisbrooke
Camberley GU16 . . . . 56 D8
Netley SO31 . . . . 315 C7
Poole BH13 . . . . 402 E7
Carisbrooke Ave
PO14 . . . . 367 B7
Carisbrooke Cl
Basingstoke RG23 . . . 68 C6
Havant PO9 . . . . 324 B2
New Alresford SO24 . . 179 D4
Carisbrooke Cres
Chandler's Ford
SO53 . . . . .243 E5
Hamworthy BH15 . . . 389 D3
Carisbrooke Ct
1 Christchurch
BH23 . . . . 397 B7
1 Knowle Village
PO17 . . . . 318 E7
New Milton BH25 . . . 382 F3
Romsey SO51 . . . . . . 216 A1
Carisbrooke Dr
SO19 . . . . 291 F6
Carisbrooke Rd
Gosport PO13 . . . . . . 343 C2
Portsmouth PO4 . . . . 371 A4
Carisbrooke Way
BH23 . . . . 381 E1
Carless Cl PO13 . . . . . 368 D7
Carleton Cl RG27 . . . .50 F1
Carlinford **5** BH5 . . . 393 F3
Carlings GU34 . . . . . . 139 E2
Carlin Pl **3** GU15 . . . 36 A4
Carlinwark Dr GU15 . . 36 D7
Carlisle Cl RG23 . . . . . 68 A8
Carlisle Ct **3** SO16 . . 290 B8
Carlisle Rd
Portsmouth PO5 . . . . 404 C3
Rushmoor GU10 . . . . 144 F7
Southampton SO16 . . 290 B8
Carlton Ave BH25 . . . 397 D8
Carlton Cl GU15 . . . . .36 D5
Carlton Commerce Ctr
The SO14 . . . . 291 B7
Carlton Cres
Fleet GU52 . . . . 74 F7
Southampton SO15 . . 290 F6
Carlton Ct **6** SO15 . . 290 F8
Carlton Gr BH12 . . . . 391 D5
Carlton Ho **4** SO41 . 385 E4
Carlton Mount BH2 . . 392 E2
Carlton Pl SO15 . . . . . 290 F6
Carlton Rd
Bournemouth BH1 . . . 393 C4
Gosport PO12 . . . . . . 369 C6
Headley SO45 . . . . . . 166 A5
Portchester PO16 . . . 320 E1
Southampton SO15 . . 290 F7
Carlton Way **7**
PO12 . . . . 369 C6
Carlyle Rd
Bournemouth BH6 . . . 394 D6
Gosport PO12 . . . . . . 369 B6
Carlyn Dr SO53 . . . . . 243 D7
Carlyon Cl
Farnborough GU14 . . . 56 A4
Mytchett GU16 . . . . . . 56 F2
Carmans La SO21 . . . 219 D8
Carmarthen Ave
PO6 . . . . 346 B8
Carmarthen Cl GU14 . .55 E7
Carmel Cl BH15 . . . . . 389 D2
Carmichael Way
RG22 . . . . 91 C8
Carmine Ct **5** PO13 . 368 C4
Carnarvon Rd
4 Bournemouth
BH1 . . . . 393 E4
Gosport PO12 . . . . . . 369 A5
Portsmouth PO2 . . . . 370 F4
Carnation Rd SO16 . . 267 C4
Carne Cl SO53 . . . . . . 243 C6
Carnegie Cl BH12 . . . 391 D5
Carnegie Rd RG14 . . . 1 E2
Carne Pl PO6 . . . . 345 A7
Carolina Pl RG40 . . . . 16 C7
Caroline Ave BH23 . . . 395 F6
Caroline Cl
Basingstoke RG21 . . . 68 F1
Southampton SO15 . . 290 B7
Caroline Gdns PO15 . 318 C2
Caroline Pl PO12 . . . . 369 B7
Caroline Rd BH11 . . . 377 B2
Caroline Way SO16 . . 36 D1
Carolyn Cl SO19 . . . . 291 E2
Carpathia Cl SO18 . . . 268 A2
Carpenter Cl
4 Portsmouth
PO4 . . . . 371 A3
Hythe SO45 . . . . 314 A4
Lymington SO41 . . . . 385 D5
Carpenters Cl SO24 . . 179 D5
Carpenters Ct
Basingstoke RG22 . . . 68 D3

Carpenters Ct continued
Mortimer RG7 . . . . . . 11 E6
Carpenter's Down
RG24 . . . . 48 C2
Carradale BH23 . . . . . 396 B6
Carran Wlk PO14 . . . . 342 E7
Carraway PO15 . . . . . 317 D7
Carrbridge Cl BH3 . . . 392 D7
Carrbridge Gdns
BH3 . . . . 392 D7
Carrbridge Rd BH3 . . 392 D7
Carrick La GU46 . . . . . 34 C6
Carrick Way BH25 . . . 383 C2
Carrington Cl SO41 . . 399 E5
Carrington Cres RG26 26 F8
Carrington Cvn Pk
SO41 . . . . 399 F3
Carrington Ho **28**
SO17 . . . . 267 A1
Carrington La
Ash Vale GU12 . . . . . . 77 E8
Milford on S SO41 . . . 399 E4
Carrol Cl SO50 . . . . . . 245 D1
Carroll Ave BH22 . . . . 353 E5
Carroll Cl BH12 . . . . . 392 A6
Carronades The **3**
SO14 . . . . 291 A5
Carronade Wlk PO3 . . 345 F5
Carshalton Ave PO6 . . 346 B8
Carshalton Rd **1**
GU15 . . . . .36 E8
Carsworth Way
BH17 . . . . 376 A2
Cartel Bsns Ctr RG24. 69 E8
Carter Com Sch
BH15 . . . . 389 F2
Carter Ho
15 Portsmouth
PO1 . . . . 370 A5
Gosport PO13 . . . . . . 343 B5
Carters Ave BH15 . . . 389 D4
Carter's Cl SP6 . . . . . . 235 D3
Carter's Clay Rd
SO51 . . . . 214 B5
Carter's Copse Nature
Trail★ PO13 . . . . 368 C5
Carter's La **9** BH15 . 390 C2
Cartersland SO30 . . . . 209 F3
Carter's Mdw SP10 . . .82 E2
Carters Wlk GU9 . . . . 99 B8
Carthage Cl SO53 . . . 243 F8
Carthagena SO21 . . . 131 D4
Carthona Dr GU52 . . . 74 F7
Cartref Cl BH31 . . . . . 302 F6
Cartwright Cl BH10 . . 377 C4
Cartwright Dr PO15 . . 317 F2
Carvers Ind Est
BH24 . . . . 329 A7
Carvers La BH24 . . . . . 329 A7
Carwarden House Com
Sch GU15 . . . . .36 F3
Cary Cl RG14 . . . . . . .5 B6
Carysfort Rd BH1 . . . . 393 D4
Cascades App PO1 . . . 404 B4
Cascades Sh Ctr
PO1 . . . . 404 B4
Cases Bakery Cl
PO17 . . . . 296 A4
Cashmoor Cl **4**
BH12 . . . . 391 F7
Caslake Cl BH25 . . . . 382 F1
Caspar John Cl
PO14 . . . . 367 B6
Caspian Cl PO15 . . . . 317 B7
Cassel Ave BH13 . . . . 392 B1
Casselles Ct **6**
BH25 . . . . 383 A2
Cassino Cl GU11 . . . .76 F2
Casterbridge Ct **5**
BH4 . . . . 392 C3
Casterbridge La SP11 81 D2
Casterbridge Rd
BH22 . . . . 353 C3
Castle Ave
Christchurch BH23 . . 396 E8
Havant PO9 . . . . 324 B1
Winchester SO23 . . . 403 D6
Castle Bridge Cotts
RG29 . . . . 72 C4
Castle Cl
Camberley GU15 . . . . 36 D4
Farnborough GU14 . . . 56 C2
Milford on S SO41 . . . 399 E4
Portsmouth PO5 . . . . 404 B1
Castle Court Prep Sch
BH21 . . . . 374 B7
Castlecraig Ct **2**
GU47 . . . . .35 B7
Castle Ct
2 Bitterne Pk
SO18 . . . . .267 F1
2 Christchurch
BH23 . . . . 397 A7
Southampton,Millbrook
SO15 . . . . 290 A6
Castledene Cres
BH14 . . . . 391 A2
Castle Farm La PO17 296 B2
Castle Field SO23 . . . .98 E3
Castle Gate Cl BH8 . . 378 C2
Castle Gdns GU32 . . . 228 E3
Castle Gr
Newbury RG14 . . . . . . 1 D5
Portchester PO16 . . . 344 D7
Castle Hill
Farley Hill RG7 . . . . . 15 A7
Farnham GU9 . . . . 98 F3

Castle Hill continued
Winchester SO22 . . . . 403 D6
Castle Hill Inf Sch
RG23 . . . . 68 C5
Castle Hill Jun Sch
RG23 . . . . 68 C5
Castle Hill La
Burley BH24 . . . . 330 E3
Edmondsham BH21 . . 279 A7
Castle Hts **1** SO18 . . 267 F1
Castle Ind Pk RG14 . . .2 A5
Castle La
1 Southampton
SO14 . . . . 290 F3
Calshot SO45 . . . . . . 366 F7
Chandler's Ford SO53 243 B4
Donnington RG14 . . . . 1 C6
North Baddesley
SO52 . . . . .242 D4
Castle Lane E BH7 . . . 394 C8
Castle La W BH9 . . . . 378 C2
Castlemain Ave BH6 . 394 C5
Castle Malwood Lodge
SO43 . . . . 286 B5
Castleman Ct BH22 . . 353 B2
Castlemans La PO11 . 348 A1
Castleman Way
BH24 . . . . 329 A6
Castle Marina PO13 . 367 F1
Castle Mdw SP5 . . . . 234 F7
Castlemews BH24 . . . 328 C5
Castle Mews SO41 . . . 290 F3
Castle of Mey Ho
GU27 . . . . .189 D6
Castle Par BH7 . . . . . 394 C8
Castlepoint BH8 . . . . 378 E4
Castle Prim Sch
PO16 . . . . 344 D7
Castle Rd
Aldershot GU11 . . . . . 76 C4
Basingstoke RG21 . . . 69 B3
Bournemouth BH9 . . . 378 A1
Camberley GU15 . . . . 36 D4
Netley SO31 . . . . 315 B6
Portsmouth PO5 . . . . 404 B1
Rowlands Castle PO9 301 B1
Southampton SO18 . . 267 E2
Southwick PO17 . . . . 320 F6
Castle Rise
Kings Worthy SO23 . . 154 C1
North Warnborough
RG29 . . . . 72 C4
Castle Sch The RG14 . .1 B6
Castleshaw Cl SO16 . 289 F7
Castle Sq
3 Southampton
SO14 . . . . 290 F3
Basingstoke RG21 . . . 69 B5
Castle St
Christchurch BH23 . . 395 B6
Farnham GU9 . . . . 98 F3
Fleet GU52 . . . . 74 F7
Medstead GU34 . . . . 159 E7
Poole BH15 . . . . 390 C1
Portchester PO16 . . . 344 D7
Southampton SO14 . . 291 A4
Castleton Ave BH10 . 377 D6
Castleton Ct PO5 . . . . 404 A1
Castle Trad Est
PO16 . . . . 344 E8
Castle View PO12 . . . 369 B9
Castle View Rd
PO16 . . . . 344 E6
Castleway PO9 . . . . . . 324 B1
Castle Way SO14 . . . . 290 F3
Castlewood BH24 . . . 328 D5
Castle Woods SP5 . . . 235 D6
Caston's Yd RG21 . . . .69 B4
Castor Ct
Fleet GU52 . . . . 75 B5
Yateley GU46 . . . . 33 F7
Caswall Ride GU46 . . . 34 D5
Caswell Cl GU14 . . . . 55 D6
Catalina Dr BH23 . . . 396 A6
Catalina Dr BH15 . . . 390 E1
Catamaran Cl SO31 . . 316 C1
Cateran Cl SO16 . . . . 289 F8
Catesby Gdns GU46 . . 33 E5
Cathay Gdns SO45 . . 313 C3
Cathedral View **4**
SO23 . . . . .403 F4
Catherine Cl SO30 . . 268 C2
Catherine Cres SP5 . . 234 D7
Catherine Ct **1** GU11 76 D1
Catherine Gdns
SO30 . . . . .268 E2
Catherine Rd GU11 . . 1 E2
Catherines Wlk SP11 104 F3
Catherine Villas
GU27 . . . . .189 F6
Catherine Wheel Gdns
BH23 . . . . 379 E3
Catherington CE Inf Sch
PO8 . . . . 276 B1
Catherington La
Horndean,Catherington
PO8 . . . . 276 B1
Horndean PO8 . . . . . . 300 B7
Catherington Way
PO9 . . . . 323 F3
Catisfield Ho **3** PO1 404 C4
Catisfield La PO15 . . . 318 B1
Catisfield Rd
Fareham PO15 . . . . . . 318 C2
Portsmouth PO4 . . . . 371 B4
Catkin Cl RG24 . . . . . .48 F7
Catmint Cl SO53 . . . . 242 F7
Caton Cl BH12 . . . . . . 392 B8

Cattistock Rd BH8 .. 378 E2
Cattle La SP11 .... 104 E5
Catways SO21 ...... 218 B7
Caunter Rd RG14 ....1 B4
Causeway SO51 .... 240 D6
Causeway Cres
SO40 .... 289 A8
Causeway Ct 5
SO18 .... 291 E8
Causeway Farm PO8 300 B6
Causeway The
Heckfield RG27 ...... 31 A7
Middle Winterslow
SP5 .... 168 A7
Nether Wallop SO20 . 147 F6
Petersfield GU31 .... 228 E1
Portchester PO16 .... 319 E1
Causton Gdns SO50 . 244 A3
Causton Rd RG22 .....91 B4
Cavalier Cl
Hythe SO45 .... 313 D3
Newbury RG14 .... 2 A5
Old Basing RG24 ..... 70 C6
Cavalier Ct PO6 .... 346 D8
Cavalier Rd RG24 .... 70 C6
Cavalier Way GU34 .. 139 D2
Cavalry Ct 4 GU11 ... 76 C2
Cavalry Ho GU11 .... 76 D2
Cavan Cres BH17 .... 375 B1
Cavanna Cl PO13 .... 343 B3
Cavan's Rd GU11 .... 77 A6
C Ave SO45 .... 338 D5
Cavel Ct RG24 .... 70 A8
Cavell Dr PO6 ...... 321 E1
Cavendish Cl
Romsey SO51 ...... 216 B2
Waterlooville PO7 ... 322 F8
Cavendish Corner Mobile
Home Pk 3 BH24 . 329 B8
Cavendish Ct
9 Bournemouth
BH4 .... 392 C3
Blackwater GU17 .... 35 B3
Newbury RG14 .... 2 C5
Cavendish Dr PO7 ... 322 F8
Cavendish Gdns GU52 74 E4
Cavendish Gr
Southampton SO17 .. 290 F8
Winchester SO23 ... 176 B3
Cavendish Hall BH1 . 393 A5
Cavendish Mews
3 Southampton
SO15 .... 290 F8
Aldershot GU11 ...... 76 E1
Cavendish Pk GU47 .. 35 C6
Cavendish Pl BH1 ... 393 A5
Cavendish Rd
Aldershot GU11 ..... 76 E1
Bournemouth BH1 ... 393 A5
Fleet GU52 .... 74 F4
Portsmouth PO5 .... 404 C1
Caversham Cl
Hamworthy BH15 ... 389 E3
Southampton SO19 .. 292 A4
West End SO30 ..... 268 D1
Caves Farm Cl GU47 ...34 E8
Cawdor Rd BH3 ..... 392 D7
Cawett Dr 5 GU51 ....53 E3
Cawte Rd SO15 ..... 290 D6
Cawte's Pl PO16 .... 319 D1
Caxton Ave SO19 .... 292 B6
Caxton Cl
Andover SP10 .... 82 C1
Christchurch BH23 .. 396 A7
Cayman Cl RG24 ..... 48 D1
Cecil Ave
Ashurst SO40 ...... 288 C2
Bournemouth BH8 ... 393 C8
Southampton SO16 .. 266 B1
Cecil Cl BH21 ...... 374 E6
Cecil Ct BH8 .... 393 B8
Cecil Gr PO5 .... 404 A1
Cecil Hill BH8 ..... 393 B8
Cecil Pl PO5 .... 404 A1
Cecil Rd
Bournemouth BH5 ... 393 E4
Poole BH12 .... 391 D6
Southampton SO19 .. 291 F3
Cecil Villas SO17 ... 267 C1
Cedar Ave
Blackwater GU17 .... 35 B5
Bournemouth BH10 .. 377 D6
Christchurch BH23 .. 394 D8
Southampton SO15 .. 290 D8
St Leonards BH24 ... 327 E3
Cedar Cl
Aldershot GU12 ..... 100 C8
Bursledon SO31 ..... 315 F8
Gosport PO12 ...... 344 A1
Hedge End SO30 .... 293 C7
Kings Worthy SO23 .. 176 B8
Tadley RG26 .... 27 B7
Upton BH16 .... 389 B8
Waterlooville PO7 ... 322 E6
Cedar Court Pk RG19 ...6 A7
Cedar Cres
North Baddesley
SO52 .... 241 F5
Waterlooville PO8 ... 300 C5
Cedar Ct
10 Fareham PO16 .... 319 C1
Bishop's Waltham
SO32 .... 271 D8
Bournemouth BH4 ... 392 B2
Haslemere GU27 .... 189 F6
Portsmouth PO5 .... 404 C1
Cedar Dr
Fleet GU51 .... 54 C1
Cedar Dr *continued*
Hordle SO41 .... 399 D8
Kingsclere RG20 ..... 24 C2
Wimborne Minster
BH21 .... 352 A5
Cedar Gdns
Havant PO9 .... 324 A2
Old Milton BH25 .... 382 F1
Southampton SO14 .. 291 A8
Cedar Gr PO3 .... 371 B7
Cedar Grange 18
BH13 .... 392 A4
Cedar La GU16 ....56 B8
Cedar Lawn SO51 ... 216 C1
Cedar Manor BH4 ... 392 C3
Cedarmount SO43 .. 309 F4
Cedar Mount RG14 ......5 D8
Cedar Pl BH23 ...... 357 B1
Cedar Rd
Eastleigh SO50 ..... 243 E1
Farnborough GU14 ... 56 A3
Hythe SO45 .... 338 A7
Southampton SO14 .. 291 A7
Cedar Rise RG19 ....7 F5
Cedar Sch The SO16 265 E4
Cedars Cl GU47 ...... 34 D8
Cedars Sch RG7 .... 9 E7
Cedars The
Bournemouth BH4 ... 392 C4
Fareham PO16 ...... 318 F3
Fleet GU51 .... 75 B8
Greenham RG19 ...... 6 A7
Cedars View SP5 .... 191 E7
Cedar Terr RG27 ......52 B5
Cedar Trad Pk BH21 . 352 F6
Cedar Tree Cl RG23 .. 90 A8
Cedar View GU52 .....75 B6
Cedar Way
Basingstoke RG23 .... 68 D6
Fareham PO14 ...... 342 E8
Ferndown BH22 ..... 353 C8
Cedarways GU9 ..... 121 F7
Cedar Wlk
Andover SP10 ...... 105 D6
Winchester SO22 ... 403 C5
Cedarwood
Chineham RG24 ...... 48 E3
Kings Worthy SO23 .. 176 C7
Cedar Wood Cl
Fair Oak SO50 ...... 245 E2
Totton SO40 .... 288 C8
Cedarwood Lodge 6
PO16 .... 319 B2
Ceder Ho SO14 ..... 291 B3
Cedric Cl SO45 ...... 365 F8
Celandine Ave
Locks Heath SO31 ... 316 F2
Waterlooville PO8 ... 300 B3
Celandine Cl
Chandler's Ford
SO53 .... 242 F5
Christchurch BH23 .. 396 B8
Celandine Ct GU46 ....33 F7
Celia Cl PO7 .... 323 B8
Cellars Farm Rd
BH6 .... 395 A3
Celtic Dr SP10 ...... 105 E6
Cement Terr 2
SO14 .... 290 F3
Cemetery Ave BH15 . 390 F6
Cemetery Hill RG29 ...72 E2
Cemetery Junc BH2 . 392 F5
Cemetery La
Denmead PO7 ...... 298 F5
Upton Grey RG25 ..... 94 B5
Westbourne PO10 ... 325 D3
Cemetery Rd
Fleet GU51 .... 74 E7
Southampton SO15 .. 290 F8
Wimborne Minster
BH21 .... 351 B5
Centaur St PO2 ..... 370 D8
Centaury Gdns SO50 269 C7
Centenary Cl SO41 .. 360 C2
Centenary Gdns PO9 323 F2
Centenary Ho BH23 . 395 B7
Centenary Way BH1 . 393 E5
Central Ave
Corfe Mullen BH21 .. 374 D7
Poole BH12 .... 391 E6
Central Bridge SO14 291 B3
Central Dr
Bournemouth BH2 ... 392 E5
West Moors BH24 ... 354 B8
Central Point PO3 .. 371 B6
Central Prec The
SO53 .... 243 C5
Central Rd
Bordon GU35 .... 164 D6
Cosham PO6 .... 346 C7
Portchester PO16 ... 344 B7
Southampton SO14 .. 291 A2
Central Sq PO1 ..... 370 A4
Central St PO1 ..... 404 C4
Central Station Bridge
SO15 .... 290 E5
Central Way SP10 .....83 E2
Central Way N SO45 . 339 E2
Centre Dr RG24 ....48 F1
Centre La SO41 ..... 384 E1
Centre Pl BH24 ..... 328 F7
Centreprise Ho RG19 ...6 E4
Centre Terrace Rd
GU14 ....76 E8
Centre Way SO31 ... 317 A3
Centurion Cl 5 GU47 .35 B8
Centurion Ct 24 PO1 370 A4
Centurion Gate PO4 . 371 D3
Centurion Ho SO18 .. 291 C7
Centurion Ind Pk
SO18 .... 291 C7
Centurion Way RG22 ..91 B7
Century Cl RG25 ..... 92 A7
Century Farm Ind Units
GU9 .... 99 D5
Cerdic Mews SO31 .. 316 A4
Cerne Abbas BH13 .. 392 A1
Cerne Cl
Bournemouth BH9 ... 378 B4
North Baddesley
SO52 .... 241 F4
West End SO18 ..... 268 B1
Cessac Ho PO12 .... 369 C2
Chadderton Gdns
PO1 .... 370 B3
Chaddesley Glen
BH13 .... 402 E6
Chaddesley Grange
BH13 .... 402 F6
Chaddesley Pines
BH13 .... 402 E6
Chaddesley Wood Rd
BH13 .... 402 E5
Chadswell Mdw PO9 323 D1
Chadwell Ave SO19 . 292 B4
Chadwick Rd SO50 .. 243 F2
Chadwick Way SO31 315 F2
Chafen Rd SO18 ..... 291 D7
Chaffers Cl RG29 ..... 95 D3
Chaffey Cl BH24 .... 329 C8
Chaffinch Cl
Basingstoke RG22 .... 91 A8
Broadstone BH17 ... 374 F2
New Milton BH25 ... 382 F2
Sandhurst GU47 ..... 35 B8
Totton SO40 .... 288 C8
Chaffinch Gn PO8 ... 299 E4
Chaffinch Way
Lee-on-t-S PO13 .... 367 F4
Portchester PO16 ... 343 F8
Chalbury Cl BH17 ... 376 A2
Chalbury Ct 2 BH14 391 B4
Chalcraft Cl GU30 ... 187 E4
Chalcrafts GU34 .... 140 A5
Chalcroft Distribution Pk
SO30 .... 269 B5
Chaldecott Gdns
BH10 .... 377 C4
Chaldon Rd BH17 ... 375 F2
Chale Cl PO13 ...... 343 C2
Chalet Ct GU35 ..... 164 D3
Chalet Hill GU35 .... 164 D3
Chalewood Rd SO45 . 365 E7
Chalfont Ave BH23 .. 379 D3
Chalfont Ct 7 SO16 . 266 A1
Chalfont Dr GU14 .... 56 A2
Chalford Rd RG14 ......1 C2
Chalice Cl BH14 ..... 391 A4
Chalice Ct SO30 ..... 293 B6
Chalk Cl GU34 ...... 160 B2
Chalkcroft La
Penton Grafton SP11 .. 81 F4
Penton Mewsey SP11 . 82 A4
Chalk Down SP9 ..... 79 A7
Chalk Hill
Little Somborne
SO20 .... 172 F5
Soberton SO32 ..... 273 C5
West End SO18 ..... 268 C1
Chalk Hill Rd PO8 ... 300 C8
Chalk La PO17 ...... 319 B7
Chalk Pit Cotts PO17 319 B7
Chalkpit La SP11 .... 104 D5
Chalk Pit La SP5 .... 169 B1
Chalkpit Rd PO6 ... 321 B1
Chalk Ridge
Horndean PO8 ...... 276 D3
Winchester SO23 ... 198 D7
Chalk Ridge Prim Sch
RG22 ....68 F1
Chalkridge Rd PO6 .. 322 A1
Chalk's Cl SP5 ...... 235 D7
Chalk Vale
King's Somborne
SO20 .... 172 F4
Old Basing RG24 ..... 70 C5
Chalky Copse RG27 .. 51 A2
Chalky Hill GU34 .... 159 A6
Chalky La
Bishop's Waltham
SO32 .... 271 D8
Dogmersfield RG27 ... 73 E3
Challenge Ent Ctr The
PO3 .... 346 B3
Challenger Dr PO12 . 369 C8
Challenger Way
SO45 .... 313 D2
Challenor Cl RG40 ... 16 D7
Challis Cl RG22 ...... 68 C2
Challis Ct
10 Southampton
SO14 .... 291 A3
Ludgershall SP11 ..... 57 A2
Challoner Cl RG22 ... 68 D3
Chalmers Way SO31 . 315 E3
Chaloner Cres SO45 . 314 A1
Chalton Cres PO9 ... 323 D4
Chalton Ho PO1 ..... 404 B4
Chalton La PO8 ..... 276 D6
Chalvington Ct SO53 243 C5
Chalvington Rd
SO53 .... 243 D4
Chalwyn Ind Est BH15,
BH12 .... 391 A7
Chalybeate Cl SO16 . 266 B2
Chalybeate Hospl
SO16 .... 266 B2
Chamberhouse Mill La
RG19 ....7 D8
Chamber La GU10 ... 121 A7
Chamberlain Gr
PO14 .... 343 A8
Chamberlain Hall
SO16 .... 267 A4
Chamberlain Rd
SO17 .... 267 A3
Chamberlains Mdw
RG27 ....31 B5
Chamberlayne Ct
SO52 .... 242 B4
Chamberlayne Ho
SO31 .... 315 B6
Chamberlayne Park Sch
SO19 .... 292 A1
Chamberlayne Rd
Bursledon SO31 ..... 315 F8
Eastleigh SO50 ..... 244 A2
Netley SO31 .... 315 B6
Chambers Ave SO51 . 241 B7
Chambers Cl SO16 .. 265 C5
Chambers Rd GU12 ...77 F6
Chamomile Gdns
GU14 .... 55 A5
Champion Cl SO41 .. 399 F4
Champion Way GU52 . 75 A5
Champney Cl GU35 .. 164 C1
Chancellors La SO32 269 F4
Chancel Rd SO31 ... 317 B3
Chanctonbury Ho
PO5 .... 404 B1
Chander Cl BH22 .... 353 E4
Chandler Rd RG21 ... 69 A2
Chandlers Cl
Bournemouth BH7 ... 394 B8
South Hayling PO11 . 373 C2
Chandlers Ct 29
SO14 .... 291 A3
Chandler's Ford Ind Est
SO53 .... 243 B5
Chandler's Ford Inf Sch
SO53 .... 243 D6
Chandler's Ford Sta
SO53 .... 243 C6
Chandlers La GU46 ....34 B7
Chandlers Pl SO31 .. 315 B6
Chandlers Rd GU12 ...77 F4
Chandlers Way SO31 317 B6
Chandos Ave BH12 .. 392 A8
Chandos Ho 3
SO14 .... 291 A3
Chandos Rd RG14 .....5 D8
Chandos St 12 SO14 . 291 A3
Chandos Terr SO21 .. 177 E5
Channel Ct
Barton on S BH25 ... 397 E7
Bournemouth BH6 ... 394 D3
Channel Mouth Rd
SO45 .... 339 F1
Channels Farm Rd
SO16 .... 267 D5
Channel Way SO14 .. 291 C3
Channon Ct 11 SO15 290 E7
Channon Ret Pk
SO50 .... 243 E3
Chant Cl
Christchurch BH23 .. 395 D7
Wherwell SP11 ..... 128 F6
Chantrell Wlk PO15 . 318 D3
Chantreys GU51 ..... 74 D8
Chantry Cl
Christchurch BH23 .. 381 F1
Hook RG27 .... 72 A8
Chantry Ct GU16 ......36 B1
Chantry Ctr The
SP10 .... 106 A8
Chantry Mead SO22 . 403 C7
Chantry Mews RG22 ...91 B7
Chantry Rd
Gosport PO12 ...... 369 A8
Horndean PO8 ...... 300 B7
Southampton SO14 .. 291 B3
Chantrys Ct GU9 .....98 E1
Chantry St SP10 .... 106 A8
Chantrys The GU9 ....98 E1
Chantry The
Bournemouth BH1 ... 393 A4
Locks Heath PO14 ... 317 C3
Chapel Cl
Amport SP11 .... 104 B6
Braishfield SO51 ... 216 C6
Corfe Mullen BH21 .. 374 C6
Dummer RG25 .... 90 D1
Houghton SO20 ..... 171 C4
Old Basing RG24 ..... 70 B7
West End SO30 ..... 268 D2
Chapel Cres SO19 .. 292 A4
Chapel Ct
1 Portsmouth
PO1 .... 370 C7
Broughton SO20 .... 170 B7
Wherwell SP11 ..... 128 F6
Chapel Dro
Hedge End SO30 .... 293 B6
Horton Heath SO50 .. 269 C7
Chapel Field SO21 .. 177 A4
Chapel Gate BH23 .. 378 C8
Chapel Gdns GU35 .. 164 F5
Chapel Hill RG21 ......69 B6
Chapel La
5 Waterlooville
PO7 .... 322 E7
Aldermaston RG7 ..... 10 D5
Ashford Hill RG19 ..... 8 D1
Chapel La *continued*
Baughurst RG26 ..... 26 C7
Bishopstone SP5 .... 210 B7
Blackfield SO45 .... 365 E8
Bransgore BH23 .... 381 A8
Broughton SO20 .... 170 B7
Burley BH24 .... 331 B3
Corfe Mullen BH21 .. 374 C5
Curdridge SO32 .... 294 E8
East Boldre SO42 ... 363 D6
East Parley BH23 ... 378 C8
Enham Alamein SP11 . 83 B6
Farnborough GU14 ... 55 D8
Fawley SO45 .... 339 A2
Grateley SP11 ...... 125 B8
Itchen Abbas SO21 .. 177 A2
Lockerley SO51 ..... 214 A5
Lyndhurst SO43 .... 309 F4
Michelmersh SO51 .. 215 D8
Nomansland SP5 ... 261 C7
Otterbourne SO21 .. 219 B1
Poole BH15 .... 390 C2
Redlynch SP5 ...... 235 E6
Riseley RG7 .... 14 A3
Stoke SP11 .... 61 C4
Sway SO41 .... 360 D1
Totton SO40 .... 288 E5
Wimborne Minster
BH21 .... 351 B5
Wolverton Common
RG26 .... 25 E4
Chapel Lodge RG40 .. 16 C6
Chapel Mead RG27 ... 33 C8
Chapel Pond Dr RG29 72 C3
Chapel Rd
Camberley GU15 ..... 35 F5
Droxford SO32 ..... 249 C3
Poole BH14 .... 391 A4
Rowledge GU10 ..... 121 C3
Sarisbury SO31 ..... 316 E6
Silchester RG7 ...... 11 A5
Soberton SO32 ..... 273 B2
Southampton SO14 .. 291 B4
Swanmore SO32 .... 272 B5
West End SO30 ..... 268 E2
Chapel Rise BH24 ... 328 D2
Chapel River Cl
SP10 .... 105 E7
Chapel Row RG27 .... 52 D7
Chapelside PO14 .... 342 A8
Chapel Sq
Gosport PO12 ...... 368 F7
Sandhurst GU15 ..... 35 D6
Chapel St
3 Portsmouth
PO5 .... 404 A1
East Meon GU32 .... 226 D1
Farnborough GU14 ... 56 B6
Gosport PO12 ...... 369 B9
North Waltham RG25 .. 89 E1
Petersfield GU32 ... 228 F3
Portsmouth,Buckland
PO2 .... 370 D8
Southampton SO14 .. 291 B4
Chaplains Ave PO8 .. 299 D3
Chaplains Cl PO8 ... 299 D3
Chapman Wlk RG18 ....2 F4
Chappell Cl GU30 ... 188 A4
Chapter Ct 2 GU34 . 139 F4
Chapter Terr RG27 ... 52 D6
Charborough Rd
BH18 .... 375 B3
Charden Ct SO18 ... 292 B7
Charden Rd
Bishopstoke SO50 ... 245 A2
Gosport PO13 ...... 368 D8
Charfield Cl
Fareham PO14 ...... 342 D8
Winchester SO22 ... 403 C3
Charing Cl BH24 ... 329 A6
Charity View PO17 .. 318 E7
Chark La PO13 ..... 367 F5
Charlcot Cl RG28 .... 86 C3
Charlcot Lawn PO9 . 323 D6
Charldon Gn RG24 ... 70 A8
Charlecote Cl GU14 ...56 B3
Charlecote Dr SO53 . 243 A8
Charlecote Ho SO15 . 290 D5
Charlecote Mews 14
SO22 .... 403 D6
Charledown Cl RG25 . 88 A7
Charledown Rd RG25 . 88 A7
Charlemont Dr 2
PO16 .... 319 D1
Charlesbury Ave
PO12 .... 368 F4
Charles Cl
Hook RG27 .... 51 A1
Waterlooville PO7 ... 322 D6
Winchester SO23 ... 403 F8
Charles Cres BH25 .. 383 B5
Charles Dalton Ct
SP10 .... 106 A7
Charles Dickens
Birthplace Mus★
PO1 .... 370 C7
Charles Dickens Inf Sch
PO1 .... 370 D7
Charles Dickens Jun Sch
PO1 .... 370 D7
Charles Dickens St
PO1 .... 404 B3
Charles Gdns BH10 . 377 D2
Charles Ho PO12 .... 369 E6
Charles Keightley Ct
BH21 .... 351 D4
Charles Kingsley's CE
Prim Sch RG27 ..... 33 A8
Charles Knott Gdns
SO15 .... 290 F7
Charles Ley Ct SO45 . 339 B3
Charles Miller Ct 9
SO15 .... 290 F8
Charles Norton-Thomas
Ct 4 PO1 .... 370 B5
Charles Rd
Christchurch BH23 .. 395 F8
Poole BH15 .... 390 D3
Charles Richards Cl
RG21 .... 69 A3
Charles's La BH24 ... 329 E3
Charles St
Basingstoke RG22 .... 68 E4
Camberley GU15 ..... 36 A6
Newbury RG14 ....5 B6
Petersfield GU32 .... 228 E3
Portsmouth PO1 .... 404 C4
Southampton SO14 .. 291 A3
Charleston Cl PO11 . 372 E4
Charleston Rd SO45 . 338 D8
Charles Watts Way
SO30 .... 293 B8
Charlesworth Dr
PO7 .... 299 D2
Charlesworth Gdns
PO7 .... 299 D1
Charles Wyatt Ho 3
SO14 .... 291 A7
Charliejoy Gdns 1
SO14 .... 291 C6
Charlie Soar Ct 1
SO50 .... 244 A2
Charlott Ct PO5 .... 404 B1
Charlotte Cl
3 New Milton
BH25 .... 383 A2
Andover SP10 ...... 106 D8
Christchurch BH23 .. 396 A6
Farnham GU9 .... 99 B8
Poole BH12 .... 392 C7
Charlotte Ct
Chandler's Ford
SO53 .... 243 E7
Southampton SO19 .. 291 F2
Charlotte Dr PO12 .. 369 C8
Charlotte Ho 4 RG21 69 C6
Charlotte Mews
Farnborough GU14 ... 56 B5
Gosport PO12 ...... 369 A3
Charlotte Pl SO14 .. 291 A6
Charlotte St PO1 .... 404 B4
Charlton Cl
Bournemouth BH9 ... 378 C4
Finchampstead RG40 . 16 D8
Hordle SO41 .... 383 F3
Charlton Down SP11 ..59 E1
Charlton Dr GU31 ... 229 A5
Charlton La RG7 ..... 14 A5
Charlton Pl RG14 ......1 E4
Charlton Rd
Andover SP10 ...... 106 A8
Andover SP10 .... 82 E1
Andover SP10 .... 82 F1
Southampton SO15 .. 290 D7
Charlton Sp and L Ctr
SP10 .... 82 C1
Charltons The BH2 .. 392 F5
Charlwood La SO24 . 182 D4
Charminster 6 PO5 . 370 E2
Charminster Ave
BH9 .... 378 B1
Charminster Cl
Bournemouth BH8 ... 378 B2
Waterlooville PO7 ... 322 E8
Charminster Pl BH8 . 378 C2
Charminster Rd BH8 393 B7
Charmouth Gr BH14 . 391 A4
Charmouth Terr 6
SO16 .... 266 A1
Charmus Rd SO40 ... 264 B2
Charmwen Cres
SO30 .... 268 C2
Charmwood Cl RG14 ..1 D5
Charnock Cl SO41 ... 383 F3
Charnwood PO13 ... 343 D2
Charnwood Ave BH9 378 B3
Charnwood Cl
Andover SP10 ...... 106 B6
Basingstoke RG22 .... 68 B3
Chandler's Ford SO53 218 C2
Totton SO40 .... 264 D1
West Moors BH22 ... 326 E2
Charnwood Cres
SO53 .... 218 C2
Charnwood Dr SP6 .. 257 E3
Charnwood Gdns
SO53 .... 218 C2
Charnwood Way
SO45 .... 365 E7
Chartcombe BH13 ... 402 E8
Chartergrove Ho 12
GU31 .... 228 F3
Charter Ho 2 PO5 .. 404 A2
Charterhouse Way
SO30 .... 269 C1
Charter Rd
Bournemouth BH11 .. 376 D6
Newbury RG14 .... 5 D7
Charters Ct GU12 ... 100 A8
Chart House Rd GU12 .77 E7
Chartwell
5 Poole BH13 ..... 392 B3
Camberley GU16 ..... 56 D6

Chartwell continued
Farnham GU9 . . . . . 121 D6
Chartwell Cl
Eastleigh SO50 . . . . 244 B6
Titchfield PO14 . . . . 317 C1
Chartwell Dr PO9 . . 324 C3
Chartwell Gdns GU11. 77 A7
Chase Cl GU33 . . . . . 208 A4
Chase Com Hospl
GU35. . . . . 164 D2
Chase Ct GU35. . . . . 164 F5
Chase Farm Cl SO32 271 E3
Chase Field GU34 . . 161 D2
Chase Gr SO32. . . . . 271 E3
Chase Plain GU26 . . 167 A1
Chase Rd
Lindford GU35 . . . . 164 F5
Liss GU33 . . . . 208 A4
Chaseside BH7 . . . . 394 A8
Chase The
Churt GU10 . . . . . . 144 C3
Donnington RG14 . . . . . 1 D7
Farnborough GU14 . . 56 B6
Gosport PO12 . . . . . 368 F4
St Leonards BH24 . . 328 D5
Titchfield PO14 . . . . 317 D2
Verwood BH31. . . . . 303 C5
Chasewater Ave
PO3 . . . . 371 A7
Chasewater Ct 8
GU11 . . . . 76 E1
Chatburn Ave PO8 . . 299 F3
Chatfield Ave PO2 . . 370 A8
Chatfield Cl GU14. . . 56 A2
Chatfield Ho 10 PO1. 404 C4
Chatfield Rd PO13 . . 343 B3
Chatham Cl PO12 . . 369 C8
Chatham Dr PO1. . . . 370 B3
Chatham Rd SO22. . . 403 A3
Chatsworth GU33 . . 208 B1
Chatsworth Ave
Cosham PO6 . . . . . . 346 A6
Portsmouth PO6 . . . 345 F6
Chatsworth Cl PO15. 318 C1
Chatsworth Ct PO5. . 404 B1
Chatsworth Dr SP10. 105 E7
Chatsworth Gn RG22 . 91 C6
Chatsworth Gr GU9 . . 98 F6
Chatsworth Hts GU15 . 36 F7
Chatsworth Rd
Bournemouth BH8. . 393 C6
Eastleigh SO50 . . . . 244 B8
Farnborough GU14 . . 56 C3
Poole BH14 . . . . 391 B5
Southampton SO19 . 292 A6
Chatsworth Way
BH25 . . . . 382 F3
Chatter La RG28 . . . . 86 C5
Chatters The RG7 . . . 15 A7
Chattis Hill Stables
SO20 . . . . 148 F3
Chaucer Ave
Andover SP10 . . . . . . 82 D1
Portchester PO6 . . . 320 E1
Chaucer Bsns Pk
SO23 . . . . 176 C3
Chaucer Cl
Basingstoke RG24. . . 48 C1
Fareham PO16. . . . . 318 F2
South Wonston SO21. 153 E5
Waterlooville PO7 . . 299 E2
Wimborne Minster
BH21 . . . . 351 C6
Chaucer Cres RG14 . . . 1 C5
Chaucer Dr SO41 . . . 399 D5
Chaucer Gr GU15 . . . . 36 B5
Chaucer Rd
Farnborough GU14 . . 55 D6
Poole BH13 . . . . 402 F8
Southampton SO19 . 291 E6
Chaucombe Pl BH25 382 F1
Chaundler Rd SO23 . 403 E8
Chaundlers Croft
GU10 . . . . 97 D5
Chauntsingers Cotts 5
GU34 . . . . 139 F4
Chauntsingers Rd
GU34 . . . . 139 F4
Chavasse Way GU14 . . 55 B5
Chaveney Cl SO45 . . 313 C1
Chavy Water SO51 . . 244 E6
Chawton CE Prim Sch
GU34 . . . . 161 D7
Chawton Cl
Fleet GU51 . . . . 53 C3
Southampton SO18 . 292 D8
Winchester SO22 . . 175 D4
Chawton End Cl
GU34 . . . . 160 C3
Chawton Park Rd
GU34 . . . . 139 D1
Cheam Rd BH18 . . . 374 F4
Cheam Sch RG19 . . . . 24 B8
Cheam Way SO40 . . 264 D1
Cheap St RG14. . . . . . . 1 E2
Cheater's La SP6 . . . 280 C8
Cheavley Cl SP10 . . . 105 C8
Cheddar Cl SO19 . . . 291 E3
Cheddington Rd
BH9 . . . . 378 A4
Chedington Cl BH17. 375 E2
Chedworth Cres
PO6 . . . . 321 A1
Cheeryble Ho 10
PO1 . . . . 370 D7

Cheesecombe Farm La
GU33 . . . . 206 F6
Chellowdene SO53 . . 243 C5
Chelmer Ct 1 RG21. . 69 D5
Chelmsford Rd
Portsmouth PO2 . . . 345 F2
Upton BH16 . . . . . . 389 A7
Chelsea Ho 1 RG21. . 69 B5
Chelsea Rd PO5. . . . 404 C1
Cheltenham Cres
PO13 . . . . 367 F4
Cheltenham Ct 19
SO17 . . . . 267 A1
Cheltenham Gdns
SO30 . . . . 269 C3
Cheltenham Rd
Cosham PO6 . . . . . . 345 C8
Poole BH12 . . . . 391 C5
Chelveston Cres
SO16 . . . . 266 A4
Chelwood Gate
SO16 . . . . 266 F5
Chene Rd BH21 . . . . 351 D4
Cheping Gdns SO30. 294 A6
Chepstow Cl
Chandler's Ford
SO53. . . . . 243 B6
Totton SO40. . . . . . 288 C8
Chepstow Ct PO7 . . 300 B1
Chequers Ho 4
PO16 . . . . 319 B1
Chequer La RG7 . . . . 13 C2
Chequers Cl SO41. . 385 B3
Chequers La RG21 . . 33 C7
Chequers Quay 8
PO10 . . . . 349 A8
Chequers Rd RG21. . 69 C5
Cherberry Cl GU51 . . 54 B4
Cherbourg Prim Sch
SO50. . . . . 244 A1
Cherbourg Rd SO50. 244 A1
Cherford Rd BH11. . 377 B2
Cherita Cl BH15. . . . 390 F6
Cheriton 7 BH4 . . . 392 C2
Cheriton Ave
Bournemouth BH7 . . 394 C8
Southampton SO18 . 292 D7
Cheriton Cl
1 Tadley RG26 . . . . 26 F7
Havant PO9 . . . . . . 323 D4
Horndean PO8. . . . 300 B7
Newbury RG14 . . . . . . 5 E1
Winchester SO22 . . 403 B7
Cheriton Ct 5 SO15. 290 C6
Cheriton La SO24 . . 181 A6
Cheriton Lodge GU51 53 C4
Cheriton Prim Sch
SO24. . . . . 201 C6
Cheriton Rd
Eastleigh SO50 . . . . 243 F1
Gosport PO12 . . . . . 368 F4
Portsmouth PO4 . . . 371 C4
Winchester SO22 . . 403 C6
Cheriton Way
Blackwater GU17 . . . 35 B5
Wimborne Minster
BH21 . . . . 351 C6
Cherque La PO13 . . 368 A8
Cherque Way PO13 . 368 A7
Cherrett Cl BH11. . . 376 F4
Cherries Dr BH9 . . . 377 E2
Cherrimans Orch
GU27 . . . . 189 D6
Cherry Blossom Ct 19
PO1 . . . . 370 D7
Cherry Cl
Hook RG27. . . . . 51 B2
Lee-on-t-S PO13 . . . 367 F2
Newbury RG14 . . . . . 1 D4
Poole BH14 . . . . 391 B4
South Wonston SO21 153 D4
Cherry Ct
16 Southampton
SO17 . . . . 291 A8
Poole BH14 . . . . 391 B5
Cherry Dro SO50. . . 269 D6
Cherrygarth Rd
PO15 . . . . 318 C1
Cherry Gdns SO32. . 271 D7
Cherry Gr RG22 . . . 353 C6
Cherry Hill Gdns
BH16 . . . . 389 B6
Cherryhill Gr 6 GU11 76 D1
Cherry Hill Gr BH16 . 389 B6
Cherry Lodge 5
GU12 . . . . 76 F1
Cherry Orch RG28. . . 86 D3
Cherryton Gdns
SO45 . . . . 338 B3
Cherry Tree Ave
Fareham PO14. . . . . 342 D8
Haslemere GU27. . . 189 D7
North Tidworth SP9. . 79 A7
Waterlooville PO8 . . 300 B2
Cherry Tree Cl
Farnborough GU14 . . 55 A5
Farnham GU9 . . . . . . 99 A3
Hordle SO41 . . . . . . 399 D8
St Leonards BH24 . . 327 D3
Cherry Tree Ct 4
BH25 . . . . 383 B1
Cherry Tree Dr BH25 382 E5
Cherry Tree Rd
Andover SP10 . . . . . . 82 E1
Rowledge GU10. . . . 121 C3
Cherry Tree Wlk
Basingstoke RG21. . . 69 C8
Rowledge GU10. . . . 121 C3

Cherryway GU34 . . . 139 F5
Cherry Wlk SO15. . . 290 C8
Cherrywood
Chineham RG24. . . . . 48 E3
Hedge End SO30 . . . 293 B6
Cherrywood Com Prim
Sch GU14 . . . . 55 E6
Cherrywood Gdns
South Hayling PO11. . 373 A4
Totton SO40. . . . . . 288 C7
Cherrywood Rd GU14 .55 E7
Chertsey St GU51 . . . 53 E3
Chervil Cl
Chandler's Ford
SO53. . . . . 242 F6
Horndean PO8. . . . 276 C1
Cherville Ct SO51 . . 240 E7
Cherville Mews
SO51 . . . . 240 E8
Cherville St SO51 . . 240 E8
Cherwell Cres SO16. 289 E8
Cherwell Gdns SO53 243 D5
Cherwell Ho SO16.. 289 E8
Cheshire Cl PO15 . . 317 F5
Cheshire Dr BH8 . . . 379 A2
Cheshire Way PO10 . 325 D2
Chesilbourne Gr
BH8 . . . . 378 D3
Chesildene Ave BH8 378 D3
Chesildene Dr BH8. . 378 D3
Cheslyn Gdns BH12. 391 B8
Chesil St SO23. . . . 403 F5
Chesil Terr SO23 . . . 403 F5
Chesilton Cres GU52 . 75 A5
Chesil Wood SO23 . 198 C2
Chessel Ave
Bournemouth BH5. . 393 C4
Southampton SO19 . 291 E6
Chessel Cres SO19 . 291 F7
Chester Cl
Ash GU12. . . . . 77 F2
Newbury RG14 . . . . . 2 A1
Chester Cres SO53 . 368 B4
Chester Cl SO16 . . . 266 C2
Chester Cts 8 PO12. 369 C5
Chesterfield Cl BH13 402 F8
Chesterfield Ct BH1. 393 C3
Chesterfield Rd
Basingstoke RG21. . 69 C3
Newbury RG14 . . . . . 1 E1
Portsmouth PO3 . . . 371 A8
Chester Pl
7 Portsmouth
PO5 . . . . 370 D2
Basingstoke RG21. . . 69 A4
Chester Rd
Ash GU12. . . . . 77 F3
Poole BH13 . . . . 392 A2
Southampton SO18 . 268 A1
Winchester SO23 . . 403 F6
Chesters Rd GU15. . . 36 F5
Chesterton Gdns
PO8 . . . . 299 E3
Chesterton Pl PO15 . 317 C8
Chester Way GU10 . 100 D6
Chestnut Ave
2 Colden Common
SO21. . . . . 219 F1
Aldershot GU12. . . . 100 C8
Andover SP10 . . . . . 105 C5
Barton on S BH25 . . 398 A8
Bournemouth BH6. . 394 C4
Camberley GU15 . . . . 36 E6
Christchurch BH23 . . 394 D8
Eastleigh SO50 . . . . 243 F1
Eastleigh SO53 . . . . 243 D1
Ellingham BH24. . . . 304 B6
Farnham GU9 . . . . . 121 E8
Havant PO9 . . . . . . 323 B3
Littleton SO22 . . . . 175 C4
North Tidworth SP9. . 79 A7
Portsmouth PO4 . . . 370 F4
Waterlooville PO8 . . 300 C5
Chestnut Bank RG24 .70 B2
Chestnut Cl
Alton GU34 . . . . . . 139 E5
Blackwater GU17 . . . 35 C4
Chandler's Ford SO53 243 C2
Denmead PO7 . . . . 298 F4
Fleet GU51 . . . . 54 C4
Grayshott GU26. . . . 167 A3
Liphook GU30 . . . . . 188 B3
Romsey SO51 . . . . . 241 D6
West End SO30 . . . . 268 D3
Chestnut Cres SO41. . 1 E4
Chestnut Ct
7 Newbury RG14. . . . 1 E4
Aldershot GU12. . . . . 77 B2
Bordon GU35. . . . . 164 E2
Durrants PO9 . . . . . 324 B8
Southampton SO17 . 267 B2
Chestnut Dr
Ashurst SO40 . . . . . 288 C3
Petersfield GU31 . . 228 F1
Chestnut End GU35 . 165 E4
Chestnut Gr
Ferndown BH21. . . . 352 E6
Fleet GU51 . . . . 54 B2
Chestnut Lodge 4
SO16 . . . . 266 E3
Chestnut Pl SO20 . . 126 B4
Chestnut Rd
Brockenhurst SO42. 334 A1
Farnborough GU14 . . 55 B5
Southampton SO16 . 266 A2
Chestnut Rise
Droxford SO32. . . . 249 B2
Eastleigh SO53 . . . 243 D1

Cherryway GU34 . . . 139 F5
Chestnut Sq SO20. . 126 B4
Chestnuts The SO31. 317 A2
Chestnut Way
Burton BH23 . . . . . 380 C2
Titchfield PO14 . . . . 317 C1
Chestnut Wlk
Botley SO30. . . . . . 293 F8
Gosport PO12 . . . . 344 A1
New Alresford SO24 . 179 D5
Cheswell Gdns GU51. .74 E6
Chetnole Cl BH17. . . 376 A1
Chettle Rd SO19 . . . 292 C5
Chetwode Pl GU11 . . 100 A7
Chetwode Terr GU11. 76 C1
Chetwynd Dr SO16. . 266 F4
Chetwynd Rd
Portsmouth PO4 . . . 370 E3
Southampton SO16 . 266 F5
Chevening Ct 4
PO4 . . . . 371 B5
Cheviot Cl
Basingstoke RG22. . 68 B3
Farnborough GU14 . . 55 C7
Newbury RG14 . . . . . 5 A5
Cheviot Court Flats
BH23 . . . . 395 F8
Cheviot Cres SO16 . 289 E8
Cheviot Dr
Fleet SO45 . . . . 54 B4
Hythe SO45 . . . . . . 313 D3
Cheviot Gn SO31 . . 340 D10
Cheviot Rd SO16 . . . 289 E8
Cheviots The BH14 . 391 C3
Cheviot Way BH31 . . 302 F5
Cheviot Wlk PO14 . . 342 F7
Chevron Bsns Pk
SO45. . . . . 338 B6
Chewter Cl PO4. . . . 370 E1
Chewton Common Rd
BH23 . . . . 397 B8
Chewton Farm Rd
BH23 . . . . 382 C1
Chewton Lodge
BH23 . . . . 397 B8
Chewton Mews
BH23 . . . . 382 A1
Chewton Way BH23 . 382 B1
Cheyne Gdns BH4. . . 392 C2
Cheyne Way
Farnborough GU14 . . 55 D7
Lee-on-t-S PO13 . . . 367 F2
Chicheley Ct GU14 . . .55 F6
Chichester Ave
PO11 . . . . 373 A3
Chichester Cl
Andover SP10 . . . . 105 D8
Gosport PO13 . . . . 343 B2
Hedge End SO30 . . . 269 C1
Sarisbury SO31 . . . . 316 E3
West Wellow SO51. . 239 B2
Chichester Ho PO4 . . 371 B5
Chichester Pl RG22 . .68 E2
Chichester Rd
Ash GU12. . . . . 77 E3
North Hayling PO11. . 348 C1
Portsmouth PO2 . . . 370 E8
Ringwood BH24 . . . 305 C1
Southampton SO18 . 292 A7
Chichester Way
BH23 . . . . 396 A5
Chichester Wlk
BH21 . . . . 351 E1
Chickenhall La SO50 244 C2
Chickerell Cl BH9 . . 378 A4
Chidden Cl GU32. . . 226 D1
Chidden Holt SO53. . 243 A5
Chideock Cl BH12. . 391 E6
Chidham Cl PO9 . . . 323 C2
Chidham Dr PO9 . . . 323 C2
Chidham Rd PO6. . . 322 A1
Chidham Sq PO9 . . . 323 C2
Chidham Wlk 2
PO9 . . . . 323 C2
Chigwell Rd BH8. . . 378 B1
Chilbolton Ave SO22 403 A6
Chilbolton Cl
1 Havant PO9 . . . . 324 B6
Winchester SO22 . . 403 A5
Chilcomb Cl PO13. . 367 F3
Chilcombe Cl PO9 . . 323 F3
Chilcombe Hts SO23 403 F5
Chilcombe Rd BH6. . 394 B5
Chilcomb La
Chilcomb SO23 . . . 198 E5
Winchester SO23 . . 198 C5
Chilcomb Rd SO18 . 292 C8
Chilcote Rd PO3 . . . 371 A7
Chilcroft La GU27 . . 189 F1
Chilcroft Rd GU27. . 189 D1
Chilcrofts Rd GU27. 189 E1
Childerstone Cl
GU30 . . . . 187 F4
Childe Sq PO2 . . . . 345 C2
Chilfrome Cl BH17 . . 375 C1
Chilgrove Rd PO6. . 346 C8
Chilham Cl
Camberley GU16 . . . 56 D8
Eastleigh SO50 . . . . 244 A4
Chillandham La
Itchen Abbas SO21.. 155 C2
Itchen Abbas SO21. . 155 C5
Chilland La SO21. . . 177 C6
Chillenden Ct SO40 . 288 C4
Chillerton SO31. . . 315 C3
Chillingham Way
GU15 . . . . 36 A4
Chilling La SO31 . . . 340 F1

Chillington Gdns 5
SO53 . . . . 218 B1
Chilly Hill SP6 . . . . 282 F7
Chilmark Ct GU33 . . 207 F4
Chilsdown Way PO7. 322 E4
Chiltern Ave GU14 . . .55 B4
Chiltern Cl
Farnborough GU14 . . 55 B4
Fleet GU52 . . . . 75 B6
Haslemere GU27. . . 189 F5
Newbury RG14 . . . . . 5 A5
Old Milton BH25 . . . 382 E1
Poole BH4 . . . . 392 B5
Totton SO40. . . . . . 288 D5
Chiltern Ct
2 Portsmouth
PO5 . . . . 370 D1
5 Christchurch BH23 395 F8
Gosport PO12 . . . . 369 B6
New Alresford SO24 . 179 D5
Chiltern Dr
Barton on S BH25 . . 397 E8
Verwood BH31. . . . . 302 F6
Chiltern Gn SO16 . . 289 E8
Chiltern Prim Sch
RG22. . . . . 68 B4
Chiltern Way RG22. . .68 B3
Chiltern Wlk PO14 . . 342 F7
Chiltlee Cl GU30 . . . 188 A3
Chiltlee Manor
GU30 . . . . 188 A3
Chiltley La GU30 . . . 188 B2
Chiltley Way GU30 . . 188 A2
Chilton Farm Pk
GU14 . . . . 55 A4
Chilton Ridge RG22 . .91 B5
Chilworth Cl SO16 . . 242 D1
Chilworth Dro SO16. 242 D1
Chilworth Gdns PO8 276 D4
Chilworth Gr PO12 . 369 A6
Chilworth Old Village
SO16 . . . . 242 C2
Chilworth Rd SO16.. 242 E1
Chimes The BH4 . . . 392 B3
Chine Ave SO19. . . . 291 E6
Chine Cl SO31 . . . . 317 A4
Chine Cres BH2. . . . 392 D2
Chine Crescent Rd
BH2 . . . . 392 D2
Chineham Bsns Pk
RG24. . . . . 48 E4
Chineham District Ctr
RG24. . . . . 48 F1
Chineham La
Basingstoke RG24. . . 69 D8
Sherborne St John
RG24 . . . . 48 A1
Chineham Park Ct
RG24. . . . . 69 D8
Chineham Park Prim Sch
RG24. . . . . 69 D8
Chine The
Farnham GU10 . . . . 121 D5
Gosport PO13 . . . . 343 C6
Chine Wlk BH22 . . . 353 E1
Chingford Ave GU14 . .56 B5
Chinham Rd SO40. . . 287 C6
Chinnock Cl GU52. . . .74 F7
Chippendale Cl
3 Pamber Heath
RG26 . . . . 9 C1
Blackwater GU17 . . . 35 C4
Chipstead Ho 9
PO6 . . . . 345 F8
Chipstead Rd 8
PO6 . . . . 345 F8
Chirk Pl SO51. . . . . 241 A7
Chisels La BH23. . . . 381 B6
Chisholm Cl SO16. . 265 F5
Chislehurst 16 BH4. . 392 C3
Chislett Gdns GU47. . 34 D8
Chiswell Rd BH17 . . 375 D1
Chiswick Ho RG21 . . .69 B5
Chitty Rd PO4 . . . . 371 A2
Chive Cl 2 GU14. . . . 55 A4
Chivers Cl
Basingstoke RG22. . 68 C3
Portsmouth PO5 . . . 404 B1
Chivers Dr RG40 . . . . 16 C7
Chloe Gdns BH12 . . 391 D7
Chobham Rd GU16. . 36 D2
Cholderton Rd
Grateley SP11 . . . . 124 E7
Newton Tony SP4. . . 123 A7
Shipton Bellinger
SP11. . . . . 102 D3
Cholseley Dr GU51. . .53 E3
Chopin Rd RG22 . . . . 91 D8
Chorley Cl BH15 . . . 390 C6
Chris Cres BH16 . . . 389 C4
Chrismas Ave GU12. . 77 A1
Chrismas Pl GU12. . . 77 A1
Christchurch Bay Rd
BH25 . . . . 397 F7
Christchurch By-Pass
BH23 . . . . 395 D8
Christchurch Castle ★
BH23 . . . . 395 B6
Christchurch Cl 2
GU52 . . . . .74 F4
Christchurch Dr GU47 35 B5
Christchurch Gdns
1 Winchester
SO23 . . . . 403 D3
Cosham PO7 . . . . . 322 B2
Christchurch Hospl
BH23 . . . . 394 F8

Christchurch Jun Sch
BH23 . . . . 395 A7
Christchurch Prim Sch
BH23 . . . . 395 A7
Christchurch Priory ★
BH23 . . . . 395 C6
Christchurch Rd
Barton on S BH25 . . 397 D8
Bournemouth,Boscombe
BH1,BH7. . . . . 393 D4
Bournemouth,Iford
BH7 . . . . 394 B6
Ferndown BH22. . . 353 C1
Hordle SO41 . . . . . 399 C8
Hurn BH23. . . . . . . 379 C5
Ringwood BH24 . . . 328 F7
Ringwood,Moortown
BH24 . . . . 329 A4
Winchester SO23 . . 403 D4
Winchester SO23 . . 403 D5
Christchurch Sta
BH23 . . . . 395 A7
Christie Ave PO15. . 317 C8
Christie Hts RG14 . . . . 5 F8
Christie Wlk GU46 . . . 34 A4
Christine Cl GU12. . . 77 D1
Christine Ct 8 SO18 291 E8
Christine Ho 6 GU11 .76 F2
Christmas Hill SO21. 153 B4
Christopher Cres
BH15 . . . . 390 C6
Christopher Ho GU14 . .1 F2
Christopher Way
PO10 . . . . 324 F2
Christ's Hospital 13
SO23 . . . . 403 D5
Christ the King RC Prim
Sch BH11. . . . . 377 A5
Christy Ct RG26 . . . . 27 A7
Christy Est GU12. . . . 77 C2
Christyne Ct PO7 . . 322 D4
Chudleigh Ct 5 GU14 .55 F4
Church Ave GU14 . . . 56 A3
Church Bank Rd
SO21 . . . . 133 F4
Church Brook RG26 . .26 E6
Church Circ GU14. . . 56 A1
Church Cl
Andover SP10 . . . . 106 B8
Bishopstoke SO50. . 244 D4
Clanfield PO8. . . . . 276 B6
Enborne RG20. . . . . . 4 C6
Locks Heath SO31 . . 317 B3
Minstead SO43 . . . 286 C2
North Baddesley
SO52. . . . . 242 A4
Church Cotts
Blackmoor GU33 . . . 185 F7
Farnham GU9 . . . . . . 99 E6
Ropley SO24 . . . . . . 181 D4
Church Ct 3 GU51. . . .53 F1
Churchdale 15 GU11 . 76 E1
Church End SO15 . . . 290 C6
Churcher Cl PO12. . . 368 D3
Churcher Rd PO10 . . 325 B4
Churcher's Coll
GU31. . . . . 229 A4
Churchers Coll Jun Sch
GU32. . . . . 228 E3
Churcher's Coll Jun Sch
GU30. . . . . 188 B2
Churcher Wlk 2
PO12 . . . . 368 D3
Church Farm RG7 . . 281 F8
Church Farm Barns
RG7 . . . . 12 B5
Church Farm Cl
Hythe SO45 . . . . . . 313 B6
North Waltham RG25.. 89 E2
Churchfield BH31. . . 302 E6
Churchfield Cres
BH15 . . . . 390 E4
Churchfield Ct
2 Poole BH15 . . . . 390 E3
Liphook GU30 . . . . . 187 F3
Churchfield La BH24 281 E2
Churchfield Rd
Petersfield GU31. . . 229 B4
Poole BH15 . . . . 390 E3
Churchfields
Fawley SO45 . . . . . 339 B3
Kingsley GU35. . . . . 142 B1
Twyford SO21 . . . . . 220 A6
Church Fields GU35 . 165 B5
Churchfields Rd
SO21 . . . . 220 A6
Church Gr GU51 . . . . .53 E2
Church Hams RG40 . . 16 B6
Church Hatch SP5 . . 235 B4
Church Hill
Camberley GU15 . . . . 36 C5
Milford on S SO41. . . 399 E4
Nether Wallop SO20. 148 A5
Redlynch SP5 . . . . . 235 F5
Verwood BH31. . . . . 302 E6
West End SO30 . . . . 268 C3
Church Hill Terr
GU10 . . . . 97 C6
Churchill Ave
Aldershot GU12. . . 100 A8
Bishop's Waltham
SO32. . . . . 247 A1
Odiham RG29. . . . . . 95 D8
Churchill Cl
Alderholt SP6 . . . . 280 E5
Alton GU34 . . . . . . 139 F2
Farnborough GU14 . . 55 F8
Four Marks GU34 . . 160 B3

Churchill Cl continued
Hartley Wintney RG27 . **52** B7
Kings Worthy SO23 . . . **154** B1
North Tidworth SP9 . . . **78** D8
Odiham RG29 . . . . **95** D8
Tadley RG26 . . . . **27** B7
Titchfield PO14 . . . . . . **317** C1

Churchill Cres
Farnborough GU14 . . . **55** F8
Headley GU35 . . . . . **165** D4
Poole BH12 . . . . **391** C6

Churchill Ct
Farlington PO6 . . . . . **346** E8
New Milton BH25 . . . . **382** F2
Waterlooville PO8 . . . . **300** A6
Churchill Dr PO10.. **324** F4
Churchill Dro PO7 . . **279** C2
Churchill Gdns BH12 **391** C5
Churchill Ho SO18 . . **292** C8
Churchill Mews
PO12 . . . . **369** A7
Churchill Rd
Bournemouth BH1.. . **393** E5
Poole BH12 . . . . **391** D6
Wimborne Minster
BH21 . . . . **351** E3
Churchill Sq 3 PO4. **371** B2
Churchill Way
Andover SP10 . . . . . . **83** C1
Basingstoke RG21 . . . **69** B5
Churchill Way E RG21 **69** C5
Churchill Way W
Andover SP10 . . . . . **82** D2
Basingstoke RG22 . . . **68** E5
Churchill Yard Ind Est
PO7. . . . . **299** E1
Church La
12 Southampton
SO14. . . . . **290** F3
Alton GU34 . . . . **140** C7
Ash GU12. . . . . **77** F2
Awbridge SO51 . . . . . **214** E3
Basingstoke RG21 . . . **69** B5
Basingstoke, Worting
RG23 . . . . **68** A4
Bentley GU10. . . . . . **120** A6
Bishop's Sutton SO24 **180** B4
Botley SO30 . . . . . . **294** A5
Braishfield SO51 . . . . **216** A3
Bramdean SO24 . . . . **202** C4
Bramshott GU30 . . . **188** A4
Brimpton RG7 . . . . **8** D6
Brockenhurst SO42 . . **361** B8
Burghclere RG20. . . . . **22** E7
Burley BH24 . . . . . . **331** B3
Bursledon SO31. . . . . **316** B8
Buttermere SN8 . . . . **18** C7
Christchurch BH23 . . **395** B6
Cliddesden RG25 . . . . **92** A7
Colden Common SO21 **244** F8
Combe RG17 . . . . **19** C6
Compton PO18. . . . . **278** F2
Curdridge SO32. . . . . **294** D8
Damerham SP6 . . . . . **256** D4
Durley SO32 . . . . . . **269** F6
East Boldre SO42 . . . **363** D5
Ellisfield RG25. . . . . **115** C8
Empshott GU33 . . . . **185** B3
Enborne RG20 . . . . **4** D7
Ewshot GU10. . . . . . . **98** B8
Farley Hill RG7 . . . . . **15** B6
Farnborough GU14 . . . **55** C4
Farnham GU10 . . . . . **121** D7
Fawley SO45 . . . . . . **339** A3
Ferndown BH22 . . . . . **377** F7
Finchampstead RG40.. **16** C4
Goodworth Clatford
SP11. . . . . **106** B1
Grayshott GU26. . . . . **167** A3
Greatham GU33. . . . . **185** E2
Hambledon PO7.. . . . **274** D3
Hartley Wintney RG27. **52** D5
Havant PO9. . . . . . . **348** B8
Headley GU35 . . . . . **165** C6
Heckfield RG27. . . . . . **31** A6
Hedge End SO30 . . . . **293** B5
Highfield SO17 . . . . . **267** B2
Houghton SO20 . . . . **171** C6
Kings Worthy SO23 . . **176** C6
Littleton SO22 . . . . . **175** A6
Lymington SO41 . . . . **385** E3
Lyndhurst SO43 . . . . **309** F5
Martyr Worthy SO21 . . **177** B6
Medstead GU34. . . . . **159** F7
Meonstoke SO32 . . . **249** C2
Mottisfont SO51 . . . . **192** F2
Newbury RG14 . . . . **1** B4
North Hayling PO11. . . **348** U3
Nursling SO16. . . . . **264** F6
Old Basing RG24 . . . . **70** B6
Old Milton BH25 . . . **382** F1
Pilley SO41 . . . . . . **361** F2
Plaitford SO51. . . . . **238** B5
Romsey SO51 . . . . . . **240** E7
Ropley SO24 . . . . . . **181** C4
Rowledge GU10. . . . . **121** C3
Sherfield English
SO51. . . . . **213** D3
Silchester RG7. . . . . . **28** B8
South Tidworth SP9. . . **78** F4
Sparsholt SO21 . . . . **174** C3
Swanmore SO32 . . . . **272** C6
Sway SO41 . . . . **360** B1
Twyford SO21 . . . . . **220** A7
Vernham Dean SP11.. . **38** D8
West Meon GU32 . . . **225** B5
Wolverton RG26 . . . . **25** C2

Church La continued
Woolton Hill RG20. . . . **21** B8
Church La E GU11. . . . **99** F8
Churchlands GU11 . . . . **99** F8
Church La W GU11 . . . **76** E1
Church Leat SP5 . . . . **235** B4
Church Mdws SP9 . . . **101** B8
Church Mead 9
SO41 . . . . **385** E2
Church Mews
Anna Valley SP11 . . . **105** C4
Yateley GU46. . . . . . . **34** B7
Churchmoor Rd
BH21 . . . . **352** A5
Church Pas GU9 . . . . **98** C1
Church Path
1 Emsworth PO10 . . **348** F8
Ash GU12. . . . . **77** E3
Fareham PO16. . . . . . **319** C1
Gosport PO12 . . . . . **369** D5
Hook RG27. . . . . **71** F8
Horndean PO8. . . . . **300** C8
Titchfield PO14 . . . . **342** A8
Church Path N PO1 . **404** B4
Church Pl
Fareham PO16. . . . . **319** C2
Romsey SO51 . . . . . **240** E7
Church Rd
Aldermaston RG7 . . . . . **9** F7
Aldershot GU11. . . . . **100** A8
Bishopstoke SO50. . . **244** B5
Bournemouth BH6.. . **394** F3
Bramshott GU30 . . . **188** A6
Ferndown BH22. . . . . **353** C5
Fleet GU51 . . . . **53** F2
Fleet GU51 . . . . **54** A1
Frimley GU16. . . . . . . **36** B1
Gosport PO12 . . . . . **369** A3
Haslemere GU27. . . . **189** D6
King's Somborne
SO20. . . . . **172** A4
Locks Heath SO31. . . **317** B3
Longstock SO20. . . . **149** D7
Michelmersh SO51 . . **193** D2
Nether Wallop SO20 . **148** A5
Newbury RG14 . . . . **1** F7
North Waltham RG25. . **89** E1
Overton RG25 . . . . . . **88** A8
Pamber Heath RG26 . . **10** C1
Poole BH14 . . . . . . **391** A4
Portchester PO16 . . . **344** E6
Portsmouth PO1 . . . . **404** C4
Privett SO32 . . . . . . **204** C3
Romsey SO51 . . . . . **240** E7
Sandhurst GU15 . . . . **35** D7
Shedfield SO32 . . . . **295** E7
Silchester RG7. . . . . . **11** A4
Soberton PO17 . . . . **297** C6
Southampton SO19 . . **291** D2
Southbourne PO10 . . **349** E8
South Hayling PO11. . **373** A5
Steep GU32 . . . . . . **228** T3
Swallowfield RG7 . . . . **14** B6
Swanmore SO32 . . . . **272** B5
Tadley RG26. . . . . . . **26** F5
Thorney Island PO10 **349** U1
Three Legged Cross
BH21 . . . . **302** E1
Upper Farringdon
GU34 . . . . **161** E3
Warsash SO31. . . . . **340** D10
Westbourne PO10 . . . **325** B3
Church Rd E GU14 . . . **56** B2
Church Rd W GU14. . . **56** A1
Church Sq RG21 . . . . **69** B5
Church St
6 Wimborne Minster
BH21 . . . . **351** B5
Aldershot GU11. . . . . . **76** D1
Alton GU34 . . . . **139** F4
Basingstoke RG21 . . . **69** B4
Basingstoke RG21 . . . **69** B5
Bentworth GU34 . . . **138** A5
Christchurch BH23 . . **395** B6
Crondall GU10. . . . . . **97** C6
East Meon GU32 . . . **226** E1
Fordingbridge SP6.. . **281** F8
Hurstbourne Tarrant
SP11. . . . . **60** E6
Liss GU33 . . . . **207** E6
Micheldever GU33. . . **133** A3
Odiham RG29. . . . . . . **72** E2
Poole BH15 . . . . . . **390** B1
Portsmouth PO1 . . . . **404** C4
Romsey SO51 . . . . . **240** E7
Ropley SO24 . . . . . . **181** D4
Southampton SO15 . . **266** C1
Titchfield PO14 . . . . **342** A8
Upham SO32 . . . . . . **246** F6
Wherwell SP11 . . . . **129** A6
Whitchurch RG28 . . . . **86** C4
Woolton Hill RG20. . . **21** B8
Church View
Ash GU12. . . . . **77** E2
Hartley Wintney RG27. **52** D5
Hook RG27. . . . . **51** B1
Portsmouth PO4 . . . . **371** A5
Shedfield SO32 . . . . **295** F7
Southampton SO19 . . **291** D2
South Warnborough
RG29 . . . . **94** F3
Upper Clatford SP11. **105** E4
Westbourne PO10 . . . **325** B3
Yateley GU46. . . . . . . **34** B7
Church View Cl
SO19 . . . . **292** A3

Churchward Gdns
SO30 . . . . **269** C2
Churchyard Cotts
SO24 . . . . **179** D6
Churn Cl RG24 . . . . . **70** B7
Churt Rd
Barford GU10 . . . . . . **166** B8
Beacon Hill GU26 . . . **166** E7
Headley GU10 . . . . . **165** F7
Churt Wynde GU26.. . **167** B7
Chute Cl RG26 . . . . . **28** F4
Chute Cswy SP11 . . . . **37** B3
Chute Hill SO21. . . . **174** A4
Cibbons Rd RG24 . . . **48** F3
Cinderford Cl 21
PO6 . . . . **321** B1
Cinnamon Ct 3
SO15 . . . . **290** E6
Cinnamon La 7
BH15 . . . . **390** B1
Circle The
3 Bournemouth
BH9 . . . . **378** A4
Poole BH13 . . . . . . **402** F7
Portsmouth PO5 . . . . **370** D2
Wickham PO17 . . . . **296** A4
Circular Rd PO1 . . . . **370** C7
Circus The PO6 . . . . **321** A2
Cirrus Gdns SO31 . . . **315** F2
City Bldgs PO1.. . . . **404** B4
City Bsns Ctr SO23. . **403** E6
City Commerce Ctr 6
SO14 . . . . **291** B3
City Ct 27 SO14 . . . . **291** A3
City Ind Pk SO15. . . . **290** E4
**City of Portsmouth Boys
Sch** PO2. . . . . . . **345** E4
**City of Portsmouth Girls'
Sch** PO1. . . . . . . **370** E6
City of Toronto Homes
SO16 . . . . **289** F8
City Rd SO23. . . . . . **403** E6
Civic Centre Rd
Havant PO9. . . . . . . **323** F2
Southampton SO14 . . **290** F5
Civic Way PO16 . . . . **319** C1
Clacton Rd SO18 . . . **345** D8
Claire Ct
1 Andover SP10 . . **105** E9
6 Christchurch
BH23 . . . . **397** A7
Claire Gdns PO8 . . . . **276** C2
Clamp Gn SO21 . . . . **244** F8
Clandon Cl GU14.. . . **56** B3
Clandon Dr SO50. . . . **243** F5
Clanfield Dr SO53. . . **243** D6
Clanfield Ho 7 PO1. . **404** C4
Clanfield Jun Sch
PO8. . . . . **276** B7
Clanfield Rd SO18.. . **292** C7
Clanfield Ride GU17.. . **35** B5
Clanfield Way SO53 . **243** D6
Clanwilliam Rd PO13 **367** F3
Clappers Farm Rd
RG7 . . . . **11** E1
Clapps Gate Rd RG26 . **10** A7
Clarance Ct 3 SP10. **106** A7
Clare Cl PO14. . . . . . **317** C2
Clare Ct 14 GU51 . . . **54** A1
Clare Gdns
Blackfield SO45. . . . . **365** F7
Petersfield GU31. . . . **229** C3
Clare Ho PO12 . . . . . **369** D6
Clare Lodge Cl BH23 **357** A1
Clare Mead GU10 . . . **121** D4
Claremont Ave
Bournemouth BH9. . . **378** B2
Camberley GU15 . . . . **36** D5
Claremont Cl SO50.. . **244** A6
Claremont Cres
Newbury RG14 . . . . **2** B4
Southampton SO15 . . **290** A7
Claremont Gdns
PO7 . . . . **322** E4
Claremont Rd
Bournemouth BH9. . . **378** B2
Portsmouth PO1 . . . . **404** D3
Southampton SO15 . . **290** A7
Clarence Cl GU12 . . . . **77** E2
Clarence Ct 3 GU51 . **54** A1
Clarence Dr GU15.. . . **36** F7
Clarence Espl PO5 . . **370** C1
Clarence Ho 3
SO14 . . . . **291** C6
Clarence Par PO5. . . **370** C2
Clarence Park Rd
BH7 . . . . **394** A6
Clarence Pl BH23 . . . **394** F8
Clarence Rd
3 Poole BH14 . . . **391** A3
Fleet GU51 . . . . **54** A1
Gosport PO12 . . . . . **369** D6
Lyndhurst SO43 . . . . **309** F5
Portsmouth PO5 . . . . **370** D1
Clarence St PO1 . . . . **404** B4
Clarendon Ave SP10 **105** E6
Clarendon Cl
10 Romsey SO51.. . **216** B1
Broadstone BH18 . . . **375** A4
Denmead PO7 . . . . . **298** F5
Clarendon Cres
PO14 . . . . **317** C1
Clarendon Ct
3 Bournemouth
BH2 . . . . **392** D2
4 North Tidworth SP9 **78** F7

Clarendon Ct continued
6 Portsmouth PO5. . **370** D1
Blackwater GU17 . . . . **35** B3
Clarendon Gdns RG14 . **1** E4
Clarendon Ho 1
GU51 . . . . **53** F1
**Clarendon Jun & Inf
Schs** SP9. . . . . . . **78** F6
Clarendon Pk SO41 . **385** D2
Clarendon Pl
1 Portsmouth PO1 . **404** B3
Portsmouth PO1 . . . . **404** C4
Clarendon Rd
Bournemouth BH4.. . **392** D3
Broadstone BH18 . . . **374** F4
Christchurch BH23 . . **395** A7
Havant PO9. . . . . . . **323** E1
Portsmouth, Southsea
PO5. . . . . **370** D1
Southampton SO16 . . **290** A8
Clarendon St PO1.. . **404** C4
Clare Wlk RG14 . . . . . **5** A5
Clarewood Dr GU15 . . **36** C6
Clarewood Ho GU15.. **36** C7
Clarke Cres GU15 . . . **35** C7
Clarke's La SP11. . . . **58** F6
Clarkes Rd PO1 . . . . **370** F6
Clark Mews RG28 . . . **86** C4
Clark's Cl BH24 . . . . **329** A7
Clarks Hill GU10. . . . . **98** B1
Clatford CE Prim Sch
SP11. . . . . **106** A1
Clatford Manor
SP11. . . . . **105** E4
Clatford Manor Ho
SP11. . . . . **105** E4
Claude Ashby Cl
SO18 . . . . **267** E4
Claudeen Cl SO18. . . **267** E5
Claudeen Ct SO19. . . **292** E6
Claudia Ct PO12 . . . . **368** F6
Claudius Cl
Andover SP10 . . . . . . **83** B4
Chandler's Ford SO53 **243** F7
Claudius Dr RG23 . . . **68** C7
Claudius Gdns SO53. **243** F7
Clausentum Cl SO53 **243** E7
Clausentum Ho
SO18 . . . . **291** C7
Clausentum Rd
Southampton SO14 . . **291** B7
Winchester SO23 . . . **403** D3
Clausen Way SO41 . . **385** C1
Claxton St PO1 . . . . **404** C3
Claybank Rd PO3 . . . **346** A1
Claybank Spur PO3 . . **346** A1
Claycart Rd
Aldershot GU11. . . . . **76** B4
Aldershot GU11. . . . . **76** B5
Claydon Ave PO4 . . . **371** A4
Claydon Gdns GU17. . . **35** E1
Clayford Ave BH22 . . **353** B7
Clayford Cl BH17. . . . **375** D2
Clayhall Rd PO12 . . . **369** B3
Clay Hill SO43 . . . . . **310** A3
Clay Hill Ho GU27. . . **189** E6
Claylake Dr BH31 . . . **303** A4
Claylands Ct SO32 . . **271** B8
Claylands Rd SO32 . . **271** B8
Claylands Road Ind Est
SO32. . . . . **271** B8
Claypit Rd SO51. . . . **217** C6
Claypits La SO45 . . . **313** D4
Claypitt La GU32. . . . **205** D6
Clay's La
Binsted GU34 . . . . . **141** A6
East Worldham GU34 **140** E2
Clay St SP5 . . . . **212** A3
Claythorpe Rd RG22. . **68** C3
Clayton Cl RG27. . . . **52** C5
Clayton Rd GU14. . . . **35** D1
Clearwater Apartments
5 PO5 . . . . **370** C1
Cleasby Cl SO16 . . . **289** E7
Cleasby Grange 2
BH5 . . . . **393** F3
Clease Way SO21 . . . **219** C2
Cleaver Rd RG22 . . . . **68** C3
Clee Ave PO14 . . . . **342** D8
Cleek Dr SO16 . . . . **266** F5
Cleethorpes Rd
SO19 . . . . **292** B4
Cleeve Cl PO6 . . . . . **321** B1
Cleeve Ho BH25. . . . **397** F7
Cleeves Cl BH12 . . . . **376** D4
Cleeves The SO40. . . **288** C6
Clegg Rd PO4. . . . . . **371** A3
Clematis Cl BH23 . . . **396** C8
Clement Attlee Way
PO6 . . . . **345** B8
Clement Mews BH4. **392** B3
Clements Cl GU34. . . **141** E7
Clements Gdns RG28. **86** C5
Clem's Way SO51 . . . **192** A1
Clere Ct RG20. . . . . **24** C2
Clere Gdns RG24 . . . **48** F2
Clere Sch The RG20 . . **22** E7
Clerewater Pl RG19 . . **2** D3
Cleric Ct PO14 . . . . . **317** C3
Clevedge Way RG29.. **72** C4
Clevedon Cres
PO14 . . . . **317** C1
Clevedon Ct
3 Bournemouth
BH2 . . . . **392** D2
4 Camberley GU16 . . **56** E8
Farnborough GU14 . . **56** B3
Cleveland Cl
Barton on S BH25 . . **397** D7
Basingstoke RG22 . . . **68** B2

Cleveland Ct
3 Southampton
SO18. . . . . **268** A1
4 Bournemouth BH2 **392** D2
Cleveland Dr
Fareham PO14.. . . . . **342** D8
Hythe SO45 . . . . . . **313** D2
Cleveland Gdns BH1 **393** D5
Cleveland Gr RG14 . . . . **1** D3
Cleveland Rd
Bournemouth BH1.. . **393** D5
Gosport PO12 . . . . . **369** B4
Portsmouth PO5 . . . . **404** D2
Southampton SO18 . . **267** F1
Clevelands Cl SO53 . . **218** B1
Cleverley Ho 28 PO1 **370** A5
Cleves La RG25 . . . . . **94** B6
Clewborough Dr
GU15. . . . . **36** F6
Clewborough House Sch
GU16. . . . . **56** F5
Clewers Hill SO32.. . **271** D4
Clewers La SO32.. . . **271** E4
Cliddesden Ct RG21.. **69** B2
Cliddesden La RG22.. . **91** D6
Cliddesden Prim Sch
RG25. . . . . **92** A7
Cliddesden Rd
Basingstoke, Cranbourne
RG21 . . . . **69** B2
Basingstoke, Kings Furlong
RG21 . . . . **69** B3
Cliff Cres BH25 . . . . **397** F7
Cliffdale Gdns PO6.. **322** A1
Cliffdale Prim Sch
PO2. . . . . **345** F2
Cliff Dr
Christchurch BH23 . . **396** C6
Poole BH13 . . . . . . **402** E6
Cliffe Ave SO18 . . . . **315** C3
Cliffe Rd BH25 . . . . **397** E7
Clifford Dibben Mews 1
SO14 . . . . **291** A8
Clifford Pl SO50 . . . . **245** C2
Clifford Rd BH9 . . . . **378** A1
Clifford St SO14 . . . . **291** B5
Cliff Rd
Milford on S SO41 . . . **399** B4
Southampton SO15 . . **290** D5
Stubbington PO14 . . . **341** F1
Cliff The SO19 . . . . . **291** D3
Cliff Way SO21 . . . . . **219** D2
Cliff Wlk 17 BH4 . . . . **392** C2
Clifton Cl
1 Gosport PO12 . . . **368** F6
Waterlooville PO8 . . . **300** B4
Clifton Ct
1 Bournemouth
BH7 . . . . **393** F4
2 Southampton
SO15. . . . . **290** A8
3 New Milton BH25. **383** A1
Hamworthy BH15 . . . **389** D4
Clifton Gdns
1 Bournemouth
SO15. . . . . **290** A8
Camberley GU16 . . . . **56** D8
Ferndown BH22. . . . . **353** C4
West End SO18 . . . . **268** C1
Clifton Hill SO22 . . . **403** B6
Clifton Lodge SO15 . **290** A8
Clifton Lodge No 1 18
SO22 . . . . **403** D6
Clifton Lodge No 2 19
SO22 . . . . **403** D6
Clifton Rd
10 Portsmouth
PO5 . . . . **370** C2
Bournemouth BH6.. . **394** D3
Lee-on-t-S PO13 . . . **368** A4
Newbury RG14 . . . . . . **1** C2
Poole BH14 . . . . . . **391** E2
Southampton SO15 . . **290** A8
Winchester SO22 . . . **403** D6
Clifton St
Gosport PO12 . . . . . **368** F6
Portsmouth PO1 . . . . **404** D4
Clifton Terr
11 Portsmouth
PO5 . . . . **370** C2
1 Basingstoke RG21 . **69** B6
Winchester SO22 . . . **403** D6
Clifton Wlk 8 RG21.. **69** B5
Clingan Rd BH6. . . . . **394** D7
Clinton Cl BH23 . . . . **382** B2
Clinton Rd
Lymington SO41 . . . . **385** E5
Waterlooville PO7 . . . **299** C2
Clipper Cl SO31 . . . . **316** E1
Clitheroe Cotts SO42 **336** F1
Clitheroe Rd GU17 . . . **34** D1
Clive Ct 23 BH4 . . . . **392** C3
Cliveden Cl BH22 . . . **353** C7
Clive Gr PO16. . . . . . **344** C7
Clive Rd
Aldershot GU12. . . . . **77** B1
Bournemouth BH9. . . **377** F1
Christchurch BH23 . . **381** E2
Portsmouth PO1 . . . . **370** E6
Clock Ho 4 PO7 . . . . **322** E7
Clockhouse Rd GU14 **55** F4
Clockhouse The
SO21 . . . . **133** F6
Clock House The
SO40 . . . . **264** A2
Clock St 7 PO1 . . . . . **370** A5
Clocktower Dr 1
PO4 . . . . **371** B2

Cloisters The
3 Christchurch
BH23 . . . . **395** B6
3 Romsey SO51 . . . **240** E8
4 Andover SP10 . . . **106** E4
Alton GU34 . . . . **139** E4
Fareham PO15. . . . . **318** C2
Frimley GU16. . . . . . . **36** B1
Lymington SO41 . . . . **385** E3
Ringwood BH24. . . . . **329** C6
Southampton SO16 . . **267** A3
Close Bellfield The
PO14 . . . . **341** F7
Close The
Barton on S BH25 . . **398** B8
Broadstone BH18 . . . **374** E3
Camberley GU16 . . . . **56** A8
Colden Common
SO50. . . . . **219** D1
Cosham PO6 . . . . . . **346** A7
Farnham GU9 . . . . . . **99** B1
Fordingbridge SP6.. . **282** C7
Hamble-le-R SO31.. . **316** A4
Hatherden SP11 . . . . **59** C2
Hedge End SO30 . . . **293** B6
Holbury SO45 . . . . . **338** D4
Langrish GU32. . . . . **227** C3
Liphook GU30 . . . . . **188** A2
Monk Sherborne RG26 **47** B6
Portchester PO16 . . . **344** C8
Redlynch SP5. . . . . . **235** D7
Ringwood BH24. . . . . **328** F7
Sandhurst GU47 . . . . **35** C8
Southampton SO18 . . **292** D7
St Leonards, Avon Castle
BH24 . . . . **328** A4
St Leonards, St Ives
BH24 . . . . **328** A4
Sway SO41 . . . . . . **360** A2
Thatcham RG18. . . . . . **2** F1
Whitsbury SP6. . . . . **233** B3
Closewood Rd PO7.. **299** A2
Closeworth Rd GU14 . **77** C8
Clough La BH24. . . . . **330** F3
Clough's Rd BH24. . . **329** B7
Clouston Rd GU14. . . . **55** D5
Clovelly Dr GU26. . . . **167** A7
Clovelly Pk GU26. . . . **167** A7
Clovelly Rd
Beacon Hill GU26 . . . **167** A7
Breach PO10. . . . . . **325** D1
Emsworth PO10. . . . **348** C4
North Hayling PO11. . **348** C4
Portsmouth PO4 . . . . **371** A4
Southampton SO14 . . **291** B6
Cloverbank SO23 . . . **154** B2
Clover Cl
Christchurch BH23 . . **396** B8
Gosport PO13 . . . . . **343** B3
Lindford GU35 . . . . . **165** A5
Locks Heath SO31. . . **316** E2
Clover Ct
New Milton BH25 . . . **383** D4
Waterlooville PO7 . . . **323** A6
Clover Dr BH17 . . . . **374** F1
Clover Field RG24. . . **69** F3
Clover La GU46 . . . . . **34** B7
Clover Leaf Way RG24 **70** B4
Clover Mews 4
SP10 . . . . **106** B7
Clover Nooke SO15 . **289** C8
Clovers The BH12 . . **392** A8
Clover Way
Hedge End SO30 . . . **293** A6
Romsey SO51 . . . . . **241** C8
Clowes Ave BH6 . . . . **395** B3
Club Cotts GU30 . . . **165** C1
Clubhouse La SO32 . . **271** D3
Clubhouse Rd GU11.. **76** D5
Club La SP9 . . . . **78** E4
Clump Hill BH21 . . . . **302** B1
Clumps Rd GU10. . . . **122** C4
Cluster Ind Est PO4. **371** A5
Clydebank Rd PO2 . . **370** D8
Clyde Ct
18 Andover SP10 . . **83** C2
Aldershot GU12. . . . . **100** C8
Gosport PO12 . . . . . **368** F6
Clyde Ho 7 SO14 . . . **291** C5
Clyde Rd
Gosport PO12 . . . . . **368** F6
Poole BH17 . . . . . . **375** D2
Clydes Dale Ct 5
SO17 . . . . **267** B2
Clydesdale Rd PO15. **317** B7
Clydesdale Way
SO40 . . . . **288** B8
Coach Hill
Chute Forest SP11 . . . **58** D7
Titchfield PO14 . . . . **341** F8
Coach Hill Cl SO53. . **243** D7
Coach Hill La BH24. . **330** E5
Coach Ho The SO22. **175** B7
Coach House Cl GU16 **36** C3
Coach House Gdns
GU51 . . . . **54** A3
Coach House Mews
BH22 . . . . **353** F7
Coach-House Mews
PO4. . . . . **371** C4
Coach House Pl BH1 **393** D6
Coachmakers Mews 6
SO51 . . . . **240** E7
Coachmans Copse
SO18 . . . . **268** A2

Coachman's Ct RG14....1 F5
Coachmans Gr GU47 ..34 F7
Coachmans Halt
PO7 ....274 C2
Coach Rd S031 .....315 E3
Coach Rd The SP5 ...191 C7
Coachways SP10.....106 A6
Coal Park La S031 ..316 D8
Coalville Rd S019....292 B4
Coastguard Cl PO12. 368 F2
Coastguard Cotts
Barton on S BH25 ...397 E8
Exbury S045 ....366 A2
Langstone PO9 .....347 F6
Lymington S041 ....386 A2
Coastguard Way
BH23 ....395 F5
Coate Dr S021 ......153 C2
Coates Cl RG22......68 F1
Coates Rd S019.....292 D4
Coates Way PO7 ....322 E5
Coat Gdns S045.....314 A3
Cobalt Ct 3 PO13..368 C6
Cobbett Cl S022 ....403 A3
Cobbett Ct 3 S018.291 E7
Cobbett Gn RG22 ...68 E2
Cobbett Rd S018....291 E8
Cobbett's La GU46,
GU9...............34 D5
Cobbetts Mews 4
GU9..............98 F2
Cobbetts Way GU9 121 D6
Cobbett Way S030 ..293 F7
Cobblers Cnr S041..361 B3
Cobblewood PO10 ..324 F3
Cobb Mews SP11 ...104 B6
Cobbs La BH15.......390 E6
Cobb's Rd BH21.....351 E6
Cobden Ave
Portsmouth PO3 ....371 A8
Southampton S018 .291 F8
Cobden Cres S018 ..291 F8
Cobden Ct S018 ....291 E8
Cobden Dell 4
S018..............291 E8
Cobden Gdns S018..267 E1
Cobden Hts S018....267 E1
Cobden Marine Ct
S017..............291 D8
Cobden Rise S018 ..267 E1
Cobden St PO12 ....369 B6
Cobham Gr PO15....317 F5
Cobham Rd
Bournemouth BH9.. 378 A3
Ferndown BH21.....353 A8
Cobham Way BH21...351 E1
Cob Tree Cotts RG25 ..70 E4
Coburg Ho 6 S014 .291 C6
Coburg St
Portsmouth PO1 ....404 C4
Southampton S014...291 C6
Cochcrane Ct PO13 .368 D6
Cochrane Ho 13
PO1...............370 A5
Cock-A-Dobby GU47..34 E8
Cockerell Cl
Locks Heath PO15...317 C5
Merley BH21........351 F1
Cocket's Mead S021 177 A4
Cockleshell Cl S031. 316 E1
Cockleshell Gdns
PO4...............371 C3
Cockleshell Sq
PO12..............369 D6
Cocklydown La
S040..............288 E5
Cockshott La GU32...206 C6
Codogan Ct 3 BH1 .393 B3
Cody Cl GU12.......77 D5
Cody Rd GU14 ......55 D3
Cody Tech Pk
Farnborough GU14 ..55 B1
Farnborough GU51...54 E1
Coe Cl GU11.......76 E1
Cogdean Cl BH21 ...374 E8
Cogdeane Rd BH17 .375 D2
Cogdean Way BH21..374 E8
Cogdean Wlk BH21..374 E8
Coghlan Cl PO16....319 B2
Cokenor Wood
GU10..............121 D6
Coker Cl S022 ......403 C6
Colbeck GU52 ....75 D4
Colborne Ave BH21 .351 F6
Colborne Cl
Lymington S041 ....385 E5
Poole BH15 ....390 D1
Colbourne Cl BH23. 381 A8
Colbourne Ct 7
S023..............403 E8
Colbred Cnr GU51...54 C4
Colburn Cl S016....265 D2
Colbury Gr PO9 .....323 C4
Colchester Ave
S050..............244 E4
Colchester Rd PO6.. 321 E1
Coldeast Cl S031....316 E5
Coldeast Hospl S031 316 F5
Coldeast Way S031. 316 F5
Colden Common Prim
Sch S021..........244 F8
Colden La S024.....158 A3
Coldharbour RG25...89 E1

Cold Harbour Cl
PO17..............295 F4
Cold Harbour Ct 9
SP10..............106 B7
Coldharbour Farm Rd
PO10..............324 F1
Coldharbour La S016,
S051..............265 B8
Cold Harbour La
GU14..............55 D8
Coldhill La PO8.....299 F7
Coldrey Cotts GU34 119 D4
Cole Ave GU11......76 D3
Colebrook Ave
Portsmouth PO3 ....371 B7
Southampton S015 ..266 C1
Colebrook Pl S023..403 F5
Colebrook Rd S023.. 403 E6
Colebrook Way
SP10..............105 D7
Coleford Bridge Rd
GU16..............56 C4
Coleford Cl GU16 ...56 D3
Coleford Paddocks
GU16..............56 D4
Cole Hill S032 ......273 C5
Colehill Cres BH9...378 B3
Colehill Fst Sch
BH21..............352 A7
Colehill La
Colehill BH21.......351 F8
Wimborne Minster
BH21............352 A8
Coleman Cl RG21...69 C7
Coleman Rd
Aldershot GU12.....77 B1
Bournemouth BH11..377 A3
Colemere Gdns
BH23 ....396 F8
Colemore Rd BH7...394 C7
Colemore Sq PO9...323 F4
Colenso Rd PO16....319 A2
Colenzo Dr SP10....83 C1
Coleridge Ave GU46..34 C5
Coleridge Cl S031...316 D1
Coleridge Ct S019 ..292 D5
Coleridge Gdns PO9 299 F4
Coleridge Gn BH23.. 395 F8
Coleridge Rd PO6....320 F1
Coles Ave BH15.....389 E2
Colesbourne Rd PO6 321 B1
Coles Cl S021.......220 A7
Coles Gdns BH15....389 E2
Coles Mede S021 ...219 B3
Coleson Hill Rd
GU10..............121 D5
Coleson Rd S018 ...291 E8
Coles's La GU35....236 E5
Coleville Ave S045..339 B3
Coleville Rd GU14...55 D5
Coley La S020 ......128 F4
Colin Cl BH21.......374 D5
Colinton Ave PO16..320 D1
Coliseum Bsns Ctr
GU15..............35 E3
Collard Way 4
GU33..............207 F4
College Cl
Camberley GU15.....36 B7
Hamble-le-R S031...315 F2
Rowlands Castle PO9 301 C1
College Cres GU47...35 C8
College Gdns GU9...98 F2
College Keep S014.. 291 B3
College La
Portsmouth 28
PO1.............370 A5
Ellisfield RG25.....115 B6
College Mews SP10 .106 A8
College Park Inf Sch
PO2...............345 E1
College Piece RG7 ..11 D6
College Pl 9
Southampton
S015............291 A6
Farnham GU9 ......99 A1
College Rd
Ash GU12..........77 F3
Basingstoke RG21...68 F5
Bournemouth BH5...394 A4
Portsmouth PO1 ....370 A5
Ringwood BH24....329 A4
Sandhurst GU47 ....35 C7
Southampton S019 .291 E4
Waterlooville PO7...322 F3
College Ride GU15...36 B7
College St
Petersfield GU32...228 F3
Portsmouth PO1 ....370 A5
Southampton S014 .291 A3
Winchester S023 ...403 E5
College Town Jun & Inf
Schs GU47 ....35 C8
College Wlk S023...403 E4
Collett Cl S030 .....269 B2
Colley Cl S023......176 A3
Collier Cl
Farnborough GU14 ..55 B5
Southampton S017..291 C8
Collingbourne Ave
BH6...............394 D7
Collingbourne Dr
S053..............243 A6
Collington Cres PO6 321 B1
Collingwood GU14 ..56 C2

Collingwood Coll
GU15..............36 E8
Collingwood Grange Cl
GU15..............36 F8
Collingwood Ho
PO15..............318 D2
Collingwood Mount
GU15..............36 E6
Collingwood Pl GU15..36 F8
Collingwood Rd
Portsmouth PO5 ....370 D2
West Moors BH21...326 E6
Collingwood Ret Pk
PO14..............343 B6
Collingwood Rise
GU15..............36 E7
Collingwood Way
GU31..............229 A5
Collingwood Wlk
SP10..............106 D8
Collingworth Cl
S031..............317 B6
Collingworth Rise
S031..............317 B6
Collins Cl
Andover SP10 ......82 E3
Chandler's Ford S053 242 F6
Newbury RG14 ......2 A4
Collins Ct 1 SP9....78 E8
Collins Gdns GU12 ..77 F2
Collins La
Compton GU31 .....254 F7
Ringwood BH24.....329 A7
Collins' La S021 ....218 C7
Collins Rd PO4......371 A2
Collis Rd PO3.......371 A8
Coll of Air Traffic
Control BH25.......378 F7
Collwood Cl BH15...390 C7
Collyers Cres GU30.. 188 C4
Collyers Rd S042 ...360 F7
Colman Ct BH1 .....393 C3
Colne Ave S016.....265 D2
Colne Ct S016 ......265 E2
Colne Way
25 Basingstoke
RG21............69 D5
Ash GU12..........77 E1
Colonnade Rd 3
BH5...............394 A5
Colonnade Road W 2
BH5...............394 A5
Colonnade The
S019..............291 D3
Colpoy St PO5 ......404 A2
Colson Ct S023 .....403 F6
Colson Rd S023.....403 F6
Colt Cl
Rownhams S016....265 F5
Wimborne Minster
BH21............352 B6
Colton Copse S053.. 242 F6
Coltsfoot Cl S030 ...293 B7
Coltsfoot Dr
PO7...............322 F5
Locks Heath S031...316 E2
Coltsfoot Pl RG27...51 C2
Coltsfoot Rd GU35 .165 A5
Coltsfoot Wlk S051 .216 C1
Coltsmead PO6 .....344 F8
Colts Rd S016.......265 E7
Columbia Ct RG40 ..16 C8
Columbian Way
BH10..............377 C2
Columbia Rd BH10.. 377 C2
Columbia Trees La
BH10..............377 C1
Columbine Cl BH23. 381 B1
Columbus Dr GU14.. 55 A4
Columbus Way SP10 .83 E1
Colvedene Ct S021.. 219 F1
Colville Cl 4 BH5...394 A5
Colville Dr S032 ....271 D8
Colville Rd
5 Bournemouth
BH5.............394 A5
Cosham PO6 ....346 A8
Colvin Cl SP10......106 B7
Colvin Gdns S053...243 B8
Colwell Cl S016.....289 D8
Colwell Rd PO6.....345 F7
Colwyn Cl GU46.....34 A6
Colyer Cl RG22......68 C3
Combe Down S031.. 219 E7
Combe La GU14.....55 E6
Combe Rd GU33 ....208 B1
Combe Rise GU10...122 B5
Combe St GU10.....219 D8
Comber Rd 1 BH9..378 A3
Comet Cl GU12 .....77 D5
Comet Ho RG7.......9 C2
Comet Rd GU14.....55 A1
Comet Way BH23...396 A6
Comfrey Cl
Farnborough GU14 ..55 A5
Horndean PO8......276 C1
Romsey S051 ......216 C1
Comines Way S030 .292 F7
Comley Ct 1 S051..240 E7
Comley Hill PO9.....324 D5
Comley Rd BH9 .....377 F2
Commercial Ctr The
SP11..............84 A3
Commercial Rd
Aldershot GU12.....100 A8
Bournemouth BH2...392 E3

Commercial Rd continued
Poole BH14 ....391 A4
Portsmouth PO1 ....404 B4
Southampton S014..290 F5
Southampton S015..290 E5
Totton S040........289 A7
Commercial St S018 292 B7
Commodore Ct
1 Southampton
S014............291 B3
Farnborough GU14 ..76 F8
Commodore Pl
PO7...............369 D7
Common Barn La
Lee-on-t-S PO13 ...367 F4
Lee-on-t-S PO13 ...368 A5
Common Cl S053 ...243 C8
Commonfield La
RG40..............15 F8
Common Gdns S053 243 C8
Common Hill GU34..159 D6
Common Hill Rd
S051..............216 D6
Common La
Southwick PO17....320 E7
Titchfield PO14 ....341 E8
Common Rd
Chandler's Ford
S053............243 C8
Emsworth PO10....325 F5
Headley, Nr Greenham
RG19............7 D1
Headley RG19 .....24 C8
Whiteparish SP5 ...212 D2
Commonside PO10.. 325 B5
Common St PO1 ....404 C4
Common The
Damerham SP6 .....256 D3
Longparish SP11 ...108 C4
Middle Winterslow
SP5.............168 B6
Ramsdell RG26 .....26 E1
Common Vale SP5 ..168 A6
Communications Rd
RG19..............6 D5
Compass Cl
Gosport PO13 ......368 D6
Southampton S019..292 A4
Compass Ct 21 S017 267 A1
Compass Field RG27 .51 B1
Compass Point
Fareham PO16.......343 A8
Hamble-le-R S031...315 E2
Compass Rd PO6 ...345 B8
Complins GU34......140 C6
Compton Acres Gdns★
BH13..............402 E7
Compton All Saints CE
Prim Sch S021.....219 D8
Compton Ave BH14 .391 D1
Compton Beeches
BH24..............328 A5
Compton Cl
9 Lee-on-t-S PO13..367 F3
Eastleigh S050 .....243 F6
Fleet GU52 ....75 B5
Havant PO9 ....323 F3
Hook RG27.........51 B1
Verwood BH31......302 F6
Winchester S022 ...197 B3
Compton Cotts
Compton S020......193 D7
Minstead S043 .....286 B3
Compton Cres BH22. 327 B1
Compton Ct
4 Bournemouth
BH6.............394 F4
4 Havant PO9 ....323 E2
Poole BH14........391 D3
Compton Dr BH14...391 C2
Compton Gdns BH14 391 C2
Compton Ho
6 Southampton
S016............290 B8
7 Farnborough PO9 ..99 A2
Compton Lo 28 BH4. 392 C3
Compton Place Bsns Ctr
GU15..............35 E4
Compton Rd
Fleet GU52 ....75 B5
New Milton BH25 ...383 A2
North Tidworth SP9...78 F6
Portsmouth PO2 ...345 A4
Totton S040........289 A8
Winchester S023 ...403 D5
Compton's Cnr SP4 .101 E2
Compton's Dr S051. 238 A6
Compton Sq SP10...83 C3
Compton St S021 ...219 D8
Compton & Up Marden
CE Prim Sch PO18.. 278 F2
Compton Way
Farnham GU10 .....99 F1
Sherfield on L RG27..49 B5
Winchester S022 ...197 B3
Compton Wlk 1
S014..............291 A5
Conan Rd PO2 ......345 E4
Concorde Cl PO15...317 C5
Concorde Rd GU14.. 55 A1
Concorde Way PO15 317 C5
Conde Way GU35....164 D2
Condor Ave PO16....343 F8
Condor Cl
Southampton S019..291 D3
Three Legged Cross
BH21............327 B5
Coneygar La BH22 .. 353 B3

Coney Gn 5 S023..403 E8
Conference Dr S031 317 B3
Conference Pl 5
S041..............385 F2
Conford Ct PO9......323 D6
Congleton Cl S043 ..286 C3
Congreve Cl RG7....9 E5
Conholt Hill SP11....37 F4
Conholt La SP11....38 B4
Conholt Rd SP10 ...106 A5
Conifer Ave BH14 ..391 B2
Conifer Cl
Bordon GU35.......164 C1
Christchurch BH23 .379 D3
Ferndown BH22....353 F1
Fleet GU52 ....74 F5
Hythe S045 ....313 F3
Pamber Heath RG26..9 C2
St Leonards BH24...327 C4
Waterlooville PO8 ..300 A2
Winchester S022 ...403 D7
Conifer Cres S041 ..385 B3
Conifer Crest GU14. 5 A4
Conifer Dr GU15....36 E6
Conifer Gr PO13 ....343 C4
Conifer Mews PO16. 320 D1
Conifer Rd S016.....266 A4
Conifers 4 BH13...392 B3
Conigar Rd PO10....324 F3
Coniston Ave
4 Portsmouth
PO3.............371 A8
Bournemouth BH11..376 F6
Coniston Cl
Farnborough GU14 ..55 C3
Thatcham RG19......2 E3
Verwood BH31......302 E5
Coniston Ct
8 Newbury RG14...1 E4
Ash Vale GU12......77 D4
Coniston Dr GU9 ....98 F6
Coniston Gdns S030 293 E6
Coniston Gr S024 ...179 C4
Coniston Ho 8 PO6. 321 B1
Coniston Rd
Basingstoke RG22...68 B1
Bordon GU35.......164 D5
Eastleigh S050 .....243 F2
Ringwood BH24.....329 B6
Southampton S016..289 C8
Coniston Way GU52..74 E5
Coniston Wlk PO14..342 E7
Connaught Cl
7 Bordon GU35....164 D2
Old Milton BH25 ...382 E1
Yateley GU46.......34 A6
Connaught Cres
BH12..............391 E6
Connaught Hall
S018..............267 D4
Connaught La PO6 .. 344 F8
Connaught Pl 3
PO9...............324 A1
Connaught Rd
Aldershot GU12.....77 B2
Bournemouth BH5...394 B5
Camberley GU15....36 D5
Fleet GU51 ....54 A1
Havant PO9 ....324 A1
Newbury RG14 .....1 F3
North Tidworth SP9...79 A6
Portsmouth PO2 ...345 D2
Worthy Down Camp
S021............153 D2
Connaught Sch The
GU12..............100 C7
Connaught Way
GU34..............139 D1
Connection The RG14..1 E6
Connell Rd BH15....390 C5
Connemara Cres
PO15..............317 B7
Connigar Ct S023 ...368 C7
Connop Way GU16...36 D3
Conqueror Way
PO14..............367 D6
Conrad Gdns PO15.. 317 C8
Conservatory The 6
S023..............403 F5
Consort Cl
Eastleigh S050 .....244 B5
Poole BH12........391 C5
Consort Ct 5 PO16. 319 C1
Consort Ho
3 Portsmouth
PO1.............370 D7
Ferndown BH22....353 D6
Consort Mews 7
PO17..............318 E7
Consort Pl 9 GU51. 54 A1
Consort Rd S050....244 B5
Constable Cl
Basingstoke RG21...69 D3
Ferndown BH22....353 C4
Gosport PO12 ......369 C2
Southampton S019 .292 C2
Constable St SP10 ..83 A1
Constable's Gate 10
S023..............403 D5
Constable Way GU47 35 C6
Constantine Ave
S053..............243 F6
Constantine Cl S053 243 F6
Constantine Way
RG22..............91 A6
Constantius Ct 11
GU52..............74 E4
Constant Rd GU51...54 E2

Constitution Hill Gdns
BH14..............391 A5
Constitution Hill Rd
BH14..............391 A5
Consulate Ho 3
S014..............291 B3
Convent Ct PO10....348 E8
Convent Meadow Mobile
Home Site BH23...395 C5
Conway Cl
Chandler's Ford
S053............243 B3
Frimley GU16.......36 D1
New Milton BH25 ...383 B3
Conway Ct 10 BH25 383 B3
Conway Dr
Farnborough GU14 ..55 B4
Thatcham RG18......2 F5
Conways Dr BH14...391 A4
Cook Cl BH24.......329 C8
Cooke Gdns BH12...391 F6
Cooke Rd BH12 .....391 F6
Cook Row BH21.....351 E6
Cooks La
Awbridge S051.....215 A4
Breach PO10 ....325 E1
Lockerley S051.....191 F1
Lockerley S051.....213 E8
Totton S040........264 C2
Cook St S014 ....291 A4
Coolarne Rise GU15..36 E6
Coolers Farm S020 .170 C6
Cooley Ho PO13 ....343 B5
Coolhurst BH14.....402 C7
Coombe Ave BH10 ..377 E3
Coombe Cl GU16....56 B8
Coombedale S031 ..317 B2
Coombe Dr GU51 ...54 C1
Coombe Farm Ave
PO16..............343 A8
Coombe Gdns BH10. 377 E2
Coombehurst Dr
RG21..............69 B2
Coombe La
Awbridge S051.....214 F3
Sway S041 ....384 D8
West Meon GU32 ..225 E4
Coombe Rd
East Meon GU32 ...251 D8
Gosport PO12 ......369 B8
Yateley GU46.......33 F8
Coombe Road Terr
GU32..............251 D8
Coombs Cl PO8.....276 C1
Cooperage The 3
GU34..............139 E3
Cooper Ct GU14.....56 A4
Cooper Dean Dr
BH8...............378 F1
Cooper Dean Rdbt The
BH7,BH8 ....379 A1
Cooper Gr PO16.....344 D6
Cooper Ho 5 GU35. 164 D2
Cooper Rd
Ashurst S040 ......288 C3
Portsmouth PO3 ...371 B8
Coopers Cl S021 ...153 D2
Cooper's Cl
West End S018 .....268 C1
West Wellow S051 .239 B2
Coopers Ct
20 Southampton
S014............291 A3
Bramley RG26 .....28 F3
Cooper's Hill RG27...33 C4
Coopers La
Bramley RG26 .....28 F3
Verwood BH31......302 F6
Cooper's La S019 ...291 D3
Coopers Rise PO8...300 D3
Cooper's Terr GU9...99 A3
Cope Hall La RG14...5 A7
Copeland Dr BH14...391 B2
Copeland Rd S016...265 D1
Copenhagen Twrs
S019..............314 F8
Copes La RG27......31 F7
Copinger Cl S040 ...288 C6
Copland Cl RG22....91 C8
Copnor RG20........21 B7
Copnor Bridge Bsns Ctr
PO3...............371 D7
Copnor RG20.........21 B7
Copnor Inf & Jun Sch
PO3...............346 A1
Copnor Rd PO2 .....345 F3
Copper Beech Cl
BH13..............392 A4
Copper Beech Dr
PO6...............346 E8
Copper Beeches
2 Bournemouth
BH2.............392 A4
Blackfield S045.....338 F2
Copper Beech Gdns
BH10..............377 D2
Copperbeech Pl RG14..5 B4
Coppercourt Leaze 5
BH21..............351 C4
Copperfield Ho 17
PO1...............370 D7
Copperfield Rd
S016..............267 A5
Copperfields S040 ..288 B7
Coppers Cl SP6.....281 A6
Copper St 5 PO5...404 A1
Coppice Ave BH22 .. 353 B7

Coppice Cl
Baughurst RG26 .... 26 B8
Farnham GU9 ...... 99 C6
Newbury RG14 .... 5 F8
New Milton BH25 .. 383 D4
St Leonards BH24 ... 327 F4
Winchester SO22 ... 403 A7
Coppice Gdns GU46 .. 34 A5
Coppice Hill SO32.... 271 D7
Coppice Mews RG23 . 68 C6
Coppice Rd
Kingsclere RG20 .... 24 E2
Totton SO40........ 264 C2
Coppice The
Brockenhurst SO42.. 333 D1
Christchurch BH23 .. 396 B6
Fleet GU52 .... 75 A6
Gosport PO13 ...... 343 D2
Netley SO31........ 315 C5
Waterlooville PO8 ... 300 A6
Coppice View
Bournemouth BH10.. 377 E3
Whiteley PO15...... 317 D7
Coppice Way PO15 .. 318 D3
Coppins Gr PO16.... 344 C6
Copse Ave
Farnham GU9 ...... 99 C8
New Milton BH25 .. 383 B2
Copse Cl
Camberley GU15 .... 36 E6
Liss GU33 .... 208 A4
North Baddesley
SO52........ 241 F4
Otterbourne SO21.... 219 C4
Petersfield GU31.... 229 C4
Poole BH14 .... 390 F3
Totton SO40........ 288 F6
Waterlooville PO7 ... 322 D2
Copse Cvn Pk The
SO40 .... 287 D5
Copse End
Camberley GU15 .... 36 E6
Fleet GU51 .... 74 D8
Copse Field RG24 .... 70 A8
Copse La
Brown Candover
SO24......... 134 F3
Chilworth SO16 .... 242 F1
Crookham Village
GU52 .... 74 E5
Gosport PO13 ...... 343 D1
Hamble-le-R SO31... 363 A4
Long Sutton RG29 ... 95 D3
North Hayling PO11.. 373 A8
Copse Rd
Burley BH24 .... 330 F2
Haslemere GU27 .... 189 B5
New Milton BH25 .. 383 B2
Overton RG25 ...... 66 B2
Southampton SO18.. 268 A2
Verwood BH31...... 302 F6
Copse The
Basingstoke RG23... 90 D3
Chandler's Ford SO53 243 E5
Fareham PO15...... 318 D4
Farnborough GU14 .. 55 B3
Romsey SO51 ...... 216 C1
Rowledge GU10 .... 121 D4
Tadley RG26........ 26 E8
West Moors BH24 ... 354 C8
Copse View SO19 .... 292 E5
Copse View Cl RG24.. 49 A4
Copse Way
Christchurch BH23 .. 396 E8
Farnham GU10 .... 121 D6
Finchampstead RG40.. 16 C7
Copsewood Ave BH8 378 E1
Copsewood Rd
Ashurst SO40 ...... 288 C3
Hythe SO45 .... 313 F3
Southampton SO18.. 267 C4
Copsey Cl PO6...... 346 D8
Copsey Gr PO6...... 346 D8
Copthall Ho 5 GU11 .76 F2
Copthorne Cotts
SO45 .... 339 C3
Copthorne La SO45 .. 339 B3
Copythorne CE Inf Sch
SO40........ 263 B2
Copythorne Cl BH8. 378 D2
Copythorne Cres
SO40 .... 263 C3
Copythorn Rd PO2... 345 F1
Coracle Cl PO16..... 316 F1
Coral Cl PO16....... 344 C6
Coral Ct
2 Poole BH13 .... 392 A4
6 Gosport PO13 ... 368 C6
Coralin Gr PO7 ...... 300 B1
Coram Cl 3 SO23.... 403 E6
Corbar Rd BH23..... 394 E8
Corbett Rd PO7..... 322 D5
Corbiere Ave BH12.. 376 E3
Corbiere Cl SO16.... 265 E3
Corbin Ave BH22.... 354 A6
Corbin Cl SO41 ..... 385 B2
Corbin Rd SO41..... 385 B2
Corbould Rd SO45 .. 337 F8
Corby Cres PO3..... 346 B4
Cordale Rd RG21.... 69 A3
Cordelia Cl SO45.... 313 D3
Cordelia Gdns GU12.. 56 D1
Cordwalles Jun Sch
GU15......... 36 D8
Corfe Cl
New Alresford
SO24.......... 179 D4
Stubbington PO14... 367 A7

Corfe Gdns GU16 .... 36 D1
Corfe Halt Cl BH21... 350 E1
Corfe Hills Sch BH18 374 F6
Corfe Lodge Rd
BH18........ 374 D3
Corfe Mews BH15.... 390 D4
Corfe View Rd
Corfe Mullen BH21... 374 C5
Poole BH14 .... 391 C3
Corfe Way
Broadstone BH18 ... 374 E3
Farnborough GU14 .. 56 C1
Corfe Wlk RG23..... 68 C6
Corfield Cl SO53.... 242 F6
Corfu BH13 .... 402 E6
Corhampton Cres
PO9 .... 323 D4
Corhampton Ho 11
PO1 .... 404 C4
Corhampton La
Droxford SO32...... 248 D6
Meonstoke SO32 ... 248 D6
Corhampton Rd BH6 394 C6
Coriander Cl GU14 .. 55 A4
Coriander Dr SO40 .. 288 C7
Coriander Way
PO15 .... 317 D8
Corinna Gdns SO45 . 313 D3
Corinthian Cl
Andover SP10 ...... 83 B4
Basingstoke RG22... 91 C7
Corinthian Rd SO53. 243 E7
Cork La SO40 ...... 289 F2
Cormorant Cl
Basingstoke RG22... 90 F8
Portchester PO16 ... 343 F8
Cormorant Dr SO45 . 314 C2
Cormorant Pl GU47 . 35 C7
Cormorant Wlk
PO13 .... 343 B2
Cornaway La PO16... 344 B8
Cornbrook Gr PO7... 300 C1
Cornbunting Cl 8
GU47......... 35 B8
Cornelia Cl SO14.....55 B3
Cornelia Cres BH12 . 392 A6
Cornelius Dr PO7 ... 300 B1
Cornel Rd SO19..... 291 F5
Corner Cotts 2
GU26 .... 167 B3
Corner Mead PO7... 298 F4
Corner The SO22.... 403 C7
Cornerways GU26... 167 B6
Cornerways Ct 3
BH25 .... 383 B2
Cornes Cl SO22 .... 403 B5
Cornfield PO16 ..... 319 B4
Cornfield Cl SO53... 242 F6
Cornfield Rd PO13 .. 367 F4
Cornfields
Andover SP10 ...... 106 C6
Yateley GU46....... 33 F4
Cornfields The RG22 . 91 C7
Cornflower Cl SO31. 316 E3
Cornflower Dr BH23. 396 C8
Conford Way BH21.. 396 D8
Conforth Rd SO40.. 264 C4
Cornish Cl SO32.... 68 C3
Cornish Gdns BH10 . 377 D1
Cornmarket Cl 7
BH21 .... 351 B5
Corn Mkt SO51 ..... 240 E7
Cornpits La SP6..... 256 C5
Cornwall Cl
4 Southampton
SO18........ 268 A2
Camberley GU15 .... 36 D7
Cornwall Cres SO18. 267 F2
Cornwall Ho RG24... 68 D8
Cornwallis Cres PO1 404 C4
Cornwallis Ho SO41 . 399 B4
Cornwall Rd
Bordon GU35....... 164 D1
Chandler's Ford SO53 243 C3
Portsmouth PO1 .... 370 E5
Southampton SO18.. 267 F2
Cornwell Cl
Gosport PO13 ...... 368 D7
Portsmouth PO2 .... 345 B2
Coronado Rd PO12.. 369 B8
Coronation Ave
Bournemouth BH9... 377 F2
Upton BH16........ 389 B7
Coronation Cl
Burghclere RG20 .... 22 D7
Odiham RG29....... 72 F3
Verwood BH31...... 302 F7
Coronation Eventide
Homes 4 PO2 .... 345 E4
Coronation Homes
SO18......... 292 D8
Coronation Par
SO31 .... 315 E3
Coronation Rd
Aldershot GU11..... 99 F7
Basingstoke RG21... 69 C6
Ludgershall SP11..... 57 A2
North Tidworth SP9.. 78 E8
South Hayling PO11.. 373 F4
Swanmore SO32 ... 272 B5
Verwood BH31...... 302 F7
Waterlooville PO7 ... 322 C8
Yateley GU46....... 34 C7
Coronation Terr SP6 257 A2
Corporation Cotts 1
RG14 .... 1 E4
Corporation Rd BH1 393 C5

Corpus Christi RC Prim
Sch
Bournemouth BH5... 394 A5
Portsmouth PO2 .... 345 D2
Correlli Rd RG22....91 F8
Corringway GU52 ....75 B6
Corry Rd GU26...... 167 A6
Corsair Dr SO45 .... 313 D3
Corscombe Cl BH17. 375 D4
Cortina Way SO30... 293 C5
Cortmerron 20 BH4 . 392 C2
Cortry Cl BH12...... 392 A7
Cort Way PO15...... 318 C4
Corunna Main SP10.. 83 B1
Corvette Ave SO31 .. 316 F1
Corylus Ct SO40 .... 264 B1
Cosford Cl SO50 .... 245 A2
Cosham Park Ave
PO6 .... 345 F7
Cosham Sta PO6 .... 345 F7
Cossack Gn 1 SO14. 291 A4
Cossack La 23 SO23. 403 E6
Cossack Lane Ho 26
SO23 .... 403 E6
Cossaton Rise SO20. 126 A3
Costello Technology Coll
RG21......... 69 C4
Coster Cl RG14......1 B5
Cosworth Dr SO45 .. 313 D3
Cotes Ave BH14..... 391 A5
Cotes Ct BH14...... 391 A5
Cotlands Rd BH8.... 393 B4
Cotsalls SO50....... 245 D1
Cotswold Cl
Basingstoke RG22... 68 B4
Farnborough GU14 .. 55 C7
Hythe SO45 .... 313 D3
Verwood BH31...... 302 E6
Cotswold Ct
11 Fleet GU51..... 53 F1
5 Southampton
SO17.......... 267 A1
6 Christchurch BH23 395 F4
Cotswold Ho 3 PO6 345 C8
Cotswold Rd SO16 .. 289 F8
Cotswold Wlk 1
PO14 .... 342 F7
Cottage Cl PO7..... 298 F3
Cottage Gdns
Farnborough GU14 .. 55 D4
Poole BH12 .... 391 C5
Cottage Gn
Goodworth Clatford
SP11.......... 128 A8
Hartley Wintney RG27. 52 D5
Cottage Gr
Gosport PO12 ...... 369 B6
Portsmouth PO5 .... 404 B2
Cottage Grove Prim Sch
PO5.......... 404 B1
Cottage La GU32,
GU33 .... 206 F3
Cottage Mews PO14. 367 B6
Cottage Rd SO20.... 147 C8
Cottagers La SO41 .. 384 A4
Cottage View PO1 .. 404 C3
Cotteridge Ho 1
PO5.......... 404 C2
Cottes Way PO14.... 367 B6
Cottesway E PO14... 367 B6
Cottington Cl RG20.. 24 E2
Cott La BH24....... 331 B2
Cottle Cl RG21...... 69 A2
Cotton Cl
Aldershot GU11..... 76 D3
Bishopstoke SO50... 244 E3
Corfe Mullen BH18 .. 374 F5
Cotton Dr PO10..... 324 E3
Cotton Ho
PO5.......... 404 C4
Cottonworth Cotts
SP11.......... 128 D4
Cottrell Ct GU52 .... 74 F4
Cottrell Flats GU14.. 77 B8
Cott St SO32....... 272 D4
Cott Street La SO32. 272 E4
Cotwell Ave PO8.... 300 B4
Couch Gn SO21..... 177 C7
Coulmere Rd PO12.. 369 A7
Coulsdon Rd SO30.. 293 C6
Coultas Rd SO53.... 218 E2
Council Hos
Farley Hill RG7 ..... 15 B5
Horton Heath BH21.. 302 A1
Lockerley SO51..... 214 B5
Sopley BH23 ...... 355 F2
Up Sombourne SO20. 173 B5
Council Hos The
Penwood RG20 ..... 21 E7
Wolverton Common
RG26 .... 25 E4
Council Houses The
RG26 .... 8 F1
Council Rd RG21....69 B4
Countess Cl BH21... 375 E8
Countess Gdns BH7. 393 F8
Country View
Stubbington PO14... 342 B4
West Wellow SO51 . 238 E3
County Gates La 10
BH4.......... 392 B4
County Gdns PO14.. 342 C8
Course Park Cres
PO14 .... 317 D2
Court Barn Cl PO13. 367 F4
Court Barn La PO13. 367 F4
Court Cl
2 Liphook GU30.... 188 A3

Court Cl continued
3 Christchurch
BH23 .... 395 E7
Cosham PO6 .... 346 B7
Lymington SO41 ... 385 D2
Southampton SO18 .. 292 A6
Totton SO40........ 264 D2
Court Dr GU52 ..... 75 A7
Court Dro RG25.....64 F7
Courtenay Dr BH21 . 351 C6
Courtenay Pl SO41.. 385 D4
Courtenay Rd
Farnham GU9 ...... 99 C7
Poole BH14 .... 391 B4
Winchester SO23 ... 176 A3
Court Farm RG7 ....10 B6
Court Gdns GU15 ... 36 B5
Court Hill SP6 ..... 256 F5
Courthill Fst Sch
BH14......... 391 D4
Courthill Rd BH14... 391 D4
Court House Cl
SO45 .... 314 A4
Courtier Cl SO45.... 313 C3
Court La
Cosham PO6 .... 346 B7
Gilbert Street SO24.. 181 D6
Up Sombourne SO20. 173 B6
Court Lane Inf Sch
PO6.......... 346 A7
Court Lane Jun Sch
PO6.......... 346 A7
Courtleigh Manor 6
BH5 .... 393 D4
Court Mead PO6.... 346 B7
Courtmoor Ave GU52. 75 A7
Courtmoor Sch GU52 74 F7
Court Moor Sch GU52 74 F7
Courtnay Cl PO15... 317 D3
Courtney Ho 1 GU15 . 35 F3
Courtney Pl BH21... 374 C5
Court Rd
Aldershot GU11..... 76 E2
Bournemouth BH9... 378 B1
Kings Worthy SO23 .. 176 C5
Lee-on-t-S PO13 ... 367 E4
Southampton SO15 .. 290 F7
Court Royal Mews
SO15 .... 290 F8
Courts Hill Rd GU27. 189 F6
Courts Mount Rd
GU27......... 189 F6
Court The SO41..... 385 D2
Courtyard Cl SO42 .. 333 F1
Courtyard Mews
SO42 .... 333 F1
Courtyard The
11 Petersfield
GU31 .... 228 F3
4 Romsey SO51 ... 240 F7
Christchurch BH23 .. 395 D6
Finchdean PO8 ..... 301 B3
Linchmere GU27 ... 188 F2
Poole BH12 .... 376 C1
Wimborne Minster
BH21 .... 352 A1
Cousins Gr PO4..... 370 F2
Cove Inf Sch GU14 .. 55 C6
Cove Jun Sch GU14 . 55 C5
Covena Rd BH6..... 394 E6
Coventry Cl
Basingstoke RG22... 91 B8
Corfe Mullen BH21.. 374 C4
Coventry Cres BH17. 375 A4
Coventry Ct
8 Winchester
SO23.......... 403 E8
Gosport PO13 ...... 368 D6
Coventry Rd SO15... 290 F6
Coverack Way PO6.. 345 B7
Cove Rd
Bournemouth BH10.. 377 C2
Farnborough GU14 .. 55 D4
Fleet GU51 .... 54 C3
Covert Gr PO7...... 323 A5
Coverts Cl GU9 ..... 99 C4
Coverts The RG26... 26 F6
Covert The
Farnborough GU14 .. 55 C8
Romsey SO51 ...... 241 B6
Cove Sch GU14 .... 55 C5
Covey Cl GU14 .....55 F4
Covey Way SO24 ... 179 B4
Covindale Ho 2
PO4.......... 371 A3
Covington Rd PO10 . 325 B5
Cowan Rd PO7...... 322 D5
Coward Rd PO12.... 368 F2
Cowdown Farm Cotts
SP11.......... 106 F5
Cowdown La
Compton PO18...... 278 D4
Goodworth Clatford
SP11.......... 106 D3
Cowdray Ho
25 Winchester
SO23.......... 403 D6
Portsmouth PO1 .... 404 C4
Cowdray Pk
Alton GU34 .... 139 F2

Cowdray Pk continued
Stubbington PO14... 367 A7
Cowdray Gdns BH8 . 378 E2
Cowdrey Hts RG24 .. 69 E6
Cowdrey Sq SP10 ...83 B3
Cow Drove Hill
SO20......... 172 A3
Cowdrys Field 2
BH21 .... 351 B6
Cowell Dr BH7 ..... 394 B8
Cowes La SO31..... 340 D8
Cowfold La RG27.....51 B6
Cowgrove Rd BH21.. 350 F5
Cow La
Cosham PO6 .... 345 D7
Kimpton SP11 ...... 80 B4
Portchester PO16 ... 344 D7
Cowleas Cl SO51.... 214 E5
Cowleas Cotts SO51. 214 E5
Cowley Cl SO16..... 265 E2
Cowley Dr SO21..... 153 D2
Cowley Rd
Lymington SO41 ... 385 C4
Poole BH17 .... 390 D8
Cowleys Rd BH23... 380 C2
Cowper Ave BH25... 383 A1
Cowper Rd
Bournemouth BH9... 377 F2
Portsmouth PO1 .... 370 E7
Southampton SO19 .. 292 D6
Cowpitts La BH24... 305 D2
Cowplain Com Sch
PO8.......... 299 F2
Cowslade RG14 ..... 1 B8
Cowslip Bank RG24 . 69 F8
Cowslip Cl
Gosport PO13 ...... 343 C2
Lindford GU35...... 165 A4
Locks Heath SO31... 316 E2
Cowslip Way SO51 . 216 C1
Cox Ave BH9........ 378 B4
Coxbridge Mdws GU9. 98 E1
Coxbridge Rdbt GU9 121 D8
Cox Cl BH9 .... 378 B4
Cox Dale PO14...... 317 C1
Coxes Mdw GU32... 228 E5
Coxgreen GU47 .....35 B6
Coxheath Rd GU51,
GU52......... 74 C5
Coxmoor Cl GU52 .. 75 C5
Cox Row SO53 ..... 243 D3
Cox's Dr SO19 ..... 292 B2
Cox's Hill SO21 .... 220 A8
Cox's La SO19 ..... 291 D3
Coxstone La 2
BH24 .... 329 A6
Coy Pond Rd BH12.. 392 B5
Cozens Cl SO19 .... 291 E1
Crabapple Cl SO40.. 288 C7
Crabbe Ct PO5...... 404 B2
Crabbs Hill RG26 ... 25 C1
Crabbs Way SO40... 288 B7
Crabbswood La
SO41......... 383 E8
Crabden La PO8 .... 276 E1
Crableck La SO31... 316 D5
Crab Orchard Way
PO14 .... 302 F2
Crabthorn Farm La
PO14 .... 367 B8
Crabton Close Rd
BH5 .... 393 F4
Crabtree SO16...... 265 F1
Crabtree Cl BH23 ... 380 C2
Crabtree Gdns GU35 165 D5
Crabtree La
Churt GU10 .... 144 E2
Headley GU35...... 165 C5
Crabtree Rd GU15...35 F2
Crabtree Way RG24 . 70 B4
Crabwood Cl SO16.. 265 F2
Crabwood Ct PO9... 323 D7
Crabwood Dr SO30.. 268 E1
Crabwood Rd SO16. 265 E2
Cracknore Hard
Marchwood SO40 ...290 A1
Marchwood SO40 ...290 A1
Cracknore Hard La
SO43 .... 309 F6
Cracknore Rd SO15. 290 D5
Craddock Ho
11 Portsmouth
PO1 .... 370 A5
2 Winchester SO23 198 C8
Cradle La GU35..... 143 A4
Crafts La GU31...... 229 A5
Craig Ho 3 PO5 .... 370 D2
Craigmoor Ave BH8. 378 F1
Craigmoor Cl BH8 .. 378 F1
Craigmoor Way BH8 378 E2
Craigside Rd BH24 .. 327 D4
Craigwell Rd PO7... 322 E4
Craigwood Dr BH22. 353 E4
Crake Pl GU47...... 35 B8
Crampmoor La SO51 216 E1
Cramptons GU34.... 139 A2
Cranberry Cl SO40.. 289 F1
Cranberry Wlk GU17 . 35 D3
Cranborne Cres
BH12 .... 391 E8
Cranborne Ct
17 Bournemouth,
Westbourne BH4 . 392 C3

Cranborne Ct continued
Bournemouth,Winton
BH9.......... 393 B8
Cranborne Gdns 8
SO53 .... 218 B1
Cranborne Pl BH25.. 382 E3
Cranborne Rd
Alderholt SP6 ...... 280 A5
Bournemouth BH2... 392 E2
Cosham PO6 .... 322 A1
Wimborne Minster
BH21 .... 351 C7
Cranborne Wlk
PO14 .... 342 E7
Cranbourne Bsns & Ent
Coll RG21 .... 68 F3
Cranbourne Cl SO15 266 D1
Cranbourne Ct
Basingstoke RG21.... 69 A2
Poole BH17 .... 376 A2
Cranbourne Dr SO21 319 B3
Cranbourne La RG21 .68 F2
Cranbourne Pk
SO30 .... 293 C4
Cranbourne Rd
PO12 .... 369 C4
Cranbrook Ct GU51. 54 A3
Cranbrook Mews
BH12 .... 391 B6
Cranbrook Rd BH12. 391 B6
Cranbury Ave SO14. 291 B6
Cranbury Cl
Downton SP5....... 234 F6
Otterbourne SO21... 219 B3
Cranbury Ct SO19... 291 F3
Cranbury Gdns SO31 292 F1
Cranbury Pl SO14... 291 A6
Cranbury Rd
Eastleigh SO50 ..... 244 A1
Eastleigh SO50 ..... 244 A2
Southampton SO19 .. 291 F3
Cranbury Terr 5
SO14 .... 291 A6
Cranbury The 4
SO14 .... 291 A6
Cranbury Twrs 6
SO14 .... 291 A6
Crane Cl
Gosport PO13 ...... 343 B2
Verwood BH31...... 302 E6
Crane Ct GU47......35 B8
Crane Dr BH31...... 302 E6
Cranemoor Ave
BH23 .... 381 E2
Cranemoor Cl BH23. 381 E2
Cranemoor Gdns
BH23 .... 381 F2
Cranesfield RG24 ...47 E4
Cranes Mews BH15 . 390 D3
Cranes Rd RG24 .... 47 D4
Craneswater Ave
PO4.......... 370 F2
Craneswater Gate 10
PO4.......... 370 E1
Craneswater Jun Sch
PO4.......... 370 F2
Craneswater Mews 5
PO4.......... 370 E2
Craneswater Pk PO4 370 E2
Crane Way BH21.... 327 B6
Cranfield Ave SO51. 351 D5
Cranford Ave GU52...74 F5
Cranford Dr GU34... 140 C6
Cranford Gdns SO53 243 B8
Cranford Ho 6
SO17.......... 267 A2
Cranford Park Dr
GU46......... 34 B6
Cranford Rd GU32... 228 E2
Cranford Way SO17. 267 A2
Cranleigh Ave PO1.. 370 E6
Cranleigh Ct
Bournemouth BH6... 394 E5
Farnborough GU14 .. 55 D4
Cranleigh Gdns BH6 394 E5
Cranleigh Ho
Hedge End SO30 ... 269 C3
Southampton SO17 . 291 A8
Cranleigh Paddock
SO43 .... 309 F6
Cranleigh Rd
Bournemouth BH6... 394 D5
Hedge End SO30 ... 293 C6
Portchester PO16 ... 344 A7
Portsmouth PO1 .... 370 E6
Cranmer Dr SO16 ... 265 C5
Cranmer Lodge 2
GU15......... 36 C6
Cranmer Rd BH9.... 392 F8
Cranmore SO31..... 315 C7
Cranmore Cl GU11... 76 C1
Cranmore Ct GU16 .. 56 D4
Cranmore Gdns GU11 76 C1
Cranmore La GU11... 76 C1
Cranmore Rd GU16 .. 56 E4
Cransley Ct
4 Bournemouth
BH4.......... 392 C2
Bournemouth BH4... 392 C2
Crantock Gr BH8.... 378 F2
Cranwell Cl
Bournemouth BH11.. 376 E4
Bransgore BH23 .... 357 B1
Cranwell Ct SO16... 265 F5
Cranworth Rd SO22. 403 D7

Crasswell St PO1 ... 404 C4
Craven Cl GU10 ..... 122 A6
Craven Ct
 Camberley GU15 ..... 35 D4
 Fareham PO15...... 318 D3
Craven Dene RG14 .... 1 F4
Craven Ho 7 GU9....98 F2
Craven Rd
 Chandler's Ford
 SO53.......... 243 D6
 Newbury RG14 .... 1 C2
Craven St 9 SO14 .. 291 A5
Crawford Cl SO16... 265 D5
Crawford Dr PO16 .. 318 F3
Crawford Gdns GU15...35 F5
Crawford Pl RG14...... 1 D3
Crawlboys La SP11....57 B3
Crawley Ave PO9 ... 324 A6
Crawley Cotts SO21 . 152 B2
Crawley Dr GU15..... 36 D6
Crawley Hill
 Camberley GU15 ..... 36 D5
 West Wellow SO51 .... 238 F2
Crawley Lo 3 GU16... 36 E7
Crawley Ridge GU15 .. 36 D7
Crawley Ridgel Inf Sch
 GU15............. 36 D7
Crawley Ridge Jun Sch
 GU15............. 36 D7
Crawley Rise 4 GU15 .36 E7
Crawley Wood Cl
 GU15............. 36 D5
Crawshaw Rd BH14 . 391 B2
Crawte Ave SO45 .... 338 D2
Crawters La 6 GU31 228 F3
Crawts Rd RG25....... 88 A7
Craydown La SO20 .. 125 E2
Cray Ho PO12....... 369 D5
Creasey Rd BH11... 377 A5
Credenhill Rd PO6 .. 321 C1
Credon Cl GU14...... 55 D5
Creech Rd BH12 .... 391 C5
Creech View PO7 ... 298 E4
Creech Wood Forest
 Walk★ PO7 ...... 298 D3
Creedy Dr BH23.... 395 B5
Creedy Gdns SO18 .. 268 A3
Creek End PO10 .... 348 F7
Creekmoor La BH17. 390 A8
Creek Rd
 Gosport PO12 ...... 369 D5
 South Hayling PO11.. 373 D1
Creighton Rd SO15.. 289 F6
Cremorne Pl 7
 GU32............ 228 F4
Cremyll Cl PO14 .... 367 C7
Crerar Cl GU14 ...... 55 B3
Crescent Cl SO22 ... 197 B4
Crescent Ct
 14 Bournemouth
 BH2............ 392 D2
 Barton on S BH25 .... 397 F7
Crescent Dr BH25... 397 F7
Crescent Ho SO50.... 244 B3
Crescent La GU12....77 F5
Crescent Prim Sch The
 SO50............ 244 A3
Crescent Rd
 Bournemouth BH2... 392 E3
 Fareham PO16...... 319 A1
 Gosport PO12 ...... 369 A2
 Locks Heath SO31... 316 F2
 North Baddesley
 SO52............ 241 F5
 Poole BH14 .... 391 E4
 Verwood BH31...... 303 A6
 Wimborne Minster
 BH21........... 351 C4
Crescent The
 3 Bournemouth
 BH1............ 393 E4
 Andover SP10 ...... 105 C7
 Barton on S BH25 .... 397 D8
 Basingstoke RG24.... 68 D8
 Bramley RG26 .... 28 E3
 Crookham Village
 GU51............ 74 C6
 Eastleigh SO50 .... 244 B4
 Exbury SO45 ...... 345 B5
 Farnborough GU14 .... 56 A3
 Farnham GU9 ..... 99 B8
 Four Marks GU34 ... 160 B4
 Goodworth Clatford
 SP11........... 105 F1
 Hurstbourne Tarrant
 SP11........... 60 E7
 Marchwood SO40 ... 289 C1
 Mortimer RG7 ..... 11 D6
 Netley SO31....... 315 C6
 Romsey SO51 ..... 241 B8
 Southampton SO19 .. 292 A2
 Southbourne PO10 .. 349 D8
 Twyford SO21 ..... 220 A6
 Upham SO32 ...... 246 C2
 Waterlooville PO7 ... 322 C4
 West Moors BH24 ... 354 B8
 Yateley GU46...... 48 E6
Crescent Wlk BH22 . 353 E2
Cressey Rd SO51.... 240 F7
Cress Gdns SP10.... 105 F6
Cresswell Rd RG14.... 1 B4
Cressy Rd PO2...... 370 D7
Cresta Ct 6 PO4... 370 F2
Cresta Gdns BH22... 353 E2

Crest Cl PO16...... 319 D1
Crestland Cl PO8 ... 300 B3
Crest Rd BH12 ... 391 C6
Crest The PO7 ..... 322 C2
Crest Way SO19..... 292 C4
**Crestwood Coll for Bsns
 & Enterprise** SO50.. 243 F5
Creswell RG27...... 51 D1
Crete Cotts SO45.... 313 E1
Crete La SO45 ...... 313 F1
Crete Rd SO45 ...... 313 F1
Cribb Cl BH17...... 390 E7
Crichel Mount Rd
 BH14............ 402 C7
Crichel Rd BH9 .... 393 A8
Crichton Ct RG7 ......11 E6
Crichton Ho SO31.... 315 B6
Cricket Chambers
 BH1............. 393 A4
Cricket Cl
 Beacon Hill GU26 ... 167 B6
 Christchurch BH23 .. 395 F5
 Crawley SO21 ...... 152 B2
Cricket Dr PO8 ..... 300 A5
Cricket Green La
 RG27............. 52 D6
Cricket Hill RG40 ... 16 D2
Cricket Hill La GU46.. 34 C4
Cricket La GU10 .... 122 B6
Cricket Lea GU35 ... 165 C5
Cricklade Coll SP10. 106 A8
Cricklade Pl SP10.....82 F1
Cricklemede SO32 .. 271 D7
Cricklewood Cl
 SO32............ 271 D7
Crigdon Cl SO16.... 289 E8
Crimea Rd
 Aldershot GU11..... 76 F2
 Bournemouth BH9... 392 F7
Cringle Ave BH6 .... 395 A4
Crinoline Gdns PO4 . 371 B2
Cripley Rd GU14.....55 D5
Cripple Gate La
 SO42............ 363 D5
Crispin Cl
 Christchurch BH23 .. 396 F8
 Horton Heath SO50.. 269 C6
 Locks Heath SO31... 317 B4
Crispstead La SO23 . 403 D3
Crisspyn Cl PO8..... 300 B6
Criswick Cl SP11.... 104 F2
Critchmere Hill
 GU27............ 189 C7
Critchmere La GU27. 189 C6
Critchmere Vale
 GU27............ 189 C6
Criterion Arc 10 BH1 392 F3
Crittall Cl SO41 .... 360 C2
Croad Ct 4 PO16 ... 319 C1
Crockford Cl BH25 .. 383 B5
Crockford Ho 1
 SO24............ 179 D6
Crockford La
 Basingstoke RG24.... 48 D1
 Basingstoke RG24.... 48 D2
Crockford Rd PO10 . 325 B4
Croft Av SP10....... 106 A6
Croft Cl BH21....... 374 D7
Crofter's Cl GU47....34 E8
Crofters Mdw RG24 ..69 F8
Croft Gdns
 Alton GU34 .... 139 E4
 Andover SP10 ...... 106 A6
Croft Hts SP5....... 212 B3
Croft La
 Crondall GU10...... 97 C5
 Newbury RG14 .... 1 C4
 Stoke PO11 .... 347 F1
 Yateley GU46...... 34 B7
Croftlands Ave PO14 367 C8
Crofton GU27...... 189 D7
**Crofton Anne Dale Inf
 Sch** PO14.......... 367 C7
**Crofton Anne Dale Jun
 Sch** PO14.......... 367 C7
Crofton Ave PO13... 367 C5
Crofton Cl
 Christchurch BH23 .. 379 E1
 Southampton SO17.. 267 A1
 Waterlooville PO7... 322 D5
Crofton Ct PO14 .... 367 C7
**Crofton Hammond Inf
 Sch** PO14.......... 367 C7
**Crofton Hammond Jun
 Sch** PO14.......... 367 C7
Crofton La PO14 .... 367 B6
Crofton Rd
 Portsmouth,Milton
 PO4............ 371 B5
 Portsmouth,North End
 PO2............ 345 E2
Crofton Sch PO14... 367 E7
Crofton Way
 Swanmore SO32 .... 272 A5
 Warsash SO31...... 316 C1
Croft Rd
 Aldershot GU11......99 F8
 Bournemouth BH9... 377 F2
 Bransgore BH23 .... 381 B6
 Christchurch BH23 .. 395 F7
 Mortimer RG7 ..... 11 D6
 Newbury RG14 ...... 5 D8
 Oakley RG23 .... 67 B2
 Poole BH12 .... 391 B6
 Portsmouth PO2 .... 345 D1
 Ringwood BH24... 305 C1
Crofts The RG22.... 91 C6

Croft The
 7 Eastleigh SO50... 244 A2
 Bishopstone SP5.... 210 B8
 Chandler's Ford SO53 243 C3
 Fleet GU51 .... 74 D8
 Newton Tony SP4... 123 B5
 Stubbington PO14 .. 342 C4
 Totton SO40........ 264 C2
Croft Way GU16...... 36 D2
Cromalt Cl SO45..... 313 D2
Cromarty Ave PO4 .. 371 B8
Cromarty Cl PO14... 342 B4
Cromarty Rd SO16 .. 265 E5
Crombie Cl PO8...... 299 F4
Cromer Gdns BH12.. 391 F5
Cromer Rd
 Bournemouth BH8... 393 D7
 Poole BH12 .... 391 F5
 Portsmouth PO6 .... 321 E1
 Southampton SO16.. 265 D1
Cromhall Cl PO14 ... 342 C8
Crompton Way PO15 317 C5
Cromwell Cl RG24....70 B6
Cromwell Gdns
 GU34............ 139 F4
Cromwell Pl
 2 Bournemouth
 BH5............ 394 B5
 Newbury RG14 .... 1 E3
Cromwell Rd
 4 Wimborne Minster
 BH21........... 351 D4
 Basingstoke RG21.... 69 A6
 Bournemouth BH5... 394 B5
 Camberley GU15 .... 36 B7
 Newbury RG14 ...... 2 A5
 Poole BH12 .... 391 D5
 Portsmouth PO4 .... 371 B2
 Southampton SO15 .. 290 F7
 Winchester SO22 ... 403 C4
Cromwell Terr RG14 .. 1 B5
Cromwell Way GU14 ..55 F7
Crondall Ave PO9 ... 323 E6
Crondall Ct GU15 .... 35 F4
Crondall End GU46.... 34 A7
Crondall La GU9,GU10 98 C2
Crondall Prim Sch
 GU10............. 97 D6
Crondall Rd
 Bentley GU10....... 120 E6
 Crookham Village GU51
 GU51............ 74 C3
Crooked Hays Cl
 SO40............ 289 F1
Crooked Walk La
 PO17............ 320 F4
Crookham CE Inf Sch
 GU52............. 74 F4
Crookham Cl
 Havant PO9 .... 323 C4
 Tadley RG26........ 26 F6
Crookham Common Rd
 Brimpton RG7 ...... 8 B5
 Thatcham RG19 ...... 7 E1
Crookham Hill RG19 ...7 C7
Crookham Jun Sch
 GU52............. 75 B4
Crookham Pk RG19 ...7 F6
Crookham Rd
 Fleet GU51,GU52.... 74 E7
 Southampton SO19 . 314 F8
Crookham Reach
 GU52............. 74 E5
**Crookhorn Coll of
 Technology** PO7... 322 F4
Crookhorn La
 Soberton SO32 .... 273 C8
 Waterlooville PO7... 322 E3
Crooksbury Rd GU10 100 A3
Cropmark Way RG22 .91 B7
Crosby Gdns GU46 ...33 E7
Crosby Hill Dr GU15.. 36 D7
Crosby Rd BH4...... 392 C1
Crosby Way GU9.....98 E1
Crosfield Cl SO51... 239 B2
Crossbill Cl PO8..... 300 A7
Crossborough Gdns
 RG21............. 69 C4
Crossborough Hill
 RG21............. 69 C4
Cross Droves SN8.... 17 D3
Cross Farm Inf Sch
 GU16............. 56 C6
Crossfell Wlk PO14.. 342 E7
Cross Gdns GU16 .... 56 D6
Cross House Ctr
 SO14............ 291 C3
Crosshouse Rd SO14 291 C3
Cross Keys Pas 6
 SO23............ 403 E5
Cross La
 Andover SP10 ...... 105 F8
 Ashmansworth RG20.. 41 A8
 Beech Hill RG7 ..... 13 A7
 Bishop's Waltham
 SO32........... 247 A2
 Camberley GU16 .... 56 D6
 Stratfield Mortimer
 RG7............ 12 F8
 Waterlooville PO8... 300 A5
Crossland Cl PO12 .. 369 C4
Crossland Dr PO9 ... 324 A3
Cross Lanes BH24... 305 C7
Crossley Ct 2 SO15. 290 C6
Crossley Pl 5 SO15. 290 E6
Crossmead Ave
 BH25............ 383 A2

Cross & Pillory La 9
 GU34............ 139 F3
Cross Rd
 Ash GU12........... 77 F3
 Farnborough GU14 ... 55 C1
 Lee-on-t-S PO13 ... 368 A4
 Southampton SO19 . 291 E7
Cross St
 1 Bishop's Waltham
 SO32........... 271 C7
 Aldershot GU11..... 76 E2
 Basingstoke RG21.... 69 B5
 Farnborough GU14 ... 77 A8
 Portsmouth PO5 ... 404 C2
 Portsmouth,Portsea
 PO1............ 370 A6
 Winchester SO23 ... 403 D6
Cross The
 Bishopstone SP5.... 210 B7
 Burley BH24 ...... 331 A3
 East Meon GU32 ... 226 D1
 King's Somborne
 SO20........... 172 A3
Cross Trees SP6 .... 233 F1
Crosswater La GU10. 144 D4
Cross Way
 Christchurch BH23 .. 379 D1
 Compton SO21...... 219 D5
 Havant PO9 .... 323 E2
Crossways
 Aldershot GU12..... 77 A1
 Churt GU10 .... 144 C1
 Crookham Village
 GU51............ 74 C6
 Everton SO41 ...... 384 D1
 Whitchurch RG28 .... 86 C6
Cross Ways BH23 ... 357 D5
Crossways GU35 .... 234 E7
Crossways Rd GU26. 167 B3
Crossways The
 Andover SP10 ...... 105 F8
 Denmead PO7 ...... 299 B7
 Gosport PO12 ...... 369 B7
 Upton BH16........ 389 C7
Crossway The PO16. 344 C8
Crosswell Cl SO19 .. 292 C5
Croucher's Croft
 SO22............ 403 A7
Crouch La PO8....... 300 A7
Crow Arch La BH24 . 329 B6
Crow Arch Lane Ind Est
 BH24............ 329 B5
Crow Cotts BH24.... 329 D4
Crowdale Dr 4 GU51 .53 E3
Crowders Gn SO21... 244 F8
Crowder Terr SO22 . 403 D5
Crowe Hill Ct 2
 BH15............ 390 E4
Crowfield Dr RG19 ....2 F3
Crow Hill Top BH24 . 330 A4
Crowholt GU10 ..... 121 D5
Crow La BH24 ...... 329 C5
Crowley Dr GU34 ... 140 A3
Crowlin Ho 1 PO17. 318 E8
Crown Cl
 Poole BH12 .... 391 C5
 Waterlooville PO7... 322 E3
Crown Cl Mews
 GU34............ 139 F3
Crown Cres RG24 ... 70 A6
Crown Ct
 4 Wimborne Minster
 BH21........... 351 B5
 Portsmouth PO1 ... 404 C4
Crown Dr GU9 ...... 99 C5
Crownfields
 RG29............. 72 D2
Crown Gdns GU51....75 B8
Crown Hts RG21..... 69 B5
Crown La
 Farnham GU9 ...... 99 E5
 Newnham RG27..... 71 C8
 Old Basing RG24 .... 70 B6
Crown Mead BH21 .. 351 C4
Crown Mews 1
 PO12............ 369 D5
Crown St
 Portsmouth PO1 ... 404 C4
 Southampton SO15 .. 290 B8
Crown Way RG19 .... 83 D1
Crowsbury Cl PO10 . 324 E3
Crows La GU34 ..... 161 E3
Crows Nest La SO32. 269 F1
Crowsport SO31 .... 316 A3
Crowther Cl SO19 .. 292 C4
Croxton Rd PO1..... 370 B3
Croyde Cl GU14......55 E6
Croydon Cl SO16.... 266 A4
Croye Cl SP10 ..... 105 F9
Cruikshank Lea GU47 35 C6
Crumlins Bsns Ct
 RG29............. 72 C3
Crummock Rd SO53 . 243 A8
Crundles GU31...... 229 B3
Crundwell Ct GU9.... 99 B3
Crusader Ct
 3 Bournemouth
 BH4............ 392 B4
 4 Gosport PO12 ... 369 C8
Crusader Rd
 Bournemouth BH11.. 376 D4
 Hedge End SO30 .... 293 D6
Crusaders Way SO53 242 F6
Cruse Cl SO41 ..... 360 B2
Cruxton Farm Ctyd
 BH21............ 351 D2
Crystal Way PO7... 323 B8

Cucklington Gdns
 BH9............. 378 B4
Cuckmere La SO16.. 289 D8
Cuckoo Bushes La
 SO53............ 243 C8
Cuckoo Cl RG25......89 E1
Cuckoo Hill Rly★
 SP6............. 282 C1
Cuckoo Hill Way
 BH23............ 357 C1
Cuckoo La
 17 Southampton
 SO14........... 290 F3
 Stubbington PO14 .. 367 B8
Cuckoo Rd BH12.... 391 A8
Cudbury Dr 8 GU51..53 E3
Cudnell Ave BH11... 377 A6
Cudworth Mead
 SO30............ 269 D1
Cufaude Bsns Pk
 RG26............. 48 D8
Cufaude La
 Bramley RG26 ..... 28 D1
 Cufaude RG26 ...... 48 E6
Cuffelle Cl RG24 .... 49 A3
Cuffnells Cl BH24 ... 305 B8
Cul-De-Sac PO14 ... 397 C8
Culford Ave SO40 ... 288 F6
Culford Cl BH8...... 378 F2
Culford Ct 1 BH8... 393 A5
Culford Way SO40... 288 F6
Cull Cl BH12 .... 392 C8
Cullen Cl GU46...... 34 A5
Cullens Mews 6
 GU11............. 76 E1
Culley View SO24 ... 179 D4
Culliford Cres BH17. 375 E2
Culloden Cl PO15 ... 318 E2
Culloden Rd PO14.. 342 F6
Cullwood La BH25 .. 383 B5
Cully Terr PO13 .... 343 C4
Culver Cl SO31 ..... 315 C7
Culver Cl SO16..... 265 D2
Culver Dr PO11 .... 373 C1
Culverhayes Ct 5
 BH21............ 351 B4
Culverhayes Pl BH21 351 B6
Culverhayes Rd
 BH21............ 351 B6
Culverin Sq PO3 .... 346 A4
Culverlands Bsns Pk
 SO32............ 295 E6
Culverlands Cl SO32 295 E7
Culverlands Cres
 GU12............. 77 E3
Culverley Cl SO40 .. 333 F1
Culver Mews SO23 . 403 E5
Culver Rd
 2 Portsmouth
 PO4............ 371 C2
 Basingstoke RG21.... 69 A3
 Newbury RG14 ...... 5 D8
 New Milton BH25 .. 382 F2
 Winchester SO23 ... 403 D4
Culverwell Gdns 6
 SO23............ 403 D5
Culvery Gdns SO18.. 268 B2
Cumberland Ave
 Basingstoke RG22.... 68 E1
 Chandler's Ford SO53 243 E6
 Emsworth PO10...... 324 F4
Cumberland Bsns Ctr
 PO1............. 404 C3
Cumberland Cl SO53 243 E6
Cumberland Ho PO1 370 A6
**Cumberland House
 Natural History Mus★**
 PO4............. 370 F1
Cumberland Inf Sch
 PO4............. 371 A3
Cumberland Pl SO15 290 F5
Cumberland Rd PO5 404 D3
Cumberland St
 Portsmouth PO1 ... 370 A6
 Southampton SO14 .. 291 B4
Cumberland Way
 SO45............ 313 D3
Cumber Rd SO31.... 316 E3
Cumbria Ct GU14 .... 56 C1
Cumbrian Way SO16 289 F8
Cummins Cl GU10 .. 106 C7
Cummins Gn SO31.. 293 A1
Cumnor Rd BH1 .... 393 A3
Cunard Ave SO15 ... 290 C8
Cunard Rd SO14 .... 291 A2
Cundell Way SO23 .. 154 B1
Cunningham Ave
 SO32............ 271 A8
Cunningham Cl
 Bournemouth BH11.. 377 A3
 Christchurch BH23 .. 396 A6
 Portsmouth PO2 .... 345 D4
 Ringwood BH24 .... 329 C6
Cunningham Cres
 Bournemouth BH11.. 377 A3
 Southampton SO19 . 292 B4
Cunningham Ct
 18 Portsmouth
 PO5............ 370 D2
 New Milton BH25 .. 382 F2
Cunningham Dr
 Gosport PO13 ...... 343 D4
 Locks Heath SO31... 317 A4
Cunningham Gdns
 SO31............ 315 F8

Cunningham Ho
 4 North Tidworth
 SP9............. 78 E8
 Bishop's Waltham
 SO32........... 271 B8
Cunningham Pl
 BH11............ 377 A3
Cunningham Rd
 Horndean PO8....... 300 C7
 Waterlooville PO7... 322 D5
Cunnington Rd GU14. 56 C2
Cupernham Cl SO51. 216 A1
Cupernham Inf Sch
 SO51............ 216 B1
Cupernham Jun Sch
 SO51............ 216 B1
Cupernham La SO51 216 A2
Curdridge Cl 2 PO9 324 A5
Curdridge La SO32.. 271 C3
Curdridge Prim Sch
 SO32............ 294 D8
Curlew Cl
 Basingstoke RG22.... 68 A1
 Emsworth PO10..... 348 E7
 Ferndown BH22...... 353 B7
 Hythe SO45 .... 314 B2
 Southampton SO16 . 266 B5
Curlew Ct GU11......99 E7
Curlew Dr
 Hythe SO45 .... 314 B2
 Portchester PO16 ... 343 F8
Curlew Gdns PO8 ... 299 F4
Curlew Path 3 PO4. 371 B5
Curlew Rd
 Bournemouth BH8... 378 D2
 Christchurch BH23 .. 396 A6
Curlews GU34 ..... 139 F6
Curlew Sq SO50..... 243 C7
Curlews The BH31 .. 303 A5
Curlew Wlk
 Gosport PO13 ...... 343 A3
 Hythe SO45 .... 314 B2
Curlieu Rd BH15.... 390 E6
Curling Way RG14..... 2 A4
Curly Bridge Cl GU14. 55 D8
Curlys Way RG7...... 14 B6
Curnock Ct RG14...... 1 C1
Curtis Cl GU35 ..... 165 C5
Curtis Ct GU52 ..... 75 A6
Curtis La GU35...... 165 C6
Curtis Mead PO2.... 345 F4
Curtis Mus★ GU34 . 139 F3
Curtis Rd
 Alton GU34 .... 140 A2
 Poole BH12 .... 391 C5
Curtiss Gdns PO12 .. 368 F4
Curve The
 Gosport PO13 ...... 343 B2
 Horndean PO8...... 299 F6
Curzon Ct
 46 Bournemouth
 BH4............ 392 C3
 Southampton SO16 . 266 D4
Curzon Dr GU52 .... 75 A5
Curzon Howe Rd
 PO1............. 370 A5
Curzon Pl SO41 .... 385 D2
Curzon Rd
 Bournemouth BH1... 393 D6
 Poole BH14 .... 391 A3
 Waterlooville PO7... 322 E2
Curzon Way BH23... 396 D8
Cusden Dr SP10 .... 83 A2
Custards Rd SO43.... 309 F6
Custards The SO43.. 310 A6
Cutbush La
 Southampton SO18.. 292 B8
 West End SO18 .... 268 A1
Cuthbert Rd
 Ash Vale GU12...... 77 F6
 Portsmouth PO1 ... 370 F6
Cuthburga Rd BH21. 351 C4
Cuthbury Cl BH21... 351 A4
Cuthbury Gdns BH21 351 A5
Cutler Cl
 New Milton BH25 ... 383 C3
 Poole BH12 .... 392 C7
Cutlers La PO14..... 367 C8
Cutlers Pl BH21..... 352 A5
Cutter Ave SO31 ... 316 E1
Cut Throat La
 Droxford SO32...... 249 B2
 Swanmore SO32 ... 272 C6
Cutts Arch SO32 ... 273 B7
Cutts Rd GU11.......77 B7
Cuxhaven Way SP10.. 82 F3
Cygnet Cl RG19 ...... 2 F3
Cygnet Ct
 Fleet GU51 .... 54 B3
 Newbury RG14 ...... 1 D3
 Portchester PO16 ... 343 F8
Cygnet Ho PO12 .... 369 B8
Cygnet Rd PO6 .... 346 F7
Cygnus Gdns SO45 . 313 F2
Cynthia Cl BH12 .... 391 B7
Cynthia Ho BH12... 391 B7
Cynthia Rd BH12... 391 B7
Cypress Ave SO19... 291 F5
Cypress Cl RG40......16 E8
Cypress Cres PO8... 300 A5
Cypress Dr GU51..... 54 C1
Cypress Gdns
 Botley SO30........ 294 A7
 Totton SO40....... 288 C7
Cypress Gr
 Andover SP10 ...... 105 C7
 Ash Vale GU12...... 77 D7
 Hordle SO41 ...... 399 D8

Cypress Hill Ct GU14 . . 35 D1
Cypress Ho **3** RG14 . . . . 1 C2
Cypress Rd GU35 . . . . 164 A2
Cypress Way
 Blackwater GU17 . . . . . 34 F5
 Grayshott GU26 . . . . . 167 B2
Cyprus Rd
 Basingstoke RG22 . . . . 91 C5
 Portsmouth PO2 . . . . 370 E8
 Titchfield PO14 . . . . . 317 C1
Cyril Rd BH8 . . . . 393 C6
Cyril Vokins Rd RG14 . . . 2 C2

D

Dacombe Cl BH16 . . . 389 C7
Dacombe Dr BH16 . . . 389 C7
Dacre Cl SP10 . . . . 82 D3
Dacres Wlk **3** SO41 . 399 D5
Daffodil Rd GU22 . . . . . 91 A8
Daffodil Rd SO16 . . . . 267 C4
Daggons Rd SP6 . . . . 280 D6
Dagmar Mews **24**
 PO5 . . . . 370 C2
Dahlia Cl RG22 . . . . . . .91 B8
Dahlia Cl BH15 . . . . . 390 E6
Dahlia Rd SO16 . . . . . 267 C4
Daintree Cl SO19 . . . . 292 D3
Dairy Cl
 Christchurch BH23 . . . 395 D7
 Corfe Mullen BH21 . . 374 B4
 Redlynch SP5 . . . . . 235 D8
Dairy Gate Rd GU14 . . 76 F8
Dairy Ho SP11 . . . . . . 57 A2
Dairy La SO16 . . . . . . 265 B5
Dairymoor PO17 . . . . 296 A4
Dairy Wlk RG27 . . . . . . 52 D6
Daisy Cl BH15 . . . . . 390 E6
Daisy La
 Gosport PO12 . . . . . 369 B5
 Locks Heath SO31 . . 317 C3
Daisy Mead PO7 . . . . 323 A7
Daisy Rd SO16 . . . . . 267 B4
Dakota Cl BH23 . . . . . 396 B7
Dalby Cres RG14 . . . . . .6 A8
Dale Cl
 Farnham GU10 . . . . . 121 D7
 Littleton SO22 . . . . . 175 A5
 Poole BH15 . . . . 390 F6
Dale Dr PO13 . . . . . . 343 B5
Dale Gdns GU47 . . . . . 34 E8
Dale Gn SO53 . . . . . . 243 B8
Dale Park Ho **4**
 PO1 . . . . 404 B3
Dale Rd
 Hythe SO45 . . . . . . 313 C3
 Poole BH15 . . . . . . 390 F6
 Southampton SO16 . . 266 C2
 Stubbington PO14 . . 367 D8
Dales Cl BH21 . . . . . 352 C6
Dales Dr BH21 . . . . . 352 B5
Dales Way SO40 . . . . 288 B8
Dale The PO7 . . . . . . 322 D2
Dale Valley Cl SO16 . . 266 C2
Dale Valley Gdns
 SO16 . . . . 266 C2
Dale Valley Rd
 Poole BH15 . . . . 390 F7
 Southampton SO16 . . 266 C3
Dale View GU27 . . . . 189 D5
Dalewood RG22 . . . . . 68 A3
Dalewood Ave BH11 . 376 E5
Dalewood Rd PO15 . . 318 D1
Dalkeith Arc BH1 . . . 392 F3
Dalkeith Rd
 Corfe Mullen BH21 . . 374 D4
 Poole BH13 . . . . . . 392 A4
Dallence Ho RG25 . . . 88 A7
Dalley Ct GU47 . . . . . . 35 B7
Dalley Way GU33 . . . 207 F4
Dalling Rd BH12 . . . . 392 A5
Dallington Cl PO14 . . 367 F8
Dalmally Gdns SO18 . 291 F8
Dalmeny Rd BH6 . . . 395 A4
Dalzell **19** SO23 . . . . 403 E8
Damask Gdns PO7 . . . 300 B5
Dame Elizabeth Kelly Ct
 3 PO2 . . . . 345 E4
Damen Cl SO30 . . . . 293 A5
Damerham Rd BH8 . . 378 D3
Damerham Trout Lakes★
 SP6 . . . . 256 D2
Dampier Cl SP10 . . . 368 C7
Damsel La RG25 . . . . 114 D2
Damsel Path **14** RG21 69 D5
Damson Cres SO50 . . 245 B1
Damson Hill SO32 . . . 248 B1
Danbury Ct PO10 . . . 325 A2
Dancers Mdw RG24 . . .47 F3
Dances Cl SP10 . . . . . .83 B1
Dances La RG28 . . . . . 86 D6
Dances Way PO14 . . . 372 E4
Dandelion Cl PO13 . . 343 B2
Dando Rd PO7 . . . . . 299 A4
Dandy's Ford La
 SO51 . . . . 213 F1
Danebury Cl PO9 . . . 323 E6
Danebury Gdns
 SO53 . . . . 243 A4
Danebury Rd RG22 . . 91 C6
Danebury Ring★
 SO20 . . . . 148 E8
Danebury Wlk SO16 265 D3
Danebury Wlk SO16 . . 56 D8
Dane Cl SO45 . . . . . . 338 F1
Danecourt Cl BH14 . . 390 F4

Danecourt Rd BH14 . . 390 F4
Danecrest Rd SO41 . . 383 F3
Dane Dr BH22 . . . . . 353 E3
Danegeld Cl SP10 . . . .83 B4
Danehurst Cl SO41 . . 399 A6
Danehurst New Rd
 SO41 . . . . 383 C8
Danehurst Pl
 Andover SP10 . . . . . 105 C8
 Locks Heath SO31 . . 317 C3
Danemark Ct **5**
 SO23 . . . . 403 E6
Dane Rd SO41 . . . . . 399 E6
Danesbrook La PO7 . . 323 A7
Danesbury Ave BH6 . 394 F4
Danesbury Mdws
 BH25 . . . . 383 C5
Daneshill Dr RG24 . . 70 A8
Daneshill East Ind Est
 RG24 . . . . 69 E7
Daneshill Rdbt RG24 . .69 E7
Daneshill Sch RG27 . . 30 D4
Daneshill West Ind Est
 RG24 . . . . 69 D8
Danes Rd
 4 Winchester
   SO23 . . . . 403 E7
 Awbridge SO51 . . . 214 D3
 Portchester PO16 . . 320 B1
Danestead Ho **3**
 BH25 . . . . 383 A3
Danes The RG21 . . . . 69 C5
Danestream Cl SO41 399 D4
Danestream Ct SO41 399 E4
Daneswood Rd
 BH25 . . . . 383 C3
Daniel Gdns **2**
 BH15 . . . . 390 F7
Daniell's Cl SO41 . . . 385 E3
Daniell's Wlk SO41 . . 385 E3
Daniel Rd RG28 . . . . 86 D4
Danley La GU27 . . . . 188 E3
Dansie Cl BH14 . . . . 391 B4
Danvers Dr GU52 . . . 74 E4
Daphne Dr GU52 . . . . 74 E3
Dapple Pl SO40 . . . . 264 B1
Darby Green La GU17 .34 F6
Darby Green Rd GU17 .34 F5
Darby's Cl BH15 . . . . 390 D6
Darby's Cnr BH17 . . . 375 C2
Darby's La BH17 . . . . 375 C2
Darby's La N BH17 . . 390 D8
Darcy Cl RG21 . . . . . 69 C7
Darcy Ho RG22 . . . . . 68 C3
Darent Ct **22** RG21 . . 69 D5
Dares Farm GU10 . . . .74 E1
Dare's La GU10 . . . . . 74 F1
Dark La
 Blackfield SO45 . . . . 338 F1
 Cheriton SO24 . . . . 201 D5
 Hinton BH23 . . . . . . 382 A4
 New Alresford SO24 . 179 F2
 Sherborne St John
   RG24 . . . . 47 E3
Darley Rd BH22 . . . . 353 C3
Darlington Gdns
 SO16 . . . . 266 D1
Darlington Rd
 Basingstoke RG21 . . . 69 A7
 Portsmouth PO4 . . . 370 B7
Darnan Rd **6** SO14 . . 291 A7
Darracott Cl GU15 . . 36 F8
Darracott Rd BH5 . . . 394 B5
Darren Cl PO14 . . . . 342 D4
Darren Ct **9** PO16 . . . 319 B2
Darrington GU15 . . . 36 E5
Darset Ave GU51 . . . 54 A2
Dart Cl
 Finchampstead RG40 . 16 D6
 Thatcham RG19 . . . . . .2 F5
Dart Ct **19** SP10 . . . . 83 D3
Dart Ho SO18 . . . . . 291 F6
Dartington Rd SO50 . 244 F5
Dartmoor Wlk RG22 . . 68 D3
Dartmoor Bldgs **5**
 PO14 . . . . 343 A6
Dartmouth Cl **6**
 PO12 . . . . 369 C8
Dartmouth Ct **5**
 PO12 . . . . 369 C8
Dartmouth Mews
 PO5 . . . . 404 A1
Dartmouth Rd PO3 . . 346 A2
Dartmouth Way RG22 68 C3
Dartmouth Wlk RG22 . 68 C3
Dart Rd
 Farnborough GU14 . . 55 B6
 West End SO18 . . . . 268 B3
Darvill Rd SO41 . . . . 181 A5
Darvills La GU9 . . . . . .99 B2
Darwin Ave BH23 . . . 379 E1
Darwin Cl PO13 . . . . 367 F4
Darwin Ct
 2 Camberley GU15 . . 35 F3
 4 Poole BH13 . . . . . 392 A4
Darwin Gr GU11 . . . . 77 A3
Darwin Ho PO1 . . . . 404 C4
Darwin Rd
 Eastleigh SO50 . . . . 244 B4
 Southampton SO15 . . 290 E7
Darwin Way PO13 . . . 368 D6
Dashwood Cl GU34 . . 139 D2
Dasna Rd SP9 . . . . . . 78 D5

Daubney Gdns PO9 . . 323 C6
Daulston Rd PO1 . . . 370 F7
Daunch Cl SP9 . . . . . . 78 D7
Dauntsey Dro SP11 . . 81 A2
Dauntsey La SP11 . . . 81 A1
D Ave SO45 . . . . 338 E5
Davenport Cl
 Gosport PO13 . . . . . 368 C6
 Upton BH16 . . . . . . 389 C7
Daventry La PO3 . . . 346 C4
David Cowan Ho **23**
 SO23 . . . . 403 D6
David Ct SO51 . . . . . 241 A6
David Hart Bsns Ctr
 SP5 . . . . 234 E8
Davidia Ct PO7 . . . . 323 A6
David Newberry Dr
 PO13 . . . . 368 A6
David's La BH24 . . . . 328 D5
Davidson Cl SO43 . . . 314 B4
Davidson Ct **42** PO1 . 370 A1
David Way BH15 . . . . 389 D2
Davis Cl PO13 . . . . . 368 C8
Davis Ct BH12 . . . . . 391 E5
Davis Field BH25 . . . 382 F2
Davis Gdns GU47 . . . 35 C7
Davis Rd BH12 . . . . . 391 E5
Davis Way PO14 . . . . 343 A6
Davy Cl RG22 . . . . . . 68 C3
Dawkins Bsns Ctr
 BH15 . . . . 389 D3
Dawkins Rd BH15 . . . 389 D3
Dawkins Way BH25 . . 383 A2
Daw La PO11 . . . . . . 372 F8
Dawlish Ave SO40 . . . 290 D8
Dawnay Cl SO16 . . . . 267 C5
Dawnay Rd
 Camberley GU15 . . . 36 A8
 Sandhurst GU15 . . . 35 F7
Dawn Cl BH10 . . . . . 377 C5
Dawn Ct SO15 . . . . . 36 D7
Dawn Gdns SO22 . . . 403 A4
Daws Ave BH11 . . . . 377 B2
Dawson Rd SO19 . . . 292 C2
Daylesford BH14 . . . 391 A2
Dayrell Cl SO40 . . . . 264 B1
Day's Ct BH21 . . . . . 351 D4
Dayshes Cl PO13 . . . 343 B3
Dayslondon Rd PO7 . 323 A5
Days Meadow RG20 . . 21 A7
Daytona BH14 . . . . . 402 C7
D-Day Mus★ PO5 . . . 370 C1
Deacon Cl SO19 . . . . 292 A5
Deacon Cres SO19 . . 292 A5
Deacon Gdns BH11 . . 377 A5
Deacon Rd
 Bournemouth BH11 . 377 A5
 Kimpton SP11 . . . . . 80 C4
 Locks Heath SO31 . . 317 B8
 Southampton SO19 . . 292 A5
Deacon Trad Est
 SO50 . . . . 244 C2
Deadbrook La GU12 . . 77 C3
Deadman Hill SP6 . . . 259 D5
Deadmans La RG14,
 RG19 . . . . .5 F6
Deadmoor La RG20 . . .5 C1
Deakin Cl SO53 . . . . 243 C5
Deal Cl PO14 . . . . . . 342 C4
Deal Rd PO6 . . . . . . 321 E1
Dean Cl
 Hamworthy BH15 . . 389 E3
 Winchester SO22 . . 403 A8
Dean Court
 (Bournemouth FC)
 BH7 . . . . 393 F6
Dean Ct
 3 Southampton,Bitterne
   Manor SO18 . . . . 291 E8
 Hedge End SO30 . . . 293 C7
 Southampton SO18 . 292 A8
Deane Cotts RG25 . . . 66 A1
Deane Ct **22** PO9 . . . 324 B5
Deane Down Dro
 SO22 . . . . 175 B4
Deane Gdns **5** PO13 367 F3
Deanery The SO53 . . 243 B8
Deanes Cl RG21 . . . . 69 C6
Deane's Park Rd
 PO16 . . . . 319 D1
Dean Farm PO17 . . . 319 A5
Deanfield Cl SO31 . . 315 D7
Deanfields Ct SO18 . 292 A8
Dean La
 Bishop's Waltham
   SO32 . . . . 247 E3
 Finchdean PO8,PO9 . 301 D5
 Whiteparish SP5 . . . 212 B4
 Winchester SO22 . . 175 B2
Dean Par GU15 . . . . 36 D8
Dean Park Cres BH1 . 392 F4
Dean Park Rd BH1 . . 392 F4
Dean Pl SO53 . . . . . 243 C6
Dean Rd
 Cosham PO6 . . . . . 345 F8
 Fair Oak SO50 . . . . 245 C1
 Southampton SO18 . 292 A7
 West Dean SP5 . . . . 190 B2
 West Tytherley SP5 . 190 E5
Dean Rise SP11 . . . . . 60 F7
Deans Cl SP9 . . . . . . .78 F4
Deans Court La
 BH21 . . . . 351 C4
Deanscroft Rd BH10 . 377 E4
Deans Cl SO41 . . . . 399 D5
Deans Dell GU32 . . . 205 E1
Deansfield Cl SO51 . . 241 B8

Deans Gate PO14 . . . 367 C6
Deans Gr BH21 . . . . 351 C4
Dean Side GU15 . . . . 36 D8
Deansleigh Rd BH7 . . 379 B1
Dean's Rd **6** BH5 . . . 394 B5
Dean St PO1 . . . . . . 370 A5
Deans Sta SP5 . . . . . 190 D3
Deans The BH1 . . . . 392 F4
Dean Swift Cres
 BH14 . . . . 402 C8
Deanswood Dr PO7 . 299 E1
Deanswood Rd RG26 .26 E8
Dean Terr SP11 . . . . 38 C5
Dean Villas PO17 . . . 318 E7
Dear Hay La BH15 . . 390 C2
Dearing Cl SO43 . . . . 309 F4
Debney Lodge PO7 . . 322 F7
Decies Rd BH14 . . . . 391 B5
De Courtenai Cl
 BH11 . . . . 376 E5
Decoutere Cl GU52 . . 74 E4
Dee Cl SO53 . . . . . . 243 A5
Deedman Cl GU12 . . . 77 E2
Deep Dell PO8 . . . . . 300 B5
Deepdene
 Farnham GU10 . . . . 122 B7
 Haslemere GU27 . . . 189 C6
Deepdene La BH11 . . 376 E5
Deeping Cl SO19 . . . 291 F1
Deeping Gate PO7 . . 323 A7
Deep La RG21 . . . . . . 68 F5
Deep Well Dr GU15 . . 36 C5
Deerfield Cl RG26 . . . 29 B2
Deerhurst Cl SO40 . . 288 D6
Deerhurst Cres PO6 . 321 A1
Deerhurst Ho **3**
 PO6 . . . . 321 A1
Deerleap GU35 . . . . 166 A4
Deer Leap PO15 . . . . 318 D5
Deerleap Cl SO45 . . . 314 A3
Deerleap La SO40 . . . 288 D2
Deerleap Way
 Hythe SO45 . . . . . . 314 A3
 New Milton BH25 . . 383 B6
Deer Park Cl BH25 . . 382 F4
Deer Park Farm Ind Est
 SO50 . . . . 245 C4
Deer Park View RG29 72 C3
Deer Rock Rd GU15 . . 36 D6
Deer Wlk SO30 . . . . 293 D8
Dee Way BH15 . . . . . 390 B1
Defender Rd SO19 . . 291 D3
Defender Wlk SO19 . 291 D3
Defiant Rd GU14 . . . . 76 D8
Defoe Cl PO15 . . . . . 317 C8
De Grouchy La SO17 267 A1
De Haviland Cl BH21 351 F2
De Havilland Ho
 BH23 . . . . 396 A6
De Havilland Way
 BH23 . . . . 396 A6
Dehlia Cl **4** SP10 . . . 105 D6
Delamere Gdns
 BH10 . . . . 377 E3
Delamere Rd PO4 . . . 370 E3
Delaval Ho **2** PO1 . . 370 B5
De La Warr Rd SO41 399 C4
Delft Cl SO31 . . . . . 316 F3
Delft Gdns PO8 . . . . 299 F2
Delft Mews BH23 . . . 395 D6
Delhi Cl BH14 . . . . . 391 D3
Delhi Rd BH9 . . . . . 377 F2
Delibes Rd RG22 . . . .91 F8
Delilah Rd BH15 . . . . 389 D2
De Lisle Cl PO2 . . . . 345 F4
De Lisle Rd BH3 . . . . 392 F7
Delius Ave SO19 . . . . 292 D3
Delius Cl RG22 . . . . . .68 E1
Delius Wlk PO7 . . . . 322 E5
Delkeith Ct BH22 . . . 353 D4
Dellands RG25 . . . . . . 88 A7
Dellands La RG25 . . . 88 A7
Dell Cl
 Broadstone BH18 . . 374 E4
 Cosham PO7 . . . . . 322 B2
 Fair Oak SO50 . . . . 245 C1
 Haslemere GU27 . . . 189 E7
Dell Cotts SO24 . . . . 202 F1
Dellcrest Path PO6 . . 322 B2
Dellfield
 High Cross GU32 . . . 205 E2
 Oakley RG23 . . . . . . 67 B3
Dellfield Cl **11** PO6 . 321 A1
Dell Gr GU16 . . . . . . 36 D2
Dell Piece E PO8 . . . 300 C5
Dell Piece W PO8 . . . 300 C5
Dell Quay Cl PO13 . . 343 B2
Dell Rd
 Andover SP10 . . . . . 82 F1
 Finchampstead RG40. 16 E3
 Southampton SO18 . 267 C4
 Winchester SO23 . . . 198 C6
Dell The
 Barton on S BH23 . . 397 F8
 Farnham GU9 . . . . . .99 B7
 Grateley SP11 . . . . . 103 B1
 Havant PO9 . . . . . . 326 E6
 Kingsclere RG20 . . . 24 D2
 Old Basing RG24 . . . 70 C5
 Portchester PO16 . . 319 D1
 Southampton SO15 . 290 E6
 Vernham Dean SP11 . 38 B6
 Yateley GU46 . . . . . 34 C3
Delme Ct **4** PO16 . . . 319 A1
Delme Dr PO16 . . . . . 319 D2
Delme Sq **7** PO16 . . 319 B1

Delphi Way PO7 . . . . 322 F2
Delph Rd BH21 . . . . 375 D8
Delph Woods Woodland
 Trail★ BH18,BH21 . . 375 C7
Delta Bsns Pk
 Alton GU34 . . . . . . 140 B3
 Fareham PO16 . . . . 343 B7
Delta Cl BH23 . . . . . 396 A7
De-Lucy Ave SO17 . . 179 B5
Delunn Bldgs **8**
 SO23 . . . . 403 E6
Delville Cl GU14 . . . . 55 B3
De Mauley Cl BH13 . 402 E8
De Mauley Rd BH13 . 402 E8
De Montfort Rd
 Merley BH21 . . . . . 351 D1
 Newbury RG14 . . . . 1 C5
De Mowbray Way
 SO41 . . . . 385 D2
Dempsey Cl SO19 . . 292 B4
Dempster Ho GU9 . . .99 B8
Denbigh Cl
 Eastleigh SO50 . . . . 243 F5
 Totton SO40 . . . . . . 288 D5
Denbigh Dr PO16 . . . 318 F2
Denbigh Gdns SO16 . 266 F4
Denby Cl **4** GU14 . . . 56 A1
Denby Rd BH15 . . . . 390 E4
Dene Cl
 3 Camberley GU15 . . 36 E8
 Bordon GU35 . . . . . 164 D2
 Chilworth SO16 . . . . 266 F7
 Farnham GU10 . . . . 122 C6
 Ringwood BH24 . . . . 305 C1
 Sarisbury SO31 . . . . 316 E4
Denecote Lodge
 BH13 . . . . 402 H8
Dene Ct SP10 . . . . . 106 B7
Dene Hollow PO6 . . . 346 D8
Dene La GU10 . . . . . 122 C6
Dene La W GU10 . . . 122 C5
Dene Path SP10 . . . . 106 A7
Dene Rd
 Andover SP10 . . . . . 106 B7
 Ashurst SO40 . . . . . 288 C6
 Farnborough GU14 . . 55 D3
Deneside Copse
 SO41 . . . . 385 B1
Dene Terr SO31 . . . . 181 A5
Dene The
 Poole BH13 . . . . . . 392 A4
 Ropley SO24 . . . . . 181 A5
Deneve Ave BH17 . . 375 C1
Dene Way
 Ashurst SO40 . . . . . 288 C3
 Donnington RG14 . . . 1 E5
Dene Wlk
 Farnham GU10 . . . . 122 B6
 Ferndown BH22 . . . 353 E1
Denewood Copse
 BH22 . . . . 326 D3
Denewood Rd
 Bournemouth BH4 . . 392 B3
 West Moors BH22 . . 326 D4
Denewulf Cl **2**
 SO32 . . . . 271 C8
Denham Cl
 Poole BH17 . . . . . . 375 E3
 Stubbington PO14 . . 367 B7
 Winchester SO23 . . 403 D8
Denham Dr
 Basingstoke RG22 . . 68 C2
 Christchurch BH23 . . 381 F1
 Yateley GU46 . . . . . 34 B5
Denham Fields SO50 245 B3
Denham Gdns SO31 . 315 B5
Denham's Cnr SO32 . 269 D5
Denham's La SP11 . . 61 F2
Denhill Cl PO11 . . . . 372 E5
Denholm Cl BH24 . . . 305 D1
Denison Rd BH17 . . . 375 C1
Denman Cl GU51 . . . 54 C1
Denmark La BH15 . . 390 D3
Denmark Rd
 Bournemouth BH9 . . 377 F1
 Newbury RG14 . . . . 1 E3
 Poole BH15 . . . . . . 390 D3
Denmark Sq GU12 . . 77 C2
Denmark St GU12 . . .77 B2
Denmark Terr BH1 . . 393 E6
Denmead BH25 . . . . 383 D4
Denmead Ho PO1 . . 404 C4
Denmead Inf Sch
 PO7 . . . . 299 A4
Denmead Jun Sch
 PO7 . . . . 299 A4
Denmead Pk PO7 . . . 299 A4
Denmead Rd
 Bournemouth BH6 . . 394 D7
 Southampton SO18 . 292 C8
 Tadley RG26 . . . . . . 26 F8
Dennet Ho SO23 . . . 176 D1
Denning Cl GU51 . . . .74 E7
Denning Mead SP10. 105 F7
Denning Mews PO5 . 404 B3
Dennis Rd BH21 . . . . 374 D5
Dennison Ct **18**
 SO15 . . . . 290 B8
Dennistoun Ave
 BH23 . . . . 395 F7
Dennistoun Cl GU15. .36 B5
Denny Cl SO45 . . . . . 339 B3
Densome Cnr SP6 . . 259 A6
Denton Way GU16 . . .36 B2

Denvale Trade Pk
 RG14 . . . . .2 B2
Denvale Trad Pk
 RG21 . . . . 68 F6
Denville Ave PO16 . . 344 D6
Denville Cl PO6 . . . . 346 F8
Denvilles Cl PO9 . . . 324 B2
Denyers Cotts GU34 138 A4
Denzil Ave
 Netley SO31 . . . . . . 315 C6
 Southampton SO14 . 291 B6
Depden Gdns SO45 . . 313 D1
Depedene Cl SO45 . . 338 B4
De Port Hts SO32 . . . 249 C6
Deptford La RG29 . . . 72 A3
Derby Ct **12** PO13 . . 368 C6
Derby Fields RG29 . . 72 C6
Derby Gate SP10 . . . . 82 B1
Derby Ho SO50 . . . . 244 A1
Derby Rd
 Bournemouth BH1 . . 393 C4
 Eastleigh SO50 . . . . 243 F2
 Haslemere GU27 . . . 189 F7
 Newbury RG14 . . . . . 1 D1
 Portsmouth PO2 . . . 345 C1
 Southampton SO14 . 291 B6
De Redvers Rd BH14 391 C2
Dereham Way BH12 . 391 F6
Derek Horn Ct GU15 . 35 F6
Deridene Cl SO40 . . . 288 C6
Derlyn Rd PO16 . . . . 319 A1
Derritt La BH23 . . . . 380 D8
Derrybrian Gdns
 BH25 . . . . 383 A2
Derry Cl GU12 . . . . . . 77 D5
Derry Rd GU14 . . . . . 55 D8
Dersingham Cl PO6 . 321 E1
Derwent Ave GU12 . . 77 D4
Derwent Cl
 Bordon GU35 . . . . . 164 D5
 Bournemouth BH9 . . 378 A2
 Farnborough GU14 . . 55 C3
 Farnham GU9 . . . . . 98 E6
 Ferndown BH22 . . . 354 A6
 Horndean PO8 . . . . 276 C2
 Stubbington PO14 . . 342 D4
 West End SO18 . . . . 268 B1
Derwent Ct **20** SP10 . 83 C2
Derwent Dr SO40 . . . 288 B8
Derwent Gdns SO24 179 D4
Derwent Rd
 Basingstoke RG22 . . 68 A1
 Lee-on-t-S PO13 . . . 367 F3
 New Milton BH25 . . 383 B5
 Southampton SO16 . 265 D1
 Thatcham RG19 . . . . .2 E3
Derwentwater Rd
 BH21 . . . . 351 C2
Desborough Cl
 6 Portsmouth
   PO6 . . . . 321 A1
 Newbury RG14 . . . . 2 C5
Desborough Rd
 SO50 . . . . 244 A2
Devenish Rd SO22 . . 175 D3
Dever Cl SO21 . . . . . 133 A3
Deverel Cl BH23 . . . . 395 A8
Deverell Pl PO7 . . . . 322 C3
Dever Way RG23 . . . . 67 B1
Devils La GU30 . . . . 188 C3
Devine Gdns SO50 . . 244 E2
Devizes Ho **7** SP9 . . .78 F7
Devon Cl
 Chandler's Ford
   SO53 . . . . 243 C5
 Fleet GU51 . . . . 54 B4
 Sandhurst GU47 . . . 35 B5
Devon Dr SO53 . . . . 243 C5
Devon Ho RG24 . . . . 68 D8
Devon Mews **6**
 SO15 . . . . 290 E5
Devon Rd
 Bordon GU35 . . . . . 164 D5
 Christchurch BH23 . . 394 E8
 Farnborough GU14 . . 76 D7
 Poole BH15 . . . . . . 390 E5
 Portsmouth PO3 . . . 346 A3
Devonshire Ave PO4 371 A4
Devonshire Dr GU15 . 36 D7
Devonshire Gdns
 Bursledon SO31 . . . 293 A2
 Hythe SO45 . . . . . . 338 A8
Devonshire Inf Sch
 PO4 . . . . 370 F4
Devonshire Mans **10**
 SO15 . . . . 290 F6
Devonshire Pl
 6 Basingstoke
   RG21 . . . . 69 A4
 Aldershot GU11 . . . . 76 D1
Devonshire Rd SO15 290 F6
Devonshire Sq PO4 . 370 F4
Devonshire Way
 PO14 . . . . 342 C8
Dewar Cl PO15 . . . . 317 C5
Deweys La BH24 . . . 328 F2
Dew La SO50 . . . . . . 243 F5
Dewlands Pk BH31 . . 302 D6
Dewlands Rd BH31 . . 302 D6
Dewlands Way BH31 302 E6
Dewlish Cl BH17 . . . . 376 A2
Dewpond Wlk RG24 . . 69 C1
Dewsbury Ct **3**
 SO18 . . . . 268 A2
Dexter Sq SP10 . . . . 83 C3

Dexter Way GU51 54 B4
Dhekelia Ct PO1 404 C4
Dial Cl BH23 357 D2
Diamond Cl SP6 281 E8
Diamond Ct
2 Waterlooville PO7 322 E8
Fordingbridge SP6 281 E8
Diamond Hill GU15 36 C7
Diamond Ho GU12 77 D6
Diamond Ridge GU15 36 C7
Diamond St 2 PO5 404 A1
Diamond Way GU14 76 C8
Diana Cl
Basingstoke RG22 68 E3
Emsworth PO10 324 E4
Ferndown BH22 353 D6
Gosport PO12 368 E4
Diana Ct 7 BH23 397 A7
Diana Way BH21 374 E7
Dibben Wlk SO51 216 C1
Dibble Dr SO52 241 F3
Dibden Cl
Bournemouth BH8 378 D3
Havant PO9 323 C4
Dibden Lodge Cl SO45 313 F5
Dibles Pk SO31 316 E1
Dibles Rd
Locks Heath SO31 316 D1
Locks Heath SO31 316 E1
Dibley Cl RG22 68 C3
Dickens Cl PO2 370 D7
Dickens Dell SO40 288 B7
Dickens Dr PO15 294 C1
Dickens Ho PO4 371 B4
Dickens La RG24 70 A4
Dickenson Wlk SO24 179 D4
Dickens Rd BH6 394 D7
Dickens Way GU46 34 A5
Dickens Wlk RG14 5 E8
Dicker's La GU34 140 A4
Dickins La GU31 229 A5
Dickinson Rd PO4 370 F5
Dickson Pk PO17 296 A4
Didcot Rd
Poole BH17 390 D7
Southampton SO15 266 C1
Dieppe Cres PO2 345 E4
Dieppe Gdns PO12 368 F4
Digby Rd RG14 1 C4
Digby Way GU33 186 A4
Dight Rd PO12 369 C3
Diligence Cl SO31 293 A1
Dillington Ho 4 PO7 322 E8
Dilly La
Barton on S BH25 398 A7
Hartley Wintney RG27 52 C4
Dimond Cl SO18 267 E1
Dimond Hill SO18 267 E1
Dimond Rd SO18 267 E2
Dines Cl SP11 60 E7
Dingle Rd BH5 394 B4
Dingle Way SO31 317 A4
Dingley Rd BH15 390 D6
Dingley Way GU14 76 E8
Dinham Ct BH25 383 D4
Dinham Rd BH25 383 D4
Dinorben Ave GU52 74 F7
Dinorben Beeches GU51 74 E7
Dinorben Cl GU52 74 F7
Dinwoodie Dr RG24 68 E8
Dippenhall Rd GU10 98 A2
Dippenhall St GU10 97 D6
Diprose Rd BH21 374 E7
Dirty Cnr RG28 85 F8
Disa Ho SO15 290 E6
Discovery Cl PO14 342 C5
Discovery Court Bsns Ctr BH12 376 E2
Discovery Ct 8 RG14 1 E2
Disraeli Rd BH23 395 D6
Ditcham Cres PO9 323 E4
Ditcham Park Sch GU31 277 F8
Ditchbury SO41 385 D6
Ditchfield La RG40 16 C8
Ditton Cl PO14 342 C4
Ditton Cotts SO42 336 F1
Dittons The RG40 16 D6
Divers Cl GU34 139 F6
Dixon Rd RG27 49 B6
Dixons La SO20 170 B7
Dockenfield Cl PO9 323 C4
Dockenfield St GU10 143 A6
Dock La SO42 337 A1
Dock Mill Cotts 18 PO5 370 D2
Dock Rd PO12 369 C5
Doctors Acre RG27 51 D1
Doctors Dro SP11 60 D7
Doctor's Hill SO51 214 A3
Doctors La GU32 225 C5
Dodds La SO32 272 C5
Dodgson Cl SP6 258 E8
Dodsells Well RG40 16 D8
Dodwell La SO31 293 B3
Dodwell Terr SO31 293 B1
Doe Copse Way BH25 382 E4
Doe Wlk SO30 293 D8
Dogdean BH21 351 C8
Dogflud Way GU9 99 A3
Dogkennel La PO7 91 B6
Dogmersfield CE Prim Sch RG27 74 A7
Dogwood Dell 1 PO7 322 F5
Dogwood Rd BH18 374 E2
Doiley Bottom SP11 40 D1
Doiley Hill SP11 40 C3
Dolbery Rd N BH12 376 D2
Dolbery Rd S BH12 376 C1
Dollis Ct GU9 99 B3
Dollis Dr GU9 99 B3
Dollis Gn RG26 28 F3
Dolman Rd
Gosport PO12 369 C4
Newbury RG14 1 E4
Dolomans La SP11 60 E8
Dolphin Ave BH10 377 E5
Dolphin Cl
Aldermaston RG7 9 D7
Bishopstoke SO50 244 F2
Haslemere GU27 189 C6
Dolphin Cres PO12 369 C4
Dolphin Ct
11 Portsmouth PO5 370 E1
Poole BH13 392 B2
Stubbington PO14 342 B4
Dolphin Ctr 3 BH15 390 C2
Dolphin Hill SO21 220 A6
Dolphin Mans BH25 398 A6
Dolphin Pl BH25 398 A7
Dolphin Quays 10 BH15 390 C1
Dolphin Way PO12 369 D2
Dolton Mews RG14 1 D3
Dolton Rd SO16 265 F3
Doman Rd GU15 35 E4
Dombey Ct 5 PO1 370 D7
Dome Alley SO23 403 E5
Dominica Cl RG24 48 C2
Dominie Wlk 1 PO13 367 F3
Dominion Ctr BH11 376 E3
Dominion Rd BH11 376 E3
Dominy Cl SO45 314 B4
Domitian Gdns RG24 68 C8
Domum Rd
Portsmouth PO2 345 F2
Winchester SO23 403 F4
Domvilles App PO2 345 B1
Donaldson Rd PO6 345 F6
Doncaster Rd SO50 268 A8
Donigers Cl SO32 272 A6
Donigers Dell SO32 272 A6
Donkey La SO30 294 A7
Donnelly Rd BH6 394 F5
Donnelly St PO12 369 A7
Donnington Castle* RG14 1 C7
Donnington Cl 3 GU15 35 F4
Donnington Ct 2 SO23 403 E7
Donnington Dr
Chandler's Ford SO53 243 B3
Christchurch BH23 396 B7
Donnington Gr SO17 267 C2
Donnington Hospital RG14 1 C6
Donnington Lodge RG14 1 D6
Donnington Pk RG14 1 D6
Donnington Sq RG14 1 D5
Donoughmore Rd 1 BH1 393 E4
Doras Green La GU10 98 A2
Dora's Green La
Dippenhall GU10 98 A3
Ewshot GU10 98 A5
Dorcas Cl PO7 300 A1
Dorcas Ct GU15 35 F3
Dorchester Cl RG23 68 B5
Dorchester Ct SO15 290 F8
Dorchester Gdns BH15 390 E5
Dorchester Mans BH1 393 D3
Dorchester Rd
Hook RG27 51 A1
Poole BH15 390 E6
Upton BH16 389 A7
Dorchester Way RG29 72 A4
Dore Ave PO16 320 C1
Doreen Cl GU14 55 C7
Dores La
Lower Slackstead SO51 217 B7
Winchester SO21, SO51 195 D2
Dorian Gr SO24 179 B4
Doric Cl SO53 243 F7
Dorking Cres PO6 345 F7
Dorland Gdns SO40 288 D6
Dormer Cl RG14 5 B6
Dormers The BH25 382 F1
Dormington Rd PO6 321 C1
Dormy Cl SO31 316 D3
Dormy Way PO13 343 B1
Dorney Ct 1 PO6 346 A7
Dorneywood Way RG14 2 B4
Dornie Rd BH13 402 E7
Dornmere La PO7 323 A7
Dorothy Ct
Newbury RG14 2 B4
Portsmouth PO5 404 C1
Dorothy Dymond St PO1 404 B3
Dorrel Cl RG22 91 B6
Dorrick Ct 10 SO15 290 F7
Dorrien Rd PO12 369 B8
Dorrita Ave PO8 300 A4
Dorrita Cl PO4 370 F2
Dorrits The SO40 288 B7
Dorset Ave BH22 353 D3
Dorset Cl PO8 300 B6
Dorset Ct GU15 36 D8
Dorset Grange BH23 394 F7
Dorset Heavy Horse & Animal Ctr* BH21 279 D2
Dorset Ho
Basingstoke RG24 68 E8
Poole BH13 392 A2
Dorset Lake Ave BH14 402 B8
Dorset Lake Manor BH14 391 A2
Dorset Rd
Ash Vale GU12 77 F5
Bournemouth BH4 392 C5
Chandler's Ford SO53 243 C3
Christchurch BH23 395 F8
Dorset St SO14 291 A6
Dorset Way BH17 390 E7
Dorstone Rd PO6 321 C1
Dorval Ho 6 SO15 290 E7
Dorval Manor 7 SO15 290 E7
Doswell Way RG21 69 C6
Douai Cl GU14 56 A4
Doublet Cl RG19 2 E3
Doughty Way SP10 83 E1
Douglas Ave BH23 395 A6
Douglas Cl BH16 389 C7
Douglas Cres SO19 292 D6
Douglas Gdns
Havant PO9 324 A4
Poole BH12 391 E5
Douglas Gr GU10 122 A5
Douglas Mews
Bournemouth BH6 394 C5
Upton BH16 389 C8
Douglas Pl GU14 55 E5
Douglas Rd
Andover SP11 105 B7
Bournemouth BH6 394 E4
Poole BH12 391 E5
Portsmouth PO3 370 F7
Douglas Ride RG20 21 C8
Douglas Way SO45 313 F4
Doulton Gdns BH14 391 B2
Douro Cl RG26 9 B1
Doussie Cl BH16 389 B8
Dove Cl
Andover SP10 83 B2
Basingstoke RG22 67 F1
Waterlooville PO8 299 F4
Dovecote Cotts SO21 131 C4
Dove Ct GU34 140 A6
Dove Dale SO50 243 D2
Dove Gdns 3 SO31 317 B5
Dove House Sch RG21 69 B7
Dove La SO51 217 B7
Dover Cl
Basingstoke RG23 68 D6
New Alresford SO24 179 D4
Poole BH13 392 A3
Stubbington PO14 367 B8
Dovercourt Rd PO6 346 A6
Dover Ct PO11 372 E5
Dover Rd
Poole BH13 392 A3
Portsmouth PO3 371 A8
Dover St SO14 291 A7
Doveshill Cres BH10 377 D3
Doveshill Gdns BH10 377 D3
Doveshill Mobile Home Pk BH10 377 D3
Doveton Way RG14 1 F4
Doveys Cl BH24 331 A3
Dowden Gr GU34 140 A5
Dowds Cl SO30 293 B8
Dowell Ho 10 PO4 371 B2
Dowlands Cl BH10 377 D4
Dowlands Rd BH10 377 D4
Down End PO6 322 C1
Downend Rd PO16 319 F1
Down End Rd PO6 322 C1
Downey Cl BH11 376 F2
Down Farm Cotts SP6 232 C4
Down Farm La SO22 175 E7
Down Farm Pl PO8 276 C1
Down Gate SO24 179 C4
Downham Cl PO8 299 F3
Downhouse Rd PO8 276 A4
Downing Ct PO14 317 C1
Downing St GU9 98 F2
Down La RG25 70 F3
Downland Cl
Botley SO30 293 F7
Locks Heath SO31 317 A4
Downland Pl SO30 293 B5
Downlands Cl SP5 234 F6
Downlands Pl BH17 390 F8
Downlands Rd SO22 197 B4
Downlands Way
South Wonston SO21 153 C4
South Wonston SO21 153 D4
Downley Point PO9 324 B4
Downley Rd PO9 324 B4
Down Lodge Cl SP6 281 A6
Down Rd
Horndean PO8 276 B1
Horndean PO8 300 C8
Kimpton SP11 80 B2
Downs Cl
Farnborough GU14 55 C7
Waterlooville PO7 322 F3
Downscroft Gdns SO30 293 B7
Downshill GU10 100 B4
Downside
Beacon Hill GU26 167 B7
Gosport PO13 343 D2
Downside Ave SO19 292 A6
Downside Cotts SP11 124 F7
Downside Rd
Waterlooville PO7 322 C3
Winchester SO22 175 B2
Downs La SN8 18 B7
Downsland Par RG21 68 F4
Downsland Rd RG21 69 A4
Down's Park Ave SO40 289 A6
Down's Park Cres SO40 289 A5
Down's Park Rd SO40 289 A6
Downs Rd
Over Wallop SO20 125 D3
South Wonston SO21 153 D4
Down St RG25 90 D1
Downs View GU34 140 E7
Downsview Rd GU35 166 A5
Downsview Way SP11 79 D6
Downs Way GU34 139 D2
Downsway The PO16 344 C8
Downton CE Prim Sch SP5 234 E8
Downton Cl BH8 378 D3
Downton Cvn Pk SO41 399 A6
Downton Hill SP5 235 D7
Downton Ho 2 PO6 345 C8
Downton La SO41 398 F7
Downton Rd SO18 267 F2
Downton Sch SP5 234 E7
Downview Cl GU26 167 B6
Downview Rd SP6 231 A4
Downwood Cl
Fordingbridge SP6 257 D2
Hythe SO45 313 C2
Downwood Way PO8 276 C1
Doyen Ct RG14 1 F3
Doyle Ave PO2 345 E3
Doyle Cl PO2 345 E4
Doyle Ct
1 Portsmouth PO2 345 E3
Southampton SO19 291 F1
Doyle Gdns GU46 34 A5
Doyle Ho PO9 323 B3
Doyne Rd BH14 391 E4
Dradfield La SO32 297 C8
Dragon Est PO6 346 E7
Dragonfly Dr RG24 69 F8
Dragon La BH23 356 B7
Dragon St GU31 228 F3
Dragoon Cl SO19 292 C4
Dragoon Ct 10 GU11 76 C2
Dragoon Ho PO7 299 C1
Dragoon Way BH23 394 F7
Drake Ave GU16 56 E1
Drake Cl
Christchurch BH23 395 F6
Finchampstead RG40 16 C7
Locks Heath SO31 317 B5
Marchwood SO40 290 A2
New Milton BH25 382 F3
Ringwood BH24 305 D1
Drake Ct
4 Poole BH15 390 C1
Andover SP10 83 D1
Lee-on-t-S PO13 367 D4
Drake Ho 3 PO1 370 A5
Drakeleys Field GU30 209 F2
Drake Rd
Bishopstoke SO50 244 E4
Lee-on-t-S PO13 367 D4
Poole BH15 390 C1
Drakes Cl SO45 313 F2
Drakes Ct SO40 290 A3
Drakes Rd BH22 353 F3
Draper Rd
Bournemouth BH11 377 A4
Christchurch BH23 395 E7
Drapers Copse Mobile Home Pk SO45 313 D4
Draycote Rd PO8 276 C3
Draycott Rd BH10 377 D2
Drayman's Way GU34 139 F3
Drayton Cl SO19 314 F8
Drayton La PO6 322 B1
Drayton Pk SO21 108 D2
Drayton Pl SO40 288 D7
Drayton Rd PO2 345 E1
Drayton St SO22 403 A4
Draytons View RG19 6 B7
Dreadnought Rd PO14 342 F5
Dresden Dr PO8 299 E3
Dreswick Cl BH23 379 D4
Drew Cl BH12 392 C7
Drew Grange BH15 389 E4
Drewitt Ind Est BH11 376 E3
Drift Rd
Bordon GU33,GU35 186 A8
Chilbolton SO20 129 F2
Clanfield PO8 276 C4
Fareham PO16 319 D2
Drift The
Bentley GU10 120 A4
Rowlands Castle PO9 301 B1
Driftway Rd RG27 51 C1
Driftwood Gdns
Portsmouth PO4 371 C2
Totton SO40 288 C6
Drill Shed Rd PO2 345 B1
Drinkwater Cl SO50 243 F3
Drive The
Fareham PO16 319 A1
Farnham GU9 121 F7
Gosport PO13 343 A2
Havant PO9 323 F3
Newbury RG14 5 C8
Oakley RG23 67 B1
Poole,Lilliput BH13 402 D7
Poole,Upper Parkstone BH12 391 D5
Sherfield English SO51 213 B1
Southbourne PO10 349 D8
Totton SO40 288 F5
West End SO18 268 B3
West Wellow SO51 239 B2
Droffatts Ho SO15 290 D7
Drove Cl SO21 219 F5
Drove Cotts GU34 162 F8
Drove Hill SO20 129 A3
Drove La SO24 179 B5
Drove Rd
Chilbolton SP11 129 B3
Southampton SO19 292 B4
Southwick PO17 321 A4
Drovers End GU51 54 C4
Drovers Way GU9 98 E6
Drove The
Andover SP10 105 D8
Blackfield SO45 338 E1
Durley SO32 270 D8
Headley, Nr Greenham RG19 7 F1
Horton Heath SO50 269 D6
Redlynch SP5 235 D6
Southampton SO18 292 A7
Swanmore SO32 272 B5
Totton SO40 264 B1
Twyford SO21 219 F5
West End SO30 268 F3
West Wellow SO51 238 E3
Droxford Cl 2 PO12 368 F4
Droxford Cres RG26 26 E7
Droxford Jun Sch SO32 249 A1
Droxford Rd
Bournemouth BH6 394 B6
East Meon GU32 251 D3
Swanmore SO32 272 D5
Druids Cl BH22 353 D2
Druitt Rd BH23 395 F8
Drum La GU32 228 F3
Drumlanrig Terr 4 PO12 369 C9
Drum Mead GU32 228 E3
Drummond Cl
Four Marks GU34 159 F2
Winchester SO22 403 C3
Drummond Ct
Eastleigh SO50 244 B5
Hythe SO45 314 A5
Southampton SO19 291 E3
Drummond Dr SO14 291 C8
Drummond Rd
Bournemouth BH1 393 D4
Hedge End SO30 269 C1
Hythe SO45 314 A4
Portsmouth PO1 404 C4
Titchfield PO15 317 D4
Drummond Way SO53 243 B8
Drum Rd SO50 243 F2
Drury Cl RG28 108 D8
Drury La
Bentworth GU34 138 B6
Mortimer RG7 11 E5
Drury Rd BH4 392 B2
Dryden Ave PO6 320 E1
Dryden Cl
Basingstoke RG24 48 C1
Fareham PO16 319 A1
St Leonards BH24 327 E5
Waterlooville PO7 299 E2
Dryden Pl 4 SO41 399 D5
Dryden Rd
Farnborough GU14 55 D6
Southampton SO19 292 E5
Dryden Way GU30 187 E5
Drysdale Mews 7 PO4 371 B2
Duart Ct BH25 383 C3
Duchess Cl GU34 139 E3
Ducking Stool La BH23 395 B6
Duck Island La 5 BH24 329 A6
Duck La BH11 376 F4
Ducklands GU35 164 E2
Duckmead La GU33 208 B5
Ducks La SO20 147 F5
Duckworth Ho 34 PO1 370 A5
Duddon Cl SO18 268 B2
Duddon Way RG21 69 D5
Dudleston Heath Dr PO8 300 B2
Dudley Ave
Fordingbridge SP6 257 F3
Hordle SO41 383 F3
Dudley Cl
Basingstoke RG23 68 B5
Bordon GU35 164 D1
Dudley Ct GU52 75 A5
Dudley Gdns BH10 377 D5
Dudley Pl 3 BH25 383 B1
Dudley Rd
Bournemouth BH10 377 D5
Portsmouth PO3 371 A7
Dudley Terr GU33 208 A5
Dudmoor Farm Rd BH23 379 F4
Dudmoor La BH23 379 F3
Dudsbury Ave BH22 353 D4
Dudsbury Cres BH22 353 E4
Dudsbury Gdns BH22 377 E8
Dudsbury Rd BH22 353 D1
Dudsway Ct BH22 353 D4
Duffield La PO10 325 E3
Dugald Drummond St PO1 404 B3
Dugdell Cl BH22 353 F6
Duisburg Way PO5 370 B2
Duke Cl SP10 83 D1
Duke Cres PO1 370 D7
Duke of Connaughts Rd GU11 77 B5
Duke of Cornwall Ave GU15 36 B8
Duke of Edinburgh Ho PO1 370 A6
Duke Rd SO30 293 D5
Dukes Cl
Alton GU34 139 D2
Bournemouth BH6 394 D6
Farnham GU9 98 E6
Petersfield GU32 228 D4
Westbourne PO10 325 B3
Dukes Ct
4 Bishop's Waltham SO32 271 C8
Farnborough GU14 55 F3
Verwood BH31 302 F7
Dukes Dr BH11 376 E5
Dukesfield BH23 379 D2
Dukes Mead GU51 53 D1
Dukes Mill 12 SO51 240 E7
Dukes Pk GU11 77 B6
Dukes Rd
Gosport PO12 369 A7
Southampton SO14 291 B7
Dukes Ride RG7 27 E8
Duke St
Micheldever SO21 133 B3
Southampton SO14 291 B3
Dukes Wlk
7 Waterlooville PO7 322 E7
Farnham GU9 98 E6
Dukes Wlk Service Rd 6 PO7 322 E7
Dukeswood Dr SO45 314 A1
Duke Terr PO9 323 D4
Dulsie Rd BH3 392 C7
Dumas Cl GU46 34 A5
Du Maurier Cl GU52 74 E3
Dumbarton Cl PO2 370 D8
Dumbleton Cl SO19 292 F5
Dumbleton's Twrs SO19 292 E4
Dummer Ct PO9 323 D6
Dummer Down La RG25 113 C7
Dummer La SP11 37 A2
Dummer Mews 5 SO23 403 D5
Dummers Rd SO51 216 D7
Dumpers Dro SO50 269 D7
Dump Rd GU14 55 C1
Dumpton Sch BH21 351 D8
Dunbar Cl SO16 265 F5
Dunbar Cres BH23 381 F2
Dunbar Rd
Bournemouth BH3 392 E6
Camberley GU16 56 D7
Portsmouth PO4 371 B4
Dunbridge La
Awbridge SO51 214 F7
Chilton Candover SO24 135 D5
Dunbridge SO51 192 D1
Dunbridge Sta SO51 192 D1
Duncan Cl SO19 291 E1
Duncan Cooper Ho PO7 322 D7
Duncan Ct
Andover SP10 106 C7
Southampton SO19 292 C4
Duncan Ho 5 RG21 69 C6
Duncan Rd
Locks Heath SO31 317 B6
New Milton BH25 383 D4
Portsmouth PO5 370 D2
Duncan's Cl SP11 80 E2
Duncans Dr PO14 342 B8
Duncliff Rd BH6 395 A4
Duncombe Dr BH24 304 C3
Duncombe Rd GU32 251 D8
Duncton Rd PO8 276 D5
Duncton Way PO13 343 C3

Dundaff Cl GU15 36 E5
Dundas Cl PO3 346 B2
Dundas La PO3 346 B1
Dundas Rd BH17 390 E8
Dundas Spur PO3 346 B2
Dundee Cl PO15 318 E3
Dundee Gdns RG22 68 B4
Dundee Rd SO17 267 C1
Dundonald Cl
Southampton SO19 291 D1
South Hayling PO11 373 A5
Dundridge La SO32 248 C2
Dundry Way SO30 293 C7
Dune Crest BH13 402 C3
Dunedin Cl BH22 353 B3
Dunedin Dr BH22 353 B3
Dunedin Gdns BH22 353 B3
Dunedin Gr BH23 396 C7
Dunfield Way SO45 338 F2
Dunford Cl
Barton on S BH25 397 E8
Old Milton BH25 382 E1
Dunford Rd BH12 391 D5
Dungells Farm Cl
GU46 34 B4
Dungells La GU46 34 A4
Dunhills La SP11 83 C8
Dunhurst Cl PO9 324 A3
Dunhurst Sch (Bedales Jun Sch) GU32 228 E6
Dunkeld Rd
Bournemouth BH3 392 E6
Gosport PO12 369 A8
Dunkirk Cl SO16 266 D4
Dunkirk Rd SO16 266 D4
Dunkirt La SP11 104 E3
Dunley Dr [1] GU51 53 C3
Dunley's Hill RG29 72 C3
Dunlin Cl
Christchurch BH23 396 B5
Portsmouth PO4 371 D5
Dunmow Hill GU51 54 A2
Dunmow Rd SP10 106 B6
Dunn Cl PO4 371 B3
Dunnings La SO52 241 F5
Dunnock Cl
Ferndown BH22 353 B8
Rowlands Castle PO9 301 B1
Dunsbury Way PO9 323 E5
Dunsell's Cl SO24 181 D5
Dunsell's La SO24 181 D5
Dunsford Cres RG23 68 C7
Dunsmore Cl PO5 404 B2
Dunsmore Gdns GU46 33 E5
Dunstable Wlk PO14 342 D7
Dunstall Pk GU14 55 E7
Dunstans La BH15 391 A6
Dunster Cl SO16 266 C5
Dunston's Dro SP11 39 C1
Dunvegan Dr SO16 266 C5
Dunyeats Rd BH18 375 B4
Dunyeats Rdbt BH18 375 D5
Duplock Ho BH25 383 A3
Dupree Dr PO4 371 A3
Durban Cl SO51 216 A1
Durban Ct [9] SO15 290 E7
Durban Ho PO1 404 C4
Durban Rd PO1 370 F7
Durbidges RG19 24 C8
Durdells Ave BH11 377 A5
Durdells Gdns BH11 377 A5
Durford Ct PO9 323 D6
Durford Rd GU31 229 C3
Durham Gdns PO7 322 F5
Durham St
Gosport PO12 369 A7
Portsmouth PO1 404 B3
Durham Way RG22 91 B8
Durland Cl BH25 383 A1
Durlands Rd PO8 300 C8
Durley Ave PO8 299 F3
Durley Brook Rd
SO32 270 A6
Durley CE Prim Sch
SO32 270 A6
Durley Chine Ct [12]
BH2 392 D2
Durley Chine Rd
BH2 392 D2
Durley Chine Rd S
BH2 392 D2
Durley Cl SP10 105 E7
Durley Cres SO40 288 D5
Durley Gdns BH2 392 D2
Durley Hall La SO32 246 C1
Durley Rd
Bournemouth BH2 392 E2
Durley SO32,SO50 269 E7
Gosport PO12 369 A7
Durley Rdbt BH2 392 E2
Durley St SO32 270 C7
Durlston Court Sch
BH25 398 A8
Durlston Cres BH23 379 D4
Durlston Rd
Poole BH14 391 C2
Southampton SO16 265 D1
Durnford Cl SO20 129 A4
Durnford Rd SO14 291 B6
Durngate Pl SO23 403 F6
Durngate Terr [5]
SO23 403 F6
Durnsford Ave GU52 75 A7
Durnstown SO41 360 C2
Durrant Rd
Bournemouth BH2 392 E4
Poole BH14 391 C3
Durrants Gdns PO9 324 B8
Durrants PRU PO9 324 B8
Durrants Rd PO9 324 B7
Durrant Way SO41 360 B2
Durrington Pl BH7 394 B6
Durrington Rd BH7 394 B7
Dursley Cres PO6 345 D8
Durweston Cl BH9 378 B3
Dutton La SO50 244 B3
Dutton's Rd SO51 240 E8
Dyer Rd SO15 290 C7
Dymchurch Ho [3]
PO6 345 E8
Dymewood Rd BH21 326 E7
Dymoke St PO10 324 E4
Dymott Cl SO15 290 D5
Dyneley Gn SO18 268 A1
Dyram Cl SO50 243 F5
Dysart Ave PO6 346 B7
Dyserth Cl SO19 292 B1
Dyson Dr SO23 403 E8
Dysons Cl RG14 1 C3

E

Eadens La SO40 287 D7
Eagle Ave PO8 299 E4
Eagle Cl
Alton GU34 139 F6
Basingstoke RG22 90 F8
Chandler's Ford SO53 243 B4
Portchester PO16 343 F8
Eagle Ct
[8] Winchester SO23 403 D6
Basingstoke RG24 69 F6
Eagle Rd
Bishop's Green RG20 6 E2
Lee-on-t-S PO13 367 D4
Poole BH13 392 A4
Eagle Rise BH8 378 D1
Eaglhurst [5] BH13 392 A4
Eame's Cotts GU32 226 E1
Eames La GU33 206 F8
Eardley Ave SP10 82 D1
Earle Ho [1] SO23 198 D8
Earle Rd BH4 392 C1
Earley Ct SO41 385 F4
Earlham Dr BH14 391 C4
Earlsbourne GU52 75 B4
Earls Cl SO50 245 A2
Earlsdon St PO5 404 B2
Earlsdon Way BH23 396 F8
Earlsdown [9] SO23 403 F5
Earls Gr GU15 36 C6
Earls Rd
Fareham PO16 343 B7
Southampton SO14 291 A7
Earlswood [16] BH4 392 C2
Earlswood Dr SP6 280 F5
Earlswood Pk BH25 383 C4
Early Lands RG7 27 F8
Earnley Rd PO11 373 F2
Earthpits La SP5 230 B1
Eastacre SO22 403 C7
East Ave
Barton on S BH25 397 C7
Bournemouth BH3 392 D6
Farnham GU9 99 B6
East Avenue Rdbt
BH3 392 E6
East Bank Rd SO42 361 A8
East Bargate [6]
SO14 291 A4
East Bldg PO1 370 A5
East Boldre Rd SO42 363 C6
East Borough BH21 351 B5
Eastbourne Ave
Gosport PO12 368 F8
Southampton SO15 290 D8
Eastbourne Rd PO3 371 A8
Eastbrook Cl
Gosport PO12 368 F8
Locks Heath SO31 317 A5
Eastbrooke Rd GU34 140 A4
Eastbrook Row
BH21 351 C4
Eastbury Ct BH23 395 F4
East Cams Cl PO16 319 F1
Eastchurch Cl SO16 265 F4
East Cl BH25 397 D8
East Cliff [8] BH2 392 F4
Eastcliff Cl PO13 367 E4
East Cliff Way BH23 396 C7
East Cosham Rd
PO6 346 B8
Eastcot Cl SO45 338 C3
Eastcott Cl BH7 394 A8
Eastcroft Rd PO12 368 F5
East Ct
Cosham PO6 346 B8
Portsmouth PO1 370 E7
East Dean Rd SO51 191 E2
East Dorset Trade Pk
BH21 352 F6
East Dr
Bishopstoke SO50 244 E3
West Moors BH24 354 B7
Eastend Cotts SP11 59 D6
Eastern Ave
Andover SP10 106 B7
Portsmouth PO4 371 B6
Eastern Ind Ctr PO6 346 C6
Eastern Par
Fareham PO16 343 B7
Portsmouth PO4 370 F2
Eastern Rd
Aldershot GU12 77 C2
Eastern Rd *continued*
Bordon GU35 164 D6
Fawley SO45 339 E2
Havant PO9 324 A2
Lymington SO41 385 D4
Portsmouth,Anchorage Park PO6 346 C4
Portsmouth,Baffins PO3 371 C7
Portsmouth,Whale Island PO2 345 B1
West End SO30 268 D1
Eastern Terr [3] PO4 371 A2
Eastern Villas Rd
PO4 370 D1
Eastern Way
Fareham PO16 319 C1
Milford on S SO41 399 F4
Easter Rd BH9 378 A2
Eastfield Ave
Basingstoke RG21 69 C5
Fareham PO14 342 F7
Eastfield Cl SP10 106 C8
East Field Cl PO10 325 E2
Eastfield Ct BH24 329 C7
Eastfield Ho SP10 106 C7
Eastfield La
Ringwood,Hightown BH24 329 C7
Ringwood,Poulner BH24 329 C8
Eastfield Lodge [2]
SP10 106 B7
Eastfield Rd
Andover SP10 106 B8
Portsmouth,Eastney PO4 371 A3
Portsmouth,Ports Down PO6 321 C2
Southampton SO17 291 C8
Eastfields PO5 404 C1
Eastgate St
Southampton SO14 291 A3
Winchester SO23 403 F5
East Gn GU17 35 A4
East Hayling Light Rly★
PO11 373 A2
East Hill
Lymington SO41 385 E4
Winchester SO23 403 F4
East Hill Cl PO16 319 D2
East Hill Dr GU33 208 A3
East Hoe Rd PO7 274 A4
East House Ave
PO14 367 D7
East Howe La BH10 377 C4
East Hundreds GU51 53 E3
East La
Everton SO41 384 E1
Ovington SO24 178 F4
Eastlake Ave BH12 391 C6
Eastlake Cl GU31 229 C3
Eastlake Hts PO4 371 D3
Eastlands BH25 383 B1
Eastleigh Coll SO50 244 A1
Eastleigh Coll of F Ed
SO50 244 A2
Eastleigh Lakeside Rly★
SO50 267 F8
Eastleigh Rd
Fair Oak SO50 245 C1
Havant PO9 324 D4
Eastleigh Sta SO50 244 B3
Eastleigh Town Mus★
SO50 244 A2
East Links SO53 243 C2
East Lodge
Fareham PO15 318 C1
Lee-on-t-S PO13 367 E2
East Lodge Pk PO6 346 F8
Eastlyn Rd RG26 10 C1
Eastman Cl SP5 235 A6
Eastmans Field
SO20 129 A3
Eastmead
Farnborough GU14 55 F3
Farnborough GU14 55 F4
Eastmeare Ct SO40 288 C6
East Meon CE Prim Sch
GU32 226 D1
East Meon Rd PO8 276 B6
East Mews [5] PO17 318 E7
Eastney Farm Rd
PO4 371 C3
Eastney Rd PO4 371 B3
Eastney St [6] PO4 371 A2
Eastoke Ave PO11 373 E2
Eastoke Corner Sta★
PO11 373 B2
Easton Common Hill
SP5 168 C6
Easton La
Easton SO21 176 E3
Easton SO21 177 A5
Winchester SO23 176 C1
Easton Lane Bsns Ctr
SO23 403 F6
East Overcliff Dr
BH1 393 C3
Eastover Ct PO9 323 D6
East Park Terr SO14 291 A5
East Portway SP10 82 C1
East Quay [11] BH15 390 C1
East Quay Rd BH15 390 C1
East Rd
Barton Stacey SO21 130 E7
Southwick PO17 321 A6
East Ring GU10 100 E7
Eastrop La RG21 69 C5
Eastrop Rdbt RG21 69 C5
Eastrop Way RG21 69 C5
East Shore Sch PO4 371 B6
East St
Andover SP10 106 B7
Andover SP10 106 B8
Fareham PO16 319 C1
Farnham GU9 99 A3
Hambledon PO7 274 D3
Havant PO9 323 F1
New Alresford SO24 179 D6
Poole BH15 390 C1
Portchester PO16 344 E8
Portsmouth PO1 370 A4
Southampton SO14 291 A4
Titchfield PO14 342 A8
Westbourne PO10 325 B3
Wimborne Minster BH21 351 C4
East Station Rd GU12 76 F1
East Street Ctr [9]
SO14 291 A4
East Surrey St PO1 404 B3
Eastview RG23 68 A4
East View RG27 52 B4
Eastview Gdns GU34 161 E3
East View Rd BH24 329 B7
East View Terr [9]
PO9 323 F1
Eastville SP11 81 C7
Eastville Rd SO50 245 C1
East Way
Bournemouth BH8 378 C1
Corfe Mullen BH21 374 D5
Eastways SO32 271 C7
Eastwood SO51 213 C1
Eastwood Ave BH22 353 E6
Eastwood Cl PO11 373 B5
East Woodhay Rd
SO22 175 D4
Eastwood Rd [5] PO2 345 E4
Eastworth Rd BH31 302 E7
Eaton Ct [6] GU15 35 F5
Eaton Rd
Camberley GU15 35 F4
Poole BH13 392 A2
E Ave SO45 338 F5
Ebblake Cl BH31 303 C3
Ebblake Ent Pk
BH31 303 C5
Ebblake Ind Est
BH31 303 C4
Ebble Cl SP9 78 F7
Ebden Rd SO23 403 F6
Ebenezer La BH24 328 F7
Ebery Gr PO3 371 C7
Ebor Cl BH22 353 E2
Ebor Rd BH12 391 D6
Ebury Ct [7] BH4 392 C3
Ecchinswell Rd
Ecchinswell RG20 23 E3
Kingsclere RG20 24 B2
Ecchinswell & Sydmonton CE Prim Sch RG20 23 E4
Eccles Rd BH15 390 A2
Echo Barn La GU10 121 D5
Ecton La PO3 346 C3
Eddeys Cl GU35 165 F6
Eddeys La GU35 165 F5
Eddy Rd GU12 77 A1
Eddystone Ct GU10 144 D1
Eddystone Rd SO40 264 D2
Edelvale Rd SO18 268 B1
Edenbridge Rd PO4 371 C5
Edenbridge Way
SO31 316 F6
Eden Ct
[11] Bournemouth, Westbourne BH4 392 C2
[9] Bournemouth BH1 393 B3
Eden Gr BH21 351 D3
Eden Grange [5]
SO14 291 A7
Edenhurst [12] BH4 392 C3
Eden Rd SO18 268 B2
Eden Rise PO16 343 B8
Eden St PO1 404 B4
Eden Terr [1] PO2 345 D2
Eden Wlk SO53 243 A5
Edgar Cl SP10 83 B4
Edgar Cres PO16 344 D6
Edgar Rd SO23 403 D4
Edgarton Rd BH17 375 D3
Edgar Villas SO23 403 D4
Edgbaston Ho PO5 404 B2
Edgeborough Sch
GU10 122 A3
Edgecombe Cres
PO13 368 C8
Edgecombe La RG14 2 A5
Edgefield Gr PO7 300 C1
Edgehill Cl
Basingstoke RG22 68 C4
Newbury RG14 2 C5
Edgehill Rd
Bournemouth BH9 377 F1
Southampton SO18 267 F1
Edgell Rd PO10 325 B4
Edgemoor Rd BH22 327 B1
Edgerly Gdns PO6 345 F6
Edgeware Rd PO4 371 B5
Edgewood Ct GU33 208 B2
Edifred Rd BH9 378 A4
Edinburgh Cl GU12 77 E5
Edinburgh Ct [2]
SO15 290 A6
Edinburgh Ho [4]
SO22 403 D6
Edinburgh Rd
Kings Worthy SO23 154 C1
Portsmouth PO1 404 A3
Edington Cl SO32 271 B8
Edington Rd SO23 403 E7
Edison Rd RG21 68 E7
Edith Haisman Cl
SO15 290 D5
Edmondsham Ho [16]
BH2 392 E3
Edmondsham House Gardens★ BH21 279 A4
Edmondsham Rd
BH31 302 E8
Edmund Rd PO4 370 F3
Edmunds Cl
[8] Old Milton BH25 383 A1
Hedge End SO30 293 D5
Edney Cl GU52 75 B6
Edneys La PO7 299 B6
Edrich Sq SP10 83 B2
Edric's Gn SP4 101 D1
Edward Ave
Bishopstoke SO50 244 D4
Camberley GU15 35 E5
Edward Cl SO45 338 E1
Edward Ct
[5] Aldershot GU11 76 E1
Farnborough GU14 55 E4
Edward Gdns PO9 323 C1
Edward Gr PO16 320 E1
Edward May Ct
BH11 377 A4
Edward Rd
Alton GU34 140 A5
Bournemouth BH11 377 B3
Christchurch BH23 395 F8
Farnham GU9 122 A7
Hythe SO45 314 A4
Poole BH14 391 C5
Southampton SO15 290 C7
Winchester SO23 403 D3
Edwards Cl
Lymington SO41 385 B3
Waterlooville PO8 299 F2
Edward's Cl [18] PO6 321 B1
Edwards Ct BH23 397 A8
Edward St GU11 76 D2
Edward Terr SO24 179 E5
Edwina Cl
North Baddesley SO52 242 B4
Ringwood BH24 305 C1
Southampton SO19 292 A6
Edwina Dr BH17 375 B2
Edwina Ho SO18 267 E4
Edwin Jones Gn
SO15 290 E8
Edwins Ct GU14 56 A7
Eeklo Pl RG14 1 E1
Eelmoor Plain Rd
GU11 76 B5
Eelmoor Rd
Aldershot GU14 76 B5
Farnborough GU14 55 D2
Eelmoor Trad Est
GU14 55 D2
Effingham Gdns
SO19 292 C4
Efford Ct SO41 385 B2
Efford Farm Cotts
SO41 385 A1
Efford Way SO41 385 B2
Egan Cl PO2 345 F3
Egbert Rd SO23 403 E7
Egbury Rd SP11 62 B2
Egdon Cl BH22 353 B3
Egdon Ct BH16 389 B7
Egdon Dr BH21 375 E8
Egerton Ct BH8 393 D6
Egerton Gdns BH8 393 D6
Egerton Rd
Bournemouth BH8 393 D6
Sandhurst GU15 35 D7
Eggars Cl GU34 140 B4
Eggar's Ct [6] GU12 76 F1
Eggars Field GU10 120 B5
Eggar's Hill GU11 99 E8
Eggar's Sch GU34 140 B6
Eggleton Cl GU52 74 E5
Eglantine Cl PO8 300 B4
Eglantine Wlk PO8 300 C4
Eglinton Rd GU10 144 F6
Egmont Cl BH24 328 D2
Egmont Dr BH24 328 D2
Egmont Gdns BH24 328 D2
Egmont Rd BH16 389 B4
Egret Gdns GU11 99 E7
Eight Acres
Beacon Hill GU26 167 A7
Romsey SO51 241 B7
Eight Bells RG14 1 D2
Eights The SP11 104 B6
Eileen Beard Ho [1]
PO9 324 A5
Elaine Gdns PO8 300 A5
Elan Cl SO18 268 B1
Eland Rd GU12 77 B1
Elane Ho SP11 57 A2
Elbe Way SP10 82 F3
Elbow Cnr RG21 69 B5
Elcombes Cl SO43 309 F5
Elderberry Bank RG24 69 F8
Elderberry Cl
Clanfield PO8 276 D4
Fair Oak SO50 245 B1
Elderberry La BH23 395 F6
Elderberry Rd GU35 165 A4
Elderberry Way PO8 300 C4
Elder Cl
Locks Heath SO31 316 F2
Marchwood SO40 290 A1
Winchester SO22 403 A2
Elder Cres SP10 105 D7
Elderfield Cl PO10 325 A3
Elderfield Rd PO9 323 D7
Elder Gn SO21 245 A8
Eldergrove GU14 56 C2
Elder Rd PO9 324 B3
Eldon Ave BH25 397 E8
Eldon Cl
Barton on S BH25 397 E8
King's Somborne SO20 172 A2
Eldon Ct
[5] Poole BH14 391 A4
Portsmouth PO5 404 B2
Eldon Dr GU10 122 B5
Eldon Ho [9] SO14 291 A3
Eldon Pl BH4 392 B3
Eldon Rd
Bournemouth BH9 377 E1
King's Somborne SO20 194 A5
Eldon St PO5 404 B2
Eldridge Gdns SO51 240 F8
Eleanor Cl GU30 187 B8
Eleanor Ct BH25 382 F1
Eleanor Dr BH11 376 D5
Eleanor Gdns BH23 394 E8
Electron Way SO53 243 C5
Elettra Ave PO7 322 C8
Eleven Cross SP6 256 B5
Elfin Ct [11] SO17 291 A8
Elfin Dr BH22 353 C7
Elgar Cl
Basingstoke RG22 91 E8
Gosport PO12 369 A3
Portchester PO6 344 E8
Southampton SO19 292 C3
Elgar Ct SO41 385 F4
Elgar Rd
Bournemouth BH10 377 D4
Southampton SO19 292 C3
Elgarth Dr RG40 16 D8
Elgar Wlk PO7 322 F5
Elgin Cl
Fareham PO15 318 F2
Hythe SO45 314 A3
Elgin Rd
Bournemouth BH4 392 D6
Cosham PO6 345 F6
Hawley GU17 34 C1
Poole BH14 391 C2
Southampton SO15 290 D5
Elgin Way GU16 56 D8
Elijah Cl BH15 389 E2
Eling Cl SO22 175 D3
Eling Ct PO9 323 D6
Elingfield Ct SO40 289 A7
Eling Hill SO40 289 B5
Eling Inf Sch SO40 289 A6
Eling La SO40 289 A6
Eling Tide Mill★
SO40 289 A6
Eling View SO15 289 C7
Eling Wharf SO40 289 B6
Eliot Cl GU15 36 F7
Eliot Dr GU27 189 C6
Eliot Ho
[8] New Milton BH25 383 A2
Southampton SO17 267 C2
Elise Cl BH7 394 B8
Elizabethan Rise
RG25 89 E1
Elizabeth Ave
Christchurch BH23 394 F8
Newbury RG14 5 B7
Elizabeth Cl
Downton SP5 234 D7
Kings Worthy SO23 154 B1
West End SO30 268 D1
Wickham PO17 295 F4
Elizabeth Cres SO41 384 B2
Elizabeth Ct
[1] Bournemouth BH1 393 B3
[3] Cosham PO6 345 F8
[4] Gosport PO12 369 A7
[8] New Milton BH25 383 B2
Aldermoor SO16 266 A3
Eastleigh SO50 244 A4
Fareham PO14 342 F7
Ferndown BH22 353 D6
Penton Corner SP11 82 A1
Portswood SO17 267 C1
West End SO30 268 D1
Elizabeth Dr GU52 75 A5
Elizabeth Gdns
Christchurch BH23 396 D7
Hythe SO45 314 A1
Portsmouth PO4 370 F2
Elizabeth Ho SO40 264 B2
Elizabeth Par GU46 34 B4
Elizabeth Rd
Basingstoke RG22 68 E3
Poole BH15 390 D3
Stubbington PO14 367 D7
Upton BH16 389 C7
Waterlooville PO7 322 E5

Elizabeth Rd *continued*
Wickham PO17 . . . . . **296** A4
Wimborne Minster
BH21 . . . . **351** C5
Elizabeth Sq SP9. . . . . . **79** A7
Elizabeth Way
Bishop's Waltham
SO32. . . . . **271** B7
Eastleigh SO50 . . . . **244** B5
Eliza Pl **6** PO12 . . . **369** C6
Elkhams Cl SO41. . . . **384** D1
Elkington Cl RG20. . . . . **22** E7
Elkstone Rd PO6. . . . **321** B1
Ellachie Gdns PO12. **369** B2
Ellachie Mews PO12 **369** B2
Ellachie Rd PO12 . . . **369** B2
Elland Cl SO50 . . . . . **245** C1
Elldene Ct SO40. . . . **288** E5
Ellen Dr GU51 . . . . . . **54** C4
Ellen Gdns
Bramley RG26 . . . . . **28** E3
Chandler's Ford SO53 **243** A5
Ellen Wren Ho SO18. **267** E4
Elleray Cl GU12. . . . . . **77** E5
Ellerslie Cl PO14. . . . **367** A6
Ellery Gr SO41 . . . . . **385** E5
Elles Cl GU14 . . . . **55** F3
Ellesfield Dr BH22 . . **353** D2
Ellesmere Orch
PO10. . . . . **325** B5
Elles Rd GU14 . . . . . . **55** E2
Ellingham Cl SO24 . . **179** D5
Ellingham Cross
BH24 . . . . **304** F5
Ellingham Dr BH24. . **304** D5
Ellingham Dro BH24. **305** B3
Ellingham Rd BH25. **397** D8
Ellington Cl SP11 . . . **105** B7
Ellington Dr RG22. . . . **91** C7
Elliot Cl SO40 . . . . . **288** D7
Elliot Rise SO30. . . . **269** C2
Elliott Park Ind Est
GU12. . . . . **77** C2
Elliott Rd BH11 . . . . **376** F3
Ellisfield Rd PO9. . . . **323** E4
Ellison Way GU10 . . . **100** D7
Ellis Rd SO19 . . . . . . **292** E5
Ellwood Ave SO19. . . **292** E5
Ellwood Cl SO19 . . . . **292** E6
Elm Ave
Christchurch BH23 . . **379** E1
Lymington SO41 . . . **385** C1
New Milton BH25 . . **383** A2
Elmay Ho SP11 . . . . . . **57** B1
Elm Bank GU46 . . . . . . **34** A7
Elm Bank Rd SP10 . . **106** A6
Elm Bottom Cross
RG24 . . . . **47** D2
Elm Cl
Bordon GU35 . . . . . **164** E3
Ludgershall SP11. . . . **57** B2
Southampton SO16 . . **266** F4
South Hayling PO11. . **373** A3
Thruxton SP11 . . . . **103** D8
Elm Close Est PO11 . **372** F3
Elm Cotts
Ringwood BH24 . . . . **329** A7
Woolton Hill RG20. . . . **4** D1
Elm Cres
Farnham GU9 . . . . . . **99** B7
Hythe SO45 . . . . . . **338** A4
Upham SO32 . . . . . **246** E5
Elmcroft GU16 . . . . . . **56** D7
Elm Ct
24 Westwood Park
SO17. . . . . **267** A1
5 New Milton BH25. **383** A2
Andover SP10 . . . . . **106** A4
Chandler's Ford SO53 **218** C1
Southampton,Sholing
SO19. . . . . **291** F3
Winchester SO22 . . . **403** C6
Elmdale GU31 . . . . . **229** A4
Elmdale Cl SO31 . . . **340** D10
Elmdale Gr SO51. . . . **239** B1
Elm Dr GU31. . . . . . . **228** C1
Elmers Way BH21 . . . **357** B1
Elmes Dr SO15. . . . . **289** F7
Elmes Rd BH9 . . . . . **377** F2
Elmeswelle Rd PO8 . **300** A6
Elmfield GU35 . . . . . **165** A5
Elmfield Cl SP5 . . . . **235** D5
Elmfield Ct GU35. . . . **164** F5
Elmfield Gdns RG14 . . **1** C4
Elmfield La SO45. . . . **366** F2
Elmfield North Block
SO15 . . . . **290** D5
Elmfield West Block
SO15 . . . . **290** D5
Elmgate Dr BH7 . . . . **394** A7
Elm Gdns
Bournemouth BH4 . . **392** C5
West End SO30 . . . . **268** D3
Elm Gr
Eastleigh SO50 . . . . **243** F2
Farnham GU9 . . . . . . **99** A7
Gosport PO12 . . . . . **369** B6
Kingsclere RG20 . . . . **24** D2
Portsmouth PO5 . . . **404** B1
South Hayling PO11. . **373** A3
Elm Grove Cvn Pk
RG18 . . . . **2** F5
Elm Grove Flats RG20 **24** D2
Elm Grove Fm RG20. . **24** D2
Elm Grove Rd GU14 . . **55** F4

Elmhurst RG26. . . . . . **27** A7
Elmhurst Rd
Bournemouth BH11. . **377** A5
Fareham PO16. . . . . **343** B8
Gosport PO12 . . . . . **369** C5
Thatcham RG18 . . . . . . **2** E5
West Moors BH22 . . **326** F2
Elmhurst Way BH22 . **326** F1
Elm La
Havant PO9 . . . . . . **323** F1
Tongham GU10 . . . . **100** D8
Elmleigh Rd PO9. . . . **323** F2
Elm Lodge PO5 . . . . **404** C1
Elmore Ave PO13 . . . **368** A5
Elmore Cl PO13 . . . . **367** F2
Elmore Dr BH24 . . . . **327** E6
Elmore Rd PO13 . . . . **367** F2
Elm Park Rd PO9 . . . **323** F2
Elm Piece Ho RG25 . . **88** B7
Elm Pl GU11 . . . . . . **100** A8
Elm Rd
Bishop's Waltham
SO32. . . . . **271** E8
Farnham GU9 . . . . . . **99** B7
Havant PO9 . . . . . . **348** A8
New Alresford SO24 . **179** D5
Overton RG25 . . . . . . **65** B2
Sherborne St John
RG24 . . . . **47** E2
Winchester SO22 . . . **403** C6
Elmrise Prim Sch
BH11. . . . . **377** A4
Elms Ave BH14 . . . . . **391** A1
Elms Cl
Fordingbridge SP6. . . **257** B2
Poole BH14 . . . . . . **391** A1
Elmsdown Ct BH24. . **328** F7
Elmsleigh Ct SO17 . . **267** A4
Elmsleigh Gdns
SO16 . . . . **267** A4
Elmsleigh Rd GU14. . . **55** D4
Elmsley Ct GU14 . . . . **55** D4
Elmslie Gdns SO31. . **292** F1
Elms Rd
Aldershot GU11. . . . . **76** E1
Fareham PO16. . . . . **343** B7
Fleet GU51 . . . . **75** C8
Hook RG27. . . . . **51** A1
Elm St
Portsmouth PO5 . . . **404** A1
Southampton SO14 . . **291** B4
Elm Terr
Liss GU33 . . . . **207** E5
Southampton SO14 . . **291** B3
Elm Tree Cl SO40 . . . **288** B2
Elmtree Gdns SO51 . **241** C6
Elmtree Rd PO6. . . . **346** E8
Elm Tree Wlk BH22 . **377** E8
Elm View GU12. . . . . . **77** F3
Elmwood RG24 . . . . . **48** E3
Elmwood Ave
Fordingbridge SP6. . . **257** D2
Waterlooville PO7 . . . **322** E6
Elmwood Cl GU34 . . **139** D2
Elmwood Cl SO16. . . **266** B2
Elmwood Lodge **2**
PO16 . . . . **319** B2
Elmwood Par RG23 . . **68** C7
Elmwood Rd PO2 . . . **345** E4
Elmwood Way
Basingstoke RG23. . . . **68** C7
Christchurch BH23 . . **397** A7
Elphinstone Rd
Portsmouth PO5 . . . **370** C2
Walkford BH23 . . . . **382** B1
Elsenwood Cres GU15 **36** E6
Elsenwood Dr GU15. . **36** E7
Elsfred Rd PO14 . . . . **367** A6
Elsley Cl GU16 . . . . . . **56** D6
Elson Inf Sch PO12. . **369** A9
Elson Jun Sch PO12. **369** A9
Elson La PO12 . . . . . **369** A9
Elson Rd PO12 . . . . . **369** A9
Elstead Gdns PO7. . . **322** C4
Elstead Rd GU10 . . . **100** F2
Elston Pl GU12 . . . . **100** A8
Elston Rd GU12 . . . . **100** A8
Elstree Rd SO19. . . . **291** E5
Eltham Cl BH7 . . . . . **394** B8
Eltham Cl GU51 . . . . . **54** A3
Eltham Cres SO31 . . . **53** D3
Eltham Heath Prim
Sch GU51 . . . . **53** D3
Eltham La RG27. . . . . . **53** A8
Eltham Pl GU51. . . . . . **53** E3
Eltham Rd GU51 . . . . . **53** E3
Elvin Cl SO41 . . . . . . **383** F3
Elwell Gn PO11 . . . . **372** F3
Elwyn Rd BH1,BH8. . . **393** C5
Ely Cl GU10 . . . . **56** E7
Ely Gr RG14. . . . . **2** C5
Elysium Ct BH22 . . . **353** E4
Emanuel St PO2 . . . . **370** D7
Embankment Way
BH24 . . . . **329** B6
Embassy Ct PO4 . . . **404** D2

Emberley Cl BH22. . . **354** A6
Embleton Rd GU35 . . **165** F6
Embley Cl SO40. . . . . **264** D2
Embley La SO51. . . . **239** E7
Embley Park Ind Est
SO51. . . . . **239** E7
Embley Park Jun Sch
SO51. . . . . **240** E7
Embley Park Sch
SO51. . . . . **239** E6
Embsay Rd SO31. . . . **316** B8
Emden Rd SP10. . . . . . **82** F3
Emerald Cl
Southampton SO19 . . **292** B6
St Leonards BH24 . . **327** E6
Waterlooville PO7 . . . **322** D7
Emerald Cres SO45 . **314** B4
Emer Cl SO52. . . . . . **212** A6
Emerson Cl **12** BH15. **390** C2
Emerson Rd BH15. . . **390** C2
Emery Down Dr **3**
GU51 . . . . **53** C3
Emily Cl BH23 . . . . . **380** A1
Emily Ct
Poole BH15 . . . . . . **391** E5
Tadley RG26. . . . . . . **27** A6
Emmadale Ct **7**
SO14 . . . . **291** A6
Emmanuel CE Mid Sch
BH31. . . . . **302** E5
Emmanuel Cl PO14. . **317** C2
Emmett Rd SO16. . . . **265** F5
Emmons Cl SO31. . . . **316** A1
Emperor Ho SO18. . . **291** C7
Empire Ct **6** PO9 . . . **323** F1
Empress Ave GU14. . . . **55** F5
Empress Pk SO14 . . . **291** B7
Empress Rd
Lyndhurst SO43. . . . **309** F5
Southampton,Bevois Valley
SO14. . . . . **291** B7
Empshott Rd PO4 . . . **370** F4
Empson Wlk PO13 . . . **367** F4
Emsbrook Dr PO10. . **342** F1
Emsworth Common Rd
PO10 . . . . **324** F6
Emsworth House Cl
PO10 . . . . **324** E1
Emsworth Mus★
PO10. . . . . **348** F8
Emsworth Prim Sch
PO10. . . . . **324** E1
Emsworth Rd
Havant PO9 . . . . . . **324** B1
Lymington SO41 . . . **385** E4
Portsmouth PO2 . . . **345** E4
Thorney Island PO10. . **349** B2
Emsworth Sta PO10. **324** F1
Elms Way BH6 . . . . . **394** E4
Enborne CE Prim Sch
RG20. . . . . **4** C6
Enborne Gate RG14 . . . **1** B1
Enborne Gr RG14 . . . . . **1** C2
Enborne Lodge La
RG14 . . . . **5** A6
Enborne Pl RG14. . . . . . **1** C2
Enborne Rd RG14 . . . . . **1** C1
Enborne St
Enborne RG20 . . . . . . **4** A6
Newbury RG14 . . . . . . **5** A6
Enborne Way RG7. . . . . **8** D6
Encombe Cl BH12 . . . **391** F8
Endeavour Bsns Pk
PO9. . . . . **347** E7
Endeavour Cl
Gosport PO12 . . . . . **369** D5
Southampton SO15 . . **290** B4
Endeavour Ct **5**
SO14 . . . . **291** B3
Endeavour Pk BH24. **329** B6
Endeavour Way
SO45 . . . . **314** A5
Enderleigh Ho PO9. . **323** E1
Enderwood Ct SO40. **288** B8
Endfield Cl BH23. . . . **379** F1
Endfield Rd
Bournemouth BH9. . . **378** A2
Christchurch BH23 . . **379** F1
Endle St SO14 . . . . . **291** C3
Endofield Cl PO14. . . **342** F4
Enfield Ave BH15 . . . **390** E6
Enfield Cres BH15. . . **390** E6
Enfield Gr SO19. . . . . **291** E3
Enfield Rd
Ash Vale GU12. . . . . . **77** F5
Poole BH15 . . . . . . **390** E6
Engineer's Rd RG19 . . **6** E5
Englands Way BH11. **376** D5
Englefield Ct SO31. . **315** A6
Englefield Rd SO18 . **291** D7
English Ct
15 Bournemouth
BH2 . . . . **392** D4
7 Romsey SO51. . . **240** F7
English Rd SO15 . . . . **290** B7
English Wood RG24 . . **64** C7
Enham Alamein Mus★
SP11. . . . . **83** B7
Enham La
Andover,Charlton
SP10. . . . . **82** D9
Andover,Knights Enham
SP10. . . . . **83** A5
Enmill La SO22 . . . . **196** E5
Ennel Copse SO52 . . **242** A4
Ennerdale Cl
Basingstoke RG22. . . . **68** B2
Horndean PO8. . . . . **276** C2

Ennerdale Gdns
New Alresford
SO24. . . . . **179** D4
West End SO18 . . . . **268** B1
Ennerdale Gr GU9 . . . . **98** E6
Ennerdale Rd
Bordon GU35. . . . . . **164** D5
Southampton SO16 . . **265** E2
Stubbington PO14 . . . **342** D4
Ennerdale Way RG19 . . **2** E3
Ensbury Ave BH10 . . **377** D1
Ensbury Cl BH10 . . . **377** D1
Ensbury Ct BH10 . . . **377** E2
Ensbury Park Rd
BH9 . . . . **377** E2
Ensign Dr PO13 . . . . **368** D6
Ensign Park SO31. . . **315** E2
Ensign Way SO31 . . . **315** E2
Enterprise Cl SO31. . **316** E1
Enterprise Ct RG24. . . **69** D7
Enterprise Est GU12. . **77** D7
Enterprise Ho
Aldershot GU11. . . . . **76** F2
Basingstoke RG22. . . . **68** B4
Enterprise Ind Est
PO8. . . . . **300** C8
Enterprise Pk PO16 . **319** E2
Enterprise Rd
Chilworth SO16. . . . . **242** C1
Horndean PO8. . . . . **300** C8
Enterprise Way
BH23 . . . . **378** E4
Eperston Rd PO8. . . . **300** A6
Epiphany CE Prim Sch
The BH9 . . . . **378** B4
Epping Cl SO18 . . . . **268** B1
Epsom Cl
Camberley GU15 . . . . **36** A8
Horton Heath SO50 . . **269** D7
Epsom Cres RG14. . . . . . **1** F1
Epsom Ct PO15 . . . . **317** C8
Epsom Down GU34. . **139** F2
Epworth Rd PO2 . . . . **345** F1
Equine Way RG14. . . . . **5** F7
Erasmus Park Student
Village SO23 . . . . . **176** C1
Erica Cl
Locks Heath SO31. . . **316** F3
Waterlooville PO8 . . . **300** B3
Erica Cotts GU26. . . . **167** A6
Erica Dr PO21 . . . . . **374** D6
Erica Way PO8. . . . . **300** B3
Ericksen Rd BH11. . . **377** C3
Eric Rd PO14 . . . . . . **367** D7
Erinbank Mans BH1. **393** C3
Erleigh Dene RG14 . . . **1** D1
Erles Rd GU30 . . . . . **188** A4
Ermin Wlk RG19 . . . . . . **2** F3
Ernest Cl
Emsworth PO10. . . . **324** F1
Farnham GU10 . . . . **121** F6
Ernest Rd
Havant PO9 . . . . . . **323** C3
Portsmouth PO1 . . . **370** E7
Erpingham Rd BH12 . **392** A5
Errington Ho **3**
SO50 . . . . **244** A2
Erskine Cl RG26. . . . . **10** D1
Erskine Cl SO16. . . . . **265** F5
Erskine Rd SO22 . . . **403** C5
Escombe Rd SO50. . . **244** D3
Escur Cl PO22 . . . . . **345** F4
Esdaile La BH24. . . . **330** F3
Esher Cl RG22 . . . . . . **68** D1
Esher Gr PO7 . . . . . . **299** C2
Eshott Hill Cross
GU10 . . . . **98** A7
Eskdale Cl PO8 . . . . **276** C2
Eskdale Ct GU12 . . . . **77** D4
Eskdale Ho **5** PO6. . **321** F1
Esmond Cl PO10 . . . **348** F8
Esmonde Cl PO13 . . **367** F3
Esmonde Way BH17. **390** F8
Esplanade
Poole BH13 . . . . . . **402** F7
Portsmouth PO4 . . . **371** B2
Esplanade Gdns
PO4 . . . . **371** C2
Esplanade The PO12 **369** E5
Essex Ave BH23 . . . . **379** F1
Essex Cl
Bordon GU35 . . . . . **164** D4
Camberley GU16 . . . . **56** E7
Essex Gn SO53 . . . . **243** C2
Essex Rd
Basingstoke RG21. . . . **69** A5
Bordon GU35. . . . . . **164** D4
Portsmouth PO4 . . . **371** A4
Essex St RG14 . . . . **5** B7
Esslemont Rd PO4 . . **370** F3
Estancia Cl PO13. . . . **367** F4
Estella Rd PO2. . . . . **370** D8
Estridge Cl SO31. . . . **293** A1
Ethelbert Dr SP10. . . . **82** D3
Ethelbert Rd BH21 . . **351** D4
Ethelburt Ave SO16 . **267** C5
Ethel Rd PO1 . . . . . . **370** E6
Ethelred Gdns SO40. **288** C6
Eton Cl RG22 . . . . **91** A6
Eton Gdns BH4 . . . . **392** C4
Eton Mans **2** BH6 . . **394** E3
Eton Pl GU12 . . . . **98** F7
Eton Rd PO5 . . . . . . **404** D2
Etps Rd GU14 . . . . **76** F8
Ettrick Cl GU14 . . . . . **76** F8
Ettrick Rd BH13 . . . . **392** A1
Etwall SP11. . . . . . . **103** D4

Exford Dr SO18 . . . . **292** C7
Exleigh Cl SO18 . . . . **292** B6
Exmoor Cl
Basingstoke RG22. . . . **68** B3
Swanwick PO15. . . . **317** B7
Totton SO40. . . . . . **288** B7
Exmoor Rd SO14 . . . **291** B6
Exmouth Gdns SO50. **269** C7
Exmouth Rd
Gosport PO12 . . . . . **369** A9
Portsmouth PO5 . . . **370** D2
Exmouth St SO14 . . . **291** A5
Explosion Mus of Naval
Firepower★ PO12. . **369** D8
Express Way RG14. . . . . **2** C2
Exton Gdns PO16 . . . **320** C2
Exton Rd
Bournemouth BH6. . . **394** C7
Havant PO9. . . . . . . **324** B5
Eyebright Cl SO50. . . **269** E5
Eyeworth Wlk SO45 . **313** C4
Eynham Ave SO19 . . **292** C6
Eynham Cl SO19 . . . . **292** B6
Eynon Mews BH24 . . **328** F6
Eyre Cl SO40. . . . . . **288** D6

F

Faber Cl PO9 . . . . . . **324** A4
Faber Mews SO51. . . **241** B8
Fabers Yd **12** SO22 . . **403** D6
Fabian Cl
2 Basingstoke
RG21 . . . . **69** A4
Waterlooville PO7 . . . **323** A8
Factory Cotts GU10 . . **98** A1
Factory Rd
Eastleigh SO50 . . . . **244** A2
Upton BH16. . . . . . . **389** C6
Factory The GU10. . . . **98** B2
Fairacre RG20 . . . . . . **21** D8
Fairacre Rise PO14. . **342** B8
Fairacres GU10 . . . . **121** D4
Fairacre Wlk PO14 . . **342** B8
Fairbairn Wlk SO53 . **242** F6
Fairbourne Cl PO8 . . **299** E2
Fairclose RG28 . . . . . **86** C4
Fairclose Dr SO22. . . **175** B5
Fair Close Ho **3** RG14. . **1** E2
Fairclose Terr RG28. . **86** C4
Faircourt **8** BH25. . . **383** B3
Faircross Cl SO45. . . **338** C3
Fairdown Rd SO23. . . **198** C7
Fairfax Cl SO22 . . . . **197** B5
Fairfax St SO19 . . . . **292** E6
Fairfax Ind Est GU12. . **77** C2
Fairfax Mews
Farnborough GU14 . . . **56** B2
Southampton SO19 . . **292** E6
Fairfax Pl RG14 . . . . . . **2** C5
Fairfax Rd GU14 . . . . . **56** A7
Fairfield
Christchurch BH23 . . **395** B7
Denmead PO7 . . . . . **298** F5
Whitchurch RG28 . . . . **86** C6
Fair Field SO51 . . . . **216** A1
Fairfield Ave PO14 . . **342** F7
Fairfield Cl
Christchurch BH23 . . **395** B7
Emsworth PO10. . . . **324** A1
Hythe SO45 . . . . . . **313** F4
Lymington SO41 . . . **385** E3
Wimborne Minster
BH21 . . . . **351** F5
Fairfield Dr GU16 . . . . **36** C3
Fairfield Gn GU34 . . **160** C3
Fairfield Inf Sch
BH21 . . . . **351** F5
Fairfield Mobile Home
Pk RG7 . . . . **11** D5
Fairfield Rd
Barton on S BH25 . . **397** E7
Compton SO21. . . . . **219** D5
Havant PO9. . . . . . . **323** F1
Wimborne Minster
BH21 . . . . **351** D4
Winchester SO22 . . . **403** D7
Fairfields Ct RG21. . . . **69** B4
Fairfields Prim Sch
RG21. . . . . **69** B4
Fairfield Sq PO6 . . . . **345** E8
Fairfields Rd RG21. . . **69** B3
Fairfield Terr **7**
PO9 . . . . **323** F1
Fairfield The GU9 . . . . **99** A2
Fairgate Ctr The
SP6. . . . . **258** A4
Fair Gn SO19 . . . . . . **292** B5
Fairground Craft &
Design Ctr The★
SP11. . . . . **81** D2
Fairground The SP11. **81** D2
Fairhaven Ct **1** BH5 **393** E4
Fairholme Ct **1**
SO50 . . . . **244** A3
Fairholme Gdns GU9 **99** A1
Fairholme Par **4**
RG27 . . . . **51** A1
Fairhome Cl PO12. . . **369** B8
Fairies Dr BH22 . . . . **353** F3
Fair Isle Cl PO14 . . . **367** B8
Fairisle Inf Sch
SO16. . . . . **265** E4
Fairisle Jun Sch
SO16. . . . . **265** E4
Fairisle Rd SO16 . . . **265** E4

Fair La
Chilcomb SO21 . . . . . 198 F8
Itchen Abbas SO21 . . . 177 A1
Fairland Cl GU52 . . . . .75 B8
Fairlands GU35 . . . . 166 B5
Fairlawn BH22 . . . . . 353 D5
Fairlawn Cl SO16 . . . . 265 F6
Fairlawn Ho 9
SO22 . . . . 403 D5
Fairlawn Rd RG26 . . . . .27 B7
Fair Lea BH2 . . . . . . 392 E2
Fairlead Dr PO13 . . . . 368 D6
Fairlea Grange 3
SO16 . . . . 266 F4
Fairlea Rd
Emsworth PO10 . . . . 324 F3
Lymington SO41 . . . 385 E5
Fairlie BH24 . . . . . . 305 C1
Fairlie Cl SO30 . . . . . 269 C3
Fairlie Pk BH24 . . . . 305 C1
Fairlight Gdns GU34 . . 160 C3
Fairlight Holiday Chalets
PO11 . . . . 373 C2
Fairlight La SO41 . . . . 383 D8
Fairmead Cl GU47 . . . . .35 C7
Fairmead Ct
1 Camberley GU15 . . .36 A4
Locks Heath SO31 . . 316 C1
South Hayling PO11 . . 372 E3
Fairmead Way SO40 . . 288 E5
Fairmead Wlk PO8 . . . 300 B3
Fairmile GU52 . . . . . . .75 A6
Fairmile Par BH23 . . . 379 F1
Fairmile Rd BH23 . . . 379 F1
Fair Oak Ct
5 Gosport PO12 . . . 368 D3
Fair Oak SO50 . . . . 245 D2
Fair Oak Dr PO9 . . . . 323 F3
Fair Oak Inf Sch
SO50 . . . . 245 C1
Fair Oak Jun Sch
SO50 . . . . 245 C1
Fair Oak La RG7 . . . . . 29 D7
Fairoak Rd
Bishopstoke SO50 . . 244 E2
Bishopstoke SO50 . . 244 F2
Fair Oak SO50 . . . . 245 B2
Fair Oak Rd PO4 . . . . 371 C4
Fairoak Way RG26 . . . . 9 B1
Fair Piece SP11 . . . . . 128 F6
Fairthorn Ct 3 BH2 . . 392 F4
Fairthorne Gdns
PO12 . . . . 369 A5
Fairthorne Ho RG22 . . .68 E3
Fairthorne Rise RG24 . . 70 C5
Fairview RG14 . . . . . . 5 C8
Fair View
2 Eastleigh SO50 . . 244 A3
New Alresford SO24 . . 179 C4
Fairview Cl
Hythe SO45 . . . . . 314 A3
Romsey SO51 . . . . 216 B1
Fairview Cres BH18 . . 375 A5
Fairview Ct PO12 . . . . 368 E4
Fairview Dr
Broadstone BH18 . . 375 A4
Hythe SO45 . . . . . 314 A3
Romsey SO51 . . . . 216 B1
Fairview Gdns GU9 . . . .99 A5
Fairview Mdw RG23 . . .90 B8
Fairview Par 1
SO45 . . . . 314 A2
Fairview Pk BH14 . . . 391 C3
Fairview Rd
Ash GU12 . . . . . . .77 F3
Broadstone BH18 . . 375 A5
Headley GU35 . . . . 166 A5
Penton Grafton SP11 . 81 C2
Fairview Terr GU35 . . 165 E6
Fairwater Cl PO13 . . . 343 B1
Fairway Bsns Ctr
PO3 . . . . 346 C2
Fairway Cl GU30 . . . . 187 B3
Fairway Dr BH23 . . . . 394 F6
Fairway Gdns SO16 . . 265 E5
Fairway Hts GU15 . . . .36 F6
Fairway Rd
Hythe SO45 . . . . . 313 F4
Poole BH14 . . . . . . 402 C8
Fairways
Beacon Hill GU26 . . 166 F6
Ferndown BH22 . . . 353 F6
Weyhill SP11 . . . . . .81 B2
Fairway The
Barton on S BH25 . . 398 B7
Bordon GU35 . . . . 164 B1
Farnborough GU51 . . .54 E1
Farnham GU9 . . . . . .99 B1
Fleet GU14 . . . . . . .75 F8
Frimley GU15 . . . . . .36 E1
Gosport PO13 . . . . 343 C1
Locks Heath SO31 . . 316 F1
Portchester PO16 . . 344 C8
Rowlands Castle PO9 301 C2
Fairwinds BH13 . . . . 402 B3
Fairwood Rd BH31 . . . 303 C5
Fairy Cross Way
PO8 . . . . 300 B2
Faithfulls Dro SO20 . . 171 B4
Falaise Cl
Aldershot GU11 . . . . .76 F2
Southampton SO16 . . 266 C4
Falaise Rd SO20 . . . . 126 A4
Falcon Bsns Pk RG40 . .15 E6
Falcon Cl
2 Gosport PO12 . . . 369 C8

Falcon Cl continued
Basingstoke RG22 . . . .67 F1
Portchester PO16 . . . 343 F8
Falcon Coppice RG20 . 21 D8
Falcon Ct
Alton GU34 . . . . . . 139 F6
Denmead PO7 . . . . . 298 F3
Frimley GU16 . . . . . . .36 B1
Falcon Dr BH23 . . . . . 396 A5
Falconer Ct SO45 . . . . 338 C6
Falconer Dr BH15 . . . 389 E4
Falcon Fields
Fawley SO45 . . . . . 339 B3
Pamber Heath RG26 . . .9 F3
Falcon House Gdns
RG20 . . . . .4 C1
Falcon Rd PO8 . . . . . 300 A7
Falcon Sq SO50 . . . . 243 E5
Falcon View SO22 . . . 403 A2
Falcon Way
Botley SO30 . . . . . 269 F1
Yateley GU46 . . . . . .33 F6
Falconwood Cl SP6 . . 257 D1
Falkland Ct
Chandler's Ford
SO53 . . . . 243 C3
Farnborough GU14 . . .77 C8
Falkland Dr RG14 . . . . .5 B8
Falkland Garth RG14 . . .5 B7
Falkland Prim Sch
RG14 . . . . .5 B8
Falkland Rd
1 Portsmouth PO2 . . 345 E4
Basingstoke RG24 . . . 48 C1
Chandler's Ford SO53 243 C3
Newbury RG14 . . . . .5 B6
Falklands Cl GU34 . . . 367 F4
Falkland Sq 2 BH15 . . 390 C2
Falkner Ct 3 GU9 . . . .99 A2
Falkner Ho GU9 . . . . . 54 C4
Falkner Rd GU9 . . . . . .98 F2
Falkners Cl GU51 . . . . .54 C4
Fallow Cres SO30 . . . . 293 D8
Fallowfield
Fleet GU51 . . . . . . .54 C4
Yateley GU46 . . . . . .33 F7
Fallow Field SO21 . . . 403 E8
Fallows The BH25 . . . 383 B5
Falmouth Cl GU15 . . . .36 E4
Falmouth Rd PO6 . . . 320 F1
Falstaff Way SO40 . . . 288 E5
Fancy Rd BH12 . . . . . 391 B8
Fanshawe St SO14 . . . 291 A6
Fantails GU34 . . . . . . 139 F6
Faraday Cl RG21 . . . . .15 C7
Faraday Ct RG24 . . . . .69 D8
Faraday Office Pk
RG24 . . . . .69 D8
Faraday Pk SP10 . . . . .82 B1
Faraday Rd
Basingstoke RG24 . . . 69 D8
Farnborough GU14 . . .56 A6
Newbury RG14 . . . . 1 F3
Faraday Way RG2 . . . .15 E8
Farcroft Rd BH12 . . . . 391 B5
Farcrosse Cl GU47 . . . .35 A8
Farefield Ho GU15 . . . .36 E5
Faregrove Ct 8
PO16 . . . . 319 E1
Fareham Coll PO14 . . . 318 E1
Fareham Dr GU46 . . . .33 F7
Fareham Ent Ctr 3
PO14 . . . . 343 A6
Fareham Hts PO16 . . . 319 D3
Fareham Ind Pk
PO16 . . . . 319 C3
Fareham Park Rd
PO15 . . . . 318 C3
Fareham Rd
Gosport PO13 . . . . . 343 D4
Southwick PO17 . . . 320 E6
Wickham PO17 . . . . 296 A3
Fareham Sta PO15 . . . 318 F1
Far Ends 4 BH14 . . . . 391 B4
Faringdon Ct 17
SO23 . . . . 403 E8
Faringdon Rd SO18 . . 292 D7
Farleigh Cl PO9 . . . . . 323 D5
Farleigh La RG22 . . . . .91 B2
Farleigh Rd RG25 . . . . 92 A7
Farleigh Rise RG21 . . . .69 C2
Farleigh Sch RG25 . . . 383 B5
Farleigh Wallop Dr 4
GU51 . . . . .53 C3
Farley Cl
Fair Oak SO50 . . . . 245 D1
Winchester SO22 . . . 197 B4
Farley Ct
Farley Hill RG7 . . . . 15 A5
Farnborough GU14 . . .56 D2
Southampton SO16 . . 266 D2
Farley Hill Prim Sch
RG7 . . . . 15 B5
Farley La SO51 . . . . . 194 E2
Farley Mount Ctry Pk ★
SO21 . . . . 196 B3
Farley Mount Rd
SO21 . . . . 196 A3
Farley St SO51 . . . . . 147 F6
Farlington Ave PO6 . . 322 D1
Farlington Marshes
(Nature Reserve) ★
PO6 . . . . 346 E5
Farlington Rd PO2 . . . 370 E8
Farm Cl
Hamble-le-R SO31 . . 316 A2

Farm Cl continued
Ringwood BH24 . . . . 329 A8
Yateley GU46 . . . . . . 34 B5
Farm Cotts RG24 . . . . .68 D8
Farm Ct
Frimley GU16 . . . . . . 36 D2
Wimborne Minster
BH21 . . . . 352 A4
Farmdene Cl BH23 . . . 396 D8
Farm Dr GU51 . . . . . .54 B4
Far Meadow Way
PO10 . . . . 348 D8
Farm Edge Rd PO14 . . 367 C6
Farmers Gdn RG25 . . .88 B7
Farmers Wlk
1 Wimborne Minster
BH21 . . . . 351 B6
Hordle SO41 . . . . . 399 D8
Farmery Cl SO18 . . . . 267 D4
Farm Ground Cl RG27 51 C1
Farm House Cl PO14 . 342 C5
Farmhouse Way
Crookham Village
GU52 . . . . 74 E5
Waterlooville PO8 . . . 300 A5
Farm La
Christchurch BH23 . . 396 A5
Crondall GU10 . . . . .97 C5
Southbourne PO10 . . 348 F7
Farm La N BH25 . . . . 398 A8
Farm Lane Cl PO7 . . . 322 D6
Farmlea Rd PO6 . . . . . 345 A8
Farm Rd
Abbotts Ann SP11 . . 105 A6
Aldershot GU12 . . . . 77 C3
Frimley GU16 . . . . . .36 D2
Sparsholt SO21 . . . . 174 A5
Titchfield PO15 . . . . 317 C2
West Moors BH22 . . 326 D2
Farmside Gdns PO3 . . 345 F4
Farm View
Emsworth PO10 . . . . 324 F3
Yateley GU46 . . . . . . 34 B5
Farm View Ave PO8 . . 276 B5
Farm View Dr RG24 . . . 49 A4
Farnborough Airport
GU14 . . . . 55 C1
Farnborough Air
Sciences Trust (Mus) ★
GU14 . . . . 55 F1
Farnborough Bsns Ctr
GU14 . . . . 55 D2
Farnborough Bsns Pk
GU14 . . . . 55 F2
Farnborough Coll of
Tech GU14 . . . . 56 A2
Farnborough Gate Ret
Pk GU14 . . . . 56 A7
Farnborough Grange Inf
Sch GU14 . . . . 55 E8
Farnborough Hill (Girls
Sch) GU14 . . . . 56 A5
Farnborough Ind Est
GU14 . . . . 55 E3
Farnborough North Sta
GU14 . . . . 56 B6
Farnborough Rd
Aldershot GU11 . . . . 76 D3
Farnborough,F'rnboro Gn
GU14 . . . . 56 A6
Farnham GU9 . . . . . .99 B7
Farnborough St GU14 .56 B6
Farnborough Sta
GU14 . . . . .55 F5
Farnham Bsns Ctr
GU9 . . . . 99 A3
Farnham Bsns Pk
GU9 . . . . .98 F1
Farnham By-Pass
GU9 . . . . .99 B3
Farnham Castle ★
GU9 . . . . 98 F3
Farnham Coll GU9 . . . 99 A1
Farnham Heath End Sch
GU9 . . . . 99 C6
Farnham Hospl GU9 . . 99 A2
Farnham La GU27 . . . 189 E7
Farnham Mus ★ GU9 . .98 F2
Farnham Park Cl GU9 .98 F6
Farnham Park Dr GU9 98 F6
Farnham Rd
Bordon GU35 . . . . 164 D6
Churt GU10 . . . . . 144 B3
Crondall GU10 . . . . .74 A1
Fleet GU51 . . . . . . .75 D8
Liss GU33 . . . . 207 E4
Odiham RG29,RG27,
GU10 . . . . 73 D2
Poole BH12 . . . . . . 392 A7
Steep GU32 . . . . . . 229 B7
Farnham Sta GU9 . . . 99 A2
Farnham Trad Est
GU9 . . . . 99 D4
Farnleys Mead SO41 385 E2
Faroe Cl PO14 . . . . . . 367 B8
Faroes Cl PO14 . . . . . 367 B8
Farrell Cl GU15 . . . . . 36 A1
Farren Ho GU14 . . . . .56 A1
Farrier Pl GU47 . . . . .34 F7
Farriers Cl
Bramley RG26 . . . . . 28 F3
Crookham Village
GU52 . . . . 74 E3
Wimborne Minster
BH21 . . . . 352 B6
Farriers Ct 4 PO5 . . . 370 D2
Farrier's Field RG25 . 115 A8

Farriers La SO20 . . . . 126 B4
Farriers Way PO7 . . . . 300 C1
Farriers Wlk PO12 . . . 369 D6
Farrier Way PO16 . . . . 343 B6
Farringdon Bsns Pk
GU34 . . . . 161 C3
Farringdon Ind Est
GU34 . . . . 161 C2
Farringdon Rd PO9 . . 324 A3
Farringdon Way RG26 . 26 F7
Farringford Rd
SO19 . . . . 292 D5
Farrington 24 BH4 . . . 392 C2
Farrs Ave PO12 . . . . . 106 B7
Farthingale Terr 1
PO1 . . . . 370 A3
Farthing Cl PO12 . . . . 369 A6
Farthingfield Ho GU9 . 99 A3
Farthing Fields
GU35 . . . . 165 C5
Farthing La PO1 . . . . 370 A3
Farthings Ct The 13
BH1 . . . . 393 A3
Farthings Gate PO7 . . 322 E3
Farthings The PO14 . . 341 C8
Farwell Cl BH23 . . . . 380 C3
Farwell Rd BH12 . . . . 376 C2
Fastnet Cl SO16 . . . . 265 C5
Fastnet Ho 9 PO5 . . . 370 D1
Fastnet Way PO14 . . . 342 B4
Fathersfield SO42 . . . 333 F2
Fathoms Reach
PO11 . . . . 372 F4
Faulkner's Cross
RG28 . . . . 85 C1
Faulston Cotts SP5 . . 210 D8
F Ave SO45 . . . . 338 A6
Faversham 9 BH2 . . . 392 D2
Fawcett Rd
New Milton BH25 . . . 382 F2
Portsmouth PO4 . . . 404 D2
Fawconer Rd RG20 . . 24 C2
Fawley Bsns Ctr
SO45 . . . . 339 A3
Fawley By Pass
SO45 . . . . 339 B3
Fawley Ct 24 PO9 . . . 324 B5
Fawley Gn BH8 . . . . . 378 D3
Fawley Inf Sch SO45 . 339 A3
Fawley La
Owslebury SO21 . . . 221 A8
Privett GU34 . . . . . 204 B4
Fawley Rd
Fawley SO45 . . . . . 338 E3
Hythe,Buttsash SO45 338 B8
Hythe SO45 . . . . . 314 A2
Portsmouth PO2 . . . 345 E5
Southampton SO15 . . 290 A6
Fawn Cres SO30 . . . . 293 D8
Fawn Dr GU12 . . . . . 77 C3
Fawn Gdns BH25 . . . . 382 F4
Fay Cl PO14 . . . . 367 C7
Fayre Rd PO16 . . . . . 343 A6
Fayrewood Chase
RG22 . . . . .91 B7
Fayrewood Cl BH31 . . 302 F7
Fearon Rd PO2 . . . . . 345 E1
Feathers La 5 RG21 . . .69 B4
Feathers Yd 8 RG21 . .69 B4
Feilden Ct RG20 . . . . . 24 D1
Felbridge Cl GU16 . . . 36 D1
Felders Mead RG27 . . .51 D3
Feld Way RG24 . . . . . 70 A8
Felix Rd PO12 . . . . . 369 D6
Fell Cl SO31 . . . . 317 A4
Fell Dr PO13 . . . . 367 F3
Fellows Rd GU14 . . . . .56 B1
Felmer Dr SO23 . . . . 176 C7
Feltham Cl SO51 . . . . 241 C8
Felton Cres BH23 . . . 396 F8
Felton Ct BH14 . . . . . 390 F5
Felton Rd BH14 . . . . . 390 F5
Feltons Pl PO3 . . . . . 345 F5
Feltre Pl 11 RG14 . . . . .1 D7
Fen Ave PO16 . . . . . . 343 B7
Fencott Pl RG21 . . . . .69 B6
Fenleigh Cl BH25 . . . . 383 B1
Fennel Cl
Chineham RG24 . . . . 49 A4
Farnborough GU14 . . .54 F4
Newbury RG14 . . . . .2 B5
Fennel Gdns SO41 . . . 385 E5
Fennell Cl PO7 . . . . . 299 D1
Fenn's Yd 8 RG21 . . . .98 E1
Fenton Lodge 3
GU15 . . . . .36 C6
Fenton Rd BH6 . . . . . 394 C5
Fenwick Ct BH8 . . . . . 393 B5
Fenwick Hospl SO43 . 309 E6
Ferbies GU52 . . . . . . 75 A6
Ferden Hts GU27 . . . . 189 F2
Ferguson Cl RG21 . . . .69 B2
Fermor Dr GU11 . . . . .76 D3
Fernacre Bsns Pk
SO51 . . . . 215 E1
Fernbank RG40 . . . . . .16 B6
Fern Bank
5 Bournemouth
BH2 . . . . 392 F3
Three Legged Cross
BH21 . . . . 326 E7
Fern Barrow BH12 . . . 392 B7
Fernbrae Cl GU10 . . . 121 F3
Fern Cl
Alderholt SP6 . . . . . 281 A5
Burton BH23 . . . . . 380 C2
Frimley GU16 . . . . . . 36 F3
Petersfield GU31 . . . 229 C3

Ferncote Rd GU35 . . . 164 E3
Fern Cotts 2 PO16 . . . 319 C2
Ferncroft Cl PO14 . . . 367 C6
Ferncroft Gdns
BH10 . . . . 377 D5
Ferncroft Rd BH10 . . . 377 D5
Fern Ct
Ash GU12 . . . . 77 D1
Southampton SO18 . . 291 E7
Ferndale
Hedge End SO30 . . . 293 D5
Waterlooville PO7 . . 323 A8
Ferndale Gdns RG27 . . 51 A2
Ferndale Mews
PO13 . . . . 343 B4
Ferndale Rd
Andover SP10 . . . . . 82 E1
Fleet GU52 . . . . . . 74 F5
Marchwood SO40 . . 289 C1
New Milton BH25 . . . 383 B4
Ferndene Way SO18 . . 291 F6
Ferndene La GU27 . . . 189 F3
Ferndown Cl RG22 . . . .91 A4
Ferndown Ct
Alton GU34 . . . . . . 140 A4
Farnham GU10 . . . . 122 B5
Ferndown Fst Sch
BH22 . . . . 353 C5
Ferndown Gdns GU14 55 C4
Ferndown Ind Est
BH21 . . . . 352 F7
Ferndown Mid Sch
BH22 . . . . 353 C5
Ferndown Upper Sch
BH22 . . . . 353 B6
Fern Dr
Fleet GU51 . . . . . . 74 E6
Havant PO9 . . . . . . 324 A2
Ferneham Rd PO15 . . 318 C2
Ferney Cl GU34 . . . . . 161 D7
Fernglade BH25 . . . . 383 A4
Fernheath Cl BH11 . . . 377 A3
Fernheath Rd BH11 . . 377 A3
Fernhill SO53 . . . . . . 243 E6
Fernhill Cl
Farnborough GU17 . . 35 C1
Farnham GU9 . . . . . 98 F6
Poole BH17 . . . . . . 376 A2
Fernhill Dr GU9 . . . . .98 F6
Fernhill Flats 6
BH2 . . . . 392 F3
Fernhill Gate BH25 . . 383 A4
Fernhill La
Farnborough GU17 . . 35 C1
Farnham GU9 . . . . . 98 F6
New Milton BH25 . . . 383 A4
Fern Hill La SO51 . . . 216 E8
Fernhill Lodge GU14 . 55 C7
Fernhill Pl RG27 . . . . .49 B5
Fernhill Prim Sch
GU14 . . . . 35 D1
Fernhill Rd
Farnborough,Cove
GU14 . . . . 55 C6
Farnborough,Hawley
GU14 . . . . 35 C2
New Milton BH25 . . . 383 A3
Fernhills Rd SO45 . . . 314 B5
Fernhill Wlk GU17 . . . 35 D1
Fernhurst Jun Sch
PO4 . . . . 370 F4
Fernhurst Rd PO4 . . . 370 F4
Fernie Cl PO14 . . . . . 367 B7
Ferniehurst GU15 . . . .36 F4
Fernlea
Bordon GU35 . . . . 164 B1
Christchurch BH23 . . 395 D6
Fern Lea GU9 . . . . . . .99 F6
Fernlea Ave BH22 . . . 353 D4
Fernlea Cl
Ferndown BH22 . . . 353 D4
St Leonards BH24 . . 327 E4
Fernlea Gdns
Ferndown BH22 . . . 353 D4
Southampton SO16 . . 266 C4
Fernlea Way SO45 . . . 313 D3
Fernleigh Ct 9 GU14 . .55 F4
Fern Rd
Hythe SO45 . . . . . 313 F3
Southampton SO19 . . 291 F2
Fernside Ave BH14 . . . 390 F4
Fernside Bsns Pk
BH22 . . . . 353 A7
Fernside Cl
Holbury SO45 . . . . . 338 C3
Southampton SO18 . . 289 F8
Fernside Ct BH15 . . . 390 E4
Fernside Rd
Bournemouth BH9 . . 392 E8
Poole BH15 . . . . . . 390 E4
West Moors BH22 . . 326 E2
Fernside Way SO50 . . 245 C6
Fernside Wlk SO50 . . 245 E2
Ferns Mead GU9 . . . . .98 E1
Ferns The
3 Farnborough
GU14 . . . . 77 B8
Farnham GU9 . . . . . 99 A7
Fern Way PO15 . . . . . 317 C5
Fernway Cl BH21 . . . . 352 B4
Fernwood Cl BH24 . . . 328 B3
Fernwood Cres
SO18 . . . . 291 D4
Fernwood Ho PO8 . . . 300 A2
Ferrell Field RG27 . . . . .50 F1
Ferrier Gr RG14 . . . . . .5 F8
Ferris Ave BH8 . . . . . 378 D2
Ferris Cl BH8 . . . . . . 378 D2
Ferris Pl BH8 . . . . . . 378 D2
Ferrol Rd PO12 . . . . . 369 C7
Ferrybridge Gn 4
SO30 . . . . 293 C6
Ferrymans Quay
SO31 . . . . 315 B5
Ferrypoint SO41 . . . . 386 A4
Ferry Rd
Bournemouth BH6 . . 394 F3
Hythe SO45 . . . . . 313 F3
Poole BH19 . . . . . . 402 A1
Poole,Lower Hamworthy
BH15 . . . . 390 B1
Portsmouth PO4 . . . 371 E4
South Hayling PO11 . 372 B4
Ferry Way BH13 . . . . 402 B3
Festing Bldgs 1
PO4 . . . . 370 F2
Festing Gr PO4 . . . . . 371 A2
Festing Mews 2
PO4 . . . . 370 F2
Festing Rd PO4 . . . . . 370 F2
Festival Pl RG21 . . . . 69 B5
Feversham Ave BH8 . . 378 C1
Fey Rd PO12 . . . . . . 369 C6
Fibbards Rd SO42 . . . 333 F1
Fiddlers Field SO41 . . 139 B8
Field Cl
Compton SO21 . . . . 219 C6
Gosport PO13 . . . . . 343 B5
Locks Heath SO31 . . 317 A2
Romsey SO51 . . . . 241 A7
Southampton SO16 . . 267 C5
Fielden Cl SO52 . . . . 241 F4
Field End
Farnham GU9 . . . . . 99 D4
Kings Worthy SO23 . . 176 C7
Fielder Dr 1 PO14 . . . 343 A6
Fielders Ct
Alton GU34 . . . . . . 139 F3
Waterlooville PO7 . . 322 C4
West End SO18 . . . . 268 C1
Fielders The RG27 . . . 33 C8
Fielders' Way SO51 . . 239 B2
Fieldfare Ave 2 GU46 33 F6
Fieldfare Cl PO8 . . . . 276 C4
Fieldfare Ct SO40 . . . 288 E3
Fieldgate Ctr RG20 . . 24 C2
Field Gate Dr RG20 . . 24 C2
Fieldhouse Dr PO13 . . 367 F4
Fielding Rd GU47 . . . . 35 C6
Field La GU16 . . . . . . 36 C1
Fieldmore Rd PO12 . . 369 B8
Field Path GU11 . . . . 35 D1
Field Pl
Barton on S BH25 . . 397 D8
Liphook GU30 . . . . 188 A3
Verwood BH31 . . . . 302 E7
Field Rd GU14 . . . . . . 35 D1
Fieldridge RG14 . . . . .2 B5
Fields Cl SO45 . . . . . 338 E1
Fields The BH31 . . . . 302 F7
Field Stores App
GU11 . . . . 77 A3
Field View SO53 . . . . 242 F6
Fieldway
Fleet GU51 . . . . . . 74 D8
Ringwood BH24 . . . . 329 B8
Field Way
Aldershot GU12 . . . . 77 C3
Christchurch BH23 . . 381 D1
Compton SO21 . . . . 219 C6
Corfe Mullen BH21 . . 374 E8
Denmead PO7 . . . . 298 F4
Godshill SP6 . . . . . 258 D2
Tongham GU10 . . . . 100 D7
Field Wlk SO41 . . . . . 385 D5
Fifehead Cotts SO20 . 147 C8
Fifield La GU10 . . . . . 122 B2
Fifth Ave
Cosham PO6 . . . . . 345 E8
Havant PO9 . . . . . . 324 B2
Fifth Rd RG14 . . . . . .1 C1
Fifth St
Greenham RG19 . . . . 6 D5
Portsmouth PO1 . . . 370 F6
Filmer Cl PO13 . . . . . 368 D8
Filmorehill La GU34 . . 204 B3
Filton Cl SO40 . . . . . 264 C1
Filton Rd SO41 . . . . . 385 D4
Finchampstead Prim Sch
RG40 . . . . 16 C3
Finchampstead Rd
RG40 . . . . 16 D6
Finch Cl RG26 . . . . . 27 A7
Finchdean Rd
Havant PO9 . . . . . . 323 D4
Rowlands Castle PO9 301 D3
Finches Gn GU34 . . . . 139 F6
Finches The SO17 . . . 267 B2
Finchfield Ave BH11 . . 376 F6
Finch Ho 11 PO4 . . . . 371 B2
Finchmead La GU32 . . 228 B4
Finch Rd PO4 . . . . . . 371 D3
Finch's La PO12 . . . . 369 C8
Finchwood Farm Ind
Units PO13 . . . . . . 348 B1
Findhorn Cl 4 GU47 . .35 B7
Findings The GU14 . . . 55 C8
Findon Rd PO12 . . . . 369 B9

Fineshade 7 BH13.. **402** F7
Fingle Dr SP10...... **105** E8
Finisterre Cl PO14 .. **342** B4
Finkley Down Farm Pk★
 SP11............. **83** E3
Finkley Rd SP11 ..... **84** C7
Finlay Cl SO19...... **292** C4
Finley Cl SO40 ...... **264** B1
Finns Ind Pk GU10 ... **74** B2
Fintry Pl GU14 ...... **55** C7
Fintry Wlk GU14 ..... **55** C7
Finzi Cl SO19 .... **292** C3
Fiona Cl SO23 ...... **198** C8
Fir Acre Rd GU12 .....**77** E6
Fir Ave BH25........ **383** B2
Firbank Rd BH9..... **393** B8
Fir Cl
 Fleet GU51 .... **74** F8
 Lyndhurst SO43.... **309** F4
 Thatcham RG19.......**7** F5
 West Moors BH22... **326** E3
Fir Copse Rd PO7 ... **322** D4
Fir Cottage Rd RG40 . **16** C8
Fir Croft Dr SO53 .... **243** D5
Fircrofts 5 GU51....**53** F1
Fir Dr GU17.......**35** B3
Firecrest Cl SO16 .... **266** B6
Firecrest Rd RG22....**90** F6
Firefly Cl PO13....... **368** A5
Fire Station Rd GU11..**76** F9
Fire Thorn Cl GU52...**75** A7
Firfield Rd GU9 ..... **121** E7
Firglen Dr GU46 ......**34** B7
Fir Gr GU35......... **164** B1
Firgrove Cl SO52.... **241** F4
Firgrove Cres PO3 .. **345** F5
Firgrove Ct
 8 Farnborough
 GU14 .... **55** F4
 Farnham GU9 ...... **99** A1
 Southampton SO15 . **290** C7
Firgrove Hill GU9 .... **99** A1
Firgrove La PO17 .... **296** F2
Firgrove Manor RG27 **33** D6
Firgrove Par 7 GU14 .**55** F4
Firgrove Rd
 6 Farnborough
 GU14 .... **55** F4
 Bordon GU35....... **164** B1
 North Baddesley
 SO52........... **242** A5
 Southampton SO15 . **290** C7
 Yateley RG27,GU46... **33** E6
Firlands Ave GU15 ... **36** B5
Firlands Rise PO9.... **323** A4
Firmain Rd BH12..... **376** D1
Firmount Cl SO41.... **384** C1
Firmstone Rd SO23 .. **198** C8
Fir Rd SO40......... **288** B2
Firs Ave PO8......... **299** F2
Firs Cl
 Farnborough GU14 ... **56** A2
 Finchampstead RG40... **16** D7
Firs Cres SO23 ..... **176** B8
Firs Dr SO30........ **293** A5
Firs End RG7 .... **11** D6
Firs Glen Rd
 Bournemouth BH9... **392** C8
 Verwood BH31...... **303** A4
 West Moors BH22... **326** E2
Firshill BH23........ **396** E8
Firside Rd BH21..... **374** C4
Firs La
 Odiham RG29....... **72** C1
 Poole BH14 .... **402** B8
Firs Pk GU31........ **229** C3
First Ave
 Aldermaston RG7 .... **10** B2
 Cosham PO6 ...... **345** F8
 Farlington PO6 ..... **346** E8
 Havant PO9 .... **324** B2
 Horndean PO8...... **276** E2
 Southampton SO15 . **289** D7
 Southbourne PO10 .. **349** D8
Firs The
 Andover SP10 ..... **105** E8
 Bournemouth BH1... **393** A4
 Chandler's Ford SO53 **243** C3
 Gosport PO13 ..... **343** D1
 Liphook GU30 ..... **187** F3
 Southampton SO16 .. **266** F4
 Thatcham RG18.......**2** F4
 Winchester SO22 ... **403** C7
First Marine Ave
 BH25............. **397** F7
First St
 Fawley SO45...... **338** E8
 Greenham RG19 ......**6** E5
Firsway
 Upton BH16........ **389** C7
 Whitchurch RG28 .... **86** C5
Firs Way RG23........**68** B7
Firth Cl RG7 .... **27** F8
Fir Tree Alley 12
 GU11............ **290** E6
Fir Tree Ave GU27... **189** B6
Firtree Cl GU47 ..... **34** D8
Fir Tree Cl
 Horton Heath SO50.. **269** C7
 St Leonards BH24.... **327** D2
Fir Tree Cnr 13 RG26 ..**9** C2
Fir Tree Cotts GU33 . **208** E8
Firtree Cres SO41... **383** F3
Fir Tree Ct SO18 .... **292** B8
Firtree Gdns PO8 ... **300** C5

Fir Tree Gdns PO8 .. **300** C5
Fir Tree Hill SP6..... **281** A6
Fir Tree La
 Christchurch BH23 .. **381** D1
 Horton Heath SO50.. **269** B7
 Newbury RG14 ...... **2** C4
Fir Tree Piece RG26.. **45** A4
Fir Tree Prim Sch
 RG14..............**2** C4
Fir Tree Rd
 Bartley SO40....... **287** A7
 South Hayling PO11.. **373** A3
Firtree Way
 Fleet GU52 .... **75** B8
 Southampton SO19 .. **292** B5
Fir Vale Rd BH1...... **392** F3
Firview GU30 .... **187** F3
Firway GU30 .... **166** C5
Firwood Cl SO53.... **243** D8
Firwood Ct GU15..... **36** A5
Firwood Dr GU15 .... **36** A5
Fisgard Rd PO12..... **369** B8
Fisher Cl
 Andover SP10 ..... **106** C7
 Stubbington PO14 .. **367** B8
Fisher Ho 5 RG14 ......**1** D2
Fisherman's Ave
 BH5 .... **394** B4
Fisherman's Bank
 BH23 .... **395** E5
Fishermans Rd
 BH15 .... **390** C1
Fishermans The
 PO10 .... **349** A8
Fishermans Wlk
 PO11 .... **373** E2
Fisherman's Wlk
 BH5 .... **394** B4
Fishermen's Cl GU11. **77** C5
Fisher Rd PO13 ..... **343** C3
Fishers Gr PO6 ..... **346** E7
Fishers Hill PO15 ... **318** B2
Fisher's Rd SO40.... **289** A6
Fishery La PO11 .... **373** C2
Fish La SO21........ **176** E5
Fishlake Mdws SO51 **215** F1
Fiske Cl RG22....... **68** C4
Fiske Ct GU46 ...... **34** C6
Fitzgerald Cl PO15 .. **317** C8
Fitzgerald Ct RG14......**1** D3
Fitzharris Ave BH9 .. **393** A7
Fitzherbert Rd PO6 .. **346** D7
Fitzherbert Spur
 PO6 .... **346** E7
Fitzherbert St PO1.. **404** B4
Fitzhugh Ho 8 SO15 **290** E6
Fitzhugh Pl SO15 ... **290** F7
Fitzhugh St 8 SO15. **290** F5
Fitzmaurice Rd
 BH23 .... **394** E8
Fitzpain Cl BH22 .... **353** D2
Fitzpain Rd BH22 ... **353** D2
Fitzpatrick Ct PO6 .. **321** D1
Fitzroy Cl SO16 ..... **266** F7
Fitzroy Dr PO13..... **368** A7
Fitzroy Rd GU51 .... **53** D1
Fitzroy Wlk PO1 .... **404** C4
Fitzwilliam Ave
 PO14 .... **367** A7
Fitzwilliam Cl BH11 . **376** E5
Fitzworth Ave BH16 **389** C4
Fitzwygram Cres
 PO9 .... **323** F3
Five Acres Cl GU35.. **164** F5
Five Ash Rd GU34 ... **160** A4
Five Bells La SO20 .. **147** E5
Five Bridges Rd
 SO23 .... **403** C1
Five Elms Dr SO51 .. **241** C6
Fivefields Cl SO23.. **198** C6
Fivefields Rd SO23 . **198** C7
Five Heads Rd PO8.. **300** C8
Five Lanes SP11 ......**61** E1
Five Lanes End RG25 **71** B1
Five Post La PO12... **369** B7
Fiveways
 Basingstoke RG22.... **68** A2
 Camberley GU15 .... **36** C5
Flaghead BH13 ..... **402** E6
Flaghead Chine Rd
 BH13 .... **402** E6
Flaghead Rd BH13... **402** E7
Flagstaff Gn PO12.. **369** D7
Flag Wlk PO8........ **299** F5
Flambard Ave BH23. **380** A1
Flambard Rd BH14 .. **391** C2
Flamborough Cl
 SO16 .... **265** D3
Flamingo Ct PO16... **343** F7
Flamstone St SP5... **210** B8
Flanders Ho 1
 PO14 .... **342** E8
Flanders Ind Pk
 SO30............. **293** B8
Flanders Rd SO30... **293** B8
Flashett The SP5.... **168** B6
Flathouse Rd PO1... **370** C7
Flats The GU17......**34** F4
Flaxfield Ct RG21... **69** A5
Flaxfield Rd RG21... **69** A5
Flaxfields End SP6.. **257** E1
Flazen Cl BH11...... **376** D3
Fleet Bsns Pk GU52. **75** B3
Fleet Cl PO13 .... **343** D1
Fleet Com Hospl
 GU51............. **53** E2

Fleet End Bottom
 SO31............. **340** F10
Fleetend Cl PO9 .... **323** E6
Fleet End Rd
 Locks Heath SO31... **316** F1
 Warsash SO31...... **340** F10
Fleet Farm Cvn &
 Camping Ctr PO11. **373** A8
Fleet Hill RG40......**16** B3
Fleet Inf Sch GU52... **75** C7
Fleet La RG40........**15** F2
Fleet Pond (Nature
 Reserve)★ GU51.... **54** C3
Fleet Rd
 Aldershot GU11..... **76** C6
 Farnborough GU14 ... **55** B4
 Fleet GU51 .... **54** A2
 Hartley Wintney RG27 **52** E5
Fleetsbridge Bsns Ctr
 BH17............. **390** B7
Fleet's Cnr BH17.... **390** B7
Fleets Est BH15..... **390** B6
Fleets La BH15...... **390** C6
Fleetspoint Bsns Ctr
 BH15............. **390** B5
Fleet Sta GU51...... **54** B3
Fleet Terr SO21..... **219** B1
Fleet Way PO1...... **370** B6
Fleetwood Cl RG14....**2** B5
Fleetwood Dr BH15 . **390** C7
Fleming Ave SO52 .. **242** B4
Fleming Cl
 Arborfield Garrison
 RG2 .... **15** C7
 Farnborough GU14 ... **56** B6
 Titchfield PO15 ..... **317** D4
Fleming Ct
 North Baddesley
 SO52........... **242** B4
 Southampton SO19 . **291** D2
Fleming Pl
 1 Romsey SO51..... **240** F7
 Colden Common SO21 **219** F1
Fleming Rd
 Newbury RG14 ...... **1** F3
 Southampton SO16 . **267** A7
 Winchester SO22 ... **175** C3
Flensburg Cl SP10 ...**82** F3
Fletcher Cl
 Basingstoke RG21.... **68** F4
 Bournemouth BH10.. **377** D3
 Hythe SO45 .... **313** D3
Fletcher Rd BH10 ... **377** D3
Fletchers Field
 GU30 .... **188** A3
Fletchers Ho GU30 . **187** F3
Fletchwood La
 Totton SO40........ **288** B4
 Woodlands SO40.... **287** F2
Fleur de Lys Mobile
 Home Pk SO41..... **361** F1
Fleuret Cl SO45...... **314** A1
Flexditch RG7 ....**27** F8
Flexford Cl
 Chandler's Ford
 SO53........... **218** A1
 Highclere RG20 ..... **21** B2
Flexford Gdns PO9.. **324** A3
Flexford La SO41.... **384** C6
Flexford Rd SO52,
 SO53........... **242** E7
Flinders Cl SP10 .....**83** F1
Flinders Ct 4 PO4.. **371** B2
Flint Cl
 Andover SP10 ..... **105** E6
 Southampton SO19 . **292** E4
Flint La SP11 ....**81** E8
Flint St PO5 .... **404** A1
Floating Bridge Rd
 SO14 .... **291** C3
Floral Farm BH21 ... **352** A2
Floral Way SP10 .... **105** D7
Floreat Gdns RG14....**1** C1
Florence Cl
 West Wellow SO51 .. **239** B2
 Yateley GU46....... **34** A6
Florence Ct
 2 Southampton
 SO18........... **291** E8
 Andover SP10 ..... **105** E8
Florence Gdns RG18 ..**2** E5
Florence Portal Cl
 RG28.............. **87** B5
Florence Rd
 Bournemouth BH5... **393** F4
 Fleet GU52 .... **75** B7
 Poole BH14 .... **391** D4
 Portsmouth PO5.... **370** D1
 Sandhurst GU47 .... **35** F7
 Southampton SO19 . **291** D2
Florence Way
 Alton GU34 .... **139** D1
 Sherborne St John
 RG24 .... **68** C8
Florentine Way PO7. **323** A8
Florins The
 Locks Heath PO14... **317** A1
 Waterlooville PO7 .. **322** E3
Floriston Gdns BH25 **380** D3
Florrie Pl GU34 ..... **161** D3
Floud La GU32...... **225** B5
Flower Ct BH21..... **351** D3
Flowerdew Ct SP10 . **106** A5
Flowerdown Cl
 SO40............. **288** C8
Flowerdown Ho
 SO22 .... **175** C4

Flowerdown Mobile
 Home Pk SO22 .... **175** C5
Flowers Cl SO31 .... **315** E3
Flowers La SO51 .... **238** D6
Flume Rd SO45 ..... **339** C4
Flushards SO41..... **385** F3
Flying Bull Cl 3
 PO2............. **370** D8
Flying Bull La PO2 .. **370** D8
Flying Bull Prim Sch
 PO2............. **370** D8
Focus 303 SP10 .....**83** E1
Focus Way SP10 .....**83** E1
Foden Rd GU11.....**76** E1
Foldsgate Cl SO43 .. **309** F6
Foley Ho PO1........ **404** B4
Folkestone Rd PO3.. **371** A8
Folland Cl SO52..... **242** A4
Folly Cl GU52....... **75** A7
Folly Cotts RG20 .....**22** E7
Folly Farm La BH24 . **328** C6
Folly Field SO32 .... **271** D7
Folly Hill GU9........**98** F5
Folly Hill Inf Sch GU9 **98** E6
Folly La
 Bramley RG26...... **29** B4
 Petersfield GU32.... **228** F3
Folly La N GU9.......**98** F6
Folly La S GU9.......**98** E5
Folly Mkt 7 GU31... **228** F3
Folly The RG14 ....**1** F1
Font Cl PO14 .... **317** C3
Fontley Rd PO15 .... **318** A5
Fontmell Rd BH18... **375** C3
Fontwell Cl
 Aldershot GU12..... **77** B2
 Totton SO40........ **264** C1
Fontwell Dr GU34 ... **139** F2
Fontwell Gdns SO50. **269** C4
Fontwell Mews 5
 PO7............. **300** B1
Fontwell Rd
 5 Portsmouth
 PO5........... **370** D2
 Newbury RG14 ....**1** F1
Foord Rd SO30...... **293** B5
Football Gn SO43 ... **286** D3
Footner Cl SO51 .... **216** C2
Footners La BH23... **380** C2
Forbes Almshouses
 GU32 .... **226** E1
Forbes Chase 8
 GU47.............. **35** B7
Forbes Cl SO16 ..... **265** F6
Forbes Rd SO23 .... **176** B8
Forbury La RG20 .....**3** A7
Forbury Rd 2 PO5.. **404** C2
Forburys GU9....... **121** F8
Ford Ave SO53...... **243** D4
Ford Cl BH22 .... **353** F7
Fordingbridge Bsns Pk
 SP6............. **257** D5
Fordingbridge Hospl
 SP6............. **257** F1
Fordingbridge Inf Sch
 SP6............. **257** F3
Fordingbridge Jun Sch
 SP6............. **257** F3
Fordingbridge Rd
 Alderholt SP6 ..... **281** B7
 Portsmouth PO4.... **371** B3
Fordington Ave
 SO22 .... **403** C6
Fordington Rd SO22. **403** C7
Ford La
 Farnham GU10 ..... **121** F6
 Ferndown BH22..... **354** A7
 Lower Common RG27 **14** E2
 Odiham RG29....... **95** A6
 South Warnborough
 RG29 .... **94** F8
Ford Rd PO12....... **368** F6
Fore Bridge GU31... **228** F2
Forefield Dr RG22 ... **91** A5
Forehead The RG7... **12** D4
Foreland Cl BH23 ... **379** D4
Foreland Ct PO11... **373** C2
Foreland Rd BH16... **389** C4
Forelle Ctr The
 BH31............. **303** C4
Foreman Pk GU12... **77** F2
Foreman Rd GU12 .. **77** F1
Foremans Cotts
 PO12 .... **369** E3
Foreshore N SO45 .. **339** B6
Foreshore S SO45... **339** B6
Forest Ave PO8 ..... **299** F5
Forest Cl
 Chandler's Ford
 SO53........... **243** C8
 Christchurch BH23 .. **381** D1
 North Baddesley
 SO52........... **241** E5
 Pamber Heath RG26 .. **9** C2
 Verwood BH31...... **303** D4
 Waltham Chase SO32 **271** D3
 Waterlooville PO8 .. **299** F3
Forest Cnr GU33 ... **208** A7
Forest Ct
 3 North Tidworth
 SP9............. **79** A7
Forest Dean GU51.... **54** C4

Forest Dr
 Chineham RG24..... **48** F4
 Gong Hill GU10 .... **122** A4
 North Tidworth SP9....**79** A7
Forest Edge
 Fawley SO45....... **339** B3
 New Milton BH25 ... **383** C4
Forest Edge Cl
 St Leonards BH24... **327** D5
 Sway SO41 .... **360** A3
Forest Edge Dr
 BH24 .... **327** D6
Forest Edge Rd
 BH24 .... **329** E5
Forest Edge Sch
 SO40............. **288** E7
Forest End
 Fleet GU52 .... **74** F6
 Waterlooville PO7 .. **322** D7
Forest End Rd GU47...**34** E8
Forester Rd SO32 ... **273** B1
Foresters Gate SO45 **365** D7
Foresters Pk SO23 . **176** A4
Foresters Rd SO45.. **338** F2
Forest Front SO45 .. **338** A8
Forest Gate SO45 .. **365** F7
Forest Gate Gdns
 SO41............. **385** D1
Forest Gdns
 Lyndhurst SO43..... **309** F5
 Waltham Chase SO32 **271** E3
Forest Glade GU10.. **121** B3
Forest Glade Cl
 SO42............. **333** D1
Forest Hall SO42.... **334** A1
Forest Hills GU15 ... **35** F4
Forest Hills Ct BH24. **329** D6
Forest Hills Dr SO18. **267** F3
Forest Hill Way
 SO45............. **313** D6
Forest Ho 14 BH1... **393** A3
Forest La
 Andover SP11 ..... **106** F6
 Fareham PO17...... **319** B8
 Hardley SO45....... **338** B6
 Lindford GU35...... **165** A6
 Ringwood BH24..... **329** F6
 Tadley RG26....... **27** B6
 Upper Chute SP11... **57** F7
 Verwood BH31...... **302** E7
Forestlake Ave
 BH24 .... **329** D6
Forest Lane Cl GU30 **187** E4
Forest Links Rd
 BH22............. **326** B1
Forest Mdw SO45 .. **338** A8
Forest Mead PO7 ... **298** F3
Forest Oak Dr BH25. **383** A5
Forest Park Rd SO42 **333** E2
Forest Pines BH25 . **383** A4
Forest Rd
 Bordon GU35....... **164** D2
 Bordon,Whitehill
 GU35 .... **164** D1
 Bransgore BH23 ... **357** F4
 Burley Street BH24.. **330** F5
 Chandler's Ford
 SO53........... **243** D8
 Denmead PO7 ..... **298** D4
 Greatham GU33..... **185** F1
 Liss GU33 .... **208** A6
 Nomansland SP5.... **261** C2
 Poole BH13 .... **392** A2
 Waltham Chase SO32 **271** F3
 West Moors BH22... **326** F3
 Woodgreen SP6..... **235** E3
Forest Rise
 Christchurch BH23 .. **381** C2
 Liss GU33 .... **208** A6
Forest Sh Ctr The
 GU35............. **164** E3
Forestside Ave PO9 **324** A5
Forest Side Gdns
 BH24 .... **305** C1
Forestside The
 BH31............. **303** D5
Forest View
 4 Southampton
 SO14........... **290** F4
 Beckley BH25 ..... **382** D5
 Brockenhurst SO42.. **333** D1
Forest View Cl BH9 . **378** A2
Forest View Dr
 BH21............. **353** A5
Forest View Rd BH9. **378** A3
Forest Way
 Christchurch BH23 .. **381** D1
 Everton SO41...... **384** D1
 Ferndown BH21..... **353** A5
 Gosport PO13 ..... **343** D1
 Totton SO40........ **264** A2
Forest Wlks
 (Blackwater)★
 SO42............. **332** C6
Forge Cl
 Bramley RG26...... **29** A2
 Bursledon SO31.... **293** A1
 Farnham GU9 ...... **99** B3
 King's Somborne
 SO20........... **172** A2
Forge Ct GU46......**34** B7
Forge Field SP10 .....**83** B1
Forge La
 Farnborough GU11 .. **76** D2
 Fawley SO45 ...... **339** A1

Forge Rd continued
 Sleaford GU35...... **142** E1
Forneth Gdns PO15 . **342** B8
Forres Sandle Manor
 SP6............. **257** D2
Forster Rd SO14 .... **291** B7
Forsters RG7 ....**9** D7
Forsters Farm Ct RG7 .**9** D6
Forsyth Gdns BH10.. **377** C1
Forsythia Cl
 Havant PO9 .... **324** C4
 Hedge End SO30.... **293** B8
 Hythe SO45 .... **338** A7
Forsythia Pl SO19 ... **291** F5
Forsythia Wlk RG21 . **69** C8
Fort Brockhurst★
 PO12............. **343** F1
Fort Cumberland★
 PO4............. **371** E3
Fort Cumberland Cl
 BH15............. **389** D2
Fort Cumberland Rd
 PO4............. **371** D3
Fortescue Rd
 Bournemouth BH3... **393** A6
 Poole BH12 .... **391** D6
Fort Fareham Ind Est
 PO14............. **343** A6
Fort Fareham Rd
 PO14............. **342** F6
Forth Cl
 Chandler's Ford
 SO53............. **243** B5
 Farnborough GU14 .. **55** B6
 Stubbington PO14 .. **367** B8
Forth Ct 21 SP10.....**83** C2
Forth Ho 11 SO14... **291** C5
Fort Hill Com Sch
 RG23.............. **68** C6
Fort Hill Dr RG23..... **68** C6
Forties PO14 .... **342** B4
Fort Narrien GU15 ... **35** D7
Fort Nelson★ PO17. **320** B3
Forton Cl BH10 ..... **377** E4
Forton Lodge 3
 PO12 .... **369** C6
Forton Rd
 Gosport PO12 ..... **369** B2
 Portsmouth PO1 ... **370** E6
Fort Rd
 Gosport PO12 ..... **369** B2
 Southampton SO19 . **291** E3
Fortrose Cl GU47 ....**35** B7
Fortuna Ct 1 RG7....**9** C2
Fortune Cl SO53 .... **243** C6
Fortune Ho PO12 ... **369** A6
Fortunes Way PO9 . **322** F1
Fort Wallington Ind Est
 PO16............. **319** D2
Fort Widley Married
 Quarters PO6..... **321** F1
Forty Acre La GU31 . **254** D3
Forum Cl RG23........**68** B5
Forum The 6 PO9... **323** E2
Forward Dr SO41.... **385** C2
Fossewood Dr GU15...**36** B7
Foster Cl PO14...... **342** C4
Foster Rd
 Gosport PO12 ..... **369** B4
 Portsmouth PO1 ... **404** C4
Fosters Bsns Pk RG27 **71** E8
Foul La GU34........ **159** F7
Founders Way PO13. **343** D2
Foundry Cl RG27..... **51** A1
Foundry Cres SO31.. **315** F8
Foundry Ct 23 PO1.. **370** A5
Foundry La
 Haslemere GU27.... **189** E6
 Southampton SO15 . **290** B7
Foundry Lane Prim Sch
 SO15............. **290** B7
Foundry Rd
 Anna Valley SP11 ... **105** D4
 Redlynch SP5...... **235** D7
Fountain Cl
 4 Colden Common
 SO21........... **219** F1
 Hedge End SO30 ... **293** B6
 Poole BH13 .... **392** B2
Fountain Rdbt BH23. **395** B6
Fountains Cl RG24 .. **48** A1
Fountains Pk SO31.. **315** A7
Fountain Sq PO11... **372** E4
Fountain St PO1 .... **404** B3
Fountain Way BH23. **395** B6
Four Acre SO30...... **294** A6
Four Acre Coppice
 RG27............. **51** C2
Four Cnrs SP6....... **256** A4
Four Houses Cnr RG7 **11** C8
Four Houses Cnr Cvn
 Site RG7............ **11** C8
Four Lanes Cl RG24 . **49** A3
Four Lanes End
 Chineham RG24..... **49** A3
 Odiham RG29....... **95** B5
Four Lanes Inf & Com
 Jun Schs RG24 .....**48** F3
Four Marks CE Prim Sch
 GU34............. **182** B8
Four Marks Gn 3
 PO9 .... **324** B6
Four Oaks RG20...... **21** D6
Fourposts Hill 3
 SO15............. **290** E5
Fourshells Cl SO45.. **338** F2

Fourth Ave
Cosham PO6 . . . . . . **345** E8
Havant PO9 . . . . **324** B2
Fourth St
Greenham RG19 . . . . . . **6** D5
Portsmouth PO1 . . . . **370** F6
Four Ways GU10 . . **142** F8
Four Wells Rd BH21. **352** A7
Fowey PO13 . . . . . . **243** B6
Fowey The SO45 . . . . **338** E2
Fowler Ave GU14 . . . . . **55** F2
Fowler Rd GU14 . . . . **55** D3
Fowlers Rd SO30 . . . . **293** B8
Fowler's Rd GU11 . . . . **77** B6
Fowlers Wlk SO16 . . . . **242** D2
Foxborough RG7 . . . . . **14** B6
Foxbury Cl SO45 . . . . **314** A2
Foxbury Gr PO16 . . . . **344** B7
Foxbury La
Gosport PO13 . . . . . **343** D4
Westbourne PO10 . . . **325** D4
Foxbury Rd BH24 . . . . **354** F8
Fox Cl SO50 . . . . . . **244** F2
Foxcombe Cl SO32 . . **272** A5
Foxcote RG40 . . . . **16** E7
Foxcote Gdns BH25 . . **382** F7
Foxcote Ho 6 PO6 . . **320** F2
Foxcott Cl SO19 . . . . **314** F8
Foxcotte Cl SP10 . . . . . . **82** D2
Foxcotte La SP10 . . . . . **82** C3
Foxcotte Rd SP10 . . . . . **82** D2
Foxcott Gr PO9 . . . . . **323** F5
Fox Court Mobile Homes
GU47 . . . . **35** A8
Fox Cover The SO20. **126** B4
Fox Croft GU52 . . . . . . **75** A5
Foxcroft Dr
Holbury SO45 . . . . . . **338** B3
Wimborne Minster
BH21 . . . . **352** B5
Fox Ct GU12 . . . . **77** C3
Foxdale Ct 17 BH2 . . **392** E3
Foxdown RG25 . . . . **65** B2
Foxdown Cl GU15 . . . . . **36** A5
Fox Dr GU46 . . . . **34** B7
Foxes
Verwood BH31 . . . . . **302** F5
Waterlooville PO7 . . **322** E6
Foxes La SO51 . . . . . **238** F5
Fox Farm SP11 . . . . . **103** E3
Fox Field SO41 . . . . . **384** D1
Foxglade SO45 . . . . . **365** F7
Foxglove Cl
Basingstoke RG22 . . . **91** A7
Christchurch BH23 . . **396** C8
Foxglove Dr GU35 . . **164** E2
Foxglove Pl BH25 . . **383** D4
Foxgloves
Fareham PO16 . . . . . . **319** C3
Upton BH16 . . . . **389** B7
Foxgloves The SO30 . **293** D5
Foxhayes La SO45 . . **365** F7
Fox Heath GU14 . . . . . **55** A3
Foxhill Cres GU15 . . . . . **36** F8
Foxhills
Ashurst SO40 . . . . . . **288** D4
Verwood BH31 . . . . . **303** B6
Foxhills Cl SO40 . . . . **288** C4
Foxhills Inf Sch
SO40 . . . . **288** D4
Foxhills Jun Sch
SO40 . . . . **288** D4
Foxholes 1 BH6 . . . **394** E4
Foxholes Rd
Bournemouth BH6 . . . **394** E4
Poole BH15 . . . . . . **390** F6
Foxhunter Way RG19 . . **2** D3
Foxhurst Rd GU12 . . . **77** E4
Fox La
Eversley Cross RG27 . . **33** D8
Oakley RG23 . . . . **67** C3
Wimborne Minster
BH21 . . . . **352** C5
Winchester SO22 . . . **403** A3
Foxlands SO45 . . . . . **365** F7
Foxlea 1 SO15 . . . . . **290** E7
Foxlea Gdns PO12 . . **369** B8
Foxlease Terr SO43 . **309** F4
Foxley Cl GU17 . . . . . . **35** C5
Foxley Dr PO3 . . . . . **346** B4
Foxmoor Cl RG23 . . . . **67** C3
Fox Pond La SO41 . . . **385** D1
Fox Rd
Farnham GU10 . . . . . **122** A7
Haslemere GU27 . . . **189** C6
Foxs Furlong RG24 . . . **49** B4
Fox's La RG20 . . . . **24** C2
Fox's Wlk SO45 . . . . . **365** F7
Foxtail Dr SO45 . . . . **313** F1
Fox Way GU10 . . . . **98** B8
Foxwood BH23 . . . . . . **395** F5
Foxwood Ave BH23 . . **395** F5
Fox Yd GU9 . . . . **98** F2
Foxy Paddock SO45 . **365** F7
Foye La GU52 . . . . **75** B5
Foyes Ct SO15 . . . . . **290** D6
Foy Gdns SO31 . . . . . **316** C1
Foyle Pk RG21 . . . . **69** B2
Foyle Rd
Chandler's Ford
SO53 . . . . **243** B6
Kimpton SP11 . . . . . . **80** C4
Frampton Cl
1 Colden Common
SO21 . . . . **219** F1
New Milton BH25 . . . **383** C5
Frampton Pl BH24 . . **329** A7
Frampton Rd BH9 . . . **393** A8

Frampton Way
Kings Worthy SO23 . . **176** C7
Totton SO40 . . . . **288** F6
France Hill Dr GU15 . . **36** A5
Francesca Ct 5
BH23 . . . . **395** E7
Francesca Grange 4
BH23 . . . . **395** E7
Francesca Lo 1
BH23 . . . . **395** E6
Frances Ct 7 BH23 . **397** B7
Frances Rd
Basingstoke RG21 . . . **69** A4
Bournemouth BH1 . . **393** C4
Waterlooville PO7 . . **322** D3
Frances Sheldon Ct
SO22 . . . . **403** C5
Francis Ave
Bournemouth BH11 . **376** D3
Portsmouth PO4 . . . . **370** F3
Francis Avenue Ind Est
BH11 . . . . **376** D3
Francis Cl PO13 . . . . **368** A5
Francis Ct GU14 . . . . . **55** D4
Francis Gdns SO23 . . **176** B3
Francis Pl PO14 . . . . **367** D7
Francis Rd
Horndean PO8 . . . . . **276** C3
Poole BH12 . . . . . . **391** E5
Francis Way GU15 . . . **36** F4
Franconia Dr SO16 . . **265** B3
Frank Judd Ct 35
PO1 . . . . **370** A4
Frankland Cres
BH14 . . . . **391** E3
Frankland Terr 4
PO10 . . . . **349** A8
Franklin Ave
Hartley Wintney
RG27 . . . . **52** C7
Pamber Heath RG26 . . **9** E1
Franklin Ct 6 GU14 . . **55** A4
Franklin Rd
Bournemouth BH9 . . **378** A3
Gosport PO13 . . . . . **368** A7
New Milton BH25 . . . **383** C4
Twyford SO21 . . . . . **220** A7
Franklyn Ave SO19 . . **292** A4
Franklyn Cl BH16 . . . **389** B7
Frank Miles Ho 1
PO5 . . . . **404** B2
Frankston Rd BH6 . . **394** C4
Franks Way BH12 . . . **390** E4
Frankton Way PO12 . . **369** D6
Frank Wareham Cottage
Homes The BH9 . . **378** A4
Frarydene PO10 . . . . **349** D8
Fraser Cl
Old Basing RG24 . . . . . **70** B6
Southampton SO16 . . **265** F4
Fraser Ct BH25 . . . . **382** E3
Fraser Gdns PO10 . . **325** E2
Fraser Mead GU47 . . . **35** C6
Fraser Rd
Gosport PO13 . . . . . **343** C4
Havant PO9 . . . . **323** D2
Kings Worthy SO23 . . **176** C3
Poole BH12 . . . . . . **391** F8
Portsmouth PO5 . . . . **404** C2
Portsmouth,Whale Island
PO2 . . . . **345** B2
Frater La PO14 . . . . **344** A1
Fratton Ct PO1. . . . . **404** E3
Fratton Park
(Portsmouth FC)
PO4 . . . . **371** A5
Fratton Rd PO1 . . . . **404** E4
Fratton Sta PO1 . . . . **370** E5
Fratton Way
Fair Oak SO50 . . . . . **245** C1
Portsmouth PO4 . . . . **370** F4
Fratton Ind Est PO4 **371** A5
Fraynes Croft GU51 . **74** B8
Frayslea 4 SO45 . . . **314** A2
Freda Rd BH23 . . . . . **394** F6
Freda Routh Gdns
SO50 . . . . **245** D2
Frederica Rd BH9 . . **392** E8
Frederick Ho 6 RG21 **69** C6
Frederick St
Aldershot GU11 . . . . **76** E2
Portsmouth PO1 . . . **404** B4
Southampton SO14 . . **291** B6
Freedom Ct SO45 . . . **314** A3
Freefolk Gn 1 PO9 . . **324** B5
Freegrounds Ave
SO30 . . . . **293** C6
Freegrounds Cl 1
SO30 . . . . **293** C6
Freegrounds Inf Sch
SO30 . . . . **293** C6
Freegrounds Jun Sch
SO30 . . . . **293** C6
Freegrounds Rd
SO30 . . . . **293** C6
Freelands Dr GU52 . . **74** E5
Freeman Ct RG14 . . . . **1** D3
Freemans Cl BH21 . . **352** B6
Freemans La BH21 . . **352** B5
Freemantle Bsns Ctr
SO15 . . . . **290** C5
Freemantle CE Inf Sch
SO15 . . . . **290** C6
Freemantle Common Rd
SO19 . . . . **291** F6

Freemantle Rd PO12 **369** B8
Free St SO32 . . . . . . **271** D8
Freestone Rd 10
PO5 . . . . **370** D2
Fremantle Rd SP11 . . **79** D7
Fremington Ct 6
BH25 . . . . **383** B3
Frenches La SO51 . . . **239** C8
French Gdns GU17 . . . **35** A4
Frenchies View PO7. **298** E4
Frenchmans Creek 10
GU52 . . . . **74** E4
Frenchmans Rd
GU32 . . . . **228** E4
Frenchmoor La
East Dean SP5 . . . . . **190** F2
West Tytherley SP5 . . **190** F4
French Rd
Greatham GU33 . . . . **186** D3
Poole BH17 . . . . . . **375** B1
French's Farm Rd
BH16 . . . . **389** A7
French St
8 Portsmouth
PO1 . . . . **370** A3
Southampton SO14 . . **290** F3
Frendstaple Rd PO7. **323** A6
Frensham Ave GU51. . **54** C1
Frensham Cl
Bournemouth BH10. **377** E3
Hedge End SO30 . . . **293** C6
Yateley GU46 . . . . . . **33** F6
Frensham Country Pk★
GU10 . . . . **144** C5
Frensham Ct
Hedge End SO30 . . . **293** C6
Portsmouth PO4 . . . . **370** F4
Rowledge GU10 . . . . **121** F4
Frensham Heights Rd
GU10 . . . . **121** E2
Frensham Heights Sch
GU10 . . . . **121** E2
Frensham La
Headley GU10 . . . . . **143** E2
Lindford GU35 . . . . . **165** B6
Frensham Rd
Farnham GU9,GU10. . **122** B5
Portsmouth PO4 . . . . **370** F4
Frensham Vale
GU10 . . . . **122** A4
Frere Ave GU51 . . . . **74** B8
Frescade Cres RG21. . **69** D5
Freshfield Gdns PO7 **322** E8
Freshfield Rd SO15 . **290** A7
Freshfield Sq SO15. . **290** B7
Freshwater Ct
Chandler's Ford
SO53 . . . . **218** E1
Lee-on-t-S PO13 . . . **367** E3
Freshwater Dr BH15 **389** D3
Freshwater Rd
Christchurch BH23 . . **396** C6
Cosham PO6 . . . . . . **345** C2
Freshwood Dr GU46. . **34** B4
Frewen Lily PO1. . . . **370** B4
Friarscroft SO31 . . . **315** B7
Friars Croft SO40 . . **264** C2
Friars Ct
Farnham GU9 . . . . . . **99** B7
Sandhurst GU47 . . . . **34** D8
Friar's Field GU9. . . . **98** E3
Friarsgate SO23 . . . . **403** E6
Friars Gate BH23. . . **396** C4
Friars Oak GU34 . . . **160** C4
Friars Pond Rd
PO15 . . . . **318** C2
Friars Rd
Christchurch BH23 . . **396** B6
Eastleigh SO50 . . . . **243** F1
Newbury RG14 . . . . . . **5** E8
Friars Way SO18 . . . **267** D4
Friars Wlk BH25 . . . . **398** A8
Friary Cl 6 PO5 . . . . **370** D2
Friary Gdns 7 SO23. **403** D5
Friary The 5 PO5 . . . **370** C2
Friday's St BH24 . . . **328** F7
Friend Ave GU12 . . . . **77** B1
Friendly Societies'
Homes PO4 . . . . **371** B3
Friendship St PO5 . . **404** B1
Friends Provident St
Mary's Stadium
(Southampton FC) The
SO14 . . . . **291** B5
Friesian Cl PO11 . . . **54** B4
Frimley Bsns Pk
Camberley GU16 . . . **249** C4
Farnborough GU14 . . **55** F8
Frimley CE Jun Sch
GU16 . . . . **56** C7
Frimley Green Rd
GU16 . . . . **56** C7
Frimley Grove Gdns
GU16 . . . . **56** C7
Frimley Hall Dr GU15. **36** D6
Frimley High St
Camberley GU16 . . . . **56** A8
Frimley GU16 . . . . . . **36** B1
Frimley Park Hospl
GU16 . . . . **36** B2
Frimley Rd
Ash Vale GU12 . . . . . **77** E8
Camberley GU15 . . . . **35** F4
Frimley GU16 . . . . . . **36** A1
Frimley Sq GU16 . . . . **36** C1
Frimley Sta GU16 . . . . **36** B1
Frinton Ct 2 BH14. . **391** A4
Fritham Cl SO40 . . . . **288** C7

Fritham Gdns BH8 . . **378** D3
Fritham Rd SO18 . . . **292** D8
Frith End Rd GU35,
GU34 . . . . **142** E6
Frith Hill Rd GU16 . . **36** E1
Frith La PO17 . . . . . **296** B7
Frith Lane End PO17 **296** B8
Frithmead Cl RG21 . . **69** A2
Frobisher Ave BH12. **376** F1
Frobisher Cl
Christchurch BH23 . . **395** F6
Gosport PO13 . . . . . **368** C6
Ringwood BH24 . . . . **305** C1
Frobisher Ct SO40 . . **290** A3
Frobisher Gdns
6 Emsworth PO10. . **348** F8
Southampton SO19 . . **292** C4
Frobisher Gr PO16 . . **344** C7
Frobisher Ho 6
PO1 . . . . **370** A5
SO51 . . . . **215** E1
Froddington Rd PO5 **404** C2
Frogall SO45 . . . . . . **314** A1
Frogham Cross SP6. **282** E6
Frogham Gn PO9 . . . **323** D6
Frogham Hill SP6 . . . **282** D6
Froghole La SO20 . . . **171** F2
Frog La
Bramley RG26 . . . . . . **28** A5
Fordingbridge SP6. . . **281** E7
Little London RG26 . . **27** F5
Mapledurwell RG25 . . **70** F4
Rotherwick RG27 . . . . **50** D6
Titchfield PO15 . . . . **342** A8
Frogmore PO14 . . . . **342** C8
Frogmore Com Coll
GU46 . . . . **34** D5
Frogmore Ct GU17 . . . **35** A4
Frogmore Gr GU17 . . . **35** A4
Frogmore Jun & Inf Schs
GU17 . . . . **34** D5
Frogmore La
Nursling SO16 . . . . . **265** D3
Waterlooville PO8 . . **300** A6
Frogmore Park Dr
GU17 . . . . **35** B4
Frogmore Rd GU17. . . **35** A4
Frogs Hole RG20 . . . . **24** C2
Frome Cl
Basingstoke RG21 . . . **69** D5
Farnborough GU14 . . **55** B6
Marchwood SO40 . . . **290** A1
Oakley RG23 . . . . **67** C1
Frome Rd SO18 . . . . **268** A3
Fromond Cl SO41 . . . **385** E5
Fromond Rd SO22 . . **175** D3
Front Lawn Inf Sch
PO9. . . . . **323** F5
Front Lawn Jun Sch
PO9. . . . . **323** F5
Froome Pl RG24 . . . . . **48** E2
Frosthole Cl PO15. . . **318** E3
Frosthole Cres PO15 **318** E3
Frost La SO45 . . . . . **314** B1
Frost Rd BH11 . . . . . **376** F3
Froude Ave PO12 . . . **369** C3
Froude Rd PO12 . . . . **369** D3
Frouds Cl RG27 . . . . . **71** F8
Froud Way BH21 . . . . **374** C4
Froyle Ct 19 PO9 . . . **324** B5
Froyle Ho GU34 . . . . **119** A2
Froyle La RG29 . . . . . **95** A3
Fry Cl
Blackfield SO45 . . . . **338** F2
Hamble-le-R SO31. . . **316** A4
Fryer Cl BH11 . . . . . **377** B5
Fryern Arc SO53 . . . **243** E6
Fryern Court Rd SP6 **257** E5
Fryern Ct SO53 . . . . **243** E6
Fryern Inf Sch SO53. **243** E6
Fryern Jun Sch
SO53. . . . . **243** E6
Fryers Cl SO23 . . . . **176** C8
Fryers Copse BH21 . **352** C6
Fryers Rd BH21 . . . . **326** D8
Fry's Acre GU12. . . . . **77** E3
Frys Cl SO41 . . . . . . **384** D1
Fry's La
Meonstoke SO32 . . . **249** C6
Yateley GU46. . . . . . . **34** C7
Fry Sq SP10 . . . . **83** B2
Fuchsia Gdns SO15 . **266** D2
Fugelmere Rd GU51. . **54** C2
Fulbrook Way RG29 . . **95** D8
Fulcrum Ctr The
BH12. . . . . **378** C2
Fulflood 2 SO22 . . . **403** E6
Fulflood Rd PO9 . . . . **323** E5
Fullegar Cotts SO32. **272** B6
Fullers La RG20 . . . . . **21** A8
Fullers Rd GU10 . . . . **121** B4
Fullers Vale GU35. . . **165** D5
Fullerton Cl
14 Fleet GU51 . . . **53** C3
7 Havant PO9 . . . **324** B5
Southampton SO19 . . **314** E8
Fullerton Rd
Goodworth Clatford
SP11 . . . . **127** D7
Lymington SO41 . . . **385** C4

Wherwell SP11 . . . . **128** E5
Fullerton Way RG26 . . **27** A7
Fulmar Cl
Basingstoke RG22 . . . **90** F7
Southampton SO16 . . **266** A5
Fulmar Dr SO45 . . . . **314** B2
Fulmar Rd BH23 . . . . **396** A5
Fulmar Wlk PO13 . . . **343** A3
Fulmer Wlk PO8 . . . . **299** E4
Fulwood Ave BH11. . **376** E5
Funtington Rd PO2. . **370** D4
Funtley Ct PO16. . . . **318** E4
Funtley Hill PO16 . . . **318** E4
Funtley La PO17 . . . . **318** E5
Funtley Rd PO17 . . . . **318** E5
Furdies PO7 . . . . **298** E4
Furley Cl 8 SO23 . . **403** F6
Furlong BH24 . . . . . . **328** F7
Furlonge Ho PO10 . . **324** E1
Furlong Mews BH24. **328** F7
Furlong The BH24. . . **328** F7
Furneaux Gdns
PO16 . . . . **319** B3
Furnell Rd BH15 . . . **390** D1
Furness Rd 18 PO5. **370** D1
Furness Way PO11. . **372** B3
Furniss Way PO13 . . **367** B8
Furnston Gr PO10 . . **325** D4
Furrows The SO20 . . **126** B4
Furse Hill Rd SP9 . . . **78** F5
Further Vell-Mead
GU52 . . . . **74** E5
Further Vel-Mead
GU52 . . . . **74** E5
Fury Way PO14 . . . . **367** B8
Furzebrook Cl BH17. **375** E3
Furze Cl
Ash Vale GU12. . . . . . **77** E7
Southampton SO19 . . **292** A5
Furze Croft BH25 . . **383** A2
Furzedale Gdns
SO45 . . . . **314** B1
Furzedale Pk SO45. . **314** B1
Furzedown Cotts
SO20 . . . . **194** B7
Furzedown Cres 4
PO9 . . . . **324** A5
Furzedown Ho SO20 **194** B6
Furzedown La SP11. **103** F5
Furzedown Mews 2
SO45 . . . . **314** B1
Furzedown Rd
King's Somborne
SO20. . . . . **194** B8
Southampton SO17 . . **267** A2
Furze Dr SP11 . . . . . . **79** D6
Furze Hall Rd PO16. . **319** B4
Furzehall Ave PO16 . **319** B3
Furzehill BH21 . . . . . **351** C8
Furze Hill Dr BH14 . . **391** C1
Furze Hill Rd GU35. . **166** A4
Furze La PO4 . . . . . . **371** D4
Furzelands Rd BH21. **326** E8
Furzeley Rd PO7 . . . **298** F2
Furzen La RG25 . . . . **115** B7
Furze Rd
Pamber Heath RG26 . . **9** D2
Southampton SO19 . . **292** A5
Furze Vale Rd GU35. **166** A4
Furzey Ave SO45 . . . **314** B2
Furzey Cl SO45 . . . . **338** F1
Furzey Gdns★ SO43. **286** A3
Furzey La SO42 . . . . **336** B1
Furzey Rd BH16 . . . . **389** B6
Furzley Ct PO9. . . . . **323** C6
Furzley La SO43 . . . **262** D6
Furzley Rd SO40 . . . **262** E3
Furzy Whistlers Cl
BH23 . . . . **357** B1
Fushia Cl PO9 . . . . . **324** C4
Futcher Sch The
PO6. . . . . **346** C8
Fuzzy Dro RG22 . . . . **90** F8
Fyeford Cl SO16 . . . **265** F6
Fyfield Cl
Blackwater GU17 . . . **35** B5
Swanwick PO15 . . . . **317** C8
Fyfield La SP11 . . . . . **81** A3
Fyfield Rd SP11 . . . . . **81** B2
Fyfield Way
Littleton SO22 . . . . . **175** D5
North Tidworth SP11. . **79** D6
Fylingdales Cl RG22 . **68** B3
Fyning St PO1 . . . . . **404** C4

G

Gable End
10 Aldershot GU11 . . **76** F2
3 Farnborough GU14. **55** F4
Gablehurst BH16 . . . **389** C7
Gable Mews PO11. . . **373** A4
Gables Cl
Ash Vale GU12. . . . . . **77** E5
Farnborough GU14 . . **55** E4
Gables Ct SO16 . . . . **266** F5
Gables Rd GU52. . . . . **74** F4
Gables The
10 Grayshott GU26 . **167** B3
Whitchurch RG28 . . . . **86** E5
Gabriel Dr GU15 . . . . **36** F4
Gabriels The RG14 . . . **5** B5
Gadbridge Ct 14
BH4 . . . . **392** C2
Gaffney Cl GU11 . . . **77** B7
Gage Cl
Marchwood SO40 . . . **290** A2

Gage Cl continued
Old Basing RG24 . . . . **69** F7
Gaiger Ave RG27 . . . . **49** B5
Gainsborough Ave
BH25 . . . . **383** B5
Gainsborough Cl
Camberley GU15 . . . . **36** D7
Farnborough GU14 . . **56** B2
Southampton SO19 . . **292** C2
Gainsborough Ct
4 Bournemouth
BH5 . . . . **394** B5
5 Fleet GU51 . . . . **54** A2
Andover SP10 . . . . . . **82** F1
Farnborough GU14 . . **77** A8
Lymington SO41 . . . **385** D2
North Baddesley
SO52 . . . . **242** B4
Gainsborough Ho
2 Portsmouth PO4. **370** E2
Barton on S BH25 . . **398** A6
Gainsborough Mews
PO14 . . . . **341** F8
Gainsborough Rd
Basingstoke RG21 . . . **69** C2
Bournemouth BH7 . . **393** F7
St Leonards BH24 . . **327** F5
Gainsford Rd SO19. . **291** E5
Gain's Rd PO4 . . . . . **370** E2
Galahad Cl SP10 . . . . **83** A3
Galaxie Rd PO8 . . . . **300** B4
Galaxy Ho RG19 . . . . . **6** E5
Gale Moor Ave PO12 **368** D4
Gales Ct SP16 . . . . . **106** A7
Galileo Pk SP10 . . . . **82** C1
Gallaghers Mead
SP10 . . . . **105** C8
Galleon Cl SO31 . . . **316** F1
Galleries The 8
GU11 . . . . **76** E2
Galley La RG19 . . . . . **24** C8
Gallia Ct SO17 . . . . **266** F1
Gallops The PO14 . . **317** D2
Gallop The GU46 . . . . **34** B7
Gallop Way BH12 . . . **392** C7
Galloway
Basingstoke RG22 . . . **68** B3
Fleet GU51 . . . . **54** C2
Galloway Ctr The RG14 **2** C2
Galloway Rd BH15 . . **389** D4
Gallows Dr BH22 . . . **353** E1
Gallwey Rd GU11. . . . **77** A3
Gally Hill Rd GU52 . . **74** E5
Galsworthy Rd SO40 **288** D7
Galton Ave BH23 . . . **394** F6
Galt Rd PO6 . . . . **346** D8
Galway Rd GU46 . . . . **34** A4
Gamble Cl SO19 . . . . **291** F4
Gambledon La SO51. **213** F5
Gamble Rd PO2 . . . . **370** D8
Gamblins La SO32. . . **295** D8
Gander Dr RG24 . . . . . **68** C8
Ganders Cl GU34 . . . **184** E8
Gangbridge La SP11. . **61** E3
Ganger Farm La
SO51 . . . . **216** C2
Ganger Rd SO51 . . . **216** C2
Gannet Cl
Basingstoke RG22 . . . **90** F8
Hythe SO45 . . . . . . **314** B2
Southampton SO16 . . **266** B5
Gannets The PO14 . . **367** B8
Garage Cotts SO32 . **228** E4
Garbett Rd SO23 . . . **198** C8
Garbetts Way GU10. **100** D6
Garden City SO45 . . **313** A6
Garden Cl
3 Andover SP10 . . **106** B7
Axford RG25 . . . . . . **114** B1
Farnborough GU14 . . **55** C3
Hook RG27. . . . . **50** F1
Kingsclere RG20 . . . . **24** D2
Lyndhurst SO43 . . . . **309** E5
New Milton BH25 . . . **383** A1
South Hayling PO11 . **372** F3
Garden Close La RG14. **5** B4
Garden Cotts RG29 . . **95** F1
Garden Court Cotts
BH22 . . . . **326** D3
Garden Ct
Bournemouth BH1. . **393** D6
Portchester PO16 . . **344** D8
Sutton Scotney SO21. **131** C3
Gardeners Cotts
BH24 . . . . **329** A4
Gardeners Gn SP9 . . **101** D7
Gardener's Hill Rd
GU10 . . . . **121** F4
Gardeners La SO51. . **240** A4
Garden Ho 6 BH1 . . **393** B3
Gardenia Dr PO15. . . **317** E3
Garden La
25 Winchester
SO23. . . . . **403** E6
Portsmouth PO5 . . . **404** B1
Garden-La BH24 . . . **327** E3
Garden Mews
10 Petersfield
GU32 . . . . **228** F3
Warsash SO31. . . . . **316** C1
Garden Rd BH24 . . . . **330** F3
Gardens Cres BH14 . **402** B8
Gardens Ct 5 BH15. **390** E3
Gardens Rd BH14 . . **402** B8

Gardens The
Broughton SO20 . . . . . . **170** B7
Fareham PO16. . . . . **319** C3
Hambledon PO7. . . . **274** C3
Havant PO9. . . . . **324** B1
Tongham GU10 . . . . **100** D7
Garden Terr 14 PO5 . **370** D2
Garden Wlk BH22 . . . **353** E7
Gardiner Cl SO40 . . . . **290** A2
Gardiners Cnr SO51 . . **216** D6
Gardner Cl BH23 . . . **394** E8
Gardner Rd
Christchurch BH23 . . **394** E8
Ringwood BH24. . . . **329** B6
Titchfield PO14 . . . . **341** F7
Gardner Way SO53 . . **243** B8
Garendon Ct SP6 . . . **257** E2
Garfield Ave BH1 . . . **393** D5
Garfield Cl SO32 . . . **271** C8
Garfield Rd
Bishop's Waltham
SO32. . . . . **271** C8
Camberley GU15 . . . . **36** A5
Netley SO31. . . . . . . **315** A4
Portsmouth PO2 . . . . **370** D8
Southampton SO19 . . **291** E7
Garford Cres RG14. . . **5** B8
Garland Ave PO10. . . **324** F3
Garland Ct
5 Gosport PO12 . . . **369** B6
Newbury RG14 . . . . . . **1** D2
Garland Rd BH15. . . **390** D4
Garland Way SO40 . . **288** B8
Garnet Field GU46 . . . **33** E5
Garnet Rd GU35. . . . **164** E2
Garnett Cl PO14. . . . **342** C4
Garnier Pk PO17 . . . **296** A4
Garnier Rd SO23 . . . **403** E3
Garnier St PO1 . . . . **404** D3
Garnock Rd SO19 . . . **291** D2
Garratt Cl SO30 . . . . **269** D2
Garrett Cl
Kingsclere RG20 . . . . **24** C3
Southampton SO19 . . **292** A1
Garrett Mews 7
GU11. . . . . **76** E1
Garrick Gdns SO19 . . **292** B2
Garrick Ho 4 PO2 . . **345** F4
Garrick Way GU16 . . . **56** C7
Garrison Hill SO32 . . . **249** B2
Garrow Dr SO41 . . . . **385** E5
Garsdale Cl BH11 . . . **377** A6
Garsons Rd PO10 . . . **349** D8
Gar St SO23 . . . . . . **403** D5
Garston Cl GU32 . . . . **251** D8
Garston Mede SO20 . . **129** A3
Garstons Cl PO14 . . . **341** F8
Garstons Rd PO14. . . **341** F8
Garstons Tk SO21 . . . **174** B5
Garth Cl
Bordon GU35. . . . . . **164** D4
Farnham GU9 . . . . . . **121** E7
St Leonards BH24 . . . **327** D4
Garth Rd
Bournemouth BH9 . . . **378** A1
Mortimer RG7. . . . . . . **11** E5
Garth The
Alton GU34 . . . . **140** A4
Ash GU12. . . . . **77** D1
Farnborough GU14 . . . **56** B4
Hythe SO45. . . . . . . **313** F2
Garton Rd SO19 . . . **291** D3
Gascoigne La SO24 . . **181** C5
Gashouse Hill SO31 . . **315** C5
Gaskell Cl GU34. . . . **140** C6
Gaskell Mews RG14 . . . **5** F8
Gason Hill Rd SP9. . . . **78** E8
Gaston Gdns SO51 . . **240** F8
Gaston La
South Warnborough
RG29 . . . . **95** A5
Upper Farringdon
GU34 . . . . **161** F4
Gaston's Wood Ind Est
RG24. . . . . **69** D8
Gatcombe SO31. . . . **315** C7
Gatcombe Ave PO3 . . **346** A4
Gatcombe Dr PO2. . . **345** F3
Gatcombe Gdns
Fareham PO14. . . . . **342** B8
West End SO18 . . . . **268** A2
Gatcombe Park Prim Sch
PO2. . . . . **345** F3
Gate House Rd PO16 **344** A7
Gatehouse The
11 Southampton
SO18. . . . . **291** E8
West End SO30 . . . . **268** C2
Gatekeeper Cl 7
SO23. . . . . **198** C8
Gates The GU51. . . . . **54** C4
Gateway The BH13 . . **391** F4
Gatwick Cl SO16 . . . **266** A4
Gaulter Cl PO9. . . . . **324** A3
Gauvain Cl GU34 . . . **140** A2
Gavan St SO19 . . . . **292** D5
G Ave SO45 . . . . . . **338** F6
Gawaine Cl SP10. . . . **83** A4
Gawn Pl PO12 . . . . . **369** D3
Gaydon Rise BH11 . . **376** E4
Gaylyn Way PO14 . . . **342** B8
Gaywood Dr RG14. . . **2** B4
Gaza Ave SO42. . . . . **363** C6
Gaza Ho PO15 . . . . . **318** D3

Gazelle Cl PO13 . . . . **368** D5
Gazing La SO51 . . . . **238** E3
Gazings The SO51. . . **238** E3
Geale's Almshouses 6
GU34 . . . . **139** F4
Geale's Cres GU34 . . . **140** A5
Geale's Ct GU34 . . . . **140** A5
Geddes Way GU31 . . . **229** C4
Geffery's Fields RG21 **69** C5
Geffery's Ho RG27 . . . **51** B2
Gemini Cl SO16 . . . . **265** F4
General Johnson Ct 4
SO22 . . . . **403** A4
Geneva Ave BH6 . . . . **394** D5
Genoa Cl SO41. . . . . **385** C1
Genoa Ct
Andover SP10 . . . . . . **83** B3
Andover SP10 . . . . . . **83** B4
Genoa Ho PO6. . . . . **345** A7
Gentles La GU30 . . . **165** E3
Gento Cl SO30 . . . . . **293** E6
Geoffrey Ave PO7. . . **322** B2
Geoffrey Cres PO16 . **343** B6
George Byng Way
PO2 . . . . **370** C8
George Ct PO5. . . . . **370** D2
George Ct The 10
PO1 . . . . **370** A3
George Curl Way
SO18 . . . . **267** F6
George Eyston Dr
SO22 . . . . **403** B4
George Gdns
Aldershot GU11,
GU12 . . . . **100** A7
Fleet GU51 . . . . **54** B1
George Mews The
BH24 . . . . **328** F7
George Rd
Fleet GU51 . . . . **54** B1
Milford on S SO41. . . **399** C5
George Rdbt The
BH15 . . . . **390** C3
Georges Mews BH21 **374** D7
George St
Basingstoke RG21. . . . **68** F5
Eastleigh SO50 . . . . **244** B3
Gosport PO12 . . . . . **369** C6
Kingsclere RG20 . . . . **24** D2
Portsmouth PO1,PO2 **370** F7
George VI Rd SP9. . . . **78** E8
George Wright Cl
SO50 . . . . **243** F2
George Yd SP10 . . . . **106** B7
George Yd The
SO24 . . . . **179** D6
Georgia Cl
Andover SP10 . . . . . **105** E6
Havant PO9. . . . . . . **323** E3
Lee-on-t-S PO13 . . . **367** F4
Georgia La SP11 . . . . **103** F2
Georgian Cl
Camberley GU15 . . . . **36** C7
Ringwood BH24. . . . **329** A8
Georgian Way BH10 . **377** F4
Georgina Cl
Poole BH12 . . . . **392** C8
Totton SO40. . . . . . **264** B1
Georgina Ct 4 GU51. **54** A1
Georgina Gdns RG26 **27** B8
Georgina Talbot Ho
BH12 . . . . **392** B8
Gerald Rd BH3. . . . . **393** A6
Gerald Sq GU34. . . . **140** A6
Gerard Cres SO19. . . **292** D6
Gerard Ho 6 PO2. . . **345** F4
Germaine Cl BH23 . . **396** F8
German Rd RG26. . . . **29** A2
Gerring Rd RG2. . . . . **15** D7
Gershwin Cl RG22. . . **91** C8
Gershwin Rd RG22 . . **91** C7
Gervis Cres BH14 . . . **391** A4
Gervis Pl BH1. . . . . . **392** F3
Gervis Rd BH1. . . . . **393** B3
Gibbet La GU15. . . . . **36** E7
Gibbons Cl GU47. . . . **35** A8
Gibbs Cl
Finchampstead RG40. . **16** C6
Hythe SO45. . . . . . . **338** A8
Gibbs' La GU35 . . . . **164** A6
Gibbs Rd SO14. . . . . **290** F5
Gibbs Way GU46 . . . . **33** F4
Giblet Ore PO14 . . . . **367** A6
Gibraltar Cl PO15 . . . **318** D4
Gibraltar Rd
Fareham PO14. . . . . **342** F6
Portsmouth PO4 . . . **371** D3
Gibson Cl
Lee-on-t-S PO13 . . . **367** F4
Whiteley PO15. . . . . **317** E5
Gibson Rd BH17 . . . . **390** E7
Giddylake BH21. . . . **351** D6
Gid La GU34. . . . . . . **119** B3
Giffard Dr GU14. . . . **55** D5
Giffard La GU51. . . . **53** E3
Giffards Mdw GU9 . . . **99** C1
Gifford Cl PO15 . . . . **318** B3
Gilbard Ct RG24. . . . . **49** A3
Gilbert Cl
Alderholt SP6 . . . . . **281** B6
Basingstoke RG24. . . **48** C1
Gosport PO13 . . . . . **368** D8
Lymington SO41. . . . **385** D2
Gilbert Mead PO11. . **372** E4
Gilbert Rd
Bournemouth BH8. . . **393** D6
Camberley GU16. . . . **36** A2
Gilbert's Gn SP9 . . . **101** E7

Gilberts Mead Cl
SP11 . . . . **105** C4
Gilbert St SO24 . . . . **181** E6
Gilbert Way
Finchampstead RG40. . **16** C8
Waterlooville PO7 . . **322** E5
Gilbert White Way
GU34 . . . . **139** F6
Gilbury Cl SO18 . . . . **267** E4
Gilchrist Gdns SO31. **340** C9
Giles Cl
Fareham PO16. . . . . **319** B3
Gosport PO12 . . . . . **369** A7
Hedge End SO30 . . . **269** D1
Newbury RG14 . . . . . . **1** C2
Giles Ct RG26. . . . . . . **27** A8
Giles La SP5 . . . . . . **238** A4
Giles Rd RG26 . . . . . **27** A8
Gilkicker Rd PO12. . . **369** C2
Gillam Rd BH10. . . . **377** D5
Gillcrest PO14 . . . . . **317** C4
Gillett Rd BH12 . . . . **392** C7
Gillham's La GU27 . . **188** D5
Gillian Ave GU14. . . . **100** B8
Gillian Cl GU12 . . . . **100** B8
Gillies Dr RG24 . . . . . **68** C8
Gillies The 6 PO16 . **319** A1
Gillingham Cl
Bournemouth BH9. . . **378** C4
Kings Worthy SO23 . . **176** C7
Gillingham Rd SO41. **399** D4
Gillion Ct 2 BH23. . . **395** E6
Gilman Rd PO6. . . . . **322** C1
Gilmour Gdns GU34. **140** A6
Gilpin Cl
Pilley SO41 . . . . **361** F1
Southampton SO19 . . **292** E5
Gilpin Hill SO41. . . . **360** B2
Gilpins Folly SO41 . . **360** A3
Gilroy Cl RG14 . . . . . . **5** A6
Gins La SO42 . . . . . . **364** E1
Girton Cl PO14 . . . . **317** C1
Gisors Rd PO4. . . . . **371** B4
Gitsham Gdns PO7 . . **322** C3
Gladdis Rd BH11. . . . **376** F3
Glade Cl RG24 . . . . . . **48** F2
Gladelands Cl BH18 . **374** E4
Gladelands Pk BH22. **353** F7
Gladelands Way
BH18 . . . . **374** E4
Glades The SO31. . . **317** A4
Glade The
Binsted GU10 . . . . . **120** F1
Blackfield SO45. . . . **365** E7
Chandler's Ford SO53 **218** F1
Christchurch BH23 . . **379** E1
Fareham PO15. . . . . **318** D4
Farnham GU9 . . . . . . **99** B7
Mytchett GU16 . . . . . **56** E2
Newbury RG14 . . . . . . **5** D7
South Hayling PO11. . **373** C1
St Leonards BH24 . . . **327** E5
Waterlooville PO7 . . . **323** A8
Gladiator Way GU14. . **76** E8
Gladstone Cl BH23 . . **395** D6
Gladstone Gdns
PO16 . . . . **344** C7
Gladstone Pl 4 PO2 . **370** D8
Gladstone Rd
Bournemouth BH7 . . **393** F5
Gosport PO12 . . . . . **369** A8
Poole BH12 . . . . **391** C5
Gladstone Rd E BH7. **393** F5
Gladstone Rd W
BH1 . . . . **393** E5
Gladstone St SO23 . . **403** D6
Gladstone Terr SP11 **108** B5
Gladys Ave
Portsmouth PO2 . . . **345** D2
Waterlooville PO8 . . . **300** A4
Glamis Ave BH10. . . **377** E5
Glamis Cl
Camberley GU16 . . . . **56** D7
Oakley RG23 . . . . . . **67** B2
Waterlooville PO7 . . . **323** A8
Glamis Ct PO14 . . . . **367** C8
Glamorgan Rd PO6 . . **276** B3
Glasgow Rd PO4 . . . **371** B3
Glasslaw Rd SO18. . . **292** A8
Glasspool PO7. . . . . **298** E5
Glastonbury Cl RG24 **69** A8
Glaston Hill Rd RG27 **33** A8
Glayshers Hill GU35. **165** F6
Gleadowe Ave BH23. **395** A6
Glebe Cl
Bentworth GU34 . . . **138** A8
Dummer RG25. . . . . . **90** D1
South Hayling PO11. . **372** E5
Tadley RG26. . . . . . . **27** A7
Glebe Cnr PO17. . . . **296** B3
Glebe Cotts SO21 . . **132** B3
Glebe Ct
Botley SO30. . . . . . **294** A8
Fair Oak SO50 . . . . **245** D2
Fleet GU51 . . . . **53** F1
Southampton SO17 . . **267** A2
Glebe Dr PO13 . . . . . **343** C1
Glebefield Gdns 1
PO6 . . . . **345** E8
Glebefields
6 Milford on S
SO41. . . . . **399** D3
Newbury RG14 . . . . . . **1** F5
Glebe Fields GU34 . . **138** B5
Glebe La
Basingstoke RG23. . . **68** A4
Hartley Wintney RG27. **52** D5

Glebe La continued
Landford SP5. . . . . . **237** D4
Glebeland Rd GU15 . . **35** C4
Glebelands SP11. . . . **106** B1
Glebe Mdw
East Dean SP5. . . . . **191** A2
Overton RG25 . . . . . . **88** A8
Glebe Park Ave PO9. **323** A1
Glebe Rd
Buriton GU31. . . . . . **253** D5
Crondall GU10 . . . . . . **97** C6
Farnborough GU14 . . . **55** D5
Headley GU35 . . . . . **165** C5
Southampton SO14 . . **291** B3
Glebe The
Blackwater GU17 . . . . **35** C4
Stubbington PO14 . . . **367** C6
Glenair Ave BH14 . . . **391** A3
Glenair Cres BH14 . . **391** A3
Glenair Rd BH14 . . . **391** A3
Glenapp Grange RG7. **11** D6
Glenavon BH25 . . . . **383** C2
Glenavon Gdns GU46. .**34** B4
Glenavon Rd BH23 . . **381** F1
Glenbrook Wlk
PO14 . . . . **342** C8
Glencarron Way 3
SO16 . . . . **266** E3
Glen Cl
Andover SP10 . . . . . **105** E8
Barton on S BH25 . . . **397** D8
Beacon Hill GU26 . . . **167** A6
Glencoe Cl GU16. . . . . **56** E8
Glencoe Rd
Bournemouth BH7 . . . **393** F7
Poole BH12 . . . . **391** D5
Portsmouth PO1 . . . **370** F7
Glencoyne Gdns
SO16 . . . . **265** F2
Glen Ct GU26 . . . . . **167** A6
Glenda Cl SO31. . . . **340** D10
Glendale
Locks Heath SO31. . . **317** B2
Swanmore SO32 . . . . **272** B4
Glen Dale PO9. . . . . **301** C1
Glendale Ave
Ferndown BH22. . . . **353** E6
Newbury RG14 . . . . . . **5** A5
Glendale Cl
Christchurch BH23 . . **379** D3
Wimborne Minster
BH21. . . . . **351** C5
Glendale Ct BH23 . . **379** D3
Glendale Pk GU51. . . **53** D2
Glendale Rd
Bournemouth BH6. . . **395** A4
Pamber Heath RG26 . . . **9** E1
Glendeep SO23 . . . . **176** B6
Glendon Ave BH10 . . **377** C6
Glendowan Rd SO53 **243** A7
Glendrive BH25 . . . . **397** C8
Gleneagles
Christchurch BH23 . . **394** F6
Poole BH13 . . . . **392** B2
Gleneagles Ave
BH14 . . . . **391** D2
Gleneagles Cl
Basingstoke RG22. . . **91** A3
Ferndown BH22. . . . **353** F6
Gleneagles Dr
Farnborough GU14 . . . **55** A3
Waterlooville PO7 . . . **300** B2
Glenelg PO15 . . . . . **318** F2
Glenesha Gdns
PO15 . . . . **318** D2
Glen Eyre Cl SO16. . . **267** A4
Glen Eyre Dr SO16. . . **267** A5
Glen Eyre Hall SO16. **267** A5
Glen Eyre Rd SO16 . . **266** F5
Glen Eyre Way SO16 **267** A4
Glenferness Ave
BH4 . . . . **392** D5
Glen Fern Rd BH1. . . **393** A3
Glenfield Ave SO18. . **291** F7
Glenfield Cl SP5 . . . . **168** B6
Glenfield Cres SO18. **291** F7
Glenfield Inf Sch
SO18. . . . . **291** F7
Glenfield Way SO18 . **291** F7
Glengariff Rd BH14 . **391** C2
Glengarry PO5. . . . . **383** C2
Glengarry Way BH23 **396** C6
Glen Ho PO12. . . . . . **368** F3
Glenhurst Cl GU17 . . . **35** C4
Glenhurst Sch PO9. . **324** A1
Glenives Cl BH24. . . **328** A4
Glenlea Cl GU26 . . . **167** C1
Glenlea Cl SO30. . . . **268** D1
Glenlea Dr SO30 . . . **268** D1
Glenleigh Ave 6
PO6 . . . . **345** F7
Glenleigh Ct 5 PO6. **345** F7
Glenleigh Pk PO9 . . . **324** B2
Glenmeadows Dr
BH10 . . . . **377** B5
Glenmoor Cl BH10 . . **377** D1
Glenmoor Rd
Bournemouth BH9 . . . **392** E8
Ferndown BH22. . . . **353** D3
Glenmoor Sch BH10 **377** D1
Glenmore Bsns Pk
SP10 . . . . **105** C3
Glenmore Ct SO17 . . **291** A8
Glenmore Gdns PO8 **299** F2
Glenmount Dr BH14. **391** B4
Glenn Rd SO30. . . . . **268** C2
Glenny Cl PO13 . . . . **368** A6

Glen Park Mobile Home
Pk SO21. . . . . **245** B8
Glen Rd
Beacon Hill GU26 . . . **167** B6
Bournemouth BH5. . . **393** F4
Fleet GU51 . . . . **74** F8
Grayshott GU26. . . . **167** B3
Poole BH14 . . . . **391** B4
Sarisbury SO31 . . . . **316** F6
Southampton SO19 . . **291** D2
Glenroyd Gdns BH6 . **394** E4
Glenside
Barton on S BH23,
BH25 . . . . **397** B7
Hythe SO45. . . . . . . **313** F3
Glenside Ave SO19 . . **292** D4
Glen Spey BH25. . . . **383** D2
Glen The
Farnham GU9 . . . . . . **99** A6
Gosport PO13 . . . . . **343** E1
Poole BH14 . . . . **391** D6
Poole,Canford Cliffs
BH13 . . . . **402** E8
Glenthorne Cl PO14 . **367** D6
Glenthorne Mdw
GU32. . . . . **226** E1
Glenthorne Rd PO3 . **346** A1
Glenville Cl BH23. . . **382** B2
Glenville Gdns
Bournemouth BH10. . **377** C2
Hindhead GU26 . . . . **167** D4
Glenville Rd
Bournemouth BH10. . **377** C2
Walkford BH23. . . . . **382** B2
Glenwood GU9 . . . . . **99** A6
Glenwood Ave SO16. **262** A5
Glenwood Cl BH22 . . **326** E2
Glenwood Ct SO50 . . **245** E2
Glenwood Gdns PO8 **299** F3
Glenwood La BH22. . **326** E2
Glenwood Rd
Breach PO10 . . . . . . **325** E1
Verwood BH31. . . . . **302** F5
West Moors BH22. . . **326** E2
Woodlands Sch SO10 **324** F1
Glenwood Way BH22 **326** E2
Glidden Cl PO1 . . . . **404** C3
Glidden La PO7. . . . . **274** C1
Glissons BH22 . . . . . **353** A2
Globe Farm La GU17 . . **34** F5
Globe La BH15. . . . . **390** C2
Glorney Mead GU9 . . . **99** E6
Gloster Cl GU12. . . . . **77** D5
Gloster Ct PO15. . . . **317** C5
Gloucester Cl
Camberley GU16 . . . . **56** C6
Four Marks GU34 . . . **160** A2
Petersfield GU32. . . . **228** D3
Gloucester Ct 3
GU32. . . . . **228** F4
Gloucester Dr RG22 . .**91** B8
Gloucester Ho 1
PO12 . . . . **369** C5
Gloucester Mews
PO5 . . . . **404** B2
Gloucester Pl PO5 . . **404** B1
Gloucester Rd
Aldershot GU11. . . . . **100** A7
Bournemouth BH7 . . . **393** F5
Newbury RG14 . . . . . . **1** C2
Poole BH15 . . . . **391** E5
Portsmouth PO1 . . . **370** A4
Waterlooville PO7 . . . **322** F6
Gloucester Sq 28
SO14 . . . . **291** A3
Gloucester Terr PO5 **404** B1
Gloucester View
PO5 . . . . **404** B2
Glovers Field GU27. . **189** D6
Glovers Ho GU27. . . **189** D6
Glyn Dr PO14 . . . . . **367** C7
Glyn Jones Cl SO45. . **338** F2
Glynswood
Frimley GU15. . . . . . **36** D3
Rowledge GU10. . . . **121** E4
Glynville Cl BH21 . . . **352** A7
Glynville Ct BH21 . . . **352** A7
Glynville Rd BH21. . . **352** A7
Glyn Way PO14 . . . . **367** C7
Goatacre Rd GU34 . . **159** C4
Goathorn Cl BH16. . . **389** D4
Goathouse La PO17 . **297** B4
Goat La RG21 . . . . . . **69** C5
Goch Way SP10 . . . . **82** E2
Goddard Cl SO51. . . **238** E3
Goddards Cl RG27 . . . **49** D8
Goddards Firs RG23. . **90** C3
Goddards La
Camberley GU15 . . . . **35** F3
Sherfield on L RG27 . . **49** C8
Goddards Mead
SP10 . . . . **105** E7
Goddard Sq 1 SP10 . **83** C2
Godfrey Cl GU47 . . . . **35** B7
Godfrey Olson Ho
SO50 . . . . **244** B3
Godfrey Pink Way
SO32 . . . . **271** D2
Godiva Lawn PO4 . . . **371** C3
Godmanston Cl
BH17 . . . . **376** A1
Godshill Cl BH8. . . . **378** D3
Godson Ho 27 SO23 . **403** E6
Godwin Cl
Emsworth PO10 . . . . **324** C1
Winchester SO22 . . . **175** D3
Godwin Cres PO8 . . . **276** C3

Godwins Field SO21 . **219** C8
Godwit Cl PO12 . . . . **369** B9
Godwit Rd PO4 . . . . **371** C6
Gofton Ave PO6. . . . **346** B7
Gogg's La SP5 . . . . . **235** F6
Goldcrest Cl
1 Yateley GU46 . . . . **33** F6
Fareham PO16. . . . . **343** E8
Horndean PO8 . . . . . **300** A7
Goldcrest Gdns
SO16 . . . . **266** A5
Goldcrest La SO40 . . **288** C7
Golden Cres SO41. . . **384** D1
Golden Ct
Waterlooville PO7 . . . **322** E7
West End SO30 . . . . **268** F3
Goldenfields GU30 . . **188** B3
Goldenfields Cl
GU30. . . . . **188** B3
Golden Gates BH13 . **402** B3
Golden Gr SO14. . . . **291** B5
Golden Hind Pk
SO45 . . . . **313** F2
Goldenleas Ct BH11. **376** D3
Goldenleas Dr BH11. **376** D3
Golden Lion Rdbt
RG21 . . . . **69** B2
Golden Sands BH13 . **402** B3
Goldfinch Cl
Aldershot GU11. . . . . **99** E8
New Milton BH25 . . . **382** F2
Goldfinch Gdns RG22. .**90** F6
Goldfinch La
Bishop's Green RG20 . . .**6** E3
Lee-on-t-S PO13 . . . **367** F4
Goldfinch Rd BH17. . **389** E8
Goldfinch Way SO21 **153** E5
Goldhill GU10. . . . . **122** B6
Gold Hill GU35 . . . . **142** C1
Gold La GU11. . . . . . **77** C4
Gold Mead Cl 5
SO41 . . . . **385** E2
Goldney Rd GU15 . . . . **36** F4
Gold Oak SP5. . . . . . **279** F7
Goldring Cl PO11 . . . **373** A3
Goldsmith Ave PO4 . **370** F4
Goldsmith Cl SO40 . . **288** D7
Goldsmith Inf Sch
PO4. . . . . **370** E4
Goldsmith Rd SO50 . **243** F1
Goldsmiths Ct 17
SO14 . . . . **291** A3
Gold St PO5 . . . . . . **404** A1
Goldwell Dr RG14 . . . **1** D3
Goldwire Dr SO53. . . **242** F5
Golf Course Rd
SO16 . . . . **266** E6
Golf Dr GU15 . . . . . . **36** C4
Golf La GU35 . . . . . **164** B1
Golf Links Ave GU26. **166** F6
Golf Links Rd
Broadstone BH18 . . . **375** B5
Ferndown BH22. . . . **353** E4
Goliath Rd BH15. . . . **389** D2
Gomer Ct PO12 . . . . **368** E3
Gomer Inf Sch PO12 **368** E3
Gomer Jun Sch
PO12. . . . . **368** E3
Gomer La PO12 . . . . **368** E3
Gondreville Gdns
GU52. . . . . **74** E4
Gong Hill GU10 . . . . **122** B4
Gong Hill Dr GU10 . . **122** B4
Goodacre Dr SO53 . . **242** F5
Goodall Ct 13 PO16 . **319** B1
Goodboy's La RG7 . . . **12** E8
Goodden Cres GU14. . **55** D3
Goodens The SO24 . . **201** C5
Goodfellow Ho 6
GU34 . . . . **139** F3
Goodison Cl SO50. . . **245** B1
Goodlands Vale
SO30 . . . . **293** A7
Goodman Cl RG21. . . **68** F4
Good Rd BH12. . . . . **391** C7
Goodsell Cl PO14 . . . **367** B7
Goodwin Cl SO16 . . . **265** D2
Goodwin Wlk RG14. . .**5** A6
Goodwood Cl
Alton GU34 . . . . **139** F2
Camberley GU15 . . . . **36** A8
Gosport PO12 . . . . . **369** B9
Titchfield PO14 . . . . **317** D2
Waterlooville PO8 . . . **300** B1
Goodwood Ct PO10 . **349** E8
Goodwood Gdns
SO40 . . . . **288** C8
Goodwood Pl GU14 . . **56** C3
Goodwood Rd
Eastleigh SO50 . . . . **243** E4
Gosport PO12 . . . . . **369** B9
Portsmouth PO5 . . . **404** D1
Goodwood Way RG14 . .**2** A1
Goodwyns Cl SP11 . . **101** D7
Goodwyns Gn GU34. . **140** A3
Goodyers GU34 . . . . **140** A3
Gooseberry La BH24 **328** F7
Goose Gn RG27 . . . . . **50** F2
Goose La RG27. . . . . **51** A2
Gooserye Ct GU30. . . **187** F3
Gordleton Ind Pk
SO41. . . . . **384** F5
Gordon Ave
Camberley GU15 . . . . **35** F4
Fleet GU52 . . . . **75** B6
Southampton SO14 . . **291** B4
Winchester SO23 . . . **198** C6
Winchester SO23 . . . **198** C7

Gordon Bldgs SO15 . 290 C8
Gordon Cl RG21...... 69 C6
Gordon Cres GU15 ... 36 A4
Gordon Ct
 [1] Newbury RG14.......1 F2
 [7] Bournemouth BH4 392 C4
Gordon Mount BH23 397 B8
Gordon Palmer Cl
 RG7................12 B5
Gordon Rd
 Aldershot GU11...... 76 E1
 Bournemouth BH1.. 393 D4
 Camberley GU15 .... 36 A5
 Chandler's Ford
 SO53............218 D1
 Christchurch BH23.. 397 A8
 Curdridge SO32..... 271 A1
 Emsworth PO10..... 349 B8
 Fareham PO16....... 319 A1
 Farnborough GU14 .. 77 B8
 Gosport PO12...... 369 A5
 Lymington SO41 ... 385 C3
 Newbury RG14 ....1 F2
 Poole BH12......... 392 A5
 Portsmouth PO1 ... 370 B3
 Thatcham RG18....... 2 E5
 Waterlooville PO7 .. 322 D6
 Wimborne Minster
 BH21 .... 351 E4
 Winchester SO23 ... 403 E6
Gordon Rd S BH12 .. 392 A5
Gordon Terr SO19 ... 292 A2
Gordon Watson Ho
 SO23............403 D3
Gordon Way BH23 .. 380 D1
Gordon Wlk GU46... 34 D5
Gore End Rd RG20 ....3 F3
Gore Grange BH25.. 382 E2
Gore Rd BH25........ 382 E2
Gore Rd Ind Est
 BH25............382 F2
Gorey Rd BH12 .... 376 D1
Goring Ave PO8..... 276 D4
Goring Field SO22 ... 403 A7
Gorleston Rd BH12.. 391 F5
Gorley Cross SP6 ... 282 B4
Gorley Ct PO9....... 323 C6
Gorley Lynch SP6 ... 282 D4
Gorley Rd BH24..... 305 C1
Gorran Ave PO13.... 343 C1
Gorrings The SO20.. 172 A2
Gorse Cl
 Farnham GU10 ..... 121 F6
 Locks Heath SO31... 316 F2
 New Milton BH25 ... 383 D4
 St Leonards BH24... 327 D4
Gorsecliff Ct [7] BH5 393 D4
Gorsecliff Rd BH10.. 377 D1
Gorse Cotts
 Haslemere GU27 ... 189 A8
 Shortfield Common
 GU10...........122 A1
Gorse Down SO21... 221 B4
Gorsedown Cl GU35. 164 B1
Gorsefield Rd BH25. 383 B4
Gorse Hill Cl BH15 .. 390 F5
Gorse Hill Cres
 BH15............390 E5
Gorse Hill Rd BH15.. 390 E5
Gorse Knoll Dr BH31 302 E7
Gorse La
 Farnham GU10 ..... 121 F6
 Upton BH16......... 389 D7
Gorseland Ct BH22.. 353 E3
Gorselands
 Farnham GU9 ...... 99 A7
 Newbury RG14 ....5 B5
 Pamber Heath RG26 ...9 F1
 Tadley RG26.......... 27 A8
Gorselands Cl
 Ash Vale GU12....... 77 E5
 Headley GU35...... 166 A4
Gorselands Rd SO18 268 B1
Gorselands Way
 PO13............368 D8
Gorse Rd
 Corfe Mullen BH21.. 374 C5
 Frimley GU16......... 36 C2
 Petersfield GU31.... 229 C3
Gorse Ride Jun & Inf Sch
 RG40.............16 C7
Gorse Ride N RG40... 16 C7
Gorse Ride S RG40.. 16 C6
Gorseway
 Fleet GU52 ...... 75 A7
 South Hayling PO11. 372 D3
Gorseway The PO11. 372 D3
Gort Cl GU11....... 77 C7
Gort Cres SO19 .... 292 B4
Gort Rd
 Bournemouth BH11.. 377 B3
 Poole BH17....... 375 A1
Goscombs La SO24.. 180 E8
Gosling Cl BH17 .... 390 F2
Goslings Croft GU34 184 E8
Gosport Ho [29] PO9.. 324 B5
Gosport La SO43.... 310 A4
Gosport Mus ★ PO12 369 D5
Gosport Rd
 Fareham PO16...... 343 B7
 Lee-on-t-S PO13 ... 367 F2
 Lower Farringdon
 GU34...........161 D2
 Stubbington PO14... 367 F7
Gosport Sh Prec [6]
 PO12............369 D5
Gosport St SO41.... 385 F4
Gothic Ct GU47 ...... 34 F7

Gough Cres BH17 ... 375 B2
Gough Rd GU51..... 69 C6
Gough's Mdw RG47...34 F7
Gould Cl RG14 .... 1 F2
Government House Rd
 GU11,GU14.......76 F7
Government Rd GU11 77 C4
Gover Rd SO16..... 289 C8
Gower Cl RG21.......69 B7
Gower Cres RG27 ... 51 B1
Gower Pk GU47...... 35 B7
Goyda Ho PO12 .... 368 F6
Grace Bennett Cl
 GU14............55 E7
Grace Ct [15] PO5 ... 370 C2
Grace Darling Ho
 BH15............390 D1
Grace Dieu Gdns
 SO31............292 F1
Gracefields PO15 ... 342 B8
Grace Gdns GU51....74 F8
Grace La SP6........ 258 E8
Gracemere Cres RG22 90 F7
Grace Reynolds Wlk [3]
 GU15............ 36 A6
Grace Sq [3] SP10 ... 83 C2
Gracious St GU34 .. 184 D8
Graddidge Way
 SO40............288 D6
Gradwell La GU34... 182 A8
Graemar Cotts SO51 213 C3
Graemar La SO51.... 213 C2
Grafton Cl
 Bordon GU35....... 164 E2
 Bournemouth BH3.. 393 A7
 Christchurch BH23.. 395 D6
 Gosport PO12...... 369 C8
Grafton Gdns
 Lymington SO41.... 385 C1
 Southampton SO16. 288 D2
Grafton Ho [2] SP10. 106 A7
Grafton Pl SP11.......81 F3
Grafton Rd
 Bournemouth BH3.. 393 A6
 Winchester SO23 .. 403 D4
Grafton St PO2..... 370 D7
Grafton Way RG22 ... 68 D7
Graham Ct SO19.... 292 B6
Graham Ho [4] SO14. 291 C6
Graham Norris Bsns Ctr
 The SO45.......... 338 E1
Graham Rd
 Gosport PO12...... 369 A8
 Portsmouth PO4 ... 370 D7
 Southampton SO14. 291 B6
Graham St SO14.... 291 C6
Grainger Cl RG22 .... 68 E1
Grainger Gdns SO19 292 C3
Grammar School La
 BH21............351 B4
Grammarsham La
 RG25.............92 A2
Grampian Way RG22..68 B3
Granada Cl PO8..... 308 A2
Granada Pl SP10..... 83 D1
Granada Rd
 Hedge End SO30 ... 293 B6
 Portsmouth PO4 ... 370 D7
Granary Mews BH24. 328 F7
Granary The
 Newbury RG14 ..... 1 D3
 Ringwood BH24..... 328 F4
Granby Gr SO17.... 267 B3
Granby Rd BH9 .... 378 A4
Grand Ave
 Bournemouth BH6.. 394 C4
 Camberley GU15 ... 36 A6
Grand Division Row [1]
 PO4............371 B3
Grand Par
 [13] Poole BH15 ... 390 B1
 [3] Hook RG27..... 51 A1
 Portsmouth PO1 ... 370 A3
 South Hayling PO11. 373 A4
Grand Trunk Rd SP9 . 78 D4
Grange Cl
 Fyfield SP11....... 80 F2
 Gosport PO12...... 368 F6
 Havant PO9........ 324 B2
 Hordle SO41....... 399 E8
 New Alresford SO24 179 C5
 Southampton SO18. 267 E4
 Winchester SO23 .. 403 C2
Grange Com Jun Sch
 GU14............55 E7
Grange Cotts SO30.. 293 E7
Grange Cres PO12 .. 368 F6
Grange Ct
 [5] Bournemouth
 BH1............393 B3
 Netley SO31....... 315 B7
 Newbury RG14 ..... 1 F2
 Tongham GU10 .... 100 C6
Grange Dr SO30 ... 293 C8
Grange Farm GU34.. 184 D8
Grange Farm Rd
 GU12............77 E3
Grange Gdns
 Newbury RG14 ..... 5 A5
 Poole BH12....... 391 E8
Grange Inf Sch
 PO13............368 C7
Grange Jun Sch
 PO13............368 C7
Grange La
 Gosport PO13 ... 368 C7
 Hartley Wintney RG27. 52 B5

Grange Mews SO51. 216 C1
Grange Park Mobile
 Homes SO30...... 269 C1
Grange Rd
 [2] Southampton
 SO16............266 B1
 Ash GU12.......... 77 F1
 Bournemouth BH6.. 394 D3
 Broadstone BH18 .. 375 A4
 Camberley GU15 ... 36 C5
 Christchurch BH23.. 396 B7
 Farnborough GU14 .. 55 F7
 Fleet GU52 .... 74 F5
 Gosport PO13...... 368 D6
 Hedge End SO30 .. 293 C8
 Netley SO31....... 315 B7
 New Alresford SO24. 179 C5
 Petersfield GU32.... 228 E2
 Portsmouth PO2 ... 345 D1
 Rushmoor GU14 ... 144 F8
 St Leonards BH24.. 327 E1
 Tongham GU10 .... 100 C6
 Winchester SO23 .. 403 C1
Grange Road Bsns Ctr
 BH23............396 A7
Grange Sch The
 BH23............395 E7
Grange The
 [1] Southampton
 SO16............266 B1
 Frensham GU10.... 144 B7
 Hordle SO41....... 399 E8
 Newbury RG14 ..... 5 A5
 Northington SO24.. 156 E5
Grangewood Ct
 SO50............245 B2
Grangewood Gdns
 SO50............245 B2
Grangewood Hall
 BH21............351 D5
Grantham Ave SO31. 315 E3
Grantham Ct [9]
 SO50............244 A2
Grantham Dr GU14.. 55 B5
Grantham Rd
 Bournemouth BH1.. 393 E5
 Eastleigh SO50 .... 243 F2
 Southampton SO19. 291 F6
Grantley Dr GU52 ...74 F7
Grantley Rd [3] BH5. 393 F4
Grantly Ct GU10..... 121 D6
Grant Rd PO6....... 346 D8
Grant's Ave BH1 ... 393 E6
Grants Cl BH1 ..... 393 E6
Granville Cl PO9 ... 348 A8
Granville Ct SO15... 290 E7
Granville Pl
 [9] Bournemouth
 BH1.............392 F3
 Winchester SO23 .. 403 F4
Granville Rd
 Bournemouth BH5.. 394 A5
 Poole BH12....... 391 E8
Granville St SO14... 291 B4
Grasdean Cl [1]
 SO18............268 A1
Grasmere SO50..... 243 F2
Grasmere Cl
 Bordon GU35...... 164 E4
 Christchurch BH23.. 379 D3
 West End SO18 .... 268 B1
Grasmere Ct SO16.. 265 E2
Grasmere Gdns
 BH25............383 B5
Grasmere Ho [7]
 PO6............321 B1
Grasmere Rd
 Bournemouth BH5.. 394 A4
 Farnborough GU14 ... 55 C4
 Farnham GU9 ..... 98 E6
 Poole BH13........ 442 D4
Grasmere Way PO14 342 D4
Graspan Rd SP11.....57 B1
Grassmere Way PO7. 300 C1
Grassymead PO14.. 317 C4
Grateley Bsns Pk
 SP11............124 E7
Grateley Cl SP19 ... 314 E8
Grateley Cres PO9 .. 323 C6
Grateley Dro
 Amport SP11....... 103 D3
 Grateley SP11....... 103 A1
Grateley House Sch
 SP11............125 B8
Grateley Prim Sch
 SP11............125 B8
Grateley Rd SP11 .. 101 D1
Grateley Sta SP11.. 124 F7
Gratton Cl SO21.... 131 D4
Gravel Cl
 Brown Candover
 SO24............135 C4
 Downton SP5...... 234 E8
Gravel Hill
 Broadstone BH17,BH18,
 BH21............375 D5
 Swanmore SO32... 272 D5
Gravel Hill Rd GU10. 120 E4
Gravel La
 Barton Stacey
 SO21............130 D7
 Ringwood BH24.... 328 F8
 Ropley SO24....... 159 E1
Gravellhill Cotts
 SO20............129 C5
Gravelly La
 Ball Hill RG20 ....3 E3
 Tadley RG26........ 27 A6

Gravel Rd
 Farnborough GU14 .. 77 B8
 Farnham GU9 ..... 98 F7
 Fleet GU52 .... 75 B6
Graveney Sq SP10...83 B2
Gray Cl
 Locks Heath SO31.. 316 F2
 Poole BH17....... 390 D1
Graycot Cl BH10 ... 377 C5
Grayland Cl PO11 .. 372 E4
Grayling Mead SO51 215 F1
Grays Ave SO45.... 314 B3
Grays Cl
 Colden Common
 SO21............244 F8
 Gosport PO12...... 368 E3
 Romsey SO51 ..... 241 E1
Grays Ct PO1 ..... 370 A4
Grayshot Dr GU17... 35 A3
Grayshott CE Prim Sch
 GU26............166 F4
Grayshott Cl SO22.. 175 D4
Grayshott Laurels
 GU35............165 A5
Grayshott Rd
 Gosport PO12...... 368 E4
 Headley GU35..... 166 B5
 Portsmouth PO4 ... 370 B1
Grayson Cl PO13.... 368 A6
Grayswood Dr GU16.. 36 E2
Gray's Yd [5] BH15. 390 C1
Great Austins GU9 .. 122 B8
Great Austins Ho
 GU9............122 C8
Great Binfields Cres
 RG24.............70 A8
Great Binfields Prim Sch
 RG24.............49 A1
Great Binfields Rd
 Chineham RG24.... 48 F1
 Old Basing RG24... 49 A1
Greatbridge Rd
 SO51............215 E1
Great Copse Dr RG24 323 E6
Great Elms Cl SO45. 338 B3
Greater Horseshoe Way
 [3] PO17.......... 318 E8
Great Farm Rd SO50 243 F3
Greatfield Cl GU14 ... 55 E7
Greatfield Rd GU14 .. 55 E8
Great Field Rd RG22. 175 D3
Greatfield Way PO9. 301 B3
Great Gays PO14.... 341 F1
Great Hanger GU31. 229 B3
Great La RG28 ..... 86 C5
Great Marlow RG27 . 51 D1
Great Mead
 Denmead PO7 ..... 299 A3
 Lyndhurst SO43.... 309 F4
Great Minster St [2]
 SO23............403 E5
Great Oaks Chase
 RG24.............48 E2
Great Posbrook Cotts
 PO14............341 E6
Great Sheldons Coppice
 RG27.............51 A2
Great Southsea St
 PO5............404 B1
Great Well Dr SO51. 241 A8
Greatwood Cl SO45. 314 A2
Greaves Cl BH10 ... 377 C3
Grebe Cl
 Aldershot GU11..... 99 E7
 Alton GU34........ 139 E6
 Basingstoke RG22 .. 90 F7
 Broadstone BH17 .. 389 E8
 Christchurch BH23.. 396 A6
 Milford on S SO41... 399 E4
 Portchester PO16... 343 F8
 Waterlooville PO8... 299 E4
 Westbourne PO10... 325 B4
Greenacre
 Barton on S BH25 .. 398 E6
 Broughton SO20 ... 170 B6
 Kingsclere RG20 ... 24 D2
Green Acre GU11... 76 D1
Greenacre Ct BH16. 389 C6
Greenacre Gdns
 PO7............322 D4
Greenacres
 [32] Bournemouth
 BH4............392 C3
 Bordon GU35...... 164 F4
 Downton SP5...... 234 D8
 Runfold GU10..... 100 A2
 Woolton Hill RG20... 21 C8
Green Acres
 Barton Stacey
 SO21............130 C6
 Christchurch BH23 .. 395 F7
Greenacres Cl BH10. 377 E6
Green Acres
 BH24............328 D5
Greenacres Dr SO21 219 C3
Greenaway La
 Locks Heath SO31.. 316 E2
 Warsash SO31..... 316 D2
Greenaways The
 RG23.............67 C2
Greenbank Cres
 SO16............266 F5
Greenbanks Cl SO41 399 D5
Greenbanks Gdns
 PO16............319 D2
Greenbank Way GU16.36 B2

Greenbirch Cl RG22...90 F7
Green Bottom BH21. 352 A7
Greenbury Cl RG23... 68 C5
Green Cl
 Hythe SO45....... 314 A4
 Kings Worthy SO23. 176 A5
 Old Alresford SO24. 157 D1
 South Wonston SO21 153 E4
 Whiteparish SP5 ... 212 B4
 Woodlands SO40... 287 F4
Greenclose Rd BH1. 351 D4
Green Cres PO13.... 343 C1
Greencroft [2] GU14 ..55 F4
Green Croft GU9 .... 99 F6
Green Cross La
 GU10............144 E1
Greendale Cl
 Chandler's Ford
 SO53............243 E6
 Fareham PO15..... 318 C4
Greendale The PO15 318 D4
Green Dr SP6...... 281 B6
Green Dro SP11.......60 B1
Green End GU46 .... 34 D7
Green Farm Gdns
 PO3............346 D3
Greenfield Cl GU30. 188 A5
Greenfield Cres PO8 300 C4
Greenfield Gdns
 BH25............398 B8
Greenfield Rd
 Farnham GU9 ..... 121 E7
 Poole BH15....... 390 F7
Greenfield Rise PO8 300 B3
Greenfields
 [1] Poole BH12 .... 391 F7
 Enham Alamein SP11. 83 C8
 Liss GU33 .... 208 A4
Greenfields Ave
 Alton GU34........ 139 E4
 Totton SO40....... 264 F1
Greenfields Cl SO40. 264 F1
Greenfields Jun Sch
 RG27.............52 C5
Greenfinch Cl
 Broadstone BH17 .. 374 F1
 Eastleigh SO50 .... 243 D1
 Sandhurst GU47 ... 35 B8
Greenfinch Wlk
 BH24............329 C6
Green Gdns BH15... 390 C6
Green Glades GU52 . 74 A7
Greenham Cl RG19...6 B8
Greenham Court Com
 Prim Sch RG14.....5 F8
Greenham Mill RG14 . 1 F3
Greenham Rd
 Greenham RG14,RG19.. 6 A7
 Newbury RG14 ..... 1 F1
Greenhanger GU10.. 166 F4
Greenhaven GU46....33 F5
Greenhayes BH18... 375 C2
Greenhays Rise
 BH21............351 C5
Greenhill Ave SO22. 403 E6
Greenhill Cl
 Farnham GU9 ..... 121 E7
 Wimborne Minster
 BH21............351 D6
Greenhill La
 Rownhams SO16... 265 E8
 Wimborne Minster
 BH21............351 D6
Greenhill Rd
 Farnham GU9 ..... 122 B8
 Wimborne Minster
 BH21............351 D6
 Winchester SO22 .. 403 B6
Greenhills GU9 .... 122 C8
Greenhill Terr SO22. 403 C6
Greenhill Way GU14. 55 E7
Green Hollow Cl
 PO16............318 F4
Greenidge Ct [8]
 SO15............290 F8
Green Jacket Cl
 SO22............403 C3
Green La
 Ampfield SO51..... 241 E8
 Barton on S BH25 .. 398 B8
 Beacon Hill GU10 .. 167 A8
 Bishop's Sutton SO24 180 C5
 Bishop's Waltham
 SO32............271 D7
 Blackfield SO45.... 365 F4
 Blackwater,Darby Green
 GU17.............34 F4
 Blackwater,Hawley
 GU17.............35 C4
 Bournemouth BH10. 377 D3
 Burridge SO31..... 294 A1
 Bursledon SO31... 292 F1
 Chilworth SO16.... 242 F1
 Churt GU10....... 144 E1
 Clanfield PO8...... 276 D5
 Denmead PO7 .... 298 E4
 Dockenfield GU10.. 143 C6
 Downton SP5...... 234 F8
 Ellisfield RG25..... 115 A7
 Farnham,Weybourne
 GU9.............99 D5
 Farnham,Wrecclesham
 GU9.............121 E7
 Ferndown BH22.... 353 A1
 Fordingbridge SP6.. 257 F2

Green La continued
 Four Marks GU34 ... 182 A8
 Gosport,Alverstoke
 PO12............369 A5
 Gosport,Elson PO12. 369 C9
 Hambledon PO7.... 274 B4
 Hamble-le-R SO31.. 316 A2
 Hartley Wintney RG27. 52 D5
 Haslemere GU27 ... 189 F4
 High Cross GU32... 205 F5
 Locks Heath SO31.. 316 F1
 Lower Swanwick
 SO31............316 D8
 Monxton SP11..... 104 C5
 Newbury RG14 ..... 1 C2
 Ossemsley BH25... 382 E8
 Pamber End RG26.. 27 C4
 Portsmouth PO3 ... 346 A3
 Ringwood BH24.... 329 A7
 Ringwood,Upper Kingston
 BH24............329 C4
 Rotherwick RG27... 50 E5
 Sandhurst GU47 ... 35 A7
 Soberton PO7 ..... 274 C7
 Southampton SO16. 265 E2
 South Hayling PO11. 372 E3
 Stratfield Saye RG7... 29 C8
 Swanmore SO32... 272 D7
 Totton SO40....... 264 B4
 Whitsbury SP6..... 257 C7
 Yateley GU46....... 33 F6
Greenlands RG20 .... 4 C1
Greenlands Rd
 Camberley GU15 ... 35 F1
 Kingsclere RG20 ... 24 D2
 Newbury RG14 ..... 1 E3
Green Lane Cl GU15. 36 A7
Green Lane Cotts
 GU10............144 E1
Greenlea Cl PO7 ... 322 B2
Greenlea Cres SO16. 267 D5
Greenlea Rd PO12.. 368 F7
Greenleas GU14 .... 55 D6
Greenleas Cl GU46... 34 A7
Green Leys GU52.....74 F4
Green Loaning BH23 395 F5
Greenmead Ave
 SO41............384 D1
Green Meadows La
 SP11............106 A2
Green Park Cl SO23. 403 F8
Green Park Rd SO16 289 E7
Green Pastures Cvn Site
 SO51............263 E4
Green Pk BH1 ..... 393 D3
Green Pond Cnr [2]
 PO9............324 B1
Green Pond La SO51 217 C3
Green Rd
 Bournemouth BH9.. 393 A8
 Gosport PO12...... 369 A3
 Poole BH15....... 390 D1
 Portsmouth PO5 ... 404 B2
 Stubbington PO14 .. 342 C4
Greenride Cl RG27....32 B4
Greens Cl SO32 .... 271 E8
Green's Cl SO50.... 245 A1
Greensey SP11.......81 B6
Greenside Ct PO13.. 358 B6
Greensleeves Ave
 BH18............375 B6
Greens Meade SP5.. 235 D6
Greensome Dr BH22 353 F6
Green Springs GU10. 97 D7
Green's School La
 GU14............55 E4
Green St GU35 .... 163 E8
Green Stile GU34 .. 159 E7
Green The
 Amport SP11...... 104 A5
 Andover SP10 ..... 82 E7
 Barton Stacey SO21. 130 E7
 Blackwater GU17 ... 35 A4
 Burton BH23....... 380 D2
 Camberley GU16 ... 56 D6
 East Meon GU32... 226 D1
 Farnham,Badshot Grn 99 E6
 Farnham,Upper Hale
 GU9.............99 A6
 Kimpton SP11..... 80 C2
 Liss GU33 .... 207 E5
 Middle Wallop SO20. 126 B4
 Overton RG25 ..... 88 B8
 Romsey SO51 ..... 216 C1
 Rowlands Castle PO9 301 C2
 Sarisbury SO31.... 316 E6
 Tadley RG26........ 27 A6
 The Sands GU10 ... 100 C1
 Whitchurch RG28 .. 86 D5
 Whiteparish SP5 ... 212 B4
Greenway
 East Meon GU32.... 226 C1
 Sherfield on L RG27. 49 D8
Green Way GU12.... 77 C2
Greenway Cl SO41.. 385 C3
Greenway Cres
 BH16............389 A7
Greenway La GU51. 253 C6
Greenway Rd PO12. 369 C6
Greenways
 Chandler's Ford
 SO53............243 E6
 Christchurch BH23.. 396 F8
 Fleet GU52 .... 74 F6
 Milford on S SO41.. 399 C5

Greenways continued
  Southampton SO16 . . . . **267** D5
Greenways Ave BH8. . **378** C3
Greenways Ct BH22 . . . **353** E3
Greenways Ho [4] RG14 . 1 C2
Greenways Rd SO42 . . **334** A1
Greenway The PO10. **324** F4
Greenwich The
  [24] Southampton
  SO14. . . . . **291** A3
  Blackfield SO45. . . . . **338** E2
Greenwich Way SP10. **83** A2
Green Wlk PO15 . . . . **318** E3
Greenwood Ave
  Cosham PO6 . . . . . **345** D8
  Ferndown BH22. . . . **353** E6
  Poole BH14. . . . . . **402** C8
  Rownhams SO16. . . **265** D6
Greenwood Cl
  Eastleigh SO50 . . . . **243** F1
  Fareham PO16. . . . . **319** A4
  Romsey SO51. . . . . **241** A8
Greenwood Copse
  BH24 . . . . **328** A4
Greenwood Dr RG24 . . **48** F4
Greenwood La SO32 . **270** A8
Greenwood Manor
  GU51 . . . . **53** F2
Greenwood Rd BH9 . **392** E8
Greenwoods
  [6] New Milton
  BH25 . . . . **383** B1
  Whitchurch RG28 . . . **86** C6
Greenwood Way
  BH24 . . . . **328** A4
Greetham St PO5 . . . **404** B3
Gregan Ct [2] GU11 . . . **76** D1
Gregg Sch The SO18 **268** A3
Gregory Cl RG21 . . . . . **69** C7
Gregory Gdns SO40 . . **264** C5
Gregory Ho [1] RG27. . **51** A1
Gregory La SO32. . . . **270** C5
Gregson Ave PO13. . . **343** C4
Gregson Cl PO13. . . . **343** C3
Grenadier Cl SO31. . . **317** B2
Grenadier Rd GU12 . . **77** F2
Grenadiers Way GU14 **55** A3
Grendon Cl SO16. . . . **267** B5
Grenehurst Way
  GU31 . . . . **228** F4
Grenfell Rd BH9 . . . . **377** F3
Grenfield Ct PO10. . . . **324** F3
Grensell Ct RG27. . . . . **33** C8
Grenville Cl
  Liphook GU30 . . . . . **188** A4
  Ringwood BH24. . . . **305** D1
Grenville Ct
  [11] Bournemouth
  BH4. . . . . **392** D4
  [15] Poole BH15 . . . . **390** C2
  Bitterne Pk SO18. . . **267** F3
Grenville Dr GU51. . . . **74** E7
Grenville Gdns
  Camberley GU16 . . . . **56** C6
  Hythe SO45 . . . . . . **314** A1
Grenville Ho [32] PO1. **370** A5
Grenville Rd
  Portsmouth PO4 . . . **404** D1
  Wimborne Minster
  BH21 . . . . **351** D4
Gresham Ct [3] GU14 . . **77** A8
Gresham Ind Est
  GU12. . . . . **77** C2
Gresham Rd BH9. . . . **378** B1
Gresham Way GU16. . . **56** C6
Gresley Gdns SO30. . **269** C2
Gresley Rd RG21 . . . . . **69** D6
Grevillea Ave PO15. . **317** E3
Greville Cl GU11 . . . . . **76** D2
Greville Gn PO10. . . . **324** E3
Greville Rd SO15. . . . **290** D7
Greyberry Copse Rd
  RG19 . . . . **6** B8
Greycot Cl BH21 . . . . **326** E8
Greyfriars [2] SO23 . . **403** F6
Greyfriars Ct PO5 . . . **404** B1
Greyfriars Rd PO15. . **318** C2
Greyhound Cl
  Ash GU12. . . . . **77** D1
  Hedge End SO30 . . . **269** B3
Greyhound La RG25. . . **88** A7
Grey House Sch The
  RG27. . . . . **52** D6
Greyladyes SO31. . . . **316** B7
Greys Ct [6] GU11 . . . . **76** C2
Greys Farm Cl SO24 . **201** D4
Greyshott Ave SO16 . **265** C4
Greystoke Ave BH11. . **376** E5
Greystead Pk GU10 . . **121** C5
Greywell Ave SO16. . . **266** C4
Greywell Cl RG26 . . . . **26** E8
Greywell Ct SO16 . . . **266** C4
Greywell Rd
  Mapledurwell RG24,
  RG25 . . . . **70** E5
  Old Basing RG24 . . . . **70** D5
  Up Nately RG27. . . . . **71** C4
Greywell Sq PO9. . . . **323** F5
Grieg Cl RG22 . . . . **68** E1
Grieve Cl GU10 . . . . **100** C7
Griffen Cl SO50 . . . . **244** E2
Griffin Ct
  Southampton SO17 . . **291** C8

Griffin Ct continued
  Wimborne Minster
  BH21 . . . . **351** D3
Griffin Ind Pk SO40 . **264** E2
Griffin Way N RG27 . . . **51** B2
Griffin Way S RG27. . . **72** B8
Griffin Wlk PO13. . . . **368** C6
Griffiths Gdns BH10. . **377** B5
Griffon Cl
  Bursledon SO31. . . . **293** A2
  Farnborough GU14 . . . **55** B3
Grigg La SO42 . . . . . **334** A1
Grindle Cl PO16. . . . **320** C1
Gritanwood Rd PO4. . **371** B3
Groombridge Pl RG14 . .**1** C6
Grosvenor Cl
  Basingstoke RG22. . . . **91** B5
  North Tidworth SP9. . . **79** A6
  Southampton SO17 . . **267** C2
  St Leonards BH24 . . **327** D5
Grosvenor Ct
  [1] Southampton
  SO17. . . . . **267** C1
  [2] Bournemouth,
  Springbourne BH1 . **393** D4
  [8] Bournemouth BH1 **393** C3
  Blackwater GU17 . . . . **35** B3
  Christchurch BH23 . . **397** B8
  Farlington PO6 . . . . **346** F8
  Romsey SO51 . . . . . **241** C7
  Stubbington PO14 . . **367** D7
Grosvenor Dr SO23. . **403** F8
Grosvenor Gdns
  Bournemouth BH1. . **393** E4
  Southampton SO17 . . **267** C2
  West End SO30 . . . . **292** D8
Grosvenor Ho
  [12] Southampton
  SO15. . . . . **290** F6
  [1] Farnborough GU14. . **77** B8
  [4] Portsmouth PO5. . **404** B2
  [6] Bournemouth BH4 **392** C3
Grosvenor Lawn [6]
  RG14 . . . . **1** C2
Grosvenor Lo [8]
  BH4 . . . . **392** C3
Grosvenor Lodge [5]
  SO17. . . . . **267** C1
Grosvenor Mews
  [3] Southampton
  SO17. . . . . **267** C1
  [5] Gosport PO12 . . . **369** C6
  [7] Highfield SO17. . . **267** C2
  Lymington SO41 . . . **385** D5
Grosvenor Pines [13]
  BH4 . . . . **392** C3
Grosvenor Rd
  Aldershot GU11. . . . . **76** E1
  Bournemouth BH4. . . **392** C3
  Chandler's Ford SO53 **218** E1
  Medstead GU34. . . . **159** F1
  Southampton SO17 . . **267** C2
Grosvenor Sq SO15 . **290** F6
Grosvenor St PO5 . . **404** B2
Grove Ave
  Gosport PO12 . . . . **369** C6
  Portchester PO16 . . . **344** C6
Grovebell Ind Est
  GU9 . . . . **121** D7
Grove Bldgs [7]
  PO12 . . . . **369** C5
Grovebury SO31 . . . **317** A2
Grove Cl RG21 . . . . . . **69** C3
Grove Cross Rd GU16 .**36** B1
Grove Ct
  [5] Havant PO9 . . . . **323** F1
  Newbury RG14 . . . . . **5** E8
Grove End Rd GU9 . . **121** F8
Grove Farm Pk GU16. **56** D1
Grovefields Ave GU16 .**36** B1
Grove Gdns
  Barton on S BH25 . . **398** A7
  Southampton SO19 . . **292** B4
Grove Ho
  Portsmouth PO5 . . . **404** B1
  Portsmouth PO5 . . . **404** C1
Grove La SP5 . . . . . . **235** F7
Groveland Rd RG14 . . .**1** B5
Grovelands GU10 . . . **122** C4
Grovelands Cl SO45. **164** D1
Grovelands Rd SO22 **175** B1
Groveley Bsns Ctr
  BH23. . . . . **395** E6
Groveley Rd
  Bournemouth BH4. . **392** B2
  Christchurch BH23 . . **395** E6
Groveley Way SO51. **216** E1
Grovely Ave BH5 . . . **393** F3
Grove Mans [10] BH1 . **393** B3
Grove Mews SO19 . . **292** B4
Grove Park Ind Est
  GU34. . . . . **140** B4
Grove Pastures
  SO41 . . . . **385** C2
Grove Pl
  Lymington SO41 . . . **385** E3
  Southampton SO19 . . **292** B2
Grove Prim Sch The
  GU16. . . . . **36** C2
Grove Rd
  Alton GU34 . . . . . **139** F2
  Ash GU12. . . . . **77** E3
  Barton on S BH25 . . **398** A7
  Basingstoke RG21. . . . **69** C3
  Beacon Hill GU26 . . . **167** A6
  Bournemouth BH1. . . **393** B3
  Camberley GU15 . . . . **36** D5
  Compton SO21. . . . . **219** D5

Grove Rd continued
  Cosham PO6 . . . . . **346** C7
  Fareham PO16. . . . . **319** A1
  Fleet GU52 . . . . **75** B5
  Gosport PO12 . . . . **369** B8
  Havant PO9 . . . . . . **323** F1
  Lee-on-t-S PO13 . . . **367** A3
  Lymington SO41 . . . **385** F3
  Newbury RG14 . . . . . **1** C5
  Poole BH12 . . . . . . **391** B6
  Southampton SO15 . . **290** C7
  Wimborne Minster
  BH21 . . . . **351** D4
Grove Rd N PO5. . . . **404** B1
Grove Rd S PO5. . . . **404** B1
Grove Road E BH23 . **395** A8
Grove Road W BH23. **394** F8
Groves Cl SO21 . . . . **153** C4
Groves Down SO51. . **238** E4
Groves Lea RG7. . . . . **11** D6
Groves Orch RG28 . . **26** B5
Grove St SO14 . . . . . **291** B4
Grove The
  Aldershot GU11. . . . . **76** E1
  Bournemouth BH9. . . **377** F3
  Bursledon SO31. . . . **293** A1
  Christchurch BH23 . . **379** E1
  Farnborough GU14 . . . **56** B1
  Ferndown BH22. . . . **353** C4
  Frimley GU16. . . . . . **36** B1
  Hartley Wintney RG27. **52** C5
  Liphook GU30 . . . . **187** F4
  Netley SO31. . . . . . **315** D7
  Penton Grafton SP11. . **81** F4
  Southampton SO19 . . **292** B1
  Stubbington PO14 . . **367** B7
  Verwood BH31. . . . . **303** A5
  Westbourne PO10. . . **325** B3
Grove Villas GU12. . . . **77** E4
Grower Gdns BH11. . **377** A4
Gruneisen Rd PO2 . . **345** C2
Guardhouse Rd PO1 . **370** B7
Guardian Ct [25] SO17 **267** A1
Guardroom Rd PO2 . **345** B1
Gudge Heath La
  PO15 . . . . **318** E2
Guelders The PO7. . . **322** E3
Guernsey Cl
  Basingstoke RG24 . . . **48** C2
  Southampton SO16 . . **265** E3
Guernsey Dr GU51 . . . **54** B4
Guernsey Rd BH12 . . **376** D1
Guessens La PO14 . . **341** F8
Guest Ave BH12. . . . **392** A6
Guest Cl BH12 . . . . . **392** A6
Guest Rd
  Bishopstoke SO50 . . **244** D3
  Upton BH16 . . . . . . **389** A7
Guildford Cl PO10. . . **325** C1
Guildford Ct
  [15] Gosport PO13 . . **368** D5
  [2] Bournemouth BH4 **392** C4
Guildford Dr SO53 . . **243** C4
Guildford Rd
  Aldershot GU12. . . . **100** B7
  Ash GU12. . . . . **77** F2
  Farnham,Badshot
  GU10 . . . . **99** E4
  Farnham GU9 . . . . . **99** E4
  Fleet GU51 . . . . **54** C1
  Mytchett GU16 . . . . . **56** E5
  Portsmouth PO1 . . . **370** E6
  Runfold GU10 . . . . **100** A4
Guildford Rd E GU14 .**56** A1
Guildford Rd Ind Est
  GU9 . . . . **99** C3
Guildford Rd W GU14 **56** A1
Guildford Road Trad Est
  GU9 . . . . **99** B3
Guildford St [1]
  SO14 . . . . **291** C5
Guildhall Ct BH15 . . . **390** B2
Guildhall Mus★
  BH15. . . . . **390** B2
Guildhall Sq PO1. . . **404** B3
Guildhall Wlk PO1 . . **404** A3
Guildhill Rd BH6 . . . **394** E4
Guild Ho [18] SO14 . . **291** A3
Guillemont Jun Sch
  GU14. . . . . **55** A6
Guillemot Cl SO45 . . **314** B2
Guillemot Gdns
  PO13 . . . . **343** B3
Guinea Ct RG24 . . . . . **49** A4
Gull Cl PO13 . . . . . . **343** B2
Gulley Rd GU14 . . . . **76** E8
Gulliver Cl BH14 . . . **402** D8
Gulliver Ct [1] BH21 . **351** C5
Gulls The SO40 . . . . **289** F2
Gullycroft Mead
  SO30. . . . . **293** B7
Gun Hill GU11 . . . . . **100** B7
Gunners Bldgs PO3 . **345** F4
Gunners La SO24 . . . **135** A5
Gunners Mews SO32 **271** E8
Gunners Pk SO32 . . . **271** E7
Gunners Row PO4 . . **371** B2
Gunners Way PO12. . **343** F1
Gunns Farm GU30. . . **188** A2
Gunstore Rd PO3 . . . **346** A4
Gunville Cres BH9 . . **378** A3
Gunville Hill SP5 . . . **168** B6
Gunville Rd SP5 . . . . **168** B6
Gunwharf Quays
  PO1. . . . . **369** F6
Gunwharf Quays (Sh Ctr)
  PO1. . . . . **370** A4
Gunwharf Rd PO1. . . **370** A4

Gurdons GU34 . . . . . **139** D1
Gurjun Cl BH16 . . . . **389** A8
Gurkha Mus The★
  SO23. . . . . **403** D5
Gurkha Sq GU51 . . . . **74** F8
Gurnard Rd PO6 . . . . **345** E7
Gurnays Mead SO51 . **238** C2
Gurney Ct RG29. . . . . **72** E2
Gurney Rd
  Corfe Mullen BH21 . . **374** E6
  Portsmouth PO4 . . . **371** B4
  Southampton SO15 . . **290** C8
Gussage Rd BH12. . . **391** F8
Gutner La PO11 . . . . **348** C1
Guttridge Dro SO51 . **217** B7
Guttridge La RG26 . . . **26** E8
Guy's Cl BH24 . . . . . **329** B6
Gwatkin Cl PO9. . . . **323** C3
Gwenlyn Rd BH16. . . **389** C6
Gwen-Rhian Ct [4]
  SO15. . . . . **290** F7
Gwessin Terr [6]
  PO12 . . . . **369** C5
Gwyn Cl RG14. . . . . . . **5** C8
Gwynne Rd BH12. . . **391** E5
Gypsy La
  Ringwood BH24. . . . **329** B8
  Waterlooville PO8 . . . **299** F5

H

Haarlem Mews
  BH23 . . . . **395** D7
Haccupps La SO51 . **193** D1
Hack Dr SO21. . . . . . **244** F8
Hacketts La SO32 . . **248** F2
Hackett Way [2]
  PO14. . . . . **343** A6
Hackleys La SO51 . . **239** B5
Hacks La SO21 . . . . **152** B3
Hackwood Cl SO10 . . **105** D7
Hackwood Cotts
  RG21 . . . . **69** C2
Hackwood La RG25 . . **92** C6
Hackwood Rd RG21 . . **69** C3
Hackwood Rdbt RG21 **69** C3
Hackworth Gdns
  SO30. . . . . **269** C3
Hadden Rd BH8. . . . **393** D8
Haddon Cl PO14 . . . **318** E1
Haddon Dr SO50 . . . **244** A5
Haddons Dr BH21 . . **326** D7
Hadleigh Gdns
  Camberley GU16 . . . . **56** C6
  Eastleigh SO50 . . . . **244** A5
Hadleigh Pl [1] RG21 . . **69** A5
Hadleigh Rd [3] PO6. **345** D8
Hadley Field SO45 . . **338** B5
Hadley Way BH18 . . **374** E3
Hadow Rd BH10. . . . **377** C3
Hadrian Cl BH22 . . . **353** D2
Hadrian Rd SP10. . . . **83** B3
Hadrians GU9. . . . . . **99** C4
Hadrians Cl SO53 . . **243** E7
Hadrians Way RG23 . . **68** C7
Hadrian Way
  Chilworth SO16 . . . . **266** C7
  Corfe Mullen BH21 . . **374** C6
Haflinger Dr PO15 . . **317** B8
Haglane Copse
  SO41 . . . . **385** C2
Hagley Rd GU51 . . . . **53** C2
Hahnemann Rd BH2. **392** E2
Haig Ave BH13 . . . . **391** E1
Haig Ct [6] PO2 . . . . **345** E3
Haig La GU52 . . . . . . **75** B5
Haig Rd
  Aldershot GU12. . . . . **77** A1
  Andover SP10 . . . . **105** E8
  Bishopstoke SO50. . . **245** A1
  New Alresford SO24 . **179** D6
  Sandhurst GU15 . . . . **35** D5
Haileybury Gdns
  SO30. . . . . **269** C1
Hailstone Rd RG21 . . .**69** B8
Hainault Dr BH31 . . . **303** A6
Haining Gdns GU16 . . **56** E3
Haking Rd BH23 . . . **395** D7
Halcyon Cl BH15 . . . **390** C6
Halcyon Dr SP11. . . . **103** E8
Halden Cl [2] SO51 . . **216** B1
Hale Ave BH25 . . . . **383** B2
Hale Cl SO24 . . . . . **181** C5
Hale Ct PO1 . . . . . . **370** E7
Hale Farm Flats GU9 . .**99** B5
Hale Gdns BH25 . . . **383** B2
Hale Ho GU11 . . . . . **100** C5
Hale La
  Farnham GU9 . . . . . **99** B4
  Woodgreen SP6. . . . **258** E8
Hale Rdbt GU9. . . . . . **99** C5
Hale Reeds GU9 . . . . **99** C6
Hale St N PO1 . . . . **404** C4
Hale St S PO1. . . . . **404** C4
Hale Sch GU9. . . . . . **98** F7
Hales Dr SO30. . . . . **293** A6
Halesowen Ho [4]
  PO5. . . . . **404** A2
Hale Way GU16 . . . . . **56** B8
Halewood Way BH23 **394** F8
Half Moon St [1]
  PO1 . . . . **370** A5

Halfpenny La PO1 . . **370** A3
Half Way Cotts GU10 . **98** A3
Halfway Rd SO45. . . . **339** E1
Halifax Cl
  Andover SP10 . . . . . **82** F1
  Farnborough GU14 . . . **55** D3
Halifax Ct SO30 . . . **268** C2
Halifax Rise PO7. . . **322** F3
Halifax Way BH23 . . **396** B7
Halimote Rd GU11 . . .**76** E1
Hall Cl
  Bishop's Waltham
  SO32. . . . . **271** D8
  Camberley GU15 . . . . **36** C6
Hall Ct SO32 . . . . . . **295** A7
Hall Dr GU52. . . . . . . **75** B6
Hallet Cl SO18 . . . . **268** A3
Hallett Rd PO9 . . . . **324** B2
Halletts Cl PO14 . . . **367** C8
Hall Farm Cres GU46 . . **34** A5
Halliards The PO16. . **343** B7
Halliday Cl
  Basingstoke RG21 . . . **69** A2
  Gosport PO12 . . . . **369** B6
Halliday Cres PO4 . . **371** C3
Halliday Ho [12] PO4. **371** B2
Hall La
  Hartley Mauditt
  GU34 . . . . **162** B2
  Yateley GU46 . . . . . . **34** A6
Hall Lands La SO50. . **245** D2
Hallmark Cl GU47 . . . **35** C8
Hall of Aviation (Mus)★
  SO14. . . . . **291** B3
Hallowell Ho PO1 . . **404** B4
Hall Rd
  Alton GU34 . . . . . . **140** A6
  Bournemouth BH11. . **376** B3
  Farnborough GU14 . . . **55** F2
Halls Farm Cl SO22 . **175** B3
Hall Way The SO22. . **175** B6
Halpin Ho RG7. . . . . **14** A3
Halsey Cl PO12 . . . . **368** F3
Halstead Rd
  Cosham PO6 . . . . . **345** D8
  Southampton SO18 . . **267** F2
Halstock Cres BH17 . **375** D7
Halter Path BH15 . . **389** E3
Halter Rise BH21 . . . **352** C6
Halters End GU26 . . **166** E3
Halters The RG14 . . . . **5** F7
Halterworth Cl SO51 **241** B7
Halterworth Com Prim
  Sch SO51. . . . . . . **241** C7
Halterworth La
  SO51 . . . . **241** C7
Halton Cl BH23 . . . . **381** B8
Halton Rd SP11 . . . . **79** D7
Haltons Cl SO40 . . . **264** C1
Halyard Ct PO13 . . . **368** D7
Halyards SO31. . . . . **316** A4
Hambert Way SO40 . **288** C5
Hamble Ave GU17 . . . **35** B5
Hamble Cl
  Oakley RG23 . . . . . . **67** B1
  Warsash SO31. . . . . **316** C1
Hamblecliff Ho
  SO31. . . . . **315** D3
Hamble Com Sports Coll
  SO31. . . . . **315** E5
Hamble Court Bsns Pk
  SO31. . . . . **315** E3
Hamble Ct
  [16] Basingstoke
  RG21 . . . . **69** D5
  [23] Andover SP10 . . . **83** C2
  [3] Waterlooville PO8 **299** F4
  Chandler's Ford
  SO53. . . . . **243** D5
  Stubbington PO14 . . **367** B8
Hambledon Cl SO22 **175** D6
Hambledon Gdns
  BH6 . . . . **394** C6
Hambledon Inf Sch
  PO7. . . . . **274** D3
Hambledon La PO7,
  SO32. . . . . **273** D3
Hambledon Par PO7 **299** C2
Hambledon Rd
  Bournemouth BH7. . **394** B7
  Bournemouth,West
  Southbourne BH6. . **394** C6
  Clanfield PO8. . . . . **276** B6
  Denmead PO7. . . . . **299** C3
  Hambledon PO7. . . **298** D8
  Waterlooville PO7. . . **322** F9
Hambledon Way
  RG27. . . . . **49** B5
Hamble Dr RG26 . . . . **27** B8
Hamble Ho PO16. . . . **343** A4
Hamble House Gdns
  SO31. . . . . **316** A2
Hamble La
  Bursledon SO31. . . . **292** F2
  Bursledon SO31. . . . **315** F8
  Waterlooville PO7. . . **322** E5
Hamble Manor SO31 **316** A2
Hamble Pk SO31 . . . **316** F1
Hamble Prim Sch
  SO31. . . . . **315** E4
Hamble Rd
  Gosport PO12 . . . . **368** F2
  Poole BH15 . . . . . . **391** A6
Hambleside Ct SO31 **315** F2
Hamble Springs
  SO32 . . . . **271** D7
Hamble Sta SO31 . . **315** E5

Hambleton Cl GU16 . . **36** F3
Hamblewood SO30. . **294** A6
Hamblewood Ct
  SO30 . . . . **294** A6
Hamblin Way BH8. . . **378** E2
Hambridge La RG14. . . **2** C2
Hambrook Rd [1]
  PO12 . . . . **369** A7
Hambrook St PO5. . . **404** A1
Hamburg Cl SP10 . . . . **82** F3
Hamdown Cres
  SO51 . . . . **239** B2
Hameldon Cl SO16 . . **289** E7
Hamelyn Cl [5] RG21. . **69** A4
Hamelyn Rd RG21. . . . **69** A4
Hamesmoor Rd GU16 **56** D4
Hamesmoor Way
  GU16. . . . . **56** D4
Hamfield Dr PO11. . . **372** A2
Hamilton Bsns Pk
  BH25. . . . . **382** E2
Hamilton Cl
  Basingstoke RG21. . . **68** E7
  Bordon GU35. . . . . **164** F4
  Bournemouth BH1. . . **393** D5
  Christchurch BH23 . . **395** F4
  Hamworthy BH15 . . . **389** E2
  Langstone PO9 . . . . **347** F8
Hamilton Cres BH15. **389** E2
Hamilton Ct
  [16] Portsmouth
  PO5. . . . . **370** C2
  [18] Southampton
  SO17. . . . . **267** A1
  [1] Bournemouth BH8 **393** B5
  [1] Wimborne Minster
  BH21 . . . . **351** B5
  Farnborough GU17 . . . **35** C1
  Milford on S SO41. . . **399** C4
  Newbury RG14 . . . . . **5** F8
  South Tidworth SP9 . . **78** E5
Hamilton Gn SP9 . . . . **78** E5
Hamilton Gr PO13 . . **343** B2
Hamilton Ho PO1 . . . **404** D4
Hamilton Mews
  [4] Hythe SO45 . . . . **314** B1
  Bransgore BH23 . . . **381** B8
  Lymington SO41 . . . **385** F4
Hamilton Pk SP5. . . . **235** A8
Hamilton Pl
  Aldershot GU11. . . . . **76** D1
  Lymington SO41 . . . **385** D3
Hamilton Rd
  Bishopstoke SO50. . . **244** D3
  Bournemouth BH1. . . **393** D4
  Corfe Mullen BH21 . . **374** E5
  Fleet GU52 . . . . **75** B6
  Greatham GU33. . . . **186** D2
  Hamworthy BH15 . . . **389** E2
  Hythe SO45 . . . . . . **338** B8
  Portchester PO6 . . . **344** E8
  Portsmouth PO5 . . . **370** D2
Hamilton Way BH25. **382** E2
Ham La
  Gosport PO12 . . . . **344** A1
  Hampreston BH21. . . **352** E3
  Horndean PO8. . . . . **300** A8
  Southbourne PO10 . . **349** D7
  Wimborne Minster
  BH21 . . . . **352** C5
  Wolverton Common
  RG26 . . . . **25** F5
Hamlash Cotts GU10 **122** A2
Hamlash La GU10 . . **122** A2
Hamlet Cl SO45. . . . **339** B3
Hamlet Gdns SP11. . . .**83** B6
Hamlet Way PO12. . . **344** A1
Hammer Hill GU27 . . **189** A4
Hammer La
  Bramshott GU27 . . . **188** F6
  Haslemere GU26 . . . **189** A8
  Haslemere GU27 . . . **189** A5
  Headley GU26 . . . . **166** C6
Hammersley Rd GU11 **77** A6
Hammer Vale GU27 . **189** A6
Hammerwood Copse
  GU27. . . . . **189** B5
Hammond Cl PO15 . . **318** D2
Hammond Ho [9]
  PO12 . . . . **369** E5
Hammond Ind Pk
  PO14. . . . . **367** D6
Hammond Rd
  [3] Basingstoke
  RG21 . . . . **69** A3
  Fareham PO15. . . . . **318** E2
Hammonds Cl SO40 . **288** E8
Hammond's Gn
  SO40 . . . . **288** D8
Hammonds Heath
  RG7 . . . . **11** F6
Hammonds La SO40. **288** E8
Hammond's La SO24 **181** C4
Hammond Sq SO17. . .**83** B2
Hammonds Way
  SO40 . . . . **288** D8
Hampage Gn PO9 . . **323** D7
Hampden La BH6 . . . **394** E6
Hampdens The RG14 . .**5** A6
Hampreston CE Fst Sch
  BH21. . . . . **352** E3
Hampshire Cl
  Aldershot GU12. . . . **100** B7
  Basingstoke RG22. . . **68** A3
  Christchurch BH23 . . **379** F2
Hampshire Corporate Pk
  SO53. . . . . **243** B2

Hampshire Cross SP9 78 E5
Hampshire Ct
3 Bournemouth BH2 392 F3
Chandler's Ford SO53 243 C3
Hampshire Hatches La BH24 329 A4
Hampshire Ho
2 Bournemouth BH2 392 F3
Basingstoke RG24 68 E8
Liphook GU30 187 F7
Hampshire Int Bsns Pk RG24 48 E4
Hampshire Rd
Bordon GU35 164 D4
Camberley GU15 36 D8
Hampshire St PO1 370 E7
Hampshire Terr PO1 404 A2
Hampstead Ho RG21 69 B5
Hampton Cl
Blackfield SO45 365 E8
Fleet GU52 75 A4
Waterlooville PO7 323 A7
Hampton Ct
5 Bournemouth BH2 392 D4
Basingstoke RG23 68 D6
Hampton Dr BH24 305 B1
Hampton Farm La SO32 272 A6
Hampton Gdns SO45 365 E8
Hampton Gr PO15 318 B1
Hampton Hill SO32 272 B6
Hampton La
Blackfield SO45 338 E1
Winchester SO22 403 A7
Hampton Rd
Farnham GU9 98 F6
Newbury RG14 1 D1
Hampton Terr GU26 167 A6
Hampton Twrs SO19 314 E8
Hamptworth Rd SP5 236 D4
Hams Cnr RG27 49 E7
Hamtun Cres SO40 264 E1
Hamtun Gdns SO40 264 E1
Hamtun Rd SO19 292 C3
Hamtun St 6 SO14 290 F3
Hamwic Ho 3 SO14 291 A6
Hamworthy Fst Sch BH15 389 F1
Hamworthy Lodge BH15 389 F2
Hamworthy Mid Sch BH15 389 F1
Hamworthy Sta BH16 389 D4
Hanbidge Cres PO13 343 D4
Hanbidge Wlk PO13 343 D4
Hanbury Sq GU31 229 A5
Hanbury Way GU15 36 A3
Handcroft Cl GU10 97 D7
Handel Cl RG22 68 E1
Handel Rd SO15 290 F5
Handel Terr SO15 290 E6
Handford La GU46 34 B5
Handford Pl 2 SO15 290 F6
Handley Ct BH24 328 F7
Handley Lodge 2 BH12 391 F7
Handley Rd PO12 368 F6
Handsworth Ho PO5 404 C2
Handy Villas 22 SO23 403 E6
Hangerfield Cl GU46 34 A5
Hanger Rd RG26 9 D1
Hangers The SO32 247 E2
Hanger The GU35 165 D7
Hanger Way GU31 229 B3
Hanham Ct BH12 392 B8
Hanham Rd
Corfe Mullen BH21 374 D5
Wimborne Minster BH21 351 C5
Hankinson Rd BH9 393 A8
Hanley Rd SO15 290 D8
Hanlon Cl BH11 377 B4
Hanmore Rd RG24 48 E3
Hannah Gdns PO7 322 F8
Hannah Way SO41 384 F5
Hannam's Farm Cl GU10 97 C6
Hannay Rise SO19 292 D5
Hannington Pl BH7 394 A5
Hannington Rd
Bournemouth BH7 394 A5
Havant PO9 323 D7
Hann Rd SO16 265 E6
Hanns Way SO50 244 A2
Hanover Bldgs SO14 291 A4
Hanover Cl
7 Andover SP10 105 D6
Frimley GU16 36 C1
Yateley GU46 34 B7
Hanover Cotts SO32 224 E3
Hanover Ct
7 Portsmouth PO1 370 A4
Hythe SO45 314 A4
Liphook GU30 187 F5
Hanover Dr GU51 54 C4
Hanover Gdns
Basingstoke RG21 69 A2
Fareham PO16 319 B3
Farnborough GU14 55 C6
Hanover Gn BH17 390 F7
Hanover Ho
6 Andover SP10 106 B7
Hanover Ho *continued*
7 Southampton SO14 291 A4
Gosport PO13 343 B5
Poole BH15 390 D3
Totton SO40 289 A8
Hanoverian Way PO15 317 C7
Hanover Lodge SO23 403 D4
Hanover Mead RG14 5 B6
Hanover St PO1 370 A5
Hanson Cl GU15 36 F7
Hanson Rd SP10 82 E1
Hanway Rd PO1,PO2 370 E7
Ha'penny Dell PO7 322 E3
Harbeck Rd BH8 378 C3
Harborough Rd SO15 290 F6
Harbour Cl
Farnborough GU14 55 E8
Marchwood SO40 290 C2
Poole BH13 402 D6
Harbour Cres BH23 395 E5
Harbour Ct
8 Emsworth PO10 348 F8
Barton on S BH25 397 E7
Christchurch BH23 395 E6
Poole BH13 402 E6
Harbourgate Bsns Pk PO6 345 B8
Harbour Hill Cres BH15 390 E5
Harbour Hill Rd BH15 390 E5
Harbour Hospl The BH15 390 D3
Harbour Lights BH15 390 E4
Harbourne Gdns SO18 268 B2
Harbour Par SO15 290 F4
Harbour Prospect BH14 402 C8
Harbour Rd
Bournemouth BH6 395 A3
Gosport PO1 369 E6
South Hayling PO11 372 C4
Harbourside PO9 347 F6
Harbour Side Cvn & Camping Site PO3 346 D1
Harbour Twr 10 PO12 369 E5
Harbour View PO16 344 C6
Harbour View Cl BH14 391 A5
Harbour View Ct BH23 395 B5
Harbour View Rd BH14 391 A5
Harbour Watch BH14 402 C7
Harbour Way
Emsworth PO10 349 A8
Portsmouth PO2 345 C2
Harbridge Ct
Havant PO9 323 D7
Verwood BH24 303 F6
Harbridge Dro BH24 281 C3
Harbury Ct RG14 1 E2
Harcombe Cl BH17 375 E3
Harcourt Cl PO8 300 A4
Harcourt Mews 6 BH5 394 A5
Harcourt Rd
Bournemouth BH5 394 A5
Camberley GU15 35 F5
Fareham PO14 342 B7
Gosport PO12 369 A6
Portsmouth PO1 370 E7
Southampton SO18 291 E8
Harding La SO50 245 B3
Harding Rd PO12 368 F6
Hardings La RG27 52 D6
Hardley Ind Est SO45 338 B6
Hardley La SO45 338 B8
Hardley Rdbt SO45 338 B6
Hardley Sch & Sixth Form SO45 338 C5
Hardman Ct PO3 346 B4
Hard The PO1 370 A5
Hardwicke Cl SO16 265 F2
Hardwicke Way SO31 315 E3
Hardwick Rd SO53 243 D6
Hardy Ave
Petersfield GU31 229 A5
Yateley GU46 34 A4
Hardy Cl
Locks Heath SO31 317 B4
New Milton BH25 382 F3
Southampton SO15 290 B6
West Moors BH22 326 F1
Hardy Cres BH21 351 D4
Hardy Dr SO45 314 B1
Hardyfair Cl SP11 81 D2
Hardy La RG21 69 A4
Hardy Rd
Eastleigh SO50 244 A1
Farlington PO6 346 E7
Poole BH14 391 D4
West Moors BH22 326 F1
Hardys Field RG20 24 C3
Harebell Cl
Fareham PO16 319 C3
Hartley Wintney RG27 52 D7
Harebell Gdns RG27 52 D7
Harefield Ct SO51 241 B8
Harefield Inf Sch SO18 292 B8
Harefield Jun Sch SO18 292 B8
Harefield Rd SO17 267 C3
Hare La
Alderholt BH21 279 F5
New Milton BH25, SO41 383 E3
Twyford SO21 220 A4
Hares Gn BH7 394 A8
Hare's La RG27 52 E8
Harestock Cl SO22 175 D5
Harestock Cnr SO22 175 C3
Harestock Prim Sch SO22 175 D3
Harestock Rd
Havant PO9 323 D3
Winchester SO22 175 C4
Hare Warren Cotts RG28 43 B2
Harewood Ave BH7 394 A6
Harewood Cl SO50 244 A5
Harewood Cres BH7 393 F8
Harewood Forest Ind Est SP11 107 E3
Harewood Gdns BH7 393 F7
Harewood Gn SO41 400 A4
Harewood Mobile Home Pk SP11 83 F1
Harewood Pl BH7 394 B6
Harfield Cl RG27 51 A1
Harford Cl SO41 385 C1
Harford Rd BH12 391 C8
Harkness Dr PO7 323 B8
Harkwood Dr BH15 389 E4
Harland Cres SO15 266 D1
Harland Rd BH6 395 A3
Harlaxton Cl SO50 243 F5
Harlech Cl RG23 68 C5
Harlech Dr SO53 243 A4
Harlech Rd GU17 35 B4
Harlequin Gr PO15 318 F1
Harlequin Ho GU26 167 A3
Harleston Rd PO6 321 D1
Harleston Villas 5 BH21 351 D4
Harley Ct SO31 316 D1
Harley Wlk PO1 404 C4
Harlington Way GU51 53 F1
Harlyn Rd SO16 265 F1
Harman Rd PO13 343 C3
Harmes Way GU11 77 B7
Harmsworth Rd RG26 26 F8
Harness Cl BH21 352 B6
Harold Cl SO40 288 C6
Harold Gdns GU34 140 A5
Harold Jackson Terr RG21 69 C4
Harold Rd
Portsmouth PO4 370 E3
Southampton SO15 290 C7
South Hayling PO11 373 B2
Stubbington PO14 367 D8
Westbourne PO10 325 B4
Harold Terr PO10 324 F1
Harpdon Par GU46 34 B7
Harper Way 15 PO16 319 B1
Harpton Cl GU46 34 B7
Harpway La BH23 380 C6
Harraby Gn BH18 375 A3
Harrage The SO51 240 F7
Harrier Cl
Horndean PO8 300 A7
Lee-on-t-S PO13 367 F3
Southampton SO16 266 B6
Harrier Dr BH21 351 D2
Harrier Gn SO45 338 B6
Harrier Mews SO31 315 E3
Harrier Rd GU14 55 A1
Harriers Cl BH23 396 D8
Harrier Way
Hardley SO45 338 B6
Petersfield GU31 229 C2
Harriet Cl PO14 367 B7
Harriet Ct 2 GU12 76 F1
Harrington Cl RG14 2 C5
Harrington Ct BH23 396 F7
Harris Ave SO30 293 C8
Harris Ct GU30 187 F2
Harris Hill RG22 91 B7
Harris La PO8 277 E5
Harrison Ave BH1 393 D6
Harrison Cl BH23 380 C3
Harrison Ho 3 PO2 345 D2
Harrison Prim Sch PO16 319 B2
Harrison Rd
Fareham PO16 319 B2
Southampton SO17 267 C3
Harrison's Cut SO14 291 A4
Harrison Way BH22 326 E3
Harris Rd PO13 343 C3
Harris Way
New Milton BH25 383 B6
North Baddesley SO52 242 A4
Harroway RG28 85 D7
Harrow Cl BH23 381 B7
Harrow Down SO22 403 B2
Harrowgate La PO7, PO8 275 B1
Harrow La
Fleet GU51 53 F4
Penton Corner SP11 82 A2
Petersfield GU32 228 F6
Harrow Rd
Bransgore BH23 381 B6
Portsmouth PO5 404 D2
Harrow Way
Andover SP10 82 D1
Oakley RG23 66 E3
Penton Corner SP11 82 A1
Harrow Way Com Sch SP10 82 D2
Harrow Way The RG21, RG22 69 A1
Harry Barrow Cl 1 BH24 329 A6
Harry Law Hall PO1 404 B3
Hart Cl
Farnborough GU14 55 C8
New Milton BH25 382 F4
Hart Ct SO19 291 F3
Hart Ctr 9 GU51 53 F1
Hartfield Ho 2 GU51 53 F1
Hartford Bridge Flats RG27,GU17 33 C2
Hartford Ct RG27 52 C6
Hartford Ho PO1 404 A1
Hartford Rd
Fleet GU51 53 F3
Hartley Wintney RG27 52 D7
Hartford Rise GU15 36 B6
Hartford Terr RG27 52 D6
Hart Hill SO45 314 C2
Harthill Dro SP5 235 E6
Harting Cl PO8 276 D4
Harting Down GU31 229 B4
Harting Gdns PO16 320 C1
Harting Rd BH6 394 D7
Hartington Rd
Gosport PO12 368 F6
Southampton SO14 291 B6
Hartland Ct PO10 325 D1
Hartland Pl GU14 55 E6
Hartland's Rd PO16 319 B1
Hartley Ave SO17 267 B3
Hartley Cl
Bishopstoke SO50 245 A1
Blackwater GU17 34 F5
Hythe SO45 314 A1
Hartley Ct 5 SO17 291 A8
Hartley Gdns 5 RG26 26 F7
Hartley Gr SO16 267 A4
Hartley Grange RG27 52 B6
Hartley La
Hartley Wespall RG27 30 A1
Sherfield on L RG27 29 F2
Hartley Mdw RG28 86 B5
Hartley Mews RG27 52 D7
Hartley Park Bsns Ctr GU34 162 D4
Hartley Rd
Bishopstoke SO50 245 A1
Portsmouth PO2 345 E3
Hartleys RG7 27 F8
Hartley Wlk 1 SO45 314 A1
Hart Mews GU46 33 F6
Hartnell Ct BH21 374 D5
Hart Plain Ave
Waterlooville PO8 299 D3
Waterlooville PO8 299 F2
Hart Plain Jun & Inf Schs PO7,PO8 299 E2
Hartsbourne Dr BH7 394 B8
Harts Cotts RG20 22 C6
Harts Farm Way PO9 347 C8
Hartsgrove Ave SO45 338 E1
Hartsgrove Cl SO45 338 E1
Hartshill Rd 3 RG26 9 D1
Harts La RG20 22 D6
Hartsleaf Cl GU51 74 F8
Harts Leap Cl GU47 34 F8
Harts Leap Rd GU47 34 E8
Harts Way SO41 384 D1
Hartswood RG24 48 F2
Harts Yd GU9 98 F2
Hart The GU9 98 F2
Hartvale Ct GU15 36 E8
Hartwell Rd PO3 346 B4
Hartwood Gdns PO8 299 E2
Harvard Cl PO13 368 A5
Harvest Cl
Winchester SO22 403 B2
Yateley GU46 33 F4
Harvest Cres GU51 54 B5
Harvester Dr PO15 318 B1
Harvester Way SO41 385 D6
Harvestgate Wlk PO9 323 D6
Harvest Gn RG14 1 C1
Harvesting La GU32 252 C5
Harvest La SP5 210 C8
Harvest Rd
Chandler's Ford SO53 242 F6
Denmead PO7 298 E4
Harvest Way
Middle Wallop SO20 126 B4
Old Basing RG24 69 F8
Harvey Brown Ho PO11 373 A5
Harvey Cres SO31 316 F2
Harvey Ct SO45 338 E2
Harvey Gdns SO45 314 B3
Harvey Ho 13 PO4 371 B2
Harvey Pl SP10 106 D8
Harvey Rd
Bishopstoke SO50 244 E2
Harvey Rd *continued*
Bournemouth BH5 394 A5
Farnborough GU14 55 A5
Oakley BH21 375 E8
Harveys Field RG25 88 A8
Harvey Villas GU30 187 B8
Harwell Rd BH17 390 D7
Harwich Rd PO6 321 D1
Harwood Cl
Gosport PO13 343 C4
Totton SO40 288 D8
Harwood Ct BH25 382 F3
Harwood Pl SO23 176 C8
Harwood Rd PO13 343 C4
Harwood Rise
Woolton Hill,Broad Laying RG20 4 D1
Woolton Hill,Slade Hill RG20 4 D2
Haselbury Rd SO40 288 F7
Haselfoot Gdns SO30 292 E7
Haselworth Dr PO12 369 B2
Haselworth Prim Sch PO12 369 B4
Haskells Cl SO43 309 E4
Haskells Rd BH12 391 B7
Haslar Cres PO7 299 D2
Haslar Marina PO12 369 E4
Haslar Rd
Gosport,Clayhall PO12 369 D3
Gosport,Newtown PO12 369 E5
Haslar Terr PO12 369 D3
Hasle Dr GU27 189 F6
Haslegrave Ho 2 PO2 370 D8
Haslemere Ave BH23 397 A8
Haslemere Gdns PO11 373 F2
Haslemere Pl BH23 397 A8
Haslemere Rd
Breach PO10 325 D2
Liphook GU30 188 B4
Marley Heights GU27 189 F1
Portsmouth PO4 370 F3
Haslemere Sta GU27 189 F6
Hasler Rd BH17 375 D2
Haslop Rd BH21 352 A7
Hassocks The 7 PO7 323 A7
Hassocks Workshops The RG24 69 E7
Hastards La GU34 184 E8
Hasted Dr SO24 179 C4
Hastings Ave PO12 368 F8
Hastings Cl
Basingstoke RG23 68 B5
Camberley GU16 56 E7
Hastings Ho 3 PO2 345 C2
Hastings Rd
Bournemouth BH8 378 F2
Poole BH17 375 B2
Hatchbury La SP11 38 C6
Hatch Ct PO9 323 C7
Hatchers La SO21 221 A5
Hatchery Hill SO21 174 B5
Hatches The
Camberley GU16 56 D6
Farnham GU9 121 D8
Hatchet Cl SP6 235 D3
Hatchet La
Beaulieu SO42 363 D8
Hatherden SP11 59 B1
Hatchetts Dr GU27 189 B7
Hatchgate Mead RG27 51 A2
Hatch Hill GU27 189 F1
Hatch La
Kingsley Green GU27 189 F2
Liss GU33 208 C4
Old Basing RG24 70 C5
Hatchley La SO32 246 B5
Hatch Mead SO30 268 C2
Hatch Pond Rd BH17 390 C8
Hatchwarren Cotts RG22 91 C7
Hatchwarren Gdns RG22 91 E7
Hatch Warren Inf Sch RG22 91 C7
Hatch Warren Jun Sch RG22 91 C7
Hatchwarren La RG22 91 C7
Hatch Warren La RG22 91 F8
Hatch Warren Ret Pk RG22 91 A6
Hatfield Ct
4 Camberley GU17 35 F5
New Milton BH25 382 E3
Hatfield Gdns
Bournemouth BH7 394 B8
Farnborough GU14 56 C3
Hatfield Ho GU12 77 D5
Hatfield Rd 1 PO4 371 A3
Hathaway Cl SO50 244 B4
Hathaway Gdns
Basingstoke RG24 69 C8
Waterlooville PO7 300 B1
Hathaway Rd BH6 394 D4
Hatherden SP11 59 C1
Hatherden Ave BH14 390 F5
Hatherden CE Prim Sch SP11 59 C1
Hatherden Cl 1 SP10 106 B7
Hatherell Cl SO30 268 D1
Hatherley Cres PO16 344 B8
Hatherley Dr PO16 344 B8
Hatherley Mans 4 SO15 290 C7
Hatherley Rd
Portsmouth PO6 321 A1
Winchester SO22 403 D7
Hatherwood GU46 34 D5
Hatley Rd SO18 292 B8
Hattem Pl SP10 82 F3
Hattingley Rd GU34 159 C7
Hatt La SO51 192 E2
Haughton Ho GU27 189 F6
Haughurst Hill
Axmansford RG26 25 F8
Pamber Heath RG26 9 A1
Havant Bsns Ctr PO9 347 D8
Havant-by-pass PO9 348 A8
Havant Coll PO9 323 E2
Havant Education PRU PO8 299 F2
Havant Farm Cl PO9 323 F3
Havant Mus & Arts Ctr★ PO9 324 A1
Havant Rd
Cosham PO6 345 F8
Emsworth PO10 348 D8
Farlington PO6 346 D8
Horndean PO8 300 D6
North Hayling,Fleet PO11 373 A7
North Hayling PO11 348 A5
Portsmouth PO2 345 E1
Stoke PO11 347 F2
Havant Ret Pk PO9 323 B1
Havant St PO1 370 A5
Havant Sta PO9 323 F2
Havant War Meml Hospl PO9 323 E2
H Ave SO45 338 F6
Havelock Ct SO31 316 C1
Havelock Ho GU14 77 A8
Havelock Mans PO5 404 D2
Havelock Rd
Poole BH12 392 A5
Portsmouth PO5 404 C2
Southampton SO14 290 F5
Warsash SO31 316 C1
Havelock Way BH23 381 D2
Haven Cotts BH23 396 A4
Haven Cres PO14 341 F1
Haven Ct
4 Milford on S SO41 399 C4
Poole BH13 402 B3
Havendale SO30 293 D5
Haven Gdns BH25 383 B2
Havenhurst BH13 402 E6
Haven Rd
Corfe Mullen BH21 374 C6
Poole BH13 402 E7
South Hayling PO11 373 E1
Havenstone Way SO18 267 E4
Haven The
Eastleigh SO50 244 B5
Gosport PO12 369 B3
Locks Heath SO31 317 B4
Portsmouth PO4 371 B5
Southampton SO19 291 E4
Haven Way GU9 99 B4
Haverstock Rd BH9 378 B2
Haviland Mews BH7 393 F5
Haviland Rd
Bournemouth BH7 393 F5
Ferndown BH21 353 A7
Haviland Rd E BH7 393 F5
Haviland Rd W BH1 393 F5
Havisham Rd PO2 370 C7
Havre Twrs SO19 314 E8
Hawden Rd BH11 377 A1
Haweswater Cl
Bordon GU35 164 D5
Southampton SO16 265 F1
Haweswater Ct GU12 77 D5
Hawfinch Cl SO16 266 B6
Hawkchurch Gdns BH17 375 E2
Hawk Cl
Basingstoke RG22 90 F8
Stubbington PO14 367 B7
Wimborne Minster BH21 352 A7
Hawk Conservancy The★ SP11 104 B8
Hawke Cl SP10 83 D1
Hawker Cl BH21 351 F1
Hawker Rd GU12 77 D5
Hawkers Cl SO40 264 E1
Hawkes Cl RG27 52 C7
Hawke St PO1 370 A5
Hawkeswood Rd SO18 291 C7
Hawkewood Ave PO7 299 D2
Hawkfield La RG21 69 A3
Hawkhill SO45 313 C3
Hawkhurst Cl SO19 292 A1

Hawkins Cl
Ringwood BH24.....305 C1
Yateley GU46........33 F5
Hawkins Ct SO40....289 F3
Hawkins Gr GU51....74 D6
Hawkins Rd
Gosport PO13.....343 D2
Poole BH12........376 F1
Hawkins Way GU52..75 C8
Hawkley Cl PO9.....323 E6
Hawkley Dr RG26....27 A7
Hawkley Gn SO19...314 F8
Hawkley Rd GU33...207 C5
Hawkley Way GU51..53 C3
Hawkshaw Cl GU30..188 B4
Hawks Mead GU33...207 E5
Hawkswood Ave
GU16.............36 D2
Hawkwell
Fleet GU52........75 B4
Portchester PO16...343 F8
Hawkwood Rd BH1,
BH5.............393 F4
Hawley Ct GU14.....55 C8
Hawley Garden Cotts
GU17.............35 B4
Hawley Gn GU17.....35 C3
Hawley Gr GU17.....35 C2
Hawley Green Farm
GU17.............35 D3
Hawley La GU14.....55 F8
Hawley Lodge GU17..35 D2
Hawley Place Sch
GU17.............35 C1
Hawley Prim Sch
GU17.............35 C3
Hawley Rd GU17.....35 C3
Haworth Cl BH23....380 A1
Hawstead Gn PO9...323 D6
Hawthorn Cl
Aldershot GU12....100 C8
Colden Common
SO21...........245 A8
Fair Oak SO50.....245 C2
Hedge End SO30....293 D6
Micheldever SO21...133 B2
New Alresford SO24..179 D5
New Milton BH25....383 C4
Portchester PO16...320 B1
Hawthorn Cres PO6..346 B6
Hawthorn Ct
Farnborough GU14...77 A8
Petersfield GU31....229 C3
Hawthorn Dr
Broadstone BH17...374 F1
Sway SO41.........360 B2
Hawthorne Cl SP11..103 B1
Hawthorne Cres
GU17.............35 C4
Hawthorne Gr PO11..373 B4
Hawthorne Rd SO40..288 D8
Hawthorn La
Four Marks GU34...182 E8
Rowledge GU10.....121 D3
Sarisbury SO31.....316 E5
Hawthorn Rd
Bournemouth BH9...392 F8
Burton BH23.......380 E4
Denmead PO7.......298 E4
Four Marks GU34...182 C8
Frimley GU16.......36 D2
Horndean PO8.......276 C2
Hythe SO45........313 F3
Newbury RG14.......1 E4
North Tidworth SP9...79 A7
Southampton SO17...267 A2
Hawthorn Rise RG27..51 B2
Hawthorns GU34....139 E5
Hawthorns The
Baughurst RG26....26 C8
Bishop's Waltham
SO32............271 A8
Christchurch BH23...395 F6
Eastleigh SO50.....243 E1
Marchwood SO40...290 A1
Hawthorns The Urban
Wildlife Ctr★ SO15..290 F8
Hawthorn Way RG23..68 C7
Hawthorn Wlk 6
PO13.............367 F3
Hayburn Rd SO16....265 D2
Haydens Cl SO41....385 F4
Haydn Cl SO23......176 B8
Haydn Rd RG22.......91 D8
Haydock Cl
Alton GU34........139 F2
Totton SO40.......288 C8
Haydock Mews PO7..300 B1
Haydon Pl GU46.....34 C6
Haydon Rd BH13....392 B1
Hay Down La SP11...103 E5
Haydown Leas SP11..38 C6
Hayes Ave BH7......393 E6
Hayes Cl
Fareham PO15......318 D3
King's Somborne
SO20............171 F2
Wimborne Minster
BH21............352 A4
Hayes La BH21......352 B5
Hayes Mead SO45...338 B6
Hayeswood Fst Sch
BH21............352 B6

Hayeswood Rd BH21..352 A6
Hayle Rd SO18.......268 B2
Hayley Cl SO45......337 F8
Hayley La RG29......95 C4
Hayling Ave PO3....371 B7
Hayling Billy Bsns Ctr
PO11.............372 D4
Hayling Cl
Fareham PO14......342 D8
Gosport PO12......369 C9
Hayling Sch The
PO11.............373 A5
Haymoor Mid Sch
BH17.............375 E1
Haymoor Rd BH15...391 A7
Haynes Ave BH15....390 D4
Haynes Way SO45...313 E1
Hays Cotts GU32....228 D7
Haysoms Cl BH25...383 B1
Haysoms Dr RG19....5 F7
Hayter Gdns SO51...241 A8
Hayters Way SP6....281 A6
Hayton Ct 2 SO40..288 F7
Hayward Bsns Ctr
PO9.............324 B3
Hayward Cl SO40....288 D7
Hayward Cres BH31..302 E5
Hayward Ct SO45....338 C4
Haywarden Pl RG27..52 D7
Haywards Ct 11 PO1..370 A4
Haywards Farm Cl
BH31.............302 E5
Haywards La BH21...374 C7
Hayward Way BH31..302 E5
Haywood Dr GU52....75 A7
Hazel Ave GU14.....55 D3
Hazelbank RG40.....16 C6
Hazelbank Cl
Liphook GU30......188 B4
Petersfield GU31....229 B4
Hazelbank Mews
GU30.............188 A4
Hazel Cl
Alderholt SP6......281 A5
Andover SP10......105 D6
Chandler's Ford SO53.218 C1
Christchurch BH23...381 C1
Colden Common
SO21...........245 A8
Oakley RG23.......67 B1
Hazelcombe RG25....88 B7
Hazel Coppice RG27..51 B2
Hazel Ct
1 New Milton
BH25............383 B1
Bournemouth BH9...378 C4
Portsmouth PO4....370 F4
Winchester SO22...403 A8
Hazeldale Villas
SO45.............314 A5
Hazeldean Ct PO9...301 B1
Hazeldean Dr PO9...301 B1
Hazeldene RG24.....48 F2
Hazeldene Gdns
SO21.............177 D3
Hazeldene Rd GU30..187 B4
Hazeldown Rd SO16..265 E5
Hazel Dr BH22......353 D8
Hazeleigh Ave SO19..291 E2
Hazeley Cl RG27.....52 C7
Hazeley Dr 5 GU51..53 C3
Hazeley Farm Cotts
SO21.............220 E7
Hazeley Gn PO9.....324 B5
Hazeley Lea RG27....31 F4
Hazeley Rd SO21....220 D6
Hazel Farm Rd SO40.288 C7
Hazel Gn RG26.......9 B1
Hazel Gr
Haslemere GU26...167 C2
Locks Heath SO31...317 B2
Winchester SO22...403 B3
Woodlands SO40....287 F3
Hazelgrove PO8.....276 C5
Hazelholt Dr PO9...323 D3
Hazell Ave SO40....377 B2
Hazell Rd GU9......98 D1
Hazel Rd
Clanfield PO8......276 C5
Four Marks GU34...160 C3
Lymington SO41....385 A4
Mytchett GU16......56 E2
Southampton SO19...291 D3
Hazelton Cl BH7....394 A8
Hazel Wlk GU31.....228 F1
Hazelwood
Chineham RG24.....48 E4
Stubbington PO14...342 B5
Hazelwood Ave
Havant PO9........323 B3
New Milton BH25...382 F4
Hazelwood Cl RG23..68 D7
Hazelwood Ct GU14..55 C8
Hazelwood Dr
Basingstoke RG23...68 D7
Verwood BH31.....303 B4
Hazel Wood Inf Sch
SO40.............288 C7
Hazelwood Rd SO18..268 A1
Hazlebury Rd BH17..390 F4
Hazlemere Dr RG24..327 E3
Hazleton Way PO8...300 B4
Headbourne Worthy Ho
SO23.............176 B5
Head Down GU31....229 B3
Headinglea 9 BH4...392 B3
Headington Cl RG22..91 D7
Headland Dr SO31...317 A4

Headlands Bsns Pk
BH24.............305 A2
Headlands The SP5..234 E7
Headless Cross
BH10.............377 D5
Headley Cl
Lee-on-t-S PO13...367 F3
New Alresford SO24..179 D4
Headley Fields SO15..165 C4
Headley Hill Rd
GU35.............165 E5
Headley La GU30....165 E5
Headley Rd
Grayshott GU26....166 E3
Lindford GU35......165 A5
Liphook GU30......187 F5
Headmore La GU34..160 E1
Headon Ct GU9......99 B1
Headon View GU32..225 C5
Heads Farm Cl BH10.377 E5
Head's La BH10.....377 E5
Headswell Ave BH10.377 E4
Headswell Cres
BH10.............377 E4
Headswell Gdns
BH10.............377 E4
Heanor Cl BH10....377 C2
Hearmon Cl GU46...34 C6
Hearne Gdns SO32..272 A1
Hearn Vale GU35....165 E7
Hearsey Gdns GU17..34 F6
Hearts of Oak Mews
SO41.............385 D4
Heath Ave BH15....390 D6
Heath Cl
Beacon Hill GU26..167 A7
Fair Oak SO50.....245 D1
Farnham GU9.......99 A7
Horndean PO8......300 B7
Wimborne Minster
BH21............352 B7
Heathcote Cl GU12..77 E3
Heathcote Ct 2 BH7.393 F4
Heathcote Pl SO21..218 B7
Heathcote Rd
Ash GU12.........77 F3
Bordon GU35......164 E3
Bournemouth BH5,
BH7............393 F4
Camberley GU15...36 B5
Chandler's Ford
SO53............243 D6
Portsmouth PO2....345 F1
Heath Cotts
Beacon Hill GU26..167 A6
Edgeborough GU10..122 B3
Heath Ct
Pamber Heath RG26..9 C1
Petersfield GU31....228 F7
Heath End Farm RG26.9 C1
Heath End Rd RG26..9 C1
Heathen St SO32....270 B4
Heatherbank GU16..167 C4
Heatherbank Rd
BH4.............392 C3
Heatherbrae Gdns
SO52.............241 F4
Heatherbrae La
BH16.............389 E4
Heather Chase SO50.245 A2
Heather Cl
Aldershot GU11....76 C1
Ash Vale GU12.....77 F5
Bordon GU35......164 B1
Bournemouth BH8...378 D4
Corfe Mullen BH21..374 E6
Farnham GU9......121 D6
Finchampstead RG40.16 C7
Gosport PO13......343 B2
Hordle SO41.......384 A3
St Leonards BH24...327 A4
Totton SO40.......288 E7
Walkford BH23.....382 A2
Waterlooville PO7...322 F6
Heather Cotts GU12..77 E7
Heather Ct
12 Aldershot GU11..76 C1
Hindhead GU26....167 A6
Southampton SO18..292 D7
Heatherdale Rd GU15.36 B4
Heatherdeane Rd
SO17.............267 A4
Heatherdell BH16...389 B6
Heatherdene Rd
SO53.............218 E1
Heatherdown Rd
BH22.............327 A1
Heatherdown Way
BH22.............327 A1
Heather Dr
Andover SP10......105 F8
Ferndown BH22.....353 D7
Fleet GU52........74 F5
Lindford GU35......164 F5
Pamber Heath RG26.9 D2
Heatherfield GU31...253 D5
Heather Gdns
Fareham PO15......318 D3
Farnborough GU14...55 B3
Newbury RG14......5 C7
Heather Gr RG27....52 C7
Heather La RG27.....71 C5
Heather Rd
Haslemere GU27...189 B5
Hordle SO41.......383 F3
Locks Heath SO31...317 A3
North Baddesley
SO52............242 A3
Pamber Heath RG26..10 C1
Petersfield GU31....229 A3
Soberton SO32.....273 A1
Southampton SO19...292 A5
St Leonards BH24...327 D4
Walkford BH23.....382 B1

Heatherlands Rise
BH12.............391 D5
Heatherlea Rd BH6..394 D4
Heatherley Cl 8
GU15.............35 F5
Heatherley Ct PO5..404 C1
Heatherley Mews
GU30.............188 A2
Heatherley Rd GU15..35 F5
Heather Lo 1 BH25..383 A3
Heather Mead GU16..36 D2
Heather Mead Ct
GU16.............36 D2
Heather Rd
Blackfield SO45....338 F2
Bournemouth BH10..377 D3
Petersfield GU31....229 C3
Heather Row La
Newnham RG27.....71 C4
Up Nately RG27.....71 E6
Heatherside Jun & Inf
Schs GU51........75 A8
Heatherstone Ave
Dibden Purlieu
SO45............313 F1
Hythe SO45........314 A1
Heatherton Mews
PO10.............324 F2
Heatherview Cl
SO52.............241 F5
Heather View Rd
BH12.............391 F7
Heather Way
Basingstoke RG22...91 A7
Ferndown BH22.....353 D7
Hindhead GU26....167 D4
Heath Farm Cl BH22.353 C3
Heath Farm Rd
BH22.............353 C3
Heath Farm Way
BH22.............353 C3
Heath End Bsns Ctr
SO30.............269 B1
Hedge End Rd SP10.106 D6
Hedge End Ret Pk
SO30.............293 A7
Hedge End Sta
SO30.............269 D3
Hedge End Trad Pk
SO30.............269 A1
Hedge End Wlk 7
PO9.............324 B6
Hedgehog La GU27..189 F5
Hedgerley RG25.....88 B8
Hedgerow Cl SO16...265 E7
Hedgerow Dr SO18..268 B1
Hedgerow Gdns
PO10.............324 F2
Hedgerows The RG24.70 A8
Hedges Cl SP9......101 D7
Hedgeway RG14.......2 A4
Hedley Cl SO45.....338 E1
Hedley Gdns SO30..269 B2
Heenan Cl GU16.....56 C7
Heidelberg Rd PO4..370 F4
Heights App BH16...389 C7
Heights Rd BH16....389 C8
Heights The
Camberley GU15....36 C5
Fareham PO16......319 D2
Hedge End SO30....293 A6
Heinz Burt Cl SO50..243 F3
Hele Cl RG21........69 A2
Helena Ho 2 RG21...69 C6
Helena Rd PO4......370 F2
Helen Ct
2 Newbury RG14....1 D2
Farnborough GU14...55 F4
Helford Ct 22 PO10..83 C2
Helford Gdns SO18..268 B2
Helic Ho 2 BH21...351 C5
Helix Bsns Pk GU15..35 F3
Hellyer Rd PO4.....371 A3
Helm Cl PO13.......368 D6
Helsby Cl PO14.....342 E8
Helsted Cl PO12.....368 E4
Helston Cl GU16....56 E7
Helston Dr PO10....324 F2
Helston Rd PO6.....320 F1
Helvellyn Rd SO16..289 F8
Helyar Rd BH8......378 F2
Hemdean Gdns
SO30.............268 D1
Hemlock Rd PO8....299 E4
Hemlock Way SO53..242 F5
Hemming Cl SO40...288 E6
Hemmingway Gdns
PO15.............317 C8
Hempland La GU34..204 C4
Hempsted Rd PO6...367 B1
Hemsley Wlk PO8...300 A4
Henbest Cl BH21....352 C5
Henbury Cl
Corfe Mullen BH21..374 D6
Poole BH17........376 A2
Henbury Rise BH21..374 D6
Henbury View Fst Sch
BH21.............374 C6
Henbury View Rd
BH21.............374 D6
Henchard Cl BH22..353 C2
Henderson Pk PO4..371 C3
Henderson Rd PO4..371 C3
Hendford Gdns
BH10.............377 D2
Hendford Rd BH10..377 D2
Hendon Rd GU35...164 D2
Hendren Sq 2 SP10.83 C2
Hendy Cl PO5......404 B1

Henery St 10 PO12..369 C5
Hengest Cl SP10....82 D3
Hengistbury Head Nature
Reserve★ BH6......395 E2
Hengistbury Head Nature
Trail★ BH6........395 C3
Hengistbury Rd
Barton on S BH25...397 E8
Bournemouth BH6...395 A3
Hengist Cvn Pk BH6.395 B4
Hengist Rd BH1.....393 D4
Henley Cl GU14.....55 C8
Henley Ct SO41.....399 E3
Henley Dr GU16.....56 C7
Henley Gdns
Bournemouth BH7..394 A7
Fareham PO15......318 D4
Yateley GU46.......34 B5
Henley Rd PO4.....370 F3
Henning's Park Rd
BH15.............390 E5
Henry Beaufort Sch
SO22.............175 E3
Henry Cl SO45......338 B6
Henry Cort Com Coll The
PO15.............318 D3
Henry Cort Dr PO15.318 C3
Henry Ct GU12......56 E1
Henry Player Ave
PO12.............369 D7
Henry Randell's
Almshouses GU17..35 C3
Henry Rd
Bishopstoke SO50..244 D4
Southampton SO15..290 C7
Henry St SO15......290 F6
Henry Tyndale Sch
GU14.............56 B6
Henshaw Cres RG14..5 B8
Henstead Ct 9 SO15.290 F6
Henstead Rd SO15..290 F6
Hensting La SO50...220 E2
Henty Rd SO16......290 B8
Henville Cl PO13....368 D8
Henville Rd 6 BH8..393 C5
Henwick Cl RG18....2 F6
Henwick La RG18....2 E4
Henwood Down
GU31.............229 A3
Hepplewhite Cl 2
RG26.............9 C1
Hepplewhite Dr RG22.91 A7
Hepworth Cl
Andover SP10......83 A1
Southampton SO19..292 C2
Hepworth Croft GU47.35 C6
Herald Ct 4 GU12..76 F1
Herald Ind Est SO30.269 B1
Herald Rd SO30....269 B1
Herbert Ave BH12...391 D7
Herbert Ct BH12....391 D7
Herbert Hospl BH4..392 B2
Herberton Rd BH6..394 C5
Herbert Rd
Fleet GU51........53 E1
Gosport PO12......368 F5
New Milton BH25...383 B3
Poole BH4.........392 B2
Portsmouth PO4....370 E2
Redlynch SP5......235 D6
Herbert St PO1.....370 C7
Herbert Walker Ave
Southampton SO15..290 C4
Southampton SO15..290 E3
Herbs End GU14....55 A5
Hercules Rd BH15...389 D3
Hercules St PO2....370 D8
Hereford Cl RG29...72 C2
Hereford Ct
10 Gosport PO13..368 C6
Portsmouth PO5....404 C1
Hereford Ho GU11..76 E1
Hereford La GU9.....98 F7
Hereford Mead GU51.54 B4
Hereford Rd
Basingstoke RG23...68 C5
Portsmouth PO5....404 C1
Hereward Ct SO51..241 B7
Herewood Cl RG14...1 D4
Heriot Ct GU15......36 B3
Heritage Bsns Pk
PO12.............343 F1
Heritage Ct BH13...402 F7
Heritage Gdns PO16.344 A2
Heritage Pk RG22...91 B5
Heritage View RG22..91 B5
Heritage Way PO12.343 F1
Heritage Way,Priddy's
Hard PO12........369 C9
Hermes Cl GU51....54 C1
Hermes Ct 10 PO12.369 C9
Hermes Rd PO13....367 D4
Hermitage Cl
Alton GU34........139 E2
Bishop's Waltham
SO32............271 A8
Farnborough GU14...56 B1
Frimley GU16......36 D1
Havant PO9........323 E4
Three Legged Cross
BH21.............322 E8
Hermitage Gdns
PO7.............322 F8
Hermitage Rd BH14.391 A5
Hermitage The
BH14.............391 A5
Herm Rd BH12......376 D1
Herne Jun Sch GU31.229 A4

Herne Rd
Cosham PO6 . . . . . **345** E8
Petersfield GU31 . . . . **229** A3
Hern La SP6 . . . . . . **282** B6
Heron Cl
Alton GU34 . . . . . . **139** F6
Fleet GU52 . . . . . . **75** C6
Mytchett GU16 . . . . **56** D4
Portsmouth PO4 . . . . **371** B5
Sway SO41 . . . . . . **360** B4
Heron Court Rd BH3,
BH9 . . . . **393** A7
Heron Ct GU47 . . . . . **35** A7
Herondale GU27 . . . . **189** C6
Heron Dr BH21 . . . . . **352** A8
Heron Ho
1 Portsmouth PO5 . . **370** E2
Newbury RG14 . . . . **2** B3
Heron Ind Est RG7 . . . **13** E8
Heron La SO51 . . . . . **215** D6
Heron Pk
Chineham RG24 . . . . . . **48** F1
Old Basing RG24 . . . . **69** F8
Heron Quay PO10 . . . . **349** A7
Herons Cl PO14 . . . . . **342** C4
Herons Ct PO11 . . . . . **373** B5
Heron Sq SO50 . . . . . **243** E2
Herons Rise SP10 . . . **106** B6
Heronswood
Odiham RG29 . . . . **72** F4
Totton SO40 . . . . . . **264** D2
Heron Way
Basingstoke RG22 . . . . **90** F8
Gosport PO13 . . . . . **343** B3
Thatcham RG19 . . . . **2** F3
Heron Wood Rd
GU12 . . . . **100** B7
Herretts Gdns GU12 . . . **77** B1
Herrett St GU12 . . . . . **100** B8
Herriard Pl RG22 . . . . . **91** A5
Herriard Way RG26 . . . **27** A7
Herrick Cl SO19 . . . . . **292** D4
Herridge Cl RG26 . . . . **29** B2
Herriot Cl GU46 . . . . . **34** A4
Herriot Ho PO8 . . . . . **300** A4
Herriott Cl PO8 . . . . . **300** A5
Herstone Cl BH17 . . . . **375** F4
Hertford Cl SP6 . . . . . **257** F3
Hertford Ct 6 BH23 . . **397** B7
Hertford Pl PO1 . . . . . **370** D7
Hertsfield PO14 . . . . . **317** C4
Hesketh Cl BH24 . . . . **328** A5
Hesketh Ho 4 SO15. **290** C6
Hestan Cl BH23 . . . . . **379** D4
Hester Rd PO4 . . . . . . **371** B4
Hesters View RG29 . . . . **95** D2
Hestia Cl SO51 . . . . . **241** C8
Heston Way BH22 . . . . **326** D3
Heston Wlk PO12 . . . . **368** E3
Hewett Cl PO14 . . . . . **341** F7
Hewett Ho PO14 . . . . . **341** F7
Hewett Rd
Portsmouth PO2 . . . . **345** E2
Titchfield PO14 . . . . **341** F7
Hewetts Rise SO31. **340** C10
Hewitt Cl PO12 . . . . . **369** E4
Hewitt Rd BH15 . . . . . **389** E4
Hewitt's Rd SO15 . . . . **290** C4
Hewshott Gr GU30 . . . **188** C5
Hewshott La GU30 . . . **188** C5
Hexagon The 6
SP10 . . . . **105** D6
Heyes Dr SO19 . . . . . **292** C3
Heysham Rd
Broadstone BH18 . . . **375** A4
Southampton SO15 . . . **290** B7
Heyshott Gdns PO8 . . . **276** D4
Heyshott Rd PO4. . . . . **370** F4
Heytesbury Rd BH6 . . . **394** D5
Heyward Rd PO4 . . . . . **370** E4
Heywood Gdns PO9 . . . **323** D6
Heywood Gn SO19 . . . **292** E5
Hibbard Ct BH10 . . . . **377** C2
Hibberds Field BH21 **279** A7
Hibberd Way BH10 . . . **377** D1
Hibbs Cl BH16 . . . . . . **389** C7
Hibiscus Cres SP10 . . . **105** C7
Hibiscus Gr GU35 . . . . **164** E2
Hickes Cl BH11 . . . . . **376** F4
Hickory Cl BH16 . . . . . **389** A8
Hickory Dr SO22 . . . . . **175** C4
Hickory Gdns SO30. . . . **268** C3
Hicks Cl RG26 . . . . **27** A7
Hicks La GU17 . . . . . . **34** F5
Hides Cl RG28 . . . . **86** C4
Highams Cl PO7 . . . . . **322** C3
Highbank Ave PO7 . . . . **322** C3
Highbank Gdns SP6 . . . **257** F1
High Barn Cotts
SO32 . . . . **224** F3
High Beeches GU16 . . . . **36** B2
High Beech Gdns
SP10 . . . . **106** C7
Highbridge Rd
Colden Common,
Highbridge SO50 . . . **244** D7
Colden Common, Twyford
SO21 . . . . **219** F2
Poole BH14 . . . . . . **391** C4
High Brow BH22 . . . . . **353** D6
Highbury Bldgs PO6. **345** E6
Highbury Cl
Fair Oak SO50 . . . . . **245** C1
New Milton BH25 . . . **383** B2
Highbury Coll PO6. . **346** A6
Highbury Cres GU15 . . . **36** E8
Highbury Gr
Cosham PO6 . . . . . . **346** A6

Highbury Gr continued
Portsmouth PO6 . . . . **345** F6
Highbury Prim Sch
PO6. . . . . **346** A6
Highbury Rd SP11. . . . **105** D4
Highbury St 6 PO1 . **370** A4
Highbury Way PO6. . . . **345** D6
Highclere Ave PO9. . . . **323** E4
Highclere Castle ★
RG20 . . . . **21** F2
Highclere Dr GU15 . . . . **36** E7
Highclere Rd
Aldershot GU12 . . . . **100** B8
Southampton SO16 . . **266** D3
Highclere St RG20 . . . . **21** C3
Highclere Way SO53 . . **243** B3
Highcliff Ave SO14 . . . **291** A8
Highcliffe Castle ★
BH23 . . . . **396** E7
Highcliffe Cnr BH23. **397** B8
Highcliffe Ct SO50 . . . . **244** A7
Highcliffe Rd
Christchurch BH23 . . . **396** C7
Gosport PO12 . . . . . **368** F4
Southampton SO19 . . **292** D4
Highcliffe St Mark's
Prim Sch BH23 . . . **381** F1
Highcliffe Sch BH23. **381** D1
High Copse GU9 . . . . . **98** E5
High Crissels 3 GU47 **35** B8
Highcroft GU26 . . . . . **167** B6
Highcroft Ind Est
PO8. . . . . **300** C8
Highcroft Rd PO8 . . . . **300** C7
High Cross GU32 . . . . **205** D2
High Cross La GU32 . . . **205** D1
Highcrown Mews
SO17 . . . . **267** A2
Highcrown St SO17 . **267** A2
High Ct PO4 . . . . **371** A3
Highdown GU51 . . . . . **54** A2
Highdowns RG22 . . . . . **91** C6
High Dr
Basingstoke RG22 . . . . **68** D2
Gosport PO13 . . . . . **343** C1
Higher Blandford Rd
BH18,BH21 . . . . . . **374** F6
Higher Mead RG24 . . . . **69** F7
Higher Merley La
BH21 . . . . **374** E8
Highfield
Ashmansworth RG20. . . **40** F7
Lymington SO41 . . . . **385** D4
Twyford SO21 . . . . . **220** A5
Highfield Ave
Aldershot GU11 . . . . . **99** E8
Fareham PO14 . . . . . **342** F8
Lymington SO41 . . . . **385** C3
Newbury RG14 . . . . **1** E2
Ringwood BH24 . . . . **329** A8
Southampton SO17 . . **266** F3
Twyford SO21 . . . . . **220** A5
Waterlooville PO7 . . . **299** F1
Highfield Campus (Univ
of Southampton)
SO17 . . . . **267** A3
Highfield CE Prim Sch
(Inf) SO17 . . . . . **267** B2
Highfield CE Prim Sch
(Jun) SO17 . . . . . **267** A2
Highfield Chase RG21 **68** F5
Highfield Cl
Aldershot GU11 . . . . . **99** F8
Chandler's Ford SO53 **243** E6
Corfe Mullen BH21 . . **374** E5
Farnborough GU14 . . . **55** D4
Farnham GU9 . . . . . **121** F7
Southampton SO17 . . **267** A2
Sway SO41 . . . . . . **360** B4
Waterlooville PO7 . . . **299** F1
Highfield Cres
Hindhead GU26 . . . . **167** D4
Southampton SO17 . . **267** B2
Highfield Ct SO32 . . . . **271** B8
Highfield Dr BH24 . . . . **329** A8
Highfield Gdns
Aldershot GU11 . . . . . **99** F8
Liss GU33 . . . . **208** B4
Sway SO41 . . . . . . **360** B2
Highfield Hall SO17 . **267** A2
Highfield Ho 3
BH14 . . . . **391** B4
Highfield La
Liphook GU30 . . . . . **188** C3
Redlynch SP5 . . . . . **235** D5
Southampton SO17 . . **267** B2
Highfield Lodge 3
SO17 . . . . **267** A2
Highfield Par PO7. . **300** A1
Highfield Path GU14 . **55** D4
Highfield Pk (Cvn Pk)
RG2 . . . . **15** B8
Highfield Rd
Bournemouth BH9. . . **377** E2
Chandler's Ford SO53 **243** E6
Corfe Mullen BH21 . . **374** E5
Farnborough GU14 . . . **55** D4
Gosport PO12 . . . . . **368** F6
Lymington SO41 . . . . **385** C3
Newbury RG14 . . . . **1** D1
Petersfield GU32 . . . . **228** F4
Portsmouth PO1 . . . . **404** C3
Ringwood BH24 . . . . **329** A8
Southampton SO17 . . **267** A2
West Moors BH22 . . . **326** D9
Highfields
Locks Heath SO31. . . **316** F1
Overton RG25 . . . . . . **88** B7

Highfield Sch GU30 . . **188** C2
Highfield Terr 1
SO22 . . . . **403** D5
High Firs Gdns SO51 **241** C7
High Firs Rd
Romsey SO51 . . . . . **241** C7
Southampton SO19 . . **292** C6
Highgate Ct GU14 . . . . **56** A5
Highgate La GU14 . . . . **56** A5
Highgate Rd PO3 . . . . **346** A1
Highgrove SO14 . . . . . **291** A3
Highgrove Cl SO40 . . . **288** D5
Highgrove Ind Pk
PO3. . . . . **346** B3
Highgrove Rd PO3 . . . . **371** B8
High Howe Cl BH11 . . . **376** E4
High Howe Gdns
BH11 . . . . **376** E4
High Howe La BH11 . . . **376** E4
Highland Ave BH23 . . . **382** B1
Highland Cl PO10 . . . . **348** E8
Highland Dr
Fleet GU51 . . . . **54** C4
Oakley RG23 . . . . **67** A2
Highland Rd
Aldershot GU12 . . . . . **77** B2
Camberley GU15 . . . . **36** B8
Emsworth PO10 . . . . **324** E1
Poole BH14 . . . . . . **391** B5
Portsmouth PO4 . . . . **371** A3
Wimborne Minster
BH21 . . . . **351** D6
Highlands RG14. . . . . . . **5** C7
Highlands Cl
Farnham GU9 . . . . . **121** F7
Hythe SO45 . . . . . . **314** A2
North Baddesley
SO52 . . . . **241** E5
Winchester SO23 . . . **403** D6
Winchester SO23 . . . **403** E5
Winchester SO23 . . . **403** F5
Woodgreen SP6. . . . . **258** E7
Highlands Cres
BH10 . . . . **377** C4
Highlands Ho SO19 . . . **291** D3
Highlands Rd
Andover SP10 . . . . . **106** C7
Barton on S BH25 . . . **398** A8
Basingstoke RG22. . . . **68** A3
Fareham PO15,PO16 . . **318** D3
Farlington PO6 . . . . . **346** D8
Farnham GU9 . . . . . . **99** A7
Highland St 4 PO4 . . **371** A3
Highlands Way
Hythe SO45 . . . . . . **313** F2
Whiteparish SP5 . . . . **212** B4
Highland Terr PO4 . . . **370** F3
Highland View Cl
BH21 . . . . **351** D5
High Lawn Way PO9. . . **323** F5
High Marryats BH25. **398** A7
High Mdw SO19. . . . . **292** C6
High Mead
Fareham PO15. . . . . **318** E4
Ferndown BH22. . . . . **353** D4
High Mead La BH22 . . . **353** A1
Highmoor Cl
Corfe Mullen BH21 . . **374** D5
Poole BH14 . . . . . . **391** B3
Highmoor Rd
Bournemouth BH11. . **377** A1
Corfe Mullen BH21 . . **374** D5
Poole BH14 . . . . . . **391** B3
Highmoors RG24. . . . . . **48** F3
Highmount Cl SO23 . . . **198** C7
Highnam Gdns SO31 **316** F4
High Oaks Cl SO31 . . . **317** A3
High Oaks Gdns
BH11 . . . . **376** E4
High Park Rd
Broadstone BH18 . . . **374** E4
Farnham GU9 . . . . . . **99** A3
Highpath Way RG24. . **68** C8
High Pines BH23 . . . . . **396** D7
High Pitfold GU26. . . . **167** B1
High Point SO18 . . . . . **291** E8
High Rd
Bishopstone SP5 . . . . **210** B8
Southampton SO16 . . **267** D4
Highridge GU34. . . . . . **139** D2
High Ridge Cres
BH25 . . . . **383** C2
High St N BH15 . . . . . **390** D3
High St
16 Southampton
SO14 . . . . **291** A3
Aldershot GU11 . . . . . **76** F2
Alton GU34 . . . . . . **139** F3
Andover SP10 . . . . . **106** A8
Beaulieu SO42 . . . . . **336** F1
Bishop's Waltham
SO32 . . . . **271** C7
Bordon GU35 . . . . . **164** D3
Botley SO30 . . . . . . **294** A7
Broughton SO20 . . . **170** B7
Buriton SU31 . . . . . **253** D5
Bursledon SO31 . . . . **316** B4
Camberley GU15 . . . . **36** B6
Christchurch BH23 . . . **395** B6
Cosham PO6 . . . . . **345** F7
Damerham SP6 . . . . **256** C5
Downton SP6 . . . . . **235** A8
Droxford SO32 . . . . . **249** B1
Eastleigh SO50 . . . . **244** A4
East Meon GU32 . . . . **226** E1
Emsworth PO10 . . . . **348** E8
Fareham PO16 . . . . . **318** D7
Farnborough GU14 . . . **77** B8
Fordingbridge SP6. . . **257** F1
Gosport PO12 . . . . . **369** D5
Grately SP11 . . . . . **125** B8
Hambledon PO7. . . . **274** D3

High St continued
Hamble-le-R SO31. . . **316** A2
Hartley Wintney RG27. **52** D6
Headley GU35 . . . . . **165** C5
Hythe SO45 . . . . . . **314** A5
Lee-on-t-S PO13 . . . . **367** E2
Lymington SO41 . . . . **385** E4
Lyndhurst SO43 . . . . **309** F4
Medstead GU34. . . . . **159** F7
Meonstoke SO32. . . . **249** C4
Milford on S SO41 . . . **399** D4
Nether Wallop SO20 . . **148** A5
Odiham RG29. . . . . . **72** E3
Overton RG25 . . . . . . **88** A8
Petersfield GU32 . . . . **228** F3
Poole BH15 . . . . . . **390** C2
Portsmouth PO1 . . . . **370** A3
Ringwood BH24 . . . . **328** F7
Rowledge GU10. . . . . **121** C4
Sandhurst GU47 . . . . . **34** A8
Selborne GU34 . . . . . **184** E8
Shedfield SO32 . . . . **295** F7
Shipton Bellinger SP9 **101** E7
Soberton SO32 . . . . . **273** B4
Southwick PO17 . . . . **320** F6
St Leonards BH24 . . . **327** F6
Stockbridge SO20 . . . **149** E3
Titchfield PO14 . . . . . **341** F8
Totton SO40 . . . . . . **289** A7
Twyford SO21 . . . . . **220** A7
Twyford SO21 . . . . . **220** A5
West End SO30 . . . . . **268** D1
West Meon GU32 . . . **225** C5
Wimborne Minster
BH21 . . . . **351** B4
Winchester SO23 . . . **403** D6
Winchester SO23 . . . **403** E5
Winchester SO23 . . . **403** F5
Woodgreen SP6. . . . . **258** E7
High Thicket Rd
GU10 . . . . **143** B5
Hightown Gdns
BH24 . . . . **329** C6
Hightown Hill BH24 . . **329** F7
Hightown Ind Est
BH24. . . . . **329** B6
Hightown Prim Sch
SO19. . . . . **292** E4
Hightown Rd
Ringwood,Hightown
BH24 . . . . **329** C6
Ringwood,Moortown
BH24 . . . . **329** A6
Hightown Twrs
SO19 . . . . **292** E4
High Trees
Fair Oak SO50 . . . . . **245** E2
Poole BH13 . . . . . . **402** G8
Waterlooville PO7 . . . **322** F8
Hightrees Ave BH8 . . . **378** F1
High Trees Dr SO22. **403** C8
High Trees Wlk
BH22 . . . . **353** D7
High View PO16. . . . . **320** C1
Highview Bsns Ctr
GU35. . . . . **164** C3
Highview Bsns Pk
RG27. . . . . **71** D8
High View Cl GU14. . . . **55** E4
Highview Gdns
BH12 . . . . **391** C7
High View Lodge 7
GU11 . . . . **76** E2
High View Rd GU14 . . . **55** E4
High View Way SO18 **291** E8
High Walls PO16 . . . . . **319** C1
High Way BH11 . . . . . **374** F3
Highways Rd SO21 . . . **219** C5
High Wlk PO15. . . . . . **318** E3
Highwood Cl
Alderholt SP6. . . . . **280** D6
Newbury RG14 . . . . . . **1** F6
Yateley GU46. . . . . . . **34** B4
Highwood La
North Baddesley
SO51 . . . . **241** D7
Ringwood BH24 . . . . **305** E3
Highwood Lawn
PO9 . . . . **323** D7
Highwood Rd
Brockenhurst SO42 . . **360** F8
Gosport PO13 . . . . . **368** C7
Poole BH14 . . . . . . **391** E4
Highwood Ridge
RG22 . . . . **91** B6
Highworth Cotts RG26. **9** A1
Higworth Cvn Site
PO11 . . . . **372** F5
Higworth La PO11. . . . **372** F5
Hilary Ave PO6 . . . . . **346** A7
Hilary Ct PO13 . . . . . **368** D6
Hilary Ho 2 RG14. . . . **1** C4
Hilary Rd BH17 . . . . . **375** C1
Hilborn Way RG2 . . . . **15** B8
Hilda Cl 1 SO15 . . . . **290** F4
Hilda Gdns PO7 . . . . . **299** A4
Hilda Pl 3 SO14 . . . . **291** C5
Hilda Rd BH12 . . . . . **391** E7
Hilden Ct PO11 . . . . . **372** F3
Hilden Way SO22 . . . . **175** B5
Hilder Gdns GU14. . . . **56** B3
Hiley Rd BH15 . . . . . . **390** C6
Hilfield GU46 . . . . **34** D5
Hilland Rise GU35 . . . **165** D5
Hillary Cl
Fareham PO16 . . . . . **318** F2

Hillary Cl continued
Farnham GU9 . . . . . **121** F7
Lyndhurst SO43 . . . . **310** A3
Hillary Rd
Basingstoke RG21. . . . **69** A3
Christchurch BH23 . . . **395** E8
Farnham GU9 . . . . . **121** F7
Hill Barn La SO21 . . . **131** A5
Hillborough Cres 2
PO5 . . . . **404** C1
Hillborough Ct 1
PO5 . . . . **404** C1
Hillbourne Com Fst &
Mid Schs BH17 . . . **375** B2
Hillbourne Rd BH17. . . **375** B2
Hillbrook Rise GU9. . . . **98** F6
Hill Brow Cl PO9 . . . . **301** B1
Hillbrow Rd BH6 . . . . . **394** B6
Hill Brow Rd GU33 . . . **208** B2
Hillbury Ave SP10 . . . **105** E6
Hillbury Pk SP6 . . . . . **281** B5
Hillbury Rd SP6 . . . . . **281** B5
Hill Cl
Bransgore BH23 . . . . **381** A8
Fair Oak SO50 . . . . . **245** C5
Newbury RG14 . . . . . . **5** B7
Hill Corner Farm Est
GU14 . . . . **55** B7
Hillcrest
Farnham GU9 . . . . . . **99** B8
Fleet GU51 . . . . **54** A3
Pamber Heath RG26 . . **9** F1
Hillcrest Ave
Chandler's Ford
SO53 . . . . **243** E6
Ferndown BH22. . . . . **353** C8
Hillcrest Cl
Bournemouth BH9. . . **378** A3
North Baddesley
SO52 . . . . **241** F5
Hillcrest Cotts RG14. . . . **1** D7
Hillcrest Ct RG25. . . . . . **68** B6
Hillcrest Dr SO53 . . . . **243** D6
Hill Crest Dr GU10 . . . **121** D6
Hillcrest Gdns SO32. . **271** E4
Hillcrest Hospl
BH10. . . . . **377** D1
Hillcrest Rd
Bournemouth BH9. . . **378** A3
Camberley GU15 . . . . **36** F7
Corfe Mullen BH21 . . **374** C5
Poole BH12 . . . . . . **391** A5
Hillcrest Wlk RG23 . . . **68** C6
Hillcroft SP5. . . . . . . **235** D6
Hill Croft PO15. . . . . . **317** E3
Hillcroft Cl SO41 . . . . **385** E4
Hill Ct GU27 . . . . **189** F6
Hilldene Way SO30. . . **268** E1
Hilldown Rd SO17. . . . **267** B2
Hilldowns Ave PO2. . . **345** C2
Hill Dr PO15 . . . . **318** D3
Hiller Wlk 2 PO13 . . **367** F3
Hill Farm Cl GU27. . . . **189** D5
Hill Farm Rd
Southampton SO15 . . **290** E6
West Tisted SO24,
GU34 . . . . **182** C2
Hillgarth GU26 . . . . . **167** B5
Hill Grove La SO32 . . . **272** C5
Hillgrove Rd SO18 . . . **267** F3
Hill Head Rd PO14 . . . **367** A6
Hill Ho GU26 . . . . **167** A6
Hill House Nfld GU30 **187** E6
Hillhouse La
Headley,Goose Hill
RG19 . . . . **7** E2
Headley, Nr Greenham
RG19 . . . . **7** E1
Headley RG19 . . . . . **24** D1
Hill Houses Sch SO41 **361** D1
Hill Houses SO24. . . . **201** B6
Hillier Way SO23 . . . . **403** E8
Hill La
Bransgore BH23 . . . . **381** A8
Burton BH23 . . . . . . **380** F2
Colden Common SO21 **219** F1
Southampton SO15 . . **266** E2
Hillman Rd BH14. . . . . **391** D5
Hill Mdw RG25. . . . . . . **65** A2
Hill Pl SO31 . . . . **316** B8
Hill Rd
Beacon Hill GU26 . . . **167** A6
Farnham GU9 . . . . . . **99** B7
Grayshott GU26. . . . **167** A3
Newbury RG14 . . . . . **1** C4
Oakley RG23 . . . . . . **90** B8
Portchester PO16 . . . **320** D1
Hill Rise
Meonstoke SO32. . . . **249** C5
Twyford SO21 . . . . . **220** A5
Hillsborough Ct GU14 **55** C8
Hillsborough Cl SO53 **218** D1
Hillsea Mkt PO2 . . . . . **345** E5
Hillside
Abbotts Ann SP11. . . **104** F4
Baughurst RG26 . . . . **26** A4
Curdridge SO32. . . . **294** F8
Littleton SO22 . . . . . **175** C5
Sandhurst GU15 . . . . **35** D7
Upton SP11 . . . . . . **38** F2
Whitchurch RG28 . . . **86** E5

Hillside Ave
Romsey SO51 . . . . . **241** A7
Southampton SO18 . . **267** E1
Waterlooville PO7 . . . **322** B2
Hillside Cl
Alton GU34 . . . . . . **139** F5
Chandler's Ford
SO53 . . . . **243** D6
Crookham Village
GU51 . . . . **74** C6
Headley SO53 . . . . . **165** E6
Horndean PO8 . . . . . **276** C3
West Dean SP5 . . . . . **190** D2
Winchester SO22 . . . **403** A8
Hillside Cotts
Hill Brow GU33 . . . . **208** B2
Sparsholt SO21 . . . . **174** B4
Hillside Cres
Camberley GU16 . . . . **56** D7
Portchester PO6 . . . . **320** F1
Hillside Ct SP10. . . . . **105** F7
Hillside Dr BH23 . . . . **379** D3
Hillside Flats GU26. . . **167** B6
Hillside Fst Sch
BH31. . . . . **302** F7
Hillside Gdns BH21. . . **374** C4
Hillside Ind Est PO8. **300** C8
Hillside La GU9 . . . . . . **99** B8
Hillside Mews BH21. **374** C4
Hillside Rd
Aldershot GU11. . . . . **99** E8
Ash GU12 . . . . **77** C3
Corfe Mullen BH21 . . **374** C5
Edgeborough GU10 . . **122** A3
Farnham,Weybourne
GU9 . . . . **99** C7
Haslemere GU27 . . . **189** D5
Lymington SO41 . . . . **385** C3
Odiham RG29. . . . . . **72** F3
Poole BH12 . . . . . . **376** F1
Sparsholt SO21 . . . . **174** B4
Verwood BH31. . . . . **302** F7
Winchester SO22 . . . **403** A7
Woodlands Common
BH21 . . . . **302** A6
Hillside Villas SP10 . . **82** E2
Hillside Wlk BH21. . . . **302** A6
Hillsley Rd PO6 . . . . . **320** F2
Hillson Dr PO15 . . . . . **318** C3
Hillson Ho PO15 . . . . . **318** D3
Hillsons Rd SO30. . . . . **294** B7
Hill Sq RG24 . . . . **49** A1
Hill St
Poole BH15 . . . . . . **390** C2
Totton SO40 . . . . . . **264** C5
Hillstead Ct RG21 . . . . **69** B3
Hill Terr
Fair Oak SO50 . . . . . **245** C5
New Alresford SO24. . **179** D6
Wimborne Minster
BH21 . . . . **352** A2
Hilltop SO22 . . . . **175** C5
Hilltop Cl BH22 . . . . . **353** B7
Hilltop Cres PO6 . . . . **322** C2
Hilltop Dr SO19 . . . . . **292** B4
Hilltop Gdns PO8 . . . . **276** D3
Hilltop Rd
Corfe Mullen BH21 . . **374** E5
Ferndown BH22. . . . . **353** B7
Overton RG25 . . . . . . **65** B2
Portsmouth PO6 . . . . **321** A4
Hilltop View GU46 . . . . **33** F5
Hillview PO8. . . . . **300** C9
Hill View GU32 . . . . . **226** D1
Hill View Cvn Pk
SO50 . . . . **245** B5
Hill View Prim Sch
BH10. . . . . **377** E3
Hillview Rd
Bournemouth BH10. . **377** D1
Hythe SO45 . . . . . . **313** F3
Hill View Rd
Basingstoke RG22 . . . **68** E3
Braishfield SO51 . . . **216** C6
Farnham GU9 . . . . . . **98** D2
Ferndown BH22. . . . . **353** C7
Michelmersh SO51 . . **215** C8
Portchester PO16 . . . **320** D1
Hill Way BH24 . . . . . . **327** F5
Hillway The
Chandler's Ford
SO53 . . . . **243** D7
Portchester PO16 . . . **344** C8
Hill Wlk PO15 . . . . . . **318** D3
Hilly Cl SO21 . . . . **221** B4
Hillyfields SO16. . . . . **265** C3
Hilsea Cres PO2 . . . . . **345** E5
Hilsea Mkt PO2 . . . . . **345** E5
Hilsea Sta PO3. . . . . . **346** A4
Hiltingbury Cl SO53 **218** D1
Hiltingbury Ct 4
SO53 . . . . **218** B1
Hiltingbury Inf Sch
SO53 . . . . **218** C1
Hiltingbury Jun Sch
SO53 . . . . **218** C1
Hiltingbury Rd
3 Havant PO9 . . . . **324** A5
Chandler's Ford
SO53 . . . . **218** D1
Hiltom Rd BH24 . . . . . **329** B7
Hilton Cl BH15 . . . . . . **391** A6
Hilton Rd
Gosport PO12 . . . . . **369** C4

Hilton Rd *continued*
Hedge End SO30 ... 293 C7
New Milton BH25 ... 383 B4
Hinaidi Way GU14 ... 76 D8
Hinchliffe Cl BH15 ... 389 F2
Hinchliffe Rd BH15 ... 389 F2
Hindell Cl GU14 ... 55 E8
Hindhead Commons Nature Trails★ GU26 ... 167 E4
Hindhead Ho GU26 ... 167 D4
Hindhead Rd GU26 ... 167 D2
Hinkler Ct SO19 ... 292 D4
Hinkler Rd SO19 ... 292 E5
Hinstock Cl GU14 ... 55 E3
Hinton Admiral Mews BH23 ... 381 E2
Hinton Admiral Sta BH23 ... 381 E2
Hinton Ampner Ho★ SO24 ... 201 E3
Hinton Cl
Havant PO9 ... 323 C4
Tadley RG26 ... 26 F7
Hinton Cres SO19 ... 292 E4
Hinton Fields SO23 ... 176 C6
Hinton Hill SO24 ... 201 F4
Hinton Ho 3 PO7 ... 322 E8
Hinton House Dr SO23 ... 176 C6
Hinton Manor La PO8 ... 275 F2
Hinton Rd BH1 ... 392 F3
Hinton Wood BH1 ... 393 A2
Hinton Wood Ave BH23 ... 381 E1
Hintonwood La BH23 ... 381 E2
Hinwood Cl SO20 ... 170 B7
Hipley Rd PO9 ... 324 A3
Hirst Copse SP11 ... 62 A2
Hirst Rd SO45 ... 314 B3
Hispano Ave PO15 ... 317 C7
Hitches La GU51 ... 74 C7
Hither Gn PO10 ... 325 E2
Hitherwood Cl 9 PO7 ... 300 B1
Hive Gdns BH13 ... 402 D6
Hives Way SO41 ... 385 D6
H Jones Cres GU11 ... 77 A3
HMS Victory★ PO1 ... 369 F7
HMS Warrior★ PO1 ... 369 F6
Hoadlands GU31 ... 229 B4
Hoad's Hill PO17 ... 296 B2
Hobart Dr SO45 ... 314 B3
Hobart Rd BH25 ... 382 F2
Hobb La SO30 ... 293 D6
Hobbs Cl SO24 ... 180 C4
Hobbs Ct 2 PO12 ... 369 E5
Hobbs Pk BH24 ... 327 F4
Hobbs Rd BH12 ... 391 C8
Hobbs Sq 4 SP10 ... 83 C2
Hobby Cl
Portsmouth PO3 ... 346 A4
Waterlooville PO8 ... 299 E4
Hobson Way SO45 ... 338 D3
Hoburne Ct BH23 ... 381 C1
Hoburne Cvn Pk BH23 ... 396 C8
Hoburne Gdns BH23 ... 381 C1
Hoburne La BH23 ... 396 C8
Hockford La RG19 ... 8 E3
Hockham Ct PO9 ... 323 C7
Hockley Cl 4 PO6 ... 345 D8
Hockley Cotts
Cheriton SO24 ... 200 E3
Twyford SO21 ... 220 A8
Hockley Link SO21 ... 197 E1
Hockleys La RG25 ... 116 C7
Hocombe Dr SO53 ... 218 B2
Hocombe Park Cl SO53 ... 218 B2
Hocombe Rd SO53 ... 218 D2
Hocombe Wood Rd SO53 ... 218 B2
Hodder Cl SO53 ... 243 B5
Hoddington Cotts RG25 ... 94 C4
Hodges Cl
Havant PO9 ... 324 A3
Poole BH17 ... 390 E7
Hoeford Cl PO16 ... 343 B6
Hoe La SO51,SO52 ... 241 D3
Hoe Rd SO32 ... 271 E7
Hoe St PO7 ... 297 F7
Hoe The PO13 ... 343 E1
Hogarth Cl
7 Romsey SO51 ... 216 B1
Basingstoke RG21 ... 69 E4
Sandhurst GU47 ... 35 C6
Southampton SO19 ... 292 C2
Hogarth Ct SP10 ... 82 F1
Hogarth Way BH8 ... 379 A2
Hoggarth Cl GU31 ... 229 A4
Hoghatch La GU9 ... 98 E6
Hogmoor Rd GU35 ... 164 B3
Hogs Lodge La PO8 ... 276 E8
Hogue Ave BH10 ... 377 D5
Hogwood Ind Est RG40 ... 15 E6
Hogwood La
Arborfield Garrison RG40 ... 15 E6
West End SO30 ... 268 E6
Holbeach Cl PO6 ... 321 E1
Holbeche Cl GU46 ... 33 E6
Holbein Cl RG21 ... 69 D3
Holbein Lodge SO41 ... 386 B3
Holborne Cl RG14 ... 5 A5
Holbrook Cl GU9 ... 99 D8
Holbrook Pl 3 SO51 ... 240 E7
Holbrook Prim Sch PO13 ... 343 C3
Holbrook Rd
Fareham PO16 ... 343 B8
Portsmouth PO1 ... 404 C3
Holbrook Way GU11 ... 99 F7
Holburne Naish BH25 ... 397 D8
Holbury Cl BH8 ... 378 E3
Holbury Ct 6 PO9 ... 324 B5
Holbury Dro SO45 ... 338 C4
Holbury La SO51 ... 191 D3
Holbury Prim Sch SO45 ... 338 C3
Holcombe Rd BH16 ... 389 B6
Holcot La PO3 ... 346 C4
Holcroft Rd SO19 ... 292 E5
Holdaway Cl SO23 ... 176 C7
Holdenbury Ct PO3 ... 346 C5
Holdenhurst Ave BH7 ... 394 C7
Holdenhurst Cl PO8 ... 276 C1
Holdenhurst Rd
Bournemouth BH8 ... 393 C5
Bournemouth,Holdenhurst BH8 ... 379 B3
Holden La SO24 ... 222 F7
Holder Rd GU12 ... 77 C1
Holdings The BH24 ... 329 B5
Hole La
Bentley GU10 ... 120 A5
Curdridge SO32 ... 271 A1
Soberton PO7 ... 298 A8
Holes Bay North Rdbt BH17 ... 390 A6
Holes Bay Pk BH15 ... 390 B4
Holes Bay Rd BH15 ... 390 B4
Holes Bay Rdbt BH15 ... 390 B5
Holes Cl SO41 ... 383 F4
Holkham Cl SO16 ... 265 E3
Hollam Cl PO14 ... 342 B8
Hollam Cres PO14 ... 342 B8
Hollam Dr PO14 ... 342 B8
Hollam Rd PO4 ... 371 B4
Holland Cl
Chandler's Ford SO53 ... 243 C3
Farnham GU9 ... 99 C1
Holland Dr SP10 ... 82 F3
Holland Gdns GU51 ... 75 A8
Holland Pk SO31 ... 316 F3
Holland Pl
Gosport PO13 ... 343 D2
Southampton SO16 ... 266 B1
Holland Rd
Portsmouth PO4 ... 404 D2
Southampton SO19 ... 291 D2
Totton SO40 ... 288 C7
Hollands Cl SO22 ... 175 B5
Hollands Wood Cvn & Camping Site SO42 ... 334 A4
Hollands Wood Dr BH25 ... 383 B5
Holland Way BH18 ... 374 F5
Hollenden 9 BH13 ... 392 A4
Hollies Cl SO41 ... 360 B1
Hollies The
Hartley Wintney RG27 ... 52 C4
Horndean PO8 ... 276 C2
Newbury RG14 ... 5 B5
West Wellow SO51 ... 238 E2
Hollingbourne Cl SO18 ... 291 D8
Hollington La RG20 ... 21 A3
Hollin's Wlk 9 RG21 ... 69 B5
Hollis Wood Dr GU10 ... 121 C5
Hollman Dr SO51 ... 240 D7
Holloway Ave BH11 ... 376 F5
Hollow La
Headley GU35 ... 165 C6
South Hayling PO11 ... 372 F3
Hollowshot La RG20 ... 24 C1
Hollow The
Broughton SO20 ... 170 D5
Kingsclere RG20 ... 24 C2
Holly Acre GU46 ... 34 B5
Holly Ave GU16 ... 36 F3
Hollybank PO13 ... 367 F2
Hollybank Cl SO45 ... 314 A3
Holly Bank Cl PO8 ... 300 C5
Hollybank Cres SO45 ... 313 F4
Hollybank La PO10 ... 324 F4
Hollybank Rd SO45 ... 313 F4
Hollybrook Appartments PO16 ... 344 B8
Hollybrook Ave SO16 ... 266 C3
Hollybrook Cl SO16 ... 266 B2
Hollybrook Ct GU35 ... 164 E3
Hollybrook Gdns SO31 ... 317 A5
Hollybrook Inf Sch SO16 ... 266 D3
Hollybrook Jun Sch SO16 ... 266 D3
Hollybrook Pk GU35 ... 164 E3
Hollybrook Rd SO16 ... 266 C2
Holly Bush Cotts RG26 ... 26 B1
Hollybush Ind Pk GU11 ... 77 C5
Hollybush La
Eversley Cross RG27 ... 33 C7
Farnborough GU11 ... 77 C6
Ramsdell RG26 ... 26 D2
Holly Bush La RG27 ... 71 E7
Holly Cl
Aldershot GU12 ... 77 A2
Bramley RG26 ... 29 A2
Eversley Centre RG27 ... 33 C8
Farnborough GU14 ... 55 E4
Headley GU35 ... 166 A5
Hythe SO45 ... 338 A7
Sarisbury SO31 ... 316 E3
St Leonards BH24 ... 327 D4
Thatcham RG19 ... 7 F6
Upton BH16 ... 389 A7
West Moors BH22 ... 326 D2
Holly Cnr RG7 ... 14 F7
Hollycombe Cl GU30 ... 188 A2
Hollycroft RG19 ... 8 D1
Holly Cross RG26 ... 28 F4
Holly Ct
Lymington SO41 ... 385 B2
Poole BH15 ... 390 D4
West Moors BH22 ... 326 D2
Holly Dell SO16 ... 266 E5
Hollydene Villas SO45 ... 314 A4
Holly Dr
Old Basing RG24 ... 70 C6
Waterlooville PO7 ... 323 A6
Hollyfields Cl GU15 ... 35 F5
Holly Gdns
Burton BH23 ... 380 D1
Milford on S SO41 ... 399 C5
West End SO30 ... 268 D3
Holly Gr
Fareham PO16 ... 318 E4
Verwood BH31 ... 302 E5
Holly Green Rise BH11 ... 376 E4
Holly Hatch Rd SO40 ... 288 E6
Holly Hedge Cl GU16 ... 36 C2
Holly Hedge La BH17 ... 390 C8
Holly Hedge Rd GU16 ... 36 C2
Holly Hill SO16 ... 266 E5
Holly Hill Cl SO16 ... 266 E5
Holly Hill La SO31 ... 316 C4
Holly Hill Mans SO31 ... 316 E4
Holly Hill Woodland Pk★ SO31 ... 316 C4
Holly Ho SO19 ... 291 E2
Hollyhock Cl RG22 ... 91 A8
Holly La
Boldre SO41 ... 362 B1
New Milton BH25 ... 383 C4
Silchester RG7 ... 27 F8
Walkford BH23 ... 382 C2
Holly Lo 13 BH13 ... 392 A4
Holly Lodge
Chandler's Ford SO53 ... 243 C3
Southampton SO17 ... 267 B1
Holly Lodge Prim Sch GU12 ... 77 D8
Holly Mdws SO22 ... 403 A8
Holly Oak Ct SO16 ... 266 A4
Holly Oak Rd SO16 ... 266 A3
Holly Rd
Aldershot GU12 ... 77 B1
Ashurst SO40 ... 288 B2
Blackfield SO45 ... 365 E8
Farnborough GU14 ... 55 E4
Hollyridge GU27 ... 189 F6
Holly St PO12 ... 369 C5
Hollytree Gdns GU16 ... 56 B8
Holly Tree Pk SO21 ... 131 C4
Hollytrees GU51 ... 74 E6
Hollywater Rd
Bordon GU35 ... 164 F2
Liphook GU30 ... 187 A8
Holly Way GU17 ... 35 B4
Hollywell Dr PO6 ... 345 B7
Holly Wlk SP10 ... 105 D6
Hollywood Cl SO52 ... 241 F4
Hollywood Ct SO41 ... 385 D5
Hollywood La SO41 ... 385 D5
Holman Cl
Bramley RG26 ... 29 B2
Waterlooville PO8 ... 300 A2
Holmbrook Cl GU14 ... 55 A4
Holmbrook Gdns 7 GU14 ... 55 A4
Holmbush Ct PO5 ... 404 B1
Holm Cl BH24 ... 305 C1
Holm Ct PO11 ... 372 F2
Holmdale Rd PO12 ... 368 F7
Holme CE Prim Sch The GU35 ... 165 C6
Holmefield Ave PO14 ... 342 F7
Holme Rd BH23 ... 397 B8
Holmes Cl
Basingstoke RG22 ... 91 C6
Netley SO31 ... 315 B6
Holmes Ct
13 Grayshott GU26 ... 167 B3
Andover SP10 ... 105 E7
Holmesland Dr SO30 ... 293 F7
Holmesland La SO30 ... 293 F8
Holmesland Wlk SO30 ... 293 F7
Holmfield Ave BH7 ... 394 C7
Holmgrove PO14 ... 317 C3
Holm Hill La BH23, BH25 ... 382 B7
Holmhurst Ave BH23 ... 381 F1
Holm Oak Cl
Littleton SO22 ... 175 B5
Verwood BH31 ... 302 E8
Holmsley Cl
Lymington SO41 ... 385 B2
Southampton SO18 ... 292 C7
Holmsley Ct SO40 ... 288 B8
Holmsley Pas BH24 ... 358 C7
Holmsley Rd BH25 ... 358 E2
Holmwood Cotts GU10 ... 119 F4
Holmwood Ct SO16 ... 267 A4
Holmwood Garth BH24 ... 329 D6
Holmwood Terr RG27 ... 52 C6
Holne Ct PO4 ... 371 C3
Holnest Rd BH17 ... 375 D1
Holst Cl RG22 ... 91 E7
Holst Way PO7 ... 322 E5
Holt Barns GU35 ... 142 E5
Holt Cl
Farnborough GU14 ... 56 A7
Lee-on-t-S PO13 ... 368 A6
Wickham PO17 ... 295 F4
Holt Cotts RG19 ... 25 D8
Holt Ct SO19 ... 314 E8
Holt Down GU31 ... 229 B3
Holt End La GU34 ... 138 A4
Holt Gdns PO9 ... 301 B3
Holt Ho BH8 ... 393 D5
Holt La
Hook RG27 ... 51 C1
Tangley SP11 ... 59 B7
Wolverton Common RG26 ... 25 D4
Holt Pl BH22 ... 353 F7
Holt Pound La GU10 ... 121 A5
Holt Rd
Poole BH12 ... 391 F6
Southampton SO15 ... 290 F6
Three Legged Cross BH21 ... 326 D8
Holt View SO50 ... 244 F2
Holt Way RG27 ... 51 C2
Holtwood Rd RG20 ... 3 F6
Holworth Cl BH11 ... 376 E3
Holy Barn Cl RG22 ... 68 A1
Holyborne Rd SO51 ... 241 B7
Holybourne Rd PO9 ... 323 F3
Holy Cross Hospl GU27 ... 189 C7
Holy Family RC Prim Sch SO16 ... 265 D2
Holyrood Ave SO17 ... 267 B2
Holyrood Cl
2 Waterlooville PO7 ... 323 A7
Poole BH17 ... 390 A8
Holyrood Ct RG22 ... 68 B3
Holy Rood Est SO14 ... 291 A3
Holyrood Ho 5 SO14 ... 291 A3
Holy Rood Pl 1 SO14 ... 291 A3
Holywell Cl
Farnborough GU14 ... 55 E7
Poole BH17 ... 375 D3
Homeborough Ho SO45 ... 314 A5
Homebridge Ho 2 SP6 ... 257 F2
Home Cl SO24 ... 136 F2
Homecliffe Ho BH23 ... 397 B8
Homecorfe Ho BH18 ... 375 B5
Homedale Ho BH2 ... 392 F5
Homedene Ho BH15 ... 390 D3
Home Farm BH25 ... 398 E8
Home Farm Bsns Ctr SO51 ... 191 E5
Home Farm Cl
Farnborough GU14 ... 56 B6
Hythe SO45 ... 314 B3
Home Farm Gdns SP10 ... 82 D3
Home Farm Office Village PO16 ... 343 D8
Home Farm Rd
Hartley Wintney RG27 ... 53 B6
Verwood BH31 ... 302 E7
Home Farm Way BH31 ... 302 E6
Homefayre Ho 3 PO16 ... 319 B1
Homefield
Romsey SO51 ... 216 A1
St Mary Bourne SP11 ... 61 F2
Homefield Cotts
East Tisted GU34 ... 183 D5
Hawkley GU33 ... 206 E7
Liss GU33 ... 207 E5
Home Field Dr SO16 ... 265 C5
Homefield Ho 7 BH25 ... 383 A2
Homefield Ind Prep Sch BH6 ... 394 F5
Homefield Rd
Cosham PO6 ... 346 C7
Westbourne PO10 ... 325 B4
Homefield Way
Clanfield PO8 ... 276 B6
Sherborne St John RG24 ... 47 D1
Homeforde Ho SO42 ... 334 A1
Homefort Ho 2 PO12 ... 369 B5
Homegrange Ho SO41 ... 399 D4
Homegreen Ho GU27 ... 189 E6
Homegrove Ho PO5 ... 404 C1
Homeheights 8 PO5 ... 370 C2
Home La SO21 ... 174 D3
Homelake Ho BH14 ... 391 B3
Homelands GU27 ... 189 F1
Homelands Est BH23 ... 394 F6
Homelands Ho BH22 ... 353 D5
Homelea Cl GU14 ... 55 F8
Homeleigh Cres GU12 ... 77 E8
Homeleigh Ho 5 BH8 ... 393 A5
Homelife Ho BH8 ... 393 B4
Home Mead
Denmead PO7 ... 298 F4
North Waltham RG25 ... 89 F1
Home Mead Cl RG14 ... 5 C8
Homemead Ho SO51 ... 240 E6
Homemill Ho 5 BH25 ... 383 A3
Homeoaks Ho BH2 ... 392 F5
Homepark Ho GU9 ... 99 A2
Home Park Rd GU46 ... 34 B5
Homepoint Ho SO18 ... 292 A7
Homer Cl
Gosport PO13 ... 368 B8
Waterlooville PO8 ... 299 E2
Home Rd BH11 ... 377 B6
Homer Farm La SO45 ... 365 E6
Homerise Ho 1 SO23 ... 403 E6
Homer Mobile Home Pk SO45 ... 365 E6
Homerose Ho PO5 ... 404 B2
Home Rule Rd SO31 ... 317 B4
Homeryde Ho PO13 ... 367 E2
Homesea Ho PO5 ... 404 B2
Homeside Rd BH9 ... 378 A2
Homespinney Ho SO18 ... 267 D1
Homestead Rd GU34 ... 159 E5
Homesteads Rd RG22 ... 91 B8
Homestour Ho 1 BH23 ... 395 A6
Hometide Ho PO13 ... 367 E2
Homeview Ho BH15 ... 390 D3
Homewater Ho 8 PO7 ... 322 E8
Home Way GU31 ... 229 C3
Homeway Cotts SO40 ... 289 B5
Homewell PO9 ... 323 F1
Homewood Cl BH25 ... 383 C3
Homewood Ho SO41 ... 385 C2
Homington Rd SP5 ... 211 F8
Hone Hill GU47 ... 34 F8
Hones Yard Bsns Pk GU9 ... 99 B2
Honey Bottom Rd RG26 ... 9 F1
Honeybourne Cres BH6 ... 395 A4
Honeycritch La GU32 ... 206 C3
Honeyhanger GU26 ... 167 D1
Honey La
Burley BH24 ... 330 E2
Fareham PO15 ... 318 D5
Selborne GU34 ... 185 A8
Honeyleaze RG22 ... 91 A5
Honeysuckle Cl
Basingstoke RG22 ... 91 A8
Gosport PO13 ... 343 B3
Locks Heath SO31 ... 317 A5
Winchester SO22 ... 403 C2
Yateley GU46 ... 33 E6
Honeysuckle Ct
3 Southampton SO18 ... 292 B7
Locks Heath SO31 ... 317 A5
Waterlooville PO7 ... 323 A5
Winchester SO22 ... 175 C3
Honeysuckle Gdns
Andover SP10 ... 105 C7
Everton SO41 ... 384 C1
Honeysuckle La
Broadstone BH17 ... 374 F1
Headley GU35 ... 165 F5
Honeysuckle Rd SO16 ... 267 B4
Honeysuckle Way
Chandler's Ford SO53 ... 243 A6
Christchurch BH23 ... 396 B8
Honeywood Cl
Portsmouth PO3 ... 345 F4
Totton SO40 ... 264 D1
Honeywood Ho BH14 ... 402 C7
Honister Cl SO16 ... 289 E8
Honister Gdns GU51 ... 54 C2
Hood Cl
Andover SP10 ... 106 C7
Bournemouth BH10 ... 377 B1
Locks Heath SO31 ... 317 B4
Hood Cres BH10 ... 377 B1
Hood Rd SO18 ... 292 A8
Hook Cl
Chandler's Ford SO51 ... 218 A2
Greenham RG19 ... 6 A7
Hook Comm RG29 ... 71 F7
Hook Cotts SO31 ... 340 F9
Hook Cres SO51 ... 218 A2
Hooke Cl BH17 ... 376 A2
Hook Inf Sch RG27 ... 51 B1
Hook Jun Sch RG27 ... 51 B1
Hook La
Axmansford RG26 ... 25 F7
Locks Heath PO14, SO31 ... 341 B8
Ropley SO24 ... 181 A4
Wooton St Lawrence RG23, RG26 ... 67 A8
Hook Par 2 RG27 ... 51 A1
Hook Park Rd SO31 ... 340 E8
Hookpit Farm La SO23 ... 176 B8
Hook Rd
Ampfield SO51 ... 217 F2
Greywell RG29 ... 72 A5
Hook RG27 ... 72 A7
Kingsclere RG20 ... 24 E2
North Warnborough RG29 ... 72 C4
Rotherwick RG27 ... 51 A5
Hook's Farm Way PO9 ... 323 D3
Hook's La PO9 ... 323 D3
Hook Sta RG27 ... 72 B8
Hookstile La GU9 ... 99 A1
Hook Water Cl SO53 ... 218 B2
Hook Water Rd SO53 ... 218 B2
Hook with Warsash CE Prim Sch SO31 ... 340 D10
Hookwood La
Ampfield SO51 ... 217 F2
Upper Chute SP11 ... 58 A7
Hoopersmead RG25 ... 92 A7
Hoopers Way RG23 ... 67 B1
Hop Cl BH16 ... 389 A7
Hope Fountain GU15 ... 36 D4
Hope Grant's Rd GU11 ... 76 F3
Hope La GU9 ... 98 F6
Hope Lodge Sch SO18 ... 291 E7
Hopeman Cl GU47 ... 35 B7
Hope Rd SO30 ... 268 E2
Hope St PO1 ... 404 B4
Hopeswood GU33 ... 186 A2
Hope Way GU11 ... 76 D3
Hopfield Cl PO7 ... 322 E7
Hopfield Ho PO7 ... 322 E6
Hopfield Mews PO7 ... 322 E6
Hopfield Rd RG27 ... 52 C5
Hop Garden Rd RG27 ... 50 F4
Hop Gdn GU52 ... 74 E4
Hop Gdns The SP5 ... 212 A3
Hop Kiln The GU9 ... 121 F8
Hopkins Cl
Bournemouth BH8 ... 379 A2
Portchester PO6 ... 344 E8
Hopkins Ct PO4 ... 371 B2
Hopkinson Way SP10 ... 82 B1
Hopton Garth RG24 ... 49 A1
Hopwood Cl RG14 ... 2 B4
Hopwood Ct PO16 ... 318 F3
Horace Rd 7 BH5 ... 393 E4
Horder Cl SO16 ... 266 F3
Hordle CE Prim Sch SO41 ... 384 A3
Hordle La SO41 ... 384 A2
Hordle Rd PO9 ... 323 C4
Hordle Walhampton Sch SO41 ... 386 A6
Horizon West Ind Est RG14 ... 2 B3
Horlock Rd SO42 ... 334 A2
Hornbeam Cl
2 Hedge End SO30 ... 293 D6
3 Farnborough GU14 ... 55 A5
South Wonston SO21 ... 153 E4
Hornbeam Gdns SO30 ... 268 D3
Hornbeam Pl RG27 ... 51 B2
Hornbeam Rd
Chandler's Ford SO53 ... 242 F6
Havant PO9 ... 324 B3
Hornbeams RG7 ... 14 A6
Hornbeam Sq BH15 ... 390 D2
Hornbeam Way BH21 ... 351 E5
Hornby Cl SO31 ... 340 D10
Hornby Halt★ PO11 ... 373 A2
Hornchurch Rd SO16 ... 265 F4
Horndean CE Jun Sch PO8 ... 300 C7
Horndean Ho 6 PO1 ... 404 C4
Horndean Inf Sch PO8 ... 300 C7
Horndean Prec PO8 ... 300 D7
Horndean Rd PO9 ... 324 E3
Horndean Tech Coll PO8 ... 300 B7
Hornes Field Ct 4 GU52 ... 74 E4
Hornet Cl
Fareham PO15 ... 318 D2
Gosport PO12 ... 369 C4
Hornet Rd
Fareham PO14 ... 342 F5
Thorney Island PO10 ... 349 A3
Horning Rd BH12 ... 391 F5
Horn Rd GU14 ... 55 C5

Horns Dro SO16..... 265 E6
Horns Hill
　Nursling SO16...... 265 D6
　Soberton SO32 ..... 273 B2
Horns Hill Cl SO16 .. 265 D6
Horris Hill Sch RG20 ...5 C3
Horsa Cl BH6 ...... 394 E4
Horsa Ct BH6 .... 394 E4
Horsa Rd BH6 .... 394 E4
Horsea La PO2...... 345 E4
Horsea Rd PO2...... 345 E5
Horsebridge Rd
　Broughton SO20 .... 170 D4
　Havant PO9....... 324 A4
　Houghton SO20..... 171 B3
Horsebridge Way
　SO16 .... 265 C6
Horsecroft SO51 .... 240 F8
Horsefair Mews
　SO51 .... 240 E7
Horsefair The SO51 .. 240 E7
Horse La SO24...... 181 D7
Horsepost La PO7,
　PO8 .... 275 B2
Horse Sands Cl PO4. 371 D3
Horseshoe Bend
　GU26 .... 166 F3
Horseshoe Bridge
　SO14 .... 291 C8
Horseshoe Cl
　Camberley GU15 .... 36 D8
　Titchfield PO14 .... 317 D2
　Wimborne Minster
　BH21 .... 352 B6
Horseshoe Common
　Rdbt BH1 .... 392 F3
Horseshoe Cres
　Bordon GU35...... 164 E3
　Camberley GU15 .... 36 D8
Horseshoe Ct
　5 Bournemouth
　BH1 .... 392 F4
　Downton SP5....... 234 F7
Horseshoe Dr
　Romsey SO51 ...... 216 B2
　Totton SO40....... 264 A2
Horseshoe End RG14 ...5 F7
Horseshoe La
　Ash Vale GU12...... 77 E7
　Hurstbourne Tarrant
　SP11 .... 60 D8
Horseshoe Lodge
　SO31 .... 316 F1
Horseshoe Paddocks
　Bsns Ctr PO15 .... 318 B6
Horseshoe The
　BH13 .... 402 C4
Horsham Ave BH10.. 377 C6
Horton Cl BH9 ...... 378 C3
Horton Ho BH22 .... 353 F7
Horton Rd
　Gosport PO13 ..... 343 C4
　Horton Heath BH21.. 302 B1
　Ringwood BH24 .... 328 C6
　St Leonards BH24 ... 327 E6
Horton Way
　Bishopstoke SO50 ... 244 F1
　Verwood BH31...... 302 D5
Horwood Gdns RG21 ..68 F2
Hosker Rd BH5 ..... 394 B5
Hosketts La SO20 ... 147 E5
Hoskins Ho PO1 .... 370 B6
Hoskins Place Ind Est 3
　GU15............... 35 F3
Hospital Hill SO18 ...76 E3
Hospital La PO16.... 344 F6
Hospital Rd
　Aldershot GU11..... 76 E3
　Shirrell Heath PO17,
　SO32............. 296 B8
Hostel Rd GU14.....76 F8
Hotspur Cl SO45.... 313 F5
Houchin St SO32.... 271 C7
Houghton Cl 1 PO9. 324 B6
Houghton Lodge Gdns★
　SO20............. 171 C7
Houlton Rd BH15 ... 390 E4
Hound Cl SO31..... 315 D5
Hound Farm SO31 ... 315 E6
Hound Green Cl RG27.31 B3
Hound Manor SO31. 315 E6
Houndmills Rd RG21 ..68 E6
Houndmills Rdbt
　RG21................68 F7
Hound Rd SO31..... 315 D6
Hound Road Gdns
　SO31 .... 315 D6
Hounds Way BH21 . 352 B5
Hound Way SO31 ... 315 D6
Houndwell Pl SO14. 291 A4
Housedown Ave
　SO40............. 288 F4
Housedown Bsns Pk
　SO40............. 289 A3
Housedown Cl SO40. 288 F5
Housedown Sch
　SO40............. 288 F4
Hounslow Cl BH15 .. 389 F1
Hoursome Ct RG22...91 B4
House Farm Rd
　PO12............. 368 E4
Houseman Rd GU14.. 55 D6
House Plat Ct 3
　GU52...............74 E4
Hove Ct PO13...... 367 E3
Hoverfly Cl PO13.... 368 A5
Hoveton Gr SO53.... 243 B8

Howard Cl
　Burley BH24 .... 331 A3
　Chandler's Ford
　SO53.............. 243 D4
　Christchurch BH23 .. 395 F6
　Fair Oak SO50 ..... 245 C2
　Fleet GU51 ....54 C1
　Lee-on-t-S PO13.... 368 A7
　Southampton SO18 .. 267 E4
Howard Cole Way
　GU11 ....76 C2
Howard Dr GU14.....54 F4
Howard Lo 20 PO5 .. 370 C2
Howard Oliver Ho
　SO45 .... 314 B3
Howard Rd
　Basingstoke RG21.... 69 C3
　Bournemouth BH8.. 393 C8
　Newbury RG14 ....1 E1
　Portsmouth PO2 ... 345 E4
　Southampton SO15 .. 290 D6
　Verwood BH31...... 302 F2
Howard's Gr SO15 .. 290 C8
Howard's La GU34 .. 140 C7
Howards Mead SO41. 385 E4
Howard View RG22 .. 68 D3
Howarth Ct RG14 .....5 F8
Howberry Chase
　GU27 .... 189 F6
Howe Cl
　Christchurch BH23 .. 395 F5
　New Milton BH25 ... 382 F5
Howe La BH31 ...... 302 F5
Howell Cl
　Arborfield Garrison
　RG2 .... 15 C8
　Southampton SO14 . 291 C8
Howell Ho PO11 .... 351 F7
Howe Rd PO13...... 368 C5
Howerts Cl SO31.... 340 D10
Howes Gdns GU51 ...74 E6
Howeth Cl BH10 .... 377 D3
Howeth Rd BH10 ... 377 D3
Howf The GU14.......54 F1
Howlett Cl SO41 .... 385 C4
Howton Cl BH10 .... 377 C5
Howton Rd BH10 ... 377 C5
Hoxley Rd BH10.... 377 D4
Hoyal Rd BH15..... 389 D4
Hoylake Cl PO13 ... 343 C1
Hoylake Rd PO6 .... 322 C1
Hoyle Cl SO32...... 271 C7
Hoylecroft Cl PO15.. 318 E3
HTH Complex GU12. 100 C8
Hubbard Rd RG21....68 F7
Hubert Rd SO23..... 403 C7
Huckers La SO20.... 184 E8
Huddington Glade
　GU46 ....33 E5
Hudson Cl
　Gosport PO13 ..... 368 C6
　Liphook GU30 ..... 188 A3
　Poole BH12....... 376 C2
　Ringwood BH24 ... 329 C8
Hudson Ct SO40 .... 288 D6
Hudson Davies Cl
　SO41 .... 361 F1
Hudson Rd PO5..... 404 C2
Hudsons Mdw RG27..31 B3
Hugh De Port La
　GU26 .... 167 C4
Hughes Bsns Ctr
　BH23............. 396 A7
Hughes Cl SO45..... 338 C1
Huish La RG24 ....70 B3
Hulbert Jun Sch
　PO7............... 322 F6
Hulbert Rd
　Havant PO9....... 323 B4
　Waterlooville PO7 .. 322 F7
Hulbert Way RG22 ... 68 C2
Hulfords La RG27 .....32 E1
Hullam La GU34..... 184 B5
Hull Cres BH11 .... 376 D4
Hulles Way SO52.... 241 F4
Hull Rd BH11 ...... 376 E4
Hull Way BH11..... 376 E4
Hulse Lodge 5
　SO15 .... 290 F8
Hulse Rd SO15 ..... 290 F8
Hulton Cl SO19 .... 291 D1
Humber Cl
　Stubbington PO14 .. 367 B8
　Thatcham RG18 ....2 F5
Humber Ct 24 SP10 ..83 C2
Humber Gdns SO31.. 293 A1
Humber La SP9...... 78 D3
Humber Rd BH22 ... 354 A6
Humberstone Rd
　SP10............. 106 A6
Humbers View SO20 172 A1
Humber Way GU47...35 B8
Hummicks The SO42 364 C8
Humming Bird Ct
　RG22...............90 F8
Humphrey Pk GU52 .. 74 F3
Hundred Acre Cnr
　SP10.............. 105 C8
Hundred Acres PO17 296 F4
Hundred Acres Rd
　PO17............. 296 E4
Hundred La SO41 ... 386 A7
Hundred The
　5 Fordingbridge
　SP6................ 257 F1
　Romsey SO51 ..... 240 E7
　Waterlooville PO7... 299 D1
Hungerfield Cl BH23 357 A1

Hungerford SO31 ... 316 A7
Hungerford Cl GU47... 35 A8
Hungerford Hill SP6 282 D5
Hungerford La
　Enham Alamein SP11.. 82 F8
　Hampshire Gate SP11.. 37 E1
Hungerford Rd
　Bournemouth BH8.. 378 D3
　Buttermere SN8 .... 18 A6
Hunger Hill PO1 .... 370 C2
Hunnels Cl GU52.....74 E4
Hunt Ave SO31..... 315 C6
Hunt Cl SO21...... 153 E4
Hunter Cl
　Christchurch BH23 .. 396 A7
　Gosport PO13 ..... 368 D7
　Hardley SO45 ..... 338 B6
　King's Somborne
　SO20............. 172 A1
　Wimborne Minster
　BH21 .... 352 C6
Hunter Ct 4 SO16 .. 266 F3
Hunter Rd
　Farnborough GU14 ... 55 D3
　Portsmouth PO4 ... 370 F3
　Thorney Island PO10. 349 A3
Hunters Chase
　Liphook GU30 ..... 187 F5
　Swanmore SO32 ... 272 C3
Hunters Cl
　Oakley RG23 ....67 B3
　Verwood BH31..... 303 C5
Hunters Cres
　Romsey SO51 ..... 216 C1
　Totton SO40....... 288 B6
Hunters Ct SO31 ... 293 B3
Hunters Hill SO40 .. 288 D3
Hunters Lodge PO15 318 B1
Hunters Mews GU11. 76 C2
Hunters Rd GU33 ... 186 D2
Hunters Ride PO7... 322 E6
Hunters Way SO50 .. 245 C4
Huntfield Rd BH9 ... 378 B2
Huntingdon Cl
　Titchfield PO14 .... 317 C1
　Totton SO40....... 264 E1
Huntingdon Gdns
　Christchurch BH23 .. 380 A2
　Horton Heath SO50.. 269 D7
　Newbury RG14 ....2 C5
Huntingdon House Dr
　GU26 .... 167 C4
Huntingford Cl
　GU26 .... 167 A7
Hunting Gate SP10.. 105 C8
Huntley Ct 19 PO6.. 321 B1
Huntly Rd BH3 ..... 392 D7
Huntly Way SO18 ... 291 F7
Hunton Cl SO16..... 266 D3
Hunton Down La
　SO21 .... 132 C6
Hunton La SO21 .... 132 A4
Hunt Rd
　Christchurch BH23 .. 395 F8
　Poole BH15....... 390 E4
Huntsbottom La
　GU33 .... 208 B3
Hunts Cl RG27 ......51 C1
Hunts Cotts RG27 ... 52 D7
Hunt's Cotts RG14 ...1 C6
Huntsman Ct PO8 .. 299 F5
Huntsman's Mews
　GU16 ....76 C2
Huntsmead GU34 ... 140 A3
Huntsmoor Rd RG26. 26 D8
Hunts Pond Rd
　SO31 .... 317 C3
Huntvale Rd BH9 ... 378 B3
Hurdles Mead SO41. 399 D3
Hurdles The
　Christchurch BH23 .. 394 E8
　Titchfield PO14 .... 317 D2
Hurdle Way SO21 ... 219 C7
Hurland La GU35 ... 165 D3
Hurlands Bsns Ctr
　GU9 .... 99 D4
Hurlands Cl GU9 .... 99 D4
Hurlands Pl GU9 .... 99 D4
Hurlingham Gdns
　SO16 .... 267 A5
Hurn Cl BH24 ...... 328 D6
Hurn Court La BH23. 378 F6
Hurn Ct
　12 Havant PO9 .... 323 B4
　Bournemouth BH8.. 379 A4
Hurne Ct 20 RG21 ... 69 D5
Hurn La BH24...... 328 D6
Hurn Rd
　Christchurch BH23 .. 379 D3
　St Leonards BH24 .. 328 D3
Hurn Way BH23 .... 379 D1
Huron Dr GU30 .... 188 B3
Hurricane Dr SO16.. 265 E6
Hursley Cl BH7 ..... 394 F8
Hursley Cl 2 SO53.. 218 B1
Hursley Dr
　7 Fleet GU51...... 53 C3
　Blackfield SO45.... 365 C7
Hursley Park Rd
　SO21 .... 218 A6
Hursley Rd
　Chandler's Ford
　SO53.............. 243 C7
　Havant PO9....... 323 D5
Hurstbourne Ave
　BH23............. 381 E1

Hurstbourne Cl PO9. 323 D5
Hurstbourne Pl
　SO19 .... 314 F8
Hurstbourne Tarrant CE
　Prim Sch SP11 .... 60 E6
Hurst Castle★ SO41 400 D1
Hurst Cl
　Barton on S BH25 .. 397 D8
　Chandler's Ford SO53 243 A4
　Liphook GU30 ..... 187 E5
　Stubbington PO14 .. 367 A6
　Totton SO40....... 288 F8
　Walkford BH23 .... 382 C2
Hurst Com Sch The
　RG26................9 B1
Hurst Ct
　4 Christchurch
　BH23............. 397 A7
　5 Milford on S SO41 399 C4
Hurstdene Rd BH8 .. 378 C2
Hurst Gn PO13...... 343 B2
Hurst Green Cl
　Southampton SO19 . 291 A4
　Waterlooville PO8 .. 300 B2
Hurst Hill BH14 .... 402 C8
Hurst La
　Colden Common SO21,
　SO50............. 246 A7
　High Cross GU34... 205 B3
Hurstly La SO41 ... 361 B4
Hurstmere Cl GU34. 167 B3
Hurstmere Ho 8
　GU26 .... 167 B3
Hurst Rd
　Aldershot GU11..... 77 A4
　Farnborough GU14 .. 55 F8
　Milford on S SO41.. 399 E3
　Ringwood BH24 ... 305 A1
Hurst The RG27......73 F8
Hurstville Dr PO7... 322 F6
Hurstwood Ave
　PO10............. 325 E1
Hussar Rd BH23 .... 394 F7
Hussar Ct
　1 Aldershot GU11 .. 76 C2
　Waterlooville PO7 .. 299 C1
Hussell La GU34 ... 160 A7
Hussey Cl 2 SO23 .. 403 E8
Husseys La GU34... 119 D5
Hutfield Cl 1 PO12 . 369 B6
Hutton Cl RG14 ....1 F4
Hutton Rd GU12 ....77 E6
Hutton Sq 5 SP10 .. 83 C2
Hutwood Rd SO16.. 267 A8
Huxley Cl SO31 .... 317 B2
Huxley Ct SO45 .... 313 C2
Hyacinth Cl
　Basingstoke RG22... 91 A8
　Broadstone BH17 .. 374 F1
Hyde Abbey Rd
　SO23 .... 403 E6
Hyde CE Prim Sch
　SP6............... 282 D5
Hyde Church La
　SO23 .... 403 E7
Hyde Church Path 6
　SO23 .... 403 E7
Hyde Cl
　Southampton SO15 . 266 C1
　Sway SO41 .... 360 B2
　Totton SO40....... 288 B2
　Winchester SO23 .. 403 E7
Hyde End Rd PO8 .....8 B5
Hyde Farm Cotts
　RG29................95 E2
Hyde Gate 10 SO23. 403 E7
Hyde House Gdns 5
　SO23 .... 403 E7
Hyde La
　Bishop's Green RG20 ...6 E1
　Crondall GU10..... 97 C8
　Ecchinswell RG20 .. 23 F7
　Fordingbridge SP6.. 282 C6
Hyde Lodge SO23 .. 403 D7
Hyden Cross SO32 . 251 E2
Hyden Farm La
　East Meon GU32 ... 251 D1
　Hambledon PO8.... 275 D7
Hyde Wood GU32 .. 251 E2
Hyde Park Ho PO5.. 404 B3
Hyde Park Rd PO5.. 404 B3
Hyde Rd BH10 ..... 377 C5
Hydes Platt RG7 .....27 E8
Hyde St
　Portsmouth PO5 ... 404 B2
　Winchester SO23 .. 403 E7
Hyde The BH25 .... 382 E4
Hylton Ct RG26 ..... 27 A8
Hylton Rd GU32.... 228 F3
Hymans Way SO40.. 288 F2
Hynesbury Rd BH23. 396 C6
Hynes Ct 1 SO17 .. 291 B8
Hyson Cres SP11.....57 B2
Hyssop Cl PO15.... 317 D7
Hythe By Pass SO45. 337 E8
Hythe Cl RG26 ......26 F7
Hythe Hosp SO45... 314 A4
Hythe Prim Sch
　SO45............. 314 A4
Hythe Rd
　Cosham PO6 ..... 345 E8
　Marchwood SO40 .. 312 F8
　Poole BH15....... 391 A7

Ibbertson Cl BH8 ... 378 F2

Ibbertson Rd BH8 .. 378 F2
Ibbertson Way BH8. 378 F2
Ibbett Rd BH10 .... 377 C3
Ibbotson Way SO40. 288 D5
Iberian Way GU15....36 F3
Ibsen Cl PO15...... 317 C8
Ibsley Cl BH8 ...... 393 C6
Ibsley Dro BH24.... 282 B1
Ibsley Gr PO9...... 323 C9
Ibworth La
　Fleet GU51 ....53 C3
　Hannington RG26 ... 45 C3
Icarus Ct PO7...... 322 F2
Icknield Ho SP10.... 83 D2
Icknield Sch SP10... 83 D2
Icknield Way SP10 ...83 B4
Iddesleigh Rd BH3 .. 393 A6
Ideal Park Homes Cvn Pk
　SO50............. 244 E6
Iden Ct SO32...... 139 F3
Idlefield Cotts GU10. 120 D5
Idsworth Cl PO8 ... 300 E6
Idsworth Ho PO1... 404 B4
Idsworth Rd
　Portsmouth PO3 ... 371 A8
　Waterlooville PO8 .. 300 B2
Iford Bridge Home Pk
　BH6 .... 394 D7
Iford Cl 15 PO9 .... 324 B6
Iford Gdns BH7 .... 394 C7
Iford La BH6....... 394 D5
Ilchester Ct 7 RG14 ...1 E8
Ilex Cl
　Kings Worthy SO23 . 176 B8
　Pamber Heath RG26 . 10 C1
　Yateley GU46....... 33 F6
Ilex Cres SO31..... 317 A3
Ilex Wlk PO11...... 373 C2
Ilford Cl BH6 ...... 394 F5
Illingworth Cl RG26...29 B2
Illustrious Rd PO13. 367 B6
Imadene Cl GU35... 164 F4
Imadene Cres GU35. 164 F4
Imber Dr BH23..... 396 F8
Imber Ho SP10..... 105 E8
Imber Rd SO23..... 198 C6
Imber Way SO19 ... 292 C4
Imbrecourt BH13 ... 402 E7
Imjin Cl GU11.......76 F3
Imperial Appartments 8
　SO14 .... 291 B8
Imperial Ave SO15 . 290 B7
Imperial Ct
　4 Poole BH13 .... 402 F7
　7 Newbury RG14... 1 D2
　Andover SP10 ..... 83 E1
Imperial Pk SO14 .. 291 B7
Imperial Rd SO14 .. 291 B7
Imperial Way SO15.. 290 C5
Implacable Rd PO13. 367 A4
Impstone Rd RG26 .. 10 D1
Imran Ct GU12..... 100 A8
Inadown Bglws
　GU34 .... 183 E8
Ingarth 7 BH6...... 394 E3
Ingersley Rise SO30. 268 D1
Ingle Dell GU35......36 B4
Ingledene Cl
　Gosport PO12..... 369 B5
　Havant PO9....... 323 D2
Ingle Glen
　Finchampstead RG40. 16 C1
　Hythe SO45....... 314 A1
Ingle Gn SO40 ..... 264 B1
Inglegreen Cl BH25. 382 F1
Inglesham Way
　BH15 .... 389 E4
Ingleside SO31..... 315 C2
Ingleside Cl PO14 .. 342 B8
Ingleton Rd SO16 .. 265 D1
Inglewood Ave BH8. 378 F1
Inglewood Dr
　Basingstoke RG22... 91 B6
　New Milton BH25 .. 383 B8
Inglewood Gdns
　SO50............. 245 C3
Inglis Rd PO5...... 404 D1
Ingoldfield La PO17,
　SO32............. 297 C7
Ingram Ct SO17.... 291 C8
Ingram Wlk 1 BH21 351 D4
Ings Cl GU34...... 139 F2
Ingworth Rd BH12 . 392 A5
Inhams La PO7..... 298 D5
Inhams Rd GU34 ... 140 D6
Inhams Way RG7.....27 E8
Inholmes Dr 9 SO41 .53 E3
Inhurst La
　Baughurst RG26 .... 26 A8
　Pamber Heath RG26 . 9 A1
Inhurst Rd PO2 .... 345 E2
Inhurst Way 2 RG26 ...9 B1
Inkerman Rd SO19 . 291 D3
Inkpen Gdns RG24 .. 70 A8
Inkpen Wlk PO9 ... 323 D7
Inlands Rd PO18.... 349 E6
Inman La SO32..... 229 B5
Innisfail Gdns GU11.. 99 D8
Insley Cres BH18... 374 E5
Institute Rd GU12....77 B1
Instow Gdns GU14.. 55 E6
Intec Bsns Ctr RG24. 69 E8
Intech★ SO21...... 199 B7
International Pk
　SO18.............. 267 F6
International Way
　SO19 .... 314 F8

Hor–Ivo 439

Inveravon BH23 .... 395 F4
Inverclyde Ho BH14. 391 B4
Inverclyde Rd BH14. 391 C4
Invergordon Ave
　PO6 .... 346 B7
Inverkip Cl PO13.... 367 E4
Inverleigh Rd BH6 .. 394 C6
Inverness Ave PO15. 318 E3
Inverness Rd
　Gosport PO12..... 369 A7
　Poole BH13....... 402 E7
　Portsmouth PO1 ... 370 E7
Inverness Way GU47 ..35 B7
Invincible Rd
　Farnborough GU14 .. 55 E3
　Stubbington PO14 .. 367 B6
Inwood Ct 5 SU34.. 139 F3
Inwood Rd GU33 ... 208 A4
I O Ctr The PO15 ... 317 E2
Ionic Cl SO53...... 243 F7
Iping Ave PO9 ..... 323 E4
Ipley Way SO45.... 314 A2
Ipoh Cl SO20...... 126 A5
Ipsley Lodge GU10. 100 C5
Ipswich Rd BH12... 392 B4
Ireland Way PO7 ... 322 E5
Irene Ct SO16...... 266 B2
Irequois Ct SO14 .. 291 B7
Iris Ct RG22....... 91 A7
Iris Rd
　Bournemouth BH9 . 377 F1
　Southampton SO16 . 267 B4
Ironbridge Cres
　SO31 .... 317 A6
Ironbridge La PO4 . 371 C4
Iron Mill Cl PO15... 318 D3
Ironmill La PO15.... 318 B5
Ironside Ct 7 SO14. 290 F3
Irvine Cl PO16..... 319 A3
Irvine Dr GU14......55 C8
Irvine Way BH23... 395 E8
Irving La BH6...... 394 D5
Irving Rd
　Bournemouth BH6.. 394 D5
　Southampton SO16 . 265 F1
Irwell Cl
　24 Basingstoke
　RG21............... 69 D5
　Chandler's Ford SO53 243 A5
Irwin Hts PO12..... 369 A9
Isaac Newton Rd RG2 .15 E8
Isaacs Cl BH12..... 392 B7
Isambard Brunel Jun Sch
　PO2.............. 370 E8
Isambard Brunel Rd
　PO1.............. 404 B3
Isington La GU34... 119 E2
Isington Rd GU34... 119 E1
Isis Cl SO16....... 289 E8
Isis Way GU47......35 B8
Island Cl PO11..... 348 A3
Island Farm Rd RG7 .11 C8
Island Point SO41 .. 385 F4
Island View SO41 .. 360 B3
Island View Ave
　BH23............. 396 B5
Island View Cl SO41. 399 E3
Island View Gdns
　SO41 .... 399 E4
Island View Rd BH25 397 C7
Island View Terr
　PO2.............. 345 C1
Island View Wlk
　PO16............. 320 C1
Islay Gdns PO6..... 321 F1
Itchel La GU10...... 97 C7
Itchell Dr 10 GU51...53 E3
Itchen Abbas Prim Sch
　SO21............. 177 F6
Itchen Ave SO50 ... 244 F2
Itchen Cl
　Oakley RG23 ....67 B1
　Petersfield GU31... 228 E2
　West Wellow SO51 . 238 D3
Itchen Coll SO19 ... 292 A5
Itchen Ct
　28 Andover SP10 ... 83 C2
　3 Winchester SO23. 403 F6
　4 Waterlooville PO8 299 F4
Itchenor Rd PO11 .. 373 C2
Itchen Rd PO8...... 324 B6
Itchenside Cl SO18.. 267 F4
Itchen Valley Ctry Pk★
　SO30............. 268 C5
Itchen Valley Ctry Pk
　Visitor Ctr★ SO30.. 268 C5
Itchen View
　Itchen Stoke SO24 . 178 D5
　Southampton SO18 . 267 E4
Itchin Cl SO40..... 288 D6
Ithica Rd PO11 .... 373 A4
Ivamy Pl BH11..... 376 F4
Ivanhoe Rd
　Arborfield Garrison
　RG40............... 15 E6
　Southampton SO15 . 266 D1
Ivar Gdns RG24 .... 49 A1
Ively Rd GU14......55 B2
Ively Rdbt GU14.... 55 C2
Ives Cl GU46.......33 F7
Ivor Cl SO45....... 338 C4
Ivor Rd
　Corfe Mullen BH21 . 374 D4
　Poole BH15....... 390 A1

Ivy CI
St Leonards BH24 . . . . **327** D4
Totton SO40 . . . . **264** E2
Winchester SO22 . . . **403** C3
Ivy Cotts SO21 . . . **219** A1
Ivy Ct
🔲 Whiteley PO15 . . . **317** D8
Southampton SO16 . . **266** D3
Waterlooville PO7 . . . **322** D4
Ivy Dene SO19 . . . . **292** C4
Ivydene Gdns PO8 . . **300** A4
Ivy Down La RG23 . . . .**66** E3
Ivy Ho 🔲 PO12 . . . . . **369** C5
Ivyhole Hill RG27 . . . .**53** B8
Ivyhouse La GU32 . . **205** E3
Ivy La
Farnham GU9 . . . .**98** F2
Portsmouth PO1 . . . . **370** A6
Ringwood BH24 . . . . . **305** B4
West End SO30 . . . . . **268** C2
Ivy Orch PO8 . . . . . . **276** B6
Ivy Rd
Aldershot GU12 . . . . . .**77** C2
Oakley RG23 . . . . **375** D8
Southampton SO17 . . **291** C6
Iwerne CI BH9 . . . . . **378** B4

J

Jacaranda CI PO15 . . **317** E3
Jacaranda Rd GU35 . **164** D2
Jacey Ho 🔲 BH1 . . . . **393** A3
Jack CI SO53 . . . . . . **242** E6
Jack Cockerill Way 🔲
PO5 . . . . **370** D1
Jackdaw CI
Basingstoke RG22 . . . .**90** F8
Waterlooville PO8 . . . **299** E4
Jackdaw Rise SO50 . **243** D1
Jackie Wigg Gdns
SO40 . . . . **289** A7
Jacklin CI BH18 . . . . **375** B5
Jacklyns CI SO24 . . . **179** C4
Jacklyns La SO24 . . . **179** C5
Jackmans CI SO19 . . **291** D3
Jackman's Hill SO21 **221** A6
Jackson CI PO6 . . . . **346** C6
Jackson Gdns BH12 . **391** C6
Jackson Rd BH12 . . . **391** C6
Jack St RG14 . . . .**1** E3
Jacmar Ct 🔲 BH25 . . **383** B2
Jacobean CI BH23 . . . **382** B1
Jacob Rd GU15 . . . . . .**35** D7
Jacobs CI
Clanfield PO8 . . . . . . **276** C5
Romsey SO51 . . . . . . **241** A7
Jacobs Ct PO9 . . . . . **323** E1
Jacob's Gutter La
SO40 . . . . **289** A4
Jacobs Rd BH15 . . . . **389** E2
Jacob's St PO1 . . . . . **404** B4
Jacobs Wlk SO40 . . . **288** E5
Jacob's Yd 🔲 RG21 . . . .**69** B4
Jacomb PI PO13 . . . . **343** D2
Jacqueline Ave PO7 . **322** D4
Jacqueline Rd BH12 . **391** C7
Jade Ct
🔲 Gosport PO13 . . . **368** C6
🔲 Waterlooville PO7 . **322** E8
Jagdalik Rd SP9 . . . . . .**78** E4
Jago Ct RG14 . . . .**5** E8
Jago Rd PO1 . . . . **369** F7
Jamaica PI PO12 . . . **369** C5
Jamaica Rd PO12 . . . **369** D6
James Butcher Ct 🔲
PO5 . . . . **370** D1
James Callaghan Dr
PO6 . . . . **321** B2
James CI
Gosport PO13 . . . . . . **343** C4
South Hayling PO11 . . **372** E4
James Copse Rd
PO8 . . . . **299** F5
James Ct SO51 . . . . . **241** A6
James Grieve Ave
SO31 . . . . **317** B2
James Howell Ct
PO7 . . . . **298** F4
Jameson Ho GU51 . . . .**74** F8
Jameson Rd
Bournemouth BH9 . . . **377** F1
Southampton SO19 . . **291** F3
James PI RG26 . . . .**27** A8
James Rd
Camberley GU15 . . . . .**36** F2
Gosport PO13 . . . . . . **343** C4
Havant PO9 . . . . **323** E2
Poole BH12 . . . . **392** A5
James St SO14 . . . . . **291** B4
James Watt Rd
Arborfield Garrison
RG2 . . . .**15** D7
Arborfield Garrison
RG2 . . . .**15** E8
James Way GU15 . . . . .**35** F2
Jamrud Rd SP9 . . . . . .**78** D5
Janaway Gdns SO17 . **291** D8
Jane Austen's Ho
(Mus)★ SO24 . . . . . . **161** D8
Janes CI SO45 . . . . . **365** E8
Janred Ct BH25 . . . . . **397** E7
Jan Smuts CI GU33 . **186** D2
Janson Rd SO15 . . . . **290** D8
Japonica Ct GU12 . . . .**77** D1

Japonica Way PO9 . . **324** C4
Jardine Sq 🔲 SP10 . . .**83** C2
Jarndyce Wlk PO2 . . **370** D7
Jarvis CI RG27 . . . .**33** B8
Jarvis Fields SO31 . . **316** B8
Jasmine Ct
🔲 Andover SP10 . . . **105** E6
🔲 Southampton
SO15 . . . . **290** F8
🔲 Gosport PO13 . . . **368** C6
Lymington SO41 . . . . **385** C4
Whiteley PO15 . . . . . **294** D1
Jasmine Gr PO7 . . . . **323** A6
Jasmine Rd
Basingstoke RG22 . . . .**91** B8
Hedge End SO30 . . . . **293** B8
Jasmine Way
Bordon GU35 . . . . . . **164** E2
Clanfield PO8 . . . . . . **276** C5
Thatcham RG19 . . . .**7** F6
Jasmine Wlk 🔲
PO14 . . . . **342** E8
Jasmond Rd PO6 . . . . **345** F6
Jason PI PO7 . . . . **322** E2
Jason Way PO12 . . . . **368** F3
Jaundrells CI BH25 . . **383** C3
Java Dr PO15 . . . . . . **317** C7
Javelin Rd PO10 . . . . **349** A3
Jay CI
Horndean PO8 . . . . . **300** A7
Stubbington PO14 . . . **342** B5
Jays CI RG22 . . . .**69** A1
Jay's Ct BH23 . . . . . . **397** E8
Jays Nest CI GU17 . . . .**35** B4
Jealous La SO41 . . . . **361** A2
Jean Orr Ct GU52 . . . .**75** A5
Jefferson Ave BH1 . . **393** D6
Jefferson Rd RG21 . . . .**69** C7
Jeffries CI SO16 . . . . **265** E5
Jellicoe Ave PO12 . . **368** F3
Jellicoe CI BH14 . . . . **390** F5
Jellicoe Ct SP10 . . . . . .**83** D1
Jellicoe Dr BH23 . . . . **395** F6
Jellicoe Ho 🔲 PO1 . . **404** C4
Jenkins Dr PO3 . . . . . **371** B7
Jenkins PI GU14 . . . . . .**77** B8
Jenkyns CI SO30 . . . . **294** A7
Jenner CI BH31 . . . . . **302** E7
Jenner Way
Alton GU34 . . . . **140** A6
Romsey SO51 . . . . . . **241** C8
Jennie Green La
Bentworth GU34 . . . . **137** F1
Medstead GU34 . . . . . **160** B8
Jennings Rd
Poole BH14 . . . . **391** C2
Totton SO40 . . . . **289** A8
Jenny's Wlk GU46 . . . .**34** C6
Jensen Ct SO15 . . . . **290** F7
Jenson Gdns SP10 . . **105** E7
Jephcote Rd BH11 . . . **376** F4
Jermyns La SO51 . . . **216** E4
Jerome Ct SO19 . . . . **292** D6
Jerram CI PO12 . . . . . **368** F3
Jerrett's La SO16 . . . **265** D3
Jerrymoor Hill RG40 . .**16** D8
Jersey CI
Basingstoke RG24 . . . .**48** C2
Fleet GU51 . . . .**54** B4
Poole BH12 . . . . **376** D1
Southampton SO16 . . **265** E3
Stubbington PO14 . . . **367** D6
Jersey Rd
Poole BH12 . . . . **376** D1
Portsmouth PO2 . . . . **370** D8
Jervis Court La
SO32 . . . . **272** A7
Jervis Ct SP10 . . . .**83** D1
Jervis Dr PO12 . . . . . **369** B7
Jervis Rd PO2 . . . . . . **345** C2
Jesmond Ave BH23 . . **396** F8
Jesmond Dene RG14 . . .**1** D4
Jesmond Gr SO31 . . . **317** A1
Jessamine Rd SO16 . **266** B2
Jesse Rd GU46 . . . .**34** D5
Jessett Dr GU52 . . . . . .**74** E4
Jessica Ave BH31 . . . **302** D7
Jessica CI 🔲 PO7 . . . **300** B1
Jessica Cres SO40 . . **264** B1
Jessie Rd
Gosport PO12 . . . . . . **369** A5
Havant PO9 . . . . **323** C3
Portsmouth PO4 . . . . **370** E4
Jessie Terr 🔲 SO14 . **291** A3
Jessop CI SO45 . . . . . **313** F5
Jessopp CI BH10 . . . . **377** F4
Jessopp Ho 🔲 PO31 . **351** C2
Jessopp Rd BH21 . . . **352** B6
Jessop Wlk SO45 . . . **313** F5
Jesty Rd SO24 . . . . . . **179** B4
Jetty Rd SO45 . . . . . . **339** C5
Jewell Rd BH8 . . . . . . **379** A2
Jewry St SO23 . . . . . . **403** E6
Jex Blake CI SO16 . . . **266** B4
Jibbs Mdw RG26 . . . . . .**28** F3
Jimmy Brown Ave
BH21 . . . . **326** F5
Jinny La SO51 . . . . . . **215** E5
Joanna CI SP5 . . . . . . **234** D7
Jo Benson Ct 🔲
PO4 . . . . **370** F2
Jobson Rd RG28 . . . . . .**86** C5
Jockey La SO50 . . . . . **244** E5
Jodrell CI PO8 . . . . . . **300** C1
Joe Bigwood CI
SO16 . . . . **265** D5
John Boys Ho RG14 . . . .**5** A6

John Bunyan CI
PO15 . . . . **317** C8
John Childs CI RG14 . . . .**1** E1
John CI GU11 . . . .**99** C8
John Darling Mall
SO50 . . . . **244** A4
John Eddie Ct RG22 . . .**68** C3
John Eggars Sq
GU34 . . . . **140** B5
John Hanson Com Sch
SP10 . . . . **105** D7
John Hunt of Everest
Com Sch RG24 . . . .**48** C1
John Keble CE Prim Sch
SO21 . . . . **218** B6
John Kimber's
Almshouses RG14 . . . . .**1** D2
John King Shipyard 🔟
PO10 . . . . **349** A8
John Morgan CI RG27 . .**51** A2
John Norgate Ho RG14 **2** C3
John Pounds Ho 🔲
GU35 . . . . **164** D2
John Rankin Inf Sch
RG14 . . . .**5** B8
John Rankin Jun Sch
RG14 . . . .**5** B8
Johnson Dr RG40 . . . . .**16** F7
Johnson Rd BH21 . . . **353** A8
Johnson St 🔲 SO14 . **291** A4
Johnson View PO15 . **317** E6
Johnson Way GU52 . . . .**75** A5
Johns Rd PO16 . . . . . **343** B7
John's Rd SO19 . . . . . **291** D3
John St SO14 . . . . **291** A3
Johnstone Rd BH23 . . **395** E6
Johnston Rd BH15 . . . **390** D7
Joices Yd 🔲 RG21 . . . .**69** B4
Jolliffe Ave BH15 . . . **390** D4
Jolliffe Ct 🔢 GU32 . . **228** F3
Jolliffe Rd BH15 . . . . **390** D4
Jonas Nichols Sq
SO14 . . . . **291** B4
Jonathan CI SO41 . . . **385** E5
Jonathan Hill RG20 . . . .**5** F3
Jonathan Rd PO15 . . **318** E1
Jones La SO45 . . . . . . **314** A5
Jopps Cnr BH23 . . . . **380** C4
Jordan Ho SO15 . . . . **290** C5
Jordans La
Portmore SO41 . . . . . **386** B8
Sway SO41 . . . . **360** C2
Joseph Nye Ct 🔲
PO1 . . . . **370** A5
Joseph St 🔲 PO12 . . **369** C5
Joshua CI BH15 . . . . . **389** E2
Josian Wlk SO14 . . . . **291** B5
Jouldings La RG7 . . . . .**15** B4
Joule Rd
Andover SP10 . . . .**82** B1
Basingstoke RG22 . . . .**68** F7
Jowitt Dr BH25 . . . . . **382** F2
Joyce Dickson CI
BH24 . . . . **329** B6
Joys La SO41 . . . . **386** E8
Joy's La SO20 . . . . . . **129** A4
Joys Rd BH21 . . . . . . **326** E8
Jubilee Ave PO16 . . . **344** E8
Jubilee Bsns Ctr
PO7 . . . . **322** E8
Jubilee Cir RG21 . . . . . .**69** B5
Jubilee CI
Corfe Mullen BH21 . . **374** E7
Eastleigh SO50 . . . . . **243** F1
Farnborough GU14 . . . .**54** A4
Fordingbridge SP6 . . . **257** C1
Litchfield RG28 . . . .**42** C1
Pamber Heath RG26 . . .**10** C1
Ringwood BH24 . . . . . **329** C8
Jubilee Cotts
Riseley RG7 . . . .**14** A3
West Meon GU32 . . . **205** E7
Jubilee Cres BH12 . . . **391** D5
Jubilee Ct
Alderholt SP6 . . . . . . **280** E5
Fareham PO14 . . . . . . **343** A7
North Tidworth SP9 . . . .**78** F7
Sway SO41 . . . . **360** B1
Thatcham RG19 . . . .**2** E8
Jubilee Dr GU12 . . . . . .**77** E6
Jubilee Gdns
Bournemouth BH10 . . **377** D2
Southampton SO30 . . **292** B7
Jubilee Hall Rd GU14. **56** A4
Jubilee Ho
Bordon GU35 . . . . . . **164** E4
Emsworth PO10 . . . . . **324** E1
Jubilee La
Farnham GU10 . . . . . **121** E5
Grayshott GU26 . . . . **167** A3
Jubilee Mews PO10 . **349** C8
Jubilee Rd
Aldershot GU11 . . . . . .**99** F7
Basingstoke RG21 . . . .**69** B4
Corfe Mullen BH21 . . **374** E7
Finchampstead RG40 . .**16** D4
Fordingbridge SP6 . . . **257** C1
Gosport PO12 . . . . . . **369** B6
Mytchett GU16 . . . .**56** E2
Newbury RG14 . . . .**1** F2
Poole BH12 . . . . **391** D5
Portchester PO16 . . . **344** D7
Portsmouth PO4 . . . . **370** F3
Romsey SO51 . . . . . . **240** E8
Waterlooville PO7 . . . **299** E1
Jubilee Terr
Portsmouth PO5 . . . . **404** A1

Jubilee Terr continued
Westbourne PO10 . . . **325** B3
Jukes Wlk SO30 . . . . **268** F2
Julia CI BH23 . . . . **396** F8
Julian CI SO16 . . . . . . **266** F6
Julian Ct SO18 . . . . . . **267** E2
Julian Rd SO19 . . . . . **292** B3
Julian's Rd BH21 . . . . **351** A4
Julie Ave PO15 . . . . . **318** E1
Juliet Ct PO7 . . . . **323** A8
Julius CI
Basingstoke RG24 . . . .**68** C8
Chandler's Ford SO53 **243** E6
Julyan Ave BH12 . . . . **392** A8
Jumar CI SO31 . . . . . . **340** D9
Jumpers Ave BH23 . . **394** E8
Jumpers Rd BH23 . . . **394** F8
Jumps Rd GU10 . . . . **144** E3
Junction PI GU27 . . . **189** D6
Junction Rd
Andover SP10 . . . . . . **106** A8
Bournemouth BH9 . . . **392** F8
Hamworthy BH16 . . . **389** D4
Totton SO40 . . . . **289** A7
Junction Terr RG14 . . . .**2** A2
June Dr RG23 . . . .**68** B5
Juniper CI
Andover SP10 . . . . . . **105** D7
Bordon GU35 . . . . . . **164** A2
Chineham RG24 . . . . . .**49** A4
Ferndown BH22 . . . . **353** C8
Lymington SO41 . . . . **385** B2
North Baddesley
SO52 . . . . **241** F5
Three Legged Cross
BH21 . . . . **326** E8
Winchester SO22 . . . **403** B3
Juniper Ct
🔲 Southampton
SO18 . . . . **291** E7
🔲 North Tidworth SP9 **79** A7
Juniper Flats BH23 . . **394** E8
Juniper PI RG19 . . . .**7** E6
Juniper Rd
Farnborough GU14 . . . .**55** A5
Horndean PO8 . . . . . **276** C1
Southampton SO18 . . **291** F7
Juniper Sq PO9 . . . . . **347** F8
Juno Ho RG7 . . . .**9** C2
Jupiter CI SO16 . . . . . **265** E3
Jupiter Ct PO1 . . . . . . **370** A4
Jupiter Ho 🔲 RG7 . . . . .**9** C2
Jupiter Way BH21 . . . **374** E8
Jura CI PO6 . . . . **322** A1
Jurds Lake Way
SO19 . . . . **291** E1
Jurd Way SO31 . . . . . **292** F1
Justin CI
Fareham PO14 . . . . . . **342** E8
Gosport PO12 . . . . . . **369** D7
Justine Ct 🔲 SO18 . . **292** B7
Justin Gdns BH10 . . . **377** E4
Justinian CI SO53 . . . **243** F7
Jute CI PO16 . . . . **320** B1
Jutland CI PO15 . . . . . **317** B7
Jutland Cres SP10 . . . .**82** F4
Juventu CI PO9 . . . . . **324** A3

K

Kalis Cnr SP11 . . . .**80** E5
Kamptee Copse
BH25 . . . . **383** B6
Kanes Hill SO19 . . . . **292** F5
Kanes Hill Cvn Site
SO19 . . . . **292** E6
Kanes Hill Prim Sch
SO19 . . . . **292** E6
Kangaw PI BH15 . . . . **389** D2
Karachi CI SP9 . . . .**78** E7
Karen Ave PO6 . . . . . **346** C6
Kashmir Ct 🔲 GU14 . . .**56** A1
Kassassin St PO4 . . . **371** A2
Kassel CI PO7 . . . . . . **323** B8
Katherine Chance CI
BH23 . . . . **380** C3
Katherine Ct 🔲 GU15 . .**36** B5
Kathleen CI RG21 . . . . .**69** A2
Kathleen Rd SO19 . . . **292** B4
Kathryn CI SO40 . . . . **264** B1
Katrina Gdns PO11 . . **373** A5
Katrine Cres SO53 . . **243** A8
Katterns CI BH23 . . . **379** E2
Kayak CI SO31 . . . . . . **316** E1
Kay CI BH23 . . . . **395** E6
Kay Cres GU35 . . . . . **165** F6
Kayleigh CI SO40 . . . **288** D6
K&B Est BH17 . . . . . . **390** B8
Keable Rd GU10 . . . . **121** D7
Kealy Rd PO12 . . . . . . **369** A7
Kearsney Ave PO2 . . **345** E2
Keast Wlk PO13 . . . . **343** D7
Keats Ave
Milford on S SO41 . . . **399** D5
Portchester PO6 . . . . **320** E1
Keats CI
Basingstoke RG22 . . . .**69** C8
South Wonston SO21 . **153** D4
Swanwick PO15 . . . . **294** B1
Waterlooville PO8 . . . **299** F4
Winchester SO22 . . . **403** A4
Keats Gdns GU51 . . . . .**54** B1
Keats Ho
🔲 New Milton
BH25 . . . . **383** A1
Havant PO9 . . . . **323** F4
Keats Rd SO19 . . . . . **292** C6

Keats Way GU46 . . . . . .**33** F4
Keble CI
Chandler's Ford
SO53 . . . . **243** C4
Hursley SO21 . . . . . . **218** B8
Keble Rd SO53 . . . . . **243** C4
Keble St SO22 . . . . . . **403** A4
Keeble CI BH10 . . . . . **377** D6
Keeble Cres BH10 . . . **377** D6
Keeble Rd BH10 . . . . **377** D6
Keelan CI PO5 . . . . . . **370** D2
Keel CI
Gosport PO13 . . . . . . **368** D7
Portsmouth PO3 . . . . **346** E4
Keenans Cotts GU33 **207** E5
Keepers CI SO53 . . . . **243** B6
Keeper's Hill SP11 . . **104** A5
Keepers La
Dunbridge SO51 . . . . **192** C2
Wimborne Minster
BH21 . . . . **352** F4
Keeps Mead RG20 . . . .**24** C3
Keep The PO16 . . . . . **344** D7
Kefford CI PO8 . . . . . . **300** B6
Keighley Ave BH18 . . **374** F1
Keith CI PO12 . . . . **369** B7
Keith Ho 🔢 PO1 . . . . . **370** B7
Keith Lucas Rd GU14 . **55** D7
Keith Rd BH3 . . . . **392** D7
Kelburn CI SO53 . . . . **243** B6
Kellaway Rd BH17 . . . **390** F8
Kellett Rd SO15 . . . . . **290** E8
Kelly CI
🔟 Fareham PO16 . . . **319** D2
🔲 Southampton,Bitterne
SO18 . . . . **291** E8
Southampton SO16 . . **266** C5
Kelly Ho SO18 . . . . . . **267** E4
Kellynch CI GU34 . . . **139** E4
Kelly Rd PO7 . . . . **322** E5
Kellys Wlk SP10 . . . . **105** E7
Kelmscott Gdns
SO53 . . . . **218** B1
Kelsall Gdns BH25 . . **383** A3
Kelsey CI
Breach PO10 . . . . **325** C1
Finchampstead RG40 . .**16** C4
Kelsey Gr GU46 . . . . . .**34** C5
Kelsey Head PO13 . . **345** A7
Kelston CI SO15 . . . . **290** A7
Kelvin CI
Arborfield Garrison
RG2 . . . .**15** C7
Hythe SO45 . . . . **314** A1
Kelvin Gr
Netley SO31 . . . . **315** C6
Portchester PO16 . . . **344** D8
Kelvin Hill RG22 . . . . . .**68** C2
Kelvin Rd
Eastleigh SO50 . . . . . **243** F2
Newbury RG14 . . . .**1** F4
Kembers La RG25 . . . . .**70** E4
Kemmitt Way SP10 . . **105** E6
Kempfelt Ho 🔢 PO1 . . **370** A5
Kemp Rd BH9 . . . . **392** F8
Kempshott Gdns
RG22 . . . .**91** A8
Kempshott Gr RG22 . . .**68** A4
Kempshott Inf Sch
RG22 . . . .**91** A8
Kempshott Jun Sch
RG22 . . . .**91** A8
Kempshott La RG22 . . .**91** A8
Kempshott Park Ind Est
RG23 . . . .**90** F3
Kempshott Rdbt RG22 **91** B7
Kemps Quay Ind Pk
SO18 . . . . **291** D7
Kempton CI
Alton GU34 . . . . **139** D7
Newbury RG14 . . . .**2** A1
Kempton Ct
Farnborough GU14 . . . .**55** D2
Swanwick PO15 . . . . **317** C8
Kempton Pk 🔢 PO7 . . **300** B1
Kemp Welch Ct
BH12 . . . . **392** B8
Kemshott Ct PO9 . . . **323** D6
Kemys Gdns SP10 . . **105** E6
Ken Berry Ct PO9 . . . **324** B6
Kench The PO11 . . . . **371** F4
Kendal Ave
Portsmouth PO3 . . . . **346** A1
Southampton SO16 . . **289** D8
Kendal CI
Chandler's Ford
SO53 . . . . **243** D7
Farnborough GU14 . . . .**55** C4
Waterlooville PO8 . . . **300** A4
Kendal Ct SO16 . . . . . **265** D1
Kendal Gdns RG22 . . . .**68** B2
Kendall Court Bsns Pk
GU15 . . . .**35** D4
Kendrick Rd RG14 . . . . .**5** B5
Kenilworth CI
Lee-on-t-S PO13 . . . **367** F4
New Milton BH25 . . . **383** B3
Kenilworth Cres
GU51 . . . .**54** C2
Kenilworth Ct
🔲 Poole BH15 . . . . . **402** F8
🔲 Christchurch
BH23 . . . . **395** A7
🔲 Winchester SO23 . **403** E8

Kenilworth Dr SO50 . **244** A6
Kenilworth Gdns
SO30 . . . . **268** E1
Kenilworth Ho 🔢
SO14 . . . . **291** C6
Kenilworth Rd
Basingstoke RG23 . . . .**68** C6
Farnborough GU14 . . . .**55** A5
Fleet GU51 . . . .**54** B1
Fleet GU51 . . . .**54** C2
Portsmouth PO5 . . . . **370** D1
Southampton SO15 . . **290** F6
Kenley Rd GU35 . . . . . **166** A5
Kenmore CI
Camberley GU16 . . . . . .**56** B8
Fleet GU52 . . . .**75** B5
Totton SO40 . . . . **288** E5
Kennard Ct BH25 . . . . **382** F3
Kennard Rd BH25 . . . . **382** F3
Kennedy Ave PO15 . . **318** E3
Kennedy CI
Newbury RG14 . . . .**5** B6
Waterlooville PO7 . . . **322** E4
Kennedy Cres PO12 . **368** F2
Kennedy Rd SO16 . . . **265** F3
Kennel La
Littleton SO22 . . . . . . **175** C4
Shortfield Common
GU10 . . . . **122** A2
Kennels La GU14 . . . . . .**55** D4
Kennet CI
🔢 Basingstoke
RG21 . . . .**69** D5
Ash GU12 . . . .**77** E1
Farnborough GU14 . . . .**55** B6
Gosport PO12 . . . . . . **369** B2
West End SO18 . . . . . **268** B3
Kennet Ct
🔲 Newbury RG14 . . . . .**1** E1
🔢 Andover SP10 . . . . .**83** C2
Kennet Ctr The RG14 . . .**1** E2
Kenneth CI
🔢 Christchurch
BH23 . . . . **397** E7
Farnborough GU14 . . . .**55** D4
Kennet PI 🔲 RG14 . . . . .**1** F4
Kennet Rd
Newbury RG14 . . . .**1** D2
North Tidworth SP9 . . . .**79** A7
Petersfield GU31 . . . . **228** E2
Kennet Side RG14 . . . . .**2** A3
Kennett CI SO51 . . . . **241** C7
Kennett Rd SO51 . . . . **241** C7
Kennet Way RG23 . . . . .**67** B5
Kennington La SO40 **287** B7
Kennington Rd
BH17 . . . . **390** D8
Ken Rd BH6 . . . . **394** E4
Kensington CI SO50 . **244** A6
Kensington Ct
🔢 Gosport PO12 . . . **369** C9
🔢 Poole BH13 . . . . . **392** B3
🔢 Southampton
SO17 . . . . **267** C2
Fleet GU51 . . . .**53** C4
Kensington Dr 🔲
BH2 . . . . **392** D4
Kensington Fields
SO45 . . . . **313** D2
Kensington Gdns
PO14 . . . . **317** C2
Kensington Ho 🔲
RG21 . . . .**69** B5
Kensington Pk SO41 **399** C4
Kensington Rd
Gosport PO12 . . . . . . **369** C4
Portsmouth PO2 . . . . **345** F1
Kenson Gdns SO19 . . **292** A4
Kent Cotts RG7 . . . .**14** A3
Kent Gdns SO40 . . . . **288** D5
Kent Gr PO16 . . . . **344** E4
Kent Ho
🔢 Bournemouth
BH4 . . . . **392** C3
🔲 Southampton
SO14 . . . . **291** C5
Kentidge Rd PO7 . . . **322** D5
Kentish Rd SO15 . . . . **290** C7
Kent La BH24 . . . . **281** D1
Kenton CI GU16 . . . .**36** D1
Kent Rd
Bordon GU35 . . . . . . **164** D2
Chandler's Ford SO53 **243** C3
Fleet GU51 . . . .**54** B1
Gosport PO13 . . . . . . **343** B4
Poole BH12 . . . . **391** E6
Portsmouth PO5 . . . . **404** B1
Southampton SO17 . . **267** C1
Kent St
Portsmouth PO1 . . . . **370** A5
Southampton SO14 . . **291** C6
Kenward Bglws
RG25 . . . . **114** C3
Kenwith Ave GU51 . . . .**54** C1
Kenwood Bsns Pk
PO9 . . . . **324** A2
Kenwood Rd PO16 . . **344** D6
Kenwyn CI SO18 . . . . **268** B2
Kenya Rd PO16 . . . . . **344** B7
Kenyon CI BH15 . . . . . **390** E7
Kenyon Rd
Poole BH15 . . . . **390** E7
Portsmouth PO2 . . . . **345** F2
Kenyons Yd SP10 . . . **105** E8
Keogh Barracks GU12 **56** F1
Keogh CI GU12 . . . .**56** F2
Keppel CI BH24 . . . . . **329** B7

Kerchers Field RG25 . 88 A7
Kerfield Way RG27 . . . . .51 B1
Kerley Rd BH2 . . . . . . 392 E2
Kern Cl SO16 . . . . 265 F3
Kernells Ct **2** BH4 . . 392 B4
Kerrfield SO22. . . . . . 403 B5
Kerrfield Mews
  SO22. . . . . 403 B5
Kerridge Ind Est
  GU34. . . . . 140 A4
Kerrigan Ct SO17 . . . 291 A7
Kerry Cl
  Chandler's Ford
    SO53. . . . . 243 C6
  Fleet GU51 . . . . 54 B5
  Lymington SO41 . . . . 385 C3
Kerry Gdns SP6 . . . . . 257 B2
Kersey Cres RG14 . . . . 1 C5
Kersley Cres RG29 . . . 95 C8
Kersley Gdns SO19 . . 292 A4
Kersten Cl RG14 . . . . . . 6 A8
Kesteven Way SO18 . . 268 B1
Kestrel Cl
  Bishop's Waltham
    SO32. . . . . 271 A8
  Botley SO32. . . . . . . 269 F1
  Clanfield PO8. . . . . . 276 C4
  Ewshot GU10. . . . . . . 98 B7
  Ferndown BH22. . . . . 353 B7
  Marchwood SO40 . . . 289 E1
  Southampton SO16 . . 266 B5
  Stubbington PO14 . . . 342 B4
  Thatcham RG19 . . . . . . 2 F3
  Upton BH16. . . . . . . 389 B8
  Winchester SO22 . . . 403 B2
Kestrel Ct
  Alton GU34 . . . . 139 F5
  Ringwood BH24. . . . . 329 A8
Kestrel Dr BH23. . . . . 396 A6
Kestrel Ho GU9 . . . . . 121 E8
Kestrel Pl PO6 . . . . . . 346 F7
Kestrel Rd
  Basingstoke RG22. . . . 67 F1
  Eastleigh SO50 . . . . . 243 E2
  Farnborough GU14 . . . 55 F2
  Portsmouth PO3 . . . . 346 A4
Kestrels Mead RG26. . . . 9 F2
Kestrels The SO31 . . . 315 F8
Kestrel Way SP6 . . . . 281 B5
Keswick Ave PO3 . . . . 371 A8
Keswick Ct BH25. . . . . 383 B5
Keswick Rd
  Bournemouth BH5. . . 393 F4
  New Milton BH25 . . . 383 B5
  Southampton SO19 . . 291 D2
Keswick Way BH31. . . 302 E5
Ketchers Field GU34 184 F6
Ketelbey Rise RG22 . . .91 F7
Kettering Terr PO2. . . 370 C8
Keverstone Ct BH1. . . 393 D3
Kevin Cl RG20 . . . . . . 24 F2
Kevins Dr GU46 . . . . . 34 C7
Kevins Gr GU51. . . . . . 54 B1
Kevlyn Cres SO31 . . . 292 F1
Kew Cotts RG14. . . . . . 1 C1
Kew La SO31 . . . . 316 A7
Kewlake La SO40 . . . . 262 D1
Kew Wlk SP10 . . . . . . 105 E7
Keydell Ave PO8 . . . . 300 A5
Keydell Cl PO8. . . . . . 300 A5
Keyes Cl
  Christchurch BH23 . . 395 F6
  Gosport PO13 . . . . . 343 C3
  Poole BH12. . . . . . . 376 F1
Keyes Ct **4** PO5 . . . . 404 C1
Keyes Rd PO13. . . . . . 343 C3
Keyhaven Cl PO13. . . 343 A2
Keyhaven Cotts
  SO20 . . . . 125 C2
Keyhaven Dr PO9 . . . 323 D5
Keyhaven Rd SO41. . . 400 A5
Keynes Cl GU52. . . . . .75 B4
Keynsham Rd SO19 . . 292 B3
Keysworth Ave BH25 397 F8
Keysworth Rd BH16. . 389 C4
Keytech Ctr The RG23 68 E2
Key The GU51. . . . . . . 53 D3
Khandala Gdns PO7. . 322 F4
Khartoum Rd SO17. . . 267 A2
Khyber Rd BH12 . . . . 391 D5
Kidmore La PO7 . . . . 298 F6
Kidson Ct PO2 . . . . . . 370 D8
Kielder Cl SO53. . . . . 243 D2
Kielder Gr PO13 . . . . 343 D2
Kiel Dr SP10 . . . . .82 F3
Kilbride Path **5**
  PO2 . . . . 370 D8
Kildare Cl GU35. . . . . 164 D4
Kildare Rd GU35 . . . . 164 D4
Kilderkin Dr PO8. . . . 300 D7
Kilford Ct SO30 . . . . . 294 A6
Kilham La SO22. . . . . 197 B6
Killarney Cl SO19 . . . 292 E3
Killock **6** BH13. . . . . 402 F7
Kilmarnock Rd BH9 . . 377 F1
Kilmartin Gdns GU16 . 36 D1
Kilmeston Cl PO9 . . . 323 F6
Kilmeston Rd
  Cheriton SO24. . . . . 201 D4
  Kilmeston SO24. . . . 201 D4
Kilmington Way
  BH23. . . . . 396 F8
Kilmiston Cl PO1. . . . 404 B3
Kilmiston Dr PO16. . . 320 C1
Kilmore Dr GU51. . . . .35 B7
Kilmuir Cl **3** GU47. . .35 B7
Kiln Acre PO16 . . . . . 319 B3

Kiln Cl
  Corfe Mullen BH21 . . 374 C4
  Hythe SO45 . . . . 313 E3
Kiln Field GU33 . . . . . 207 E5
Kiln Gdns RG27 . . . . . . 52 C6
Kiln Gn SO21 . . . . 245 A8
Kiln Hill
  Arborfield Garrison
    RG7 . . . . 14 F7
  Soberton SO32 . . . . 297 B8
Kiln La
  Braishfield SO51 . . . 216 C6
  Buriton GU31. . . . . . 253 D5
  Farnham GU10 . . . . . 122 A6
  Monk Sherborne RG26 47 B5
  Old Alresford SO24 . . 157 D1
  Otterbourne SO21 . . 219 C2
  Redlynch SP5. . . . . . 235 E7
  Southwick PO7. . . . . 297 D4
  Stratfield Mortimer
    RG7 . . . . 12 A5
Kiln Rd
  Fareham PO16. . . . . . 319 A3
  Newbury RG14 . . . . . . 2 A1
  Portsmouth PO3 . . . . 346 A1
  Sherborne St John
    RG24 . . . . 47 F3
Kiln Ride RG40. . . . . . .16 E8
Kiln Ride Extension
  RG40 . . . . 16 E6
Kilnside PO7. . . . . 298 F3
Kilns The
  Alton GU34 . . . . 140 B3
  Bucks Horn Oak GU35 142 E5
  Farnham GU9 . . . . 99 D3
Kiln Way
  Aldershot GU11. . . . . .99 F7
  Grayshott GU26. . . . . 166 C5
  Verwood BH31. . . . . . 303 C3
Kiln Workshops GU51 74 C6
Kilnyard Cl SO40 . . . . 264 D1
Kilpatrick Cl **6** PO2. 370 D8
Kilsby Flats SP9 . . . . . 101 E8
Kilwich Way PO16. . . . 344 B6
Kimbell Rd RG22. . . . . .68 F2
Kimber Ct RG24. . . . . . .48 F2
Kimberley Cl
  Andover SP10 . . . . . . .82 D2
  Christchurch BH23 . . 394 F8
  Fair Oak SO50. . . . . . 245 D2
  Hedge End SO30 . . . . 293 B5
Kimberley Ct SO19 . . 291 E2
Kimberley Rd
  Basingstoke RG22. . . . 68 E3
  Bournemouth BH6. . . 394 C5
  Greatham GU33. . . . . 186 C2
  Poole BH14 . . . . 391 B3
  Portsmouth PO4 . . . . 371 A2
Kimber Rd BH11 . . . . . 376 F3
Kimbers GU32. . . . . . . 228 E4
Kimber's Cl SO23 . . . . . 1 D3
Kimbers Dr RG14 . . . . . 1 A5
Kimbers La
  Farnham GU9 . . . . 99 B3
  Pamber End PO2. . . . . 28 B5
Kimbolton Rd PO3 . . . 371 A6
Kimmeridge Ave
  BH12. . . . . 391 C8
Kimpton Cl PO13 . . . . 367 F3
Kimpton Ct **9** PO9. . 324 B6
Kimpton Dr **10** GU51 . 53 C3
Kimpton, Thruxton &
  Fyfield CE Prim Sch
  SP11. . . . . 80 D1
Kindersley Pk Homes
  SP11 . . . . 105 B3
Kineton Rd SO15. . . . . 266 E1
King Albert Ct PO1. . . 404 C4
King Albert St PO1. . . 404 C4
King Alfred Pl SO23. . 403 E7
King Alfred Terr
  13 Winchester
    SO23. . . . . 403 E7
  Kingsclere RG20 . . . . 24 D2
King Arthur's Ct
  PO6. . . . . 346 D8
King Arthur's Way
  SP10 . . . . .83 A1
King Charles St **9**
  PO1. . . . . 370 A4
King Cl BH24 . . . . 327 F4
Kingcome Ho PO1 . . . 404 B4
Kingcup Cl BH18. . . . . 374 E2
Kingdom Cl PO15 . . . . 317 D5
Kingdom Ho **4** GU14. .77 B8
Kingdons Mews
  GU34 . . . . 139 F3
King Edward Ave
  Bournemouth BH9. . . 378 A2
  Southampton SO16 . . 290 A8
King Edward Cres
  PO2. . . . . 345 D2
King Edward Ct BH9 377 F2
King Edward Cvn Pk The
  SO52 . . . . 218 A1
King Edward Pk (Cvn Pk)
  SO52 . . . . 243 A8
King Edward VI Sch
  SO15. . . . . 290 E8
Kingfisher
  Basingstoke RG22 . . . 67 F1
  Bordon GU35. . . . . . 164 E2
  Bournemouth BH6. . . 394 E6

Kingfisher Cl continued
  Farnborough GU14 . . . 55 B6
  Fleet GU52. . . . . .75 A5
  Hamble-le-R SO31 . . . 316 A4
  Rowlands Castle PO9 301 B1
  South Hayling PO11. . 373 C2
  Waterlooville PO8. . . 299 E4
  West Moors BH22. . . . 326 F2
  Whitchurch RG28 . . . . 86 C5
Kingfisher Copse
  SO31 . . . . 317 B3
Kingfisher Court Ind Est
  RG14. . . . . 2 B3
Kingfisher Ct
  1 Southampton
    SO17. . . . . 267 A2
  Alton GU34 . . . . 139 F6
  Basingstoke RG21. . . . 69 A6
  Bournemouth BH8. . . 393 D6
  Fleet GU51 . . . . 74 F8
  Havant PO9. . . . . . . 324 D2
  Portsmouth PO3 . . . . 346 A4
Kingfisher Cvn Pk
  PO13 . . . . 368 C3
Kingfisher Dr
  Westbourne PO10. . . 325 B4
  Yateley GU46. . . . . . . 33 F6
Kingfisher Ho **3**
  RG21 . . . . 69 C7
Kingfisher Par GU17 . 34 F5
Kingfisher Park Homes
  3 BH10 . . . . 377 C4
Kingfisher Pk BH21 . . 326 E6
Kingfisher Rd SO50 . 243 E2
Kingfishers
  4 Christchurch
    BH23 . . . . 395 A5
  Portchester PO16 . . . 343 F8
  Shipton Bellinger SP9 101 C1
Kingfishers The
  BH31 . . . . 303 A5
Kingfisher Way
  Christchurch BH23 . . 396 A5
  Marchwood SO40 . . . 289 E1
  Ringwood BH24. . . . . 305 B1
  Romsey SO51 . . . . . . 240 F8
Kingfisher Wlk GU12. 77 D2
King George Ave
  Bournemouth BH9. . . 377 F2
  Petersfield GU32. . . . 228 F4
King George Cl GU14. .56 B2
King George Mews **4**
  GU32 . . . . 228 F4
King George Mobile
  Home Pk BH25 . . . . . 382 F1
King George Rd
  Andover SP10 . . . . . . 105 E8
  Portchester PO16 . . . 344 D7
King George's Ave
  SO15 . . . . 289 F7
Kingham Pl **17** GU9 . .98 F7
King Harold St SO23 403 D4
King Henry 1 St PO1 404 A3
King Henry Rd **1**. . .53 F3
King James Terr **2**
  PO1 . . . . 370 A3
King John Ave
  Bournemouth BH11. . 376 D5
  Portchester PO16 . . . 344 B7
King John Cl BH11 . . . 376 D6
King John Ct RG20 . . . 24 D2
King John Rd RG20 . . . 24 D2
King Johns Rd RG29 . 72 C4
King John St GU51 . . .53 F3
King La
  Froxfield Green
    GU32 . . . . 227 F8
  Over Wallop SO20 . . . 125 C3
Kingland Cres **4**
  BH15 . . . . 390 C2
Kingland Rd BH15. . . . 390 C2
King Lane Cotts
  SO20 . . . . 125 C2
King Richard 1 Rd
  PO1 . . . . 404 A3
King Richard Cl PO6 345 D8
King Richard Dr
  BH11 . . . . 376 D5
King Richard Sec Sch
  PO6. . . . . 344 F4
Kings Acre SO20 . . . . 172 A3
Kings Apartments **2**
  GU15 . . . . 36 A4
Kings Arms La BH24 . 328 F7
Kings Arms Row
  BH24 . . . . 328 F7
Kings Ave
  Hamble-le-R SO31 . . . 315 E3
  Poole BH14 . . . . 391 D2
  Tongham GU10 . . . . . 100 D8
  Winchester SO22 . . . 403 C3
King's Ave BH23 . . . . 394 F6
Kings Bench Alley **19**
  PO1 . . . . 370 A5
Kingsbere Ave BH10 377 B2
Kingsbere Gdns
  BH23 . . . . 397 A8
Kingsbere Rd BH15 . 390 E5
Kingsbridge Copse
  RG27 . . . . .71 E8
Kingsbridge Hill RG7. .13 E6
Kingsbridge Rd
  Newbury RG14 . . . . . . 1 C1
  Poole BH14. . . . . 391 D4
Kingsbury Rd SO14. . . 291 B7
Kingsbury's La BH24 328 F7
Kings Chase SP10. . . . 105 E7

Kings Cl
  Lymington SO41 . . . . 385 D4
  Lyndhurst SO43. . . . . 309 F5
  Poole BH15 . . . . 390 D5
  Rowlands Castle PO9 301 A1
  Twyford SO21 . . . . . . 220 A7
  West Moors BH22. . . . 326 E1
King's Cl
  Chandler's Ford
    SO53. . . . . 243 D7
  Kings Worthy SO23 . . 154 B1
Kingsclear Pk GU15. . .36 B4
Kingsclere Ave
  Havant PO9. . . . . . . 323 D5
  Southampton SO19 . . 314 F8
Kingsclere CE Prim Sch
  RG20. . . . . 24 D2
Kingsclere Cl SO19. . 291 F1
Kingsclere Pk RG20 . . 24 C3
Kingsclere Rd
  Basingstoke RG21. . . . 68 F7
  Basingstoke RG21. . . . 69 A6
  Overton RG25 . . . . . . 65 A1
  Upper Wootton RG26. . 46 E2
Kings Copse Ave
  SO30 . . . . 293 D5
Kings Copse Prim Sch
  SO30 . . . . 293 C5
Kings Copse Rd
  SO30 . . . . 293 D5
King's Copse Rd
  SO45 . . . . 365 D5
Kingscote Ho **7**
  PO6 . . . . 320 F2
Kingscote Rd
  Portchester PO6 . . . . 320 F2
  Waterlooville PO8. . . 299 D5
Kings Cote Villas **3**
  PO5 . . . . 370 E1
Kings Court Sch
  PO8. . . . . 276 A1
Kings Cres SO41 . . . . 385 D4
King's Cres
  Camberley GU15 . . . . 36 A8
  Poole BH14 . . . . 391 E2
Kingscroft GU51 . . . . .75 A8
Kingscroft Ct PO9. . . 323 D1
King's Croft La PO9 . 323 C2
Kings Ct
  1 Farnborough
    GU14 . . . . 77 A8
  Fordingbridge SP6. . . 257 F1
  King's Ct GU10. . . . . 100 C8
Kingsdale Ct **9**
  SO22 . . . . 403 D6
Kingsdown Pl PO1 . . . 404 D3
Kingsdown Rd PO7 . . 299 C2
Kingsdown Way
  SO18 . . . . 268 A2
King's Elms SO21 . . . 130 D7
Kingsey Ave PO10. . . 348 E8
Kingsfernsden La GU31,
  GU32 . . . . 229 A5
Kingsfield
  Lymington SO41 . . . . 386 A1
  Ringwood BH24. . . . . 329 A7
Kings Field SO31. . . . 293 A4
Kings Field Gdns
  SO31 . . . . 293 A1
Kingsfold Ave SO18 . 267 E4
Kingsford Cl SP5. . . . 235 D5
Kings Furlong Ctr
  RG21 . . . . 69 A3
Kings Furlong Dr
  RG21. . . . . .68 F3
Kings Furlong Inf Sch
  RG21. . . . . .68 F3
Kings Furlong Jun Sch
  RG21. . . . . .68 F3
Kingsgate **10** BH13 . 392 B3
Kingsgate Rd SO23 . . 403 D6
Kingsgate St SO23 . . 403 E4
Kings Glade GU46. . . . 34 D6
Kings Grange **11**
  BH4 . . . . 392 D2
Kingsgrove Ind Est
  GU14. . . . . .55 E3
Kings Head Yd **1**
  SO23 . . . . 403 E5
Kings High Sch
  BH10. . . . . 377 C3
King's Hill GU34 . . . . 138 D1
King's Ho **6** SO14 . . 291 A3
Kingshott Cotts
  GU33 . . . . 185 D3
Kings Huts SO41 . . . . 385 A3
Kings International Coll
  for Buisness & Arts
  GU16. . . . . 36 A2
Kings Keep GU52 . . . . 75 A6
Kings La
  Chilcomb SO21 . . . . 198 C7
  Farnham GU10 . . . . . 121 D6
  Sway SO41 . . . . 384 E8
King's La GU32 . . . . . 205 D4
Kingsland Cl PO6 . . . 321 C1
Kingsland Ct
  3 Southampton
    SO14. . . . . 291 A4
  Poole BH13. . . . . . . 402 F7
Kingsland Grange
  RG14 . . . . 5 C8
Kingsland Ho **4**
  SO14 . . . . 291 A5
Kingsland Ind Pk
  RG24. . . . . .48 E1
Kingsland Mkt SO14. 291 A4
Kingsland Rd GU34. . 139 E3

Kingsland Sq **5**
  SO14 . . . . 291 A4
Kingsleigh Prim Sch
  BH10. . . . . 377 C3
Kingsley Ave
  Bournemouth BH6. . . 395 A4
  Camberley GU15 . . . . 36 C3
Kingsley Bglws
  SO24 . . . . 179 B4
Kingsley Bsns Pk
  GU35. . . . . 142 C1
Kingsley Cl
  Bournemouth BH6. . . 395 A4
  Newbury RG14 . . . . . . 1 F6
Kingsley Gdns SO40 288 B7
Kingsley Gn PO9 . . . 323 E6
Kingsley Pk RG28 . . . 86 C6
Kingsley Pl SO22. . . . 403 C3
Kingsley Rd
  Eversley Centre
    RG27 . . . . 33 A8
  Farnborough GU14 . . . 55 D6
  Gosport PO12 . . . . . 368 F7
  Portsmouth PO4 . . . . 371 C4
  Southampton SO15 . . 290 B7
Kingsley Sq GU51 . . . 53 C4
Kings Mdw SP10 . . . . 106 B7
King's Mdw RG25 . . . . 88 B3
Kingsmead
  Alton GU34 . . . . 140 A3
  Anna Valley SP11 . . . 105 C4
  Camberley GU16 . . . . 56 C7
  Farnborough GU14 . . . 55 F3
  Soberton PO17 . . . . . 296 D8
Kings Mead RG14 . . . . 5 A5
Kingsmead Ave
  PO14 . . . . 367 D6
Kingsmead Cotts
  Alton GU34 . . . . 140 A4
  Soberton PO17 . . . . . 296 C7
Kingsmead Ct
  5 Wimborne Minster
    BH21 . . . . 351 B4
  7 Southampton
    SO15. . . . . 266 B1
Kings Meadow SP10 . 106 A7
Kingsmead Sh Ctr **13**
  GU14. . . . . .55 F4
Kings Mede PO8 . . . . 300 B5
Kings Mews
  Camberley GU16 . . . . 56 D6
  Portsmouth PO5 . . . . 370 D2
Kingsmill Cl PO12. . . . 368 F4
Kingsmill Rd
  Basingstoke RG21. . . . 69 A2
  Poole BH17 . . . . 390 E7
Kings Orch RG23 . . . . 90 B8
Kings Par **4** GU51 . . 54 A2
Kings Park Com Hospl
  BH7. . . . . 393 E6
King's Park Dr BH7,
  BH1 . . . . 393 E6
King's Park Prim Sch
  BH1. . . . . 393 E5
Kings Park Rd SO15 . 291 A6
King's Park Rd BH7 . 393 E6
Kings Peace The
  RG26 . . . . 167 A3
Kings Pightle RG24 . . .48 F3
King's Prim Sch The
  SO30 . . . . 268 E3
Kings Rd
  Aldershot GU11. . . . . .76 D1
  Alton GU34 . . . . 139 D4
  Chandler's Ford
    SO53. . . . . 243 D6
  Enham Alamein SP11 . 83 B7
  Fleet GU51 . . . . 54 B1
  Gosport PO12 . . . . . 369 B6
  Lymington SO41 . . . . 385 D4
  Newbury RG14 . . . . . . 1 F2
  New Milton BH25 . . . 383 C3
  Petersfield GU32. . . . 228 D4
  Silchester RG7. . . . . . 10 F2
  South Hayling PO11. . 373 A5
  Winchester SO22 . . . 403 A4
King's Rd
  Basingstoke RG22. . . . 68 E3
  Bournemouth BH3. . . 393 A4
  Emsworth PO10. . . . . 348 E8
  Fareham PO16. . . . . . 319 D4
  Haslemere GU27 . . . . 189 C6
  Lee-on-t-S PO13 . . . . 367 E4
  Portsmouth PO5 . . . . 404 B1
  Waterlooville PO8. . . 299 D5
Kings Rd W RG14 . . . . 1 E2
Kings Ride SO45 . . . . 365 D5
King's Ride GU15 . . . . 36 B7
Kings Road Ind Est
  GU27. . . . . 189 C6
Kings Row **3** SO22. 403 D6
King's Royal Hussars
  Mus The **4** SO23 . . 403 D5
King's Saltern Rd
  SO41 . . . . 386 A2
Kings' Sch **2** PO17 . 197 B7
Kings Sch The SO50. . 245 B1
King's Sch The RG8 . . 69 A4
King's Somborne CE
  Prim Sch SO20 . . . . . 171 F2
Kings Somborne Rd
  SO51 . . . . 194 D2
King St
  Emsworth PO10. . . . . 349 A4
  Gosport PO12 . . . . . 369 D6
  Mortimer RG7 . . . . . . 11 C4
  Odiham RG29. . . . . . . 72 C2
  Portsmouth PO5 . . . . 404 B2

Ker–Kip 441

King St continued
  Southampton SO14 . . 291 A3
  Westbourne PO10. . . 325 B3
  Wimborne Minster
    BH21 . . . . 351 B4
King's Terr
  4 Emsworth PO10. . 348 E8
  Portsmouth PO1,PO5 404 A1
Kingston SO31 . . . . . . 315 C7
Kingston Cl SP10 . . . . 105 E5
Kingston Cres PO2. . . 370 D8
Kingston Cross PO2. . 370 D8
Kingston Ct SO16 . . . 265 F3
Kingston Gdns PO15 318 D4
Kingston Lacy House ★
  BH21 . . . . 350 B7
Kingston Pk
  Lymington SO41 . . . . 385 D2
  West Wellow SO51 . . . 262 E8
Kingston Rd
  Camberley GU15 . . . . 36 D8
  Gosport PO12 . . . . . 368 F5
  Poole BH15 . . . . 390 D4
  Portsmouth PO1,PO2 370 E8
  Southampton SO15 . . 290 D6
Kingstons Ind Est
  GU12. . . . . .77 C2
Kingsvale Ct RG21 . . . .68 E3
Kingsway
  Aldershot GU11. . . . . .76 C1
  Andover SP10 . . . . . . 83 E2
  Blackwater GU17 . . . . 35 C5
  Chandler's Ford SO53 243 D6
  Chandler's Ford SO53 243 D6
  Ferndown BH22. . . . . 353 B8
  North Hayling PO11. . 348 A3
  Southampton SO14 . . 291 A5
Kings Way PO9 . . . . . 301 A1
Kingsway Cl BH23 . . . 379 F1
Kingsway Ct SO53 . . . 243 F8
Kingsway Gdns
  Andover SP10 . . . . . . 83 A3
  Chandler's Ford SO53 243 A3
Kingsway The PO16 . . 344 C8
Kingswell Cl BH10 . . 377 D2
Kingswell Gdns
  BH10 . . . . 377 B2
Kingswell Gr BH10 . . 377 B2
Kingswell Path PO1 . 404 B4
Kingswell Rd BH10 . . 377 C2
Kingswell St PO1 . . . 404 B3
Kings Wlk RG28. . . . . 86 C5
King's Wlk **8** SO23 . 403 E5
Kings Wlk GU15 . . . . 35 C6
Kingswood
  15 Bournemouth
    BH4 . . . . 392 C2
  Grayshott GU26. . . . . 167 B2
  Marchwood SO40 . . . 290 A1
Kingswood Cl PO15 . . 317 D8
Kingswood Ct
  3 Whiteley PO15. . . 317 D8
  6 Fleet GU51. . . . . . 54 A1
Kingswood Firs
  GU26 . . . . 167 A2
Kingswood La GU26. . 167 A2
Kingswood Pl PO17. . 318 E7
Kingswood Rise
  GU34 . . . . 159 F2
Kings Worthy Prim Sch
  SO23. . . . . 176 C6
Kingsworthy Rd PO9 323 F3
Kings Worthy Rd **9**
  GU51. . . . . .53 C3
Kings Yd SP10 . . . . . . 106 A7
King's Yd SP10 . . . . . 106 B8
King William St PO1 370 A6
Kinloss Ct SO16. . . . . 266 A5
Kinnell Cl PO10 . . . . . 348 F8
Kinross Cres PO6 . . . 346 E7
Kinross Rd
  Bournemouth BH3. . . 392 E6
  Totton SO40. . . . . . . 288 F7
Kinsbourne Ave
  BH10 . . . . 377 D2
Kinsbourne Cl SO19. . 292 E6
Kinsbourne Rise
  SO19 . . . . 292 F5
Kinsbourne Way
  SO19 . . . . 292 E6
Kinsford Ct SO42. . . . 333 F1
Kinson Ave BH15. . . . 391 A7
Kinson Gr BH10 . . . . 377 C6
Kinson Park Rd
  BH10 . . . . 377 D6
Kinson Pottery Ind Est
  BH14. . . . . 391 A6
Kinson Prim Sch
  BH11. . . . . 377 B5
Kinson Rd BH10 . . . . 377 C3
Kintbury Cl GU51 . . . 53 C3
Kinterbury Ct **10**
  SO17. . . . . 291 A8
Kintyre Cl RG23 . . . . . 67 A2
Kintyre Rd PO6 . . . . . 321 F1
Kinver Cl SO51. . . . . . 216 D1
Kiosks The **9** BH15 . 390 C1
Kipling Bldgs **3**
  PO2. . . . . 345 E3
Kipling Cl
  Swanwick PO15. . . . . 294 B1
  Yateley GU46. . . . . . . 34 A4
Kipling Ct SO19 . . . . . 291 F1
Kipling Rd
  Alton GU34 . . . . 139 D1

Kipling Rd continued
Eastleigh SO50 . . . . . 243 F3
Poole BH14 . . . . 391 B5
Portsmouth PO2 . . . . 345 E3
Kipling Wlk RG21 . . . . .68 F3
Kirby Cl BH15 . . . . . . 390 F6
Kirby Ct 4 PO2 . . . . . 345 E2
Kirby Rd PO2 . . . . 345 F2
Kirby Way BH6 . . . . . 394 D4
Kirkby Ct GU16 . . . . . . 36 C1
Kirkee Rd SP9 . . . . . . .78 E5
Kirk Gdns SO40 . . . . . 288 F5
Kirkham Ave BH23 . . . 380 C3
Kirk Knoll GU35 . . . . . 165 D5
Kirkstall Rd PO4 . . . . 370 E1
Kirkway BH15 . . . . . . 375 B4
Kirpal Rd PO3 . . . . . . 371 B6
Kirtle Dr GU34 . . . . . . 160 A2
Kirtley Cl PO6 . . . . . . 346 C6
Kirton Rd PO6 . . . . . . 346 C7
Kitchener Cres BH17 375 B2
Kitchener Rd
Farnborough GU11 . . . .77 B6
Greatham GU33 . . . . . 186 D2
Southampton SO17 . . . 267 C2
Kitchers SO41 . . . . . . 360 B2
Kitcombe La GU34 . . . 161 C1
Kite Cl PO8 . . . . 299 E4
Kites Croft Bsns Pk
SO31 . . . . 317 E2
Kites Croft BH14 . . . . 225 B5
Kitnocks Hill SO32 . . . 294 F8
Kitscroft Rd BH10 . . . 377 C5
Kittiwake Cl
Bournemouth BH6 . . . 394 D6
Gosport PO13 . . . . . . 343 B2
Kitt's La GU32,SO24 . . 203 C2
Kitwalls La SO41 . . . . 399 D5
Kitwood Gn 26 PO9 . . 324 B5
Kitwood La SO24,
GU34 . . . . 182 C7
Kitwood Rd GU34,
GU34 . . . . 182 C7
Kivernell Pl 1
SO41 . . . . 399 C4
Kivernell Rd SO41 . . . 399 D4
Kiwi Cl BH15 . . . . 390 E3
Kleves Ct SO19 . . . . . 292 B6
Knapp Cl BH23 . . . . . 395 A8
Knapp La
Ampfield SO51 . . . . . . 217 D4
Tadley RG26 . . . . 27 B4
Knapp Mill Ave
BH23 . . . . 395 A8
Knapps Hard GU32 . . . 225 B5
Knatchbull Cl SO51 . . 240 F7
Knellers La SO40 . . . . 288 D4
Knight Cl
Crookham Village
GU51 . . . . .74 C6
Winchester SO23 . . . 403 E8
Knightcrest Rd SO41 384 E1
Knight Gdns PO6 . . . . 346 E7
Knighton Cnr PO8 . . . 300 C7
Knighton Cvn Pk
SO41 . . . . 384 E1
Knighton Heath Cl
BH11 . . . . 376 E4
Knighton Heath Ind Est
BH11 . . . . 376 E4
Knighton Heath Rd
BH11 . . . . 376 E4
Knighton La BH21 . . . 376 D7
Knighton Pk BH25 . . . 397 F8
Knighton Rd SO19 . . . 291 F4
Knights Bank Rd
PO14 . . . . 341 F1
Knightsbridge Ct
BH2 . . . . 392 E2
Knightsbridge Dr RG19 6 B3
Knightsbridge Rd
Camberley GU15 . . . . .36 C2
Enham Alamein SP11 . .83 C7
Knights Cl SO31 . . . . . 316 E1
Knights Ct SP10 . . . . . 83 B1
Knights Enham Dr 8
GU51 . . . . .53 C3
Knights Enham Inf Sch
SP10 . . . . .83 A3
Knights Enham Jun Sch
SP10 . . . . .83 A3
Knightsfield GU32. . . . 228 E3
Knights La RG20 . . . . . .4 F3
Knights Lea RG20 . . . . .3 F3
Knights Park Rd RG21 68 F7
Knights Rd
Bournemouth BH11 . . 376 D5
Farnham GU9 . . . . 99 C7
Knight St RG21 . . . . . .68 F4
Knightstone Ct 3
PO2 . . . . 345 F4
Knightstone Gr
BH22 . . . . 326 D2
Knightstone Grange 2
SO45 . . . . 314 A2
Knights Way
Alton GU34 . . . . 139 D3
Frimley GU15 . . . . .36 F4
Knightwood Ave
Havant PO9 . . . . 324 A5
Lyndhurst SO43 . . . . . 309 F5
Knightwood Cl
Ashurst SO40 . . . . . . 288 B2
Christchurch BH23 . . 396 D8

Knightwood Cl continued
Farnborough GU14 . . . 56 C2
Lyndhurst SO43 . . . . . 309 F5
Knightwood Glade
SO53 . . . . 242 F7
Knightwood Oak★
SO43 . . . . 308 F1
Knightwood Prim Sch
SO53 . . . . 242 F7
Knightwood Rd
Chandler's Ford
SO53 . . . . 243 A6
Hythe SO45 . . . . 314 B3
Knightwood View
SO53 . . . . 243 C5
Knobcrook Rd 3
BH21 . . . . 351 B6
Knockhundred La
GU26 . . . . 189 A8
Knockwood La SO20 147 F7
Knole Cl 5 BH1 . . . . . 393 D4
Knole Gdns BH1 . . . . . 393 D4
Knole Rd BH1 . . . . . . 393 D4
Knoll Cl SO51 . . . . 54 A2
Knoll Ct SO51 . . . . . . .54 A3
Knoll Gdns
Enborne Row RG20 . . . .4 E4
Ferndown BH21 . . . . . 352 F4
St Leonards BH24 . . . 327 F4
Knoll La BH21 . . . . . . 374 B7
Knoll Manor BH2 . . . . 392 F5
Knoll Rd
Camberley GU15 . . . . .36 B6
Fleet GU51 . . . . 54 A2
Knoll Wlk GU15 . . . . . .36 B6
Knollys Rd
Aldershot GU11 . . . . . .76 D3
Pamber Heath RG26 . . 10 D1
Knook The 6 GU47 . . .35 B7
Knotgrass Rd SO31 . . . 316 E2
Knowland Dr SO41 . . . 399 D5
Knowle Ave PO17 . . . . 318 E4
Knowle Cres RG20 . . . 24 D2
Knowle Hill SO50 . . . . 244 B4
Knowle La SO50 . . . . . 245 E1
Knowle Rd
Brockenhurst SO42 . . 333 E2
Fareham PO17 . . . . . . 319 A7
Knowle Village PO17 . 318 F4
Knowles Cl
Bordon GU35 . . . . . . 164 D2
Christchurch BH23 . . 395 E7
Nursling SO16 . . . . . . 265 D5
Knowles Mdw GU33 . . 208 B1
Knowle The GU35 . . . 165 F6
Knowle Village Bsns Pk
PO17 . . . . 318 D8
Knowlings The RG28 . . 86 D4
Knowlton Gdns BH9 . . 378 B3
Knowlton Rd BH11 . . . 375 F2
Knowsley Cres PO6 . . 346 A7
Knowsley Rd PO6 . . . . 345 F7
Knox Cl GU52 . . . . .74 E5
Knox Rd
Havant PO9 . . . . 323 D1
Portsmouth PO2 . . . . 345 C1
Knox Terr GU34 . . . . . 140 A4
Knyght Cl SO51 . . . . . 241 A6
Knyveton Ho BH1 . . . . 393 B4
Knyveton Rd BH1 . . . . 393 C4
Kohat Cl SP9 . . . . .78 D7
Kohat Cl 2 GU11 . . . . .76 D2
Kohat Rd SP9 . . . . . . .78 E5
Kohima Cl GU11 . . . . . .76 F2
Kootenay Ave SO18 . . 292 E7
Kooyong GU51 . . . . . . 239 B2
Kornwestheim Way
SO50 . . . . 243 E3
Krooner Rd GU15 . . . . .35 F3
Kurnool Mortar Cross
Roads 35 E6
Kyftle Ct RG14 . . . . .1 D2
Kynegils Rd SO22 . . . . 403 B8
Kynon Ct 2 PO12 . . . . 369 C9
Kyoto Wlk PO9 . . . . . . 324 A3
Kyrchil La BH21 . . . . . 351 F6
Kyrchil Way BH21 . . . . 351 F7
Kytes La SO32 . . . . . . 270 C6

L

Labrador Dr BH15 . . . . 390 D1
Laburnam Gdns GU52 .75 B5
Laburnam Rise RG19 . . .7 F5
Laburnum Ave PO6 . . . 346 C7
Laburnum Cl
Aldershot GU11 . . . . . .76 E1
Ferndown BH22 . . . . . 353 B6
North Baddesley
SO52 . . . . 242 A5
Verwood BH31 . . . . . . 303 C5
Laburnum Cres
SO45 . . . . 338 B8
Laburnum Ct SO19 . . . 291 D3
Laburnum Dr
Everton SO41 . . . . . . 399 D8
Kings Worthy SO23 . . 176 B8
Laburnum Gr
Eastleigh SO50 . . . . . 244 A4
Newbury RG14 . . . . . . .1 E4
Portsmouth PO2 . . . . 345 E1
South Hayling PO11. . 373 B4
Laburnum Ho
8 Bournemouth
BH10 . . . . 377 F4
Hedge End SO30 . . . . 293 D6

Laburnum Pas 1
GU11 . . . . .76 E1
Laburnum Rd
Aldershot GU11 . . . . . .76 E1
Fareham PO16 . . . . . . 343 B6
Farnham GU9 . . . . 99 C7
Hedge End SO30 . . . . 293 D6
Southampton SO16 . . 289 F8
Waterlooville PO7 . . . 322 D6
Laburnums The GU17 .34 F5
Laburnum Way RG23 . . 68 D7
Lacey Cres BH15 . . . . 391 A6
Lackford Ave SO40 . . . 288 C6
Lackland Ct 14 GU51 . .53 E3
Lacon Cl SO18 . . . . . . 291 E8
Lacy Cl BH21 . . . . 351 C6
Lacy Dr BH21 . . . . 351 C6
Ladram Rd PO12 . . . . . 368 E4
Ladwell Cl RG14 . . . . . .5 B5
Lady Betty's Dr PO15 317 E5
Ladybridge Rd PO7 . . 322 C4
Ladycross Rd SO45 . . 314 A2
Ladygate Dr GU26 . . . 166 E3
Lady Godley Cl SP9 . . .78 E5
Ladyplace Ct 7
GU34 . . . . 139 F3
Ladysmith Cl BH23 . . 395 E7
Ladysmith Pl GU35 . . 164 C5
Ladysmith Terr
SO32 . . . . 271 C7
Ladywell La SO24 . . . 179 D6
Ladywood SO50 . . . . . 243 F6
Ladywood Ave GU14 . . 55 A4
Ladywood Ct GU10 . . 121 D6
Ladywood Ho PO5 . . . 404 B2
Laffans Rd RG29 . . . . . .95 E8
Laffan's Rd GU11 . . . . .76 C6
Lagado Cl BH14 . . . . . 402 C8
Lagland Cl 14 BH15 . . 390 C2
Lagland St BH15 . . . . 390 C2
Lagoon Cl BH14 . . . . . 402 B8
Lagoon Rd BH14 . . . . 402 B8
Lahore Cl SP9 . . . . . . .78 E7
Lahore Rd SP9 . . . . . . .78 E5
Laidlaw Cl BH12 . . . . . 392 B8
Laidlaw Gdns SO53 . . 218 B1
Lainston Cl SO22 . . . . 403 A8
Lake Ave BH15 . . . . . . 389 D1
Lake Cres BH15 . . . . . 389 E3
Lake Ct RG26 . . . . .27 B8
Lake Dr
Bordon GU35 . . . . . . 164 E3
Hamworthy BH15 . . . 389 D1
Poole BH15 . . . . 389 D2
Winchester SO22 . . . 197 B3
Lake Farm Cl
Ferndown BH22 . . . . . 377 B8
Hedge End SO30 . . . . 293 C8
Lake Grove Rd BH25 . 383 A4
Lake Ho SO15 . . . . . . 290 C6
Lake La GU10 . . . . 143 C6
Lakeland Dr GU16 . . . . 36 C1
Lakeland Gdns SO40 289 E1
Lakelands RG26 . . . . . .26 B8
Lakelands Dr SO15 . . 290 C6
Lake Rd
Bournemouth BH11 . . 377 C6
Camberley GU16 . . . . .56 F6
Chandler's Ford SO53 243 E8
Curdridge SO32 . . . . 294 F8
Hamworthy BH15 . . . 389 E2
Portsmouth PO1 . . . . 404 C4
Southampton SO19 . . 291 D2
Verwood BH31 . . . . . . 303 B5
Laker Ho SO15 . . . . . . 290 F7
Laker Sq 8 SP10 . . . . .83 C2
Lakeside
Fareham PO16 . . . . . . 318 E5
Lee-on-t-S PO13 . . . . 367 F1
Ower SO51 . . . . 263 D6
Ringwood BH24 . . . . . 329 C6
Lakeside Ave
Portsmouth PO3 . . . . 371 B7
Rownhams SO16 . . . . 265 E5
Lakeside Bsns Pk
GU47 . . . . 34 E7
Lakeside Cl
Andover SP10 . . . . . . .82 D2
Ash Vale GU12 . . . . . . 77 D4
SO50 . . . . 267 F8
Lakeside Country Park★
SO50 . . . . 267 F8
Lakeside Ct
Fleet GU51 . . . . 54 B3
Portsmouth PO3 . . . . 370 F2
Lakeside Dr RG27 . . . .32 B4
Lakeside Gdns
Farnborough GU14 . . . 55 B7
Havant PO9 . . . . 324 A2
Lakeside Pines
BH25 . . . . 383 A4
Lakeside Prim Sch
GU16 . . . . 36 D1
Lakeside Rd
Ash Vale GU12 . . . . . . 77 D4
Farnborough GU14 . . . 76 E7
Poole BH13 . . . . 392 A2
Lakeside Sch SO53 . . 243 F8
Lake Side The PO17 . . 318 E5
Lakesmere Rd PO8 . . . 300 C6
Lakes The SO32 . . . . . 272 A4
Lakeview Dr BH24 . . . 329 D6
Lake View Manor
BH25 . . . . 383 A4
Lakewood Cl SO53 . . . 243 D8
Lakewood Rd
Ashurst SO40 . . . . . . 288 C3
Chandler's Ford SO53 218 E1
Chandler's Ford SO53 243 D8

Lakewood Rd continued
Christchurch BH23 . . 381 F1
Lamb Cl SP10 . . . . 106 C8
Lambdens Wlk RG26 . . 26 F8
Lambdown App SP11 . . 79 C6
Lambdown Terr SP11 . 79 C7
Lamberhurst Cl
SO19 . . . . 315 A8
Lambert Cl PO7 . . . . . 322 E5
Lambert Cres GU17 . . . 35 A4
Lambert Dr RG14 . . . . .2 C5
Lambourn Cl PO14 . . . 342 D8
Lambourn Ct RG14 . . . . .1 F5
Lambourne Cl
Dibden Purlieu
SO45 . . . . 313 D1
Sparsholt SO21 . . . . . 174 C3
Thruxton SP11 . . . . . . 103 E8
Lambourne Dr SO31 . . 317 B3
Lambourne Ho SO30 293 A6
Lambourne Rd SO18 . . 268 B2
Lambourne Way
Thruxton SP11 . . . . . . 103 E8
Tongham GU10 . . . . . 100 D7
Lambourn Rd RG20 . . . .1 B5
Lambourn Sq SO53 . . . 243 B6
Lambs Cl
Overton RG25 . . . . . . .88 B8
Poole BH17 . . . . 375 C1
Lambs Farm Bsns Pk
RG7 . . . . .13 F7
Lambsgreen La
BH21 . . . . 350 F2
Lamb's Lane Prim Sch
RG7 . . . . .13 E8
Lambs Lease GU33 . . 208 A3
Lambs Row RG24 . . . . .69 F7
Lamerton Cl GU35 . . . 164 D4
Lamerton Rd GU35 . . . 164 D4
Lamiarra Way RG14 . . .6 B8
Lammas Rd SO45 . . . . 314 B2
Lampacres RG14 . . . . . .1 F5
Lampard La GU10 . . . . 144 C2
Lampards Cl RG27 . . . .50 F6
Lampeter Ave PO6 . . . 346 B8
Lampool Ho RG25 . . . .88 B8
Lamport Ct GU9 . . . . . 99 A1
Lamports The GU34 . . 140 A4
Lampton Gdns 5
BH9 . . . . 377 F3
Lamwath Mans 1
SO14 . . . . 291 A7
Lanark Cl
Frimley GU16 . . . . 36 C2
Hamworthy BH15 . . . 389 E2
Lancashire Cotts
SP11 . . . . 59 C1
Lancaster Ave GU9 . . 122 B8
Lancaster Cl
Andover SP10 . . . . . . .82 F1
Ash Vale GU12 . . . . . . 77 D5
Bursledon SO31 . . . . 293 A1
Christchurch BH23 . . 396 C7
Corfe Mullen BH18 . . 374 F5
Lee-on-t-S PO13 . . . . 368 B4
Portchester PO16 . . . 320 B1
Lancaster Ct SO30 . . . 268 C2
Lancaster Dr
Camberley GU15 . . . . .36 B6
Corfe Mullen BH18 . . 374 F5
Verwood BH31 . . . . . . 302 E6
Lancaster Rd
Basingstoke RG21 . . . 69 A6
Farnborough GU14 . . . 55 F1
Ferndown BH21 . . . . . 353 A8
Southampton SO16 . . 265 F3
Lancaster Way
Farnborough GU14 . . . 56 A7
Waterlooville PO7 . . . 322 F6
Lancer Cl BH23 . . . . . 394 F7
Lancer Ct 5 GU11 . . . .76 C2
Lancer Ho PO7 . . . . . . 299 C1
Lance's Hill SO18 . . . . 291 F7
Landale Cl SP11 . . . . . .83 B7
Lander Cl BH15 . . . . . 390 C1
Landford CE Prim Sch
SP5 . . . . 237 D4
Landford Common Farm
SP5 . . . . 237 E2
Landford Gdns BH8 . . 378 A4
Landford Way BH8 . . . 378 D2
Landguard Rd
Portsmouth PO4 . . . . 371 A3
Southampton SO15 . . 290 D6
Landon Ct PO12 . . . . . 369 A3
Landon Rd PO13 . . . . 343 D1
Landport St
Portsmouth PO1 . . . . 404 C4
Portsmouth,Southsea
PO5 . . . . 404 A2
Landport Terr PO1 . . . 404 A2
Landport View PO1 . . 404 B4
Landsdowne St PO5. . 404 A2
Landseer Cl
Basingstoke RG21 . . . 69 D3
Sandhurst GU47 . . . . .35 C6
Landseer Ct SP10 . . . .82 F1
Landseer Rd
1 Bournemouth
BH4 . . . . 392 D4
Southampton SO19 . . 292 C3
Lands End La GU35 . . 164 E4
Lands End Rd SO31 . . 316 C0
Lane End
Bramley RG26 . . . . . . 29 A2
West Tisted SO24 . . . 204 C8

Lane End Bglws
SO21 . . . . 133 B3
Lane End Cotts SP5 . . 237 D3
Lane End Dr PO10 . . . 348 F8
Lanehays Rd SO45 . . . 313 D3
Lane Lowther Gdns The
4 BH8 . . . . 393 C5
Lanesbridge Cl SO40 287 F5
Lanes End
Chineham RG24 . . . . . 49 A3
Stubbington PO14 . . . 367 C7
Lanes The BH25 . . . . . 383 A5
Laneswood RG7 . . . . . 11 C5
Lane The
Fawley SO45 . . . . 339 B3
Gosport PO12 . . . . . . 369 A2
Portsmouth PO4 . . . . 370 F2
Tadley RG26 . . . . 27 A8
Langbar Cl SO19 . . . . 291 E6
Langbrook Cl PO9 . . . 347 F8
Langdale Ave PO6 . . . 346 B7
Langdale Cl
Farnborough GU14 . . . 55 C4
Southampton SO16 . . 289 F8
Langdale Ct GU12 . . . .77 D5
Langdon Cl BH14 . . . . 391 D4
Langdon Rd BH14 . . . 391 D4
Langdown Firs SO45 . 314 A3
Langdown Lawn
SO45 . . . . 314 A2
Langdown Lawn Cl
SO45 . . . . 314 A2
Langdown Rd SO45 . . 314 B3
Langford Cl 12 PO16 319 B1
Langford La SP5 . . . . . 235 E8
Langford Rd PO1 . . . . 370 F7
Langham Cl SO52 . . . 241 F4
Langham Ct
Christchurch BH23 . . 379 F1
Farnham GU9 . . . . 122 A7
Langham Rd GU34 . . . 139 E3
Langhorn Rd SO16 . . . 267 C4
Langley Chase BH24 . 328 A5
Langley Cl 1 GU52 . . .74 F7
Langley Dr
Aldershot GU11 . . . . . .99 E8
Camberley GU15 . . . . .36 B6
Langley Gdn SP6 . . . . 258 A3
Langley Lodge Gdns
SO45 . . . . 365 F7
Langley Rd
Christchurch BH23 . . 381 E1
Poole BH14 . . . . 391 F4
Portsmouth PO2 . . . . 370 E1
Southampton SO15 . . 290 A6
Langrish Cl PO9 . . . . . 324 A6
Langrish Prim Sch
GU32 . . . . 228 A3
Langrish Rd SO16 . . . 266 B4
Langside Ave BH12 . . 392 A8
Langside Sch BH12 . . 392 A8
Langstone Ave PO9 . . 347 F7
Langstone Harbour
Nature Reserve★
PO9 . . . . 347 A3
Langstone High St
PO9 . . . . 347 F6
Langstone Ho
Fareham PO16 . . . . . . 343 A4
Havant PO9 . . . . 324 A3
Langstone Inf Sch
PO3 . . . . 371 A7
Langstone Jun Sch
PO3 . . . . 371 A7
Langstone Marina Hts
PO4 . . . . 371 D3
Langstone Rd
Langstone PO9 . . . . . 347 F7
Portsmouth PO3 . . . . 371 A7
Langstone Wlk
Fareham PO14 . . . . . . 342 C8
Gosport PO13 . . . . . . 343 B2
Langton Cl
Barton on S BH25 . . . 398 B8
Lee-on-t-S PO13 . . . . 368 A6
Winchester SO22 . . . 403 C7
Langton Dr GU35 . . . . 165 E7
Langton Farm Gdns
PO1 . . . . 370 E7
Langton Rd
Bishop's Waltham
SO32 . . . . 271 C8
Bournemouth BH7 . . 393 F5
Langtons Ct SO24 . . . 179 E5
Lanham La SO22 . . . . 175 B1
Lankhills Rd SO23 . . . 403 E7
Lansdell Ct 4 BH15 . . 390 E3
Lansdown Ave PO16 . 344 D6
Lansdowne Ave
Andover SP10 . . . . . . 105 E6
Waterlooville PO7 . . . 322 B2
Winchester SO23 . . . 403 D3
Lansdowne Cl 2
SO51 . . . . 240 E8
Lansdowne Cres
BH1 . . . . 393 B3
Lansdowne Ct
1 Romsey SO51 . . . . 240 E8
3 Winchester SO23 403 D3
Lansdowne Gdns
Bournemouth BH1 . . 393 A4
Romsey SO51 . . . . . . 240 E8
Lansdowne Hill 4
SO14 . . . . 290 F3
Lansdowne Ho 3
PO12 . . . . 369 F7
Lansdowne Rd
Aldershot GU11 . . . . . .76 D1

Lansdowne Rd continued
Alton GU34 . . . . 140 A5
Bournemouth BH1 . . 393 A5
Camberley GU16 . . . . 56 E8
Southampton SO15 . . 290 A7
Lansdowne Rdbt The
BH1 . . . . 393 A3
Lansdown Terr PO10 325 B5
Lansley Rd RG21 . . . . .69 B8
Lantana Cl PO7 . . . . . 322 F6
Lantarra Way RG14,
RG19 . . . . .6 A8
Lantern Ct SO23 . . . . 403 C4
Lanyard Dr PO13 . . . . 368 D6
Lapin La RG22 . . . . . . .91 B5
Lapthorn Cl PO13 . . . 343 B4
Lapwing Cl
Basingstoke RG22 . . . .90 F7
Gosport PO12 . . . . . . 369 B8
Horndean PO8 . . . . . . 300 A7
Lapwing Dr SO40 . . . . 288 C8
Lapwing Gr PO16 . . . . 343 F4
Lapwing Rd
Portsmouth PO4 . . . . 371 C5
Wimborne Minster
BH21 . . . . 352 A7
Lapwing Rise RG28. . . .86 B5
Lara Cl BH8 . . . . 378 D3
Larch Ave SO45 . . . . . 338 C7
Larch Cl
Broadstone BH17 . . . 374 E1
Camberley GU15 . . . . 36 C8
Hordle SO41 . . . . 383 F3
Kings Worthy SO23 . . 154 B1
Lee-on-t-S PO13 . . . . 368 A5
Liphook GU30 . . . . . . 187 F3
Newbury RG14 . . . . . . .1 B5
St Leonards BH24 . . . 328 A4
West End SO30 . . . . . 268 D2
Larch Ct PO1 . . . . 404 C4
Larchdale Cl SO31 . . . 340 D10
Larch Dr
Andover SP10 . . . . . . 105 C7
Kingsclere RG20 . . . . 24 D2
Thatcham RG19 . . . . . .7 F6
Larches Gdns PO15 . . 318 C1
Larches Way GU17 . . . .34 F5
Larchfield Rd GU52 . . 75 B7
Larchfield Way PO8 . . 300 C5
Larch Rd
Headley GU35 . . . . . . 165 F6
Southampton SO16 . . 266 A3
Larch Row SP6 . . . . . 258 D2
Larch Way
Bursledon SO31 . . . . 315 F8
Farnborough GU14 . . . 55 A3
Ferndown BH22 . . . . . 353 C7
Larchwood RG24 . . . . .48 E3
Larchwood Ave PO9 . 323 B4
Larchwood Glade
GU15 . . . . 36 E7
Larchwood Rd SO40 . 288 C6
Larcombe Rd GU32 . . 228 D2
Larg Dr SO22 . . . . 175 C4
Lark Cl
Andover SP10 . . . . . . 83 B2
Basingstoke RG22 . . . .90 F8
Larkfield RG24 . . . . . . .48 F3
Larkfield Cl GU9 . . . . .98 D2
Larkfield Rd GU9 . . . . .98 D2
Larkhill Rd PO3 . . . . . 345 F4
Lark Hill Rise SO22 . . 403 B2
Larkin Cl SP11 . . . . . . .57 A2
Lark Rd BH23 . . . . . . 396 A6
Lark Rise GU30 . . . . . 187 E5
Larks Barrow Hill
RG28 . . . . 63 C2
Larks Cl BH22. . . . . . . 353 B7
Larksfield Ave BH9. . . 378 C3
Larkshill Cl BH25 . . . . 383 B4
Larkspur Chase
SO19 . . . . 292 E5
Larkspur Cl
Aldershot GU11 . . . . . .99 E7
Locks Heath SO31 . . . 316 F2
Swanmore SO32 . . . . 272 A5
Larkspur Dr
Chandler's Ford
SO53 . . . . 242 F6
Marchwood SO40 . . . 312 F8
Larkspur Gdns
7 Hedge End
SO30. . . . . 293 C6
Holbury SO45 . . . . . . 338 B4
Larks Rise BH22 . . . . . 353 B7
Lark Way PO10 . . . . . 325 C4
Larkwhistle Farm Rd
PO9 . . . . 111 D1
Larkwhistle Wlk
PO9 . . . . 323 C4
Larmer Cl GU51 . . . . . 74 D7
Larwood Sq 10 SP10 . 83 C2
Lascelles Ct 1 BH7 . . 394 B6
Lascelles Rd BH7 . . . . 394 B6
Laser Cl SO31. . . . . . . 316 E1
Lasham Gn 28 PO9 . . 324 B5
Lasham Ho 5 SO16 . . 290 B8
Lasham Rd GU51. . . . . 53 C4
Lasham Wlk PO14. . . . 342 D7
Lashly Mdw PO7 . . . . 274 C3
Latch Farm Ave
BH23 . . . . 395 A8
Latchmore Dr SO45 . . 313 C4
Latchmore Forest Gr
PO8 . . . . 300 A3
Latchmore Gdns
PO8 . . . . 299 F3
Latchwood La GU10 . 122 B5

Latelie Cl SO31 ..... 315 C5
Latham Ave GU16 ..... 36 C2
Latham Cl SO50 ..... 245 B2
Latham Ct SO15 ..... 290 B7
Latham Rd
Fair Oak SO50 ..... 245 B2
Romsey SO51 ..... 241 A8
Latimer Ct
4 Southampton SO17 ..... 267 A1
Portsmouth PO3 ..... 346 B4
Latimer Gate 22 SO14 ..... 291 A3
Latimer Ho
11 Fleet GU51 ..... 53 E3
5 Southampton SO15 ..... 290 F5
Latimer Rd BH9 ..... 392 F8
Latimers Cl BH23 ..... 381 F1
Latimer St
Romsey SO51 ..... 240 E7
Southampton SO14 ..... 291 A3
Laud Cl RG14 ..... 2 B5
Lauder Cl
Breach PO10 ..... 325 D2
Frimley GU16 ..... 36 C2
Lauderdale GU14 ..... 55 B3
Launcelot Cl SP10 ..... 83 A3
Launcelyn Cl SO52 ..... 241 F3
Launceston Cl 3 PO12 ..... 369 C8
Launceston Dr SO50 243 F5
Laundry Bglws SP4 . 101 F1
Laundry Ct 8 RG14 ..... 1 F2
Laundry La
Heckfield RG27 ..... 31 B5
Milford on S SO41 ..... 399 E4
Sandhurst GU47 ..... 35 C5
Laundry Rd SO16 ..... 266 B2
Laundry Yd RG28 ..... 86 C5
Laurel Ave RG19 ..... 7 E5
Laurel Cl
8 Gosport PO12 ..... 369 C8
Camberley GU15 ..... 36 B4
Christchurch BH23 ..... 381 D1
Corfe Mullen BH21 ..... 374 D6
Farnborough GU14 ..... 55 A3
Hordle SO41 ..... 383 E4
Hythe SO45 ..... 313 F3
Locks Heath SO31 ..... 317 B4
North Warnborough RG29 ..... 72 C3
Oakley RG23 ..... 67 B1
Southampton SO19 ..... 291 D3
St Leonards BH24 ..... 327 E3
Laurel Dr BH18 ..... 375 C4
Laurel Gdns
Aldershot GU11 ..... 99 E7
Broadstone BH18 ..... 375 C4
Locks Heath SO31 ..... 317 B4
Laurel Gr GU10 ..... 121 D5
Laurel La BH24 ..... 327 E3
Laurel Rd
Locks Heath SO31 ..... 317 B4
Waterlooville PO8 ..... 300 C4
Laurels The
Andover SP10 ..... 82 E1
Basingstoke RG21 ..... 69 C6
Broadstone BH18 ..... 375 B4
Brockenhurst SO42 ..... 360 F8
Farnham GU9 ..... 99 D7
Ferndown BH22 ..... 353 C7
Fleet GU51 ..... 54 A1
Laurence Ct SO50 ..... 245 C2
Laurence Gn PO10 ..... 324 F4
Laurence Mews SO51 ..... 240 F8
Lauren Mews PO11 ..... 372 E2
Lauren Way SO40 ..... 264 B1
Laureston 2 GU15 ..... 36 E7
Lauriston Dr 7 SO53 ..... 218 B1
Laurus Cl PO7 ..... 323 A5
Laurus Wlk 4 PO13 ..... 367 F3
Lavant Cl PO8 ..... 300 B1
Lavant Ct GU32 ..... 228 E4
Lavant Dr PO9 ..... 324 A3
Lavant Field GU34 ..... 161 E8
Lavant St GU32 ..... 228 E3
Lavell's La RG7 ..... 29 B8
Lavender Cl
Southampton SO19 ..... 291 F5
Verwood BH31 ..... 303 C5
Lavender Ct 2 SP10 105 E6
Lavender Gdns GU35 ..... 164 D3
Lavender La GU10 ..... 121 D4
Lavender Rd
Basingstoke RG22 ..... 91 A7
Bournemouth BH8 ..... 378 D4
Hordle SO41 ..... 383 E3
Waterlooville PO7 ..... 323 A6
Lavender Villas BH23 ..... 397 A8
Lavender Way BH18 . 374 D3
Lavender Wlk BH8 ..... 378 D4
Laverock Lea PO16 ..... 320 C1
Laverstock 3 BH5 ..... 393 F3
Laverstoke Cl
Fleet GU51 ..... 53 C4
Rownhams SO16 ..... 265 E6
Laverstoke La RG28 ..... 87 B3
Lavey's La PO15 ..... 318 B6
Lavington Gdns SO52 ..... 241 F3
Lavinia Rd
Gosport PO12 ..... 369 B6
Poole BH12 ..... 391 C7
Lawday Link GU9 ..... 98 E7
Lawday Pl GU9 ..... 98 E7
Lawday Place La GU9 . 98 E7
Lawford Cres GU46 ..... 34 B6
Lawford Rd BH9 ..... 378 A4
Lawford Way SO40 ..... 288 E7
Lawn Cl
Gosport PO13 ..... 368 D8
Milford on S SO41 ..... 399 E4
Lawn Ct
13 Bournemouth BH2 ..... 392 D4
Southampton SO17 ..... 291 A7
Lawn Dr SO31 ..... 317 A2
Lawn Ho 24 SO23 ..... 403 E6
Lawn Rd
Eastleigh SO50 ..... 244 B5
Littleton SO22 ..... 175 C5
Lymington SO41 ..... 385 B3
Milford on S SO41 ..... 399 E4
Southampton SO17 ..... 291 B8
Lawns Cl BH21 ..... 352 C6
Lawnside Rd SO15 ..... 290 A8
Lawns Rd BH21 ..... 352 B6
Lawn St SO23 ..... 403 E6
Lawns The
Christchurch BH23 ..... 397 B8
Farnborough GU14 ..... 55 C3
Lawnswood SO50 ..... 245 D1
Lawnswood Cl
Dibden Purlieu SO45 ..... 313 E1
Waterlooville PO8 ..... 299 F2
Lawn View BH25 ..... 382 D5
Lawrence Ave PO8 ..... 299 E2
Lawrence Cl
Andover SP10 ..... 82 F2
Basingstoke RG24 ..... 48 C1
Lawrence Ct
Bournemouth BH8 ..... 393 C6
Southampton SO19 ..... 291 F2
Lawrence Dale Ct RG21 ..... 68 F4
Lawrence Dr BH13 ..... 391 E1
Lawrence Gr SO19 ..... 291 F2
Lawrence Ho SO45 ..... 314 B4
Lawrence Hos SP11 ..... 103 B1
Lawrence La SP6 ..... 282 B4
Lawrence Lo GU15 ..... 36 E7
Lawrence Mans PO5 404 D1
Lawrence Pl RG14 ..... 2 A5
Lawrence Rd
Fareham PO15 ..... 318 F2
Fleet GU52 ..... 74 F8
Portsmouth PO5 ..... 404 D1
Ringwood BH24 ..... 305 D2
Lawrence Sq 3 PO12 ..... 369 D5
Lawrence Way
4 Winchester SO23 ..... 403 E8
Camberley GU15 ..... 35 D4
Lawrence Wlk PO13 . 368 D6
Lawson Cl SO31 ..... 316 D8
Lawson Ct 3 SO16 ..... 266 B1
Lawson Rd
Poole BH12 ..... 391 B6
Portsmouth PO5 ..... 404 D2
Laws Terr GU11 ..... 77 A2
Laxton Cl
Locks Heath SO31 ..... 317 B3
Southampton SO19 ..... 292 A2
Layard Dr BH21 ..... 351 D1
Lay Field RG27 ..... 50 F1
Laymoor La BH21 ..... 352 D5
Layton Ct BH12 ..... 391 D5
Layton Rd
Gosport PO13 ..... 343 C3
Poole BH12 ..... 391 D5
Lazy Acre PO10 ..... 349 D8
Leabrook SO31 ..... 317 A5
Lea Cl
Ash GU12 ..... 77 E1
Basingstoke RG21 ..... 69 D5
Farnham GU9 ..... 99 E6
Leacock Cl SO32 ..... 272 B5
Lea Ct GU9 ..... 99 D7
Leaden Vere RG29 ..... 95 D4
Leafy La PO15 ..... 317 E6
Leafy Oak Farm GU17 34 E4
Lealand Gr PO6 ..... 346 D8
Lealand Rd PO6 ..... 346 D7
Leamington Cres PO13 ..... 367 F3
Leamington Ho 9 PO5 ..... 404 B2
Leamington Rd BH9 . 393 A7
Leander Cl SO50 ..... 244 A5
Leander Dr 7 PO12 . 369 C8
Lea-Oak Gdns PO15 . 318 D3
Leaphill Rd BH7 ..... 394 B6
Lea Rd
Blackfield SO45 ..... 365 E7
Camberley GU15 ..... 35 F2
Learoyd Rd BH17 ..... 390 E7
Lear Rd PO12 ..... 369 B6
Leaside Way SO16 ..... 267 C5
Lea Springs GU51 ..... 74 D7
Lea The
Finchampstead RG40 ..... 16 D8
Fleet GU51 ..... 74 E7
Verwood BH31 ..... 303 A5
Leatherhead Gdns SO30 ..... 269 D2
Lea Way
Aldershot GU12 ..... 77 D3
Bournemouth BH11 ..... 376 E6
Leaway The PO16 ..... 344 D8
Lea Wood Rd GU51 ..... 74 E7
Lebanon Rd SO15 ..... 289 D7
Lebern Ho SO30 ..... 293 D7
Le Borowe GU52 ..... 74 E4
Lechlade Gdns
Bournemouth BH7 ..... 394 B8
Fareham PO15 ..... 318 E4
Leckford SO20 ..... 150 D8
Leckford Cl
Portchester PO16 ..... 320 B2
Southampton SO18 ..... 292 D8
Leckford La SO20 ..... 150 B6
Leckford Rd PO9 ..... 324 B6
Ledbury Rd
Christchurch BH23 ..... 395 F5
Portsmouth PO6 ..... 321 C1
Lederle La PO13 ..... 343 C5
Ledgard Cl BH14 ..... 391 B4
Ledwell Ct PO12 ..... 369 D7
Lee Church La SO51 . 264 F8
Lee Ct
Aldershot GU11 ..... 100 A8
Ferndown BH22 ..... 353 D4
Leedam Rd BH10 ..... 377 D4
Lee Dro SO51 ..... 241 B1
Lee Ground PO15 ..... 317 F5
Lee La SO16,SO51 ..... 241 A2
Lee Lands SO41 ..... 385 D1
Lee-on-the-Solent Inf Sch PO13 ..... 367 F2
Lee-on-the-Solent Jun Sch PO13 ..... 367 F2
Leep La PO12 ..... 369 B3
Lee Rd
Aldershot GU11 ..... 76 C2
Gosport PO12 ..... 369 A7
Lees Cl BH23 ..... 379 D4
Lees Hill RG29 ..... 94 E4
Lees La PO12 ..... 369 B6
Leesland CE Inf Sch PO12 ..... 369 A5
Leesland CE Jun Sch PO12 ..... 369 B5
Leesland Rd PO12 ..... 369 A6
Lees Lane N 9 PO12 ..... 369 B6
Lees Mdw RG27 ..... 51 C1
Leeson Dr BH22 ..... 353 B8
Leeson Rd BH7 ..... 393 E7
Le Freth Dr 12 GU51 ..... 53 E3
Lefroy Ave RG21 ..... 69 C7
Lefroy Pk GU51 ..... 53 F1
Lefroy's Field GU10 ..... 97 D8
Leger Cl GU52 ..... 74 E5
Legge Cres GU11 ..... 76 C1
Legg La BH21 ..... 351 D4
Legion Cl
Hamworthy BH15 ..... 389 E2
Southampton SO16 ..... 267 C4
Legion La SO23 ..... 176 C7
Legion Rd
Hamworthy BH15 ..... 389 E2
South Hayling PO11 ..... 373 A4
Lehar Cl RG22 ..... 91 D8
Leicester Ct 11 PO13 ..... 368 D5
Leicester Pl SP10 ..... 106 A7
Leicester Rd
Poole BH13 ..... 391 F3
Southampton SO15 ..... 266 D2
Leicester Way SO23 . 176 C1
Leigham Vale Rd BH6 ..... 394 D4
Leigh Cl
Andover SP10 ..... 106 C7
Wimborne Minster BH21 ..... 351 E4
Leigh Comm BH21 ..... 351 E5
Leigh Cotts PO9 ..... 324 A4
Leigh Ct SO50 ..... 243 E3
Leigh Field RG7 ..... 11 D6
Leigh Gdns
Andover SP10 ..... 106 C7
Wimborne Minster BH21 ..... 351 D4
Leigh House Hospl SO21 ..... 198 E7
Leigh La
Farnham GU9 ..... 122 C8
Wimborne Minster BH21 ..... 351 F5
Leigh Mans 2 SO17 . 267 A1
Leigh Pk SO41 ..... 385 C3
Leigh Rd
Andover SP10 ..... 106 C7
Eastleigh SO50 ..... 243 E3
Fareham PO16 ..... 319 A2
Havant PO9 ..... 323 F2
New Milton BH25 ..... 383 A3
Southampton SO17 ..... 267 A1
Wimborne Minster BH21 ..... 351 E4
Leighton Ave 19 SO15 ..... 290 B8
Leighton Lo 3 BH2 . 392 D4
Leighton Rd SO19 ..... 291 F3
Leipzig Rd GU52 ..... 75 B3
Leisure The PO13 ..... 343 D4
Leith Ave PO16 ..... 320 E1
Leith Dr GU11 ..... 76 D3
Le Marchant Rd GU16 36 D3
Lemon Gr GU35 ..... 164 C1
Lemon Rd SO15 ..... 290 B7
Lendorber Ave PO6 . 346 A8
Lendore Rd GU16 ..... 56 B8
Lennel Gdns GU52 ..... 75 C6
Lennon Way RG22 ..... 91 C8
Lennox Cl
Chandler's Ford SO53 ..... 243 E7
Gosport PO12 ..... 369 C2
Southampton SO16 ..... 265 F5
Lennox Ct 9 PO5 ..... 370 D2
Lennox Mans PO5 ..... 370 D1
Lennox Rd RG22 ..... 68 F2
Lennox Rd N PO5 ..... 370 D2
Lennox Rd S PO5 ..... 370 D2
Len Smart Ct 2 RG21 69 C7
Lensyd Gdns PO8 ..... 299 F6
Lenten St GU34 ..... 139 E3
Lentham Cl BH17 ..... 375 D1
Lent Hill Ct SO22 ..... 403 B4
Lentune Way SO41 ..... 385 D2
Len Williams Terr PO2 ..... 370 E7
Leofric Ct PO4 ..... 371 C3
Leominster Ho PO6 ..... 321 B1
Leominster Rd PO6 ..... 321 B1
Leonard Cl GU16 ..... 56 B8
Leonard Rd PO12 ..... 369 C6
Leonards Ct SO16 ..... 289 C8
Leonardslee Cres RG14 2 B4
Leopold Ave GU14 ..... 55 F5
Leopold Dr SO32 ..... 271 B7
Leopold St PO4 ..... 370 E2
Le Patourel Cl BH23 . 395 D7
Lepe Ctry Pk* SO45 366 B2
Lepe Rd SO45 ..... 366 A3
Leroux Cl SO15 ..... 290 F5
Lerryn Rd PO13 ..... 343 D2
Leslie Loader Ct SO50 ..... 244 A4
Leslie Loader Ho SO19 ..... 291 E5
Leslie Rd
Bournemouth BH9 ..... 392 F7
Poole BH14 ..... 391 A3
Leslie Southern Ct 1 RG14 ..... 1 F4
Lesser Horseshoe Cl 2 PO17 ..... 318 E8
Lester Ave PO9 ..... 323 C2
Lester Rd PO12 ..... 368 F5
Lester Sq BH24 ..... 331 C3
Lestock Way GU51 ..... 54 C1
Le Tissier Ct 6 SO15 ..... 290 E6
Leven Ave BH4 ..... 392 D5
Leven Cl
Bournemouth BH4 ..... 392 D4
Chandler's Ford SO53 243 A7
Leventhorpe Ct PO12 ..... 369 C5
Leveret Cl PO12 ..... 369 C9
Levern Dr GU9 ..... 99 A6
Leveson Cl PO12 ..... 368 F3
Levet's La 4 BH15 ..... 390 B1
Leviathan Cl PO14 ..... 367 D7
Levignen Cl GU52 ..... 74 D5
Lewendon Rd RG14 ..... 1 C5
Lewens Cl BH21 ..... 351 C4
Lewens La BH21 ..... 351 C4
Lewes Cl SO50 ..... 244 A6
Lewesdon Dr BH18 ..... 374 F4
Lewin Cl SO21 ..... 244 F8
Lewins Wlk SO31 ..... 292 F1
Lewis Cl
4 Basingstoke RG21 ..... 69 C7
Hythe SO45 ..... 313 C2
Lewis Ho 5 SO14 ..... 291 A5
Lewis Rd PO10 ..... 325 A3
Lewis Silkin Way SO16 ..... 266 A4
Lewis Wlk RG14 ..... 5 A6
Lewry Cl SO30 ..... 293 C7
Lexby Rd SO40 ..... 289 A6
Lexden Gdns PO11 ..... 372 E4
Leybourne Ave
Bournemouth BH10 ..... 377 D4
Southampton SO18 ..... 292 A8
Leybourne Cl BH10 ..... 377 C5
Leydene Ave BH8 ..... 378 F1
Leydene Cl BH8 ..... 378 F1
Leydene Pk GU32 ..... 251 E3
Leyland Cl PO12 ..... 369 B4
Leyland Rd BH12 ..... 376 E2
Ley Rd GU14 ..... 55 E8
Leys Gdns RG14 ..... 1 D4
Leyside BH23 ..... 395 F6
Leyton Conyers 11 BH13 ..... 402 F7
Leyton Rd SO14 ..... 291 C6
Leyton Way SP10 ..... 105 E6
Liam Cl PO9 ..... 324 A4
Liberty Cl BH21 ..... 327 B6
Liberty Ct BH23 ..... 394 F7
Liberty Ho RG19 ..... 6 E5
Liberty Rd PO17 ..... 297 A8
Liberty Row SO31 ..... 316 A2
Liberty The PO7 ..... 298 E3
Library Gdns PO9 ..... 323 E3
Library La SO21 ..... 174 B4
Library Mews BH12 . 391 D5
Library Rd
Bournemouth BH9 ..... 377 F1
Ferndown BH22 ..... 353 D5
Poole BH12 ..... 391 E5
Totton SO40 ..... 289 A7
Lichen Way SO40 ..... 289 F2
Lichfield Ct 4 PO13 . 368 D5
Lichfield Dr PO12 ..... 369 C8
Lichfield Rd
Locks Heath PO14 ..... 317 C3
Portsmouth PO3 ..... 371 A6
Lickfolds Rd GU10 ..... 121 C3
Liddell Cl RG40 ..... 16 C3
Liddel Way SO53 ..... 243 B5
Liddiard Gdns PO4 ..... 371 B2
Liddiards Way PO7 ..... 322 E3
Lidiard Gdns PO4 ..... 371 B2
Liederbach Dr BH31 . 303 C4
Lightfoot Gr RG21 ..... 69 B2
Lightfoot Lawn PO4 . 371 C3
Lighthouse The 18 PO1 ..... 370 A4
Lightning Cl SO45 ..... 338 F2
Lights Cl BH23 ..... 395 B7
Lightsfield RG23 ..... 67 B2
Lilac Cl
Andover SP10 ..... 105 D7
Bordon GU35 ..... 164 D2
Havant PO9 ..... 324 C3
Ringwood BH24 ..... 329 B8
Lilac Rd SO16 ..... 267 B4
Lilac Way RG23 ..... 68 D6
Lilac Wlk RG19 ..... 7 F5
Lilian Pl GU34 ..... 161 D3
Lilley Cl SO40 ..... 289 F2
Lillies The SO50 ..... 269 D7
Lilliput CE Fst Sch BH14 ..... 402 C8
Lilliput Ct BH14 ..... 391 B3
Lilliput Rd BH14 ..... 402 D8
Lillywhite Cres SP10 ..... 83 B4
Lily Ave PO7 ..... 322 B2
Lily Cl RG22 ..... 91 A7
Limberline Rd PO3 . 346 A4
Limberline Spur PO3 ..... 346 A5
Limbrey Hill RG25 ..... 94 C5
Lime Ave
Alton GU34 ..... 139 E5
Camberley GU15 ..... 36 E6
Southampton SO19 ..... 292 A5
Lime Cl
Colden Common SO21 ..... 245 A8
Hythe SO45 ..... 313 E2
Newbury RG14 ..... 2 B4
Poole BH15 ..... 390 F6
Southampton SO19 ..... 292 A5
Thatcham RG19 ..... 7 E5
Lime Cres GU12 ..... 77 F2
Limecroft GU46 ..... 34 A5
Lime Dr GU51 ..... 54 B4
Lime Gdns
Basingstoke RG21 ..... 69 E5
West End SO30 ..... 268 D3
Lime Gr
Alton GU34 ..... 139 E5
Hordle SO41 ..... 399 D8
Portsmouth PO6 ..... 321 B1
South Hayling PO11 ..... 372 C3
Lime Kiln Cotts The RG20 ..... 42 D8
Limekiln La
Bishop's Waltham SO32 ..... 247 F4
East Meon GU32 ..... 252 D6
Lime Kiln La SO45 ..... 338 B5
Lime Kiln Lane Estate Mobile Home Pk SO45 ..... 338 B5
Limekiln Rd SP11 ..... 58 B4
Lime Rd SO24 ..... 179 D5
Lime St Rdbt GU11 ..... 76 D2
Limes Ave RG20 ..... 22 E7
Limes Cl
Bramshott GU30 ..... 188 A7
Liss GU33 ..... 207 F4
Limes Rd GU14 ..... 55 A5
Lime St
Aldershot GU11 ..... 76 D2
Southampton SO14 ..... 291 A3
Limes The
Amport SP11 ..... 104 B8
Basingstoke RG22 ..... 91 A8
Bramley RG26 ..... 29 B2
Gosport PO13 ..... 343 D1
Haslemere GU27 ..... 189 E6
Langstone PO9 ..... 347 F8
Marchwood SO40 ..... 290 A1
Waterlooville PO7 ..... 322 D3
Limetree Ave RG20 ..... 21 F2
Lime Tree Cl SP6 ..... 280 F6
Lime Tree Ho 1 SO41 ..... 385 E4
Lime Tree Way RG24 ..... 48 E4
Limetree Wlk 3 SO23 ..... 198 D8
Lime Tree Wlk GU14 . 77 C8
Lime Wlk
Andover SP10 ..... 105 D6
Botley SO30 ..... 293 F7
Hythe SO45 ..... 313 E2
Limington House Sch RG22 ..... 68 D3
Limited Rd BH9 ..... 378 A1
Linacre Rd SO19 ..... 292 D5
Linbrook Ct BH24 ..... 305 A1
Lin Brook Dr BH24 ..... 305 C2
Linchmere Rd
Haslemere GU27 ..... 189 B5
Linchmere GU27 ..... 189 A4
Lincoln Ave
Bournemouth BH1 ..... 393 D5
Christchurch BH23 ..... 379 F2
Lincoln Cl
Ash Vale GU12 ..... 77 D5
Basingstoke RG22 ..... 91 B8
Frimley GU15 ..... 36 F4
Locks Heath PO14 ..... 317 C3
Lincoln Cl *continued*
Romsey SO51 ..... 216 B1
Lincoln Ct
2 Liphook GU30 ..... 188 A4
9 Gosport PO13 ..... 368 D5
Newbury RG14 ..... 1 D2
Southampton SO15 ..... 266 E2
West End SO30 ..... 268 C2
Lincoln Gn GU34 ..... 139 E2
Lincoln Pl SO53 ..... 243 D4
Lincoln Rd
Farnborough GU14 ..... 76 F8
Poole BH12 ..... 391 D7
Portsmouth PO1 ..... 370 E5
Lincoln Rise PO8 ..... 300 B4
Lincolns Rise SO50 ..... 219 B1
Linda Gr PO8 ..... 299 F3
Lindal Ct SO30 ..... 293 C7
Linda Rd SO45 ..... 339 B3
Lindbergh Cl PO13 ..... 368 D5
Lindbergh Rd BH21 . 353 A8
Lindbergh Rise PO15 ..... 317 E6
Lind Cl PO7 ..... 322 F3
Linden Ave
Odiham RG29 ..... 72 F4
Old Basing RG24 ..... 70 B5
Linden Cl
Ferndown BH22 ..... 353 D1
Ludgershall SP11 ..... 57 A2
Newbury RG14 ..... 1 D4
Waltham Chase SO32 271 E3
Linden Ct
6 Romsey SO51 ..... 240 F7
Camberley GU15 ..... 36 D7
Locks Heath SO31 ..... 317 C4
Old Basing RG24 ..... 70 B5
Ringwood BH24 ..... 328 F8
West End SO18 ..... 268 B3
Linden Dr GU33 ..... 207 F4
Linden Gdns
Hedge End SO30 ..... 293 D5
Ringwood BH24 ..... 328 F8
Linden Gr
Chandler's Ford SO53 ..... 243 C8
Gosport PO12 ..... 369 B4
South Hayling PO11 ..... 373 A3
Linden Ho 13 GU34 ..... 139 F3
Linden Lea PO16 ..... 320 C1
Lindenmuth way RG19 . 6 D5
Linden Rd
Bishop's Green RG20 ..... 6 D3
Bournemouth BH9 ..... 378 A3
Ferndown BH22 ..... 353 D1
Headley GU35 ..... 166 A5
Poole BH12 ..... 391 C6
Romsey SO51 ..... 240 F7
Southampton SO16 ..... 266 A4
Lindens Cl PO10 ..... 324 F2
Lindens The
Burton BH23 ..... 380 D3
Farnham GU9 ..... 99 B1
Lindford GU35 ..... 164 F6
Linden Way
Havant PO9 ..... 323 F3
Lymington SO41 ..... 385 C4
Waterlooville PO8 ..... 300 C5
Linden Wlk SO52 ..... 241 F5
Lindenwood RG24 ..... 48 E4
Lindford Chase GU35 ..... 164 F5
Lindford Rd
Lindford GU35 ..... 164 E6
Ringwood BH24 ..... 305 D1
Lindford Wey GU35 . 164 F5
Lindisfarne Cl PO6 ..... 346 A7
Lindley Ave PO4 ..... 371 A2
Lindley Cl SP9 ..... 78 F6
Lindley Gdns SO24 ..... 179 D4
Lindon Ct PO4 ..... 370 F4
Lind Rd PO12 ..... 369 C2
Lindsay Ct 19 BH13 ..... 392 A4
Lindsay Ho 8 PO5 ..... 370 D2
Lindsay Manor 11 BH13 ..... 392 A4
Lindsay Pk 15 BH13 ..... 392 A4
Lindsay Rd
Poole BH13 ..... 391 F4
Southampton SO19 ..... 292 E6
Lindum Ct 3 BH13 ..... 392 A4
Lindum Dene GU11 ..... 76 E1
Lindway SO31 ..... 317 A5
Liners Ind Est SO15 ..... 290 C6
Lineside BH23 ..... 395 C8
Lines Rd GU11 ..... 77 B7
Lines The RG20 ..... 24 D3
Linford Cl BH25 ..... 383 B4
Linford Cres SO16 ..... 266 D3
Linford Ct
Fair Oak SO50 ..... 245 C2
Havant PO9 ..... 323 D7
Linford Ho BH24 ..... 305 F3
Linford Rd BH24 ..... 305 D1
Ling Cres GU35 ..... 165 F6
Ling Dale SO16 ..... 266 F7
Lingdale Pl 3 SO17 ..... 291 A8
Lingdale Rd BH6 ..... 394 D6
Lingen Cl SP10 ..... 82 F3
Lingfield GU51 ..... 54 A3
Lingfield Cl
Alton GU34 ..... 139 F2
Old Basing RG24 ..... 70 C5
Lingfield Ct PO1 ..... 370 B3
Lingfield Gdns SO18 267 F2

Lingfield Grange **11**
　BH13 . . . . **392** B3
Lingfield Rd RG14 . . . .**6** A8
Lingmala Gr GU52 . . . . .**75** B5
Ling Rd BH12 . . . . . **376** B1
Lingwood Ave BH23 . **395** F6
Lingwood Cl SO16 . . . **266** F7
Lingwood Wlk SO16 . **266** F7
Linhorns La BH25 . . . **383** A5
Linkenholt Way PO9 **323** C4
Link Ho
　4 Newbury RG14 . . . . . .**1** E2
　Portsmouth PO3 . . . **346** B3
Linklater Path PO1 . . **370** D7
Linklater's Cotts GU17 **54** F5
Link Rd
　Alton GU34 . . . . **140** A6
　Farnborough GU14 . . . **55** B1
　Kingsclere RG20 . . . **24** E2
　Newbury RG14 . . . .**1** E2
　Portsmouth PO6 . . . **321** B2
　Ringwood BH24 . . . . **329** C8
　Southampton SO16 . . **265** F3
Link Rise BH21 . . . . **374** E6
Links Cl PO9 . . . . . . **301** B1
Links Cotts SO24 . . . **179** D4
Links Dr BH23 . . . . . **379** D1
Linkside Ave BH7 . . . **393** F8
Linkside E GU26 . . . . **167** A7
Linkside N GU26 . . . **166** F7
Linkside S GU26 . . . **167** A6
Linkside W
　Beacon Hill GU26 . . . **167** A6
　Hindhead GU26 . . . . **166** F6
Links La
　Rowlands Castle
　PO9 . . . . **301** B2
　South Hayling PO11 . **372** C3
Links Rd
　Poole BH14 . . . . **391** D2
　Winchester SO22 . . . **403** B7
Links The
　Bordon GU35 . . . . . . **164** B1
　Gosport PO13 . . . . . **343** C1
Links View Ave
　BH14 . . . . **391** E2
Links View Way
　SO16 . . . . **266** F6
Links Way GU14 . . . . .**55** A3
Link The
　Andover SP10 . . . . . **105** C8
　Waterlooville PO7 . . . **300** A1
　Yateley GU46 . . . .**34** A7
Link View RG14 . . . . . .**1** D7
Linkway
　Camberley GU15 . . . .**36** A4
　Fleet GU52 . . . . **75** A6
　Stubbington PO14 . . . **367** C6
Link Way
　Oakley RG23 . . . . **67** F2
　Thatcham RG18 . . . . . .**2** F4
Linkway Par GU52 . . . .**74** F6
Linmead Dr BH11 . . . **377** A6
Linnet Cl
　Basingstoke RG22 . . . .**68** A2
　Petersfield GU31 . . . **229** C2
　Ringwood BH24 . . . . **329** C6
　Waterlooville PO8 . . . **299** E4
Linnet Ct
　Gosport PO12 . . . . . **368** F6
　New Milton BH25 . . . **382** F3
Linnet La RG20 . . . .**6** D3
Linnet Rd BH17 . . . . **389** F8
Linnet Sq SO50 . . . . **243** D1
Linnets Rd SO24 . . . . **179** D4
Linnets The
　Portchester PO16 . . . **343** F8
　Totton SO40 . . . . . . **288** C8
Linnets Way GU34 . . . **139** F5
Linnies La SO41 . . . . **384** B7
Linsford Bsns Pk
　GU16 . . . .**56** D3
Linsford La GU16 . . . . .**56** D3
Linstead La GU35 . . . **165** B7
Linthorpe Rd BH15 . . **390** E4
Linton Cl RG26 . . . .**27** B7
Linton Dr SP10 . . . . . .**83** A1
Linton Lawns BH22 . . **353** E3
Linwood Cl SO45 . . . **314** A4
Linwood Rd BH9 . . . . **393** B7
Linwood Rd BH9 . . . . **393** B7
Lion And Lamb Way **5**
　GU9 . . . .**98** F2
Lion and Lamb Yd **13**
　GU9 . . . .**98** F2
Lion Brewery The **1**
　PO2 . . . . **370** D8
Lion Cl
　Haslemere GU27 . . . . **189** D7
　Overton RG25 . . . . . . **88** A7
Lion Ct RG24 . . . .**69** F6
Lion Gn GU27 . . . . . **189** D6
Lionheart Cl BH11 . . . **376** D5
Lionheart Way SO31 **293** A1
Lion Ho PO17 . . . . . **296** A4
Lion La GU27 . . . . . . **189** D7
Lion Mead GU27 . . . . **189** D6
Lion Rd PO1 . . . . **369** F6
Lions Field GU35 . . . . **163** D4
Lions Hall **4** SO22 . . **403** E6
Lions La BH24 . . . . . **327** D5
Lion St PO1 . . . . **370** B5
Lions Wood BH24 . . . **327** E4
Lion Terr PO1 . . . . . . **370** B5

Lion Way GU52 . . . . . .**75** B5
Liphook CE Jun Sch
　GU30 . . . . **187** F4
Liphook Ho **30** PO9 . . **324** B5
Liphook Inf Sch
　GU30 . . . . **187** F4
Liphook Rd
　Bordon GU35 . . . . . . **186** D8
　Haslemere GU27 . . . . **189** D6
　Headley GU35 . . . . . **165** C3
　Linchmere GU27 . . . . **188** E4
　Lindford GU35 . . . . . **164** F5
　Liphook Sta GU30 . . . **188** A2
Lipizzaner Fields
　PO15 . . . . **317** B8
Lippen La SO32 . . . . . **224** F4
Lipscombe Cl
　Newbury RG14 . . . . . .**1** C2
　Southrope RG25 . . . . **116** C6
Lipscombe Rise
　GU34 . . . . **139** F5
Lisa Ct **1** RG21 . . . . .**69** A4
Lisbon Rd SO15 . . . . **290** D6
Liskeard Dr GU14 . . . . .**55** E6
Lisle Cl
　Lymington SO41 . . . . **385** D3
　Newbury RG14 . . . .**1** D5
　Winchester SO22 . . . **197** A3
Lisle Court Rd SO41 . . **386** C3
Lisle Way PO10 . . . . . **324** E3
Lismoyne Cl GU51 . . . .**53** F2
Liss Dr **11** GU51 . . . . . .**53** C3
Lissenden **8** GU35 . . **392** B3
Liss Inf & Jun Schs
　GU33 . . . . **208** A3
Liss Rd PO4 . . . . **370** F4
Liss Sta GU33 . . . . . **207** F4
Lister Rd RG22 . . . .**68** F2
Litchfield Cl SP10 . . . .**82** D3
Litchfield Cres SO18 **267** F1
Litchfield Dr GU51 . . . .**53** C3
Litchfield Ho **2** RG26 .**26** F8
Litchfield Rd
　Southampton SO18 . . **267** F1
　Winchester SO22 . . . **175** D4
Litchford Rd BH25 . . . **383** C3
Lith Ave PO8 . . . . . . **300** C8
Lith La PO8 . . . . **276** C1
Litten The RG20 . . . . . .**24** D2
Little Abshot Rd
　PO14 . . . . **341** B8
Little Aldershot La
　Ashford Hill RG26 . . . . .**8** F2
　Pamber Heath RG26 . . . .**9** A2
Little Anglesey PO12 **369** B3
Little Anglesey Rd
　PO12 . . . . **369** A3
Little-Ann Bridge Farm
　SP11 . . . . **105** C6
Little Arthur St PO2 . . **370** E7
Little Ashton La
　SO32 . . . . **247** E4
Little Austins Rd
　GU9 . . . . **122** B8
Little Barn Pl GU33 . . **208** B4
Little Barrs Dr BH25 . **383** B4
Little Basing RG24 . . . .**70** A7
Little Binfields RG24 . . **49** A4
Little Bull La SO32 . . . **271** D4
Little Burn SO41 . . . . **360** B2
Little Cnr PO7 . . . . . . **299** A3
Little Coburg St PO1 **404** C3
Little Copse
　Andover SP10 . . . . . **105** C4
　Fleet GU52 . . . .**74** F7
　Yateley GU46 . . . .**34** B7
Little Copse Chase
　RG24 . . . .**48** E2
Little Croft GU46 . . . . .**34** B4
Littlecroft Ave BH9 . . **378** B3
Little Croft Rd BH23 . **391** B6
Little Ct
　Poole BH14 . . . . **402** C7
　Poole,Canford Cliffs
　BH13 . . . . **402** F8
Little Dean Ct SO20 . . **150** A3
Little Dean Ho SO20 **150** A3
Little Dean La RG25 . . .**94** E6
Little Dene Copse
　SO41 . . . . **385** B2
Little Dewlands
　BH31 . . . . **302** D6
Littledown Ave BH7 . . **393** F7
Littledown Dr BH7 . . . **393** F7
Little Dro SP6 . . . . . . **258** E7
Little Drove Rd
　SO20 . . . . **129** A3
Little Fallow RG24 . . . .**70** A8
Littlefield Cres SO53 **242** E6
Littlefield Gdns GU12 .**77** E1
Littlefield Rd GU34 . . **140** A6
Little Forest Mans **12**
　BH1 . . . . **393** A3
Little Forest Rd BH4 **392** E5
Little Fosters BH13 . . **402** E6
Little Fox Dr **2**
　SO31 . . . . **317** B5
Little Foxes RG40 . . . . .**16** E7
Little Gays PO15 . . . . **214** D5
Little George St PO1 **370** E7
Little Gn PO12 . . . . . **369** A3
Littlegreen Ave PO9 . **324** B4
Little Green La GU9 . . **121** E6
Little Green Orch
　PO12 . . . . **369** A3

Littlegreen Sch
　PO18 . . . . **278** E4
Little Hambrook St **6**
　PO5 . . . . **404** A1
Little Hartleys RG27 . . .**51** D1
Little Hatherden SP11 .**59** E2
Little Hayes La SO21 **177** F7
Little Hoddington Cl
　SO30 . . . .**94** C5
Little Holbury Park
　Homes Mobile Home
　Pk SO45 . . . . **338** B5
Little Hyden La PO8 . **276** B7
Little Kimble Wlk **3**
　SO30 . . . . **293** C6
Little Knowl Hill RG20 **24** F4
Little La PO12 . . . . . . **369** A3
Little Lance's Hill
　SO19 . . . . **291** F6
Little London Rd RG7 .**27** F8
Little Lonnen
　Colehill BH21 . . . . . **351** F8
　Wimborne Minster
　BH21 . . . . **352** A8
Little Mead PO7 . . . . **299** A3
Littlemead Cl BH17 . . **390** A7
Littlemeads SO51 . . . **240** D7
Littlemill La SP6 . . . . **256** C6
Little Minster St
　SO23 . . . . **403** E5
Littlemoor Ave
　BH11 . . . . **376** D4
Little Oak Rd SO16 . . **266** F4
Little Paddock SO51 . . .**36** E8
Littlepark Ave PO9 . . **323** B3
Little Park Cl SO30 . . **293** B6
Little Park Farm Rd
　PO15 . . . . **317** C5
Little Park Mans
　PO17 . . . . **295** E4
Little Quob La SO30 . **268** E2
Little Reynolds
　SO40 . . . . **288** D5
Little Shore La SO32 **271** D7
Little Southsea St
　PO5 . . . . **404** A1
Little Stodham Ho
　GU33 . . . . **207** D2
Little Thurbans Cl
　GU9 . . . . **121** E6
Little Toller SO16 . . . **266** F7
Littleton Cotts SP11 . . .**80** C4
Littleton Gr PO9 . . . . **323** F4
Littleton La SO21,
　SO22 . . . . **175** A5
Littleton Rd SO22 . . . **175** B4
Little Vigo GU46 . . . . . .**33** F4
Little Wellington St
　GU11 . . . .**76** E2
Littlewood SO51 . . . . **238** F3
Little Woodfalls Dr
　SP5 . . . . **235** D4
Littlewood Gdns
　Sarisbury SO31 . . . . **316** C3
　West End SO30 . . . . **268** D1
Little Woodham La
　PO13 . . . . **368** C5
Littleworth Rd GU10 **100** D1
Litton Gdns RG23 . . . .**67** B1
Liverpool Ct **2**
　PO13 . . . . **368** D5
Liverpool Rd
　Fareham PO14 . . . . . **342** F6
　Portsmouth PO1 . . . . **370** E5
Liverpool St SO14 . . . **291** A7
Livery Rd SP5 . . . . . . **168** A2
Livesay Gdns PO1 . . **370** F6
Livia Cl SP10 . . . .**83** B4
Livingstone Ct PO13 . **368** D6
Livingstone Rd
　Andover SP10 . . . .**83** E1
　Bournemouth BH5 . . . **394** B5
　Christchurch BH23 . . **395** D7
　Newbury RG14 . . . .**1** F2
　Poole BH12 . . . . **391** C6
　Portsmouth PO5 . . . . **404** C1
　Southampton SO14 . . **291** A8
Llewellin Ct BH16 . . . **389** C7
Llewelyn Cl BH16 . . . **389** C7
Lloyd Ave SO40 . . . . **289** E1
Lloyd's La RG26 . . . . . .**46** B6
Loader Cl SO23 . . . . . **176** C7
Loaders Cl BH9 . . . . . **393** A8
Loane Rd SO19 . . . . . **291** F3
Lobelia Ct PO7 . . . . . **323** A6
Lobelia Rd SO16 . . . . **267** C5
Locarno Rd PO2 . . . . **346** A2
Loch Rd BH14 . . . . . . **391** E5
Lock App PO6 . . . . . . **345** A7
Locke Cl SP11 . . . . . . **124** F7
Locke Rd
　Hedge End SO30 . . . **293** C8
　Liphook GU30 . . . . . **188** B4
Lockerley CE Prim Sch
　SO51 . . . . **192** A1
Lockerley Cl SO41 . . . **385** E2
Lockerley Cres SO16 **265** F1
Lockerley Rd
　Awbridge SO51 . . . . **214** D5
　Dunbridge SO51 . . . **192** D1
　Dunbridge SO51 . . . **214** C8
　Havant PO9 . . . . **324** A1
　Lockerley SO51 . . . . **192** A1
Lockham's Dro SP6 . . **258** E7
Lockram La RG7 . . . . . .**12** B8

Lock Rd GU11 . . . .**77** B5
Lock's Cotts SO45 . . . **313** D5
Locksheath Cl PO9 . . **323** D6
Locks Heath Ctr
　SO31 . . . . **317** A3
Locks Heath Jun & Inf
　Schs SO31 . . . . **317** A1
Locksheath Park Rd
　SO31 . . . . **317** B2
Locksley Ct SO15 . . . **290** F7
Locksley Dr BH22 . . . **353** C3
Locksmead **9** RG21 . . .**69** D5
Lock Sq **12** SP10 . . . . .**83** C2
Locks Rd SO31 . . . . . **317** A3
Locksway Rd PO4 . . . **371** C4
Lockswood Keep
　SO31 . . . . **317** A4
Lockswood Rd SO31 **316** F3
Lock View PO6 . . . . . **345** A7
Lockwood Cl GU14 . . . .**55** C8
Lockyer Ct GU32 . . . . **229** B5
Lockyers Dr BH22 . . . **353** F6
Lockyer's Mid Sch
　BH21 . . . . **374** D8
Lockyers Rd BH21 . . . **374** E8
Loddon Bsns Ctr The
　RG24 . . . .**69** E7
Loddon Cl GU15 . . . . . .**36** E6
Loddon Court Farm Park
　Homes RG7 . . . .**13** D7
Loddon Ct RG21 . . . . . .**69** C2
Loddon Ctr RG24 . . . . . .**69** E8
Loddon Dr RG21 . . . . . .**69** D5
Loddon Mall **16** RG21 .**69** B5
Loddon Rd GU14 . . . . . .**55** B6
Loddon Sch The
　RG27 . . . .**49** D5
Loddon Way GU12 . . . .**77** E1
Lode Hill SP5 . . . . . . **235** B8
Loders Cl BH17 . . . . . **375** D3
Lodgebury Ct PO10. . **349** E8
Lodge Ave PO6 . . . . . **346** A8
Lodge Cl
　Aldershot GU11 . . . . **100** A8
　Andover SP10 . . . . . **105** E8
　Poole BH14 . . . . **391** E4
Lodge Ct BH14 . . . . . **391** E4
Lodge Dr
　Hythe SO45 . . . . . . **314** A1
　Penton Grafton SP11 . . **81** D2
Lodge Dro SP5 . . . . . **235** D4
Lodge Gdns PO12 . . . **369** A4
Lodge Gr GU46 . . . .**34** D6
Lodge Hill PO17 . . . . **297** B6
Lodge Hill Cl GU10 . . **122** C6
Lodge Hill Rd GU10 . **122** C6
Lodge La SP11 . . . .**58** B4
Lodge Rd
　Christchurch BH23 . . **394** E8
　Havant PO9 . . . . **323** B1
　Locks Heath SO31 . . **317** B3
　Lymington SO41 . . . . **385** B3
　Southampton SO14 . . **291** A7
Lodge The
　Bournemouth BH2 . . . **392** E4
　Farnham GU9 . . . .**99** C4
　Newbury RG14 . . . .**1** F4
　Southampton SO15 . . **290** F7
　Waterlooville PO7 . . . **323** B3
Lodge Vale SO51 . . . . **239** B1
Lodsworth GU14 . . . . . .**55** B3
Lodsworth Cl PO8 . . . **276** D4
Lodsworth Ho PO1 . . **404** C4
Loewy Cres BH12 . . . **376** D2
Lofting Cl SO50 . . . . **244** A2
Logan Cl SO16 . . . . . **265** F5
Loggon Rd RG21 . . . . . .**69** A1
Loman Rd GU16 . . . . . .**56** E4
Lomax Cl SO30 . . . . . **269** C1
Lombard Ave BH6 . . . **394** D5
Lombard Ct **8** PO1 . . **370** A4
Lombard St PO1 . . . . **370** A3
Lombardy Cl
　Gosport PO13 . . . . . **343** E2
　Verwood BH31 . . . . . **303** B5
Lombardy Rise PO7 . . **322** F5
Lomer La BH24 . . . . . **281** C3
Lomond Cl
　Oakley RG23 . . . .**67** A2
　Portsmouth PO2 . . . . **370** D8
Londesborough Rd
　PO4 . . . . **370** E3
Londlandes GU52 . . . . .**74** F4
London Ave PO2 . . . . **345** D2
London Ct SO14 . . . . . .**2** A3
London La BH23 . . . . **355** F2
London Rd
　Alton GU34 . . . . **140** D6
　Andover SP10 . . . . . **106** C8
　Basingstoke RG21 . . . .**69** C4
　Blendworth PO8 . . . . **300** D8
　Camberley GU15 . . . . .**36** C7
　Clanfield PO8 . . . . . **276** D4
　Clanfield PO8 . . . . . **276** E5
　Cosham PO6 . . . . . . **345** F8
　Hartley Wintney RG27 .**52** C6
　Hill Brow SO23 . . . . **208** B1
　Hindhead GU26 . . . . **167** D4
　Hook RG27 . . . .**51** D2
　Horndean PO8 . . . . . **276** D2
　Kings Worthy SO23 . . **176** B5
　Laverstoke RG28 . . . . .**87** B6
　Liphook GU30 . . . . . **188** A5
　Newbury,Shaw RG18 . . .**2** B3

London Rd continued
　Newbury,Speenhamland
　RG14 . . . .**1** E4
　Odiham,Colt Hill RG29. .**72** F3
　Odiham RG29. . . . .**72** F5
　Old Basing RG24,RG27 **70** D5
　Overton RG25 . . . .**88** B8
　Petersfield GU31 . . . . **229** D6
　Picket Piece SP10 . . . .**84** B1
　Portsmouth PO2 . . . . **345** E6
　Sandhurst GU17,GU15 **35** D5
　Southampton SO15 . . **291** A6
　Stockbridge SO20 . . . **150** D4
　Waterlooville PO7,
　PO8 . . . . **299** F1
　Waterlooville,Purbrook
　PO7 . . . . **322** C4
　Whitchurch RG28 . . . . .**86** E5
London St
　Andover SP10 . . . . . **106** B7
　Basingstoke RG21 . . . .**69** C4
　Whitchurch RG28 . . . . .**86** C5
London Tavern Cvn Pk
　The BH24 . . . . **329** C8
Lone Barn La SO32 . . **248** E7
Lone Pine Dr BH22 . . **353** E3
Lone Pine Pk BH22 . . **353** F3
Lone Pine Way BH22 **353** F2
Lone Valley PO7 . . . . **322** C3
Longacre
　Ash GU12 . . . .**77** E2
　Newbury RG14 . . . .**5** B8
Longacre Cl GU33 . . . **208** A4
Long Acre Ct PO1 . . . **370** E7
Longacre Dr BH22 . . . **353** C4
Longacre Rise RG24 . . .**48** E2
Longacres PO1 . . . . . **370** E7
Long Barn Rd SO21 . . **174** B5
Longbarrow Cl
　Bournemouth BH8 . . . **379** A1
　South Wonston SO21 **153** C4
Long Beech Dr
　Farnborough GU14 . . . .**55** A3
　Totton SO40 . . . . . . **288** D6
Long Bottom SP11 . . . .**57** F3
Long Bridge GU9 . . . . . .**99** A2
Longbridge Cl
　Sherfield on L RG27 . . .**29** E1
　Totton SO40 . . . . . . **264** D2
Longbridge Ct SO40 **264** D2
Longbridge Ho **8**
　PO5 . . . . **404** B2
Longbridge Ind Pk
　SO14 . . . . **291** C3
Longbridge Rd RG26 . .**28** F3
Long Cl SO23 . . . . . . **403** C3
Longclose Rd SO30 . **293** D7
Long Cl W SP5 . . . . . **234** E8
Long Copse SO45 . . . **338** E3
Long Copse Chase
　RG24 . . . .**48** E3
Long Copse Ct PO10 **324** F4
Long Copse La PO10 **325** A4
Longcroft
　Bentley GU10 . . . . . . **120** A5
　Havant PO9 . . . . **323** E1
Longcroft Cl **3** RG21 . .**69** A4
Longcroft Rd RG20. . . .**24** C3
Long Cross Hill
　GU35 . . . . **165** C6
Long Cross La RG22 . . .**91** A6
Long Curtain Rd
　PO5 . . . . **370** A2
Longdean Cl **1** PO6 . **321** A1
Longdene Rd GU27 . . **189** F6
Longdon Dr PO13 . . . **367** F4
Longdown GU52 . . . . . .**74** F6
Long Down SO21 . . . **229** B4
Longdown Activity
　Farm ★ SO40 . . . . . **288** D2
Longdown Cl GU10 . . **122** A6
Longdown Lodge
　GU47 . . . .**34** F8
Longdown Rd GU10 . **122** A5
Long Dr
　Gosport PO13 . . . . . **343** C1
　West End SO30 . . . . **268** E2
Longespee Rd BH21 . **375** E8
Longfellow Par RG24 .**69** C8
Longfield RG23 . . . .**67** B3
Longfield Cl
　Farnborough GU14 . . . .**55** E8
　North Waltham RG25. . .**89** E1
　Portsmouth PO4 . . . . **371** C5
Longfield Dr
　Bournemouth BH11. . . **377** A6
　Ferndown BH22. . . . . **377** E8
Longfield Rd
　Ash GU12. . . . .**77** E2
　Emsworth PO10. . . . . **324** E3
　Fair Oak SO50 . . . . . **245** D1
　Hordle SO41 . . . . . . **384** B2
　Winchester SO23 . . . **198** D8
Longfleet CE Comb Sch
　BH15. . . . . **390** D4
Longfleet Rd BH15 . . **390** E4
Longford Cl GU15 . . . . .**36** E4
Longford Pl SO41 . . . **385** D1
Long Garden Mews **11**
　GU9 . . . .**98** F2
Long Garden Way
　GU9 . . . .**98** F2
Long Garden Wlk
　GU9 . . . .**98** F2
Long Garden Wlk E
　GU9 . . . .**98** F2

Long Garden Wlk W
　GU9 . . . .**98** F2
Long Gdn Way GU9 . . .**98** E1
Long Gdn Wlk GU9 . . . .**98** E1
Long Gdn Wlk E GU9 . .**98** E1
Long Gdn Wlk W GU9 **98** E1
Long Gr RG26 . . . .**9** B7
Longham Bsns Ctr
　BH22 . . . . **353** B2
Long Hill GU10 . . . . . **100** C1
Longhope Dr GU10. . . **121** E6
Longhouse Gn **6**
　SO23 . . . . **198** C8
Long Island GU35 . . . **164** D3
Long La
　Bursl023 . . . . **293** A1
　Bursledon SO31 . . . . **293** A1
　Colehill BH21 . . . . . **351** E8
　Holbury SO45 . . . . . **338** C5
　Long Sutton RG29 . . . .**96** A5
　Marchwood SO40 . . . **289** D1
　Newbury RG14 . . . .**2** B7
　Old Basing RG24 . . . . .**49** A2
　Ringwood BH24 . . . . **329** B4
Longlands Rd PO10 . . **349** D8
Long Lane Cl SO45 . . **338** D3
Longleat Gdns
　New Milton BH25 . . . **382** E3
　Southampton SO16 . . **266** B4
Longleat Sq GU14 . . . . .**56** B3
Long Leaze SP11 . . . . .**61** C4
Longley Rd GU9 . . . .**99** B1
Longman Dr **23** PO5 . **370** C2
Longmead
　Fleet GU52 . . . . **75** A6
　Liss GU33 . . . . **207** F4
　Woolton Hill RG20 . . . .**4** D1
Longmead Ave SO50 **244** D4
Longmead Ct **1** **347** F7
Longmead Gdns
　PO9 . . . . **347** F7
Longmeadow GU16 . . .**36** D3
Longmeadow Gdns
　SO45 . . . . **314** A4
Long Meadow Ind Est
　BH21. . . . . **326** F2
Longmeadow La
　BH17 . . . . **389** E8
Longmead Rd
　1 Southampton
　SO18. . . . . **268** A4
　Burley Street BH24 . . **330** F4
Longmoor Cl RG40. . . . .**16** B1
Longmoor Dr GU30 . . **187** B4
Longmoor La RG7. . . . **11** E7
Longmoor Rd
　Basingstoke RG21 . . . .**69** A4
　Greatham GU33. . . . . **186** A3
　Liphook GU30 . . . . . **187** D4
Longmore Ave SO19 **291** D2
Longmore Cres
　SO19 . . . . **291** D2
Longmynd Dr PO14 . . **356** A8
Longparish CE Prim Sch
　SP11 . . . . **108** B4
Longparish Ct **8**
　SP10 . . . . **106** B7
Longparish Rd
　Hurstbourne Priors
　RG28 . . . .**85** D1
　Longparish SP11 . . . **107** E2
Long Priors GU32 . . . **225** B5
Long Rd
　Bournemouth BH10. . . **377** C5
　Petersfield GU32. . . . **229** A5
　Soberton SO32 . . . . **273** D6
Long Rd The GU10 . . . **121** E3
Longridge Rd SO30 . . **293** C6
Longroden La RG25 . . . .**93** C7
Longs Ct RG28 . . . .**86** C5
Longshore Way PO4 **371** D4
Longs La PO14 . . . . . **367** C8
Longspee Sch BH17 . **390** F4
Longstaff Gdns
　PO16 . . . . **318** F3
Long Steeple La
　SP6 . . . . **233** D2
Longstock Cl
　Andover SP10 . . . . . **105** E7
　Chineham RG24. . . . . .**49** B4
　Southampton SO19 . . **315** A8
Longstock Cres
　SO40 . . . . **288** C2
Longstock Ct **7**
　SP10 . . . . **106** B7
Longstock Rd
　Goodworth Clatford
　SP11. . . . . **127** A4
　Havant PO9 . . . . **324** B6
Long Sutton CE Prim Sch
　RG29. . . . .**95** B3
Long Sutton Dr GU51 .**53** C4
Longs Wlk PO1 . . . . . **371** C7
Long Water Dr PO12 **369** C2
Longwater La
　Eversley Cross RG27. . .**33** C8
　Finchampstead RG40. . .**16** C2
Longwater Rd RG40 . . .**16** C2
Long Wlk SO21 . . . . . **176** E3
Longwood Copse La
　RG23 . . . .**90** F4
Longwood Dean La
　SO21 . . . . **222** B5
Longwood Rd SO21 . **221** C5
Longworthy **3** SO45 **313** E1
Lonnen Rd BH21 . . . . **352** A8
Lonnen Wood Cl
　BH21 . . . . **352** A8

Lonsdale Ave
Cosham PO6 346 A7
Portchester PO16 344 D6
Lonsdale Rd BH3 392 F6
Loosehanger SP5, SP6 235 F3
Lopcombe Cnr SP5 146 B3
Loperwood SO40 264 A2
Loperwood La SO40 264 A3
Loraine Ave BH23 397 C8
Lord Cl BH17 390 F7
Lord Denning Ct RG28 86 C5
Lordington Cl PO6 346 B8
Lord Montgomery Way 1 PO1 404 A2
Lord Mountbatten Cl SO18 267 E4
Lords Ct PO1 404 C4
Lordsfield Gdns RG25 88 A8
Lord's Hill Ctr E SO16 265 F4
Lord's Hill Ctr W SO16 265 F4
Lord's Hill District Ctr SO16 265 F4
Lordshill Rdbt SO16 265 E4
Lord's Hill Way SO16 266 B5
Lords St PO1 404 C4
Lordswood
Colden Common SO50 244 E7
Silchester RG7 27 E8
Lordswood Cl SO16 266 D4
Lordswood Ct SO16 266 C4
Lordswood Gdns SO16 266 D4
Lordswood Rd SO16 266 C4
Lord Wandsworth Coll RG29 95 F1
Lord Wilson Sch SO31 316 F4
Loreille Gdns SO16 265 E7
Loring Ho 7 PO2 345 E4
Lorne Park Rd BH1 393 A3
Lorne Pl SO18 292 A7
Lorne Rd PO5 404 D1
Lorraine Rd GU15 36 D8
Lorraine Sch GU15 36 C8
Lortemore Pl 5 SO51 240 E7
Loughwood Cl SO50 244 A6
Louisburg Rd GU35 164 D6
Louise Margaret Rd GU11 76 F3
Louis Flagg Ho 2 PO5 404 B2
Loundyes Cl RG18 2 F4
Lovage Gdns SO40 288 C7
Lovage Rd PO15 317 D7
Lovage Way PO8 276 C1
Lovatt Gr PO15 318 D3
Lovedean La
Horndean PO8 299 F6
Waterlooville PO8 300 A4
Lovedon La SO23 176 C7
Lovegroves RG24 49 B3
Love La
Andover SP10 106 B7
Kingsclere RG20 24 D2
Milford on S SO41 399 D5
Newbury RG14 1 E6
Odiham RG29 72 D1
Petersfield GU31 229 A4
Petersfield GU31 229 B4
Romsey SO51 240 E7
Twyford SO21 220 B5
Upham SO24,SO32 223 B4
West Meon GU32 225 C4
Woodgreen SP6 258 E8
Lovell Cl
South Wonston SO21 153 E4
Thruxton SP11 103 D7
Lovells Wlk SO24 179 C5
Lovelock Terr 13 PO13 368 C6
Loveridge Cl
Andover SP10 83 B4
Basingstoke RG21 69 A2
Loveridge Way SO50 244 A3
Lovers La GU10 144 A7
Loves Wood RG7 11 D5
Lovett Ho 2 GU9 98 F2
Lovett Rd PO3 346 A3
Lovett Wlk SO22 175 C3
Lovington La SO21, SO24 178 C4
Lowa Rd SP9 78 E6
Lowcay Rd PO5 370 E2
Lowden Cl SO22 403 B2
Lowe Cl GU11 76 D3
Lower Alfred St SO14 291 B6
Lower Ashley Rd BH25 383 D2
Lower Banister St 7 SO15 290 F6
Lower Bartons SP6 257 F1
Lower Baybridge La SO21 221 C2
Lower Bellfield PO14 341 F7
Lower Bere Wood PO7 322 F7
Lower Blandford Rd BH18 375 B3
Lower Brookfield Rd PO1 370 E6
Lower Brook St
Basingstoke RG21 68 F5
Winchester SO23 403 E6
Lower Brownhill Rd SO16 265 D3
Lower Buckland Rd SO41 385 D5
Lower Canal Wlk SO14 291 A3
Lower Canes GU46 33 E6
Lower Charles St GU15 36 A6
Lower Chase Rd SO32 271 F4
Lower Chestnut Dr RG21 68 F3
Lower Church La 16 GU9 98 F2
Lower Church Path PO1 404 B3
Lower Church Rd
Locks Heath PO14 317 C3
Yateley GU47 34 C8
Lower Comm RG27 15 D1
Lower Common La BH21 327 A7
Lower Common Rd SO51 238 E3
Lower Crabbick La PO7 298 B5
Lower Densome Wood SP6 258 E8
Lower Derby Rd PO2 345 C1
Lower Drayton La PO6 346 C7
Lower Duncan Rd SO31 317 B5
Lower Evingar Rd RG28 86 C5
Lower Farlington Rd PO6 346 E8
Lower Farm Ct RG18, RG19 2 D1
Lower Farm Dr PO6 345 E7
Lower Farm La SO51 217 B3
Lower Farnham Rd GU11, GU12 100 A8
Lower Forbury Rd PO5 404 C2
Lower Golf Links Rd BH18 375 B5
Lower Gr SP6 233 B2
Lower Grove Rd PO9 348 A8
Lower Hanger GU27 189 B6
Lower Henwick Farm RG18 2 D5
Lower Heyshott GU31 229 A3
Lower La SO32 271 C8
Lower Lamborough La SO24 201 D5
Lower Mead
Middle Wallop SO20 126 B4
Petersfield GU31 229 B4
Lower Mead End Rd SO41 359 F1
Lower Moor GU46 34 B5
Lower Moors Rd SO21 219 F1
Lower Mortimer Rd SO19 291 D3
Lower Mount St 4 GU51 53 D3
Lower Mullin's La SO45 313 E4
Lower Neatham Mill La
Alton GU34 140 D6
Alton,Neatham GU34 140 E6
Lower Nelson St 1 GU11 76 E2
Lower Newport Rd GU12 77 B1
Lower New Rd SO30 268 D2
Lower Northam Rd SO30 293 C7
Lower Paice La GU34 159 C4
Lower Pennington La SO41 400 D7
Lower Pool Rd RG27 32 B4
Lower Preshaw La SO32 247 F8
Lower Quay PO16 343 B8
Lower Quay Cl PO16 343 B8
Lower Quay Rd PO16 343 B8
Lower Raymond Almshouses 10 RG14 1 D2
Lower Rd
Havant PO9 323 C1
South Wonston SO21 153 C4
Lower St Helens Rd SO30 293 C5
Lower Sandhurst Rd RG40 16 E2
Lower Sandy Down La SO41 361 C3
Lower South View GU9 99 A3
Lower Spinney SO31 340 C9
Lower St
Braishfield SO51 216 B7
Haslemere GU27 189 F6
Lower Stanmore La SO23 403 C3
Lower Swanwick Rd SO31 316 D8
Lower Terrace Rd GU14 76 E8
Lower Turk St GU34 139 F3
Lower Tye Cvn & Camping Ctr PO11 348 C1
Lower Vicarage Rd SO19 291 D3
Lower Wardown GU31 229 B4
Lower Way RG19 2 E3
Lower Weybourne La GU9 99 E6
Lower William St Ind Est SO14 291 D6
Lower William St SO14 291 D6
Lower Wingfield St PO1 404 C4
Lower Woodside SO41 400 E8
Lower York St SO14 291 D6
Lowesmore Ct BH14 391 C4
Lowestoft Rd PO6 321 D1
Loweswater Gdns GU35 164 D5
Loweswater Ho 10 PO6 321 B1
Lowford Hill Cl SO31 293 A1
Lowicks Rd GU10 144 F6
Low La GU9 99 F6
Lowland Rd PO7 298 E4
Lowlands Rd
Basingstoke RG22 68 A3
Blackwater GU17 35 A4
Lowndes Bldgs GU9 98 E3
Lowry Cl GU47 35 B6
Lowry Ct SP10 82 F1
Lowry Gdns SO19 292 C2
Lowther Gdns 3 BH8 393 C5
Lowther Rd BH8 393 B6
Loxwood Ave GU51 74 E7
Loxwood Rd PO8 299 F6
Loyalty La RG24 70 C6
Loyd-Lindsay Sq SO22 403 B8
Luard Ct 4 PO9 324 B1
Lubeck Dr SP10 82 F3
Lucas Cl
Rownhams SO16 265 F5
Yateley GU46 34 B5
Lucas Field GU27 189 C6
Lucas Rd
Poole BH15 390 B1
Poole,Upper Parkstone BH12 391 C6
Luccombe Pl SO15 266 D2
Luccombe Rd SO15 266 D2
Lucerne Ave
Bournemouth BH6 394 D5
Waterlooville PO7 299 D2
Lucerne Gdns SO30 293 B7
Lucerne Rd SO41 399 D4
Lucia Foster Welch Coll Student Village 7 SO14 291 B3
Luckham Cl BH9 378 B2
Luckham Gdns BH9 378 C2
Luckham Pl BH9 378 B2
Luckham Rd BH9 378 B2
Luckham Rd E BH9 378 B2
Lucknow St PO1 404 D3
Lucky La SO41 362 A1
Ludcombe PO7 298 F5
Ludgershall Castle Prim Sch SP11 57 A2
Ludgershall Rd SP9 79 A8
Ludlow Cl
Basingstoke RG23 68 C5
Camberley GU16 56 E7
Newbury RG14 2 C4
Ludlow Gdns RG23 68 D5
Ludlow Inf Sch SO19 291 E4
Ludlow Jun Sch SO19 291 E4
Ludlow Pl RG26 27 A8
Ludlow Rd
Portsmouth PO6 321 C1
Southampton SO19 291 E4
Ludshott Gr GU35 165 F5
Ludshott Manor GU30 166 A1
Ludwell's La SO32 271 F4
Lugano Cl PO7 299 D1
Luke Rd GU11 99 C8
Luke Rd E GU11 99 C8
Lukes Cl SO31 316 A2
Lukin Dr SO16 265 C6
Lulworth Ave BH15 389 E1
Lulworth Bsns Ctr SO40 264 E2
Lulworth Cl
Chandler's Ford SO53 243 B3
Farnborough GU14 55 E7
Hamworthy BH15 389 E1
Southampton SO16 265 E2
South Hayling PO11 373 A5
Lulworth Cres BH15 389 E1
Lulworth Ct BH15 389 E2
Lulworth Gn SO16 265 E2
Lulworth Rd PO13 367 E2
Lumby Dr BH24 329 B8
Lumby Drive Mobile Home Pk 2 BH24 329 B8
Lumley Gdns PO10 349 A8
Lumley Path 7 PO10 349 A8
Lumley Rd PO10 325 A1
Lumley Terr PO10 325 A1
Lumsden Ave SO15 290 D7
Lumsden Mans 3 SO15 290 C7
Lumsden Rd PO4 371 D3
Lundy Cl
Basingstoke RG24 48 D1
Southampton SO16 265 E5
Lundy Wlk PO14 367 B8
Lune Cl 4 RG21 69 D5
Lune Ct 26 SP10 83 C2
Lunedale Rd SO45 337 E8
Lunn Cotts GU26 167 D4
Lupin Cl RG22 91 A8
Lupin Gdns SO22 175 B2
Lupin Rd SO16 267 C5
Luscombe Rd BH14 391 C2
Luther Rd BH9 392 F8
Lutman St PO10 324 E4
Luton Rd SO19 292 B4
Lutyens Cl
Basingstoke RG24 69 F8
Chineham RG24 48 F1
Lutyens Ind Ctr RG24 48 E1
Luxor Pk PO9 347 E7
Luxton Cl SO30 293 F8
Luzborough La SO51 241 D6
Lyall Pl GU9 98 F7
Lyburn Cl SO16 266 C4
Lyburn Ct SO16 266 C4
Lyburn Ho SP5 261 B7
Lyburn Rd
Nomansland SP5 261 B8
Redlynch SP5 236 F1
Lych Gate Cl GU47 34 D8
Lych Gate Ct BH24 329 C6
Lychgate Dr PO8 300 B7
Lychgate Gn PO14 342 C5
Lydden Ct PO13 343 D2
Lyde Cl RG23 67 B1
Lydford Cl
Camberley GU16 56 E7
Farnborough GU14 55 E7
Lydford Gdns BH11 377 A2
Lydford Rd BH11 377 A2
Lydgate
Milford on S SO41 399 A5
Totton SO40 288 D7
Lydgate Cl SO19 292 D4
Lydgate Gn SO19 292 D4
Lydgate Rd SO19 292 D4
Lydiard Cl SO50 244 A5
Lydlinch Cl BH22 353 D1
Lydlynch Inf Sch SO40 288 E7
Lydlynch Rd SO40 288 F7
Lydney Cl PO6 345 C8
Lydney Rd SO31 316 F3
Lydwell Cl BH11 376 F5
Lye Copse Ave GU14 55 F8
Lyell Rd BH12 391 C6
Lyeway La SO24, GU34 182 C4
Lyeway Rd SO24 182 A5
Lyford Rd RG21 69 B6
Lymbourn Rd PO9 324 A1
Lyme Cl SO50 243 F5
Lyme Cres BH23 396 F8
Lymefields SO41 399 E6
Lymer La SO16 265 C6
Lymer Villas SO16 265 C6
Lymington Ave GU46 34 A5
Lymington Bottom GU34 160 B1
Lymington Bottom Rd GU34 160 A3
Lymington CE Inf Sch SO41 385 D4
Lymington Cl
Basingstoke RG22 91 B7
Four Marks GU34 160 B2
Lymington Farm Ind Est GU34 160 A3
Lymington Hospl SO41 385 D4
Lymington Jun Sch SO41 385 D4
Lymington Pier Sta SO41 386 A3
Lymington Rd
Brockenhurst SO42 334 A1
Christchurch BH23 396 F7
East End SO41 387 B7
Milford on S SO41 399 E6
New Milton BH25 383 C1
Lymington Rehabilitation Unit SO41 385 E4
Lymington Rise GU34 160 B2
Lymington Town Sta SO41 385 F4
Lymington Vineyard* SO41 385 B2
Lymore La SO41 399 F6
Lymore Valley SO41 399 E6
Lynams GU52 74 E3
Lynchborough Rd GU30 187 B8
Lynch Cl SO22 403 C8
Lynchford La GU14 77 C8
Lynchford Rd GU14 77 B8
Lynch Hill RG28 86 C5
Lynch Hill Pk RG28 86 D5
Lynch La GU32 225 C4
Lynch Rd GU9 99 C2
Lynch The
Overton RG25 87 E8
Whitchurch RG28 86 D5
Lyn Ct 5 RG21 69 D5
Lyndale Cl SO41 399 E5
Lyndale Dr GU51 54 D1
Lyndale Rd SO31 317 C4
Lynden Cl PO14 342 B8
Lynden Gate SO19 292 A3
Lyndford Terr GU52 74 F7
Lyndhurst Ave
Aldershot GU11 100 A6
Blackwater GU17 35 A6
Lyndhurst Cl
South Hayling PO11 373 A3
Winchester SO22 175 D4
Lyndhurst Dr RG22 91 C6
Lyndhurst Ho PO9 323 E6
Lyndhurst Jun Sch PO2 345 F1
Lyndhurst Rd
Ashurst SO40 288 B2
Bransgore BH23 381 D6
Brockenhurst SO42 334 A2
Burley BH24 331 C5
Cadnam SO40 286 E7
Christchurch BH23 381 D2
Fleet GU51 53 C4
Gosport PO12 369 A5
Landford SP5 237 D3
Portsmouth PO2 345 F1
Lyndhurst Sch GU15 35 F5
Lyndock Cl SO19 291 E2
Lyndock Pl SO19 291 E2
Lyndon Ct BH23 379 F1
Lyndons The GU30 187 B8
Lyndsey Cl GU14 54 F4
Lyndum Cl GU32 228 F4
Lyne Pl PO8 300 B6
Lynes La BH24 328 F7
Lynford Ave SO22 403 C8
Lynford Way SO22 403 C8
Lynn Cl SO18 268 B3
Lynn Rd
Poole BH17 375 F1
Portsmouth PO2 370 F8
Lynn Way
Farnborough GU14 55 D7
Kings Worthy SO23 176 C7
Lynric Cl BH25 398 A7
Lynton Cl GU9 121 E7
Lynton Cres BH23 379 D3
Lynton Ct
Newbury RG14 1 E4
Totton SO40 288 E6
Lynton Gdns PO16 318 F3
Lynton Gr PO3 371 A8
Lynton Mdw SO20 129 A4
Lynton Rd
Bordon GU35 164 D3
Hedge End SO30 293 C7
Petersfield GU32 228 E4
Lynwood Ave PO8 299 D3
Lynwood Cl
Ferndown BH22 353 D7
Lindford GU35 165 A5
Lynwood Ct
Lymington SO41 385 D3
Winchester SO22 403 D8
Lynwood Dr
Andover SP10 105 E8
Mytchett GU16 56 E3
Oakley BH21 375 E8
Lynwood Gdns RG27 51 A1
Lynx Cl SO50 244 F2
Lyon Ave BH25 383 B3
Lyon Rd BH12 376 E2
Lyons Pl SO30 293 B5
Lyon St SO14 291 A6
Lyon Way GU16 36 A1
Lyon Way Ind Est GU16 36 A1
Lysander Cl BH23 396 C7
Lysander Ct 21 PO1 370 A4
Lysander Way
Farnborough GU14 55 F1
Waterlooville PO7 323 A8
Lyse Ct GU33 207 F4
Lysons Ave GU12 77 D8
Lysons Rd GU11 76 E1
Lysons Way GU12 77 E7
Lysses Ct PO16 319 C1
Lyster Rd SP6 258 A2
Lystra Rd BH9 378 A3
Lytchett Dr BH18 374 F2
Lytchett Way BH16 389 B6
Lyteltane Rd SO41 385 D2
Lytham Cl GU35 164 B2
Lytham Rd
Broadstone BH18 375 A3
Southampton SO18 268 A1
Lythe La GU32 228 A5
Lyttell Combe RG27 51 D1
Lytton Rd
Basingstoke RG21 69 D5
Bournemouth BH1, BH8 393 C5
Hythe SO45 314 B2

M

Mabbs La RG27 52 C4
Mabelmyll Croft RG27 51 D2
Mabett Cl RG2 15 C8
Mabey Ave BH10 377 D2
Mabey Cl PO12 369 C3
Mablethorpe Rd PO6 321 E1
MacAdam Way SP10 82 B1
MacAndrew Rd BH13 402 F7
MacArthur Cres SO18 292 A8
MacAulay Ave PO6 320 F1
MacAulay Rd BH18 375 A4
MacCallum Rd SP11 83 B8
McCarthy Way RG40 16 D8
McCartney Wlk RG22 91 C7
MacDonald Rd GU9 98 F7
McDonald's Almshouses 2 GU9 98 E1
McFauld Way RG28 86 D4
McGovern Mews SO31 340 D10
McIntyre Rd BH23 379 A8
McKay Cl GU11 77 A3
McKernan Ct GU47 34 D8
McKinley Rd BH4 392 C2
Macklin Ho 21 SO22 403 D6
MacLaren Rd BH9 377 F3
Maclay Ho SP11 83 B7
Maclean Rd BH11 376 F3
Macnaghten Rd SO18 291 D8
Macnaghten Woods 1 GU15 36 C6
McNaughton Cl GU14 55 B3
Macrae Rd GU46 34 A6
McWilliam Cl BH12 392 C8
McWilliam Rd 2 BH9 378 A2
Madden Cl PO12 368 F3
Maddison St 5 SO14 290 F4
Maddocks Hill SO24 181 B4
Maddoxford La SO32 270 A1
Maddoxford Way SO32 269 F2
Madeira Cl RG24 48 D1
Madeira Ct GU14 55 C5
Madeira Pl 5 RG14 1 E2
Madeira Rd
Bournemouth BH1 393 A4
Poole BH14 391 D5
Portsmouth PO2 345 F3
Madeley Rd GU52 75 B6
Madeline Cl BH12 391 B7
Madeline Cres BH12 391 B7
Madeline Rd GU31 228 F4
Madison Ave BH1 393 D6
Madison Cl PO13 368 E8
Madison Ct 8 PO16 319 C1
Madox Brown End GU47 35 C6
Madrid Rd SP10 83 C1
Madrisa Ct SO41 385 E4
Mafeking Rd PO4 370 F3
Maffey Ct SO30 294 A7
Magazine La SO40 290 A3
Magazine Rd GU14 76 B8
Magdala Rd
Cosham PO6 345 F7
South Hayling PO11 372 E3
Magdalen Ct 4 PO2 345 E3
Magdalene Way PO14 317 C2
Magdalen Hill SO23 403 F5
Magdalen La BH23 395 A6
Magdalen Mews 8 SO23 403 F5
Magdalen Rd PO2 345 E3
Magellan Cl SP10 83 E1
Magennis Cl PO13 368 D7
Magenta Ct 4 PO13 368 C6
Magister Dr PO13 368 A5
Magna Cl BH11 376 F6
Magna Gdns BH11 376 F6
Magna Rd BH21 376 C7
Magnolia Cl
Andover SP10 105 E7
Bournemouth BH6 395 A5
Fareham PO14 342 E8
Hythe SO45 313 C4
Verwood BH31 303 C4
Magnolia Ct RG19 7 F6
Magnolia Gr SO50 245 E2
Magnolia Ho
6 Bournemouth BH10 377 F4
Basingstoke RG24 48 A1
Magnolia Rd SO19 291 F5
Magnolia Terr PO7 322 E6
Magnolia Way
Fleet GU52 75 A7
Waterlooville PO8 300 C4
Magnus Dr RG22 91 B7
Magpie Cl
Basingstoke RG22 90 F8
Bordon GU35 164 E2
Bournemouth BH8 378 C3
Ewshot GU10 98 B8
Fareham PO16 343 E8
Thatcham RG19 2 F3
Magpie Cotts PO8 301 C4
Magpie Dr SO40 288 C7

Magpie Gdns SO19 292 C4
Magpie Gr BH25 382 F2
Magpie La
Eastleigh SO50 243 E1
Lee-on-t-S PO13 367 F4
Magpie Rd PO8 301 C5
Magpie Wlk PO8 299 D4
Mag's Barrow BH22 353 E2
Mahler Cl RG22 91 F8
Maida Rd GU11 76 F4
Maidenhead Ho 6
RG14 1 D2
Maiden La SO41 385 F1
Maidenthorn La RG25 90 A1
Maidford Gr PO3 346 C4
Maidment Cl BH11 376 E4
Maidstone Cres PO6 321 E1
Main Dr PO17 321 A6
Mainline Bsns Ctr
GU33 207 F4
Main Rd
Colden Common
SO21 220 A1
East End SO41 387 B8
Gosport PO13 343 D5
Hardley SO45 338 C6
Hermitage PO10,
PO18 349 D8
Hythe SO45 313 C5
Littleton SO22 175 B5
Marchwood SO40 289 F1
Marchwood SO40,
SO45 313 A6
Otterbourne SO21 219 C3
Owslebury SO21 221 B3
Portmore SO41 386 B7
Portsmouth PO1 369 F7
Tadley RG26 27 B6
Totton SO40 288 E4
Twyford SO21 219 F2
Mainsail Dr PO16 343 B8
Main St RG19 6 E5
Mainstone SO51 240 D6
Mainstream Ct SO50 244 D3
Maisemore Gdns
PO10 348 D8
Maitland Ct SO41 385 D3
Maitland Rd GU14 76 F8
Maitlands Cl GU10 100 D6
Maitland St PO1 370 D7
Maitlands The 2
BH2 392 D2
Maizemore Wlk 7
PO13 367 F3
Majendie Cl RG14 1 B5
Majestic Rd
Basingstoke RG22 91 A5
Nursling SO16 265 B4
Majoram Way PO15 317 D7
Majorca Ave SP10 83 C1
Majorca Mans 4
BH2 392 E3
Major Ct PO12 369 B8
Makins Ct SO24 179 C5
Malan Cl BH17 390 E8
Malcolm Cl
Chandler's Ford
SO53 218 E1
Locks Heath SO31 317 B3
Malcolm Rd SO53 218 E1
Malcomb Cl BH6 395 A3
Malcroft Mews
SO40 290 A1
Maldive Rd RG24 48 D1
Maldon Cl SO50 244 D3
Maldon Rd
2 Cosham PO6 345 D8
Southampton SO19 291 E4
Malham Gdns RG22 91 B5
Malibres Rd SO53 243 F8
Malin Cl
Southampton SO16 265 E4
Stubbington PO14 367 B8
Malins Rd PO2 370 D8
Malins Road Apts 18
PO2 370 D7
Mallard Bldgs 6
BH25 383 A3
Mallard Cl
Andover SP10 83 B2
Ash GU12 77 D2
Basingstoke RG22 90 F7
Bishop's Waltham
SO32 271 A8
Bournemouth BH8 378 C1
Christchurch BH23 396 A6
Haslemere GU27 189 C6
Hordle SO41 384 A3
New Alresford SO24 179 D6
Romsey SO51 240 F8
Mallard Ct
Aldershot GU11 99 E7
Newbury RG14 1 D3
Mallard Gdns
Gosport PO13 343 B2
Hedge End SO30 269 C2
Mallard Rd
Bournemouth BH8 378 D1
Portsmouth PO4 371 B5
Rowlands Castle PO9 301 B1
Wimborne Minster
BH21 352 A7
Mallards GU34 139 F5
Mallards Rd SO31 315 F8
Mallards The
Fareham PO16 319 A3
Frimley GU16 36 D2
Langstone PO9 347 F7
Mallard Way
4 Yateley GU46 33 F6
Westbourne PO10 325 C4
Mallett Cl SO30 269 E2
Mallory Cl BH23 395 F8
Mallory Cres PO16 319 A3
Mallow Cl
2 Cosham PO6 345 F8
Broadstone BH18 374 E3
Christchurch BH23 396 C8
Lindford GU35 165 A5
Locks Heath SO31 316 F2
Waterlooville PO7 322 F6
Mallow Rd SO30 293 A6
Mallows The BH25 383 D4
Mall The
Andover SP10 106 A7
Burley BH24 331 A3
Chandler's Ford SO53 243 E7
Portsmouth PO2 345 D1
South Tidworth SP9 78 C4
Malmesbury Cl
SO50 245 C2
Malmesbury Ct BH8 393 C6
Malmesbury Gdns
SO22 403 B8
Malmesbury Ho 2
SP9 79 A6
Malmesbury Park Pl 7
BH8 393 C5
Malmesbury Park Prim
Sch BH8 393 B5
Malmesbury Park Rd
BH8 393 B6
Malmesbury Pl
SO15 290 D7
Malmesbury Rd
Romsey SO51 240 E8
Southampton SO15 290 D7
St Leonards BH24 327 E3
Malmsbury Cl 6
BH23 395 A5
Malmsbury Rd GU35 164 D2
Maloney Mews PO11 373 E1
Maloren Way BH22 327 A1
Malory Cl SO19 292 D6
Malpass Rd SO21 153 C2
Malshanger Cotts
RG23 66 E6
Malshanger La RG23 67 A3
Malta Cl RG24 48 B1
Malta Rd PO2 370 E8
Maltbys GU34 184 E8
Malthouse 7 BH15 390 C2
Malthouse Bridge Cotts
GU51 74 D5
Malthouse Cl
Crookham Village
GU52 74 E5
Itchen Abbas SO21 176 F4
Romsey SO51 240 E8
Malthouse Cotts
Lee SO51 265 A8
North Warnborough
RG29 72 C3
Penton Mewsey SP11 82 A3
Malthouse Ct GU30 188 A4
Malthouse Gdns
SO40 289 F1
Malthouse La
Bighton SO24 158 C1
Fareham PO16 319 B1
Tadley RG26 27 B6
Upper Chute SP11 58 A8
Malt House La SP11 83 D7
Malthouse Mdws
GU30 188 A4
Malthouse Mews
GU34 140 C6
Malthouse Rd PO2 370 D8
Maltings Cl GU34 139 F3
Maltings The
3 Poole BH15 390 E3
Bournemouth BH11 376 F6
Bramley RG26 28 F2
Fareham PO16 319 D2
Liphook GU30 188 B4
Petersfield GU31 228 F3
Malt La SO32 271 C7
Malus Cl PO14 342 F7
Malvern Ave PO14 342 E8
Malvern Bsns Ctr
SO15 266 D2
Malvern Cl
Basingstoke RG22 68 A3
Bishop's Waltham
SO32 271 D7
Bournemouth BH9 378 A3
Malvern Ct
2 Christchurch
BH23 395 F8
4 Bournemouth BH9 378 A2
Newbury RG14 1 D1
Malvern Dr SO45 313 D3
Malvern Gdns SO30 269 D2
Malvern Mews PO10 324 F1
Malvern Rd
Bournemouth BH9 378 A2
Farnborough GU14 55 B7
Gosport PO12 368 F5
Hawley GU17 34 D1
Hill Brow GU33 208 B2
Portsmouth PO5 370 D1
Southampton SO16 266 C2
Malvern Terr SO16 266 D2
Malwood Ave SO16 266 D3
Malwood Cl PO9 324 A6
Malwood Gdns SO40 288 C8
Malwood Rd SO45 314 A4
Malwood Rd W SO45 313 F4
Manaton Way SO30 269 B1
Manchester Ct 10
PO13 368 D5
Manchester Rd
Netley SO31 315 A5
Portsmouth PO1 370 E5
Sway SO41 360 B3
Manchester Terr
PO10 325 B4
Mancroft Ave PO14 367 C7
Mandalay Cl BH31 302 E5
Mandale Cl BH11 377 A4
Mandale Rd BH11 376 F3
Mandarin Cl
Farnham GU9 99 B5
Newbury RG14 2 A2
Mandarin Dr RG14 6 A8
Mandarin Way PO13 368 C6
Mandela Way SO15 290 E5
Manderley SO41 399 E3
Mandora Rd GU11 76 F4
Manfield Rd GU12 77 E2
Manica Cl GU35 164 D3
Manington Hall 5
BH4 392 C2
Manley Bridge Rd
GU10 121 C5
Manley James Cl
RG29 72 E3
Manley Rd SO31 292 F1
Mann Cl RG28 86 D4
Manners La PO4 370 E4
Manners Rd PO4 370 E4
Manning Ave BH23 381 C1
Manningford Cl
SO23 176 A3
Mannings Heath Rd
BH12 376 B1
Mannings Heath Rdbt
BH17 376 B2
Mannings Heath Ret Pk
BH12 391 A8
Mannington Pl 12
BH2 392 E3
Mannington Way
BH22 326 D2
Manns Cl SO18 268 C2
Mannyngham Way
SO51 215 D7
Manor Ave BH12 376 C1
Manor Bridge Ct SP9 78 F7
Manor Cl
7 Winchester
SO23 403 F6
8 Havant PO9 323 F1
Abbotts Ann SP11 105 A3
Alton GU34 140 A6
Basingstoke RG22 91 A6
Bursledon SO31 292 F1
Ferndown BH22 353 E5
Fordingbridge SP6 257 F1
Haslemere GU27 189 C6
Milford on S SO41 399 D6
Shipton Bellinger SP9 101 E7
Tongham GU10 100 D7
Totton SO40 288 E6
Wickham PO17 296 A3
Manor Copse SP10 83 B5
Manor Cotts RG28 87 B6
Manor Cres
Bursledon SO31 292 F1
Cosham PO6 346 B7
Haslemere GU27 189 C6
Manor Ct
Fleet GU52 75 A4
Havant PO9 323 D1
Ringwood BH24 328 F8
Titchfield PO15 317 D4
Verwood BH31 302 F6
Manor Farm SO24 201 D1
Manor Farm Bsns Ctr
GU10 100 D5
Manor Farm Cl
Ash GU12 77 D1
Bishopstoke SO50 244 E2
Old Milton BH25 382 F1
Manor Farm Cotts
Exton SO32 249 C7
Rockbourne SP6 232 E2
South Hayling PO11 373 A6
Sutton Scotney SO21 131 B2
Whitsbury SP6 233 A5
Manor Farm Ctry Pk★
SO31 293 D3
Manor Farm Gn
SO21 219 F5
Manor Farm Gr
SO50 244 E2
Manor Farm La
SO51 193 E1
Manor Farm Mus★
SO30 293 F4
Manor Farm Rd
Bournemouth BH10 377 C7
Fordingbridge SP6 257 C1
Southampton SO18 267 D2
Manor Farmyard
BH8 379 B3
Manor Field Inf Sch
RG22 91 E7
Manor Field Jun Sch
RG22 91 E7
Manor Fields
Liphook GU30 188 B4
Seale GU10 100 F4
Manor Flats SO21 219 F5
Manor Gdns
Breach PO10 325 D1
Farnham GU10 122 B5
Ringwood BH24 328 F8
Verwood BH31 302 F6
Manor Ho BH18 375 A4
Manor Ho The
Camberley GU15 36 B6
Fleet GU51 53 F1
Manor House Ave
SO15 289 E6
Manor House Farm
SO24 180 E3
Manor House Flats
GU10 100 D6
Manor Inf Sch
Farnborough GU14 55 C6
Holbury SO45 338 B4
Portsmouth PO1 370 E7
Manor Jun Sch GU14 55 D6
Manor La
Brimpton RG7 8 A6
Newbury RG18 2 C5
Old Basing RG24 70 B6
Verwood BH31 302 F5
Manor Lea GU27 189 C6
Manor Lodge Rd
PO9 301 A1
Manor Mews PO6 346 C8
Manor Park Ave 5
PO3 371 A8
Manor Park Cotts
GU34 140 A3
Manor Park Dr
Finchampstead RG40 16 C6
Yateley GU46 34 B5
Yateley GU46 34 C6
Manor Park Ho 1
SO18 291 E7
Manor Park Ind Est
GU12 77 A1
Manor Pk BH15 390 B5
Manor Pl RG14 1 B5
Manor Quay SO18 291 D7
Manor Rd
Aldershot GU11 99 E8
Alton GU34 140 A6
Andover SP10 82 F1
Bishopstoke SO50 244 E2
Bournemouth BH1 393 C3
Breach PO10 325 D1
Chilworth SO16 242 D1
Christchurch BH23 395 A6
Durley SO32 270 D7
East Tytherley SP5 191 E7
Farnborough GU14 56 B3
Farnham GU9 99 C4
Holbury SO45 338 C4
Hythe SO45 313 A4
Milford on S SO41 399 D6
New Milton BH25 383 B3
Portsmouth PO1 370 E7
Ringwood BH24 329 B7
Sherborne St John
RG24 47 E3
South Hayling PO11 372 F5
Tongham GU10,GU12 100 D8
Twyford SO21 219 F5
Verwood BH31 302 F6
Manor Rd N SO19 291 E4
Manor Rd S SO19 291 E3
Manor Rise SP11 105 E4
Manor Rise Flats
SP11 105 E4
Manorside Comb Sch
BH12 376 D1
Manor Terr
Bursledon SO31 292 E1
Durley SO32 270 E7
Manor View RG7 8 D7
Manor Villas PO17 296 A3
Manor Way
Breach PO10 325 D1
Lee-on-t-S PO13 367 E3
South Hayling PO11 373 A2
Verwood BH31 302 F7
Manor Wharf SO18 291 C7
Manor Wks SO40 289 B7
Manor Wlk GU12 76 F6
Mansard Ct BH13 402 B3
Mansbridge Cotts
SO18 267 F4
Mansbridge Prim Sch
SO18 267 E4
Mansbridge Rd
Eastleigh SO50 244 A1
Southampton SO18 267 F4
Manse La RG26 27 B6
Mansel Cl BH12 392 C7
Mansel Ct SO16 265 E2
Mansel Inf Sch
SO16 265 D2
Mansel Jun Sch
SO16 265 D2
Mansell Cl SO45 313 E1
Mansell Dr RG14 5 A5
Mansel Rd E SO16 265 E1
Mansel Rd W SO16 265 D2
Mansergh Wlk SO40 288 B8
Mansfield Ave BH14 391 C4
Mansfield Bsns Pk
GU34 160 B3
Mansfield Cl
Ferndown BH22 353 D2
Mansfield Cl *continued*
Poole BH14 391 C4
Mansfield La SO32 295 B4
Mansfield Rd
Basingstoke RG22 68 E2
Bournemouth BH9 377 E1
Gosport PO13 368 C8
Poole BH14 391 C4
Ringwood BH24 328 F7
Mansion Ct 6 PO4 370 E1
Mansion Dr RG27 32 B4
Mansion House St 2
RG14 1 E3
Mansion Rd
Portsmouth PO4 370 E1
Southampton SO15 290 D6
Manston Ct SO16 265 F4
Mansvid Ave PO6 346 B7
Mantle Cl PO13 368 D7
Mantle Sq PO2 345 B2
Manton Cl BH15 389 E3
Manton Rd BH15 389 E3
Maple Bsns Pk BH21 352 F7
Maple Cl
Alton GU34 139 F5
Ash Vale GU12 77 D7
Barton on S BH25 398 B7
Blackwater GU17 35 A5
Bursledon SO31 315 F8
Christchurch BH23 396 F7
Emsworth PO10 324 F2
Fareham PO15 318 C1
Lee-on-t-S PO13 367 F2
New Alresford SO24 179 C4
Romsey SO51 241 C6
Maple Cres
Basingstoke RG21 69 B7
Clanfield PO8 276 D6
Ludgershall SP11 57 B2
Newbury RG14 1 E4
Maple Ct
Basingstoke RG22 68 B4
Lymington SO41 385 B2
Southampton,Sholing
SO19 292 B4
Southampton,Woolston
SO19 291 E2
Maple Dr
Denmead PO7 299 A4
Ferndown BH22 353 C8
Kings Worthy SO23 176 B8
Maple Gdns
Totton SO40 288 C6
Yateley GU46 34 B5
Maple Gr RG26 26 F8
Maple Ho
Havant PO9 324 A2
Southampton SO16 266 F7
Maplehurst Chase
RG22 91 B6
Maple Leaf Cl GU14 55 D3
Maple Leaf Dr GU35 164 D4
Mapleleaf Gdns 5
SO50 244 A2
Maple Lo BH16 389 C7
Maple Rd
Bournemouth BH9 392 F8
Hythe SO45 338 B8
Poole BH15 390 D3
Portsmouth PO5 370 D2
Southampton SO18 291 E7
Maple Ridge Sch
RG21 69 A7
Maplers Dr 13 GU51 53 E3
Maplespeen Ct RG14 1 D4
Maple Sq SO50 243 E1
Maples The SO53 243 C8
Maple Terr 4 SP9 79 A7
Mapleton Rd SO30 293 D6
Mapletons The RG29 72 F3
Mapletree Ave PO8 300 C4
Maple Way GU35 165 F6
Maple Wlk
9 Andover SP10 105 D6
Aldershot GU12 100 B8
Petersfield GU31 228 F1
Maplewood RG24 48 A5
Maple Wood PO9 323 B1
Maplewood Cl SO40 288 C6
Maplin Rd SO16 265 D2
Mapperton Cl BH17 375 F2
Marabout Cl BH23 395 D7
Maralyn Ave PO7 322 E6
Marathon Pl SO50 245 B2
Marazan Rd PO3 346 B2
Marbrean Cl SP6 257 C2
Marchant Cl RG19 6 B7
Marchant Rd SP10 105 E7
March Cl SP10 83 B1
Marchesi Ct PO14 342 C4
Marchwood By Pass
Marchwood SO40 312 E8
Totton SO40 289 B3
Marchwood CE Inf Sch
SO40 312 E8
Marchwood Ct 8
PO12 368 D3
Marchwood Ho GU51 53 C3
Marchwood Ind Pk
SO40 290 A3
Marchwood Jun Sch
SO40 289 F1
Marchwood Priory Hospl
SO40 313 A7
Marchwood Rd
Bournemouth BH10 377 C3
Havant PO9 323 E6
Southampton SO15 290 B6
Marchwood Rd *continued*
Totton SO15 289 C4
Marchwood Terr
SO40 289 F2
Marconi Rd RG14 1 F4
Marcus Cl SO50 245 B2
Mardale Rd SO16 289 D8
Mardale Wlk SO16 289 D8
Marden Paddock
SO42 333 F1
Marden Way GU31 229 A3
Mardon Cl SO18 267 E5
Mare La SO21 220 F6
Mareth Cl GU11 76 F2
Margam Ave SO19 291 F5
Margards La BH31 302 E5
Margaret Cl PO7 299 D1
Margaret Rd RG22 68 D4
Margaret Rule Hall 5
PO1 404 B3
Margarita Rd PO15 318 E2
Margate Rd PO5 404 C2
Margery's Ct 31 PO1 370 A5
Marguerite Cl RG26 28 F3
Marian Cl BH21 374 C4
Marianne Cl SO15 289 F6
Marianne Rd
Poole BH12 392 C8
Wimborne Minster
BH21 352 A7
Marian Rd BH21 374 C4
Marie Ave SP5 234 D7
Marie Cl BH12 391 D7
Marie Ct 6 PO7 322 E8
Marie Rd SO19 292 C3
Marigold Cl
Basingstoke RG22 91 A8
Fareham PO15 318 E2
Marina Bldgs 3
PO12 369 B5
Marina Cl PO10 349 A7
Marina Ct
2 Bournemouth
BH5 393 E3
Christchurch BH23 397 A7
Marina Dr
Hamble-le-R SO31 316 A2
Poole BH14 391 B1
Marina Gr
Portchester PO16 344 C6
Portsmouth PO3 371 B7
Marina Keep PO6 345 A6
Marina The BH5 393 E3
Marina Twrs 5 BH5 393 E3
Marina View
1 Christchurch
BH23 395 A5
Netley SO31 314 F7
Marine Cotts 7
PO12 369 B6
Marine Ct
Barton on S BH25 397 D7
Portsmouth PO4 371 A2
Marine Dr BH25 397 E7
Marine Dr E BH25 398 A6
Marine Drive W
BH25 397 E7
Marine Par SO14 291 B4
Marine Par E PO13 367 F2
Marine Par W PO13 367 D4
Marine Point BH25 397 F7
Marine Prospect
BH25 397 F7
Marine Rd BH6 394 D3
Mariners Cl RG26 27 B6
Mariner's Cl SO31 316 A4
Mariners Ct
Christchurch BH23 396 A6
Lymington SO41 385 F2
South Hayling PO11 373 D1
Mariners Dr GU14 56 A6
Mariners Mews
SO45 314 A4
Mariners Reach
BH25 398 A6
Mariners The SO31 315 B6
Mariners Way
Gosport PO12 369 D4
Warsash SO31 316 C1
Mariners Wlk PO4 371 B5
Marine Wlk PO11 373 D3
Marino Way RG40 15 E6
Marion Rd PO4 370 E2
Maritime Ave SO40 290 A3
Maritime Chambers
SO14 291 B2
Maritime Way SO14 291 A2
Maritime Wlk SO14 291 B2
Marjoram Cl GU14 54 F4
Marjoram Cres PO8 300 B3
Markall Cl SO24 201 D5
Mark Anthony Ct
PO11 372 F3
Mark Cl
Portsmouth PO3 345 F4
Southampton SO15 290 A7
Mark Ct PO7 322 E8
Marken Cl SO31 316 E3
Market Bldgs SO16 267 D4
Market Cl BH15 390 C2
Market La SO23 403 E5
Market Par PO9 323 F1
Market Pl
19 Southampton
SO14 291 A3
5 Newbury RG14 1 E3
Basingstoke RG21 69 B4
Fordingbridge SP6 257 F1

Market Pl *continued*
Ringwood BH24 . . . . . **328** F7
Romsey SO51 . . . . . **240** E2
Market Sq **8** GU34. . **139** F3
Market St
Alton GU34 . . . . **139** F3
Eastleigh SO50 . . . . . **244** B1
Eastleigh SO50 . . . . . **244** B2
Newbury RG14 . . . .**1** E2
Poole BH15 . . . . **390** B2
Winchester SO23 . . . . **403** E5
Marketway PO1. . . . . **404** B4
Market Way BH21. . . . **351** E4
Markham Ave BH10 . . **377** D7
Markham Cl BH10. . . **377** D6
Markham Ct GU15 . . . . .**36** B6
Markham Rd BH9 . . . **393** A8
Mark La **3** RG21. . . . . . .**69** B4
Mark's La BH25 . . . . **383** A6
Markson Rd SO21. . . **153** C4
Marks Rd BH9 . . . . . **377** F3
Mark's Rd PO14 . . . . **367** E7
Marks Terr SO32 . . . . **271** B8
Marks Tey Rd PO14 . **342** C5
Mark Way SO51 . . . . **191** D3
Markway Cl PO10 . . . **324** D1
Mark Way Sch The
SP10 . . . . **106** C8
Marlands Lawn PO9. **323** C6
Marlands Sh Ctr
SO14. . . . . **290** F4
Marlborough Cl
Fleet GU51 . . . .**75** D8
Waterlooville PO7 . . . **322** D5
Marlborough Ct
15 Gosport PO12 . . **369** C9
30 Bournemouth BH4 **392** C2
3 Wimborne Minster
BH21 . . . . **351** C5
Chandler's Ford SO53 **243** A4
Hythe SO45 . . . . **313** E2
Marlborough Gdns
Hedge End SO30 . . . . **269** C3
Oakley RG23 . . . .**67** B2
Marlborough Gr
PO16 . . . . **344** C7
Marlborough Ho
3 Highfield SO17. . . **267** A1
Southampton SO15 . . **290** F8
Marlborough Inf Sch
GU11. . . . .**77** A7
Marlborough Mans **2**
BH7 . . . . **394** B6
Marlborough Pines **25**
BH4 . . . . **392** C3
Marlborough Pk
PO9 . . . . **324** C3
Marlborough Pl
Lymington SO41 . . . . **385** D5
Wimborne Minster
BH21 . . . . **351** D5
Marlborough Rd
Bournemouth BH4 . . . **392** C3
Chandler's Ford SO53 **218** F1
Gosport PO12 . . . . . . **368** F6
Poole BH14 . . . . **391** C4
Southampton SO15,
SO16. . . . . **290** B8
Marlborough Rise
GU15 . . . .**36** C6
Marlborough Row
PO1. . . . . **370** A6
Marlborough St
SP10 . . . . **106** A8
Marlborough Trad Mews
RG24. . . . .**48** D2
Marlborough View
GU14 . . . .**55** A5
Marldell Cl PO9. . . . . **324** A5
Marler Ho **9** BH4 . . . **392** B4
Marles Cl PO13 . . . . **368** D8
Marley Ave BH25. . . . **382** F3
Marley Cl BH25 . . . . **382** F3
Marley Combe Rd
GU27 . . . . **189** D4
Marley Hanger GU27 **189** E3
Marley La GU27 . . . . **189** D3
Marley Mount SO41 . **359** E1
Marlhill Cl SO18 . . . . **267** F2
Marlin Cl PO13 . . . . . **368** D6
Marline Rd BH12. . . . **391** D6
Marl La SP6 . . . . **257** D2
Marlott Rd BH15 . . . **390** C5
Marlow Cl PO15. . . . **318** E4
Marlow Dr BH23 . . . . **379** E3
Marlowe Cl RG24 . . . . .**69** C4
Marlowe Ct
Southampton SO19 . . **291** F1
Waterlooville PO7 . . . **299** D1
Marlowes The RG14. . . .**5** D7
Marlow Rd SO32 . . . . **271** A8
Marlpit Dr BH23 . . . . **382** A2
Marlpit La BH25 . . . . **383** A8
Marl's La RG24 . . . .**48** B4
Marls Rd SO30. . . . . . **293** E2
Marmion Ave PO5. . . **370** D2
Marmion Gn BH23 . . **395** F7
Marmion Rd PO5 . . . **370** D2
Marne Ho **8** PO14 . . **342** E8
Marnel Inf & Jun Schs
RG24. . . . .**48** C1
Marne Rd SO18 . . . . **292** A4
Marnhull Rd PO14 . . **390** D4
Marnhull Rise SO22 . **403** A5
Marpet Cl BH11 . . . . **376** F6
Marples Way PO9. . . **323** D1
Marquis Way BH11 . . **376** D5
Marram Cl SO41 . . . **385** E5

Marrelswood Gdns
PO7 . . . . **322** C4
Marrowbrook Cl
GU14 . . . .**55** E4
Marrowbrook La
GU14 . . . .**55** E3
Marrow Meade GU51. .**53** E3
Marryat Ct
Christchurch BH23 . . **397** B7
New Milton BH25 . . . **382** F3
Marryat Rd BH25. . . . **382** F3
Marsden Ct RG28 . . . . .**87** C6
Marsden Rd PO6. . . . **345** B8
Marshal Cl GU34 . . . . **139** E2
Marshall Cl GU43 . . . . . .**7** A1
Marshall Ct **10** SO15. **290** F8
Marshall Dr SO30 . . . **268** F1
Marshall Gdns RG21. . .**69** B7
Marshall Pl **1** SO16. **266** E3
Marshall Rd
Sandhurst GU47 . . . . . .**35** C6
South Hayling PO11. . **373** C2
Marshalls Cl RG14 . . . . .**1** B5
Marshalls St GU9 . . . **121** F8
Marshall Sq
13 Andover SP10 . . . .**83** C2
Southampton SO15 . . **290** F8
Marshal Rd BH17 . . . **375** B1
Marsh Cl
Bordon GU35. . . . . . . **164** F3
Cosham PO6 . . . . **346** C6
Marshcourt RG24 . . . . .**69** F8
Marsh Farm Bsns Ctr
GU10. . . . .**74** D1
Marshfield BH21 . . . . **351** F7
Marshfield SO18 . . . . **289** D1
Marshfield Ho PO6. . . **346** C7
Marsh Gdns SO30 . . . **269** C2
Marsh Ho **8** SO14 . . **291** A3
Marsh La
Breamore SP6. . . . . . **258** A8
Christchurch BH23 . . **379** F2
Eversley Cross RG27. . .**33** D7
Fawley SO45 . . . . . . **339** B4
Lymington SO41 . . . . **385** E5
Newbury RG14 . . . .**1** E3
Southampton SO14 . . **291** B3
Upton BH16. . . . . . . **389** A7
Marshlands Cl BH23. . **395** D6
Marshlands Rd PO6 . . **346** D7
Marshlands Spur
PO6 . . . . **346** E7
Mars Ho **10** RG7. . . . . . .**9** C2
Marsh Par SO45 . . . . **314** A4
Marsh The SO45 . . . . **314** A4
Marshwood Ave
Poole BH17 . . . . **375** F3
Waterlooville PO7. . . **323** A7
Marston Cl BH25. . . . **383** B5
Marston Dr
Farnborough GU14 . . . .**55** F7
Newbury RG14 . . . .**2** B5
Marston Gate **6**
SO23 . . . . **403** E6
Marston Gr BH23 . . . **381** E1
Marston La PO3. . . . . **346** B4
Marston Rd
Farnham GU9 . . . .**98** D2
New Milton BH25 . . . **383** B6
Poole BH15 . . . . **390** B2
Southampton SO19 . . **292** E5
Marsum Cl SP10 . . . . . .**82** F4
Martello Cl PO12 . . . **368** D3
Martello Ho **5** BH13 **402** F8
Martello Pk BH13 . . . **402** F7
Martello Rd BH13 . . . **391** F1
Martello Rd S BH13 . . **402** F8
Martello Twrs BH13 . . **402** F7
Martells Ct **1** PO1. . . **370** A4
Martells The BH25 . . **398** B7
Martin Ave
Denmead PO7 . . . . . . **299** A4
Stubbington PO14 . . . **367** D7
Martin Cl
Basingstoke RG21. . . . .**69** C7
Broadstone BH17 . . . **389** F8
Lee-on-t-S PO13 . . . . **367** F4
Swanmore SO32 . . . . **272** B4
Martindale Ave
BH21 . . . . **352** B5
Martindale Terr **1**
SO16 . . . . **289** E7
**Martin Down National
Nature Reserve** ★ SP5,
SP6. . . . . **230** C3
Martingale Chase
RG14 . . . .**2** A4
Martingale Cl BH16 . **389** D7
Martingale Ct **8**
GU11. . . . .**76** C2
Martin Rd
Havant PO9 . . . . **324** A4
Portsmouth PO3 . . . . **371** C4
Stubbington PO14 . . . **367** D7
Martins Cl
Alton GU34 . . . . **140** A5
Blackwater GU17 . . . . .**35** B4
Ferndown BH22. . . . . **353** E7
Portsmouth PO4 . . . . **371** A3
Southampton SO19 . . **292** A3
Martins Dr BH22 . . . . **353** E7
Martins Fields SO21. **197** C1
Martins Hill Cl BH23 **380** C1
Martins Hill La BH23 **380** C1
Martins La SO20 . . . . **129** C2
Martins Pk GU14 . . . . .**55** B7
Martin's Rd SO32 . . . **271** B7
Martins Rise SP5 . . . **212** A3
Martin St SO32 . . . . **271** B7
Martins The SO50 . . . **245** D1

Martins Way BH22 . . **353** E7
Martins Wood RG24. . .**48** F3
Martin Way
Andover SP10 . . . .**83** B2
Frimley GU16. . . . .**36** C2
Martlet Cl PO13 . . . . **368** A5
Martley Gdns SO30. . **269** D2
Marvic Ct PO9 . . . . . . **323** E6
Marvin Cl SO30 . . . . **293** D7
Marvin Way
Hedge End SO30 . . . . **293** D7
Southampton SO18 . . **292** C6
Marwell Cl BH7 . . . . **394** A7
Marwell Rd GU51 . . . . .**53** C4
Marwell Zoological Pk ★
SO21. . . . . **245** A3
Marybridge Cl SO40. . **288** E6
Mary Coombs Ct
PO11 . . . . **373** A3
Marycourt Sch PO12 **369** A2
Maryfield SO14 . . . . **291** B4
Mary La
Newton Valence
GU34 . . . . **183** B8
North Waltham RG25. . .**89** E2
West Moors BH22 . . . **326** D2
Maryland RG40 . . . .**16** C8
Maryland SO18 . . . . . **267** E5
Maryland Ct **3** SO41 **399** B4
Maryland Gdns SO41 **399** B4
Maryland Rd BH16 . . **389** C4
Mary Mitchell Cl
BH24 . . . . **328** F7
Mary Rose ★ PO1 . . . **369** F7
Mary Rose Cl PO15. . **318** E3
Mary Rose St PO21. . . .**68** F4
Mary Rose Mews
GU34 . . . . **140** A5
Mary Rose St The
PO1 . . . . **404** B3
Masdar Gdns RG40. . . .**16** C8
Masefield Ave PO6. . . **320** F1
Masefield Cl SO53 . . **243** F3
Masefield Cres PO8 . **299** F4
Masefield Gn SO19. . **292** D6
Maskell Way GU14 . . . .**55** A3
Mason Cl GU46 . . . .**34** C5
Mason Ct RG20 . . . .**4** D1
Mason Moor Prim Sch
SO16. . . . . **289** F8
Mason Pl GU47 . . . .**34** D8
Mason Rd GU14. . . . . . .**55** C6
Mason Way GU11 . . . . .**99** F7
Masseys La SO42. . . . **363** C7
Masten Cres PO13 . . . **368** C8
Masten Mews RG22 . . .**91** D7
Masters Ct BH4 . . . . **392** D3
Masterson Cl BH23. . **395** D7
Matapan Rd PO2. . . . **345** E4
Matchams Cl BH24. . **355** B7
Matchams La BH24. . **355** B4
Matheson Rd SO16. . **266** A5
Mathews Cl GU14 . . . .**77** B8
Mathew Terr GU11. . . .**77** A2
Mathias Wlk RG22 . . . .**91** D7
Matilda Dr RG22 . . . . .**91** B7
Matilda Pl **4** SO23 . . **403** E6
Matley Gdns SO40 . . **288** B7
Matlock Rd BH22 . . . **353** C3
Matthew Rd GU11. . . .**99** C8
Matthews Cl
Havant PO9 . . . . **323** C3
Thatcham RG19 . . . .**2** F4
Matthews La SO42 . . **363** C6
Matthews Pl PO7 . . . **322** E6
Matthews Rd GU15. . . .**36** A8
Matthews Way RG21 . .**67** C1
Mattingley Dr **12**
GU51 . . . .**53** C3
Mattock Way RG24. . . .**48** F3
Maturin Cl SO41 . . . **385** D3
Maultway Cl GU15 . . . .**36** F8
Maultway Cres GU15 . .**36** F8
Maultway N GU15. . . . .**36** F8
Maultway The GU15. . .**36** F8
Maundeville Cres
BH23 . . . . **394** E8
Maundeville Rd
BH23 . . . . **394** E8
Maunsell Way SO30. **269** D2
Maureen Cl BH12 . . . **391** B8
Maurepas Way PO7. . **322** D7
Mauretania Ho **13**
SO14 . . . . **291** C6
Mauretania Rd SO16 **265** B4
Maurice Rd
Bournemouth BH8. . . **393** D8
Portsmouth PO4 . . . . **371** C4
Maury's La SO51 . . . **238** D4
Mavins Rd GU9 . . . . . **122** B8
Mavis Cres PO9 . . . . **323** F2
Mavis Rd BH9 . . . . . . **378** B1
Maw Cl RG22 . . . .**91** F8
Maxstoke Cl PO5. . . . **404** C3
Maxwell Rd
Bournemouth BH9 . . **393** D8
Broadstone BH18 . . . **374** E3
Poole BH13 . . . . **402** F7
Portsmouth PO4 . . . . **371** A3
Southampton SO19 . . **292** A3
May Ave SO41 . . . . . **385** D5
Maybray King Way SO18,
SO19 . . . . **292** A7
Maybrook SO40 . . . . . .**48** F4
Maybury Cl GU16 . . . . .**56** B8
Maybush Ct **2** SO16 **266** A1
May Bush La SO32 . . **273** B1

Maybush Rd SO16. . . **265** F2
May Cl
Headley SO45 . . . . . . **165** D4
Holbury SO45 . . . . . . **338** D3
Old Basing RG24 . . . . . .**70** C6
Sandhurst GU47 . . . . . .**35** B8
May Copse SO45 . . . . **338** D3
May Cres
Ash GU12. . . . .**77** C1
Holbury SO45 . . . . . . **338** D3
Maycroft Ct **4** SO15 **290** F8
Mayday Ct SO40 . . . . **289** A7
Maydman Sq PO3 . . . **371** A6
Mayfair BH4 . . . . **392** C2
Mayfair Ct
Botley SO30. . . . . . . **294** A7
Fleet GU51 . . . .**53** D4
Poole BH13 . . . . **392** B2
Mayfair Dr RG14 . . . . . .**1** C1
Mayfair Gdns
Bournemouth BH11. . **377** A4
Southampton SO15 . . **290** F7
Mayfair Ho **10** RG21 . .**69** B5
Mayfield
Lee-on-t-S PO13 . . . . **367** E2
Rowledge GU10. . . . . **121** D3
Mayfield Ave
Poole BH14 . . . . **391** E3
Totton SO40. . . . . . . **288** F4
Mayfield Ave Ind Pk
SP11 . . . .**81** A2
Mayfield Cl
Farnham GU9 . . . .**99** F6
Ferndown BH22. . . . . **353** C6
Shipton Bellinger SP9 **101** D7
Stubbington PO14 . . . **367** D8
Mayfield Ct RG27 . . . . .**33** E8
Mayfield Dr BH22 . . . **353** C6
Mayfield Rd
Bournemouth BH9 . . . **378** A2
Camberley GU15 . . . . . .**35** F1
Farnborough GU14 . . . .**55** D6
Gosport PO12 . . . . . . **369** C4
Portsmouth PO2 . . . . **345** F2
Southampton SO17 . . **267** C3
Mayfield Ridge RG22 . .**91** C5
Mayfield Sch PO2. . . **345** F2
Mayfield Way BH22 . . **353** C6
Mayflower Cl
Chandler's Ford
SO53 . . . . **243** C6
Chineham RG24 . . . . . .**48** E2
Lymington SO41 . . . . **386** A2
Stubbington PO14 . . . **367** C6
Mayflower Ct
10 Southampton
SO16. . . . . **290** B8
7 Southampton,Banister's
Park SO15 . . . . . . **290** F7
Mayflower Dr
Portsmouth PO4 . . . . **371** C5
Yateley GU46. . . . .**33** F7
Mayflower Rd
Bordon GU35. . . . . . . **164** C1
Southampton SO15 . . **290** B8
Mayflowers The
SO16 . . . . **267** A4
Mayfly Cl SP6. . . . . . **257** F2
Mayford Rd BH12 . . . **392** B6
May Gdns
Bournemouth BH11. . **376** A4
Walkford BH23 . . . . . **382** B2
Mayhall Rd PO3. . . . . **346** A1
Mayhill Jun Sch RG29 **72** D2
Mayhill La SO32. . . . . **272** E8
May La SO41 . . . . **362** A1
Maylands Ave PO4 . . **371** A5
Maylands Rd PO9 . . . **323** D2
Mayles Cl PO17 . . . . . **296** A3
Mayles Cnr PO17. . . . **318** D8
Mayles La
Knowle Village
PO17 . . . . **318** E8
Wickham PO17 . . . . . **295** F1
Mayles Rd PO4 . . . . . **371** B5
Maylings Farm Rd
PO16 . . . . **318** F3
Maylyn Rd BH16 . . . . **374** A2
Maynard Pl PO13 . . . **343** C4
Maynard Pl PO8 . . . . **300** B7
Maynard Rd SO40 . . . **288** F7
Maynard's Wood
RG24 . . . .**48** E2
Mayo Cl PO1. . . . . . . **370** D7
Mayors La RG14 . . . .**1** E2
May Pl RG21. . . . .**69** B4
Maypole Villas SO50 **244** B8
May Rd SO15 . . . . . . **290** C7
Mayridge PO14 . . . . **317** C3
Mays Firs SP6 . . . . . **235** F2
Mays La PO14. . . . . . **342** C4
May's La RG7 . . . .**10** E7
May St RG21. . . . .**68** F5
Mays Yd PO8 . . . . . . **300** C8
Maytree Cl
Fair Oak SO50 . . . . . **245** D2
Locks Heath SO31. . . **317** A3
May Tree Cl SO22 . . . **403** A2
Maytree Gdns PO8 . . **299** E3
Maytree Inf Sch
SO14. . . . . **291** B6
Maytree Rd
5 Fareham PO16. . **319** A1
Chandler's Ford
SO53 . . . . **218** D2
Southampton SO18 . . **292** A4
Waterlooville PO8 . . . **299** E3

May Tree Rd SP10 . . . .**82** D1
Mayvale Cl SO40 . . . . **289** F7
Mayville High Sch
PO5. . . . . **370** D2
Maywood Dr GU15 . . . .**36** E7
Meacher Cl SO40 . . . . **288** E8
Mead Cl
Andover SP10 . . . . . . **105** F7
Broadstone BH18 . . . **375** A1
Romsey SO51 . . . . . . **241** B7
Mead Cres SO18 . . . . **267** D3
Meadcrest Wood
SO42 . . . . **333** D1
Mead Ct
Chandler's Ford
SO53 . . . . **243** C6
Southampton SO16 . . **266** A3
Meadend Cl PO9. . . . **324** B5
Mead End Rd
Denmead PO7 . . . . . . **299** A3
Sway SO41 . . . . **359** F2
Meade Rd SP11. . . . . . .**57** A2
Mead Gdns RG27. . . . . .**52** B7
Meadham La RG26 . . . . .**44** E4
Mead Hedges SP10 . . **105** E6
Mead Hedges Footpath
SP10 . . . . **105** F7
Mead La GU9 . . . .**98** F2
Meadow Ave
Fordingbridge SP6. . . **257** E2
Locks Heath SO31. . . **317** A4
Meadowbank
Sparsholt SO21 . . . . **174** A5
Upton BH16. . . . . . . **389** C8
Meadow Bank GU9. . . .**98** E1
Meadowbank Rd
SO16 . . . . **266** A3
Meadow Cl
Ash Vale GU12. . . . . . .**56** D1
Blackwater GU17 . . . . .**35** B4
Bransgore BH23 . . . . **381** A8
Burley BH24 . . . . **330** F2
Ferndown BH22. . . . . **353** C6
Fordingbridge SP6. . . **257** E2
Liphook GU30 . . . . . . **188** A4
New Alresford SO24 . . **179** D5
North Baddesley
SO52. . . . . **242** A3
Ringwood BH24 . . . . **329** B8
Sopley BH23 . . . . **380** B7
Stoke PO11 . . . . **347** F3
Totton SO40. . . . . . . **288** F5
Waltham Chase SO32 **271** E4
West End SO30 . . . . . **268** C2
Meadow Court Cl
BH9 . . . . **378** A3
Meadowcroft Cl
SO21 . . . . **219** C3
Meadow Ct
2 Bournemouth
BH9 . . . . **378** A3
2 Emsworth PO10. . **348** F8
3 Wimborne Minster
BH21 . . . . **351** D4
7 Fleet GU51. . . . . . .**53** F1
Farnborough GU14 . . . .**55** D4
Fordingbridge SP6. . . **257** E2
Verwood BH31. . . . . . **303** A4
Whiteparish SP5 . . . . **212** C4
Meadow Dr SP11 . . . . **127** F8
Meadow Edge PO7. . . **322** B2
Meadow End GU30. . . **188** A5
Meadow Farm La
BH21 . . . . **374** D8
Meadow Gate Ave
GU14 . . . .**55** D2
Meadow Gdns SO32. **271** E4
Meadow Gr
Chandler's Ford
SO53 . . . . **243** C6
Verwood BH31. . . . . . **303** D5
Meadowhead Rd
SO16 . . . . **266** F3
Meadow Hts **7**
SP10 . . . . **106** B8
Meadow La
Burton BH23 . . . . . . **380** C5
Eastleigh SO50 . . . . **244** A2
Hamble-le-R SO31. . . **316** A2
Hartley Wintney RG27. .**52** C6
Meadowland
Chineham RG24 . . . . . .**48** B3
Christchurch BH23 . . **395** F6
Kings Worthy SO23 . . **176** B3
Meadowlands
Havant PO9 . . . . **324** A1
Lymington SO41 . . . . **385** C4
Ringwood BH24 . . . . **329** A4
Rowlands Castle PO9 **301** C3
**Meadowlands Jun & Inf
Schs** PO8. . . . . . . **299** E5
Meadowmead Ave
SO15 . . . . **290** A4
Meadow Rd
Basingstoke RG21. . . . .**69** A4
Farnborough GU14 . . . .**55** F7
Lymington SO41 . . . . **385** C2
Newbury RG14 . . . .**5** D8
New Milton BH25 . . . **383** B4
Ringwood BH24. . . . . **329** B6
Meadowridge RG22 . . . .**91** C6
Meadow Rise
Corfe Mullen BH18 . . **374** F5
North Waltham RG25. . .**89** F1
Waterlooville PO8 . . . **300** B3

Meadows Bsns Pk The
GU17. . . . .**35** C5
Meadow Sch The
GU35. . . . . **165** A4
Meadows Cl BH16. . . **389** C7
Meadows Dr BH16 . . **389** C7
Meadowside Cl
SO18 . . . . **267** E4
Meadows Sh Ctr The
GU47. . . . .**35** C5
Meadow St PO5. . . . . **404** A2
Meadows The
Ash GU12. . . . .**77** F2
Churt GU10 . . . . **144** D1
Fareham PO16. . . . . . **319** C3
Lyndhurst SO43 . . . . **310** A4
Waterlooville PO7 . . . **322** C8
Meadowsweet PO7 . . **300** C1
Meadowsweet Rd
BH17 . . . . **389** E8
Meadowsweet Way
Horton Heath SO50. . **269** C6
Portsmouth PO6 . . . . **321** D1
Meadow Terr **1**
PO16 . . . . **319** A1
Meadow The
Denmead PO7 . . . . . . **298** F4
Romsey SO51 . . . . . . **215** F1
Sherfield on L RG27 . . .**29** A4
Meadow Vale GU27 . . **189** E6
Meadowview SO21. . . **174** A5
Meadow View
Bordon GU35. . . . . . . **164** E3
Crookham Village
GU52 . . . .**74** E5
Micheldever SO21. . . **133** B3
Ropley SO24 . . . . . . **181** C5
Whitchurch RG28 . . . . .**86** B5
Meadowview Cl SP11 **79** D6
Meadow View Rd
BH11 . . . . **376** E4
Meadow Way
Aldershot GU12. . . . . . .**77** D3
Andover SP10 . . . . . . **105** D8
Barton on S BH25 . . . **398** A7
Blackwater GU17 . . . . .**35** A5
Fawley SO45 . . . . . . **339** B3
Liphook GU30 . . . . . . **188** A5
Ringwood BH24 . . . . **329** B8
Rowledge GU10. . . . . **121** D3
Verwood BH31. . . . . . **303** B5
Winchester SO22 . . . **403** A2
Meadow Wlk
1 Liss GU33. . . . . . **207** F4
Fleet GU51. . . . .**74** D7
Gosport PO13 . . . . . . **343** B5
Portsmouth PO1 . . . . **404** B4
Mead Park Sq SO20 . **126** B4
Mead Rd
Andover SP10 . . . . . . **105** F7
Chandler's Ford SO53 **243** C6
Hindhead GU26 . . . . **167** D4
Lymington SO41 . . . . **385** B2
Winchester SO23 . . . **403** C2
Meads The
Chandler's Ford
SO53 . . . . **243** A5
Haslemere GU27 . . . **189** D6
Romsey SO51 . . . . . . **240** D7
Meadsview Ct **4**
GU14 . . . .**55** F4
Mead The
Farnborough GU14 . . . .**55** F3
Gosport PO13 . . . . . . **343** B3
Hythe SO45 . . . . **313** F3
Liphook GU30 . . . . . . **187** F5
Liss GU33 . . . . **207** F4
Old Basing RG24 . . . . . .**70** B6
Petersfield GU32. . . . **228** D2
Meadway
Frimley GU16. . . . .**36** C2
Haslemere GU27 . . . **189** D6
Waterlooville PO7 . . . **300** A1
Mead Way PO16 . . . . **319** B3
Meadway The BH23 . . **381** D2
Mears Rd SO50 . . . . . **245** D1
Measures Gate SO21 **132** B3
Meath Cl PO11. . . . . . **373** C1
Mede Cl RG25 . . . .**88** B7
Medina Cl SO53. . . . . **243** E5
Medina Ct
27 Andover SP10 . . . .**83** C2
Lee-on-t-S PO13 . . . . **367** D4
Medina Gdns RG23 . . . .**67** B1
Medina Ho PO16 . . . . **343** A7
Medina Prim Sch
PO6. . . . . **345** E7
Medina Rd
Cosham PO6 . . . . **345** E8
Southampton SO15 . . **266** B1
Medina Way BH23 . . **396** C6
Medlar Cl
1 Hedge End
SO30. . . . . **293** D6
Burton BH23 . . . . . . **380** D1
Medlar Dr GU17. . . . . . .**35** D3
Medley Pl SO15 . . . . **290** A7
Medlicott Way SO32 **272** A4
Medonte Cl GU52 . . . . .**75** B8
Medstead CE Prim Sch
GU34. . . . . **159** F6
Medstead Dr **8** GU51 **53** D3
**Medstead & Four Marks
Sta** GU34 . . . . **160** B3

Medstead Rd
Beech GU34. . . . . . . **139** A2
Havant PO9. . . . . **323** F3
Medwall Gn SO19. . . . **292** D5
Medway Ave RG23 . . . **67** B2
Medway Cl RG18. . . . . **2** F5
Medway Ct
15 Basingstoke
RG21 . . . . **69** D5
29 Andover SP10 . . . **83** C2
Medway Dr
Chandler's Ford
SO53. . . . . **243** A8
Farnborough GU14 . . . **55** C7
Medway Rd BH22 . . . . **354** A6
Meerut Rd
Brockenhurst SO42 . . . **333** F2
North Tidworth SP9 . . . **78** E6
Meeting House La
BH24 . . . . **328** F7
Megana Way SO51 . . . **216** C5
Megan Ct 7 PO6 . . . . . **345** F7
Megan Rd SO30. . . . . . **268** D2
Meggeson Ave SO18 **268** A2
Megson Dr PO13. . . . . . **368** A6
Meitner Cl RG26 . . . . . . **28** F4
Melbourne Gdns 6
SO30 . . . . **293** C6
Melbourne Ho PO1. . . **404** B3
Melbourne Pl PO5 . . . . **404** B2
Melbourne Rd
5 Hedge End
SO30. . . . . **293** C6
Bournemouth BH8. . . . **393** C6
Christchurch BH23 . . . **379** E1
Melbourne St SO14 . . . **291** B4
Melbury Ave BH12 . . . **391** E7
Melbury Cl
Ferndown BH22 . . . . . **353** D4
Lymington SO41 . . . . . **385** D3
Melbury Ct 12 SO17 . . **267** A1
Melchet Cl SO51 . . . . . **213** B1
Melchet Ct GU51. . . . . . **53** C4
Melchet Rd SO18 . . . **292** C8
Meldrum Cl RG14 . . . . . **5** A6
Melford Ct BH1 . . . . **393** A3
Melford Gdns RG22 . . . **68** A2
Melick Cl SO40 . . . . **289** F2
Meliot Rise SO51 . . . . . . **83** A4
Melksham Ho 1 SP9 . **78** F6
Mellersh Cl GU52. . . . . **74** E4
Mellor Cl 1 PO6 . . . . . **345** D8
Mellstock Rd BH15 . . . **390** D5
Melrose Ave GU14 . . . . **55** A4
Melrose Cl
Bordon GU35. . . . . **164** D2
Portsmouth PO4 . . . . . **371** B4
Melrose Ct
New Milton BH25 . . . . **383** C3
Totton SO40. . . . . **264** C1
Melrose Gdns PO12 . . . **368** F7
Melrose Rd SO15 . . . . . **266** D2
Melrose Wlk RG24 . . . . **69** A8
Melton Ct BH13 . . . . . . **391** F4
Melverley Gdns
BH21 . . . . **351** D5
Melville Ave GU16. . . . . **36** D1
Melville Cl SO16 . . . . . **266** C5
Melville Rd
Bournemouth BH9. . . . **392** C6
Gosport PO12 . . . . . . **369** B8
Portsmouth PO4 . . . . . **371** D3
Melville Terr 1 GU9 . . **98** F2
Melvin Jones Ho
PO14 . . . . **342** C4
Membury Cl GU16. . . . . **56** E7
Memorial Bglws PO15 . **385** E5
Memorial Rd RG27 . . . . **72** A8
Mendip Cl
Basingstoke RG22. . . . **68** A3
New Milton BH25 . . . **383** B2
Verwood BH31. . . . . . **302** F5
Mendip Ct 4 BH23 . . . **395** F8
Mendip Gdns SO45. . . **313** D2
Mendip Rd
Farnborough GU14 . . . **55** C7
Southampton SO16 . . . **289** F8
Verwood BH31. . . . . . **302** F6
Mendips Rd PO14 . . . . **342** E8
Mendips Wlk PO14. . . **342** D8
Mengham Ave PO11. . . **373** A3
Mengham Ct PO11 . . . **373** B3
Mengham Inf Sch
PO11. . . . . **373** A4
Mengham Jun Sch
PO11. . . . . **373** A4
Mengham La PO11. . . . **373** A3
Mengham Rd PO11. . . . **373** A3
Menin Ho PO15 . . . . . . **318** C2
Menin Way GU9. . . . . . . **99** B1
Menslands La
Hambledon PO7. . . . . **274** B1
Soberton PO7 . . . . . . **297** F8
Mentone Rd 2
BH14 . . . . **391** A4
Menzies Cl SO16. . . . . **265** F5
Meon Cl
Clanfield PO8. . . . . . . **276** D4
Farnborough GU14 . . . **55** B6
Gosport PO13 . . . . . . **369** A8
Pamber Heath RG26 . . . **9** E1
Petersfield GU32. . . . . **228** E4
Romsey SO51 . . . . . . **241** C7
Meon Cres SO53 . . . **243** D5

Meoncross Sch
PO14. . . . . **342** D4
Meon Gdns SO32. . . . **272** B5
Meon Ho
Fareham PO16. . . . . . . **343** A7
Winchester SO23 . . . **403** F4
Meon Jun & Inf Schs
PO4. . . . . **371** B4
Meon Rd
Bournemouth BH7. . . . **394** B7
Oakley RG23 . . . . **67** B1
Portsmouth PO4 . . . . . **371** B5
Romsey SO51 . . . . . . **241** C7
Meon Shore Chalets
PO14 . . . . **341** D2
Meonside CE Inf Sch
SO32. . . . . **249** C4
Meonstoke CE Inf Sch
SO32. . . . . **249** C4
Meonwara Cres
GU32. . . . . **225** D5
Meon Wlk RG21 . . . . . . **69** C5
Mercer Cl RG22. . . . . . . **68** C4
Mercer Way SO51. . . . **241** A8
Merchants Pl 19
SO23 . . . . **403** E6
Merchants Row 6
PO1. . . . . **370** A3
Merchants Wlk 18
SO14 . . . . **290** F3
Merchistoun Rd
PO8 . . . . **300** C7
Mercia Ave SP10 . . . . . **82** D3
Mercury Cl
Bordon GU35. . . . . **164** E3
Southampton SO16 . . . **265** F4
Mercury Gdns SO31 . . **316** A4
Mercury Ho RG7 . . . . . . **9** C2
Mercury Pl PO7. . . . . . **322** E2
Merdon Ave SO53. . . . **243** D8
Merdon Cl SO53 . . . . . **243** D8
Merdon Ct SO53 . . . . . **243** D7
Merdon Jun Sch
SO53. . . . . **243** D7
Mere Croft PO15 . . . . **317** D3
Meredith Cl BH23 . . . . **395** D7
Meredith Gdns SO40 **288** D6
Meredith Inf Sch
PO2. . . . . **370** E8
Meredith Lodge 5
PO7 . . . . **323** A7
Meredith Rd PO2 . . . . **345** E3
Meredun Cl SO21 . . . . **218** B7
Merepond La GU34. . . **204** F3
Merganser Cl PO12 . . **369** B8
Meriden Cl BH13. . . . . **405** A2
Meriden Ct 11 SO23 . . **403** E8
Meriden Rd PO5 . . . . . **404** A2
Meridian Ctr 12 PO9 **323** F1
Meridians The BH23 **394** F6
Merino Way BH21. . . . **326** F1
Merivale GU51. . . . . **74** D8
Merlewood Cl BH2. . . **392** F4
Merlewood Ct 9
BH25 . . . . **383** B3
Merley Court Touring Pk
BH21 . . . . **351** C1
Merley Dr BH23. . . . . . **397** A8
Merley Fst Sch
BH21. . . . . **351** C1
Merley Gdns BH21 . . . **351** C1
Merley Ho BH21 . . . . . **351** B1
Merley House Holiday Pk
BH21 . . . . **351** B1
Merley House La
BH21 . . . . **351** C1
Merley La BH21 . . . . . . **351** E1
Merley Park Rd
Ashington BH21. . . . . **375** B8
Corfe Mullen BH21 . . **374** F8
Merley BH21 . . . . **351** C1
Merley Ways BH21 . . . **351** D2
Merlin Cl
Bishop's Waltham
SO32. . . . . **271** B8
Ringwood BH24 . . . . . **329** C6
Waterlooville PO8 . . . **299** E4
Merlin Cotts SO45 . . . **339** B3
Merlin Court Flats
GU34 . . . . **160** B2
Merlin Ct GU16 . . . . . . **36** B1
Merlin Dr PO3 . . . . **346** A4
Merlin Gdns
Hedge End SO30 . . . . **293** B7
Portchester PO16 . . . . **320** B1
Merlin Lodge SO19. . . **291** D3
Merlin Mead RG22 . . . . **90** F6
Merlin Mews 4
SO32 . . . . **271** C2
Merlin Rd
Farnborough GU14 . . . **55** F2
Four Marks GU34 . . . . **160** B2
Merlins Cl GU9 . . . . **99** A1
Merlin Way
Chandler's Ford
SO53. . . . . **242** F7
Christchurch BH23 . . . **396** A5
Farnborough GU14 . . . **55** B3
Mermaid Cl 3 BH5 . . . **393** E3
Mermaid Rd PO16. . . . **342** F5
Mermaid Way SO14 . . **291** B2
Merriatt Cl RG21. . . . . . **69** B2
Merrick Way SO53. . . . **243** A8
Merridale Rd SO19. . . . **291** E5
Merriefield Ave
BH18 . . . . **375** B5
Merriefield Cl BH18. . . **375** B6

Merriefield Dr BH18. . **375** B6
Merrieleas Cl SO53. . . **243** C7
Merrieleas Dr SO53. . . **243** C7
Merriemeade Cl 2
SO45. . . . . **313** E1
Merriemeade Par 1
SO45. . . . . **313** E1
Merrifield
Chineham RG24. . . . . . **48** E3
Locks Heath PO14 . . . **317** C4
Merrifield Ave PO9 . . **323** D5
Merrifield Cl
Bransgore BH23 . . . . . **381** A8
Verwood BH31. . . . . . **302** F6
Merrifield Ct BH10. . . . **377** C4
Merrifield La BH10 . . . **377** C4
Merrifield Rd GU31 . . . **229** B4
Merry Gdns SO52 . . . . **242** A5
Merryoak Gn SO19. . . **291** F5
Merryoak Rd SO19 . . . **291** F5
Merrytree Cl SO51. . . . **238** E3
Merryweather Est
BH24 . . . . **329** C8
Merrywood Pk GU15. . . **36** D4
Merryworth Cl GU12 . **77** D1
Mersea Gdns SO19. . . **292** A4
Mersey Cl 33 SP10 . . . **83** C2
Mersey Way RG18. . . . . **2** F5
Mersham Gdns
SO18 . . . . **292** A7
Merstone Rd PO13 . . . **343** C2
Merthyr Ave PO6. . . . . **346** B8
Merton Ave PO16 . . . . **344** D6
Merton Cl SP6 . . . . **257** F3
Merton Cres PO16 . . . . **344** D6
Merton Ct
2 Christchurch
BH23 . . . . **397** B7
3 Poole BH15 . . . . . **390** B4
3 Portsmouth PO5. . **404** C1
Merton Gr BH24 . . . . . . **328** F8
Merton Inf Sch RG24. . . **69** A8
Merton Jun Sch RG24 **69** A8
Merton Rd
Basingstoke RG21. . . . **69** A6
Portsmouth PO5 . . . . . **404** C1
Southampton SO17 . . . **267** B3
Merville Gdns BH9 . . . **392** F8
Meryl Rd PO4. . . . . **371** C4
Meryon Rd SO24 . . . . . **179** C4
Mesh Pond SP5. . . . . . **234** D7
Mesh Rd SO51 . . . . . . **193** B2
Metcalfe Ave PO14. . . **362** B8
Meteor Rd PO10 . . . . . **349** A3
Meteor Way GU14. . . . . **55** F1
Methuen Cl 2 BH8 . . . **393** C5
Methuen Rd
Bournemouth BH8. . . . **393** B5
Greatham GU33. . . . . **186** C3
Poole BH17 . . . . **375** B2
Portsmouth PO4 . . . . . **371** A3
Methuen St SO14 . . . . **291** A7
Metuchen Way SO30 **293** C4
Meudon Ave GU14 . . . **55** F3
Mews Ct SO21 . . . . **219** B3
Mewsey Ct PO9 . . . . . . **323** D7
Mews La SO22 . . . . **403** C5
Mews The
7 Gosport PO12 . . . **369** E5
3 Farnham GU9. . . . **98** F2
Andover SP10 . . . . . . **106** B6
Blackfield SO45. . . . . **365** F7
Bournemouth BH2 . . . **392** D3
Bramley RG26 . . . . **29** B2
Chandler's Ford SO53 **243** C3
Farley Hill RG7 . . . . . . **15** A7
Havant PO9 . . . . **323** E4
New Alresford SO24 . . **179** C6
Newbury RG14 . . . . **1** C2
Petersfield GU31. . . . . **229** A4
Rownhams SO16. . . . . **265** F6
Southampton SO19 . . . **292** D4
Verwood BH31. . . . . . **303** A4
Mey Cl PO7. . . . . **323** A7
Meynell Cl SO50 . . . . . **243** F3
Meyrick Cl BH23 . . . . . **381** A7
Meyrick Dr RG14. . . . . . **5** A5
Meyrick Ho 1 PO2. . . . **345** C1
Meyrick Park Cres
BH3 . . . . **392** F6
Meyrick Park Mans 7
BH2 . . . . **392** F4
Meyrick Rd
Bournemouth BH1. . . . **393** B3
Havant PO9 . . . . **323** D1
Portsmouth PO2 . . . . . **345** C1
Micawber Ho 23
PO1. . . . . **370** D7
Michael Crook Cl
PO9 . . . . **323** C3
Michael Ho SP11. . . . . . **83** B8
Michaelmas Cl GU46 . . **34** B4

Michaelmas Dro SP11 **81** B1
Michaels Way SO50 . . **245** D2
Michael's Way SO45 . **313** F4
Micheldever CE Prim
Sch SO21. . . . . **133** A3
Micheldever Cl RG28. . **86** D3
Micheldever Dr 13
GU51. . . . . **53** C3
Micheldever Gdns
RG28 . . . . **86** D3
Micheldever Rd
Andover SP11 . . . . . . **106** D7
Whitchurch RG28 . . . . **86** E3
Micheldever Sta
SO21 . . . . **111** B2
Michelgrove Rd BH5 **393** E3
Michelmersh Cl
SO16 . . . . **265** E5
Michelmersh Gn
BH8 . . . . **378** D2
Michigan Way SO40. . **288** B8
Mickleham Cl BH12 . . **392** B8
Midanbury Cres
SO18 . . . . **267** F1
Midanbury Ct 9
SO18 . . . . **291** E8
Midanbury La SO18 . . **267** F1
Midanbury Wlk
SO18 . . . . **291** F8
Midas Cl PO7. . . . . **322** F4
Midas Ho 3 RG7. . . . . . . **9** C2
Middle Ave GU9 . . . . . **122** B8
Middlebere Cres
BH16 . . . . **389** C4
Middle Bourne La
GU10 . . . . **122** A7
Middlebridge St
SO51 . . . . **240** E6
Middlebrook 3
SO32 . . . . **271** C8
Middle Brook BH11. . . **377** A6
Middle Brook St
SO23 . . . . **403** E6
Middle Church La 15
GU9 . . . . **98** F2
Middle Cl
Frimley GU15. . . . . **36** F6
Newbury RG14 . . . . **5** B7
Middle Common Rd
SO41 . . . . **385** A3
Middle Conholt SP11 . . **37** F3
Middlecroft La PO12 **368** F6
Middle Cl PO1 . . . . **370** E7
Middlefield GU9 . . . . . **121** E7
Middlefield Cl GU9. . . **121** E8
Middle Gordon Rd
GU15. . . . . **36** B5
Middle Hill GU11. . . . . . **76** E3
Middlehill Dr BH21. . . **352** B6
Middlehill Rd BH21 . . **352** A6
Middle La BH24 . . . . . . **329** A7
Middle Mdw GU33 . . . **208** A4
Middle Mead
Fareham PO14. . . . . . **342** B8
Hook RG27. . . . . **51** A1
Middlemoor Rd
Camberley GU16. . . . . **56** C8
Frimley GU16. . . . . **36** C1
Middle Old Pk GU9. . . **98** D4
Middle Park Way
PO9 . . . . **323** D6
Middle Rd
Bournemouth BH10. . . **377** C5
Locks Heath SO31. . . . **317** B5
Lymington SO41 . . . . . **385** D3
North Baddesley
SO52. . . . . **242** A4
Poole BH15 . . . . **390** E6
Southampton SO19 . . . **292** A4
Sway SO41. . . . . **360** B2
Tiptoe SO41. . . . . **383** E8
Winchester SO22 . . . . **403** C6
Middlesex Rd PO4 . . . **371** B3
Middle St
Portsmouth PO5 . . . . . **404** B2
Southampton SO14 . . . **291** A7
Middleton Cl
Fareham PO14. . . . . . **342** E7
Southampton SO18 . . . **268** A1
Middleton Ct RG14. . . . . **2** C5
Middleton Gdns
Basingstoke RG21. . . . **69** B7
Farnborough GU14 . . . **55** C6
Middleton Mews
Locks Heath SO31. . . . **317** B5
Old Milton BH25 . . . . **382** F1
Middleton Rd
Bournemouth BH9. . . . **377** E2
Camberley GU15 . . . . . **36** D7
Middle Winterslow
SP5. . . . . **168** A6
Ringwood BH24. . . . . **329** A8
Middleton Rise PO8. . **276** D4
Middleton Wlk 1
PO14 . . . . **342** E7
Middle Wallop Airfield
SO20. . . . . **126** A2
Middleway The
SP11 . . . . **107** D6
Midfield Cl PO14 . . . . . **342** F7
Midgham Farm Cotts
SP6. . . . . **281** D6
Mid Hants Railway
Watercress Line★
GU34. . . . . **160** D4

Mid Hants Rly
Watercress Line★
SO24. . . . . **179** E5
Midhurst Ho PO1 . . . . **404** C4
Midhurst Rd
Haslemere GU27. . . . . **189** F5
Liphook GU30 . . . . . . **188** A2
Midland Rd BH9 . . . . . **377** F1
Midlands Est SO30 . . . **268** C1
Midlane Cl RG21 . . . . . . **69** A2
Midlington Barns
SO32 . . . . **273** A7
Midlington Hill
SO32 . . . . **273** A7
Midlington Ho SO32. . **273** A7
Midlington Rd SO32. . **273** B8
Midway SO45 . . . . **313** F3
Midway Path SO31 . . . **402** C3
Midway Rd PO2. . . . . . **345** C3
Midways PO11 . . . . **367** C6
Midwood Ave BH8 . . . **378** F1
Mike Hawthorn Dr
GU9 . . . . **99** A3
Milam Cl RG2. . . . . **15** C8
Milbeck Cl PO8 . . . . . . **300** A3
Milborne Cres BH12. . **391** E8
Milbourne Rd BH22 . . **353** C6
Milburn Cl 3 BH4 . . . . **392** C4
Milburn Rd BH4 . . . . . . **392** B4
Milburns The SO51. . . **215** D7
Milbury Cres SO18 . . . **292** A6
Milbury Ho PO6. . . . . . **321** A2
Milden Cl GU16 . . . . **56** E6
Milden Gdns SO16 . . . . **56** D6
Mildenhall 5 BH2 . . . **392** C2
Mildmay Ct
2 Winchester
SO23. . . . . **403** F5
Odiham RG29 . . . . **72** E3
Mildmay St SO22. . . . **403** B3
Mildmay Terr RG27 . . . **52** D6
Milebush Rd PO4 . . . . **371** C5
Mile End Rd PO2. . . . . **370** C7
Miles Ct
3 Aldershot GU11 . . **76** D1
South Hayling PO11. . . **373** D1
Miles Rd GU12 . . . . **77** F3
Miles's La SP5 . . . . **212** C5
Milestone Point 1
PO9 . . . . **323** F1
Milestone Rd BH15. . . **390** D7
Milestones Living History
Mus★ RG22 . . . . **68** E3
Milford Cl
Havant PO9 . . . . **323** D3
West Moors BH22. . . . **326** F2
Milford Cres SO41 . . . **399** E4
Milford Ct
1 Gosport PO12 . . . **368** D3
4 Portsmouth PO4. . **371** B4
Milford Dr BH11 . . . . . **376** F5
Milford Gdns SO53. . . **243** C6
Milford Ho
Milford on S SO41. . . . **399** E5
Southampton SO19 . . . **292** B6
Winchester SO23 . . . **403** B5
Milford on Sea CE Prim
Sch SO41. . . . . **399** E6
Milford Rd
Barton on S BH25 . . . **398** C7
Lymington SO41 . . . . . **385** C1
Portsmouth PO1 . . . . . **404** C3
Milford Trad Est
SO41 . . . . **399** E4
Military Rd
Fareham PO16. . . . . . **319** D2
Gosport,Alverstoke
PO12 . . . . **369** A2
Gosport,Alverstoke
PO12 . . . . **369** B1
Gosport,Brockhurst
PO12 . . . . **368** E6
Gosport,Clayhall
PO12 . . . . **369** C2
Portsmouth,Hilsea
PO3 . . . . **345** F5
Portsmouth,Landport
PO1 . . . . **370** B7
Milkingpen La RG24. . . **70** B6
Milkwood Ct SO40 . . . **288** C7
Milky Down Back La
BH24 . . . . **329** C2
Millais Rd SO19. . . . . . **291** E3
Milland Cl GU30 . . . . . **209** E5
Milland Rd SO23. . . . . **403** F4
Millard Cl RG21. . . . . . . **68** F7
Millbank Ho
14 Southampton
SO19. . . . . **291** C6
5 Wimborne Minster
BH21 . . . . **351** C5
Millbank St SO14 . . . . **291** C5
Millbridge Gdns
SO19 . . . . **292** B4
Millbridge Rd GU46 . . . **33** F8
Millbrook Cl
Chandler's Ford
SO53. . . . . **243** B5
Liss GU33 . . . . **208** A4
Millbrook Com Sch
SO16. . . . . **265** E3
Millbrook Dr PO9 . . . . **324** A6
Millbrook Flyover
SO15 . . . . **289** E7
Millbrook Point Rd
SO15 . . . . **290** A6

Millbrook Rd W
SO15 . . . . **289** F6
Millbrook Road E
SO15 . . . . **290** D5
Millbrook Road W
SO15 . . . . **290** A6
Millbrook Sta SO15 . . **290** B6
Millbrook Trad Est
SO15 . . . . **289** D7
Mill Chase Com Sch
GU35. . . . . **164** F3
Mill Chase Rd GU35 . . **164** F4
Mill Cl
Denmead PO7 . . . . . . **299** B4
Haslemere GU27. . . . . **189** C6
Nursling SO16 . . . . . . **265** D5
Sherfield on L RG27. . . **29** E1
Stoke PO11 . . . . **347** F2
Mill Cnr GU51 . . . . **54** C4
Mill Copse Rd GU27. . **189** F4
Millcourt SO50. . . . . . . **245** D2
Mill Cross PO7. . . . . . . **299** B4
Mill Ct
4 Southampton
SO17. . . . . **267** C2
Fordingbridge SP6. . . . **257** E1
Milldown Ho RG25 . . . . **88** A7
Mill End
Damerham SP6 . . . . . **256** D4
Emsworth PO10. . . . . **349** B8
Millennium Ct
Basingstoke RG21. . . . **68** F5
Waterlooville PO7 . . . . **322** E5
Millennium Ctr GU9. . . **98** E1
Millennium Sq 11
PO16 . . . . **319** B1
Miller Cl BH25 . . . . **383** C4
Miller Dr PO16. . . . . . . **318** F3
Miller Rd BH23 . . . . . . **395** D7
Millers La SO22 . . . . . **196** F3
Miller's Pond Gdns
SO19 . . . . **291** F3
Millers Quay Ho
PO16 . . . . **343** B8
Millers Rd RG26. . . . . . . **26** F8
Millers Way SO45 . . . . **313** F2
Millers Yd SO21. . . . . . **131** C4
Millfield
New Milton BH25 . . . **382** E3
Poole BH17 . . . . **390** A7
Millgate Ct GU9. . . . . . . **99** B3
Mill Gate Ho 30 PO1. **370** A5
Millgreen La PO7 . . . . . . **7** D3
Mill Hall Sch RG19. . . . . **6** B8
Millhams Cl BH10 . . . . **377** B6
Millhams Dr BH10. . . . **377** B6
Millhams Rd BH10 . . . **377** B6
Millhams St BH23 . . . . **395** B6
Millhams Street N 2
BH23 . . . . **395** B6
Mill Hill
Botley SO30. . . . . **294** B6
New Alresford SO24 . . **179** D6
Mill Hill Ave SP9 . . . . . **78** E8
Mill Hill Cl BH14 . . . . . **391** B3
Mill Ho SO18 . . . . **268** A4
Mill House Bsns Ctr
SO19. . . . . **291** D4
Mill House Ctr SO40 **289** A7
Mill House Lodge
SO50 . . . . **244** C3
Milliken Cl SO45 . . . . . **338** F2
Mill La
Alton GU34 . . . . **140** B4
Bishop's Sutton SO24 **180** A5
Bishopstone SP5 . . . . **210** C8
Brockbridge SO32. . . . **249** C2
Brockenhurst SO42 . . **334** B1
Burley BH24 . . . . **331** C4
Christchurch BH23 . . . **397** B8
Droxford SO32. . . . . . **249** B1
Durley SO32. . . . . **270** C2
Ecchinswell RG20 . . . . **23** E4
Emsworth PO10. . . . . **325** B2
Frensham GU10. . . . . **143** F7
Gosport PO12 . . . . . . **369** B7
Havant,Bedhampton
PO9 . . . . **323** C1
Hawkley GU33 . . . . . . **184** F1
Headley GU35 . . . . . . **165** B5
Hurn BH23 . . . . **379** B6
Kings Worthy SO21 . . **176** D6
Langstone PO9 . . . . . **347** F6
Lindford GU35 . . . . . . **165** A4
Longparish SP11 . . . . **108** C3
Lymington SO41 . . . . . **385** C1
Middle Winterslow
SP5. . . . . **168** B7
Minstead SO43 . . . . . **286** E2
Newbury RG14 . . . . **1** F3
North Warnborough
RG29 . . . . **72** B5
Nursling SO16. . . . . . **264** C4
Petersfield GU32. . . . **229** B6
Poole BH14 . . . . **391** B3
Portsmouth,Landport
PO1 . . . . **370** C7
Portsmouth,Wymering PO6,
PO7 . . . . **321** F3
Romsey SO51 . . . . . . **240** D7
Rotherwick RG27. . . . . **50** C6
Sherfield English
SO51. . . . . **213** E1
South Baddesley
SO41. . . . . **386** F4
Steep Marsh GU32 . . **206** F1
Stratfield Saye RG7,RG27,
RG26 . . . . **29** C4

Mill La continued
Sway SO41 . . . . **384** E7
Titchfield PO15 . . . . . . **318** A2
Wickham PO17 . . . . **296** A5
Wimborne Minster
BH21 . . . . **351** C5
Yateley GU46 . . . . **34** B7
Mill Lane Ind Est
GU34 . . . . **140** B4
Mill Mdw SO41 . . . . . **399** D5
Millmere GU46 . . . . . . **34** B7
Mill Pond Rd PO12 . . **369** B7
Mill Pond The SO45 . **338** B6
Mill Quay PO10 . . . . . **349** A7
Mill Race View SP5 . . **234** F8
Mill Rd
Basingstoke RG24 . . . **68** C8
Christchurch BH23 . . **395** A8
Denmead PO7 . . . . . **299** A4
Fareham PO16 . . . . . **343** A8
Gosport PO12 . . . . . **369** A7
Liss GU33 . . . . **208** A5
Southampton SO15 . . **290** A7
Totton SO40 . . . . . **289** A7
Waterlooville PO7 . . **322** E6
Westbourne PO10 . . **325** B4
Mill Rd N BH8 . . . . . . **378** E3
Mill Rd S BH8 . . . . . . **378** D2
Mill Reef Cl RG19 . . . . **2** E7
Mill Rise SO51 . . . . . . **192** D1
Mill Rythe Inf Sch
PO11 . . . . **373** B6
Mill Rythe Jun Sch
PO11 . . . . **373** B6
Mill Rythe La PO11 . . **373** A7
Mills Ho GU12 . . . . . . **77** B2
Mills Rd PO2 . . . . **345** D1
Mill St
Corfe Mullen BH21 . . **350** A1
Eastleigh SO50 . . . **244** B4
Mills The BH12 . . . . . **391** E7
Mill Stream GU9 . . . . **99** C6
Millstream Cl
Andover SP10 . . . . . **105** F6
Poole BH17 . . . . . . **390** A7
Wimborne Minster
BH21 . . . . **351** C4
Millstream Ho RG14 . . . **2** B3
Millstream Rise
SO51 . . . . **240** D7
Millstream The
BH24 . . . . **329** A5
Mill Vale Mdws
GU30 . . . . **209** F3
Millverton Ct [1]
SO18 . . . . **292** B7
Mill View RG29 . . . . . . **71** F2
Millvina Cl SO40 . . . . **287** F4
Millway SO32 . . . . . . **270** B5
Mill Way SO40 . . . . . . **288** E5
Millway Cl SP10 . . . . . **105** E7
Millway Rd SP10 . . . . **105** E7
Mill Yd The SO16 . . . . **265** C5
Millyford Cl BH25 . . . **397** D8
Milman Ct [12] SO23 . . **403** E6
Milne Cl SO45 . . . . . . **313** C1
Milner Ct SO15 . . . . . **290** C8
Milne Rd BH17 . . . . . **375** B1
Milner Rd PO22 . . . . . **403** C4
Milner Rd BH4 . . . . . . **392** C1
Milnthorpe La SO31 . . **402** D3
Milsons The SO20 . . . **149** F2
Milton Ave SP10 . . . . . **82** D1
Milton Bsns Ctr
BH25 . . . . **382** E2
Milton Cl
Basingstoke RG24 . . . **69** C8
Poole BH14 . . . . . . **391** D3
Miltoncross Sch
PO3 . . . . **371** A6
Milton Ct
[3] Portsmouth
PO4 . . . . **371** A5
Ferndown BH22 . . . **353** D5
Milton Gr
Locks Heath SO31 . . **317** B2
New Milton BH25 . . **383** B2
Milton Grange GU12 . . **77** E5
Milton La PO4 . . . . . . **371** A4
Milton Mead BH25 . . . **382** F2
Milton Par PO8 . . . . . **299** E2
Milton Park Ave [1]
PO4 . . . . **371** B4
Milton Park Jun & Inf
Schs PO4 . . . . **371** B4
Milton Rd
Bournemouth BH8 . . **393** A4
Eastleigh SO50 . . . **244** B5
Poole BH14 . . . . . . **391** D3
Portsmouth PO4 . . . **371** A5
Southampton SO15 . . **290** F6
Waterlooville PO7,
PO8 . . . . **299** E3
Wimborne Minster
BH21 . . . . **351** C6
Milton Villas BH8 . . . . **393** A5
Milverton Cl
Christchurch BH23 . . **381** E1
Totton SO40 . . . . . **289** A6
Milverton Ho PO5 . . . **404** B2
Milverton Rd
Totton SO40 . . . . . **289** A6
Winchester SO22 . . . **403** C6
Milvil Ct PO13 . . . . . **367** E3
Milvil Rd PO13 . . . . . **367** E3
Mimosa Ave BH21 . . . **375** E8

Mimosa Cl
Lindford GU35 . . . . . **165** A5
Titchfield PO15 . . . . **317** E3
Mimosa Ct [3] SP10 . . **105** D6
Mimosa Dr SO50 . . . . **245** E2
Minchens La RG26 . . . **28** E4
Mincingfield La
SO32 . . . . **270** D5
Mincingfield Terr
SO32 . . . . **270** D5
Minden Cl
Andover SP10 . . . . . **82** F3
Chineham RG24 . . . . **48** E2
Minden Ho
Fareham PO14 . . . . **342** F8
Romsey SO51 . . . . . **241** B7
Minden Way SO22 . . . **403** A3
Minehurst Rd GU16 . . **56** D4
Minerva Cl PO7 . . . . . **322** E2
Minerva Cres [20]
PO1 . . . . **370** A4
Minerva Ct [2] PO4 . . **370** E1
Minerva Dr [9] PO12 . . **369** C8
Minerva Ho [5] RG7 . . . **9** C2
Ministry Rd RG19 . . . . **6** E5
Minley Cl GU14 . . . . . **55** C4
Minley Ct [16] PO9 . . . **324** B5
Minley Gr GU51 . . . . . **54** B3
Minley Rd
Farnborough GU14 . . **55** B5
Fleet GU51 . . . . . . **54** B4
Hawley GU17 . . . . . **34** C1
Yateley GU14 . . . . . **54** E7
Minnitt Rd PO12 . . . . **369** E5
Minores Rd SP9 . . . . . **79** A6
Minshull Ct [6] PO10 . . **105** F8
Minstead Ave SO18 . . **292** D8
Minstead Cl
Tadley RG26 . . . . . . **26** F6
Winchester SO22 . . . **175** D4
Minstead Ct [4] SO17 . **291** A8
Minstead Dr GU46 . . . **34** A5
Minstead Rd
Bournemouth BH10 . . **377** C3
Portsmouth PO4 . . . **371** B3
Minster Cl
Fareham PO15 . . . . . **318** C2
Farnborough GU14 . . **56** B1
Minster Ct
[9] Southampton
SO15 . . . . **290** C6
Camberley GU15 . . . **36** B7
Camberley,York Town
GU15 . . . . **35** D4
Minster La [3] SO23 . . **403** E5
Minster Pk BH21 . . . . **326** E5
Minster The BH21 . . . **351** B4
Minster View BH21 . . . **351** C5
Minster Way BH16 . . . **389** B7
Minter Ct [17] RG26 . . . **9** D1
Mintern Cl SO50 . . . . **244** D5
Minterne Grange
BH14 . . . . **402** C7
Minterne Rd
[3] Bournemouth
BH9 . . . . **378** A2
Christchurch BH23 . . **395** E5
Poole BH14 . . . . . . **402** C4
Minters Ct [28] SO23 . . **403** D6
Minter's Lepe PO7 . . . **322** E3
Minton Mews BH2 . . . **392** F5
Mint Rd GU33 . . . . . . **208** B6
Mint The GU31,GU32 . **228** F2
Mintys Hill SP6 . . . . . **256** F8
Mintys Yd [4] BH24 . . **329** A6
Mirabella Cl SO19 . . . **291** D2
Mirror Cl SO31 . . . . . **316** F1
Mislingford Rd
SO32 . . . . **272** D3
Missenden Acres
SO30 . . . . **293** C8
Missenden Pl SO50 . . **244** A1
Mission La
Broadstone BH18 . . **375** A2
Waterlooville PO8 . . **300** A3
Mission Rd BH18 . . . . **375** A2
Misslebrook La SO16,
SO52 . . . . **242** D3
Mistletoe Gdns
SO31 . . . . **316** E6
Mistletoe Rd GU46 . . . **34** B4
Mistral [11] SO14 . . . . **291** B3
Mitcham Rd GU15 . . . **36** E8
Mitchell Ave RG27 . . . **52** C5
Mitchell Bldgs GU46 . **33** F5
Mitchell Cl
Andover SP10 . . . . . **82** C1
Barton on S BH25 . . **398** A7
Locks Heath PO15 . . **317** D5
Mitchell Dr SO50 . . . . **245** C2
Mitchell Gdns RG21 . . **91** C7
Mitchell Point SO31 . . **315** F2
Mitchell Rd
Eastleigh SO50 . . . **244** B2
Ferndown BH21 . . . **353** A7
Havant PO9 . . . . . . **323** B3
Poole BH17 . . . . . . **390** F8
Mitchells Cl
Redlynch SP5 . . . . . **235** D6
Romsey SO51 . . . . . **240** F7
Mitchell Way
Eastleigh SO18,
SO50 . . . . **268** A8
Portsmouth PO3 . . . **346** B3
Mitford Rd SO24 . . . . **179** C4
Mitre Copse SO50 . . . **244** F2

Mitre Ct
[5] Christchurch
BH23 . . . . **395** A7
[5] Fareham PO14 . . **342** E7
Mizen Ho PO6 . . . . . . **345** A7
Mizen Way PO13 . . . . **368** D6
Mizpah Villas SO32 . . **271** C3
Moat Cl
Bramley RG26 . . . . . **28** F4
Holbury SO45 . . . . . **338** B3
Moat Ct
Bournemouth BH4 . . **392** C5
Gosport PO12 . . . . . **368** D4
Moat Dr PO12 . . . . . . **368** D3
Moat Hill SO18 . . . . . **267** F3
Moat La BH25 . . . . . . **397** F8
Moat Wlk PO12 . . . . . **368** D3
Mockbeggar La
BH24 . . . . **305** A7
Moffat Rd BH23 . . . . **395** D7
Moffatts Cl GU47 . . . . **34** E8
Moggs Mead GU31 . . . **229** A3
Mole Cl GU14 . . . . . . **55** B6
Mole Hill PO7 . . . . . . **322** F5
Molesworth Rd
PO12 . . . . **369** C4
Mollison Rise PO15 . . **317** D6
Molyneux Rd BH25 . . **383** D3
Momford Rd SO22 . . . **197** B3
Monachus La RG27 . . . **52** D7
Monaco Ct BH9 . . . . . **393** B8
Monarch Cl
[3] Waterlooville
PO7 . . . . **323** A7
Basingstoke RG22 . . . **91** A6
Locks Heath SO31 . . **317** A4
Monarch Ct [29] BH4 . **392** C3
Monarch Way
West End SO30 . . . . **268** F2
Winchester SO22 . . . **403** A4
Monastery Rd SO18 . . **291** E7
Monckton Rd
Gosport PO12 . . . . . **369** B2
Portsmouth PO3 . . . **346** A2
Mon Cres SO18 . . . . . **292** C7
Moneyer Rd SP10 . . . . **82** F3
Moneyfield Ave PO3 . . **346** B1
Moneyfield La [3]
PO3 . . . . **371** A8
Moneyfly Rd BH31 . . . **303** B5
Mongers Piece RG24 . **49** A4
Monier Williams Rd
SP11 . . . . **108** B3
Moniton Trad Est
RG22 . . . . **68** B4
Monkey Puzzle Rdbt
GU14 . . . . **55** C3
Monks Brook Cl
SO50 . . . . **243** E1
Monks Brook Ind Pk
SO53 . . . . **243** B5
Monks Cl
Farnborough GU14 . . **56** A4
North Tidworth SP9 . . **78** E7
West Moors BH22 . . **354** A8
Monks Ct SO41 . . . . . **385** F2
Monkshanger GU9 . . . **99** C2
Monk Sherborne Ho
RG26 . . . . **47** B5
Monk Sherborne Rd
RG26 . . . . **46** A8
Monks Hill PO13 . . . . **367** C5
Monk's Hill PO10 . . . . **325** B5
Monkshood Cl BH23 . . **381** B1
Monks La RG14 . . . . . . **5** D7
Monk's La RG14 . . . . . **5** C7
Monks Orch GU32 . . . **228** F5
Monks Pl SO40 . . . . . **288** D6
Monks Rd
Netley SO31 . . . . . . **315** B6
Winchester SO23 . . . **403** E7
Monks Rise GU51 . . . . **53** D1
Monks Way
Bournemouth BH11 . . **376** D5
Eastleigh SO50 . . . **243** F1
Southampton SO18 . . **267** E4
Stubbington PO14 . . **367** B5
Monks' Well GU10 . . . **99** F1
Monkswell Dn RG23 . . **395** D6
Monks Wlk SO45 . . . . **337** E8
Monk's Wlk GU9 . . . . **122** D8
Monks Wood GU32 . . **228** F5
Monkswood Cl RG14 . . **5** C7
Monks Wood Cl
SO16 . . . . **267** B6
Monks Wood Cres
RG26 . . . . **26** F7
Monkton Cl RG23 . . . **353** D6
Monkton Cres BH12 . . **391** E8
Monkton La
Farnham GU9 . . . . . **99** C5
Totton SO40 . . . . . **288** C6
Monkton Pk GU9 . . . . **99** D4
Monkwood Cl PO9 . . . **323** D5
Monkworthy Dr
BH24 . . . . **327** F5
Monmouth Cl
Chandler's Ford
SO53 . . . . **243** B6
Verwood BH31 . . . . **303** B4
Monmouth Ct
Lymington SO41 . . . **385** E3
Ringwood BH24 . . . **329** C5
Monmouth Dr BH31 . . **303** B4
Monmouth Gdns
SO40 . . . . **288** D5

Monmouth Rd PO2 . . **345** D1
Monmouth Sq SO22 . . **197** B5
Monnow Gdns SO18 . . **268** B1
Monroe Cl PO12 . . . . **368** E3
Monsal Ave BH22 . . . **353** C3
Mons Cl GU11 . . . . . . **77** C7
Mons The [17] SO23 . . **403** D6
Montacute Cl GU14 . . . **56** B4
Montacute Sch
BH17 . . . . **375** C2
Montacute Way
BH21 . . . . **375** E8
Montagu Cl PO12 . . . **369** E7
Montague Ave SO19 . . **292** D3
Montague Cl
Camberley GU15 . . . **35** F5
Southampton SO19 . . **292** D3
Southampton SO45 . . **337** E8
Montague Gdns
GU31 . . . . **229** B3
Montague Pl [1] RG21 . **69** B3
Montague Rd
Bishopstoke SO50 . . **244** D3
Bournemouth BH5 . . **394** B4
Portsmouth PO2 . . . **345** E1
Montague Terr RG14 . . **5** E8
Montague Wallis [40]
PO1 . . . . **370** A5
Montagu Pk BH23 . . . **397** A7
Montagu Rd BH23 . . . **397** B8
Montana Ct PO7 . . . . **323** A6
Monteagle La
Yateley GU46 . . . . . **33** E6
Yateley GU46 . . . . . **33** F5
Montefiore Ho SO18 . **267** D4
Monteray Dr SO41 . . . **383** F4
Monterey Dr
Havant PO9 . . . . . . **324** A4
Locks Heath SO31 . . **317** A2
Montfort Cl SO51 . . . **241** C7
Montfort College
SO51 . . . . **241** C7
Montfort Hts SO51 . . . **241** C7
Montfort Rd SO51 . . . **241** C6
Montgomerie Rd
PO5 . . . . **404** C2
Montgomery Ave
Bournemouth BH11 . . **377** B3
Totton SO40 . . . . . **288** D8
Montgomery Cl
Sandhurst GU47 . . . **34** F8
Winchester SO22 . . . **403** A3
Montgomery Ho [5]
SP9 . . . . **78** E8
Montgomery Rd
Enham Alamein SP11 . **83** B6
Farnborough GU14 . . **55** D3
Gosport PO13 . . . . . **343** C3
Havant PO9 . . . . . . **324** A1
Newbury RG14 . . . . **5** C8
Southampton SO18 . . **292** A8
Montgomery Way
SO53 . . . . **243** B3
Montgomery Wlk
PO7 . . . . **322** D5
Montpelier Cl SO31 . . **317** C3
Montreal Wlk GU30 . . **188** A3
Montrose Ave PO16 . . **320** C5
Montrose Cl
Bordon GU35 . . . . . **164** E1
Fleet GU51 . . . . . . **75** B8
Frimley GU16 . . . . . **36** C2
Hedge End SO30 . . . **293** E6
Verwood BH31 . . . . **302** F6
Montrose Dr BH10 . . **377** B2
Montserrat Pl RG24 . . **48** C2
Montserrat Rd
Basingstoke RG24 . . **48** C2
Lee-on-t-S PO13 . . . **367** E3
Monument Chase
GU35 . . . . **164** E1
Monument Cl RG14 . . . **5** B7
Monument Ct SO14 . . **291** A4
Monument La
Portchester PO17 . . **320** B4
Walhampton SO41 . . **386** A5
Woodmancott PO18 . **203** D1
Monxton Gn [13] PO9 . **324** B6
Monxton Rd
Andover SP11 . . . . . **105** C8
Grateley SP11 . . . . . **103** D2
Monxton SP11 . . . . **105** A7
Moody Rd PO14 . . . . **367** C6
Moody's Hill SP5 . . . . **190** C2
Moon Cl SO40 . . . . . . **289** E1
Moonhills La SO42 . . . **337** B2
Moonrakers Way
BH23 . . . . **381** E1
Moonscross Ave
SO40 . . . . **288** F4
Moons Hill GU10 . . . . **122** A4
Moor Cl
Bordon GU35 . . . . . **164** B3
Finchampstead RG40 . **16** C7
Moor Court La SO21 . . **174** B3
Moorcroft Ave BH23 . **380** C7
Moorcroft Cl SO21 . . . **131** D3
Moordown BH9 . . . . . **378 A4
Moordown St John's CE
Prim Sch BH9 . . . . **377** F1
Moore Ave BH11 . . . . **377** A4
Moore Cl
Andover SP10 . . . . . **83** A1
Fleet GU52 . . . . . . **75** D5
Old Milton BH25 . . . **382** F1
Tongham GU10 . . . . **100** D8
Moore Cres SO31 . . . **315** C7
Moore Gdns PO12 . . . **368** F4

Moore Rd GU52 . . . . . **75** A5
Moorfield GU27 . . . . . **189** D5
Moorfield Gr BH9 . . . . **377** F2
Moorfields Rd BH13 . . **402** F8
Moorfoot Gdns RG22 . . **68** B3
Moorgreen Hospl
SO30 . . . . **268** E1
Moorgreen Rd
Havant PO9 . . . . . . **324** A5
West End SO30 . . . . **268** F2
Moorhams Ave RG22 . **91** A4
Moorhaven BH22 . . . . **353** D6
Moorhead Ct SO14 . . **291** C2
Moorhill Gdns SO18 . . **292** E7
Moorhill Rd
Burley BH24 . . . . . . **331** A2
West End SO18,SO30 **292** D8
Moorhills Cl BH15 . . . **389** F1
Moorings The
[2] Christchurch
BH23 . . . . **395** A5
Basingstoke RG21 . . **69** D5
Fareham PO16 . . . . **343** B7
Hindhead GU26 . . . **167** C3
Moorings Way Inf Sch
PO4 . . . . **371** C6
Moor La
Newbury RG14 . . . . . **1** C3
Whiteparish SP5 . . . **236** C8
Moorland Ave BH25 . **397** F8
Moorland Cl
Hythe SO45 . . . . . . **313** D3
Locks Heath SO31 . . **317** A4
Moorland Cres BH16 . **389** B7
Moorland Ct BH22 . . . **326** D2
Moorland Gate
BH24 . . . . **329** A5
Moorland Par BH16 . . **389** B7
Moorland Rd
Bournemouth BH11 . . **393** D4
Portsmouth PO1 . . . **370** E4
Moorlands Cl
Brockenhurst SO42 . **333** D1
Fleet GU51 . . . . . . **75** B8
Hindhead GU26 . . . **167** C4
Moorlands Coll
BH23 . . . . **380** B6
Moorlands Cres
SO18 . . . . **292** B8
Moorlands Inf Sch
SO18 . . . . **268** B1
Moorlands Pl GU15 . . **35** E4
Moorlands Rd
Camberley GU15 . . . **35** F4
Swanmore SO32 . . . **272** A7
Verwood BH31 . . . . **302** F7
West Moors BH22 . . **326** E3
Moorlands Rise
BH22 . . . . **326** F3
Moorland Way BH16 . **389** B7
Moorlea [2] BH8 . . . . . **393** B6
Moor Park La GU9 . . . **99** D3
Moor Park Way GU9 . . **99** D3
Moor Pk PO7 . . . . . . **300** B1
Moor Place Farm
RG27 . . . . **32** A6
Moor Rd
Broadstone BH18 . . **375** B5
Camberley GU16 . . . **56** D8
Farnborough GU14 . . **55** E8
Greatham GU33 . . . **186** C1
Haslemere GU27 . . . **189** A5
Moors Cl
Colden Common
SO21 . . . . **219** F1
Hurn BH23 . . . . . . **379** B7
Moors Ct RG40 . . . . . **16** C8
Moor Side BH24 . . . . **354** B8
Moorside Gdns
BH11 . . . . **377** B3
Moorside Rd
Bournemouth BH11 . . **377** B3
Corfe Mullen BH21 . . **374** D5
West Moors BH22 . . **326** E3
Winchester SO23 . . . **176** C2
Moors The GU10 . . . . **100** D7
Moors Valley Ctry Park
Visitor Ctr ★ BH24 . . **327** D8
Moors Valley Ctry Pk ★
BH24 . . . . **303** D1
Moors Valley Railway ★
BH24 . . . . **303** C1
Moortown Ave PO6 . . **322** D1
Moortown Dr
Bournemouth BH21 . . **376** B8
Wimborne Minster
BH21 . . . . **352** B1
Moortown Farm
BH21 . . . . **376** B8
Moortown Ho BH24 . . **329** A5
Moortown La BH24 . . **329** A5
Moorvale Rd BH9 . . . **378** A4
Moor View BH9 . . . . . **70** B7
Moor View Rd BH15 . . **390** E6
Moot Cl
Andover SP10 . . . . . **83** A4
Downton SP5 . . . . . **235** A7
Moot Garden The ★
SP5 . . . . **235** A7
Moot Gdns SP5 . . . . . **234** F6
Moot La SP5 . . . . **234** F5
Mopley SO45 . . . . . . **365** C5
Mopley Cl SO45 . . . . **365** C5

Morant Ct [4] BH25 . . **383** B3
Morant Rd BH24 . . . . **305** B1
Morant Ct [1] PO8 . . . **369** C9
Moraunt Dr PO16 . . . **344** B6
Moray Ave GU47 . . . . **35** B7
Moray Ct [11] BH21 . . **351** B5
Mordaunt Rd SO14 . . **291** A7
Morden Ave BH22 . . . **353** C4
Morden Rd BH9 . . . . **377** F4
Morecombe Ct [4]
PO5 . . . . **404** C2
More House Sch
GU10 . . . . **122** A2
Moreland Cl GU34 . . . **140** A2
Moreland Rd PO12 . . **369** B6
Morelands Cl PO7 . . . **322** F4
Morelands Prim Sch
PO7 . . . . **322** E2
Morelands Rd PO7 . . . **322** E2
Moresby Ct [5] PO16 . **319** B3
Morestead Rd
Winchester SO21 . . . **198** E3
Winchester SO23 . . . **403** F2
Moreton Cl
Churt GU10 . . . . . . **144** C1
Fleet GU52 . . . . **74** F4
Moreton Rd BH9 . . . . **378** B4
Morgan Ct [3] GU14 . . **55** A4
Morgan Le Fay Dr
SO53 . . . . **242** F7
Morgan Rd
Hedge End SO30 . . . **293** C5
Portsmouth PO4 . . . **371** C4
Morgans Dr PO14 . . . **342** C5
Morgan's La SP5 . . . . **230** A1
Morgans Rise Rd
SP5 . . . . **235** D7
Morgans Vale Rd
SP5 . . . . **235** D6
Morgan's Vale &
Woodfalls CE Prim Sch
SP5 . . . . **235** D7
Morgaston Rd RG26 . . **48** A7
Moriconium Quay
BH15 . . . . **389** D1
Morington Ct [8]
BH8 . . . . **393** A5
Morland Rd
Aldershot GU11 . . . **100** A6
Southampton SO15 . . **266** C1
Morland's Rd GU11 . . **77** B5
Morley Cl
Bournemouth BH5 . . **394** A5
Burton BH23 . . . . . **380** C3
Southampton SO19 . . **291** F6
Yateley GU46 . . . . . **33** F5
Morley Cres PO8 . . . . **300** A3
Morley Dr SO32 . . . . **271** C8
Morley Gdns SO53 . . **243** C8
Morley Rd
Basingstoke RG21 . . . **69** A1
Bournemouth BH5 . . **394** A5
Farnham GU9 . . . . . . **99** B1
Portsmouth PO4 . . . **371** A2
Morleys La SO51 . . . . **217** C3
Morley Way PO12 . . . **353** F3
Morningside Ave
PO16 . . . . **320** E1
Mornington Ave
RG40 . . . . **16** D8
Mornington Dr SO22 **403** A4
Mornington Rd
GU35 . . . . **164** A2
Mornish Rd BH13 . . . **391** F2
Morpeth Ave SO40 . . **288** F8
Morris Cl
Gosport PO13 . . . . . **343** B5
Hythe SO45 . . . . . . **313** D4
Morris Ho [5] GU14 . . **77** B8
Morrison Ave BH12 . . **391** F6
Morris Rd
Farnborough GU14 . . **77** B8
Poole BH17 . . . . . . **390** D8
Southampton SO15 . . **290** D8
Morris Rise RG24 . . . **48** E2
Morris St RG27 . . . . . **71** E8
Morse Ct SO31 . . . . . **315** A6
Morse Rd RG22 . . . . . **68** E4
Morshead Cres
PO16 . . . . **318** F3
Mortimer Cl
Christchurch BH23 . . **396** A6
Hartley Wintney RG27 . **52** B4
Kings Worthy SO23 . . **176** C6
Netley SO31 . . . . . . **315** B6
Totton SO40 . . . . . **264** D1
Mortimer Gdns RG26 . **27** A7
Mortimer Hall RG7 . . **12** A5
Mortimer La
[2] Basingstoke
RG21 . . . . **69** A5
Stratfield Mortimer
RG7 . . . . **12** B7
Stratfield Saye RG7 . . **29** B7
Mortimer Lawn PO9 . **323** D7
Mortimer Rd
Botley SO30 . . . . . . **294** A6
Bournemouth BH8 . . **378** B1
Portsmouth PO6 . . . **321** C1
Southampton SO19 . . **291** E4
Mortimer St John's CE
Sch RG7 . . . . **11** E5

Mortimers Dr SO50 . 245 D2
Mortimer's Ind Units
  SO51............ 263 E5
Mortimers La SO50.. 245 E2
Mortimer Sta RG7 ... 12 C5
Mortimer Way SO52. 241 F3
Mortimore Rd PO12. 368 F6
Morton Cl GU16..... 56 D7
Morval Cl GU14..... 55 C4
Morval Rd GU17 .... 34 D1
Mosaic Cl SO19..... 292 F4
Moscrop Ct 8 RG21.. 69 A4
Mosdell Rd PO10.... 349 E8
Mosedale Wlk 2
  SO16............ 289 E7
Moselle Cl GU14.....55 B5
Moselle Ct SO15 .... 290 C5
Mosquito Way GU14.. 55 D1
Moss Cl GU33...... 208 A4
Moss Dr SO40...... 289 F2
Mossleigh Ave SO16 265 F5
Mossley Ave
  Poole BH12......377 A1
  Poole BH14 ......392 A8
Moss Rd SO23...... 403 F6
Motcombe Rd BH13.. 392 A2
Mothes Ho RG26..... 27 A7
Mottisfont Abbey Gdns*
  SO51............ 192 F3
Mottisfont Abbey (NT)*
  SO51............ 192 F3
Mottisfont Cl 1
  SO15............ 290 A6
Mottisfont Lodge 5
  SO51............ 240 F7
Mottisfont Rd SO50.. 244 A4
Moulin Ave PO5 .... 370 E2
Moulsham Copse La
  GU46............33 F7
Moulsham La GU46 ..33 F7
Mound Cl PO12..... 369 A4
Mountain Ash Cl
  SO18............ 292 C7
Mount Ave BH25.... 383 A1
Mountbatten Ave
  SO51............ 240 F7
Mountbatten Bsns Ctr
  SO15............ 290 E5
Mountbatten Bsns Pk
  PO6............ 346 C6
Mountbatten Cl
  Christchurch BH23.. 396 A5
  Gosport PO13.... 343 C4
  Newbury RG14 .... 2 A5
Mountbatten Ct
  13 Aldershot GU11 .. 76 E2
  Andover SP10...... 83 D1
  New Milton BH25... 382 F3
  Winchester SO22 ... 175 E3
Mountbatten Dr
  Ferndown BH22.... 353 C5
  Waterlooville PO7 .. 322 D6
Mountbatten Gdns
  BH8............ 378 F2
Mountbatten Pl
  SO23............ 176 C8
Mountbatten Rd
  Eastleigh SO50 .... 244 A5
  Poole BH13...... 392 B1
  Totton SO40...... 288 C6
Mountbatten Sch &
  Language Coll The
  SO51............ 241 C6
Mountbatten Sq 6
  PO4............ 371 B2
Mountbatten Way
  Portsmouth PO1 ... 370 B7
  Southampton SO15.. 290 C5
Mount Carmel Rd
  SP11............ 124 C5
Mount Cl
  Highclere RG20..... 21 D6
  Newbury RG14 ......1 E1
  New Milton BH25 ... 383 A1
  Winchester SO22 ... 175 E3
Mount Dr
  Chandler's Ford
  SO53............ 243 E4
  Fareham PO15..... 342 B8
Mounters La GU34.. 139 D1
Mounter's La GU34.. 139 D1
Mountfield SO45.... 313 E4
Mount Grace Dr
  BH14............ 402 D7
Mount Heatherbank 7
  BH1............ 392 F3
Mount Hermon Rd
  SP11............ 124 E6
Mount Hospl The
  SO50............ 244 D5
Mount House Cl
  SO45............ 314 A5
Mount Hts SP5...... 146 C3
Mountjoy Cl BH21... 351 F2
Mountjoy Ct 4 PO1. 370 A3
Mount La SO51 ..... 213 F7
Mount Pleasant
  Amport SP11...... 104 B6
  Christchurch BH23.. 396 A5
  Denmead PO7 ..... 298 F2
  Farnham GU9...... 98 E1
  Hartley Wintney RG27. 52 D6
  Kings Worthy SO23.. 176 C6
  Laverstoke RG28.... 87 B6
  Ringwood BH24.... 329 A7

Mount Pleasant continued
  Romsey SO51 .... 240 E6
  Tadley RG26...... 26 E8
Mount Pleasant Dr
  Bournemouth BH8... 378 F1
  Bransgore BH23 ... 357 C1
  Tadley RG26...... 26 E8
Mount Pleasant Ind Pk
  SO14............ 291 B8
Mount Pleasant Jun Sch
  SO14............ 291 B7
Mount Pleasant La
  SO41............ 385 A7
Mount Pleasant Rd
  Aldershot GU12.... 77 A1
  Alton GU34...... 139 F2
  Gosport PO12..... 369 B4
  Lindford GU35..... 164 F5
  Poole BH15...... 390 D3
  Southampton SO14 .. 291 B6
Mount Rd
  Bournemouth BH11.. 378 F2
  Highclere RG20..... 21 D7
  Poole BH14....... 391 B5
Mountsom's La GU34 161 F3
Mounts Way GU51 ... 53 C3
Mount Temple SO51 241 A7
Mount The
  5 Bassett SO16.... 266 F4
  9 Old Shirley SO16.. 266 A1
  Fleet GU51 .... 54 A2
  Gosport PO13 ..... 343 E1
  Headley GU35..... 165 E6
  Highclere RG20..... 21 D7
  Ringwood BH24.... 329 D8
Mount View
  Aldershot GU11..... 76 E1
  Eastleigh SO50 .... 244 B4
Mountview Ave
  PO16............ 320 E1
Mount View Rd
  SO22............ 197 B4
Mountwood Rd
  PO10............ 325 D1
Mourne Cl RG22.....68 B4
Mousehole La
  Hythe SO45...... 314 A3
  Southampton SO18 .. 291 F8
Mousehole Rd PO6.. 320 F1
Mowatt Rd GU26.... 167 B2
Mowbray Rd SO19... 292 B4
Moxhams SP6...... 257 F1
Moyles Court Sch
  BH24............ 305 C5
Mozart Cl RG22......91 E8
Muccleshell Cl PO9. 324 A4
Muddyford Rd SP5.. 235 D8
Mudeford Com Inf Sch
  BH23............ 395 E6
Mudeford Green Cl
  BH23............ 395 F5
Mudeford Jun Sch
  BH23............ 395 F6
Mudeford La BH23 .. 395 F6
Mude Gdns BH23 ... 396 A5
Mud La RG27 ...... 15 D1
Muira Est SO14 .... 291 C5
Muir Ho SO45...... 313 E1
Mulberries The GU9.. 99 D4
Mulberry Ave
  Cosham PO6 ...... 346 A7
  Stubbington PO14... 367 C6
Mulberry Cl
  1 Sandhurst GU47... 35 B8
  Ash Vale GU12..... 77 E4
  Gosport PO12 ..... 369 B5
Mulberry Ct
  4 Christchurch
  BH23............ 395 A7
  Four Marks GU34 .. 160 C3
  Newbury RG14 ......1 D3
Mulberry Gdns SP6.. 281 E8
Mulberry Gr SO41... 399 D8
Mulberry Ho 2
  SP10............ 106 B8
Mulberry La
  Cosham PO6 ...... 346 A7
  Sarisbury SO31.... 316 E5
Mulberry Mead RG28. 86 C5
Mulberry Mews SP6. 281 E8
Mulberry Rd SO40... 289 F1
Mulberry Way RG24.. 48 F3
Mulberry Wlk SO15.. 290 C8
Mulfords Hill
  Pamber Heath RG26...9 F1
  Tadley RG26...... 27 A8
Mulgrave Rd GU16... 36 D2
Mull Cl RG23....... 67 A2
Mullen Cl SO19 .... 291 E4
Mullenscote Mobile
  Home Pk SP11..... 81 A1
Mullins Cl
  Basingstoke RG21... 69 B8
Mullion Cl PO6..... 345 B7
Mulroy Dr GU15..... 36 E6
Mumby Rd PO12.... 369 D6
Mundays Row PO8 .. 276 C1
Munnings Cl RG21... 69 D3
Munnings Ct SP10 ...82 F1
Munnings Dr GU47... 35 C6
Munro Cres SO15 ... 289 F7
Munro Way GU11....77 B8
Munster Rd
  Poole BH14...... 391 D3
  Portsmouth PO2... 345 D2
Murefield Rd PO1... 404 C3
Muriel Rd PO7...... 322 E8

Murley Rd BH9 ..... 393 A8
Murray Cl
  Andover SP10..... 105 F5
  Fareham PO15..... 318 E2
  Southampton SO19 .. 292 E6
Murray Cotts SO32.. 295 D7
Murray Rd
  Farnborough GU14 .. 55 D3
  Waterlooville PO8 .. 300 B6
Murray's La PO1.... 369 F7
Murray's Rd PO1.....77 B5
Murrell Green Bsns Pk
  RG27............ 51 E2
Murrell Rd GU12.....77 E3
Murrells La GU15 ... 35 F3
Murrills Est PO16 ... 344 E8
Muscliffe Ct 8 PO9. 324 B5
Muscliffe La BH9 ... 324 B5
Muscliffe Rd BH9 ... 377 F1
Muscliff Prim Sch
  BH9............. 378 C4
Muscott Cl SP9..... 101 D7
Museum of
  Archaeology*
  SO14............ 291 A2
Museum of the Iron
  Age* SP10...... 106 A7
Museum Rd PO1.... 370 B4
Musgrave Cl RG22 .. 91 D7
Musgrove Gdns
  GU34............ 139 E4
Musket Copse RG24.. 70 A6
Mus of Army Flying
  Explorers' World*
  SO20............ 126 A2
Mus of Electricity*
  BH23............ 395 B7
Mussett Cl SO40.... 288 E7
Muss La SO20...... 172 A3
Mustang Ave PO15.. 317 C2
Myers Cl SO32 ..... 272 B5
Mylen Bsns Ctr SP10 105 E8
Mylen Rd SP10......82 E1
Myllers Lond RG27.. 51 D1
My Lords La PO11... 373 B3
Myrtle Ave
  Portchester PO16 .. 344 D7
  Totton SO40...... 288 D6
Myrtle Cl
  Gosport PO13 ..... 343 B3
  Hordle SO41...... 383 F4
Myrtle Dr GU17 ..... 35 B5
Myrtle Gr PO3 ..... 371 B7
Myrtle Rd
  Bournemouth BH8... 393 C6
  Southampton SO16.. 266 B4
Mytchett Farm Cvn Pk
  GU16............ 56 D2
Mytchett Heath GU16 .56 E3
Mytchett Lake Rd
  GU16............ 56 E1
Mytchett Place Rd
  GU16............ 56 E2
Mytchett Prim Sch
  GU16............ 56 D4
Mytchett Rd GU16... 56 D3
Myvern Cl SO45..... 338 D3

N

Naafi Rdbt GU11.....76 F2
Nada Rd BH23 ..... 381 D1
Nadder Rd SP9...... 78 F6
Nailsworth Rd PO6.. 321 B1
Nairn Cl GU16...... 36 C2
Nairn Ct BH3 ...... 392 E7
Nairn Rd
  Bournemouth BH3 .. 392 E6
  Poole BH13....... 402 E7
Naish Cl PO9....... 323 C7
Naish Dr PO12...... 344 A1
Naish Rd BH25..... 397 E7
Namu Rd BH9...... 377 E1
Nancy Rd PO1 ..... 404 D3
Nansen Ave BH15 .. 390 D5
Napier Cl
  Farnborough GU11 .. 77 C7
  Gosport PO13 ..... 368 D5
Napier Cres PO15 .. 318 C1
Napier Dr GU15......36 E7
Napier La GU12 .....77 E4
Napier Rd
  Hamworthy BH15 .. 389 C3
  Horndean PO8..... 300 C6
  Portsmouth PO5... 370 D2
  Southampton SO19 .. 292 E5
Napier Wlk SP10.... 83 D1
Napoleon Ave GU14.. 55 D4
Napoleon Dr RG23 .. 68 C7
Narrow La
  9 Romsey SO51.... 240 E7
  Ringwood,North Poulner
  BH24............ 305 D1
  Ringwood,Poulner
  BH24............ 329 D8
Narvik Rd PO2...... 345 D4
Naseby Cl BH9..... 378 A2
Naseby Rise RG14....2 B5
Nash Cl
  Basingstoke RG21... 69 C7
  Dibden Purlieu SO45 313 D1
  Farnborough GU14... 55 D4
Nashe Cl PO15..... 318 D3
Nashe Ho PO15..... 318 C3
Nashe Way PO15.... 318 C3
Nash Grove La RG40. 16 D8

Nash Mdws RG29 ... 95 A4
Nash Rd SO45...... 313 D2
Nasmith Cl PO12.... 368 D4
Natanbury SP5...... 235 A7
Nately Rd RG29......71 E2
Nat Gonella Sq 4
  PO12............ 369 D5
Nathen Gdns BH15.. 389 D3
National Air Traffic
  Services Hq PO15.. 317 F8
National Motor Mus
  The* SO42...... 336 E2
Nations Hill SO23 .. 176 B6
Navarac Ct BH14.... 391 C3
Navigator's Way
  SO30............ 293 C8
Navy Rd PO1....... 370 A6
Naylors The RG7 .... 11 A8
Nea Cl BH23 ...... 396 D8
Nea Dr BH24....... 304 B5
Nea Rd BH23 ...... 396 E8
Neath Rd RG21 ..... 69 D5
Neath Way SO53.... 243 A5
Needles Cl 11 SO50 240 F8
Needles Ho PO16 ... 343 A7
Needles Point SO41. 399 D3
Neelands Gr PO6 ... 344 E8
Neelem Ct 6 GU14.. 56 A1
Neighbourhood Ctr
  BH17............ 375 E2
Neilson Cl SO53..... 243 C7
Nelson Ave
  Portchester PO16 .. 344 B8
  Portsmouth PO2... 345 D2
Nelson Cl
  Aldershot GU12.... 77 B1
  Farnham GU9 ..... 99 B8
  Holbury SO45 ..... 338 C3
  New Milton BH25 .. 382 F3
  Romsey SO51 ..... 240 F8
  Stockbridge SO20 .. 149 F2
Nelson Cres PO8.... 300 C7
Nelson Ct
  13 Poole BH15 .... 390 C2
  1 Hythe SO45 .... 314 B1
  8 Portsmouth PO1.. 370 D7
  Fareham PO14..... 342 F6
Nelson Ctr The PO3. 346 B2
Nelson Dr BH23 .... 395 F6
Nelson Ho
  2 Aldershot GU11 .. 76 C2
  8 Gosport PO12 ... 369 E5
Nelson Ind Pk SO30. 269 E1
Nelson La PO17 .... 320 C2
Nelson Pl SO41 .... 385 F3
Nelson Rd
  Bishopstoke SO50.. 244 D4
  Farnham GU9 ..... 99 B8
  Gosport PO12 ..... 369 B5
  Portsmouth,Landport
  PO1............ 370 D7
  Portsmouth PO5 ... 404 C1
  Southampton SO15.. 290 C6
  Winchester SO23 .. 198 C6
Nelsons Gdns SO30. 269 C3
Nelson St GU11.....76 E2
Nelson Way GU15 ... 35 D4
Nelson Wlk SP10.... 83 D1
Nene Ct 10 SP10 ... 83 C2
Nepaul Rd SP9......78 E7
Nepean Ct PO12 ... 369 B2
Neptune Ct
  14 Portsmouth
  PO1............ 370 A4
  Southampton SO16.. 265 F4
Neptune Ho
  1 Cosham PO6 .... 345 F8
  Southampton SO14 .. 291 B2
Neptune Rd
  Bordon GU35...... 164 E2
  Fareham,Hill Park
  PO15............ 318 C2
  Fareham,West End
  PO14............ 342 F5
Neptune Way SO14.. 291 B2
Nerissa Cl PO7..... 323 B8
Nerquis Cl SO51 ... 241 B8
Nesbitt Cl PO13..... 343 B3
Nessus St PO2...... 370 D8
Nestor Cl PO15......82 F1
Nethercliffe Sch
  SO22............ 403 C7
Netherfield Cl
  Alton GU34...... 139 E4
  Havant PO9....... 324 A1
Netherhall Gdns
  BH4............ 392 C3
Netherhill SO32.... 270 C3
Netherhill La SO32.. 270 B2
Netherhouse Ct GU51 74 D6
Netherhouse Moor
  GU51............ 74 D6
Nether St 7 GU34 .. 139 F4
Netherton Rd PO12. 368 F7
Nether Vell-Mead
  GU52............74 E3
Netherwood Pl
  BH21............ 351 A5
Netley Abbey*
  SO31............ 315 A7
Netley Abbey Inf Sch
  SO31............ 315 B7
Netley Abbey Jun Sch
  SO31............ 315 B7

Netley Cl
  Chandler's Ford
  SO53............ 243 B3
  Poole BH15 ...... 391 A4
Netley Cliff SO31.... 315 B5
Netley Court Sch
  SO31............ 315 B5
Netley Ct 8 PO12... 369 C9
Netley Firs Rd
  Hedge End SO19 ... 292 F4
  Hedge End SO30... 293 A6
Netley Hill Est SO19. 292 F4
Netley Lodge Cl
  SO31............ 315 C5
Netley Mans 10 PO5. 370 D1
Netley Marsh CE Inf Sch
  SO40............ 288 A7
Netley Marsh Workshops
  SO40............ 288 A7
Netley Rd
  13 Portsmouth
  PO5............ 370 C2
  Titchfield PO14 ... 317 C1
Netley St GU14...... 77 A8
Netley Sta SO31 ... 315 C6
Netley Terr 14 PO5.. 370 C2
Nettlebeds La SO24. 158 B2
Nettlecombe Ave
  PO4............ 370 E1
Nettlestone SO31... 315 C7
Nettlestone Rd 1
  PO4............ 371 A2
Nettleton Cl BH17... 390 E4
Netton Cl SP5...... 210 B8
Netton St SP5...... 210 C8
Neuvic Way RG28... 86 D4
Nevada Cl GU14......55 B5
Neva Rd SO18...... 291 F8
Neville Ave PO16.... 344 D6
Neville Cl
  Andover SP10..... 106 B6
  Basingstoke RG21... 69 B2
Neville Dr SO51 .... 215 F1
Neville Duke Rd
  GU14............ 55 D8
Neville Gdns PO10 .. 324 E3
Neville Lovett Com Sch
  The PO14........ 342 F8
Neville Shute Rd
  PO3............ 346 A3
Newall Rd SP11..... 105 A7
Newark Rd GU17.... 34 C2
New Barn Cl GU51 .. 74 D7
New Barn Cotts
  SO21............ 152 E3
Newbarn La PO18... 325 F8
New Barn La
  Alton GU34...... 139 F2
  Wherwell SP11 .... 128 F8
Newbarn Rd
  Buriton GU31..... 253 C2
  Havant PO9....... 323 C3
New Bldgs SP11 .... 58 D7
Newbold Rd RG14....1 B5
Newbolt Cl PO8 .... 299 E3
Newbolt Rd PO6 ... 320 F1
New Borough Rd
  BH21............ 351 B2
Newbridge SO31.... 315 C6
Newbridge Jun Sch
  PO2............ 370 F7
New Bridge La 10
  RG21............ 69 D5
Newbridge Rd
  Cadnam SO40 .... 263 A1
  Newbridge SO40... 262 F3
Newbridge Way
  SO41............ 385 C1
New Brighton Rd
  PO10............ 324 F7
Newbroke Rd PO13. 368 E8
Newburgh St SO23.. 403 D6
Newbury Cl SO50 .. 245 B2
Newbury Coll RG14 ...5 F7
Newbury Dr BH10... 377 D1
Newbury Ho RG14....5 B6
Newbury Pl SO31... 316 F7
Newbury Racecourse Sta
  RG14............2 A2
Newbury Rd
  Andover SP10,SP11... 83 B5
  Kingsclere RG20... 24 B4
  Southampton SO15.. 266 C1
  Whitchurch RG28... 86 D7
Newbury St
  Andover SP10..... 106 B3
  Whitchurch RG28... 86 C5
Newbury Sta RG14....1 E2
Newchurch Rd RG26...9 E1
New Cliffe Gdns
  SO30............ 293 B6
New Cliff Ho SO19 .. 291 E1
New Coll (Univ of
  Southampton)
  SO15............ 290 F7
Newcomb Cl SP10 .. 106 A5
Newcombe Rd
  Bournemouth BH6... 394 E5
  Southampton SO15.. 290 E6
  West Moors BH22... 326 D3
Newcome Ct 8
  PO2............ 345 E2
Newcomen Rd PO2. 345 C2
Newcome Pl GU12 .. 100 B3
Newcome Rd
  Farnham GU9 ..... 99 C6

Newcome Rd continued
  Portsmouth PO1 ... 370 E6
New Cotts
  Ashurst SO40..... 311 F7
  Exbury SO45 ..... 365 B5
  Fareham PO16 .... 343 A8
  Hampreston BH21... 352 E2
  King's Somborne
  SO20............ 172 A2
  Liphook GU30..... 187 C8
  Nursling SO16..... 265 C2
  South Baddesley
  SO41............ 387 A5
  South Warnborough
  RG29............ 95 A4
  Sutton Scotney SO21. 131 C4
Newcroft Gdns
  BH23............ 395 A8
New Ct
  Ringwood BH24.... 328 E7
  Sutton Scotney SO21. 131 C3
New Cut PO11 ..... 347 F3
New Dawn Cl GU14 ...55 B3
New Down La PO6,
  PO7............ 322 A2
Newenham Rd SO41 385 E2
New Farm Cotts RG29 95 C1
New Farm Rd
  East Stratton SO21.. 134 A4
  New Alresford SO24. 179 B3
Newfield Ave GU14.. 55 C6
Newfield Rd
  Ash Vale GU12.... 77 E6
  Liss GU33 ...... 208 A6
New Fields Bsns Pk
  BH17............ 390 D8
New Forest Dr SO42. 333 D1
New Forest Ent Ctr
  SO40............ 288 E5
New Forest Mus &
  Visitor Ctr* SO43. 310 A3
New Forest Otter, Owl &
  Wildlife Pk* SO40. 311 E8
New Forest Reptile Ctr*
  SO43............ 309 A3
Newfoundland Dr
  BH15............ 390 D2
Newfoundland Drive
  Rdbt BH15....... 390 D1
Newgate La PO14 .. 343 A4
Newgate Lane Ind Est
  PO14............ 343 B4
New Greenham Pk
  RG19............6 E5
New Harbour Rd
  BH15............ 390 B1
New Harbour Rd S
  BH15............ 401 B8
New Harbour Road W
  BH15............ 390 A1
New Horizon Ho RG19..6 E4
New Hos RG20...... 23 E6
Newhouse SO24 ... 156 B6
New House La SP11. 81 B8
New Inn Cotts SO42. 363 C5
New Inn La
  Bartley SO40...... 287 B6
  East Boldre SO42 .. 363 C5
New Inn Rd SO40 .. 287 B7
Newitt Pl SO16..... 266 F6
New La
  Bashley BH25 .... 382 F6
  Havant PO9....... 324 A4
  King's Somborne
  SO20............ 172 B3
  Milford on S SO41.. 399 F3
Newland Ave PO12.. 369 A5
Newlands
  Fareham PO15..... 318 C1
  Fleet GU52 ...... 75 A6
Newlands Ave SO15. 290 D7
Newlands Cl
  Blackfield SO45.... 338 E1
  Chandler's Ford SO53 242 E5
  Yateley GU46...... 34 B5
Newlands Copse
  SO45............ 338 F1
Newlands Dr GU12...77 F4
Newlands La
  Denmead PO7 .... 299 A1
  Waterlooville PO7 .. 322 A6
Newlands Manor
  SO41............ 399 D7
Newlands Prim Sch
  Southampton SO16.. 265 E1
  Yateley GU46...... 34 A5
Newlands Rd
  Blackfield SO45.... 338 E2
  Bournemouth BH7... 394 A6
  Camberley GU15.... 35 F1
  Christchurch BH23.. 395 F7
  New Milton BH25... 383 B1
  Waterlooville PO7 .. 322 D5
Newlands The 2
  SO17............ 267 C2
Newlands Way BH18 374 D3
Newlease Rd PO7... 322 F5
Newlyn Way
  Poole BH12...... 391 E7
  Portsmouth PO6... 345 A7
Newlyn Wlk SO51... 216 A1
Newman La GU34... 140 B5
Newmans Cl
  West Moors BH21... 326 E5
  Wimborne Minster
  BH21............ 351 D3
Newmans Copse Rd
  SO40............ 289 A4

New–Nor 451

Newmans Ct GU9 98 E7
Newmans Hill PO17 272 D1
Newman's La BH22 326 C4
Newman St 2 SO16 290 B8
Newmarket Cl SO50 269 D7
New Marsh Ho SO45 314 A4
Newmer Ct PO9 323 C6
New Merrifield
BH21 351 F7
New Mill La RG27 15 C2
New Mill Rd RG40 15 C3
New Milton Inf Sch
BH25 383 A1
New Milton Jun Sch
BH25 383 A1
New Milton Sta
BH25 383 A3
Newmorton Rd BH9 378 A4
Newney Cl PO2 345 F4
Newnham Ct PO9 324 B5
Newnham La
Newnham RG27 50 A1
Old Basing RG24,RG27 49 E1
Newnham Pk RG27 71 F8
Newnham Rd RG27 71 E8
New North Dr RG27 49 E7
New Odiham Rd
GU34 139 D6
New Orchard BH15 390 B2
New Paddock Cl
GU34 140 C6
New Par
Bournemouth BH10 377 E3
Portchester PO16 344 D8
New Park Rd BH6 394 C4
New Poplars The
GU12 77 E1
Newport Cl
Chandler's Ford
SO53 243 A4
Newbury RG14 1 F4
Newport Jun Sch
GU12 77 B1
Newport La SO51 216 C6
Newport Rd
Aldershot GU12 77 B1
Gosport PO12 368 F5
Newbury RG14 1 F4
New Quay Rd BH15 390 B1
New Rd
Ashurst SO40 288 C2
Basingstoke RG21 69 B4
Bishop's Waltham
SO32 247 D2
Blackfield SO45 338 E1
Blackwater GU17 35 C4
Bordon GU35 164 D1
Bournemouth BH10 377 E7
Clanfield PO8 276 C5
Colden Common SO21 219 F1
Eversley Cross RG27 33 C7
Fair Oak SO50 245 B2
Fareham PO16 319 A1
Ferndown BH22 353 E3
Fleet GU52 75 B6
Greenham RG19 6 B8
Hartley Wintney RG27 52 D6
Haslemere GU27 189 D5
Havant PO9 323 E2
Holbury SO45 338 C7
Hook RG27 72 A8
Horndean PO8 299 E6
Hythe,Buttsash SO45 338 B7
Hythe SO45 314 A4
Ibsley BH24 305 B8
Landford SP5 237 F2
Littleton SO22 175 B6
Meonstoke SO32 249 D3
Micheldever SO21 111 B2
Michelmersh SO51 215 D8
Milford on S SO41 400 A4
Netley SO31 315 B6
Newbury RG14 2 A1
North Warnborough
RG29 72 C4
Over Wallop SO20 147 D8
Pamber End RG26 27 D3
Poole BH12 391 D6
Portsmouth PO2 370 F7
Ringwood BH24 329 A4
Rockbourne SP6 232 E1
Romsey SO51 241 A8
Sandhurst GU47 34 E8
Southampton SO14 291 A5
Southbourne PO10 349 E8
Stratfield Mortimer
RG7 12 B8
Swanmore SO32 272 A5
Swanwick SO31 316 F8
Tadley RG26 26 E7
Tongham GU10 100 D6
Warsash SO31 340 E10
Westbourne PO10 325 B3
Woodlands Common
BH21 302 A6
New Rd Cotts GU34 184 E8
New Rd E PO2 370 F8
New St
5 Poole BH15 390 B1
Andover SP10 106 B8
Lymington SO41 385 E4
Ringwood BH24 329 A6
Stockbridge SO20 149 F3
Stratfield Saye RG7 29 E8
Newstead Rd BH6 394 D4
New Street Mews
SO41 385 E4
Newton Bglws SP5 212 A3
Newton Cl
Stubbington PO14 342 C4
Whiteparish SP5 212 A3
Newton Ct RG24 69 D7
Newton La
Newton Valence
GU34 183 E8
Romsey SO51 240 E6
Whiteparish SP5 212 A3
Newton Morrell
BH14 391 D3
Newton Pk SP10 82 B1
Newton Pl PO13 367 E4
Newton Rd
Barton on S BH25 398 B8
Farnborough GU14 56 B6
Poole BH13 402 F8
Southampton SO18 267 E1
Twyford SO21 220 A7
Newton Toney CE Sch
SP4 123 B5
Newton Villas SP11 57 B1
Newton Way GU10 100 D7
Newtown RG26 9 E1
New Town PO16 344 D8
Newtown Bsns Ctr
BH12 391 A7
Newtown CE Prim Sch
PO12 369 C6
Newtown Cl SP10 105 E7
Newtown Ct SO31 316 C1
Newtown La
Corfe Mullen BH21 374 D8
Ibsley BH24,SP26 282 C1
South Hayling PO11 372 E4
Verwood BH31 303 A5
Newtown Rd
Eastleigh SO50 244 A3
Liphook GU30 188 A3
Newbury RG14 5 E8
Newbury RG14,RG19,
RG20 5 E6
Sandhurst GU47 34 F8
Sherfield English
SO51 214 B3
Southampton SO19 292 B1
Verwood BH31 303 A5
Verwood BH31 303 A6
Warsash SO31 340 C10
Newtown Soberton Inf
Sch PO17 297 C6
New Valley Rd SO41 399 C5
New Villas RG20 3 F3
Nexus Pk GU12 77 D8
Nichola Ct BH12 391 B7
Nicholas Cl BH23 382 B2
Nicholas Cres PO15 318 F2
Nicholas Ct
Lee-on-t-S PO13 367 E2
South Hayling PO11 372 E3
Nicholas Gdns BH10 377 C2
Nicholas Rd SO45 365 F7
Nicholl Pl PO13 343 C2
Nichol Rd SO53 218 D1
Nicholson Cl BH17 390 E8
Nicholson Gdns 1
PO1 404 C3
Nicholson Pl SO24 179 B5
Nicholson Way PO9 323 E3
Nicholson Wlk SO16 265 D6
Nichols Rd SO14 291 B5
Nickel Cl SO23 403 F6
Nickel St 4 PO5 404 A1
Nickleby Gdns SO40 288 B7
Nickleby Ho 10 PO1 370 D7
Nickleby Rd PO8 276 B6
Nickson Cl SO53 243 B8
Nicola Ct GU12 77 B2
Nicotiana Ct 5 GU52 74 E4
Nightingale Ave
SO50 243 D1
Nightingale Cl
5 Winchester
SO22 403 A4
Bursledon SO31 315 F8
Farnborough GU14 55 A6
Gosport PO12 368 F6
Romsey SO51 241 B7
Rowlands Castle PO9 301 A1
Verwood BH31 303 A5
West Wellow SO51 238 D3
Nightingale Cres
SO32 295 F8
Nightingale Ct
Cosham PO6 346 B8
Southampton SO16 266 A4
Westbourne PO10 325 B4
Nightingale Dr
Mytchett GU16 56 E3
Totton SO40 288 C8
Nightingale Gdns
Hook RG27 51 A2
Sandhurst GU47 34 F8
Sherborne St John
RG24 68 C8
Nightingale Gr SO15 290 C7
Nightingale Ho
SO51 241 A8
Nightingale La
Mortimer RG7 11 F7
Stratfield Mortimer
RG7 12 A6
Nightingale Mews
Locks Heath SO31 317 B3
Netley SO31 315 C5
Nightingale Pk 1
PO9 324 B1
Nightingale Prim Sch
SO50 243 D1
Nightingale Rd
Bordon GU35 164 E2
Petersfield GU32 228 E4
Portsmouth PO5 370 B2
Southampton SO15 290 C7
Nightingale Rise
RG25 88 B7
Nightingales The RG14 5 F8
Nightingale Wlk
SO31 315 C4
Nightingdale Ct 3
SO15 290 C6
Nightjar Cl
Broadstone BH17 389 F8
Ewshot GU10 98 B8
Waterlooville PO8 300 A6
Night Owls RG19 6 A7
Nile Rd SO17 267 A2
Nile St PO10 348 F8
Nimrod Dr PO13 368 D6
Nimrod Way BH21 352 F6
Nine Acres GU32 207 B1
Nine Elms La PO17 319 E4
Nine Mile Ride RG40 16 C6
Nine Mile Ride Ind
RG40 16 B5
Nine Mile Ride Prim Sch
RG40 16 D6
Ninfield Dr RG19 6 A7
Ninian Cl SO50 245 C1
Ninian Park Rd PO3 346 A2
Nirvana Mans 12
PO5 370 D1
Niton Cl PO13 343 C2
Noads Cl SO45 313 F2
Noads Way SO45 313 E2
Noadswood Sec Sch
SO45 313 E2
Nobbs La PO1 370 A4
Nobes Ave PO13 343 C3
Nobes Cl PO13 343 D2
Noble Cl BH11 376 F1
Noble Rd SO30 293 D6
Nobs Crook RG27 51 C1
Nob's Crook SO50 245 A7
Noctule Ct PO17 318 D7
Noel Cl SO42 334 A1
Noel Rd BH10 377 B2
Noel The BH25 383 C3
Nomad Cl SO18 268 B1
Nomansland &
Hamptworth CE Prim
Sch SP5 261 C8
Nook The
Eastleigh SO50 244 B5
Gosport PO13 343 E1
Noon Gdns BH31 303 B6
Noon Hill Dr BH31 303 B6
Noon Hill Rd BH31 303 B6
Norbury Cl SO53 243 B7
Norbury Gdns SO31 315 E2
Norcliffe Cl BH11 377 B3
Norcliffe Rd SO17 291 A8
Norcroft Ct SO15 266 C2
Norden Cl RG21 69 B6
Nordik Gdns SO30 293 C5
Nore Cres PO10 324 D1
Nore Farm Ave
PO10 324 D1
Noreuil Rd GU32 228 D3
Norfolk Ave BH23 379 F2
Norfolk Cres PO11 372 E2
Norfolk Ct SO53 243 C3
Norfolk Ho 2 PO9 324 A1
Norfolk Mews PO11 372 E2
Norfolk Rd
Gosport PO12 368 F7
Southampton SO15 290 D7
Norfolk St PO5 404 B2
Norgett Way PO16 344 B7
Norham Ave SO16 266 C2
Norham Cl SO16 266 C2
Norland Rd PO4 404 D1
Norlands Dr SO21 219 C4
Norley Cl PO9 323 E5
Norleywood BH23 396 F8
Norleywood Rd
SO41 386 E8
Norman Ave BH12 392 A6
Norman Cl
Bordon GU35 164 E3
Portchester PO16 344 D6
Norman Court La
Goodworth Clatford
SP11 106 A3
Upper Clatford SP11 105 F4
Norman Court Sch
SP5 168 F2
Norman Ct
4 Portsmouth PO4 370 E2
Farnham GU9 99 A1
Normandy Cl
Rownhams SO16 265 E6
Sway SO41 360 A2
Normandy Ct
Warsash SO31 316 C1
Wickham PO17 296 B4
Normandy Dr BH23 395 D7
Normandy Gdns 1
PO12 368 F4
Normandy Ho SO51 241 B7
Normandy La SO41 386 A1
Normandy Rd PO2 345 E4
Normandy St GU34 140 A4
Normandy Way
Fordingbridge SP6 257 E1
Normandy Way *continued*
Hamworthy BH15 389 D2
Marchwood SO40 290 A1
Norman Gate Sch
SP10 83 C1
Norman Gdns
Hedge End SO30 293 A5
Poole BH12 392 A6
Norman Ho 16 SO14 291 C6
Normanhurst Ave
BH8 378 E1
Norman Rd
Blackfield SO45 365 F8
Gosport PO12 369 A6
Portsmouth PO4 370 E3
Southampton SO15 290 D5
South Hayling PO11 373 B2
Winchester SO23 403 D4
Normans SO23 403 D4
Normanton Cl BH23 379 F1
Normanton Rd RG21 69 B7
Norman Way PO9 323 C2
Normay Rise RG14 5 A5
Norn Hill RG21 69 C7
Norn Hill Cl RG21 69 C6
Norris Cl
Bordon GU35 164 B1
Romsey SO51 216 C2
St Leonards BH24 327 E4
Norris Gdns
Havant PO9 348 A8
New Milton BH25 383 A1
South Wonston SO21 153 D4
Norrish Ct PO2 370 E7
Norris Hill SO18 267 E1
Norris Hill Rd GU51 75 D7
Norris Ho RG25 88 B8
Norrish Rd BH12 391 C5
Norset Rd PO15 318 D2
North Acre SP11 108 C6
Northam Bsns Ctr 21
SO14 291 C6
Northam Mews PO1 404 C3
Northampton La
SO45 365 E8
Northam Rd SO14 291 B5
Northam St PO1 404 C3
Northanger Cl GU34 139 E4
Northarbour Rd PO6 345 D7
Northarbour Spur
PO6 345 D8
North Ave
Bournemouth BH10 377 D6
Farnham GU9 99 B7
Portsmouth PO2 345 E5
North Baddesley Inf Sch
SO52 242 B4
North Baddesley Jun Sch
SO52 242 B4
North Battery Rd
PO2 345 B2
North Bay PO10 349 A3
Northbourne Ave
BH10 377 D5
Northbourne Cl 5
SO45 314 A1
Northbourne Gdns
BH10 377 E5
Northbourne Pl 3
BH10 377 D5
Northbourne Rdbt
BH10 377 E5
Northbrook SO21 132 F4
Northbrook Ave
SO23 198 C7
Northbrook Bower
SO32 271 D8
Northbrook Cl
Portsmouth PO1 370 D7
Winchester SO23 198 C7
Northbrooke Ct
SO23 198 C7
Northbrook Ho
SO32 271 D8
Northbrook Ind Est
SO16 266 C2
Northbrook Pl RG14 1 E3
Northbrook Rd
Aldershot GU11 99 F8
Broadstone BH18 375 A2
Southampton SO14 291 B5
Northbrook Springs
Vineyard* SO32 247 C1
Northbrook St RG14 1 E3
North Camp Sta GU12 77 D8
North Cl
Aldershot GU12 77 C1
Farnborough GU14 55 E8
Gosport PO12 368 F4
Havant PO9 348 A8
Lymington SO41 385 E4
Romsey SO51 216 C1
North Common La
Landford SP5 237 B6
Sway SO41 384 F7
Northcote Gdns
PO10 349 E8
Northcote Rd
Ash Vale GU12 77 E7
Bournemouth BH1 393 C4
Farnborough GU14 55 D6
Portsmouth PO4 370 E3
Southampton SO17 267 C2
Northcott Cl PO12 368 F3
Northcott Gdns GU14 55 B5
North Cres PO11 373 B3
Northcroft Ct RG29 95 A3
Northcroft La RG14 1 D3
Northcroft Rd PO12 368 F6
Northcroft Terr RG14 1 D3
North Cross St PO12 369 D5
North Ct
Finchampstead RG40 16 D4
Portsmouth PO1 370 E7
Northdene Rd SO53 243 C5
North Dr
Littleton SO22 175 B5
Ossemsley BH25 382 E8
Southwick PO17 320 F6
West Moors BH24 354 B8
North East Cl SO19 292 C5
North East Rd SO19 292 B4
North End SO20 170 B7
North End Ave PO2 345 D2
North End Cl SO53 243 C4
North End Farm Cotts
SO24 201 C7
North End Gr PO2 345 D2
Northend La SO32 249 B2
North End La
Cheriton SO24 201 D7
Ibsley BH24,SP6 281 D4
Northern Access Rd
SO45 339 D2
Northern Anchorage
SO19 291 D3
Northern Ave
Andover SP10 83 A1
Donnington RG14 1 E6
Northern Bldgs 10
PO6 345 F8
Northern Galleries 4
PO14 343 A6
Northern Inf Sch
PO16 320 C1
Northern Jun Com Sch
PO16 320 C1
Northern Par PO2 345 E3
Northern Parade Inf Sch
PO2 345 E3
Northern Parade Jun
Sch PO2 345 E3
Northern Rd
Cosham PO6 345 F7
Cosham PO6 345 F8
Fawley SO45 339 E2
Northern Way PO1 369 F8
Northerwood Ave
SO43 309 E5
Northerwood Cl
SO52 241 F4
Northerwood Ho
SO43 309 E6
Northesk Ho PO1 404 C4
Northey Rd BH6 394 E6
North Farm Cl GU14 55 D8
North Farm Rd GU14 55 D8
North Farnborough Inf
Sch GU14 56 B5
North Field RG25 65 A1
Northfield Ave PO14 342 F7
Northfield Cl
Aldershot GU12 77 B1
Bishop's Waltham
SO32 247 A1
Fleet GU52 75 B6
Horndean PO8 276 C2
Northfield Ho RG21 69 C7
Northfield La GU34 161 C8
Northfield Pk PO16 320 B1
Northfield Rd
Fleet GU52 75 C6
Milford on S SO41 399 F4
Ringwood BH24 305 B1
Sherfield on L RG27 29 D1
Southampton SO18 267 F2
Thatcham RG18 2 F4
North Fields Cotts
SO21 220 A7
Northfields Farm La
PO17 296 B5
North Fryerne GU46 34 B8
Northgate Ave PO2 370 F8
Northgate Chambers 10
SO23 403 E6
Northgate Dr GU15 36 E7
Northgate La RG25 92 B1
Northgate Lodge 2
SO23 403 E6
Northgate Way RG22 91 A6
North Greenlands
SO41 385 C2
North Hampshire Hospl
The RG24 68 E8
North Head SO41 399 A5
North Hill
Fareham PO16 319 B3
Portsmouth PO6 321 B2
North Hill Cl SO22 403 D8
North Hill Ct SO22 403 D7
Northington Cnr
SO21 134 B3
Northington Rd
Itchen Abbas SO21 177 F8
Northington SO24 156 C3
North La
Aldershot GU12 77 B2
Beaulieu SO42 336 E5
Buriton GU31 253 E5
Clanfield PO8 276 C7
East Meon PO8 252 C2
Nomansland SP5 261 C7
West Tytherley SP5 169 A2
Northlands Cl SO40 288 D8
Northlands Dr SO23 403 E8
Northlands Gdns
SO15 290 E7
Northlands Rd
Eastleigh SO50 244 A3
Romsey SO51 241 C6
Southampton SO15 290 E8
Totton SO40 288 E8
Northleigh Cnr SO18 267 E5
Northleigh La BH21 351 E6
North Lodge Ind Pk
GU30 188 B1
North Lodge Rd
BH14 391 E4
Northmead GU14 55 F4
Northmead Dr BH17 389 F8
Northmere Dr BH12 391 F7
Northmere Rd BH12 391 F7
North Millers Dale
SO53 243 B8
Northmore Cl SO31 317 B5
Northmore Rd SO31 317 B5
Northney La PO11 348 C4
Northney Rd PO11 348 B4
Northolt Gdns SO16 266 A5
Northover BH3 392 F6
Northover La SO41 383 E7
Northover Rd
Lymington SO41 385 A4
Portsmouth PO3 371 B8
North Par GU35 164 D6
North Park Bsns Ctr
PO17 318 D8
North Poulner Rd
BH24 305 B2
North Rd
Ash Vale GU12 77 D4
Bournemouth BH7 393 E5
Brockenhurst SO42 334 A1
Dibden Purlieu SO45 313 E1
Farnborough GU11 77 B7
Horndean PO8 276 C2
Kings Worthy SO23 154 B1
Petersfield GU32 228 F4
Poole BH14 391 A4
Portsmouth PO6 321 A2
Southampton SO17 291 C8
North Road E PO17 321 A6
North Road W PO17 321 A6
North Row RG26 28 F4
Northshore BH13 402 C4
North Shore Rd
PO11 372 D4
North Side GU10 100 D7
Northside La SO24 180 E6
North Sq 2 PO17 318 E7
North St
Bishop's Sutton
SO24 180 C5
Emsworth PO10 324 F1
Gosport PO12 369 D6
Havant,Bedhampton
PO9 323 D2
Havant PO9 323 F1
Kingsclere RG20 24 D2
Lymington SO41 385 C2
Poole BH15 390 C2
Portsmouth PO1 404 C4
Portsmouth,Portsea
PO1 370 A5
Westbourne PO10 325 B4
North Street Arc 11
PO9 323 F1
North Stroud La
GU32 227 E3
Northtown Trad Est
GU12 77 C1
North Trestle Rd
SO45 339 C6
Northumberland Ct
BH24 328 F7
Northumberland Rd
Bordon GU35 164 D1
Portsmouth PO5 404 D3
Southampton SO14 291 B6
North View SO22 403 C6
North View Gdns 2
RG14 1 F4
North View Rd RG26 27 B7
North Wallington
PO16 319 C3
North Walls SO23 403 E6
North Waltham Prim Sch
RG25 89 E1
North Warnborough St
RG29 72 B3
Northway
Gosport PO13 343 C4
Newbury RG14 1 F2
Titchfield PO15 317 E3
North Way
Andover SP10 83 D2
Havant PO9 323 E1
Northways PO14 367 D7
North Weirs SO42 333 D1
Northwick RG27 33 C7
Northwood Cl SO16 267 A6
Northwood Dr RG14 2 A4
Northwood La PO11 348 A1
Northwood Rd PO2 345 E4
Northwood Sq 8
PO16 319 B2
Nortoft Rd BH8 393 B6
Norton Cl
Christchurch BH23 395 D7
Newbury RG14 5 A6

Norton Cl *continued*
Southampton SO19 291 E3
Southwick PO17 320 F6
Waterlooville PO7 322 D7
Norton Cotts SO21 131 D7
Norton Dr PO16 319 A3
Norton Gdns BH9 377 E1
Norton Rd
Bournemouth BH9 392 E8
Riseley RG7 14 A3
Southwick PO17 320 F6
Norton Ride RG24 69 F7
Norton Way BH15 390 A1
Norton Welch Cl
SO52 242 B4
Norway Cl 3 BH9 377 F1
Norway Rd PO3 346 A4
Norwich Ave
Bournemouth BH2 392 D3
Camberley GU15 36 C3
Norwich Ave W BH2 392 D3
Norwich Cl
Basingstoke RG22 91 B7
Sarisbury SO31 316 E4
Norwich Ct 5 BH2 392 E3
Norwich Mans BH2 392 D3
Norwich Pl PO13 367 E4
Norwich Rd
Bournemouth BH2 392 E3
Portsmouth PO6 321 D1
Southampton SO18 267 F2
Norwood Pl BH5 394 B5
Norwood Prim Sch
SO50 244 A3
Nottingham Pl PO13 367 E4
Nouale La BH24 329 D8
Novello Cl RG22 91 D7
Novello Gdns PO7 322 E6
Noyce Dr SO50 245 D1
Noyce Gdns BH8 379 B2
Nuffield Ind Est
BH17 390 D8
Nuffield Rd
Arborfield Garrison
RG2 15 E8
Poole BH17 390 D7
Nugent Rd BH6 395 A4
Nunns Pk SP5 212 B4
Nuns Rd SO23 403 E7
Nuns Wlk SO23 403 F8
Nursery Cl
Camberley GU16 56 D7
Chineham RG24 49 A3
Emsworth PO10 324 F3
Fleet GU51 75 D8
Gosport PO13 343 B3
Hook RG27 51 A2
Nursery Cotts SP6 234 E1
Nursery Field GU33 207 E3
Nursery Gdns
Chandler's Ford
SO53 243 C3
Romsey SO51 241 A7
Southampton SO19 292 B6
Waterlooville PO8 300 A5
Winchester SO22 403 B6
Nursery Gr SO30 293 C5
Nursery Ho SO53 243 C6
Nursery La PO14 367 C6
Nursery Rd
Alton GU34 140 A4
Bournemouth BH9 378 A3
Havant PO9 323 C2
New Alresford SO24 179 D5
Ringwood BH24 329 A6
Southampton SO18 267 D1
Nursery Terr RG29 72 C4
Nurse's Path SO21 220 A5
Nursling CE Prim Sch
SO16 265 C5
Nursling Cres PO9 324 A5
Nursling Gn BH8 378 D2
Nursling Ind Est
SO16 265 B4
Nursling St SO16 265 C5
Nutash PO14 317 C4
Nutbane Cl SP10 105 E7
Nutbane La SP11 81 F8
Nutbean La RG7 14 D3
Nutbeem Rd SO50 244 A2
Nutbourne GU9 99 C7
Nutbourne Ho PO6 346 D7
Nutbourne Pk PO18 349 F7
Nutbourne Rd
Farlington PO6 346 D7
South Hayling PO11 373 E1
Nutburn Rd SO52 242 B5
Nutchers Dro SO20 172 A3
Nutcombe Ht GU26 167 D4
Nutcombe La GU26 167 C1
Nutfield Ct
Camberley GU15 36 B7
Southampton SO16 265 E3
Nutfield Pl PO1 404 C4
Nutfield Rd SO16 265 D6
Nuthatch Cl
Basingstoke RG22 90 F6
Broadstone BH17 389 F8
Ewshot GU10 98 B7
Ferndown BH22 353 B8
Rowlands Castle PO9 301 B1
Nutley Cl
Bordon GU35 164 D2
Bournemouth BH11 376 F4
Yateley GU46 34 B5
Nutley Dr 6 GU51 53 D3
Nutley La RG25 90 F1
Nutley Rd PO9 323 D5
Nutley Way BH11 376 F4
Nutmeg Ct GU14 55 A5
Nutsey Ave SO40 264 D2
Nutsey Cl SO40 264 E3
Nutsey La SO40 264 E2
Nutshalling Ave
SO16 265 E5
Nutshalling Cl SO40 264 C2
Nutshell La GU9 99 A6
Nutter's La RG2 14 E8
Nutwick Rd PO9 324 B3
Nutwood Way SO40 264 E2
Nyewood Ave PO16 320 D1
Nyria Way PO12 369 D5

O

Oakapple Gdns PO6 346 E8
Oak Ave BH23 394 D8
Oak Bank SP10 106 A6
Oakbank Rd
Bishopstoke SO50 244 D3
Southampton SO19 291 D3
Oak Cl
Basingstoke RG21 69 D5
Baughurst RG26 26 B8
Corfe Mullen BH21 374 C5
Dibden Purlieu SO45 313 E1
Ferndown BH22 353 E1
Kingsclere RG20 24 E2
Lyndhurst SO43 309 F4
North Tidworth SP9 79 A7
Oakley RG23 67 B1
Overton RG25 88 A7
Southampton SO15 289 C8
Upham SO32 246 F5
Waterlooville PO8 299 E2
Oak Coppice Cl
SO50 245 A2
Oak Coppice Rd
PO15 317 D8
Oak Cott 9 GU26 167 B3
Oak Cotts GU27 189 C6
Oakcroft La PO14 342 C5
Oak Ct
Fareham PO15 318 C2
Farnborough GU14 56 C1
Farnham GU9 98 F1
Lymington SO41 385 C2
Oakdale Rd BH15 390 E6
Oakdale South Road Mid
Sch BH15 390 C5
Oakdean Rd PO4 371 C4
Oakdene
Alton GU34 139 E5
Gosport PO13 343 D1
Southampton SO17 267 B2
Totton SO40 288 C7
Oakdene Cl BH21 351 D5
Oakdene Gdns SO50 245 C2
Oakdown Rd PO14 367 D8
Oak Dr
Fair Oak SO50 245 C1
Newbury RG14 1 D1
Petersfield GU31 228 E1
Poole BH15 390 D2
Oaken Botton Cvn Site
BH25 359 E5
Oakenbrow
Hythe SO45 313 D2
Sway SO41 360 A2
Oaken Copse GU52 75 B4
Oaken Copse Cres
GU14 55 F7
Oaken Gr RG14 5 B8
Oakes The PO14 342 B4
Oak Farm Cl GU17 35 A5
Oak Farm Com Sch
GU14 55 D6
Oakfield Ct 13 PO9 324 B5
Oakfield Pl GU14 55 A4
Oakfield Prim Sch
SO40 264 E1
Oakfield Rd
Bartley SO40 287 B7
Blackwater GU17 35 D3
Pamber Heath RG26 10 C1
Poole BH15 390 C6
Totton SO40 288 F7
Oakfields
5 Camberley GU15 35 F5
Basingstoke RG24 69 F8
Eastleigh SO50 244 A7
Oakfields Cl RG20 23 D4
Oakford Ct BH8 378 D3
Oak Gdns
Bournemouth BH11 377 B1
Hordle SO41 399 D8
Oakgreen Par GU34 160 C3
Oak Green Way
SO18 292 A8
Oak Grove Cres GU15 35 D6
Oakgrove Gdns
SO50 244 E2
Oakgrove Rd SO50 244 E2
Oakham Grange
BH22 353 E5
Oak Hanger Cl RG27 51 B1
Oakhanger Ho GU51 53 C3
Oakhanger Rd GU35 164 B5
Oakhill SO31 293 B1
Oak Hill SO24 179 D5
Oakhill Cl
Bursledon SO31 293 B1
Oakhill Cl *continued*
Chandler's Ford SO53 243 E5
Oakhill Ct SO53 243 E5
Oakhill Rd GU35 165 F5
Oakhill Terr SO31 293 B1
Oak Ho
1 Farnborough
GU14 55 F7
7 Grayshott GU26 167 B3
Oakhurst
Christchurch BH23 395 F7
Grayshott GU26 167 B3
Oakhurst Cl
Netley SO31 315 C6
West Moors BH22 326 F2
Oakhurst Com Fst Sch
BH22 326 F2
Oakhurst Dr PO7 323 A8
Oakhurst Gdns PO7 322 B2
Oakhurst La BH22 326 F2
Oakhurst Rd
Southampton SO17 267 A3
West Moors BH22 326 F2
Oakhurst Way SO31 315 C6
Oak La BH24 329 B8
Oakland Ave GU9 99 C7
Oakland Dr SO40 289 F1
Oakland Rd RG28 86 C5
Oaklands
14 Chandler's Ford
SO53 218 B1
Hartley Wintney RG27 52 C5
Hook RG27 71 E7
Lymington SO41 385 F2
South Wonston SO21 153 D4
Waterlooville PO7 323 A6
Yateley GU46 34 B6
Oaklands Ave SO40 288 F8
Oaklands Cl
6 Winchester
SO22 403 A4
Fordingbridge SP6 257 E2
Verwood BH31 302 E6
Oaklands Com Sch
SO16 265 F5
Oaklands Gdns
PO14 317 C1
Oaklands Gr PO8 299 E3
Oaklands Ho 9 PO6 320 F2
Oaklands RC Sch
PO7 322 F5
Oaklands Rd
Havant PO9 324 A1
Petersfield GU32 228 E4
Oaklands The SO53 243 C3
Oaklands Way
Basingstoke RG23 68 C7
Hythe SO45 313 D2
Southampton SO16 266 F4
Titchfield PO14 317 C1
Oakland Terr RG27 52 D6
Oakland Wlk BH22 353 F1
Oaklea GU12 77 E5
Oaklea Cl PO7 322 B2
Oaklea Dr RG27 15 C2
Oak Leaf Cl SO40 312 E8
Oakleafe Pl SO53 243 C6
Oaklea Gdns RG26 29 B2
Oaklea Ho 4 GU26 167 B3
Oakleigh Cres SO40 288 E6
Oakleigh Dr SP5 261 D8
Oakleigh Gdns SO51 241 A7
Oakleigh Way BH23 396 F7
Oakley CE Jun Sch
RG23 67 A1
Oakley Cl SO45 338 C4
Oakley Ct 11 SO16 290 B8
Oakley Dr GU51 75 A8
Oakley Gdns BH16 389 A7
Oakley Hill BH21 351 D2
Oakley Ho
12 Southampton
SO15 290 B8
3 Southampton,Banister's
Pk SO15 290 F7
Portsmouth PO5 404 B1
Oakley Inf Sch RG23 67 A1
Oakley La
Merley BH21 351 E2
Mottisfont SO51 192 F4
Oakley RG23 67 B2
Wimborne Minster
BH21 352 A2
Oakley Pl RG27 52 D6
Oakley Rd
Bordon GU35 164 D5
Camberley GU15 35 F4
Hannington RG26 44 F2
Havant PO9 323 D5
Mottisfont SO51 192 E3
Newbury RG14 2 B4
Southampton,Shirley
SO16 290 A8
Southampton,Wimpson
SO16 289 F8
Wimborne Minster
BH21 351 D2
Oakley Sh Ctr BH21 351 E1
Oakley Straight
BH21 351 E1
Oak Lodge
2 Bordon GU35 164 D2
4 Portsmouth PO2 345 C2
Oak Lodge Specl Sch
SO45 313 C3
Oakmead RG26 28 E3
Oakmead Coll of Tech
BH11 376 F4
Oakmead Gdns BH11 376 F4
Oak Meadow CE Prim
Sch PO15 318 C3
Oakmeadow Cl
PO10 325 A3
Oakmead Rd BH17 389 F7
Oak Mews BH12 391 C5
Oakmont Dr PO8 299 F2
Oakmount Ave
Chandler's Ford
SO53 243 D4
Southampton SO17 267 A1
Totton SO40 288 F8
Oakmount Mans
SO17 266 F1
Oakmount Rd SO53 243 E5
Oak Park Dr PO9 324 A3
Oak Park Ind Est
PO6 345 D8
Oak Rd
Alderholt SP6 280 F5
Bishop's Waltham
SO32 271 E8
Bournemouth BH8 393 C6
Bursledon SO31 315 F8
Clanfield PO8 276 C5
Dibden Purlieu SO45 313 E1
Fareham PO15 318 D2
Farnborough GU14 56 A3
New Milton BH25 383 C3
Southampton SO19 291 E2
Upton BH16 389 C6
Oak Ridge Cl RG14 5 C8
Oakridge Inf Sch
RG21 69 A7
Oakridge Jun Sch
RG21 69 A7
Oakridge Rd
Basingstoke RG21 69 B8
Southampton SO15 289 D8
Oakridge Towers 1
RG21 69 C7
Oaks Coppice PO8 300 A6
Oaks Cvn Pk The
GU33 185 F2
Oaks Dr BH24 327 D3
Oakshott Dr PO9 324 A5
Oaks Mead BH31 303 A6
Oak St PO12 369 C5
Oaks The
Andover SP10 105 E8
Blackwater GU17 35 C3
Bursledon SO31 315 F8
Farnborough GU14 55 B3
Fleet GU51 53 D1
Medstead GU34 160 A7
Newbury RG14 5 E7
Southampton SO19 291 F5
Tadley RG26 26 E8
Verwood BH31 302 E7
Waterlooville PO8 300 A2
Yateley GU46 34 B5
Oakthorn Cl PO13 368 C6
Oaktree Ave RG19 7 F5
Oak Tree Cl
Aldershot GU12 100 C8
Ash Vale GU12 56 D1
Chilbolton SO20 129 A3
Colden Common SO21 244 F8
Headley GU35 165 D4
Oak Tree Cotts RG25 70 E5
Oaktree Ct
Milford on S SO41 399 C4
Southampton SO16 266 E3
Oak Tree Dr
Emsworth PO10 324 F4
Hook RG27 51 B2
Liss GU33 208 A4
Oak Tree Gdns SO30 293 B6
Oak Tree La GU27 189 B6
Oaktree Par BH23 357 B1
Oaktree Pk SO30 268 C4
Oaktree Rd SO18 267 E2
Oak Tree Rd GU35 164 C1
Oaktrees
Ash GU12 77 D1
Farnham GU9 98 F6
Oaktrees Ct GU12 77 D1
Oak Tree View GU9 99 C6
Oak Tree Way SO50 244 A5
Oakum Ho PO3 371 A6
Oak Vale SO18 268 B3
Oakville Mans 11
SO15 290 F6
Oakway
Aldershot GU12 100 C8
Bentley GU10 120 A5
Oakway Dr GU16 36 C1
Oak Wlk SO50 245 C1
Oakwood
Bournemouth BH3 392 E7
Chineham RG24 48 F3
Fleet GU52 75 A4
Oakwood Ave
Havant PO9 323 B3
New Milton BH25 383 C4
Otterbourne SO21 219 C3
Oakwood Cl
Bournemouth BH9 378 B2
Chandler's Ford
SO53 218 D1
Otterbourne SO21 219 C4
Romsey SO51 216 C1
Warsash SO31 340 D10
Oakwood Ct
Chandler's Ford
SO53 218 D1
New Milton BH25 383 B3
Oakwood Ct *continued*
West End SO30 268 E2
Oakwood Ctr The
PO9 324 B3
Oakwood Dr
Alton GU34 139 E2
Southampton SO16 266 C5
Oakwood House
SO21 219 C4
Oakwood Inf Sch
Hartley Wintney
RG27 52 D5
Southampton SO16 266 B5
Oakwood Jun Sch
SO16 266 B5
Oakwood Lodge
SO21 219 C4
Oakwood Rd
Bournemouth BH9 378 B2
Chandler's Ford
SO53 243 D8
Christchurch BH23 381 E1
Portsmouth PO2 345 E4
South Hayling PO11 372 F3
Oakwood Way SO31 316 A3
Oasis Mews BH16 389 A7
Oasis The 12 BH13 392 A4
Oast House Cres GU9 99 B6
Oasthouse Dr GU51 54 C4
Oast House La GU9 99 B6
Oast La GU11 99 F7
Oasts The RG29 95 D4
Oates Mus, Gilbert
White's Ho★ GU34 184 E8
Oates Rd BH9 377 E1
Oatfield Gdns SO40 264 C1
Oatlands SO51 240 F8
Oatlands Cl SO32 269 F1
Oatlands Rd SO32 269 F1
Oban Cl RG23 67 A2
Oban Rd BH3 392 E7
O'bee Gdns RG26 9 C1
Obelisk Ct SO19 291 D2
Obelisk Rd SO19 291 E2
Obelisk Way GU15 36 A6
Oberfield Rd SO42 333 D1
Oberland Ct SO41 385 D4
Oberon Cl PO7 323 A8
Ober Rd SO42 333 E2
Oberursel Way GU11 76 D2
Occupation La PO14 341 E7
Oceana Cres RG23 90 F4
Oceana Ho SO15 290 E5
Oceanarium★ BH2 392 F2
Ocean Cl PO15 318 D2
Ocean Ct PO11 372 E3
Ocean Hts 4 BH5 393 F3
Ocean Pk PO3 346 B1
Ocean Rd
Fareham PO14 342 F5
Southampton SO14 291 A1
Ocean Way SO14 291 B2
Ochil Cl RG22 68 B3
Ockendon Cl PO5 404 B2
Ockham Hall GU35 142 B1
Ocknell Camping Site
SO43 285 B6
Ocknell Gr SO45 313 C3
O'connell Rd SO50 243 F2
O'connor Rd GU11 77 C7
Octavia Gdns SO53 243 F7
Octavia Hill SO22 403 B4
Octavian Cl RG22 91 B7
Octavia Rd SO18 267 E4
Octavius Ct 2 PO7 300 B1
Oddfellows Rd RG14 1 D2
Odell Cl PO16 318 F3
Odeon Bldgs 7 PO6 345 F8
Odette Gdns RG26 10 A1
Odiham Cl
Chandler's Ford
SO53 243 B3
Southampton SO16 265 F4
Odiham Cottage Hospl
RG29 72 E2
Odiham Rd
Ewshot GU10 98 B7
Farnham GU10 98 D7
Heckfield RG7 14 A2
Odiham RG29 72 F6
Winchfield RG27,RG29 73 A8
Officers Quarters The
PO12 369 D6
Officers Row RG26 29 B1
Oglander Rd SO23 403 E8
Ogle Rd SO14 290 F4
O'Gorman Ave GU14 55 F2
O' Jays Ind Pk PO3 346 A2
Okeford Rd BH18 375 C2
Okement Cl SO18 268 B2
OK Mobile Home Pk
BH23 396 B8
Olaf Cl SP10 83 B4
Olave Cl PO13 367 E3
Old Acre Rd GU34 139 F2
Old Agwi Rd SO45 339 C5
Old Auction Ho 13
PO12 369 E5
Old Aylesfield Bldgs
GU34 117 E3
Oldbarn Cl SO40 264 C2
Old Barn Cl
Christchurch BH23 379 D2
North Waltham RG25 89 E1
Ringwood BH24 329 C7
Old Barn Cres PO7 274 C2
Old Barn Farm Rd
BH21 327 B6
Old Barn Gdns PO8 299 F6
Old Barn La GU10 144 F1
Old Barn Rd BH23 379 D2
Old Basing Inf Sch
RG24 70 B6
Old Basing Mall 14
RG21 69 B5
Old Bath Rd RG14 1 D4
Old Beggarwood La
RG22 91 A5
Oldberg Gdns RG22 91 F8
Old Bisley Rd GU16 36 F3
Old Bound Rd BH16 389 C6
Old Brewery The 10
BH15 390 C2
Old Brickfield Rd
GU11 99 F7
Old Brick Kiln Trad Est
The RG26 46 E7
Old Brickyard Rd
SP6 257 B2
Old Bridge Cl SO31 316 B8
Old Bridge House Rd
SO31 316 B8
Old Bridge Rd
Bournemouth BH6 394 D7
Portsmouth PO4 370 E2
Oldbury Cl GU16 56 D8
Oldbury Ct SO16 265 D2
Oldbury Ho 6 PO5 404 B2
Oldbury Way PO14 342 C8
Old Canal 8 PO4 371 B4
Old Canal Pl RG21 69 D5
Old Chapel La GU12 77 E1
Old Christchurch La 12
BH1 392 F3
Old Christchurch Rd
Bournemouth BH1 392 F3
Everton SO41 384 D1
Old Church La GU9 122 B7
Old Coach Mews
BH14 391 A4
Old Coach Rd
Kimpton SP11 79 E1
Shipton Bellinger SP9 102 B8
Old Coastguard Cotts
SO41 400 A3
Old Coastguard Rd
BH13 402 B4
Old College Rd RG14 1 D4
Old Commercial Rd
PO1 370 C7
Old Common SO31 317 A4
Old Common Gdns
SO31 317 A4
Old Common Rd
RG21 69 D4
Old Common Way
SP11 57 A2
Old Compton La GU9 99 D2
Old Contemptibles Ave
GU11 76 C2
Old Convent The
GU10 143 B3
Old Copse Rd PO9 324 A3
Oldcorne Hollow
GU46 33 E5
Old Cottage Cl SO51 238 E3
Old Cove Rd GU51 54 B3
Old Cracknore Cl
SO40 289 F2
Old Cricket Mews
SO15 290 F8
Old Ct RG29 72 E2
Old Dairy Cl 1 GU51 54 A1
Old Dairy The SO21 177 A5
Old Dean Rd GU15 36 B7
Old Down Cl RG22 68 A1
Old Down Rd SP10 82 F1
Olde Farm Dr GU17 34 F5
Oldenburg PO15 317 B8
Oldenburg Cl SP10 82 F3
Old English Dr SP10 82 F4
Old Farm Cl BH24 305 C2
Old Farm Copse
SO51 238 F3
Old Farm Dr SO18 267 F3
Old Farmhouse Cl
SP9 101 E7
Old Farmhouse Mews
SO41 385 E5
Old Farm La
Stubbington PO14 367 C6
Westbourne PO10 325 D3
Old Farm Pl
Ash Vale GU12 77 D5
Ash Vale GU12 77 D5
Old Farm Rd BH15 390 E6
Old Farm Way PO6 346 E7
Old Farm Wlk SO41 385 D3
Old Farnham La
Bentley GU10 97 E1
Farnham GU9 122 A8
Oldfield View RG27 52 C5
Old Forge Cl SP6 280 F6
Old Forge Ct SO41 385 D2
Old Forge End GU47 34 F7
Old Forge Gdn SO20 170 B7
Old Forge Rd
Crookham Village
GU52 74 E3
Ferndown BH21 352 F6
Old Forge The SO32 295 D7
Old Frensham Rd
GU10 122 C4
Old Fromans Farm
SO20 172 A3
Old Garden Cl SO31 317 C2

Old–Pad 453

Oldgate Gdns 1 PO2 345 F4
Old Gdns SO22 403 D8
Old Generator Ho The BH12 392 A5
Old Gosport Rd PO16 343 B8
Old Granary The SP5 234 F8
Old Green La GU15 36 A7
Old Guildford Rd GU16 56 F5
Old Ham La BH21 352 D4
Old Heath Way GU9 99 A7
Old Highway Mews BH21 351 D4
Old Hillside Rd SO22 403 A8
Old Hill The SP11 128 F6
Oldhouse La SO51 238 E7
Old Infirmary Ho 13 PO1 370 A4
Old Iron Foundry The SO20 171 F3
Old Ively Rd GU14, GU51 75 F8
Old Ivy La SO30 268 B2
Old Kempshott La RG22 68 A3
Old Kennels Cl SO22 197 A3
Old Kennels La SO22 197 B3
Old Kiln GU9 98 E2
Old Kiln Cl GU10 144 D2
Old Kiln Ctyd 12 GU9 98 F2
Old Kiln La GU10 144 D2
Old Kiln Rd BH16 389 D6
Old La
Aldershot GU11 99 E7
Ashford Hill RG19 8 D1
Dockenfield GU10 143 D4
Hamstead Marshall RG20 3 C8
Old Laundry The SO21 220 A5
Old Lifeboat House* BH15 390 C1
Old Litten La GU32 206 D3
Old London Rd
Portsmouth PO2 345 F4
Stockbridge SO20 150 A3
Old Lyndhurst Rd SO40 286 F8
Old Magazine Cl SO40 289 F2
Old Maltings The SO41 385 D3
Old Manor Cl BH21 351 D4
Old Manor Farm PO9 323 B1
Old Manor Way PO6 346 B7
Old Market Rd
Corfe Mullen BH21 374 A8
Cosham PO6 345 F8
Old Micheldever Rd SP11 107 B5
Old Mill Ho BH24 328 F6
Old Mill La
Denmead PO7,PO8 299 B8
Hambledon PO8 275 D3
Petersfield GU31 229 C5
Old Mill Pl GU27 189 D7
Old Mill Way SO16 266 A1
Old Milton Gn BH25 382 F1
Old Milton Rd BH25 383 A2
Old Monteagle La GU46 33 F6
Old Mulberry Cl BH10 377 A1
Old Newtown Rd RG14 1 D1
Old Odiham Rd GU34 139 E6
Old Orchard BH15 390 C1
Old Orchards SO41 385 E2
Old Orchard The GU9 121 E7
Old Orch The RG29 94 F4
Old Palace Farm SO20 172 A2
Old Park Cl GU9 98 E6
Old Park Farm GU35 142 C1
Old Park La
Farnham GU9 98 E5
Farnham,Hog Hatch GU10 98 D6
Middle Wallop SO20 126 B4
Old Park Rd SO24 180 E2
Old Parsonage Ct SO21 219 C3
Old Pasture Rd GU16 36 D3
Old Pines Cl BH22 353 E4
Old Pond Cl GU16 36 A1
Old Portsmouth Rd GU15 36 E5
Old Potbridge Rd RG27 52 B2
Old Priory Cl SO31 316 A2
Old Priory Rd BH6 394 F4
Old Pumphouse Cl GU51 54 B2
Old Quarry The GU27 189 D4
Old Rd
Gosport PO12 369 C4
Romsey SO51 241 A7
Southampton SO14 291 B2
Wimborne Minster BH21 351 B5
Old Rd The PO6 345 F6
Old Reading Rd RG21 69 C6
Old Rectory Cl
Corfe Mullen BH21 374 D8
Westbourne PO10 325 B3
Old Rectory Ct SO40 289 B5
Old Rectory Dr GU12 77 F2
Old Rectory Gdns
Farnborough GU14 56 B4
Kings Worthy SO21 176 D6
Old Rectory La SO21 220 A6
Old Rectory Rd PO6 346 F8
Old Rectory The SO20 150 C8
Old Redbridge Rd SO15 289 C8
Old Reservoir Rd PO6 346 D7
Old Riseley Stores The RG7 14 A3
Old River PO7 298 F3
Old Romsey Rd SO40 286 E8
Old Ropewalk BH15 390 A1
Old Rope Wlk The BH15 389 F1
Old St John's Mews BH9 377 F3
Old Salisbury La SO51 215 B2
Old Salisbury Rd
Abbotts Ann SP11 105 B3
Ower SO51 263 F7
Old Sandpit La BH16 374 A2
Old Sawmill Cl BH31 302 E7
Old School Cl
Ash GU12 77 E3
Ferndown BH22 353 C5
Fleet GU51 54 A1
Hardley SO45 338 B6
Hartley Wintney RG27 52 D6
Netley SO31 315 D7
Poole BH14 391 A4
Old School Dr PO11 373 B2
Old School Gdns SO30 268 E2
Old School Ho SO24 135 C4
Old School La GU46 34 A6
Old School Rd
Liss GU33 207 F4
Newnham RG27 71 E8
Old School Terr 8 GU51 54 A1
Old Shamblehurst La SO30 269 C2
Old Spring La SO32 272 B5
Old St
Stubbington,Hill Head PO14 367 A7
Stubbington PO14 342 B4
Old Stacks Gdns BH24 329 C6
Old Star Pl 2 PO1 370 A5
Old Station App SO23 403 F5
Old Station Rd SO21 177 E6
Old Station Way GU35 164 A5
Old Stockbridge Rd SO20 125 C6
Old Stoke Rd SO21 154 A6
Old Swanwick La SO31 316 D8
Old Tannery The SP5 235 A8
Old Thornford Rd RG19 7 C6
Old Timbers PO11 372 F3
Old Town Mews
8 Poole BH15 390 C2
Farnham GU9 98 E2
Old Turnpike PO16 319 B3
Old Van Diemens Rd PO7 322 C5
Old Vicarage Cl BH10 377 E6
Old Vicarage La
King's Somborne SO20 172 A3
Sway SO41 384 C8
Old Vicarage The GU10 121 D7
Old Vineries The SP6 257 D1
Old Vyne La RG26 26 D1
Old Wareham Rd
Corfe Mullen BH16, BH21 374 A3
Poole BH12 391 A7
Old Well Cl The SO19 292 C3
Old Welmore GU46 34 C5
Old Winchester Hill La
Warnford SO32 225 B2
West Meon GU32 225 D2
Old Winchester Hill Nature Reserve* SO32 250 C6
Old Winchester Hill Nature Trail* GU32 250 D6
Old Winton Rd SP10 106 B6
Oldwood Chase GU14 55 A3
Old Worting Rd RG22 68 C4
Old Wymering La PO6 345 E8
Oleander Cl SO31 317 A5
Oleander Dr SO40 288 B8
Olinda St PO1 370 E6
Olive Cres PO16 344 D6
Olive Rd SO16 266 A3
Oliver Rd
Lymington SO41 385 C3
Portsmouth PO4 371 A3
Southampton SO18 267 D3
Oliver Rise GU34 139 F4
Oliver's Battery Cres SO22 197 B4
Oliver's Battery Gdns SO22 197 B3
Oliver's Battery Prim Sch SO22 403 A1
Oliver's Battery Rd N SO22 197 B5
Oliver's Battery Rd S SO22 197 B4
Olivers Cl
Bramley RG26 29 A2
Totton SO40 288 B7
Olivers Ct PO2 370 E8
Oliver's La RG26 29 A4
Olivers Rd BH21 352 A6
Olivers Way BH21 352 A6
Oliver's Wlk RG24 69 F7
Olivia Cl PO7 300 A1
Olympic Way SO50 245 B2
Omdurman Ct 2 SO17 267 A2
Omdurman Rd SO17 267 A2
Omega Ho PO5 404 C3
Omega Pk GU34 140 B3
Omega St PO5 404 C3
Omni Bsns Ctr GU34 140 B3
Onibury Cl SO18 268 A1
Onibury Rd SO18 268 A1
Onslow Cl RG24 48 E1
Onslow Gdns BH21 351 D6
Onslow Ho BH21 351 D6
Onslow Rd
4 Portsmouth PO5 370 D1
Southampton SO14 291 A6
Ontario Way GU30 188 A3
Openfields GU35 165 C6
Ophir Gdns 1 BH8 393 C5
Ophir Rd
Bournemouth BH8 393 B5
Portsmouth PO2 345 E3
Optrex Bsns Pk RG27 50 D4
Oracle Dr PO7 322 E3
Orange Gr
Gosport PO13 343 D1
Over Wallop SP11 124 E5
Orange La SO20 125 D1
Orange Row PO10 348 F8
Oratory Gdns BH13 402 F8
Orbit Cl RG40 16 C6
Orchard Ave
Bishopstoke SO50 244 F1
Poole BH14 390 F2
Orchard Bglws PO17 297 A2
Orchard Cl
Ash Vale GU12 77 E5
Christchurch BH23 395 A6
Colden Common SO21 219 F1
Corfe Mullen BH21 374 D7
Edmondsham BH21 279 A4
Farnborough GU17 35 D1
Farnham GU9 99 E6
Fawley SO45 339 B3
Ferndown BH22 353 E5
Fordingbridge SP6 257 F2
Gosport PO12 344 A1
Haslemere GU27 189 D5
Horndean PO8 300 C6
New Alresford SO24 179 D4
Newbury RG14 2 A5
North Baddesley SO52 241 F5
Ringwood BH24 329 A8
South Hayling PO11 372 F2
South Wonston SO21 153 C4
Totton SO40 288 F5
Orchard Cotts SP11 58 B4
Orchard Ct
Cadnam SO40 286 F8
Camberley GU15 35 F2
Crondall GU10 97 D6
Hedge End SO30 293 E7
Verwood BH31 303 A5
Orchard Cvn Pk The SO40 287 D5
Orchard Dr GU35 165 A4
Orchard End GU10 121 D3
Orchardene RG14 1 F4
Orchard Fields GU51 53 F1
Orchard Gate GU47 34 F8
Orchard Gdns
1 Fordingbridge SP6 257 F1
Aldershot GU12 100 A8
Orchard Gr
New Milton BH25 383 A1
Portchester PO16 344 B7
Waterlooville PO8 299 F3
Orchard Ho
4 Southampton SO14 291 A3
Alton GU34 140 A3
Tongham GU10 100 D7
Winchester SO22 403 C5
Orchard Inf Sch SO45 313 E2
Orchard Jun Sch SO45 313 E3
Orchard La
Alton GU34 140 A3
Orchard La *continued*
Corfe Mullen BH21 374 D7
Emsworth PO10 349 A8
Romsey SO51 240 E7
Southampton SO14 291 A3
Orchardlea SO32 272 C3
Orchard Lea Inf Sch PO15 318 E4
Orchard Lea Jun Sch PO15 318 E4
Orchard Leigh 2 BH25 383 B2
Orchard Mead 2 BH24 329 A8
Orchard Mews 2 BH23 395 A6
Orchard Mount 3 BH24 329 A8
Orchard Pl SO14 291 A3
Orchard Rd
Andover SP10 82 E1
Basingstoke RG22 68 C4
Fair Oak SO50 245 C2
Farnborough, Cove Green GU14 55 E4
Farnham GU9 99 E6
Gosport PO12 369 D7
Havant PO9 347 F8
Locks Heath SO31 316 F2
Mortimer RG7 11 F5
Portsmouth PO4 370 E4
Redlynch SP5 235 D6
South Hayling PO11 373 A2
South Wonston SO21 153 C4
Orchard St BH2 392 E3
Orchards Way
Southampton SO17 267 A2
West End SO30 268 D1
Orchard Terr GU34 140 A4
Orchard The
Bournemouth BH11 376 D6
Bransgore BH23 381 C8
Chilworth SO16 242 E1
Cosham PO6 345 F7
Denmead PO7 298 F4
Hook RG27 51 A2
Kingsclere RG20 24 C1
Milford on S SO41 399 D4
Overton RG25 88 B7
Shipton Bellinger SP9 101 D7
Southampton SO16 267 B5
Tadley RG26 27 B8
Orchard Way
Aldershot GU12 100 A8
Camberley GU15 35 F2
Hythe SO45 313 F2
Orchard Wlk
15 Bournemouth BH2 392 E3
Winchester SO22 403 B8
Orcheston Rd BH8 393 C6
Orchid Ct 2 SP10 105 D6
Orchid Way BH23 395 C7
Ordnance Ct PO3 346 A5
Ordnance Rd
Aldershot GU11 77 A3
Gosport PO12 369 D5
North Tidworth SP9 78 F6
Southampton SO15 291 A6
Ordnance Rdbt GU11 76 F2
Ordnance Row PO1 370 A5
Ordnance Way SO40 290 A3
Oregon Cl SO19 292 A4
Oregon Wlk RG40 16 C7
Orestes Gate BH23 396 A5
Orford Cl BH23 379 D4
Orford Ct 4 PO6 345 F7
Oriana Way SO16 265 B4
Oriel Dr PO14 317 B1
Oriel Hill GU15 36 B4
Oriel Rd PO2 345 D2
Orient Dr SO22 175 C3
Orion Ave PO12 369 C8
Orion Cl
Southampton SO16 265 F4
Stubbington PO14 367 D7
Orion Ind Ctr SO18 267 E5
Orkney Cl
Basingstoke RG24 48 D1
Southampton SO16 265 E4
Orkney Rd PO6 321 F1
Ormesby Dr SO53 243 B8
Ormond Cl SO50 245 B2
Ormonde Rd BH13 392 A2
Ormsby Rd PO5 404 B1
Orpen Rd SO19 292 C4
Orpheus Ho 2 RG7 9 C2
Orpine Cl PO15 317 F3
Orsmond Cl PO7 322 F6
Orts Rd RG14 1 F2
Orwell Cl
Farnborough GU14 55 C6
Gosport PO12 369 C8
Southampton SO16 265 E1
Orwell Cres PO14 317 C2
Orwell Rd GU31 228 E2
Osborn Cres PO13 343 B4
Osborn Ct PO3 346 B4
Osborne Cl
1 Waterlooville PO7 323 A7
Alton GU34 139 D3
Basingstoke RG21 69 A7
Camberley GU16 56 D8
Netley SO31 315 C5
Osborne Ct
7 Milford on S SO41 399 C4
Osborne Ct *continued*
Farnborough GU14 77 A8
Fleet GU51 74 F8
Southampton SO17 267 C1
Osborne Dr
Chandler's Ford SO53 243 E5
Fleet GU52 75 B7
Osborne Gdns
Fair Oak SO50 245 E1
Southampton SO17 267 C1
Osborne Ho
Southampton SO14 291 B3
West Wellow SO51 238 E3
Osborne Rd
Andover SP10 106 A7
Bournemouth BH9 392 E8
Farnborough GU14 77 A8
Gosport PO12 369 D6
Lee-on-t-S PO13 367 E3
New Milton BH25 383 B3
Petersfield GU32 228 F4
Poole BH14 391 B3
Portsmouth PO5 370 C2
Totton SO40 289 A7
Warsash SO31 340 D10
Wimborne Minster BH21 351 D4
Osborne Rd N SO17 267 C1
Osborne Rd S SO17 291 C8
Osborne Sch SO23 403 D7
Osborne View Rd PO14 367 A6
Osborn Mall 3 PO16 319 C1
Osborn Rd
Fareham PO16 319 B1
Farnham GU9 99 B4
Osborn Rd S PO16 319 B1
Osborn Sq 2 PO16 319 C1
Osborn Way RG27 72 B8
Osbourne Ho 4 BH25 383 A3
Osgood Ct GU10 100 C8
Osier Cl PO2 345 C3
Osier Ho 9 RG26 26 F8
Osier Rd GU31 228 D1
Oslands La SO31 316 D7
Osler Cl RG26 28 F3
Oslo Twrs SO19 314 E8
Osnaburgh Hill GU15 35 F5
Osprey Cl
Christchurch BH23 396 A5
Farlington PO6 346 E7
Marchwood SO40 289 E1
Southampton SO16 266 B5
Osprey Ct PO16 343 F8
Osprey Dr PO11 373 B3
Osprey Gdns
Aldershot GU11 99 E7
Lee-on-t-S PO13 367 F3
Osprey Quay PO10 349 B7
Osprey Rd RG22 67 F1
Ossemsley Manor Ho BH23 382 D6
Ossemsley South Dr BH25 382 F8
Osterley Cl SO30 293 E6
Osterley Ct BH23 395 A8
Osterley Rd SO19 291 E5
Ostlers The SO41 384 A3
Oswald Cl BH9 377 E2
Oswald Rd BH9 377 F2
Othello Dr PO7 323 A8
Ottawa Dr GU30 188 A3
Otterbourne 14 BH2 392 D4
Otterbourne CE Prim Sch SO21 219 B2
Otterbourne Cres
Havant PO9 323 D5
Tadley RG26 26 F6
Otterbourne Hill SO21 219 B2
Otterbourne Ho SO21 219 B2
Otterbourne House Gdns SO21 219 B2
Otterbourne Rd
Compton SO21 197 E1
Compton SO21 219 D6
Otterbourne Wlk RG27 49 B5
Otter Cl
3 Gosport PO13 368 D5
Bishopstoke SO50 245 A2
Upton BH16 389 B6
Verwood BH31 303 A5
Otter Rd BH15 390 F6
Otters Wlk BH25 383 C5
Our Lady & St Joseph RC Prim Sch SO41 385 A4
Ouse Cl SO53 243 A8
Ouse Ct 32 SP10 83 C2
Outer Circ SO16 266 A4
Outlands La SO30 294 D7
Outram Rd PO5 404 C1
Outwick Cross SP6 257 F8
Oval Gdns PO12 368 F4
Oval Rd SO51 192 A1
Oval The
Andover SP10 83 C3
Liss GU33 207 F4
Oven Camping Site The PO11 372 F5
Overbecks RG14 2 B4
Overbridge Sq RG14 2 C3
Overbrook SO45 313 F2
Overbrook Way SO52 241 E5
Overbury Manor BH12 392 B5
Overbury Rd BH14 391 C3
Overcliffe Mans BH1 393 C3
Overcliff Rise SO16 266 E4
Overcombe Cl BH17 375 E2
Overdale Pl GU35 164 D1
Overdale Rise GU16 36 C3
Overdale Wlk GU35 164 D1
Overdell Ct 8 SO15 290 E7
Over Links Dr BH14 391 D2
Overlord Cl GU15 36 A8
Overstand Cres SO41 399 D3
Overton CE Prim Sch RG25 65 A1
Overton Cl GU11 100 A6
Overton Cres PO9 323 D5
Overton Ho RG25 88 B8
Overton Rd
Breach PO10 325 E1
Micheldever SO21 111 C3
Overton Sta RG25 65 B2
Oviat Cl SO40 288 B7
Ovington Ave BH7 394 C7
Ovington Ct SO18 292 D8
Ovington Dr 9 GU51 53 D3
Ovington Gdns BH7 394 C7
Ovington Rd SO50 244 A1
Owen Cl PO13 368 C7
Owen Rd
Eastleigh SO50 243 F2
Newbury RG14 1 F6
Owen's Rd SO22 403 D7
Owen St PO4 371 A2
Ower La SO45 366 E8
Owletts Gr RG14 2 B4
Owlshotts BH13 402 F7
Owlsmoor Rd GU47 35 B8
Owls Rd
Bournemouth BH5 393 E3
Verwood BH31 303 A5
Owslebury Bottom SO21 221 A5
Owslebury Gr PO9 323 F5
Owslebury Prim Sch SO21 221 A4
Oxburgh Cl SO50 243 F5
Ox Dro
Kimpton SP11 79 F2
Picket Piece SP10,SP11 83 F1
South Wonston SO21 153 F4
Ox Drove Rise SP11 84 B3
Ox Drove Way SO24 137 A1
Oxenden Ct GU10 100 C8
Oxenden Rd GU10 100 D8
Oxendown SO32 249 C4
Oxenwood Gn PO9 323 D6
Oxey Cl BH25 383 A1
Oxford Ave
Bournemouth BH6 394 B5
Southampton SO14 291 B6
Oxford Cl PO16 319 A2
Oxford La
Bournemouth BH11 377 B6
Swanmore SO32 272 F7
Oxford Rd
Bournemouth BH8 393 B4
Farnborough GU14 56 A1
Gosport PO12 368 F5
Newbury RG14 1 D5
Portsmouth PO5 404 D1
Southampton SO14 291 A7
Sutton Scotney SO21 131 C4
Oxford St
Newbury RG14 1 D4
Southampton SO14 291 A3
Oxford Terr SO41 360 C2
Oxlease Cl SO51 216 A1
Oxleys Cl PO14 342 B8
Oxted Ct 5 PO4 371 B5
Oyster Cl RG22 91 B7
Oyster Ct PO13 367 D4
Oyster Est The PO6 346 C6
Oyster Mews
5 Emsworth PO10 348 F8
7 Portsmouth PO1 370 A3
Oyster Quay PO6 345 B7
Oyster St PO1 370 A3
Ozier Rd SO18 268 A2

P

Pacific Cl SO14 291 C2
Packenham Rd RG21 68 F3
Pack La RG23 67 D2
Packridge La SO51, SO52 241 F1
Packway GU9,GU10 122 C7
Padbury Cl PO2 345 F4
Paddington Cl BH11 376 D4
Paddington Gr BH11 376 D3
Paddington Ho 7 RG21 69 B5
Paddington Rd PO2 345 F1
Paddock Cl
Camberley GU15 36 E6
Ferndown BH21 353 A5
Poole BH12 391 B7
South Wonston SO21 153 E4
St Leonards BH24 327 F4
Paddock Ct RG27 52 C5

Paddock End PO7... 298 F3
Paddock Field
Chilbolton SO20.... 129 B5
Monk Sherborne RG26 47 B5
Paddockfields RG24.... 70 B8
Paddock Gdns SO41. 385 D5
Paddock Gr BH31 ... 303 A5
Paddock Rd
Basingstoke RG22.... 68 D3
Newbury RG14 ...... 5 D8
Paddocks The
Bournemouth BH10.. 377 D4
Fawley SO45 .... 339 B3
Paddock The
Brockenhurst SO42.. 333 F1
Eastleigh SO50 ..... 244 B6
Farnham GU10 ..... 121 D4
Fordingbridge SP6.. 282 E6
Gosport PO12 ...... 369 A4
Grayshott GU26.... 166 F4
Hartley Wintney RG27. 52 D7
Haslemere GU27.... 189 E8
Headley GU35 ..... 165 C5
Kingsclere RG20 .... 24 C2
Kings Worthy SO23.. 176 C5
Newbury RG14 ...... 2 A2
Stubbington PO14... 342 C4
Totton SO40....... 264 C2
West Moors BH24... 354 C8
Paddock Way
Liphook GU30 ...... 188 A5
New Alresford SO24. 179 C4
Petersfield GU32.... 228 D2
Paddock Wlk
Basingstoke RG22.... 68 D3
Portchester PO6.... 345 A8
Padfield Cl BH6..... 394 E6
Padget Rd BH24 .... 305 C1
Padnell Ave PO8.... 300 A4
Padnell Inf Sch PO8. 300 A3
Padnell Jun Sch
PO8............. 300 B3
Padnell Pl PO8 ..... 300 B2
Padnell Rd PO8..... 300 B4
Padstow Pl SP6..... 281 E8
Padwell Rd SO14.... 291 A7
Padwick Ave PO6 ... 346 A8
Padwick Cl RG21.... 69 A4
Padwick Ct PO11.... 372 E3
Padworth Rd RG7.... 11 B8
Paffard Cl PO13..... 368 C7
Page Cl SO45 ...... 338 D2
Pages La SO42..... 363 C6
Pages Yd RG28 ..... 86 C4
Paget Cl
Camberley GU15..... 36 F7
North Tidworth SP9... 78 D8
Wimborne Minster
BH21........... 352 A7
Paget Rd
Bournemouth BH11.. 377 A4
Gosport PO12 ...... 369 A3
Paget St SO14 ...... 291 B4
Pagham Cl PO11.... 349 A8
Pagham Gdns PO11. 373 F2
Paice La GU34 ..... 159 E4
Paignton Ave PO3... 371 A8
Paignton Rd SO16... 265 F1
Paimpol Pl SO51..... 240 E6
Pain's Rd PO5...... 404 C2
Painswick Cl
Cosham PO6 ...... 345 C8
Sarisbury SO31..... 316 F6
Painter Cl PO3..... 346 B3
Painters Field SO23. 403 C2
Painters Pightle RG27 50 F1
Paisley Rd BH6..... 394 C5
Pakenham Dr GU11.. 76 D3
Palace Cl SO30..... 171 F2
Palace Gate RG29.... 72 D3
Palace Gate Farm
RG29............ 72 D3
Palace Ho★ SO42.. 336 F2
Palace La SO42..... 336 F1
Palace Mews SO32.. 271 C7
Pale La
Fleet RG27.......... 53 A2
Hartley Wintney RG27. 53 D4
Palestine Rd SP11.. 124 D5
Palfrey Rd BH10 .... 377 C6
Paling Bsns Pk SO30 293 B4
Palk Rd PO9........ 323 D1
Pallant Gdns PO16.. 319 D2
Pallant The PO9.... 323 F1
Pallet Cl SO21...... 244 F8
Palliser Ct GU26.... 167 A6
Pallot Cl SO31...... 292 F1
Palma Ct BH23...... 397 A7
Palm Ct 17 PO5..... 370 C2
Palmer Dr SP10..... 106 D8
Palmer Pl BH25..... 383 A4
Palmer Rd BH15 .... 390 C5
Palmers Cl SO50.... 245 D1
Palmer's Rd PO10.. 324 F1
Palmerston Ave
Christchurch BH23 . 395 D6
Fareham PO16...... 319 E4
Palmerston Bsns Pk
PO14............. 343 B7
Palmerston Cl
Farnborough GU14... 55 B3
Upton BH16........ 389 D7

Palmerston Ct
26 Portsmouth
PO5............ 370 C2
Palmerston Dr PO14 343 A7
Palmerston Mans 3
PO5............ 370 C2
Palmerston Pl SP10. 106 E7
Palmerston Rd
Bournemouth BH1... 393 E5
Poole BH14 .... 391 D4
Portsmouth PO5 .... 370 C2
Southampton SO14 . 291 A4
South Hayling PO11.. 373 A4
Upton BH16........ 389 C7
Palmerston Road Prec 4
PO5............ 370 C2
Palmerston St SO51. 240 F7
Palmerston Way
PO12............ 368 F2
Palmers Yd RG20.... 23 E6
Palm Hall Cl SO23... 403 F5
Palm Rd SO16...... 266 A3
Palmyra Rd PO12.... 369 A8
Palomino Dr PO15 .. 317 B7
Pamber Dr 5 GU51.. 53 D3
Pamber Heath Rd
RG26............ 10 C1
Pamber Rd
Charter Alley RG26... 46 F8
Silchester RG7...... 10 F1
Pamela Ave PO6.... 320 F1
Pamphill CE Fst Sch
BH21............ 350 E5
Pamplyn Cl SO41... 385 C4
Pangbourne Ave
PO6............ 346 B7
Pangbourne Cl SO19 292 A4
Pankridge St GU10... 97 D7
Pannall Rd PO12.... 369 A8
Pannells GU10 ..... 122 B5
Panorama Ct PO13.. 367 E3
Panorama Rd BH13 . 402 B2
Pans Cnr BH22...... 353 F3
Pan's Gdns GU15.... 36 D4
Pan St PO1........ 404 B4
Pansy Rd SO16...... 267 A4
Pantheon Rd SO53... 243 F7
Pantile Dr RG27..... 51 C1
Pantiles The PO6.... 257 D1
Pantings La RG20 ... 21 D7
Panton Cl PO10 .... 324 E3
Pantull Rd SO18.... 292 A7
Papermakers RG25... 88 B7
Paper Mill La GU34 . 140 A4
Parade Ct PO2...... 345 E5
Parade The
3 Pamber Heath
RG26 .... 9 F1
4 Bournemouth BH6 394 E3
Ash Vale GU12...... 77 E4
Basingstoke RG21.... 66 C6
Cadnam SO40 ..... 286 F8
New Milton BH25 ... 383 D3
Old Milton BH25 ... 382 F1
Poole BH17 .... 375 B1
Portsmouth PO1 .... 370 A6
Paradise La
Bartley SO40....... 287 D6
Bishop's Waltham
SO32........... 271 F6
Fareham PO16...... 319 E2
Westbourne PO10 .. 325 B4
Paradise St
14 Poole BH15 ..... 390 B1
Portsmouth PO1 .... 403 A6
Parchment St SO23 . 403 E6
Parchment The PO9. 323 F1
Pardoe Cl SO30..... 293 C5
Pardys Hill BH21.... 374 D8
Parfitts Cl GU9...... 98 E2
Parham Cl BH25..... 382 E3
Parham Dr SO50.... 243 F4
Parham Rd
Bournemouth BH10.. 377 C2
Gosport PO12 ...... 369 C7
Parish Cl
Ash GU12........... 77 F1
Farnham GU9....... 98 E6
Parish Rd SO41..... 385 E4
Parish Rd
Farnborough GU14... 77 A8
Poole BH15 .... 390 E3
Park App PO17...... 318 E7
Park Ave
Bournemouth BH10.. 377 C6
Camberley GU15..... 36 B4
Lymington SO41..... 385 D4
Old Basing RG24 .... 70 B5
Waterlooville PO7... 322 C3
Winchester SO23 ... 403 E6
Park Cl
8 Aldershot GU12... 77 A1
Binsted GU10 ..... 120 E2
Brockenhurst SO42.. 334 A2
Burton BH23 ...... 380 C3
Gosport PO12 ..... 368 F6
Hythe SO45........ 314 B4
Kingsley GU35..... 142 C1
Lyndhurst SO43..... 310 A3
Marchwood SO40 .. 289 D1
Milford on S SO41... 399 E4
New Milton BH25 ... 383 C5
Oakley RG23....... 67 B2
Park Close Rd GU34. 140 A5
Park Com Sch PO9.. 323 C5
Park Corner Rd RG27. 52 D7

Park Cotts
4 Camberley GU15 .. 35 F3
Wickham PO17 .... 296 A3
Park Court Flats 7
SO15 .... 290 C6
Park Cres PO10..... 324 D1
Park Ct
12 Poole BH13 ..... 392 B3
14 Milford on S SO41 399 C4
1 Petersfield GU32.. 228 F3
1 Winchester SO23 . 403 E8
Farnham GU9 .... 99 B3
Portsmouth PO5 .... 404 B1
Park Dr BH31....... 302 E7
Park Dro SO20..... 125 E3
Park End RG14...... 1 E4
Parker Cl PO12 .... 344 A1
Parker Gdns PO7... 322 C3
Parker Rd BH9...... 392 F7
Parkers Cl BH24.... 305 C1
Park Farm GU9..... 99 E5
Park Farm Ave PO15 318 D3
Park Farm Cl PO15.. 318 D3
Park Farm Ind Est
GU16............. 36 A1
Parkfield Ho 11 PO6. 320 F2
Parkfields GU46..... 34 B6
Park Gate BH25..... 383 A2
Park Gate Bsns Ctr
SO31........... 317 B6
Park Gate Mews 7
BH2 .... 392 E3
Park Gate Prim Sch
SO31........... 317 B6
Park Gdns
Basingstoke RG21.... 69 C3
Christchurch BH23 .. 395 E7
Park Glen SO31..... 317 C4
Park Gr PO6....... 345 F7
Park Heritage Ctr The★
SO31........... 315 C4
Park Hill GU52...... 74 F5
Parkhill Cl GU17..... 35 B4
Park Hill Cl SO45.... 338 C3
Parkhill Farm Cotts
SO21........... 133 F7
Parkhill Rd GU17.... 35 B4
Park Ho
2 Aldershot GU11... 76 E1
9 Portsmouth PO5.. 370 C2
Winchester SO23 ... 403 E6
Park Homer Dr
BH21........... 352 A6
Park Homer Rd
BH21........... 351 F6
Parkhouse Cnr SP4. 101 E3
Park House Cotts
RG20 .... 44 C8
Parkhouse Cross
SP4............ 101 D4
Parkhouse Farm Way
PO9............ 323 C5
Park House Mews
SP4............ 101 E4
Parkhouse Rd SP9 . 101 D7
Portsmouth PO1 .... 370 A6
Park House Sch & Sports
Coll RG14.......... 5 C6
Parkhurst Cotts
GU10........... 166 D8
Parkhurst Fields
GU10........... 144 D1
Park La
1 Southampton
SO15........... 290 F5
Alderholt SP6 ..... 280 F6
Arborfield Garrison
RG40 .... 15 F5
Bournemouth BH10.. 377 E2
Bucklers Hard SO42. 388 B7
Camberley GU15 ... 36 A5
Cosham PO6 ...... 346 A7
Droxford SO32...... 249 B1
Hamstead Marshall
RG20 .... 3 F8
Havant,Bedhampton
PO9............ 323 C3
Havant PO9........ 323 C7
Kings Worthy SO21.. 176 D6
Lower Froyle GU34 . 119 C5
Marchwood SO40 .. 289 C7
Milford on S SO41... 399 D4
Newbury RG14 ...... 1 E4
Old Basing RG24 .... 70 B5
Otterbourne SO21... 244 B8
Quarley SP11....... 103 A4
Ropley SO24 ...... 181 B3
Rowland's Castle
PO10........... 325 C8
Silchester RG7...... 12 A2
Stratfield Saye RG7... 13 A2
Stubbington PO14... 367 C8
Swanmore SO32 ... 248 D1
Swanmore SO32 ... 272 B8
Twyford SO21 ..... 220 A5
Waterlooville PO8... 300 A2
West Dean SP5 .... 190 B8
Wimborne Minster
BH21........... 351 C4
Park Lake Rd BH15. 390 E2
Parkland Cl BH31... 303 D4
Parkland Dr BH25... 397 F8
Parkland Gr GU9.... 99 D8

Parkland Pl
15 Southampton
SO17........... 291 A8
New Milton BH25 ... 383 A2
Parklands
11 Bournemouth
BH4 .... 392 C3
Haslemere GU26.... 167 C1
Locks Heath SO31... 317 A4
Southampton SO18 . 267 E1
Totton SO40....... 289 A4
Parklands Ave PO8.. 300 A5
Parklands Bsns Pk
PO7............ 298 F3
Parklands Cl
Chandler's Ford
SO53........... 243 C7
Gosport PO12 ..... 369 B7
Havant PO9........ 323 C1
Newbury RG14 ...... 1 E3
West Moors BH24... 326 E2
Parkway Dr BH8.... 393 E8
Parkway Gdns SO53. 243 C7
Parkway S Rdbt
PO15........... 317 D7
Parkway The
Gosport PO13 ..... 343 B2
Southampton SO16 . 267 B5
Park Wlk
Fareham PO15...... 318 D3
Southampton SO14 . 291 A5
Parkwood Cl
Chineham RG24..... 48 F4
Hedge End SO30 ... 293 C7
Parkwood Ctr PO7.. 322 E8
Parkwood La 7 BH5 394 B5
Parkwood Rd
Bournemouth BH5.. 394 A4
Wimborne Minster
BH21........... 351 C4
Parley Cl BH22..... 353 F1
Parley Cross BH22 . 377 E8
Parley Fst Sch BH22 353 D3
Parley Green La
BH23........... 378 B7
Parley La BH23..... 378 D7
Parley Rd BH9...... 378 A2
Parliament Pl SO22. 403 A2
Parmiter Dr BH21... 351 E4
Parmiter Ho 6
SO23........... 403 F6
Parmiter Rd BH21.. 351 E4
Parmiter Way BH21. 351 E4
Parnell Ct SP10..... 82 C1
Parnell Rd SO50.... 243 F2
Parr Ho 1 BH14 ... 391 A4
Parr Rd PO6....... 345 D8
Parr St BH14....... 391 A4
Parry Cl PO6....... 344 E8
Parry Rd SO19...... 292 D4
Parsonage Barn La
BH24........... 329 B7
Parsonage Cl
Fordingbridge SP6.. 257 F2
Petersfield GU32.... 229 B5
Upper Farringdon
GU34........... 161 E3
Parsonage Ct 9
BH8 .... 393 A5
Parsonage Farm Inf Sch
GU14........... 55 A5
Parsonage La SO32. 270 B5
Parsonage Park Dr
SP6............ 257 E2
Parsonage Rd
Bournemouth BH1.. 393 A3
Southampton SO14 . 291 C6
Parsonage Way GU16 36 C1
Parsons Cl
Arborfield Garrison
RG2 .... 15 E8
Fleet GU52 .... 74 F5
Newbury RG14 ..... 1 C2
Portsmouth PO3 ... 345 F5
Parsons Down Inf & Jun
Schs RG19........ 2 E3
Parsons Field GU47.. 34 F8
Parsons La GU26... 167 B6
Part La RG7........ 14 C4
Partridge Ave GU46.. 33 F6
Partridge Cl
Barton Stacey
SO21........... 130 D7
Basingstoke RG22... 90 F7
Christchurch BH23 . 396 A5
Ewshot GU10....... 98 B8
Fareham PO16...... 343 E8
Frimley GU16...... 36 C1
Partridge Down
SO22........... 197 B3
Partridge Dr BH14 . 391 C1
Partridge Gdns PO8. 299 D4
Partridge Gn
Alton GU34 .... 139 F5
New Milton BH25 ... 383 B6
Partridge Hill SP5 .. 238 A3
Partridge Rd
Brockenhurst SO42.. 360 F8
Dibden Purlieu SO45. 313 F1
Partridge Wlk BH14. 391 B1
Partry Cl SO53..... 243 A8
Paschal Rd GU15.... 36 D8
Pascoe Cl BH14.... 391 A4
Passage La SO31... 316 B1
Passfield Ave SO50. 243 E2
Passfield Cl SO50... 243 E2
Passfield Ent Ctr
GU30........... 187 B8

Parkview Cl SP10....82 E2
Park View Ct BH8... 393 E2
Park View Inf Sch
RG22........... 68 C2
Park View Jun Sch
RG22........... 68 C2
Park View Mews
BH25........... 383 A2
Park Villas SO32.... 249 B1
Parkville Rd SO16... 267 D4
Park Vista SO32.... 226 D1
Parkwater Rd SP5 .. 212 D2
Parkway
Camberley GU15.... 36 A3
Whiteley PO15...... 317 F7
Park Way
Fair Oak SO50 ..... 245 E2
Havant PO9........ 323 E1
Newbury RG14 ...... 1 E3
West Moors BH24... 326 E2
Paston Ho 10 PO17. 318 E7
Pastures The
6 Eastleigh SO50... 244 A2
Cheriton SO24...... 201 C6
Denmead PO7...... 298 E3
Kings Worthy SO23 . 154 B1
Locks Heath PO14... 317 C4
Pat Bear Cl SO15... 289 C8
Patchins Rd BH16... 389 B4
Patchins The BH14.. 402 C8
Pathway Dr PO14 .. 342 D8
Paternoster Ho 4
SO23........... 403 E5
Paternoster Row 5
SO23........... 403 E5
Paterson Cl RG22.... 91 C7
Paterson Rd GU33.. 186 C2
Pathfinders The GU14 55 A3
Patricia Cl SO30.... 268 C2
Patricia Dr SO30.... 293 D7
Patrick Howard-Dobson
Ct 6 PO8......... 299 F4
Patrick's Cl GU33... 208 A4
Patrick's Copse Rd
GU33........... 208 A4
Patten Ave GU46.... 34 A5
Patterdale Ho 6
PO6............ 321 B1
Pattinson Cres SP11 105 A7
Paul Cl GU11 .... 99 C8
Paulet Cl SO18...... 268 A1
Paulet Lacave Ave
SO16........... 265 D6
Paulet Pl
Old Basing RG24 .... 70 B6
Winchester SO22 ... 403 C3
Pauletts La SO40.... 264 B3
Paul's Field RG27.... 33 C8
Paulsgrove Ent Ctr
PO6............ 345 B8
Paulsgrove Ind Ctr
PO6............ 345 B8
Paulsgrove Prim Sch
PO6............ 345 C8
Paulsgrove Rd PO2. 370 F8
Pauls La SO41...... 384 E8
Paulson Cl SO53.... 243 C8
Paultons Park★
SO51........... 263 C6
Pauncefoot Hill
SO51........... 240 C5
Pauncefote Rd BH5. 394 A5
Pauntley Rd BH23... 395 E5
Pavan Gdns BH10... 377 C2
Pavilion Cl SO50.... 269 D8
Pavilion Ct 4 SO15. 290 E7
Pavilion Rd
Aldershot GU11..... 76 C1
Farnborough GU11... 76 B7
Hedge End SO30 ... 293 D8
Pavilions End The
GU15............ 36 B3
Pavilion The 23 BH4. 392 C4
Pavilion Way PO12 . 369 D6
Paviors GU9........ 99 A3
Pawley Cl GU10..... 100 C7
Pawmers Mead GU52 74 E3
Pax Hill GU10....... 119 F4
Paxton Cl
Basingstoke RG22... 91 B3
Hedge End SO30 ... 293 D5
Paxton Ct SO31..... 317 A2
Paxton Rd PO14.... 343 A8
Payne Cl PO2....... 326 E5
Paynes Cl
Broughton SO20 ... 170 B7
Headley RG19...... 24 C8
Paynesdown Rd RG19 2 F4
Paynes Hay Rd
Braishfield SO51.... 194 C1
Braishfield SO51.... 216 C8
Payne's La SO50 ... 245 C3
Payne's Mdw RG24.. 70 A8
Payne's Rd SO15.... 290 C6
Peabody Rd GU14.... 77 B8
Peace Cl BH23...... 381 A8
Peach Gr SP11..... 124 C5
Peach Rd SO16..... 266 A4
Peach Tree Cl SU14.. 55 E7
Peacock Cl PO16.... 343 E8
Peacock La PO1 .... 370 A3
Peacock Pl 4 SO23. 198 C8
Peak Cl SO16....... 289 F8
Peak Dr PO14...... 342 D8
Peake Cl RG24...... 69 F7
Peaked Post SP5.... 230 A1
Peake New Rd SO32. 249 F8
Peakfield
Denmead PO7...... 298 E3
Frensham GU10..... 144 A7
Peak La
Fareham PO14...... 342 D7
Upham SO32....... 247 B4
Peak Rd PO8....... 276 A5
Peak The PO9...... 301 C2
Pealsham Gdns SP6. 257 E2
Pearce Ave BH14... 391 A1
Pearce Ct PO12..... 369 C6

Pearce Gdns BH14 . . 391 A1
Pearce Rd BH16 . . . 389 B6
Pearce-Smith Ct
 BH25 . . . . 397 E7
Pearces Pl RG20 . . . 24 D1
Pear Cl BH12 . . . . . 392 B4
Pearl Gdns BH10 . . . 377 C4
Pearl Ho SP11 . . . . . 57 A2
Pearl Rd BH10 . . . . 377 C4
Pearmain Dr [6]
 SO41 . . . . 385 E2
Pearman Ct SO41 . . 385 E2
Pearman Dr SP10 . . 106 D8
Pears Gr PO10 . . . . 349 D8
Pearson Ave BH14 . . 391 B5
Pearson Gdns BH10 . 377 C4
Peartree Ave SO19 . 291 E5
Pear Tree Ave [4]
 GU51 . . . . .53 F2
Peartree Cl
 Southampton SO19 . 291 D4
 Stubbington PO14 . . 367 D8
 West Wellow SO51 . . 238 C3
Pear Tree Cl
 Alderholt SP6 . . . . 280 F6
 Botley SO32 . . . . . 269 F2
 Bransgore BH23 . . . 381 B8
 Lindford GU35 . . . . 164 F4
Peartree Ct
 [7] Lymington SO41 . 385 E2
 Southampton SO19 . 291 E4
Pear Tree Ct GU15 . . .36 F8
Pear Tree Dr SP5 . . . 261 D8
Pear Tree Hts GU35 . 164 F4
Pear Tree La
 Newbury RG14 . . . . . 2 A5
 Rowledge GU10 . . . 121 D3
Peartree Rd
 Hythe SO45 . . . . . 313 E2
 Southampton SO19 . 291 D4
Pear Tree Rd GU35 . 164 F4
Peatmoor Cl GU51 . . .53 E2
Pebble Cl PO11 . . . . 373 B2
Pebble Ct
 Marchwood SO40 . . 289 F2
 South Hayling PO11 . 373 D1
Pebmarsh Rd [5]
 PO6 . . . . 345 D8
Pecche Rd RG14 . . . . 49 A2
Peckham Ave BH25 . 383 A4
Peckham Ct PO17 . . 317 C2
Peckmoor Dr RG19 . . . 6 A7
Peddlars Gr GU46 . . . 34 C6
Pedlars Wlk BH24 . . 328 F7
Pedula Way SO50 . . 244 E5
Peeks Mews BH6 . . 394 F5
Peel Ave GU16 . . . . .56 E7
Peel Cl
 Poole BH12 . . . . . 391 C5
 Romsey SO51 . . . . 216 C1
 Verwood BH31 . . . . 302 E7
Peel Common Inf Sch
 PO13 . . . . 343 B2
Peel Common Jun Sch
 PO13 . . . . 343 B2
Peel Ct
 Farnborough GU14 . . 77 A8
 Hartley Wintney RG27 . 52 C6
Peelers Gate [10] PO6 . 345 C7
Peel Gdns RG20 . . . . 24 C3
Peel Pl PO5 . . . . . . 404 B2
Peel Rd PO12 . . . . . 369 C5
Peel St SO14 . . . . . 291 C5
Peewit Hill SO31 . . . 293 A3
Peewit Hill Cl SO31 . 293 B3
Pegasus Ave
 Aldershot GU12 . . . . 77 C2
 Hordle SO41 . . . . . 384 B2
Pegasus Cl
 Gosport PO13 . . . . 368 D5
 Hamble-le-R SO31 . . 315 C3
 Haslemere GU27 . . 189 B5
 Southampton SO16 . . . 2 E4
 Thatcham RG19 . . . . 2 E4
Pegasus Ct
 [8] New Milton
 BH25 . . . . 383 A3
 Aldershot GU12 . . . . 77 C1
 Bournemouth BH1 . . 393 A5
 Farnborough GU14 . . 56 C1
 Fleet GU51 . . . . . . 53 F2
 Whitchurch RG28 . . . 86 C6
Pegasus Lodge
 BH22 . . . . 353 D5
Pegasus Rd GU14 . . . 55 D7
Peggotty Ho [22] PO1 . 370 D7
Pegham Bsns Ctr
 PO15 . . . . 318 B6
Pegham Coppice
 PO15 . . . . 318 B6
Pegham Ind Pk
 PO15 . . . . 318 B6
Peked Mede RG27 . . . 51 D1
Pelham [21] BH13 . . 392 A4
Pelham Cl
 Bordon GU35 . . . . 164 D1
 Christchurch BH23 . . 395 D6
 Old Basing RG24 . . . . 70 B5
Pelham Pl GU10 . . . 121 E4
Pelham Rd
 Gosport PO12 . . . . 369 B6
 Portsmouth PO5 . . . 404 B1
Pelham Terr [3]
 PO10 . . . . 349 A8
Pelican Cl PO15 . . . 318 D2
Pelican Ct
 Andover SP10 . . . . . 83 B1

Pelican Ct continued
 Hursley SO21 . . . . 218 B7
Pelican La RG14 . . . . 1 E4
Pelican Mead BH24 . 329 C6
Pelican Rd
 Fareham PO14 . . . . 342 F5
 Pamber Heath RG26 . 10 C2
Pelton Rd RG21 . . . . 68 F6
Pembers Cl SO50 . . 243 D2
Pemberton Rd SO43 . 310 A5
Pembridge Rd PO6 . . 258 A2
Pembroke Bwy GU15 . 36 A5
Pembroke Cl
 Eastleigh SO50 . . . 243 F5
 Portsmouth PO1 . . . 370 A3
 Romsey SO51 . . . . 240 F7
 Totton SO40 . . . . . 289 A8
Pembroke Cres
 PO14 . . . . 367 A7
Pembroke Ct
 [4] Christchurch
 BH23 . . . . 397 B7
 Andover SP10 . . . . 106 A7
 Gosport PO13 . . . . 343 C1
 Southampton SO17 . . 267 B1
Pembroke Rd
 Basingstoke RG23 . . 68 B5
 Bournemouth BH4 . . 392 B2
 Newbury RG14 . . . . . 1 D3
 Poole BH12 . . . . . 391 D7
 Portsmouth PO1 . . . 370 A3
 Southampton SO19 . . 292 B4
Pembury Pl GU12 . . . 77 A1
Pembury Rd
 Havant PO9 . . . . . 348 A8
 Stubbington PO14 . . 342 D4
Pemerton Rd
 Basingstoke RG21 . . 69 C7
 Winchester SO22 . . 175 D3
Penarth Ave PO6 . . 346 B8
Penarth Ct SO19 . . 292 D1
Pen Cl SP10 . . . . . 106 C7
Pen Craig [2] BH13 . 392 B3
Pendennis Cl RG23 . . .68 B6
Pendennis Rd PO6 . . 320 F1
Pendle Cl SO16 . . . 289 F8
Pendle Gn SO51 . . . 191 F1
Pendleton Gdns
 SO45 . . . . 338 E1
Penelope Ct [12]
 BH23 . . . . 397 B7
Penelope Gdns SO31 . 292 F2
Penfold Croft GU9 . . . 99 D4
Penfords Paddock
 SO32 . . . . 271 D7
Pengelly Ave BH10 . 377 E5
Pengilly Rd GU9 . . . . 98 F1
Penhale Gdns PO14 . 317 B1
Penhale Inf Sch PO1 . 370 E1
Penhale Rd PO1 . . . 370 E1
Penhale Way SO40 . . 288 E5
Penhurst Rd PO9 . . 323 B2
Peninsular Cl GU15 . . .36 F7
Peninsula Rd SO22 . 403 C5
Peninsula Sq SO23 . 403 D5
Penistone Cl SO19 . 292 B1
Penjar Ave PO7 . . . 322 C4
Penk Ridge PO9 . . . 346 F8
Pennant Hills PO9 . . 323 B2
Pennant Way BH21 . 395 F7
Pennard Way SO53 . 243 A4
Penn Cl BH25 . . . . 382 E1
Penn Ct BH22 . . . . 326 D2
Pennefather's Rd
 GU11 . . . . 76 D3
Pennels Cl GU30 . . 209 F2
Pennerly Ct PO9 . . 323 D7
Penner Rd PO9 . . . 347 E7
Penn Hill Ave BH14 . 391 D3
Pennine Ct RG22 . . . .68 B3
Pennine Ct [8] BH23 . 395 F8
Pennine Gdns SO45 . 313 D2
Pennine Ho SO16 . . 289 F7
Pennine Rd SO16 . . 289 F8
Pennine Way
 Basingstoke RG22 . . 68 B3
 Chandler's Ford
 SO53 . . . . 243 D4
 Farnborough GU14 . . 55 C7
 Lee-on-t-S PO13 . . 368 A4
 Verwood BH31 . . . 302 F5
Pennine Wlk PO14 . . 342 F1
Pennings Dro SP5 . . 211 E8
Pennings Rd SP9 . . . .78 E5
Pennington CE Jun Sch
 SO41 . . . . 385 C3
Pennington Cl
 Colden Common
 SO21 . . . . 244 F8
 Lymington SO41 . . . 385 C2
 West Moors BH22 . . 326 D1
Pennington Cres
 BH22 . . . . 326 D2
Pennington Cross
 SO41 . . . . 385 D2
Pennington Ho [6]
 BH4 . . . . 392 D2
Pennington Inf Sch
 SO41 . . . . 385 C3
Pennington Oval
 SO41 . . . . 385 B2
Pennington Rd
 BH22 . . . . 326 D2
Pennington Way
 PO15 . . . . 318 D3
Penn Rd RG14 . . . . . 1 B5

Penns Pl GU31 . . . 229 D3
Penns Rd GU32 . . . 228 E4
Penns Wood GU14 . . 56 B1
Penns Yd GU9 . . . . . .98 F2
Penn Way PO12 . . . 368 E3
Pennycress SO31 . . 316 C2
Penny Ct
 [2] Gosport PO12 . . 369 C6
 [5] Petersfield GU31 . 228 F3
Penny Hedge BH25 . . 398 B8
Penny La
 Emsworth PO10 . . . 349 B8
 Stockbridge SO20 . . 150 A1
Penny Pl PO7 . . . . 322 E3
Penny's Cl SP6 . . . 257 F3
Penny's Cnr SO41 . . 383 D4
Penny's Cres SP6 . . 257 F3
Penny's Ct BH22 . . 353 C5
Penny's Hatch RG20 . .24 E2
Pennys La SP6 . . . 257 F3
Penny St PO1 . . . . 370 A3
Penny's Wlk BH22 . . 353 C5
Penny Way BH23 . . 396 C6
Pennywell Gdns
 BH25 . . . . 383 D4
Penrhyn Ave PO6 . . 346 B8
Penrhyn Cl
 Aldershot GU11 . . . . 76 F1
 Eastleigh SO50 . . . 243 F5
Penrith Cl BH31 . . . 302 F5
Penrith Ct SO16 . . . 289 E7
Penrith Rd
 Basingstoke RG21 . . 69 A4
 Bournemouth BH5 . . 394 A4
Penrose Cl
 [2] Portsmouth
 PO2 . . . . 345 D2
 Newbury RG14 . . . . . 1 D5
Penrose Gdns GU12 . .77 E6
Penrose Rd BH12 . . 353 D6
Penrose Way SO34 . 160 A2
Penryn Dr GU35 . . . 166 A5
Penshurst Rise GU16 . 56 D8
Penshurst Way
 SO50 . . . . 244 A6
Pentagon The SO45 . 339 A2
Pentangle The RG14 . 1 E4
Pentere Rd PO8 . . . 300 A6
Pentire Ave SO15 . . 266 D2
Pentire Way SO15 . . 266 D2
Pentland Cl
 Basingstoke RG22 . . 68 B3
 Hythe SO45 . . . . . 313 D2
Pentland Pl GU14 . . .55 B7
Pentland Rise PO16 . 320 D1
Penton Ct PO9 . . . . 324 B6
Penton La
 Penton Grafton SP11 . 81 F5
 Penton Mewsey SP11 . 82 A1
Penton Pl [8] SO23 . . 403 F4
Penton Rd SO21 . . . 220 A7
Pentons Hill SP6 . . 282 D6
Pentridge Way SO40 . 288 E5
Penwith Dr GU27 . . 189 C5
Penwood Gn [15] PO9 . 322 B1
Penwood Hts RG20 . .21 E8
Penwood Rd RG20 . . . .5 A3
Peper Harow Rd PO1 . 300 B6
Peppard Cl SO18 . . 292 A7
Pepper Cl PO11 . . . 373 A5
Peppercorn Cl BH23 . 395 E8
Peppercorn Way
 SO30 . . . . 269 B3
Pepys Ave SO19 . . . 292 D5
Pepys Cl
 Gosport PO12 . . . . 369 B2
 Portsmouth PO4 . . . 370 F3
Percival Rd
 PO1 . . . . 404 C4
Percy Cl SO45 . . . . 313 F5
Percy Rd
 Bournemouth BH5 . . 393 F4
 Gosport PO12 . . . . 369 C5
 Portsmouth PO4 . . . 370 E4
 Southampton SO16 . . 290 A8
Peregrine Cl SO40 . . 288 C6
Peregrine Rd BH23 . . 396 A5
Peregrines The
 PO16 . . . . 343 F8
Peregrins GU12 . . . .77 E2
Pergin Cres BH17 . . 390 B7
Pergin Way BH17 . . 390 B7
Perham Cres SP11 . . 57 A2
Perins Cl SO24 . . . . 179 B4
Perins Sch SO24 . . . 179 C5
Periwinkle Cl GU35 . 165 A5
Perkins Ho [3] PO1 . . 370 B5
Pern Dr SO30 . . . . 294 A7
Peronne Cl PO3 . . . 345 D5
Peronne Rd PO3 . . . 345 D5
Perowne St GU11 . . . 76 D2
Perran Rd SO16 . . . 265 D1
Perring Ave GU14 . . 55 D8
Perring Rd GU14 . . . 55 C2
Perry Dr GU51 . . . . 53 D1
Perryfield Gdns BH7 . 394 B8
Perry Gdns BH15 . . 390 C1
Perry Way
 Farnham GU9 . . . . . 98 F7
 Headley GU35 . . . . 165 D4
Perrywood Cl SO45 . 338 C3
Perrywood Gdns
 SO40 . . . . 288 B8
Perseus Pl PO7 . . . 322 E3

Perseus Terr [15] PO1 . 370 A4
Pershore Cl SO31 . . 317 B3
Pershore Rd RG24 . . .48 B1
Persian Dr PO15 . . 317 C3
Persley Rd BH10 . . . 377 E4
Perth Cl BH23 . . . . 379 C1
Perth Ho PO1 . . . . 404 C3
Perth Rd
 Gosport PO13 . . . . 343 D3
 North Tidworth SP11 . .79 D7
 Portsmouth PO4 . . . 371 B4
Pervin Rd PO6 . . . . 345 F8
Peshawar Cl SP9 . . . .78 D7
Pest Hos GU32 . . . 203 C1
Peststead La SO32 . 273 C4
Peter Ashley Activity Ctr
 PO6 . . . . 322 D1
Peter Ashley Rd
 PO6 . . . . 322 D1
Peterborough Ct [12]
 PO13 . . . . 368 D5
Peterborough Rd
 Portsmouth PO6 . . . 321 E1
 Southampton SO14 . . 291 A7
Peter Grant Way
 BH22 . . . . 353 C5
Peters Cl
 Sarisbury SO31 . . . 316 E3
 Upton BH16 . . . . . 389 C6
Peterscroft Ave
 SO40 . . . . 288 D7
Petersfield Bsns Pk
 GU32 . . . . 228 D3
Petersfield Cl RG24 . . 49 B4
Petersfield Gn SP9 . . .78 E5
Petersfield Ho PO1 . 404 C4
Petersfield Hospl
 GU32 . . . . 228 E3
Petersfield Inf Sch
 GU32 . . . . 228 E3
Petersfield La PO8 . . 276 C6
Petersfield Mus ★
Petersfield Pl BH7 . . 394 B7
Petersfield Rd
 Bordon GU33,GU35 . 186 B6
 Bournemouth BH7 . . 394 B7
 Bramdean SO24 . . . 202 B5
 Buriton GU31 . . . . 253 D6
 Cheriton SO24 . . . . 201 D4
 Chilcomb SO21 . . . 198 D7
 Clanfield PO8 . . . . 276 C6
 East Tisted GU34,
 SO24 . . . . 182 D2
 Greatham GU33 . . . 185 F2
 Havant PO9 . . . . . 324 A6
 Ropley SO24 . . . . . 181 D3
 Winchester SO23 . . 198 C7
Petersfield Sch The
 GU32 . . . . 228 E2
Petersfield Sta GU32 . 228 E4
Petersgate Inf Sch
 PO8 . . . . 276 C4
Petersham Cl PO7 . . 299 D1
Petersham Ho [5]
 PO5 . . . . 404 C4
Petersham Rd BH17 . 390 A4
Peters Rd
 Ferndown BH22 . . . 353 F3
 Locks Heath SO31 . . 316 F3
Peter Symonds Coll
 SO22 . . . . 403 D7
Petit Rd BH9 . . . . . 378 A3
Petrel Croft RG22 . . . .90 F8
Petrel Wlk PO13 . . . 343 B2
Petrie Rd PO13 . . . 367 F3
Petticoat La SP5 . . . 235 E7
Pettinger Gdns
 SO17 . . . . 291 D8
Petty Cl SO31 . . . . 241 A6
Pettycot Cres PO13 . 343 B3
Petty's Brook Rd
 RG24 . . . . 49 A4
Petunia Cl RG22 . . . 91 A8
Peveral Way RG22 . . 68 D3
Peveral Wlk RG22 . . 68 D3
Peverel Cl GU30 . . . 187 C5
Peverell Rd BH16 . . 389 B4
Peverells Rd SO53 . . 243 E4
Peverells Wood Ave
 SO53 . . . . 243 F6
Peverells Wood Cl
 SO53 . . . . 243 F6
Peveril Cl BH24 . . . 327 F6
Peveril Rd SO19 . . . 291 E4
Pewsey Ho [4] SP9 . . 78 E5
Pewsey Pl SO15 . . . 266 D2
Pexalls Cl RG27 . . . 51 D1
Phaleron Cotts RG20 . 24 D1
Pheabens Field RG26 . 28 E3
Pheasant Cl
 Barton Stacey SO21 . 130 E7
 Basingstoke RG22 . . 90 F8
Pheasant Copse GU51 . 53 E2
Pheasant La RG20 . . . .6 D3
Pheasantry Dr RG27 . .32 B4

Pheby Rd RG22 . . . . 68 D2
Phelipps Rd BH21 . . 374 E6
Pheonix Way PO13 . . 343 C1
Philip Green Meml Sch
 BH21 . . . . 255 B2
Philip Rd PO7 . . . . 322 F5
Philips Ho GU35 . . . 166 F3
Phillimore Rd SO16 . 267 D4
Phillips Cl
 Headley GU35 . . . . 165 D5
 Rownhams SO16 . . . 265 E6
 Tongham GU10 . . . 100 C8
Phillips Cres SO53 . . 165 D5
Philpott Dr SO40 . . 289 F1
Phoenix Cl SO31 . . . 293 A3
Phoenix Ct
 [3] Aldershot GU11 . 76 E1
 Hartley Wintney RG27 . 52 B4
 Kingsclere RG20 . . . 24 D2
Phoenix Ctr The
 SO40 . . . . 264 D2
Phoenix Park Terr
 RG21 . . . . 69 B6
Phoenix Pk SO50 . . 244 C2
Phoenix Sq PO2 . . . 345 E4
Phoenix Terr RG27 . .52 B4
Phoenix Wlk RG14 . . 5 A6
Phyldon Cl BH12 . . . 391 B5
Phyldon Rd BH12 . . 391 B6
Pickard Rd BH22 . . 353 F7
Pickaxe La RG29 . . 118 A6
Pickering Dr BH18 . . 375 A2
Picket Cl SP6 . . . . 257 F2
Picket Twenty SP11 . 106 E7
Pickford Rd BH9 . . . 377 E1
Pickford St GU11 . . . .76 F2
Pickwick Cl
 Southampton SO40 . 288 B7
Pickwick Gdns GU15 . 36 F4
Pickwick Ho [12] PO1 . 370 D7
Picton Cl GU15 . . . . .36 F7
Picton Ho
 [10] Portsmouth PO5 . 404 B2
 Waterlooville PO7 . . 299 C1
Picton Rd SP10 . . . 106 A5
Pier Head Rd PO2 . . 345 B1
Pier Rd PO1 . . . . . 370 B3
Pierrefondes Ave
 GU14 . . . . 55 F5
Pier St PO13 . . . . . 367 E3
Pigeon Cl RG26 . . . 29 A2
Pigeonhouse Cotts
 SO21 . . . . 131 C4
Pigeonhouse Field
 SO21 . . . . 131 C4
Pigeon House La
 PO7 . . . . 321 D4
Pigeonhouse Yd
 SO21 . . . . 131 C4
Pigeons Farm Rd RG19 . 6 B8
Pig Shoot La BH23 . . 378 F5
Pike Cl GU11 . . . . . 77 A2
Pikes Hill SO43 . . . 309 F6
Pikes Hill Ave SO43 . 309 F6
Pike St RG14 . . . . . 1 F4
Pilbrow Ct [8] PO12 . 368 F4
Pilchards Ave SO50 . 245 B3
Pilcot Rd GU51,RG27 . 74 C2
Pilford Heath Rd
 BH21 . . . . 352 B7
Pilgrim Park Homes
 BH24 . . . . 329 C8
Pilgrim Pl
 Lymington SO41 . . . 385 E3
 Southampton SO18 . 267 E4
Pilgrims Cl
 Chandler's Ford
 SO53 . . . . 243 A4
 Farnham GU9 . . . . 121 E8
Pilgrim's Cl BH25 . . 383 C3
Pilgrims Gate
 Bishop's Waltham
 SO32 . . . . 271 B8
 Winchester SO22 . . 403 C7
Pilgrims Sch The
 SO23 . . . . 403 E5
Pilgrims Way
 Andover SP10 . . . . 83 C1
 Headley GU35 . . . . 165 C5
 Poole BH17 . . . . . 390 A7
 Stubbington PO14 . . 367 B6
Pilgrims' Way Sch The
 GU9 . . . . 121 F8
Pilley Bailey SO41 . . 362 A2
Pilley Gn SO41 . . . . 362 A1
Pilley Hill SO41 . . . 361 F1
Pilley St SO41 . . . . 362 A1
Pill Hill SP5 . . . . . 212 A4
Pilning Cl PO14 . . . 342 C8
Pilot Hight Rd BH11 . 377 A4
Pilsdon Dr BH17 . . . 375 E3
Pimpern Cl BH17 . . 375 F2
Pimpernel Cl SO31 . 316 C2
Pimpernel Way [4]
 RG19 . . . . 5 F7
Pinchington La RG14,
 RG19 . . . . 5 F7
Pindar Pl RG14 . . . . .2 C5
Pine Ave
 Bournemouth BH6 . . 394 C4
 Camberley GU15 . . . 36 D1
 Poole BH12 . . . . . 391 F6
Pine Bank GU26 . . . 167 C4
Pinebeach Ct BH13 . 402 G8
Pine Cl
 Ashurst SO40 . . . . 288 C3
 Ash Vale GU12 . . . . .77 E6
 Barton on S BH25 . . 397 E8

Pine Cl continued
 Ferndown BH22 . . . 353 C7
 Hythe SO45 . . . . . 313 F2
 Landford SP5 . . . . 237 D2
 North Baddesley
 SO52 . . . . 241 F5
 Sandhurst GU15 . . . 35 C7
 South Wonston SO21 . 153 E4
 Winchester SO22 . . 197 B3
Pinecliffe Ave BH6 . . 394 C4
Pinecliffe Rd BH25 . . 397 C7
Pinecliff Rd BH13 . . 402 G8
Pine Cotts GU33 . . 208 A7
Pine Cres
 Chandler's Ford
 SO53 . . . . 218 C1
 Christchurch BH23 . . 396 E8
Pinecrest GU17 . . . 35 C1
Pine Ct PO10 . . . . 324 F4
Pine Dr
 Blackwater GU17 . . 35 C3
 Clanfield PO8 . . . . 276 C5
 Finchampstead RG40 . 16 E7
 Mortimer RG7 . . . . 11 D6
 Poole BH13 . . . . . 391 F3
 Southampton SO18 . 292 D7
 St Leonards BH24 . . 327 F4
Pine Dr E SO18 . . . 292 F7
Pine End BH22 . . . . 353 F3
Pinefield Rd SO18 . . 267 F2
Pine Glen Ave BH22 . 353 C8
Pine Gr
 Farnham GU10 . . . 122 C6
 Fleet GU52 . . . . . 75 B6
 Havant PO9 . . . . . 324 A1
Pine Grange [4] BH1 . 393 A3
Pinegrove Rd SO19 . 291 F4
Pinehill Rd GU35 . . 164 D2
Pinehill Rise GU47 . . 35 A8
Pine Ho
 New Milton BH25 . . 383 A3
 Southampton SO16 . 266 F7
Pineholt Cl BH24 . . 328 A5
Pinehurst
 [10] Milford on S
 SO41 . . . . 399 C4
 [6] Southampton
 SO17 . . . . 267 A1
 Tadley RG26 . . . . . 26 F7
Pinehurst Ave
 Christchurch BH23 . . 395 F5
 Farnborough GU14 . 55 F2
Pinehurst Cl PO7 . . 300 C2
Pinehurst Cotts GU14 . 55 F2
Pinehurst Pk BH22 . 353 F8
Pinehurst Rd
 Farnborough GU14 . 55 F2
 Southampton SO16 . 266 F7
 West Moors BH22 . . 326 F1
Pinelands Cl SO16 . . 266 C4
Pinelands Cvn Pk
 RG7 . . . . 10 D4
Pinelands Rd SO16 . 266 F6
Pine Lodge [10] BH13 . 402 F7
Pine Manor Rd
 BH24 . . . . 327 D5
Pine Mans [3] BH1 . . 393 D4
Pine Mount Rd GU15 . 36 B4
Pine Park Mans [16]
 BH13 . . . . 392 A4
Pine Rd
 Alderholt SP6 . . . . 280 F5
 Bishop's Waltham
 SO32 . . . . 271 D8
 Bournemouth BH9 . . 393 A8
 Chandler's Ford SO53 . 243 C3
 East End BH21 . . . 350 F1
 Four Marks GU34 . . 160 C3
 Romsey SO51 . . . . 241 C6
Pine Ridge RG14 . . . 2 A5
Pine Ridge Dr GU10 . 122 A8
Pineside BH9 . . . . 393 A8
Pinesprings Dr BH18 374 E2
Pines Rd
 Fleet GU51 . . . . . 53 F2
 Liphook GU30 . . . . 187 C4
Pines The
 Andover SP10 . . . . 105 F8
 Camberley GU15 . . . 36 D7
 Godshill SP6 . . . . 258 E2
 Poole BH13 . . . . . 392 A2
 Portchester PO16 . . 320 A1
 Southampton SO16 . 266 B3
Pine Top Cvn Site
 BH25 . . . . 359 F5
Pinetops Cl SO41 . . 385 B3
Pine Tree Cl BH21 . . 351 D5
Pine Tree Gdns PO8 . 300 A2
Pine Tree Glen BH4 . 392 C3
Pinetree Ho [6] SP9 . .79 A7
Pine Trees Cl PO14 . 342 D8
Pinetree Wlk BH17 . 389 F8
Pine Vale Cres BH10 377 F3
Pineview GU14 . . . . .55 E4
Pine View GU35 . . . 166 A6
Pineview Cl SO31 . . 293 A1
Pine View Cl
 Farnham GU9 . . . . 99 E5
 Redlynch SP5 . . . . 235 D4
 Upton BH16 . . . . . 389 C6
 Verwood BH31 . . . 302 D7
Pine View Rd BH31 . 302 D7
Pine Way SO16 . . . 266 F7
Pine Wlk
 [8] Andover SP10 . . 105 D6

Pine Wlk continued
Chilworth SO16 . . . . . 266 F7
Liss GU33 . . . . 208 A6
Locks Heath SO31 . . . 317 A5
Verwood BH31 . . . . . . 303 B5
West Moors BH22 . . . . 326 E3
Pinewood
Chineham RG24 . . . . . . 48 E3
Gosport PO13 . . . . . . 343 E1
Southampton SO16 . . . 266 F6
Pinewood Ave
Bournemouth BH10 . . . 377 D5
Havant PO9 . . . . 323 B3
Pinewood Cl
Bournemouth BH10 . . . 377 D5
Pamber Heath RG26 . . . . 9 B1
Romsey SO51 . . . . . . 216 C1
Sandhurst GU47 . . . . . 34 D8
Stubbington PO14 . . . . 342 D4
Upton BH16 . . . . 389 A7
Walkford BH23 . . . . . 382 A2
Pinewood Cres
Farnborough GU14 . . . . 55 A5
Hythe SO45 . . . . 314 B2
Pinewood Ct
2 Fleet GU51 . . . . . . 54 A2
West Moors BH22 . . . . 326 D2
Pinewood Dr
Burghclere RG20 . . . . . . 5 E2
Hythe SO45 . . . . 314 B1
Pinewood Gdns
BH22 . . . . 353 D7
Pinewood Hill GU51 . . 54 A2
Pinewood Inf Sch
GU14 . . . . 55 B7
Pinewood Lodge **5**
PO16 . . . . 319 B2
Pinewood Pk
Farnborough GU14 . . . . 55 A7
Southampton SO19 . . . 292 F5
Pinewood Rd
Christchurch BH23 . . . 381 F1
Ferndown BH22 . . . . . 353 C7
Hordle SO41 . . . . 383 F3
Poole BH13 . . . . 392 B1
St Leonards BH24 . . . . 327 F4
Upton BH16 . . . . 389 B7
Pinkerton Rd GU52 . . . 68 D2
Pinkney La SO43 . . . . 309 E3
Pink Rd PO2 . . . . 370 E8
Pinks Hill PO16 . . . . 319 D2
Pinks La RG26 . . . . 9 C1
Pinnacle The **7**
BH1 . . . . 393 A3
Pinnell Cl RG22 . . . . . 91 A6
Pinsley Dr PO17 . . . . 321 B5
Pintail Ct RG22 . . . . . 90 F7
Pinto Cl PO15 . . . . . . 317 C7
Pipers Ash BH24 . . . . 289 B5
Pipers Ct SO40 . . . . . 288 D6
Pipers Croft GU52 . . . . 75 A4
Pipers Dr BH23 . . . . . 396 A7
Pipers Mead PO8 . . . . 276 A5
Pipers Patch **1** GU14 . . 55 F4
Pipers Wood Ind Est
PO7 . . . . 322 C8
Piping Cl SO21 . . . . . 244 F8
Piping Gn SO21 . . . . . 244 F8
Piping Rd SO21 . . . . . 244 F8
Pipistrelle Wlk **4**
PO17 . . . . 318 E8
Pipit Cl
Gosport PO12 . . . . . . 369 B8
Thatcham RG19 . . . . 2 F3
Waterlooville PO8 . . . . 300 A6
Pippin Cl
8 Lymington SO41 . . . 385 E2
Christchurch BH23 . . . 379 E2
Pipsons Cl GU46 . . . . . 34 B6
Pirbright Rd GU14 . . . . 56 A3
Pirelli St SO15 . . . . . 290 F4
Pirelli Way SO50 . . . . 244 A2
Pirrie Cl SO15 . . . . . . 266 D1
Pitcairn Cl RG24 . . . . . 48 D2
Pitcairn Mews **8**
PO4 . . . . 371 B2
Pitchponds Rd
SO31 . . . . 340 C10
Pitcot Lane SO21 . . . . 221 B3
Pitcroft La GU31 . . . . 253 F5
Pitcroft Rd PO2 . . . . . 345 D1
Pitfield La
Mortimer RG7 . . . . 11 F3
Stratfield Mortimer
RG7 . . . . 12 A4
Pitfold Ave GU27 . . . . 189 B6
Pitfold Cl GU27 . . . . . 189 C6
Pither Rd RG29 . . . . . . 95 C8
Pithouse La RG19 . . . . 25 D6
Pitman Cl RG22 . . . . . . 68 B2
Pitmore Cl SO50 . . . . 244 B8
Pitmore La
Sway,Bowling Green
SO41 . . . . 384 F7
Sway,Durns Town
SO41 . . . . 360 D1
Pitmore Rd SO50 . . . . 244 B8
Pitreavie Rd PO6 . . . . 345 F6
Pittard Rd RG21 . . . . . 68 F3
Pitter Cl SO22 . . . . . . 175 B5
Pitt Hall Cotts RG26 . . 45 F5
Pitt Hill La PO7 . . . . . 274 F1
Pitthouse La RG18 . . . 379 D8
Pitt La GU10 . . . . 143 E6
Pittmore Rd BH23 . . . 380 C2

Pitt Rd SO15 . . . . 290 C6
Pitt Rdbt SO22 . . . . . . 197 B5
Pitts Deep La SO41 . . . 387 C4
Pitts La
Andover SP10 . . . . . . 106 A6
Bishopstone SP5 . . . . 210 C8
Pitts Pl BH25 . . . . 383 D2
Pitts Rd GU11 . . . . 76 F4
Pitt Way GU14 . . . . . . 55 D5
Pitwines Cl BH15 . . . . 390 D2
Pit Wlk SP4 . . . . 123 D7
Pitymoor La PO17 . . . 321 B4
Place Cres PO7 . . . . . 322 F5
Place Ct GU11 . . . . . . 100 A7
Place House Cl
PO15 . . . . 318 C1
Place La SO21 . . . . . . 219 E8
Plaitford Gr PO9 . . . . 323 C5
Plaitford Wlk SO16 . . . 265 F1
Plantagenet Cres
BH11 . . . . 376 D5
Plantation Ct
Lymington SO41 . . . . 385 D4
Poole BH17 . . . . 375 C1
Plantation Dr
Marchwood SO40 . . . 289 E1
Walkford BH23 . . . . . 382 A2
Plantation Farm Cotts
RG26 . . . . 45 A7
Plantation Rd
Andover SP10 . . . . . . 105 E7
Hill Brow GU33 . . . . . 208 B2
Pamber Heath RG26 . . . 9 D2
Poole BH17 . . . . 375 C1
South Tidworth SP9 . . . . 78 F5
West Wellow SO51 . . . 262 D8
Plantation Row SO15 . . 35 F5
Plantation The
Curdridge SO32 . . . . 270 E2
Sherfield on L RG27 . . 49 D8
Plantation Way
GU35 . . . . 164 A1
Plant Cl SO51 . . . . . . 239 B2
Plant Park Rd BH24 . . 328 C2
Plassey Cres BH10 . . . 377 C5
Plassey Rd SP9 . . . . . . 78 F7
Platform Rd SO14 . . . 291 A2
Platoff Rd SO41 . . . . 400 E8
Player Ct SP6 . . . . . . 257 F3
Players Cres SO40 . . . 288 E5
Playfair Rd PO5 . . . . 404 C2
Playfields Dr SO19 . . . 291 E8
Plaza Mews **3** SO51 . 240 F7
Plaza Par **4** SO51 . . . 240 F7
Pleasance Way
BH25 . . . . 382 F3
Pleasant Hill RG26 . . . 26 F8
Pleasant La PO10 . . . . 349 C1
Pleasant Rd PO4 . . . . 371 B4
Plecy Cl BH22 . . . . . . 353 D8
Plemont Cl BH12 . . . . 376 E1
Pless Rd SO41 . . . . . . 399 B5
Plough Gdns SO20 . . . 170 B6
Plough La
Bramshill RG27 . . . . . 32 A6
Soberton SO32 . . . . . 273 C2
Plough Rd GU46 . . . . . 34 C7
Plough Way SO22 . . . 403 B2
Plover Cl
Andover SP10 . . . . . . 83 B2
Basingstoke RG22 . . . 68 A1
Southampton SO16 . . . 266 B5
Stubbington PO14 . . . . 367 B7
Plover Dr SO41 . . . . . 399 F4
Plover La RG27 . . . . . . 15 C1
Plover Rd SO40 . . . . . 288 C2
Plover Reach PO4 . . . 371 B5
Plovers Down SO22 . . 197 B3
Plovers Rd PO8 . . . . . 300 A6
Plovers Way GU34 . . . 140 A5
P.L.P.H. Rd SO45 . . . . 339 B5
Plumer Rd
Greatham GU33 . . . . . 186 C3
Poole BH17 . . . . 375 A1
Plum Fell La GU34 . . . 184 E7
Plumley Wlk PO9 . . . 323 D7
Plumpton Gdns PO3 . . 346 B3
Plumpton Gr **4** PO7 . . 300 B1
Plumpton Rd RG14 . . . . 2 A1
Plumpton Way GU34 . . 139 F2
Pluto Rd SO50 . . . . . . 243 F3
Plymouth Dr PO14 . . . 367 B8
Plymouth St PO5 . . . . 404 B2
Poachers End RG29 . . 95 A3
Pococks La GU33 . . . . 206 F7
Poets Way SO22 . . . . 403 B6
Poinsettia Cl PO15 . . . 317 C3
Pointout Cl SO16 . . . . 266 E3
Pointout Rd SO16 . . . . 266 E3
Point The BH5 . . . . . . 393 E3
Pokesdown Com Prim
Sch BH5 . . . . 394 B5
Pokesdown Sta BH7 . . 394 A5
Poland La RG29 . . . . . . 72 E6
Polden Cl GU14 . . . . . . 55 C7
Polecat Cnr RG24 . . . . 70 E1
Polesden Cl SO53 . . . 243 B8
Poles La
Hursley SO21 . . . . . . 218 D6
Lymington SO41 . . . . 385 E1
Otterbourne SO21 . . . 219 B5
Police Station La
SO32 . . . . 249 B1
Police Training Ctr
SO31 . . . . 315 D5
Polkerris Way GU52 . . 75 B4

Pollards Moor Rd
SO40 . . . . 263 B1
Pollards The GU10 . . . 120 A4
Pollen's Almhouses
SP10 . . . . 106 A8
Polmear Cl GU52 . . . . 75 B4
Polygon Ct SO15 . . . . 290 E5
Polygon Sch The
SO15 . . . . 290 E6
Polygon The SO15 . . . 290 E5
Pomlingbroke RG27 . . 51 F1
Pomona BH22 . . . . . . 353 D6
Pompey Ctr PO4 . . . . 370 F5
Pompey Ctr Trad Pk The
PO4 . . . . 370 F5
Pompey's Cnr BH21 . . 353 A4
Pompey's La BH22 . . . 353 B2
Pond Cl
Marchwood SO40 . . . 289 F2
Newbury RG14 . . . . 5 B7
New Milton BH25 . . . 383 A3
Overton RG25 . . . . . . 88 A6
Pond Cotts GU32 . . . . 227 C1
Pond Croft GU46 . . . . . 34 C6
Pondhead Cl SO45 . . . 338 C3
Pond La
Churt GU10 . . . . 144 B4
Clanfield PO8 . . . . . . 276 B6
Grateley SP11,SO20 . . 125 B7
Pondpenny La GU51 . . 54 L1
Pond Piece PO7 . . . . . 298 F3
Pond Rd
Bramley RG26 . . . . . . 29 A2
Farnborough GU14 . . . 55 F2
Headley GU35 . . . . . . 165 F4
Sarisbury SO31 . . . . . 316 F6
Pondside Flats SO42 . . 336 F1
Pondside La SO32 . . . 271 C8
Pondtail Cl GU51 . . . . 75 C8
Pondtail Gdns GU51 . . 75 C8
Pondtail Rd GU51 . . . . 75 C8
Pondview Cl GU51 . . . . 54 C2
Ponsonby Ho PO5 . . . 404 B2
Ponsonby Rd BH14 . . . 391 D4
Pony Dr BH16 . . . . . . 389 D7
Pook La
Fareham PO17 . . . . . 319 C4
Havant PO9 . . . . 348 A8
Pooksgreen SO40 . . . 289 D1
Poole Aquarium &
Serpentarium ★
BH15 . . . . 390 C1
Poole Commerce Ctr
BH12 . . . . 391 F5
Poole Gram Sch
BH17 . . . . 375 D2
Poole High Sch
BH15 . . . . 390 C4
Poole Hill BH2 . . . . . . 392 D3
Poole Hospl BH15 . . . 390 D3
Poole La BH11 . . . . . . 377 B5
Poole Rd
Bournemouth BH4 . . . 392 C4
Poole BH13 . . . . 392 A4
Southampton SO19 . . . 291 E4
Upton BH16 . . . . 389 D7
Poole Sta BH15 . . . . . 390 C3
Pool Lane Rdbt
BH11 . . . . 376 E4
Pool Rd
Aldershot GU11 . . . . . 100 A7
Hartley Wintney RG27 . . 52 C7
Poors Farm Rd RG24 . . 70 E8
Popes Hill RG20 . . . . . 24 C2
Popes La
Totton SO40 . . . . 288 F7
Upham SO32 . . . . . . 246 C4
Popes Rd BH15 . . . . . 390 D6
Popham Ct PO9 . . . . . 323 C6
Popham La RG25 . . . . 112 F8
Poplar Cl
3 Poole BH15 . . . . . 390 B1
Baughurst RG26 . . . . . 26 B8
Bransgore BH23 . . . . 381 C8
Christchurch BH23 . . . 397 B8
Mytchett GU16 . . . . . . 86 B3
Sherfield on L RG27 . . 29 D1
Thatcham RG19 . . . . . . 7 E6
Wimborne Minster
BH21 . . . . 351 D5
Poplar Cotts GU16 . . . 56 D6
Poplar Cres BH24 . . . 329 B7
Poplar Dr
Fareham PO14 . . . . . 342 E8
Marchwood SO40 . . . 289 D1
Poplar Gr PO11 . . . . . 373 A4
Poplar La BH23 . . . . . 381 C8
Poplar Pl RG14 . . . . . . 1 E5
Poplar Rd
New Milton BH25 . . . 383 D4
Southampton SO19 . . . 291 F6
Poplars Cl GU14 . . . . . 55 A5
Poplars The SO32 . . . 271 E3
Poplar Way
Hedge End SO30 . . . . 293 D6
North Baddesley
SO52 . . . . 241 F5
Ringwood BH24 . . . . 329 B7
Poplar Wlk
Farnham GU9 . . . . . . 99 B7
Petersfield GU31 . . . . 228 C1
Popley Way RG24 . . . . 48 B1
Poppy Cl
Andover SP10 . . . . . . 105 C7
Christchurch BH23 . . . 396 C8
Locks Heath SO31 . . . 316 F2

Poppyfields SO53 . . . 243 A6
Poppy Fields RG24 . . . 70 A8
Poppyhills Rd BH15 . . . 36 D8
Poppy Rd SO16 . . . . . 267 C5
Porchester Cl SP10 . . . 82 D3
Porchester Rd
Newbury RG14 . . . . 1 E1
Southampton SO19 . . . 291 E3
Porchester Sq **12**
RG21 . . . . 69 B5
Porlock Rd SO16 . . . . 265 D2
Portacre Rise RG21 . . . 68 F3
Portadene **1** BH4 . . . 392 C2
Portal Cl SP11 . . . . . . 105 B7
Portal Rd
Bishopstoke SO50 . . . 244 D3
Gosport PO13 . . . . . . 343 C3
Southampton SO19 . . . 292 B4
Winchester SO23 . . . . 403 F4
Portarlington Cl
BH4 . . . . 392 D2
Portarlington Ct **44**
BH4 . . . . 392 C3
Portarlington Rd
BH4 . . . . 392 C2
Porchester Bsns Ctr
PO16 . . . . 344 D8
Porchester Castle ★
PO16 . . . . 344 F6
Porchester Com Sch
PO16 . . . . 344 D7
Porchester Ct **3**
BH8 . . . . 393 B5
Porchester Ho **5**
PO17 . . . . 318 E8
Porchester Hts
PO16 . . . . 320 D1
Porchester La PO17 . . 320 D4
Porchester Pl BH8 . . . 393 B5
Porchester Rd
Bournemouth BH8 . . . 393 A5
Porchester PO16 . . . . 344 A8
Portsmouth PO2 . . . . 370 E8
Porchester Rise
SO50 . . . . 244 A7
Porchester Sch
BH7 . . . . 394 A7
Porchester Sta
PO16 . . . . 344 D8
Portcreek Cotts PO6 . . 346 B5
Portelet Cl BH12 . . . . 376 D2
Portelet Pl SO30 . . . . 293 C5
Porteous Cres SO53 . . 243 F6
Porter Cl RG29 . . . . . . 95 C8
Porter End RG14 . . . . . . 5 F8
Porter Rd
Basingstoke RG22 . . . 68 F1
Poole BH17 . . . . 390 B7
Portersbridge Mews **1**
SO51 . . . . 240 E7
Portersbridge St
SO51 . . . . 240 E7
Porters Cl
Andover SP10 . . . . . . 82 D1
Dummer RG25 . . . . . . 90 D1
Porters La BH21 . . . . 352 C6
Porter's La SO14 . . . . 290 F3
Portesbery Hill Dr
GU15 . . . . 36 C6
Portesbery Rd GU15 . . 36 C6
Portesbery Sch GU15 . . 36 B6
Portesham Gdns
BH9 . . . . 378 B4
Portesham Way
BH17 . . . . 375 E3
Portfield Cl BH23 . . . . 395 A7
Portfield Rd
Christchurch BH23 . . . 395 A7
Portsmouth PO3 . . . . 346 B3
Portfield Sch
Christchurch BH23 . . . 395 A6
East Parley BH23 . . . . 378 B6
Portiere Ho BH11 . . . . 377 A4
Portiswood Ct RG26 . . 27 B8
Port La
Hursley SO21 . . . . . . 218 C8
Standon SO21,SO22 . . 196 E1
Winchester SO22 . . . . 197 A2
Portland Bldgs **5**
PO12 . . . . 369 C5
Portland Dr
Fleet GU52 . . . . 74 F4
Gosport PO12 . . . . . . 368 D3
Portland Gr SP10 . . . . 106 A8
Portland Ho **7**
PO12 . . . . 369 D5
Portland Pl BH2 . . . . . 392 F4
Portland Rd
Bournemouth BH9 . . . 393 A8
Waterlooville PO7 . . . 322 E7
Portland's Cl GU32 . . . 229 B8
Portland Sq **5** GU33 207 F4
Portland St
Portsmouth PO1 . . . . 370 B5
Southampton SO14 . . . 290 F4
Portland Terr
2 Portsmouth
PO5 . . . . 370 C2
Southampton SO14 . . . 290 F4
Portman Cres BH5 . . . 394 B4
Portman Rd BH7 . . . . 393 F5
Portman Terr BH5 . . . 394 B4
Portobello Gr PO16 . . 320 D1
Port Royal St PO5 . . . 404 C3

Portsdown Ave PO6 . . 346 C8
Portsdown Hill Rd
Cosham PO6 . . . . 322 C1
Havant PO9 . . . . 323 A1
Portchester PO17 . . . . 320 D2
Portsmouth PO6 . . . . 321 E1
Portsdown Prim Sch
PO6 . . . . 345 F8
Portsdown Rd PO16 . . 344 E8
Portside SO40 . . . . . . 290 A3
Portsmouth Cath (CE)
PO1 . . . . 370 A4
Portsmouth City Mus &
Art Gallery ★ PO1 . 370 B3
Portsmouth Cl GU34 . . 139 D1
Portsmouth Coll
PO3 . . . . 371 C7
Portsmouth Cres
RG22 . . . . 68 D2
Portsmouth Ent Ctr
PO3 . . . . 346 D2
Portsmouth Gram Sch
The PO1 . . . . 370 B3
Portsmouth Harbour Sta
PO1 . . . . 369 F6
Portsmouth High Sch for
Girls PO5 . . . . 404 A1
Portsmouth High Sch for
Girls (Juns) PO5 . . . 370 C4
Portsmouth Hospl
(Bupa) PO9 . . . . . . 324 D5
Portsmouth RC Cath ★
PO1 . . . . 404 A4
Portsmouth Rd
Bursledon SO31 . . . . 293 A1
Colden Common
SO50 . . . . 245 C6
Cosham PO6 . . . . 345 F6
Frimley GU16 . . . . . . 36 D4
Hindhead GU8 . . . . . 167 F6
Hindhead,Nutcombe
GU26 . . . . 167 C2
Horndean PO8 . . . . . 300 C6
Lee-on-t-S PO13 . . . . 368 A4
Liphook GU30 . . . . . 187 F2
Southampton SO19 . . . 292 C2
Portsmouth & Southsea
Sta PO1 . . . . 404 B3
Portsmouth Way
RG22 . . . . 68 D2
Portsmouth Wlk
RG22 . . . . 68 D2
Portsview Ave PO16 . . 344 E8
Portsview Gdns
PO16 . . . . 320 D1
Portswood Ave
SO17 . . . . 291 B8
Portswood Ctr SO17 . . 267 B1
Portswood Dr **2**
BH10 . . . . 378 A4
Portswood Pk SO17 . . 291 B8
Portswood Prim Sch
SO17 . . . . 267 C2
Portswood Rd
Havant PO9 . . . . 323 D6
Portsmouth PO2 . . . . 345 E5
Southampton SO17 . . . 267 C2
Portuguese Fireplace ★
SO43 . . . . 308 F4
Portview Rd SO18 . . . 267 F1
Portway
Pamber Heath RG26 . . 9 C1
Riseley RG7 . . . . 14 A2
Port Way PO6 . . . . . . 345 B7
Portway Cl
Andover SP10 . . . . . . 105 D8
Southampton SO18 . . . 292 B4
Portway Ind Est SP10 . 82 B1
Portway Inf Sch
SP10 . . . . 105 C8
Portway Jun Sch
SP10 . . . . 105 C8
Portway Pl RG23 . . . . 68 B5
Posbrooke La PO14 . . 341 E6
Posbrooke Rd PO4 . . . 371 B4
Postern Cl PO16 . . . . 344 D8
Postern Ct **9** SO14 . . 290 F3
Post Horn La RG27 . . . 50 D5
Posting House Mews
RG14 . . . . 1 C4
Post Office Bldgs
BH9 . . . . 392 F8
Post Office La
Dummer RG25 . . . . . . 90 D1
St Leonards BH24 . . . 328 A5
Post Office Rd
18 Bournemouth
BH1 . . . . 392 F3
Waterlooville PO7 . . . 322 C5
Potash Terr PO9 . . . . 323 C1
Potbridge Rd RG29 . . . 72 F7
Pot La RG24 . . . . 70 F8
Potley Hill Prim Sch
GU46 . . . . 34 C5
Potley Hill Rd GU46 . . 34 D5
Potteries La GU16 . . . . 56 D3
Potteries The
Fareham PO16 . . . . . 319 B3
Farnborough GU14 . . . 55 B6
Potterne Way BH21 . . 303 A4
Potterne Wood Cl
BH31 . . . . 303 C4
Potters Ave PO16 . . . . 319 A4
Potters Cres GU12 . . . 77 F2
Potter's Cross SP4 . . . 101 F4
Potters Field GU33 . . . 208 A4
Potters Gate GU9 . . . . 98 E2

Potters Gate CE Prim
Sch GU9 . . . . 98 E2
Potters Heron Cl
SO51 . . . . 217 E3
Potters Heron La
SO51 . . . . 217 E3
Potters Ind Pk GU52 . . 75 C5
Potters La RG27 . . . . . 29 C3
Potters Way BH14 . . . 391 C2
Pottery Cl GU10 . . . . 121 D6
Pottery Junc BH14 . . . 391 E5
Pottery La GU10 . . . . 121 D6
Pottery Rd BH14 . . . . 391 B2
Poulner Cl SO19 . . . . 292 A1
Poulner Ct BH8 . . . . . 393 C6
Poulner Hill BH24 . . . 329 E8
Poulner Inf & Jun Schs
BH24 . . . . 305 C2
Poulner Pk BH24 . . . . 305 C1
Poultons Cl RG25 . . . . 88 A7
Poultons Rd RG25 . . . . 88 A7
Poundbury Ct SO31 . . 317 A6
Pound Cl
Bramley RG26 . . . . . . 28 E3
Gosport PO13 . . . . . . 368 D8
Headley GU35 . . . . . . 165 D5
Over Wallop SO20 . . . 125 C2
Poole BH15 . . . . 390 F5
Ringwood BH24 . . . . 329 A8
Upper Wield SO24 . . . 137 A2
Pound Cotts SO32 . . . 249 D5
Pound Ct SO18 . . . . . 292 A7
Pound Farm Barns
GU34 . . . . 161 D8
Pound Gate GU34 . . . 140 A5
Pound Gate Dr PO14 . 317 C1
Pound Hill
New Alresford
SO24 . . . . 179 D6
Plaitford SO51 . . . . . 238 C5
Pound La
1 Christchurch
BH23 . . . . 395 B6
Ampfield SO51 . . . . . 217 B2
Ashurst SO40 . . . . . . 288 C3
Burghclere RG20 . . . . 22 C6
Burley BH24 . . . . 330 F2
Cadnam SO40 . . . . . 263 C1
Damerham SP6 . . . . . 256 C1
Meonstoke SO32 . . . 249 D5
Newbury RG14 . . . . . . 1 D4
Plaitford SO51 . . . . . 238 C5
Poole BH15 . . . . 390 E5
Sherfield English
SO51 . . . . 213 F2
Thatcham RG19 . . . . . . 2 E3
Pound Lea PO11 . . . . 373 A5
Pound Mdw
Sherfield on L RG27 . . 49 E8
Whitchurch RG28 . . . 86 D5
Pound Rd
3 Aldershot GU12 . . . 77 A1
Bursledon SO31 . . . . 292 E1
Kings Worthy SO23 . . 176 C8
Lymington SO41 . . . . 385 B2
Overton RG25 . . . . . . 88 B7
Over Wallop SO20 . . . 125 C2
Portsmouth PO6 . . . . 321 B2
Pound St
Newbury RG14 . . . . . . 1 D2
Southampton SO18 . . . 292 A7
Pounds Terr PO1 . . . . 370 A6
Pound The SO20 . . . . 170 B6
Pound Tree Rd
SO14 . . . . 291 A4
Pound View SP11 . . . . 83 F7
Poveys Mead RG20 . . . 24 C1
Powell Cres SO40 . . . 288 F5
Powell Rd BH14 . . . . . 391 B3
Powell Sq **8** PO1 . . . 370 A5
Power Ho RG24 . . . . . 70 B7
Power Rd PO1 . . . . . . 370 E6
Powerscourt Rd
Barton on S BH25 . . . 397 E7
Portsmouth PO2 . . . . 370 E8
Powis Cl BH25 . . . . . . 383 B3
Powlett Rd SO41 . . . . 385 E3
Poyle Rd GU10 . . . . . 100 C7
Poyner Cl PO16 . . . . . 319 B2
Poynings Cres RG21 . . 69 C2
Poynings Pl PO1 . . . . 370 A3
Poynters Cl SP10 . . . . 82 F2
Poyntz Rd RG25 . . . . . 88 A8
Pragnells Cotts SP5 . . 169 A1
Precinct The
Holbury SO45 . . . . . 338 C4
Waterlooville PO7 . . . 322 E5
Precosa Rd SO30 . . . . 293 E6
Prelate Way PO14 . . . 317 D2
Premier Ct RG27 . . . . 29 D1
Premier Ctr The
SO51 . . . . 241 D5
Premier Par SO18 . . . 267 F3
Premier Way SO51 . . . 241 D5
Prentice Cl GU14 . . . . 55 F8
Prescelly Cl RG22 . . . . 68 B4
Preshaw Cl SO16 . . . . 266 B4
Preshaw Est SO32 . . . 223 B3
Presidents Ct **12**
PO12 . . . . 369 C9
Presseys Cnr SP6 . . . 281 D7
Preston Candover CE
Prim Sch RG25 . . . 136 B8
Preston Cl BH16 . . . . 389 C7
Preston La BH23 . . . . 380 D3
Preston Pl RG14 . . . . . . 2 B5

Preston Rd
Poole BH15 ... 390 C6
Portsmouth PO2 ... 370 F8
Preston Way BH23 ... 396 D8
Prestwood Cl BH25 ... 382 F1
Prestwood Rd SO30 ... 293 C6
Pretoria Cl GU33 ... 186 D2
Pretoria Rd
Hedge End SO30 ... 293 B5
Ludgershall SP11 ... 57 B1
Portsmouth PO4 ... 370 F3
Prettyjohn Ho 14
PO4 ... 371 B2
Preymead Ind Est
GU11 ... 99 F7
Pricketts Hill PO17,
SO32 ... 296 A6
Prideaux-Brune Ave
PO13 ... 343 C4
Priest Croft SO45 ... 338 E2
Priest Croft Dr SO45 338 E2
Priest Down RG22 ... 91 B5
Priestfields PO14 ... 317 C2
Priest La BH23 ... 380 B7
Priestlands SO51 ... 240 E8
Priestlands Cl SO40 ... 288 A6
Priestlands La SO41 ... 385 C3
Priestlands Pl SO41 ... 385 D3
Priestlands Rd SO41 385 C3
Priestlands Sch
SO41 ... 385 D2
Priestley Cl SO40 ... 288 D7
Priestley Rd
Basingstoke RG21,
RG24 ... 68 E8
Bournemouth BH10 ... 377 B1
Priest's House Mus & Gdns★ BH21 ... 351 B4
Priestwood Cl SO18 ... 292 D7
Primate Rd PO14 ... 317 D2
Primrose Cl
Chandler's Ford
SO53 ... 242 F4
Gosport PO13 ... 343 C5
Hedge End SO30 ... 293 C5
Primrose Ct
1 Andover SP10 ... 105 D6
Waterlooville PO7 ... 323 A6
Primrose Dr RG27 ... 52 D7
Primrose Gdns
Basingstoke RG22 ... 91 B5
Broadstone BH17 ... 374 F1
Farnborough GU14 ... 55 C3
Primrose La
Rake GU33 ... 208 D4
Redlynch SP5 ... 235 C6
Primrose Rd SO16 ... 267 A4
Primrose Terr SO32 ... 247 D2
Primrose Way
Christchurch BH23 ... 396 C8
Corfe Mullen BH21 ... 374 E7
Locks Heath SO31 ... 316 F2
Romsey SO51 ... 216 C1
Primrose Wlk
3 Fleet GU51 ... 53 F2
Yateley GU46 ... 33 F6
Primula Rd GU35 ... 164 E3
Prince Albert Gdns 1
SP10 ... 106 A7
Prince Albert Rd
PO4 ... 371 A3
Prince Alfred St
PO12 ... 369 B4
Prince Charles Cres
GU14 ... 56 A7
Prince Cl SP10 ... 83 D2
Prince George St
Havant PO9 ... 323 F1
Portsmouth PO1 ... 370 A5
Prince Hold Rd RG19 ... 2 E3
Prince Of Wales Ave
SO15 ... 290 A8
Prince Of Wales Cl 4
PO7 ... 323 A7
Prince Of Wales Rd
3 Gosport PO12 ... 369 C5
Bournemouth BH4 ... 392 C4
Prince of Wales Wlk 4
GU15 ... 36 A6
Prince Rd
Fareham PO14 ... 342 F6
Rownhams SO16 ... 265 E6
Prince Regent Ct
PO5 ... 404 B2
Prince's Ave GU11 ... 77 A5
Prince's Bldgs 21
SO23 ... 403 E6
Princes Cl
Bishop's Waltham
SO32 ... 271 B8
Bordon GU35 ... 164 C1
Redlynch SP5 ... 235 E7
Princes Cotts GU32 ... 251 D8
Princes Cres SO43 ... 310 B5
Princes' Cres RG22 ... 68 E3
Princes Ct
2 Southampton
SO14 ... 291 C6
8 Poole BH13 ... 392 A4
Lyndhurst SO43 ... 310 B5
Prince's Ct
4 Portsmouth
PO1 ... 370 D7
Ferndown BH22 ... 353 D5
Princes Ct SP9 ... 78 F7
Princes Dr PO7 ... 300 A1
Princes Hill SP5 ... 235 E7
Princes Ho
3 Southampton
SO14 ... 291 C6
Portsmouth PO5 ... 404 A1
Princes Mead GU14 ... 55 F3
Prince's Mead Sch
SO21 ... 176 E6
Princes Pl SO22 ... 403 C3
Prince's Pl
1 Portsmouth
PO1 ... 370 D7
New Milton BH25 ... 383 C3
Princes Rd
Ferndown BH22 ... 353 D5
Petersfield GU32 ... 228 D4
Southampton SO15 ... 290 D6
Prince's Rd SO51 ... 240 E8
Princess Anne Hospl
SO16 ... 266 B3
Princess Ave BH23 ... 395 B6
Princess Cl SO30 ... 268 E2
Princess Ct
11 Winchester
SO23 ... 403 E6
2 Farnborough GU14 ... 77 A8
Princess Dr GU34 ... 139 D3
Princess Gdns PO8 ... 300 C7
Princess Louise Sq
GU34 ... 139 D1
Princess Marina Dr
Arborfield Garrison
RG2 ... 15 D8
Arborfield Garrison RG2,
RG40 ... 15 F8
Princess Rd
Ashurst SO40 ... 288 B2
Bournemouth BH4 ... 392 B4
Poole BH13 ... 392 A4
Prince's St
Portsmouth PO1 ... 370 D7
Southampton SO14 ... 291 C6
Princess Way GU15 ... 36 A6
Princes Way GU11 ... 76 E2
Prince William Ct
SO50 ... 244 F2
Pringles Cl BH22 ... 353 E5
Pringles Dr BH22 ... 353 E5
Prinstead Cl 6
SO23 ... 403 F4
Prinsted Cres PO6 ... 346 D7
Prinsted La PO10 ... 349 D7
Prinsted Wlk PO14 ... 342 D8
Printers Row 13
SO23 ... 403 D6
Prior Croft Cl GU15 ... 36 E4
Prior End GU15 ... 36 E5
Prior Heath Com Inf Sch
GU15 ... 36 E5
Prior Place Cross Rds
GU15 ... 36 F4
Prior Rd GU15 ... 36 E5
Priors Barton SO23 ... 403 D3
Priors Cl
Breach PO10 ... 325 E1
Christchurch BH23 ... 396 C7
Farnborough GU14 ... 55 F8
Kingsclere RG20 ... 24 D2
Priors Ct GU12 ... 77 C1
Priorsdean Ave PO3 ... 371 A6
Priorsdean Cres
PO9 ... 323 D3
Priors Dean Rd
SO22 ... 175 D4
Priors Hill La SO31 ... 315 E8
Priors Keep GU52 ... 75 B8
Prior's La GU17 ... 34 E5
Priors Leaze La
PO18 ... 325 F1
Priors Rd
Pamber Heath RG26 ... 9 E1
Poole BH17 ... 390 A8
Priors Row RG29 ... 72 C4
Priors Way SO22 ... 197 B3
Priors Way The
SO24 ... 182 B1
Priors Wlk 3 BH21 ... 351 B5
Priors Wood GU27 ... 189 D6
Priory Ave SO17 ... 267 D1
Priory CE Prim Sch The
BH23 ... 395 B6
Priory Cl
Bishop's Waltham
SO32 ... 271 B8
Fleet GU51 ... 74 D8
Southampton SO17 ... 267 D1
Priory Cotts RG7 ... 13 A4
Priory Cres PO4 ... 371 A4
Priory Ct
Bishop's Waltham
SO32 ... 271 B8
Farnham GU9 ... 122 A8
Portchester PO6 ... 344 E8
Portsmouth PO5 ... 404 D2
Sandhurst GU15 ... 35 D5
Priory Gdns
13 Winchester
SO23 ... 403 E6
Old Basing RG24 ... 70 B7
Portchester PO16 ... 344 C7
Waterlooville PO7 ... 299 E1
West Moors BH22 ... 354 A8
Priory Ho
6 Southampton
SO14 ... 291 A5
Christchurch BH23 ... 395 C5
Priory Ind Pk BH23 ... 396 B7
Priory La
Frensham GU10 ... 144 C8
Priory La *continued*
Hartley Wintney RG27 ... 52 C4
Laverstoke RG28 ... 87 A6
Priory Pl RG19 ... 5 F6
Priory Prim Sch The
RG26 ... 27 B1
Priory Quay BH23 ... 395 C5
Priory Rd
5 Portsmouth
PO4 ... 371 A2
Bournemouth BH2 ... 392 E2
Eastleigh SO50 ... 243 F1
Fareham PO15 ... 318 D2
Gosport PO12 ... 369 B9
Gosport PO12 ... 369 C9
Netley SO31 ... 315 B6
Newbury RG14 ... 1 E1
Southampton,Portswood
SO17 ... 267 D1
Southampton,St Denys
SO17 ... 291 C8
Southwick PO17 ... 321 A6
West Moors BH22 ... 354 A8
Priory Sch SO32 ... 271 B8
Priory Sch (Sports Coll)
PO4 ... 404 D2
Priory St GU14 ... 56 B4
Priory The SO32 ... 271 B7
Priory View Ct 4
BH23 ... 395 B6
Priory View Pl 3
BH9 ... 378 A3
Priory View Rd
Bournemouth BH9 ... 378 A3
Burton BH23 ... 380 C2
Pritchard Cl RG19 ... 6 B7
Private Rd SO41 ... 385 E5
Privet La SP11 ... 80 F5
Privet Rd
Bournemouth BH9 ... 392 F8
Lindford GU35 ... 165 A5
Privett Cl RG24 ... 70 A8
Privett Ho PO1 ... 370 A6
Privett Pl PO12 ... 368 E4
Privett Rd
Fareham PO15 ... 318 C2
Gosport PO12,PO13 ... 368 D3
High Cross GU32 ... 205 E2
Waterlooville PO7 ... 322 D3
Prochurch Rd PO8 ... 300 B4
Proctor Cl SO19 ... 292 D5
Proctor Dr SO52 ... 241 F3
Proctor La PO1 ... 370 F5
Project Workshops
SP11 ... 103 A5
Promenade BH23 ... 396 B5
Promenade Ct PO13 ... 367 E3
Promenade The
5 Portsmouth
PO2 ... 345 D1
Emsworth PO10 ... 348 F7
Hythe SO45 ... 314 A5
Propeller Rd GU14 ... 55 F2
Prospect Ave GU14 ... 55 F6
Prospect Bsns Ctr
SO24 ... 179 C4
Prospect Cotts GU12 ... 77 E4
Prospect Hill GU35 ... 165 C8
Prospect La
Durrants PO9 ... 324 B7
Havant PO9 ... 324 B5
Prospect Pl
Chandler's Ford
SO53 ... 243 C6
Hythe SO45 ... 314 A5
Newbury RG14 ... 1 E1
Prospect Rd
Ash Vale GU12 ... 77 E5
Farnborough GU14 ... 55 E5
New Alresford SO24 ... 179 C4
Portsmouth PO1 ... 370 C7
Rowledge GU10 ... 121 C3
Prosperous St 1
BH15 ... 390 C1
Protea Gdns PO14 ... 318 A1
Provene Cl SO32 ... 271 E4
Provene Gdns SO32 ... 271 E4
Providence Ct 2
PO1 ... 370 C7
Providence Hill
SO31 ... 293 A2
Providence Pk SO16 266 F5
Providence Pl 6 GU9 99 A2
Provost St SP6 ... 257 F1
Pruetts La GU31 ... 207 F1
Prunus Cl
Ferndown BH22 ... 353 B7
Southampton SO16 ... 266 C5
Prunus Dr BH22 ... 353 B7
Puckridge Gate Rd
GU11 ... 76 C6
Pudbrooke Gdns
SO30 ... 293 B8
Pudbrook Ho SO30 ... 294 A6
Pudding La SO23 ... 176 B5
Puddleslosh La SP6 ... 257 D3
Puddletown Cres
BH17 ... 375 F2
Puffers Way 1 RG14 ... 1 C2
Puffin Cl
Basingstoke RG22 ... 90 F6
Southampton SO16 ... 266 B5
Puffin Cres PO14 ... 342 B4
Puffin Gdns PO13 ... 343 B3
Puffin Wlk PO8 ... 299 D4
Pug's Hole SP5 ... 191 B7
Pulens Cres GU31 ... 229 C4
Pulens La GU31 ... 229 B4
Pullman Bsns Pk
BH24 ... 329 B6
Pullman Ct BH22 ... 326 D2
Pullman Way BH24 ... 329 B6
Pump La
Gosport PO13 ... 343 C1
Waterlooville PO8 ... 300 A5
Pundle Green Est
SO40 ... 287 B6
Punsholt La SO24 ... 203 F5
Purbeck Ave BH15 ... 389 E1
Purbeck Cl BH16 ... 389 B7
Purbeck Ct
3 Christchurch
BH23 ... 395 F8
Bournemouth BH5 ... 394 B3
Purbeck Dr
Fareham PO14 ... 342 D8
Verwood BH31 ... 302 F5
Purbeck Gdns BH14 ... 390 F5
Purbeck Hts BH14 ... 391 B5
Purbeck Rd
Barton on S BH25 ... 397 D7
Bournemouth BH2 ... 392 E2
Purbeck Wlk PO14 ... 342 D7
Purbrook Chase Prec
PO7 ... 322 E3
Purbrook Cl SO16 ... 266 C4
Purbrook Gdns PO7 ... 322 C5
Purbrook Heath Rd
PO7 ... 322 B5
Purbrook Ho PO7 ... 322 C5
Purbrook Inf Sch
PO7 ... 322 D5
Purbrook Jun Sch
PO7 ... 322 D5
Purbrook Park Sch
PO7 ... 322 D3
Purbrook Rd
Portsmouth PO1 ... 370 E5
Tadley RG26 ... 26 E8
Purbrook Way
Havant PO9 ... 323 C4
Waterlooville PO7 ... 322 F4
Purcell Cl
Basingstoke RG22 ... 68 F1
Waterlooville PO7 ... 322 E5
Purcell Rd SO19 ... 292 D4
Purchase Rd BH12 ... 392 C7
Purdy Ho BH11 ... 377 A4
Purewell BH23 ... 395 D6
Purewell Cl BH23 ... 395 E6
Purewell Cross
BH23 ... 395 E6
Purewell Cross Rd
BH23 ... 395 D7
Purewell Ct 2 BH23 395 E7
Purewell Rdbt BH23 ... 395 E6
Purkess Cl SO53 ... 243 D7
Purkiss Cl SO40 ... 287 C5
Purley Way
Camberley GU16 ... 56 C8
Plaitford SO51 ... 238 B3
Purlieu La SP6 ... 258 F3
Purmerend Cl 1
GU14 ... 55 A5
Purrocks The GU32 ... 228 F5
Purslane Gdns PO15 317 E3
Purvis Gdns SO19 ... 292 B2
Pussex La BH23 ... 379 A7
Putmans La GU31 ... 254 F7
Puttenham Rd
Chineham RG24 ... 49 A3
Seale GU10 ... 100 F4
Puttocks Cl GU27 ... 189 B5
Pycroft Cl
North Hayling PO11 ... 348 C3
Southampton SO19 ... 292 A5
Pye Cl BH21 ... 374 E7
Pye Cnr BH21 ... 351 B4
Pye La
Alderholt BH21 ... 279 E6
Wimborne Minster
BH21 ... 351 B4
Pye St PO1 ... 404 B4
Pyestock Cres GU14 ... 55 A4
Pyland's La SO31 ... 293 B3
Pyle Cl PO8 ... 300 A4
Pylehill SO50 ... 245 C3
Pyle Hill RG14 ... 1 F1
Pylewell Park Gdns★
SO41 ... 386 E4
Pylewell Rd SO45 ... 314 A4
Pyotts Copse RG24 ... 49 A1
Pyotts Ct RG24 ... 49 A1
Pyotts Hill RG24 ... 49 A1
Pyramid Ctr PO3 ... 346 B3
Pyramids L Ctr The
PO5 ... 370 D1
Pyrford Cl
Gosport PO12 ... 368 E3
Waterlooville PO7 ... 299 E2
Pyrford Gdns 3
SO41 ... 385 E2
Pyrford Mews SO41 ... 385 E2
Pytchley Cl PO14 ... 367 A7

Q

Quadrangle The
Bramshill RG27 ... 32 B4
Eastleigh SO50 ... 244 A4
Romsey SO51 ... 241 D6
Quadrant SP6 ... 281 E8
Quadrant Ctr The
BH1 ... 392 F3
Quadrant The GU12 ... 77 E4
Quadra Point PO3 ... 346 B3
Quail Way PO8 ... 300 A6
Quaker Ct BH24 ... 328 F6
Quantock Cl RG22 ... 68 B3
Quantock Ct 7
BH23 ... 395 F8
Quantock Rd SO16 ... 289 E8
Quantocks The
SO45 ... 313 D2
Quarely Rd PO9 ... 323 C6
Quarr Ho SO41 ... 360 A3
Quarry Chase 4
BH4 ... 392 C3
Quarry Cl BH21 ... 352 B7
Quarry Cotts RG20 ... 43 B8
Quarry Dr BH21 ... 352 B7
Quarry La GU46 ... 34 C5
Quarry Rd
Wimborne Minster
BH21 ... 352 B7
Winchester SO23 ... 198 C7
Quarterdeck Ave
PO2 ... 345 B1
Quarterdeck The
PO1 ... 369 E6
Quarterjack Mews 1
BH21 ... 351 C4
Quartremaine Rd
PO3 ... 346 B3
Quavey Rd SP5 ... 235 E6
Quay 2000 SO14 ... 291 C8
Quay Haven SO31 ... 316 D8
Quay Hill SO41 ... 385 F4
Quay Ho SO31 ... 316 B1
Quay La PO12 ... 344 B1
Quayle Dr BH11 ... 376 F6
Quay Point
8 Poole BH15 ... 390 C1
Portsmouth PO6 ... 345 C8
Quay Rd
Christchurch BH23 ... 395 B6
Lymington SO41 ... 385 F4
Quayside SO30 ... 294 A6
Quayside Commerce Ctr
PO16 ... 343 B8
Quayside Rd
Fawley SO45 ... 339 F1
Southampton SO18 ... 291 D7
Quayside Wlk SO40 ... 289 F3
Quay St
Fareham PO16 ... 319 C1
Fareham PO16 ... 343 B8
Lymington SO41 ... 385 F4
Quay The
Hamble-le-R SO31 ... 316 A2
Poole BH15 ... 390 C1
Quebec Cl GU30 ... 188 A3
Quebec Gdns
Blackwater GU17 ... 35 B4
Bursledon SO31 ... 292 F1
Queen Alexandra Hospl
PO6 ... 345 F8
Queen Anne Dr
Oakley BH21 ... 375 E8
Wimborne Minster
BH21 ... 352 A1
Queen Anne's Dr
PO9 ... 323 C2
Queen Annes Gate
GU9 ... 99 B7
Queen Anne's Sq 18
RG21 ... 69 B5
Queen Anne's Wlk 2
RG21 ... 69 B5
Queen Elizabeth Ave
SO41 ... 385 D4
Queen Elizabeth Cl
GU12 ... 77 E2
Queen Elizabeth Country Park★ GU31 ... 253 B3
Queen Elizabeth Country Park Visitor Ctr★
PO8 ... 252 F4
Queen Elizabeth Ct
Southampton SO17 ... 267 C3
Wimborne Minster
BH21 ... 351 B4
Queen Elizabeth Dr
GU11 ... 76 D2
Queen Elizabeth's Sch
BH21 ... 350 F6
Queen Katherine Rd
SO41 ... 385 F3
Queen Mary Ave
Basingstoke RG21 ... 69 B6
Bournemouth BH9 ... 377 F2
Camberley GU15 ... 35 E5
Queen Mary Cl GU51 ... 53 F3
Queen Mary Rd
PO16 ... 344 D7
Queen Mary's Coll
RG21 ... 69 B3
Queen Rd PO14 ... 342 F6
Queens Ave
Aldershot GU11 ... 76 F4
Andover SP10 ... 106 A8
Queen's Ave BH23 ... 395 B5
Queensbury Mans 9
BH1 ... 393 A3
Queensbury Pl GU17 ... 35 A3
Queens Cl
Hythe SO45 ... 314 B3
Lee-on-t-S PO13 ... 367 E3
West Moors BH22 ... 326 D1
Queen's Cl
Farnborough GU14 ... 76 F8
Romsey SO51 ... 241 A7
Queens Cotts SP11 ... 61 E2
Queens Cres
Horndean PO8 ... 300 C7
Stubbington PO14 ... 367 D8
Queen's Cres PO5 ... 404 B1
Queens Ct
12 Winchester
SO23 ... 403 D5
16 Bournemouth BH4 392 D4
Bournemouth,Charminster
BH8 ... 393 B8
Farnham GU9 ... 98 F7
Newbury RG14 ... 1 E1
New Milton BH25 ... 383 D3
Queen's Ct
Farnborough GU14 ... 77 A8
Southampton SO15 ... 290 E5
Queensdale Ct RG21 ... 69 A3
Queensfield RG25 ... 90 D1
Queensgate GU14 ... 55 F3
Queens Gate PO1 ... 370 B2
Queen's Gate Rd
GU14 ... 76 F8
Queens Gdns
Bournemouth BH2 ... 392 D4
Fordingbridge SP6 ... 257 F2
Queens Gr
New Milton BH25 ... 383 C4
Waterlooville PO7 ... 322 D5
Queen's Gr PO5 ... 404 B1
Queens Ho 2 SO14 ... 291 A3
Queen's Inclosure Prim Sch PO7 ... 300 A1
Queens Keep
22 Portsmouth
PO5 ... 370 C2
4 Southampton
SO15 ... 290 F5
5 Camberley GU15 ... 36 B5
Queens La GU9 ... 98 F7
Queensland Rd BH5 ... 394 A5
Queensmead
4 Wimborne Minster
BH21 ... 351 C5
Burton BH23 ... 380 A1
Farnborough GU14 ... 55 F3
Queens Mead SO22 ... 403 A4
Queens Mead Gdns
RG29 ... 72 D3
Queen's Par
1 Waterlooville
PO7 ... 322 E7
Basingstoke RG21 ... 69 B4
Lyndhurst SO43 ... 309 F5
Queen's Park Ave
BH8 ... 393 D8
Queen's Park Gdns
BH8 ... 393 D7
Queen's Park Inf Sch
BH8 ... 378 C1
Queen's Park Jun Sch
BH8 ... 378 B1
Queen's Park Rd
BH8 ... 393 D7
Queen's Park South Dr
BH8 ... 393 D7
Queen's Park West Dr
BH8 ... 393 D7
Queen's Pl PO5 ... 404 B1
Queens Rd
Aldershot GU11 ... 76 D2
Camberley GU15 ... 35 F4
Farnborough GU14 ... 77 B8
Farnham GU9 ... 99 A6
Ferndown BH22 ... 353 D7
Fleet GU52 ... 75 A7
Kingsclere RG20 ... 24 E1
Lee-on-t-S PO13 ... 367 F1
Liphook GU30 ... 187 A3
Lyndhurst SO43 ... 310 B5
North Warnborough
RG29 ... 72 C3
Petersfield GU32 ... 228 D4
Whitchurch RG28 ... 86 D3
Queen's Rd
Alton GU34 ... 139 E3
Basingstoke RG21 ... 68 F5
Bournemouth BH3 ... 392 D4
Chandler's Ford
SO53 ... 218 D1
Christchurch BH23 ... 395 E6
Corfe Mullen BH21 ... 374 D5
Fareham PO16 ... 319 B1
Gosport PO12 ... 369 C5
Newbury RG14 ... 1 F2
Poole BH14 ... 391 D4
Portsmouth,Buckland
PO2 ... 370 E8
Portsmouth PO1 ... 369 F7
Southampton SO15 ... 266 C2
Warsash SO31 ... 340 C10
Waterlooville PO7 ... 299 F1
Winchester SO22 ... 403 B5
Queen's Rdbt GU11,
GU14 ... 76 F7
Queens Ride SO52 ... 241 E4
Queen St
Aldershot GU12 ... 77 B2
Emsworth PO10 ... 349 A8
Lymington SO41 ... 385 D3
Portsmouth PO1 ... 370 A5
Twyford SO21 ... 219 F5
Woodgreen SP6 ... 235 B2
Queen's Terr PO5 ... 404 B1
Queen's Terr SO14 ... 291 A3

Queenstown Rd
SO15 . . . . 290 D6
Queens View SO31 . . 315 B6
Queensway
Andover SP10 . . . . . . 83 D2
Camberley GU16 . . . . . 56 E7
New Milton BH25 . . 382 E3
North Hayling PO11. . 348 A3
Southampton SO14 . . 291 A3
Queens Way BH24 . . . 329 B7
Queen's Way PO5 . . . 404 B1
Queensway The
PO16 . . . . 344 B8
Queenswood Ave
BH8 . . . . 378 E1
Queenswood Dr
BH22 . . . . 353 D7
Queen Victoria Cross
Roads GU15 . . . . . 35 E6
Queen Victoria Ct
GU14 . . . . 55 F5
Queen Victoria's Wlk
GU15 . . . . 35 D6
Queenwood Rd
SO20 . . . . 170 B6
Queenwood Rise
SO20 . . . . 170 B6
Quennells Hill GU10. 121 D5
Querida SO31 . . . . . . 316 D8
Quetta Pk GU10. . . . . 75 B2
Quilter Cl SO19 . . . . 292 D4
Quilter Rd RG22. . . . . 68 D1
Quince La BH21 . . . . . 351 E6
Quince Tree Way
RG27 . . . . 51 B1
Quinnettes GU10. . . . 144 D1
Quinneys GU14 . . . . . 56 A1
Quintin Cl BH23 . . . . 396 F8
Quinton Cl PO5 . . . . . 404 C2
Quintrell Ave PO16. . 344 A8
Quob Farm Cl SO30 . 268 E3
Quob La SO30 . . . . . . 268 E3
Quomp The BH24 . . . . 329 A7
Quorn Terr GU33. . . . 186 C3
Quoyne Cl SO51 . . . . 240 E7

R

Racecourse La PO6 . 345 B8
Race Course Rd RG14 . . 1 F1
Racecourse View
SO43 . . . . 309 F6
Racedown Cotts
SP11 . . . . 102 F6
Raceview Bsns Ctr
RG14 . . . . 1 F2
Rachel Cl
Fair Oak SO50 . . . . . 245 B2
Poole BH12 . . . . 391 C7
Rachel Madocks Sch
PO8 . . . . 299 D4
Rack Cl SP10 . . . . . . 106 B8
Rack Close Rd GU34. 139 E3
Rackfield GU27 . . . . 189 B7
Rack & Manger Cotts
SO21 . . . . 174 A4
Rackstraw Rd GU47 . . 35 B8
Racton Ave PO6 . . . . 346 B7
Racton Rd PO10 . . . . 324 F3
Radar Rd GU14 . . . . . . 55 B1
Radcliffe Cl GU16 . . . 56 F7
Radcliffe Ct SO14 . . . 291 B5
Radcliffe Rd SO14. . . 291 B6
Radclyffe Rd PO16 . . 319 C2
Radford Cl GU9. . . . . . 99 C5
Radford Gdns RG21. . . 68 F2
Radical Ride RG40 . . . 16 D7
Radipole Rd BH17. . . 376 A2
Radleigh Gdns SO40 288 E8
Radley Cl SO30 . . . . . 269 C1
Radnor St PO5 . . . . . 404 B2
Radstock Rd SO19 . . 291 E3
Radway Rd SO15. . . . 266 E1
Raeburn Cl SO24. . . . 201 D5
Raeburn Dr SO30 . . . 293 C7
Raeburn Way GU47 . . 35 B6
Rae Rd GU14 . . . . 55 F1
RAF Gate Rd GU14 . . . 55 F1
Raghill RG7. . . . . 10 B6
Raglan Cl
Aldershot GU12. . . . . 77 A1
Camberley GU16 . . . . 56 E8
Chandler's Ford SO53 243 A4
Raglan Ct
Basingstoke RG22 . . . . 91 C8
Eastleigh SO50 . . . . 244 A6
Gosport PO12 . . . . . 369 A5
Locks Heath SO31 . . 317 C6
Raglan Gdns BH11 . . 377 A2
Raglan St PO5 . . . . . . 404 B2
Raglan Terr PO10 . . . 325 A1
Ragmore La GU32. . . 205 E5
Rails La PO11 . . . . . . 373 C2
Railton 2 GU15. . . . . . 36 B6
Railway Cotts
Bordon GU35. . . . . . 164 A5
East Tisted GU34. . . . 183 D5
Southampton SO15 . . 289 C8
West Dean SP5 . . . . . 190 D3
West Meon GU32 . . . 225 C4
West Tisted SO24 . . . 204 C6
Railway Flats PO1. . . 370 E5

Railway Rd
Greatham GU33. . . . . 186 D3
Newbury RG14 . . . . 1 F1
Railway Terr
Brockenhurst SO42 . . 360 F8
Stratfield Mortimer
RG7 . . . . 12 C5
Railway Triangle Ind Est
PO6. . . . . 346 B6
Railway View PO1. . . 404 C3
Railway View Rd
SO17. . . . . 291 C8
Rainbow Cl RG24 . . . . 70 C5
Rainbow Pl SO15 . . . 290 C6
Rainham Cl RG22. . . . . 90 F7
Rake Bsns Pk GU33 . 208 E4
Rake CE Fst Sch
GU33. . . . . 208 E4
Rakemakers GU34 . . 140 D7
Rake Rd
Liss GU33 . . . . 208 B4
Milland GU30. . . . . . 209 E2
Raleigh Cl
Christchurch BH23 . . 395 F6
New Milton BH25 . . . 382 F3
Ringwood BH24. . . . . 329 C8
Raleigh Rd BH12. . . . 376 E1
Raleigh Way GU16 . . . 36 D3
Raleigh Wlk PO13. . . 368 D6
Raley Rd SO31 . . . . . 317 A2
Ralph Ct GU10 . . . . . . 97 D5
Ralph Jessop Ct
BH12 . . . . 391 D7
Ralph La SO51 . . . . . 216 A1
Ralph Rd BH21. . . . . . 374 E7
Ram Alley
Ashford Hill RG19 . . . . 8 B1
Fair Oak RG19 . . . . . 25 A8
Ramalley La SO53 . . 243 B8
Rambler Dr PO13 . . . 368 C6
Ramblers Way PO7. . 300 C1
Ramillies Cl GU11. . . . 77 C7
Ramillies Ho
16 Gosport PO12 . . . 369 C5
3 Fareham PO14 . . . 342 E7
Ramillies Rd GU11. . . . 77 B5
Ramley Rd SO41 . . . . 385 B3
Rampart Gdns PO3. . 345 F5
Rampart Rd SO18 . . . 291 D7
Rampart Row PO12 . 369 F4
Ramparts The SP10 . 105 E5
Rampart Way SO41 . 385 D5
Rampton Rd RG28 . . . 86 D4
Ramridge Ho SP11 . . . 81 C4
Ramsay Cl GU15 . . . . . 36 F7
Ramsay Pl PO13 . . . . 343 C2
Ramsay Rd SO23. . . . 176 C8
Ramsdale Ave PO9. . 323 C5
Ramsdean Rd GU32 . 227 E2
Ramsdell Cl RG26. . . . . 26 F7
Ramsdell Rd
Fleet GU51 . . . . 53 D4
Pamber End RG26 . . . 27 B1
Wolverton RG26 . . . . 25 D1
Ramsey Ct BH25 . . . . 382 F3
Ramsey Rd PO11. . . . 373 A3
Ramshill GU31. . . . . . 229 A4
Ramsholt Cl RG25. . . . 89 E1
Rams Wlk GU32 . . . . 228 F3
Rances Way SO22. . . 403 C3
Randall Cl SO40. . . . . 264 C2
Randall Rd SO53 . . . . 218 D2
Randall's La BH24 . . . 330 E5
Randell Cl GU17 . . . . . 35 C1
Randolph Dr GU14 . . . 55 A3
Randolph Rd
2 Bournemouth
BH1 . . . . 393 E4
Poole BH14 . . . . 391 C5
Portsmouth PO2 . . . . 345 E2
Randolph St SO15. . . 290 C7
Ranelagh Ct **9**
SO17. . . . . 291 A8
Ranelagh Gdns SO15 290 E7
Ranelagh Rd
Christchurch BH23 . . 396 F7
Havant PO9 . . . . 323 D1
Portsmouth PO2 . . . . 345 C1
Winchester SO23 . . . 403 E8
Ranfurly Gdns SO45. 313 E1
Range Gdns SO19 . . . 292 B3
Range Gn PO2 . . . . . . 345 C3
Ranger Ct SO14 . . . . 291 B2
Range Rd
Farnborough GU14 . . . 55 C1
Finchampstead RG40. . 16 F7
Range Ride GU15 . . . . 35 D7
Range View GU47 . . . 35 D7
Rankine Cl GU9 . . . . . . 99 E6
Rankine Rd RG24 . . . . 69 D8
Rank The
Fyfield SP11 . . . . 80 E2
Hurstbourne Tarrant
SP11 . . . . 60 F7
Penton Grafton SP11. . 81 D2
Ranmore Ct SO45 . . . 313 C4
Rannoch Cl PO15 . . . 318 E3
Ransome Ct PO14 . . . 341 F7
Ranvilles Jun & Inf Schs
PO14. . . . . 342 C8
Ranvilles La PO14 . . 342 B7
Rapallo Cl GU14 . . . . . 56 A4
Raphael Cl RG21 . . . . 69 D3
Rapley Cl GU15 . . . . . 36 D8
Rapley Ct PO11 . . . . . 372 E3

Rapson Cl PO6. . . . . . 321 C1
Raptor & Reptile Ctr ★
BH24. . . . . 329 C5
Rareridge La SO32. . . 271 E8
Rashleigh Ct GU52 . . . 75 B4
Rashley Mews SO41. 385 E3
Rasset Mead GU52 . . 74 B3
Ratcliffe Rd
Dibden Purlieu
SO45. . . . . 313 F1
Farnborough GU14 . . . 55 B8
Hedge End SO30 . . . 293 C7
Rathdora Mews
SO31 . . . . 315 F8
Ratlake La SO21 . . . . 217 F4
Rattigan Gdns PO15 . 317 C8
Ravana Ct **4** BH8 . . . 393 A5
Ravel Cl RG22. . . . . 68 C1
Ravelin Ct GU10. . . . . . 97 D5
Raven Cl
5 Yateley GU46 . . . . 33 F6
Gosport PO13 . . . . . 368 C6
Raven Croft PO5 . . . . 404 B1
Raven Rd
Hook RG27 . . . . 51 A1
Southampton SO14 . . 291 B6
Ravens Cl PO14 . . . . . 367 D7
Ravenscote Com Jun Sch
GU16. . . . . 36 E3
Ravenscourt Rd
Bournemouth BH6. . . 394 C5
Lymington SO41 . . . . 385 D2
Ravenscroft RG27. . . . 51 C1
Ravenscroft Cl SO31 292 F1
Ravenscroft Way
SO32 . . . . 269 F1
Ravensdale Cl BH3 . . 391 C6
Ravensdale Cotts
GU26 . . . . 167 A1
Ravenshall **7** BH2 . . 392 C4
Raven Sq
Alton GU34 . . . . 139 F6
Eastleigh SO50 . . . . 243 D2
Ravens Way SO41 . . . 399 D4
Ravenswing Pk RG7. . 10 B3
Ravenswood PO14 . . 341 F7
Ravenswood Dr GU15 . 36 E5
Ravenswood Gdns **12**
PO5 . . . . 370 D2
Ravenswood House
Hospl PO14 . . . . 341 F7
Ravensworth Rd RG7. 11 C5
Raven Way BH23. . . . 396 A5
Ravine Cl BH13 . . . . . 402 F7
Ravine Gdns **5**
BH13 . . . . 402 F7
Ravine Rd
Bournemouth BH5. . . 394 B4
Poole BH13 . . . . 402 F8
Rawdon Rise GU15 . . 36 E6
Rawlings Rd RG27 . . . 72 B8
Rawlinson Rd
Farnborough GU11 . . . 77 A5
Sandhurst GU15 . . . . 35 E6
Rawlinson Terr PO1. 370 A6
Raygnoldes GU52. . . . 74 A3
Rayleigh Rd RG21. . . . 69 A5
Raymond Cl
Holbury SO45 . . . . . 338 D3
Verwood BH31. . . . . 303 B6
West End SO30 . . . . 268 F3
Raymond Rd
Portchester PO6. . . . 320 E1
Southampton SO15 . . 290 D7
Rayner Dr RG2. . . . . . . 15 C3
Rayners Dr BH12 . . . . 391 D6
Rayners Gdns SO16 . 267 D4
Raynes Rd PO13 . . . . 368 A4
Rays Cl RG26 . . . . 27 A8
Rayscliff **21** BH4 . . . . 392 C2
Reading Dr N GU51 . . 53 E1
Reading Dr S RG27. . . 32 B4
Reading Rd
Aldermaston RG7 . . . . 10 D5
Chineham RG24 . . . . 48 F2
Eversley Centre RG27 . 33 B8
Farley Hill RG40 . . . . 15 D3
Farnborough GU14 . . . 56 A1
Hook RG27 . . . . 51 A2
Padworth RG7 . . . . . 11 D8
Rotherwick RG27. . . . 51 B5
Sherfield on L RG27 . . 49 D8
Yateley GU46. . . . . . 34 D6
Reading Rd N GU51 . . 53 E1
Reading Rd S GU52 . . 75 A6
Reading Room La
SO32 . . . . 294 D8
Readon Cl GU31 . . . . 229 A4
Readon Ho GU31. . . . 229 A4
Read's Field GU34 . . 160 B2
Rebbeck Rd BH7. . . . 394 A6
Rebecca Cl GU52 . . . . 74 E3
Recess The SO50 . . . 244 B5
Record Rd PO10 . . . . 324 E1
Recreation Cl GU14 . . 35 D1
Recreation Cotts
SO51 . . . . 238 E3
Recreation Rd
Andover SP10 . . . . . 106 B8
Odiham RG29. . . . . . . 72 D2
Poole BH12 . . . . 391 E6
Rowledge GU10. . . . . 121 C3
Rectory Ave
Corfe Mullen BH21 . . 350 D1
Farlington PO6 . . . . . 346 F8
Rectory Cl
Gosport PO12 . . . . . 369 A3
Newbury RG14 . . . . 1 D2

Rectory Cl continued
Sandhurst GU47 . . . . . 34 D8
Stubbington PO14 . . 367 C8
Tadley RG26 . . . . 27 A6
Rectory Ct SO30 . . . . 293 F7
Rectory Hill
West Dean SP5 . . . . 190 D3
West Tytherley SP5. . 169 A1
Rectory La
Bentley GU10. . . . . . 120 B4
Bramshott SO20 . . . . 188 B7
Breamore SP6. . . . . 234 B1
Broughton SO20 . . . 170 B7
Hannington RG26 . . . 45 A8
Itchen Abbas SO21 . . 178 A7
Meonstoke SO32 . . . 270 E7
Rectory Pl SP11. . . . . . 81 D2
Rectory Rd
Farnborough GU14 . . . 56 B4
Hook RG27. . . . . 72 A8
Langstone PO9 . . . . 347 F8
Oakley RG23. . . . . . . 66 F1
Padworth RG7 . . . . . . 10 D7
Poole BH15 . . . . 390 C6
Rectory Row RG25. . . 92 A7
Redan Cl BH23. . . . . . 396 F7
Redan Gdns **1** GU12 . 77 A1
Redan Hill Est GU12. . 77 A2
Redan Rd GU12 . . . . . . 77 A2
Redan The PO12 . . . . 369 C2
Red Barn Ave PO16 . 320 C1
Red Barn Com Prim Sch
PO16. . . . . 318 E4
Red Barn La PO16. . . 318 E4
Redbreast Rd BH9 . . 378 A3
Redbreast Rd N BH9 . 378 A3
Redbridge Com Sch
SO16. . . . . 289 D8
Redbridge Cswy SO15,
SO16,SO40. . . . . . . 289 B8
Redbridge Dr SP10. . 105 F6
Redbridge Flyover
SO16 . . . . 289 C8
Redbridge Gr PO9 . . 323 D3
Redbridge Hill SO16 265 F1
Redbridge La
Nursling SO16. . . . . 265 D4
Old Basing RG24. . . . 69 F5
Ropley SO24 . . . . . . 182 A4
Southampton SO16 . . 265 C2
Redbridge Prim Sch
SO15. . . . . 289 C8
Redbridge Rd SO15 . 289 D8
Redbridge Sta SO15. 289 C8
Redbridge Towers
SO16 . . . . 289 C8
Redbrook Cotts SP6. 282 A7
Redcar Ave PO3 . . . . 346 A1
Redcliffe Cl BH23 . . . 380 C2
Redcote Cl SO18 . . . . 292 B7
Redcotts La BH21 . . . 351 B5
Redcotts Rd BH21 . . . 351 B5
Redcourt **2** SO16 . . . 266 F4
Redcrest Gdns GU15 . 36 D5
Redcroft La SO31 . . . 293 A1
Red Deer Ct **4**
SO22 . . . . 403 C6
Rede Ct **5** GU11 . . . . 56 A1
Redenham Dro SP11 . 81 A8
Redes Cl RG27 . . . . . . 51 D1
Redfield Ct RG14. . . . . 2 B4
Redfields La GU10,
GU52 . . . . 74 E2
Redfields Pk GU52 . . . 74 E2
Redfords The SO40 . 264 E1
Redgauntlet RG40. . . . 16 C6
Redgrave Ct GU12 . . . 77 D2
Redhearne Fields
GU10. . . . . 144 C1
Redhill SO16. . . . . 266 E4
Red Hill
Ashmansworth RG20. . 41 B7
Four Marks GU34 . . . 160 B5
Mattingley RG27 . . . . 31 E2
Redhill Ave BH9 . . . . 377 E4
Redhill Cl
Bournemouth BH10. . 377 E3
Southampton SO16 . . 266 C4
Redhill Cres BH9. . . . 377 F3
Redhill Ct **1** BH10 . . 378 A4
Redhill Dr BH10. . . . . 377 E3
Redhill Ho PO1 . . . . . 404 C2
Redhill Park Homes **1**
BH10 . . . . 377 F4
Redhill Rd PO9 . . . . . 301 B1
Redhill Rdbt BH10 . . 377 F4
Red Hill Way SO16. . 266 E4
Redhoave Rd BH17 . . 375 E2
Red Horn Cl BH16. . . 389 C4
Redhouse Mews
GU30 . . . . 188 A2
Red House Mews
SO41 . . . . 385 E3
Red House Mus & Gdns ★
BH23. . . . . 395 B6
Redhouse Park Gdns
PO12 . . . . 368 F7
Red La
Aldermaston RG7 . . . 10 B5
Corfe Mullen BH21 . . 374 A8
Ellisfield RG25. . . . . 115 C4
Headley GU35. . . . . 165 F7
Upham SO32 . . . . . . 246 B6
Redlands
Christchurch BH23 . . 396 A7

Redlands continued
Poole BH12 . . . . 391 F5
Redlands Dr SO19. . . 291 F6
Redlands Gr PO4. . . . 371 C4
Redlands La
Crondall GU10. . . . . . 97 E7
Emsworth PO10. . . . 324 F4
Ewshot GU10. . . . . . . 98 A7
Fareham PO14,PO16. 343 A8
Redlands Prim Sch
PO16. . . . . 343 B7
Redlane Hill RG7. . . . . 10 A6
Red Leaves SO32. . . 271 E2
Red Lion La
Basingstoke RG21. . . 69 B4
Farnham GU9 . . . . . . 98 F1
Overton RG25. . . . . . 88 A8
Red Lion Mews RG29 . 72 E3
Red Lodge SO53 . . . 243 B3
Red Lodge Sch SO16 266 E4
Redlynch CE Prim Sch
SP5. . . . . 236 A5
Redlynch Cl PO9 . . . 324 E4
Redmans View BH31. 302 E6
Redmoor Cl SO19 . . . 291 F6
Rednal Ho PO5 . . . . . 404 C3
Red Oaks GU10 . . . . . 121 B3
Red Oaks Cl BH23. . . 351 B7
Red Oaks Dr SO31. . . 317 B5
Redon Way SO15 . . . . 82 F1
Redoubt Ct PO14. . . . 342 F6
Red Post Bridge
SP11. . . . . 104 F7
Red Post La SP11 . . . 104 F7
Red Rice Rd SP10 . . 105 C2
Redrise Cl SO45. . . . . 338 B3
Redsails BH13 . . . . . . 402 B3
Redshank Cl BH17 . . 374 F1
Redshank Ct RG19 . . . . 2 E3
Redshank PO8. . . . . . 300 A7
Redvers Buller Rd
GU11. . . . . 77 B7
Redvers Cl SO41 . . . 385 D2
Redvers Rd BH23 . . . 395 E7
Red Villas SP9 . . . . . 101 E8
Redward Rd SO16. . . 265 F5
Redwing Ct PO4 . . . . 371 C5
Redwing Gdns SO40. 288 C8
Redwing Rd
Basingstoke RG22. . . . 90 F7
Clanfield PO8. . . . . . 276 C4
Redwood Cl
Hythe SO45. . . . . . . 313 C3
Lymington SO41 . . . . 385 D5
Ringwood BH24. . . . . 329 B7
West End SO30 . . . . 268 C2
Redwood Ct
5 Waterlooville
PO7 . . . . 322 E8
Bassett SO16. . . . . . 267 A6
Redwood Dr
Ferndown BH22. . . . 353 C8
Portchester PO16. . . 344 B8
Redwood Gdns
SO40 . . . . 288 C7
Redwood Gr PO9 . . . 324 A4
Redwood La SO24 . . 160 A8
Redwood Lodge **4**
PO16 . . . . 319 B2
Redwood Park Sch
PO6. . . . . 346 A6
Redwood Rd BH16 . . 389 A8
Redwoods Way GU52. 75 B5
Redwood Way SO16. 267 A6
Reed Cl GU11. . . . . 77 B5
Reed Dr SO40. . . . . . . 289 F2
Reeder Dr PO4. . . . . . 371 C5
Reedling Dr PO4. . . . 371 C5
Reedmace Ct PO7. . . 323 A6
Reeds La GU33. . . . . . 208 D6
Reeds Mdw GU32 . . . 227 D4
Reed's Pl SO40 . . . . . 289 B7
Reeds Rd PO12 . . . . . 369 B8
Reeds Rd The GU10. 122 D3
Reed Wlk RG14 . . . . . . 2 A4
Rees Rd SO21. . . . . . . 153 C2
Reeves Cl SO51 . . . . 238 E3
Reeves Rd GU12 . . . . . 77 A1
Reeves Way SO31. . . 292 F1
Regal Cl PO6. . . . . 345 F8
Regal Ct **3** RG14 . . . . . 1 F2
Regency Cres BH23 . 394 F8
Regency Ct **12** PO1. . 370 A4
Regency Gdns PO7. . 322 D6
Regency Pl
Fareham PO15. . . . . 318 E1
Ringwood BH24. . . . 329 A8
Regent Cl
Fleet GU52 . . . . 75 A8
Otterbourne SO21. . . 219 C4
Regent Ct
17 Southampton
SO17. . . . . 267 A1
18 Winchester SO23. 403 E8
2 Portsmouth PO1. . 370 D7
7 Aldershot GU11. . . 76 F2
Basingstoke RG21. . . 69 C6
Fleet GU51 . . . . 74 F8
Regent Dr BH7. . . . . . 393 F8
Regent Mews GU32 . 228 D4
Regent Pl PO5 . . . . . . 404 A1
Regents Ct
11 Knowle Village
PO17 . . . . 318 E7
8 Southampton
SO16. . . . . 290 B8

Regents Ct continued
Andover SP10 . . . . . . 83 E1
Langstone PO9 . . . . 347 F8
Newbury RG14 . . . . 1 D3
Newbury RG14 . . . . 1 F3
Regents Gate SO31. . 316 E5
Regent's Gr **1** SO16 290 B8
Regents Park Com Coll
SO16. . . . . 290 A8
Regent's Park Gdns
SO15 . . . . 290 B7
Regent's Park Rd
SO15 . . . . 290 A7
Regents Pl
Gosport PO12 . . . . . 369 D7
Sandhurst GU47 . . . . 35 A8
Regent St
Fleet GU51 . . . . 75 A8
Portsmouth PO1 . . . . 370 C7
Southampton SO14 . . 290 F4
Regent Way
Christchurch BH23 . . 395 B6
Frimley GU16. . . . . . . 36 E1
Regiment Cl GU14 . . . 55 A3
Reginald Rd PO4. . . . 371 A3
Regnum Dr RG14 . . . . . 1 F5
Reid St BH23 . . . . 395 A8
Reigate Ho PO1. . . . . 404 C4
Reith Way SP10 . . . . . 82 B1
Relay Rd PO7 . . . . 322 D8
Reldas The **9** PO1 . . 370 A4
Reliant Cl SO53 . . . . 243 B4
Rembrandt Cl RG21. . 69 D4
Remembrance Gdns
RG24 . . . . 48 F2
Remembrance Rd
RG14 . . . . 1 C2
R.E.M.E. Mus ★ RG2. . 15 E8
Rempstone Rd BH21 375 D8
Renault Dr BH18. . . . 375 A1
Renda Rd SO45. . . . . 338 C4
Rennie Ct RG14 . . . . . . 1 D4
Renny Rd PO1. . . . . . 370 F5
Renoir Cl RG21 . . . . . . 69 D3
Renouf Cl SO41 . . . . 385 C3
Renown Cl SO53 . . . 243 B5
Renown Gdns PO8. . 299 F5
Renown Ho **15** PO12. 369 C5
Renown Way RG24 . . 48 F4
Repton Cl PO12 . . . . 368 E4
Repton Gdns SO30 . 269 D2
Reservoir La
Hedge End SO30 . . . 293 A6
Petersfield GU32. . . . 228 A6
Reservoir Rd GU14 . . 55 B1
Resolution Ho **14**
PO12 . . . . 369 C5
Rest-A-Wyle Ave
PO11 . . . . 373 A5
Restharrow BH1 . . . . 393 A4
Restormel Cl RG23 . . 68 B6
Restynge Ho BH31 . . 302 F7
Retreat Rd BH21 . . . 351 D4
Retreat The
Eastleigh SO50 . . . . 244 A4
Portsmouth PO5 . . . . 404 B1
Totton SO40. . . . . . . 289 A5
Reuben's Cres RG26. . 26 F7
Revelstoke Ave GU14. 55 F6
Revenge Cl PO4 . . . . 371 C6
Revenge Ho **13**
PO12 . . . . 369 C5
Rewlands Dr SO22 . . 175 C4
Rex Cl GU27 . . . . 189 D6
Rex Est SO53 . . . . . . 243 D5
Reynard Ct BH15. . . . 390 F3
Reynards Rd RG26. . . 26 F7
Reynolds Cl RG21 . . . 69 D4
Reynolds Ct
Andover SP10 . . . . . . 82 F1
Romsey SO51 . . . . . 241 A6
Reynolds Dale SO40. 288 D5
Reynolds Ho GU47 . . 35 B6
Reynolds Ho RG22 . . 68 C2
Reynolds Rd
Fair Oak SO50 . . . . . 245 D1
Gosport PO12 . . . . . 369 C5
Southampton SO15 . . 290 C8
Reyntiens View RG29. 72 E2
Rhine Banks GU14 . . 55 B5
Rhinefield Cl
Bishopstoke SO50. . . 244 A4
Brockenhurst SO42. . 333 E1
Havant PO9 . . . . 323 C4
Rhinefield Forest
Walks ★ SO42. . . . . 333 A2
Rhinefield Ornamental
Dr ★ SO42 . . . . 332 F6
Rhinefield Rd
Brockenhurst SO42. . 333 C2
New Milton BH25 . . . 358 E2
Rhiners Cl SO41 . . . . 360 B2
Rhodes Sq SP10 . . . . 83 C3
Rhododendron Cnr
RG40 . . . . 16 E4
Rhododendron Rd
Camberley GU16 . . . . 56 F8
Frimley GU16. . . . . . . 36 F1
Rhododendron Wlk
RG19 . . . . 7 F5
Rhyll Gdns GU11 . . . . 76 D1
Rhyme Hall Mews
SO45 . . . . 339 B3
Rhys Ct PO4 . . . . 371 A4
Ribble Cl
Broadstone BH18 . . . 375 A2
Chandler's Ford
SO53. . . . . 243 D5

Ribble Ct
34 Andover SP10 . . . . . . 83 C2
Southampton SO16 . . . 265 E1
Ribble Pl GU14. . . . . . . 55 C6
Ribble Way 17 RG21. . 69 D5
Ribbonwood Hts
BH14 . . . . 391 B4
Ricardo Cres BH23. . . 396 A6
Ricardo Way SO41 . . . 385 D7
Rice Gdns BH16. . . . . . 389 D4
Rice Terr BH16 . . . . . . 389 D4
Richard Cl
Fleet GU51 . . . . 74 E7
Upton BH16 . . . . 389 B8
Richard Gr PO12 . . . . . 344 A1
Richard Moss Ho 9
SO23 . . . . 403 E6
Richards Cl
Ash Vale GU12. . . . . . 77 E5
Blackfield SO45 . . . . 338 F2
Locks Heath SO31 . . . 317 B3
Richards Ct 6 SO16 . . 266 B1
Richards Field RG24 . . 49 A2
Richardson Cl RG26. . . 28 F2
Richard Taunton Pl
SO17 . . . . 267 A2
Richborough Dr SP10 82 C3
Riches Mews 9
PO16 . . . . 319 A1
Richlans Rd SO30 . . . 293 C6
Richmond Ave RG19 . . 2 E3
Richmond Cl
Bordon GU35. . . . . . . 164 D2
Chandler's Ford SO53 218 C1
Farnborough GU14 . . 55 B3
Fleet GU52 . . . . 74 F6
Frimley GU16. . . . . . . 36 D1
South Hayling PO11. . 372 E4
Totton SO40. . . . . 264 B1
Richmond Cres SP9 . . 79 A6
Richmond Ct
12 Milford on S
SO41. . . . . 399 C4
7 New Milton BH25. 383 A3
Richmond Dr PO11 . . . 372 E4
Richmond Gdns
Bournemouth BH1. . . 392 F3
Southampton SO17 . . 267 B8
Waterlooville PO7. . . 322 C5
Richmond Hall 6
SO17 . . . . 267 C2
Richmond Hill BH2. . 392 F3
Richmond Hill Dr
BH2. . . . . 392 F3
Richmond Ho
1 Southampton
SO15. . . . . 290 C6
5 Winchester SO22 403 D6
Sandhurst GU47 . . . . 35 C7
Richmond La SO51 . . 216 A1
Richmond Park Ave
BH8 . . . . 393 C7
Richmond Park Cl
BH8 . . . . 393 D6
Richmond Park Cres
BH8 . . . . 393 C7
Richmond Park Rd
BH8 . . . . 393 C7
Richmond Pk SO21. . . 219 D4
Richmond Pl
Portsmouth,Portsea
PO1. . . . . 370 B5
Portsmouth,Southsea
PO5. . . . . 370 C2
Richmond Rd
Basingstoke RG21. . . 69 A6
Gosport PO12 . . . . . . 369 A5
Lee-on-t-S PO13 . . . . 367 D3
Poole BH14 . . . . 391 C4
Portsmouth PO5. . . . . 370 D2
Sandhurst GU47. . . . . 35 C8
Southampton SO15. . . 290 C6
Wimborne Minster
BH21 . . . . 351 D4
Richmond Rise
Bournemouth BH8. . . 393 D6
Portchester PO16. . . . 320 C1
Richmond St SO14 . . 291 B3
Richmond Terr 12
PO5. . . . . 370 C2
Richmond Wood Rd
BH8 . . . . 393 C7
Richville Rd SO16. . . . 290 A8
Ridding Cl SO15 . . . . 266 C1
Riddings La RG19 . . . . .8 A2
Riders Inf Sch PO9. . 323 C5
Riders Jun Sch PO9. 323 C5
Riders La PO9 . . . . . . 323 E4
Rideway Cl GU15. . . . .35 F4
Ridge Cl
Basingstoke RG22. . . 91 C5
Clanfield PO8 . . . . . . 276 C4
Ridge Common La
GU32 . . . . 228 C6
Ridgefield Gdns
BH23 . . . . 396 D8
Ridge La
Curbridge SO30. . . . . 294 D3
Newnham RG27. . . . . 50 E1
Romsey SO51 . . . . . . 264 C8
Ridgemede Jun Sch
SO32. . . . . 271 D8
Ridgemoor Cl GU26. . 167 C5
Ridgemount Ave
SO16 . . . . 266 F5
Ridgemount Gdns
BH15 . . . . 389 E3

Ridgemount La
SO16 . . . . 266 F5
Ridges Cl SP11 . . . . . . 83 D8
Ridges View SP11. . . . 83 D8
Ridge The SP5. . . . . . 235 D5
Ridge Top La
Froxfield Green
GU32 . . . . 227 E6
Froxfield Green GU32 228 B8
Ridgeway
Broadstone BH18 . . . 375 B4
Corfe Mullen BH21. . 374 D8
Ferndown BH22. . . . . 377 E8
Winchester SO22 . . . 403 A3
Ridgeway Cl
Chandler's Ford
SO53. . . . . 243 E5
Fair Oak SO50. . . . . . 245 C4
Portchester PO6. . . . . 320 F1
Ridgeway Com Sch The
GU9 . . . . 122 A7
Ridgeway Hill Rd
GU9 . . . . 122 A8
Ridgeway House Sch
SO19. . . . . 291 F5
Ridgeway La SO41 . . 385 D1
Ridgeway Par GU52 . . 75 A5
Ridgeway The
Alton GU34 . . . . 139 F2
Portchester PO16. . . . 319 E1
Ridgeway Wlk SO53. . 243 E5
Ridgewood Cl SO45. . 313 C4
Ridgway PO9 . . . . 323 D1
Ridgway Rd GU9 . . . . 122 A8
Ridings The
Fair Oak SO50. . . . . . 245 A2
Frimley GU16. . . . . . . 36 F6
Liss GU33 . . . . 208 B4
Portsmouth PO2 . . . . 345 F3
Waltham Chase SO32 271 E4
Ridley Cl
Fleet GU52 . . . . 74 F7
Holbury SO45 . . . . . . 338 C4
Ridley Rd BH9. . . . . . . 392 F4
Ridleys Piece RG29 . . 95 A4
Ridout Cl BH10 . . . . . 377 B1
Rifle Way GU14 . . . . . 55 A3
Rigby Rd SO17. . . . . . 291 B8
Riggs Gdns BH11 . . . 376 F2
Rigler Rd BH15 . . . . . 390 A2
Riley La RG24 . . . . . . 70 B7
Riley Rd SO21 . . . . . . 153 F3
Rimbault Cl GU11. . . . 77 B7
Rimbury Way BH23. . 395 A8
Rimes's La RG26 . . . . 26 D6
Rimington Gdns 1
SO51 . . . . 216 B1
Rimington Rd PO8. . . 299 E3
Rindle Cl 4 GU14. . . . 55 A4
Ringbury SO41. . . . . . 385 D6
Ringlet Way 5
SO23 . . . . 198 C8
Ringshall Gdns RG26. .28 E3
Ring The SO16 . . . . . . 266 E7
Ringway Ctr The
RG21. . . . . .68 F7
Ringway E RG21 . . . . .69 E6
Ringway N RG21. . . . .69 B8
Ringway S RG21. . . . .69 B3
Ringway W RG21,RG22,
RG23 . . . . .68 C5
Ringwood CE Inf Sch
BH24 . . . . 329 A7
Ringwood Dr SO52. . 241 E4
Ringwood Ho PO9 . . 323 F5
Ringwood Jun Sch
BH24. . . . . 329 A6
Ringwood Rd
Alderholt SP6 . . . . . . 281 A4
Blackwater GU17 . . . . 35 A6
Bournemouth BH11. . 376 E4
Bransgore BH23 . . . . 381 D5
Burley Street BH24. . 330 E5
Farnborough GU14 . . 56 A7
Ferndown BH22. . . . . 353 C4
Fordingbridge SP6. . . 282 A4
Fordingbridge SP6. . . 282 C4
Poole BH12 . . . . 391 B7
Portsmouth PO4 . . . . 371 B3
Ringwood BH24. . . . . 328 C6
Sopley BH23 . . . . 380 A4
St Leonards BH24. . . 327 D2
Three Legged Cross
BH21 . . . . 327 B7
Totton SO40. . . . . 288 C7
Verwood BH31. . . . . . 303 F5
Walkford BH23 . . . . . 382 B1
West Moors BH22. . . 354 A8
Ringwood Rd Nature
Reserve BH11 . . . . 376 E5
Ringwood Road Ret Pk
BH11. . . . . 376 E5
Ringwood Sch BH24 329 A7
Ringwood Terr SO42 334 A2
Ringwood Trad Est
BH24. . . . . 329 A6
Ringwood Waldorf Sch
BH24. . . . . 328 D6
Ripley Ct BH22. . . . . . 353 F7
Ripley Gr PO3 . . . . . . 371 A8
Ripon Cl SO50 . . . . . . 269 D7
Ripon Gdns 6 PO7. . 300 B1
Ripon Rd
Bournemouth BH9. . . 378 A4
Hawley GU17. . . . . . . 34 D1
Ripplesmore Cl GU47 .34 F1
Ripplewood SO40. . . 290 A1
Ripstone Gdns SO17 267 B3

Riseley Bsns Ctr RG7. 14 A3
Rise The
Brockenhurst SO42. . 333 F1
Finchampstead RG40. 15 E2
Waterlooville PO7. . . 322 D2
Ritchie Ct PO11 . . . . . 373 A3
Ritchie Ct SO19 . . . . . 292 B4
Ritchie Pl BH22 . . . . . 326 D4
Ritchie Rd BH11 . . . . 377 B4
Rival Moor Rd GU31. 229 C2
Rivendell Ct GU14. . . 55 C4
Riverbourne Ct
SO18 . . . . 291 D8
River Cl
Four Marks GU34 . . . 160 B2
Wimborne Minster
BH21 . . . . 351 C6
River Ct SO41. . . . . . . 385 F4
Riverdale GU10 . . . . . 121 C7
Riverdale Ave PO7 . . 323 A7
Riverdale Cl SP6 . . . . 257 F2
Riverdale Cotts
PO16 . . . . 319 D3
Riverdale Ct RG14. . . . 2 A1
Riverdale La BH23 . . 395 A6
Riverdene Pl SO18 . . 291 D8
River Gdns SO41 . . . . 399 E4
River Gn SO31 . . . . . . 316 A2
Riverhead SO24 . . . . 180 C4
Riverhead Cl PO4 . . . 371 B1
River Ho 38 SP10. . . . 83 C2
River La
Fareham PO15. . . . . . 318 C6
Farnham GU9 . . . . . . 121 C7
Riverland Ct 4
BH23 . . . . 395 A6
Riverlea Rd BH23 . . . 395 A6
Rivermead Cl SO51. . 240 D7
Rivermead Ct PO10 . 325 A3
Rivermead Gdns
BH23 . . . . 379 E2
Rivermead Rd GU15. . 35 C2
Rivermede GU35 . . . . 164 E4
River Mews SO50 . . . 244 D3
Riverpark Ct SO18 . . 267 D1
River Park Ind Est
RG14. . . . . 1 F3
River Pk BH6 . . . . 394 F6
River Rd
Godshill SP6 . . . . 258 D2
Yateley GU46. . . . . . . 33 F8
River Row Cotts
SO40 . . . . 121 D8
Rivers Cl GU14. . . . . . 56 C1
Riversdale 8 BH23. . 351 C4
Riversdale Cl SO19. . 314 E8
Riversdale Gdns
PO9 . . . . 323 F2
Riversdale Rd BH6. . 395 A4
Riverside
4 Bournemouth
BH10 . . . . 377 F4
Bishopstoke SO50. . . 244 E4
Ringwood BH24. . . . . 328 F6
Riverside Ave
Bournemouth BH7. . . 379 C1
Fareham PO16. . . . . . 319 D3
Riverside Bsns Pk
Farnham GU9 . . . . . . 99 B3
Lymington SO41 . . . . 385 F4
Riverside Cl
Bartley SO40. . . . . . . 287 C6
Farnborough GU14 . . 55 D5
Liss GU33 . . . . 207 F4
Old Basing RG24 . . . . 70 B8
Overton RG25 . . . . . . 88 B8
Riverside Cotts
Twyford SO21. . . . . . . 219 F6
Whitchurch RG28 . . . 86 B2
Riverside Ct
7 Bournemouth
BH4 . . . . 392 D4
Farnham GU9 . . . . . . 99 A3
Southampton,Bitterne
Manor SO18. . . . . . . 291 C4
Southampton,Bitterne
SO18. . . . . 291 D8
West Moors BH22. . . 326 D3
Riverside Gdns SO51 240 E6
Riverside Gn SO20 . . 172 A3
Riverside Ho 4
SO23 . . . . 403 F6
Riverside Ind Pk GU9 99 B3
Riverside Mews
PO17. . . . . 296 A3
Riverside Pk Cvn &
Campsite SO31. . . . 316 A5
Riverside Pk Ind Est
BH21. . . . . 351 D3
Riverside Pl SP6 . . . . 257 F1
Riverside Rd
Bournemouth BH6. . . 394 F5
West Moors BH22. . . 326 D2
Riverside Sch PO7 . . 322 F4
Riverside Terr 5
PO10 . . . . 349 A8
Riverside Way SO15. .35 E3
Riverslea Mews
BH23 . . . . 395 D6
Riversmeet Ct BH23. 395 D6
Rivers Reach SO41. . 385 F3
River's St PO5. . . . . . . 404 C2
River View PO10. . . . . 325 B4
Riverview SO40 . . . . . 288 F5
River View Cl SO20. . 128 C1

River View Cotts
GU34. . . . . 140 A4
River View Ho SO19 291 D3
River View Rd SO18. 267 D2
Riverview Terr SO31 316 D8
River Way
Andover SP10 . . . . . . 83 C2
Christchurch BH23 . . 379 D2
Havant PO9 . . . . 324 A3
Riverwey Ind Est
GU34. . . . . 140 B4
River Wlk
Newbury RG14 . . . . . . 2 A4
Southampton SO18 . . 267 E3
Riviera 11 BH1. . . . . . 393 B3
Riviera Ct
3 Poole BH13. . . . . 402 F7
Bournemouth BH2. . 392 D3
R L Stevenson Ave
BH4 . . . . 392 B3
RNLI Mus ★ BH15. . 390 C2
RN Submarine Mus &
HMS Alliance ★
PO12. . . . . 369 E4
Roads Hill PO8. . . . . . 276 A1
Road View PO2 . . . . . 370 C8
Robann Cvn Pk
SO31 . . . . 317 D3
Robere Ho SO19 . . . . 291 D3
Robert Cecil Ave
SO18 . . . . 267 A4
Robert Mack Ct 39
PO1 . . . . 370 A5
Robert Mays Rd RG29 72 C2
Robert May's Sch
RG29. . . . . 72 C3
Robert Sandilands Prim
Sch RG14. . . . . .1 C4
Roberts Cl
Everton SO41 . . . . . . 384 E1
Kings Worthy SO23 . . 154 B1
Wickham PO17 . . . . . 296 A4
Robertsfield RG19 . . . .2 D3
Robertshaw Ho
SO43 . . . . 309 F6
Roberts La BH17. . . . 389 F7
Robertson Cl
Alton GU34 . . . . 139 D1
Newbury RG14 . . . . . .5 F8
Robertson Rd SO14 . 291 C4
Robertson Way GU12. 77 D1
Roberts Rd
Aldershot GU12. . . . . 77 B1
Barton Stacey SO21 . 130 E8
Bournemouth BH7. . . 394 A6
Gosport PO12 . . . . . . 368 F6
Greatham GU33. . . . . 186 C2
Hythe SO45 . . . . 313 F4
Poole BH17 . . . . 375 B1
Sandhurst GU15 . . . . 35 E6
Southampton SO15 . . 290 E5
Totton SO40. . . . . 288 F6
Robert Way GU16 . . . 56 D3
Robert Whitworth Dr
SO51 . . . . 215 F1
Robina Cl PO7 . . . . . . 323 A7
Robin Cl
Alton GU34 . . . . 140 A6
Ash Vale GU12. . . . . . 77 E6
Basingstoke RG22 . . 91 A6
Robin Cres BH25 . . . 382 D5
Robin Ct SO15 . . . . . . 290 F8
Robin Gdns
Christchurch BH23 . . 395 A6
Totton SO40. . . . . 288 C8
Waterlooville PO8 . . . 299 D4
Robin Gr BH25. . . . . . 382 F2
Robin Hill Dr GU15. . 36 E3
Robin Hood Cl GU14 . 55 E7
Robinia Gn SO16. . . . 266 C5
Robin La
Bishop's Green RG20 . 6 D3
Sandhurst GU47 . . . . 34 F7
Robin's Bow GU15 . . 35 F4
Robins Cl
Newbury RG14 . . . . . 5 D7
Stubbington PO14 . . 367 C8
Robins Ct 7 BH21 . . 351 C4
Robins Grove Cres
GU46 . . . . 33 F6
Robins Mdw PO14 . . 317 C1
Robins Nest 1 GU34 139 F4
Robinson Crusoe Pk
RG40. . . . . 15 F6
Robinson Ct
Lee-on-t-S PO13 . . . . 367 E2
Portchester PO16. . . . 320 C1
Robinson Rd PO14 . . 367 B6
Robinson Way
Bordon GU35. . . . . . . 164 E2
Portsmouth PO3 . . . . 346 C3
Robin Sq SO50. . . . . . 243 C2
Robins Way BH23 . . . 396 A5
Robinswood Dr
BH22. . . . . 353 D7
Robin Way SP10 . . . . 83 D2
Robsall Cl BH12. . . . . 391 E7
Robville Ct 3 BH7 . . 394 B6
Rochester Cl RG22 . . 91 B8
Rochester Ct 1
PO13 . . . . 368 D5
Rochester Gr GU51. . 75 A8
Rochester Rd
Bournemouth BH11. . 377 D4
Portsmouth PO4 . . . . 370 F3
Rochester St SO14 . . 291 C5
Rochford Rd
Basingstoke RG21. . . 69 A5

Rochford Rd continued
Cosham PO6 . . . . 345 D8
Rockall PO7 . . . . 323 A7
Rockbourne Cl PO9 . 323 C4
Rockbourne Gdns
BH25 . . . . 397 D8
Rockbourne La SP6 . 256 D7
Rockbourne Rd
SO22 . . . . 175 D4
Rockbourne Roman
Villa ★ SP6 . . . . . . 256 F7
Rockdale 5 GU26. . . 167 B3
Rockdale Dr GU26 . . 167 B3
Rockdale Ho 6
GU26 . . . . 167 B3
Rockery Cl SO45 . . . . 313 C4
Rockery The GU14 . . 55 C3
Rocket Rd GU14 . . . . 55 B1
Rockfield Way 7
GU47. . . . . .35 B8
Rockford Cl BH6 . . . . 394 F3
Rockford Ho SO50 . . 245 B1
Rockingham Rd RG14 .1 D2
Rockingham Way
PO16 . . . . 344 B8
Rock La GU10. . . . . . . 76 D1
Rockleigh Dr SO40. . 288 D5
Rockleigh Rd SO16. . 266 D3
Rockley Mews BH15. 389 E2
Rockley Pk Cvn Est BH15,
BH16. . . . . 389 B8
Rockley Rd BH15. . . . 389 E1
Rockmoor La SP11. . . 18 D2
Rockpit Cotts GU33. . 208 B4
Rockram Cl SO40 . . . 287 B7
Rockram Gdns SO45 313 C4
Rockrose Way PO6. . 321 A2
Rockstone Ct 2
SO14 . . . . 291 A6
Rockstone La SO14 . 291 A6
Rockstone Pl SO15 . 290 F6
Rockville Dr PO7. . . . 322 E7
Rodbard Ho SO31 . . 292 F1
Rodbourne Ct SO41 399 D8
Rodfield La SO21,
SO24 . . . . 200 C5
Roding Ct RG21. . . . . 69 C5
Rodlease La SO41. . . 361 E2
Rodmel Ct GU14 . . . . 56 C1
Rodney Cl
Gosport PO13 . . . . . . 368 D6
Poole BH12 . . . . 392 A8
Rodney Ct
7 Poole BH15. . . . . 390 C1
Andover SP10 . . . . . . 83 D1
Christchurch BH23 . . 396 A6
Southampton SO19 . . 292 C4
Rodney Dr BH23 . . . . 396 A6
Rodney Ho 10 PO12 369 D5
Rodney Rd PO4 . . . . . 371 A5
Rodney Way PO8 . . . 300 B6
Rodway RG21. . . . . . . 351 C4
Rodwell Cl BH10 . . . 377 C6
Roebuck Ave PO15. . 318 C5
Roebuck Cl
Cosham PO6 . . . . 345 F7
New Milton BH25 . . . 383 B3
Roebuck Dr PO12 . . . 369 C8
Roebuts Cl RG14 . . . .5 D8
Roedeer Copse
GU27. . . . . 189 C6
Roe Downs Rd GU34 160 A5
Roentgen Rd RG24 . .69 F7
Roeshot Cres BH23 . 381 E1
Roeshot Hill BH23 . . 381 C2
Roewood Cl SO45 . . . 338 C3
Roewood Rd SO45 . . 338 C3
Rogate Gdns PO16 . . 320 C1
Rogate Ho 1 PO1. . . 404 C4
Roger Penny Way
Brook SO43 . . . . 261 C2
Fordingbridge,Bramshaw,
SP5. . . . . 260 D6
Fordingbridge,Godshill
SP6. . . . . 259 B5
Rogers Cl
Bishopstoke SO50. . . 244 E4
Gosport PO12 . . . . . . 369 B7
Rogers Ct 1 GU34 . . 139 F3
Rogers Ho PO13 . . . . 367 F2
Rogers Mead PO11. . 348 A3
Rogers Rd SO50 . . . . 244 E4
Roi-mar Home Pk
BH8 . . . . 378 D4
Rokeby Cl RG14. . . . . 5 F7
Roke La RG29. . . . . . . 96 B8
Roker Way SO50 . . . . 245 B1
Rokes Pl GU46 . . . . . .33 E6
Roland Cl PO8 . . . . . . 300 B6
Rollesbrook Gdns
SO15 . . . . 290 E6
Rollestone St SO45 . 338 C2
Rolls Dr BH6. . . . . 395 B3
Rolston Ho GU27. . . . 189 D6
Roman Cl SO33 . . . . . 243 E7
Roman Ct PO10 . . . . . 325 D1
Roman Dr SO16. . . . . 266 E7
Roman Gdns SO45 . . 313 C4
Roman Gn PO7 . . . . . 298 E4
Roman Ho SO18 . . . . 291 C7
Roman Hts BH21. . . . 374 F8
Roman Mdw SP5. . . . 234 F7
Romano Ct 2 BH4. . 392 C1
Roman Quay SP6 . . . 257 F1
Roman Rd
Basingstoke RG23 . . 68 B6

Rib–Roo 459
Roman Rd continued
Chilworth SO16. . . . . 266 E8
Corfe Mullen BH18. . 374 E5
Dibden Purlieu,Applemore
SO45. . . . . 337 E8
Dibden Purlieu SO45 337 E8
Hardley SO45 . . . . . . 338 B6
Havant PO10 . . . . 324 C1
Stockbridge SO20 . . . 149 D3
Twyford SO21 . . . . . . 220 A5
Roman Row SO32. . . 271 D8
Romans Bsns Pk GU9 99 B3
Romans Field RG7 . . 10 F1
Romans Gate RG26. . 10 D1
Romans Ind Pk GU9. 99 B3
Romans' Rd SO23. . . 403 D4
Roman Way
Andover SP10 . . . . . . 83 B3
Barton Stacey SO21 . 130 E8
Basingstoke RG23 . . 68 A3
Dibden Purlieu SO45 313 D1
Farnham GU9 . . . . . . 99 C3
Havant PO9 . . . . 323 C2
Pamphill BH21. . . . . . 350 C5
Thatcham RG18. . . . . 2 F4
Roman Way Prim Sch
SP10. . . . . 83 B4
Romany The GU51 . . 54 E1
Romayne Ct GU14 . . 55 E5
Romford Rd SO31 . . . 340 D10
Romill Ct SO18. . . . . . 268 B3
Romley Ct GU9 . . . . . 99 B1
Romney Cl BH10 . . . . 377 E3
Romney Ct 51 BH4 . . 392 C1
Romney Rd
Bournemouth BH10. . 377 E4
Farnborough GU14 . . 55 C1
Romsey Abbey ★
SO51. . . . . 240 E7
Romsey Abbey CE Prim
Sch SO51. . . . . 240 E7
Romsey Ave
Portchester PO16. . . . 344 A8
Portsmouth PO3 . . . 371 B6
Romsey Cl
Aldershot GU11. . . . . 100 A6
Basingstoke RG24. . . 48 A1
Blackwater GU17 . . . 35 A6
Eastleigh SO50. . . . . 244 A3
Romsey Ct SO15 . . . . 290 D6
Romsey Hospl SO51. 241 A7
Romsey Ind Est
SO51. . . . . 240 F8
Romsey Inf Sch
SO51. . . . . 240 F7
Romsey Jun Sch
SO51. . . . . 241 A8
Romsey Lodge 8
SO16 . . . . 266 A1
Romsey Rd
Awbridge SO51 . . . . . 214 E4
Broughton SO20 . . . . 170 B5
Cadnam SO40,SO51. . 263 C3
Eastleigh SO50. . . . . 244 A4
Horndean PO8. . . . . . 276 C2
King's Somborne
SO20. . . . . 171 F1
Lyndhurst SO43. . . . . 309 F5
Nether Wallop SO20 . 147 A4
Ower SO51 . . . . 263 F6
Southampton SO16. . 266 A1
West Wellow SO51 . . 239 A3
Wherwell SP11,SO20 128 C3
Whiteparish SP5 . . . . 212 F3
Winchester SO22 . . . 403 A4
Romsey Sch The
SO51. . . . . 240 E8
Romsey Sta SO51 . . 240 F8
Romyns Ct PO14. . . . 318 F1
Ronald Bowker Ct 1
SO22 . . . . 403 C6
Ronald Pugh Ct
SO18 . . . . 267 E4
Rookcliff 13 SO41. . . 399 C4
Rookcliff Way SO41. 399 C4
Rooke Ho 17 PO1 . . . 370 A5
Rookery Ave PO15,
SO31. . . . . 317 B7
Rookery Ct RG40. . . . 15 E6
Rookery Grange
SO31. . . . . 317 B7
Rookery La
Breamore SP6. . . . . . 233 F1
Broughton SO20 . . . . 170 D6
Rookery The
Lumley PO10 . . . . 325 A1
West Dean SP5. . . . . 190 D3
Whitchurch RG28 . . . 86 C5
Rookesbury Park Sch
PO17. . . . . 296 C4
Rookesbury Pk Cvn Club
Site PO17. . . . . 296 D5
Rookes Cl PO8 . . . . . 300 B6
Rookes La SO41. . . . . 385 C2
Rookes Mews GU31. 229 A4
Rook Hill Rd BH23 . . 396 B6
Rook La SO21 . . . . . . 133 A3
Rookley SO31. . . . . . . 315 C7
Rooksbridge SO45 . . 313 C4
Rooksbury Croft
PO9 . . . . 324 A5
Rooksbury Rd SP10. 105 E6
Rooksdown Ave RG24 68 C8
Rooksdown La RG24. 47 C1

Rooks Down Rd
SO22 ... 403 B3
Rooksfield RG20 ... 6 E2
Rooksway Gr PO16 .. 343 F8
Rookswood GU34 ... 139 F5
Rookswood Cl RG27 .. 51 B1
Rookwood 3 SO41 . 399 C4
Rookwood Cl SO50 .. 244 B6
Rookwood Gdns
SP6 ... 257 D1
Rookwood La GU34 . 159 C1
Rookwood Sch SP10 105 F7
Rookwood View PO7 298 F5
Room Cotts SO20 ... 129 A5
Roosevelt Cres BH11 377 B6
Rope Hill SO41 ... 361 D1
Ropers La BH16 ... 389 D7
Ropewalk Ho 7
SO23 ... 403 E6
Rope Wlk SO31 ... 316 A2
Rope Wlk The PO16 . 343 B8
Ropley CE Prim Sch
SO24 ... 181 C4
Ropley Cl
Southampton SO19 . 315 A8
Tadley RG26 ... 26 F7
Ropley Rd
25 Havant PO9 ... 324 B5
Bournemouth BH7 .. 394 C7
East Tisted GU34 ... 183 A4
Ropley Sta★ SO24 .. 180 F5
Rorkes Drift GU16 ... 56 E4
Rosa Ct SP10 ... 105 D7
Rosalind Hill Ho
SO20 ... 149 F3
Rosamund Ave BH21 351 E1
Rosary Gdns GU46 ... 34 B6
Roscrea Cl BH6 ... 395 B4
Roscrea Dr BH6 ... 395 B4
Rosebank Cl
6 Tadley RG26 ... 26 F8
Rownhams SO16 ... 265 E5
Rosebank Lodge
SO16 ... 265 E5
Rosebay Cl SO50 ... 269 C6
Rosebay Ct 2 PO7 .. 322 F5
Rosebay Gdns RG27 .. 51 C1
Roseberry Cl RG22 ... 91 B5
Rosebery Ave
Cosham PO6 ... 346 A7
Hythe SO45 ... 314 A2
Rosebery Cl BH31 ... 303 C5
Rosebery Cres SO50. 244 B6
Rosebery Rd
Bournemouth BH5 ... 394 A5
New Alresford SO24 . 179 C5
Rose Bowl The★
SO30 ... 268 F1
Rosebrook Ct 4
SO18 ... 291 E7
Rosebud Ave 1 BH9 378 A2
Rose Cl
Basingstoke RG22 ... 91 B8
Hedge End SO30 ... 293 C8
Hythe SO45 ... 314 A2
Rose Cott PO8 ... 300 D7
Rose Cotts GU12 ... 77 E2
Rosecrae Cl BH25 ... 382 F4
Rose Cres BH15 ... 390 F6
Rose Ct BH15 ... 390 E3
Rosedale GU12 ... 77 A2
Rosedale Ave SO51 . 241 A7
Rosedale Cl
3 Christchurch
BH23 ... 395 E6
Titchfield PO14 ... 341 F8
Rosedene Gdns GU51 . 53 F2
Rosedene La 9 GU47 . 35 B7
Rose Est The RG27 ... 72 B8
Rose Farm Cl BH22 ... 353 B3
Rosefield Ct RG27 ... 52 D7
Rose Gdns
Bournemouth BH9 ... 378 A3
Farnborough GU14 ... 55 C3
Rose Gdn The BH23 . 379 D1
Rose Hill PO8 ... 300 A5
Rosehill Cl BH23 ... 357 B1
Rosehill Dr BH23 ... 357 B1
Rosehip Cl SO50 ... 245 A1
Rosehip Way RG24 ... 69 F4
Rose Hodson Pl RG23 68 C7
Roselands
Waterlooville PO8 ... 300 A5
West End SO30 ... 292 D8
Roselands Cl SO50 .. 245 B3
Roselands Gdns
SO17 ... 267 A2
Roseleigh Dr SO40 .. 288 E6
Rosemary Ave GU12 ... 77 E8
Rosemary Cl GU14 ... 55 B4
Rosemary Ct 8
BH23 ... 397 B7
Rosemary Dr RG26 ... 26 F6
Rosemary Gdns
Blackwater GU17 ... 35 B5
Hedge End SO30 ... 293 C5
Poole BH12 ... 391 B7
Whiteley PO15 ... 317 D8
Rosemary La
29 Portsmouth
PO1 ... 370 A5
Blackwater GU17 ... 35 B5
Rowledge GU10 ... 121 C4
Rosemary Rd BH12 .. 391 C7
Rosemary Terr RG14 ... 1 C2
Rosemary Way PO8 . 300 B5
Rosemary Wlk 3
PO13 ... 367 F3
Rosemoor Gdns RG14 .. 2 A4
Rosemoor Gr SO53 .. 218 B1
Rosemount Rd BH4 . 392 B2
Rosendale Rd SO53 . 243 D4
Rose Rd
Southampton SO14 .. 291 A8
Totton SO40 ... 289 A6
Rosery The PO12 ... 369 B2
Rosetree Cotts
GU34 ... 140 A4
Rosetta Rd PO4 ... 371 B4
Rosewall Rd SO16 .. 265 F3
Rosewarne Ct 9
SO23 ... 403 E7
Rose Wlk GU51 ... 53 F2
Rosewood
Chineham RG24 ... 48 E3
Gosport PO13 ... 343 E1
Mytchett GU16 ... 56 E4
Rosewood Ct 1 SP9 . 79 A7
Rosewood Gdns
Clanfield PO8 ... 276 C5
Marchwood SO40 ... 290 A1
New Milton BH25 ... 382 F4
Rosewood Rd GU35 . 165 A5
Rosida Gdns SO15 .. 290 E6
Rosina Cl PO7 ... 323 B8
Roslin Gdns BH3 ... 392 D7
Roslin Rd BH3 ... 392 E7
Roslin Rd S BH3 ... 392 E7
Roslyn Ho PO5 ... 404 B1
Rosoman Ct SO19 ... 291 F4
Rosoman Ho SO19 .. 291 F4
Rosoman Rd SO19 .. 291 F4
Rossan Ave SO31 ... 340 D9
Ross Cl RG21 ... 69 A2
Ross Gdns
Bournemouth BH11 .. 376 C5
Southampton SO16 .. 266 A2
Ross Glades BH3 ... 392 E6
Rossington Ave
SO18 ... 291 F8
Rossington Way
SO18 ... 291 F7
Rossini Cl RG22 ... 91 E8
Rossiters La SO40 ... 287 E5
Rossiters Quay
BH23 ... 395 C6
Rossley Cl BH23 ... 381 E2
Rosslyn Cl SO52 ... 242 A4
Ross Mews SO31 ... 315 A6
Rossmore Com Coll
BH12 ... 391 D8
Rossmore Gdns GU11 76 D1
Rossmore Par BH12 . 391 B8
Rossmore Rd BH12 .. 391 D7
Ross Rd BH24 ... 305 C1
Ross Terr 2 RG14 ... 1 D1
Ross Way PO13 ... 367 F4
Rostrevor La 9 PO4 370 E1
Rostrevor Mans 8
PO4 ... 370 E1
Rostron Cl SO18 ... 268 A3
Rosyth Rd SO18 ... 291 F7
Rotary Cl BH21 ... 351 F7
Rotary Ct SO31 ... 315 B6
Rotary Ho SO15 ... 290 D8
Rothay Ct 18 RG21 ... 69 D5
Rothbury Cl
Southampton SO19 .. 292 A4
Totton SO40 ... 264 D1
Rothbury Pk BH25 .. 383 B2
Rotherbank Farm La
GU33 ... 208 A6
Rother Cl
Petersfield GU31 ... 229 C4
Sandhurst GU47 ... 35 A8
West End SO18 ... 268 B1
Rothercombe La
GU32 ... 228 A4
Rother Dale SO19 ... 292 E3
Rotherfield Rd
Bournemouth BH5 ... 394 B3
Walkford BH23 ... 382 A1
Rother Ho GU33 ... 207 F3
Rotherley GU32 ... 228 E4
Rother Rd GU14 ... 55 C7
Rotherwick Cl PO9 .. 324 B5
Rotherwick Ct GU14 .. 77 A8
Rotherwick Ho GU51 . 53 D4
Rotherwick La RG27 .. 50 C8
Rotherwick Rd RG26 . 27 A7
Rothesay Dr BH23 ... 396 E7
Rothesay Rd
Bournemouth BH4 ... 392 C5
Gosport PO12 ... 369 A8
Rothsbury Dr SO53 .. 243 B6
Rothschild Cl SO19 .. 291 E1
Rothville Pl SO53 ... 218 B2
Rothwell Cl 9 PO6 .. 321 A1
Rotten Green Rd
RG27 ... 53 E6
Rotten Hill RG25,RG28 . 87 E6
Rotterdam Dr BH23 . 395 D7
Rotterdam Twrs
SO19 ... 314 F8
Rotunda Est The 11
GU11 ... 76 F2
Roughdown La SO45 338 C1
Roumelia La BH1,
BH5 ... 393 E4
Roundabouts The
GU33 ... 208 A5
Roundaway La SP11 .. 58 F3
Round Cl GU46 ... 34 D5
Roundcopse SO45 .. 313 C3
Round End RG14 ... 5 B5
Roundhaye Gdns
BH11 ... 376 F6
Roundhaye Rd BH11 376 F6
Round Hill SP6 ... 257 F1
Roundhill Cl SO18 ... 268 A1
Roundhill Cross SP6 233 E1
Roundhouse Ct
Lymington SO41 ... 385 D3
South Hayling PO11 .. 373 B2
Roundhouse Dr
SO40 ... 288 C6
Roundhouse Mdw
PO10 ... 349 A7
Roundhuts Rise 3
SO23 ... 198 C8
Roundmead Rd RG21. 69 A4
Roundway PO7 ... 322 F8
Roundway Ct SP10 .. 105 E8
Roundways BH11 ... 376 F3
Rounton Rd GU52 ... 75 A5
Routs Way SO16 ... 265 F7
Rowallan Ave PO13 . 368 C8
Rowan Ave PO8 ... 300 B2
Rowan Chase GU10 . 121 E5
Rowan Cl
Bursledon SO31 ... 315 F8
Camberley GU15 ... 36 D8
Christchurch BH23 .. 396 D8
Fleet GU51 ... 54 C1
Lee-on-t-S PO13 ... 367 F2
Romsey SO51 ... 241 C6
Southampton SO16 .. 266 A3
South Wonston SO21. 153 E4
St Leonards BH24 ... 327 D4
Swanmore SO32 ... 272 B4
Sway SO41 ... 360 B1
Tadley RG26 ... 27 A8
Totton SO40 ... 288 D6
Rowan Ct
9 North Tidworth
SP9 ... 78 F7
Portsmouth PO4 ... 370 F4
Southampton SO19 .. 291 F3
Rowan Dale GU52 ... 74 F5
Rowan Dr
Broadstone BH17 ... 374 E1
Christchurch BH23 .. 396 D8
Newbury RG14 ... 1 E5
Verwood BH31 ... 303 B4
Rowan Gdns SO30 .. 293 D6
Rowan Rd
Havant PO9 ... 324 C3
Tadley RG26 ... 27 B8
Rowans Cl GU14 ... 55 C8
Rowanside Cl GU35 . 166 A4
Rowans Pk SO41 ... 385 D3
Rowans The
Andover SP10 ... 82 E1
Grayshott GU26 ... 167 B2
Marchwood SO40 ... 289 E1
Rowan Tree Cl GU33 208 A4
Rowan Way PO14 ... 342 C7
Rowanwood RG40 ... 15 E6
Rowbarrow Cl BH17. 375 E2
Rowborough Rd
SO18 ... 291 F8
Rowbury Rd PO9 ... 323 D6
Rowcroft Cl GU12 ... 77 F6
Rowcroft Rd RG2 ... 15 D7
Rowdell Cotts SO24 . 181 C5
Rowden Cl SO51 ... 238 E2
Rowe Asheway SO31 316 F3
Rowe Gdns 6 BH12 . 391 F7
Rowena Ct PO5 ... 404 C2
Rowena Rd BH6 ... 394 F5
Rowes La SO41 ... 387 B7
Rowhay La SO32 ... 246 C5
Rowhill Ave GU11 ... 99 D8
Rowhill Cl 5 GU14 ... 55 A4
Rowhill Cres GU11 ... 99 D8
Rowhill Dr SO45 ... 313 C3
Rowhill Nature Trail★
GU11 ... 99 B8
Rowhills GU9 ... 99 B8
Rowhills Cl GU9 ... 99 D7
Rowin Cl PO11 ... 373 D2
Rowland Ave BH15 .. 390 E6
Rowland Rd
Fareham PO15 ... 318 F2
Portchester PO6 ... 320 E1
Rowlands Ave PO7 .. 299 E1
Rowlands Castle Rd
Blendworth PO8 ... 300 E6
Blendworth PO8 ... 300 F7
Rowlands Castle St
John's CE Prim Sch
PO9 ... 324 B8
Rowlands Castle Sta
PO9 ... 301 C2
Rowlands Cl SO53 ... 243 A4
Rowland's Cl RG7 ... 11 A5
Rowlands Hill BH21 . 351 D6
Rowlands Wlk 2
SO18 ... 268 A2
Rowledge CE Prim Sch
GU10 ... 121 C3
Rowley Cl SO30 ... 293 F8
Rowley Dr SO30 ... 293 F8
Rowlings Rd SO22 .. 175 D3
Rowner Cl PO13 ... 343 C1
Rowner Inf Schs
PO13 ... 343 D1
Rowner Jun Sch
PO13 ... 343 D1
Rowner La PO13 ... 343 D1
Rowner Rd PO13 ... 368 D8
Rownhams Cl SO16 . 265 E6
Rownhams Ct SO16 . 265 F3
Rownhams La
North Baddesley
SO52 ... 241 F5
Rownhams SO16 ... 265 F7
Rownhams,Toot Hill SO16,
SO52 ... 241 F1
Rownhams Pk SO16 . 265 E8
Rownhams Rd
Bournemouth BH8 .. 378 D3
Havant PO9 ... 323 D5
North Baddesley
SO52 ... 242 A4
Southampton SO16 .. 265 F3
Rownhams Rd N
SO16 ... 265 F5
Rownhams St John's CE
Prim Sch SO16 ... 265 E6
Rownhams Way
SO16 ... 265 E6
Rowse Cl SO51 ... 215 F1
Row The
Avington SO21 ... 177 E5
Redlynch SP5 ... 235 D7
Row Wood La PO13 . 343 B1
Roxan Ct 5 SO15 ... 290 F7
Roxbee Cox Rd GU51 .. 54 E1
Roxborough 47 BH4. 392 C3
Roxburghe Cl GU35 . 164 D2
Roxburgh Ho SO31 .. 317 A3
Royal Arc 5 BH1 ... 393 E4
Royal Armouries Mus of
Artillery★ PO17 ... 320 B3
Royal Bournemouth Gen
Hospl The BH7 ... 379 B1
Royal Crescent The 8
SP9 ... 79 A7
Royal Cl RG22 ... 91 A5
Royal Crescent Rd 10
SO14 ... 291 B3
Royal Ct
Chandler's Ford
SO53 ... 243 C6
Southampton SO17 .. 267 C2
Royale Cl GU11 ... 100 A8
Royal Gate PO4 ... 371 B2
Royal Gdns
Rowlands Castle
PO9 ... 301 A1
Southampton SO15 .. 289 F7
Royal Greenjackets
Mus★ SO23 ... 403 D5
Royal Hampshire Cty
Hospl SO22 ... 403 C5
Royal Hampshire
Regiment Mus★
SO23 ... 403 D5
Royal Hospl Haslar
PO12 ... 369 D3
Royal Huts Ave
GU26 ... 167 D4
Royal Junior Sch The
GU26 ... 167 C2
Royal London Pk
SO30 ... 293 B8
Royal Marines Mus★
PO4 ... 371 B2
Royal Mews 15 PO5 . 370 D2
Royal Military Academy
Hospl GU15 ... 35 E8
Royal Military Ct The 2
GU11 ... 76 F2
Royal Naval Cotts
PO17 ... 320 F6
Royal Naval Mus★
PO1 ... 369 F7
Royal Oak Cl GU46 ... 34 C6
Royal Oak Rd BH10 .. 377 C5
Royal Par GU26 ... 167 D4
Royal Sch The GU27 . 167 E2
Royal South Hants Hospl
SO14 ... 291 A6
Royal Sovereign Ave
PO14 ... 343 A5
Royal The PO11 ... 372 E2
Royal Victoria Ctry Pk★
SO31 ... 315 C4
Royal Victoria Mews
BH4 ... 392 D3
Royal Way PO7 ... 323 A7
Royal Winchester Mews
SO22 ... 403 A5
Royce Cl SP10 ... 82 B1
Roycroft La RG40 ... 16 C8
Royden La SO41 ... 361 D3
Roydon Cl SO22 ... 403 C3
Roy's La SO32 ... 297 D8
Royster Cl BH17 ... 375 C1
Royston Ave SO50 ... 244 A5
Royston Cl SO17 ... 267 B2
Royston Ct SO40 ... 264 E1
Royston Ctr GU12 ... 77 D8
Royston Dr BH21 ... 351 D5
Royston Pl BH25 ... 398 B8
Rozel Ct SO16 ... 265 E3
Rozeldene GU26 ... 167 C3
Rozelle Cl SO22 ... 175 A5
Rozelle Rd BH14 ... 391 C4
Rozel Manor BH13 .. 392 B2
Ruben Dr BH15 ... 389 D2
Rubens Cl
Basingstoke RG21 ... 69 D2
New Milton BH25 ... 383 B3
Ruby Cl SO40 ... 264 B1
Ruby Ct 1 PO7 ... 322 E8
Ruby Rd SO19 ... 292 A6
Rucstall Ctr RG21 ... 69 D3
Rucstall Prim Sch
RG21 ... 69 D3
Rudd Hall Rise GU15 . 36 B3
Rudd La SO51 ... 215 E7
Rudgwick Cl PO16 .. 344 B8
Rudmore Ct 3 PO2 . 345 C1
Rudmore Rd PO2 ... 370 C8
Rudmore Sq PO2 ... 370 C8
Rudolph Ct PO7 ... 322 C5
Ruffield Cl SO22 ... 403 A8
Rufford Cl
Eastleigh SO50 ... 244 A6
Fleet GU52 ... 75 A6
Rufford Gdns BH6 ... 394 E5
Rufus Cl
Chandler's Ford
SO53 ... 243 E8
Rownhams SO16 ... 265 D6
Rufus Ct SO43 ... 310 A5
Rufus Gdns SO40 ... 288 C7
Rufus Stone★ SO43 . 286 A6
Rugby Rd
Poole BH17 ... 375 A1
Portsmouth PO5 ... 404 D2
Rumbridge Ct SO40 . 289 A6
Rumbridge Gdns
SO40 ... 289 A7
Rumbridge St SO40 . 289 A6
Rune Dr SP10 ... 82 F4
Runfold-St George
GU10 ... 99 F5
Runnymede
Fareham PO15 ... 318 D4
West End SO30 ... 268 D1
Runnymede Ave
BH11 ... 376 E6
Runnymede Ct 1
GU14 ... 55 E7
Runnymede Ho 5
SP10 ... 106 B7
Runton Rd BH12 ... 391 F5
Runway The BH23 ... 396 B7
Runwick La GU10 ... 98 B1
Rupert Rd RG14 ... 5 D7
Rural Cl GU9 ... 121 D6
Rural Life Ctr Mus★
GU10 ... 122 D3
Rushall La BH21 ... 374 A5
Rushcombe Fst Sch
BH21 ... 374 D5
Rushcombe Way
BH21 ... 374 E6
Rushden Way GU9 ... 99 B7
Rushes Ct GU32 ... 228 E4
Rushes Farm GU32 .. 228 E4
Rushes Rd GU32 ... 228 E4
Rushes The
12 Basingstoke
RG21 ... 69 D5
Marchwood SO40 ... 289 F2
Rushfield Rd GU33 .. 207 F3
Rushford Warren
BH23 ... 395 F5
Rushington Ave
SO40 ... 288 F6
Rushington Bsns Pk
SO40 ... 288 E5
Rushington La SO40. 288 E6
Rushin Ho PO16 ... 344 D8
Rushmere Gate PO7. 274 C2
Rushmere La PO7 ... 298 E8
Rushmere Rd BH6 .. 394 D7
Rushmere Wlk PO9 . 323 D6
Rushmoor Cl GU52 .. 75 A7
Rushmoor Ct GU14 ... 77 A8
Rushmoor Ind Sch
GU14 ... 56 A1
Rushmoor Rd GU11 ... 76 B4
Rushpole Ct SO45 ... 313 C3
Rushton Cres BH3 ... 392 F6
Ruskin Ave BH9 ... 378 B3
Ruskin Cl RG21 ... 69 E3
Ruskin Rd
Eastleigh SO50 ... 244 B5
Portsmouth PO4 ... 371 A4
Ruskin Way PO8 ... 299 F4
Rusland Cl SO53 ... 243 B7
Russell Bldgs PO16 . 344 C7
Russell Churcher Ct
PO12 ... 368 F7
Russell Cl PO13 ... 367 F3
Russell Cotes Art Gall &
Mus★ BH1 ... 393 A2
Russell Cotes Rd
BH1 ... 393 A2
Russell Ct
2 New Milton
BH25 ... 383 A3
Blackwater GU17 ... 35 B5
Hindhead GU26 ... 167 D4
Russell Dr
Christchurch BH23 .. 395 D6
Dunbridge SO51 ... 192 D1
Russell Gdns
Hamworthy BH16 ... 389 C4
St Leonards BH24 ... 328 B5
Russell Pl
Fareham PO16 ... 319 A1
Southampton SO17 .. 267 B1
Russell Rd
Basingstoke RG21 ... 69 B3
Havant PO9 ... 323 F2
Lee-on-t-S PO13 ... 367 F3
Newbury RG14 ... 1 C2
Winchester SO23 ... 403 E8
Russell St
11 Southampton
SO14 ... 291 A3
Russell St *continued*
Gosport PO12 ... 369 A7
Russell Way GU31 ... 229 A2
Russel Rd BH10 ... 377 C6
Russet Cl
3 Lymington SO41 .. 385 F2
Ferndown BH22 ... 353 D6
New Alresford SO24 . 179 C4
Tongham GU10 ... 100 C7
Russet Gdns
Camberley GU15 ... 36 B3
Emsworth PO10 ... 349 B8
Russet Glade GU11 ... 99 C8
Russet Ho SO30 ... 293 A6
Russett Cl SO32 ... 272 B4
Russett Rd GU34 ... 140 A3
Russetts Dr GU51 ... 75 A8
Rustan Cl
Fair Oak SO50 ... 245 D2
Hedge End SO30 ... 293 B6
Rustic Glen GU52 ... 74 F5
Rustington Ho 3
PO1 ... 404 B3
Rustlings Mews PO8 300 B7
Ruth Cl GU14 ... 55 A5
Rutherford Ct RG20 .. 21 D5
Rutherford Rd RG24 .. 69 D8
Rutland Cl GU11 ... 76 E3
Rutland Ct SO18 ... 292 A7
Rutland Gdns SO31 . 293 A1
Rutland Manor 10
BH13 ... 392 A4
Rutland Rd
Bournemouth BH9 ... 393 B8
Christchurch BH23 ... 379 F1
Rutland Way SO18 ... 268 A1
Ruxley Cl SO45 ... 338 C4
Ryall Rd BH17 ... 375 D1
Ryan Cl BH22 ... 353 C7
Ryan Gdns
Bournemouth BH11 .. 377 B6
Ferndown BH22 ... 353 C7
Ryan Mount GU47 ... 34 E8
Rycroft Mdw RG22 ... 91 A4
Rydal Cl
9 Portsmouth PO6 . 321 B1
Basingstoke RG22 ... 68 A2
Bordon GU35 ... 164 D5
Christchurch BH23 .. 379 D4
Farnborough GU14 ... 55 B3
Rydal Dr
Crookham Village
GU52 ... 74 E5
Thatcham RG19 ... 2 E3
Rydal Ho
11 Portsmouth PO6 . 321 B1
2 Bournemouth BH4 392 C2
Rydal Mews BH21 ... 351 D5
Rydal Rd PO12 ... 369 A9
Ryde Ct 10 GU11 ... 77 A1
Ryde Gdns GU46 ... 33 F6
Ryde Pl PO13 ... 368 A4
Ryde Terr SO14 ... 291 B3
Ryebeck Rd GU52 ... 75 A5
Rye Cl
Chandler's Ford
SO53 ... 242 F6
Farnborough GU14 ... 55 C7
Fleet GU51 ... 54 C5
Ryecroft
Havant PO9 ... 324 B1
Titchfield PO14 ... 317 C2
Rye Croft 6 GU52 ... 74 E4
Ryecroft Ave BH11 .. 376 E5
Ryecroft Gdns GU17 .. 35 C4
Rye Dale SO40 ... 288 C3
Ryedown La SO51 ... 239 E4
Ryefield Cl GU31 ... 229 C3
Ryeland Cl GU51 ... 54 C5
Ryelaw Rd GU52 ... 75 A5
Rye Paddock La
SO45 ... 339 B4
Rylandes Ct SO16 ... 265 F3
Ryle Rd GU9 ... 121 F8
Ryon Cl SP10 ... 83 A4
Ryves Ave GU46 ... 33 E5

S

Sabre Ct 3 GU11 ... 76 C2
Sabre Rd PO10 ... 349 A3
Sackville St PO5 ... 404 B2
Saddleback Rd GU15. 36 C8
Saddleback Way
GU51 ... 54 B4
Saddle Cl BH21 ... 352 C6
Saddler Cnr GU47 ... 34 F7
Saddlers Cl
2 Fordingbridge
SP6 ... 257 F1
Eastleigh SO50 ... 244 A6
Sutton Scotney SO21. 131 C4
Saddlers Ct RG14 ... 1 D4
Saddlers Scarp
GU26 ... 166 E4
Saddlewood GU15 ... 36 A4
Sadlers La SO45 ... 314 A1
Sadlers Wlk 9 PO10 349 A8
Saffron Cl
Chineham RG24 ... 49 A4
Newbury RG14 ... 1 D3
Saffron Ct
1 Farnborough
GU14 ... 55 A4
Bournemouth BH11 . 376 D3
Locks Heath SO31 ... 316 E2
Saffron Dr BH23 ... 396 B8

Saffron Way
Bournemouth BH11..376 D3
Whiteley PO15......317 D8
Sage Cl PO7.......323 A6
Sages La GU34.....204 D5
Sailors La SO32....248 C8
Sailor's La SO32....223 E1
Sainfoin La RG23.....90 B8
Sainsbury Cl SP10...105 F6
Sainsbury Lodge
PO1.............404 D3
St Adlem's CE Comb Sch
BH12..........392 A6
St Agatha's Rd SO31 316 A4
St Agathas Way PO1 404 B4
St Alban's Ave BH8..393 C7
St Alban's CE Prim Sch
PO9............392 A8
St Alban's Cres BH8..393 B8
St Albans Ct 14
PO13...........368 D5
St Albans Rd PO4...370 F3
St Alban's Rd
Bournemouth BH8...393 B7
Havant PO9........324 A4
Southampton SO14...291 B5
St Albans Rdbt GU14..77 A8
St Aldhelm's BH14..391 F4
St Aldhelm's Cl
BH13...........391 F3
St Aldhelm's Pl
BH13...........391 F4
St Aldhelm's Rd
BH13...........391 F4
St Alphege Gdns
SP10...........82 F2
St Andrew Cl PO8...276 C2
St Andrews 3 BH23..395 A6
St Andrew's Bldgs
SO31...........316 A2
St Andrew's CE Inf Sch
GU9............98 F3
St Andrews Cl
Michelmersh SO51...215 D6
North Baddesley
SO52...........241 E5
St Andrew's Ct 4
GU9............99 A2
St Andrews Gn SO32 249 C5
St Andrews Ho 3
SO17...........291 B8
St Andrews Pk SO50 269 D6
St Andrews Rd
Bordon GU35......164 B2
Broadstone BH18....375 A5
North Tidworth SP9...78 E6
Southampton SO14...291 A5
St Andrew's Rd
Basingstoke RG22...68 D3
Farlington PO6.....346 F8
Gosport PO12......369 B5
Portsmouth PO5.....404 C2
South Hayling PO11..373 B2
St Andrew's Way
GU16...........56 D7
St Anne's Ave BH6..394 E5
St Annes Cl
Goodworth Clatford
SP11...........106 A1
Winchester SO22....403 A2
St Annes Gdns SO41 385 D3
St Anne's Gdns SO19 291 E2
St Anne's Gr.......342 F7
St Annes Ho SO51...240 E6
St Annes La SO32...295 C2
St Annes Mews 18
SO14...........291 A8
St Anne's RC Prim Sch
RG22...........68 D3
St Anne's RC Sch
SO15...........290 F6
St Anne's Rd
Southampton SO19..291 E2
Upton BH16........389 B7
St Anne's Rd PO13..367 E3
St Ann's Cl SP10....105 F7
St Ann's Cres PO12..369 A7
St Anns Ct SO17....262 B7
St Ann's Ct 1 BH1..393 E5
St Ann's Hospl BH13 402 E6
St Ann's Rd
Horndean PO8.....300 C7
Portsmouth PO4....370 F3
St Anthony's RC Prim
Sch PO14.......317 D1
St Anthony's Rd BH2 392 F5
St Antony's 6 BH4..392 D2
St Aubin's Ave SO19. 292 B5
St Aubins Cl GU34...160 B2
St Aubin's Pk PO11..372 C3
St Aubyns Ct BH15..390 B2
St Aubyns La BH24..305 C4
St Augustine Gdns
SO17...........267 D1
St Augustine Rd PO4 370 F3
St Augustine's Cl
GU12...........77 B1
St Augustine's RC Prim
Sch GU16.......36 D2
St Augustin's Rd
BH2............392 F5
St Austell Cl SO50...244 E3
St Austins GU32....167 B3
St Barbara's Cl RG26..29 B2
St Barbara Way PO2 345 F4
St Barbe Cl SO51....241 A6
St Barbe Mus ★
SO41...........385 E4

St Bartholomew Sch
RG14.............1 C1
St Bartholomew's Gdns
PO5............404 C1
St Bede CE Prim Sch
SO23...........403 E6
St Bede's 8 SO23 403 E7
St Bede's RC Prim Sch
RG24...........48 B1
St Benedicts Cl GU11.76 E1
St Benedict's Convent
Sch SP11.......82 A3
St Bernadette RC Prim
Sch GU14.......55 E5
St Bernard Ho 15
SO14...........291 A3
St Birinus Gdns SP10..82 F3
St Birinus Rd SP5....235 D6
St Birstan Gdns SP10..82 F2
St Blaize Rd SO23...241 C8
St Boniface Ct SO52..242 B3
St Bonnet Dr SO32...271 C8
St Brelade Pl SO16...265 D3
St Brelades Ave
BH12...........376 D1
St Catherines BH21..351 C4
St Catherines Ct
PO11...........372 C3
St Catherine's Hill
RG7.............11 C6
St Catherine's Par
BH23...........379 F1
St Catherine's RC Prim
Sch BH21.......352 B6
St Catherines Rd
Camberley GU16....56 E8
Eastleigh SO50.....244 A5
Frimley GU16......36 D1
St Catherine's Rd
Bournemouth BH6...394 F3
Eastleigh SO50.....244 A5
Southampton SO18..267 C1
South Hayling PO11..372 C4
Winchester SO23....403 F4
St Catherine St PO5. 370 D1
St Catherines View
SO30...........293 A6
St Catherines Way
PO16...........319 E1
St Catherine's Way
BH23...........379 D3
St Catherines Wood
GU15...........36 A4
St Chad's Ave PO2..345 E4
St Christopher Ave
PO16...........319 C3
St Christopher Ct 1
PO5............370 E1
St Christophers Cl
Aldershot GU12....77 B2
Basingstoke RG22...68 C3
Haslemere GU27....189 E6
North Baddesley
SO52...........242 A4
St Christophers Gdns
PO13...........343 C2
St Christopher's Gn
GU27...........189 E6
St Christophers Hospl
PO16...........319 E3
St Christophers Mobile
Home Pk PO8....276 D3
St Christophers Pl
GU14...........55 D3
St Christophers Rd
GU14...........55 E3
St Christopher's Rd
Farnborough GU14..55 E3
Haslemere GU27....189 E6
Havant PO9........323 C4
St Christophers Sch
SO18...........291 E8
St Clair Rd BH13....402 F7
St Clares Ave PO9...323 D7
St Cleeve Way RG42. 353 C3
St Clements Cl SO51 240 E8
St Clements Ct GU14.55 F7
St Clement's Gdns
BH1............393 D5
St Clements Rd
BH15...........391 A7
St Clement's Rd BH1 393 D5
St Clement's & St John's
CE Inf Sch BH1...393 D5
St Clement St 2
SO23...........403 D5
St Colman's Ave
PO6............346 A8
St Contest Way
SO40...........312 F8
St Cross Ct 4 SO23. 403 D3
St Cross Hospital ★
SO23...........403 D2
St Cross Mede SO23. 403 C2
St Cross Rd
Camberley GU16....56 F7
Crondall GU10......97 D5
Farnham GU9.......99 A3
Winchester SO23....403 D3
St Cuthberts Cl
SO31...........317 B4
St Cuthberts La
SO31...........317 B4
St Cyres Memorial Cotts
SO41...........385 F5
St Davids Rd GU29...72 C2
St David's Cl
Farnborough GU14..55 D8

St David's Cl *continued*
Farnham GU9.......99 C7
Totton SO40.......264 C1
St David's Ct 3 BH1 393 E5
St David's Ct GU11...76 F1
St David's Ct
Gosport PO13......368 C6
North Baddesley
SO52...........242 A4
St Davids Rd SO31..316 F3
St David's Rd
Basingstoke RG22...68 C3
Clanfield PO8......276 C5
Newbury RG14......1 D2
Portsmouth PO5....404 C2
Upton BH16.......389 B7
St Denys 2 BH25...383 B1
St Denys Prim Sch
SO17...........267 C1
St Denys Rd SO17...267 C1
St Denys' Sta SO17..291 C8
St Denys Wlk PO9...323 D6
St Donats Pl RG14....1 E2
St Edmondsbury Ct 6
PO13...........368 D5
St Edmund Cl PO14. 317 D1
St Edmunds RC Sch
PO1............404 C3
St Edmund's Rd
SO16...........290 B8
St Edmund's Sch
GU26...........167 B3
St Edward's RC/CE Sch
BH15...........390 F7
St Edwards Rd SO31 315 B7
St Edward's Rd
Gosport PO12......369 B5
Portsmouth PO5....404 C2
St Edward's Sch
SO51...........213 A1
St Edward's Terr 6
PO12...........369 A7
St Elizabeth's Ave
SO18...........292 B7
St Evox Cl SO16.....265 F5
St Faith Cl GU34....160 B2
St Faith's CE Prim Sch
SO22...........403 D3
St Faith's Cl PO12...369 A6
St Faith's Rd
Portsmouth PO1....404 B4
Winchester SO23....403 D3
St Francis Ave SO18. 292 B8
St Francis CE Prim Sch
SO53...........243 A5
St Francis Cl SO45..365 E7
St Francis Ct
2 Portsmouth PO2. 345 E4
Locks Heath PO14...317 C3
St Francis Pl PO9...323 E3
St Francis Rd
Blackfield SO45.....365 E7
Gosport PO12......369 C2
St Francis Specl Sch
PO14...........342 C8
St Gabriels Ct 7
GU15...........36 B5
St Gabriels Lea RG24. 49 A3
St Gabriel's Rd SO18 292 B7
St Gabriel's Sch RG20..5 F5
St George Cl SO31...292 F7
St George RC Sch (Boys)
SO17...........267 C6
St George's Almshs 6
BH15...........390 B4
St Georges Ave RG14..1 C1
St George's Ave
Bournemouth BH8...393 C8
Havant PO9........324 A1
Newbury RG14......1 C2
Poole BH12........391 B8
St George's Beneficial CE
Prim Sch PO1....370 A5
St George's Bsns Ctr 44
PO1............370 A5
St George's Cl
Bournemouth BH8...393 C8
Christchurch BH23...396 D8
Farnham GU9.......99 F6
St George's Cl SP9...78 E6
St Georges Cotts
Martin SP6.........231 C3
Woodgreen SP6.....258 D8
St George's Cotts
SP6............235 D3
St Georges Cres
SP6............257 F3
St Georges Ct
Fareham PO16......343 B8
Ferndown PO16.....353 E5
St George's Ct
2 Bournemouth
BH1............393 E5
7 Portsmouth PO5..404 A1
North Baddesley
SO52...........242 A3
St George's Ct BH12 391 B8
St Georges Dr
Bournemouth BH11..376 D3
Bransgore BH23....381 B8
St George's Dr BH22 353 C4
St Georges Ho 4
SO17...........291 B8
St George's Ho 18
SO23...........403 E6
St Georges Ind Est
Camberley GU15....35 F3
Portsmouth PO4....371 A5

St Georges Mans 5
BH15...........393 F4
St Georges Mews
GU9............99 A3
St George's Rd
Aldershot GU11.....76 F1
Camberley GU15....36 B6
Cosham PO6.......345 F8
Farnham GU9.......99 B1
Portsmouth,Eastney
PO4............371 A2
Portsmouth,Old Portsmouth
PO1............370 A4
South Hayling PO11..372 D3
St George's Rd E
GU12...........76 F1
St Georges Sq PO1.. 370 A5
St George's Sq 2
SO32...........271 C7
St Georges St SO14. 291 A4
St Georges St SO23. 403 E6
St George's Way
PO1............370 A5
St Georges Wlk
PO16...........369 D6
St George's Wlk 3
PO7............322 E7
St Georges Yd GU9...99 A2
St Giles Cl SO23....403 F5
St Giles Hill SO23...403 F5
St Giles Way PO8...276 C2
St Helena Gdns
SO18...........267 F3
St Helena Way PO16 344 C8
St Helens Cl PO4....370 F2
St Helens Cres GU47..34 F8
St Helen's Mans 7
PO4............370 E1
St Helens Mews
SO50...........245 D2
St Helen's Par PO4.. 370 E1
St Helen's Rd
Gosport PO12......368 C3
South Hayling PO11..372 D3
St Helier Rd
Gosport PO12......369 C9
Poole BH12........391 A8
St Hellen's Rd PO6..346 D8
St Hermans Cvn Est
PO11...........373 C2
St Hermans Mans
PO11...........373 C2
St Hermans Rd
PO11...........373 C2
St Hilda Ave PO8....276 C2
St Hubert Rd
Andover SP10......105 E7
Horndean PO8......276 C2
St Ives End La BH24. 328 A4
St Ives Fst Sch BH24 328 B5
St Ives La BH24.....392 F5
St Ives Pk BH24.....328 A5
St Ives Wood BH24.. 328 A5
St James' Ave GU9...99 B3
St James CE Fst Sch
SP6............281 A6
St James CE Prim Sch
PO10...........324 F2
St James' CE Prim Sch
West End SO30.....268 F2
St James Cl
2 Poole BH15.....390 B1
Bramley RG26......29 B1
Clanfield PO8......276 C4
Southampton SO15..266 C1
St James Ct
Farnham GU9.......99 A3
Fleet GU51........74 F7
St James Cvn Pk
SO52...........218 A1
St James Ho 14
SO14...........291 A3
St James Hospl PO4 371 C6
St James' La SO22,
SO23...........403 D5
St James Park Rd
SO16...........266 C2
St James Pk (Cvn Pk)
SO52...........243 A8
St James Rd
Ferndown BH22....353 A6
Finchampstead RG40..16 C8
Fleet GU51........74 F7
Sway SO41........360 C2
Upper Shirley SO15..266 C1
West End SO30.....268 C4
St James' Rd PO10.. 324 F1
St James' Sq BH5...394 A5
St James's St PO1...370 B5
St James' Terr
Farnham GU9.......99 A3
Winchester SO22,
SO23...........403 D5
St James' Villas
SO23...........403 D5
St James Way PO16. 344 C8
St John Cl RG26.....29 A2

St John's Ave PO7...322 E3
St Johns CE Fst Sch
BH21...........351 D4
St John's CE Inf Sch
GU10...........144 C1
St Johns Cl
Hook RG27........51 B1
Rownhams SO16....265 E7
South Hayling PO11..372 F2
St Johns Cl
Gosport PO12......369 B8
Wimborne Minster
BH21...........351 D4
St John's Cl
Gosport PO12......369 B8
St John's Coll PO5...404 C1
St Johns Cotts RG27..71 E8
St John's Cross
SP11...........105 A2
St Johns Ct SO40...289 F1
St John's Ct
12 Fleet GU51.....54 A1
2 Portsmouth PO2. 345 C1
4 Farnborough BH1 393 E5
Farnborough GU14..55 B5
North Baddesley
SO52...........242 A4
St Johns Ctr SO30...293 B6
St Johns Dr SO40...289 E1
St Johns Gdns SO51 240 F8
St John's Gdns
1 Newbury RG14...1 D1
2 Bournemouth BH9 377 F1
St Johns Glebe SO16 265 F6
St Johns Gr GU9....121 F8
St John's Hill BH21..351 D5
St John's Hospital
(Almshouses)(N) 1
SO23...........403 F6
St John's Hospital
(Almshouses)(S) 3
SO23...........403 F5
St Johns Inf Sch
SO14...........290 F3
St Johns La SO32....295 E7
St Johns Mews
Locks Heath SO31...317 C3
Portsmouth PO5....404 C1
St John's Piece RG23 .90 B8
St Johns RC Prim Sch
PO1............404 C3
St John's Rd
Bashley BH25......383 A7
Hartley Wintney RG27. 52 D5
St John's Rd
Andover SP10......106 B8
Bournemouth BH5...393 E4
Breach PO10.......325 D1
Christchurch BH23...395 A6
Cosham PO6.......346 A8
Eastleigh SO50.....244 B4
Farnborough GU14..55 C5
Farnham GU9.......121 F8
Havant PO9........323 C4
Hedge End SO19,
SO30...........293 B5
Locks Heath SO31...317 B2
Mortimer RG7......11 E5
Newbury RG14......1 E1
Oakley RG23.......67 C2
Poole BH15........390 D4
Sandhurst GU47....34 F7
Winchester SO23....403 F5
St Johns Sq 6 PO12 369 B6
St John's St
Hythe SO45.......314 A4
Winchester SO23....403 F5
St John's Wlk 13
RG21...........69 B5
St John the Baptist CE
Prim Sch
Titchfield PO14.....317 C2
Waltham Chase SO32 271 E2
St John the Baptist RC
Prim Sch SP10....105 D7
St John the Evangelist
CE Inf Sch RG14....1 D1
St Joseph Cl SO31...317 B3
St Joseph's Cres
RG24...........48 F2
St Josephs Ct RG14...1 F4
St Josephs Mews
PO5............404 C1
St Josephs RC Comb
Sch BH12.......391 E7
St Josephs RC Prim Sch
GU11...........99 E8
St Joseph's RC Prim Sch
Christchurch BH23...396 A4
Newbury RG14......1 F4
St Joseph's Rd GU12..76 E1
St Jude's CE Prim Sch
PO1............370 B3
St Judes Cl PO5.....404 B3
St Jude's RC Prim Sch
PO14...........318 E1
St Julien's Hospl
(Almhouses) SO14. 291 C4
St Just Cl
Ferndown BH22....353 C4
Newton Tony SP4...123 B5
St Katharine's CE Prim
Sch BH6........395 B4
St Kitts Ho 4 PO6.. 320 F2
St Lawrence CE Prim
Sch GU34.......139 F4

St Lawrence Cl
SO30...........269 D2
St Lawrence Rd
2 Southampton
SO14...........291 B3
Alton GU34........139 F4
Eastleigh SO50.....244 A4
St Ledger's Pl BH8..393 D6
St Ledger's Rd BH8.. 393 D6
St Leger Ct RG14.....1 C4
St Leonard's Ave
Chineham RG24....49 A3
South Hayling PO11..373 A3
St Leonards Cl
South Wonston
SO21...........153 D4
Titchfield PO15.....317 E3
St Leonards Farm Pk
BH22...........354 A8
St Leonards Hospl
BH24...........327 C1
St Leonards Rd
SO41...........387 B8
St Leonard's Rd
Bournemouth BH8...393 B6
Winchester SO23....198 C6
St Leonards Way
BH24...........327 D4
St Lucia Ho 2 PO6.. 320 F2
Saint Lucia Pk GU35 164 E5
St Luke's CE Prim Sch
Bournemouth BH9...392 F8
Sway SO41........360 B1
St Luke's CE Sec Sch
PO5............404 B3
St Lukes Cl
Basingstoke RG22...68 C3
Hedge End SO30....269 C1
St Luke's Rd
Bournemouth BH3...392 F7
Gosport PO12......369 A7
St Maradox La BH9.. 377 F2
St Margarets
Bournemouth BH2...392 F5
Penton Grafton SP11..81 E8
St Margaret's
Almshouses BH21. 351 A5
St Margarets Ave
BH23...........395 B5
St Margarets Cl
BH21...........351 A5
St Margaret's Cl
SO18...........292 B7
St Margaret's Cotts
SO32...........247 D2
St Margarets Hill
BH21...........351 A5
St Margaret's Hill
BH21...........351 A6
St Margarets La
PO14...........317 E1
St Margarets Rd
PO11...........373 A3
St Margaret's Rd
Bishopstoke SO50...244 D4
Bournemouth BH10..377 C2
Poole BH15........390 D4
St Mark's CE Jun Sch
SO15...........290 D7
St Mark's CE Prim Sch
Basingstoke RG22...91 B6
Bournemouth BH10..377 C2
Farnborough GU14..77 B8
St Marks Cl
Bramley RG26......29 A2
Chandler's Ford SO53 218 F1
Farnborough GU14..56 A1
St Mark's Cl PO12...369 A6
St Marks Ct 2 PO12 369 A6
St Marks Pl GU14....98 F7
St Mark's Pl PO12...369 B8
St Marks Rd
Lymington SO41....385 B3
Southampton SO14..291 B5
St Mark's Rd
Bournemouth BH11..377 B3
Gosport PO12......369 A3
Portsmouth PO2....345 D1
St Martins Cl SO50.. 244 D4
St Martin's Cl
Southampton SO16..265 E3
Winchester SO23...403 F4
St Martin's East
Woodhay CE Prim Sch
RG20...........20 E7
St Martins Ho 1
PO5............370 D1
St Martins Rd BH16. 389 A7
St Martins Trad Pk
SO23...........403 F6
St Mary Bourne Prim Sch
SP11...........61 D2
St Mary Gr SO41....384 B2
St Mary Magdalen
Almshouses 4
SO23...........403 F5
St Mary's SO51.....240 E6
St Mary's Almshouses 13
RG14...........1 D2
St Mary's Ave
Bramley RG26......29 B2
Gosport PO12......369 B5
St Marys Bentworth CE
Prim Sch GU34...138 B5

St Mary's CE Inf Sch
GU10 . . . . 144 B7
St Mary's CE Jun Sch
Old Basing RG24 . . . . 70 B6
Stratfield Mortimer
RG7 . . . . 12 B5
St Mary's CE Prim Sch
SO14 . . . . 291 B4
St Mary's Church Cl
SO18 . . . . 267 D4
St Marys Cl
Alton GU34 . . . . 139 F3
Bransgore BH23 . . . . 381 C8
Sandhurst GU47 . . . . . 35 A8
St Mary's Cl
Droxford SO32 . . . . . 249 B1
Kings Worthy SO21 . . 176 C5
Old Basing RG24 . . . . 70 B6
Redlynch SP5 . . . . 235 F4
St Mary's Coll SO18 . 291 F8
St Mary's Cotts
GU10 . . . . 144 A7
St Mary's Ct
4 Newbury RG14 . . . . . .1 E4
Basingstoke RG21 . . . 69 C5
Bournemouth BH6 . . . 394 E3
Bramley RG26 . . . . 29 B2
St Mary's Ho PO1 . . 370 F6
St Mary's Hospl East
Wing PO3 . . . . 371 A4
St Mary's Hospl West
Wing PO1 . . . . 370 F6
St Mary's Maternity
Hospl BH15 . . . . 390 D3
St Mary's Mdw SP11 . 105 A4
St Mary's Mews
BH22 . . . . 353 D4
St Mary's Pl
Farnham GU9 . . . . 99 A3
Newbury RG14 . . . . . . .1 E4
Southampton SO14 . . 291 A4
St Mary's RC Comb Sch
BH15 . . . . 390 E5
St Mary's RC Prim Sch
PO12 . . . . 369 A6
St Mary's Rd
Ash Vale GU12 . . . . . . 77 E5
Bishopstoke SO50 . . . 244 D4
Bournemouth BH1 . . . 393 D6
Camberley GU15 . . . . . 36 A6
Ferndown BH22 . . . . . 353 C5
Hartley Wintney RG27 . 52 C5
Kingsclere RG20 . . . . . 24 D2
Liss GU33 . . . . 207 F4
Mortimer RG7 . . . . 11 E5
Netley SO31 . . . . 315 C6
Newbury RG14 . . . . . . .1 E4
Poole BH15 . . . . 390 E4
Portsmouth PO1 . . . . 370 F6
Southampton SO14 . . 291 A6
South Hayling PO11 . . 372 F3
Stubbington PO14 . . . 342 C4
St Mary St
Southampton SO14 . . 291 A4
Winchester SO22 . . . 403 B3
St Mary's Terr SO22 . 220 A6
St Mathews Rd SO22 403 B8
St Matthew's CE Prim
Sch GU33 . . . . 186 A8
St Matthews Cl 2
SO14 . . . . 291 A5
St Matthews Ct
PO12 . . . . 369 D6
St Matthew's Rd
PO6 . . . . 345 F8
St Merrin's Cl BH10 . 377 C4
St Michael & All Angels
CE Inf Sch SO43 . . . . 309 F5
St Michael's BH2 . . . 392 D3
St Michaels Ave SP9 . .78 E5
St Michael's CE Inf Sch
GU11 . . . . .99 F8
St Michael's CE Jun Sch
GU11 . . . . 100 A8
St Michael's CE Mid Sch
BH21 . . . . 351 E7
St Michael's CE Prim Sch
Bournemouth BH2 . . . 392 D3
Sandhurst GU47 . . . . . 34 D8
St Michaels Cl
Blackfield SO45 . . . . . 338 F1
Fleet GU51 . . . . 75 C8
Hamworthy BH15 . . . 389 C4
Verwood BH31 . . . . . 302 F5
St Michael's Cl RG25 .89 E1
St Michaels Ct 1
BH6 . . . . 394 C4
St Michael's Ct 17
PO6 . . . . 321 B1
St Michael's Gdns 8
SO23 . . . . 403 D6
St Michaels Gn SP9 . .78 E5
St Michael's Gr PO14 342 F7
St Michael's Hall
GU11 . . . . .99 F8
St Michael's Ho
PO14 . . . . 342 F7
St Michael's Mews 9
BH2 . . . . 392 E3
St Michael's Pas
SO23 . . . . 403 E4
St Michael's Pl
11 Bournemouth
BH2 . . . . 392 D3
2 Camberley GU15 . . 35 F5

St Michaels Rd
Camberley GU15 . . . . . 35 F5
Locks Heath SO31 . . . 317 A2
Totton SO40 . . . . 288 F8
Verwood BH31 . . . . . 302 F4
St Michael's Rd
Aldershot GU12 . . . . . 76 F1
Basingstoke RG22 . . . 68 C3
Bournemouth BH2 . . . 392 E2
Farnborough GU14 . . . 55 F6
Havant PO9 . . . . 323 C3
Newbury RG14 . . . . . . .1 D2
Portsmouth PO1 . . . . 404 A2
Sandhurst GU47 . . . . . 34 D8
Winchester SO23 . . . 403 D4
St Michael's Rdbt
BH4 . . . . 392 D3
St Michael's Sch
RG20 . . . . 22 D6
St Michael's Sq 11
SO14 . . . . 290 F3
St Michael's St 13
SO14 . . . . 290 F3
St Michaels View SP9 .78 F7
St Michaels Way
PO8 . . . . 276 C2
St Monica Inf Sch
SO19 . . . . 292 A3
St Monica Jun Sch
SO19 . . . . 292 A3
St Monica Rd SO19 . 292 A3
St Neot's Rd RG27 . . 32 D8
St Neot's Rd RG27 . . 32 C8
St Nicholas Ave
PO13 . . . . 368 C7
St Nicholas Cl
Fleet GU51 . . . . 53 F1
Ludgershall SP11 . . . . 57 B2
St Nicholas Ct RG22 . 68 D4
St Nicholas Flats 3
PO2 . . . . 345 D1
St Nicholas Rd RG14 . .1 D2
St Nicholas' Rd
Havant PO9 . . . . 323 C3
Newbury RG14 . . . . . . .1 D2
St Nicholas Rise
SO23 . . . . 176 B6
St Nicholas Row
PO17 . . . . 296 A3
St Nicholas Sch GU52 74 E2
St Nicholas St PO2 . . 345 A3
St Nicolas CE Jun Sch
RG14 . . . . .1 E2
St Osmund's Rd
BH14 . . . . 391 D3
St Patricks Ave SP9 . .78 E5
St Patrick's Ct SO52 . 242 A3
St Patrick's La GU33 208 D5
St Patrick's RC Prim Sch
Farnborough GU14 . . . 56 B4
Southampton SO19 . . 291 E3
St Patrick's Rd RG22 .68 E3
St Paul's CE Inf Sch
GU10 . . . . 100 E7
St Pauls Cl GU10 . . . 100 D7
St Pauls Ct 15 SO22 . 403 D6
St Paul's Hill SO22 . . 403 D6
St Pauls Pl 26 SO23 . 403 D6
St Paul's Pl BH8 . . . . 393 B4
St Pauls RC Prim Sch
PO6 . . . . 345 B8
St Paul's Rd
Basingstoke RG22 . . . 68 E3
Bournemouth BH8 . . . 393 B4
Portsmouth PO5 . . . . 404 A2
Sarisbury SO31 . . . . . 316 E4
St Paul's Sq PO5 . . . . 404 A2
St Peter's Ave PO11 . 348 C2
St Peter's CE Jun Sch
Farnborough GU14 . . . 56 A4
Yateley GU46 . . . . 34 C6
St Peter's CE Prim Sch
Appleshaw SP11 . . . . . 81 B7
Farnham GU9 . . . . 121 E6
St Peters Cl
Curdridge SO32 . . . . . 294 D8
Headley RG19 . . . . .7 B1
Shipton Bellinger SP9 101 E7
St Peter's Cl
Goodworth Clatford
SP11 . . . . 106 B1
Tadley RG26 . . . . 26 F7
St Peters Ct
1 Emsworth PO10 . . 349 A8
3 Bournemouth BH1 393 A3
St Peter's Ct
14 Petersfield
GU32 . . . . 228 F3
3 Poole BH14 . . . . 391 A4
St Peter's Gate 13
BH1 . . . . 392 F3
St Peter's Gdns
Farnham GU10 . . . . . 121 D6
Yateley GU46 . . . . 34 B6
St Peter's Gr PO5 . . . 404 C1
St Peters Mead GU12 .77 F2
St Peters Pk GU11 . . .99 C8
St Peter's RC Comp Sch
BH6 . . . . 394 F4
St Peters RC Prim Sch
PO7 . . . . 322 F6
St Peter's RC Prim Sch
SO22 . . . . 197 B5
St Peter's RC Sch
BH7 . . . . 394 B8
St Peters Rd PO11 . . 348 C2

St Peter's Rd
Basingstoke RG22 . . . 68 D4
Bournemouth BH1 . . . 393 A3
Petersfield GU32 . . . . 228 F3
Poole BH14 . . . . 391 A4
St Peter's Sq 7
PO10 . . . . 348 F8
St Peter St SO32 . . . 271 C8
St Peter St SO23 . . . 403 E6
St Peter's Way GU16 . 56 D7
St Peter's Wlk 15
BH1 . . . . 392 F3
St Philips Ct 3 GU51 . 54 A2
St Philip's Way SO18 292 B7
St Pirans Ave PO3 . . 371 A7
St Polycarp's RC Prim
Sch GU9 . . . . .99 B1
St Quentin Ho 2
PO14 . . . . 342 E7
St Richards Gdns
PO7 . . . . 322 C5
St Richards Rd RG14 . .1 F5
St Ronan's Ave PO4 . 370 D2
St Ronan's Rd PO4 . . 370 E2
St Saviours Cl BH7 . . 394 C7
Saints Cl BH21 . . . . . 326 E4
St Sebastian Cres
PO16 . . . . 319 B3
St Simon Cl SO31 . . . 317 B3
St Simons Rd PO5 . . . 370 D2
St Stephens Cl RG27 . 189 D6
St Stephen's Cl BH2 . 392 E4
St Stephens La
BH31 . . . . 303 A7
St Stephens Rd PO2 . 370 E8
St Stephen's Rd
Bournemouth BH2 . . . 392 E3
Winchester SO22 . . . 403 B8
St Stephen's Way 4
BH2 . . . . 392 F3
St Swithin Way SP10 . .82 F2
St Swithun Cl SO32 . 271 B8
St Swithun's Cl
SO51 . . . . 216 D1
St Swithuns Ct 8
SO14 . . . . 291 A6
St Swithun's RC Prim
Sch PO5 . . . . 370 D2
St Swithuns Rd BH1 393 B4
St Swithun's Rdbt
BH1 . . . . 393 B3
St Swithun's Rd S
BH1 . . . . 393 B4
St Swithun's Sch
SO21 . . . . 198 D8
St Swithun Wells RC
Prim Sch SO53 . . . . . 243 E5
St Theresas Ct PO9 . . 323 C3
St Thomas Ave
PO11 . . . . 372 D4
St Thomas' CE Inf Sch
RG20 . . . . 21 B8
St Thomas Cl
Andover SP10 . . . . 82 E3
Bournemouth BH10 . . 377 D2
Fareham PO16 . . . . . . 319 C3
St Thomas' Cl RG21 . .69 A7
St Thomas Ct SO50 . 245 D2
St Thomas Garnet's RC
Sch BH5 . . . . 394 A5
St Thomas Mews 3
SO23 . . . . 403 D5
St Thomas More's RC
Prim Sch PO9 . . . . . . 323 D3
St Thomas Pk SO41 . 385 D3
St Thomas's Ct 5
PO1 . . . . 370 A4
St Thomas's Rd
PO12 . . . . 369 B9
St Thomas's St
Lymington SO41 . . . . 385 E3
Portsmouth PO1 . . . . 370 A3
St Thomas Cl SO23 . . 403 D5
St Tristan Cl SO31 . . 317 B2
St Ursula Gr PO5 . . . 404 C1
St Valerie Rd
Bournemouth BH2 . . . 392 F5
Gosport PO12 . . . . . . 369 B8
St Vigor Way SO21 . . 244 F8
St Vincent Coll PO12 369 B6
St Vincent Cres PO8 300 B6
St Vincent Rd
Gosport PO12 . . . . . . 369 B7
Portsmouth PO5 . . . . 370 D7
St Vincent St PO5 . . . 404 C1
St Walburga's RC Prim
Sch BH9 . . . . 378 B1
St Winifred's Rd
Bournemouth BH2 . . . 392 F5
Southampton SO16 . . 266 C2
St Winifred's Sch
SO17 . . . . 267 A1
Salamander Ct 5
SP9 . . . . .78 F7
Salcombe Ave PO3 . . 346 A1
Salcombe Cl SO53 . . 243 B4
Salcombe Cres SO40 288 E6
Salcombe Rd
Newbury RG14 . . . . . . .1 C1
Southampton SO15 . . 290 C2
Totton SO40 . . . . 288 D6
Salcot Rd SO23 . . . . 403 E8
Salem St SO15 . . . . . 266 C1
Salerno Cl GU11 . . . . .76 E2

Salerno Dr PO12 . . . . 368 F4
Salerno Ho
Fareham PO14 . . . . . . 342 F7
Romsey SO51 . . . . 241 B7
Salerno Pl BH15 . . . . 389 D2
Salerno Rd
Portsmouth PO2 . . . . 345 D4
Southampton SO16 . . 266 C5
Sales Ct 9 GU11 . . . . .76 E1
Salesian Coll GU14 . . 56 B1
Salesian View GU14 . 77 C8
Salet Way PO7 . . . . . 300 D1
Salisbury Cl
Alton GU34 . . . . 140 A2
Eastleigh SO50 . . . . . 244 B4
Odiham RG29 . . . . 72 C2
Salisbury Ct 1 SO50 244 B4
Salisbury Gdns RG22 . 68 C4
Salisbury Gr GU16 . . .56 E3
Salisbury Ho 1 SP5 . .78 F7
Salisbury La SO20 . . . 147 C8
Salisbury Rd
Abbotts Ann SP11 . . . 105 B3
Andover SP10 . . . . . . 105 E6
Ash GU12 . . . . 77 E2
Awbridge SO51 . . . . . 240 B6
Blackwater GU17 . . . . 35 A5
Bournemouth BH1 . . . 393 E4
Breamore SP6 . . . . . . 234 C2
Broughton SO20 . . . . 169 F8
Burton BH23 . . . . 380 D2
Cosham PO6 . . . . 346 A7
Ellingham BH24 . . . . . 284 F5
Farnborough GU14 . . . 56 A3
Fordingbridge SP6 . . 258 A5
Ibsley BH24 . . . . 282 A1
New Alresford SO24 . 179 D5
Over Wallop SP11 . . . 124 F6
Ower SO51 . . . . 263 D8
Ower,Stonyford SO51 263 F4
Poole BH14 . . . . 391 C5
Portsmouth PO4 . . . . 370 F2
Ringwood BH24 . . . . 328 F8
Shipton Bellinger SP9 101 E6
Sopley,Winkton BH23 380 B5
Southampton SO17 . . 267 A3
Totton SO40 . . . . 264 C3
West Wellow SO51 . . 239 B1
Salisbury Road Arc 4
SO40 . . . . 288 F7
Salisbury St
6 Southampton
SO15 . . . . 290 F6
Fordingbridge SP6 . . 257 F1
Salisbury Terr
Lee-on-t-S PO13 . . . . 367 F2
Mytchett GU16 . . . . . . 56 E3
Salmon Dr SO50 . . . . 244 F2
Salmond Rd SP11 . . . 105 E4
Salmon Rd GU11 . . . .77 B5
Salmons Rd RG29 . . . 72 C2
Salterne Ho 2 SO41 385 E2
Salterns Ave PO4 . . . 371 B6
Salterns Cl PO11 . . . . 373 C3
Salterns Ct BH14 . . . 402 B8
Salterns Est PO16 . . . 343 B7
Salterns La
Bursledon SO31 . . . . 316 A7
Fareham PO16 . . . . . . 343 B7
South Hayling PO11 . . 373 C4
Salterns Point BH14 . 402 B8
Salterns Quay BH14 . 402 B8
Salterns Rd
Poole BH14 . . . . 391 A3
Stubbington PO13,
PO14 . . . . 367 B5
Salterns Sch SO40 . . 289 A7
Salterns Way BH14 . . 402 B8
Salter Rd BH13 . . . . . 402 C3
Salters Acres SO22 . . 175 C3
Salters Heath Rd
RG26 . . . . .47 B7
Salters La SO22 . . . . 175 B2
Saltgrass La SO41 . . . 400 A3
Saltings Rd BH16 . . . 389 B6
Saltings The
Farlington PO6 . . . . . 346 E7
Langstone PO9 . . . . . 347 F6
Salt La SO24,SO32 . . 222 E3
Saltmarsh La PO11 . . 372 E5
Saltmarsh Rd SO14 . . 291 B3
Saltmead SO17 . . . . . 267 C1
Salt Meat La PO12 . . 369 D7
Saltram Rd GU14 . . . 56 C2
Salvia Cl PO7 . . . . . . 323 A6
Salwey Rd SO30 . . . . 293 D5
Samantha Cl BH23 . . 380 A1
Samarkand Cl GU15 . .36 F4
Samber Cl SO41 . . . . 385 C4
Sammy Miller
Motorcycle Mus** ★**
BH25 . . . . 382 E5
Sampan Cl SO31 . . . . 316 E1
Sampford Cl SO41 . . . 385 E5
Samples Way BH17 . . 390 E6
Sampson Bsns Pk
GU15 . . . . 35 F3
Sampson Rd
Fareham PO14 . . . . . . 342 F6
Portsmouth PO1 . . . . 369 F7
Sampson's Almshouses
3 GU9 . . . . .98 E1
Samson Cl PO13 . . . . 368 D7
Samson Rd BH15 . . . 389 D2
Samuel Cody Ho
GU12 . . . . .77 D7
Samuel Cody Sch The
GU14 . . . . .76 F7

Samuel Rd PO1 . . . . 370 F6
Sam Whites Hill
SP11 . . . . 105 E4
San Carlos App GU11 . 77 A2
Sancreed Rd BH12 . . 391 E7
Sancroft Ho BH21 . . . 352 A1
Sandbanks Bsns Ctr
BH13 . . . . 402 B3
Sandbanks Dr RG22 . .91 B7
Sandbanks Rd BH14,
BH15 . . . . 391 A2
Sandbourne Rd
Bournemouth BH4 . . . 392 C1
Poole BH15 . . . . 390 D4
Sand Cl SO51 . . . . . . 238 E3
Sandcroft Cl PO12 . . 368 E3
Sandecotes Rd
BH14 . . . . 391 C3
Sandell Ct SO16 . . . . 267 B5
Sanderling Rd PO4 . . 371 D5
Sanderlings BH24 . . . 329 C6
Sanderlings The
PO11 . . . . 373 A2
Sandford Ave PO12 . . 368 D4
Sandford Cl
Bournemouth BH9 . . . 378 C3
Kingsclere RG20 . . . . 24 F2
Sandford Ct GU11 . . . 76 D1
Sandford Ho RG20 . . 24 F4
Sandford Rd
Aldershot GU11 . . . . . 76 D1
Farnham GU9 . . . . 98 F7
Tadley RG26 . . . . 26 E8
Sandford Way BH18 . 374 F2
Sandham Memorial
Chapel ★ RG20 . . . . 22 C6
Sandheath Rd GU26 . 167 A7
Sand Hill GU14 . . . . . .55 F7
Sand Hill Ct GU14 . . . .55 F7
Sandhill La PO13 . . . 368 A6
Sandhills Cl BH17 . . . 375 D2
Sandhurst GU10 . . . . 100 A4
Sandhurst Ct PO5 . . . 404 C1
Sandhurst Dr BH21 . . 327 A7
Sandhurst La GU17 . . .34 F6
Sandhurst Rd
Finchampstead RG40 . 16 F3
Sandhurst GU46 . . . . 34 D7
Southampton SO15 . . 290 E6
Sandhurst Royal Military
Acad GU15 . . . . 17 D6
Sandhurst Sch GU47 . 35 B8
Sandhurst Sta GU47 . 34 E7
San Diego Rd PO12 . . 369 B7
Sandilands Way 7
SO45 . . . . 314 A1
Sandisplatt PO14 . . . 342 C8
Sandle Copse SP6 . . . 257 B2
Sandleford Lodge Pk
RG19 . . . . .5 F6
Sandleford Rd PO9 . . 323 D7
Sandleheath Ind Est
SP6 . . . . 257 B2
Sandleheath Rd SP6 280 B8
Sandlewood Cl
Clanfield PO8 . . . . 276 C5
Totton SO40 . . . . 288 C8
Sandmartin Cl BH25 . 397 F7
Sandown Cl
Alton GU34 . . . . 140 A2
Blackwater GU17 . . . . 35 B5
Gosport PO12 . . . . . . 368 D3
Sandown Cres GU11 . .99 F7
Sandown Dr GU16 . . . 36 C2
Sandown Rd
Christchurch BH23 . . . 395 E6
Cosham PO6 . . . . 345 E7
Southampton SO15 . . 266 B1
Sandown Way RG14 . . .2 A1
Sandpiper Cl
Broadstone BH17 . . . 374 F1
Horndean PO8 . . . . . . 300 A7
Marchwood SO40 . . . 289 E1
Sandpiper Rd SO16 . . 266 B6
Sandpipers PO6 . . . . 346 E2
Sandpiper Way RG22 . .90 F7
Sandpit Cotts GU10 . .75 B1
Sandpit Hill RG20 . . . .5 A4
Sandpit La
Arborfield Garrison
RG7 . . . . 14 F5
East End SO41 . . . . . . 387 D5
Sandport Gr PO16 . . . 344 B7
Sark Rd BH12 . . . . . . 391 D8
Sarnia Ct SO16 . . . . . 265 C4
Sarson Cl SP11 . . . . . 104 B6
Sarson La
Amport SP11 . . . . 104 B7
Weyhill SP11 . . . . 81 B1
Sarsons Barns SP11 . 104 C5
Sarum Ave BH22 . . . . 326 E4
Sarum Cl
Over Wallop SO20 . . . 147 D8
Shipton Bellinger SP9 101 D8
Winchester SO22 . . . 403 A5
Sarum Ct
Poole BH14 . . . . 391 C4
Winchester SO22 . . . 403 B5
Sarum Hill RG21 . . . . 69 A4
Sarum Ho 6 SP10 . . 106 A7
Sarum Rd
Chandler's Ford
SO53 . . . . 243 E6
Pamber Heath RG26 . .9 D1
Winchester SO22 . . . 197 B7
Sarum Road Hospl
SO22 . . . . 403 A5

Sandringham Sch
GU16 . . . . 56 D7
Sandringham Way
GU16 . . . . 56 D7
Sandrock Hill Rd
GU10 . . . . 121 E5
Sandsbury La GU32 . . 228 C5
Sands Cl GU10 . . . . . 100 C2
Sands Rd GU10 . . . . . 100 B2
Sands The GU35 . . . . 164 A2
Sandy Balls Holiday Ctr
SP6 . . . . 258 D2
Sandy Beach Est
PO11 . . . . 373 F1
Sandy Brow PO7 . . . . 322 D3
Sandy Cl
Petersfield GU31 . . . . 229 C3
Wimborne Minster
BH21 . . . . 352 A8
Sandy Cross GU10 . . 100 D4
Sandy Down SO41 . . . 361 C4
Sandydown Cotts
SO20 . . . . 150 F3
Sandyfield Cres PO8 299 E3
Sandy Hill Rd GU9 . . . .98 F7
Sandyhurst Cl BH17 . 375 C1
Sandy La
Abbotswood SO51 . . 216 B3
Bournemouth BH6 . . . 394 B5
Camberley GU15 . . . . 36 C6
Christchurch BH23 . . . 379 E2
Fair Oak SO50 . . . . . . 245 B2
Farnborough GU14 . . . 55 B7
Fleet GU52 . . . . 75 B4
Hartley Wintney RG27 . 52 D5
Haslemere,Nutcombe
GU26 . . . . 167 D2
Haslemere,Woolmer Hill
GU27 . . . . 189 A7
Lyndhurst SO43 . . . . . 309 F4
North Baddesley
SO52 . . . . 242 B5
Pamphill BH21 . . . . . 350 B5
Rake GU33 . . . . 208 E4
Redlynch SP5 . . . . 235 E7
Rushmoor GU10 . . . . 144 F5
Shortfield Common
GU10 . . . . 122 A1
Steep Marsh GU32 . . 229 B8
St Leonards BH24 . . . 328 A5
Tadley RG26 . . . . 27 B7
Three Legged Cross
BH21 . . . . 302 E2
Titchfield PO14 . . . . . 341 F8
Upton BH16 . . . . 389 B6
Verwood BH31 . . . . . 303 A6
Waltham Chase SO32 271 C2
Wimborne Minster
BH21 . . . . 352 A8
Sandy Mead Rd BH8 378 F1
Sandy Plot BH23 . . . . 395 C8
Sandy Point Rd
PO11 . . . . 373 E1
Sandys Cl RG22 . . . . . .68 E3
Sandys Rd RG22 . . . . .68 E4
Sandys Road Rdbt
RG22 . . . . .68 E4
Sandy Way BH10 . . . . 377 E4
Sankey La GU51 . . . . . 54 D4
San Remo Twrs 4
BH5 . . . . 393 E3
Sanross Cl PO14 . . . . 367 A6
Santina Cl GU9 . . . . . .99 B8
Santoy BH13 . . . . 402 D5
Saor Mews 3 SP10 . . 105 F8
Sapley La RG25 . . . . . 88 A7
Saplings The SO45 . . 338 B5
Sapphire Cl 1 PO12 369 C8
Sapphire Ridge PO7 323 A7
Saracen Cl SO41 . . . . 385 C1
Saracens Rd SO53 . . . 243 F7
Sarah Cl BH7 . . . . 394 B8
Sarah Robinson Ho 22
PO1 . . . . 370 A5
Sarah Sands Cl
BH23 . . . . 395 D8
Sarah Way GU14 . . . . .55 F4
Sarisbury CE Jun Sch
SO31 . . . . 316 E5
Sarisbury Cl RG26 . . . .26 E3
Sarisbury Gate 4
SO31 . . . . 317 B5
Sarisbury Inf Sch
SO31 . . . . 316 E4

Sarum St 12 BH15 . . . . 390 B1
Sarum View SO22 . . . . . 197 B7
Satchell La SO31 . . . . . 316 A4
Saturn Cl SO16 . . . . 265 F4
Saturn Ho 9 RG7 . . . . 9 C2
Saulfland Dr BH23 . . . . 396 D8
Saulfland Ho BH23 . . . . 396 D8
Saulfland Pl BH23 . . . . 396 D8
Saunders Cl PO13 . . . . 368 A7
Saunders Gdn 7
. . . . 26 F8
Saunders Ho PO6 . . . . . 320 E1
Saunders La SO51 . . . . 214 E6
Saunders Mews 5
PO4 . . . . 371 B2
Saunton Gdns GU14 . . . 55 F6
Savernake Cl
9 Romsey SO51 . . . . 216 B1
Gosport PO13 . . . . . . 343 D2
Savernake Ho 2 SP9 . 78 F4
Saville Cres GU35 . . . . 164 D3
Saville Cl
Bishopstoke SO50 . . . 244 D5
Gosport PO12 . . . . . . 368 F3
Saville Ct BH21 . . . . . . 351 E2
Saville Gdns
Fareham PO16 . . . . . . 319 A3
Frimley GU15 . . . . 36 F5
Savoy Bldgs 6 PO16 319 B1
Savoy Cl SP10 . . . . 106 B7
Savoy Ct GU15 . . . . 36 A5
Savoy Gr GU17 . . . . 35 B3
Savoy Ho SO40 . . . . . . 289 A7
Sawmills The SO32 . . . 270 B5
Sawyer Cl SO22 . . . . . . 175 B1
Sawyers Ley RG7 . . . . . 12 B8
Saxe Ct 12 PO17 . . . . . 318 E7
Saxholm Cl SO16 . . . . . 266 F6
Saxholm Dale SO16 . . . 266 F6
Saxholm Way SO16 . . . 266 F6
Saxley Ct PO9 . . . . 323 C6
Saxonbury Rd BH6 . . . . 394 E5
Saxon Cl
Horndean PO8 . . . . . . 276 C3
Locks Heath SO31 . . . 316 E1
Portchester PO16 . . . . 320 B1
Saxon Croft GU9 . . . . . . 99 A1
Saxon Ct
17 Winchester
SO23 . . . . 403 E6
1 Andover SP10 . . . . 83 A3
North Tidworth SP9 . . . 78 F6
Thatcham RG19 . . . . . . 2 E3
Saxonford Rd BH23 . . . 396 C7
Saxon Gdns SO30 . . . . 293 A5
Saxon Ho
17 Southampton
SO14 . . . . 291 C6
2 Alton GU34 . . . . . 139 F3
Saxon Hts BH6 . . . . 394 E5
Saxonhurst SP5 . . . . . . 235 A7
Saxonhurst Cl BH10 . . . 377 E6
Saxonhurst Gdns
BH10 . . . . 377 E6
Saxonhurst Rd BH10 . . 377 E6
Saxon King Gdns
BH6 . . . . 395 B4
Saxon Leas SP5 . . . . . 168 B6
Saxon Mdw SP5 . . . . . 234 F7
Saxon Mews 3
GU34 . . . . 139 F3
Saxon Pl SO41 . . . . . . 385 D6
Saxon Rd
Blackfield SO45 . . . . . 338 F1
Southampton SO15 . . . 290 D5
Winchester SO23 . . . . 403 E7
Saxon Shore Inf Sch
PO6 . . . . 344 D8
Saxon Sq Sh Ctr
BH23 . . . . 395 B6
Saxon Way
Alderholt SP6 . . . . . . 281 A5
Andover SP10 . . . . 82 F3
Old Basing RG24 . . . . . 69 F7
Romsey SO51 . . . . . . 241 C7
Saxon Wlk SO53 . . . . . 243 E5
Saxon Wood Sch
RG24 . . . . 68 B8
Saxony Cres SO51 . . . . 174 B4
Saxony Way GU46 . . . . . 34 A4
Sayers Cl
Camberley GU16 . . . . . 56 C7
Newbury RG14 . . . . 5 F8
Sayers Rd SO50 . . . . . 244 E3
Sbac Tk GU11 . . . . 76 C6
Scafell Ave SO18 . . . . . 342 D8
Scallows La SO51 . . . . 238 E6
Scamblers Mead
SP11 . . . . 81 F3
Scantabout Ave
SO53 . . . . 243 F7
Scantabout Prim Sch
SO53 . . . . 243 F7
Scarff Ct PO11 . . . . . . 373 B2
Scarf Rd BH17 . . . . 390 F7
Scarlatti Rd RG22 . . . . . 91 F8
Scarlet Oaks GU15 . . . . 36 C3
Scarlett's Rd GU11 . . . . 76 E3
Scholars' Wlk PO6 . . . . 346 C1
School Cl
Chandler's Ford
SO53 . . . . 243 B6
Vernham Dean SP11 . . . 38 C1
Verwood BH31 . . . . . . 303 A7
School Fields GU35 . . . 142 B1
School Hill
Farnham GU10 . . . . . 121 D6

School Hill continued
Seale GU10 . . . . 100 F4
Soberton SO32 . . . . . . 273 A8
School La
3 Liss GU33 . . . . 207 F3
Bentley GU10 . . . . . . 120 B5
Bishop's Sutton SO24 180 B4
Bournemouth BH11 . . . 377 B6
Bransgore BH23 . . . . . 357 E4
Broughton SO20 . . . . 170 B2
Chandler's Ford SO53 243 B5
Compton SO21 . . . . . . 278 F2
Denmead PO7 . . . . . . 298 D5
Emsworth PO10 . . . . . 348 F8
Ewshot GU10 . . . . 98 B8
Farnham GU10 . . . . . . 122 B6
Hamble-le-R SO31 . . . 316 A2
Itchen Abbas SO21 . . . 177 F7
Kings Worthy SO23 . . . 176 B3
Lymington SO41 . . . . 385 E4
Lymington,Warborne
SO41 . . . . 385 F8
Middle Wallop SO20 . . 147 F8
Milford on S SO41 . . . 399 E6
Petersfield GU32 . . . . 229 B6
Poole BH15 . . . . 390 C5
Ringwood BH24 . . . . . 329 A7
Riseley RG7 . . . . 14 C3
Ropley SO24 . . . . 181 C4
Silchester RG7 . . . . 10 F1
Southbourne PO18 . . 349 F7
St Leonards BH24 . . . . 328 A4
Three Legged Cross
BH21 . . . . 326 F7
Westbourne PO10 . . . 325 B5
Wimborne Minster
BH21 . . . . 351 B5
Yateley GU46 . . . . 33 F6
School Lane Cotts
SO20 . . . . 147 F8
School Pl SO19 . . . . . . 291 E4
School Rd
Bordon GU35 . . . . . . 164 D4
Bransgore BH23 . . . . . 357 E4
Bursledon SO31 . . . . . 316 A8
Fawley SO45 . . . . 339 B3
Gosport PO12 . . . . . . 343 F1
Grayshott GU26 . . . . . 166 F4
Haslemere GU27 . . . . 189 D5
Havant PO9 . . . . 323 E1
Hythe SO45 . . . . 314 A4
Nomansland SP5 . . . . 261 C8
Redlynch SP5 . . . . . . 236 A5
Riseley RG7 . . . . 14 C3
Romsey SO51 . . . . . . 216 C1
Rowledge GU10 . . . . . 121 C3
Totton SO40 . . . . 289 A6
Twyford SO21 . . . . . . 219 F5
West Wellow SO51 . . 238 F2
Wickham PO17 . . . . . 296 A3
Schooners Cl PO13 . . . 367 F4
Schooner Way
Locks Heath SO31 . . . 316 E1
Portsmouth PO4 . . . . 371 C6
Schroeder Cl RG21 . . . . 69 A2
Schubert Rd RG22 . . . . . 91 E8
Scimitars The PO14 . . 367 B8
Scivier's La SO32 . . . . 246 C2
Scotland Cl
Ash Vale GU12 . . . . . . 77 C5
Fair Oak SO50 . . . . . . 245 E2
Scotland Farm Rd
GU12 . . . . 77 C5
Scotland Hill GU47 . . . . 34 E8
Scotland La GU27 . . . . 189 D5
Scotlands GU27 . . . . . . 189 E5
Scotlands Dr GU27 . . . 189 E5
Scotney Ct 18 PO9 . . . 324 B6
Scotney Rd GU11 . . . . . 69 B7
Scots Ct RG27 . . . . 51 C2
Scott Cl
Andover SP10 . . . . . . 83 C1
King's Somborne
SO20 . . . . 172 A2
Poole BH12 . . . . 376 F1
Stubbington PO14 . . . 342 C4
Scotter Rd
Bishopstoke SO50 . . . 244 D3
Bournemouth BH7 . . . 394 B6
Scotter Sq SO50 . . . . . 244 D3
Scott Ho 2 PO2 . . . . . 345 C2
Scott-Paine Dr
SO45 . . . . 314 A4
Scott Rd
Eastleigh SO50 . . . . . 243 F2
Poole BH12 . . . . 376 F1
Poole BH12 . . . . 391 F8
Portsmouth,Hilsea
PO3 . . . . 345 F5
Portsmouth,Hilsea
PO3 . . . . 346 A5
Portsmouth,Portsea Island
PO1 . . . . 369 F7
Southampton SO19 . . 291 F1
Scotts Cl
Colden Common
SO21 . . . . 245 A8
Downton SP5 . . . . . . 234 E8
Scott's Ct GU14 . . . . . . 55 F7
Scotts Gn BH23 . . . . . 395 F8
Scotts Hill La BH23 . . . 395 D7
Scratchface La
Havant PO9 . . . . 323 B2
Waterlooville PO7 . . . 322 F4
Scrubbs La SO24 . . . . 180 A3
Scullards La 1
SO14 . . . . 290 F4
Scures Rd RG27 . . . . . . 50 F1

Scylla Ind Est SO23 . . . 198 C8
Seabank Cl BH16 . . . . . 389 A7
Seabird Way PO16 . . . . 343 B7
Seabourne Pl 5
BH5 . . . . 394 B5
Seabourne Rd BH5 . . . 394 B5
Sea Breeze Gdns
PO4 . . . . 371 C3
Seabreeze Way
SO41 . . . . 399 B6
Seacliff Ct BH6 . . . . . . 394 B5
Seacombe Gn SO16 . . . 265 D1
Seacombe Rd BH13 . . . 402 B3
Sea Crest Rd PO13 . . . 367 F2
Seacroft Ave PO4 . . . . 397 E8
Seafarers Wlk PO11 . . 373 F1
Seafield Cl BH25 . . . . . 397 F7
Seafield Dr BH6 . . . . . . 394 E5
Seafield Park Rd
PO14 . . . . 367 B6
Seafield Rd
Barton on S BH25 . . . 397 E8
Bournemouth BH6 . . . 394 D4
Christchurch BH23 . . . 396 C7
Portchester PO16 . . . . 344 B7
Portsmouth PO3 . . . . 346 A1
Southampton SO16 . . . 265 E3
Seafields SO16 . . . . . . 348 E8
Seafield Terr PO12 . . . 369 C4
Seafire Way 1 . . . . 76 C7
Seaford Cl SO31 . . . . . 292 F1
Sea Front PO11 . . . . . . 372 E3
Sea Front Est PO11 . . . 373 B2
Seagarth Cl SO16 . . . . 266 D3
Seagarth La SO16 . . . . 266 D3
Seager's Ct PO1 . . . . . . 369 F4
Seagrim Rd BH8 . . . . . 378 C2
Sea Grove Ave PO11 . . 373 A2
Seagrove Rd PO2 . . . . 345 D1
Seagull Cl
Basingstoke RG22 . . . . 90 F8
Portsmouth PO4 . . . . 371 C6
Seagull Ct PO10 . . . . . 324 F1
Seagull La PO10 . . . . . 324 F1
Seagull Rd BH8 . . . . . . 378 C2
Seagulls The PO13 . . . 368 A4
Seahorse Wlk PO12 . . 369 D6
Sea Kings PO14 . . . . . 367 B7
Sea La PO14 . . . . 367 C5
Sea Lark Rd PO12 . . . . 369 B8
Seale La GU10 . . . . 100 D4
Seal Rd RG21 . . . . 69 B5
Seaman's La SO43 . . . . 286 C4
Seamead PO14 . . . . . . 367 C5
Sea Mill Gdns 36
PO1 . . . . 370 A5
Seamoor La BH4 . . . . . 392 B3
Seamoor Rd BH4 . . . . . 392 B3
Sea Pines 9 SO41 . . . 399 C4
Sea Point 8 BH13 . . . . 402 F7
Sea Rd
Barton on S BH25 . . . 397 E8
Bournemouth BH5 . . . 393 E4
Bournemouth,Southbourne
BH6 . . . . 394 F3
Milford on S SO41 . . . 399 E4
Southampton SO19 . . 291 D4
Searing Way RG26 . . . . 9 E1
Searle Rd GU9 . . . . . . 122 A8
Searles Cl SO24 . . . . . 179 D5
Searles Hill SO21 . . . . 220 A4
Searl's La
Hook RG27 . . . . 51 B4
Hook RG27 . . . . 51 C2
Seathrift Cl PO13 . . . . 367 E3
Seathwaite Ho 15
PO6 . . . . 321 B1
Seaton Ave PO3 . . . . . 371 A4
Seaton Cl
Christchurch BH23 . . . 397 B8
Lymington SO41 . . . . 385 E5
Stubbington PO14 . . . 367 C7
West End SO18 . . . . . 268 C1
Seaton Rd
Camberley GU15 . . . . . 35 F5
Christchurch BH23 . . . 397 B8
Seatown Cl BH17 . . . . . 376 A1
Seaview Ave PO11 . . . . 373 D3
Sea View Cotts PO10 348 F1
Seaview Ct
9 Gosport PO12 . . . 368 D3
Lee-on-t-S PO13 . . . . 367 F2
Sea View Est SO31 . . . 315 B5
Seaview Rd
Barton on S BH25 . . . 397 D7
South Hayling PO11 . . 373 D3
Walkford BH23 . . . . . 382 C1
Sea View Rd
Cosham PO6 . . . . 322 D1
Poole BH15 . . . . 391 A6
Upton BH16 . . . . 389 A7
Sea Vixen Ind Est
BH23 . . . . 396 A8
Seaward Ave
Barton on S BH25 . . . 397 F8
Bournemouth BH6 . . . 394 B4
Seaward Gdns SO19 . . 291 E4
Seaward Rd SO19 . . . . 291 E4
Seaward Twr 11
PO12 . . . . 369 C6
Seaway Bh25 . . . . 395 B8
Seaway Ave BH23 . . . . 396 C7
Seaway Cres PO4 . . . . 371 D4
Seaway Gr PO16 . . . . . 344 C5
Seaweed Cl SO19 . . . . 314 E8
Sebastian Gr PO7 . . . . 323 A8
Sebastopol Rd GU11 . . 76 F2

Second Ave
Aldermaston RG7 . . . . . 10 A2
Cosham PO6 . . . . 345 E8
Farlington PO6 . . . . . 346 E8
Havant PO9 . . . . 324 B2
Southampton SO15 . . . 289 D7
Southbourne PO10 . . 349 D8
Second Marine Ave
BH25 . . . . 398 A6
Second St E RG19 . . . . . 6 E5
Second St W RG19 . . . . 6 E4
Second St SO45 . . . . . 338 E8
Sedbergh Ho SO16 . . . 265 D1
Sedbergh Rd SO16 . . . 265 D1
Seddon Cl BH25 . . . . . 398 B8
Seddul-Bahr SO30 . . . 268 C5
Sedgefield Cl
Portchester PO6 . . . . 344 F8
Totton SO40 . . . . 288 C8
Sedgefield Rd RG14 . . . 6 A8
Sedgeley Gr PO12 . . . . 369 A8
Sedgemead SO31 . . . . 315 B5
Sedgemead Ct SO31 . . 315 B5
Sedgemoor GU14 . . . . . 55 F7
Sedgewick Cl PO13 . . . 368 C8
Sedgewick Rd SO19 . . . 292 C5
Sedgley Cl PO5 . . . . . . 404 C2
Sedgwick Ct SO50 . . . . 244 D3
Sedgwick Rd SO50 . . . 244 D3
Seebys Oak GU47 . . . . . 35 B6
Seed Warehouse The 3
BH15 . . . . 390 D4
Seeviour's Ct RG28 . . . . 36 C5
Sefton Ho 11 GU11 . . . 76 E2
Segars La SO21 . . . . . 219 F5
Segensworth E Ind Est
PO15 . . . . 317 D5
Segensworth N Ind Est
PO15 . . . . 317 C5
Segensworth Rd
PO15 . . . . 317 E3
Segensworth W Ind Est
PO15 . . . . 317 C5
Sek Kong Cl SO20 . . . . 126 A4
Selangor Ave PO10 . . . 324 D1
Selborne Ave
Aldershot GU11 . . . . . 100 A6
Havant PO9 . . . . 323 D5
Southampton SO18 . . . 292 D1
Selborne CE Prim Sch
GU34 . . . . 184 D8
Selborne Cl
Blackwater GU17 . . . . . 35 A6
Hook RG27 . . . . 51 B1
Petersfield GU32 . . . . 228 F5
Selborne Ct 3 SO51 216 B1
Selborne Gdns
Farnham GU9 . . . . . . 121 E8
Gosport PO12 . . . . . . 369 A5
Southampton SO16 . . . 266 D3
Selborne Pl SO22 . . . . 403 B3
Selborne Rd
Alton GU34 . . . . 139 E1
Hartley Mauditt GU34 162 D5
Selborne Way GU35 . . . 164 A2
Tadley RG26 . . . . 26 F8
Selbourne Dr SO50 . . . 244 A4
Selbourne Rd
Havant PO9 . . . . 323 E1
Totton SO40 . . . . 288 D8
Selbourne Terr PO1 . . 404 D3
Selby Cl BH18 . . . . 375 A3
Selby Wlk RG24 . . . . . . 48 B1
Seldon Cl SO22 . . . . . . 197 B4
Seldown BH15 . . . . 390 D3
Seldown Bridge
BH15 . . . . 390 D2
Seldown La BH15 . . . . . 390 D3
Seldown Rd BH15 . . . . 390 D3
Self Rd BH15 . . . . 390 A2
Selfridge Ave BH6 . . . . 395 B3
Selfridge Cl BH6 . . . . . 395 B3
Selhurst Ho PO1 . . . . . 404 C4
Selhurst Way SO50 . . . 245 C1
Seliot Cl BH15 . . . . 390 D5
Selkirk Cl BH21 . . . . . . 351 E1
Sellwood Rd SO31 . . . . 315 C6
Sellwood Way BH25 . . 397 D8
Selma Cl 1 PO5 . . . . . 370 D2
Selman Cl SO45 . . . . . 314 B4
Selsdon Ave SO51 . . . . 241 B8
Selsey Ave
Gosport PO12 . . . . . . 369 A9
Portsmouth PO4 . . . . 371 A2
Selsey Cl
Southampton SO16 . . . 265 E2
South Hayling PO11 . . 373 F2
Selsmore Ave PO11 . . . 373 C3
Selsmore Rd PO11 . . . 373 B3
Selwood Pk BH10 . . . . 377 C7
Selworth La SO32 . . . . 273 A8
Selworthy Cl BH14 . . . 391 A2
Selwyn Ct 8 PO6 . . . . 345 F7
Selwyn Dr GU46 . . . . . . 33 F6
Selwyn Gdns SO50 . . . 244 A5
Sengana Cl SO30 . . . . 293 D6
Senlac Rd SO51 . . . . . 241 B7
Sennen Pl PO6 . . . . . . 345 A7
Sentinel Ct BH15 . . . . . 390 B1
Sentinel Ct PO7 . . . . . . 300 B1
Sepen Meade 8
GU52 . . . . 74 E4
Seps 4 Rd SO45 . . . . . 339 C4
September Cl SO20 . . . 308 D1
Seremban Cl SO20 . . . 126 A5
Serle Cl SO40 . . . . 288 B7

Serle Gdns SO40 . . . . . 288 D6
Sermon Rd SO22 . . . . . 403 A7
Serotine Cl PO17 . . . . . 318 E7
Serpentine Rd
7 Portsmouth
PO5 . . . . 370 C2
Fareham PO16 . . . . . 319 B2
Poole BH15 . . . . 390 C5
Waterlooville PO7 . . . 322 C5
Service Rd PO6 . . . . . . 345 D8
Setley Gdns BH8 . . . . . 378 E3
Set Oaks Cvn Site
BH25 . . . . 359 E5
Seton Dr RG27 . . . . 71 F8
Setters Cl SO21 . . . . . 244 F8
Set Thorns Rd SO41 . . 360 C2
Settle Cl 4 SO16 . . . . 290 B8
Settlers Ct PO1 . . . . . . 404 C4
Sett The GU46 . . . . 33 F5
Sevenoaks Dr BH7 . . . 394 A8
Sevenoaks Rd PO6 . . . 345 E8
Seventh St RG19 . . . . . . 6 D5
Severals Rd RG24 . . . . . 47 E3
Severn Cl
Portchester PO16 . . . . 344 A8
Portsmouth PO6 . . . . 321 B1
Sandhurst GU47 . . . . . 35 A8
Thatcham RG18 . . . . . . 2 F5
Severn Ct 35 SO10 . . . 83 C2
Severn Gdns RG23 . . . . 67 B1
Severn Rd
Farnborough GU14 . . . 55 C6
Ferndown BH22 . . . . . 354 A5
Southampton SO16 . . . 289 E8
Severn Way
29 Basingstoke
RG21 . . . . 69 D5
West End SO30 . . . . . 268 D1
Seville Cres SP10 . . . . . 83 C1
Seward Rd SO45 . . . . . 314 B3
Seward Rise SO51 . . . . 241 D8
Seymour Cl
Chandler's Ford
SO53 . . . . 243 E5
Portsmouth PO2 . . . . 370 D7
Southampton SO16 . . . 266 C2
Totton SO40 . . . . 264 C1
Seymour Ct GU15 . . . . 54 A3
Seymour Dr GU15 . . . . 36 F8
Seymour Gdns BH24 . . 305 B1
Seymour Ho SO16 . . . . 266 D3
Seymour La SO52 . . . . 241 F4
Seymour Pl RG29 . . . . 72 E3
Seymour Rd
Basingstoke RG22 . . . . 68 C2
Headley GU35 . . . . . . 166 A4
Lee-on-t-S PO13 . . . . 368 A4
Ringwood BH24 . . . . . 305 B1
Southampton SO16 . . . 266 D3
Shackleton Cl PO13 . . . 368 D8
Shackleton Ho 2
PO2 . . . . 345 E2
Shackleton Rd PO13 368 D8
Shackleton Sq
11 Andover SP10 . . . 83 C2
Bransgore BH23 . . . . . 357 B1
Shadwell Ct 9 PO2 . . . 345 D2
Shadwell Rd PO2 . . . . 345 D2
Shady Nook GU9 . . . . . 98 F6
Shafer Ct RG14 . . . . 1 E1
Shaftesbury Ave
Chandler's Ford
SO53 . . . . 243 C4
Southampton SO17 . . . 267 B2
Waterlooville PO7 . . . 322 E5
Shaftesbury Ct
3 Bordon GU35 . . . . 164 B2
Bournemouth BH3 . . . 392 F6
Farnborough GU14 . . . 77 A8
Shaftesbury Mount
GU17 . . . . 35 B3
Shaftesbury Rd
Bournemouth BH8 . . . 393 C6
Gosport PO12 . . . . . . 369 C4
Poole BH15 . . . . 390 D3
Portsmouth,Southsea
PO5 . . . . 370 C2
West Moors BH22 . . . 326 F2
Shaftesbury St SP6 . . . 257 F1
Shaftsbury Rd
Gosport PO12 . . . . . . 369 C4
Gosport PO12 . . . . . . 369 C5
Shaggs Mdw SO43 . . . 310 A5
Shakespeare Ave
Andover SP10 . . . . . . 82 D1
Southampton SO17 . . 291 B8
Shakespeare Bsns Ctr
SO50 . . . . 244 B4
Shakespeare Dr
SO40 . . . . 264 D2
Shakespeare Gdns
Farnborough GU14 . . . 55 B5
Waterlooville PO8 . . . 299 E3
Shakespeare Inf Sch
SO50 . . . . 244 A4
Shakespeare Jun Sch
SO50 . . . . 244 A4
Shakespeare Mews
PO14 . . . . 342 A8
Shakespeare Rd
Basingstoke RG24 . . . . 69 C8
Bournemouth BH6 . . . 394 D2
Eastleigh SO50 . . . . . 244 A4
Portsmouth PO1 . . . . 370 E7
Wimborne Minster
BH21 . . . . 351 C6

Shakespeare Terr 12
PO1 . . . . 370 A3
Shalbourne Rd PO12 369 A8
Shalbourne Rise
GU15 . . . . 36 B5
Shalcombe SO31 . . . . . 315 C5
Shalden La GU34 . . . . 138 F7
Shalden Rd GU12 . . . . 100 B8
Shaldon Cl SO16 . . . . . 266 C4
Shaldon Rd 8 BH9 . . . 324 B6
Shaldon Way GU51 . . . 74 D8
Shales Rd SO18 . . . . . 292 B7
Shallow La SO41 . . . . . 385 E4
Shallows The SP6 . . . . 258 C7
Shamblehurst La N
SO32 . . . . 269 D3
Shamblehurst La S
SO30 . . . . 269 C1
Shamblehurst Prim Sch
SO30 . . . . 293 C8
Shamrock Cl
Camberley GU16 . . . . . 56 B8
Gosport PO12 . . . . . . 369 D5
Shamrock Ct 2
BH21 . . . . 351 C4
Shamrock Quay
SO14 . . . . 291 D5
Shamrock Rd SO19 . . . 291 D3
Shamrock Villas 3
SO17 . . . . 267 C1
Shamrock Way
SO45 . . . . 314 A5
Shanklin Cres SO15 . . 266 D1
Shanklin Ct GU12 . . . . 77 A1
Shanklin Rd
Portsmouth PO4 . . . . 370 E4
Southampton SO15 . . . 266 D2
Shannon Ct PO15 . . . . 318 D2
Shannon Ct
36 Andover SP10 . . . 83 C2
7 Gosport PO13 . . . . 369 C9
Shannon Ho 9
SO14 . . . . 291 C5
Shannon Rd
Gosport PO14 . . . . . . 343 A5
Stubbington PO14 . . . 367 B8
Shannon Way SO53 . . 243 B6
Shapland Ave BH11 . . . 376 E5
Shapley Heath RG27 . . 52 B2
Shapley Hill RG27 . . . . 52 B2
Shapley Ho RG27 . . . . 52 A3
Shappen Hill La
BH24 . . . . 330 F1
Shapton Cl SO45 . . . . . 338 B4
Shapwick Rd BH15 . . . 390 A1
Shard Cl BH31 . . . . 303 A6
Sharland Pl 6 PO14 342 E7
Sharlands Cl BH18 . . . 375 B3
Sharlands Rd PO14 . . 343 A6
Sharon Ct 4 PO12 . . . 369 C6
Sharon Rd SO30 . . . . . 268 C2
Sharpley Cl SP6 . . . . . 257 E3
Sharpness Cl PO14 . . . 342 C8
Sharp Rd BH12 . . . . . . 392 A2
Sharps Cl PO3 . . . . . . 346 B3
Sharp's Copse Prim Sch
PO9 . . . . 324 C5
Sharps Rd PO9 . . . . . . 324 B5
Sharp's Rd PO9 . . . . . . 324 B5
Sharvells Rd SO41 . . . 399 C5
Shavard La GU32 . . . . 249 D6
Shaves La BH25 . . . . . 383 A5
Shaw Cl
Andover SP10 . . . . . . 105 C8
Totton SO40 . . . . 288 D7
West End SO18 . . . . . 268 A4
Shawcross Ind Pk
PO3 . . . . 346 A5
Shaw-cum-Donnington
CE Prim Sch RG14 . . . 1 E6
Shaw Farm Rd RG14 . . . 1 F6
Shawfield La GU12 . . . . 77 D2
Shawfield Prim Sch
GU12 . . . . 77 E3
Shawfield Rd GU12 . . . 77 E2
Shawford Cl
Southampton SO16 . . . 266 E4
Totton SO40 . . . . 288 B7
Shawford Gdns BH8 . . 378 D2
Shawford Gr PO9 . . . . 323 C4
Shawford Rd
Bournemouth BH8 . . . 378 D3
Twyford SO21 . . . . . . 219 F6
Shawford Sta SO21 . . 219 E6
Shaw Hill RG14 . . . . 1 F5
Shaw Ho SP11 . . . . 81 B6
Shaw La RG26 . . . . 26 D7
Shaw Mill RG14 . . . . . . 1 F5
Shaw Pightle RG27 . . . 50 F1
Shaw Rd
Newbury RG14 . . . . 1 F4
Ringwood BH24 . . . . . 305 C2
Shayer Rd SO15 . . . . . 266 D5
Sheardley La SO32 . . . 250 A1
Shearer Rd PO1 . . . . . 370 E7
Shear Hill GU31 . . . . . 229 B5
Shears Brook Cl
BH23 . . . . 357 B1
Shears Rd SO50 . . . . . 244 E3
Shearwater Ave
PO16 . . . . 343 E8
Shearwater Cl PO13 . 343 B2
Shearwater Ct PO11 . . 373 D1
Shearwater Dr PO6 . . . 346 F7
Sheddon Pl SO21 . . . . 174 D2

Sheep Dro SO20 .... **147** D4
Sheep Fair SP10 .... **106** C7
Sheep Fair Cl SP10.. **106** C8
Sheephatch La GU10 **122** F5
Sheephouse GU9 .... **122** A8
Sheepmoor Dr GU51 . **53** F3
Sheep Pond La SO32 **249** B3
Sheep St GU32.... **228** F3
Sheepwash La
  Burghclere RG20.......**5** E2
  Denmead PO7 ...... **321** F8
  Ramsdell RG26 ...... **46** D7
Sheerlands Rd RG2,
  RG40 .... **15** D6
Sheet Prim Sch
  GU32............. **229** B6
Sheffield Cl
  Bishopstoke SO50...**244** D5
  Farnborough GU14 .... **55** D4
Sheffield Ct 11 PO13 **368** C6
Sheffield Rd PO1 ... **404** D3
Shefford Lodge 6
  RG14 ....**1** E2
Sheiling Sch The
  BH24.............. **328** C6
Shelbourne Cl BH8.. **393** D6
Shelbourne Rd BH8.. **393** D6
Sheldon's La RG27... **51** A1
Sheldon's Rd RG27... **51** A1
Sheldrake Gdns
  Hordle SO41 ...... **384** B3
  Southampton SO16.. **266** B5
Sheldrake Rd BH23 . **396** A5
Shelford Rd PO4.... **371** B5
Shell Bay Sailing Ctr★
  BH19.............. **402** A1
Shellcroft SO31.... **340** D10
Shell Ct SO40...... **289** F2
Shelley Ave PO6.... **320** E1
Shelley Cl
  Basingstoke RG24.... **69** C8
  Bournemouth BH1... **393** E5
  Christchurch BH23 .. **396** C7
  Fleet GU51 .... **75** A8
  Itchen Abbas SO21 .. **177** E6
  St Leonards BH24 ... **327** E5
  Winchester SO22 ... **403** B6
Shelley Ct
  10 Bournemouth
  BH4 .... **392** C3
  Camberley GU15 .... **36** A5
  Ferndown BH22..... **353** D6
  Southampton SO15 .. **290** E5
Shelley Gdns
  Bournemouth BH1... **393** E5
  Waterlooville PO8... **299** E3
Shelley Hamlets
  BH23 .... **396** D7
Shelley Hill BH23 .. **396** D7
Shelley Ho 9 BH25 . **383** A2
Shelley La SO51..... **263** E8
Shelley Rd
  Bournemouth BH1... **393** E5
  Eastleigh SO50 ..... **243** F1
  Poole BH12 .... **391** D5
  Southampton SO19 .. **292** E6
  Totton SO40....... **264** D2
Shelley Rd E BH7 .. **393** F5
Shelley Rise GU14... **55** D6
Shelleys La GU34 ... **140** F1
Shelley Way SO41... **399** D5
Shell La GU34...... **183** B2
Shelton Rd BH6..... **394** C6
Shenley Cl PO15 ... **318** C2
Shenstone Cl RG40...**16** E8
Shenstone Ct 2
  BH25 .... **383** A1
Shepards Cl PO14... **342** D8
Shepheard's Way
  PO12 .... **369** C3
Shepherd Cl BH23 .. **381** E1
Shepherd & Flock Rdbt
  GU9 .... **99** C4
Shepherd Lodge
  SP10 .... **83** A1
Shepherds Cl
  Bartley SO40...... **287** B6
  Winchester SO22 ... **197** B4
Shepherds Cl GU9 ... **122** A8
Shepherds Down
  SO24 .... **179** C4
Shepherds Down Specl
  Sch SO21......... **219** C6
Shepherds Hey Rd
  SO40 .... **264** B1
Shepherds Hill BH24 **304** C6
Shepherds La
  Compton SO21..... **219** C6
  Ellingham BH24 .... **304** B6
Shepherds Purse Cl
  SO31 .... **316** F2
Shepherds Rd
  Bartley SO40...... **287** C6
  Winchester SO23 ...**198** C8
Shepherds Rise SP11. **38** C6
Shepherds Row
  SP10 .... **106** C7
Shepherds Spring Inf
  Sch SP10.......... **83** B3
Shepherds Spring Jun
  Sch SP10.......... **83** B3
Shepherds Spring La
  SP10 ....**83** B1
Shepherds Way
  Bournemouth BH7.. **394** A7

Shepherds Way continued
  Everton SO41 ...... **384** D1
  Liphook GU30 ..... **188** B3
  Nursling SO16 ..... **265** C5
Shepherds Wlk GU14. **55** C7
Sheppard Almshouses
  SP11 .... **104** A5
Sheppard Cl
  Waterlooville PO8 ... **300** A6
  Whitchurch RG28 ... **86** C4
Sheppard Rd SO21 ... **35** C4
Sheppards Field 4
  BH21............. **351** B6
Sheppard Sq 9 SP10 **83** C2
Shepperd Terr 14
  PO13 .... **368** C6
Sheraton Ave RG22 ...**91** B7
Sheraton Cl GU17 ... **35** C4
Sherborn Cres BH17 **376** A2
Sherborne Ct SO40.. **244** A6
Sherborne Dr BH22 . **353** D4
Sherborne House Sch
  SO53............. **243** D8
Sherborne Rd
  Basingstoke RG21.... **69** A7
  Sherborne St John
  RG24 .... **47** F2
  Southampton SO17 .. **267** B3
Sherborne St John CE
  Prim Sch RG24 .... **47** E3
Sherborne Way
  SO30 .... **293** C6
Sherbrooke Cl
  Kings Worthy SO23 .. **176** C8
  Lee-on-t-S PO13 ... **368** A6
Sherecroft Gdns
  SO30 .... **294** B7
Sherfield Ave PO9 .. **324** A5
Sherfield Cl BH8.... **378** D2
Sherfield English La
  SO51 .... **238** C6
Sherfield English Rd
  SP5 .... **238** B4
Sherfield Ho 10
  SO15 .... **290** E7
Sherfield Rd RG26 .. **278** A2
Sherfield Sch RG27 .. **49** E6
Sheridan Cl
  Aldershot GU11...... **99** E8
  Southampton SO19 .. **292** D5
  Winchester SO22 ... **403** A3
Sheridan Cres RG26....**9** C1
Sheridan Ct
  Camberley GU16 .... **56** B8
  Newbury RG14 ......**2** A3
Sheridan Gdns
  Swanwick PO15..... **317** C8
  Totton SO40....... **288** D7
Sheridan Rd GU16 ... **56** B8
Sheringham Rd
  Poole BH12 .... **391** F5
  Portsmouth PO6 ... **321** D1
Sherington Cl GU14...**55** C7
Sherley Gn SO31..... **293** A1
Sherlock Lea RG27... **33** C7
Sherrardmead RG14 ...**1** F5
Sherrin Cl BH15..... **390** D5
Sherringham Cl
  SO45 .... **339** B3
Sherrington Way
  RG22 .... **68** F2
Sherwin Cres GU14...**55** F8
Sherwin Wlk PO12 .. **369** A4
Sherwood Ave
  Ferndown BH22..... **353** C3
  Hedge End SO30 .... **293** C4
  Poole BH14 .... **391** A3
Sherwood Cl
  Basingstoke RG22.... **91** C6
  Christchurch BH23 .. **394** F7
  Liss GU33 .... **208** A7
  Southampton SO16 .. **266** C3
Sherwood Dr BH31.. **303** B6
Sherwood Gdns
  SO31 .... **316** E4
Sherwood Rd
  Chandler's Ford
  SO53............ **218** E1
  Gosport PO12 ..... **369** C3
Sherwood Terr
  GU34 .... **140** A3
Sherwood Way SO45 **365** E7
Shetland Cl
  Portsmouth PO6 ... **321** F1
  Totton SO40....... **288** B8
Shetland Rd RG24... **48** D1
Shetland Rise PO15 . **317** B7
Shetland View BH31 **303** A6
Shetland Way GU51.. **54** B4
Shillinglee PO7 .... **322** E4
Shillingstone Dr
  BH9.............. **378** B3
Shillingstone Gdns 3
  BH12............. **391** F7
Shillito Rd BH12 ... **391** E5
Shinewell Gdns 4
  SO16 .... **289** E8
Shingle Bank Dr
  SO41 .... **399** D4
Shinwell Ct 8 SO15. **266** B1
Ship Alley GU14...... **56** A6
Shipbuilding Rd PO1 **369** F8
Shipcote La SO32 ... **247** D2
Ship La GU14 ...... **56** A6
Ship Leopard St 12
  PO1 .... **370** A5
Shipley Cl GU34.... **140** A1
Shipley Ct 1 GU30.. **188** A3

Shipley Rd SO21 .... **220** A7
Shipstal Cl BH16 ... **389** C4
Shipton Bellinger Prim
  Sch SP9........... **101** D8
Shipton Gn PO9..... **323** D6
Shipton Way RG22 .. **68** C2
Shipwrights Wlk
  SO41 .... **400** B3
Shire Ave GU51 .... **54** C4
Shire Cl
  Swanwick PO15..... **317** B7
  Waterlooville PO7... **300** C1
Shire Ct 2 GU11.... **76** C2
Shires Cl BH24...... **329** A4
Shires Copse BH6... **394** F3
Shires Mead BH31... **303** A6
Shires The SO30 ... **293** A6
Shires Way GU46 .... **34** B7
Shires Wlk SO40.... **288** B7
Shirley Ave
  Portsmouth PO4 .... **371** C4
  Southampton SO15 .. **290** C8
Shirley Cl
  Bransgore BH23 .... **357** B1
  West Moors BH31 .. **326** E2
Shirley High St SO15,
  SO16 .... **290** B8
Shirley Holms SO41 . **361** B1
Shirley Inf Sch SO15 **266** C1
Shirley Park SO16.. **266** C2
Shirley Park Rd
  SO16 .... **290** B8
Shirley Rd
  Bournemouth BH9... **378** A1
  Poole BH12 .... **391** B6
  Portsmouth PO5 ... **370** E2
  Southampton SO15 .. **290** C7
  Upton BH16....... **389** C7
Shirley Twrs SO15 .. **290** B7
Shirley Warren Prim Sch
  SO16 .... **266** A2
Shirrel Ct 7 PO12 .. **368** D3
Shoblands Way 6
  SO45 .... **314** A1
Shoddesden La SP11. **80** C7
Shoe La
  Farnborough GU11,
  GU14 .... **76** E6
  Meonstoke SO32... **249** C6
  Upham SO32 ...... **246** F6
Sholing Ct PO9 .... **323** D6
Sholing Inf Sch
  SO19 .... **292** A5
Sholing Jun Sch
  SO19 .... **292** A5
Sholing Rd SO19 ... **291** E4
Sholing Sta SO19 ... **291** F2
Sholing Tech Coll The
  SO19 .... **292** A4
Shooters Hill Cl
  SO19 .... **292** B3
Shooters Way RG21 .. **69** C6
Shoot Hill PO7,PO17. **297** D3
Shop La PO13 ...... **368** A8
Shop La
  Donnington RG14 ....**1** C6
  Southampton SO19,
  SO31............ **292** E2
Shoreacres BH13 ... **402** C3
Shore Ave
  Portsmouth PO4 .... **371** B6
  Upton BH16....... **389** C6
Shore Cl
  Milford on S SO41.. **399** D4
  Upton BH16....... **389** C6
Shore Cres SO32.... **271** D7
Shorefield Country Pk
  SO41 .... **399** A6
Shorefield Cres
  SO41 .... **399** C5
Shorefield Rd
  Marchwood SO40 ... **289** F2
  Milford on S SO41.. **399** A6
Shorefield Way
  SO41 .... **399** C5
Shore Gdns BH16... **389** B6
Shorehaven PO6.... **344** F8
Shore Ho SO31 .... **316** C1
Shore La
  Bishop's Waltham
  SO32............ **271** D7
  Upton BH16....... **389** C6
Shore Rd
  Hythe SO45 .... **314** B3
  Poole BH13 .... **402** D6
  Warsash SO31...... **316** C1
Shorewood Cl SO31 . **316** F1
Short Cl BH12 ..... **392** A8
Shortdale Rd GU11.. **100** A6
Shortfield Rd GU10 . **122** A1
Shortheath Crest
  GU9.............. **121** D6
Shortheath Rd GU9 . **121** E6
Short Hill
  Nomansland SP5.... **261** B8
  Romsey SO51 ..... **216** C1
Short La SP11....... **82** A1
Short Rd PO14...... **367** A7
Short Row PO1 ..... **370** A6
Shorts Cl BH23 .... **380** C1
Short's Farm SO51.. **238** D7
Shorts Rd SO50 .... **245** C2
Short St
  Aldershot GU11...... **76** E2
  Ludgershall SP11.... **57** A2
Shortwood Copse La
  RG23 ....**90** F5
Shorwell SO31...... **315** C7

Shotterfield Terr
  GU33 .... **207** F4
Shottermill Inf Sch
  GU27............. **189** D7
Shottermill Jun Sch
  GU27............. **189** D7
Shottermill Pk GU27 **189** D7
Shottermill Rd GU27 **189** C5
Shotters Hill Cl
  SO30 .... **268** D1
Shotter's La GU11... **183** F6
Shottsford Rd BH15.. **390** B4
Shotts La SO41 ..... **386** C4
Shraveshill Cl SO40. **264** C1
Shrave The GU34 ... **160** E4
Shrewsbury Terr RG14 .**1** D1
Shrivenham Cl 4
  GU47............. **35** B8
Shrubbery Cl PO16.. **344** C7
Shrubbery The
  Farnborough GU14... **55** B3
  Gosport PO12 ..... **368** F7
Shrubb's Ave SO41.. **385** E4
Shrubbs Hill Gdns
  SO43 .... **309** F4
Shrubbs Hill Rd
  SO43 .... **309** F4
Shrubbs La GU10 ... **121** D4
Shrubland Cl SO18.. **292** B8
Shyshack La RG26 ....**9** D1
Sian Cl GU52........**75** B5
Sibelius Cl RG22 .... **91** E7
Sibland Cl PO14..... **342** D8
Siblings The SO19 .. **292** E6
Sicily Rd 7 PO14 .. **342** E7
Sickle Mill Ct GU27 . **189** D6
Sickle Rd GU27 .... **189** E5
Sickles La GU35..... **142** B2
Sidbury Circular Rd
  SP9 .... **78** D7
Sidbury Hill Ave SP9 .**78** D7
Siddal Cl SO19...... **292** C4
Sidestrand Rd
  Farnborough GU11 ... **76** C7
  Newbury RG14 ......**5** C7
Sidings The
  Aldershot GU11...... **77** A3
  Downton SP5....... **235** A8
  Netley SO31....... **315** D5
Sidlaw Cl RG22 ..... **68** A3
Sidlaws Rd GU14.... **55** B6
Sidlesham Cl PO11.. **373** F2
Sidmouth Ave 1
  PO3 .... **371** A4
Sidmouth Rd SP10 .. **106** C8
Sidney Gdns 2 BH9. **378** B4
Sidney Smith Ct
  BH17 .... **375** E2
Sidney St SO41 .... **384** A2
Silchester CE Prim Sch
  RG7.............. **10** F1
Silchester Cl
  Andover SP10 ..... **82** C2
  Bournemouth BH2... **392** F5
Silchester Dr 10
  GU51 .... **53** D3
Silchester Pl 11
  SO23 .... **403** E7
Silchester Rd
  Bramley RG26 ..... **28** C3
  Little London RG26 . **27** E4
  Pamber Heath RG7,
  RG26 .... **10** D2
  Portsmouth PO3 ... **371** B7
Silhouette Ct PO11.. **373** D1
Silkin Gdns SO40 .. **288** D6
Silk Mill La RG25.... **87** F8
Silkstead Ave PO9 .. **323** F6
Silkstead La
  Compton SO21..... **218** F7
  Winchester SO21,
  SO22............ **197** A1
Silkweavers Rd
  SP10 .... **106** B5
Sillen La SP6 ...... **231** A3
Silver Birch Ave
  PO14 .... **342** E8
Silver Birch Cl
  Fleet GU52 .... **74** F5
  Liss GU33 .... **208** A4
  Poole BH13 .... **392** A4
  Southampton SO19 .. **292** E4
Silver Birches SO31 . **315** F4
Silver Birch Rd SP10 .**82** E1
Silver Birch Way 1
  PO15 .... **317** D8
Silver Bsns Pk BH23 **395** F7
Silverdale
  Barton on S BH25 .. **398** B7
  Fleet GU52 .... **75** A6
Silverdale Cl BH18.. **374** E4
Silverdale Cres SP6. **281** A6
Silverdale Ct 5
  SO15 .... **290** E7
Silverdale Dr PO7 .. **299** C3
Silverdale Rd
  Pamber Heath RG26....**9** F1
  Southampton SO15 .. **290** E7
Silverglades GU46 ... **34** A4
Silver Hill
  Sandhurst GU47 .... **35** C8
  Winchester SO23 ... **403** E5
Silverlock Pl PO10 .. **325** E5
Silver Park Cl GU52...**75** B6
Silversands Gdns
  PO11 .... **373** B2

Silvers End 2 SO45. **314** A1
Silver St
  1 Portsmouth
  PO5 .... **404** A1
  5 Christchurch
  BH23 .... **395** B6
  Hordle SO41 ...... **384** C5
  Lyndhurst SO43.... **309** D5
Silvers Wood SO40.. **264** C1
Silverthorne Way
  PO7 .... **322** D8
Silvertrees
  Emsworth PO10..... **324** F2
  Sarisbury SO31 .... **316** E6
Silver Way BH23 ... **396** E7
Silverweed Cl SO31 . **242** F7
Silverweed Ct SO31. **316** C2
Silverwood Cl
  Merley BH21....... **351** D2
  Winchester SO22 ... **403** B3
Silverwood Dr GU15..**36** E7
Silvester Cl RG21 ... **69** C7
Silvester Rd PO8.... **299** F2
Silvester Way GU52...**74** E4
Silwood Cl SO22 ... **403** C7
Simmonds Cl BH15.. **390** D5
Simmondstone La
  GU10 .... **144** B2
Simmons Cl SO30... **293** C8
Simmons Gn PO11 .. **373** C3
Simmons Wlk 27
  RG21 .... **69** D5
Simms Farm La RG7 . **11** D5
Simnel St 8 SO14 .. **290** F3
Simon Cl SO18...... **292** E7
Simonds Ct 6 SO23. **403** E8
Simons Cl RG24..... **48** F2
Simons Rd RG24 .... **48** F2
Simon Way SO18.... **292** E6
Simpkins Ct 13 SO53 **218** B1
Simpson Cl PO16 ... **344** C8
Simpson Rd PO2.... **345** C1
Sims Cl RG26 ...... **29** B2
Sinah La PO11 ..... **372** C4
Sinclair Cl 4 BH14 . **391** A4
Sinclair Prim Sch
  SO16.............. **266** A5
Sinclair Rd SO16.... **266** A5
Sine Cl GU14 ....**55** F8
Singleton Dr BH10 .. **377** C2
Singleton Gdns PO8. **276** D4
Singleton Way SO40 **288** B8
Sinhurst Rd GU15 ... **35** F4
Sir Christopher Ct
  SO45 .... **314** B4
Sirdar Ho SO17 .... **267** C3
Sirdar Rd SO17 .... **267** C3
Sir Galahad Rd SO53 **242** F6
Sir George's Rd
  SO15 .... **290** D6
Sir Harold Hillier
  Gardens &
  Arboretum ★
  SO51............. **216** D4
Sirius Cl PO5 ...... **404** B2
Sirius Ho 11 PO5 .. **370** D2
Sir John's Mews
  SO32 .... **223** B3
Sir Lancelot Cl SO53 **242** F6
Siskin Cl
  Bishop's Waltham
  SO32............ **271** A8
  Ferndown BH22..... **353** B7
  Southampton SO16 .. **266** A5
Siskin Gr PO7....... **323** A6
Siskin Inf Sch PO13 **368** D6
Siskin Jun Sch PO13 **368** D6
Siskin Rd PO4 ..... **371** C5
Sissinghurst Cl
  SO19 .... **292** A1
Sissinghurst Rd
  PO16 .... **344** A7
Siward Ho GU32 .... **228** E3
Six Dials SO14 ..... **291** A5
Six Oaks Rd SO52 .. **242** A4
Sixpenny Cl
  Locks Heath PO14... **317** A1
  Poole BH12 .... **391** F7
Sixth Ave PO6 ..... **345** E8
Sixth Form Coll
  Farnborough GU14 .. **55** F6
Sixth St RG19 ....**6** D5
Sizer Way SO45..... **313** B3
Skates La RG26.......**27** B5
Skew Rd
  Portchester PO17 ... **320** D2
  Quarley SP11....... **103** B3
Skinners Green La
  RG14 ....**4** F7
Skinner St BH15 ... **390** C1
Skintle Gn SO21 ... **244** F8
Skipper Cl SO40 ... **290** A3
Skipper Way PO13 .. **368** A5
Skippetts La E RG21. **69** C2
Skippetts La W RG21. **69** B2
Skippons Cl RG14.... **5** A6
Skipton Cl BH18 ... **375** A2
Skipton Rd SO53.... **243** D4
Skye Cl PO6 .... **321** F1
Sky End La SO41 ... **384** A2
Skylark Cl RG22..... **90** F6
Skylark Ct PO4..... **371** C5
Skylark Mdws
  Fareham PO15...... **318** A6
  Whiteley PO15..... **317** F5
Skylark Rise RG28... **86** B6
Skylings RG14 ...... **2** A4
Skys Wood Rd SO53. **242** F6

Slab La
  Redlynch SP5...... **235** C6
  West Wellow SO51 . **238** E3
Slade Cl SO41 ..... **384** A3
Slade Hill Gdns RG20....**4** D2
Sladen Cnr SP11......**61** F8
Slader Bsns Pk
  BH17............. **375** E1
Slades Farm Rd
  BH10............. **377** D2
Slades Hill SO45.... **338** F2
Slade's La BH10..... **392** C8
Slade The GU32.... **205** F2
Slater App PO2 .... **345** A1
Slater Cl SO40 ..... **288** B8
Sleepbrook Cl BH31. **302** E6
Sleepers Delle Gdns
  SO22 .... **403** C4
Sleeper's Hill SO22 . **403** B4
Sleepers Hill Gdns
  SO22 .... **403** B4
Sleeper's Hill Ho
  SO22 .... **403** B4
Sleepy Hollow (Cvn Pk)
  RG26 ....**27** B7
Sleight La BH21..... **374** C8
Slepe Cres BH12 ... **391** F8
Slessor Cl SP11..... **105** B7
Slim Cl GU11 ...... **77** C7
Slim Rd GU15....... **36** A7
Slindon Cl PO8 .... **276** D5
Slindon Gdns 4
  PO9 .... **323** F1
Slindon St PO1..... **404** B3
Slingsby Cl PO1..... **404** A1
Slinn Rd BH23 ..... **395** F5
Slipper Cvn Pk PO10 **349** A8
Slipper Rd PO10 ... **349** A8
Slip Way BH15 ..... **390** B2
Slipway The PO6.... **345** A7
Sloane Ave SO45.... **338** D4
Sloane Pk SO32..... **295** D7
Sloane Stanley Ct
  PO12 .... **369** B7
Slocum Ho 18 PO12 **369** C5
Sloe Tree Cl SO31... **317** C2
Slough La BH16..... **389** A6
Small Cl GU31...... **229** A5
Smallcutts Ave
  PO10 .... **325** D1
Smallfield Dr RG27... **51** C1
Smallridge RG20......**5** A4
Smannell & Enham CE
  Prim Sch SP11..... **83** E7
Smannell Rd SP10,
  SP11 .... **83** B4
Smay Down La SN8 ...**17** B3
Smeaton Cl PO15 ... **317** E4
Smeaton Rd RG14 .....**1** C4
Smeaton St PO2 .... **345** C2
Smeeton Rd PO13... **367** F3
Smith Cl SO45...... **338** F2
Smithe Cl SO50 .... **244** A3
Smithfield La GU35,
  GU35............. **143** E1
Smithfield Pl BH9... **377** F1
Smith Gr SO30...... **293** C6
Smith La PO10 ..... **349** D1
Smith's Field RG25....**88** F3
Smith's Field SO51.. **216** A1
Smiths La SO32..... **295** F8
Smiths Mead RG25....**89** C1
Smithson Cl BH12... **392** C8
Smith St PO12 ..... **369** A6
Smithy Cl GU34.... **140** D7
Smithy La
  Bashley BH25 ..... **382** F6
  Headley GU10 ..... **143** C2
Smithy The
  Bramley RG26 ..... **28** C3
  Denmead PO7 ..... **298** E4
Smugglers La
  Colehill BH21...... **351** E7
  Ropley SO24....... **182** A2
Smugglers La N
  BH23 .... **381** E1
Smugglers La S
  BH23 .... **396** E8
Smugglers Reach
  BH23 .... **396** A5
Smugglers' Way
  GU10 .... **100** C1
Smugglers Wood Rd
  BH23 .... **381** D1
Smythe Rd SO19 ... **292** D3
Snailing La GU33.... **207** C8
Snails La BH24...... **305** B3
Snailslynch GU9 .....**99** B2
Snakemoor La SO32. **269** E5
Snapdragon Cl SO31 **316** F2
Snape Cl PO13...... **368** C8
Snellgrove Cl SO40.. **264** C1
Snellgrove Pl SO40.. **264** C2
Snell's Cnr PO8..... **276** D3
Snipe La
  Bishop's Green RG20 . **6** D2
  Marley Heights GU27 **189** E1
Snoddington Rd
  Kimpton SP11...... **80** B1
  Shipton Bellinger
  SP11............ **102** F8
Snode Hill GU34.... **139** A3
Snooks La SO41..... **386** B6
Snowberry Cres
  PO9 .... **324** C3
Snowdon Dr PO14 .. **342** E8

Snowdon Rd
Bournemouth BH4 392 C4
Farnborough GU14 55 C7
Snowdrop Cl
Basingstoke RG22 91 A8
Locks Heath SO31 316 F2
Snowdrop Gdns
BH23 381 B1
Snowdrop Wlk 2
GU51 53 F2
Soake Rd PO7 299 B3
Soalwood La GU32 205 F1
Soame's La SO24 181 E2
Sobers Sq 7 SP10 83 C2
Soberton Ho
29 Southampton
SO17 267 A1
Portsmouth PO1 404 C4
Soberton Rd
Bournemouth BH8 393 D6
Havant PO9 323 E4
Soberton Twrs SO32 273 B6
Soke Hill GU34 159 F1
Soke Rd RG7 10 D3
Soke The SO24 179 D6
Solar Ct BH13 392 A4
Solartron Rd GU14 55 F3
Solartron Retail Pk
GU14 55 E3
Solby's Rd 3 RG21 69 A5
Soldridge Cl 5 PO9 324 B6
Soldridge Rd GU34 159 F4
Solent Ave
Lymington SO41 386 A3
Southampton SO19 292 E6
Solent Breezes Cvn Site
SO31 340 F6
Solent Bsns Ctr
SO15 290 B6
Solent Bsns Pk PO15 317 E7
Solent Cl
Chandler's Ford
SO53 243 E6
Lymington SO41 385 F3
Solent Ct
25 Portsmouth
PO5 370 C2
6 Milford on S SO41 399 C4
Southampton SO19 291 E1
Stubbington PO14 367 C7
Solent Ctr PO15 317 E7
Solent Dr
Barton on S BH25 398 A7
Basingstoke RG22 91 B7
Hythe SO45 313 F4
South Hayling PO11 372 F2
Warsash SO31 340 D8
Solent Gate
12 Portsmouth PO5 370 E1
Gosport PO14 343 B5
Solent Ho
Fareham PO16 343 A7
Havant PO9 324 A3
Solent Homes SO19 292 E6
Solent Hts
Lee-on-t-S PO13 367 E2
Portsmouth PO4 371 D3
Solent Ind Ctr SO15 290 C6
Solent Ind Est SO30 269 B1
Solent Inf Sch PO6 346 D8
Solent Jun Sch PO6 346 D8
Solent Lo 5 BH25 383 A1
Solent Mdws SO31 316 A2
Solent Mead SO41 385 E3
Solent Pines 2
SO41 399 B4
Solent Rd
Barton on S BH25 397 D7
Bournemouth BH6 395 A3
Cosham PO6 346 C8
Havant PO9 323 E1
Hythe SO45 337 E8
Southampton SO15 290 E4
Stubbington PO14 367 A6
Walkford BH23 382 B2
Solent View
Bournemouth BH6 395 A3
Calshot SO45 366 F8
Lee-on-t-S PO13 367 D4
Portchester PO16 320 B1
Walhampton SO41 386 B3
Solent Village PO15 317 E6
Solent Way
Beaulieu SO42 336 F8
Gosport PO12 368 F3
Milford on S SO41 399 F4
Solihull Ho PO5 404 A2
Solly Cl BH12 391 E7
Solomons La SO32 271 F2
Solomon Way BH15 389 D2
Solona Cl SO53 243 F7
Solway Ho 10 SO14 291 C6
Somborne Ct 27
SO17 267 A1
Somborne Dr PO9 323 F5
Somborne Ho SO19 291 F1
Somborne Park Rd
SO20 172 D7
Somerby Rd BH15 390 D6
Somerford Ave
BH23 396 B8
Somerford Bsns Pk
BH23 396 A7
Somerford Cl SO19 292 A6
Somerford Ct BH23 396 E7
Somerford Prim Com
Sch BH23 395 E7
Somerford Rd BH23 395 F7
Somerford Rdbt
BH23 396 A8
Somerford Way
BH23 395 E6
Somerley Rd BH9 393 A8
Somerley View 1
BH24 329 A8
Somers Ct SO22 403 B3
Somerset Ave
Bordon GU35 164 D3
Southampton SO18 292 C7
Somerset Cres SO53 243 D3
Somerset Ct
12 Farnborough
GU14 56 A1
6 Southampton
SO15 290 C6
Somerset Ho
Basingstoke RG24 68 D8
Waterlooville PO7 299 C1
Somerset Rd
Bournemouth BH7 394 A5
Christchurch BH23 394 E8
Farnborough GU14 56 A1
Portsmouth PO5 370 D1
Southampton SO17 267 C2
Somerset Terr SO15 290 C6
Somers Park Prim Sch
PO5 404 C3
Somers Rd
Portsmouth PO5 404 C2
Portsmouth PO5 404 C3
Somers Rd N PO1 404 D3
Somerstown Flats
PO9 324 A1
Somerton Ave SO18 292 B7
Somerton Cl BH25 383 D3
Somervell Cl PO12 369 A3
Somervell Dr PO16 319 A3
Somerville Cres GU46 34 C6
Somerville Ct
Andover SP10 83 D1
New Milton BH25 382 F3
Somerville Pl 1
PO2 345 C2
Somerville Rd
Bournemouth BH2 392 D3
Kings Worthy SO23 176 C8
Ringwood BH24 329 C8
Somme Rd SP11 79 D7
Sommers Ct SO19 291 C3
Sonata Ho PO6 345 A7
Sonnet Way PO7 323 B8
Sonning Cl RG22 90 F7
Sonninge Cl GU47 35 B8
Sonning Way BH8 378 B2
Soper Gr RG21 69 B6
Sopers La
Christchurch BH23 395 A6
Poole BH17 375 B1
Sopley Cl BH25 397 D8
Sopley Common Nature
Reserve★ BH23 379 C8
Sopley Ct 16 PO9 324 B6
Sopley Farm Bldgs
BH23 380 B6
Sopley Prim Sch
BH23 356 C1
Sopwith Cl
Christchurch BH23 396 B6
King's Somborne
SO20 172 A2
Sopwith Cres BH21 351 E2
Sopwith Pk SP10 82 B1
Sopwith Rd SO50 243 F3
Sopwith Way SO31 316 F8
Sorrel Cl
2 Farnborough
GU14 55 A5
Newbury RG14 2 B5
Romsey SO51 216 C1
Waterlooville PO7 323 A6
Sorrel Dr PO15 317 D7
Sorrel Gdns BH18 374 F2
Sorrell Cl SO31 316 F2
Sorrell Ct BH23 396 B8
Sorrell's Cl RG24 48 F3
Sorrell Way BH23 396 B8
Sotherington La GU33,
GU34 185 C6
Southampton Airport
(Parkway) Sta
SO18 267 F6
Southampton Central Sta
SO15 290 E5
Southampton City Coll
SO14 291 B4
Southampton Cl
GU17 35 A6
Southampton Gen Hospl
SO16 266 B2
Southampton Hill
PO14 317 F1
Southampton Ho 6
PO9 324 A5
Southampton
International Airport
SO18 267 F6
Southampton Maritime
Mus★ SO14 290 F3
Southampton
Oceanography Ctr
SO14 291 B2
Southampton Rd
Bartley SO40 287 B7
Brockenhurst SO42,
SO41 361 A4
Cadnam SO40 286 E8
Southampton Rd *continued*
Eastleigh SO50 244 B1
Fareham PO16 319 B2
Fordingbridge SP6 258 B1
Hythe SO45 313 F4
Locks Heath PO15 317 C5
Locks Heath SO31 317 C4
Lymington SO41 385 D5
Lyndhurst SO43 310 B6
Portsmouth PO6 345 D8
Ringwood BH24 329 B8
Romsey SO51 241 A6
Titchfield PO14 317 D3
Southampton Solent
Univ SO14 291 A5
Southampton Solent
Univ Marine
Operations Ctr
SO40 290 A2
Southampton St
3 Southampton
SO15 290 F6
Farnborough GU14 76 F8
South Atlantic Dr
GU11 77 A3
South Ave
Farnham GU9 99 B6
Fawley SO45 338 E3
Holbury SO45 338 C5
New Milton BH25 383 B2
Portsmouth PO2 345 E4
South Baddesey Rd
SO41 386 B4
South Baddesley CE Prim
Sch SO41 386 E6
South Bay PO10 349 A3
Southbourne Ave
Cosham PO6 346 B7
Emsworth PO10 349 B8
Holbury SO45 338 C4
Southbourne Coast Rd
BH6 394 F3
Southbourne Cross
Roads 5 BH6 394 E3
Southbourne Gr
BH6 394 C4
Southbourne Jun & Inf
Schs PO10 349 E8
Southbourne Lane
Central 6 BH6 394 C4
Southbourne Lane E 5
BH6 394 C4
Southbourne Lane W
BH6 394 B4
Southbourne Overcliff Dr
BH6 394 D3
Southbourne Rd
Bournemouth BH6 394 C4
Lymington SO41 385 C3
Southbourne Sands
BH6 394 D3
Southbourne Sta
PO10 349 E8
Southbrook Cl
Langstone PO9 347 F8
Poole BH17 376 A2
Southbrook Cotts
SO21 133 B3
Southbrook Mews 5
SO32 271 C8
Southbrook Pl SO21 133 A3
Southbrook Rd
5 Southampton
SO15 290 E5
Langstone PO9 347 F8
Southby Dr GU51 54 B1
South Cl
Gosport PO12 368 F2
Havant PO9 348 A8
New Alresford SO24 179 B5
Romsey SO51 216 C1
Southcliff PO13 367 E4
Southcliffe Ho 1
SO14 291 A6
Southcliffe Rd
Barton on S BH25 397 D7
Christchurch BH23 396 C6
Southcliff Rd SO14 291 A7
South Cliff Rd BH2 392 F2
Southcote Dr GU15 36 E5
Southcote Rd BH1 393 C4
Southcroft Rd PO12 368 F5
South Cross St
PO12 369 D5
South Ct
Hamble-le-R SO31 315 E2
Milford on S SO41 399 E4
Southdale Ct SO53 243 C6
Southdene Rd SO53 243 C5
Southdown Ct 1
BH23 395 F8
Southdown Rd
Compton SO21 219 D5
Cosham PO6 346 A8
Horndean PO8 276 B2
Horndean PO8 276 C3
Tadley RG26 26 E8
Thatcham RG19 2 D4
Southdowns SO24 157 E1
South Downs Coll
PO7 323 A3
Southdown View
PO7 299 C2
Southdown Way
BH22 326 F1
South Dr
Awbridge SO51 215 B3
Littleton SO22 175 B4
South Dr *continued*
Sherfield on L RG27 49 D7
South Tidworth SP9 78 E4
West Moors BH24 354 B7
South East Cres
SO19 292 A4
South East Rd SO19 292 A4
South End Cl SO21 218 B7
Southend La SO32 297 D8
Southend Rd RG21 69 A5
South End Rd SP10 106 B6
Southern Ave BH22 327 A1
Southern Gdns SO40 288 E7
Southernhay PO7 298 F4
Southern Haye RG27 52 C5
Southernhay Rd
BH31 303 B6
Southern La
Barton on S BH25 397 F8
Old Milton BH25 382 F1
Southern Oaks BH25 382 F1
Southern Rd
Basingstoke RG21 69 B4
Bordon GU35 164 D5
Bournemouth BH6 394 C4
Camberley GU15 36 A6
Fawley SO45 339 F1
Lymington SO41 385 D3
Southampton SO15 290 E4
West End SO30 268 E1
Southern Way
Farnborough GU14 55 C3
Farnham GU9 99 A1
Southey Rd BH23 395 F7
South Farnborough Inf
Sch GU14 77 B8
South Farnborough Jun
Sch GU14 56 B2
South Farnham Com Jun
Sch GU9 99 B1
Southfield BH24 329 A6
Southfield La BH24 331 D2
Southfield Mews 6
BH24 329 A6
Southfields Cl SO32 271 C8
Southfield Wlk PO9 323 C7
South Front
9 Romsey SO51 240 F7
Southampton SO14 291 A4
Southgate St SO23 403 D5
Southgate Villas
SO23 403 D5
South Gr
Fleet GU51 54 C4
Lymington SO41 385 F3
South Hampshire Ind Pk
SO40 264 D2
South Ham Rd RG22 68 E4
South Haven Cl
BH16 389 B3
South Hill
Alderholt SP6 281 A6
Droxford SO32 273 A8
Southampton SO16 267 A4
Upton Grey RG25 94 C5
South Hurst GU35 164 D1
Southill Ave BH12 391 C6
Southill Gdns BH9 378 A1
Southill Rd
Bournemouth BH9 378 A1
Poole BH12 391 D7
Southington Cl RG25 87 F7
Southington La RG25 87 F8
South Kinson Dr
BH11 377 B4
South La
Ash GU12 77 F1
Breach PO10 325 E2
Buriton GU31 253 D4
Clanfield PO8 276 B6
Downton SP5 234 E7
Horndean PO8 277 B3
Nomansland SP5 261 C7
Woodmancote PO10 325 D3
Southlands
Chineham RG24 48 E3
Cosham PO6 346 A8
Lymington SO41 385 C2
Southlands Ave
Bournemouth BH6 394 F4
Corfe Mullen BH21 374 D6
Southlands Cl
Ash GU12 77 E1
Corfe Mullen BH21 374 D6
Southlands Ct BH18 375 A3
Southlands Rd GU12 77 E1
Southlands Sch & The
Wing Ctr SO41 385 F7
Southlawns Wlk
BH25 382 F1
Southlea RG25 92 A8
Southlea Ave BH6 394 F4
Southleigh Gr PO11 372 F4
Southleigh Rd
Emsworth PO10 324 F3
Havant PO9 324 C3
South Lodge
Fareham PO15 318 B1
Poole BH13 402 G7
Southmead Rd
Aldershot GU11 99 F8
Fareham PO15 318 E1
South Millers Dale
SO53 243 B7
South Mill Rd SO15 290 A7
Southmoor La PO9 347 D7
South Normandy 4
PO1 370 A4
South Par
5 Totton SO40 288 F7
Portsmouth PO5 370 D1
South Parade Pier★
PO4 370 E1
South Park Rd BH12 392 A8
South Pl PO13 368 A4
South Rd
Ash Vale GU12 77 E4
Bournemouth BH1 393 E5
Broughton SO20 170 C5
Corfe Mullen BH21 374 E6
Cosham PO6 346 C7
Horndean PO8 276 C1
Kingsclere RG20 24 E2
Liphook GU30 188 B1
New Alresford SO24 179 B5
Poole BH15 390 C2
Portsmouth,Paulsgrove
PO6 321 A2
Portsmouth,Portsea Island
PO1 370 E7
Southampton SO17 291 C8
South Hayling PO11 372 F3
Southwick PO17 321 A6
South Ridge RG29 72 E2
South Road Comb Sch
BH15 390 C2
Southrope Gn RG25 116 C7
Southsea Castle★
PO5 370 C1
Southsea Cvn Pk
PO4 371 D2
Southsea Inf Sch
PO5 370 E2
Southsea Terr PO5 404 A1
South Side GU10 100 D7
South Side Cotts
SO20 149 E4
Southside Rd SP11 108 B4
South Spur PO6 321 B2
South Sq 9 PO17 318 E7
South St
Andover SP10 106 A7
Eastleigh SO50 268 A8
Emsworth PO10 348 F8
Farnborough GU14 56 C1
Farnham GU9 99 A2
Gosport PO12 369 D5
Havant PO9 323 F1
Hythe SO45 314 A4
Lymington SO41 385 C2
Portsmouth PO5 404 A1
Ropley SO24 181 C4
Titchfield PO14 341 F8
South Stoneham Ho
SO18 267 D3
South Sway La SO41 384 D7
South Terr PO1 370 A5
South Town Rd
GU34 159 F6
South Trestle Rd
SO45 339 D5
Southview
4 Portsmouth PO4 370 F2
Droxford SO32 249 B1
South View
Bournemouth BH2 392 F5
Waterlooville PO8 300 A3
Winchester SO22 403 C6
South View Cl SO21 131 D3
Southview Cotts
GU10 122 B1
South View Cotts
Bentley GU10 120 A4
Hook RG27 72 A8
South View Gdns
4 Newbury RG14 1 F4
Andover SP10 106 B7
South View Inf Sch
RG21 69 C7
South View Jun Sch
RG21 69 C7
South View Park Homes
SO22 403 A1
South View Pl 10
BH2 392 E3
Southview Rd GU35 165 F5
South View Rd
Christchurch BH23 395 A6
Southampton SO15 290 D8
Winchester SO22 197 B4
Southview Rise
GU34 139 E5
South View Terr SP11 85 B8
Southville Rd BH5 394 B5
Southwark Cl
North Tidworth SP9 79 A6
Yateley GU46 34 A6
Southwater PO13 367 E3
Southway
Camberley GU15 35 F4
Gosport PO13 343 C3
Titchfield PO15 317 E3
South Way SP10 83 E1
Southways PO14 367 D7
South Weirs SO42 360 D8
Southwell Park Rd
GU15 36 A5
South Western Cres
BH14 391 B2
Southwick Ave PO16 320 E1
Southwick Cl SO22 175 D4
Southwick Ct PO14 343 A6
Southwick Hill Rd
PO6 321 E1
Southwick Ho 5
PO1 404 C4
Southwick Pl BH6 394 C7
Southwick Rd
Bournemouth BH6 394 C6
Denmead PO7 298 E4
Portsmouth PO6 321 C2
Wickham PO17 296 C3
South Wlk GU12 77 B2
South Wonston Prim Sch
SO21 153 D4
Southwood Ave
Bournemouth BH6 394 C4
Walkford BH23 382 B1
Southwood Cl
Ferndown BH22 353 C6
Walkford BH23 382 A1
Southwood Cres
GU14 55 B4
South Wood Gdns
SO31 316 F3
Southwood Inf Sch
GU14 55 B3
Southwood La
Farnborough GU51 54 E3
Farnborough,Southwood
GU14 55 B3
Southwood Rd
Farnborough GU14 55 C4
Hawley GU17 34 D1
Portsmouth PO2 345 E4
Shalden GU34 139 B7
South Hayling PO11 373 D1
Sovereign Ave PO12 369 C8
Sovereign Bsns Ctr
BH15 390 B6
Sovereign Cl
Bournemouth BH7 393 F8
Portsmouth PO4 371 C5
Totton SO40 288 C8
Sovereign Cres
PO14 317 A1
Sovereign Ct
13 Southampton
SO17 267 A1
4 Eastleigh SO50 244 A2
8 Fleet GU51 53 F1
Sovereign Ctr 6
BH1 393 E4
Sovereign Dr
Camberley GU15 36 F7
Hedge End SO30 293 E6
Portsmouth PO4 371 C5
Sovereign La PO7 322 E3
Sovereign Pl BH24 328 F7
Sovereign Way SO50 243 F6
Sowcroft La RG29 118 A5
Sowden Cl SO30 293 B7
Sowley La SO41 387 D5
Spain Bldgs GU32 228 E3
Spain La GU34 115 E3
Spain The GU32 228 E3
Spalding Rd SO19 292 E5
Spa Meadow Cl RG19 6 A8
Spaniard's La SO51 241 A3
Sparkford Cl
Bournemouth BH7 394 B8
Winchester SO22 403 C4
Sparkford Rd SO22 403 C5
Sparrow Cl PO8 299 F4
Sparrow Ct PO13 367 F4
Sparrowgrove SO21 219 D4
Sparrowhawk Cl
Ewshot GU10 98 B8
Portsmouth PO3 346 A4
Sparrow Sq SO50 243 D2
Sparsholt CE Prim Sch
SO21 174 D3
Sparsholt Cl PO9 323 B5
Sparsholt Coll
Hampshire SO21 174 A4
Sparsholt Rd
Southampton SO19 314 F8
Winchester SO21,
SO22 196 C3
Spartan Cl
Stubbington PO14 342 C5
Thorney Island PO10 349 A3
Spartina Dr SO41 385 E5
Sparvells RG27 33 C8
Sparvell Way GU15 36 A6
Spats La GU35 165 D8
Spear Rd SO14 291 A8
Spearywell Wood
Woodland Walk★
SO51 192 C4
Speckled Wood Rd
RG24 48 B1
Specks La PO4 371 A5
Speedfield Pk PO14 343 A5
Speedwell Cl
Chandler's Ford
SO53 243 B5
Locks Heath SO31 316 F2
Speedwell Dr BH23 396 B8
Speenhamland Ct 3
RG14 1 E4
Speenhamland Prim Sch
RG14 1 D4
Speen Hill Cl RG14 1 C4
Speen La RG14 1 B4
Speen Lodge Ct RG14 1 C4
Speen Pl RG14 1 C4
Speggs Wlk 2 SO30 293 C6
Speltham Hill PO7 274 D2
Spencer Cl
Camberley GU16 56 C6

Spencer Cl continued
Fleet GU52 . . . . 75 C5
Four Marks GU34 . . . 160 B3
Pamber Heath RG26 . . 10 C1
South Hayling PO11. . 373 A3
Spencer Ct
1 New Milton
BH25 . . . . 383 B2
2 Portsmouth PO5. . 370 D2
Stubbington PO14 . . . 367 E7
Spencer Dr PO13 . . . 367 F2
Spencer Gdns PO8 . . 299 E3
Spencer Rd
Bournemouth BH1 . . . 393 C4
Eastleigh SO50 . . . . . 243 E2
Emsworth PO10 . . . . 324 E4
Newbury RG14 . . . . 5 B6
New Milton BH25 . . . 383 B2
Poole BH13 . . . . 402 F8
Portsmouth PO4 . . . . 370 F2
Southampton SO19 . . 292 D6
Spencers Ct GU35. . . 164 D1
Spenlow Cl PO2 . . . . 370 D8
Spenser Cl
Alton GU34 . . . . 140 A3
Warsash SO31. . . . . 340 D10
Sperrin Cl RG22. . . . . .68 B3
Spetisbury Cl BH9 . . 378 B3
Spey Cl **31** SP10. . . . . 83 C2
Spice Quay **1** PO1. . 370 A3
Spicer Ho PO1. . . . . . 370 B6
Spicer La BH11 . . . . . 376 E5
Spicers GU34 . . . . . . 140 A3
Spicers Ct **2** SO22. . 403 D6
Spicer's Hill SO40. . . 288 F5
Spicer St PO1. . . . . . 404 B4
Spicer's Way SO40. . 288 E6
Spicewood PO15 . . . . 318 E2
Spiers Cl RG26. . . . . . . 27 A8
Spiers La SO24 . . . . . 135 C3
Spinacre BH25. . . . . . 398 B8
Spindle Cl
Broadstone BH18 . . . 374 F2
Havant PO9 . . . . 324 C3
Spindle Ho **1** SP10 . 106 B8
Spindle Warren PO9 324 C3
Spindlewood RG24. . . .48 E4
Spindlewood Cl
10 Old Milton BH25. . 383 A1
Southampton SO16 . . 267 A6
Spindlewood Way
SO40 . . . . 312 F8
Spinnaker Cl
Gosport PO13 . . . . . . 368 D7
South Hayling PO11. . 372 A4
Spinnaker Ct
21 Portsmouth
PO1 . . . . 370 A5
Netley SO31. . . . . . . 315 B6
Spinnaker Dr PO2. . . 345 D4
Spinnaker Grange
PO11 . . . . 348 C4
Spinnaker Ho PO6 . . 345 A7
Spinnaker Pl **6**
PO10 . . . . 349 A8
Spinnaker Quay PO1 369 F4
Spinnakers The
PO13 . . . . 367 E2
Spinnaker Twr *
PO1. . . . . 369 F5
Spinnaker View PO9 323 A1
Spinners Cl BH22 . . . 326 E1
Spinners Garden *
SO41 . . . . 361 E1
Spinney Cl
St Leonards BH24 . . . 327 D4
Waterlooville PO8 . . . 299 E3
Spinney Cvn Pk The
SO24 . . . . 179 C6
Spinney Dale SO45 . . 314 B2
Spinney Gdns SO45 . . 314 B2
Spinneys La BH22. . . 353 D5
Spinney The
8 Eastleigh SO50. . . 244 A2
Bramdean SO24 . . . . 202 C5
Compton SO21 . . . . . 219 C4
Denmead PO7 . . . . . 298 F3
Fair Oak SO50 . . . . . 245 A4
Finchampstead RG40. . 16 D8
Fleet GU51 . . . . .74 D8
Gosport PO13 . . . . . 343 D1
Grayshott GU26. . . . 166 E4
Hook RG27. . . . . .51 A2
Portchester PO16 . . . 319 F1
Southampton SO16 . . 267 A6
St Leonards BH24 . . . 327 F6
Totton SO40. . . . . . . 264 C1
Waterlooville PO8 . . . 300 A6
Yateley GU46. . . . . . . .34 A7
Spinney Way BH25. . 383 B6
Spinney Wlk SO18 . . 267 F3
Spinningfield Ho **1**
GU32. . . . . 220 A1
Spitalfields Rd GU34 139 F4
Spitalhatch GU34 . . . 140 B4
Spitfire Cl SO31. . . . . 291 D3
Spitfire End **2** SO23 198 D8
Spitfire La SO20 . . . . 148 F3
Spitfire Quay SO19 . . 291 C4
Spitfire Way
Farnborough GU14 . . .76 C7
Hamble-le-R SO31. . . 315 C4
Spithead Ave PO12 . . 369 C2
Spithead Ho PO16. . . 343 A7
Spithead Hts PO4 . . . 371 D3

Spittlefields BH24. . . 329 B7
Spoil La GU10 . . . . . . 100 D7
Spokane Cl GU11 . . . . . 99 D8
Sportsman Pl SO30 . . 268 E1
Sportsmans Ct **9**
GU11 . . . . .76 F2
Spouts La SO51. . . . . 238 D6
Sprat's Hatch La RG27 73 E7
Spray Leaze SP11. . . . .57 B2
Spreadbury Dr GU51. . .53 F3
Sprents La RG25 . . . . . .88 B7
Springbank Rd BH7 . . 393 F8
Springbourne Ct
BH1. . . . . 393 D5
Springbourne Mews
BH1. . . . . 393 C5
Spring Cl
Fair Oak SO50 . . . . . 245 C2
Sherborne St John
RG24 . . . . .47 D3
Sherborne St John
RG24 . . . . .47 E4
Southampton SO19 . . 291 F4
Verwood BH31. . . . . 302 F5
Spring Cres SO17 . . . 291 B8
Springcroft PO13 . . . 343 B5
Springcross Ave
GU17 . . . . .35 B4
Spring Ct
1 Southampton
SO15. . . . . 290 E5
Poole BH12 . . . . 391 D5
Springdale Ave
BH18 . . . . 374 F5
Springdale Ct **3**
SO40 . . . . 288 F7
Springdale Fst Sch
BH18. . . . . 374 E4
Springdale Gr BH21. 374 E4
Springdale Rd BH18,
BH21 . . . . 374 E4
Springfarm Rd GU27 189 C5
Springfield
2 Liss GU33 . . . . . 207 F4
Oakley RG23 . . . . . . .67 C2
Springfield Ave
Bournemouth BH6. . . 395 A4
Christchurch BH23 . . 379 D2
Hartley Wintney RG27. 52 C7
Holbury SO45 . . . . . 338 D3
Springfield Cl
Andover SP10 . . . . . 106 D8
Havant PO9 . . . . 323 B2
Lymington SO41 . . . 386 A3
Verwood BH31. . . . . 302 F5
Wickham PO17 . . . . 296 A4
Springfield Cres
Poole BH14 . . . . 391 B4
Redlynch SP5. . . . . . 235 D5
Springfield Ct SO19. . 291 F2
Springfield Dr SO40. . 288 E6
Springfield Gdns
BH25 . . . . 383 D2
Springfield Gr SO45. 338 C4
Springfield La
Fleet GU51 . . . . .53 E1
Newbury RG14 . . . . 5 F8
Springfield Rd
Ash Vale GU12. . . . . . .77 E5
Frimley GU15. . . . . . . .36 F5
Pamber Heath RG26 . . 10 C1
Poole BH14 . . . . 391 A4
Verwood BH31. . . . . 302 F5
Springfield Sch PO6 346 C7
Springfields Cl **3**
SO21 . . . . 219 F1
Springfield Way
PO14 . . . . 367 C6
Spring Firs SO19. . . . 291 E3
Springford Cl SO16 . . 266 B4
Springford Cres
SO16 . . . . 266 B3
Springford Gdns
SO16 . . . . 266 B4
Springford Rd SO16. 266 B4
Spring Garden La
PO12 . . . . 369 C6
Spring Gdns
2 Emsworth PO10. . 349 A8
Enborne Row RG20 . . . . 4 F3
Farnborough GU14 . . .55 E7
Frimley GU15. . . . . . . .36 F5
New Alresford SO24 . 179 C4
North Baddesley
SO52. . . . . 242 A4
Poole BH14 . . . . 391 D5
Portsmouth PO1 . . . . 404 A3
Spring Gr SO31 . . . . . 293 A1
Spring Hill La SP11 . . .62 A1
Springhill RC Prim Sch
SO15. . . . . 290 E6
Springhill Rd SO53. . 243 D6
Spring Hills SO19 . . . 292 D4
Spring Ho **9** RG21. . . .69 A4
Springholm Cl GU9 . . .99 F6
Spring House Cl
SO21 . . . . 220 A1
Spring La
Aldermaston RG7 . . . .10 A6
Bishopstoke SO50. . . 244 D3
Burghclere RG20. . . . .22 D5
Colden Common SO21 219 F1
Farnham GU9 . . . . . . .98 E7
Mortimer RG7 . . . . . . 11 E6
New Milton BH25 . . . 383 D2
Swallowfield RG7 . . . .13 F5

Spring La continued
Swallowfield,Stanford End
RG7 . . . . .13 E4
Swanmore SO32 . . . . 272 B5
Springlakes Est GU12 77 C3
Spring La W GU9. . . . . .98 E6
Spring Leaze SP11 . . . .61 C4
Springles La PO15 . . . 318 A5
Springmead Ct
GU27 . . . . 189 B5
Spring Mews SP10 . . . .83 B1
Spring Pl **2** SO51. . . 240 E7
Spring Rd
Bournemouth BH1. . . 393 D5
Hythe SO45 . . . . 314 A4
Lymington SO41 . . . 386 A2
Sarisbury SO31. . . . . 316 F6
Southampton,Itchen
SO19. . . . . 291 F4
Southampton,Merry Oak
SO19. . . . . 291 F6
Southampton SO19 . . 292 A5
Spring St PO1 . . . . . . 404 B3
Springs The RG7. . . . . .29 B8
Spring The PO7. . . . . 298 F3
Spring Vale
Swanmore SO32 . . . . 272 A4
Waterlooville PO8 . . . 300 B4
Springvale Ave
Bournemouth BH7. . . 393 F8
Kings Worthy SO23 . . 176 B6
Springvale Rd SO23 . 176 B7
Springwater Cl
BH11 . . . . 377 A3
Springwater Ct
BH23 . . . . 395 D6
Springwater Dr
BH23 . . . . 395 D6
Springwater Rd
BH11 . . . . 377 A3
Spring Way SO24 . . . 291 E3
Springwell **3** PO9 . . 323 F1
Springwell La RG27 . . .52 E8
Spring Wlk PO1. . . . . 404 B4
Springwood Ave
PO7 . . . . 322 F6
Spring Woods GU52. . .74 F7
Spruce Ave
Bordon GU35. . . . . . 164 B3
Waterlooville PO7 . . . 323 A6
Spruce Cl
Andover SP10 . . . . . 105 C7
Broadstone BH17 . . . 374 E2
South Wonston SO21 153 E4
Warsash SO31. . . . . 340 D10
Spruce Dr
Southampton SO19 . . 292 E5
Totton SO40. . . . . . . 288 B8
Spruce Way GU51. . . . .54 D1
Spruce Wlk **8** PO13. 367 F3
Spur Cl BH21 . . . . 352 C6
Spur La SO32 . . . . . . 246 F4
Stake's La SO32. . . . . 247 E8
Stakes Rd PO7. . . . . . 322 D4
Stalbridge Dr PO17 . . 319 D3
Stalbridge Rd BH17 . 390 A7
Stalham Rd BH12 . . . 391 F6
Stallard Cl PO10 . . . . 324 E1
Stallards La BH24 . . . 328 F7
Stalybridge Cl SO31. 317 A6
Stamford Ave
Frimley GU16. . . . . . . .36 D7
South Hayling PO11. . 372 E3
Stamford Lodge
PO11 . . . . 372 E3
Stamford Rd BH6 . . . 394 D5
Stamford St PO1 . . . 404 D4
Stamford Way SO50. 245 C4
Stampsey Ct **5** PO2. 345 C2
Stamshaw Ct **2**
PO2. . . . . 345 D1
Stamshaw Inf Sch
PO2. . . . . 345 D2
Stamshaw Rd PO2 . . 345 D1
Stanbridge Earls Sch
SO51. . . . . 215 B3
Stanbridge La SO51. . 215 B3
Stanbridge Rd PO9. . 324 B3
Stanbury Cl SP11 . . . 103 E8
Stanbury Rd SP11. . . . .80 D1
Stancomb Broad La
GU34 . . . . 159 C2
Stancombe La
Medstead GU34. . . . . 159 D3
Shalden GU34 . . . . . 117 D1
Standard Way PO16 . 319 D3
Standen Rd SO16 . . . 265 C5
Standford Hill GU35 . 165 A1
Standford La GU35. . 165 A3
Standford St SO41. . . 385 D2
Standing Hill SP5. . . . 190 F8
Stanfield RG26. . . . . . . .9 F1
Stanfield Cl BH12. . . 391 D7
Stanfield Rd
Bournemouth BH9. . . 392 E8
Ferndown BH22. . . . . 353 C6
Poole BH14 . . . . 391 D7
Stanford Cl PO6 . . . . 345 D8
Stanford Ct
23 Havant PO9 . . . . 324 B5
Southampton SO19 . . 292 D3
Stanford Gdns SO41. 385 D2
Stanford Hill SO41. . 385 D3
Stanford Rd
Basingstoke RG22. . . .91 C8
Lymington SO41 . . . 385 D2

Squirrel La GU14. . . . . .55 E5
Squirrel's Cl BH23 . . 379 D2
Squirrels Wlk SO45 . 313 F2
Squirrel Wlk BH31 . . 302 F5
Sqush Court Gate Rd
GU14. . . . . .55 F1
Stable Cl
Hook RG27. . . . . .50 F1
Titchfield PO14 . . . . 317 D2
Stable Cotts SO43. . . 262 A3
Stable Ct RG14. . . . . . . .1 E6
Stable La **8** GU31. . . 228 F3
Stable Rd GU35 . . . . 164 D6
Stables Rd SP9 . . . . . . .78 E4
Stables The
Bramley RG26 . . . . . . .28 F2
Christchurch BH23 . . 394 F7
Locks Heath SO31 . . . 317 A2
Stable View GU46. . . . .34 B7
Stacey Cl BH12 . . . . 391 C7
Stacey Ct
Havant PO9 . . . . 323 D7
Portsmouth PO5 . . . . 370 C1
Stacey Gdns BH8 . . . 378 F2
Staddlestones Cotts
SP11 . . . . .82 A4
Stadium Way BH15. . 390 C3
Staff Coll GU15 . . . . . .36 A6
Staff College Rd
GU15. . . . . .35 F6
Stafford Rd
Bournemouth BH1. . . 393 A4
Petersfield GU32. . . . 228 F5
Portsmouth PO5 . . . . 404 C1
Southampton SO15 . . 290 D6
Staff Rd
Aldershot GU12. . . . . .77 A2
Michelmersh SO51 . . 193 B1
Staffwise Bsns Ctr
PO6. . . . . 345 F7
Stagbrake Cl SO45 . . 338 B3
Stag Bsns Pk BH24. . 329 A5
Stag Cl
Bishopstoke SO50. . . 244 F2
New Milton BH25 . . . 382 E4
Stag Dr SO30 . . . . . . 293 D8
Stag Gates SO45 . . . 338 E1
Stag Hill RG22 . . . . . . .68 D2
Stag Oak La RG24. . . . .48 E4
Stagshorn Rd PO8 . . 300 C2
Stags La SO21 . . . . . 221 A5
Stagswood BH31. . . . 302 D6
Stag Way PO15 . . . . 318 D5
Stainer Cl SO19. . . . . 292 D3
Stainers La SO21. . . . 153 C4
Staith Cl SO19 . . . . . 292 C5
Stake La GU14 . . . . . . .55 F2
Stakes Hill Inf Sch
PO7. . . . . 322 F6
Stakes Hill Rd PO7. . 322 F6
Stakes La SO32 . . . . 246 F4

Squirrel Dr
Basingstoke RG23. . . . .90 F3
Southampton SO19 . . 292 A3

Stanhope Gate **1**
PO5 . . . . 370 C2
Stanhope Rd
Camberley GU15 . . . . .35 D4
Portsmouth PO1 . . . . 404 B3
Stanier Way SO30 . . 269 C2
Staniforth Ct BH23 . . 395 D6
Stanley Ave PO3 . . . . 371 B8
Stanley Cl
Bishopstone SP5 . . . . 210 B8
Fareham PO15. . . . . . 318 E2
Gosport PO12 . . . . . 344 A1
Verwood BH31. . . . . 303 A5
Stanley Ct
Bournemouth BH1. . . 393 C5
Poole BH15 . . . . 390 C6
Stanley Dr GU14 . . . . .55 A3
Stanley Green Cres
BH15 . . . . 390 C5
Stanley Green Fst Sch
BH15. . . . . 390 C6
Stanley Green Ind Est
BH15. . . . . 390 B5
Stanley Green Rd
Poole BH15 . . . . 390 C5
Poole BH15 . . . . 390 C6
Stanley La PO5 . . . . . 370 C2
Stanley Pearce Ho
BH17 . . . . 375 C1
Stanley Pk (Cvn & Chalet
Site) BH25 . . . . . . 383 C6
Stanley Rd
Bournemouth BH1. . . 393 C5
Christchurch BH23 . . 397 A8
Emsworth PO10. . . . . 349 A8
Holbury SO45 . . . . . 338 D4
Lymington SO41 . . . 386 A2
Newbury RG14 . . . . . . .1 F2
Poole BH15 . . . . 390 C1
Portsmouth PO2 . . . . 345 C1
Southampton SO17 . . 267 C1
Totton SO40. . . . . . . 264 D1
Stanley St PO5 . . . . . 370 C2
Stanmore Gdns RG7 . . 11 D5
Stanmore La SO22 . . 403 B3
Stanmore Prim Sch
SO22. . . . . 403 C3
Stannington Cl BH25 383 B2
Stannington Cres
SO40 . . . . 288 F8
Stannington Way
SO40 . . . . 288 F8
Stanpit BH23 . . . . . . 395 E5
Stanstead Rd SO50. . 243 F4
Stansted Cl PO9 . . . . 301 C1
Stansted Cres PO9 . . 324 B6
Stansted Ct PO9 . . . . 301 C2
Stansted Rd PO5. . . . 404 D2
Stanswood Rd
Blackfield SO45 . . . . 366 C6
Havant PO9 . . . . 323 D6
Stanton Bldgs SO15. 290 A7
Stanton Dr GU51. . . . . .74 E8
Stanton Lacy **12**
BH13 . . . . 402 F7
Stanton Rd
Bournemouth BH10. . 377 C2
Petersfield GU32. . . . 228 E4
Southampton SO15 . . 290 A7
Stanton Rd Ind Est
SO15. . . . . 290 A7
Stapehill Cres BH21. 352 C5
Stapehill Mus & Gdns *
BH21. . . . . 352 E5
Stapehill Rd BH21. . . 352 F4
Staple Ash La GU32 . 227 C2
Staple Cl PO7. . . . . . . 299 D3
Staple Close La
BH15 . . . . 390 C6
Staple Cross
Burton BH23 . . . . . . 395 B3
Southwick PO17 . . . . 320 C8
Staplecross La BH23 395 D8
Stapleford Ave BH22 353 F6
Stapleford Cl SO51. . 216 B2
Stapleford Cl SO32 . 269 F5
Staple Gdns **31**
SO23 . . . . 403 D6
Staplehurst Cl SO19. 292 B1
Staplers Reach
PO13 . . . . 343 B2
Stapleton Cl RG14 . . . .5 A6
Stapleton Rd **6** PO3 371 A4
Staplewood La
Ashurst SO40 . . . . . . 312 C2
Marchwood SO40 . . . 289 C1
Stapley La SO24 . . . . 181 D2
Star Cotts PO17. . . . . 296 A4
Stares Cl PO13. . . . . . 368 C7
Star Hill
Churt GU10 . . . . 144 B2
Hartley Wintney RG27. 32 F1
Star Hill Cvn Site
RG27 . . . . .33 A1
Star Hill Dr GU10 . . . 144 B3
Starina Gdns PO7 . . . 323 B8
Star La
Ash GU12. . . . . .77 D2
Highclere RG20 . . . . . .21 D6
Ringwood BH24. . . . . 328 F7
Starlight Farm Cl
BH31 . . . . 303 A7
Starling Cl RG22 . . . . . .90 F8
Starling Sq SO50. . . . 243 D2
Star Post Rd GU15 . . . .36 B8
Starting Gates RG14. . . .2 A1
Statham Sq SP10 . . . . .83 C3

Station App
25 Portsmouth
PO1 . . . . 370 A5
Andover SP10 . . . . . 105 F8
Ash Vale GU12. . . . . . .77 E7
Blackwater GU17 . . . . .35 C4
Broadstone BH18 . . . 375 A4
Brockenhurst SO42. . 334 A1
Four Marks GU34 . . . 160 B3
Grateley SP11 . . . . . 124 F7
Haslemere GU27 . . . 187 F6
New Alresford SO24 . 179 D5
Overton RG25 . . . . . . .65 B2
Station Cl
Itchen Abbas SO21 . . 177 E6
Wickham PO17 . . . . 296 A4
Station Cotts SO42. . 311 D1
Station Hill
Botley SO30. . . . . . . 294 C7
Bursledon SO31. . . . 316 B8
Eastleigh SO50 . . . . 244 B3
Farnham GU9 . . . . . . .99 A2
Itchen Abbas SO21 . . 177 E6
Ropley SO24 . . . . . . 180 F5
Winchester SO23 . . . 403 D6
Station Ind Est GU51. 54 A3
Station La SO53. . . . . 243 C5
Station Mall **16** RG21. .69 C8
Station Rd
32 Winchester
SO23. . . . . 403 D6
Alderholt SP6 . . . . . . 280 F6
Aldershot GU11. . . . . . .76 F2
Alton GU34 . . . . 140 A4
Bentley GU10,GU34. . 120 B3
Bishop's Waltham
SO32. . . . . 271 C7
Bordon GU35. . . . . . 164 C5
Burley BH24 . . . . . . 358 D7
Bursledon SO31. . . . 316 B8
Camberley GU16 . . . . .56 A8
Chilbolton SO20. . . . 128 F3
Christchurch BH23 . . 395 A7
Christchurch,Highcliffe
BH23 . . . . 381 E2
Cliddesden RG25. . . . .92 B7
Cosham PO6 . . . . . . 346 C2
East Tisted GU34. . . . 183 C5
Enborne Row RG20 . . . . 4 E3
Farnborough GU14 . . .55 F4
Fordingbridge SP6. . . 257 D1
Frimley GU16. . . . . . . .36 A1
Gosport PO12 . . . . . 368 F7
Grateley SP11 . . . . . 125 A8
Hook RG27. . . . . .72 A8
Liphook GU30 . . . . . 188 A2
Liss GU33 . . . . 207 F4
Locks Heath SO31. . . 317 A5
Netley SO31. . . . . . . 315 B5
New Alresford SO24 . 179 D6
Newbury RG14 . . . . . . .1 E2
Newbury,Speen RG14 . . 1 B5
New Milton BH25 . . . 383 A4
Nursling SO16. . . . . . 265 A5
Oakley RG23 . . . . . . .66 F2
Overton RG25 . . . . . . .65 B1
Over Wallop SO20 . . 125 C1
Petersfield GU32. . . . 228 E4
Poole,Lower Hamworthy
BH15 . . . . 390 A1
Poole,Lower Parkstone
BH14 . . . . 391 B4
Portchester PO16 . . . 344 D8
Portsmouth PO3 . . . . 371 A8
Romsey SO51 . . . . . 240 E7
Soberton SO32 . . . . 273 C7
Southampton,Redbridge
SO15. . . . . 289 C8
Southampton,Sholing
SO19. . . . . 291 F3
South Hayling PO11. . 372 E4
South Tidworth SP9 . . .78 F5
Stratfield Mortimer
RG7 . . . . .12 C5
Sway SO41 . . . . 360 B1
Verwood BH31. . . . . 302 D7
West Meon GU32 . . . 225 C4
West Moors BH22 . . 326 D2
Whitchurch RG28 . . . .86 C6
Wickham PO17 . . . . 296 A4
Wimborne Minster
BH21 . . . . 351 D3
Winchfield RG27 . . . . .52 D2
Station Rd E GU12 . . . .77 E7
Station Rd N SO40 . . 289 A7
Station Rd S SO40. . . 289 A7
Station Rd W GU12. . . .77 D8
Station St
Lymington SO41 . . . 385 F4
Portsmouth PO1 . . . . 404 B3
Station Terr
Twyford SO21 . . . . . 219 E6
Wimborne Minster
BH21 . . . . 351 D4
Station View GU12 . . . .77 E8
Station Yd SP6 . . . . . 280 E6
Staunton Ave PO11. . 372 D3
Staunton Ctry Pk *
PO9. . . . . 324 A7
Staunton Ctry Pk Vistors
Ctr * PO9 . . . . 324 A6
Staunton Park Com Sch
PO9. . . . . 324 B7
Staunton Rd PO9 . . . 323 E2
Staunton St PO1 . . . . 404 B4
Stavedown Rd SO21. 153 C4
Stead Cl PO11 . . . . . . 373 B3

Stedman Rd BH5.... 394 B5
Steele Cl SO53..... 243 D4
Steeles Rd GU11.....76 F4
Steels Dro SP6..... 258 E7
Steels La SP6...... 256 C4
Steel St PO5...... 404 A1
Steep CE Prim Sch
GU32.......... 228 F7
Steep Rd
Portchester PO16 ... 320 C1
Southampton SO18 .. 292 C6
Steepdene BH14.... 391 B3
Steeple Cl BH17 ... 375 D3
Steeple Dr GU34 ... 139 F4
Steepleton Rd BH18. 375 C3
Steeple Way PO14 .. 317 D3
Steepways GU26.... 166 F6
Steerforth Cl PO2... 370 D8
Steinbeck Cl PO15.. 317 C8
Stein Rd PO10...... 325 D2
Stella Ct
  13 Christchurch
    BH23........ 397 B3
  Southampton SO16 .. 266 C4
Stem La BH25...... 382 E4
Stenbury Dr RG25... 136 B8
Stenbury Way SO31.. 315 C7
Stenhurst Rd BH15.. 390 C6
Stephen Cl PO8..... 300 E2
Stephendale Rd GU9 ..99 B4
Stephen Gould Ho
  GU14.........76 F8
Stephen Langton Dr
  BH11........ 376 D5
Stephen Lodge PO5. 404 B1
Stephen Martin Gdns
  SP6......... 257 E2
Stephen Rd PO15... 318 F1
Stephen's Cl RG7 ... 11 D6
Stephens Ct SO51... 240 E6
Stephens Firs RG7 .. 11 D6
Stephenson Cl
  Andover SP10...... 82 C1
  Gosport PO12..... 369 A3
Stephenson Ct
  Farnham GU9 .... 121 E8
  Newbury RG14......1 D4
Stephenson Way
  Arborfield Garrison
    RG2......... 15 E7
  Basingstoke RG21.... 68 E6
  Totton SO40...... 264 D2
Stephenson Way
  SO30......... 269 C3
Stephens Rd RG26 ... 27 A8
Stephen's Rd RG7.... 11 D6
Stephens Wlk BH24.. 328 F7
Steplake La SO51... 213 C1
Steplake Rd SO51... 238 D7
Stepnell Reach
  BH16......... 389 D5
Stepping Stones Sch
  GU26........ 167 D4
Step Terr SO22..... 403 C6
Sterling Gdns GU47 .. 35 C8
Sterling Pk SP10.... 82 C1
Sterte Ave BH15.... 390 B4
Sterte Avenue W
  BH15........ 390 B4
Sterte Cl BH15..... 390 C4
Sterte Ct BH15..... 390 C4
Sterte Espl BH15... 390 C3
Sterte Ind Est BH15. 390 B4
Sterte Rd BH15..... 390 C4
Steuart Rd SO18.... 291 D7
Stevens Dro SO30... 171 C5
Stevens Gn SP11.... 62 A1
Stevens Hill GU46... 34 C5
Stevenson Cres
  BH14........ 391 E3
Stevenson Rd BH6... 395 A4
Stevensons Cl 3
  BH21........ 351 C4
Steventon Rd
  North Waltham RG25.. 89 E2
  Southampton SO18 .. 292 C7
Stewards Rise GU10. 121 D7
Stewart Cl 5 BH8... 393 C5
Stewart Ho SO53.... 218 C1
Stewart Pl PO1..... 370 E4
Stewart Rd
  Basingstoke RG24.... 69 E8
  Bournemouth BH8... 393 B6
Stewarts Gn PO7.... 274 C3
Stewarts Way RG23... 357 E7
Stibbs Way BH23.... 357 C7
Stile Gdns GU27.... 189 D6
Stiles Dr SP10..... 106 D8
Stillions Cl GU34... 140 A3
Stillmore Rd BH11... 376 D3
Stillwater Pk BH24.. 305 C2
Stilwell Cl GU46.... 34 B4
Stinchar Dr SO53... 243 A5
Stinsford Cl BH9.... 378 B4
Stinsford Rd BH17... 375 D1
Stirling Ave PO7.... 322 F7
Stirling Bsns Pk
  BH21........ 352 F7
Stirling Cl
  Ash Vale GU12...... 77 D5
  Farnborough GU14 ... 55 E3
  Frimley GU16...... 36 C2
  New Milton BH25... 383 B3
  Totton SO40..... 265 A1
Stirling Cres
  Hedge End SO30.... 269 C1
  Totton SO40..... 289 A8

Stirling Ct
  11 New Milton
    BH25........ 383 B3
  3 Bournemouth BH4. 392 C2
  Fareham PO15..... 318 E3
Stirling Est RG14......1 F2
Stirling St PO2..... 370 D8
Stirling Way
  Christchurch BH23 .. 396 B6
  Farnborough GU11 ... 76 C7
Stirling Wlk SO51... 240 E7
Stirrup Cl
  Newbury RG14......5 F7
  Upton BH16...... 389 D7
Stoatley Hollow
  GU27......... 189 E8
Stoatley Rise GU27.. 189 E8
Stoborough Dr
  BH18........ 375 A2
Stockbridge Cl
  Chineham RG24..... 49 B4
  Havant PO9...... 324 B5
  Poole BH17...... 376 B2
Stockbridge Dr
  GU11......... 100 A6
Stockbridge Prim Sch
  SO20......... 149 F3
Stockbridge Rd
  Fleet GU51........ 53 D4
  Goodworth Clatford
    SP11........ 127 A5
  King's Somborne
    SO20........ 172 A3
  Michelmersh SO51 .. 215 C7
  Sutton Scotney SO21. 131 C4
  Winchester SO22 ... 403 B7
Stockbridge Way
  GU46......... 34 B4
Stocker Cl RG21..... 69 A2
Stocker Pl PO13.... 343 D1
Stockers Ave SO17.. 403 B7
Stockheath La PO9.. 323 E3
Stockheath Rd PO9.. 323 F4
Stockheath Way
  PO9......... 323 F4
Stockholm Dr SO30. 293 C5
Stock La SP5...... 237 D6
Stockley Cl SO45... 338 C3
Stock's Cross SO43. 261 F4
Stocks La GU34.... 204 B2
Stock's La SO32.... 249 E5
Stockton Ave GU51... 53 F2
Stockton Cl SO30... 293 C7
Stockton House Sch
  GU51......... 53 F2
Stockton Pk GU51.... 53 F2
Stockwell Pl SO21 .. 174 D3
Stockwood Rise
  GU15......... 36 D5
Stockwood Way GU9. 99 D7
Stoddam La
  Hill Brow GU33.... 208 A2
  Liss GU33....... 207 F1
Stodham La
  Petersfield GU31.... 228 E2
  West End SO18.... 268 A3
  West Wellow SO51 .. 238 D3
Stoke Charity Rd SO21,
  SO23......... 154 B2
Stoke Common Rd
  SO50......... 244 E5
Stoke Gate SP11.... 61 C5
Stoke Gdns PO12... 369 C5
Stoke Hill SP11.....61 B3
Stoke Hills GU9.... 99 A3
Stoke Ho RG26...... 26 F8
Stoke Hts SO50.... 245 B3
Stoke La SP11.....61 B5
Stoken La RG27.....51 F8
Stokepaine RG27 ... 174 A1
Stopples La SO41... 383 B4
Storrington Rd PO8. 276 D5
Story La BH18..... 375 B4
Stourbank Rd BH23. 395 A6
Stour Cl
  Ferndown BH21.... 352 D4
  Petersfield GU31.... 228 E2
  West End SO18.... 268 A3
  West Wellow SO51 .. 238 D3
Stourcliffe Ave BH6. 394 D4
Stourcroft Dr BH23. 379 E1
Stour Ct 9 BH25... 379 E1
Stourfield Inf & Jun Schs
  BH6......... 394 D6
Stourfield Rd BH5.. 394 B4
Stourhead Cl
  Andover SP10..... 105 E7
  Farnborough GU14 ... 56 B2
Stourpaine Rd BH17. 375 D2
Stour Pk BH10..... 377 E6
Stour Rd
  Bournemouth BH8... 393 D6
  Christchurch BH23 .. 395 A6
  Oakley RG23...... 67 B1
Stour Rdbt BH23.... 394 F5
Stourton Ct 21 BH4. 392 C3
Stourvale Ave BH23. 394 D8
Stourvale Gdns
  SO53......... 243 D5
Stourvale Pl 3 BH5. 394 B5
Stourvale Rd BH6... 394 C6
Stour View Gdns
  BH21......... 350 E1
Stour Way BH23.... 379 D1
Stour Wlk
  Bournemouth BH8... 378 D4
  Wimborne Minster
    BH21........ 351 D3

Stoneham Cemetery Rd
  SO18......... 267 F4
Stoneham Cl
  Petersfield GU32.... 228 D4
  Southampton SO16 .. 267 B5
Stoneham Ct SO16.. 267 B5
Stoneham Gdns
  SO31......... 292 F1
Stoneham La SO16.. 267 D6
Stoneham Pk GU32.. 228 D4
Stoneham Way SO16,
  SO18......... 267 E5
Stonehill Pk GU35... 165 F4
Stonehill Rd GU35.. 166 A4
Stonehills
  Fawley SO45...... 339 C3
  Steventon RG25..... 89 B5
Stonehouse Rd
  GU30......... 188 B4
Stonehouse Rise
  GU16......... 36 C1
Stone La
  5 Gosport PO12 ... 369 B5
  Gosport PO12..... 369 B4
  Wimborne Minster
    BH21........ 351 A6
Stone Lane Ind Est
  BH21......... 351 B6
Stonelea Gr RG29... 72 C6
Stoneleigh 3 BH13. 486 F2
Stoneleigh Ave SO41 383 F4
Stoneleigh Cl PO13 . 344 B8
Stoneleigh Ct GU16.. 36 D1
Stoner Hill Rd SO42. 206 B1
Stoners Cl PO13 ... 343 B3
Stone Sq PO9...... 323 F4
Stone St
  Aldershot GU12.... 100 B8
  Portsmouth PO5.... 404 A1
Stone Terr SO21.... 219 A1
Stoney Bottom
  GU26......... 167 A3
Stoney Cl GU46..... 34 B4
Stoneycroft 7 GU11. 76 D1
Stoney Croft Rise
  SO53......... 243 C2
Stoney Ct SO22.... 403 C8
Stoneyfields GU9... 99 C1
Stoney La
  Four Marks GU34... 160 B4
  Newbury RG18......2 C7
  Winchester SO22 ... 403 C8
Stony La
  Burton BH23...... 380 C2
  Christchurch BH23 .. 395 C7
  Damerham SP6.... 256 B4
  Portsmouth PO1.... 370 A6
Stony Lane 3 BH23. 395 D6
Stonymoor Cl SO45. 338 C3
Stookes Way GU46... 34 F4
Stopples La SO41... 383 B4
Storrington Rd PO8. 276 D5
Story La BH18..... 375 B4
Stourbank Rd BH23. 395 A6
Stour Cl
  Ferndown BH21.... 352 D4
  Petersfield GU31.... 228 E2
  West End SO18.... 268 A3
  West Wellow SO51 .. 238 D3
Stourcliffe Ave BH6. 394 D4
Stourcroft Dr BH23. 379 E1
Stour Ct 9 BH25... 379 E1

Stratfield Dr 9
  SO53......... 218 B1
Stratfield Gdns PO9. 323 D7
Stratfield Ho 4 GU11 .76 E1
Stratfield Pk PO7... 322 C8
Stratfield Pl PO5.... 382 E3
Stratfield Rd RG21... 69 A8
Stratfield Saye Ho★
  RG7.......... 30 C8
Stratfield Saye Rd RG7,
  RG26........ 29 A5
Stratford Ct
  10 Winchester
    SO23........ 403 E8
  Farnborough GU14 ... 56 A4
  Farnham GU9 ..... 99 A1
Stratford Ho
  11 Alton GU34.... 139 F3
  Portsmouth PO5.... 404 B2
Stratford Pl
  Eastleigh SO50.... 244 B4
  Lymington SO41 ... 385 D5
Stratford Rd
  Ash Vale GU12..... 77 D8
  Waterlooville PO7... 323 A3
  BH21........ 351 A6
Strathfield Rd SP10. 106 A5
Strathmore Ct 1
  GU15......... 36 B6
Strathmore Dr BH31. 303 B6
Strathmore Rd
  Bournemouth BH9... 378 A4
  Gosport PO12..... 369 C5
Stratton Cl
  Cosham PO6..... 345 C8
  East Stratton SO21 .. 134 A4
Stratton La SO21.... 134 B3
Stratton Rd
  Basingstoke RG21... 68 F2
  Bournemouth BH9... 378 C3
  Southampton SO15 .. 266 C4
  Winchester SO23 ... 198 C7
Stratton Wlk GU14... 55 E7
Strauss Rd RG22.... 91 C8
Stravinsky Rd RG22 . 91 F8
Strawberry Fields
  Bramley RG26..... 28 F3
  East Boldre SO42.. 363 D6
  Hedge End SO30... 293 A6
Strawberry Hill
  Newbury RG14......1 D4
  Sarisbury SO31..... 316 F3
Strawberry Mead
  SO50......... 245 B1
Stream Farm Cl
  GU10......... 122 B7
Streamleaze PO14.. 317 C2
Streamside GU51... 75 A8
Stream Valley Rd
  GU10......... 122 A6
Street End
  Hartley Wintney
    RG27........ 53 B4
  North Baddesley
    SO52........ 242 B5
Streets La BH24.... 329 C4
Street The
  Aldermaston RG7 .... 9 E7
  Binsted GU34..... 141 E7
  Bramley RG26..... 28 D3
  Crookham Village
    GU51........ 74 C5
  Dockenfield GU10 .. 143 C6
  Farnham GU10.... 121 D6
  Frensham GU10.... 144 A7
  Greywell RG29..... 71 F3
  Long Sutton RG29... 95 D3
  Mortimer RG7..... 11 F5
  Old Basing RG24.... 70 B7
  Rotherwick RG27.... 50 E5
  Stratfield Mortimer
    RG7......... 12 B5
  Swallowfield RG7... 14 A6
  Tongham GU10.... 100 D6
  Whiteparish SP5.... 212 A4
Streetway Rd SP11. 124 E7
Strete Mount 1
  BH23......... 395 B4
Stretton Ct BH31... 303 B6
Stretton La SO41... 384 B4
Strettons Copse
  GU30......... 209 F2
Stride Ave PO3..... 371 B6
Strides La BH24.... 328 F7
Strides Way SO40... 288 B7
Strode Gdns BH24.. 328 B5
Strode Rd PO2..... 345 C2
Strokins Rd RG20... 24 D3
Stroller Cl RG19......2 D4
Strongs Cl SO51.... 241 B8
Stroud Cl
  Chineham RG24.... 48 F2
  Pamber Heath RG26 . 10 C1
  Portsmouth PO6.... 321 A1
  Wimborne Minster
    BH21........ 352 A6
Strouden Ave BH8... 393 C8
Strouden Court Prec
  PO9......... 323 D7
Strouden Ct PO9.... 323 D7
Stroud End SO22.... 228 B4
Strouden Rd BH9.... 378 A1
Stroud Gdns BH23.. 395 E6
Stroud Green La
  PO14......... 342 D5
Stroud La
  Blackwater GU17.... 34 A4
  Christchurch BH23 .. 395 F6
  Crookham Village
    GU51........ 74 C5

Stroudley Ave PO6.. 346 C6
Stroudley Rd RG24... 69 E8
Stroudley Way SO30. 269 D2
Stroud Park Ave
  BH23......... 395 E6
Stroud Sch SO51... 241 E8
Stroudwood Rd
  Fair Oak SO32.... 246 A4
  Havant PO9...... 324 A3
Struan Cl BH24.... 327 F6
Struan Ct BH24.... 328 A6
Struan Dr BH24.... 328 A6
Struan Gdns BH24... 327 F6
Stuart Bridgewater Ho
  SO18......... 292 A7
Stuart Cl
  Farnborough GU14 ... 55 E5
  Stubbington PO14 .. 367 C7
  Upton BH16...... 389 B7
Stuart Cres SO22... 403 C3
Stuart Ct
  2 Andover SP10.... 83 A3
  4 Cosham PO6.... 345 F8
Stuart Jones Ho
  SO53......... 243 D3
Stuart Rd
  Christchurch BH23 .. 397 B8
  Newbury RG14......5 B6
Stubbermere PO10.. 324 E7
Stubbington Ave
  Bordon GU35..... 164 C1
  Portsmouth PO2.... 345 E1
Stubbington Gn
  PO14......... 367 C8
Stubbington La
  PO14......... 367 D6
Stubbington Way
  SO50......... 245 D1
Stubbs Cl SO16..... 265 B3
Stubbs Dro SO30... 293 D7
Stubbs Folly GU47 ... 35 B7
Stubbs Ind Site GU11 77 C5
Stubbs Moor Rd
  GU14......... 55 D5
Stubbs Rd
  Basingstoke RG21... 69 C2
  Southampton SO19 .. 292 C6
Stuckton Rd SP6... 282 B8
Student Village
  BH12......... 392 D8
Studland Cl 20 BH4. 392 C3
Studland Dr SO41... 399 C5
Studland Rd
  Bournemouth BH4... 392 C1
  Lee-on-t-S PO13 ... 367 B4
  Southampton SO16 .. 265 D1
Studley Cl BH23.... 397 C8
Studley Cl BH23.... 397 D8
Stud Offices The
  SP11.......... 80 E7
Stukeley Rd RG21... 69 A4
Sturdee Cl GU16.... 36 C1
Sturgess Ct 14 PO16. 331 B8
Sturminster Ho 4
  SO16......... 266 A1
Sturminster Rd 1
  BH9......... 378 B4
Sturt Ave GU27.... 189 D5
Sturt Rd
  Camberley GU16.... 56 C5
  Farnham GU9 ..... 98 F7
  Haslemere GU27... 189 D5
Styles The SP5..... 210 C8
Stymies GU35..... 164 B1
Sudbury Rd PO6.... 345 B6
Suddern Cotts SO20. 147 C8
Suetts La SO32..... 271 A5
Suffolk Ave
  Christchurch BH23 .. 379 F2
  Southampton SO15 .. 290 D1
Suffolk Cl
  Chandler's Ford
    SO53........ 243 C2
  Wimborne Minster
    BH21........ 352 C6
Suffolk Dr
  Chandler's Ford
    SO53........ 243 C2
  Swanwick PO15.... 317 B7
Suffolk Gn SO53.... 243 C2
Suffolk Rd
  Andover SP10..... 106 A7
  Bournemouth BH2... 392 E3
  Portsmouth PO4.... 371 B3
Suffolk Rd S BH2... 392 C3
Sullivan Cl
  Farnborough GU14 .. 55 E4
  Portchester PO6.... 344 E8
Sullivan Rd
  Basingstoke RG22... 68 D1
  Basingstoke RG22... 68 F1
  Camberley GU15.... 35 E5
  Southampton SO19 .. 292 D5
Sullivan Way PO7... 322 C6
Sultan Rd
  Emsworth PO10.... 324 D1
  Portsmouth PO1,PO2 370 D7
Sulzers Rdbt GU14... 55 E7
Sumar Cl PO14.... 342 D5
Summercroft Way
  BH22......... 326 D2
Summerdown Cotts
  RG23..........66 E4
Summer Down La RG23,
  RG26..........66 E5

Summerfield Cl
  BH23......... 380 C2
Summer Field Cl
  BH21......... 352 A4
Summerfield Ct PO3. 346 B4
Summerfield Gdns
  SO16......... 267 D5
Summerfield La
  GU10......... 121 F2
Summerfields
  Bournemouth BH7... 393 F7
  Chineham RG24.... 49 A4
  Locks Heath SO31... 317 B1
Summer Flds BH31.. 302 F4
Summerhill Rd PO8. 300 A3
Summerhouse Ct 11
  GU26......... 167 B3
Summer La SO42... 364 F8
Summerlands BH22. 353 D6
Summerlands Rd
  SO50......... 245 C2
Summerlands Wlk 17
  PO9......... 324 B5
Summerlea Ct RG25. 116 C6
Summerleigh Wlk
  PO14......... 342 D5
Summers Ave BH11. 377 B6
Summersfield GU33. 207 F3
Summers La BH23 .. 380 D1
Summers St SO14... 291 C6
Summertrees Ct
  BH25......... 383 D4
Summit Ave GU14,
  GU51.......... 55 A4
Summit Cl RG40.... 16 D7
Summit Ctr GU14 ... 55 B4
Summit Way SO18.. 267 F1
Sumner Ct GU9.... 99 A3
Sumner Rd
  Buriton GU31..... 253 D5
  Farnham GU9 ..... 99 A3
Sunbeam Way PO12. 369 B4
Sun Brow GU27.... 189 E5
Sunbury Cl
  Bordon GU35..... 164 E3
  Bournemouth BH11.. 377 A6
Sunbury Ct
  24 Bournemouth
    BH4......... 392 C3
  Fareham PO15.... 318 E4
Suncourt Villas
  PO12......... 368 F8
Sun Ct PO5...... 404 A2
Sunderland Dr BH23. 396 B7
Sunderland Gdns RG14 1 B2
Sunderton La PO8... 276 C3
Sundew Cl
  Christchurch BH23 .. 381 C1
  New Milton BH25... 383 D4
Sundew Rd BH18... 374 E2
Sundowner SO14... 291 B2
Sundridge Cl PO6... 345 F8
Sunflower Rd RG22.. 91 A7
Sun Hill Cres SO24. 179 D4
Sun Hill Inf & Jun Sch
  SO24......... 179 D5
Sun La
  New Alresford
    SO24........ 179 D5
  Swallowfield RG7... 13 F2
Sunley Cl RG14.....5 B6
Sunlight Cotts SO21. 217 E8
Sunningdale
  41 Bournemouth
    BH4......... 392 C3
  6 Poole BH15.... 390 E3
  Christchurch BH23 .. 394 F6
  Colden Common SO21 219 F1
  Hythe SO45...... 313 F3
Sunningdale Cl
  Bishopstoke SO50... 244 F2
  Gosport PO13.... 343 C1
Sunningdale Cres
  BH10......... 377 C4
Sunningdale Gdns
  Broadstone BH18... 375 A5
  Southampton SO18 .. 292 B7
Sunningdale Rd
  Portchester PO16... 344 D7
  Portsmouth PO3.... 371 A7
Sunnybank SP11.... 104 E6
Sunnybank Dr BH21. 352 B6
Sunnybank Rd
  Farnborough GU14 .. 55 B6
  Wimborne Minster
    BH21........ 352 B6
Sunnybank Way
  BH21......... 352 B6
Sunnydell La GU10.. 121 E6
Sunnydown Rd SO22. 197 A3
Sunnyfield Rd BH25. 398 A8
Sunnyfield Rise
  SO31......... 293 A1
Sunnyfields PO6.... 346 C7
Sunnyheath PO9.... 323 E4
Sunny Hill Ct BH12. 391 D5
Sunnyhill Rd BH6... 394 C5
Sunny Hill Rd
  Aldershot GU11.....76 B2
  Poole BH12...... 391 D5
Sunnylands Ave BH6. 394 F4
Sunny Mead RG23... 90 B8
Sunnymead Dr PO7. 299 D2
Sunnymoor Rd BH11. 377 A4

Sunnyside
Donnington RG14 . . . . . **1** C6
Fleet GU51 . . . . **53** E2
Kingsley GU35 . . . . . **142** C1
Sunnyside Cl SP10 . . . . .**82** E2
Sunnyside Cotts RG20 **24** C1
Sunnyside Pk BH24 . **328** C5
Sunnyside Rd
Headley GU35 . . . . **166** A4
Poole BH12 . . . . **391** D6
Sunnyside Wlk PO9 . **323** D7
Sunny View Cl 7
GU12 . . . . **77** A1
Sunny Way SO40 . . . . **288** F7
Sunny Wlk PO1 . . . . **370** A6
Sun Ray Est GU47 . . **34** D8
Sunridge Cl BH12 . . . **392** A6
Sunrise Ct BH22 . . . . **353** D5
Sunset Ave SO40 . . . . **288** E8
Sunset Lo BH13 . . . . **392** A2
Sunset Rd SO40 . . . . **288** E8
Sunshine Ave PO11 . **373** B2
Sun St PO1 . . . . **370** A5
Suntrap Gdns PO11 . **373** B2
Sunvale Ave GU27 . . **189** B6
Sunvale Cl
Haslemere GU27 . . . **189** B6
Southampton SO19 . . **292** B3
Sun Valley Bsns Pk
SO23 . . . . **176** C1
Sunwood Rd PO9 . . . **323** D5
Surbiton Rd SO50 . . **244** B5
Surrey Ave GU15 . . . . **35** E4
Surrey Cl
Christchurch BH23 . . **379** F4
Totton SO40 . . . . . . **288** D5
Surrey Ct
Chandler's Ford
SO53 . . . . **243** D3
Southampton SO15 . . **290** C6
Surrey Gdns BH4 . . . **392** C4
Surrey Heath Mus★
GU15 . . . . **36** B6
Surrey Ho RG24 . . . . **68** D8
Surrey Inst of Art &
Design Coll The
GU9 . . . . **98** E2
Surrey Lo 8 BH4 . . . **392** D4
Surrey Point 7
SO16 . . . . **266** E3
Surrey Rd
Bournemouth BH4,
BH12 . . . . **392** B4
Chandler's Ford
SO53 . . . . **243** D4
Southampton SO19 . . **291** D2
Surrey Rd S BH4 . . . **392** C4
Surrey St PO1 . . . . . **404** B3
Sussex Cl BH9 . . . . . **378** B4
Sussex Ct
6 Gosport PO12 . . **369** C9
Portsmouth PO5 . . . **404** B1
Sussex Gdns
Fleet GU51 . . . . **54** B4
Petersfield GU31 . . . **228** F2
Sussex Pl
Portsmouth,Landport
PO1 . . . . **404** B4
Portsmouth PO5 . . . **404** B1
Sussex Rd
Chandler's Ford
SO53 . . . . **243** D3
Petersfield GU31 . . . **229** B1
Portsmouth PO5 . . . **404** B1
Southampton SO14 . **291** A4
Sussex St SO23 . . . . **403** D6
Sussex Terr PO5 . . . **404** B1
Sutcliffe Sq SP10 . . . **83** C3
Sutherland Ave
BH18 . . . . **374** E5
Sutherland Cl
6 Romsey SO51 . . **216** B1
Bordon GU35 . . . . . **164** D1
Sutherland Ct SP10 . **83** A1
Sutherland Rd
Portsmouth PO4 . . . **370** E4
Southampton SO16 . **265** F5
Sutherlands RG14 . . . **5** C7
Sutherlands Ct SO53 **243** C6
Sutherlands Way
SO53 . . . . **243** B6
Sutton Cl
Poole BH17 . . . . **376** B2
Portsmouth PO3 . . . **346** B4
Waterlooville PO8 . . **299** D3
Sutton Ct PO14 . . . . **318** F1
Sutton Field GU35 . . **164** C1
Sutton Gdns SO23 . . **403** E6
Sutton Hill Camping Site
BH21 . . . . **302** B8
Sutton Pl SO42 . . . . **334** A1
Sutton Rd
2 Camberley GU15 . **36** E8
Basingstoke RG21 . . . **69** B7
Bournemouth BH9 . . **378** B1
Newbury RG14 . . . . . . **1** B5
Totton SO40 . . . . . . **264** C1
Waterlooville PO8 . . **299** D3
Suttonwood La SO24 **180** F7
Swains Cl RG26 . . . . . **26** F8
Swains Rd RG26 . . . . **26** F8
Swaledale Gdns GU51 **54** B4
Swale Dr SO53 . . . . . **243** A7
Swale Rd GU14 . . . . . **55** C6

Swallow Cl
Alton GU34 . . . . . . **140** A6
Basingstoke RG22 . . . **90** F8
Broadstone BH17 . . . **389** F8
Havant PO9 . . . . . . **324** B2
North Tidworth SP9 . . **78** F6
Totton SO40 . . . . . . **288** C6
Yateley GU46 . . . . . . **33** F6
Swallow Ct
Clanfield PO8 . . . . . **276** B6
Lee-on-t-S PO13 . . . **367** F4
Swallow Dr SO41 . . . **399** E4
Swallowfield Rd
Arborfield Garrison RG2,
RG7 . . . . **14** E8
Swallowfield RG7 . . . **14** E8
Swallowfields SP10 . . **83** B2
Swallowfield St RG7 . **14** A7
Swallow Sq SO50 . . . **243** D2
Swallow Way BH21 . **352** A7
Swallow Wood PO16 **389** F8
Swanage Cl SO19 . . . **291** E3
Swanage Rd PO13 . . . **367** E3
Swan Cl
Emsworth PO10 . . . . **349** A8
Lower Swanwick
SO31 . . . . **316** D7
Swancote PO16 . . . . **343** F8
Swan Ct
4 Andover SP10 . . **106** B8
Bursledon SO31 . . . . **316** C8
Gosport PO13 . . . . . **343** B4
Hartley Wintney RG27 **52** D6
Newbury RG14 . . . . . . **1** D3
Swan Gn 3 BH23 . . . **395** A5
Swan Ho GU47 . . . . . **34** F7
Swan La
Sandhurst GU47 . . . . **34** F7
Winchester SO23 . . . **403** E6
Swanley Cl SO50 . . . **244** A5
Swan Mead BH24 . . . **329** C6
Swan Mews RG29 . . . **72** C4
Swanmore Ave SO19 **292** C3
Swanmore Bsns Pk
SO32 . . . . **271** E7
Swanmore CE Prim Sch
SO32 . . . . **272** B5
Swanmore Cl
Bournemouth BH7 . . **394** B4
Winchester SO22 . . . **175** D4
Swanmore Coll of Tech
SO32 . . . . **272** A4
Swanmore Park Ho
SO32 . . . . **272** C8
Swanmore Rd
Bournemouth BH7 . . **394** B4
Droxford SO32 . . . . . **272** E7
Havant PO9 . . . . . . **323** D7
Swanmore SO32 . . . **272** A6
Swan Quay
Portchester PO16 . . . **343** D8
Southampton SO18 . . **291** D8
Swansbury Dr BH8 . . **379** B2
Swansdown Wlk RG19 . . **2** T3
Swan St
Kingsclere RG20 . . . . **24** C1
Petersfield GU31 . . . **228** E3
Swans Wlk PO11 . . . **373** B3
Swanton Cl PO14 . . . **367** D8
Swanton Gdns SO53 **243** B7
Swan Way GU51 . . . . **74** D7
Swanwick Bsns Ctr
SO31 . . . . **316** D7
Swanwick La
Lower Swanwick
SO31 . . . . **316** E8
Swanwick SO31 . . . . **317** A8
Swanwick Nature
Reserve★ SO31 . . . **316** F8
Swanwick Shore Rd
SO31 . . . . **316** D7
Swanwick Sta SO31 . **317** B6
Swanwick Wlk 8
RG26 . . . . **26** F8
Swarraton Rd PO9 . . **324** A3
Sway Ct
20 Havant PO9 . . . . **324** B5
Sway Gdns SO41 . . . **384** C8
Sway Park Ind Est
SO41 . . . . **360** B1
Sway Rd
Brockenhurst SO42 . . **360** F7
Lymington SO41 . . . **385** B6
New Milton BH25,
SO41 . . . . **383** C6
Sway Sta SO41 . . . . **360** B1
Swaythling Prim Sch
SO17 . . . . **267** B3
Swaythling Rd
Havant PO9 . . . . . . **323** D6
West End SO30 . . . . **268** B2
Swaythling Sta
SO18 . . . . **267** D4
Swedish Hos
Norleywood SO41 . . **386** E8
Tadley RG26 . . . . **27** D4
Sweep The BH24 . . . **328** F2
Sweetbriar Gdns
PO7 . . . . **322** F5
Sweethills Cres
PO15 . . . . **317** C8
Sweetzer's Piece RG7 **11** C6
Swelling Hill SO24 . **182** A6
Sweyns Lease SO42 . **363** C6
Swift Cl
Andover SP10 . . . . . . **83** B2

Swift Cl *continued*
Broadstone BH17 . . . **389** F8
Eastleigh SO50 . . . . **243** D2
Horndean PO8 . . . . . **300** A7
Lee-on-t-S PO13 . . . **367** F4
Winchester SO22 . . . **403** B3
Swift Ct 10 GU45 . . . **54** A1
Swift Gdns SO19 . . . **291** D1
Swift Hollow SO19 . **291** D1
Swift Rd
Farnham GU9 . . . . . . **99** A7
Southampton SO19 . . **291** D1
Thorney Island PO10. **349** A3
Swift's Cl GU10 . . . . . **99** F1
Swinburn Gdns PO8. **299** F4
Swincombe Rise
SO18 . . . . **268** B1
Swindon Ho 8 SP9 . . **78** F7
Swingate Rd GU14 . . **122** B8
Swing Swang La
RG24 . . . . **69** E7
Swiss Cl GU10 . . . . . **121** E4
Swiss Ct GU17 . . . . . . **35** A4
Swiss Rd PO7 . . . . . . **322** E7
Switchback La
Rowledge GU10 . . . . **121** D4
Rowledge GU10 . . . . **121** E3
Switch House Rd
SO45 . . . . **339** E2
Swivelton La PO17 . **320** A3
Sword Cl
Clanfield PO8 . . . . . **276** B5
Gosport PO12 . . . . . **368** E2
Swordfish Dr BH23 . **396** B7
Swordfish Way GU14 **76** C7
Sword Sands Rd
PO2 . . . . **171** C1
Sycamore Ave SO53 **218** C5
Sycamore Cl
Broadstone BH17 . . . **374** F1
Bursledon SO31 . . . . **315** F8
Christchurch BH23 . . **394** D8
Clanfield PO8 . . . . . **276** D5
Frimley GU16 . . . . . . **36** C1
Gosport PO13 . . . . . **343** E1
Milford on S SO41 . . **399** C5
North Baddesley
SO52 . . . . **241** F5
North Tidworth SP9 . . **79** F4
Romsey SO51 . . . . . **241** C6
Sandhurst GU47 . . . . **34** F8
Titchfield PO14 . . . . **317** C1
Waterlooville PO8 . . **299** E3
Sycamore Cres GU51. **74** E6
Sycamore Ct
4 Fordingbridge
SP6 . . . . **257** F1
Ringwood BH24 . . . . **305** C2
Sycamore Dr
Ash Vale GU12 . . . . . **77** E7
Farnham GU10 . . . . **121** E6
Frimley GU16 . . . . . . **36** C1
Holbury SO45 . . . . . **338** B5
Kings Worthy SO23 . **176** B8
South Hayling PO11 . **372** F4
Sycamore Ho RG24 . . **49** A3
Sycamore Pk GU34 . **140** B4
Sycamore Pl SP21 . . **252** D5
Sycamore Rd
Bishop's Waltham
SO32 . . . . **271** E7
Farnborough GU14 . . **56** B2
Hordle SO41 . . . . . . **383** F4
Hythe SO45 . . . . **313** F3
Southampton SO16 . **266** A4
Sycamore Rise RG14 . . **2** A5
Sycamores The
Blackwater GU17 . . . **34** F5
Farnborough GU14 . . **56** B3
Hythe SO45 . . . . **314** A4
Sycamore Way RG23 . **68** D7
Sycamore Wlk
Andover SP10 . . . . . **105** D6
Botley SO30 . . . . . . **293** F7
Petersfield GU31 . . . **228** E1
Sydenham Ct PO1 . . **404** D3
Sydenham Terr
Portsmouth PO1 . . . **404** D3
Westbourne PO10 . . **325** B3
Sydings The RG14 . . . . **1** B5
Sydling Cl BH17 . . . . **376** B2
Sydmanton Cl SO51 . **241** A6
Sydmonton Ct 2
PO9 . . . . **324** B5
Sydney Ave SO31 . . . **315** E3
Sydney Ho PO1 . . . . **404** B4
Sydney Loader Pl
GU17 . . . .**34** E5
Sydney Rd
Bishopstoke SO50 . . **244** D4
Bordon GU35 . . . . . **164** D3
Broadstone BH18 . . . **375** A3
Christchurch BH23 . . **379** E1
Gosport PO12 . . . . . **368** B3
Southampton SO15 . **266** B1
Sydney Villas GU12. .**77** E8
Syers Cl GU33 . . . . . **207** F4
Syers Rd GU33 . . . . . **207** F4
Sylmor Gdns BH9 . . **378** A2
Sylvan Ave SO19 . . . **292** C6
Sylvan Cl
Hordle SO41 . . . . . . **384** B2
St Leonards BH24 . . **327** D4
Sylvan Ct GU14 . . . . **76** A6
Sylvan Dr SO52 . . . . **241** F3
Sylvaner Cl BH21 . . **352** A6
Sylvan Fst Sch BH12 **391** B6
Sylvan La SO31 . . . . **316** A2

Sylvan Rd BH12 . . . . **391** B6
Sylvans The SO45 . . **313** D3
Sylvan View PO7 . . . **322** F6
Sylvan Way GU52 . . . **74** F5
Sylvester Cl RG14 . . . .**1** C5
Sylvia Cl RG21 . . . . . . **69** A3
Sylvia Cres SO40 . . . **264** E1
Symes Rd
Hamworthy BH15 . . **389** E4
Romsey SO51 . . . . . **241** B7
Symonds Cl SO53 . . **243** D4
Symonds St SO23 . . . **403** E5
Synor Ho 12 SO15 . . **291** A6
Syon Pl GU14 . . . . **56** B4
Sywell Cres PO3 . . . . **346** C4

T

Tadburn Cl
Chandler's Ford
SO53 . . . . **243** D5
Romsey SO51 . . . . . **241** B7
Tadburn Gn SO51 . . . **240** E6
Tadburn Rd SO51 . . . **241** A7
Tadden Cotts BH21. . **350** D7
Tadden Wlk BH18 . . . **374** F2
Tadfield Cres SO51 . **241** A7
Tadfield Rd SO51 . . . **241** A7
Tadhurst Ho 4 PO1. **404** C2
Tadley Cl GU51 . . . . . **53** D4
Tadley Common Rd
RG26 . . . . **10** A1
Tadley Com Prim Sch
RG26 . . . . **27** A6
Tadley Hill RG26 . . . . **27** A7
Tadpole La GU10 . . . **75** B1
Taiping Rd SO20 . . . **126** A5
Tait Cl BH17 . . . . . . **390** E7
Tait Pl PO13 . . . . **343** D1
Talavera Inf & Jun Sch
GU11 . . . .**76** F3
Talbot Ave BH3 . . . . **392** E7
Talbot Cl
Havant PO9 . . . . . . **323** D3
Mytchett GU16 . . . . . **56** E4
Newbury RG14 . . . . . . **1** C5
Southampton SO16 . . **266** F4
Talbot Comb Sch
BH12 . . . . **392** B8
Talbot Ct
21 Southampton
SO14 . . . . **291** A3
Bournemouth BH9 . . **377** F1
Talbot Dr
Christchurch BH23 . . **381** F2
Poole BH12 . . . . . . **392** B8
Talbot Heath Sch
BH4 . . . . **392** C5
Talbot Hill Rd BH9 . **392** E7
Talbot House Prep Sch
BH9 . . . . **392** E7
Talbot Manor BH3 . . **392** D8
Talbot Mdws BH12 . **392** B8
Talbot Mews BH10 . **377** B1
Talbot Rd
Bournemouth BH9 . . **392** E7
Dibden Purlieu SO45. **313** E1
Farnham GU9 . . . . . **121** F8
Havant PO9 . . . . . . **323** D3
Portsmouth PO4 . . . **370** E4
Titchfield PO15 . . . . **317** E2
Talbot Rdbt BH3 . . . **392** D7
Talbot Rise BH10 . . **377** C2
Talgarth Dr GU14 . . . **56** B2
Talisman Bsns Ctr
SO31 . . . . **317** B6
Talland Rd PO14 . . . **317** B1
Tallis Gdns RG22 . . . **68** E3
Tall Pines GU52 . . . . **74** D5
Tally-Ho Lodge RG21 **69** A6
Talmey Rd RG24 . . . . **48** E3
Tamar Cl
Ferndown BH22 . . . . **354** A5
Portchester PO16 . . . **320** A1
Tamar Down PO7 . . . **323** A7
Tamar Dr RG23 . . . . . .**67** B2
Tamar Gdns SO18 . . **268** B2
Tamar Gr SO45 . . . . **313** E3
Tamarisk Cl
Basingstoke RG22 . . . **91** C5
Portsmouth PO4 . . . **371** C3
Stubbington PO14 . . **367** C6
Waterlooville PO7 . . **323** A5
Tamarisk Gdns SO18 **291** E8
Tamarisk Rd SO30 . . **293** B8
Tamella Rd SO30 . . . **290** A1
Tammys Turn PO14 . **342** E6
Tamorisk Dr SO40 . . **288** C6
Tamworth Ct 3
PO12 . . . . **369** B4
Tamworth Dr GU51. .**54** B4
Tamworth Rd
Bournemouth BH7. . **393** F5
Portsmouth PO3 . . . **371** A6
Tanfield La PO17 . . . **296** A3
Tanfield Pk PO17 . . . **296** A3
Tangier Ct 1 GU11 . . **76** D2
Tangier La SO32 . . . **271** A8
Tangier Rd PO3 . . . . **371** B7
Tanglewood
Fareham PO16. . . . . **319** A3
Finchampstead RG40 . **16** E7
Marchwood SO40 . . **290** A2
Tanglewood Ct 1
BH25 . . . . **383** B3

Tanglewood Lo
BH17 . . . . **389** F8
Tangley Wlk PO9 . . **324** B5
Tangmere Cl BH23 . **396** B6
Tangmere Dr SO16. **266** A4
Tangmere Pl BH17 . **390** E7
Tangmere Rise
SO53 . . . . **243** D4
Tangway RG24 . . . . . **48** F4
Tangyes Cl PO14 . . . **367** D8
Tanhouse Cl SO30 . . **293** D5
Tanhouse La
Alton GU34 . . . . . . **139** F3
Hedge End SO30 . . . **293** D5
Tankardale La SO23. **229** C8
Tanker Rd GU14 . . . . **55** F1
Tankerton Cl 2 PO6 **345** E8
Tankerville Rd SO19 **291** D3
Tank Rd GU15 . . . . . **35** D5
Tanner Cl RG14 . . . . . .**1** E4
Tanneries Ind Est The
PO9 . . . . **323** E1
Tanneries The PO14 . **342** A8
Tanner's Brook Inf Sch
SO15 . . . . **289** F7
Tanner's Brook Jun Sch
SO15 . . . . **289** F6
Tanner's Brook Way
SO15 . . . . **289** F6
Tanners La
Fareham PO16 . . . . **342** F5
Sandleheath SP6 . . . **256** F3
South Baddesley
SO41 . . . . **387** A4
West Wellow SO51 . . **239** D7
Tanner's La PO7 . . . **299** A5
Tanners Rd SO52 . . . **242** A3
Tanner's Ridge PO7 **322** E3
Tanner St SO23 . . . . **403** E5
Tanners The PO14 . . **317** C1
Tanners Way RG23 . . **67** B2
Tansy Cl PO7 . . . . . . **323** A6
Tansy Mdw SO53 . . . **242** F4
Tanyard Cotts GU32. **229** B6
Tanyards The SO53 . **218** B1
Taplin Dr SO30 . . . . **293** C8
Taplings Cl SO22 . . . **175** D3
Taplings Rd SO22 . . . **175** D3
Taplin's Farm La
RG27 . . . . **52** E3
Tapper Ct BH21 . . . . **351** E4
Taranto Rd SO16 . . . **266** C4
Tarbat Ct 6 GU47. . . **35** B8
Tarbery Cres PO8 . . . **300** C7
Tardif Ho SO16 . . . . **266** B2
Target Rd PO2 . . . . . **345** C2
Tarius Cl PO13 . . . . . **343** D3
Tarleton Rd PO6 . . . . **321** B1
Tarn Cl GU14 . . . . **55** C2
Tarn Dr BH17 . . . . . **389** F8
Tarn Howes Cl RG19 . . **2** E3
Tarn La RG14 . . . .**5** D8
Tarn Rd GU26 . . . . . **167** C3
Tarn Rise PO8 . . . . . **276** C2
Tarragon Cl GU14 . . . **55** A4
Tarrant Cl BH17 . . . . **375** E2
Tarrant Gdns
Hartley Wintney
RG27 . . . . **52** C4
Havant PO9 . . . . . . **323** D3
Tarrant Rd BH9 . . . . **378** B3
Tarrants The 12 BH2 **392** B4
Taskers Dr SP11 . . . . **105** C4
Tasman Cl
Christchurch BH23 . . **394** F8
Southampton SO14 . . **291** B2
Tasman Ct SO14 . . . . **291** B2
Tasmania Cl RG24. . . **48** C2
Taswell Rd PO5 . . . . **370** D2
Tatchbury La SO40. . **287** F8
Tate Ct SO15 . . . . . . **289** C7
Tate Mews SO15 . . . **289** C8
Tate Rd SO15 . . . . . . **289** C8
Tate Sq SP10 . . . . **83** C3
Tates Rd SO45 . . . . . **314** B3
Tatnam Cres BH15 . . **390** C4
Tatnam Rd BH15 . . . **390** C4
Tattenham Rd SO42. **360** F8
Tattershall Cres
PO16 . . . . **344** B7
Tatwin Cl SO19 . . . . **292** D3
Tatwin Cres SO19 . . **292** D3
Taunton Dr SO18. . . **292** B7
Taunton Row SO53 . **243** D3
Taunton's Coll SO15 **266** E1
Tavells Cl SO40 . . . . **289** E1
Tavell's La SO40 . . . **289** E1
Taverner Cl
Basingstoke RG21 . . . **69** D7
Poole BH15 . . . . . . **390** D2
Taverners Cl SO19 . . **292** D3
Tavistock Cl 4
SO51 . . . . **216** B1
Tavistock Gdns
3 Havant PO9 . . . **324** B1
Farnborough GU14 . . **55** F7
Tavistock Inf Sch
GU51 . . . . **74** D8
Tavistock Rd GU51. . **74** D8

Taylor Dr
Bournemouth BH8. . **378** A4
Bramley RG26 . . . . . **29** B2
Taylor Rd
Farnborough GU11 . . . **77** B7
Gosport PO12 . . . . . **369** C3
Taylor's Bldgs 6
BH15 . . . . **390** C1
Taylors Cl GU35 . . . . **164** F5
Taylors Cnr SO23 . . . **176** B5
Taylors La GU35 . . . . **164** F5
Taylor Way BH31. . . **303** A6
Teachers Terr 7
GU33 . . . . **207** F4
Teachers Way SO45. **338** B4
Teak Cl BH13 . . . . . **402** H8
Teal Cl
Horndean PO8 . . . . . **300** A7
Portchester PO16 . . . **343** F8
South Hayling PO11. . **373** B3
Totton SO40 . . . . . . **288** C2
Teal Cres RG22 . . . . .**90** F7
Teal Wlk PO13 . . . . . **343** B3
Teapot Row 2 PO4 . **371** B2
Teasel Way BH22 . . . **326** E1
Teazle Cl GU31 . . . . **229** C2
Tebourba Cotts
SO41 . . . . **360** B1
Tebourba Dr PO12 . . **369** A4
Tebourba Ho 6
PO14 . . . . **342** E8
Tebourba Way
Curdridge SO30 . . . . **294** D7
Southampton SO16 . . **289** F7
Technology Rd
BH17 . . . . **390** A3
Ted Bates Ct 7
SO15 . . . . **290** E6
Ted Bates Rd 9
SO14 . . . . **291** B3
Tedder Cl
Andover SP11 . . . . . **105** B7
Bournemouth BH11. . **377** B3
Tedder Gdns BH11 . **377** B3
Tedder Rd
Bournemouth BH11. . **377** B3
Gosport PO13 . . . . . **343** D3
Southampton SO18 . **292** A8
Tedder Way SO40 . . **288** D7
Teddington Rd PO4 . **371** A3
Ted Kelly Ct 43 PO1 . **370** A5
Tee Ct 10 SO51 . . . . **240** C7
Tees Cl
Chandler's Ford
SO53 . . . . **243** A7
Farnborough GU14 . . **55** C6
Tees Farm Rd SO21 . **244** F8
Tees Gn SO21. . . . . . **244** F8
Teg Down GU31. . . . **229** B4
Teg Down Meads
SO22 . . . . **403** A7
Tegg Down Rd SO24 **180** F3
Teglease Gn PO9 . . . **323** D7
Teignmouth Rd
Gosport PO12 . . . . . **368** F7
Portsmouth PO3 . . . **371** A8
Tekels Ave GU15 . . . . **36** B4
Tekels Ct GU15 . . . . . **36** C4
Tekels Way GU15 . . . . **36** D3
Telconia GU35 . . . . . **166** A4
Telegraph La GU34. . **160** D2
Telegraph Rd SO30 . **268** C1
Telegraph Way RG21 **199** B7
Telephone Rd PO4 . . **370** E4
Telford Ct RG14. . . . . . **1** D4
Telford Gate
Andover SP10 . . . . . . **82** B1
Andover SP10 . . . . . . **82** B2
Telford Gdns SO30 . **269** E2
Telford Pl SO31 . . . . **399** E4
Telford Rd
Basingstoke RG21. . . . **68** E7
Ferndown BH21 . . . . **353** A8
Portsmouth PO2 . . . **345** E3
Telford Way SO31 . . **317** C5
Teme Cres SO16 . . . **289** E8
Teme Rd SO16 . . . . . **289** E8
Temeraire 11 SO15. **290** F8
Tempest Ave PO7 . . . **323** A4
Templar Cl GU47. . . . **34** E8
Templar Ct 2 SO14 . **291** A7
Templar Lodge 12
GU12 . . . . **77** A1
Templars Mede
SO53 . . . . **243** B3
Templars Way SO53. **243** B3
Templecombe Rd
SO50 . . . . **244** F1
Temple Gdns SO19. . **291** D4
Temple La GU32 . . . **251** E8
Templemere PO14 . . **342** B7
Temple Mews BH1 . **393** D6
Templer Ave GU14. . . **55** E1
Templer Cl BH11. . . **376** F1
Temple Rd
Liss GU33 . . . . **208** A6
Southampton SO19 . . **291** F2
Temple's Cl GU10 . . **100** A1
Temple St PO1. . . . . **404** B4
Templeton Cl PO2 . . **345** E3
Templeton Ho 1
SP10 . . . . **106** A8
Temple Trees 45
BH4 . . . . **392** C3
Temple Twrs RG21. . . **69** A6
Ten Acre Wlk GU10 . **121** D4
Tenby Cl SO18 . . . . . **292** A8
Tenby Dr SO53 . . . . **243** A4

Tenby Rd GU16 . . . . . .56 E8
Tench Way SO51 . . . . 240 F8
Tennyson Cl
  Bishop's Waltham
  SO32 . . . . 271 E8
  Holbury SO45 . . . . . 338 B5
Tennyson Cres PO7 . . 299 D1
Tennyson Ct
  22 Southampton
  SO17 . . . . 267 A1
  2 Portswood SO17 . 267 B1
Tennyson Gdns
  PO16 . . . . 319 A2
Tennyson Rd
  1 Poole BH14 . . . . 391 A3
  Bournemouth BH9 . . 377 F2
  Eastleigh SO50 . . . . 243 F2
  Portsmouth PO2 . . . 370 F8
  Southampton SO17 . 267 B1
  Totton SO40 . . . . . . 264 D2
  Wimborne Minster
  BH21 . . . . 351 C6
Tennyson Way RG22 . .68 E2
Tenon Ct BH23 . . . . . 395 B7
Tensing Cl PO16 . . . . 319 A3
Tensing Rd BH23 . . . . 395 E8
Tenterten Ave SO31 . . 292 E1
Terence Ave BH17 . . . 375 C1
Terence Gdns PO4 . . . 370 E2
Terence Rd BH21 . . . . 374 C5
Terminus Terr SO14 . . 291 B3
Tern Cl
  Basingstoke RG22. . . 90 F7
  Hythe SO45 . . . . . . 314 B2
Tern Ct BH6 . . . . 394 D6
Tern Wlk
  6 Portsmouth PO4 . 371 E5
  Gosport PO13 . . . . . 343 B3
Terrace Rd BH2 . . . . . 392 E3
Terrace The ·
  Camberley GU15 . . . .35 E5
  Chawton GU34. . . . . 161 D8
  Damerham SP6 . . . . 256 D5
  Rockbourne SP6 . . . 256 F8
Terra Cotta Ct GU10. . 121 D6
Terrier Cl SO30 . . . . . 269 C3
Terrington Ave
  BH23 . . . . 381 E1
Terriote Cl SO53 . . . . 243 C7
Terry Cl RG22 . . . . . . .90 F4
Terrys Cotts RG29 . . . .72 B3
Tesimond Dr GU46 . . . .33 E5
Testbourne Ave
  SO40 . . . . 288 D7
Testbourne Cl SO40 . . 288 D7
Testbourne Com Sch
  RG28 . . . . 86 D3
Testbourne Rd SO40 . 288 D6
Testcombe Rd PO12 . . 369 B4
Test Cl GU31 . . . . 228 E2
Test Ct SP10 . . . . .83 D2
Test Ho SO23 . . . . . . 403 F4
Test House Gate Rd
  GU14 . . . . .55 F2
Test La SO16 . . . . . . 265 B2
Testlands Ave SO16 . . 265 D6
Test Mews RG28 . . . . .86 C4
Test Rd
  Southampton SO14 . . 314 B8
  Whitchurch RG28 . . . .86 C4
Test Rise SO20 . . . . . 129 A3
Test Valley Bsns Ctr
  SO16 . . . . 265 C2
Test Valley Bsns Pk
  SO52 . . . . 242 A5
Test Valley Sch
  SO20 . . . . 149 D2
Test Way RG21 . . . . . .69 D5
Testwood Ave SO40 . . 264 E1
Testwood Cres
  SO40 . . . . 264 D2
Testwood La SO40 . . . 264 F1
Testwood Pl SO40 . . . 289 A8
Testwood Rd
  Havant PO9 . . . . . . 323 D6
  Southampton SO15 . . 290 B6
Testwood Sch SO40 . . 264 F1
Tethering Dro SP6 . . . 235 D3
Tetney Cl SO16 . . . . . 265 E3
Tetsome Cotts PO17 . . 318 E2
Teviot Ho 9 SO14 . . . 291 C6
Teviot Rd SO53 . . . . . 243 A5
Tewkesbury Ave
  Fareham PO15. . . . . 318 C3
  Gosport PO12 . . . . . 369 B8
Tewkesbury Cl
  Basingstoke RG24. . . 48 B1
  Cosham PO6 . . . . . . 345 D8
Texas Dr SO22 . . . . . 197 B3
Thackeray Mall 10
  PO16 . . . . 319 B1
Thackeray Rd SO17 . . 291 B8
Thackeray Sq 1
  PO16 . . . . 319 C1
Thackham's La
  Hartley Wintney
  RG27 . . . . .52 A5
  West Green RG27 . . . 51 F5
Thacking Gn SO21 . . . 244 F8
Thames Cl
  Farnborough GU14 . . 55 C6
  Ferndown BH22 . . . . 354 A6
  West End SO18 . . . . 268 B3
Thames Ct
  1 Waterlooville
  PO8 . . . . 299 F4
  6 Basingstoke RG21 . 69 D5
  Andover SP10 . . . . . .83 D2

Thames Dr PO15 . . . . 318 D4
Thamesmead Cl
  PO12 . . . . 368 F7
Thames Mews 11
  BH15 . . . . 390 B1
Thames Rd RG18 . . . . .2 F5
Thames St BH15 . . . . 390 B1
Thatcham Nature
  Discovery Ctr★ RG19 .2 F2
Thatched Cottage Cvn Pk
  SO43 . . . . 310 B6
Thatchers La
  Norleywood SO41 . . . 386 F8
  Sopley BH23 . . . . . . 356 F3
Theatre Mews 17
  PO5 . . . . 370 D2
Theatre Rd GU14 . . . . .76 F8
Theobald Rd BH23 . . . 379 A8
Theseus Rd PO13 . . . 369 B6
Thessaly Ct 4 BH5. . . 393 F4
Thetford Gdns SO53 . . 243 A7
Thetford Rd
  Gosport PO12 . . . . . 368 F7
  Poole BH12 . . . . . . 391 F5
Thibet Rd GU47 . . . . . .35 A8
Thicket The
  Gosport PO13 . . . . . 343 E1
  Portchester PO16 . . . 319 F1
  Portsmouth PO5 . . . 404 C1
  Romsey SO51 . . . . . 241 C6
  Waterlooville PO7 . . 322 D3
Third Ave
  Aldermaston RG7 . . . 10 A2
  Cosham PO6 . . . . . . 345 E8
  Havant PO9 . . . . . . 324 A2
  Southampton SO15 . . 289 F6
Third Street E RG19 . . .6 E5
Thirlestane Ct GU26. 167 D5
Thirlmere SO50 . . . . . 243 F2
Thirlmere Cl
  Bordon GU35 . . . . . 164 D5
  Farnborough GU14 . . 55 C4
  Stubbington PO14 . . . 342 D4
Thirlmere Cres SO42. .74 E5
Thirlmere Ho 12
  PO6 . . . . 321 B1
Thirlmere Rd SO16. . . 265 B2
Thirlstane Firs SO53 243 B4
Thirsk Ct GU12 . . . . . .77 B2
Thirt Way SO20 . . . . . 129 C1
Thistlebarrow Rd
  BH7 . . . . 393 E6
Thistle Cl BH23 . . . . . 396 C8
Thistledown PO8 . . . . 300 B5
Thistledown Cl SP10 . .82 E1
Thistledowne Gdns
  PO10 . . . . 349 B8
Thistle Rd
  Chandler's Ford
  SO53. . . . . 242 F5
  Hedge End SO30 . . . 293 B6
Thomas Askew Ho
  RG14 . . . . .1 C1
Thomas Cl SO40 . . . . 288 D6
Thomas Grant Ave
  PO12 . . . . 369 D7
Thomas La RG40 . . . . 16 C8
Thomas Lewis Way
  SO17 . . . . 267 C2
Thomas Lockyer Cl
  BH31 . . . . 303 A5
Thomas Merriman Ct 1
  RG14 . . . . .1 E2
Thomas Rd
  Farnborough GU11 . . 77 B7
  North Baddesley
  SO52. . . . . 242 A4
  Petersfield GU31. . . . 229 A5
Thompsons La PO7 . . 298 C6
Thompson's La
  Colden Common,Hensting
  SO50. . . . . 245 C7
  Colden Common SO50,
  SO21. . . . . 245 E7
Thorburn Chase
  GU47 . . . . 35 C6
Thoresby Ct BH25 . . . 382 E3
Thorlands GU27 . . . . . 189 E7
Thornbrake Rd
  PO12 . . . . 369 C4
Thornbury 18 BH4 . . . 392 C4
Thornbury Ave
  Blackfield SO45 . . . . 365 F8
  Southampton SO15 . . 290 E7
Thornbury Cl PO14 . . . 342 C8
Thornbury Ho 10
  PO6 . . . . 320 F2
Thornbury Hts SO53. . 218 F1
Thornbury Rd BH6 . . . 395 A4
Thornbury Wood
  SO53 . . . . 218 F1
Thornby Dr PO3. . . . . 346 B4
Thorn Cl
  Eastleigh SO50 . . . . 244 A5
  Farnham GU10 . . . . 121 E4
  Four Marks GU34 . . . 160 C3
  Petersfield GU31. . . . 160 C3
Thorncliffe Cl PO2. . . 345 F4
Thorncombe Cl
  Bournemouth BH9 . . 378 B4
  Poole BH17 . . . . . . 375 E2
Thorn Cres SO40 . . . . 160 B2
Thorncroft Rd PO1. . . 370 E5
Thorn Ct GU34. . . . . . 160 B2
Thornden Sch SO53. 243 F8
Thorndike Cl SO16. . . 266 A3

Thorndike Rd SO16 . . 265 F2
Thorne Cl BH31 . . . . . 302 E6
Thorneley Rd RG20 . . 24 D2
Thorners Ct 8 SO15 290 F6
Thorner's Homes,Centre
  Ct 15 SO15 . . . . . . 290 B8
Thorner's Homes,North
  Ct 14 SO15 . . . . . . 290 B8
Thorner's Homes,South
  Ct 16 SO15 . . . . . . 290 B8
Thorner's Homes,West Ct
  13 SO15. . . . . 290 B8
Thorness Cl SO16 . . . 265 C1
Thorne Way BH21 . . . 327 B6
Thorney Cl PO14 . . . . 342 D8
Thorney Island Com
  Prim Sch PO10 . . . . 349 A3
Thorney Old Pk
  PO10 . . . . 349 D1
Thorney Rd PO10 . . . 349 B6
Thorney View PO11 . . 348 C2
Thornfield RG19 . . . . .7 B3
Thornfield Cl PO8. . . . 299 E8
Thornfield Dr BH23 . . 381 F1
Thornfield Gn GU17 . . 35 D3
Thornford Rd
  Greenham,Head's Hill
  RG19 . . . . .7 B5
  Headley, Nr Greenham
  RG19 . . . . .7 C3
Thorngate SP5. . . . . . 169 B1
Thorngate Ct 5
  PO12 . . . . 369 A7
Thorngate Way 5
  PO12 . . . . 369 D5
Thorngrove Sch RG20 21 C7
Thornham La SO50 . . 244 C6
Thornham Rd BH25 . . 383 D6
Thornhill Ave SO19 . . 292 D6
Thornhill Cl SO45 . . . 338 F2
Thornhill Cres SO11 . . 77 A3
Thornhill Park Rd
  SO18 . . . . 292 D7
Thornhill Prim Sch
  SO19 . . . . 292 C5
Thornhill Rd
  Aldershot GU11. . . . . 77 B4
  Blackfield SO45. . . . . 338 F2
  Southampton SO16 . . 266 D4
Thornhill Way RG24. . 49 B4
Thorni Ave PO15 . . . . 318 C3
Thornleigh Rd SO19 . . 291 E2
Thornley Rd BH10. . . . 377 D4
Thorn Rd
  Farnham GU10 . . . . 121 E5
  Poole BH17 . . . . . . 375 D3
Thorns La SO41. . . . . 387 F6
Thornton Ave SO31 . . 316 C1
Thornton Cl
  Bramley RG26 . . . . . 29 B2
  Corfe Mullen BH21 . . 374 C5
  Cosham PO7 . . . . . . 322 B2
Thornton End GU34 . . 140 C6
Thornton Rd PO12 . . . 369 B9
Thornworthy 4
  SO45 . . . . 313 E1
Thornycroft Ave
  SO19 . . . . 291 D2
Thornycroft Cl RG14 . .1 F3
Thornycroft Ind Est
  RG21. . . . . .68 F5
Thornycroft Rdbt
  RG22 . . . . .68 E5
Thornyhurst Rd GU16 .56 F4
Thorogood Ct 4
  BH15 . . . . 390 E4
Thorold Ct SO18 . . . . 267 E1
Thorold Rd
  Chandler's Ford
  SO53. . . . . 218 E1
  Farnham GU9 . . . . . 99 A3
  Southampton SO18 . . 267 E1
Thorpe Gdns GU34 . . 139 E4
Threadgill Way SP9 . . 101 D7
Threadneedle Ho 3
  SP10 . . . . 106 B8
Three Acre Dr BH25 . 397 F8
Three Acre Rd RG14 . . 5 D8
Three Acres PO7 . . . . 299 A3
Three Cross Rd
  BH21 . . . . 326 E6
Threefield La SO14 . . 291 A3
Three Horse Shoes La
  SO24 . . . . 203 E2
Three Legged Cross Fst
  Sch BH21 . . . . 302 E1
Three Lions Cl 9
  BH21 . . . . 351 B5
Three Oaks SO19 . . . 292 E5
Three Stiles Rd GU9. .98 D3
Three Tun 33 PO1 370 A5
Three Ways SO10 . . . 143 B6
Thresher Cl PO7 . . . . 300 C1
Threshers Cnr GU51. . 54 C4
Throakmead GU34 . . . 120 A2
Throgmorton Rd
  GU46. . . . . .33 E5
Throop Cl BH8. . . . . . 379 A4
Throop Rd
  Bournemouth,Holdenhurst
  BH8 . . . . 379 A4
  Bournemouth,Throop
  BH8 . . . . 378 F4
Throopside Ave BH9 378 D4
Thrush Cl BH23 . . . . . .67 F1
Thrush Rd BH12 . . . . 376 C1
Thrush Wlk PO8 . . . . 299 E4

Thruxton Ct SO19 . . . 291 E5
Thruxton Ind Est
  SP11 . . . . 103 C7
Thruxton Rd PO9 . . . 323 C5
Thumwood RG24. . . . .48 F3
Thundery Hill GU10 . . 100 D4
Thurbans Rd GU9. . . . 121 E7
Thurbern Rd PO2 . . . 345 E2
Thurmell Cl SO30 . . . 293 C4
Thurmell Wlk SO30 . . 293 C4
Thurmond Cres
  SO22 . . . . 403 A4
Thurmond Rd SO22 . . 403 A4
Thursby Rd BH23 . . . 381 F1
Thursley Ho GU27 . . . 167 E1
Thurston Cl SO53 . . . 243 D7
Thurstons GU34. . . . . 141 E7
Thwaite Rd BH12 . . . 392 B5
Thyme Ave PO15 . . . . 317 D8
Thyme Rd RG24 . . . . .49 A4
Thyme Ct
  2 Whiteley PO15 . . 317 D8
  Farnborough GU14 . . 55 A5
Tiberius Cl RG23 . . . . 68 C7
Tiberius Rd SP10 . . . . 83 B3
Tichborne Cl GU17. . . .35 B5
Tichborne Down
  SO24 . . . . 179 D3
Tichborne Gr PO9 . . . 323 D5
Tichborne Pl GU12. . . 100 B3
Tichborne Rd
  Eastleigh SO50 . . . . 268 A8
  Southampton SO18 . . 292 D8
Tichborne Way
  PO13 . . . . 343 D1
Tichbourne Cl GU16. . 36 D3
Tichbourne Ho SO30 293 C7
Tickenor Rd GU40 . . . 16 D7
Tickleford Dr SO19 . . 292 A1
Tickner Cl SO30 . . . . 293 E5
Ticonderoga Gdns
  SO19 . . . . 291 E1
Tidbury Cotts SP11. . . 109 B1
Tidcombe Gn PO9 . . . 323 C2
Tidemill Cl BH23 . . . . 395 A8
Tides End Ct GU16 . . .36 A4
Tides Reach SO18 . . . 291 D8
Tides Way SO40 . . . . 289 F2
Tideway Gdns PO4 . . 371 C4
Tidworth Rd
  Havant PO9 . . . . . . 323 F4
  Shipton Bellinger SP9 101 A8
Tiffany Cl SO41 . . . . . 383 F4
Tiffield Cl PO3. . . . . . 346 C4
Tiger Rd PO1 . . . . . . 369 F8
Tigwells Field RG29 . . 95 A4
Tilbrook Rd SO15 . . . 290 A8
Tilburg Rd BH23 . . . . 395 D7
Tilbury's Cl GU35 . . . 164 D3
Tilden Rd SO21 . . . . . 219 D5
Tile Barn Camp Site
  SO42 . . . . 361 A8
Tile Barn La SO41 . . . 55 E5
Tilebarn La SO42. . . . 361 A6
Tile Barn Row RG20 . .4 C1
Tilford Rd
  Beacon Hill GU26 . . 167 B3
  Hindhead GU26 . . . 167 D4
  Horndean PO8. . . . . 299 F6
  Tilford GU9,GU10 . . . 122 D6
Tiller Gdns BH11. . . . 377 E4
Tillingbourn PO14 . . . 317 C3
Tilling Cotts GU34 . . . 141 B1
Tillington Gdns PO8 . 276 D4
Tilmore Gdns GU32 . . 228 E5
Tilmore Rd GU32. . . . 228 E5
Tilney Cl GU34 . . . . . 139 E4
Timber Bank GU16. . . 56 E6
Timber Cl 6 GU9 . . . . 98 F2
Timbercroft GU34 160 B1
Timberlake Rd RG21 . 69 A5
Timberlane PO7 . . . . 322 D4
Timberley Ho 2
  PO1 . . . . 404 C3
Timberley La SP5 . . . 236 A5
Timberly Cl SO45. . . . 338 C4
Timbermill Dr
  Fordingbridge SP6. . . 281 F8
  Haslemere GU27. . . . 189 D6
Timbers The PO15 . . . 318 C1
Times Ho 3 GU11 . . .76 E2
Timor Cl
  Basingstoke RG24. . . 48 C1
  Swanwick PO15 . . . . 317 C8
Timothy Cl BH10 . . . . 377 D5
Timothy's Field SP11 104 F3
Timpson Rd PO1 . . . . 404 D4
Timsbury Cres PO9 . . 323 E2
Timsbury Ct SO19 . . . 291 F4
Timsbury Dr SO16. . . 265 F1
Timson Cl SO40 . . . . 288 C6
Timson Ct RG14. . . . . .1 F3
Tincleton Gdns BH9 . 378 B4
Tindal Cl GU46. . . . . .34 B6
Tindale Rd SO16 . . . . 265 E2
Tindle Ent Ctr GU35 . 164 C1
Tinker Alley SO30 . . . 268 A7
Tinker's Cnr RG20. . . .10 B4
Tinkers Cross SP6 . . . 257 E4
Tinley Gdns RG29. . . . 72 F3
Tinneys Cl SP5. . . . . 235 D4
Tintagel Cl
  Andover SP10 . . . . . 83 A3
  Basingstoke RG23. . . 68 C6
  Southampton SO16 . . 266 C6
Tintagel Dr GU16 . . . 36 D1
Tintagel Rd RG40 . . . .16 E8

Tintagel Way PO6 . . . 345 B7
Tintern Cl
  Basingstoke RG24. . . 68 F8
  Portsmouth PO6 . . . 321 A1
Tintern Rd PO12 . . . . 369 A5
Tipner Gn PO2 . . . . . 345 C3
Tipner La PO2 . . . . . . 345 C2
Tipner Rd PO2 . . . . . 345 C2
Tiptoe Gn 17 PO9 . . . 324 E6
Tiptoe Prim Sch
  SO41 . . . . 383 D8
Tiptoe Rd BH25 . . . . 359 B1
Tipton Ho PO5 . . . . . 404 B2
Tiptree Cl SO50 . . . . 244 A5
Tisbury Ct GU51 . . . . .53 E3
Tisted Ct 9 PO9 . . . . 324 B5
Titan Ho 6 RG7 . . . . . .9 C2
Titchfield Abbey★
  PO15. . . . . 318 A2
Titchfield Cl RG26. . . .27 A7
Titchfield Haven Visitor
  Ctr★ PO14 . . . . 341 F1
Titchfield Hill PO14 . . 342 A8
Titchfield La PO17 . . . 295 C3
Titchfield Park Rd
  PO15. . . . . 317 D3
Titchfield Prim Sch
  PO14. . . . . 317 F1
Titchfield Rd PO14 . . 342 B6
Tithe Barn SO41 . . . . 385 E5
Tithelands La SO24 . . 202 F4
Tithe Mdw RG22 . . . . 91 C5
Tithe Mead SO51. . . . 215 F1
Tithe The PO7 . . . . . 298 F3
Tithewood Cl SO53 . . 218 E2
Tittymouse La SP11 . . 81 C2
Titus Gdns PO7 . . . . 323 A8
Tiverton Ct
  1 Fareham PO16 . . . 319 C2
  34 Bournemouth BH4 392 C4
Tiverton Rd RG23 . . . .68 B5
Tiverton Way GU16. . . 36 D1
Tivoli Cl SO53 . . . . . 243 F7
Tivoli Ct PO2 . . . . . . 370 F8
Toad La GU17. . . . . . .35 C4
Tobago Cl RG24. . . . . 48 B1
Tobruk Cl SP11 . . . . . .83 B7
Toby St PO1 . . . . 404 B4
Tockington Ct GU46. . .34 B6
Todber Cl BH11 . . . . . 376 D3
Todmore GU33 . . . . . 185 F3
Tokar St PO4 . . . . . . 371 A2
Tokio Rd PO3 . . . . . . 346 A1
Toledo Gr SP10. . . . . .83 C1
Toledo Grove SP10. . . 83 C1
Tolefrey Gdns SO53 . 242 F6
Tollard Cl BH12 . . . . 391 E8
Tollbar Way SO30 . . . 269 B2
Tollerford Rd BH17 . . 375 D2
Tollgate SO53 . . . . . . 243 C2
Tollgate Cl RG23 . . . . .67 F1
Tollgate Ests SO51 . . 215 B3
Tollgate Rd
  Andover SP10 . . . . . 82 E1
  Lower Swanwick
  SO31. . . . . 316 D8
Tollgate The
  3 Winchester
  SO23. . . . . 403 E7
  Fareham PO16. . . . . 319 B2
Tollway RG24 . . . . . . .49 A3
Tolpuddle Gdns BH9 . 378 B4
Tolpuddle Way GU46 . 34 D5
Tolstoi Rd BH14. . . . . 391 A6
Tomkyns Cl SO53 . . . 242 F5
Tomlins Ct SO18 . . . . 267 E1
Tomlins 3 RG26 . . . . 26 E7
Tomlinscote Sch & Sixth
  Form Coll GU16. . . . 36 E2
Tomlinscote Way
  GU16 . . . . 36 E2
Tomlinson Dr RG40 . . 16 E2
Tommy Green Wlk
  SO50 . . . . 243 F3
Toms La BH24 . . . . . 306 B8
Tonbridge St PO5. . . . 370 C2
Tonge Rd BH11 . . . . . 377 B6
Tongham Mdws
  GU10 . . . . 100 D3
Tongham Rd
  Aldershot GU10 . . . . 100 B5
  Runfold GU10 . . . . . 100 A4
Tonnant Cl PO14. . . . 367 D7
Toogoods Way SO16 265 D5
Toomer Cl SO45 . . . . 338 F2
Toothill Rd SO51 . . . . 241 D1
Topaz Dr SP10 . . . . . 105 D8
Topaz Gr PO7 . . . . . . 323 B8
Topiary Gdns SO31. . . 317 D3
Topiary The
  Farnborough GU14 . . 55 C5
  Old Basing RG24 . . . 70 A8
  Poole BH14 . . . . . . 390 F5
Top La BH24 . . . . . . 329 A7
Toplady Pl GU9 . . . . . 99 A7
Top Terrace Rd GU14 .76 E8
Torbay Rd BH14 . . . . 391 C3
Torberry Dr GU31. . . . 229 B2
Torch Cl SO50 . . . . . 245 B2
Tor Cl
  Portchester PO16 . . . 319 F1
  Waterlooville PO7 . . 322 F3
Torcross Cl SO19 . . . 291 E4
Torfrida Ct PO4 . . . . . 371 C3

Tormead SO45 . . . . . 313 F3
Tornay Gr SO52 . . . . 241 F4
Toronto Pl PO12 . . . . 369 B6
Toronto Rd PO2 . . . . 370 E7
Torquay Ave
  Gosport PO12 . . . . . 369 A9
  Southampton SO15 . . 290 D8
Torque Cl SO19 . . . . . 292 E4
Tor Rd GU9 . . . . .98 D2
Torre Cl SO50. . . . . . 244 A6
Torriden Ct GU30 . . . 187 F6
Torridge Gdns SO18. . 268 B3
Torrington Cl
  Lindford GU35 . . . . . 165 A5
  Southampton SO19 . . 292 A4
Torrington Rd PO2 . . 345 F3
Tortworth Ct PO14 . . . 342 D8
Torvain Pk BH14 . . . . 391 A5
Tor Way GU31 . . . . . . 229 A3
Torwood Gdns SO50 244 F2
Tosson Cl 3 SO16 . . . 289 E8
Tothill RG20 . . . . 22 C8
Totland Cl
  Farnborough GU14 . . 55 E6
  Southampton SO16 . . 289 E8
Totland Ct 8 SO41. . . 399 C4
Totland Rd
  Cosham PO6 . . . . . . 345 E7
  Gosport PO13 . . . . . 343 C2
Totmel Rd BH17 . . . . 376 A2
Totnes Cl SO50 . . . . . 243 F5
Tottehale Cl SO52. . . . 241 F3
Tottenham Cl RG26 . . .28 F4
Tottenham Rd PO1 . . 404 D4
Totters La
  Murrell Green RG27 . . 51 F2
  Winchfield RG29 . . . . 72 F8
Totton By Pass SO40 289 A7
Totton Coll SO40. . . . 288 D8
Totton & Eling Heritage
  Ctr★ SO40 . . . . 289 A6
Totton Sta SO40 . . . . 289 A7
Totton Western By-Pass
  SO40 . . . . 288 C5
Totton Wlk PO9 . . . . 323 D6
Tournai Cl GU11 . . . . 77 C7
Tournerbury La
  PO11 . . . . 373 B4
Tourney Rd BH11 . . . 376 E6
Tovey Ct SP10 . . . . . 83 D1
Tovey Pl SO23 . . . . . 176 C3
Towans The BH13 . . . 402 C3
Tower Cl
  Andover SP10 . . . . . 82 D3
  Gosport PO12 . . . . . 368 D3
  Hindhead GU26 . . . . 167 C4
  Liphook GU30 . . . . . 187 F4
Tower Ct
  10 Winchester
  SO22. . . . . 403 D6
  Bournemouth BH2 . . 392 E2
  Warsash SO31. . . . . 316 C1
Tower Gdns 4 SO16 266 F4
Tower Hill GU14 . . . . .55 E3
Tower Hill Prim Sch
  GU14. . . . . 55 D3
Tower Ho SO19 . . . . . 291 E1
Tower Ind Est The
  SO50. . . . . 244 C2
Tower La
  Eastleigh SO50 . . . . 244 C2
  Wimborne Minster
  BH21. . . . . 351 D6
Tower Park Rdbt
  BH15 . . . . 390 F7
Tower Pl SO30 . . . . . 268 D1
Tower Rd
  Bournemouth BH1. . . 393 E5
  Hindhead GU26 . . . . 167 C4
  Liphook GU30 . . . . . 187 F4
  Poole BH13 . . . . . . 392 B2
  Portsmouth PO4 . . . 370 F3
  Winchester SO23 . . . 403 D6
Tower Rd W BH13. . . 392 A1
Towers Farm BH21 . . 374 D7
Towers Gdn PO9 . . . . 347 F6
Tower St
  Alton GU34 . . . . . . 139 F2
  Emsworth PO10. . . . 349 A8
  Portsmouth PO1 . . . 369 F4
  Winchester SO23 . . . 403 D6
Towers The SO31 . . . 315 B5
Towers Way BH21. . . 374 D7
Tower The 3 PO12 . . 369 B6
Town Cl SO24 . . . . . 181 D5
Towngate Bridge
  BH15 . . . . 390 C3
Towngate Sh Ctr 1
  BH15. . . . . 390 C2
Town Hall Ct RG28 . . 86 C5
Town Hall Rd PO9. . . 323 F1
Townhill Inf Sch
  SO18. . . . . 268 A2
Townhill Jun Sch
  SO18. . . . . 268 A2
Townhill Way SO18 . . 268 B2
Town La GU32 . . . . . 229 B5
Town Mill Rd BH25. . . 88 B8
Town Mill La RG25 . . 86 D5
Town Mills RG14. . . . .1 D3
Town Quay
  Portsmouth PO1 . . . 369 F4
  Southampton SO15 . . 290 F2
Townsend Cl
  Basingstoke RG21. . . 68 F4

Townsend Cl *continued*
Bournemouth BH11 .. 377 B6
Townsend La
Martin SP6 .... 231 A4
Pentridge SP6 ...... 230 E4
Townsend Prim Sch
BH8 .... 379 A2
Townside Pl GU15 .... 36 B6
Town Sq 8 GU15 .... 36 A6
Townsville Rd BH9 .. 378 B2
Towpath Mead PO4 . 371 C4
Toynbee Cl SO50 .... 244 A3
Toynbee Rd SO50 ... 244 A3
Toynbee Sch The
SO53 .... 243 E5
Tozer Cl BH11 ...... 376 F2
Tracey Ct 8 BH23 .. 397 A7
Trade St RG20 .... 21 B8
Trafalgar Cl
Chandler's Ford
SO53 .... 243 B5
Hermitage PO10 .... 349 D8
Trafalgar Ct
6 Portsmouth
PO5 .... 370 D2
Christchurch BH23 .. 395 F5
Fareham PO14 ...... 342 F7
Farnham GU9 .... 99 A1
Trafalgar Ho SO45 .. 314 B3
Trafalgar Pl
Lymington SO41 .... 385 F4
Portsmouth PO1 .... 404 D4
Trafalgar Rd
Bournemouth BH9 ... 392 F7
Southampton,Freemantle
SO15 .... 290 C6
Southampton SO14 .. 291 A2
Trafalgar Sq PO12 .. 369 B6
Trafalgar St SO23 ... 403 D6
Trafalgar Way
3 Hythe SO45 ..... 314 B1
Camberley GU15 ..... 35 D4
Stockbridge SO20 ... 149 F2
Trafford Rd
Camberley GU16 ..... 56 B8
Fair Oak SO50 ...... 245 B1
Trajan Wlk SP10 ..... 83 B3
Trampers La PO17 .. 297 A4
Tranby Rd SO19 ..... 291 E4
Tranmere Cl SO41 .. 385 F2
Tranmere Rd PO4 ... 371 B4
Transport Rd GU14 .... 55 F1
Travis La GU47 .... 35 A7
Treadwheel Rd PO8 . 301 B6
Treagore Rd SO40 .. 264 C1
Trearnan Cl SO16 ... 289 F8
Treasury Ct 27 SO23 . 403 D6
Treble Cl SO22 ...... 197 B4
Trebor Ave GU9 .... 99 B1
Tredegar Rd PO4 ... 371 A3
Tredenham Cl GU14 .. 77 A8
Treebys Cl BH23 .... 380 D1
Tree Hamlets BH16 . 389 C5
Treeside BH23 ...... 381 C2
Treeside Ave SO40 .. 289 A7
Treeside Dr GU9 ..... 99 C7
Treeside Rd SO15 ... 290 C8
Tree Side Way PO7 .. 299 E1
Treetops 9 BH13 ... 402 F7
Tree Tops Ave GU15 ... 36 F8
Trefoil Cl
8 Waterlooville
PO7 .... 323 A7
Hartley Wintney RG27 . 52 C7
Trefoil Way BH23 ... 396 C8
Tregantle Mews
PO12 .... 369 A5
Tregaron Ave PO6 .. 346 B7
Tregenna Ho GU30 .. 187 A5
Tregolls Dr GU14 ..... 56 A4
Tregonwell Ct 10
BH2 .... 392 E3
Tregonwell Rd BH2 . 392 E2
Trellis Dr RG24 ...... 70 A8
Treloar Coll GU34 ... 140 B6
Treloar Rd PO11 .... 373 F1
Treloar Sch GU34 ... 119 B2
Treloen Ct 3 BH8 ... 393 A5
Treloyhan Cl SO53 .. 243 D4
Tremona Ct SO16 ... 266 B2
Tremona Rd SO16 ... 266 B2
Trenchard Pk GU35 . 164 D4
Trenchard Rd SP11 .. 105 B7
Trenchmead Gdns
RG24 .... 68 C8
Trenley Cl SO45 ..... 338 C3
Trent Cl
Farnborough GU14 ... 55 C6
Southampton SO18 .. 267 F1
Trent Cres RG18 .... 2 F5
Trent Ct 37 SP10 ..... 83 C2
Trentham Ave BH7 .. 394 B8
Trentham Cl BH7 ... 394 B8
Trent Ho 8 SO14 ... 291 C5
Trenton Cl GU16 ...... 36 E1
Trent Rd SO18 ...... 267 F1
Trent Way
Basingstoke RG21 .... 69 D5
Ferndown BH22 ..... 354 A6
Lee-on-t-S PO13 .... 367 F3
West End SO30 ..... 268 D2
Trent Wlk PO16 ..... 344 A8
Tresham Cres GU46 ... 33 E6
Tresillian Cl BH23 ... 382 B2
Tresillian Gdns SO18 268 B2
Tresillian Way BH23 . 382 B2
Trevis Rd PO4 ...... 371 C4
Trevone 5 BH25 .... 383 B3
Trevone Cl SO40 .... 288 E5
Trevor Rd PO4 ...... 370 E3
Trevose Cl
Chandler's Ford
SO53 .... 243 D4
Gosport PO13 ...... 343 C1
Trevose Cres SO53 .. 243 D5
Trevose Way PO14 .. 317 B1
Triangle Gdns SO16 . 265 D3
Triangle La PO14 ... 341 E4
Triangle The
Bournemouth BH2 ... 392 E3
Greenham RG14 .... 5 F7
Upton BH16 .... 389 B7
Whiteparish SP5 .... 212 B4
Tribe Rd PO12 ...... 369 A6
Tricketts La BH22 ... 353 F6
Trigon Rd BH15 ..... 390 D7
Trilakes Ctry Pk★ GU46,
GU47 .... 34 D7
Trimaran Cl SO31 ... 316 E1
Trimaran Rd SO31 .. 316 E1
Trimmer's Almshouses
1 GU9 .... 98 E1
Trimmers Cl GU9 ..... 99 A7
Trimmer's Ct PO1 .... 369 F5
Trimmers Field GU9 . 99 C1
Trimmers Wood
GU26 .... 167 C6
Trimm's Dro SP6 ... 258 E8
Trinadad Ho 1 PO6 . 320 F2
Trinidad Cl RG24 ...... 48 B1
Trinidad Cres BH12 . 391 C8
Trinidad Ho BH12 ... 391 C8
Trinity 2 BH1 ...... 393 A3
Trinity CE Fst Sch
BH31 .... 302 F8
Trinity Cl PO12 ..... 369 E5
Trinity Ct
8 Southampton
SO15 .... 290 C6
Chandler's Ford
SO53 .... 243 D6
Totton SO40 .... 264 E2
Trinity Fields GU9 .... 98 E6
Trinity Gdns
20 Winchester
SO23 .... 403 E6
Fareham PO16 ...... 319 A1
Trinity Gn PO12 ..... 369 E5
Trinity Hill
Farnham GU9 .... 98 E6
Medstead GU34 ..... 159 E8
Trinity Ho
2 Andover SP10 ... 106 A8
North Tidworth SP9 ... 78 E7
Trinity Ind Est
Southampton SO15 .. 289 F7
Wimborne Minster
BH21 .... 351 E3
Trinity Rd
Bentworth GU34 .... 137 E1
Bournemouth BH1 ... 393 A4
Southampton SO14 .. 291 A5
Trinity Rise SP11 ...... 81 F4
Trinity Sch RG14 .... 1 F5
Trinity St PO16 ..... 319 B1
Tripps Mobile Home Pk
SO30 .... 293 D7
Tristan Cl SO45 ..... 366 E7
Tristram Cl SO53 .... 242 F4
Triton Ctr The SO51 . 241 D5
Triumph Cl PO15 .... 318 D2
Triumph Rd PO14 ... 342 F5
Troak Cl BH23 ...... 395 E8
Trojan Way PO7 .... 322 F3
Troon Cres PO6 ..... 322 C1
Troon Rd BH18 ..... 375 A5
Trooper Bottom
GU32 .... 206 B3
Trosnant Inf Sch
PO9 .... 323 E3
Trosnant Jun Sch
PO9 .... 323 E3
Trosnant Rd PO9 .... 323 E2
Trotsford Mdw GU17 . 35 A4
Trotters La BH21 .... 352 B6
Trotts La SO40 ...... 289 C3
Troublefield Nature
Reserve★ BH23 .... 379 A8
Troubridge Ct 7
PO1 .... 370 D7
Trout Rd GU27 ...... 189 C6
Trout Wlk RG14 .... 1 F4
Trowbridge Cl SO16 . 265 E5
Trowbridge Ct 18
SO23 .... 403 E6
Trowbridge Ho 2
SP9 .... 78 F7
Trowe's La
Beech Hill RG7 ...... 13 B3
Swallowfield RG7 .... 14 B5
Trueman Sq SP10 .... 83 C3
Truman Rd BH11 .... 377 B6
Trunk Rd GU14 .... 55 A5
Truro Ct PO13 ...... 368 C6
Truro Pl RG22 .... 91 B8
Truro Rd PO6 .... 320 F1
Truro Rise SO50 .... 244 E3
Truscott Ave BH9 ... 393 A7
Trussell Cl SO22 .... 175 D3
Trussell Cres SO22 . 175 D3
Trust Cl RG27 .... 50 F1
Tryplets GU52 .... 74 E3
Trystworthy 3 BH2 . 392 E3
Tubb's La
Highclere RG20 ...... 21 D6
Monk Sherborne RG26 47 A7
Tuckers La BH15 .... 389 F1
Tucks Cl BH23 ...... 381 A8
Tuckton Cl BH6 ..... 394 D4
Tuckton Rd
Bournemouth,
Southbourne BH6 .. 394 F5
Bournemouth,West
Southbourne BH6 .. 394 E4
Tuckton Rdbt BH6 .. 394 F5
Tudor Ave PO10 .... 324 F4
Tudor Cl
Alderholt SP6 ...... 281 A5
Bramley RG26 .... 28 C2
Gosport PO13 ...... 368 D8
Grayshott GU26 ..... 167 B2
Portchester PO16 ... 320 B1
South Hayling PO11 . 372 F2
Totton SO40 .... 288 C8
Tudor Cres PO6 ..... 345 F6
Tudor Ct
2 Fareham PO14 ... 342 F7
3 Andover SP10 .... 83 A3
3 Baughurst RG26 ... 26 F8
3 Portsmouth PO5 . 370 D1
5 Cosham PO6 ..... 345 F8
Basingstoke RG21 .... 69 B3
Bournemouth BH1 ... 393 A5
Fleet GU51 .... 54 C4
Poole BH15 .... 390 E6
Tudor Dr GU46 .... 34 B4
Tudor Gdns SO30 ... 293 A5
Tudor Hall GU15 ..... 36 D6
Tudor House Mus &
Gdn★ SO14 .... 290 F3
Tudor Rd
Broadstone BH18 ... 375 B4
Newbury RG14 .... 1 E1
Tudor Way
Fleet GU52 .... 75 A4
Kings Worthy SO23 .. 176 B8
Tudor Wood Cl SO16 266 F4
Tuffin Cl SO16 ...... 265 C5
Tufton Warren Cotts
RG28 .... 109 E6
Tukes Ave PO13 .... 343 B4
Tulip Cl RG22 .... 91 A7
Tulip Gdns
Havant PO9 .... 323 C1
Sarisbury SO31 ..... 316 F3
Tulip Rd SO16 ...... 267 C4
Tulls La GU35 ...... 165 B2
Tull Way RG18 .... 2 E5
Tumber Cl GU12 ...... 77 E2
Tumulus Cl SO19 .... 292 F4
Tunball La SN8 ...... 37 D8
Tunbridge Cres
GU30 .... 187 F5
Tunbridge La GU30 . 187 F6
Tunnel La RG29 .... 72 B4
Tunnel Rd GU14 ..... 55 C1
Tunstall Rd
Portsmouth PO6 .... 321 D1
Southampton SO19 .. 292 E4
Tunworth Cl GU51 .... 53 E4
Tunworth Ct
Havant PO9 .... 324 B5
Tadley RG26 .... 27 A7
Tunworth Mews RG26 27 A8
Tunworth Rd RG25 .... 70 E2
Tupman Ho 21 PO1 . 370 D7
Tuppenny La PO10 .. 349 C8
Turbary Cl BH12 .... 391 D8
Turbary Ct
Bournemouth BH12 .. 377 A1
Ferndown BH22 ..... 353 F6
Upton BH16 .... 389 C8
Turbary Gdns 2 RG26 .. 9 F1
Turbary Hts BH11 ... 376 F1
Turbary Park Ave
BH11 .... 377 A2
Turbary Rd
Ferndown BH22 ..... 353 F6
Poole BH12 .... 391 D8
Turbary Ret Pk
BH11 .... 376 E3
Turf Croft Ct BH23 .. 382 B2
Turf Hill Rd GU15 .... 36 D8
Turgis Rd GU51 ...... 53 E4
Turin Ct SP10 .... 83 B4
Turk's La
Mortimer RG7 .... 11 D4
Poole BH14 .... 391 A1
Turk St GU34 .... 139 F3
Turlin Moor Com Fst Sch
BH16 .... 389 C4
Turlin Moor Com Mid
Sch BH16 .... 389 C4
Turlin Rd BH16 ..... 389 C4
Turnberry Cl BH23 .. 394 F6
Turnberry Dr RG22 ... 91 A5
Turner Ave PO13 .... 368 E8
Turner Cl RG21 .... 69 E4
Turner Ct SP10 .... 82 F1
Turner Pl GU47 .... 35 B6
Turner Rd PO1 ...... 370 D7
Turners Ave GU51 .... 53 E4
Turners Farm Cres
SO41 .... 384 A2
Turner's Green La
Elvetham RG27 ...... 53 C5
Elvetham RG27 ...... 53 D5
Turners Oak Ct
SO15 .... 266 C1
Turners Way GU51 ... 53 D3
Turnhill Ct SP11 ...... 83 B7
Turnpike Cotts RG25 .. 88 B8
Turnpike Down
SO23 .... 198 C8
Turnpike Ind Est RG14 .. 2 B5
Turnpike Rd RG14 ...... 2 B4
Turnpike Way
Hedge End SO30 .... 293 B7
Oakley RG23 .... 67 A2
Turnstone End 3
GU46 .... 33 F6
Turnstone Gdns
SO16 .... 266 B5
Turnworth Cl BH18 .. 375 C3
Turtle Cl PO14 ...... 342 B4
Turvy King Ct PO7 .. 298 F4
Tuscam Way GU15 ... 35 D4
Tuscan Wlk SO53 ... 243 E6
Tuscany Way
Waterlooville PO7 ... 323 B8
Yateley GU46 .... 34 A4
Tussocks The SO40 . 289 F2
Tutland Rd SO52 .... 241 F4
Tutor Cl SO31 ...... 315 F3
Tutt's La SO51 ..... 238 E4
Tweedale Rd BH9 ... 378 C3
Tweed Cl
Chandler's Ford
SO53 .... 243 A7
Farnborough GU14 ... 55 C6
Tweed La SO41 ..... 385 D8
Tweedsmuir Cl
Basingstoke RG22 .... 68 B4
Farnborough GU14 ... 55 A3
Twelve Acre Cres
GU14 .... 55 C5
Twemlow Ave BH14 . 390 F3
Tweseldown Inf Sch
GU52 .... 75 B4
Tweseldown Rd GU52 . 75 B4
Twiggs End Cl SO31 . 316 F4
Twiggs La
Marchwood SO40 ... 312 E7
Marchwood SO40 ... 312 E8
Twiggs Lane End
SO40 .... 312 C5
Twinley La
Laverstoke RG28 ..... 87 B7
Whitchurch RG28 .... 64 B2
Twin Oak Pk BH23 .. 380 D6
Twin Oaks SO19 .... 291 F3
Twin Oaks Cl BH18 . 375 A3
Twisell Thorne 9
GU52 .... 74 E4
Twittens Way PO9 .. 323 F1
Two Gate La RG25 .... 88 B7
Two Gate Mdw RG25 .. 88 B8
Two Rivers Way RG14 .. 2 C3
Twoways Ct GU35 ... 164 C1
Twyford Ave
Portsmouth PO2 .... 345 D1
Southampton SO15 .. 266 C1
Twyford Cl
Bournemouth BH8 ... 378 D2
Fleet GU51 .... 53 E4
Twyford Ct 16 SO23 . 403 E8
Twyford Dr PO13 .... 367 F3
Twyford Ho
Southampton SO15 .. 290 F7
Trickett's Cross BH22 353 F6
Twyford La GU10 .... 121 F6
Twyford Rd SO50 ... 244 B5
Twyford St Mary's CE
Prim Sch SO21 ..... 219 F5
Twyford Sch SO21 .. 220 A6
Twyford Way BH17 .. 376 A2
Twynham Ave BH23 . 395 A7
Twynham Cl SP5 .... 234 F6
Twynham Rd BH6 ... 394 F4
Twynham Sch BH23 . 395 A6
Twynhams Hill SO32 296 A8
Tydehams RG14 .... 5 D7
Tyfield RG24 .... 47 E3
Tyler Ct PO9 .... 323 E5
Tyler Dr RG2 .... 15 C7
Tylers Cl SO41 ..... 385 D5
Tyleshades The
SO51 .... 241 A6
Tylney La RG27 ...... 50 D1
Tylney Wood GU26 .. 166 D7
Tylston Mdw GU30 .. 187 F5
Tyndalls GU26 ...... 167 D4
Tyne Cl
Chandler's Ford
SO53 .... 243 A5
Farnborough GU14 ... 55 C6
Tyne Ct SP10 .... 83 D2
Tynedale Cl
Bournemouth BH9 ... 378 B4
Gosport PO12 ...... 368 F8
Tyneham Ave BH12 . 391 C8
Tyne Way
Thatcham RG18 .... 2 F5
West End SO30 ..... 268 E2
Tynham Ct BH23 .... 395 C6
Tyrells Croft SP10 ... 106 C8
Tyrells La BH24 ..... 330 E4
Tyrrel Lawn PO9 .... 323 D7
Tyrrell Gdns BH8 ... 379 A2
Tyrrells Ct BH23 .... 357 B1
Tyrrel Rd SO53 ..... 243 C7
Tyseley Rd PO5 ..... 404 B2
Tytherley Gn
5 Havant PO9 ..... 324 B5
Bournemouth BH8 ... 378 D2
Tytherley Rd
Middle Winterslow
SP5 .... 168 C5
Southampton SO18 .. 292 C8

U

Ubsdell Cl BH25 .... 383 A3
Uddens Dr BH21 .... 352 D7
Uddens Trad Est
BH21 .... 352 E6
Ullswater SO50 ..... 244 A1
Ullswater Ave
Farnborough GU14 ... 55 C3
West End SO18 ..... 268 B1
Ullswater Cl
Bordon GU35 .... 164 D5
Farnham GU9 .... 98 E6
Thatcham RG19 .... 2 E3
Ullswater Ct GU12 ... 77 D5
Ullswater Gr SO24 .. 179 D4
Ullswater Ho 4 PO6 321 B1
Ullswater Rd
Southampton SO16 .. 265 E1
Wimborne Minster
BH21 .... 351 C2
Undercliff Dr BH1 ... 393 C2
Undercliff Gdns
SO16 .... 266 E4
Undercliff Rd BH5 .. 393 E3
Underdown Ave
PO7 .... 322 D2
Underhill La GU10 .. 121 F7
Undershore SO41 ... 385 E6
Undershore Rd
SO41 .... 386 A4
Underwood Ave GU12 77 D1
Underwood Cl
Poole BH17 .... 375 B1
Southampton SO16 .. 266 E4
Underwood Rd
Bishopstoke SO50 ... 244 E3
Haslemere GU27 .... 189 D7
Southampton SO16 .. 266 E4
Unicorn Rd
Lee-on-t-S PO13 .... 367 D4
Portsmouth PO1 .... 404 B4
Unicorn Trad Est The
GU27 .... 189 F6
Unicorn Training Ctr The
PO1 .... 404 A4
Union La
Droxford SO32 ...... 249 A1
Kingsclere RG20 ..... 24 D5
Union Pl PO1 .... 404 C4
Union Rd
Farnham GU9 .... 99 A2
Havant PO9 .... 323 E1
Southampton SO14 .. 291 C6
Union Rise GU33 .... 186 D2
Union St
16 Portsmouth
PO1 .... 370 A5
Aldershot GU11 ...... 76 E2
Andover SP10 ...... 106 A7
Fareham PO16 ...... 319 C1
Farnborough GU14 ... 55 F4
Winchester SO23 ... 403 F6
Union Terr GU11 ...... 76 E2
Unity Ho RG19 .... 6 E4
Univ Coll Winchester
SO22 .... 403 C5
Universal Marina
SO31 .... 316 C6
University Cres
SO17 .... 267 B3
University Parkway
SO16 .... 242 D1
University Rd SO17 .. 267 B3
University Rdbt
BH10 .... 392 C8
Univ of Portsmouth
PO1 .... 404 A3
Univ of Portsmouth
(Eldon Bldg) PO1 .. 404 B2
Univ of Portsmouth
(Langstone Campus)
PO4 .... 371 D5
Unwin Cl SO19 ..... 291 D1
Upfallow RG24 .... 70 A8
Upham CE Prim Sch
SO32 .... 246 E5
Upham St SO32 ..... 246 D5
Uphill Rd SO22 ..... 175 C5
Upland La GU33 .... 207 B7
Upland Rd GU15 ...... 36 B7
Uplands Ave BH25 .. 398 A8
Uplands Cl
Sandhurst GU47 ..... 34 F8
West Moors BH22 ... 354 A8
Uplands Cres PO16 .. 319 B2
Uplands Gdns BH8 .. 378 C2
Uplands La GU34 .... 160 A1
Uplands Prim Sch
Fareham PO16 ...... 319 A3
Sandhurst GU47 ..... 34 F8
Uplands Rd
Bournemouth BH8 ... 378 C2
Cosham PO6 .... 346 C8
Denmead PO7 ...... 298 C6
Farnham GU9 .... 99 C1
Rowlands Castle PO9 301 C2
West Moors BH22 ... 327 A1
Winchester SO22 ... 175 E3
Uplands Sch BH14 .. 391 C3
Uplands Way SO17 .. 267 A2
Uplyme Cl BH17 .... 376 A2
Upmill Cl SO18 ..... 268 B3
Upnor Cl SP11 .... 79 D7
Uppark (NT)★ GU31 278 F8
Upper Arundel St
PO1 .... 404 B3
Upper Banister St 1
SO15 .... 290 F6
Upper Barn Copse
SO50 .... 245 B3
Upper Bere Wood
PO7 .... 322 E7
Upper Bourne La
GU10 .... 121 F5
Upper Bourne Vale
GU10 .... 121 E5
Upper Brook Dr
SO31 .... 316 F2
Upper Brook St
SO23 .... 403 E6
Upper Brownhill Rd
SO16 .... 265 F3
Upper Bugle St
SO14 .... 290 F3
Upper Charles St
GU15 .... 36 A6
Upper Chestnut Dr
RG21 .... 68 F3
Upper Chobham Rd
GU15 .... 36 F3
Upper Church La 14
GU9 .... 98 F2
Upper Church Rd
SO32 .... 295 E7
Upper College Ride
GU15 .... 36 C8
Upper Common Rd
SO41 .... 384 F4
Upper Cornaway La
PO16 .... 320 B1
Upper Crabbick La
PO7 .... 298 C6
Upper Crescent Rd
SO52 .... 241 F5
Upper Deacon Rd
SO19 .... 292 C6
Upper Dro SP10 ...... 82 C1
Upper Elms Rd GU11 .. 76 E1
Upper Farm Rd RG23 .. 90 B8
Upper Froyle Dr 11
GU51 .... 53 D3
Upper Gn GU33 ..... 206 E7
Upper Golf Links Rd
BH18 .... 375 B5
Upper Gordon Rd
Camberley GU15 ..... 36 B5
Walkford BH23 ..... 382 A1
Upper Grove Rd
GU34 .... 139 F2
Upper Hale Rd GU9 .. 99 A6
Upper Heyshott
GU31 .... 229 A3
Upper High St SO23 . 403 D6
Upper Hinton Rd
BH1 .... 392 F3
Upper House Ct
PO17 .... 296 A3
Upper House Farm
SO24 .... 203 D2
Upper Lanham La
SO24 .... 158 D7
Upper Market St
SO50 .... 244 B3
Upper Mead SO20 .. 126 B4
Upper Mead Cl
SO50 .... 245 D2
Upper Moors Rd
Brambridge SO50 ... 219 F1
Colden Common SO21,
SO50 .... 244 F8
Upper Mount GU33 .. 207 E3
Upper Mount St 7
GU51 .... 53 D3
Upper Mullins La
SO45 .... 313 E3
Upper Neatham Mill La
GU34 .... 140 C6
Upper New Rd SO30 . 268 D1
Upper Northam Cl
SO30 .... 293 A6
Upper Northam Dr
SO30 .... 292 F6
Upper Northam Rd
SO30 .... 293 B6
Upper Norwich Rd 6
BH2 .... 392 E3
Upper Old Park La
GU9 .... 98 E5
Upper Old St PO14 .. 342 B4
Upper Park Rd GU15 . 36 C6
Upper Piece PO7 ... 299 A3
Upper Raymond
Almshouses 12 RG14 .1 D2
Upper Rd BH12 ..... 391 C6
Upper St Helens Rd
SO30 .... 293 B5
Upper St Michael's Gr
PO14 .... 342 F8
Upper St Michael's Rd
GU11 .... 99 F8
Upper School Dr
GU27 .... 189 D5
Upper Shaftesbury Ave
SO17 .... 267 B2
Upper Sherborne Rd
RG21 .... 69 A7
Upper Shirley Ave
SO15 .... 266 C1
Upper Soldridge Rd
GU34 .... 159 D2
Upper South View
GU9 .... 99 A3
Upper Spinney
SO31 .... 340 C10

Upper St GU51 . . . . 53 F1
Upper Stroud Cl RG24 48 E2
Upper Terrace Rd
 Bournemouth BH2 . . . 392 E3
 Farnborough GU14 . . . 76 E8
Upper Toothill Rd SO16,
SO51 . . . . 241 E1
Upper Union St 4
 GU11 . . . . 76 E2
Upper Union Terr
 GU11 . . . . 76 E2
Upper Verran Rd
 GU15 . . . . 36 B3
Upper Wardown
 GU31 . . . . 229 B4
Upper Way GU9 . . . . . 121 F8
Upper Weston La
 SO19 . . . . 292 A2
Upper Weybourne La
 GU9 . . . . 99 C7
Upper Wharf PO16 . . . 343 C8
Upper Wield Dr GU51 .53 E4
Uppleby Rd BH12 . . . 391 C6
Upron Field Cl RG22 . .91 B7
Up St
 Dummer RG25 . . . . . . 113 C8
 North Waltham RG25 . . 89 E1
Upton Cl
 Farnborough GU14 . . . 56 B3
 Havant PO9 . . . . 323 D7
 Upton BH16 . . . . 389 B7
Upton Cres
 Basingstoke RG21 . . . . 69 A7
 Upton SO16 . . . . 265 D7
Upton Cross Mobile
 Home Pk BH16 . . . . 389 C7
Upton Ct BH16 . . . . . . 389 C7
Upton Ctry Pk★
 BH17 . . . . 389 F6
Upton Grey Cl SO22 . 175 D3
Upton Grey Dr 3
 GU51 . . . . .53 E3
Upton Grey Rd RG25,
 RG29 . . . . .71 E1
Upton Heath Est
 BH16 . . . . 389 D7
Upton Ho 3 SO16 . . . 266 A1
Upton Ind Est BH16 . . 389 D6
Upton Inf Sch BH16 . 389 A7
Upton Jun Sch BH16 389 A7
Upton La SO16 . . . . . . 265 C6
Upton Rd BH17 . . . . . . 389 F7
Upton Way BH18 . . . 374 F3
Upwey Ave BH15 . . . 389 E3
Urchfont Ho 1 SP9 . . 79 A6
Usborne Cl PO13 . . . 367 F4
Utrecht Ct BH31 . . . . . 395 D7
Uxbridge Cl SO31 . . . 316 F6

V

Vadne Gdns PO12 . . . 369 B7
Vaggs La SO41 . . . . . 383 E6
Valdean Home Pk
 SO24 . . . . 179 D6
Vale Cl
 Gong Hill GU10 . . . . . 122 A4
 Poole BH14 . . . . 391 E4
Vale Ct GU12 . . . . .77 E7
Vale Dr SO18 . . . . 267 F1
Vale Gr PO12 . . . . 369 A8
Vale Lodge BH14 . . . 391 E4
Vale Mans 4 BH1 . . . 393 D4
Valencia Cl BH23 . . . 379 D4
Valencia Way SP10 . . .83 B1
Valentine Ave SO19 . 292 C3
Valentine Cl PO15 . . . 318 C2
Valentine Ct
 Southampton SO19 . . 292 C3
 Waterlooville PO7 . . . 323 A8
Valentines Inf Sch
 SO19 . . . . 292 C2
Vale Rd
 Ash Vale GU12 . . . . . . 77 E5
 Bournemouth BH1 . . . 393 D4
 Camberley GU15 . . . . 35 E4
 Poole BH14 . . . . 391 E4
 Redlynch SP5 . . . . . . 235 D6
 Winchester SO23 . . . 198 C6
Valerian Ave PO15 . . 317 F3
Valerian Cl SO50 . . . . 269 C6
Valerian Rd SO30 . . . 293 C6
Vale The
 Horndean PO8 . . . . . . 276 C1
 Hythe SO45 . . . . 313 F3
 Locks Heath SO31 . . . 317 B2
 Oakley RG23 . . . . 67 B1
 Portsmouth PO5 . . . . 370 C2
Valetta Pk PO10 . . . . 348 E8
Valetta Rd PO10 . . . . 349 D1
Valette Rd BH9 . . . . . 378 A3
Vale View Dr RG21 . . 69 C3
Vale View Pk SO41 . . 383 F7
Vale Way SO23 . . . . . 154 B1
Vale Wood Dr GU10 . 122 B4
Vale Wood La GU26 . 167 A4
Valiant Gdns PO2 . . . 345 D4
Valiant Rd PO10 . . . . 349 D1
Valiant Way
 Christchurch BH23 . . 396 B7
 Farnborough GU14 . . . 76 B8
Valley La
 Blackfield SO45 . . . . . 338 F1
 Christchurch BH23 . . 395 D6
 Colden Common SO21 244 F8
 Redlynch SP5 . . . . . . 235 D6
 Waterlooville PO7 . . . 322 C3

Valley Ct The SO22 . . 403 B4
Valleydene SO45 . . . . 313 F2
Valley La
 Bransgore BH23 . . . . 357 E4
 Farnham GU10 . . . . . 122 A7
Valley Mead SP11 . . . 105 C4
Valley Park Dr PO8 . . 276 D4
Valley Rd
 Bournemouth BH8 . . . 378 F3
 Camberley GU15 . . . . 56 F8
 Chandler's Ford SO53 243 C7
 Littleton SO22 . . . . . . 175 B5
 Newbury RG14 . . . . . . 5 C8
 Totton SO40 . . . . 288 F5
Valley Rise
 Sarisbury SO31 . . . . . 316 E4
 Upper Clatford SP11 . 105 C4
Valley Side GU30 . . . 187 F5
Valley The SO22 . . . . 403 B4
Valley View
 Poole BH12 . . . . 392 B7
 Sandhurst GU47 . . . . 34 E7
 Southampton,Sholing
 Common SO19 . . . . 292 A4
 Southampton,Sholing
 SO19 . . . . 292 A4
Valley Way RG26 . . . . 10 C1
Vallis Cl BH15 . . . . . . 390 F4
Valmeade Cl RG27 . . .51 B1
Valon Rd RG2 . . . . 15 D8
Valroy Cl GU15 . . . . . .36 B6
Valsheba Dr PO14 . . . 367 B6
Vampire Way GU11,
 GU14 . . . . 76 C8
Vanburgh Gdns RG22 .91 B7
Vanburgh Way 6
 SO53 . . . . 218 B1
Vancouver Wharf
 SO19 . . . . 291 C4
Van Dyck Cl RG21 . . . .69 E4
Vanguard Ct PO4 . . . 371 D3
Vanguard Rd
 5 Gosport PO12 . . . 369 C9
 6 Poole BH15 . . . . . 390 C4
 Bournemouth BH8 . . . 378 E1
 Southampton SO18 . . 292 A8
Vanners La RG20 . . . . . 4 B5
Vanstone Rd PO13 . . . 368 D7
Vantage Way BH12 . . 376 B2
Vardy Cl SO19 . . . . . . 292 D3
Varna Rd
 Bordon GU35 . . . . . . 164 E3
 Southampton SO15 . . 290 C6
Varndell Rd RG27 . . . .50 F1
Varney Cl GU15 . . . . . 55 C5
Varos Cl PO12 . . . . . . 369 A7
Varsity Rd PO10 . . . . 349 D1
Vaudrey Cl SO15 . . . . 266 C1
Vaughan Cl SO19 . . . 292 E5
Vaughan Rd SO45 . . . 313 C4
Vaughans GU34 . . . . 140 A3
Vauxhall Way GU32 . 228 E3
Veal's La SO40 . . . . . 313 A7
Vear's La SO21 . . . . . 245 A8
Vecta Cl BH23 . . . . . . 396 C6
Vectis Ct GU34 . . . . . 160 B2
Vectis Rd
 Barton on S BH25 . . . 397 D7
 Gosport PO12 . . . . . . 368 E3
Vectis Way PO4 . . . . 345 F7
Velder Ave PO4 . . . . . 371 B5
Vellan Ct SO16 . . . . . 265 C1
Velmead Cl GU52 . . . .75 B7
Velmead Jun Sch
 GU52 . . . . .75 B7
Velmead Rd GU52 . . . .75 B7
Velmore Rd SO53 . . . 243 B4
Velsheda Ct SO45 . . . 314 A5
Velvet Lawn Rd
 BH25 . . . . 382 F4
Venator Pl BH31 . . . . 351 C6
Venerable Rd PO14 . . 343 A5
Vengeance Rd PO13 . 367 E4
Venice Cl PO7 . . . . . . 323 A8
Venice Ct SP10 . . . . . 83 C3
Venison Terr SO20 . . 170 B7
Venning Ave BH11 . . . 376 E5
Venning Rd RG2 . . . . 15 D8
Ventnor Ct SO16 . . . . 267 C5
Ventnor Rd
 Gosport PO13 . . . . . . 343 B3
 Portsmouth PO4 . . . . 370 E4
Ventnor Terr GU12 . . .77 A1
Ventnor Way PO16 . . 319 E1
Ventry Cl BH13 . . . . . 391 F4
Ventura Ctr The
 BH16 . . . . 389 D6
Ventura Pl BH16 . . . . 389 D6
Venture Ct PO3 . . . . . 346 A5
Venture Ind Pk PO3 . 346 A5
Venture Rd SO16 . . . . 242 D1
Venture Rdbt SO16 . . 242 D1
Verbena Cres PO8 . . . 300 B4
Verbena Way PO30 . . 293 C6
Verden Way SP10 . . . .82 F3
Verdi Cl RG22 . . . . 91 D8
Verdon Ave SO31 . . . 315 F3
Verger Ct PO14 . . . . . 317 C3
Verge Wlk GU11 . . . . . 76 C5
Verica Gdns RG26 . . . 10 C2
Verity Cres BH17 . . . . 376 A1
Verity Sq SO31 . . . . . . 83 C3
Vermont Cl SO16 . . . 266 E4
Vermont Sch SO16 . . 266 E4
Vermont Woods RG40 16 C7
Vernalls Cl BH10 . . . 377 D6

Vernalls Ct BH25 . . . . 383 C5
Vernalls Gdns BH10 . 377 D5
Verner Rd BH31 . . . . . 303 A5
Verne Rd BH31 . . . . . . 303 A5
Verne The GU52 . . . . . 75 A5
Verney Cl BH11 . . . . . 377 B3
Verney Rd BH11 . . . . 377 A3
Vernham Dean Gillum's
 CE Prim Sch SP11 . . . 38 C5
Vernham Rd SO22 . . . 403 C8
Vernham Row SP11 . . 38 A7
Verno La BH23 . . . . . . 381 C1
Vernon Ave PO4 . . . . 371 A5
Vernon Cl
 Bishop's Waltham
 SO32 . . . . 247 D2
 Gosport PO12 . . . . . . 369 A6
Vernon Ct
 3 Portsmouth PO2 . . 345 E2
 Farnham GU9 . . . . 98 E1
Vernon Hill SO32 . . . 247 D2
Vernon Mews 2
 PO4 . . . . 371 A5
Vernon Rd
 Gosport PO12 . . . . . . 369 A6
 Portsmouth PO3 . . . . 346 A2
Vernon Wlk 5 SO15 . 290 F6
Verona Ave BH6 . . . . 394 D5
Verona Rd SO53 . . . . 243 F6
Veronica Cl RG22 . . . . 91 A7
Veronica Dr GU51 . . . 74 D5
Verran Rd GU15 . . . . . 36 B3
Verulam Pl 8 BH1 . . . 392 F3
Verulam Rd
 Poole BH14 . . . . 390 F4
 Southampton SO14 . . 291 B7
Verwood CE Fst Sch
 BH31 . . . . 302 C5
Verwood Cres BH6 . . 395 B4
Verwood Ind Est
 BH31 . . . . 303 A6
Verwood Rd
 Ellingham BH24 . . . . 304 A1
 Havant PO9 . . . . 324 D6
 Ringwood BH24 . . . . 328 C8
 Three Legged Cross
 BH21 . . . . 302 F1
 Woodlands Common
 BH21 . . . . 302 A7
Veryan PO14 . . . . 318 C1
Vesca Ho SO31 . . . . . 317 B6
Vesey Cl GU14 . . . . . . 55 E6
Vespasian Ct SO18 . . 291 D7
Vespasian Gdns RG24 68 C8
Vespasian Rd
 Andover SP10 . . . . 83 B3
 Southampton SO18 . . 291 D7
Vespasian Way SO53 243 E7
Vesta Way SO53 . . . . 243 E7
Vestry Cl SP10 . . . . . 105 F8
Vetch Cl BH23 . . . . . . 396 C8
Vetch Fields RG27 . . . 51 C1
Viables Ind Est RG22 . 69 A1
Viables La RG22 . . . . . .69 B1
Viables Rdbt RG21,
 RG22 . . . . .68 F1
Vian Cl PO13 . . . . 343 C4
Vian Ct BH25 . . . . 382 F3
Vian Pl SO23 . . . . 176 C8
Vian Rd PO7 . . . . 322 E5
Vicarage Cl
 Farnham GU9 . . . . . . 122 B7
 Finchampstead RG40 . 16 D6
Vicarage Cotts BH8 . 378 F3
Vicarage Dr SO30 . . . 293 B5
Vicarage Farm Bsns Pk
 SO50 . . . . 245 C5
Vicarage Gdns
 Fleet GU52 . . . . 74 F4
 Grayshott GU26 . . . . 167 A3
 Hordle SO41 . . . . 384 A2
Vicarage Hill
 Alton GU34 . . . . 139 F3
 Farnham GU9,GU10 . 122 C7
 Hartley Wintney RG27 . 52 D5
Vicarage La
 Cadnam SO40 . . . . . . 263 B1
 Curdridge SO32 . . . . 294 C8
 Farnham GU9 . . . . 98 F2
 Farnham,Lower Bourne
 GU9 . . . . 122 B7
 Farnham,Upper Hale
 GU9 . . . . 99 A7
 Hambledon PO7 . . . . 276 E3
 Haslemere GU27 . . . . 189 D6
 Hordle SO41 . . . . 384 A2
 Mattingley RG27 . . . . . 31 A2
 Ropley SO24 . . . . 181 B4
 Stubbington PO14 . . 367 A8
 Swanmore SO32 . . . 272 C6
 Yateley GU46 . . . . 34 A7
Vicarage Pk SP5 . . . . 235 D6
Vicarage Rd
 Alton GU34 . . . . 139 E2
 Blackwater GU17 . . . . 35 C4
 Bournemouth BH9 . . . 377 F1
 Marchwood SO40 . . . 289 F1
 Poole BH15 . . . . 390 C6
 Redlynch SP5 . . . . . . 236 A5
 Verwood BH31 . . . . . 302 F6
 Yateley GU46 . . . . 33 F7
Vicarage Terr PO12 . . 369 A6
Vicarage Way BH23 . 380 D2
Vice La SO43 . . . . 262 A4
Viceroy Rd SO19 . . . . 292 A3
Vickers Bsns Ctr
 RG24 . . . . 68 E8

Vickers Cl BH8 . . . . . 379 B2
Vickers Rd GU12 . . . . 77 D5
Vickery Way BH31 . . 395 D8
Victena Rd SO50 . . . . 245 C2
Victor Ct SO18 . . . . . . 292 D6
Victoria Ave
 Bournemouth BH9 . . . 377 E5
 Camberley GU15 . . . . 35 E5
 Portsmouth PO1 . . . . 370 B5
 South Hayling PO11 . 372 F3
 Waterlooville PO7 . . . 322 B3
Victoria Bldgs SO32 . 271 B8
Victoria Cl
 Corfe Mullen BH21 . . 374 D5
 Locks Heath SO31 . . 317 A1
Victoria Cottage Hospl
 PO10 . . . . 348 F8
Victoria Cotts RG20 . . 20 E7
Victoria Cres BH12 . . 391 D6
Victoria Ct
 10 Fleet GU51 . . . . . . 53 F1
 6 Portsmouth PO1 . . 370 D7
 Andover SP10 . . . . . . 105 F7
 Camberley GU15 . . . . 35 E5
 Durley SO32 . . . . 270 C7
 Netley SO31 . . . . 315 A6
 South Hayling PO11 . 372 E3
Victoria Dr GU17 . . . . 35 A4
Victoria Gdns
 6 Fleet GU51 . . . . . . 53 F1
 Farnborough GU14 . . 55 B4
 Ferndown BH22 . . . . 353 D6
 Fordingbridge SP6 . . 257 D1
 Newbury RG14 . . . . 1 E4
 Ringwood BH24 . . . . 329 A6
Victoria Glade SO31 . 315 C5
Victoria Gr
 5 Newbury RG14 . . . 1 F2
 Portsmouth PO5 . . . . 404 C1
Victoria Hill Rd GU51 .53 E1
Victoria Ho
 1 Fareham PO16 . . . 319 B1
 33 Winchester SO23 403 D6
Victoria Hospl BH21 . 351 A5
Victoria Mews 6
 PO17 . . . . 318 E7
Victoria Park Pl 4
 BH9 . . . . 377 F1
Victoria Park Rd
 BH9 . . . . 377 F1
Victoria Pl
 4 Lymington SO41 . . 385 E2
 6 Gosport PO12 . . . . 369 B5
 Basingstoke RG22 . . . 68 B4
 Bournemouth BH1,
 BH8 . . . . 393 C5
 Hurstbourne Tarrant
 SP11 . . . . 60 E7
 Romsey SO51 . . . . . . 240 E7
 Wimborne Minster
 BH21 . . . . 351 B5
Victoria Rd
 Aldershot GU11 . . . . . 76 F1
 Alton GU34 . . . . 139 F4
 Bishop's Waltham
 SO32 . . . . 271 B8
 Bournemouth BH1 . . . 393 C6
 Christchurch BH23 . . 395 E5
 Eastleigh SO50 . . . . . 244 B5
 Emsworth PO10 . . . . 324 E1
 Farnborough GU14 . . 55 E4
 Farnham GU9 . . . . 99 A2
 Fleet GU51 . . . . 53 F1
 Fordingbridge SP6 . . 257 D1
 Milford on S SO41 . . 399 C4
 Mortimer RG7 . . . . . . 11 E6
 Netley SO31 . . . . 315 A6
 Poole BH12 . . . . 391 C6
 Portsmouth PO1 . . . . 370 A6
 Southampton SO19 . . 291 D2
 Stoke PO11 . . . . 347 F2
 Waterlooville PO7 . . . 322 E7
 Wimborne Minster
 BH21 . . . . 351 B5
 Winchester SO23 . . . 403 D7
Victoria Rd E SO40 . . 140 A4
Victoria Rd N PO5 . . . 404 C2
Victoria Rd S PO5 . . . 370 D2
Victoria Sch BH13 . . . 391 F4
Victoria Sq PO13 . . . . 367 E3
Victoria St
 Basingstoke RG21 . . . 69 B4
 Gosport PO12 . . . . . . 369 C6
 Portsmouth PO1 . . . . 370 D7
 Southampton SO14 . . 291 C5
Victoria Terr
 3 Cosham PO6 . . . . 345 F7
 Grayshott GU26 . . . . 167 A3
 Lumley PO10 . . . . . . 325 A1
 Southbourne PO10 . . 349 C8
 Westbourne PO10 . . 325 B3
Victoria Tk GU11 . . . . 76 C7
Victoria Way SO30 . . 187 F4
Victoria Wlk SO30 . . 268 E2
Victor Rd
 Portsmouth PO1 . . . . 370 F7
 Thorney Island PO10 349 D1
Victor St SO15 . . . . . . 266 B1
Victor Way GU14 . . . .76 B8
Victory Ave PO8 . . . . 300 A6
Victory Cl
 Chandler's Ford
 SO53 . . . . 243 B4
 Three Legged Cross
 BH21 . . . . 327 B6
Victory Cotts SO31 . . 316 D7
Victory Cres SO15 . . . 290 B6

Victory Ct PO13 . . . . . 343 D1
Victory Gn PO2 . . . . . 345 D4
Victory Ho PO6 . . . . . 345 A7
Victory Rd
 27 Portsmouth
 PO1 . . . . 370 A5
 Southampton SO15 . 290 B6
 Stubbington PO14 . . . 367 D7
Victory Rdbt RG21 . . . 69 A5
Victory Ret Pk PO2 . . 370 C4
Victory Sq SO15 . . . . 290 B6
Victory Trad Est
 PO3 . . . . 346 B2
Victory Way SO16 . . . 265 F2
Vidlers Farm RG24 . . .47 F3
Vienna Ct GU14 . . . . . .55 E6
Viewside Cl BH21 . . . 374 C5
Vigo Inf Sch SP10 . . . 83 C1
Vigo Jun Sch SP10 . . 83 C1
Vigo La GU46 . . . . 34 A4
Vigo Rd SP10 . . . . . . 106 B8
Viking Cl
 Blackfield SO45 . . . . . 365 D5
 Bournemouth BH6 . . . 395 A4
 Southampton SO16 . . 265 E4
 Stubbington PO14 . . . 367 B8
Vikings The SO51 . . . 241 B7
Viking Way
 Andover SP10 . . . . 83 B4
 Bournemouth BH6 . . . 395 A4
 Christchurch BH23 . . 396 A5
 Horndean PO8 . . . . . 276 C3
Villa Gdns PO7 . . . . . 322 F8
Village Cl PO14 . . . . . 367 C7
Village Ctr SO40 . . . . 289 F1
Village Gate PO14 . . . 341 F8
Village Mews SO40 . . 289 F1
Village Rd PO12 . . . . 369 A3
Village St
 Bentworth GU34 . . . 138 B5
 Chilbolton SO20 . . . . 129 A4
 Petersfield GU32 . . . 229 B6
Village The
 Finchampstead RG40 . 16 C3
 Litchfield RG28 . . . . . 63 C8
 West Tytherley SP5 . . 169 B1
Village Way GU46 . . . 34 B7
Villa Pl RG7 . . . . 14 A6
Villas The BH25 . . . . 382 E5
Ville De Paris Rd
 PO14 . . . . 343 A5
Villeneuve St Georges
 Way SO50 . . . . 243 E3
Villette Cl BH23 . . . . 380 A1
Villiers Ct
 18 Portsmouth
 PO5 . . . . 370 C2
 Winchester SO23 . . . 403 D6
Villiers Rd
 Hythe SO45 . . . . 337 F8
 Portsmouth PO5 . . . . 370 C2
 Southampton SO15 . 290 C8
Villiers Way RG14 . . . . . 5 A6
Villiers Wlk RG14 . . . . . 5 A6
Vimoutiers Ct SP6 . . 257 E1
Vimy Ho 3 PO14 . . . . 342 E8
Vince Cl BH11 . . . . . . 377 B5
Vincent Ave SO16 . . . 266 C2
Vincent Cl 2 BH25 . . 383 A2
Vincent Ct 13 GU51 . . 54 A1
Vincent Dr SP10 . . . . 106 B7
Vincent Gr PO16 . . . . 344 C7
Vincent Rd
 1 New Milton
 BH25 . . . . 383 A2
 Southampton SO15 . 290 C8
Vincent's Gr SO15 . . . 290 C8
Vincent St SO15 . . . . 290 C8
Vincent's Wlk SO14 . 291 C4
Vindomis Cl GU34 . . 140 D7
Vine Bank SO18 . . . . 292 B8
Vine Cl
 Bournemouth BH7 . . . 394 A7
 Farnborough GU11 . . 76 E6
 Farnham GU10 . . . . . 121 E4
 Mytchett GU16 . . . . . 56 D1
 Warsash SO31 . . . . . 316 D3
Vine Coppice PO7 . . . 322 E4
Vine Ct
 9 Cosham PO6 . . . . 345 D7
 Newbury RG14 . . . . 1 F1
Vine Farm Cl BH12 . . 392 C8
Vine Farm Rd BH12 . 392 B8
Vinegar Hill SO41 . . . 399 D5
Vine Hill BH21 . . . . . . 350 E5
Vine Ho SO31 . . . . . . 317 A4
Vine House Cl GU16 . .56 E3
Vine La GU10 . . . . . . 121 E5
Vine Rd SO16 . . . . . . 266 B3
Vineries Cl BH21 . . . . 351 F6
Vineries The SO41 . . . 351 F6
Vine Sch The SO32 . . 294 D8
Vineside PO13 . . . . . 343 E1
Vine St GU11 . . . . .76 E1
Vine Tree Cl RG26 . . . .27 B7
Vine Way GU10 . . . . . 121 E5
Vineyard Cl SO19 . . . 291 D3
Vineyards The SO52 . 242 A4
Viney Ave SO51 . . . . . 241 B8
Viney Rd SO41 . . . . . 385 F1
Vinnells La GU32 . . . 225 D6
Vinneys Cl BH23 . . . . 380 C2
Vinns La RG25 . . . . . . .87 F1
Vinson Rd GU33 . . . . 208 A4
Violet Ave PO14 . . . . 367 B7

Violet Cl
 Basingstoke RG22 . . . 91 A7
 Chandler's Ford SO53 243 A6
Violet Farm Cl BH21 . 374 D8
Violet La
 Baughurst RG26 . . . . . 26 B6
 New Milton BH25 . . . 383 A4
Violet Rd SO16 . . . . . 267 A4
Violet Wlk BH11 . . . . 376 D5
Virginia Cl BH12 . . . . 391 C7
Virginia Gdns GU14 . 56 A2
Virginia Park Rd
 PO2 . . . . 368 F6
Viscount Cl
 Ash Vale GU12 . . . . . . 77 D5
 Bournemouth BH11 . . 376 D5
Viscount Ct BH11 . . . 376 D5
Viscount Dr BH23 . . . 396 B7
Viscounts Ct SP10 . . . .83 E1
Viscount Wlk BH11 . . 376 D5
Vista Marina BH13 . . 402 D6
Vita Rd PO2 . . . . 345 E3
Vitellius Gdns RG24 . . 68 C8
Vitre Gdns SO41 . . . . 385 E2
Vivaldi Cl RG21 . . . . . .91 E7
Vivash Rd PO1 . . . . . 404 D3
Vivian Cl GU52 . . . . . .75 B6
Vivian Rd RG21 . . . . . 69 C7
Vixen Cl PO14 . . . . . . 367 B7
Vixen Wlk BH25 . . . . 383 B5
Vockins Cl 2 SP9 . . . .78 E8
Vokes Cl SO19 . . . . . 292 B5
Vokes Cotts SO23 . . . 176 A5
Vulcan Cl
 Sandhurst GU47 . . . . 34 E7
 Southampton SO15 . 289 F7
Vulcan Ct GU47 . . . . . 34 E7
Vulcan Ho 3 RG7 . . . . 9 C2
Vulcan Rd
 Southampton SO15 . 289 F7
 Thorney Island PO10 349 D1
Vulcan The 19 PO1 . . 370 A4
Vulcan Way
 Christchurch BH23 . . 396 B7
 Sandhurst GU47 . . . . 34 F7
Vyne Cl GU14 . . . . . . 139 F4
Vyne Com Sch The
 RG21 . . . . 69 B7
Vyne Mdw RG24 . . . . .47 F4
Vyne Rd
 Basingstoke RG21 . . . 69 B6
 Bramley RG26 . . . . . . 28 C1
 Sherborne St John
 RG24 . . . . 48 B6
Vyne The★ RG24 . . . . 48 B6
Vyse La 15 SO14 . . . . 290 F3

W

Wade Court Rd PO9 . 348 A8
Wade La PO9 . . . . 348 A8
Wade Rd RG24 . . . . . .69 E8
Wadham Rd PO2 . . . . 345 D2
Wadhurst Gdns
 SO19 . . . . 315 A8
Wadhurst Rd SO30 . . 293 C6
Wadmore Cl SO45 . . 314 B4
Wadwick Bottom
 SP11 . . . . 62 B1
Waggoners Way
 GU26 . . . . 166 E4
Waggoners Wells Rd
 GU26 . . . . 166 E2
Wagner Cl RG22 . . . . .91 E8
Wagon La RG27 . . . . . .51 B2
Wagtail Dr BH25 . . . . 382 F2
Wagtail Rd PO8 . . . . . 300 A6
Wagtail Way PO16 . . 343 F8
Wainscot Rd PO4 . . . 371 A2
Wainsford Cl SO41 . . 385 B2
Wainsford Rd SO41 . 384 C2
Wainwright Cl PO6 . . 346 C6
Wainwright Gdns
 SO30 . . . . 269 C3
Waite End Prim Sch
 PO7 . . . . 322 E6
Wait End Rd PO7 . . . 322 E6
Wakefield Ave
 Bournemouth BH10 . . 377 E5
 Fareham PO16 . . . . . 318 F2
Wakefield Ct 2
 SO18 . . . . 268 A1
Wakefield Pl PO12 . . 369 A3
Wakefield Rd SO18 . . 268 A1
Wakeford Ct RG26 . . 10 C1
Wakeford Ct
 8 Romsey SO51 . . . 240 F7
 Pamber Heath RG26 . 10 C2
Wakeford Pl SO31 . . 317 A1
Wakefords Cl GU11 . .77 B6
Wakefords Copse
 GU52 . . . . .75 B3
Wakefords Pk GU52 . .75 B3
Wakefords Way PO9 324 B6
Wake Lawn PO4 . . . . 371 C2
Wakely Gdns BH11 . . 377 A5
Wakely Rd BH11 . . . . 377 B5
Wakes Cotts GU34 . . 184 E8
Walberant Bldgs 2
 PO3 . . . . 345 F4
Walberton Ave PO6 . 346 A8
Walberton Ho RG27 . 52 D6

Walburton Way P08. 276 D4
Walcheren Pl BH15. 389 C3
Walcote Pl SO23. 403 D6
Walcott Ave BH23. 379 F1
Waldegrave Cl SO19 291 D1
Waldegrave Pl RG14 . . 1 E3
Walden Gdns P08. 300 B7
Walden Rd PO2. 345 C2
Waldon Gdns SO18. 268 B2
Waldorf Hts GU17. 35 B3
Waldren Cl BH15. 390 E2
Wales St SO23. 403 F6
Walford Bldgs PO3. 371 A7
Walford Cl BH21. 351 C6
Walford Gdns BH21. 351 B6
Walford Mill Craft Ctr★
BH21. 351 B6
Walford Rd PO6. 321 C1
Walhampton Hill
SO41. 385 F5
Walker Gdns SO30. 269 C1
Walker Pl
Gosport PO13. 343 D1
Hamble-le-R SO31. 315 F2
Walker Rd PO2. 345 C2
Walkers Cl SO50. 245 D2
Walkers La N SO45. 338 F1
Walker's La S SO45. 365 F4
Walkers Rise SO20. 147 F8
Walkford La BH25. 382 D3
Walkford Rd BH23. 382 C2
Walkford Way BH23. 382 B1
Walking Field La
BH15. 390 D2
Walk The RG27. 49 E7
Walkwood Ave BH7. 394 B8
Wallace Ct BH18. 375 A3
Wallace La SO42. 363 C6
Wallace Rd
Broadstone BH18. 375 A3
Portsmouth PO2. 370 F8
Southampton SO19. 291 F1
Wallace Way GU11. 76 D1
Walled Gdn The RG7. 13 C5
Walled Mdw SP10. 106 B8
Walled Meadow
SP10. 106 A7
Waller Dr RG14. 2 C5
Wallington Ct PO14. 342 F6
Wallington Dr SO53. 243 B8
Wallington Hill ﹇3﹈
PO16. 319 C2
Wallington Rd PO2. 345 F1
Wallington Shore Rd
﹇1﹈ Portchester
PO16. 319 D1
Fareham PO16. 319 C2
Wallington Way
PO16. 319 C2
Wallins Copse RG24. 48 F2
Walliscott Rd BH11. 377 A1
Wallis Ct RG23. 68 D6
Wallisdean Ave
Fareham PO14. 342 F8
Portsmouth PO3. 371 B7
Wallisdean Jun & Inf
Schs PO14. 342 F8
Wallisdown Rd
BH10. 392 C8
Wallisdown Rdbt
BH12. 377 A1
Wallis Dr RG26. 29 B2
Wallis Gdns PO7. 299 E1
Wallis Rd
Basingstoke RG21. 69 B3
Bournemouth BH10. 377 B1
Waterlooville PO7. 299 E1
Wall La RG7. 11 B2
Wallop Dr RG22. 91 A6
Wallop Dro SO20. 147 D3
Wallop Prim Sch
SO20. 147 F8
Wallop Rd SO20,
SP11. 125 A4
Wallrock Wlk PO10. 324 F4
Walls Cvn Pk RG27. 51 D2
Walmer Cl
Camberley GU16. 56 E7
Eastleigh SO50. 244 A7
Walmer Rd PO1. 370 C4
Walnut Ave SO18. 267 E5
Walnut Cl
Aldershot GU11. 99 E8
Alton GU34. 139 F5
Chandler's Ford SO53 218 C2
New Milton BH25. 382 F3
Southampton SO16. 265 F1
Yateley GU46. 34 B4
Walnut Dr PO14. 367 B2
Walnut Gr
Southampton SO16. 265 F1
Winchester SO22. 403 B7
Walnuts The GU52. 74 E5
Walnut Tree Cl
South Hayling PO11. 372 F3
South Wonston SO21 153 D4
Walnut Tree Dr
PO10. 325 E3
Walnut Tree Ground
SP11. 80 F2
Walnut Tree Rd
SP10. 105 F7

Walpole Gdns RG27. 52 D7
Walpole Ho ﹇3﹈ GU11 . .76 F2
Walpole La SO31. 316 E3
Walpole Rd
Bournemouth BH1. 393 E5
Gosport PO12. 369 D5
Winchester SO22. 403 A3
Walpole Terr ﹇2﹈
PO12. 369 B4
Walrus Rd GU14. 76 B8
Walsall Rd PO1. 371 A6
Walsford Rd BH4. 392 C5
Walsh CE Jun Sch
GU12. 77 E1
Walsh Meml CE Inf Sch
GU12. 77 E1
Walsingham Cl PO6. 321 D1
Walsingham Dene
BH7. 393 F8
Walsingham Gdns
SO18. 267 F3
Waltham Bsns Pk
SO32. 272 A4
Waltham Cl
Droxford SO32. 249 A2
Portchester PO16. 320 C2
Waltham Cres SO16. 266 B4
Waltham Ct RG25. 88 B8
Waltham La
North Waltham RG25. 89 C2
Overton RG25. 88 D5
Waltham Rd
Bournemouth BH7. 394 B6
Overton RG25. 88 B7
Waltham St PO5. 404 A2
Walton Ct
﹇10﹈ Portsmouth
PO1. 370 A4
Fareham PO15. 318 D4
Walton Pl SU22. 403 B3
Walton Rd
Bournemouth BH10. 377 C2
Cosham PO6. 346 C5
Gosport PO12. 369 A5
Poole BH15. 391 A6
Southampton SO19. 291 D2
Waltons Ave SO45. 338 D4
Walton Way RG14. 2 A4
Walworth Ent Ctr
SP10. 83 D1
Walworth Ind Est
SP10. 83 E2
Walworth Rd
Andover SP10. 83 E2
Picket Piece SP10. 84 C4
Wandesford Pl PO12 344 A1
Wandle Cl GU12. 77 E1
Wandsdyke Cl GU16. 56 D8
Wangfield La SO32. 270 C1
Wansbeck Cl SO53. 243 B5
Wansey Gdns RG14. 2 B5
Wanstead Cl BH24. 305 B1
Wantage Rd GU47. 35 B8
Wapiti Way GU14. 76 B8
Warbler Cl
Horndean PO8. 300 A7
Southampton SO16. 266 B6
Upton BH16. 389 B8
Warbleton Rd RG24. 49 A3
Warblington Ave
PO9. 324 B1
Warblington Cl
Chandler's Ford
SO53. 243 B3
Tadley RG26. 27 A7
Warblington Ct ﹇2﹈
PO1. 370 A4
Warblington Rd
PO10. 348 E8
Warblington Sch
PO9. 324 B1
Warblington St PO1. 370 A4
Warblington Sta
PO9. 324 B1
Warborne La SO41. 385 F8
Warbrook Ct ﹇3﹈ PO9 324 B5
Warbrook La RG27. 32 C8
Warburton Cl SO19. 292 E4
Warburton Rd
Poole BH17. 390 E8
Southampton SO19. 292 E4
Ward Cl SP10. 83 A2
Ward Cres PO16. 325 A3
Ward Ct PO11. 372 E2
Warden Cl SO30. 268 D1
Wardens Cl PO11. 372 F5
Warders Ct ﹇2﹈ PO12. 369 B6
Ward Ho PO1. 370 A6
Wardle Rd SO50. 244 D7
Ward Rd PO4. 371 A2
Wardroom Rd PO2. 345 B1
Wareham Ct
Bournemouth BH7. 394 B6
Hamworthy BH15. 389 E2
Wareham Rd BH21. 374 C6
Warehouse Rd RG19. 6 D5
Warfield Ave PO7. 322 E7
Warfield Cres PO7. 322 F7
Wargrove Dr GU47. 35 B8
Warland Way BH21. 374 E7
Warlock Cl SO19. 292 D3
War Meml Hosp
Gosport PO13. 369 A5
Milford on S SO41. 399 E4

Warminster Ho ﹇6﹈
SP9. 78 F7
Warmwell Cl
Bournemouth BH9. 378 B4
Poole BH17. 375 F2
Warnborough Ct ﹇6﹈
PO9. 324 B6
Warner Ct
﹇12﹈ Winchester
SO23. 403 E8
﹇7﹈ Andover SP11. 105 F8
﹇5﹈ Sandhurst GU47. 35 B7
Warner Mews SO30. 294 A7
Warnes La BH24. 330 F2
Warnford Cl PO12. 369 A5
Warnford Cres PO9. 323 D5
Warnford Ct SO15. 290 F7
Warnford Rd
Bournemouth BH7. 394 B7
Meonstoke SO32. 249 D7
Warren Ave
Chandler's Ford
SO53. 243 E5
Christchurch BH23. 395 F5
Portsmouth PO4. 371 B5
Southampton SO16. 266 B4
Warren Cl
Bordon GU35. 164 A2
Chandler's Ford SO53 243 E5
Finchampstead RG40. 16 D6
Fleet GU52. 75 B7
Hartley Wintney RG27. 52 D5
Sandhurst GU47. 34 E8
Southampton SO16. 266 A4
South Hayling PO11. 372 C4
St Leonards BH24. 328 D5
Warren Cnr GU10. 98 A7
Warren Cres SO16. 266 A4
Warren Dr
Abbotts Ann SP11. 104 F3
St Leonards BH24. 328 D5
Warren Edge Cl BH6. 394 F3
Warren Edge Ct BH6. 394 F3
Warren Edge Rd
BH6. 394 F3
Warren Gdns SO51. 216 B1
Warren Ho GU11. 76 D1
Warren La
Bucklers Hard
SO42. 388 F2
Finchampstead RG40. 16 C5
Owslebury SO21. 221 E8
St Leonards BH24. 328 D5
Warren Corner GU32. 206 B5
Winchester SO21. 199 E1
Warren Park Prim Sch
PO9. 323 D7
Warren Pk SO41. 399 A6
Warren Pl SO40. 264 C2
Warren Rd
Bournemouth BH4. 392 B2
Greatham GU33. 186 D2
Liss GU33. 208 B7
Newbury RG14. 5 A6
Poole BH14. 391 D4
Winchester SO23. 198 C8
Warren Rise GU16. 36 D3
Warren The
Aldershot GU11. 76 D1
Farnham GU9. 99 C8
Holbury SO45. 338 B5
North Tidworth SP11. 79 D6
Tadley RG26. 26 E7
Warren Way RG22. 68 F3
Warren Wlk BH22. 353 B2
Warrington Mews
GU11. 99 C8
Warrior Bsns Ctr The
PO6. 346 E7
Warrior Cl SO53. 243 B4
Warrior Pk SO53. 243 B4
Warrys Cl SO45. 338 A8
Warsash Cl PO9. 323 E5
Warsash Ct SO31. 316 C1
Warsash Gr PO13. 343 B2
Warsash Maritime Ctr
(Southampton Solent
Univ) SO31. 340 C9
Warsash Rd
Locks Heath PO14. 341 C8
Warsash SO31. 316 E1
Warspite Cl PO2. 345 D4
Warton Cl SO42. 363 C6
Warton Rd RG21. 69 C6
Warwick Ave BH25. 383 B3
Warwick Cl
﹇14﹈ Winchester
SO23. 403 E8
Aldershot GU11. 100 A4
Chandler's Ford SO53 243 A4
Frimley GU15. 36 F3
Lee-on-t-S PO13. 38 B5
Whitchurch RG28. 86 C5
Warwick Cres PO5. 404 B2
Warwick Ct
﹇15﹈ Winchester
SO23. 403 E8
﹇3﹈ Emsworth PO10. 348 F8
Warwick Dr RG41. 1 F1
Warwick Ho ﹇19﹈
SO14. 291 C6
Warwick Pl
﹇1﹈ Bournemouth
BH7. 394 A5
West Wellow SO51. 238 E3
Warwick Rd
Ash Vale GU12. 77 E8
Basingstoke RG23. 68 C6

Warwick Rd continued
Bournemouth BH7. 394 A5
Farnborough GU14. 76 B8
Poole BH14. 391 C3
Southampton SO15. 266 D2
Totton SO40. 288 F8
Warwick Way PO17. 296 A4
Wasdale Cl PO8. 276 C2
Wash Brook RG27. 51 A2
Washbrook Rd PO6. 321 D1
Washbury Ho PO14. 5 C7
Washford Cl GU35. 164 F4
Washford La GU35. 164 F4
Washington Ave
BH1. 393 D6
Washington Ct
﹇4﹈ Portsmouth
PO4. 371 A5
Thatcham RG19. 2 E3
Washington Gdns
RG40. 16 E8
Washington Rd
Emsworth PO10. 324 F1
Portsmouth PO2. 370 D8
Wash Water RG20. 4 F3
Wasing Cnr RG7. 8 F6
Wasing La RG7. 9 C7
Wastwater Ho ﹇14﹈
PO6. 321 B1
Watchetts Lake Cl
GU15. 36 B3
Watchetts Rd GU15. 35 F4
Watchmoor Pk ﹇4﹈
GU15. 35 F5
Watchmoor Rd GU15. 35 F4
Watchmoor Trad Ctr
GU15. 35 F5
Watcombe Rd BH6. 394 D5
Waterbeech Dr
SO30. 293 C8
Waterberry Dr PO7. 299 C1
Waterbrook Rd
GU34. 140 B4
Water Cl SO23. 403 E6
Watercress Ct GU34. 140 A4
Watercress Mdw
SO24. 179 B4
Waterditch Rd BH23 381 A4
Water End La RG24. 71 A7
Water End Mobile Home
Pk RG24. 71 A7
Waterford Cl
Lymington SO41. 385 F3
Poole BH14. 391 A2
Waterford Gdns
BH23. 397 A7
Waterford La SO41. 385 F2
Waterford Lodge
BH23. 396 B6
Waterford Pl BH23. 397 B7
Waterford Rd
Christchurch BH23. 397 B7
New Milton BH25. 383 C3
Waterfront Bsns Pk
GU51. 54 B3
Waterfront Mus★
GU51. 54 B3
Watergardens BH8. 393 A5
Watergate ﹇12﹈ PO12. 369 E5
Waterhouse La SO15 290 B7
Waterhouse Mead
GU47. 35 B7
Waterhouse Way
SO15. 290 B7
Wateridge Rd RG21. 69 C8
Water La
﹇2﹈ Southampton
SO15. 290 F5
Bishop's Sutton SO24 180 C4
Bournemouth BH6. 394 D7
Farnborough GU14. 55 E7
Farnham GU9. 99 D4
Greenham RG19. 6 A8
Hythe SO45. 313 E2
Totton SO40. 288 E8
Upper Clatford SP11. 105 F5
Winchester SO23. 403 F5
Water Lane Farm
BH10. 377 E6
Waterlily Ct ﹇13﹈ RG21. 69 D5
Waterlock Gdns
PO4. 371 D4
Waterloo Ave RG23. 68 C7
Waterloo Cl
Camberley GU15. 36 F7
Waterlooville PO8. 299 C3
Waterloo Cotts
SO21. 133 A3
Waterloo Ct
Andover SP10. 106 A7
Whitchurch RG28. 86 C5
Waterloo Ho BH17. 375 B1
Waterloo Ind Est
SO30. 269 B1
Waterloo Rd
Aldershot GU12. 77 A1
Bournemouth BH9. 392 F7
Corfe Mullen BH21. 374 B5
Gosport PO12. 369 C2
Havant PO9. 323 C7
Lymington SO41. 385 F4
Poole BH17. 390 C8
Southampton SO15. 290 D6
Waterloo Sch The
PO7. 322 E7
Waterloo St PO5. 404 B2
Waterloo Terr
Anna Valley SP11. 105 D4

Waterloo Terr continued
Southampton SO15. 290 F6
Waterloo Way BH24. 329 A6
Waterman Cl GU35. 164 F2
Watermans La SO45. 313 E1
Waterman Terr PO5. 404 D1
Water Mdws The RG14. . 1 F4
Watermead ﹇5﹈ BH23 395 A5
Watermeadows Small
Industries The
GU35. 165 A4
Watermeadows The
SP10. 105 F5
Watermead Rd PO6. 346 E7
Watermill Ct ﹇2﹈ PO9 323 F1
Watermill Rd BH23. 395 A8
Watermills Cl SP10. 105 F6
Water Rede GU52. 74 E3
Water Ridges RG23. 90 B8
Watersedge PO17. 296 A4
Waters Edge
Lee-on-t-S PO13. 367 F1
Poole BH15. 402 D6
Waters Edge Gdns
PO10. 348 F8
Watersedge Rd PO6. 345 A8
Waters Gn SO42. 334 A2
Waters Green Ct
SO42. 334 A2
Watershed Ct ﹇2﹈
PO6. 321 A1
Watership Dr BH24. 329 D6
Waterside
Christchurch BH23. 395 F4
Downton SP5. 235 A7
Hythe SO45. 314 A5
Waterside Cl
Bordon GU35. 164 E4
Ringwood BH24. 305 B1
Waterside Ct
Alton GU34. 140 A4
Fleet GU51. 54 B3
Newbury RG14. 2 A1
Waterside Gdns
PO16. 319 D1
Waterside Heritage Ctr★
SO45. 314 B4
Waterside La PO16. 344 E6
Waterside Mews
GU51. 54 B3
Waterside Prim Sch
SO45. 314 B2
Waterside Rd SO51. 216 A1
Waterside Sch PO2. 345 B3
Waterside Sch (Unit)
PO4. 371 C4
Waterside Sq SO45. 313 F5
Watersmead SO23. 403 D3
Watersmeet
﹇5﹈ Winchester
SO23. 403 F5
Fareham PO16. 343 B4
Watersmeet Ct BH23 395 B5
Waters The PO17. 318 C5
Waterston Cl BH17. 375 D1
Water Tower Rd
BH18. 375 C4
Water Way ﹇11﹈ RG21. 69 D5
Waterworks Rd
Farlington PO6. 346 D7
Otterbourne SO21. 219 D4
Petersfield GU32. 229 A6
Watery La
Andover SP10. 83 B1
Christchurch BH23. 396 A8
Crookham Village
GU51. 74 E3
Hamstead Marshall
RG20. 3 D5
Upton BH16. 389 A7
Watkin Rd ﹇6﹈ Bournemouth
BH5. 393 F4
Hedge End SO30. 269 D2
Watkins Cl RG40. 16 C7
Watley Cl SO16. 265 D5
Watley La
Sparsholt SO21. 174 D4
Twyford SO21. 220 B6
Watling End RG22. 91 B7
Watson Acre SP10. 105 E8
Watson Way RG23. 68 D6
Watson Wlk SO40. 288 C7
Watt Cl SP10. 82 C1
Watton Cl SO32. 249 E2
Watton Rd SO45. 338 C5
Watts Cl SO16. 265 F3
Watts Common Rd
GU11. 76 C7
Watts Rd
Farnborough GU14. 55 D5
Hedge End SO30. 293 C2
Portsmouth PO1. 370 D7
Wavecrest Cl SO40. 290 A3
Wavell Ave BH17. 375 A1
Wavell Cl RG22. 68 E2
Wavell Ct ﹇11﹈ GU12. 77 A1
Wavell Rd
Bournemouth BH11. 377 B4
Gosport PO13. 343 D4
North Tidworth SP9. 78 D8
Southampton SO18. 292 A8
Wavell Sch The GU14. .76 F7
Wavell Way SO22. 403 A3
Wavendon Ave BH25 397 E6
Waveney Cl PO13. 367 F3

Waveney Gn SO16. 265 E1
Waverley ﹇14﹈ BH4. 392 C3
Waverley Abbey★
GU9. 122 F7
Waverley Ave
Basingstoke RG21. 69 A2
Fleet GU51. 54 A2
Netley SO31. 315 C5
Waverley Cl
Farnham GU9. 99 B2
Fordingbridge SP6. 257 F3
Frimley GU15. 36 D4
Odiham RG29. 72 F3
Romsey SO51. 216 B1
Waverley Cres BH15 390 D6
Waverley Ct SO31. 315 C5
Waverley Dr
Ash Vale GU12. 77 E6
Camberley GU15. 36 D5
South Wonston SO21. 153 F4
Waverley Gdns GU12. .77 E6
Waverley Gr PO4. 370 C2
Waverley Ho ﹇9﹈
BH25. 383 B2
Waverley La GU9. 99 C1
Waverley Path PO12 368 E3
Waverley Rd
Cosham PO6. 346 C7
Farnborough GU14. 56 B3
Fordingbridge SP6. 257 F3
New Milton BH25. 383 B2
Portsmouth PO4. 370 E2
Southampton SO15. 290 D5
Waverley Way RG40. 16 D8
Wayewood Lodge ﹇4﹈
GU9. 36 C4
Wayfarer Cl
Locks Heath SO31. 316 F1
Portsmouth PO4. 371 C5
Wayfarers PO13. 368 D7
Wayground Rd BH21 350 E1
Waylands Pl SO30. 293 B4
Wayman Rd
Corfe Mullen BH21. 374 E6
Farnborough GU14. 55 C8
Wayne Rd BH12. 391 B6
Waynflete Cl ﹇1﹈
SO30. 271 C8
Waynflete La GU9. 98 D2
Waynflete Pl SO22. 403 A4
Ways End GU15. 36 C4
Waysend Ho GU15. 36 C4
Wayside Cl SO41. 399 D5
Wayside Cotts GU10. 144 C3
Wayside Rd
Basingstoke RG23. 68 B5
Bournemouth BH6. 394 B4
St Leonards BH24. 354 F8
Wayte St PO6. 345 F7
Waytown Cl BH17. 375 D1
Weald Cl SO31. 317 A4
Weale Ct RG21. 69 B6
Weapon Rd GU14. 55 F2
Weardale Rd SO53. 243 C4
Weatherby Gdns
RG27. 52 D6
Weathermore La
GU34. 160 D2
Weaver Moss GU47. 34 F7
Weavers Cl
Andover SP10. 106 B8
Middle Winterslow
SP5. 168 A6
West Moors BH22. 326 E1
Weavers Gdns SO19. 121 D7
Weavers Gn PO9. 324 C3
Weavers Pl SO53. 243 B8
Weaver's Wlk RG14. 1 E3
Weavills Rd SO50. 245 A1
Webb Cl
Chineham RG24. 48 F2
South Hayling PO11. 373 A2
Webbers Way PO12. 369 C3
Webb La PO11. 373 A2
Webb Rd PO16. 344 D6
Webbs Cl BH24. 327 D6
Webbs Farm Cl RG28. 86 C3
Webbs Gn SO32. 273 C3
Webbs La BH24. 327 E6
Webb's Way BH11. 376 F1
Webburn Gdns SO18 268 A3
Webster Rd
Bournemouth BH9. 378 A3
Winchester SO22. 403 A7
Wedderburn Ave
RG22. 91 B5
Wedgwood Cl
Holbury SO45. 338 C4
Stubbington PO14. 367 A6
Wedgwood Way
PO8. 299 E2
Wedgwod Dr BH14. 391 A2
Wedgwood Gdns
BH23. 357 C1
Wedman's La RG27. .50 F6
Wedman's Pl RG27. .50 F6
Wedmore Cl SO22. 197 A3
Weeke Cl SP5. 234 D7
Weeke Manor Cl
SO22. 403 B8
Weeke Prim Sch
SO22. 403 B8
Weevil La PO12. 369 D7
Weir Ave GU14. 55 E3
Weir Cl GU14. 55 E3
Weir Cotts RG20. 42 E8

Weir Rd
Farnborough GU51 . . . **54** E2
Hartley Wintney RG27. . **52** B4
Weirs The 🔢 SO23. . **403** F4
Weir Rd RG28. . . . . **86** C3
Welbeck Ave SO17. . . **267** B2
Welbeck Cl GU14 . . . . **55** D3
Welbeck Ct SO17 . . . . **267** B2
Welburn Ct SO18 . . . . **268** A1
Welch Rd
Gosport PO12 . . . . . . **369** A8
Portsmouth PO4 . . . . **370** E2
Welch Way SO16. . . . . **265** F5
Welchwood Cl PO8 . . **299** F6
Weldon Ave BH11. . . . **376** E5
Weldon Cl GU52. . . . . . **75** B5
Welland Gdns SO18 . . **268** B2
Welland Gn SO16 . . . . **289** E8
Welland Rd BH21. . . . **351** D4
Wellands Rd SO43 . . . **310** A5
Wella Rd RG22. . . . . . . **68** F2
Wellbrooke Gdns
SO53. . . . . **243** B7
Wellburn Cl GU47. . . . **34** F7
Well Cl
Camberley GU15. . . . . **35** F4
New Milton BH25 . . . **382** F4
North Waltham RG25. . **89** E1
Wooton St Lawrence
RG23 . . . . **67** E7
Well Copse Cl PO8 . . **276** C1
Weller Dr
Arborfield Garrison
RG40 . . . . **15** E6
Camberley GU15 . . . . **36** A3
Weller Ho 🔢 PO1. . **370** D7
Wellers Cl SO40. . . . . **288** D7
Wellesley Ave BH23 . **396** C7
Wellesley Cl
Ash Vale GU12. . . . . . **77** D7
Waterlooville PO7 . . . **322** E7
Wellesley Ct SP10. . . **106** A5
Wellesley Gate 🔢
GU12. . . . . **76** F1
Wellesley Gdn GU9 . . **99** A4
Wellesley Rd
Aldershot GU11. . . . . . **76** C2
Andover SP10 . . . . . . **106** A6
Farnborough GU14 . . . **76** B8
Rushmoor GU10 . . . . **144** F6
Welles Rd SO53 . . . . . **243** D6
Well Hill PO7 . . . . **298** D7
Well House Cl SP6 . . **233** B3
Well House La
Kings Worthy SO22 . . **175** E5
Lower Common RG27 . . **14** F3
Wellhouse Rd GU34. . **139** A2
Wellington Ave
Aldershot GU11. . . . . . **76** D2
Bordon GU35. . . . . . . **164** D5
Christchurch BH23 . . **396** C7
Fleet GU51 . . . . **54** B4
Southampton SO18 . . **292** B7
Wellington Cl
Dibden Purlieu
SO45. . . . . **313** D1
Horndean PO8. . . . . . **300** D6
Newbury RG14 . . . . **2** A5
Sandhurst GU47 . . . . . **35** A8
Wellington Cotts RG20 . . **3** F2
Wellington Cres RG26. . . **9** B1
Wellington Ct
🔢 Havant PO9 . . . . . **323** F1
🔢 Gosport PO12 . . . **369** C9
🔢 Bournemouth,Dean Park
BH8 . . . . **393** A5
Bournemouth,Westbourne
BH2 . . . . **392** D3
New Milton BH25 . . . **383** A3
Southampton SO15 . . **290** D6
West End SO30 . . . . . **268** C4
Wellington Ctr The 🔢
GU11. . . . . **76** E2
Wellington Ctry Pk★
RG7 . . . . **14** C1
Wellington Dr PO13 . **368** A5
Wellington Gdns 🔢
GU11. . . . . **76** D1
Wellington Gr PO16 . **344** C7
Wellingtonia Cotts
RG27 . . . . **31** A7
Wellingtonia Gdns
SO41 . . . . **383** F4
Wellington La GU9 . . . **99** B7
Wellington Pk SO30 . **269** A4
Wellington Pl
Ash Vale GU12. . . . . . **77** D7
Cadnam SO40 . . . . . . **286** F8
Wellington Rd
Andover SP10 . . . . . . **82** F1
Bournemouth BH8. . . **393** A6
Poole BH14 . . . . **391** C3
Sandhurst GU47 . . . . . **35** A8
Southampton SO18 . . **267** E2
Wellington Rdbt
GU11. . . . . **76** C2
Wellington St
Aldershot GU11. . . . . . **76** E2
Portsmouth PO5 . . . . **404** E1
Wellington Terr
Basingstoke RG23. . . . **68** C7
Sandhurst GU47 . . . . . **35** A8
Wellington Way
🔢 Waterlooville
PO7 . . . . **322** E7
Farnborough GU11,
GU11 . . . . **76** B7

Well La
Godshill SP6 . . . . **258** E2
Hamble-le-R SO31. . . **316** A2
Lower Froyle GU34 . . . **119** B7
Poole BH15 . . . . **390** C4
Swanmore SO32 . . . . **272** B7
Wellman Ct 🔢 SO16. **266** E3
Wellmans Mdw RG20. . **24** C3
Well Mdw
Havant PO9 . . . . **323** E6
Newbury RG14 . . . . **1** F5
Wellowbrook Cl
SO53 . . . . **243** A6
Wellow Cl
Havant PO9 . . . . **323** D3
Southampton SO18 . . **292** C7
Wellow Cl 🔢 SO18. . **291** E8
Portchester PO16 . . . **344** B7
Romsey SO51 . . . . . . **241** B7
Wellow Dro SO51. . . . **238** E7
Wellow Gdns PO14. . . **317** C1
Wellow Ho GU51. . . . . **53** C4
Wellow's La GU51. . . . **86** B4
Wellow Sch SO51. . . . **238** F3
Wellow Wood Rd
SO51 . . . . **238** D8
Well Rd GU10. . . . . **97** C6
Wells Cl
Portsmouth PO3 . . . . **371** B6
Swanwick PO15. . . . . **317** C8
Wells Cotts GU9 . . . . **121** E7
Wellsmoor PO14. . . . . **317** C2
Wells Pl SO50. . . . . **244** B2
Wellspring Ho RG22. . **68** C2
Wells Rd SO50. . . . . . . **244** B2
Well St RG20 . . . . **22** E5
Wellswood Gdns
PO9 . . . . **301** C3
Wellsworth La PO9. . . **301** C3
Wellum Ct 🔢 SO51. . . **241** B7
Wellworthy Rd SO41 **385** D6
Welsh La RG7,RG27 . . . **13** E2
Welshman's Rd RG7 . . **10** E5
Welton Ct RG21. . . . . . **69** A5
Wembley Gr PO6. . . . . **346** B6
Wembley Way SO50. . **245** C1
Wendan Rd RG14 . . . . . **5** D8
Wendover Cl BH25. . . **382** F1
Wendover Rd PO9 . . . **323** E2
Wendy Cres BH22. . . . **353** F3
Wenlock Ct 🔢 BH23. . **395** F8
Wensley Dr GU51 . . . . **54** A3
Wensley Gdns PO10. . **324** F3
Wentwood Gdns
BH25 . . . . **383** D2
Wentworth BH14. . . . . **402** C7
Wentworth Ave BH5 . **394** B4
Wentworth Cl
Ash Vale GU12. . . . . . **77** E6
Bournemouth BH5. . . **394** B3
Farnham GU9 . . . . **99** D6
Yateley GU46. . . . . **34** B5
Wentworth Coll BH5 **394** A4
Wentworth Cres
Ash Vale GU12. . . . . . **77** E6
Basingstoke RG22. . . . **91** A5
Wentworth Ct RG14. . . **1** F1
Wentworth Dr
Broadstone BH18 . . . **375** B5
Christchurch BH23 . . **394** F6
Horndean PO8. . . . . . **300** B7
Wentworth Gdns
Alton GU34 . . . . **139** E4
Holbury SO45. . . . . . **338** D3
Southampton SO19 . . **292** B3
Wentworth Gr SO45. . **338** D3
Wentworth Grange
Ferndown BH22. . . . . **353** D7
Winchester SO22 . . . **403** C4
Wentworth Lodge 🔢
RG14 . . . . **1** C2
Wentworth Pl GU15. . **35** E4
Wescott Way BH11. . . **376** E4
Wesermarsch Rd
PO8 . . . . **300** A4
Wesley Chambers 🔢
GU11 . . . . **76** E2
Wesley Cl
🔢 Bournemouth
BH8 . . . . **393** C5
Southampton SO19 . . **292** D4
Wesley Ct PO1. . . . . . **404** D3
Wesley Gr PO3. . . . . . **346** A4
Wesley Grange 🔢
BH4 . . . . **392** C3
Wesley Ho
🔢 Winchester
SO23. . . . . **403** E6
Trickett's Cross BH22 **353** F6
Wesley Rd
Kings Worthy SO23 . . **176** C7
Poole BH12 . . . . **391** C5
Wimborne Minster
BH21. . . . . **351** E5
Wesley Wlk 🔢 RG21. . **69** B5
Wespall Ho 🔢 GU51. . **53** D3
Wessex Ave
New Milton BH25 . . . **383** A2
Odiham RG29. . . . . **72** D1
Wessex Cl
Basingstoke RG21. . . . **69** A3
Blackfield SO45 . . . . . **365** F8
Christchurch BH23 . . **396** C7
Lee-on-t-S PO13 . . . . **368** A6
Wessex Cres RG29 . . . **72** D1

Wessex Ct continued
Southampton,Sholing
SO19. . . . . **292** A4
Wessex Dr
Odiham RG29. . . . . **72** D1
Winchester SO22 . . . **403** D8
Wessex Est BH24. . . . **329** C8
Wessex Gate
🔢 Southampton
SO15. . . . . **290** E7
Bournemouth BH8. . . **393** C6
Wessex Gate Ind Est
PO8. . . . . **300** C6
Wessex Gate Ret Pk
BH15. . . . . **390** B6
Wessex Gdns
Andover SP10 . . . . . . **105** F8
Portchester PO16 . . . **344** B7
Romsey SO51 . . . . . . **241** B7
Wessex Grange RG27 . **49** E8
Wessex La SO18 . . . . . **267** D4
Wessex Mews SO20 . **149** F3
Wessex Nuffield Hospl
SO53 . . . . **219** A1
Wessex Pk SO21 . . . . **131** C5
Wessex Pl GU9 . . . . **99** A1
Wessex Rd
Farnborough GU14 . . . **55** C2
Horndean PO8. . . . . . **276** D3
Poole BH14 . . . . **391** A3
Ringwood BH24 . . . . **329** B8
Wessex Trade Ctr
BH12. . . . . **391** A7
Wessex Way
Bournemouth,
Springbourne BH8 . **393** C3
Bournemouth,Westbourne
BH2,BH4 . . . . **392** D3
Colden Common
SO21. . . . . **245** A8
West Ave
Farnham GU9 . . . . **99** B6
Three Legged Cross
BH21 . . . . **326** E8
West Bargate 🔢
SO14 . . . . **290** F4
West Battery Rd
PO2. . . . . **345** B1
West Bay Rd SO15 . . **290** C5
Westbeams Rd SO41 **360** B1
West Berkshire Com
Hospl RG18. . . . . **2** C4
West Berkshire Mus★
RG14 . . . . **1** E3
Westborn Rd PO16 . . **319** B1
West Borough BH21. **351** B5
Westbourne Ave
Emsworth PO10. . . . . **325** A2
Holbury SO45. . . . . . **338** C4
Westbourne Cl
Bournemouth BH4. . . **392** C3
Emsworth PO10. . . . . **325** A2
Westbourne Cres
SO17 . . . . **267** A1
Westbourne Ct 🔢
PO9 . . . . **323** F2
Westbourne Gate 🔢
BH4 . . . . **392** C2
Westbourne Mans 🔢
SO17 . . . . **267** A1
Westbourne Park Rd
BH4 . . . . **392** B2
Westbourne Prim Sch
PO10. . . . . **325** B4
Westbourne Rd
Portsmouth PO2 . . . . **370** F8
Sandhurst GU47 . . . . . **35** C7
Westbourne PO10. . . **325** A3
Westbourne Terr 🔢
RG14 . . . . **1** E4
Westbroke Gdns
SO51 . . . . **215** C1
Westbrook Cl
Bournemouth BH10. . **377** B3
Locks Heath SO31. . . **317** A6
Oakley RG23 . . . . **90** B8
Westbrook Ct RG22. . . **68** A4
Westbrook Ctr The 🔢
PO7 . . . . **300** B1
Westbrooke Cl
🔢 Andover SP10 . . . **106** A7
Waterlooville PO8. . . . **300** A6
Westbrooke Cotts
GU32 . . . . **226** E1
Westbrooke Rd
GU34 . . . . **139** E3
Westbrook Gr PO7. . . **322** D4
Westbrook Rd PO16. . **344** D7
Westbrook Way
SO18 . . . . **267** D4
Westbrook Wlk 🔢
GU34 . . . . **139** F3
Westburn Fields
GU34 . . . . **119** C4
Westbury Ave GU51 . . **75** D8
Westbury Cl
🔢 Portsmouth PO6 . **321** B1
Barton on S BH25 . . . **398** B8
Bransgore BH23 . . . . **381** A7
Christchurch BH23 . . **381** D1
Fleet GU51 . . . . **75** D8
Westbury Gdns
Farnham GU9 . . . . **99** C4
Fleet GU51 . . . . **75** D8
Westbury Ho 🔢 SP9 . **78** F6

Westbury Mall 🔢
PO16 . . . . **319** B1
Westbury Manor Mus★
PO16 . . . . **319** B1
Westbury Rd
Fareham PO16. . . . . . **319** B1
Ringwood BH24 . . . . **329** B7
Southampton SO15 . . **289** F7
Westbury Sq 🔢
PO16 . . . . **319** B1
Westby Rd BH5 . . . . . **393** F4
West Cl
Farnham GU9 . . . . **99** B7
Lymington SO41 . . . . **385** B2
Verwood BH31. . . . . . **302** D6
West Cliff 🔢 BH2 . . . **392** F4
Westcliff CI PO13 . . . **367** E4
West Cliff Cotts BH2 **392** C2
West Cliff Ct 🔢 BH4 **392** C3
West Cliff Gdns BH2 **392** C2
Westcliff Ho 🔢 BH4 **392** C2
Westcliff Mews
SO19 . . . . **291** D3
West Cliff Mews
BH2 . . . . **392** E2
Westcliff Palms 🔢
BH4 . . . . **392** C2
West Cliff Rd BH4. . . **392** C2
West Close Ho BH4. . **395** A4
West Comm SO45. . . . **365** E6
Westcot Rd SO45 . . . **338** B3
West Cotts GU26 . . . **167** A6
Westcroft Par 🔢
BH25 . . . . **383** B2
Westcroft Pk BH18. . **375** C4
Westcroft Rd PO12. . **368** F5
West Ct
Portsmouth,Buckland
PO1 . . . . **370** E7
Portsmouth,Eastney
PO4 . . . . **371** A3
Southampton SO19 . . **291** F1
Westdeane Ct RG21. . **68** F4
Westdown Rd BH11. . **377** A5
West Downs Cl
PO16 . . . . **319** A4
West Downs Student
Village SO22 . . . . **403** B6
West Dr
Bishopstoke SO50. . . **244** D4
West Moors BH24 . . . **354** B8
West End Rd GU24 . . . **47** D4
West End Cl SO22 . . . **403** C6
West End Cotts 🔢
PO16 . . . . **319** A1
West End Gr GU9 . . . . **98** E2
West End Ho RG14 . . . . **1** F5
West End Inf Sch
GU11. . . . . **76** D1
West End La
Medstead GU34. . . . . **159** B4
Rowledge GU10. . . . . **121** E5
West End Local History
Mus & Heritage Ctr★
SO30. . . . . **268** D1
West End Rd
Bursledon SO31. . . . . **292** F3
Mortimer RG7 . . . . **11** C5
Southampton SO18 . . **268** B2
West End Terr SO22. . **403** C6
Westerdale Dr GU16. . **36** F3
Westerham 🔢 BH13 . **392** F4
Westerham Cl PO6. . . **345** E8
Westerham Rd BH4 . . **392** B3
Westering SO51 . . . . . **241** C8
Westerleigh 🔢 BH4 . **392** C2
Westerley Cl SO31 . . **316** E1
Western Ave
Andover SP10 . . . . . . **106** A8
Barton on S BH25 . . . **397** D8
Bournemouth BH10. . **377** D4
Emsworth PO10. . . . . **348** D8
Newbury RG14 . . . . **1** D4
Poole BH13 . . . . **391** F2
Southampton SO15 . . **290** A6
Western CE Prim Sch
SO22. . . . . **403** B6
Western Cl BH10. . . . **377** D5
Western Com Hospl
SO16. . . . . **265** C1
Western Cross RG29 . **72** D2
Western Ct 🔢 PO16 . **319** A1
Western District Cut
SO15 . . . . **290** F4
Western Downland CE
Prim Sch
Damerham SP6 . . . . . **256** D4
Rockbourne SP6 . . . . **232** F1
Western End 🔢 RG14 . . **1** C2
Western Espl
Southampton SO14,
SO15. . . . . **290** F3
Southampton SO15 . . **290** E5
Westergate 🔢
BH13. . . . . **392** B3
Western La RG29 . . . . **72** D3
Western Par
Emsworth PO10. . . . . **348** E2
Portsmouth PO5 . . . . **370** B2
Western Rd
Aldershot GU11. . . . . . **76** C1
Andover SP10 . . . . . . **106** A7
Bordon GU35. . . . . . . **164** C5
Chandler's Ford SO53 **218** A1
Fareham PO16. . . . . . **319** B1
Fawley SO45. . . . . . . **339** E1

Western Rd continued
Havant PO9 . . . . **323** D1
Liss GU33 . . . . **207** F4
Lymington SO41 . . . . **385** B2
Poole BH13 . . . . **392** A2
Poole,Canford Cliffs
BH13 . . . . **402** F8
Portsmouth PO6 . . . . **345** D7
West End SO30 . . . . . **268** C4
Winchester SO22 . . . **403** C6
Western Terr PO2. . . . **345** C2
Western Way
Basingstoke RG22. . . . **68** D3
Fareham PO16. . . . . . **319** A1
Gosport PO12 . . . . . . **368** E2
Portsmouth PO1 . . . . **369** F8
Westfield 🔢 BH21 . . **351** B5
Westfield Ave
Fareham PO14. . . . . . **342** F4
South Hayling PO11. . **372** F3
Westfield Cl
Hamble-le-R SO31. . . **315** E2
Horton Heath SO50. . **269** D7
Wimborne Minster
BH21 . . . . **351** B5
West Field Rd RG26. . **27** B8
Westfield Cnr SO18 . **267** E5
Westfield Comm
SO31 . . . . **315** D2
Westfield Cres
Chandler's Ford
SO53. . . . . **243** C4
Thatcham RG18. . . . . . **2** F4
Westfield Ct
🔢 Andover SP10 . . . **106** B7
🔢 Fleet GU51 . . . . . **54** A1
Westfield Dr SO32 . . **272** D2
Westfield Dro
Beauworth SO24 . . . **201** B1
Beauworth SO24 . . . **222** F8
Westfield Ho SO18 . . **267** E4
Westfield Ind Est
Gosport PO12 . . . . . . **369** A5
Horndean PO8. . . . . . **300** D7
Westfield Jun Sch
PO6. . . . . **344** E8
Westfield La GU10 . . **121** C6
Westfield Oaks PO11 **372** F3
Westfield Rd
Basingstoke RG21. . . . **69** C3
Bournemouth BH6. . . **394** E4
Camberley GU15 . . . . **35** F2
Gosport PO12 . . . . . . **369** A5
Littleton SO22 . . . . . **175** B5
Lymington SO41 . . . . **386** A2
Portsmouth PO4 . . . . **371** A3
Southampton SO15 . . **290** A4
Thatcham RG18. . . . . . **2** F5
Totton SO40. . . . . . . **288** F8
West Field Rd SO23 . **154** C1
Westfields Inf Sch
GU46. . . . . **33** F5
Westfields Jun Sch
GU46. . . . . **33** F5
Westfield Way 🔢 RG14 **1** C2
West Fryerne GU46 . . **34** B2
Westgate PO14 . . . . . **367** C6
Westgate Cl RG23. . . . **68** B5
Westgate Ct RG14. . . . **1** C1
Westgate Mews
SO30 . . . . **268** E1
Westgate Mus★
SO23. . . . . **403** D6
Westgate Pk BH4 . . . **392** B3
Westgate Rd RG14 . . . **1** C2
Westgate Sch The
SO22. . . . . **403** C7
Westgate St 🔢 SO14 **290** F3
Westglade GU14 . . . . **55** B4
West Gn GU46 . . . . . . **33** F7
West Green House Gdn★
RG27. . . . . **51** B5
West Green Rd
Hartley Wintney
RG27 . . . . **52** B6
West Green PO27 . . . . **51** F6
Westgrove SP6 . . . . . **257** C1
Westgrove Gdns
PO10 . . . . **348** F8
Westham Cl BH17. . . **375** E3
West Ham Rd RG22 . . **68** D4
West Ham Ct RG22 . . **68** C4
West Ham Rd RG22 . . **68** C4
West Ham La
Basingstoke RG22. . . . **68** D3
Basingstoke,Worting
RG22 . . . . **68** B4
West Ham Rdbt RG22 **68** D4
West Haye Rd PO11. . **373** D1
West Hayes
Lymington SO41 . . . . **385** F3
Winchester SO22 . . . **403** B5
Westheath Rd BH18. . **375** B4
West Heath Rd GU14 . **55** D4
West Hill Ct SO15 . . . **290** E5
West Hill Dr
Hythe SO45. . . . . **313** F5
Winchester SO22 . . . **403** C6
West Hill Park Sch
PO14. . . . . **341** E8
West Hill Pk SO02. . . **403** B6
West Hill Pl 🔢 BH2 . **392** E3
West Hill Rd BH2 . . . **392** E3
West Hill Rd N SO21. **153** E5
West Hill Rd S SO21. **153** E4
West Hoe La SO32 . . **271** F7

Wei–Wes **473**

West Horton Cl
SO50 . . . . **244** F2
West Horton La
SO50 . . . . **244** F1
West Howe Ind Est
BH11. . . . . **376** E3
West Hundreds The
🔢 Fleet GU51. . . . . . **53** E3
🔢 Fleet GU51. . . . . . **53** D3
West La
Everton SO41 . . . . . . **384** C1
North Baddesley
SO52. . . . . **241** E5
North Hayling PO11. . **372** F6
Westland RG18 . . . . . . **2** F4
Westland Dr PO7 . . . **322** F4
Westland Gdns
PO12 . . . . **369** A4
Westlands Ct BH23. . **381** A8
Westlands Dr BH3 . . **402** F8
Westlands Gr PO16 . **344** C7
Westlands Ho 🔢
RG14 . . . . **69** A4
Westlands Rd RG14 . . **5** F8
Westley Cl SO22 . . . . **403** B7
Westley Court Rd
SO21 . . . . **174** A4
Westley Gr PO14 . . . **342** F4
Westley La SO21 . . . . **174** C4
Westlink SO53 . . . . . **216** A3
West Links SO53 . . . **243** C2
West Lodge PO13 . . **367** D4
Westlyn Rd RG26. . . . **10** C1
Westman Rd SO22 . . **175** D3
West Mans 🔢 BH4 . . **392** C3
Westmarch Bsns Ctr
SP10. . . . . **83** B2
Westmarch Ct 🔢
SO17 . . . . **267** C2
West Marlands Rd
SO14 . . . . **290** F5
Westmead
🔢 Farnham GU9 . . . **98** F2
Farnborough GU14. . . **55** F3
Farnborough GU14. . . **55** F4
Westmead Ct PO11. . **372** E3
Westmead Dr RG14 . . **5** D8
West Meade GU30 . . **209** F2
West Meon CE Prim Sch
GU32. . . . . **225** B5
West Mews 🔢 PO17. **318** E2
West Mills RG14 . . . . **1** D3
West Mills Rd SP6 . . **257** E1
West Mills Yd RG14 . . **1** D3
Westminster Cl
🔢 Fleet GU51. . . . . **54** A4
Basingstoke RG22. . . . **91** B7
Westminster Ct
BH25 . . . . **397** F7
Westminster Gate
SO22. . . . . **197** B3
Westminster Gdns
PO14 . . . . **317** C2
Westminster Ho 🔢
RG21. . . . . **69** B5
Westminster Pl PO1. **370** D7
Westminster Rd
Milford on S SO41. . . **399** A4
Poole BH13 . . . . **392** B1
Westminster Rd E
BH13. . . . . **392** B1
West Moors Mid Sch
BH22. . . . . **326** F1
West Moors Rd
Ferndown BH22. . . . . **353** D7
Three Legged Cross
BH21 . . . . **326** D5
West Moors St Mary's CE
Fst Sch BH22. . . . . **326** D3
Westmoreland Ct
SO41 . . . . **383** F3
Westmorland Dr
GU15. . . . . **36** F3
Westmorland Way
SO53 . . . . **243** E5
Weston Ave PO4 . . . **371** B4
Weston Cl
Southampton SO19 . . **291** F1
Upton Grey RG25. . . . **94** B5
Weston Colley Cotts
SO21 . . . . **132** D3
Weston Cres SO18 . . **292** C4
Weston Ct
Enham Alamein SP11 . **83** B8
Southampton SO19 . . **314** A8
Weston Down Rd
SO21 . . . . **132** E5
Weston Dr BH1. . . . . **393** B3
Weston Grove Rd
SO19 . . . . **291** D2
Weston Ho
Petersfield GU32. . . . **228** E3
Sherfield on L RG27 . **29** D1
Weston La
Middle Winterslow
SP5. . . . . **168** A5
Nursling SO16. . . . . . **265** A4
Southampton SO19 . . **291** F1
Weston GU32 . . . . . . **253** C8
Weston Par SO19 . . . **314** E8
Weston Park Boys Sch
SO19. . . . . **292** B1

Weston Park Inf Sch
SO19. . . . . **292** A1
Weston Park Jun Sch
SO19. . . . . **292** A1
Weston Rd
Colehill BH21. . . . . **351** F7
Eastleigh SO50 . . . . . **244** A3
Petersfield GU31. . . . **229** A3
Upton Grey RG25. . . . . **94** B4
Weston Shore Inf Sch
SO19. . . . . **314** F8
West Overcliff Dr
BH4 . . . . **392** D1
Westover La BH24 . . **328** D5
Westover Prim Sch
PO3. . . . . **371** B8
Westover Rd
Bournemouth BH1. . . **392** F3
Fleet GU51 . . . . **54** C1
Milford on S SO41. . . **399** D4
Portsmouth PO3 . . . . **371** B8
Southampton SO16 . . **289** C8
BH9. . . . . **378** A4
West Park Dr SP6. . . **256** D5
West Park La SP6. . . **256** D5
West Park Lo 30
SO17. . . . . **267** A1
West Park Rd SO15 . . **290** F5
West Pk SP11. . . . . . .**81** B6
Westpoint 3 GU15. . . .**36** B6
West Point PO13. . . . **367** E3
West Portway SP10 . . .**82** C2
West Quay SO14 . . . . **290** F4
Westquay Ho 6
PO16 . . . . **319** C3
West Quay Rd
Poole BH15 . . . . **390** B2
Southampton SO15 . . **290** E4
Westray Cl RG21. . . . . .**69** D7
Westray Hall BH4 . . . **392** C1
West Rd
Barton Stacey
SO21. . . . . **130** D7
Bournemouth BH5. . . **394** B4
Bransgore BH23 . . . . **381** A8
Camberley GU15 . . . . . .**36** B5
Dibden Purlieu SO45 . **313** D1
Emsworth PO10. . . . . **348** E8
Farnborough GU14 . . . .**55** F7
Fawley SO45 . . . . **338** C8
Hedge End SO30 . . . . **292** F6
Milford on S SO41. . . **399** A5
Southampton,Woolston
SO19. . . . . **291** E2
Southwick PO17 . . . . **321** A6
Westridge RG20 . . . . . .**21** C5
Westridge Ct 4
SO17. . . . . **267** B1
Westridge Rd
Portswood SO17 . . . . **267** B1
Southampton SO17 . . **291** B8
West Ring GU10 . . . . **100** E7
West Row BH21. . . . . **351** B4
Westrow Rd SO15. . . **290** F7
West Row Mews
BH21. . . . . **351** B4
Westrow Rd SO15. . . **290** F7
Westside Cl RG22. . . . .**68** D3
Westside View PO7 . . **299** C1
West St
Andover SP10 . . . . . . **106** A8
Burghclere RG20. . . . . .**22** C4
Emsworth PO10. . . . . **348** F8
Fareham PO16. . . . . . **319** B1
Farnham GU9 . . . .**98** C1
Fordingbridge SP6. . . **257** E1
Hambledon PO7. . . . . **274** C2
Havant,Bedhampton
PO9 . . . . **323** E1
Havant PO9 . . . . **323** F1
Hythe SO45 . . . . **326** A1
New Alresford SO24 . . **179** D6
Newbury RG14 . . . .**1** D3
Odiham RG29. . . . .**72** C2
Poole BH15 . . . . **390** B2
Portchester PO16. . . . **344** C8
Portchester PO16. . . . **344** D8
Portsmouth PO1 . . . . **369** F4
Ringwood BH24. . . . . **328** E7
Soberton SO32. . . . . **273** C5
Southampton SO14 . . **290** F3
Southwick PO17 . . . . **320** E6
Tadley RG26. . . . .**27** B8
Titchfield PO14 . . . . . **341** F8
Wimborne Minster
BH21 . . . . **351** B5
West Station Terr
BH4 . . . . **392** D3
West Street Ct RG26. . .**27** A8
West Street Ct 8
BH21 . . . . **351** B5
West Tisted Cl GU51 . . .**53** E8
West Tytherley CE Prim
Sch SP5. . . . . **191** A8
West Undercliff Prom
BH2 . . . . **392** D1
West View
Andover SP10 . . . . . . **106** A7
Bordon GU35. . . . . . . **164** B1
West View Cotts
PO10 . . . . **325** E2
West View Dr SO20 . . **129** A3
Westview Rd SO22 . . . **175** A2

West View Rd
Christchurch BH23 . . **395** E6
Headley GU35. . . . . . **166** A4
Poole BH15 . . . . **390** C4
West Walk (North)
Forest Walk★
PO17. . . . . **296** E7
West Walk (South)
Forest Walk★
PO17. . . . . **296** F5
West Way
Andover SP10 . . . .**83** D1
Bournemouth BH9. . . **378** B2
Broadstone BH18 . . . **374** F3
Lymington SO41 . . . . **385** C2
West Way Cl BH9 . . . . **378** B1
Westways
Havant PO9 . . . . **346** F8
Stubbington PO14 . . . **367** D7
Westways Cl SO16 . . . **265** D5
Westwood Ave BH22 **353** D6
Westwood Cl PO10 . . **325** A2
Westwood Ct
12 Southampton
SO17. . . . . **291** A8
Totton SO40. . . . . . . **264** E2
West End SO30 . . . . . **268** D1
Westwood Gdns
SO53 . . . . **243** E7
Westwood Mans 23
SO17. . . . . **267** A1
Westwood Rd
Lyndhurst SO43 . . . . **309** F6
Netley SO31. . . . . . . **315** B7
Newbury RG14 . . . .**6** A8
Portsmouth PO2 . . . . **345** E4
Southampton SO17 . . **291** A8
Westwood Park SO17 **267** A1
Westwoods & Glendene
Pk BH25 . . . . **382** D6
Westwood View
SO24 . . . . **201** E1
Wetherby Cl BH23 . . . **395** B4
Wetherby Ct SO40 . . . **288** D8
Wetherby Gdns
11 Farnborough
GU14 . . . .**56** A1
Andover SP10 . . . .**82** E2
Totton SO40. . . . . . . **288** C8
Wetherby Rd GU15. . . .**36** B7
Wetherdown GU31. . . **229** A3
Weybank GU10 . . . . . **120** C3
Weybank Cl GU9. . . . . .**99** A3
Weybourne Inf Sch
GU9 . . . .**99** C6
Weybourne Rd GU9. . . .**99** C6
Weybridge Cl SO31 . . **316** F6
Weybridge Mead
GU46 . . . .**34** C7
Weybrook Ct RG24 . . . .**47** D4
Wey Cl
Ash GU12. . . . .**77** E1
Camberley GU15 . . . . . .**35** F5
Weydon Farm Cotts
GU9 . . . . **121** F8
Weydon Farm La
GU9 . . . . **121** F8
Weydon Hill Cl GU9 . . **121** F8
Weydon Hill Rd GU9 **121** F8
Weydon La GU9. . . . . **121** F8
Weydon Mill La GU9 . **121** F8
Weydon Sch GU9 . . . . **121** D7
Weydown Ct GU27 . . . **189** F7
Weydown Ind Est
GU27 . . . . **189** F7
Weydown Rd GU27 . . . **189** F7
Weyford Jun & Inf Schs
GU35. . . . . **164** F4
Wey Hill GU27 . . . . . . **189** E6
Weyhill Bsns Pk SP11 . .**81** B2
Weyhill Cl
Havant PO9 . . . . **323** D5
Porchester PO16 . . . . **320** C1
Tadley RG26. . . . .**26** F7
Weyhill Gdns SP11. . . . .**81** D2
Weyhill Lodge SP11. . . .**81** D2
Weyhill Rd
Andover SP10 . . . . . . **105** D8
Penton Corner SP10,
SP11. . . . .**82** A1
Penton Grafton SP11. . .**81** E2
Weyland Cl GU30 . . . . **188** A5
Wey Lodge Cl GU30 . . **188** B4
Weyman's Ave BH10 **377** C6
Weymans Dr BH10 . . . **377** C6
Weymouth Ave PO12 **368** F8
Weymouth Rd
1 Portsmouth
PO2 . . . . **345** D1
Poole BH14 . . . . **391** C5
Weyside GU9 . . . .**99** A2
Weysprings GU27 . . . . **189** E6
Weysprings Cl 3
RG21 . . . .**69** D5
Weywood Cl GU9 . . . . . .**99** D7
Weywood La GU9 . . . . . .**99** C7
Whaddon Chase
PO14 . . . . **367** B7
Whaddon Ct PO9 . . . . **323** C6
Whaddon La
Colden Common
SO21. . . . . **246** A8
Owslebury SO21 . . . . **221** A3
Whale Island Way
PO2 . . . . **345** C1

Whalesmead Cl
SO50 . . . . **244** F1
Whalesmead Rd
SO50 . . . . **244** F1
Whaley Rd PO2. . . . . . **345** B1
Whalley Rd SO41 . . . . **391** E6
Wharfdale Rd
Bournemouth BH4. . . **392** D4
Poole BH12 . . . . **391** E6
Wharfenden Way
GU16 . . . .**56** D6
Wharf Hill SO23. . . . . **403** F4
Wharf Mill 1 SO23. . . **403** F4
Wharf Rd
Ash Vale GU12. . . . .**77** E4
Camberley GU16 . . . . . .**56** E6
Newbury RG14 . . . .**1** E3
Portsmouth PO2 . . . . **370** C8
Southampton SO19 . . **291** D3
Wharf St RG14. . . . .**1** E3
Wharf The
Newbury RG14 . . . .**1** E3
Odiham RG29. . . . .**72** F4
Wharf Way GU16. . . . . .**56** E6
Wharncliffe Ct BH23 **396** F7
Wharncliffe Gdns
BH23 . . . . **397** A7
Wharncliffe Ho
SO19 . . . . **291** D3
Wharncliffe Rd
Bournemouth BH5. . . **393** D4
Christchurch BH23 . . **397** A7
Southampton SO19 . . **291** D3
Whartons Cl SO40. . . . **288** C3
Whartons La SO40 . . . **288** C3
Whatleigh Cl BH15. . . **390** C1
Wheat Cl SO53. . . . . . **242** F6
Wheatcroft Dr SO18. **268** B1
Wheatcroft Rd PO13 **367** F3
Wheatear Dr GU31. . . **229** C2
Wheatears Dr SO51 . . **238** E3
Wheatland Cl SO22 . . **403** B3
Wheatlands PO14 . . . **317** C4
Wheatlands Ave
PO11 . . . . **373** E1
Wheatlands Cres
PO11 . . . . **373** E1
Wheatlands La RG14 . . .**4** F6
Wheatley Gn PO9 . . . **323** C6
Wheatley Ho GU51. . . . .**53** E4
Wheatley La GU35,
GU34 . . . . **142** A6
Wheatley Rd GU11. . . . .**76** D3
Wheatleys Cl RG25. . . . .**89** B4
Wheaton Grange 4
BH4 . . . . **392** D4
Wheaton Rd BH7. . . . **394** A5
Wheatplot Park Homes
2 BH10 . . . . **377** F4
Wheatsheaf Cotts
GU35. . . . . **166** E4
Wheatsheaf Ct SO30 **293** B6
Wheatsheaf Dr PO8 . . **299** D3
Wheatsheaf La RG14 . . .**1** F4
Wheatstone Rd PO4. . **370** F3
Wheeler Cl
Gosport PO12 . . . . . . **369** B7
Whitchurch RG28 . . . . .**86** C4
Wheeler Hill RG27 . . . . .**51** C1
Wheelers La BH11 . . . **376** D6
Wheelers Mdw SO31 **292** F1
Wheelers Wlk SO45 . . **365** F8
Wheelers Yard SO21 **131** C4
Wheelhouse Cvn Pk
SO52 . . . . **218** A1
Wheelside GU26 . . . . **167** C4
Wheelwright Ho 6
GU12 . . . .**77** A1
Wheelwright Mews
SP5 . . . . **234** E7
Wheelwrights La
GU26 . . . . **166** E4
Whernside Cl SO16 . . **289** F8
Wherwell Ct 14 PO9 **324** B5
Wherwell Dr 12 GU51 **53** D3
Wherwell Prim Sch
SP11. . . . . **127** A6
Whetstone Rd GU14. . . .**55** A4
Whichers Cl PO9. . . . . **324** B8
Whichers Gate Rd
PO9 . . . . **324** B8
Whimbrel Cl PO4 . . . . **371** C5
Whimbrel Ct BH23 . . **396** A6
Whinchat Cl
Fareham PO15. . . . . . **318** C4
Hartley Wintney RG27 . .**52** C7
Southampton SO16 . . **266** B6
Whincroft Cl BH22 . . **353** E7
Whincroft Dr BH22. . **353** E6
Whinfield Rd SO45. . . **337** E8
Whin Holt GU52. . . . . . .**75** A7
Whins 2 GU15 . . . .**35** F4
Whins Dr GU15 . . . .**35** F4
Whinwhistle Rd
SO51 . . . . **239** B2
Whippingham Cl
PO6 . . . . **345** D7
Whistler Cl
Basingstoke RG21. . . . .**69** D3
Southampton SO19 . . **292** C3
Whistler Gr GU47 . . . . . .**35** B6
Whistler Rd SO19 . . . **292** C3
Whistlers La RG7 . . . . . **10** F1
Whitaker Cres SO41. . **385** C3
Whitaker Ct RG18. . . . . .**2** F4
Whitby Ave BH18 . . . **375** C4
Whitby Cl
Christchurch BH23 . . **379** D4

Whitby Cl *continued*
Farnborough GU14 . . . .**56** C1
Whitby Cres BH18. . . **375** A2
Whitby Ct 4 SO41. . . **399** B4
Whitby Rd SO41 . . . . **399** B4
Whitchurch Ave
BH18 . . . . **375** C3
Whitchurch CE Prim Sch
RG28. . . . .**86** C4
Whitchurch Cl GU11 **100** B6
Whitchurch Cl SO19 **291** F3
Whitchurch Rd GU51 .**53** E3
Whitchurch Silk Mill★
RG28. . . . .**86** C4
Whitchurch Sta RG28 **86** C6
Whitcombe Cl SO40. **288** E7
Whitcombe Gdns
PO1. . . . . **370** F6
Whiteacres Cl 4
PO12 . . . . **369** B6
White Ave GU33 . . . . . **186** C2
White Barn Cres
SO41 . . . . **384** A3
Whitebeam Cl
2 Fareham PO14. . . . **342** E8
Colden Common
SO21. . . . . **245** A8
Waterlooville PO8 . . . **300** C5
Whitebeam Gdns
GU14 . . . .**55** A3
Whitebeam Rd SO30 **293** D6
White Beam Rise
PO8 . . . . **276** C5
Whitebeam Way
North Baddesley
SO52. . . . . **242** A5
Verwood BH31. . . . . . **303** B5
Whitebines GU9 . . . .**99** B2
Whitechimney Row
PO10 . . . . **325** B3
White Cl BH15 . . . . . . **391** A7
Whitecliff Cres
BH14 . . . . **391** A2
Whitecliffe Ave PO3 . **371** A7
Whitecliffe Ct 7 . . . **368** D4
Whitecliff Rd BH14. . **390** F2
White Cloud Pk PO4 **370** F3
White Cloud Pl PO4. . **370** F3
White Cottage Cl GU9 **99** B6
White Cotts SP5 . . . . . **235** D7
Whitecroft SO45 . . . . **314** A2
Whitecross BH17. . . . **375** E3
Whitecross Gdns 1
PO2. . . . . **345** F1
Whitedell La PO17 . . . **319** D5
White Dirt La PO8. . . **276** C3
Whitedown GU34 . . . **139** E2
Whitedown Cotts 1
GU34 . . . . **139** E3
Whitedown La GU34 **139** D2
Whitedown Rd RG26 . .**26** D8
Whitedown Sch
GU34. . . . . **139** E2
White Farm Cl BH10. **392** D8
White Farm La SN8 . . . .**18** B6
Whitefield Cotts RG14 . .**1** D7
Whitefield Farm
SO45. . . . . **365** F6
Whitefield Rd
Holbury SO45 . . . . . . **338** C3
New Milton BH25 . . . **383** A2
Poole BH14 . . . . **391** A2
White Gates SO32. . . . **270** B5
Whitehall BH23 . . . . . **395** B6
Whitehall Dr RG2 . . . . . .**15** D8
Whitehall Rd SO20 . . **172** F7
White Harmony Acres
Ind Est SO30. . . . . . **268** C5
Whitehart Fields
BH24 . . . . **329** C8
White Hart Ho GU17. . .**35** C4
White Hart Ind Est
GU17. . . . .**35** C4
White Hart La
Basingstoke RG21. . . . .**69** C4
Cadnam SO40 . . . . . . **286** F8
Charter Alley RG26 . . . .**46** E8
Portchester PO16 . . . **344** C7
White Hart Rd
4 Gosport PO12 . . . . **369** B5
Fair Oak SO50 . . . . . **245** C1
Portsmouth PO1 . . . . **370** A3
Whitehaugh Ct
SO50 . . . . **244** D4
Whitehaven
Horndean PO8 . . . . . **300** D6
Portchester PO16 . . . **344** B7
Whitehaven Cvn Pk
SO45. . . . . **365** E8
Whitehaven Home Pk
SO45. . . . . **365** E8
Whitehayes Cl BH23. **380** C1
Whitehayes Rd
BH23 . . . . **380** C1
Whitehead Cl RG24 . . . .**69** F7
White Heather Ct
SO45. . . . . **314** A6
White Hill
Burghclere RG20. . . . . .**22** B2
Ecchinswell RG20 . . . . .**23** D3
Kingsclere RG20 . . . . . .**44** B6
Long Sutton RG29 . . . . .**96** B2
Whitehill Cl
Camberley GU15 . . . . . .**36** B7
Southampton SO18 . . **292** C7
Whitehill Pk GU35 . . . **186** E8

Whitehill Rd
Bordon GU35. . . . . . . **164** F1
Standford GU35. . . . . **165** A1
Whitehorn Dr SP5 . . . **261** D8
White Horse Dr
BH15 . . . . **390** C5
White Horse La
Denmead PO7 . . . . . . **299** A6
Finchampstead RG40. . .**16** B5
White Horses BH25 . . **397** E4
White Ho The
Milford on S SO41. . . **399** D3
North Tidworth SP9 . . . .**78** F6
Whitehouse Cl GU14. . .**55** F6
White House Ct RG22 . .**68** C2
White House Farm
RG7. . . . .**10** B2
Whitehouse Gdns
SO15 . . . . **290** A6
White House Gdns
Petersfield GU32. . . . **228** E5
Yateley GU46. . . . .**34** A7
White House La RG7 . . **13** D8
Whitehouse Rd
BH21 . . . . **351** D2
White House Wlk
GU9 . . . .**99** B7
White Knights BH25. **397** F7
White La
Deane RG26 . . . .**66** C6
Greywell RG27. . . . .**71** D2
Twyford SO21 . . . . . . **220** A8
White Ladies SO51 . . . **216** B7
White Ladies Cl PO9 **324** A1
Whitelands
Bransgore BH23 . . . . **357** D4
Droxford SO32. . . . . . **273** B8
Whitelaw Rd SO15 . . . **290** B7
Whiteleaf La PO7 . . . . **274** C5
Whitelegg Way
BH10 . . . . **377** F5
Whiteley Farm Rdbt
PO15 . . . . **294** E1
Whiteley La
Swanwick PO15. . . . . **294** C1
Whiteley PO15. . . . . . **317** F5
Whiteley Prim Sch
PO15. . . . . **317** C7
Whiteley Sh Ctr
PO15. . . . . **317** E8
Whiteley Way PO15 . . **317** C7
White Lion Ctyd
BH24 . . . . **328** F7
White Lion Way GU46 .**34** B7
White Lion Wlk
PO12 . . . . **369** D6
White Lodge Gdns
PO16 . . . . **318** E4
Whitemoor La SO40,
SO51 . . . . **263** E3
Whitemoor Rd SO42 **333** D2
Whitenap Cl SO51. . . . **241** B6
Whitenap La SO51 . . . **241** C6
White Oaks Ct 9
SO16 . . . . **290** B8
White Oak Way
SP11 . . . . **105** C4
White Oak Wlk 12
PO9 . . . . **324** B5
White Post La GU10 . . **121** C4
White Post
Bishopstoke SO50 . . . **244** D4
Sandhurst GU15 . . . . . .**35** D6
White Rose La GU10 **121** F7
White Row SP5 . . . . . . **234** C8
Whites Cl RG14 . . . .**56** C1
Whitestone Cl SO16 **289** F8
Whitestones RG22 . . . . .**91** C6
Whiteshoot
Broughton SO20 . . . . **170** B6
Redlynch SP5,SP6. . . . **235** F4
Whiteshoot Hill SP5. **235** E4
Whiteshute La SO23. . **403** C3
Whites La SO45 . . . . . . **339** B3
Whites Rd GU14 . . . .**56** C1
White's Rd SO19 . . . . **292** A6
Whites Ct 4 PO2 . . . . **345** D1
White Swan Rd PO1. . **404** A3
Whites Hill SO21. . . . . **221** A3
Whiteshoot
Broughton SO20 . . . . **170** B6
Whitethorn Cl GU12. . . .**77** F1
Whitethorn Rd PO11 **373** B3
Whitewater CE Prim Sch
RG27. . . . .**50** E5
Whitewater Rd RG29 . .**72** C4
Whitewater Rise
Dibden Purlieu
SO45. . . . . **313** F1
Hook RG27. . . . .**51** C2
Whiteways BH21 . . . . **351** E6
Whiteways End
GU10 . . . . **100** B4
White Way The
Meonstoke SO32 . . . . **249** A7
Warnford SO32 . . . . . **224** A1
White Wings Ho
PO7 . . . . **298** F3
Whitewood Rd RG24 . . .**48** F3
Whitfield Pk BH24 . . . **328** B5
Whitgift Cl RG22 . . . . . .**91** B5
Whitehedwood Ave
SO15 . . . . **290** D8
Whithers La SO42. . . . **363** C7
Whitingham Ct 1
BH5 . . . . **394** B5
Whitlet Cl GU9. . . . .**98** F1

Whitley Cl PO10 . . . . **325** B5
Whitley Rd GU46. . . . . .**34** B4
Whitley Row PO4 . . . . **371** C5
Whitley Way BH25 . . **383** B5
Whitmarsh La RG24 . . . .**49** B3
Whitmoor Vale Rd
GU26 . . . . **166** E6
Whitmore Cl 2 GU47 . .**35** B8
Whitmore Gn GU9 . . . . .**99** C6
Whitmore Hill Cotts
GU26 . . . . **167** A4
Whitmore La BH21. . . **302** A7
Whitmore Vale
GU26 . . . . **166** D6
Whitmore Vale Rd
Grayshott GU26. . . . . **166** F4
Headley GU26 . . . . . . **166** C7
Whitney Rd RG24 . . . . . .**69** E7
Whitsbury Cl BH8 . . . **378** C4
Whitsbury Cross
SP6 . . . . **257** C8
Whitsbury Ho GU51 . . .**53** E4
Whitsbury Rd
Fordingbridge SP6. . . **257** E3
Havant PO9 . . . . **324** A5
Whitstable Rd PO6 . . **345** E8
Whittington Cl SO45 **313** F3
Whittle Ave PO15 . . . **317** C5
Whittle Cl
Ash Vale GU12. . . . .**77** D5
Finchampstead RG40. . .**16** C7
Whittle Cres GU14 . . . . .**55** D7
Whittle Rd
Andover SP10 . . . .**82** B1
Ferndown BH21. . . . . **352** F1
Whittle Rdbt GU14 . . . .**55** A1
Whittles Way BH15. . **390** B2
Whitwell SO31. . . . . . . **315** C2
Whitwell Rd PO4. . . . . **370** E1
Whitworth Cl PO12. . **369** B5
Whitworth Cres
SO18 . . . . **291** D8
Whitworth Ct SO18. . **291** D7
Whitworth Rd
Arborfield Garrison
RG2. . . . .**15** D3
Gosport PO12 . . . . . . **369** A6
Portsmouth PO2 . . . . **370** F8
Southampton SO18 . . **291** D8
Whyke St 3 PO9 . . . . **323** E2
Whynot La SP10 . . . . . **105** E8
Whyte Ave GU12 . . . . **100** B7
Whyte Cl SO45. . . . . . **338** B3
Whyteways SO50. . . . **243** F4
Wick 1 Ind Est BH25 **382** E2
Wick 2 Ind Est BH25 **382** E2
Wick Cl BH25 . . . . **382** E2
Wick Dr BH25. . . . . . . **382** E2
Wicket Hill GU10. . . . **121** E6
Wicket Rd BH10 . . . . . **377** C5
Wicket The SO45. . . . **313** F2
Wick Farm BH6 . . . . . **395** B5
Wickfield Ave BH23 . **395** B6
Wickfield Cl BH23. . . **395** B6
Wickford Ho BH23 . . **395** A6
Wickham CE Prim Sch
PO17. . . . . **296** A4
Wickham Cl
Alton GU34 . . . . **139** D2
Crookham Village
GU52 . . . .**74** E5
Tadley RG26. . . . .**26** F8
Wickham Croft
PO17. . . . . **296** A3
Wickham Ct
3 Gosport PO12 . . . . **368** D3
Ferndown BH22. . . . . **353** E6
Fleet GU52 . . . .**74** E6
Wickham Dr BH21 . . . **374** D4
Wickham Ho
10 Southampton
SO17. . . . . **267** A1
3 Portswood SO17 . . **267** B1
Wickham Pl GU52. . . . . .**74** E6
Wickham Rd
Bournemouth BH7. . . **394** A5
Camberley GU15 . . . . . .**36** C8
Droxford SO32. . . . . . **273** A5
Fareham PO16,PO17 . **319** B5
Fleet GU52 . . . .**74** E6
Wickham St PO1. . . . . **370** A5
Wickham Vineyard★
SO32. . . . . **295** B7
Wick Hill La
Finchampstead RG40. . .**16** E5
Finchampstead RG40. . .**16** E5
Wick La
Bournemouth BH6. . . **395** A5
Christchurch BH23 . . **395** B6
Downton SP5. . . . . . . **234** B8
Wicklea Rd BH6 . . . . . **395** B4
Wicklow Cl RG22. . . . . .**68** B3
Wicklow Dr SO53 . . . **243** A5
Wickmeads Rd BH6 . **395** A5
Wickor Cl PO10 . . . . . **325** A5
Wickor Way PO10 . . . **325** A2
Wick Point Mews
BH23 . . . . **395** B5
Wicor Mill La PO16. . **344** B7
Wicor Path PO16. . . . **344** D6
Wicor Prim Sch
PO16. . . . . **344** B8
Widbury Rd SP11 . . . . **385** C2
Widden Cl SO41 . . . . . **360** B2
Widdicombe Ave
BH14 . . . . **391** E2
Widecombe Dr SO45 **313** E3
Wide La SO18. . . . . . . **267** E5

Wide Lane Cl SO42 . . 333 F1
Widgeon Cl
  Gosport PO12 . . . . . 369 B8
  Southampton SO16 . . 266 B6
Widgeon Ct PO16 . . . 343 F8
Widgeons GU34 . . . . . 139 F5
Widget Cl BH11 . . . . . 377 B2
Widlers La SO32 . . . . 246 F6
Widley Court Dr
  PO6 . . . . 346 A7
Widley Ct
  3 Cosham PO6 . . . . 346 A7
  Fareham PO14 . . . . . 343 A6
Widley Gdns PO7 . . . 322 D3
Widley Rd
  Cosham PO6 . . . . . . 346 A8
  Portsmouth PO2 . . . . 345 C2
Widley Wlk PO6,PO7 . 321 F3
Widworthy Dr BH18 . 374 F5
Wield Cl PO9 . . . . 323 C4
Wield Industries
  SO24 . . . . 137 A4
Wield Rd
  Medstead GU34 . . . . 159 D7
  Upper Wield GU34 . . 137 C1
Wigan Cres PO9 . . . . 323 B2
Wigan Rd GU14 . . . . .76 B8
Wights Wlk RG22 . . . .91 B7
Wight View
  Lee-on-t-S PO13 . . . 367 D4
  South Hayling PO11 . . 373 C1
Wightway Mews
  SO31 . . . . 316 C1
Wight Wlk BH22 . . . . 353 E2
Wigmore Ho PO1 . . . 404 C4
Wigmore Rd RG26 . . . . .9 D1
Wilberforce Cl 2
  SO22 . . . . 403 A4
Wilberforce Rd
  Gosport PO12 . . . . . 369 C2
  Portsmouth PO5 . . . . 404 B1
Wilby La PO3 . . . . . . 346 C4
Wilcon Ct SO50 . . . . 269 D7
Wild Arum Way
  SO53 . . . . 242 F5
Wild Briar RG40 . . . . . 16 D7
Wildburn Cl SO40 . . . 264 C2
Wild Cherry Way
  SO53 . . . . 243 A6
Wilde Cl SO40 . . . . . 288 D7
Wildern Cl SO31 . . . . 316 F3
Wildern Ct SO30 . . . . 293 B8
Wilderness Hts
  SO18 . . . . 268 C1
Wilderness Rd GU16 . 36 C2
Wildern La SO30 . . . . 293 C7
Wildern Sch SO30 . . . 293 C7
Wilders Cl GU15 . . . . . 36 B3
Wilderton Rd BH13 . . 391 F3
Wilderton Rd W
  BH13 . . . . 392 A4
Wildfell Cl BH23 . . . . 380 A1
Wildground Inf Sch
  SO45 . . . . 313 F1
Wildground Jun Sch
  SO45 . . . . 313 F1
Wildground La 4
  SO45 . . . . 314 A1
Wild Grounds Nature
  Reserve* PO13 . . . . 368 C6
Wild Herons RG27 . . . 51 C1
Wildmoor La
  Church End RG27 . . . 49 D5
  Sherfield on L RG27 . . 49 D7
  Sherfield on L RG27 . . 49 F7
Wildmoor Wlk 4
  PO9 . . . . 324 B5
Wildown Gdns BH6 . . 395 A3
Wildown Rd BH6 . . . . 395 A3
Wild Ridings PO14 . . 342 C8
Wild Rose Cres
  SO31 . . . . 316 E2
Wildwood Dr RG26 . . . .9 B1
Wildwood Gdns GU46 34 A4
Wilfred Rd BH5 . . . . . 393 F4
Wilkins Cl PO8 . . . . . 276 B6
Wilkinson Dr BH8 . . . 379 B2
Wilkinson Ho 15
  PO4 . . . . 371 B2
Wilkins Way BH15 . . 390 B2
Wilks Cl SO16 . . . . . . 265 C5
Willems Ave GU11 . . . 76 D2
Willems Rdbt GU11 . . 76 D2
Willersley Cl PO6 . . . 321 C1
Willett Rd BH21 . . . . 351 A2
Will Hall Cl GU34 . . . 139 D3
Will Hall Farm GU34 139 D3
William Booth Ho 1
  PO1 . . . . 370 B5
William Cl
  Stubbington PO14 . . 367 D6
  Walkford BH23 . . . . 382 A2
William Cobbett Jun Sch
  GU9 . . . . 99 C6
William Ct
  11 Christchurch
    BH23 . . . . 397 B7
  3 Farnborough,South
    Farnborough GU14 . . 56 A1
  5 Portsmouth PO4 . . 371 B4
  Farnborough GU14 . . 55 F4
William Farthing Cl
  GU11 . . . . .76 E2
William George Ct
  PO13 . . . . 367 E2
William Gilpin CE Prim
  Sch SO41 . . . . 361 F1

William Hitchcock Ho 3
  GU14 . . . . .55 F7
William Ho SP11 . . . .83 B8
William Macleod Way
  SO16 . . . . 266 A1
William Panter Ct 2
  SO50 . . . . 244 A2
William Price Gdns
  PO16 . . . . 319 B2
William Rd
  Bournemouth BH7 . . 393 F7
  Lymington SO41 . . . . 385 E5
Williams Cl
  Gosport PO13 . . . . . 368 D7
  Holbury SO45 . . . . . 338 D3
William's Ind Pk
  BH25 . . . . 382 E2
Williams Rd PO3 . . . . 346 B3
William St SO14 . . . . 291 C5
Williams Way GU51 . . 54 C1
William Way GU34 . . 140 A5
Willian Pl GU26 . . . . 167 C6
Willington Cl GU15 . . 35 F6
Willis Ave SO52 . . . . 242 B4
Willis Cl GU34 . . . . . 160 E1
Willis Mus* RG21 . . . 69 B4
Willis Rd
  Gosport PO12 . . . . . 369 C5
  Portsmouth PO1 . . . 404 B3
  Southampton SO16 . . 267 D5
Willis Way SO23 . . . . 176 C6
Willis Waye SO23 . . . 176 C6
Willment Marine & Bsns
  Pk SO19 . . . . 315 A4
Willoughby Cl GU34 . 139 E4
Willoughby Way
  RG23 . . . . 68 D6
Willow Ave SP6 . . . . 257 F2
Willow Cl
  Bordon GU35 . . . . . . 164 E3
  Bournemouth BH4 . . 392 B5
  Havant PO9 . . . . 324 A1
  Hedge End SO30 . . . 293 D6
  Liphook GU30 . . . . . 188 B3
  Mytchett GU16 . . . . . 56 C4
  St Leonards BH24 . . . 327 C4
  Upton BH16 . . . . 389 D5
  West End SO30 . . . . . 268 D4
Willow Cres GU14 . . . .55 F7
Willow Ct
  Alton GU34 . . . . 139 E3
  Ash Vale GU12 . . . . . 77 E7
  Bournemouth BH7 . . 394 C6
  Fareham PO14 . . . . . 318 D1
  Frimley GU16 . . . . . . 36 B1
  Southampton SO16 . . 266 A3
Willowdale RG40 . . . . 16 D8
Willowdale Cl GU32 . 228 A4
Willowdene Cl
  Havant PO9 . . . . 323 B4
  New Milton BH25 . . . 383 C3
Willow Dr
  Christchurch BH6 . . . 395 A5
  Marchwood SO40 . . . 312 F8
  Ringwood BH24 . . . . 329 A5
  Wimborne Minster
    BH21 . . . . 352 C6
Willow Fields GU12 . . 77 F1
Willowford GU46 . . . .34 B6
Willow Gdns
  Liphook GU30 . . . . . 188 B3
  North Baddesley
    SO52 . . . . 241 F5
  Westbourne PO10 . . . 325 B4
Willow Gn SO21 . . . . 245 A8
Willow Gr
  Andover SP10 . . . . . 105 F7
  Fair Oak SO50 . . . . . 245 D2
Willow Herb Cl
  SO31 . . . . 316 E2
Willow Ho RG24 . . . . 49 A3
Willow La
  Blackwater GU17 . . . 35 B4
  Bransgore BH23 . . . . 357 D3
Willow Lo 1 BH1 . . . 393 D4
Willow Mead
  Bournemouth BH8 . . 378 D4
  Hedge End SO30 . . . 293 B8
Willowmead Cl RG14 . .5 A5
Willow Mews 2 SP9 . 79 A7
Willow Pk
  Ash GU12 . . . . 77 D2
  Poole BH14 . . . . 391 A3
Willow Pl
  Christchurch BH23 . . 395 C6
  Gosport PO12 . . . . . 369 B6
Willow Rd
  Bishop's Green RG20 . .6 D2
  Bishop's Waltham
    SO32 . . . . 271 D7
  Liss GU33 . . . . 208 A4
  Tadley RG26 . . . . 26 F8
Willows End GU47 . . .34 F8
Willows The
  Andover SP10 . . . . . 105 F6
  Barton on S BH25 . . . 398 B8
  Chandler's Ford SO53 243 C3
  Denmead PO7 . . . . . 298 F4
  North Warnborough
    RG29 . . . . 72 C4
  Runfold GU10 . . . . . 100 A4
Willow Tree Ave
  PO8 . . . . 300 B2
Willow Tree Gdns
  PO14 . . . . 342 E8
Willow Tree Ho
  SO41 . . . . 385 C2

Willow Tree Rise
  BH11 . . . . 377 B3
Willow Tree Wlk
  SO19 . . . . 292 B3
Willow View BH16 . . 389 C4
Willow Way
  Aldershot GU12 . . . . 100 C8
  Basingstoke RG23 . . . 68 D7
  Christchurch BH23 . . 395 A5
  Farnham GU9 . . . . . . 99 B6
  Ferndown BH22 . . . . 353 D7
  Sherfield on L RG27 . . 29 D1
Willow Wlk PO5 . . . . 398 B7
Willow Wood Rd
  PO11 . . . . 373 A3
Wills Cl BH21 . . . . . . 374 D4
Wills Rd BH12 . . . . . 391 F4
Wills Way SO51 . . . . 241 A6
Willwood Cl BH17 . . . 375 E3
Wilmcote Gdns 5
  PO5 . . . . 404 C3
Wilmcote Ho PO5 . . . 404 C3
Wilmer Rd SO50 . . . . 244 A2
Wilmington Cl SO18 . 267 F3
Wilmot Cl SO50 . . . . 244 E5
Wilmot Ct 10 GU14 . . 55 F4
Wilmott Cl PO12 . . . . 368 F5
Wilmott La PO12 . . . 368 F5
Wilmot Way
  Basingstoke RG23 . . . 68 D6
  Frimley GU15 . . . . . . 36 D3
Wilmot Wlk GU14 . . . .55 F4
Wilmur Cres BH15 . . 390 E6
Wilsom Cl GU34 . . . . 140 A3
Wilsom Rd GU34 . . . 140 B3
Wilson Cl SO20 . . . . 126 A4
Wilson Ct 6 SP6 . . . 257 F1
Wilson Gr PO5 . . . . . 404 C1
Wilson Ho SP9 . . . . . .78 E8
Wilson Rd
  Aldershot GU12 . . . . 77 B1
  Bournemouth BH1 . . 393 E6
  Farnborough GU14 . . 55 D3
  Poole BH14 . . . . 391 C4
  Portsmouth PO2 . . . . 345 C2
Wilsons Rd GU35 . . . 165 F5
Wilson St SO14 . . . . 291 C5
Wilson Valkenburg Ct
  RG14 . . . . .1 C4
Wilton Ave SO15 . . . 290 F6
Wilton Cl
  5 Gosport PO12 . . . 368 F4
  Christchurch BH23 . . 379 F3
Wilton Cres SO15 . . . 266 D1
Wilton Ct
  Farnborough GU14 . . 56 B3
  Southampton SO15 . . 290 F6
Wilton Dr PO8 . . . . . 300 A5
Wilton Gdns
  New Milton BH25 . . . 382 F3
  Southampton SO15 . . 266 D1
Wilton Pl
  11 Bournemouth
    BH4 . . . . 392 C2
  Basingstoke RG21 . . . 68 F4
  Portsmouth PO5 . . . . 370 D2
Wilton Rd
  Bournemouth BH7 . . 393 F5
  Camberley GU15 . . . . 35 F3
  Southampton SO15 . . 266 D1
Wilton Terr
  Portsmouth PO5 . . . . 370 D2
  Shipton Bellinger SP9 101 E7
Wiltshire Gdns BH23 380 F8
Wiltshire Ho RG24 . . 68 D8
Wiltshire Rd
  Bransgore BH23 . . . . 380 F8
  Chandler's Ford
    SO53 . . . . 243 D3
Wiltshire St PO5 . . . 404 A2
Wilverley Ave
  Bournemouth BH8 . . 378 F2
  Havant PO9 . . . . 324 A4
Wilverley Cl SO41 . . . 385 B2
Wilverley Inclosure
  Forest Walks*
    BH25 . . . . 359 C7
Wilverley Pl SO45 . . . 338 C1
Wilverley Rd
  Brockenhurst SO42 . . 333 F1
  Christchurch BH23 . . 396 A7
  New Milton BH25 . . . 358 F3
Wimbledon Park Rd
  PO5 . . . . 370 D2
Wimborne Fst Sch
  BH21 . . . . 351 B5
Wimborne Ho
  Farnborough GU14 . . 56 B2
  Southampton SO16 . . 265 F1
  Trickett's Cross BH22 353 F7
Wimborne Inf & Jun
  Schs PO4 . . . . 371 A4
Wimborne Minster
  Model Town & Gdns*
    BH21 . . . . 351 B4
Wimborne Rd
  Bournemouth,Dean Park
    BH9 . . . . 392 F5
  Bournemouth,Kinson
    BH11 . . . . 377 C6
  Bournemouth,Moordown
    BH9 . . . . 392 F8
  East End BH21 . . . . . 350 A5
  Poole,Longfleet BH15 390 D4
  Poole,Oakdale BH15 . 390 D6
  Portsmouth PO4 . . . . 371 A4
  Wimborne Minster
    BH21 . . . . 351 E6

Wimborne Rd E
  Ferndown BH22 . . . . 353 B6
  Trickett's Cross BH22 353 B6
Wimborne Rd W
  Ferndown BH21 . . . . 352 E6
  Wimborne Minster
    BH21 . . . . 352 B4
Wimbushes RG40 . . . .16 B6
Wimpole Cl PO1 . . . . 404 C4
Wimpole St PO1 . . . . 404 C4
Wimpson Gdns SO16 265 F1
Wimpson La SO16 . . . 289 E8
Wincanton Cl GU34 . 140 A2
Wincanton Way PO7 . 300 D1
Winchcombe Cl GU51 75 A8
Winchcombe Rd
  Basingstoke RG21 . . . 69 A4
  Newbury RG14 . . . . . .1 E2
  Portsmouth PO6 . . . . 321 B1
Winchelsea Specl Sch
  BH12 . . . . 376 D1
Winchester By Pass
  SO23 . . . . 176 C3
Winchester Cath* ★
  SO23 . . . . 403 E6
Winchester Christian Sch
  SO22 . . . . 403 A6
Winchester City Mill* ★
  SO23 . . . . 403 E6
Winchester Coll
  SO23 . . . . 403 E4
Winchester Ct
  12 Gosport PO13 . . . 368 D5
  5 Romsey SO51 . . . . 216 B1
  9 Newbury RG14 . . . .1 E2
  Southampton SO15 . . 266 C1
Winchester Cty Mus* ★
  SO23 . . . . 403 E5
Winchester Gdns
  SP10 . . . . 106 B6
Winchester Hill
  Romsey SO51 . . . . . 241 B8
  Sutton Scotney SO21 . 131 C3
Winchester Ho
  8 Havant PO9 . . . . . 324 A5
  Romsey SO51 . . . . . 241 A7
Winchester Mews 19
  SO17 . . . . 291 A8
Winchester Pl 5
  BH15 . . . . 390 C2
Winchester Rd
  Alton GU34 . . . . 139 E1
  Ash GU12 . . . . 77 E3
  Basingstoke RG22,
    RG23 . . . . 91 A7
  Bishop's Waltham
    SO32 . . . . 271 E8
  Chandler's Ford SO53 243 E7
  Chawton GU34 . . . . . 161 D8
  Chilbolton SO20,SP11 129 B6
  Durley SO32 . . . . . . 269 E4
  Fair Oak SO50 . . . . . 245 C4
  Four Marks GU34 . . . 160 C3
  Kingsclere RG20 . . . . 24 C1
  King's Somborne
    SO20 . . . . 172 B3
  Langrish GU32 . . . . . 227 E4
  Micheldever SO21 . . . 133 B2
  New Alresford SO24 . 179 B5
  New Milton BH25 . . . 383 C4
  North Street SO24 . . . 181 C7
  Petersfield GU32 . . . 228 D4
  Petersfield,Stroud
    GU32 . . . . 228 B4
  Portsmouth PO2 . . . . 370 E8
  Romsey SO51 . . . . . 240 F7
  Romsey,Woodley
    SO51 . . . . 216 C1
  Rushmoor GU10 . . . . 144 F7
  Shedfield SO32,PO17 295 E6
  Southampton SO16 . . 266 C2
  Upham SO21,SO32 . . 246 C3
  Upper Clatford SP11 . 106 A4
  Waltham Chase SO32 271 E2
  Wherwell SP11 . . . . 128 E7
  Whitchurch RG28 . . . 86 C3
  Wickham PO17 . . . . . 296 A3
Winchester Road Rdbt
  RG21 . . . . .68 F3
Winchester Sch of Art
  SO23 . . . . 403 F6
Winchester St
  4 Southampton
    SO15 . . . . 290 F6
  5 Andover SP10 . . . 106 A7
  7 Basingstoke RG21 . 69 B4
  Botley SO30 . . . . . . 294 A7
  Chilbolton SO20 . . . 129 B5
  Farnborough GU14 . . 77 A8
  Overton RG25 . . . . . 88 B7
  Whitchurch RG28 . . . 86 C4
Winchester Sta
  SO22 . . . . 403 D6
Winchester Trad Pk
  SO23 . . . . 176 C1
Winchester Way
  Blackwater GU17 . . . 35 A6
  Totton SO40 . . . . . . 288 C7
Winchfield Cl SO19 . . 292 A1
Winchfield Cres
  PO9 . . . . 323 C4
Winchfield Ct RG27 . . 53 A1
Winchfield Gdns
  RG26 . . . . 27 A7
Winchfield Ho 4
  PO12 . . . . 369 E5
Winchfield Sta RG27 . 52 C1

Wincombe Cl BH22 . . 353 D3
Wincombe Dr BH22 . . 353 D3
Windbury Rd SO16 . . 265 D2
Windermere Ave
  Basingstoke RG22 . . . 68 A2
  Southampton SO16 . . 265 E2
  Stubbington PO14 . . 342 D4
Windermere Cl GU14 . 55 C3
Windermere Ct GU12 . 77 D4
Windermere Gdns
  New Alresford
    SO24 . . . . 179 C6
  Totton SO40 . . . . . . 288 E8
Windermere Ho PO6 . 345 B8
Windermere Rd
  Bordon GU35 . . . . . . 164 D5
  Bournemouth BH3 . . 393 A6
  Portsmouth PO2 . . . . 345 F3
  West End SO18 . . . . . 268 B1
Windermere Way
  Farnham GU9 . . . . . . 98 E6
  Thatcham RG19 . . . . . .2 E3
Windfield Dr SO51 . . . 241 B8
Windgreen Est BH21 . 374 E7
Windham Mews
  BH1 . . . . 393 D5
Windham Rd BH1 . . . 393 D5
Winding Wood Dr
  GU15 . . . . .36 F3
Windmill Cl
  5 Milford on S
    SO41 . . . . 399 D5
  Clanfield PO8 . . . . . 276 C6
  St Leonards BH24 . . . 328 D4
Windmill Cnr RG7 . . . .11 E6
Windmill Copse
  SO45 . . . . 313 F1
Windmill Ct
  5 Aldershot GU12 . . 77 A1
  Alton GU34 . . . . 139 F2
  Mortimer RG7 . . . . . 11 E6
Windmill Dr GU35 . . . 165 F6
Windmill Field PO7 . . 299 A4
Windmill Fields
  East Worldham
    GU34 . . . . 141 A1
  Four Marks GU34 . . . 160 C3
Windmill Gr PO16 . . . 344 C6
Windmill Hill GU34 . . 140 A2
Windmill La
  Alton GU34 . . . . 140 B2
  Anna Valley SP11 . . . 105 C4
  Bursledon SO31 . . . . 293 A2
  Hurstbourne Tarrant
    SP11 . . . . 60 C7
  St Leonards BH24 . . . 328 D4
Windmill Rd
  Aldershot GU12 . . . . 77 A1
  Mortimer RG7 . . . . . 11 E6
Windmills The 14
  GU34 . . . . 139 F3
Windover Cl SO19 . . . 292 C6
Windrush Cl 28 RG21 . 69 D5
Windrush Gdns PO7 . 322 D7
Windrush Hts GU47 . .34 F8
Windrush Rd SO16 . . 289 E8
Windrush Way SO45 . 314 A3
Windsor Cl
  Alton GU34 . . . . 139 D3
  Farnborough GU14 . . 55 F4
  Hordle SO41 . . . . . . 383 E4
  St Leonards BH24 . . . 327 F4
Windsor Cres GU9 . . . .98 F6
Windsor Ct
  14 Southampton,Bevois
    Mount SO17 . . . . . 291 A8
  19 Portsmouth PO5 . . 370 C2
  2 Southampton,Bitterne
    SO18 . . . . 291 E7
  3 Christchurch
    BH23 . . . . 397 A7
  3 Southampton,Millbrook
    SO15 . . . . 290 A6
  5 Fleet GU51 . . . . . 54 A1
  6 Cosham PO6 . . . . 345 F8
  6 Southampton,Westwood
    Pk SO17 . . . . 291 A8
  Bishopstoke SO50 . . 244 D4
  Camberley GU15 . . . . 36 A3
  Newbury RG14 . . . . . .1 F2
  Poole BH14 . . . . 391 B3
Windsor Gate SO50 . . 244 A6
Windsor Gdns
  Ash GU12 . . . . 77 D1
  Basingstoke RG22 . . . 91 A6
Windsor Ho
  1 Winchester
    SO23 . . . . 403 F6
  3 Portsmouth PO1 . . 404 C3
Windsor Mans 1
  BH6 . . . . 394 E3
Windsor Pk GU34 . . . 139 F2
Windsor Rd
  Andover SP10 . . . . . 105 F6
  Bournemouth BH5 . . 393 E4
  Christchurch BH23 . . 394 E7
  Cosham PO6 . . . . . . 345 F7
  Farnborough,South
    Farnborough GU14 . . 56 B1
  Four Marks GU34 . . . 160 B4
  Gosport PO12 . . . . . 369 A5
  Lindford GU35 . . . . . 164 F5
  New Alresford SO24 . 179 C4
  Petersfield GU32 . . . 228 F4
  Poole BH14 . . . . 391 B3
  Portchester PO16 . . . 344 D6
  Waterlooville PO7 . . . 299 D2

Windsor Ride
  Finchampstead RG40 . . 16 E7
  Sandhurst GU15 . . . . 35 E8
Windsor Rise RG14 . . . .6 A8
Windsor Way
  Alderholt SP6 . . . . . 281 A6
  Aldershot GU11 . . . . . 76 F2
  Camberley GU16 . . . . 56 D8
Windsor Wlk GU35 . . 164 F4
Windward Ct 12
  PO12 . . . . 369 C5
Wine Cross PO17 . . . 297 A1
Winecross Cotts
  PO17 . . . . 297 A2
Winfield Way PO10 . . 324 F4
Winfrid Ho SO40 . . . 288 D7
Winfrith Cres BH12 . . 391 E8
Winfrith Way SO16 . . 265 D5
Wingate Ct GU11 . . . . 76 D2
Wingate Dr SO19 . . . 292 B5
Wingate La RG29 . . . . 95 D3
Wingate Rd
  Gosport PO12 . . . . . 343 F1
  Totton SO40 . . . . . . 288 D8
Wingfield Ave
  Christchurch BH23 . . 381 D1
  Poole BH15 . . . . 390 D6
Wingfield Ct BH1 . . . 393 C3
Wingfield Ho PO1 . . . 370 D7
Winghams La SO51 . . 217 B3
Wingrove Rd SO40 . . 288 C3
Wings Cl GU9 . . . . . . .98 F6
Wings Rd GU9 . . . . . .98 F6
Winifred Cl SO50 . . . 245 C3
Winifred Rd
  Poole BH15 . . . . 390 E5
  Waterlooville PO7 . . . 322 E8
Winkfield Row PO8 . . 300 B5
Winklebury Ctr RG23 . 68 C5
Winklebury Inf Sch
  RG23 . . . . 68 D6
Winklebury Jun Sch
  RG23 . . . . 68 D6
Winklebury Way
  RG23 . . . . 68 D5
Winkle St SO14 . . . . 291 A2
Winkton Cl
  Burton BH23 . . . . . . 380 C3
  Havant PO9 . . . . 323 E3
Winkton Gn BH23 . . . 380 C5
Winkton Ho BH23 . . . 380 C4
Winkworth La RG7,
  RG26 . . . . 10 A2
Winkworth Pl GU9 . . . 99 A3
Winnall Cl SO23 . . . . 176 C1
Winnall Manor Rd
  SO23 . . . . 198 C8
Winnall Prim Sch
  SO23 . . . . 198 C8
Winnall Trad Est
  Winchester SO23 . . . 176 C1
  Winchester SO23 . . . 198 C8
Winnall Valley Rd
  SO23 . . . . 198 C8
Winnards Cl BH22 . . . 353 E2
Winnards Pk SO31 . . . 316 D4
Winn Ct SO17 . . . . . . 290 E7
Winnham Dr PO16 . . . 320 A1
Winnington PO15 . . . 318 D4
Winnington Cl PO15 . 318 D4
Winnipeg Cl GU30 . . 188 A3
Winn Mans 18 SO17 . 267 A1
Winn Rd SO17 . . . . . 267 A1
Winscombe Ave
  PO8 . . . . 300 A2
Winsford Ave SO50 . . 245 A1
Winsford Cl
  Bishopstoke SO50 . . 245 A1
  Christchurch BH23 . . 381 D1
Winsford Gdns SO50 245 A1
Winslade La RG25 . . . 115 D8
Winslade Rd
  Havant PO9 . . . . 323 D5
  Winchester SO22 . . . 175 C4
Winsley Ave BH6 . . . 394 C4
Winslow Ct PO6 . . . . 346 D8
Winsor Cl PO11 . . . . 373 D1
Winsor La SO40 . . . . 287 E7
Winsor Rd
  Bartley SO40 . . . . . . 287 B8
  Cadnam SO40 . . . . . 263 D1
  Totton SO40 . . . . . . 289 A6
Winspit Cl BH15 . . . . 389 E3
Winstanley Rd
  Nursling SO16 . . . . . 265 C5
  Portsmouth PO2 . . . . 345 C1
Winston Ave
  Poole BH12 . . . . 392 A6
  Tadley RG26 . . . . 27 B6
Winston Churchill Ave
  PO5 . . . . 404 B2
Winston Cl
  Camberley GU16 . . . . 56 D6
  Eastleigh SO50 . . . . 244 A4
  Southampton SO16 . . 265 D5
  South Hayling PO11 . . 372 E3
Winston Ct
  1 Christchurch
    BH23 . . . . 395 A7
  4 Old Milton BH25 . . 383 A1
Winstone Bldgs
  SO16 . . . . 266 E3
Winstone Cres SO52 . 242 A3
Winston Gdns BH12 . 392 A6

Winston Par 6
BH25 . . . . 383 A1
Winston Pk BH12 . . . 392 A6
Winston Rd BH9 . . . . 378 A3
Winston Rise GU34. . 160 B3
Winston Way
Ringwood BH24. . . . . 329 B8
Thatcham RG19. . . . . 2 D4
Winston Wlk GU10 . . 122 A6
Winterbarrow Cotts
SO32 . . . . 224 E3
Winterbourne Cl
BH15 . . . . 390 D4
Winterbourne Ho
RG22 . . . . 68 C2
Winterbourne Rd
Poole BH15 . . . . 390 D5
Portchester PO6 . . . . 320 F1
Romsey SO51 . . . . . . 216 B1
Winterbourne Wlk
GU16 . . . . 56 D8
Winter Cl GU12 . . . . . . 77 E8
Winterdyne Mews
SP10 . . . . 105 F7
Winterhayes Cl
BH17 . . . . 375 E3
Winterhill Rd PO6 . . 345 D8
Winter Rd PO4 . . . . . 371 A3
Winters Cl SO45 . . . . 338 D3
Winters Hill SO32 . . 270 E8
Winterslow Dr PO9 . 323 E6
Winters Rd SO32 . . . 272 A1
Winterthur Way RG21 69 A5
Winterton Dr RG14 . . . 1 B5
Wintney St GU51 . . . . 53 D3
Winton Boys' Sch
BH10 . . . . 377 D1
Winton Chase SP10 . 106 D8
Winton Cl
Lymington SO41 . . . . 385 F3
South Tidworth SP9 . . . 78 F4
Winchester SO22 . . . 403 D8
Winton Cres GU46 . . . 34 C5
Winton Ct 3 Petersfield
GU32 . . . . 228 F3
West End SO30 . . . . . 268 D1
Winton Hill SO20. . . . 150 A3
Winton Prim Sch
BH9 . . . . 377 E2
Winton Rd
11 Aldershot GU11 . . . 76 E1
Petersfield GU32 . . . 228 F4
Portsmouth PO2 . . . . 345 F2
Winton Sch SP10 . . . . 106 D8
Winton Sq RG21 . . . . . 69 B4
Winton St 8 SO14 . . 291 E4
Winton Way
Bournemouth BH10 . . 377 D1
New Milton BH25 . . . 383 B8
Wiremead La SP11 . . 103 F7
Wisbech Way SO41 . . 383 F3
Wisborough Rd PO5 . 370 E2
Wises Ct 1 PO12 . . . 369 E5
Wishanger La GU10 . . 143 F2
Wishart Gdns BH9 . . 378 B5
Wishmoor Cl GU15 . . . 36 C8
Wishmoor Rd GU15 . . 36 C8
Wish Pl PO5 . . . . 404 D1
Wisley Gdns GU14 . . . 55 B2
Wisley Rd SP10 . . . . 105 E7
Wistaria Ct SP10 . . . 105 D7
Wistaria Ho 7 BH17 . 377 F4
Wistaria La GU46 . . . . 34 A5
Wisteria Ct GU9. . . . . 99 A3
Wisteria Dr
1 Bordon GU35 . . . . 164 D2
Verwood BH31 . . . . . 303 C4
Wisteria Gdns PO9 . . 324 B4
Wisteria Mews
GU34 . . . . 140 D6
Witan Cl SP10 . . . . 83 B4
Witan Ct RG28 . . . . 86 B6
Witchampton Cl
PO9 . . . . 324 A5
Witchampton Rd
BH18 . . . . 374 F2
Witham Cl SO53 . . . . 243 A6
Witherbed La PO15 . . 35 A7
Witherbed La PO15 . . 317 E5
Withermoor Rd BH9 . 392 E8
Wither Rise RG23 . . . . 67 A2
Witherslack Cl GU35 166 A4
Withewood Mans 2
SO15 . . . . 290 C7
Withies Rd PO13 . . . 368 D8
Withies The
Crondall GU10 . . . . . . 97 D6
Longparish SP11 . . . 108 B5
Withingham Rd
BH13 . . . . 391 F3
Withington Cl 3
PO6 . . . . 321 B1
Withy Cl SO51 . . . . . . 240 F8
Witley BH14 . . . . 402 C7
Witley Rd PO8 . . . . . . 299 F6
Witney Rd BH17 . . . . 375 D1
Wittcomb Terr GU35 164 C1
Wittensford La SO43 286 C8
Wittering Rd
Southampton SO16 . . 266 A4
South Hayling PO11. . 373 F4
Wittmead Rd GU16 . . . 66 A1
Witton Hill SO24 . . . . 179 D4

Witt Rd
Fair Oak SO50 . . . . . 245 C2
Middle Winterslow
SP5. . . . . 168 B5
Witts Hill SO18 . . . . 267 F1
Wivelrod Rd GU34 . . 138 C1
Wivenhoe Ho BH22 . . 353 F6
Woburn Ave GU14 . . . 56 B3
Woburn Cl
Eastleigh SO50 . . . . 244 A6
Frimley GU16 . . . . 36 E1
Woburn Ct PO13 . . . . 367 F1
Woburn Gdns RG22 . . 68 C3
Woburn Rd SO16 . . . 266 B5
Wode Cl PO8 . . . . 276 C3
Wodehouse Rd SO19 291 E4
Wokefield Row RG7. . 12 B8
Woking Rd BH14 . . . . 391 C4
Wolds The RG22 . . . . . 68 B3
Wolfe Cl
Christchurch BH23 . . 395 D7
Winchester SO22 . . . 403 A1
Wolfe Rd GU12 . . . . . . 77 A1
Wolfmere La GU33 . . 186 A2
Wolf's La GU34 . . . . . 161 E8
Wollaston Rd BH6 . . . 394 F3
Wollaton Cres BH22. . 353 C3
Wollaton Rd BH22 . . . 353 C3
Wollstonecraft Rd 11
BH5 . . . . 393 F3
Wolmer Cotts GU33 . 186 B6
Wolmer Terr GU33 . . 186 A4
Wolseley Rd
Aldershot GU11 . . . . . 76 E1
Poole BH12 . . . . 391 D6
Southampton SO15 . . 290 C7
Wolsey Way SO41 . . 399 D5
Wolterton Rd BH12 . . 392 A5
Wolverdene Specl Sch
SP10 . . . . 106 B7
Wolverley Ct
19 Bournemouth
BH4 . . . . 392 C3
Southampton SO16 . . 266 D3
Wolversdene Cl
SP10 . . . . 106 C7
Wolversdene Gdns
SP10 . . . . 106 C7
Wolversdene Rd
SP10 . . . . 106 C7
Wolverton La GU26. . . 25 D1
Wolverton Rd
Baughurst RG26 . . . . . 26 B7
Bournemouth BH7. . . 393 F5
Havant PO9 . . . . 323 E5
Southampton SO14 . . 291 B5
Wolverton Common
RG26 . . . . 25 E5
Wolverton Towns End
RG26 . . . . 25 E2
**Wolvesey Castle (Old
Bishop's Palace)** ★
SO23. . . . . 403 E3
Wolvesey Pl SO53 . . . 243 A4
Wolvesey Terr 2
SO23 . . . . 403 F4
Wonderholm Par
BH11 . . . . 377 B2
Wonston Cl SO21 . . . 131 D3
Wonston Ct PO9 . . . . 324 C6
Wonston La SO21 . . . 131 D2
Wonston Rd SO16 . . . 266 B4
Woodacre Gdns
BH22 . . . . 353 E4
Woodbarn The GU9 . . 99 A1
Woodberry La
Emsworth PO10. . . . . 325 A6
Rowlands Castle PO9 301 D1
Rowland's Castle PO9 324 F8
Woodbind Wlk SO31 316 F2
Woodbine Cl GU47 . . . 35 A7
Woodbine La RG20. . . . 5 D1
Woodbourne GU9. . . . 99 C7
Woodbourne Cl
Fareham PO15. . . . . . 318 D1
Liss GU33 . . . . 208 A4
Yateley GU46 . . . . 34 B6
Woodbridge Dr GU15 36 B4
Woodbridge Rd GU17 .34 F5
Woodbury
Bournemouth BH1. . . 393 A2
Brockenhurst SO42. . 333 D1
Woodbury Ave
Bournemouth BH8. . . 378 F2
Langstone PO9 . . . . 347 F8
Petersfield GU32. . . . 228 E5
Woodbury Cl BH23 . . 379 E3
Woodbury Ct RG7. . . . 15 B4
Woodbury Gr PO8. . . 299 F5
Woodbury Rd RG22 . . .91 B7
Wood Cl
Basingstoke RG22 . . . 91 B6
Southampton SO19 . . 292 C3
Woodcock La SO41 . . 384 B4
Woodcocks Cres
BH7 . . . . 394 A8
Woodcot Cres PO9. . 324 B5
Woodcote Cotts
Bramdean SO24 . . . . 202 D4
Sutton Scotney SO21. 131 C4
Woodcote Dr BH16. . 389 B6
Woodcote La GU51 . . . 74 D8
Woodcote La PO14. . . 343 A3
Woodcote Rd
Buttermere SN8 . . . . . 18 A7
Southampton SO17 . . 267 C3
Yateley GU46. . . . . . . 34 B4

Woodcot Prim Sch
PO13. . . . . 343 B4
Woodcott Ho
1 Tadley RG26 . . . . . 26 F8
5 Pamber Heath RG26 .9 E1
Woodcott Terr GU12 100 B8
Woodcroft RG23 . . . . .90 B8
Woodcroft Gdns
PO8 . . . . 299 F5
Woodcroft La PO8 . . . 299 F5
Woodcut Rd GU10 . . 121 D6
Woodend
1 Camberley GU15 . . 36 E7
Farnborough GU14 . . . 56 B3
Gosport PO13 . . . . . 368 C6
Sarisbury SO31 . . . . 316 F6
Wood End RG24 . . . . . 48 E2
Woodend Rd BH9 . . . 392 E8
Wood End Rd BH24 . . 329 E5
Wood End Way
SO53 . . . . 243 A6
Wooden House La
SO41 . . . . 362 B2
Wooderson Cl SO50. . 245 B3
Woodfalls Cross
SP5 . . . . 235 D4
Woodfalls Ho GU51 . . 53 E4
Woodfern SP6 . . . . . . 258 D2
Woodfield GU35 . . . . 142 B1
Woodfield Ave PO6 . . 322 F1
Woodfield Cotts
GU32 . . . . 206 B3
Woodfield Dr SO22. . . 197 B6
Woodfield Gdns
BH23 . . . . 381 D1
Woodfield Ho 7
PO2 . . . . 345 E3
Woodfield Park Rd
PO10 . . . . 349 B8
Woodfield Rd BH11 . . 377 A5
Woodford Cl BH24 . . 329 C7
Woodford Ho PO15 . . 318 D2
Woodford Rd BH1 . . . 393 C4
Woodgarston Dr
RG22 . . . . 91 A6
Woodgaston La
PO11 . . . . 348 C1
Woodgate GU51 . . . . . 54 C3
Wood Glade Cl SO40 289 F1
Woodgreen Ave
PO9 . . . . 323 D3
Woodgreen Dr BH11 376 D4
Woodgreen Rd
SO22 . . . . 175 D4
Woodgreen Wlk
SO40 . . . . 264 B1
Woodhall Way PO15 318 E3
Woodhay SO43 . . . . . 309 E5
Woodhayes Ave
BH23 . . . . 381 E2
Woodhay Wlk 19
PO9 . . . . 324 B6
Wood Hill La RG29 . . .95 E4
Woodhill Sch
Botley SO30. . . . . . . 293 F7
Chandler's Ford
SO53. . . . . 243 D7
Wood Ho 6 BH13 . . . 392 B3
Woodhouse Ct SO30 293 C8
Woodhouse La
Ashford Hill RG19 . . . . 8 C2
Finchdean PO8 . . . . . 301 A4
Hedge End SO30 . . . 293 E8
Rowlands Castle PO8,
PO9 . . . . 301 C4
Woodhouse Rd PO8. . 300 F7
Woodington Cl PO9 . . 324 A6
Woodington Rd
SO51 . . . . 239 C6
Wood La
Beech Hill RG7 . . . . . . 13 C5
Bournemouth BH11. . 376 E6
Bramdean SO24 . . . . 202 B2
Farnborough GU14 . . . 55 E3
Fleet GU51 . . . . 54 C1
Milford on S SO41. . . 399 C4
Seale GU10 . . . . 100 F5
Southwick PO17 . . . . 321 A4
Up Nately RG27 . . . . . 71 C5
Woodlake Cl BH17 . . 375 D1
Woodland Ave BH5 . . 394 A4
Woodland Cl
Southampton SO18 . . 292 D7
Verwood BH31. . . . . 302 E7
West Wellow SO51 . . 239 B2
Woodland Cres GU14. 56 A6
Woodland Ct BH7. . . 393 F5
Woodland Dr
Bramley RG26 . . . . . . 29 B2
Farnham GU10 . . . . 121 F6
Woodland Dro SO21 220 A3
Woodland Mans
BH14 . . . . 391 B5
Woodland Mews
SO30 . . . . 268 D1
Woodland Pl 1
SO15 . . . . 290 E7
Woodland Rise GU52 .74 F4
Woodlands
20 Poole BH13 . . . . . 392 A4
Andover SP10 . . . . . 106 C8
Chineham RG24. . . . . 49 A4
Fareham PO16. . . . . 319 D2
Fleet GU51 . . . . 53 F2
Overton RG25 . . . . . . 88 A8
Penwood RG20 . . . . . 21 E7
Runfold GU10 . . . . . 100 B4
Yateley GU46. . . . . . . 34 B4
Woodlands Ave
Emsworth PO10. . . . . 324 F3

Woodlands Ave continued
Farnham GU9 . . . . . . 99 D7
Hamworthy BH15 . . . 389 F3
Woodlands Bsns Village
RG21. . . . . 69 D6
Woodlands Cl
Ash Vale GU12. . . . . . 77 E5
Bransgore BH23 . . . . 381 A8
Chandler's Ford
SO53. . . . . 218 D2
Dibden Purlieu SO45. 313 F1
Farnborough GU17 . . . 35 C1
Gosport PO13 . . . . . 368 C6
Havant PO9 . . . . 324 B1
Verwood BH31. . . . . 302 F5
Woodlands Com Sch
SO18. . . . . 292 D8
Woodlands Cotts
SO24 . . . . 203 D2
Woodlands Cres
BH15 . . . . 389 F3
Woodlands Ct
1 Winchester,Hyde
SO23. . . . . 403 E7
Alton GU34 . . . . 139 D1
Dibden Purlieu SO45 . 313 F1
Poole BH12 . . . . 392 B5
Winchester,Weeke
SO22. . . . . 403 A8
Woodlands Cvn Pk
SO41 . . . . 384 A3
Woodlands Dr SO31. . 315 D6
Woodlands Dro
SO40 . . . . 288 A3
Woodlands Ed Ctr
PO8. . . . . 299 E4
Woodlands Gdns 8
SO51 . . . . 216 B1
Woodlands Gr PO7. . . 322 D5
Woodlands La
Haslemere GU27. . . . 189 D7
Hill Brow GU33 . . . . 208 B3
South Hayling PO11. . 372 F5
Woodlands Pk GU12 . 77 D1
Woodlands Rd
Barton on S BH25 . . . 397 E7
Brockenhurst SO42. . 360 F7
Camberley GU15 . . . . 35 F5
Farnborough GU14 . . . 55 B6
Pamber Heath RG26 . . 9 B1
Woodlands SO40 . . . 287 E3
Woodland St PO1 . . . 404 D4
Woodlands The
Bordon GU35 . . . . . . 186 D8
Chandler's Ford SO53 218 A1
Kings Worthy SO23 . . 176 C6
Woodlands Way
Andover SP10 . . . . . 106 C8
Bursledon SO31. . . . 315 F8
Havant PO9 . . . . 323 F4
New Milton BH25 . . . 383 B8
North Baddesley
SO52. . . . . 241 F4
Southampton SO15 . . 290 F8
St Leonards BH24 . . . 327 F4
Woodlands Wlk GU17 35 C1
Woodland View
Bursledon SO31. . . . 315 F8
Horndean PO8. . . . . 299 F6
Woodland Way
Christchurch BH23 . . 396 D8
Milford on S SO41. . . 399 C4
Woodland Wlk
Aldershot GU12. . . . . 77 C3
Bournemouth BH5. . . 394 A4
Ferndown BH22. . . . 353 F7
Woodlane Cl SO24 . . 202 D5
Woodlark Gdns
GU31 . . . . 229 C3
Woodlark Glade GU15 36 B7
Woodlarks Camp Site
GU10. . . . . 122 F7
Wood Lawn Cl BH25. 397 F8
Woodlea Cl SO22 . . . 403 C8
Woodlea Gdns SO30 268 E1
Woodlea Ho SO35. . . 243 C3
Woodlea Prim Sch
GU35. . . . . 164 D1
Woodlea Way SO51 . 217 F2
Woodleaze Cl BH18 . 375 B6
Woodleigh GU51. . . . 75 A8
Woodleigh Cl PO9 . . . 324 C5
Woodley Cl SO51 . . . 216 C2
Woodley Close Flats
SO51 . . . . 216 C2
Woodley Gdns SO41 . 385 D5
Woodley La SO51 . . . 216 B2
Woodley Rd
Gosport PO12 . . . . . 369 C5
Southampton SO19 . . 291 B8
Woodleys Rd GU20. . . 23 D4
Woodley Way SO51 . . 216 C2
Woodling Cres SP6. . 258 D2
Woodlinken Cl BH31 303 B4
Woodlinken Dr
BH31 . . . . 303 B5
Woodlinken Way
BH31 . . . . 303 C4
Wood Lodge SO40 . . 264 B1
Woodman Cl SO21 . . 174 D2
Woodmancote La
PO10 . . . . 325 E4
Woodmancote Rd
PO4 . . . . 371 A4
Woodman Ct GU51 . . .74 F8
Woodmanfield RG25 . 94 C6
Woodman La SO21. . . 174 C2
Woodmere Croft
RG22 . . . . .90 F7

Woodmill La SO18 . . 267 E2
Wood Moor RG40 . . . . 16 D2
Woodmoor Cl SO40 . . 290 A1
Woodpath PO5 . . . . . 404 B1
Woodpath Ho PO5 . . . 404 B1
Woodpecker Cl
Basingstoke RG22 . . . 90 F8
Bordon GU35 . . . . . . 164 D2
Ewshot GU10 . . . . . . 98 B8
Havant PO9 . . . . 324 B1
Verwood BH31. . . . . 302 F5
Woodpecker Copse
SO31 . . . . 317 B3
Woodpecker Dr
Broadstone BH17 . . . 389 F8
Marchwood SO40 . . . 289 E1
Woodpeckers
3 Andover SP10 . . . 106 A8
Winchester SO23 . . . 403 E8
Woodpeckers Dr
SO22 . . . . 403 A8
Woodpecker Way
Eastleigh SO50 . . . . 243 D2
Portsmouth PO3 . . . . 346 A4
Wood Pk SP11 . . . . . . 57 A2
Wood Rd
Ashurst SO40 . . . . . . 288 B2
Beacon Hill GU26 . . . 167 B6
Camberley GU15 . . . . 35 F2
Farnham GU9 . . . . . . 99 A7
Wood Ridge RG14. . . . . 5 C7
Woodridge Ho RG14 . . 5 C7
Woodridge Manor
GU15 . . . . 36 B7
Woodrising BH13 . . . 402 B3
Woodrisings The 6
BH2 . . . . 392 C4
Woodroffe Dr RG22 . . 68 C1
Woodroffe Wlk
PO10 . . . . 324 F4
Woodrow PO7 . . . . . . 298 E4
Wood Row BH9 . . . . . 378 E4
Woodruff BH23. . . . . 396 C8
Woodrush Cres
SO31 . . . . 316 E2
Wood's Cnr RG24 . . . 331 C5
Woodsedge PO7 . . . . 323 A6
Woods Edge BH18 . . 375 A2
Woods Ho 5 GU32 . . 228 F4
Woodside
Blackwater GU17 . . . . 35 A3
Brockenhurst SO42. . 361 A8
Chilworth SO16 . . . . 242 E2
Farnborough GU14 . . . 55 F7
Gosport PO13 . . . . . 343 B5
Newbury RG14 . . . . . .5 B7
Portsmouth PO5 . . . . 404 B1
Sandhurst GU15 . . . . 35 D7
Vernham Dean SP11. . 38 A5
Woodside Ave
Eastleigh SO50 . . . . 243 F4
Lymington SO41 . . . . 385 E1
Woodside Cl
10 Lymington SO41. . 385 E2
Bordon GU35 . . . . . . 164 D3
Ferndown BH22. . . . 353 E6
Finchampstead RG40. 16 C8
Marchwood SO40 . . . 289 E1
Mortimer RG7 . . . . . . 11 E6
Woodside Cotts
RG25 . . . . 112 E7
Woodside Cres
Bordon GU35 . . . . . . 164 D3
Chilworth SO16 . . . . 242 E2
Woodside Ct 5
SO17 . . . . 291 B8
Woodside Gdns
Ashurst SO40 . . . . . . 288 C3
Chineham RG24 . . . . . 49 A4
Fleet GU51 . . . . 54 C1
Woodside La
Lower Farringdon
GU34 . . . . 161 B4
Lymington SO41 . . . . 385 E1
Woodside Pk GU35. . 164 D3
Woodside Rd
Bournemouth BH5. . . 394 B4
Eastleigh SO50 . . . . 243 E4
Farnborough GU14 . . . 76 D7
Farnham GU9 . . . . . . 99 C7
Ferndown BH22. . . . 353 E6
North Baddesley
SO52. . . . . 241 F4
Poole BH14 . . . . 391 C3
Southampton SO17 . . 291 B8
West Moors BH22 . . . 326 D4
Woodside Way SO30 293 A5
Woods La RG25 . . . . . .91 F7
Wood St GU12 . . . . . . 99 D7
Woodstock Ave PO8 . 300 A5
Woodstock Cl
Fareham PO14. . . . . 318 E1
Hedge End SO30 . . . 293 D5
Poole BH14 . . . . 391 B2
Woodstock Dr SO17. . 267 A3
Woodstock La BH24 . 329 A6
Woodstock Mead
RG22 . . . . .91 B6
Woodstock Rd
Burton BH23 . . . . . . 380 D2
Gosport PO12 . . . . . 369 C4
Havant PO9 . . . . 323 D2
Poole BH14 . . . . 391 A2
Woodstocks GU14 . . . . 56 B6
Woods View Rd BH9 392 D8
Woodthorpe Gdns
SO31 . . . . 316 F6
Woodvale PO15 . . . . 318 D2

Woodvale Gdns
BH25 . . . . 383 C4
Wood View BH21 . . . 352 A8
Woodview Cl SO16 . . 267 A6
Woodview Pk SO30 . . 294 C7
Woodville Cl
Blackwater GU17 . . . . 34 F5
Chineham RG24 . . . . . 48 F2
Woodville Dr PO1 . . . 370 B3
Woodville Rd
Fawley SO45 . . . . . . 339 B3
Havant PO9 . . . . 323 B2
Woodville Rise RG24 . 48 F2
Woodward Cl PO12 . . 368 F4
Woodway GU15 . . . . . 35 F5
Woofferton Rd PO6 . 321 A1
Wooland Ct 11 GU52. .74 E4
**Wooldings Farm
Vineyard** ★ RG28 . . . 63 F1
Wooldridge Cres
RG29 . . . . 95 C8
Woolfield La GU32,
GU34 . . . . 205 B3
Woolford Cl 1
SO22 . . . . 403 A4
Woolford Way RG23. . 68 D6
Wool Gr SP10. . . . . . 106 C8
Woollards Rd GU12 . . .77 F4
Woolley Ho 7 SO14. 291 A5
Woolley Sq SP10. . . . 83 C3
Woolmead Ct GU9 . . . 99 A3
Woolmead Rd GU9. . . 99 A3
Woolmead The GU9. . 99 A3
Woolmer Cl 11 PO9 . 324 B5
Woolmer Hill Ho
GU27 . . . . 189 A6
Woolmer Hill Rd
GU27 . . . . 189 B7
Woolmer Hill Tech Coll
GU27. . . . . 189 B7
Woolmer La
Bramshott GU30 . . . . 188 A7
Ringwood BH24. . . . . 305 A2
Woolmer Rd GU33 . . 186 B3
Woolmer St PO10 . . . 324 E4
Woolmer Trad Est
GU35. . . . . 164 C3
Woolmer View 12
GU26 . . . . 167 B3
Woolmer Way GU35. 164 C2
Woolner Ave
Cosham PO6 . . . . . . 346 A8
Petersfield GU32. . . . 228 F4
Wool Rd BH12 . . . . . . 391 B8
Woolsbridge Ind Est
BH21. . . . . 327 A6
Woolsbridge Rd
BH24 . . . . 327 E5
Woolslope Rd BH22. . 326 E1
Woolslope Gdns
BH22 . . . . 326 F1
Woolslope Rd BH22 . 326 E1
Woolston Ct 4
PO12 . . . . 368 D3
Woolston Inf Sch
SO19 . . . . 291 E1
Woolston Rd
Havant PO9 . . . . 323 C6
Netley SO31. . . . . . . 315 C7
**Woolston Sch (Language
Coll)** SO19. . . . . . . 291 F2
Woolston Sta SO19. . 291 D4
Woolton Hill Jun Sch
RG20. . . . . 21 C8
Woolton Lodge Gdns
RG20. . . . . .4 D2
Woolven Cl BH14 . . . 391 A5
Woolverston SO22 . . 403 C7
Woolwich Cl SO31 . . 292 F7
Wootey Inf Sch
GU34. . . . . 139 F6
Wootey Jun Sch
GU34. . . . . 139 F6
Wooteys Way GU34 . 139 F6
Wootton SO31 . . . . . 315 C7
Wootton Farm Rd
BH25 . . . . 358 E2
Wootton Gdns BH1. . 393 A3
Wootton Mount BH1 393 A3
Wootton Rd
Lee-on-t-S PO13 . . . 368 A4
Tiptoe BH25. . . . . . . 383 D7
Wootton Rough
BH25 . . . . 383 B8
Wootton St PO6 . . . . 345 D7
Worbarrow Gdns
BH12 . . . . 391 C8
Worcester Ave RG25 .91 B8
Worcester Cl
5 Portsmouth
PO5 . . . . 404 C2
Farnborough GU14 . . . 55 F7
Worcester Ct
15 Fleet GU51 . . . . . 53 E3
9 Gosport PO13 . . . 368 D2
Worcester Ho RG24 . . 68 D8
Worcester Pl
1 Lymington SO41. . 385 F2
Southampton SO19 . . 292 B2
Wordsworth Ave
Bournemouth BH8. . . 378 E1
Portchester PO6 . . . . 320 E1
Yateley GU46. . . . . . . 33 F4
Wordsworth Cl
Basingstoke RG24. . . . 69 C8
Bishop's Waltham
SO32. . . . . 271 E8

Wordsworth Cl *continued*
Winchester SO22 ... 403 B6
Wordsworth Inf Sch
SO15............. 266 B1
Wordsworth Pl
PO15............. 294 C1
Wordsworth Rd
SO15............. 266 C1
Worgret Rd BH15.. 390 D7
Workhouse La GU32 226 D1
Workmans's La
SO31
Workshop Rd PO6 ... 321 A2
Worldham Hill GU34 141 A1
Worldham Ho GU51.. 53 E4
Worldham Rd PO9 .. 324 B6
Wormersley Rd RG19...6 B7
Worrell Dr BH12.... 391 C8
Worrell Sq SP10 .... 83 C3
Worsam Ct RG22.....68 B4
Worsley Rd
Camberley GU16 ... 56 D7
Portsmouth PO5 .... 404 B1
Worsley St PO4 .... 371 A2
Worth Apts PO5 .... 370 D1
Worthing Ave PO12 . 368 F8
Worthing Rd PO5 ... 370 D2
Worthington Cres
BH14............. 391 A3
Worthy Ho SO16 .... 266 B1
Worthy La SO23..... 403 E7
Worthy Rd
New Milton BH25 ... 383 A3
Winchester SO23 ... 403 E8
Worting Rd
Basingstoke,Buckskin
RG22............. 68 B4
Basingstoke,West Ham
RG22............. 68 E4
Worting Road Rdbt
RG22............. 68 C4
Wortley Rd BH23... 397 A7
Wote St RG21.......69 B4
Wouldham Cl SP11...79 D7
Wraxall Cl BH17 ... 375 D1
Wraysbury Park Dr
PO10............. 324 F4
Wrecclesham Hill
GU10............. 121 C5
Wrecclesham Rd
GU10............. 121 D8
Wrekin Cl RG22.....68 B3
Wrekin The GU14 ... 56 C1
Wren Cl
Alton GU34 .... 140 A5
Christchurch BH23 .. 396 B5
New Milton BH25 ... 382 F2
Ringwood BH24..... 329 C6
Winchester SO22 ... 403 B3
Yateley GU46....... 33 F6
Wren Cres BH12 .... 392 B5
Wren Ct GU12 ......77 F3
Wren Ctr The PO10.. 325 A3
Wren Gdns SP6..... 281 B5
Wren Rd SO50 ..... 243 E1
Wrenway PO16 ..... 343 F8
Wren Way GU14 .... 55 D7
Wrexham Gr PO8 ... 276 B2

Wright Cl PO15 ..... 317 F6
Wrights Cl SO21 .... 153 D4
Wright's Hill SO19 .. 292 A2
Wrights Way SO21 .. 153 D4
Wrights Wlk SO31... 292 F1
Wroxham Rd BH12 . 391 F5
Wryneck Cl SO16 ... 266 B6
Wyatt Cl [5] GU47 ....35 B7
Wyatts Cl BH21 .... 374 D6
Wyatts La BH21 .... 374 C6
Wyborn Cl PO11 ... 373 A2
Wych La PO13 ...... 343 B3
Wychwood [38] BH4 . 392 C3
Wychwood Cl
Ash GU12.......... 77 D2
Bournemouth BH2... 392 F4
Wychwood Dr
Blackfield SO45.... 365 E7
Bournemouth BH2... 392 F4
Wychwood Gr SO53 . 243 E8
Wychwood Grange [1]
BH2 .... 392 F4
Wychwood Pl GU15 ..36 F8
Wyck La
Binsted GU34 ..... 141 E6
Binsted,Wyck GU34.. 141 B3
Wycliffe Rd
Bournemouth BH9... 392 F8
Southampton SO18 . 268 A1
Wycote Rd PO13 ... 343 B4
Wye Ct SP10........ 83 D2
Wyeford Cl [4] PO9 . 324 B6
Wyelands Ave BH21. 352 D5
Wykeham Ave PO2.. 345 E1
Wykeham Cl
Netley SO31....... 315 B6
Poole BH17........ 390 E8
Southampton SO16 . 266 E4
Wykeham Ct RG29... 95 D8
Wykeham Dr RG23.. 68 A4
Wykeham Field
PO17............. 296 A3
Wykeham Ho GU14.. 77 A8
Wykeham House Sch
PO16............. 319 C1
Wykeham Ind Est The
SO23............. 176 C2
Wykeham Pk SO21 . 199 A7
Wykeham Pl
Lymington SO41 .... 385 E3
Winchester SO22 ... 403 B4
Wykeham Rd
Farnham GU9 ...... 99 A3
Netley SO31....... 315 B6
Portsmouth PO2 ... 345 E1
Wykeham Terr [7]
SO23............. 403 F4
Wyke Mark SO22.... 403 A8
Wykwood GU30 .... 188 B4
Wylde Green La
GU33............. 208 B5
Wylds La GU32..... 253 C8
Wyllie Rd PO2...... 345 E4
Wylye Ct SO18 ..... 268 B3
Wylye Rd SP9.......78 F7
Wymering Ct GU14..56 B3
Wymering La PO6... 321 E1

Wymering Manor Cl [6]
PO6 .... 345 D8
**Wymering Manor (Youth
Hostel)**★ PO6 ..... 345 D8
Wymering Rd PO2.. 370 E8
Wyncombe Rd BH5 . 394 B5
Wyndcliffe Rd PO4.. 370 E3
Wyndham Cl
Walkford BH23 .... 382 B2
Waterlooville PO8... 300 B4
Yateley GU46....... 34 B7
Wyndham Ct SO15 . 290 E5
Wyndham Mews
PO1 .... 370 A3
Wyndham Pl [4]
SO15............. 290 E5
Wyndham Rd
Andover SP10 ..... 105 F6
Newbury RG14 .....2 B5
Poole BH14 .... 391 B3
Walkford BH23 .... 382 B2
Wyndham St PO9... 77 A1
Wynfields GU16..... 56 D3
Wynford Ind Pk
SO51............. 215 F4
Wynford Rd
Bournemouth BH9.. 378 B4
Poole BH14 .... 391 C4
Wynne Cl BH18 .... 374 F4
Wynne Gdns GU52 ...75 B5
Wyn Sutcliffe Ct [3]
PO4 .... 371 A3
Wynter Cl BH7...... 393 F7
Wynter Rd SO18 ... 292 B8
Wynton Way PO15 . 318 C3
Wynyards Gap SO52. 241 F4
Wyre Cl SO53...... 243 B6
Wyvern Cl
Ash Vale GU12..... 77 D5
Chandler's Ford
SO53............. 243 C4
Poole BH12 .... 391 D7
Wyvern Tech Coll
SO50............. 245 C1

Y

Yachtsman Cl SO31. 316 C8
Yaldhurst Ct [20] PO9. 324 B6
Yaldhurst La SO41.. 385 B3
Yapton St PO1...... 404 B3
Yarborough Rd PO5. 404 B1
Yardlea Cl PO9 ..... 301 B1
Yardley Cl PO3 ..... 346 C4
Yardley Rd SO30 ... 293 C5
Yarmouth Cl BH12 . 392 A5
Yarmouth Gdns [5]
SO15............. 266 B1
Yarmouth Rd BH12.. 391 F6
Yarnhams Cl GU34.. 160 B2
Yarrell Mead SO41.. 385 B3
Yarrells Cl BH16.... 389 C6
Yarrells Dr BH16.... 389 B7
Yarrells La BH16.... 389 C6
Yarrells Sch BH16... 389 B7
Yarrow Cl BH23..... 396 B8
Yarrow Rd BH12 ... 391 A8
Yarrow Way SO31... 316 E2

Yateley Cl PO9...... 323 C5
**Yateley Common Ctry
Pk**★ GU46,GU17.... 34 D3
Yateley Inds GU46... 34 B7
Yateley Inf Sch GU46. 34 B6
Yateley Manor Sch
GU46............. 34 B6
Yateley Rd GU47 ... 34 D8
Yateley Sch GU46... 34 A6
Yatesbury Cl GU9... 121 D7
Yates Copse RG14...2 C5
Yaverland SO31..... 315 C6
Yeatmans Old Mill [10]
BH15............. 390 B1
Yeatminster Rd
BH17............. 375 F2
Yeatton Ho SO41.... 384 A1
Yellowhammer Rd
RG22.............90 F5
Yellowhammers
GU34............. 139 F5
Yelverton Ave SO45. 338 A8
Yelverton Rd [10] BH1. 392 F5
Yeo Ct PO4 .... 371 C4
Yeoman Pk SO16... 265 C1
Yeomans RG27 ..... 33 C7
Yeomans Cl
Farnborough GU14 . 55 E5
Tongham GU10 .... 100 D8
Yeomans Ind Pk
BH8.............. 378 F2
Yeomans La
Burghclere RG20..... 5 E1
Liphook GU30 ..... 187 E4
Yeomans Lodge [6]
BH25............. 383 B2
Yeomans Pl GU35... 165 C5
Yeomans Rd BH8 .. 378 E3
Yeomans Way
Bournemouth BH8.. 378 E2
Camberley GU15 ... 36 C5
Totton SO40....... 288 F8
Yeosfield RG7 ...... 14 A3
Yeovil Chase SO18 . 292 B8
Yeovil Cl SO14...... 56 B1
Yeovil Rd GU14 .... 56 C1
Yeovilton Cl SO41... 384 E1
Yerville Gdns SO41.. 383 F3
Yetminster Rd GU14. 56 B1
Yewberry Way
SO53............. 242 E6
Yew Cl PO20.......24 E2
Yew Gate RG14 .....1 D6
Yew La BH25 ...... 383 C4
Yew Rd SO18 ...... 292 A8
Yewside PO13 ..... 343 D2
Yews The PO8 ..... 300 D7
Yewtree Cl SO45.... 338 A8
Yew Tree Cl
Bramley RG26 ..... 29 A2
Fair Oak SO50..... 245 C3
Farnborough GU14 . 55 A3
Goodworth Clatford
SP11............. 106 A1
Hedge End SO30 .. 293 B6
Oakley RG23 ......90 B8
Wimborne Minster
BH21 .... 351 D5

Yew Tree Ct
[5] New Milton
BH25............. 383 B1
Fordingbridge SP6... 281 E8
Swanwick PO15..... 317 B7
Yew Tree Dr PO15 . 317 C7
Yew Tree Gdns
[3] Ringwood BH24. 329 A6
Denmead PO7 ..... 298 A4
Yewtree La SO16.... 265 C3
Yew Tree La
North Waltham RG25. 89 E1
West Tytherley SP5 . 169 B4
Yew Tree Pl GU33... 208 A4
Yew Tree Rd PO11.. 373 A8
Yew Tree Wlk GU16. 36 D1
Yoells Cres PO8 ... 299 F6
Yoells La PO8...... 299 F6
Yokesford Hill SO51. 215 E4
Yokesford Hill Est
SO51............. 215 F5
Yolland Cl GU9 .....99 A7
Yonge Cl SO50..... 244 B3
York Ave PO5...... 383 B3
York Bldgs SO14.... 291 A4
York Cl
Basingstoke RG22 .. 91 B8
Bordon GU35...... 164 D2
Broadstone BH18 .. 375 A2
Chandler's Ford SO53 242 F4
Christchurch BH23 . 394 F7
Horton Heath SO50. 269 D7
Newbury RG14 .....1 F2
Petersfield GU32... 228 D3
Southampton SO14. 291 C6
Totton SO40....... 289 A8
York Cres
Aldershot GU11..... 76 D1
Lee-on-t-S PO13 ... 368 A4
York Ct [4] SP10 ... 83 A3
Yorkdale SO31...... 316 C3
York Dro
Nomansland SP5... 261 D8
Southampton SO18 . 292 B7
York Ho
[20] Winchester
SO23............. 403 E8
[5] Aldershot GU11 . 76 D1
[7] Southampton
SO14............. 291 C6
[9] Gosport PO12... 369 D5
Basingstoke RG22... 68 E3
Fareham PO14...... 318 E1
York La RG27 ...... 52 C5
York Lodge [4] GU12. 77 A1
York Mews GU34.... 140 A4
York Pl
[7] New Milton
BH25............. 383 B3
Bournemouth BH7.. 394 A5
Camberley GU15 ... 36 B7
Portsmouth PO1 ... 370 B6
York Rd
Aldershot GU11..... 76 D1
Ash GU12.......... 77 E3
Bournemouth BH1.. 393 B4

York Rd *continued*
Broadstone BH18 .. 375 A2
Camberley GU15 ... 36 B7
Eastleigh SO50 .... 268 A8
Farnborough GU14 . 55 D1
Farnborough GU14 . 76 C8
Farnborough,South
Farnborough GU14.. 56 A1
Farnham GU9 ...... 99 A1
Netley SO31....... 315 A6
Newbury RG14 .....1 F2
Southampton SO15'. 290 C7
York Terr PO2...... 345 F5
York Terrace La GU15 35 E5
York Town Ind Est
GU15............. 35 E4
Yorktown Rd
Sandhurst,College Town
GU47.............35 C7
Sandhurst,Little Sandhurst
GU47............. 34 F7
York Way GU47.....34 F8
Yorkwood GU33 ... 207 F4
Youlden Cl GU15....36 E5
Youlden Dr GU15....36 F6
Youngbridge Ct
PO16............. 343 A7
Young Cres RG19....6 B8
Youngs Dr GU12 ...77 D2
Young's Ind Est RG7 .. 9 D4
Youngs Paddock
SP5 .... 168 A6
Youngs Rd
Alton GU34 .... 139 F4
Bournemouth BH11. 377 A5
Yves Mews PO5.... 370 D2

Z

Zamek Cl BH11 .... 377 A5
Zephyr Ho [11] RG7....9 C2
Zetland Ct BH4 .... 392 B1
Zetland Rd
Farlington PO6 .... 346 D7
Gosport PO12 ..... 369 B6
Zeus La PO7........ 322 F3
Zinnia Cl
Basingstoke RG22... 91 A7
Bournemouth BH10. 377 E2
Zion Rd SP11....... 124 D5
Zodiac Ho [12] RG7....9 C2
Zouch Ave SP9......78 E7
Zouch Cl SP9.......78 E7
Zouch Farm Rd SP9..78 E7
Zouch Mkt SP9......78 E7
Zouch Prim Sch SP9. 78 D8